Oxford Handbook of Personality Assessment

OXFORD LIBRARY OF PSYCHOLOGY

Editor-in-Chief
Peter E. Nathan

OXFORD LIBRARY OF PSYCHOLOGY

Editor-in-Chief PETER E. NATHAN

Oxford Handbook of Personality Assessment

Edited by

James N. Butcher

OXFORD
UNIVERSITY PRESS

2009

OXFORD
UNIVERSITY PRESS

Oxford University Press, Inc., publishes works that further Oxford University's objective
of excellence in research, scholarship, and education.

Oxford   New York
Auckland   Cape Town   Dar es Salaam   Hong Kong   Karachi
Kuala Lumpur   Madrid   Melbourne   Mexico City   Nairobi
New Delhi   Shanghai   Taipei   Toronto

With offices in
Argentina   Austria   Brazil   Chile   Czech Republic   France   Greece
Guatemala   Hungary   Italy   Japan   Poland   Portugal   Singapore
South Korea   Switzerland   Thailand   Turkey   Ukraine   Vietnam

Published by Oxford University Press, Inc.
198 Madison Avenue, New York, New York 10016

www.oup.com

Oxford is a registered trademark of Oxford University Press

Library of Congress Cataloging-in-Publication Data
Oxford handbook of personality assessment / edited by James N. Butcher.
p.   cm. — (Oxford library of psychology)
Includes bibliographical references and index.
ISBN 978-0-19-536687-7
1. Personality assessment—Handbooks, manuals, etc.   I. Butcher, James Neal, 1933–
BF698.4.O94 2009
155.2'8—dc22

2008037075

9 8 7 6 5 4 3 2

Printed in the United States of America
on acid-free paper

CONTENTS

OXFORD LIBRARY OF PSYCHOLOGY

The *Oxford Library of Psychology*, a landmark series of handbooks, is published by Oxford University Press, one of the world's oldest and most highly respected publishers, with a tradition of publishing significant books in psychology. The ambitious goal of the *Oxford Library of Psychology* is nothing less than to span a vibrant, wide-ranging field and, in so doing, to fill a clear market need.

Encompassing a comprehensive set of handbooks, organized hierarchically, the *Library* incorporates volumes at different levels, each designed to meet a distinct need. At one level are a set of handbooks designed broadly to survey the major subfields of psychology; at another are numerous handbooks that cover important current focal research and scholarly areas of psychology in depth and detail. Planned as a reflection of the dynamism of psychology, the *Library* will grow and expand as psychology itself develops, thereby highlighting significant new research that will impact on the field. Adding to its accessibility and ease of use, the *Library* will be published in print and, later on, electronically.

The *Library* surveys psychology's principal subfields with a set of handbooks that capture the current status and future prospects of those major subdisciplines. This initial set includes handbooks of social and personality psychology, clinical psychology, counseling psychology, school psychology, educational psychology, industrial and organizational psychology, cognitive psychology, cognitive neuroscience, methods and measurements, history, neuropsychology, personality assessment, developmental psychology, and more. Each handbook undertakes to review one of psychology's major subdisciplines with breadth, comprehensiveness, and exemplary scholarship. In addition to these broadly conceived volumes, the *Library* also includes a large number of handbooks designed to explore in depth more specialized areas of scholarship and research, such as stress, health and coping, anxiety and related disorders, cognitive development, or child and adolescent assessment. In contrast to the broad coverage of the subfield handbooks, each of these latter volumes focuses on an especially productive, more highly focused line of scholarship and research. Whether at the broadest or most specific level, however, all of the *Library* handbooks offer synthetic coverage that reviews and evaluates the relevant past and present research and anticipates research in the future. Each handbook in the *Library* includes introductory and concluding chapters written by its editor to provide a roadmap to the handbook's table of contents and to offer informed anticipations of significant future developments in that field.

An undertaking of this scope calls for handbook editors and chapter authors who are established scholars in the areas about which they write. Many of the nation's and world's most productive and best-respected psychologists have agreed to edit *Library* handbooks or write authoritative chapters in their areas of expertise.

For whom has the *Oxford Library of Psychology* been written? Because of its breadth, depth, and accessibility, the *Library* serves a diverse audience, including graduate students in psychology and their faculty mentors, scholars, researchers, and practitioners in psychology and related fields. Each will find in the *Library* the information they seek on the subfield or focal area of psychology in which they work or are interested.

Befitting its commitment to accessibility, each handbook includes a comprehensive index, as well as extensive references to help guide research. And because the *Library* was designed from its inception as an online as well as a print resource, its structure and contents will be readily and rationally searchable online. Further, once the *Library* is released online, the handbooks will be regularly and thoroughly updated.

In summary, the *Oxford Library of Psychology* will grow organically to provide a thoroughly informed perspective on the field of psychology, one that reflects both psychology's dynamism and its increasing interdisciplinarity. Once published electronically, the *Library* is also destined to become a uniquely valuable interactive tool, with extended search and browsing capabilities. As you begin to consult this handbook, we sincerely hope you will share our enthusiasm for the more than 500-year tradition of Oxford University Press for excellence, innovation, and quality, as exemplified by the *Oxford Library of Psychology*.

Peter E. Nathan
Editor-in-Chief
Oxford Library of Psychology

ABOUT THE EDITOR

James N. Butcher

James N. Butcher is Professor Emeritus in the Department of Psychology at the University of Minnesota. He received his PhD in clinical psychology from the University of North Carolina at Chapel Hill in 1964. He has devoted much of his career to personality assessment, abnormal psychology, cross-cultural personality factors, and computer-based personality assessment.

CONTRIBUTORS

JOSEPH A. BANKEN
Department of Obstetrics and Gynecology
University of Arkansas for Medical Sciences
Little Rock, AR

IRUMA BELLO
Department of Psychology
University of Hawai'i at Mānoa
Honolulu, HI

DAVID T. R. BERRY
Department of Psychology
University of Kentucky
Lexington, KY

LARRY E. BEUTLER
Pacific Graduate School of Psychology
Redwood City, CA

BRUCE BONGAR
Pacific Graduate School of Psychology
Redwood City, CA, and Department of
Psychiatry and Behavioral Sciences
Stanford University School of Medicine
Stanford, CA

SARA E. BOYD
Department of Psychology
University of Kentucky
Lexington, KY

JAMES N. BUTCHER
Department of Psychology
University of Minnesota
Minneapolis, MN

JANET F. CARLSON
Buros Center for Testing
University of Nebraska
Lincoln, NE

OLEKSANDR S. CHERNYSHENKO
Nanyang Business School
Nanyang Technological University Singapore

FANNY M. CHEUNG
Department of Psychology
The Chinese University of Hong Kong
Hong Kong

JESSICA A. CLARK
Department of Psychology
University of Kentucky
Lexington, KY

PAUL T. COSTA, JR.
National Institute on Aging
National Institutes of Health
Baltimore, MD

ANDREW C. COX
Department of Psychology
Central Michigan University
Mount Pleasant, MI

ROBERT J. CRAIG
Department of Psychology
Roosevelt University Chicago, IL

EDWARD J. CUMELLA
Remuda Programs for Eating Disorders
Wickenburg, AZ

BROOKE L. DEAN
Department of Psychology
University of Minnesota
Minneapolis, MN

FRITZ DRASGOW
Department of Psychology
University of Illinois
Champaign, IL

STEPHEN E. FINN
Center for Therapeutic Assessment
Austin, TX

CARL B. GACONO
School of Psychology
Fielding Graduate Institute
Santa Barbara, CA

CARLTON S. GASS
VA Medical Center
Miami, FL

KURT F. GEISINGER
Buros Center for Testing
University of Nebraska
Lincoln, NE

BERNADETTE GRAY-LITTLE
University of North Carolina at Chapel Hill
Chapel Hill, NC

ROGER L. GREENE
Pacific Graduate School of Psychology
Redwood City, CA

DONALD K. GUCKER
Albuquerque, NM

ALLAN R. HARKNESS
Department of Psychology
University of Tulsa
Tulsa, OK

JENNIFER L. HARRINGTON
School of Professional Psychology
Pacific University
Hillsboro, OR

T. MARK HARWOOD
Department of Psychology
Wheaton College
Wheaton, IL

STEPHEN N. HAYNES
Department of Psychology
University of Hawai'i at Mānoa
Honolulu, HI

LOWELL W. HELLERVIK
Personnel Decisions, Inc.
Minneapolis, MN

RICHARD E. HEYMAN
Department of Psychology
Stony Brook University
Stony Brook, NY

JESSICA JONES
Department of Psychology
University of Minnesota
Minneapolis, MN

KAREN KLOEZEMAN
Department of Psychology
University of Hawai'i at Mānoa
Honolulu, HI

ROBERT F. KRUEGER
Department of Psychology
Washington University
St. Louis, MO

MARTIN LEICHTMAN
Leawood, KS

ANGUS W. MacDONALD, III
Department of Psychology
University of Minnesota
Minneapolis, MN

KRISTIAN E. MARKON
Department of Psychology
University of Iowa
Iowa City, IA

ROBERT R. McCRAE
National Institute on Aging
National Institutes of Health
Baltimore, MD

EDWIN I. MEGARGEE
Havana, FL

J. REID MELOY
Department of Psychiatry
University of California
San Diego La Jolla, CA

GREGORY J. MEYER
Department of Psychology
University of Toledo
Toledo, OH

DAVID S. NICHOLS
School of Professional Psychology
Pacific University
Hillsboro, OR

JENNIFER LAFFERTY O'CONNOR
Remuda Programs for Eating Disorders
Wickenburg, AZ

MIMI OKAZAKI
Florida State Hospital
Chattahoochee, FL

SUMIE OKAZAKI
Department of Psychology
University of Illinois
Champaign, IL

RAYMOND L. OWNBY
Department of Psychiatry and Behavioral Sciences
Miller School of Medicine
University of Miami
Miami, FL

JULIA N. PERRY
VA Medical Center
Minneapolis, MN

MICHELLE B. RANSON
Fielding Graduate University
Santa Barbara, CA

DAMON ANN ROBINSON
Daphne, AL

STEVEN V. ROUSE
Seaver College
Pepperdine University
Malibu, CA

LINDSEY J. SCHIPPER
Department of Psychology
University of Kentucky
Lexington, KY

ANNE L. SHANDERA
Department of Psychology
University of Kentucky
Lexington, KY

GREGORY T. SMITH
Department of Psychology
University of Kentucky
Lexington, KY

DOUGLAS K. SNYDER
Department of Psychology
Texas A&M University
College Station, TX

MYRIAM J. SOLLMAN
Department of Psychology
University of Kentucky
Lexington, KY

SUSAN C. SOUTH
Department of Psychological Sciences
Purdue University
West Lafayette, IN

STEPHEN STARK
Department of Psychology
University of South Florida
Tampa, FL

RONALD A. STOLBERG
California School of Professional
Psychology
Alliant International University
San Diego, CA

STANLEY SUE
Department of Psychology
University of California
Davis, CA

NATHAN C. WEED
Department of Psychology
Central Michigan University
Mount Pleasant, MI

IRVING B. WEINER
University of South Florida
Tampa, FL

THOMAS A. WIDIGER
Department of Psychology
University of Kentucky
Lexington, KY

JUDITH WORELL
University of Kentucky
Lexington, KY

DAWN T. YOSHIOKA
Department of Psychology
University of Hawai'i at Mānoa
Honolulu, HI

TAMIKA C. B. ZAPOLSKI
Department of Psychology
University of Kentucky
Lexington, KY

CONTENTS

Part Seven • Interpretation and Reporting of Assessment Findings

Personality Assessment

PART 1

Overview and Introduction

Clinical Personality Assessment: History, Evolution, Contemporary Models, and Practical Applications

James N. Butcher

Abstract

Our goals in this volume are to provide a comprehensive view of the field of personality assessment from its historical roots to the major, methodological issues defining the field and that have led to numerous approaches and applications, and to the broad range of assessment techniques available today. One can find throughout history an awareness of the importance of evaluating personality and character using observation and other means of acquiring information on which to make such decisions. For over 3,000 years, an elaborate system of competitive examinations was used in China. The modern era for personality assessment began in the late nineteenth-century England with the work of Sir Francis Galton. The first self-report personality inventory used to obtain personality information was developed by Robert Woodworth during World War I. Numerous personality inventories were developed in the years that followed. One of the most successful has been the Minnesota Multiphasic Personality Inventory (MMPI) developed in the late 1930s by Starke Hathaway and J. C. McKinley. Paralleling the work on personality inventories was the development of projective assessment instruments. The most significant projective test was developed by the Swiss psychiatrist Herman Rorschach in 1922. Another projective instrument, the Thematic Apperception Test, or TAT, was developed in 1935 by Henry Murray and Christiana Morgan. These instruments came to be the most widely used assessment instruments during the expansion of applied psychology after World War II and are still the predominant tests in use today.

In this handbook, an overview of contemporary personality assessment will be provided by a number of prominent assessment psychologists who give the reader a comprehensive perspective on assessment methodology and instruments. In addition, some challenges that assessment psychology faces will be described. Discussion is provided to highlight significant assessment trends and projections about new directions for research.

Keywords: historical roots, highlights in assessment, origins, phrenology, fMRI, Rorschach, MMPI, TAT, testing standards

People have likely been making personality assessment decisions and personality appraisals since the beginning of human interactions. As an adaptive human activity, effective personality appraisal has clear survival value for our species (Buss, 1984). If our cave-dwelling ancestors happened to choose a hunting partner with the "wrong" personality and motivations, the outcome could be tragic. Or if groups from antiquity failed to evaluate whether potential leaders possessed essential personal qualities, their own survival could be threatened. Personality assessments in antiquity were probably based on diverse, if not particularly valid or reliable, sources of information. Early writings, for example, mention such factors as dreams, signs from the gods, oracular speculation, spies, traitors, direct observation, pedigree, physiognomic characteristics, and the interview as important sources of information about people. Even "tests" were employed to evaluate personality characteristics. Hathaway (1965) described an early personality screening situation from the Old Testament: For example, Gideon had collected too large an army, and now the Lord saw that the Israelites would give Him scant credit if so many men overran the Midianites camped in the valley. The Lord suggested two screening items for Gideon. The first of these items had face validity: Gideon proclaimed that all who were afraid could go home. More than two of every three did so. The second was subtle: Those who fought the Midianites were the few who drank from their cupped hands instead of stooping to drink. Altogether it was a battle decided by psychological devices, and 300 men literally scared the demoralized Midianites into headlong flight (p. 457).

Highlights in History

Efforts to appraise personality characteristics were evident in antiquity. DuBois (1970) pointed out that for over 3,000 years an elaborate system of competitive examinations was used for selecting government personnel in China. Some of these tests used were designed to assess the personal characteristics of applicants. This system of examinations was described in the year 2200 BC, when the emperor of China examined government officials every 3 years to determine their fitness for office (DuBois, 1970). In 1115 BC, candidates for government positions were examined for their proficiency in the "six arts": music, archery, horsemanship, writing, arithmetic, and the rites and ceremonies of public and private life (DuBois, 1970). Examinees were required to write for hours at a time and for a period of several days in succession. For a picture of the early testing booths, see Ben-Porath and Butcher (1991).

One can find throughout history an awareness of the importance of evaluating personality and character as using observation and other means of acquiring information on which to make such personality-based judgments. However, interest in obtaining further understanding and for evaluating underlying personality and personal qualities began to take more objective focus in the nineteenth century. Some scholars came to believe that human physical characteristics such as bumps on the head or the shape of the eyes were associated with underlying personality or character and that one could understand people by careful observation of their physical features. This phenomenon, known as phrenology, was held by a number of prominent physicians. Phrenology appealed to intellectuals who followed a biological determinism that gave promise to individuals improving themselves in life by being able to read and understand characteristics of other people from their appearance. Boring (1950) pointed out that the modern character of phrenology (as well as its name) was initially founded by Johan Spurzheim (1776–1832), a Viennese physician who studied with Franz Joseph Gall (1758–1828) in 1800 and was soon employed as his assistant. Gall, also a Viennese physician and lecturer, had been involved in the investigation of his theory that powerful memory as a characteristic in humans was reflective of having very prominent eyes and that other bodily characteristics, such as head size, were indicative of special talents for painting or music. Gall and Spurzheim were very popular speakers among upper-class intellectuals and scientists in Europe in the 1820s and influenced British physican George Combe (1788–1858), who was the most prolific British phrenologist of the nineteenth century.

During the brief period that Spurzheim and Gall worked together, Gall had hoped to have Spurzheim as his successor and included him as a co-author in a number of publications. However, they had a disagreement that prompted Spurzheim to start his own career, writing extensively about the physiognomical system. Spurzheim was highly successful in his effort to popularize phrenology throughout Europe, particularly in France and England. After leaving the tutorship of Professor Gall, he continued to expand his views and established a new and more complete topography of the skull, filling in blanks that Gall felt had not been empirically established. He also revised the terminology for the faculties used in phrenology. Once he completed the system to his satisfaction, Spurzheim set about spreading the word on phrenology in other countries. Providing lectures in Europe he influenced others such as John C. Warren (1778–1856), a professor of medicine at Harvard (also known for performing the first surgery under ether in the United States). Warren had begun the study of Gall's ideas on phrenology in 1808, but during a trip to France he studied Spurzheim's views on phrenology in 1821. When he returned to Boston, he developed a series of lectures on phrenology at Harvard and later incorporated these ideas into presentations for a broader audience at the Massachusetts Medical Society.

The most prominent promoter of phrenology in the United States during the 1820s was Charles Caldwell (1772–1853), who had also attended Spurzheim's lectures in Paris. He toured throughout the United States lecturing on phrenology and founded a number of societies that promoted phrenology. In 1832, Spurzheim traveled to the

United States to spread his views on the science of phrenology. After a lengthy series of lectures, he became ill and died with severe fever. The most notable phrenologists in the United States were the Fowler brothers who lectured and performed in public during the 1840s. Orson Squire Fowler (1809–1889) and his younger brother Lorenzo Fowler (1811–1896) wrote extensively and promoted phrenology during this period. The brothers operated a publishing house, mail-order business, and museum of human and animal skulls. They zealously promoted phrenology as a practical tool for self-improvement.

Although the phrenology movement was popular for a time, it was not widely accepted in the broader scientific community and was a short-lived phenomenon. The popularity of the movement does, however, show that the scientific community at the time was open to and interested in scientifically assessing underlying personality attributes.

Twentieth-Century Developments in Personality Assessment

One of the greatest steps in introducing personality assessment in the modern era began in the late nineteenth-century England with the work of Sir Francis Galton (1822–1911), a half-cousin and contemporary of Charles Darwin and a prolific explorer and researcher. Galton (1879, 1884) conducted a number of experiments on mental processes and devised explicit experimental procedures for measuring psychological attributes. He also proposed that human character could be studied by observation and experimentation and pointed out that such observations could be standardized and readily compared by the use of developmental norms. Sir Francis Galton initially suggested that questionnaires could be used for measuring mental traits although he did not develop a specific questionnaire for this purpose himself. The first formal use of a structured rating scale for studying human character was published by Heymans and Wiersma (1906). They constructed a 90-item rating scale and asked 3,000 physicians to rate people with whom they were well acquainted using the scale. The manual of mental and physical tests published by Whipple (1910) addressed primarily physical, motor, sensory, and perceptual tests.

The first self-report personality inventory used to obtain personality information was developed by Robert Woodworth (1919, 1920) as a means of detecting psychiatric problems for the U.S. Army in World War I. The Woodworth Personal Data Sheet included 116 items such as:

Have you ever seen a vision?
Do you make friends easily?
Do you feel tired most of the time?

The scoring on the scale was the total number of extreme item responses (based on a rational determination of adjustment problems). In addition, he included a number of "starred items" or particularly problematic behaviors (today we refer to them as critical items) which were thought to indicate particularly serious problems that require special attention. During the war, Woodworth developed the items and conducted research on a sample of draftees and returning soldiers with "shell shock" comparing the results with college students (Woodworth, 1919). The Personal Data Sheet was not, however, completed in time to be used to select out draftees who were maladjusted during the war and was published after the war was over. A few years later, Woodworth and Matthews (1924) also published a 75-item version of the inventory for children and adolescents that included some of the same items as the adult version but with additional content they thought more relevant for young people, such as:

Are you troubled with dreams about your play?
Do you find school a hard place to get along in?
Is such an idea as that you are an adopted child difficult for you to shake off?
Do you like to be tickled?

These personality inventories set the stage for broader development of psychological measures to address personality functioning (see Table 1.1). In the years that followed, a large number of personality inventories were developed to assess a variety of characteristics or temperaments. Some of those efforts persisted into the 1920s and 1930s with the development of inventories designed to measure trait-like features such as introversion, extraversion, and neuroticism, but none was used extensively in clinical settings. One exception was the Bernreuter Personality Inventory published by Robert Bernreuter (1931). This personality scale differed from the Woodworth Personal Data Sheet in that it provided scores for a number of personality characteristics, including an appraisal of neurotic tendencies, ascendance–submission, and introversion–extraversion. The Bernreuter Personality Inventory came to be widely used for counseling, clinical and personnel applications and influenced the development of other inventories that followed, such as the MMPI, that are in use today.

Table 1.1. Highlights in the History of Personality Assessment.

Year Personality Test	Reference
Personal Data Sheet 1920 Woodworth	Woodworth (1920)
1921 The Rorschach Inkblot Test	Rorschach (1921)
1924 Woodworth & Matthews Personal Data Sheet (*children and adolescent*)	Woodworth & Matthews (1924)
1933 The Bernreuter Personality Inventory	Bernreuter (1933)
1938 Thematic Apperception Test	Murray (1938)
1940 Minnesota Multiphasic Personality Inventory	Hathaway & McKinley (1940)
1956 The California Psychological Inventory	Gough (1956)
1957 The Sixteen Personality Factors Questionnaire	Cattell & Stice (1957)
1977 The Millon Clinical Multiaxial Inventory	Millon (1977)
1985 The NEO Personality Inventory	Costa & McCrae (1985)
1989 The Minnesota Multiphasic Personality Inventory (MMPI-2)	Butcher, Dahlstrom, Graham, Tellegen, & Kaemmer (1989)
1991 Personality Assessment Inventory	Morey (1991)
1992 Minnesota Multiphasic Personality Inventory-Adolescent Form (MMPI-A)	Butcher, Williams, Graham, Tellegen, et al. (1992)

Development of the Three Major Clinical Personality Assessment Instruments of the Twentieth Century: Rorschach, TAT, and MMPI

The Rorschach

The most significant event in the history of projective psychological assessment occurred during the early years of the twentieth century when the Swiss psychiatrist Herman Rorschach published his monograph *Psychodiagnostik*, which detailed the development of the "Rorschach inkblot technique." During this period, inkblots were commonly used in Europe at the time as stimuli for imagination in the popular parlor game known as *Klecksographie* or *blotto*, in which people made up responses to various inkblot designs. Although Rorschach had experimented with various types and forms of inkblots in 1911 he did not pursue these efforts until his work in 1921 that detailed the interpretation of responses to the inkblots to assess mental health symptoms and personality. This was the only work that Rorschach published on the test because he died of acute appendicitis the following year.

Subsequent developments and refinements of the Rorschach inkblot technique occurred several years later in the United States when Beck (1938), Klopfer and Tallman (1938), and Hertz (1938) began to use the Rorschach blots to understand personality and emotional characteristics of patients in a movement that was to see the publication of thousands of articles and recruitment of countless advocates who began to use the 10 blots in clinical settings—a movement that continues today. Beck, Klopfer, and Hertz also developed separate interpretation systems for the inkblots in the 1940s. The most widely used contemporary Rorschach interpretive system was published by John Exner (1983).

An important theoretical article defining this approach to personality assessment was published by L. K. Frank (1939). This article detailing the use of ambiguous stimuli like the Rorschach inkblots to assess personality provided an important theoretical explanation that came to be known as the projective method in assessment. In Frank's view, the use of ambiguous stimuli allowed people to "project" their internal meanings and feelings from their unconscious personality in their responses. This process of projection allowed an interpreter to gain a better understanding of the client's thinking. Frank's theoretical interpretation of the projective process by the projective method was influential as projective tests such as the Rorschach and TAT expanded in use during the 1940s.

The TAT

The Thematic Apperception Test, or TAT, was developed in 1935 by Henry Murray and Christiana Morgan and described in Murray's early works (1938, 1943). The TAT is a projective measure comprised of a series of pictures to which a client is asked to make up a story describing the events going on in the picture. The test allows the clinician to evaluate the client's thought patterns, attitudes, beliefs, observational capacity, and emotional responses to test stimuli that are ambiguous and unstructured. The TAT pictures consist of scenes that portray human figures in a variety of activities and situations. The subject is asked to tell the examiner a story about each card to include the following elements: the event shown in the picture; what has led up to it; what the characters in the picture are feeling and thinking; and the outcome of the event. The TAT has been administered to individuals in a variety of settings such as clinical assessment, personnel screening, and research in personality. It has been shown to be an effective means of eliciting information about a person's view of the others and his or her attitudes toward the self and expectations of relationships with peers, parents, or other authority figures.

In addition to the development of these specific projective measures to assess personality characteristics, the field of personality assessment was advanced substantially by theoretical views of personality developed during this period. Several psychologists made substantial contributions to theoretical perspectives in personality assessment during the early twentieth century. The theoretical views as to the focus of personality research, that is, nomothetic versus idiographic perspectives, can also be traced back to early twentieth-century research, when studies of traits and temperament were beginning to emerge in sufficient numbers to warrant their being reviewed by Thurstone in 1916 and Allport and Allport in 1921. For example, Allport (1937) pointed out that the movement to define the "psychology of personality" gained considerable momentum after 1920 and prompted extensive but conflicting theories and inconsistent research. Allport can be credited with bringing the issue into sharper focus by clarifying the roughly 50 definitions or descriptions of personality and providing a model for personality assessment. Shortly after Allport's classic work on personality was released, Henry Murray (1938) published another classic work *Explorations in Personality*, in which he emphasized the use of case studies that described the unique integration of various characteristics within individuals. Both Murray and Allport distinguished between idiographic and nomothetic approaches to the study of people and, in their own way, each argued for an integration of the two. They advocated an approach that would not simply judge a person against others but would contrast a person's unique features with those found in others. Allport and Murray stimulated thinking about the objectives of the psychological study of people and, in effect,

created a challenge for those interested in testing or assessment. The idea of assessing personality and psychopathology began to be of greater interest to psychologists, although they often used the two terms interchangeably. And, early on, most attempts to use tests to understand people actually did not include much personality testing, focusing instead on issues of intelligence, aptitude, achievement, and vocational interests.

The MMPI

One of the most significant achievements in personality assessment occurred with the development of the Minnesota Multiphasic Personality Inventory (MMPI) in the late 1930s. The research underlying the MMPI was initiated by Hathaway and McKinley, who were critical of the way in which personality inventories had been developed up to that time using rational scale development strategies, that is, by simply guessing as to what items would measure the variable in question. They approached the task with an empirically based method. Initially, they developed a large set of items without determining in advance which items were measuring the clinical problem areas they were interested in studying. They next defined a set of clinical problem areas such as depression, somatization, and schizophrenia by grouping together homogeneous problem cases. They then constructed their scales by determining which items actually empirically differentiated the specific clinical group (such as depressed patients) from a known sample of non-patients or "normals." The first article on the MMPI was published in 1940 introducing a novel approach to clinical personality assessment (Hathaway & McKinley, 1940). The test was published in 1943 by the University of Minnesota. In the 1940s and 1950s, numerous applications of the test were established, including medical assessment and personnel selection, as it became the most widely used personality instrument in psychology with well over 19,000 articles and books published on the MMPI and its successors MMPI-2 and MMPI-A. The MMPI went through a major revision during the 1980s. The first public discussion of the need for an MMPI revision was addressed by a panel of MMPI experts at the *Fifth MMPI Symposium on Recent Developments in the Use of the MMPI* at Minneapolis in 1969, and a book detailing the need for revising the MMPI was published in 1972 (Butcher, 1972). In 1982, the MMPI revision and data collection began after many years of discussion: The MMPI-2 Revision Committee was comprised of James Butcher, John Graham, and W. Grant Dahlstom. Auke Tellegen joined the committee a few years later at the data analysis stage. The MMPI-2 was published in 1989 and the MMPI-A (for adolescents) in 1992 (Butcher, Williams, Graham, & Ben-Porath, 1992).

Expansion of Personality Assessment During and Following World War II

The entry of the United States into World War II in 1941 brought with it an important need for psychological services in both the clinical service area and personnel selection. The military services implemented several programs in which tests like the MMPI were used in personnel selection for positions such as pilots and special services personnel (Altus, 1945; Blair, 1950; Fulkerson, Freud, & Raynor, 1958; Jennings, 1949; Melton, 1955).

Other wartime assessment efforts in the selection of special forces included those of the Office of Strategic Services or OSS, a predecessor to the present Central Intelligence Agency, which performed extensive psychological evaluations on persons who were to be assigned to secret overseas missions during the war. Henry Murray created and supervised the selection process in which over 5,000 candidates were evaluated. The psychologists involved in the program used over a hundred different psychological tests and specially designed procedures to perform the evaluations. The extensive assessment project was described, after their work was declassified when the war ended, in the OSS staff history description provided in the Office of Strategic Services Assessment Staff (1948). See also the article by Handler (2001).

Expansion of Personality Inventory Development in the Later Part of the Twentieth Century

After World War II, developments in personality assessment continued at a high rate. Most notably, shortly after the war, Cattell began working on the factor analysis of personality and published the Sixteen Personality Factors (16-PF) based upon a number of factor analyses he conducted on a large item pool of adjectives he used to construct trait names. Cattell's 16-PF included a set of 15 personality trait scales and one scale to assess intelligence which were designed to assess the full range of normal personality functioning (Cattell & Stice, 1957). This personality inventory has gained wide acceptance and use in both personnel and research applications.

In 1948, Harrison Gough, who had studied with Hathaway at Minnesota, began work on a set of personality trait scales that would assess personality characteristics in nonclinical populations. The California Psychological Inventory or CPI, published in 1956 (Gough, 1956), contained 489 items (over 200 items of which were from the original MMPI). He included an additional group of items to address personality traits that were not addressed by MMPI items. The personality scales for the CPI were grouped into four categories: (1) Poise, (2) Socialization, (3) Achievement Potential, and (4) Intelligence and Interest Modes. The CPI scales were designed to assess a broad range of personality attributes found in "normal" populations and became a standard measure for assessing personality in personnel selection and in conducting psychological research (see discussion by Megargee in Chapter 17).

In 1977, Theodore Millon developed the Millon Clinical Multiaxial Inventory (MCMI) (see Millon, 1977) to assess personality problems among clients in psychotherapy. Millon based his test development strategy upon his theory of psychopathology (a strategy that is very different from the strict empirical method followed by Hathaway and McKinley with the MMPI). Item development followed a rational strategy and his comparison samples were patients in psychotherapy rather than a "normal" population. The MCMI largely addresses Diagnostic and Statistical Manual of Mental Disorders (DSM) Axis II dimensions of personality rather than symptom disorders on AXIS I of DSM that are addressed by the MMPI.

The NEO Personality Inventory (NEO PI) was developed by Paul Costa and Robert McCrae to assess personality dimension that had been described as the "Big Five" or Five Factor Model of personality. The NEO was published in 1985 as a measure of the major personality dimensions in normal personality to assess: openness, agreeableness, neuroticism, extraversion, and conscientiousness (Costa & McCrae, 1985).

The Personality Assessment Inventory (PAI) was developed by Leslie Morey in 1991. This instrument, similar to the MMPI, was designed to address the major clinical syndromes, such as depression (Morey, 1991). The PAI contains item content and scales that are similar to the MMPI and devised to be used in the clinical assessment in a range of settings analogous to the applications of the MMPI.

Computer-Based Personality Assessment

No treatment of the history of personality assessment would be complete without mention of the beginnings of computer-based personality assessment (see discussion in Chapter 10). The automated interpretation of personality measures has revolutionized psychological testing. The first psychological test to be used in a computerized assessment program was the MMPI in 1962. A group of mental health professionals (Rome et al., 1962) at the Mayo Clinic in Rochester, Minnesota, developed the first computer interpretation program to provide personality and symptom information on all patients being evaluated at Mayo. Most personality tests today, even projective tests like the Rorschach, are interpreted by a computer. The contemporary computer interpretation option provides fast, reliable, and effective psychological results for clinical settings and for research (see discussion by Butcher, Perry, and Dean in Chapter 10).

Contemporary Approaches and Directions in Personality Assessment

The science and practice of personality assessment have expanded substantially over the past two decades both in terms of developing effective measures and in the extent of annual research on testing (Butcher, 2006; Weiner & Greene, 2008). The sheer number of research articles and journals (and that number increases by about 300 per year) devoted to personality assessment methods makes the task of keeping updated difficult in more than a few techniques. In fact, many researchers and practitioners tend to narrow their focus and rely exclusively on relatively few techniques in their assessment. Many reasons can be found for the increased rate of research publication and clinical application of personality assessment methods. First, personality assessment devices are often used as criterion measures for psychological research into abnormal behavior and psychological processes. Second, clinical assessment, the activity that accounts for the greatest use of personality tests today, appears to be becoming a more respected and engaging task for clinical practitioners today with diverse applications such as medical screening for bariatric surgery as well as traditional mental health assessment. A third reason for the increased interest in personality assessment can be seen in the broadened acceptance of psychological assessment in forensic settings. Psychological tests are more frequently requested and admitted as evidence in court today than were even a decade ago (Pope, Butcher, & Seelen, 2006). A fourth reason is that psychological assessment in industrial applications, both for conducting fitness-for-duty evaluations and

for personnel screening, has expanded greatly in recent years (Butcher, Ones, & Cullen, 2006).

The rapid growth in the field of personality assessment and broad range of techniques available guided us in developing the *Oxford Handbook of Personality and Clinical Assessment*. New areas of research have emerged in recent years requiring consideration. In developing this volume, we wanted to bring together in a single volume of personality and clinical assessment the important and diverse perspectives on personality assessment to illustrate the broad range of views and methods of study that are prominent in the field today. The task of developing this comprehensive handbook in personality and clinical assessment was made somewhat easier by beginning with a substantial core of topic areas and contributors from an earlier work. We began this volume with a number of contributors/chapters that have been at the core of the Oxford University Press's *Handbook of Clinical Assessment* published in 1995 and revised in 2002. Several of these chapters have been expanded and updated and serve as a valuable core to the present handbook. In addition, a number of additional topic areas were included in order to make this volume more comprehensive and focused on the contemporary assessment scene. In choosing additional contributors for this expanded handbook, we considered it important to provide comprehensive chapters dealing with crucial issues in the field and to focus on general theoretical perspectives as well as specific assessment techniques. We wanted to illustrate a number of varied and more recent personality assessment approaches. And finally, as is evident throughout this volume, we considered it important to try to maintain a pragmatic focus to the field of personality assessment with practical case examples and to pay attention to issues of diversity with chapters that address diverse populations. Contributors of chapters with an applied focus have been encouraged to present their ideas within a practical framework and provide case examples to illustrate the assessment process.

Human personality is infinitely varied and highly complex. The need to gain a thorough understanding of personality has prompted psychologists to approach the task of assessment through highly diverging avenues. Personality theorists have viewed personality from very different angles and have assayed different "chunks" of what we know as personality in their efforts to understand these complex human characteristics. Differing theories of personality and varying conceptions of how personality is structured have led to rather different assumptions about what data are important in understanding personality. For example, psychodynamic theorists have viewed personality as a complex and intricate system of drives and forces that cannot be understood without extensive personal historical information. The means of understanding the connections between personal history and personality can come from many sources, such as through the individual's response to intentionally ambiguous stimulus material such as the Rorschach inkblots or their response to a highly structured sentence acknowledging a clinical symptom. Other perspectives in personality have been oriented more toward "surface" behaviors. For example, a learning- or behavioral-based viewpoint may not involve such historic assumptions as the psychodynamic view but may rely more on overt, observable behaviors. Most researchers and practitioners are familiar with the "standard" sources of personality information that have been developed to appraise personality today—personality inventories, projective methods, and the clinical interview.

Goals of the Handbook

Our goal in this volume is to provide a broad-based and comprehensive view of the field of personality assessment from its historical roots to the major sources of theoretical stimuli, and the methodological issues defining the field that have led to numerous approaches and applications. This volume will serve as an introductory textbook in psychological assessment for graduate students in clinical and counseling psychology as well as a comprehensive "refresher course" for active professionals in the field. At the offset, we provide an introduction to the major sources of personality-based thought—both genetic and cultural sources of information. We next turn to presenting a framework for personality assessment and examine the methodological and conceptual factors and the psychometric considerations defining the field. We have included a number of chapters that address broad methodological issues and strategies for developing personality assessment appproaches. We also include several chapters that examine the meanings of personality assessment results. In addition, we include a number of topics that deal with issues that can impact findings or require particular attention in understanding to find meaningful results. We have tried to incorporate a broad range of personality assessment procedures and instruments to give the reader a picture of the depth of personality assessment field today. We also address factors related to a number of specific populations

that require special attention in conducting personality assessments. We examine traditional clinical personality assessment approaches and include new and expanding avenues of assessment such as behavior genetics, and functional magnetic resonance imagery (fMRI). Finally, we examine several problem areas in clinical personality assessment that require special attention because they present problems or issues that are somewhat different from mental health settings where much of the interpretive lore for clinical personality tests has evolved.

Psychological assessments are undertaken in many different settings and for many different purposes. The same psychological tests might be employed to evaluate clients in forensic settings, for example, to assist the court in determining custody of minor children in family disputes as in mental health settings to determine the nature and extent of psychological problems in pretreatment planning.

In this book, contributions were invited to provide the reader with illustrations of a number of different applications. Authors and topics were selected both to cover as many problem areas as practical. Space limitations, of course, prevent a full exploration of all the areas that might touch on assessment. It is hoped that the topics chosen will illustrate both the diversity and the effectiveness of the assessment techniques involved. In all cases, chapters were invited that would address problem-oriented assessment, and they were written by noted psychologists with substantial expertise in the assessment area in question.

Genetic and Cultural Perspectives

We begin this volume by providing two chapters that orient the readers to major sources of variance in the development of personality and important considerations for developing personality measures to assure relevance for practical assessment. A great deal of personality-based genetic research has unveiled the liklihood that many personality traits—those enduring personality characteristics—are likely to be in part inherited qualities. In Chapter 2, Susan South, Robert Krueger, and Kristian Markon focus on the genetic factors pertinent to understanding and assessing personality in the light of extensive behavior genetics research today. South, Krueger, and Markon provide a background in behavioral genetics and detail the important influences on personality assessment emanating from this rapidly growing research domain. Their chapter "Behavior genetic perspectives on clinical personality assessment" discusses how twin studies work to provide information on the genetics of personality and summarize the contributions to date for understanding personality. They describe current models for analyzing twin data and give a perspective on fruitful current directions in twin research and the implications of behavior genetics for assessment and classification theory.

However, genetic inheritance is not the whole story in personality development. The culture and family in which a person develops plays a crucial role in personality formulation, The perspective provided by Fanny Cheung addresses this second important source of variance in understanding personality and developing effective personality measures that is referred to as the cultural perspective in personality assessment. In Chapter 3, Professor Cheung points out that everyone grows up in a unique family and social environment that influences the ways they behave and view the world. She provides a rationale for understanding the well-established social and cultural forces that can form personality functioning along highly different lines. She describes the cultural factors that can impact the process of psychological assessment that need to be taken into consideration in developing or adapting psychological assessment procedures across different social or cultural boundaries. She describes the steps necessary in adapting a personality measure that crosses cultural borders. Describing, for example, adapting personality scales such as the MMPI-2 in China, she provides a perspective on the development of a personality measure specifically for Chinese populations in an effort to reduce the impact of cultural variables in personality.

Methodological and Conceptual Factors and Psychometric Considerations

Personality test results do not always mean what we think they mean at first glance. Under some conditions, test scores may not impart the information that we expect. For example, a given score on a particular scale might not reflect the same level of the measured characteristic in two different samples because the base rates for the characteristic in the two groups are different. Or, the scale might not assess the attributes in question because the test is vulnerable to measurement distortion because individuals in the particular setting may tend to dissimulate: claim extreme problems when they do not have them or deny problems when they do. Several contributors were invited to address the important question of what test scores mean or what test interpretation reflects. We initially focus attention on

discussion of a number of methodological issues and perspectives in the development of personality assessment measures. Professors Fritz Drasgow, Oleksandr Chernyshenko, and Stephen Stark have made substantial contributions to our understanding of modern test theory and applications. In Chapter 4, they provide a solid perspective on test theory and contemporary personality testing. They address a number of important related topics including a discussion of classical test theory and its pertinence for contemporary personality assessment and describe how personality constructs can be translated into measurable personality scales as well as the strategies for developing personality assessment measures (criterion-related or empirical validation, mean difference approach, factor analysis, and item response theory). They also illustrate how these methods perform in scale development. Their chapter provides an insightful perspective on test construction and test evaluation strategies in psychological assessment today. In the subsequent chapter, Chapter 5, Gregory Smith and Tamika Zapolski provide a viewpoint on the importance of demonstrating construct validity for measures of personality. In the past, Dr. Smith has contributed substantially to a contemporary understanding of this important area of thought and has generated a revival of thinking about the importance of construct validity in personality assessment. In this chapter, he and Zapolski provide an extensive description and analysis of construct validity by examining the historical basis and theoretical facets of the concept and the relationships between construct validity and other identified approaches (e.g., content validity). They detail how the construct validity model operates and provides clear illustrations of how this important validational effort can be approached and describes how researchers can incorporate material on the various means of assuring construct validity.

Having agreed upon standards by which personality test procedures can be developed and evaluated is important to a scientific field in order to assure high quality of measurement. The chapter by Kurt Geisinger and Janet Carlson (Chapter 6) addresses the importance of standards and norms in interpreting psychological test scores. This chapter describes the importance of maintaining instrument integrity in a sound research context and describes issues that can occur when traditional and well-established standards are set aside or ignored in favor of other goals. Geisinger and Carlson provide an important perspective on standards and standardization in personality measurement development.

They discuss test standardization issues and focus upon the importance of test administration factors in assessment. The authors also highlight the importance of considering differences that can emerge and accomodations that might be required in the testing of minority clients and those with disabilities. Over time, psychological assessment procedures that have been established as standards in the field for measuring aspects of personality begin to show their age or become targeted for some reason for change. After a personality inventory has become a widely used one over a number of years, its limitations may begin to be recognized and efforts to modify or surpass the existing scales with new or modified measures emerge. Are there important factors that need to be considered if standard measurement instruments or tests become altered? In Chapter 7, entitled "Changing or replacing an established standard: Issues, goals, and problem," Michelle Ranson, David Nichols, Steven Rouse, and Jennifer Harrington address these factors and discuss the issues involved in developing test revisions or modifications of instruments that have become widely used standards. They consider several factors: ethical standards, when should a measure be revised, goals for the revised measure, pragmatic concerns for widely used procedures, challenges for self-report inventories, challenges for free-response measures. They also provide a case study, viz. the MMPI by describing the MMPI-2 restandardization project and some recent changes being developed for the instrument to highlight the importance of assuring continuity to the applied psychological assessment base.

An important issue in personality assessment and prediction of behavior involves the accuracy of the assessment procedure. It is important for practitioners to consider the relative frequency of phenomena (base rates) in particular settings in order to interpret psychological test scores appropriately. One factor that influences the power of an instrument to predict behavior is the base rate of the occurrence of the phenomenon in the population. Stephen Finn, in Chapter 8, "Incorporating base rate information in daily clinical decision making," addresses this important issue. Base rates are defined for specified populations and are restricted to them. Thus, a base rate is the a priori chance or prior odds that a member of a specified population will have a certain characteristic, if we know nothing else about this person other than that he or she is a member of the population we are examining. Base rates have important implications for a wide variety of issues in clinical practice. Although rarely acknowledged, base rates affect the prediction of

behaviors (e.g., suicide), the interpretation of test data (e.g., MMPI-2 scores), and the making of diagnostic decisions.

Predicting phenomena with low base rates is difficult. In general, it is easier to increase predictive accuracy when the events to be predicted are moderately likely to occur (i.e., occur with a probability close to 50%) than when the events are unlikely to occur. Much improvement in clinical decision making can be accomplished if each of us remembered to think about base rates every time we made a clinical hypothesis. The chapter by Finn provides clear strategies for incorporating base rate information in the prediction process.

Personality assessment has been substantially advanced by theoretical conceptualization of the variables that comprise personality. The view that personality is comprised of definable factors such as personality traits (see the classical work of Allport) has made developing personality-based measures an easier task. Allan Harkness in Chapter 9, "Theory and measurement of personality traits," provides a contemporary perspective on the importance of traits in personality assessment. Harkness discusses individual differences in traits and describes the "traits versus states" debate in the search for explanatory concepts in personality assessment. He examines factors that create, develop, and maintain traits and he explores the causal source of personality variance. As an illustration, he describes the development of the MMPI-2 PSY-5 Scales and illustrates their use for assessing personality dimensions.

Computer-based test interpretation of psychological tests has a long history dating back to 1962 when psychologists at the Mayo Clinical developed the first MMPI interpretation program. In contemporary assessment psychology today, many instruments provide computer-derived reports. The extent of this medium of interpretation will be explored in Chapter 10, "Computer-based interpretation of personality scales," by James Butcher, Julia Perry, and Brooke Dean. The authors describe the issues involved in providing computer-based personality tests and discuss the professional guidelines for offering computer testing services presented. Research on the adequacy of widely used computer testing resources will be summarized.

Personality Assessment Procedures and Instruments

We next turn to an exploration of a number of personality assessment procedures and instruments that are widely used in contemporary personality assessment. We begin with a discussion of behavioral observation by Martin Leichtman in Chapter 11 who introduces the reader to topics such as the rationale and nature of the behavioral observation process and important facets for developing the standardized interview. He provides an insightful perspective on understanding behavioral observations and the personality inference process and means of incorporating descriptions from different sources of data. Throughout the process he underscores the value of subjectivity in the integration of "behavioral observations" in psychological reports and to maintaining the consumer rights and the importance of developing "humane" psychological reports. The clinical interview is the oldest and most widely used assessment procedure for obtaining assessment information in use today. The contribution by Robert Craig, in Chapter 12, provides an important overview of the use of this assessment strategy describing both the values and limitations of this approach. The widespread use and demonstrated effectiveness of behavioral therapy in contemporary clinical psychology is prefaced upon having a clear assessment of the problems in question. Sound behavioral assessment is a key ingredient to therapeutic success. Stephen Haynes, Dawn Yoshioka, Karen Kloezeman, and Iruma Bello in Chapter 13 provide an excellent introduction and exploration of behavioral assessment strategies in clinical assessment.

One of the oldest and still most widely used personality assessment instrument around the world today is the MMPI (MMPI-2 and MMPI-A). Chapter 14, by Andrew Cox, Nathan Weed, and James Butcher, addresses the history, interpretation, and clinical issues to provide an introductory overview of the use of the MMPI-2 in clinical assessment. The chapter includes exhibits illustrating historical developments and summarizing MMPI-2 measures and contain, up-to-date references and resources for readers interested in a more thorough treatment. The traditional MMPI-2 clinical, content, and supplemental scales are described and strategies for interpretation are provided. Some newer measures, such as the PSY-5 and Restructured Clinical scales, are also described. Clinical issues in the use of the MMPI-2 such as using the MMPI-2 with minority populations and international settings are described. In addition, some procedures that have produced less effective results, such as MMPI short forms, are noted.

No handbook on personality assessment would be complete without a section describing the utility of the Rorschach Inkblot Test. Weiner and Meyer provide a contemporary perspective on a major approach in clinical assessment that has a tradition dating to the early twentieth century (see Weiner & Greene, 2008)—the projective method. This chapter (Chapter 15), "Personality assessment with the Rorschach," is contributed by two of the most prominent Rorschach experts in the psychological assessment field—Irving Weiner and Gregory Meyer. This approach holds the view that clients disclose intimate and powerful descriptions of themselves through their interpretations of ambiguous stimuli, inkblots. The use of the Rorschach in personality assessment has had a strong following in both research and clinical application; the Rorschach method is one of the most widely researched and applied assessment strategies (Butcher & Rouse, 1996) and has been one of the most intriguing and widely researched personality assessment procedures in the field since the early twentieth century. The authors deal with important topics: "Is Rorschach assessment psychometrically sound?," "Does Rorschach assessment serve useful purposes?," "Is Rorschach assessment being widely taught, studied, and practiced?," "Can Rorschach assessment be applied cross-culturally?"

Two instruments that were designed to address personality characteristics in a broad range of normal populations are the NEO PI and the CPI. The view that personality can be summarized as five major dimensions or traits has been widely explored in contemporary personality assessment. Paul Costa and Robert McCrae, in Chapter 16, provide an introduction, theoretical basis, and interpretive strategies for the most widely used five-factor model instrument—the NEO PI. One of the most widely used measures in personality assessment is the CPI published by Harrison Gough (1956). This instrument is described in Chapter 17 by Edwin Megargee who had studied with Gough and later wrote a widely used textbook on the test. Megargee shares his updated perspective on the CPI in contemporary psychology and provides some key interpretive strategies for the measure.

One of the most difficult and evolving areas in the personality assessment field involves assessing personality disorders. Thomas Widiger and Sara Boyd, in Chapter 18, bring this important research and clinical area into clear focus by both presenting a theoretical perspective on the diagnosis of personality disorder and surveying the assessment instruments that make this task easier. They describe semistructured interviews based upon DSM-IV Personality Disorder Interviews as well as surveying a number of self-report inventories such as the PAI, MCMI-III, MMPI-2, and Hare Checklist. They provide a solid perspective on the issues to that need to be considered in the assessment of personality disorders including gender, culture, and ethnicity.

New psychophysiologic approaches to personality have emerged in recent years to assess personality factors or problems. Research on magnetic brain imaging has been increasing at a very rapid pace over the past 10 years. There have been numerous studies published on using fMRI to explore and identify brain processes underlying mental disorders, such as schizophrenia, and to improve the evaluation of these conditions. We have included in this handbook a chapter that addresses the emerging fMRI assessment field, entitled "Functional imaging in clinical assessment? The rise of neurodiagnostic imaging with the fMRI" (Chapter 19), by Professors Angus MacDonald, III, and Jessica Hurdelbrink. The chapter includes a description of the use of fMRI in assessing psychiatric disorders and provides an up-to-date survey of the important findings in the area. A great deal of research effort is being devoted to the psychobiology of abnormal behavior today. MacDonald and Hurdelbrink address a new, but rapidly expanding, area of assessment research and its potential in providing unique information in understanding clinical problems.

Specific Populations

By its very nature the field of personality assessment is concerned with individual differences and is enveloped in human diversity. To understand the behavior and personality of individuals, it is imperative that many "status" variables be given careful consideration. Background factors such as age, gender, and ethnicity are important, since personality is in many respects influenced by the environment or groups to which a person belongs. People may share certain characteristics of groups with which they are affiliated. In the assessment of individuals it is important to consider influences that may come from belonging to a group that has been treated differently by our social institutions than others have. Being a member of an ethnic minority group in the United States places a person at considerable risk for discrimination and diminished opportunity. Those who are cast in less dominant societal roles by fact of birth may be at risk for developing problems or adjustment difficulties that are not shared by the majority classes. To fully explore the potential problems associated with

being a minority group member in contemporary society, several contributors were asked to provide different perspectives on issues involved in the psychological assessment of minority clients. We begin our discussion in Chapter 20 with an article entitled "Clinical personality assessment with Asian Americans." Sumie Okazaki, Mimi Okazaki, and Stanley Sue contribute an informative discussion of possible factors involved in the assessment of ethnic Asian minorities that need to be considered in cross-ethnic psychological evaluations. Their work with Asian-American clients has made a substantial contribution to clinical as well as to cross-cultural psychology. In this article they provide information on the demographics of the population and a description of the recent literature on research with Asian-American populations. They describe the problem of the imposed-etic perspective in studies involving Asian-American populations. They also describe studies with overseas Asian populations and provide a critique of imposed-etic studies and provide a discussion of the alternate approach—the indigenous or emic perspective. They conclude with a framework and guidelines for conducting assessments with Asian-Americans. Professor Bernadette Gray-Little, in her chapter entitled "The assessment of psychopathology in racial and ethnic minorities" (Chapter 21), addresses factors to consider in conducting psychological evaluations on African-American clients. She describes the factors that are important in the clinical interview pertinent to understanding bias and social distance that can impact an evaluation. She examines racial and ethnic variations that can occur in symptoms of distress and addresses potential factors to consider in employing psychological tests such as the MMPI-2, the MCMI, the Rorschach Inkblot Test, the TAT, and other projective instruments.

This handbook also addresses several populations requiring the assessment psychologist to consider population-specific factors in dealing effectively with potential differences in personality assessment. Women may experience situations or activities differently because of the roles in which they may have been cast and in their lack of access to equal opportunities in society. In Chapter 22, "Issues in clinical assessment with women," Judith Worell and Damon Robinson provide valuable insights into understanding specific factors in assessment of women. They include factors related to the purposes of the assessment that is being undertaken and deals with issues related to possible gender bias in the measurement, for example, factors such as sex of clinician, psychiatric diagnosis with women, specific diagnosis and criteria, and clinical decisions. They provide a framework on contextual assessment for women and importance of screening for sexual and physical abuse. They also describe some barriers to screening as well as the need for assessing strength and well-being.

There are other important individual difference variables that require careful consideration in personality evaluation. The chapter entitled "Use of the MMPI-2 in Neuropsychological Evaluations" (Chapter 23) by Dr Carlton Gass provides information that will assist psychologists and neuropsychologists in their work with individuals who have known, suspected, or questionable brain damage. Gass describes the distinctive aspects of the MMPI-2 in neuropsychological settings and how this instrument can contribute to significant understanding of behavior and symptoms presented by neuropsychological patients. He describes special interpretive issues in neuropsychological settings including issues in diagnosing brain dysfunction, localizing brain lesions, and diagnosing neuropsychological deficits while controlling for neurological symptom reporting. He provides insights into procedures for incorporating MMPI-2 results in neuropsychological reports and factors to attend to in addressing the referral question.

Factors occurring in another subgroup of the population—couples undergoing emotional distress—require special considerations. In Chapter 24, Professors Douglas Snyder, Richard Heyman, and Stephen N. Haynes bring the pertinent issues related to marital problems into focus in their chapter entitled "Assessing couples." They begin with a discussion of important issues involved in conceptualizing couple relationship distress and explore the paramaters of couple distress. Next they focus upon the prevalence and comorbid conditions in couple distress and examine the etiological considerations and describe the implications for assessment. The authors devote a substantial portion of their discussion to assessment for issues involved in case conceptualization and treatment planning from a behavioral perspective. They also include appropriate considerations of cultural differences in couple distress. Finally they discuss effective assessment strategies and specific techniques for evaluating couple distress and the importance of monitoring progress in therapy and evaluating treatment outcome. In Chapter 25, Edward Cumella and Jennifer Lafferty provide an overview of adolescent assessment based upon the most widely used adolescent test, the MMPI-A. This chapter, "Assessing adolescents with the MMPI-A" provides an overview of special issues in the clinical assessment of adolescents and a historical introduction of the use of the MMPI in assessment of adolescents, and discusses the revision of the original instrument and publication of the MMPI for adolescents, the MMPI-A. The chapter focuses upon the use of the MMPI-A for assessing adolescents. A case example of an adolescent client will be provided and the MMPI-A performance highlighted. The use of the MMPI-A in providing test feedback to adolescents is described.

Specific Settings and Problems

In this section, we examine psychological assessment in a number of problem areas and explore their operation in different settings. In Chapter 26, Ronald Stolberg and Bruce Bongar discuss the problems and issues involved in assessment of suicide risk—an important and sometimes urgent task for a practitioner to address. They describe the recent empirical evidence on risk assessment practices and explore how risk factors are assessed through a number of psychological tests such as the Rorschach Inkblot Technique, the MMPI-2, the 16-PF, the MCMI, the MCMI-II, the TAT, the Bender Gestalt, the Beck Depression Inventory (BDI), and the Beck Hopelessness Scale (BHS). They discuss issues involved in the assessment of suicidal ideation, intent, and behavior and describe in depth assessing suicide through structured interviews and a psychological battery and discuss the limitations of theoretical orientation and DSM-IV and diagnostic formulation.

One of the most frequent psychological adjustment problems in society today involves the use and misuse of alcohol and drugs. In many instances, persons who are being seen in mental health or medical settings for problems other than substance abuse also have a hidden problem with addictive substances. Consequently, psychologists frequently find themselves involved in the determination of potential substance abuse in addition to whatever other problems clients are reporting. Because of the importance of substance abuse assessment problems in many settings, Joseph Banken and Roger Greene (Chapter 27) in "Use of self-report measures in assessing alcohol and drug abuse" address objective assessment strategies for detecting and appraising alcohol and drug problems. Banken and Greene describe the overall considerations important to conducting an effective substance abuse evaluation and the process of screening for substance abuse. They discuss several traditional personality scales that have been widely used to identify alcohol or drug problems such as the MacAndrew Alcoholism Scale (MAC-R) and the Addiction Admission and Addiction Potential Scales (MMPI-2), scales b and t on the MCMI/MCMI-II. In addition, they describe additional screening scales such as the Alcohol Use Inventory (AUI). The authors also provide a discussion on the timing of psychological assessment and the role of objective psychological tests traditionally used in alcohol or drug treatment programs.

Edwin I. Megargee, in Chapter 28, entitled "Understanding and assessing aggression and violence," discusses the issues pertinent to defining and understanding these problems in society. Dr. Megargee discusses the factors leading to aggressive behavior and violence and provides an overview of contemporary methods being used to assess and predict aggressive behavior and violence. He describes the types of assessments and deals with referral questions and assessment contexts such as not guilty by reason of insanity defense, treatment planning, and needs assessments. He details useful information on assessment tools and techniques that are effective for retrospective and prospective predictions. In his chapter, he provides an overview of violent crimes—assault and murder, domestic violence, forcible rape and sexual battery, kidnapping and hostage taking, arson, bombing, and terrorism—and describes the types of violent offenders delineated in the literature. He also highlights a conceptual framework for the analysis of aggression and violence including his "algebra of aggression" for predicting violence. He describes some personal factors that decrease the likelihood of aggression and discusses situational factors influencing the likelihood of aggression. In a related chapter (Chapter 29), "Assessing antisocial and psychopathic personalities," Carl Gacono and Reid Meloy provide a comprehensive treatment on the assessment of antisocial personality disorder. They begin with a discussion of forensic assessment and issues, and then provide a thorough overview of our knowledge of the personality disorder and a discussion of the relevant research findings on the use of the Psychopathy Checklist-Revised, the Rorschach, and the MMPI-2. They also include an overview of various measures of cognition and intelligence and their relevance to understanding antisocial personality.

The next chapter in the handbook provides an example of personality assessment in a nonclinical context, personnel selection. Chapter 30, "Clinical personality assessment in the employment context," by Butcher, Gucker, and Hellervik provides an overview of the use of personality measurement techniques in employment applications. Major goals of the chapter include the following areas of emphasis. First a rationale for the inclusion of clinical personality assessment measures in personnel decisions such as employment screening, fitness for duty evaluations, and reliability screenings for making recommendations for promotion to responsible positions or for the issuance of security clearances for sensitive applications will be provided. The history of personnel assessment is highlighted. A number of contemporary issues pertaining to clinical personnel screening will be presented. Next, a historical summary of the use of the most widely used personality measure, the MMPI-2, will be presented along with a strategy for the interpreting instruments used in employment settings. The chapter will include several practical examples of clinically based assessments in employment settings. The target audience for the article is professionals who are using personality assessment measures in these industrial-organizational (I-O) settings or are considering a career as an assessment practitioner in business/industrial settings. The strategy of interpreting psychological measures in personnel selection is illustrated with a case example. The article includes descriptive information on the most widely used measure (the MMPI-2) and contains up-to-date references and resources that interested readers wishing more thorough information can follow up on.

We next turn to a guide for the care and effective documentation of psychological test results. Regardless of one's basic approach to personality assessment, careful accumulation and analysis of information are important considerations in any psychological assessment. In this regard, the discussion by Irving Weiner (Chapter 31) provides the practitioner with important background information and a clear rationale for employing meticulous safeguards in conducting personality evaluations in order to avoid potential legal or ethical problems. Weiner, who has made substantial contributions to the field of personality assessment, provides a valuable overview of the issues and guidelines for practitioners in his chapter entitled "Anticipating ethical and legal challenges in personality assessment." In this chapter, he discusses topics such as accepting a referral, selecting the test battery for conducting the psychological evaluation, how to prepare and present a report, and factors important to managing case records in an assessment practice.

No treatment of clinical assessment would be complete without a chapter on the validity of psychological tests. This volume includes an important discussion about malingering on psychological tests by David Berry and his colleagues that highlights the importance of incorporating validity scales in any personality assessment evaluation in order to assure the credibility of the assessment. In Chapter 32, entitled "Assessment of feigned psychological symptoms," Berry and his colleagues provide an up-to-date summary and overview of research related to the credibility of the client's responses in a personality assessment. They discuss important topics such as the criteria for malingering, methodological issues in the research on malingering, the problem of base rates, and issues related to coaching to appear in particular ways on psychological tests. The authors provide a substantial research literature supporting their suggested strategy for clinical practice and assessment of malingering. They describe malingering indices on multiscale inventories and provide examples of malingering assessment using instruments such as the MMPI-2, the MCMI-III, the NEO PI-R, and the PAI as well as specific malingering measures such as the Structured Inventory of Malingered Symptomatology (SIMS), the Structured Inventory of Reported Symptoms (SIRS), and the M Test.

One of the most essential clinical tasks that practitioners are asked to perform in many clinical settings is that of conducting pretreatment planning evaluations—an activity that is often given less attention than it deserves in contemporary clinical practice. In their chapter (Chapter 33), entitled "Assessment of clients in pretreatment planning," Mark Harwood and Larry Beutler explore a number of key issues concerning this major goal of psychological assessment and provide important new insights into personality assessment in pretreatment planning. Harwood and Beutler describe a problem-solving approach in pretreatment planning that is both practical and effective. In their chapter, they focus upon important considerations in treatment planning such as subjective distress and arousal. They describe the patient's predisposition, diagnostic problems, and state variables that are important to their symptomatic picture. They also highlight the need to understand the patient expectations about treatment and the impact of the particular treatment variables inherent in the setting. An important consideration for treatment success includes factors such as important relationship variables and their impact on treatment strategies. Following this, in Chapter 34, entitled "Assessment of treatment resistance via questionnaire," Julia

Perry provides further thought about assessing personality factors in treatment planning. She focuses attention upon the concept of "resistance" and examines how resistance to undertaking psychological treatment can be assessed by objective personality measures. She describes the utility of the MMPI-2 and the Butcher Treatment Planning Inventory (BTPI).

Raymond Ownby in Chapter 35, devoted to writing clinical reports, involves the importance of viewing, summarizing, and communicating the conclusions about a patient's problem areas and personality functioning. The chapter addresses the important area of client description and developing case material in clinical reports. Issues pertinent to the practitioner's responsibility in presenting patient material are addressed and safeguards for protecting clients are described. The chapter addresses the important features of a client's interview, behavior, history, and psychological test data to be included in a forensic assessment report. He describes and provides an outline for the most pertinent case features to be included in a report and provides a case example and keys to important resources and guidelines for practitioners to follow in developing forensic reports. The related Chapter 36, "How to use computer-based reports" by James Butcher, discusses how the task of report writing and communicating personality test information can be enhanced by use of computer technology. Many practitioners use one or more computer-derived personality test interpretation programs in developing their personality assessment study of clients (see Atlis, Hahn, and Butcher (2006) for an extensive introduction to computer-based assessments). In this chapter, the clinical use of computerized exports is illustrated and cautions concerning their use provided. The value of using computer-based psychological test interpretations in developing clinical conclusions is addressed. The types of computer scorings and interpretation services are described. Several new approaches to computer-based testing are described, including computer adaptive results and Internet-based test applications. The clinical use of a computerized MMPI-2 report is illustrated and the task of providing test feedback to clients is described.

When an editor invites authors to contribute chapters to a compendium such as this, it is somewhat analogous to working a complex puzzle. Each of the component parts must mesh together to form an integrated picture. At the beginning of this project the contributions appearing here were sought to fill an important niche in the overall plan. The vastness of the field of personality assessment today does not permit all noted authorities and all perspectives to be equally represented. Some selectivity was required given the limitations of space. The reader will, of course, be the final judge as to how the many parts blend into an integral picture. As for me, I believe that the final pieces matched the initial plan quite well. A primary goal of this volume was to provide a practical and comprehensive overview of the field of personality assessment. I believe that the contributions included here provide the reader with a substantial compendium of assessment resources with diverse and interesting elements. I hope that clinicians and clinicians-in-training who are new to the field of personality assessment will be tantalized by the views and strategies presented here and will travel these paths further when this book is set aside.

Perpetuation of valuable scholarly resources for a scientific discipline is an important goal of this volume to help maintain valuable standards while at the same time incorporating new developments in the field. Following the general plan of the Oxford Handbook Series, this volume ends with a chapter, "Personality assessment: Overview and future directions" (Chapter 37), by the volume editor. An overview of the status of personality assessment as described in the contributions to this handbook will be provided and the significant contributions to future development will be summarized. Some lingering challenges to the field of personality assessment will be highlighted. Discussion is provided to highlight significant assessment trends and projections about new directions for research.

Index of Assessment Procedures

A great variety of personality assessment instruments and procedures are discussed in this volume. Because it is unlikely that readers are familiar with all of them, contributors were asked to provide a brief description of the tests they discuss in their chapter. These assessment procedures have been summarized and are described in an appendix.

References

Allport, G. W. (1937). *Personality: A psychological interpretation.* New York: Holt, Rinehart & Winston.

Allport, F. H., & Allport, G. W. (1921). Personality traits: Their classification and measurement. *The Journal of Abnormal Psychology and Social Psychology, 16,* 6–40.

Altus, W. D. (1945). The adjustment of army illiterates. *Psychological Bulletin, 42,* 461–476.

Atlis, M. M., Hahn, J., & Butcher, J. N. (2006). Computer-based assessment with the MMPI-2. In J. N. Butcher (Ed.), *MMPI-2: The practioner's handbook* (pp. 445–476). Washington, DC: American Psychological Association.

Beck, S. J. (1938). Personality structure in schizophrenia: A Rorschach investigation in 81 patients and 64 controls. *Nervous and Mental Disorders Monograph Series, 63,* ix–88.

Ben-Porath, Y. S., & Butcher, J. N. (1991). The historical development of personality assessment. In C. E. Walker (Ed.), *Clinical psychology: Historical and research roots* (pp. 121–156). New York: Plenum Publishing Corporation.

Bernreuter, R. G. (1931). *The personality inventory.* Palo Alto, CA: Consulting Psychologists Press.

Bernreuter, R. G. (1933). The theory and construction of the personality inventory. *Journal of Social Psychology, 4,* 387–405.

Blair, W. R. N. (1950). A comparative study of disciplinary offenders and non-offenders in the Canadian Army, 1948. *Canadian Journal of Psychology, 4,* 49–62.

Boring, E. G. (1950). *A history of experimental psychology* (2nd ed.). New York: Appleton-Century-Crofts.

Buss, D. M. (1984). Toward a psychology of person–environment (PE) correlation: The role of spouse selection. *Journal of Personality and Social Psychology, 47,* 361–377.

Butcher, J. N. (Ed.). (1972). *Objective personality assessment: Changing perspectives.* New York: Academic Press.

Butcher, J. N. (2006). Assessment in clinical psychology: A perspective on the past, present challenges, and future prospects. *Clinical Psychology: Research and Practice, 13*(3), 205–209.

Butcher, J. N., Dahlstrom, W. G., Graham, J. R., Tellegen, A. M., & Kaemmer, B. (1989). *Minnesota Multiphasic Personality Inventory-2 (MMPI-2): Manual for administration and scoring.* Minneapolis, MN: University of Minnesota Press.

Butcher, J. N., Ones, D. S., & Cullen, M. (2006). Personnel screening with the MMPI-2. In J. N. Butcher (Ed.), *MMPI-2: The practioner's handbook* (pp. 381–406). Washington, DC: American Psychological Association.

Butcher, J. N., & Rouse, S. V. (1996). Personality: Individual differences and clinical assessment. *Annual Review of Psychology, 47,* 87–111.

Butcher, J. N., Williams, C. L., Graham, J. R., Archer, R., Tellegen, A., Ben-Porath, Y. S., et al. (1992). *MMPI-A manual for administration, scoring, and interpretation.* Minneapolis, MN: University of Minnesota Press.

Butcher, J. N., Williams, C. L., Graham, J. R., Tellegen, A., Ben-Porath, Y. S., Archer, R. P., et al. (1992). *Manual for administration, scoring, and interpretation of the Minnesota Multiphasic Personality Inventory for Adolescents: MMPI-A.* Minneapolis, MN: University of Minnesota Press.

Cattell, R. B., & Stice, G. E. (1957). *The sixteen personality factors questionnaire.* Champaign, IL: Institute for Personality and Ability Testing.

Costa, P. T., Jr., & McCrae, R. E. (1985). *The NEO Personality Inventory manual.* Odessa, FL: Psychological Assessment Services.

DuBois, P. L. (1970). *A history of psychological testing.* Boston: Allyn & Bacon.

Exner, J. E., Jr. (1983). *The Exner report for the Rorschach Comprehensive System.* Minneapolis, MN: National Computer Systems.

Frank, L. K. (1939). Projective methods for the study of personality. *Journal of Psychology, 8,* 543–557.

Fulkerson, S. C., Freud, S. L., & Raynor, G. H. (1958). The use of the MMPI in the psychological evaluation of pilots. *Journal of Aviation Medicine, 29,* 122–129.

Galton, F. (1879). Psychometric experiments. *Brain, 2*, 179–185.

Galton, F. (1884). Measurement of character. *Fortnightly Review, 42*, 179–185.

Gough, H. G. (1956). *California Psychological Inventory*. Palo Alto, CA: Consulting Psychologists Press.

Handler, L. (2001). Assessment of men: Personality assessment goes to war by the Office of Strategic Services assessment staff. *Journal of Personality Assessment, 76*, 558–578.

Hathaway, S. R. (1965). Personality inventories. In B. B. Wolman (Ed.). *Handbook of clinical psychology* (pp. 451–476). New York: McGraw-Hill.

Hathaway, S. R., & McKinley, J. C. (1940). A multiphasic personality schedule (Minnesota): I. Construction of the schedule. *Journal of Psychology, 10*, 249–254.

Hertz, M. R. (1938). Scoring the Rorschach test with specific reference to "normal detail" category. *American Journal of Orthopsychiatry, 8*, 100–121.

Heymans, G., & Wiersma, E. (1906). Beitrage zur spezillen psychologie auf grund einer massenunterschung. *Zeitschrift Fur Psychologie, 43*, 81–127.

Jennings, L. S. (1949). Minnesota Multiphasic Personality Inventory: Differentiation of psychologically good and poor combat risks among flying personnel. *Journal of Aviation Medicine, 19*, 222–226.

Klopfer, B., & Tallman, G. (1938). A further Rorschach study of Mr. A. *Rorschach Research Exchange, 3*, 31–36.

Melton, R. S. (1955). Studies in the evaluation of the personality characteristics of successful naval aviators. *Journal of Aviation Medicine, 25*, 600–604.

Millon, T. (1977) *Millon Clinical Multiaxial Personality Inventory (MCMI)*. Minneapolis, MN: National Computer Systems.

Morey, L. C. (1991). *The Personality Assessment Inventory: Professional manual*. Odessa, FL: Psychological Assessment Resources.

Murray, H. A. (1938). *Explorations in personality*. New York: Oxford University Press.

Murray, H. A. (1943). *Manual for the Thematic Appreciation Test*. Cambridge, MA: Harvard University Press.

Office of Strategic Services Assessment Staff (1948). *Assessment of men*. New York: Rinehart.

Pope, K., Butcher. J., & Seelen, J. (2006). *The MMPI/MMPI-2/ MMPI-A in court: Assessment, testimony, and cross-examination for expert witnesses and attorneys* (3rd ed.). Washington, DC: American Psychological Association.

Rome, H. P., Swenson, W. M., Mataya, P., McCarthy, C. E., Pearson, J. S., Keating, F. R., et al. (1962). Symposium on automation techniques in personality assessment. *Proceedings of the Staff Meeting of the Mayo Clinic, 37*, 61–82.

Rorschach, H. (1921). *Psychodiagnostik*. Bern: Hans Huber.

Thurstone, L. O. (1916). Character and temperament. *Psychological Bulletin, 13*, 384–388.

Weiner, I. B., & Greene, R. L. (2008). Handbook of personality assessment. New York: Wiley.

Whipple, G. M. (1910). Manual of mental and physical tests. Baltimore, MD: Warwick & York.

Woodworth, R. S. (1919). Examination of emotional fitness for war. *Psychological Bulletin, 15*, 59–60.

Woodworth, R. S. (1920). *Personal data sheet*. Chicago: Stoelting.

Woodworth, R. S., & Matthews, E. (1924). *Personal data sheet (children and adolescent)*. Chicago: Stoelting.

PART 2

Genetic and Cultural Perspectives

Behavior Genetic Perspectives on Clinical Personality Assessment

Susan C. South, Robert F. Krueger, *and* Kristian E. Markon

Abstract

This chapter discusses how the field of behavior genetics—the genetic and environmental contributions to individual differences in human behavior—can aid and inform personality assessment. These two fields of study are often quite distinct: personality assessment applies to the study of a singular individual; behavior genetics typically is used to describe population-level individual differences. However, behavior genetic methodology has been vital in helping to understand how genetic and environmental influences transact in the development of personality. Nature *and* nurture are both important contributors to variation in human personality and newer methodologies from both behavior and molecular genetics hold great promise for understanding how different etiological factors interact in the development of personality. This chapter discusses biometric models and the important contributions from decades of behavior genetic research into personality and how research using newer biometric moderation models allows for group-specific estimates of heritability and environmental influences on personality.

Keywords: development, gene–environment interaction, genetics, personality, twins

Behavior genetics has had a profound influence on current personality research and theorizing. For much of the twentieth century, most psychologists assumed that nurture was the primary cause of personality variation. This view has been tempered by an understanding that nature and nurture work together in personality development. But what are the implications of this more integrated understanding for the assessment of personality in clinical settings? How might behavior genetic research findings impact upon the clinician's understanding of the meaning of psychological test scores? What of the extraordinary advances in research on human molecular genetics? Will we soon see the day where analysis of a client's DNA contributes directly to our assessment report?

Our task in writing this chapter was to provide a perspective on these questions—a perspective on how clinical personality assessment might be influenced by genetically informative research on personality. We begin by reviewing what has been learned about

personality from classical genetically informative research designs, such as twin and adoption studies. We then discuss the emerging field of molecular genetic personality research. We conclude with a discussion of the implications of research on the genetics of personality for assessment in clinical settings.

How Do Twin Studies Work and What Have They Taught Us about Personality?

Twins provide a fascinating natural experiment in human variability. Twins come in two basic varieties, identical (or monozygotic, MZ) and fraternal (or dizygotic, DZ). Identical twins share all of their genes, whereas fraternal twins share half of their genes, on average, of the genes that vary from person to person. In a study of MZ and DZ twins reared together, it is possible to separate the variance in a phenotype (an observed difference among people, such as a personality trait) into three sources that "add up" to account for the total variance of the phenotype.

The first source of differences among persons is what most people think of when they think of twin studies: genetic variance, also known as heritability. The heritability of a trait is the proportion of variance in the trait that can be accounted for by genetic differences in a particular sample. In a study of twins reared together, a trait is judged to be heritable if the MZ twins are found to be more similar on average than the DZ twins. The second source of variation is known as the shared or common environment. This is the extent to which twins are similar to one another by virtue of having grown up in the same families. In a study of twins reared together, the importance of the shared environment is suggested if both MZ and DZ twins are similar to their co-twins, within families, but MZ twins are no more similar than DZ twins. The third source of variation is known as the unique or nonshared environment. This is the extent to which twins are different in spite of the fact that they share rearing environments and genes. In a study of twins reared together, the importance of the unique environment is indicated if MZ twins are not phenotypically identical.

One key assumption of the twin method is known as the equal trait–relevant environments assumption. Sometimes this assumption is described simply as the equal environments assumption, but we feel this terminology is somewhat less accurate, as we explain below. The assumption can be understood as follows: If MZ twins are found to be more similar than DZ twins on a phenotype, we would like to be able to infer that this is because MZ twins are more genetically similar than DZ twins. But what if MZ twins are treated more similarly, and this makes them more similar than DZ twins in terms of the phenotypes we want to study (e.g., personality)? Then our inference of a genetic effect, based on greater MZ similarity, might be flawed. Fortunately, extensive evidence supports the validity of the equal trait–relevant environments assumption (Goodman & Stevenson, 1991; Loehlin & Nichols, 1976; Scarr & Carter-Saltzman, 1979). Although MZ twins are treated more similarly in some ways (e.g., their parents might dress them similarly), and might therefore be described as having more "equal environments," these similarities are not linked to phenotypic similarity in major individual-differences domains, such as personality.

Model-Fitting Approaches in the Analysis of Twin Data

Most twin data analyses now take advantage of the speed and power of modern computers in fitting explicit statistical models to data obtained from twins. Here we can offer only a brief description of some of these powerful approaches to understanding the genetic and environmental sources of individual differences; details and extensions can be obtained by consulting Neale and Maes (in press).

Twin data models can be usefully described as "biometric" models. The models are biological because they take into account what is known about the genetic relationships among research participants. The models are metric in that they attempt to measure genetic and environmental contributions to phenotypic variance, and also in the sense that they depend fundamentally on the precise measurement of phenotypes. That is, accurate estimation of parameters such as proportions of genetic and environmental variance in a trait demands precise measurement of the trait. Although this may seem somewhat obvious, the point is sometimes underappreciated. For example, measuring a trait using a shortened scale with reduced reliability will contribute to the apparent dissimilarity of MZ twins. This dissimilarity will be "read" as nonshared environmental variance, when in fact it is error variance. This is the reason many research reports contain the caveat that the reported nonshared variance estimates confound nonshared environment and measurement error. Although it may not always be feasible to measure constructs with high reliability, the use of measures with high reliability will improve biometric inferences. In sum, biometric inferences are constrained by psychometric considerations; biometrics and psychometrics are intimately intertwined (cf. Goldsmith, Buss, & Lemery, 1997).

A univariate (one-variable) model for data obtained from MZ and DZ twins reared together is presented in Figure 2.1. Latent variables (variables whose effects are inferred from patterns in the data) are contained in circles, and manifest variables (variables that are measured directly) are contained in squares. The model also contains lines with arrows (paths), which represent relationships among variables. The model in Figure 2.1 states that the scores of twins on a specific, measured variable result from the three influences we described previously. First, twin scores are influenced by additive genetic effects, symbolized by paths leading from the latent "A" variables to the twins' phenotypes. These are genetic effects that result from the influence of multiple genes acting independently and "adding up" to influence a phenotype. MZ twins are perfectly correlated for additive genetic effects, whereas DZ twins are correlated 0.5 for additive genetic effects. In the figure, this is symbolized by the

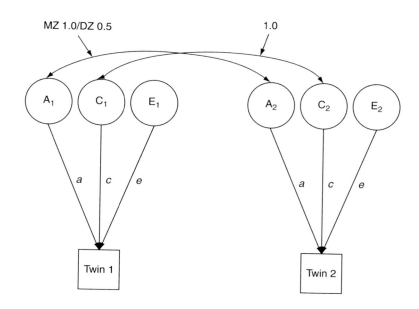

Fig. 2.1 Path model for a decomposition of variance into additive genetic (A), shared or common (C), and nonshared environmental (E) sources. Latent variables in the model (in circles) are standardized to a variance of 1.0.

curved, double-headed arrow connecting the twins' phenotypes via the latent "A" variables, set to 1.0 for MZ twins and 0.5 for DZ twins. The latent "A" variables are connected to the phenotypes by the path labeled *a*. Second, twin scores are influenced by shared environments. Because these are twins reared together, both MZ and DZ twins are perfectly correlated for shared environments (i.e., both types of twins grew up in the same families, within pairs), as reflected by the curved, double-headed arrow connecting the twins' phenotypes via the latent "C" variables, and set to 1.0 for both MZ and DZ twins. These variables are connected to the twins' scores via the path labeled *c*. Third, twin scores are influenced by nonshared environments. These effects are symbolized by the latent "E" variables, which, by definition, are not correlated across twins within pairs (note the absence of a curved, double-headed arrow connecting the twins via E). These variables are connected to the twins scores via the path labeled *e*.

The process of fitting the model in Figure 2.1 to twin data involves using a computer to search for the most likely values of *a*, *c*, and *e*, given the observed data. In the case of Figure 2.1, the data would be the scores of both halves of twin pairs (twins 1 and 2) within two different twin groups (MZ and DZ) on a single trait. This gives us two variables (twin 1 scores and twin 2 scores) within two groups (MZ and DZ), allowing us to compute two variance-covariance matrices, one for each twin group. The first matrix will be for the MZ twins, and will contain the variances of MZ twin 1 and MZ twin 2, as well as

the covariance between MZ twin 1 and MZ twin 2 (three data points). The second matrix will be for the DZ twins, and will contain the variances of DZ twin 1 and DZ twin 2, as well as the covariance between DZ twin 1 and DZ twin 2 (three more data points). That is, we observed six data points, and we have a model for the six data points that involves three unknown quantities (*a*, *c*, and *e*). Hence, model fitting to twin data on a single variable measured in twins reared together involves using a computer to try to find the most likely values of *a*, *c*, and *e* (three unknowns), given the six data points we observed and the theoretical model in Figure 2.1. The rules of path models (like the model in Figure 2.1) tell us that if we square each path coefficient and add up these squared values, we should get a value close to the variance in twins' scores (see Loehlin, 1998, for an excellent introduction to path models). We could write this as $a^2 + c^2 + e^2 = p^2$, where p^2 is the total phenotypic variance in the trait under study. Similarly, the rules of path models tell us that the covariance between twin 1 and twin 2 scores will be $a^2 + c^2$ for MZ twins and $0.5a^2 + c^2$ for DZ twins. Note that the predicted covariances for MZ and DZ twins contain a term that differs based on the different degree of relationship in MZ and DZ twins (*a*), a term that is the same by virtue of the fact that the twins all grew up in the same families, regardless of zygosity (*c*), and does not contain *e* because *e* does not contribute to the similarity of the twins. This helps to make the meanings of *a*, *c*, and *e* explicit: *a* is the extent to which twins resemble one another due to additive genes, *c* is the extent to which twins resemble one another due to shared environments, and e is the extent to which twins are different, in spite of the fact that they are biologically related and grew up together.

Although the model-fitting process is designed to find the a, c, and e values that are most likely, given the observed data, we may not perfectly reproduce the values of the data if the model in Figure 2.1 is not the best model for the data. The closeness between the data we observed (the six aforementioned data points) and the data the model predicts (the variance of the phenotype and the MZ and DZ covariances) determine the fit of the model to the data. This allows us to compare the fit of various models in an attempt to identify the model with the most optimal fit to the data we observed. For example, we could test the hypothesis that genetic factors are not important by forcing a to be zero, re-estimating the model in Figure 2.1, and comparing the resulting fit statistic with the fit for a model that includes a.

What Have We Learned from Univariate Modeling of Personality Data from Twins?

Model-fitting studies of personality traits in twins have converged on a number of key findings that would not have been predicted by many twentieth-century personality theorists. First, the vast majority of personality variables that have been studied show at least some genetic influence (i.e., the estimate of a^2 is typically significant). Moreover, distinct personality traits show similar degrees of genetic influence, with standardized values of a^2 (i.e., values of a^2 when p^2 is set to 1.0) typically estimated to be around 0.4–0.5 (see Bouchard & Loehlin (2001), Eaves, Eysenck, & Martin (1989), and Loehlin (1992) for quantitative reviews of relevant studies). This is a provocative and fundamental finding. One might readily theorize that some aspects of personality might be more heritable than others (e.g., one's typical activity level might be based more in "biological temperament" than one's interest in art and literature; cf. Cloninger, Svrakic, & Przybeck, 1993). Nevertheless, very distinctive personality traits show similar heritabilities, with remarkable regularity. For example, each of the five broad superfactors from the popular "big five" personality model (i.e., extraversion, neuroticism, agreeableness, conscientiousness, and openness to experience) shows similar heritabilities (Jang, Livesley, & Vernon, 1996; Loehlin, McCrae, Costa, & John, 1998; Riemann, Angleitner, & Strelau, 1997). Estimates of moderate to sizable genetic influences have also been found for personality disorder traits,

in adults (Torgersen et al., 2000) and children and adolescents (Coolidge, Thede, & Jang, 2001).

Second, estimates of c^2 are surprisingly low for personality traits in adulthood. To the extent that individual differences in personality are influenced by the environment, the environment is acting to make people within the same family different, rather than similar. This, too, is a provocative finding that has withstood the test of replication. Exceptions to the very small c^2 rule occasionally occur in personality domains linked to positive social behavior, such as agreeableness (Bergeman et al., 1993), altruism (Krueger, Hicks, & McGue, 2001), or romantic love styles (Waller & Shaver, 1994). Greater shared environment ($c^2 = 0.25$) has also been found when Big 5 personality traits are rated by observers who have never met the twins (Borkenau, Riemann, Angleitner, & Spinath, 2001). Nevertheless, c^2 is often estimated to be quite small, and can often be removed from the model in Figure 2.1 with no appreciable loss of fit, although results from newer biometrical moderation modeling suggest that substantial estimates of c^2 for personality traits may be found at extreme levels of certain environments (see section on current directions).

Sometimes the finding that c^2 is close to zero is taken to mean that the environment does not matter in personality development. This is unlikely to be a correct inference because estimates of e^2 are often as large as estimates of a^2. Hence, it would appear that the environment influences individual differences in personality, but is acting to make persons from the same families different. Although this is a reasonable interpretation of a significant e^2 estimate, little progress has been made in identifying specific, measured environments that account for e^2 variance (Turkheimer & Waldron, 2000). Moreover, e^2 estimates are reduced, and estimates of genetic variance increased, when multiple reporters (e.g., self and peer) contribute to ratings of target persons in genetically informative studies (Wolf, Angleitner, Spinath, Riemann, & Strelau, 2004). Apparently, what multiple reporters agree upon about a target person is highly heritable. The question is: Should we regard the greater e^2 in each individual perspective as "error" in the psychometric sense, or do individual perspectives contain reliable nongenetic variance that might be meaningfully linked to specific outcomes? This is a key topic for continued inquiry. For example, clinical considerations suggest something may be learned from the nongenetic variance in each reporter's unique perspective on a target person. Consider personality disorder constructs such as narcissism, which are defined by "discrepancies" between an individual's self-perspective and the perspectives of others regarding that individual. We may learn something about the nature of e^2 by considering how discrepancies between reporters might be linked to personality pathology and socially maladaptive behavior. For example, Colvin (1993) has shown that persons who are less "judgable" (as indexed by greater discrepancies among self, peer, and behavior ratings) are more maladjusted compared with more judgable persons.

Multivariate and Longitudinal Studies of Personality and Its Correlates in Twins

Twin studies are useful for much more than simply estimating the proportion of variance in personality attributable to additive genetic, shared, and nonshared environmental influences. An obvious extension of twin research on personality involves "multivariate biometric modeling" of multiple personality variables and their correlates. Although such models may sometimes appear daunting in their complexity, the logic of multivariate biometric modeling follows directly from univariate twin models. We have illustrated how the genetic and environmental relationships between MZ and DZ twins provide a "handle" on sources of human individual differences, allowing the investigator to decompose the variance in a phenotype into genetic and environmental

proportions. Multivariate modeling takes this logic one step further by allowing the investigator to decompose not only variance within phenotypes, but also covariance between phenotypes. That is, the investigator can ask not only, "What are the genetic and environmental contributions to variables A and B?," but also, "What are the relationships *between* the genetic and environmental contributions to variables A and B?" For example, one can determine if the genetic variance in variable A is correlated with the genetic variance in variable B by estimating the "genetic correlation" between variables A and B. Similarly, one can determine if the environmental variance in variable A is correlated with the environmental variance in variable B by estimating the "environmental correlation" between variables A and B. A "bivariate" biometric model with A and E effects is shown in Figure 2.2 (although C is not shown, it could be added to the model readily). The model in Figure 2.2 is an extension of the model in Figure 2.1 to the two-variable case. The model includes genetic and environmental effects shared between the first and second traits (A_1 and E_1), as well as genetic and environmental effects unique to the second trait (A_2 and E_2). These models are readily extended to three, four, or more personality phenotypes examined simultaneously in multivariate models.

One way in which multivariate biometric models have been employed is in investigations of the

Fig. 2.2 Path model for a bivariate decomposition of variance into additive genetic (A) and nonshared environmental (E) sources. Latent variables in the model (in circles) are standardized to a variance of 1.0.

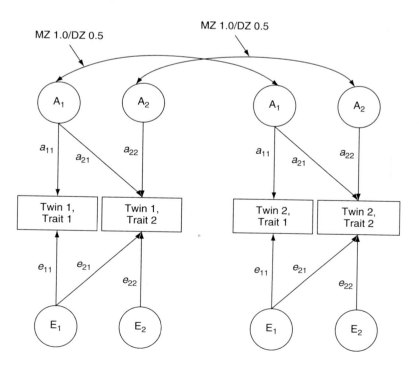

etiologic basis for the structure of personality. Personality structure is typically investigated via principal component and factor analyses, performed on phenotypic correlations among personality variables. A vexing and perennial issue involves the theoretical status of the components or factors resulting from these analyses (Block, 1995; Lykken, 1971). Are components and factors simply convenient summaries of variance, or might such analyses point us toward something deeper and theoretically richer, perhaps even toward fundamental, etiologically based dimensions of human personality variation? Multivariate biometric modeling provides a novel way to address this question. As noted earlier, these techniques allow computation of genetic and environmental correlations among variables. As a result, one can examine not only patterns of phenotypic correlations among basic, facet-level personality traits, but also patterns of genetic and environmental correlations among such traits. When this has been done (Carey & DiLalla, 1994; Krueger, 2000; Livesley, Jang, & Vernon, 1998), investigators have noted close correspondences between phenotypic, genetic, and shared environmental personality structures, although attempts to replicate the Five-Factor Model (FFM) structure in the nonshared environmental covariance have been unsuccessful, and any resemblance in nonshared environmental influences may be due to method variance (McCrae, Jang, Livesley, Riemann, & Angleitner 2001; Yamagata et al., 2006)

Jang, Livesley, Angleitner, Riemann, and Vernon (2002) further tested the etiological coherence of the personality structure of the FFM traits by comparing three different types of multivariate biometric models to NEO PI-R data from a combined German and Canadian twin sample. The three types of models were (1) the basic Cholesky decomposition model, which imposes no structure on the order of the variables; (2) an independent pathways model, which specifies direct links to the facets from one or more additive genetic and shared and nonshared environmental influences common to all the variables and unique to each individual variable; and (3) a common pathways model, in which a single latent phenotypic variable, which explains all the covariation in a set of variables, is influenced by one set of additive genetic and shared and nonshared environmental influences. The common pathways model should provide the best fit to the data if the item descriptors (or facets) are truly describing an etiologically coherent personality dimension. The common pathways model failed to provide a good fit for any of the five higher-order dimensions; each of the five domains consisted of two genetic and two nonshared environmental factors. Jang et al. concluded that their results left doubt as to the whether the higher-order personality traits actually exist as unitary psychological entities. They suggested that the FFM traits may simply be useful heuristic devices that, at best, can be associated with independent activity of many genes and multiple environmental factors. Johnson and Krueger (2004) later applied the same types of multivariate models to a nationwide sample of American twins. The common pathways model provided the best fit for extraversion and neuroticism, suggesting that these two domains come closest to being etiologically coherent latent personality constructs (Costa & McCrae, 1995). Conscientiousness and openness demonstrated looser organizational structure, while the items describing agreeableness demonstrated very little coherence.

One way to understand the divergence in results from phenotypic and genetic and environmental analysis of the structure of personality is that these differences arise because current assessment techniques do not capture genetically or environmentally homogeneous traits. This suggests the need for refinement of existing personality assessment techniques. Genetic factor analyses of existing personality measures can be used to create more genetically homogeneous (1) personality items used to measure a trait, and (2) traits that are components of higher-order factors, akin to the facets of the NEO PI. Thus, it will be possible to develop personality assessment measures that more directly capture an etiologically "pure" personality trait. This also has implications for finding measured genes for personality, which so far has been plagued by difficulties (see below). These "genetically crisp categories" (Farone, Tsuang, & Tsuang, 1999) may also lead to improvements in the ability to replicate measured gene–personality trait associations, which to date have been plagued by inconsistent results (Ebstein, 2006). Genetic factor analysis also has the potential to better elucidate the boundaries between normal and abnormal personality. The phenotypic overlap between normal personality dimensions and personality disorders (O'Connor, 2002) suggests that personality disorders may represent extremes of normal personality functioning (Miller, Lynam, Widiger, & Leukefeld, 2001). Studies with adult samples have found evidence of genetic overlap between personality disorders and normal personality functioning (Livesley et al., 1998; Markon,

Krueger, Bouchard, & Gottesman, 2002). Pergadia et al. (2006) compared the genetic and environmental contributions to both normal range and deviant levels of personality functioning in adolescents and adult samples, and concluded that shared environmental influences may show a greater contribution to deviant personality than normal-range variation for high neuroticism and high social nonconformity. Future research will need to further elucidate whether genetic and environmental influences differ in magnitude between normal and abnormal personality traits. If found, these differences have the potential to modify how we assess and conceptualize personality pathology.

Multivariate biometric models have also provided novel perspectives on the relationship between personality and its correlates. In Figure 2.2, the second variable in the model is labeled a "trait," but this could be replaced by any variable that is correlated with a specific personality variable (with this personality variable serving as trait 1 in the model). Then it would be possible to use the model in Figure 2.2 to determine *why* a personality trait is correlated with a specific outcome variable—is the correlation mediated genetically or environmentally? One application of this methodology involves modeling personality variables along with specific measures of the environment, an approach that has fundamentally redefined thinking about the environment. Beginning with the seminal work of David Rowe in the 1980s (Rowe, 1981, 1983), evidence has accumulated that so-called "environmental" measures are often heritable. For example, in Rowe's work, adolescents' reports of their parents' affection and warmth were heritable. What could this possibly mean? One possibility is that genetically influenced personality characteristics affect the ways in which people perceive and interpret the environment. As a result, the heritability of environmental measures may be traced to the heritability of personality. Stated in terms of the model in Figure 2.2, one would anticipate a large estimate for the a_{21} parameter (genetic variance shared between personality and the environmental measure) along with a small estimate for a_{22} (genetic variance unique to the environmental measure). Some pioneering multivariate biometric studies have supported the idea that genetic effects on personality account for some of the genetic effect on "environmental" measures. For example, Chipuer, Plomin, Pedersen, McClearn, and Nesselroade (1993) found that genetic effects on extraversion and neuroticism accounted for significant portions of the genetic

effect on measures of the current family environment in adult twins. Along these lines, Saudino, Pedersen, Lichtenstein, McClearn, and Plomin (1997) found that genetic effects on neuroticism, extraversion, and openness accounted for all the genetic effects on life events in older women. Spinath and O'Connor (2003) showed that genetic influences mediated the relationship between personality traits and parenting behaviors. Studies have also demonstrated that there are genetic correlations between adult personality and childhood family climate as recalled in adulthood (Krueger, Markon, & Bouchard, 2003; Lichtenstein et al., 2003; Plomin, McClearn, Pedersen, Nesselroade, & Bergeman, 1989). In other work, genetic mediating effects have been found for personality and job satisfaction (Ilies & Judge, 2003), vocational interests (Harris, Vernon, Johnson, & Jang, 2006), propensity to marry (Johnson, McGue, Krueger, 2004 & Bouchard), marital satisfaction (Spotts et al., 2005), and leadership style (Johnson, Vernon, Harris, & Jang, 2004).

Current Directions in Twin Research: Biometrical Moderation Models

Increasingly, researchers who study individual differences have become interested in the various ways that genes and environment transact to produce various behaviors. One of the most potentially important types of interplay between latent genes and measured environment is what has been variously referred to as gene–environment interaction, biometrical moderation (Purcell, 2002), or heritability–environment interaction (Moffitt, Caspi, & Rutter, 2006), but which we will refer to as biometric moderation for simplicity. The idea behind G × E, in a broader sense, is that a person's genotype serves as a blueprint for development, but the right environmental circumstances are needed for the development of a certain phenotype (i.e., personality trait). With biometric moderation models, specifically, estimates of genetic and environmental influences on a phenotype are calculated for various levels of a second, moderator phenotype, and both phenotypes have genetic and environmental aspects. The potential advantage of these models is that they can show how the etiology of personality may vary across different segments of the population. Traditionally, estimates of genetic and environmental influences on a trait or disorder have always been sample-specific population estimates. Thus, when the heritability of extraversion is reported as 50%, we interpret this as meaning that 50% of the total variance in extraversion "in that sample of a specific population" is associated with genetic influences. Essentially, traditional approaches to modeling the genetic and environmental influences on personality average over any differences within the population being studied, thus resulting in an overall account of genetic and environmental influences on a personality construct.

With biometric moderation, data obtained from specific individuals is modeled directly, instead of using sample-level summary statistics (e.g., variances and covariances). As a result, instead of averaging over the sample from which the data are drawn, estimates of genetic and environmental influences on personality can be estimated as functions of, or contingent on, other characteristics of the individual and his or her environment. Consider, as an example, the average salary of a person employed in the United States. This number would give you an overall estimate of the earning power and income of an American citizen. But this would gloss over important differences due to regional variation in availability and types of jobs. More informative, perhaps, would be to know the average income in your own state, or the average income for different types of professions. Much like understanding regional or occupational variation in income, these new behavior genetic models are able to bring heritability to a more specific level, and estimate genetic and environmental influences on personality as a function of variations that can be measured for each specific individual.

Adoption studies of biometrical moderation of personality have yet to appear, although interestingly, adoption studies of conduct disorder and aggressive behavior were the first to suggest that those with greater genetic predisposition are more vulnerable to pathogenic rearing environments (e.g., Cadoret, Yates, Troughton, Woodworth, & Stewart, 1995; Riggins-Caspers, Cadoret, Knutson, & Langbehn, 2003). Most instances of this new methodological approach to behavior genetic modeling of personality that have appeared in the literature have utilized twin samples. Many of these studies have used a measure of family environment as the moderator variable. In one study, parental bonding, family functioning, and non-assaultive traumatic events impacted genetic and environmental influences on emotional stability (similar to neuroticism), often by enhancing the impact of nonshared environmental factors (Jang, Dick, Wolf, Livesley, & Paris, 2005), while another study found that religious upbringing reduced the impact of genetic factors on disinhibitory personality

characteristics (Boomsma, de Geus, van Baal, & Koopmans, 1999). Stepping away from aspects of the family of origin, Johnson and Krueger (2006) showed that nonshared environmental factors had a greater impact on life satisfaction at lower levels of financial standing.

Despite this growing evidence of the importance of biometrical moderation, there may also be instances when influences on a personality construct are *not* moderated by an environmental variable. For instance, Kendler, Aggen, Jacobson, and Neale (2003) reported that family dysfunction did not significantly moderate genetic and environmental effects on neuroticism. We recently found that that adolescent's perceived relationships with their parents acted to both enhance and diminish genetic and environmental effects (Krueger, South, Johnson, & Iacono, 2008). For example, higher levels of perceived parental regard were associated with enhanced genetic effects on positive emotionality. This type of moderation modeling is still in its infancy, but offers the potential for important advances in our understanding of the etiology and development of personality. As experience with this type of modeling grows, there is the potential to contextualize more richly what we know about the heritability of personality, as the well-known 50% is qualified according to individual-specific demographic, family, and relationship characteristics.

What Have Adoption Studies Taught Us about Personality?

Although most behavior genetic research on personality has involved twins, adoption studies also provide a genetically informative perspective on the origins of personality variation. One particularly valuable design combines the strengths of adoption and twin studies by focusing on twins reared apart. Reared-apart twin studies provide a crucial methodological complement to studies of twins reared together because twin resemblance in such studies cannot be traced to the shared environment. Recent studies of twins reared apart conducted in Minnesota (Bouchard, 1994) and Sweden (Pedersen, Plomin, McClearn, & Friberg, 1988) agree with studies of twins reared together in finding significant heritability for personality, but also significant nonshared environmental effects.

Another powerful adoption design involves studying correlations between the personalities of parents and their adopted-away offspring. Such studies produce smaller heritability estimates than do twin studies (Loehlin, Willerman, & Horn, 1987;

Plomin, Corley, Caspi, Fulker, & DeFries, 1998). Various explanations for such findings are possible, but one prime candidate is that a portion of the genetic effect on personality may be "nonadditive," that is, traced to interactions among specific genes. Some analyses of reared-together twin studies also support this interpretation. MZ twins share all their nonadditive genetic effects (i.e., they have the same combination of genes), but DZ twins share less than half of these effects. Thus, if nonadditive genetic effects are important, one might anticipate DZ correlations that are less than half of the corresponding MZ correlation, and this is sometimes found (Finkel & McGue, 1997; Loehlin, 1992). A large-scale twin study of 11 distinctive personality traits found that an additive genetic model provided a good fit to the data when all 11 traits were modeled simultaneously (Krueger, 2000). However, the Nonshared Environment in Adolescent Development (NEAD) study, which combined information from MZ and DZ twins, full siblings, half siblings, and genetically unrelated children in the same family resulting from remarriage, found very high heritabilities, significant shared environmental estimates, and little effect of unique environment on broad domains of adjustment (Reiss et al., 2000). In a follow-up study, Loehlin, Neiderhiser, and Reiss (2003) found slightly lower heritabilities than in the original study, but confirmed the presence of significant nonadditive genetic effects. Ultimately, the complex genetic architecture of human personality may be best elucidated at the molecular level, a topic to which we now turn.

What Have Molecular Genetic Studies Taught Us about Personality?

In biometric models fit to data on relatives, genetic effects are represented as latent variables. That is, in such models we *infer* the influence of genes; we are not able to directly identify *which* genes are important in contributing to the variance of a phenotype. Nevertheless, this situation is changing rapidly, as the technology needed to directly identify genetic polymorphisms (different forms of genes) in humans has developed rapidly over the last decade. Genes are no longer only abstract entities, but rather, known quantities, described and cataloged according to numerous criteria. Details of gene sequence, structure, and variation are being elucidated, making theoretical and practical approaches to integrating molecular genetics into clinical personality assessment a reality. How to integrate molecular genetics into personality

assessment, however, depends on how individual genes' influences on behavior are mediated, because an allele whose causal pathway is complex may be difficult to interpret in an assessment context.

For example, twin and adoption studies rely fundamentally on the "polygenic" model: the hypothesis that genetic influences on behavior are mediated through multiple genes each having small effects. This model has been influential because it explains how discrete entities such as genes can give rise to continuously distributed traits such as negative mood, skin conductance, or blood pressure. The polygenic hypothesis, however, presents problems for the utilization of individual genes in personality assessment because it suggests that any given gene accounts for only a small portion of the heritability of a trait and an even smaller portion of a trait's total variance.

Evidence for Polygenic Influence

Current molecular genetic research largely supports the polygenic hypothesis. The other possible general models of genetic influence, those in which a single gene has a large effect ("monogenic" models) or a few genes have moderate effects ("oliogenic" models), have not been as well supported in the literature. In the polygenic model, many genes, each having a small effect, contribute to personality, a quantitative trait that has a continuous range and is more or less normally distributed throughout the population (cf. McCrae & Costa, 2003). The location of a gene on a chromosome is called a locus; thus the search for genes influencing a continuously distributed trait is called quantitative trait loci (QTL) analysis. In QTL analysis, researchers determine how much of the variance in a given personality trait is accounted for by the genetic markers. Support for the polygenic model derives from two lines of evidence, paralleling the two primary methods presently used to identify genes influencing behavior: "linkage analysis" and "association analysis."

The most prevalent form of linkage analysis models correlations between relatives' trait levels as a function of the probability they have inherited a stretch of chromosome from the same ancestor. This form of linkage analysis is actually an extension of the twin model discussed earlier to a specific chromosomal region and to other relative pairs. In Figure 2.1, for example, the correlation between the two additive genetic factors (i.e., 0.5 or 1) would be replaced by an index of the extent to which the members of the pair share genetic material in a specific region of a chromosome. Linkage analyses have been somewhat unsuccessful at locating specific genes affecting personality, partially because they are relatively underpowered to detect the small genetic effects predicted by polygenic theory.

The logic of association analysis is somewhat different: to determine whether individuals with different versions of a particular gene differ in their personalities. Specifically, association analysis determines whether, given a specific location on a chromosome (a "locus"), differences in genetic sequence at that location ("polymorphisms" or "alleles") are associated with differences in personality. Association analyses are more capable of detecting small genetic effects than linkage analysis (Sham, Cherny, Purcell, & Hewitt, 2000), and have not only suggested effects of specific genes on personality, but also suggested that these effects are generally small. Researchers have been industrious in the sheer number of different genes and personality traits that have been investigated, particularly in the dopaminergic and serotonergic systems, and several excellent reviews have appeared in the last few years (Ebstein, Zohar, & Benjamin et al., 2002; Ebstein, 2006; Noblett & Coccaro, 2005; Reif & Lesch, 2003; Savitz & Ramesar, 2004; Van Gestel & Van Broeckhoven, 2003). Unfortunately, results from these association studies have not been consistently replicated (Munafo et al., 2003).

The first association between a gene and a personality trait to receive substantial attention in the literature was that of the dopamine receptor type 4 (DRD4) locus and the personality trait of novelty seeking (Cloninger et al., 1993). Initial reports suggested that individuals possessing a version of the DRD4 gene in which a portion of the genetic sequence is repeated more often have greater scores on measures of novelty seeking (Benjamin et al., 1996; Ebstein et al., 1996). Attempts to replicate an association between polymorphisms of the DRD4 locus and the trait of novelty seeking, however, have been only moderately successful, with some studies reporting positive findings and others reporting negative findings (Kluger, Siegfried, & Ebstein, 2002; Schinka, Busch, & Robichaux-Keene, 2004). Although various explanations of the replication failure are plausible (Paterson, Sunohara, & Kennedy, 1999), one simple possibility is that the effect is so small that sampling fluctuations may wash it out in any given study. This interpretation, consistent with polygenic theory, is supported by a recent meta-analysis suggesting that, across 17 studies, the repeat polymorphism in question had a highly significant association with novelty seeking but accounted for only 1–2% of the variance in the trait (McGue, in press).

Small effect sizes such as this are not unique to DRD4, but extend to other alleles possibly associated with various personality traits, such as other dopamine receptor polymorphisms (Henderson et al., 2000) and polymorphisms of the serotonin transporter promoter gene (Lesch et al., 1996). The serotoin transporter gene-linked polymorphic region (5-HTTLPR) has been repeatedly linked to anxiety traits, but two meta-analyses found support only for a link with NEO PI neuroticism (Schinka, Letsch, & Crawford, 2002; Sen, Burmeister, & Ghosh, 2004). In a meta-analysis of 46 studies reporting on personality trait–gene association studies in healthy adult samples, Munafo et al. (2003) found significant associations between personality and polymorphisms in three genes: 5HTT LPR and both avoidance and aggression traits, DRD3 A1/A2 and approach traits, and DRD4 c>t and avoidance traits. When age, sex, and ethnicity were used as covariates in analyses of the 5HTT LPR and DRD4 length polymorphisms, only the association between avoidance traits and the 5HTT LPR polymorphism held up.

Mechanisms of Polygenic Influence

Beyond asking whether effects of alleles on personality are small, one can ask why this might be the case. One explanation is that variation at a locus is only weakly related to variation in a given trait—in other words, genes act additively but each allele has only a minor effect on the trait. As described earlier, the simple additive model is a good general statistical approximation of most genetic influence, and probably explains how genetic variation is related to personality for many loci. However, as also noted earlier, there may be some loci for which this explanation is not sufficient, with various forms of interaction being necessary for a complete account of their small effects. These interactive effects further complicate the interpretation and use of individual genes in personality assessment, as they suggest not only that a gene is weakly related to a trait, but also that the gene is weakly related because its effects depend on those of other genes.

At least three forms of interaction can be defined at the molecular level: intralocus interaction, or "dominance," involving variants of the same gene; interlocus interaction, or "epistasis," involving variants of different genes; and interaction among genetic and nongenetic or developmental factors, also known as "epigenesis." Currently, there is limited molecular genetic evidence for the involvement of all three forms of interactions in personality pathology (e.g., Lesch et al., 1996), supporting suggestions from some twin and adoption studies described earlier that nonadditive genetic variance contributes to personality expression.

At the chromosomal level, for example, Cloninger et al. (1998) presented evidence that a gene on the short arm of chromosome 8 is linked with harm avoidance, and that this gene interacts epistatically with other genes on chromosomes 18, 20, and 21 to influence the trait. Epistatic effects have also been observed at the level of specific polymorphisms, with Ebstein and others (Benjamin, Osher, Kotler et al., 2000; Ebstein et al., 1997, 1998; Kuhn et al., 1999), for example, reporting interactions between DRD4 repeat polymorphisms and serotonin transporter polymorphisms in predicting personality traits such as novelty seeking and reward dependence. Still others have reported interactions involving other combinations of alleles, such as polymorphisms of the catechol O-methyltransferase (COMT) gene (involved in degradation of dopamine and other neurotransmitters) and polymorphisms of the serotonin transporter gene (Benjamin, Osher, Kotler et al., 2000; Benjamin, Osher, Lichtenberg et al., 2000).

Interaction between genetic and developmental factors—that is, epigenesis—in the prediction of personality has also been reported. Evidence from studies of Turner syndrome (Donnelly et al., 2000; Skuse et al., 1997), for example, suggests that the sex differences in traits related to disinhibitedness, impulsivity, or lack of social awareness may be partially accounted for by the silencing of a protective allele in maternal X chromosomes. Individuals with Turner syndrome inherit only one complete X chromosome, either from their mother or from their father; those who inherit the complete chromosome from the mother tend to exhibit greater disinhibition than those who inherit the X chromosome from their father (Skuse et al., 1997). This pattern roughly parallels that of normal sex differences, wherein males, who inherit their X chromosome from their mother, tend to be more disinhibited than females, who inherit X chromosomes from mother and father. More detailed analyses involving individuals who inherit one complete X chromosome and part of the other suggest that the protective locus resides somewhere on the long arm or near the middle of the X chromosome (Skuse et al., 1997). The fact that the effect of this locus depends on whether it originated maternally or paternally (a phenomenon known as "imprinting"), however, points to the importance of nongenetic developmental factors in personality expression.

Finally, it is possible that a different type of interaction, gene–environment interaction, may partially explain the lack of large, replicable effects in the search for personality genes. As noted above, in a broader sense, gene–environment interaction is a term for the fact that people with different genotypes will respond differently to the same environment. Here we mean specifically behavioral variations that are due to the interaction in a measured sequence of DNA (gene) and a measured environmental variable. These types of interactions were long ignored in both behavioral and molecular genetics, due to an assumption that such an effect was relatively rare, even though research has shown that variation in response to environmental stressors is determined, in part, by individual difference variables that are genetically influenced (Moffitt et al., 2006).

Evidence for measured gene–measured environment interactions are increasingly found in medical and pharmacological research (Moffitt et al., 2006). In psychiatric genetics, these interactions have been used most famously by Caspi and colleagues in a series of studies examining developmental psychopathology. In a birth cohort of men from New Zealand, Caspi et al. (2002) found a genotype by environment interaction between variations in the monamine oxidase A (MAOA) gene (a gene coding for MAOA, a substance that metabolizes major neurotransmitters) and childhood maltreatment on antisocial behavior in adulthood. Childhood maltreatment was a risk factor for antisocial behavior but only for men with the genetic polymorphism coding for low MAOA activity. Several studies have now attempted to replicate this finding, and a recent meta-analysis confirmed a stronger relationship between maltreatment and mental health problems in boys who have the genotype conferring low MAOA activity (Kim-Cohen et al., 2006). Similarly, Caspi et al. (2003) demonstrated that variation in the serotonin transporter (5-HTT) gene predicted whether people developed depression and suicidality in respond to stressful life events. Finally, Caspi et al. (2005) found that adolescent cannabis use was a significant risk factor for psychotic symptoms and schizophreniform disorder in adulthood, but only for those carrying the valine allele of the COMT gene. In every one of these examples, the presence of the underlying diathesis (allele at the QTL) led to the expression of pathology only in the presence of a specific stressor.

Gene–environment interactions, while increasingly common in the fields of medicine and psychiatric genetics, are still relatively new in the study of personality. However, a few recent studies provide evidence for the potential of this methodology. Keltikangas-Jarvinen, Raikkonen, Ekelund, and Peltonen (2004) found an interaction between the DRD4 polymorphism and early childhood rearing environment in the prediction of novelty seeking (as assessed by the Temperament and Character Inventory, Cloninger et al., 1993), such that high scores on novelty seeking were associated with the 2- or 5-repeat DRD4 alleles only in the presence of a negative childhood family environment. Lahti et al. (2005) examined whether exposure to parental alcohol use during childhood moderated the relationship between novelty seeking in adulthood and the dopamine DRD4 receptor gene polymorphism. They found a strong association between the 2- or 5-repeat alleles of the DRD4 gene and high novelty-seeking scores, but only for those participants whose father reported more frequency alcohol consumption or drunkenness. Lahti et al. (2006) also demonstrated that 2- or 5-repeat alleles of the DRD4 polymorphism were associated with high novelty seeking in individuals with higher childhood socioeconomic levels. Gene–environment interactions are also emerging in studies of children's individual differences. Bakermans-Kranenburg and Ijzendoorn (2006) found that the DRD4–7 polymorphism interacted with maternal insensitivity to predict greater externalizing behavior in preschool-age children. It is reasonable to assume that, just as the magnitude of genetic influences on personality varies as a function of environment, the manifestation of a specific DNA sequence as a specific phenotype may also depend on the presence of a specific environment. Thus, providing for contingencies between measured genes and measured environments in the association with personality may result in more reliable and consistent linkages between genes and personality traits.

Molecular Genetics and Clinical Assessment

Alleles having large effects on personality may possibly be found in the future. However, given the complex mediation of genetic effects on behavior, it is probably more reasonable to assume that most alleles will have very small or indirect influences on behavioral variation. Such an assumption raises the question of whether it is worth introducing molecular genetics into assessment at all. A number of critics (e.g., Turkheimer, 1998) have suggested that the number of causal layers intermediate between genes and behavior are so great that individual genes are not likely to be of any use in the applied setting. If these criticisms are true, it may be that individual genes will never or rarely be utilized for assessment, being supplanted by other indicators causally closer to the phenotype. Neural imaging, for example, is likely to be refined to the point where it may have more widespread use in personality assessment. Another possibility is that protein variants themselves, rather than their coding genes, become the molecular indicators of choice in psychological assessment. Demands for precise classification in this way might engender a field of behavioral "proteomics" (Pandey & Mann, 2000).

Rather than abandoning the use of genomic information in personality assessment, however, one might also ask whether it is possible to incorporate causal complexity into the assessment process itself. If the effects of a given allele depend on the effects of a number of other alleles, or on certain environment variables, information on those other alleles or environments could be included as well. In fact, it is entirely conceivable that a clinician might genotype an individual for all known alleles having relevance to personality simultaneously, and utilize this joint allelic information in the assessment process. Just as a comprehensive multivariate approach to personality assessment has revolutionized the field at the phenotypic level, substantial gains could be made by taking a similar approach at the molecular genetic level.

Gene Microarrays

Comprehensive multivariate genomic information of the sort described above is made possible through the use of gene "microarrays" (Hacia, 1999). A microarray is a small plate, often glass or polypropylene, to which is bound a matrix of many different sets of DNA strands. Each set of DNA strands acts as a template sequence against which target DNA is matched. When a solution of an individual's DNA is passed over the microarray, if his or her sequence at a locus matches template DNA in a given location, his or her DNA binds to that template. Excess DNA is washed away, leaving the bound DNA complexes to be imaged. The sequences of an individual's DNA at numerous loci are resolved by determining at which locations in the microarray an individual's DNA binds, because a location in the array represents a certain sequence. The number of loci at which someone can be genotyped simultaneously depends on the number of template DNA strands that can be usefully bound to the microarray substrate—in other words, the size and density of the DNA template array (Southern, Mir, & Shchepinov, 1999).

In a sense, we can consider a microarray to be an inventory, analogous to personality inventories currently in use. Each location in a microarray represents a question about whether someone possesses a given allele; we ask many of these questions to get an overall picture of someone's genotypic profile. In this way, many of the principles utilized by personality inventories to overcome the complexity of assessing stable personality traits also apply to assessing genotypes.

Many of the benefits, costs, and concerns surrounding microarray use in the applied setting are likely to parallel those of personality inventories. One of the greatest practical advantages of personality inventories, for example, is their efficiency. Personality inventories typically collect a great deal of information on an individual with relatively little effort on the part of the clinician. A similar argument can be made with regard to gene microarrays. Even if complexity of genetic effects was not a factor in personality assessment, it is likely that microarrays would be commonly used anyway due to their cost and time efficiency. Automation has made the cost of genotyping someone at 500,000 loci comparable to the cost of genotyping them at just one locus.

Parallels between microarrays and personality assessment extend in other ways as well. As multivariate considerations have entered the genomic realm, researchers have begun to recognize that reliability and validity are major concerns. Basic principles of replicated measurement, familiar in psychometrics, have begun to be advocated in the genomics community (Hacia, 1999). This is the case because the signal from any given location in a microarray is unreliable: an individual's DNA can bind to template DNA that it should not bind to, or fail to bind to template DNA that it should bind to. This is particularly true when one tries to distinguish between two polymorphisms that differ only at one location in a DNA sequence. Repeating cells of a microarray increases the certainty with which we can conclude that an individual does or does not possess one polymorphism or the other, in the same way that repeated measurement of a personality trait increases the precision with which we measure the trait.

Gene Microarray Composition

Perhaps the most important implication of microarray use for personality assessment, however, is the need for a standard, predetermined set of alleles for genotyping of individuals. Currently, most clinical genotyping is done on an individual basis, the alleles to test for depending on the individual being assessed. As the identified number of clinically relevant genes increases, however, along with our understanding of their interactions, the need for comprehensive assessment of genotype with regard to a fixed set of alleles will increase as well. Standardization of microarrays, in this regard, will likely be driven as much by the complexity by which genetic effects are mediated as issues related to standardization of the clinical assessment process.

At some point, therefore, it will become necessary to initiate a discussion of what a standard clinical assessment microarray should include, and whether content should depend on other factors such as results of personality inventories. To some extent, practical or technical issues such as microarray capacity or molecular interactions (Southern et al., 1999) will constrain this discussion. Nevertheless, issues related to classification, assessment, and prediction will also predominate. It is entirely possible that a proliferation of competing microarrays will evolve, each perhaps serving a slightly different function, in much the way that personality inventories currently exist. This leads into an entire host of issues, similar in many ways to how we should assess personality— whether we should take empirical, deductive, or other approaches (Burisch, 1984) to constructing microarrays, what constitutes appropriate psychological constructs, and so on. Although some of these issues will resolve themselves as knowledge about molecular behavioral genetics increases, it is nevertheless possible to identify certain approaches to selecting polymorphisms:

1. *Selecting "critical" alleles.* Although most genes are likely to have small effect or to interact extensively with other factors in influencing personality, it is still possible that a number of "critical" alleles— those having large effect or otherwise being of critical importance in determining behavioral outcome— will be identified. Typically these alleles will be extremely rare in the population, yet reliably lead to highly abnormal personality traits or extremely poor treatment response among the individuals who possess them. One could conceivably wish to construct a microarray to screen individuals for such alleles. These screens might possibly be among the first microarrays to find extensive use in the clinical setting, as the first genes to be well characterized are those whose effects are relatively large and easily understood.

2. *Selecting alleles predictive of external criteria.* Another approach to selecting alleles for inclusion in an assessment microarray is to select alleles associated with external criteria such as diagnostic status or personality trait level. This approach is similar to that taken when screening for "critical" alleles but is different in the alleles' effect sizes and dependence on interaction with other alleles.

3. *Selecting functionally relevant alleles.* As our understanding of cellular dynamics increases, it may be possible to construct microarrays to assess the functioning of particular molecular systems. For example, we can imagine a construct of "poor serotonin transporter" activity, engendered through a number of alleles, including those coding for the transporter protein itself and the associated regulatory genes, genes coding for posttranslational modification of transporter proteins, and so on. We might then construct a microarray that includes screens for all these genes, and conceive of individuals as having more or fewer alleles contributing toward poor serotonin transporter function.

4. *Selecting alleles predictive of prognosis or treatment response.* A final approach to constructing microarrays for use in clinical assessment is to include alleles on the basis of their ability to predict treatment response or outcome, rather than diagnostic status. There will necessarily be some overlap between those alleles predicting treatment response and those correlated with behavioral classification or molecular functioning, since treatment often tends to target disrupted molecular function associated with both behavioral status and outcome. However, the overlap will probably not be complete, because individual differences in numerous variables not directly relevant to the emergence of psychopathology may nevertheless influence its progress or appearance (Harkness & Lilienfeld, 1997).

Alleles associated with psychopharmacological response have already begun to be identified, perhaps the most studied being those associated with response to clozapine, an antipsychotic medication. Polymorphisms at a number of loci have been examined for effects on clozapine response, including alleles for dopamine D3 (Scharfetter et al., 1999), D4 (Shaikh et al., 1993), and serotonin (Arranz et al., 1995, 1998) receptors. Although some of these investigations have failed to find an effect (Masellis et al., 2000), particularly those related to D4 receptor genes (Shaikh et al., 1993), and others have yet to be replicated (Scharfetter et al., 1999), meta-analyses and reviews suggest that other polymorphisms, particularly those related to serotonin

receptor genes, do have some relationship with clozapine response (Arranz et al., 1998). Arranz and colleagues (2000), moreover, recently extended the study of alleles associated with clozapine response to include numerous polymorphisms simultaneously. Six of 19 polymorphisms screened, at histamine, serotonin receptor, and serotonin transporter loci, jointly resulted in a success rate of 76.7% in classifying individuals as responders or nonresponders.

Clearly such results require replication and further scrutiny. Nevertheless, they demonstrate the utility of a multivariate molecular genetic approach to predicting treatment response. Individually, any given gene might only weakly predict response to a given treatment; in aggregate, however, the ability to predict an individual's phenotype increases. A microarray containing many alleles could be keyed, so to speak, to predict diagnostic status or responses to a particular drug or treatment of interest.

Future Directions in Molecular Genetics: Genomic Imaging

An exciting recent development in the search for neural mechanisms of personality is genomic imaging. Similar to the gene–environment interactions described above, this approach examines whether measured genes are related to personality traits in the presence of certain patterns of functional and structural activation during cognitively and affectively laden tasks. This work builds on two previous lines of research. First, there is growing evidence for associations between genetic polymorphisms and neural process of affective and cognitive inputs (Canli et al., 2005; Hariri et al., 2002). Second, findings are also emerging which suggest that individual differences in brain reactivity to emotional stimuli are correlated with personality traits (Canli et al., 2001; Canli, Sivers, Whitfield, Gotlib, & Gabrieli, 2002). By combining these two approaches, genomic imaging researchers are starting to examine the interaction between measured genes, neural substrates of behavior, and personality. Meyer-Lindenberg et al. (2006) examined the link between a common variable number tandem repeat polymorphism of the MAOA gene (associated with antisocial behavior among men who experienced childhood maltreatment in a measured gene–measured environment interaction described above; Caspi et al., 2002) and brain structures involved in emotional control using a multimodal imaging approach. When affectively salient social stimuli (angry and fearful faces) were presented to carriers of the MAOA polymorphism, participants exhibited significant structural and functional changes in brain circuitry related to affect regulation, emotional memory, and impulsivity. They further argue that the risk imparted by the MAOA variant studied here contributes to the impulsive dimension of the larger construct of antisocial and violent behavior. This type of research may eventually aid in understanding the neural substrates of personality, and the genetic etiology of both.

Implications of Behavior Genetics for Assessment and Classification Theory

How we conceive of constructing and using microarrays or any other genotyping screen is not a purely applied issue. Consider the first, second, and third approaches above, for example, the critical, predictive, and functional allele approaches to microarray construction. These three approaches to developing a microarray for use in clinical assessment imply somewhat different conceptions of what constitutes psychological abnormality and how to best discriminate between individuals within a given classification system. Just as in construction of personality inventories, a particular approach to genotyping implies certain assumptions regarding behavioral classification criteria.

The first, "critical" allele approach above, for example, assumes the abnormal personality characteristics of interest are typological or taxonic (Meehl, 1992). Under this model, discrete groups of persons having distinct, atypical phenotypes can be categorically distinguished from others. Any given individual, moreover, can be nearly perfectly classified into a group given knowledge of their status with regard to a particular locus: the genotype provides complete information about the phenotype.

The second approach to microarray construction, in contrast, relies on a measurement model in which behavioral classification may or may not be discrete in nature, and genotype is imperfectly related to phenotype. Under this model, behavioral classification rules are generated phenotypically, without use of genotypic information, and personality status is defined independently of allelic status. Genotype is treated as an external criterion with reference to personality status and vice versa.

The third, functional, approach to microarray construction described above lies somewhere intermediate between the other two. In that approach, behavioral classification rules comprise genotypic information to the extent that the latter is associated with systemic functioning. As the functioning of a

system is determined by a plurality of genetic and nongenetic factors, however, any given locus will be only imperfectly related to phenotypic status. Genotype informs behavioral classification, but does not define it perfectly; information about the two is dynamically related.

Not surprisingly, the three approaches to genotyping reflect long-standing traditions in psychology regarding the nature of assessment and abnormal behavior: whether psychopathology should be defined as statistical deviation or dysfunction, and whether personality traits are descriptive summaries of observable behavior or indirect measures of latent processes (Block, 1989; Buss & Craik, 1983). To some extent, these sorts of debates regarding descriptive versus functional definitions of abnormality and personality have been constrained by a lack of understanding of the systems underlying behavior. As the ability to obtain detailed, quantifiable information about individual physiological status increases within the realm of genetics and elsewhere, constraints on classification systems imposed by a lack of knowledge will decrease. It may eventually become possible to assign individuals to genotypic groups and to develop an entirely genotypic classification system; reconciling the phenotypic and genotypic classification of an individual will then become necessary. Nevertheless, the results of multivariate behavioral genetic analyses have suggested that the factor structure of genetic and environmental relationships among personality measures generally resemble the phenotypic factor structure (Krueger, 2000). Therefore, increased genetic information about individuals will probably reinforce the importance of phenotypic personality assessment in clinical nosology. The exciting possibility for the future is that molecular genetic research will help us both to better understand and to directly assess etiologic factors undergirding phenotypic personality profiles.

References

Arranz, M. J., Collier, D., Sodhi, M., Ball, D., Roberts, G., Price, J., et al. (1995). Association between clozapine response and allelic variation in 5-HT2A receptor gene. *Lancet, 346,* 281–282.

Arranz, M. J., Munro, J., Birkett, J., Bolonna, A., Mancama, D., Sodhi, M., et al. (2000). Pharmacogenetic prediction of clozapine response. *Lancet, 355,* 1615–1616.

Arranz, M. J., Munro, J., Sham, P., Kirov, G., Murray, R. M., Collier, D. A., et al. (1998). Meta-analysis of studies on genetic variation in 5-HT2A receptors and clozapine response. *Schizophrenia Research, 32,* 93–99.

Bakermans-Kranenburg, M. J., & Van Ijzendoorn, M. H. (2006). Gene–environment interaction of the dopamine D4 receptor (DRD4) and observed maternal insensitivity predicting externalizing behavior in preschoolers. *Developmental Psychobiology, 48*, 406–409.

Benjamin, J., Li, L., Patterson, C., Greenberg, B. D., Murphy, D. L., & Hamer, D. H. (1996). Population and familial association between the D4 dopamine receptor gene and measures of novelty seeking. *Nature Genetics, 12*, 81–84.

Benjamin, J., Osher, Y., Kotler, M., Gritsenko, I., Nemanov, L., Belmaker, R. H., et al. (2000). Association between tridimensional personality questionnaire (TPQ) traits and three functional polymorphisms: Dopamine receptor D4 (DRD4), serotonin transporter promoter region (5-HTTLPR) and catechol *O*-methyltransferase (COMT). *Molecular Psychiatry, 5*, 96–100.

Benjamin, J., Osher, Y., Lichtenberg, P., Bachner-Melman, R., Gritsenko, I., Kotler, M., et al. (2000). An interaction between the catechol *O*-methyltransferase and serotonin transporter promoter region polymorphisms contributes to tridimensional personality questionnaire persistence scores in normal subjects. *Neuropsychobiology, 41*, 48–53.

Bergeman, C. S., Chipuer, H. M., Plomin, R., Pedersen, N. L., McClearn, G. E., Nesselroade, J. R., et al. (1993). Genetic and environmental effects on openness to experience, agreeableness, and conscientiousness: An adoption/twin study. *Journal of Personality, 61*, 159–179.

Block, J. (1989). Critique of the act frequency approach to personality. *Journal of Personality and Social Psychology, 56*, 234–245.

Block, J. (1995). A contrarian view of the Five-Factor approach to personality description. *Psychological Bulletin, 117*, 187–215.

Boomsma, D., de Geus, E., van Baal, G., & Koopmans, J. (1999). A religious upbringing reduces the influence of genetic factors on disinhibition: Evidence for interaction between genotype and environment on personality. *Twin Research, 2*, 115–125.

Borkenau, P., Riemann, R., Angleitner, A., & Spinath, F. M. (2001). Genetic and environmental influences on observed personality: Evidence from the German observational study of adult twins. *Journal of Personality and Social Psychology, 80*, 655–668.

Bouchard, T. J., Jr. (1994). Genes, environment, and personality. *Science, 264*, 1700–1701.

Bouchard, T. J., Jr., & Loehlin, J. C. (2001). Genes, evolution, and personality. *Behavior Genetics, 31*, 243–273.

Burisch, M. (1984). Approaches to personality inventory construction: A comparison of merits. *American Psychologist, 39*, 214–227.

Buss, D. M., & Craik, K. H. (1983). The act frequency approach to personality. *Psychological Review, 90*, 105–126.

Cadoret, R. J., Yates, W., Troughton, E., Woodworth, G., & Stewart, M. (1995). Genetic–environmental interaction in the genesis of aggressivity and conduct disorders. *Archives of General Psychiatry, 52*, 916–924.

Canli, T., Omura, K., Haas, B. W., Fallgatter, A., Constable, R. T., & Lesch, K. P. (2005). Beyond affect: A role for genetic variation of the serotonin transporter in neural activation during a cognitive attention task. *PNAS: Proceedings of the National Academy of Sciences of the United States of America, 102*, 12224–12229.

Canli, T., Sivers, H., Whitfield, S. L., Gotlib, I. H., & Gabrieli, J. D. (2002). Amygdala response to happy faces as a function of extraversion. *Science, 296*, 2191.

Canli, T., Zhao Z., Desmond, J. E., Kang, E., Gross, J., & Gabrieli, J. D. (2001). An fMRI study of personality influences on brain reactivity to emotional stimuli. *Behavioral Neuroscience, 115*, 33–42.

Carey, G., & DiLalla, D. L. (1994). Personality and psychopathology: Genetic perspectives. *Journal of Abnormal Psychology, 103*, 32–43.

Caspi, A., McClay, J., Moffitt, T., Mill, J., Martin, J., Craig, I. W., et al. (2002). Role of genotype in the cycle of violence in maltreated children. *Science, 297*, 752–754.

Caspi, A., Moffitt, T., Cannon, M., McClay, J., Murray, R., Harrington, H., et al. (2005). Moderation of the effect of adolescent-onset cannabis use on adult psychosis by a functional polymorphism in the COMT gene: Longitudinal evidence of a gene x environment interaction. *Biological Psychiatry, 57*, 1117–1127.

Caspi, A., Sugden, K., Moffitt, T., Taylor, A., Craig, I. W., Harrington, H., et al. (2003). Influence of life stress on depression: Moderation by a polymorphism in the 5-HTT gene. *Science, 301*, 386–389.

Chipuer, H. M., Plomin, R., Pedersen, N. L., McClearn, G. E., & Nesselroade, J. R. (1993). Genetic influence on family environment: The role of personality. *Developmental Psychology, 29*, 110–118.

Cloninger, C. R., Svrakic, D. M., & Przybeck, T. R. (1993). A psychobiological model of temperament and character. *Archives of General Psychiatry, 50*, 975–990.

Cloninger, C. R., Van Eerdewegh, P., Goate, A., Edenberg, H. J., Blangero, J., Hesselbrock, V., et al. (1998). Anxiety proneness linked to epistatic loci in genome scan of human personality traits. *American Journal of Medical Genetics, 81*, 313–317.

Colvin, C. R. (1993). "Judgable" people: Personality, behavior, and competing explanations. *Journal of Personality and Social Psychology, 64*, 861–873.

Coolidge, F. L., Thede, L. L., & Jang, K. L. (2001). Heritability of personality disorders in childhood: A preliminary investigation. *Journal of Personality Disorders, 15*, 33–40.

Costa, P. T., & McCrae, R. R. (1995). Domains and facets: Hierarchical personality assessment using the Revised NEO Personality Inventory. *Journal of Personality Assessment, 64*, 21–50.

Donnelly, S. L., Wolpert, C. M., Menold, M. M., Bass, M. P., Gilbert, J. R., Cuccaro, M. L., et al. (2000). Female with autistic disorder and monosomy X (Turner syndrome): Parent-of-origin effect of the X chromosome. *American Journal of Medical Genetics, 96*, 312–316.

Eaves, L. J., Eysenck, H. J., & Martin, N. G. (1989). *Genes, culture and personality: An empirical approach.* San Diego, CA: Academic Press.

Ebstein, R. P. (2006). The molecular genetic architecture of human personality: Beyond self-report questionnaires. *Molecular Psychiatry, 11*, 427–445.

Ebstein, R. P., Levine, J., Geller, V., Auerbach, J., Gritsenko, I., & Belmaker, R. H. (1998). Dopamine D4 receptor and serotonin transporter promoter in the determination of neonatal temperament. *Molecular Psychiatry, 3*, 238–246.

Ebstein, R. P., Novick, O., Umansky, R., Priel, B., Osher, Y., Blaine, D., et al. (1996). Dopamine D4 receptor (D4DR) exon III polymorphism associated with the human personality trait of novelty seeking. *Nature Genetics, 12*, 78–80.

Ebstein, R. P., Segman, R., Benjamin, J., Osher, Y., Nemanov, L., & Belmaker, R. H. (1997). 5-HT2C (HTR2C) serotonin receptor gene polymorphism associated with the human personality trait of reward dependence: Interaction with dopamine D4 receptor (D4DR) and dopamine D3 receptor (D3DR) polymorphisms. *American Journal of Medical Genetics, 74*, 65–72.

Ebstein, R. P., Zohar, A. H., Benjamin, J., & Belmaker, R. H. (2002). An update of molecular genetic studies of human personality traits. *Applied Bioinformatics, 1,* 57–68.

Farone, S. V., Tsuang, M. T., & Tsuang, D. W. (1999). *Genetics of mental disorders.* New York: The Guilford Press.

Finkel, D., & McGue, M. (1997). Sex differences and nonadditivity in heritability of the Multidimensional Personality Questionnaire scales. *Journal of Personality and Social Psychology, 72,* 929–938.

Goldsmith, H. H., Buss, K. A., & Lemery, K. S. (1997). Toddler and childhood temperament: Expanded content, stronger genetic evidence, new evidence for the importance of environment. *Developmental Psychology, 33,* 891–905.

Goodman, R., & Stevenson, J. (1991). Parental criticism and warmth towards unrecognized monozygotic twins. *Behavior and Brain Sciences, 14,* 394–395.

Hacia, J. G. (1999). Resequencing and mutational analysis using oligonucleotide microarrays. *Nature Genetics, 21*(Suppl. 1), 42–47.

Hariri, A. R., Mattay, V. S., Tessitore, A., Kolachana, B., Fera, F., Goldman, D., et al. (2002). Serotonin transporter genetic variation and the response of the human amygdala. *Science, 297,* 400–403.

Harkness, A. R., & Lilienfeld, S. O. (1997). Individual differences science for treatment planning: Personality traits. *Psychological Assessment, 9,* 349–360.

Harris, J. A., Vernon, P. A., Johnson, A. M., & Jang, K. L. (2006). Phenotypic and genetic relationships between vocational interests and personality. *Personality and Individual Differences, 40,* 1531–1541.

Henderson, A. S., Korten, A. E., Jorm, A. F., Jacomb, P. A., Christensen, H., Rodgers, B., et al. (2000). COMT and DRD3 polymorphisms, environmental exposures, and personality traits related to common mental disorders. *American Journal of Medical Genetics, 96,* 102–107.

Ilies, R., & Judge, T. A. (2003). On the heritability of job satisfaction: The mediating role of personality. *Journal of Applied Psychology, 88,* 750–759.

Jang, K. L., Dick, D. M., Wolf, H., Livesley, W. J., & Paris, J. (2005). Psychosocial adversity and emotional instability: An application of gene–environment interaction models. *European Journal of Personality, 19,* 359–372.

Jang, K. L., Livesley, W. J., Angleitner, A., Riemann, R., & Vernon, P. A. (2002). Genetic and environmental influences on the covariance of facets defining the domains of the Five-Factor Model of personality. *Personality and Individual Differences, 33,* 83–101.

Jang, K. L., Livesley, W. J., & Vernon, P. A. (1996). Heritability of the big five personality dimensions and their facets: A twin study. *Journal of Personality, 64,* 577–591.

Johnson, A. M., Vernon, P. A., Harris, J. A., & Jang, K. L. (2004). A behavior genetic investigation of the relationship between leadership and personality. *Twin Research, 7,* 27–32.

Johnson, W., & Krueger, R. F. (2004). Genetic and environmental structure of adjectives describing the domains of the Big Five Model of personality: A nationwide US twin study. *Journal of Research in Personality, 38,* 448–472.

Johnson, W., & Krueger, R. F. (2006). How money buys happiness: Genetic and environmental processes linking finances and life satisfaction. *Journal of Personality and Social Psychology, 90,* 680–691.

Johnson, W., McGue, M., Krueger, R. F., Bouchard, T. J., Jr. (2004). Marriage and personality: A genetic analysis. *Journal of Personality and Social Psychology, 86,* 285–294.

Keltikangas-Jarvinen, L., Raikkonen, K., Ekelund, J., & Peltonen, L. (2004). Nature vs nurture in novelty seeking. *Molecular Psychiatry, 9,* 308–311.

Kendler, K. S., Aggen, S. H., Jacobson, K. C., & Neale, M. C. (2003). Does the level of family dysfunction moderate the impact of genetic factors on the personality trait of neuroticism? *Psychological Medicine, 33,* 817–825.

Kim-Cohen, J., Caspi, A., Taylor, A., Williams, B., Newcombe, R., Craig, I. W., & Moffitt, T. E. (2006). MAOA, maltreatment, and gene-environment interaction predicting children's mental health: New evidence and a meta-analysis. *Molecular Psychiatry, 11,* 903–913.

Kluger, A. N., Siegfried, Z., & Ebstein, R. P. (2002). A meta-analysis of the association between DRD4 polymorphism and novelty seeking. *Molecular Psychiatry, 7,* 712–717.

Krueger, R. F. (2000). Phenotypic, genetic, and non-shared environmental parallels in the structure of personality: A view from the Multidimensional Personality Questionnaire. *Journal of Personality and Social Psychology, 79,* 1057–1067.

Krueger, R. F., Hicks, B. M., & McGue, M. (2001). Altruism and antisocial behavior: Independent tendencies, unique personality correlates, distinct etiologies. *Psychological Science, 12,* 397–402.

Krueger, R. F., Markon, K. E., & Bouchard, T. J. (2003). The extended genotype: The heritability of personality accounts for the heritability of recalled family environments in twins reared apart. *Journal of Personality, 71,* 809–833.

Krueger, R. F., South, S. C., Johnson, W., & Iacono, W. (2008). Gene–environment interactions and correlations between personality and parenting: The heritability of personality is not always 50%. *Journal of Personality, 76,* 1485–1522.

Kuhn, K. U., Meyer, K., Nothen, M. M., Gansicke, M., Papassotiropoulos, A., & Maier, W. (1999). Allelic variants of dopamine receptor D4 (DRD4) and serotonin receptor 5HT2c (HTR2c) and temperament factors: Replication tests. *American Journal of Medical Genetics, 88,* 168–172.

Lahti, J., Raikkonen, K., Ekelund, J., Peltonen, L., Raitakari, O. T., & Keltikangas-Jarvinen, L. (2005). Novelty seeking: Interaction between parental alcohol use and dopamine D4 receptor gene exon III polymorphism over 17 years. *Psychiatric Genetics, 15,* 133–139.

Lahti, J., Raikkonen, K., Ekelund, J., Peltonen, L., Raitakari, O. T., Keltikangas-Jarvinen, L. (2006). Socio-demographic characteristics moderate the association between DRD4 and Novelty seeking. *Personality and Individual Differences, 40,* 533–543.

Lesch, K. P., Bengel, D., Heils, A., Sabol, S. Z., Greenberg, B. D., Petri, S., et al. (1996). Association of anxiety-related traits with a polymorphism in the serotonin transporter gene regulatory region. *Science, 274,* 1527–1531.

Lichtenstein, P., Ganiban, J., Neiderhiser, J. M., Pedersen, N. L., Hansson, K., Cederblad, M., et al. (2003). Remembered parental bonding in adult twins: Genetic and environmental influences. *Behavior Genetics, 33,* 397–408.

Livesley, W. J., Jang, K. L., & Vernon, P. A. (1998). Phenotypic and genetic structure of traits delineating personality disorder. *Archives of General Psychiatry, 55,* 941–948.

Loehlin, J. C. (1992). *Genes and environment in personality development.* Newbury Park, CA: Sage.

Loehlin, J. C. (1998). *Latent variable models: An introduction to factor, path, and structural analysis* (3rd ed.). Hillsdale, NJ: Erlbaum.

Loehlin, J. C., McCrae, R. R., Costa, P. T., Jr., & John, O. P. (1998). Heritabilities of common and measure-specific components of the Big Five personality factors. *Journal of Research in Personality, 32*, 431–453.

Loehlin, J. C., Neiderhiser, J. M., & Reiss, D. (2003). The behavior genetics of personality and the NEAD study. *Journal of Research in Personality, 37*, 373–387.

Loehlin, J. C., & Nichols, R. C. (1976). *Heredity, environment and personality.* Austin, TX: University of Texas Press.

Loehlin, J. C., Willerman, L., & Horn, J. M. (1987). Personality resemblance in adoptive families: A 10-year follow-up. *Journal of Personality and Social Psychology, 53*, 961–969.

Lykken, D. T. (1971). Multiple factor analysis and personality research. *Journal of Experimental Research in Personality, 5*, 161–170.

Markon, K. E., Krueger, R. F., Bouchard, T. J., Jr., & Gottesman, I. I. (2002). Normal and abnormal personality traits: Evidence for genetic and environmental relationships in the Minnesota Study of Twins Reared Apart. *Journal of Personality, 70*, 661–693.

Masellis, M., Basile, V. S., Ozdemir, V., Meltzer, H. Y., Macciardi, F. M., & Kennedy, J. L. (2000). Pharmacogenetics of antipsychotic treatment: Lessons learned from clozapine. *Biological Psychiatry, 47*, 252–266.

McCrae, R. R., & Costa, P. T. (2003). *Personality in adulthood: A Five-Factor theory perspective* (2nd ed.). New York: Guilford.

McCrae, R. R., Jang, K. L., Livesley, W. J., Riemann, R., & Angleitner, A. (2001). Sources of structure: Genetic, environmental, and artifactual influences on the covariation of personality traits. *Journal of Personality, 69*, 511–535.

McGue, M. (in press). The genetics of personality. In *Emery and Rimoin's principles and practice of medical genetics.*

Meehl, P. E. (1992). Factors and taxa, traits and types, differences of degree and differences in kind. *Journal of Personality, 60*, 117–174.

Meyer-Lindenberg, A., Buckholtz, J.W., Kolachana, B., Hariri, A.R., Pezawas, L., Blasi, G., et al. (2006). Neural mechanisms of genetic risk for impulsivity and violence in humans. *Proceedings for the National Academy of Sciences USA, 103*, 6269–6274.

Miller, J. D., Lynam, D. R., Widiger, T. A., & Leukefeld, C. (2001). Personality disorders as extreme variants of common personality dimensions: Can the Five-Factor Model adequately represent psychopathy? *Journal of Personality, 69*, 253–276.

Moffitt, T. E., Caspi, A., & Rutter, M. (2006). Measured gene–environment interactions in psychopathology: Concepts, research strategies, and implications for research, intervention, and public understanding of genetics. *Perspectives on Psychological Science, 1*, 5–27.

Munafo, M. R., Clark, T. G., Moore, L. R., Payne, E., Walton, R., & Flint, J. (2003). Genetic polymorphisms and personality in healthy adults: A systematic review and meta-analysis. *Molecular Psychiatry, 8*, 471–484.

Neale, M. C., & Maes, H. H. M. (in press). *Methodology for genetic studies of twins and families.* Dordrecht, The Netherlands: Kluwer Academic Publishers.

Noblett, K. L., & Coccaro, E. F. (2005). The psychobiology of personality disorders. In M. Rosenbluth, S. H. Kennedy, & R. M. Bagby (Eds.), *Depression and personality: Conceptual and clinical challenges* (pp. 19–42). Washington, DC: American Psychiatric Publishing, Inc.

O'Connor, B. P. (2002). The search for dimensional structure differences between normality and abnormality: A statistical review of published data on personality and psychopathology. *Journal of Personality and Social Psychology, 83*, 962–982.

Pandey, A., & Mann, M. (2000). Proteomics to study genes and genomes. *Nature, 405*, 837–846.

Paterson, A. D., Sunohara, G. A., & Kennedy, J. L. (1999). Dopamine D4 receptor gene: Novelty or nonsense? *Neuropsychopharmacology, 21*, 3–16.

Pedersen, N. L., Plomin, R., McClearn, G. E., & Friberg, L. (1988). Neuroticism, extraversion, and related traits in adult twins reared apart and reared together. *Journal of Personality and Social Psychology, 55*, 950–957.

Pergadia, M. L., Madden, P. A. F., Lessov, C. N., Todorov, A. A., Bucholz, K. K., Martin, N. G., et al. (2006). Genetic and environmental influences on extreme personality dispositions in adolescent female twins. *Journal of Child Psychology and Psychiatry, 47*, 902–909.

Pickering, A. D., & Gray, J. A. (1999). The neuroscience of personality. In L. A. Pervin & O. P. John (Eds.), *Handbook of personality: Theory and research* (2nd ed.). New York: Guilford.

Plomin, R., Corley, R., Caspi, A., Fulker, D. W., & DeFries, J. C. (1998). Adoption results for self-reported personality: Evidence for nonadditive genetic effects? *Journal of Personality and Social Psychology, 75*, 211–218.

Plomin, R., McClearn, G. E, Pedersen, N. L., Nesselroade, J. R., & Bergeman, C. S. (1989). Genetic influence on adults' ratings of their current family environment. *Journal of Marriage and the Family, 51*, 791–803.

Purcell, S. (2002). Variance components models for gene–environment interaction in twin analysis. *Twin Research, 5*, 554–571.

Reif, A., & Lesch, K.-P. (2003). Toward a molecular architecture of personality. *Behavioural Brain Research, 139*, 1–20.

Reiss, D., Neiderhiser, J. M., Hetherington, E. M., & Plomin, R. (2000). *The relationship code: Deciphering genetic and social influences on adolescent development.* Cambridge, MA: Harvard University Press.

Riemann, R., Angleitner, A., & Strelau, J. (1997). Genetic and environmental influences on personality: A study of twins reared together using the self- and peer report NEO-FFI scales. *Journal of Personality, 65*, 449–475.

Riggins-Caspers, K. M., Cadoret, R. J., Knutson, J. F., & Langbehn, D. (2003). Biology–environment interaction and evocative biology–environment correlation: Contributions of harsh discipline and parental psychopathology to problem adolescent behaviors. *Behavior Genetics, 33*, 205–220.

Rowe, D. C. (1981). Environmental and genetic influences on dimensions of perceived parenting: A twin study. *Developmental Psychology, 17*, 203–208.

Rowe, D. C. (1983). A biometrical analysis of perceptions of family environment: A study of twin and singleton sibling kinships. *Child Development, 54*, 416–423.

Saudino, K. J., Pedersen, N. L., Lichtenstein, P., McClearn, G. E., & Plomin, R. (1997). Can personality explain genetic influences on life events? *Journal of Personality and Social Psychology, 72*, 196–206.

Savitz, J. B., & Ramesar, R. S. (2004). Genetic variants implicated in personality: A review of the more promising candidates. *American Journal of Medical Genetics, 131B*, 20–32.

Scarr, S., & Carter-Saltzman, L. (1979). Twin method: Defense of a critical assumption. *Behavior Genetics, 9*, 527–542.

Scharfetter, J., Chaudhry, H. R., Hornik, K., Fuchs, K., Sieghart, W., Kasper, S., et al. (1999). Dopamine D3 receptor gene polymorphism and response to clozapine in schizophrenic

Pakastani patients. *European Neuropsychopharmacology, 10,* 17–20.

Schinka, J. A., Busch, R. M., & Robichaux-Keene, N. (2004). A meta-analysis of the association between the serotonin transporter gene polymorphism (5-HTTLPR) and trait anxiety. *Molecular Psychiatry, 9,* 197–202.

Schinka, J. A., Letsch, E. A., & Crawford, F. C. (2002). DRD4 and novelty seeking: Results of meta-analyses. *American Journal of Medical Genetics, 114,* 643–648.

Sen, S., Burmeister, M., & Ghosh, D. (2004). Meta-analysis of the association between a serotonin transporter promoter polymorphism (5-HTTLPR) and anxiety-related personality traits. *American Journal of Medical Genetics, 15,* 85–89.

Shaikh, S., Collier, D., Kerwin, R. W., Pilowsky, L. S., Gill, M., Xu, W.-M., et al. (1993). Dopamine D4 receptor subtypes and response to clozapine. *Lancet, 341,* 116.

Sham, P. C., Cherny, S. S., Purcell, S., & Hewitt, J. K. (2000). Power of linkage versus association analysis of quantitative traits, by use of variance-components models, for sibship data. *American Journal of Human Genetics, 66,* 1616–1630.

Skuse, D. H., James, R. S., Bishop, D. V., Coppin, B., Dalton, P., Aamodt-Leeper, G., et al. (1997). Evidence from Turner's syndrome of an imprinted X-linked locus affecting cognitive function. *Nature, 387,* 705–708.

Southern, E., Mir, K., & Shchepinov, M. (1999). Molecular interactions on microarrays. *Nature Genetics, 21*(Suppl. 1), 5–9.

Spinath, F. M., & O'Connor, T. G. (2003). A behavioral genetic study of the overlap between personality and parenting. *Journal of Personality, 71,* 785–808.

Spotts, E. L., Lichtenstein, P., Pedersen, N., Neiderhiser, J. M., Hansson, K., Cederblad, M., et al. (2005). Personality and marital satisfaction: A behavioural genetic analysis. *European Journal of Personality, 19,* 205–227.

Torgersen, S., Lygren, S., Oien, P. A., Skre, I., Onstad, S., Edvardsen, J., et al. (2000). A twin study of personality disorders. *Comprehensive Psychiatry, 41,* 416–425.

Turkheimer, E. (1998). Heritability and biological explanation. *Psychological Review, 105,* 782–791.

Turkheimer, E., & Waldron, M. (2000). Nonshared environment: A theoretical, methodological, and quantitative review. *Psychological Bulletin, 126,* 78–108.

Van Gestel, S., & Van Broeckhoven, C. (2003). Genetics of personality: Are we making progress? *Molecular Psychiatry, 8,* 840–852.

Waller, N. G., & Shaver, P. R. (1994). The importance of nongenetic influences on romantic love styles: A twin-family study. *Psychological Science, 5,* 268–274.

Wolf, H., Angleitner, A., Spinath, F. M., Riemann, R., & Strelau, J. (2004). Genetic and environmental influences on the EPQ-RS scales: A twin study using self- and peer reports. *Personality and Individual Differences, 37,* 579–590.

Yamagata, S., Suzuki, A., Ando, J., Ono, Y., Kijima, N., Yoshimura, K., et al. (2006). Is the genetic structure of human personality universal? A cross-cultural twin study from North America, Europe, and Asia. *Journal of Personality and Social Psychology, 90,* 987–998.

The Cultural Perspective in Personality Assessment

Fanny M. Cheung

Abstract

Culture affects personality through the ways that people are represented psychologically. Global or etic approaches to the study of culture and personality compare universal dimensions across cultures, whereas focal or emic approaches interpret and identify indigenous dimensions on the basis of local phenomena and experiences. This chapter reviews the relationship between culture and personality, and the impact of cultural factors in personality assessment. Practical and methodological issues of personality assessment across cultures, including issues of equivalence and cross-cultural validation in test translation and adaptation, using the MMPI as an example are discussed. At the theoretical level, the etic and emic approaches to personality assessment are compared, and the contributions of a combined emic–etic approach in developing culturally relevant personality assessment based on the experience of the Cross-cultural (Chinese) Personality Assessment Inventory (CPAI-2) are illustrated. These issues highlight the need for incorporating cross-cultural training as an integral part of psychology in order to enhance the cultural relevance in the practice and research in personality assessment.

Keywords: cross-cultural, validity, emic, etic, test equivalence, test translation, personality constructs, training

Prologue

At the time when I graduated from University of Minnesota in 1975 and returned to work in Hong Kong, I believed I would not be using the MMPI again. I thought that an English test with 566 items, the contents of some of which were very foreign to the Chinese people, would not be very useful there. Upon my return, I discovered that the local clinical psychologists were administering the MMPI to their patients, reading out their own translations of the items on the spot. I was not sure how many different versions of these translations there were among the practicing psychologists. I was doubtful that these versions could be taken as the standardized administration of what was expected in objective psychological assessment. I decided to do a proper translation of the MMPI into Chinese and develop the local norms.

When mainland China resumed the study of psychology in the 1980s, I collaborated with the psychologists at the Institute of Psychology to develop the standardized Chinese version of the MMPI (Cheung, 1995) and later the MMPI-2 (Cheung, Zhang, & Song, 2003) with national norms that would be applicable to Hong Kong and China. We noted cross-cultural similarities and differences in the test results and conducted a number of validation studies. Through our work, the Chinese University Press received permission from the University of Minnesota to publish the Chinese MMPI and Chinese MMPI-2.

Now and then, I received inquiries from North American practitioners about the Chinese MMPI when they were assessing ethnic Chinese clients. Those who took the initiative to inquire about the Chinese versions noted that the test results that they obtained when the English version of the MMPI was used did not always fit their clinical observations. The differences in the test results obtained when different language versions were used have serious implications for clinical and forensic decisions. I was struck by the apparent lack of familiarity among practitioners with the available measures and the knowledge base in culturally relevant personality assessment. There is a definite need for enhancing training and research in the cultural perspectives of personality assessment.

Learning about the strengths and limitations of translated instruments, our research team went on to develop an indigenously derived personality inventory suitable for the Chinese cultural context, the Chinese Personality Assessment Inventory (CPAI; Cheung et al., 1996). This is one of the few comprehensive personality measures developed in a non-English language that have been studied across cultures. Comparing the CPAI with Western personality measures and using the CPAI with non-Chinese samples enlightened our understanding of personality structure, and functioning and measurement across cultures. Work with the CPAI illustrates the reverse side of the coin in cross-cultural personality assessment, when an indigenously derived measure in the Chinese culture is compared to well-established personality measures in mainstream psychology. In a way, the English-language personality tests could also be considered as indigenous measures originating in the Western culture. This broader context offers us a more balanced view to discuss the cultural perspective in personality assessment.

There is now a growing literature on cross-cultural studies in personality and personality assessment. There are also international guidelines for adapting tests for use in various different linguistic and cultural contexts. In this chapter, I review the relationship between culture and personality, and the impact of cultural factors in personality assessment. I discuss the methodological and theoretical issues of personality assessment across cultures, and make recommendations on the training needs for enhancing the cultural perspective in personality assessment.

Culture and Personality

Buss (2001) postulated that culture poses "puzzles for personality theories that aspire to explain human nature and individual differences" at the same time (p. 975). Buss defined culture as a set of "ideas, beliefs, representations, behavior patterns, practices, artifacts, and so forth that are transmitted socially across generations within a group, resulting in patterns of within-group similarity and between-group differences" (pp. 955–956). While personality psychology seeks to integrate both human nature

and individual differences, studies of cultural differences in personality are useful in understanding whether certain prevalent features of personality are universal and common among all people, and whether the level of these personality features differs across cultures.

Approaches to Describe Culture

In their book *Social Psychology and Culture*, Chiu and Hong (2006) constructed the definition of culture as "a set of shared meanings, which provides a common frame of reference for a human group to make sense of reality, coordinate their activities in collective living, and adapt to the external environment" (pp. 16–17). They summarized different strategies that psychologists have used to describe culture: In the global approach, universal dimensions are assumed to be part of human nature and have the same meaning in all cultures. Variations along these dimensions may be found in different cultures. Cross-cultural psychologists have often referred to this approach as the "etic" approach (the term is derived from "phonetics"), which attempts to compare universal pre-established constructs across cultures. Some psychologists have criticized the Western bias in the etic approach in that most etic or "universal" dimensions originate in Western cultural traditions and are imposed on other cultures (Gergen, Gulerce, Lock, & Misra, 1996).

In contrast, the focal approach to cultural description uses local or indigenous concepts originating within a culture to interpret and organize the data for that cultural group. This approach highlights culturally relevant meanings and allows the examination of the variations of these meanings in different contexts and in response to social changes. In cross-cultural psychology, the indigenous concepts are often referred to as "emic" concepts (the term is derived from "phonemics"). The development of indigenous psychologies has adopted a bottom-up approach, building theories on the basis of local phenomena and experiences. These indigenous approaches could contribute to the development of more comprehensive universal theories in mainstream psychology (Allwood & Berry, 2006). However, at the early stage of development when cultural psychologists focus on their emic approaches, there is the danger of cultural relativity and "intellectual provincialism" that limits comparisons across cultures (Triandis, 2000).

Impact of Culture on Personality

Culture per se is not a causal agent of cultural differences in personality. Culture affects personality through the ways that people are represented psychologically, including descriptions of the self, others, and groups (Chiu & Hong, 2006). People are socialized in a unique family and social environment that influences the ways they behave and view the world. Cross-cultural psychologists have studied specific cultural features affecting these cognitive representations of persons.

Hofstede (1991) identified major cultural dimensions that differentiated organizations globally. One such dimension, individualism versus collectivism, has been studied extensively in relation to cultural differences in personality. For example, people in collectivistic cultures tend to perceive themselves as members of communal groups. Their roles and behaviors are affected by their relationships with in-group members. They would give priority to in-group goals. They focus more on the context and the situation in making attributions (Triandis, 2001). Markus and Kitayama (1991) further delineated the relationship between individualism-collectivism and personality in their model of independent versus interdependent self-construals. These two self-construals are considered overarching schemata of self-regulation and have been used to explain observed cultural differences in cognition, emotion, and motivation. Independent self-construals are commonly found in Western cultures that emphasize the inherent separateness of individuals. The view of the self is derived from each individual's unique internal attributes, which are independent from others. On the other hand, interdependent self-construals are represented in many non-Western cultures that emphasize the interconnectedness between people. The self is viewed as a part of a social relationship and is not considered as separate or differentiated from others in the group. Markus and Kitayama suggested that people who endorse independent self-construals tend to be more optimistic and more consistent in their self-perceptions, whereas those who endorse the interdependent self-construals emphasize maintaining harmony and collective goals.

People in different cultures also differ in their implicit theories of the consistency and malleability of personality. Cultures that emphasize the interdependent self-construal would expect less consistency between internal personality attributes and social behavior. Research also confirmed that East Asians from collectivistic cultures were more likely to believe that individual persons were relatively malleable whereas the world was relatively stable. Thus, they were less likely to explain social behavior in terms of global traits and were more inclined to attribute to external forces. On the other hand, North Americans who are from individualistic cultures believed more strongly in the person's unique and fixed personality traits and were more likely to make internal attributions (Chiu & Hong, 2006).

Culture and personality further interact to affect the manifestation of psychopathology in the context of behavioral environments, which consist of culturally constituted self-orientations, objects, space, time, and social norms. One dimension of cultural influence on the perception of psychopathology that has been discussed extensively in cultural psychiatry is the biased observation of somatization among Chinese persons with depressive disorders. The cultural bias in this discussion is rooted in the Western philosophical tradition of Cartesian dualism. In dualistic thinking, psychopathology is viewed in terms of distinct organic and psychological problems (Lewis-Fernandez & Kleinman, 1994). On the other hand, Chinese dialectical thinking encompasses the context and allows for the simultaneous expression of psychological distress in the form of somatic symptoms (Cheung, 1998). When the medical model of psychopathology is imposed, the somatic presentation of distress among Chinese patients is construed by Western-trained practitioners as the somatization tendency in which psychological affects were allegedly denied or suppressed. In the medical model of psychopathology, indigenous cultural beliefs are often reduced to misinformed or superstitious obstacles that interfere with proper diagnosis and treatment of real diseases. These ethnocentric assumptions in understanding psychopathology focus on the self, individual experiences and internal attributes, ignoring the social and interpersonal contexts that affect the conceptualization and manifestation of a range of physical and psychological symptoms. When practitioners understand the cultural values and holistic health beliefs of the Chinese people, somatization may be reconceptualized as a metaphor of distress in the cultural context of an illness experience with implications to social relationships, coping, and help-seeking behavior. In studies of Chinese personality and psychopathology, somatization was found to be related to culturally related personality features that emphasize harmony and traditionalism (Cheung, Gan, & Lo, 2005).

These cultural differences highlight the need to integrate a cultural perspective in understanding personality. Matsumoto (2007) proposed a comprehensive model that illustrates the interaction among human nature (universal processes), culture (via social roles and contexts), and personality (via individual role identities) on behavior. Culture mediates human nature and provides the meaning to the ecological and situational contexts in which individuals of that cultural group adopt their prescribed social roles. Individuals respond to these culturally prescribed social roles by developing their own role identities to form a core set of dispositional traits. In this multilevel model, basic human nature explains the universal psychological processes, cultural influences explains what is "true" for some people of the same group, while the individual's personality addresses what is unique to the person. This complex model may account for individual differences within cultures that contradict the expected cultural differences between cultural groups.

Recent advances in research methodology provide statistical tools to analyze cross-cultural data at the individual as well as the group level (Cheung, Leung, & Au, 2006; Van de Vijver & Leung, 1997, 2001). Since individuals are nested within cultures, cross-cultural data are hierarchically structured and multilevel analyses should be used. At the individual-level analysis, researchers focus on the cross-cultural similarities and differences to which individuals vary on the personality constructs within each culture. At the culture-level analysis, countries are the unit of analysis and comparisons focus on the means across national groups. Cross-cultural psychologists have cautioned that studies of the equivalence of a psychological construct across two or more cultures should take into account this multilevel structure.

Globalization and Cultural Diversity

Early attempts to study culture and personality in cultural anthropology have tried to describe national characters (Barnouw, 1963). The interests in these approaches have since waned, as the simplistic generalizations often led to stereotypic notions of personality (Terracciano et al., 2005). Recent studies of cross-cultural differences in personality tend to explore variations in universal dimensions of personality characteristics across cultures (McCrae & Terracciano, 2006), while indigenous approaches to personality studies try to identify culture-specific or culturally relevant dimensions that are not sufficiently covered by the universal characteristics (Cheung et al., 2001).

With the trends of globalization, migration, and cultural diversity within geographical boundaries, there is a growing recognition of the development of multicultural identities. The development of multicultural identities does not reduce the need to highlight cultural sensitivity in the study of personality. On the contrary, the greater mobility of individuals across cultures has accentuated the interaction of cultural characteristics. With globalization, psychology is rapidly becoming a popular discipline and practice in different parts of the world where professionals and professional tools still lag far behind the demand (Cheung, 2004). Use of objective tests in the guise of scientific methods of assessment enhances the status of the fledging professionals. As a result, the adoption of Western psychological tests has proliferated in these countries. With few local instruments available, most psychologists depend on the importation of well-developed Western personality tests (Cheung, 1985; Cheung et al., 1996). During the early days of test importation, practices guiding the translation and adaptation of Western instruments varied greatly. Researchers or practitioners typically translated a popular test and used it as if it were the original test. Little consideration was given to the quality of the translation or the equivalence of the translated instrument.

The challenge for multicultural assessment is not limited to psychologists in the countries where psychology is an emerging discipline. Well-trained psychologists are increasingly working in international and multicultural settings where they address psychological needs in different cultural contexts. For example, industrial-organizational psychologists working for multinational companies may be brought on site to assess personnel who are posted in different parts of the world. The personnel include locals and expatriate staff relocated to international sites. Decisions on selection and development are made on the basis of the results of the psychological assessment which may be developed originally in a different culture.

Even when they do not travel away from their own cultures, psychologists also have to attend to individuals who migrate from other cultures. Greater respect for cultural diversity also means that they now recognize the relevance of ethnic and other cultural backgrounds among members from different subgroups of their own community (Sue et al., 1991). For example, clinical psychologists practicing in California may have a clientele consisting of a majority of ethnic Asians whose first language or only language is not English. Their levels of acculturation to the host culture vary widely. Diagnostic, treatment, and forensic decisions on these clients are often made on the basis of results of objective personality tests. These cultural exchanges have increased the awareness that cultural contexts need to be taken into account in personality assessment and the study of personality. The cultural perspective is particularly relevant when we consider the widespread application of personality instruments on multicultural test users in occupational, academic, and health settings. Practitioners need to consider the basic parameters of their tools and methods: Are the existing psychological tests useful and relevant? Are there suitable language versions of these tests? Are the translated versions valid?

The broader issue behind these practical questions lies in the challenge posed by the cultural perspective to the mainstream knowledge base in personality psychology. Butcher, Mosch, Tsai, and Nezami (2006) summarized the tension between cultural influences and personality psychology in a series of questions: Is personality universal or culture-specific? Do the same personality traits manifest themselves differently across cultural contexts? How do culture and personality interact to influence behavior as well as psychopathology? Can personality be adequately measured across cultural groups? These cultural considerations can no longer be ignored in the study of personality and personality assessment. It is in this contemporary context that we discuss the impact of cultural factors on personality assessment and approaches to adapt personality assessment across cultures.

Impact of Cultural Factors on Personality Assessment

Marsella and Leong (1995) referred to two major problems of ethnocentrism in cross-cultural psychological assessment: the error of omission and the error of commission. The error of omission refers to "the failure to conduct cross-cultural comparison in reaching conclusions about human behavior" (p. 203), with the assumption that conclusions drawn from psychological studies conducted usually in Western cultures can be generalized without cultural variations. In the error of commission, researchers include different cultural groups for comparison, but neglect the cultural differences in the psychological measures that they use in making the comparison. Measures or instruments that are developed in Western cultures are imposed on the other cultural groups with the assumption that these measures are valid for all groups. Early cross-cultural studies generally adopt these imposed etic measures to identify and reify cross-cultural similarities and differences in the attributes being studied.

Recent advances have highlighted important considerations in cultural differences that need to be taken into account in cross-cultural personality assessment. In the first place, testing itself is not a universally familiar practice. Paper-and-pencil tests require test users to be able to read and write. The test users also need to respond to a forced choice format of yes or no answers or a number on a rating scale. Response bias such as the tendency toward acquiescence or extremity ratings have been noted in different cultures. For example, cultural differences have been observed in the response style of Asian participants who tend to adopt the midpoint in responding to rating scales under the influence of the moderation norm (Hamid, Lai, & Cheng, 2001). Studies with Chinese bilingual participants also showed that the Chinese version of an instrument produced more culturally accommodating responses than the English version of the same test, which could affect the results of a cross-cultural study (Ralston, Cunniff, & Gustafson, 1995).

The matching of the ethnic background of the assessor and the client is another source of administration bias that may affect the outcome of the assessment. Russell and his group of researchers (1996) have found that ethnic matching of therapist and client results in higher ratings of client functioning. Hence, difference from or unfamiliarity with the client's cultural background may limit the therapist's ability to assess optimal client functioning.

Other than response biases and therapist variables, how can differences in test results be explained? In cross-cultural applications of translated personality tests, such as the MMPI-2, differences in the mean scores among normal samples of participants have been observed. One of the inquiries I have received on the Chinese version of the MMPI-2 came from an American forensic expert working on the case of a Chinese plaintiff in a lawsuit. The psychologist described to me the difficulty he encountered when he administered the English MMPI-2 on this Chinese client before he learnt about the availability of the Chinese MMPI-2:

> VRIN was about 70T and the clinical scales did not resemble how she actually was. I consulted with a Chinese-speaking psychologist here who offered to read the items to her in Chinese and to help her understand the linguistic nuances of the questions. The result was even worse. VRIN was about 80T and now she looked overtly psychotic, which she clearly was not, and almost all the clinical scales were elevated.

This example illustrates the many problems inherent in cross-cultural assessment, including the problems of language proficiency, translation, and equivalence of the measures. Research on the Chinese MMPI with normal Chinese participants showed that the mean scores on several MMPI-2 clinical and content scales, including 2 (D), 7 (Pt), 8 (Sc), and Depression, were higher than those obtained by their American counterparts (Cheung, Song, & Zhang, 1996; Kwan, 1999). Do the elevated scores on these scales mean greater psychopathology among the Chinese normal samples? Or are there other cultural factors that affect their responses to some of the items on these scales? If that is the case, there may be a risk of overestimating psychopathology if the test scores are interpreted directly according to the original norms. Careful analyses of the contents of the MMPI scales showed that the endorsement rates of some of the items in these scales differed among Chinese and American normal participants, and the social desirability ratings of these items indicated that the items might not reflect psychopathology in the same way as in the American culture. For example, one item on scale 2 (D) that was endorsed by the majority of Chinese college students, "Most anytime I would rather sit and daydream than do anything else," was also rated by them as socially desirable, suggesting that this item does not reflect psychopathology in the Chinese cultural context (Cheung, 1985). Cultural differences in the perception of the meaning of and responses to some other items on the MMPI-2 scales suggest that these items may not reflect psychopathology among Chinese clients in the ways that they work with American clients.

These examples illustrate that cross-cultural testing is not simply presenting the test items in the local language. They point to the need for a systematic approach to the translation, adaptation, and validation of psychological measures from one culture to another before these measures could be considered cross-culturally valid.

Cross-cultural Validity of Personality Assessment

In the early stages of importing Western personality assessment measures, projective techniques had been widely adopted, given the advantage in their use of nonlinguistic stimuli that avoids the problem of translation and the requirement of literacy (Church, 2001). However, the linguistic content of the stimuli is not the only source of cultural bias. The elaborate coding and interpretive system as well as the lack of scientific support for the validity of the projective measures themselves have led to the decline in the use of these methods of assessment. The structured and standardized format of objective personality instruments and the available research database on their reliability and validity led to their popularity in cross-cultural adoption. One of the most widely translated personality measures that has been exported internationally is the MMPI. Since its first adoption in Italy in 1948 and Germany in 1954, the MMPI/MMPI-2 has been translated into over 150 versions and is used in almost 50 countries in the world (Butcher, 2004).

A number of cross-cultural psychologists have discussed the methodological considerations in translating and adapting personality assessment across cultures (Marsella, Dubanoski, Hamada, & Morse, 2000; Van de Vijver & Leung, 1997). Based on the experience of the international applications of the MMPI/MMPI-2, Butcher and his associates have formulated a comprehensive system of cross-cultural adaptation of objective personality tests. Butcher et al. (2006) outlined the major methodological problems and the technical resolutions to these problems. The key issues are summarized in this section, but readers are referred to the original chapter by Butcher et al. for a comprehensive review.

In adapting the MMPI-2 from the source culture, i.e. the United States, to a target culture, e.g. China, the greatest challenge is to assure "equivalence" between the translated version and the original version of the MMPI-2. Equivalence consists of several levels of focus: "linguistic equivalence" refers to items conveying the same literal meaning in both language versions; "construct equivalence" refers to similar concepts being conveyed in both versions of the MMPI-2; "psychometric equivalence" refers to both versions of the MMPI-2 possessing similar psychometric properties so that the reliability and validity of the original MMPI-2 could be applicable to the target culture; "psychological equivalence" refers to the similarity in meaning or cultural significance of the test items in both versions.

Linguistic Equivalence

Butcher et al. (2006) refers to linguistic equivalence as the most basic level of equivalence between translated versions of a psychological test at the level of the item and instructions. The linguistic aspects of an item include vocabulary, idioms, and grammatic structure. Accurate translation requires the use of multiple independent translators who are truly bilingual and experienced in both cultures. After the initial translation, independent translators are engaged in the process of back-translation, which involves retranslation of translated items back to the source language in order to determine if the translated items retain their meaning. Items that are difficult to translate or mistranslated are discovered and retranslated. This translation–back-translation process is repeated until the discrepancies between the items of the source language and back-translation versions are minimized.

Particular attention should be paid to idiomatic use of the language that may not be readily picked up in back-translation. For example, in the MMPI-2, expressions like "I feel blue" could be translated literally into the color blue and back-translated accurately, but the meaning of the emotional state may be lost in this literal translation. In the translation of the Chinese MMPI-2, the translators consulted the original authors to ensure that the nuances of the language were accurately reflected in the translation. Careful choice of translators who are proficient in both languages and consultation with bilingual experts have been recommended as necessary procedures in test adaptation.

Given the increasing adaptation of tests for use in various different linguistic and cultural contexts, a 13-person committee representing a number of international organizations at the International Test Commission has developed a set of guidelines. These guidelines are grouped under four main categories: the cultural context, the technicalities of instrument development and adaptation, test administration, and documentation and interpretation. For details of the guidelines, readers are referred to the *ITC Guidelines on Adapting Tests* (International Test Commission, www.intestcom.org; Hambleton, Merenda, & Spielberger, 2005; Van de Vijver & Hambleton, 1996).

Construct Equivalence

Construct equivalence or conceptual equivalence refers to the generalizability of the personality variables or constructs being examined from the source culture to the target culture. Personality variables may differ in form and quantity across cultures and constructs may not have the same psychological meaning across cultures. To test for construct equivalence in adapted personality measures, one of the recommended approaches is to use bilingual test–retest studies (Butcher et al., 2006). In these studies, a group of bilinguals in the target culture would take the original form and the translated version of the test within 1–2-week intervals

(Butcher, Nezami, & Exner, 1998). The correlations between the bilingual results may be compared to the test–retest reliability of the single-language versions to determine if the translated version could be considered to be an alternate form of the original version (Butcher, Derksen, Sloore, & Sirigatti, 2003).

In the case of the international versions of the MMPI, programs are also available to compare the differences in item endorsement between two cultural groups (Butcher & Pancheri, 1976). Items showing large discrepancies in endorsement rates between the cultural groups may suggest either errors in translation, or differences in the relevance of the item to the construct being measured. As shown in the earlier example of the item on the MMPI scale 2 (D), the higher rate of endorsement of that item among Chinese college students compared to that of the American college students, and the results that showed that the item was rated as more socially desirable by the Chinese students suggested that this item did not reflect depression in the Chinese cultural context (Cheung, 1985).

In addition to bottom-up approaches, recent studies have also adopted the top-down approach to establish construct equivalence by multilevel analysis (McCrae et al., 2005). To test for cross-cultural equivalence of the underlying structure of the constructs being measured, some researchers recommended the use of exploratory factor analysis with country-level data in addition to individual-level data (Van de Vijver & Poortinga, 2002). The use of structural equation modeling within the framework of a multilevel model provides the most rigorous approach to testing for cross-level equivalence. Structural equation modeling allows the researcher to consider both the individual and the cultural group level of the data simultaneously (Cheung et al., 2006). However, one critical restriction of this approach is the need for large samples of cross-cultural groups, which is often not the purpose for establishing construct equivalence in translating and adapting a personality test.

Psychometric Equivalence

Psychometric equivalence refers to an instrument possessing similar psychometric properties in different cultures (Butcher & Han, 1996), which includes reliability, item–scale correlation, item endorsement frequencies, inter-item correlations, inter-scale correlations, and factor structure of the scales. Butcher et al. (2006) described a variety of objective indices used to demonstrate the congruence of factors between different samples, including the congruence coefficient, factor score correlations, and confirmatory factor analysis. Item response theory has also been used in the investigation of psychometric equivalence between test translations. By examining the item characteristic curves for two different language versions of an item, it is possible to determine the equivalence of the item meanings in relation to the trait being measured.

Related to psychometric equivalence is "scalar equivalence," i.e. the scores on the translated and the original instruments express the same level of intensity of that trait (Butcher & Han, 1996). Scalar equivalence is demonstrated by administering the test to similar groups (e.g., persons with psychiatric disorders) in the two cultural samples in order to determine if similar scores on the same scales are achieved. If the two groups achieved very different levels of scores on that scale, then it may be more appropriate to collect a culture-specific norm instead of using the norms developed for the original instrument. For example, with the Chinese MMPI-2, Chinese normals scored significantly higher than American normals on a number of clinical scales, even though Chinese persons with psychiatric disorders scored even higher on these scales (Cheung, Zhang, & Song, 2003). When the Chinese norms are used, persons without psychiatric disorders scored within the normal range. Cheung et al. recommended using both the U.S. and the Chinese norms with the Chinese MMPI-2 to provide a more accurate interpretation of the clinical profile.

Psychological Equivalence

Psychological equivalence refers to the similarity in meaning or cultural significance of test items that are familiar to the real experiences of the target and source cultures (Butcher, 1996). Related to the idea of psychological equivalence is the issue of "functional equivalence," meaning that the function of a behavior depicted in the item in the source culture is equivalent to that contained in a related but different item in the target culture. For example, some of the MMPI-2 items are idioms which have specific cultural meaning. The item depicting a superstition about being careful to step over sidewalk cracks when walking is unfamiliar in the Chinese culture. To depict a similar superstitious behavior, the item is substituted by an item that describes avoiding to walk under a ladder.

The ultimate demonstration of the functional utility of the adapted instrument in the target culture lies in cross-cultural validation studies that show

similar test patterns are correlated with similar outcomes as in the source culture. Studies with international versions of the MMPI-2 show that with careful translation and adaptation, and using appropriate norms, the MMPI-2 can be used effectively for clinical assessment as it is originally intended. Butcher et al. (2006) summarized the internal validity, convergent validity, and interpretive accuracy of these international versions. In the validation of the Chinese MMPI, studies were conducted to demonstrate the usefulness of the MMPI in differentiating between psychiatric and normal groups (Cheung & Song, 1989). In additional to empirical studies, clinical case studies also provide useful illustrations of the clinical utility of the MMPI-2 in the target culture. Butcher and Cheung (2006, May) showed that there was more convergence than divergence in the clinical interpretation of cases that used computerized reports using US norms and the clinicians' observations of the cases based on the test results scored on the Chinese norms of the Chinese MMPI-2.

Even when imported constructs are demonstrated to be present in the target culture does not mean they are universally relevant in psychological meaning. For example, Cheung, Cheung et al. (2008) showed that a distinct Openness factor in the Five-Factor Model (FFM; Digman, 1990) was not found in indigenous studies of personality in the Chinese culture even though it could be extracted in imposed etic studies using translated measures of FFM. Instead, using a combined emic–etic approach, they extracted a Social Potency/Expansiveness factor in the indigenously derived CPAI-2 that combined extraversion and openness-related scales. This complex construct denoted a more interpersonal dimension that characterized dynamic and charismatic leadership, as opposed to a more introspective and individual-level construct of openness in the Five-Factor Model.

Emics versus Etics Personality Measures
Value and Limitations of Universal Constructs

International applications of the MMPI-2 illustrate the value of using common psychological measures across cultures. Cross-cultural validation of the international versions allows access to the rich research database accumulated on the MMPI-2. The range of clinical studies on the MMPI-2 provides test users the scientific basis for their assessment, which would be difficult to match if indigenous tools were developed in different cultures. The importation of well-established tests provides psychologists in countries where assessment is only beginning to develop with an efficient repertory of assessment tools (Cheung, 2004).

These imported instruments also allow for cross-cultural comparison of common personality constructs (Cheung & Leung, 1998). The personality model that has been studied most widely across culture is the FFM using the NEO PI-R (Costa & McCrae, 1992). McCrae et al. (2005) studied personality profiles of 51 cultures by using mean trait levels of culture members by asking college students from their countries to rate an individual whom they knew well. While cultural variations were found on the mean levels of the five personality factors, the FFM structure was found to be a universally valid taxonomy of personality (McCrae & Allik, 2002). McCrae asserted that these etic or universal traits are rooted in biology while culture shapes their expressions (Hofstede & McCrae, 2004).

When importing etic personality measures, cross-cultural psychologists usually ask the following questions: How well do the personality dimensions assessed by the imported tests replicate across cultures? What are the significant differences in personality traits that are identified by the imported measures? Can imported tests predict relevant criteria across cultures (Church, 2001)? Cross-cultural research on the well-established personality measures such as the MMPI-2 and the NEO PI-R have replicated the factor structure and the relationships with external correlates, supporting the relevance and usefulness of these imported measures. However, different factor structures could also be extracted in cross-cultural studies, and some of the factors in the NEO PI-R, such as Openness, did not replicate well in European and Asian cultures, suggesting that the imported measures may be imposing their model of factor structure in the new cultural context (Cheung, Cheung et al., 2008; Church, 2001). There may be other personality constructs that are important to the local cultures that are not covered in the imported measures, or are not construed in the same taxonomy that is meaningful to the local culture. The rise of indigenous movements in psychology has led to the development of emic personality measures which derive the constructs from within the culture.

Indigenous Measures of Personality

In the movement toward indigenization of psychology since the 1970s, psychologists in non-Western cultures have proposed indigenous personality theories and attempted to develop their own personality measures (Enriquez, 1993; Yang, 1997). Ho (1998) defined an indigenous psychology as "the study of human behavior and mental processes within a cultural context" in which cultural "conceptions and methodologies rooted in that cultural group [are] employed to generate knowledge" (p. 94). Personality constructs are derived from the local cultural perspective instead of being imported. Many of the indigenous personality constructs derived in Asia reflect the relational nature of human experience in a social and interpersonal context (Cheung, Cheung, Wada, & Zhang, 2003). Examples include the Chinese concepts of "harmony" and "face" (public sense of self) (Cheung et al., 2001), the Japanese concept of *amae* ("sweet indulgence"), the Korean concept of *chong* ("affection") (Kim, Park, & Park, 1999), and the concept of selflessness, or "selfless-self" in Taoism, Buddhism, and Hinduism (Verma, 1999).

Some of the early indigenous personality measures modified imported instruments by selecting relevant scales and collecting data to establish local norms. Others made use of the lexical approach to extract personality dimensions that are relevant to the local culture (Guanzon-Lapeña, Church, Carlota, & Katigbak, 1998; Isaka, 1990; Yang & Bond, 1990).

However, few of the indigenous measures have been followed through with a program of research on its development and validation that is necessary for its utility as an assessment tool. Nor have they addressed satisfactorily the questions posed by cross-cultural psychologists (Church, 2001): How culture-specific are the indigenous personality constructs and measures? Do these constructs and measures provide incremental validity beyond that provided by the imported measures? Church concluded that most indigenous measures did not identify culture-specific constructs that could not be subsumed under the universal FFM. He acknowledged that the best support for the incremental validity of indigenously derived personality measures came from the CPAI.

Combined Emic–Etic Approach

The CPAI was developed to measure Chinese personality from an indigenous perspective, using a combined emic–etic approach (Cheung et al., 1996, 2001). Universal and indigenous personality traits considered to be important in the Chinese culture were generated in a bottom-up approach to develop a set of normal personality and clinical scales for comprehensive personality assessment. Borrowing from the experience of adapting the MMPI, validity scales were included to enhance the accuracy of assessment. Four normal personality factors and two clinical factors were extracted from the CPAI scales. In a joint factor analysis between the CPAI and the NEO PI-R (Cheung et al., 2001), it was found that the indigenous Interpersonal Relatedness factor did not load on any of the NEO factors. In that study, the NEO Openness factor did not load on any of the CPAI factors.

In the subsequent revision of the CPAI, a set of indigenously derived openness scales were added (Cheung, Cheung, & Zhang, 2004; Cheung, Cheung et al., 2008). Originally, it was expected that a separate openness factor would be extracted from the CPAI-2 after adding these scales. However, some of the individually oriented openness scales loaded with extraversion to form the expanded Social Potency/ Expansiveness factor, which depicts dynamic leadership, while the other interpersonally related openness scales loaded with the Accommodation factor and the Interpersonal Relatedness factor. The replication of a four-factor structure in the CPAI-2 even after the addition of openness-related scales suggests that the lack of loading on Openness in the joint analysis between the original CPAI and the NEO PI-R may reflect cultural differences in the psychological meaning of Openness. Openness is not an inherently distinct dimension in the implicit theory and taxonomy of personality in the Chinese culture, although characteristics of people who are regarded as open could be described. Instead, these openness-related characteristics coexisted with other traits to define the personality taxonomy that is relevant to the local reality.

A program of research to validate the utility of the CPAI/CPAI-2 has been conducted to support its usefulness as a personality assessment tool in clinical and organizational settings (Cheung, 2007; Cheung, Fan, & To, 2008; Cheung, Kwong, & Zhang, 2003; Cheung, Cheung, & Leung, 2008; Kwong & Cheung, 2003). The indigenously derived CPAI-2 personality factors contributed additional value to the prediction of social behavior in the Chinese cultural context (Cheung et al., 2001, 2008). To test the cross-cultural relevance of its indigenously derived personality constructs, the CPAI has been translated into English, Korean, and Japanese, and cross-cultural samples have confirmed the congruence of the factor structure, especially among Asian and Asian-American samples (Cheung, Cheung, Leung, Ward, & Leong, 2003; Cheung, Cheung, Howard, & Lin, 2006). Lin and Church (2004) found that the indigenously derived Interpersonal

Relatedness factor replicated well among Asian-Americans and fairly well among European-Americans, supporting its cross-cultural relevance. However, Asian-Americans who were less acculturated to the American culture scored higher on this factor than the Asian-American participants who were more acculturated and the European-American participants. This result demonstrated the stronger salience of the Interpersonal Relatedness factor in traditional Chinese culture. Current research on the CPAI includes the development of an adolescent version, the CPAI-A, and studies on the cross-cultural utility of the CPAI-2/ CPAI-A in career counseling.

Although the original objective of developing the CPAI was to offer Chinese psychologists an instrument that was culturally relevant to their applied needs, cross-cultural research with the CPAI provides an opportunity to explore the emic and etic dimensions of Chinese personality. The combined emic–etic approach allows cross-cultural researchers to compare personality constructs derived from different cultural perspectives and to examine the additional contributions of indigenous constructs to existing mainstream models of personality that are mostly rooted in Western culture. Cheung (2002) observed that the CPAI "research findings have led us down a more theoretical path to look at how the cultural reality that is cut by this indigenous instrument reflects upon the imposed reality that we used to know, based on borrowed instruments and borrowed theories" (p. 155). The extension of the CPAI beyond the Chinese context has led to the renaming of the CPAI-2 as the Cross-cultural Personality Assessment Inventory. The culturally relevant personality constructs in the CPAI-2 may fill the gap in the interpersonal dimensions in Western personality theories.

The combined emic–etic approach adopted by the CPAI is currently being used as a framework in developing the national South African Personality Inventory (SAPI) as a set of comprehensive personality questionnaires for all South African language groups. The South African psychologists considered that imported questionnaires based on a Western model of independence would not be appropriate for describing the African personality in which interdependence (Ubuntu) was more salient. This ambitious project aims at deriving a culturally relevant measure for the multiethnic communities of South Africa with 11 language versions and ensuring equivalent constructs and measures for the different tribes and ethnic groups (Meiring, van de Vijver, Rothmann, & Bruin, 2008, July).

Training Needs in Enhancing the Cultural Perspective in Personality Assessment

The increasing use of personality assessment across cultures illustrates the need to develop culturally sensitive measures. Recent advances in cross-cultural psychology have introduced useful methodological and statistical tools for research in this area. The American Psychological Association has published two important documents to promote scholarship on multicultural awareness: *Guidelines on Multicultural Education, Training, Research, Practice, and Organizational Change for Psychologists* (American Psychological Association, 2003) and *Resolution on Culture and Gender Awareness in International Psychology* (American Psychological Association Council of Representatives, 2004). It has established a task force initiated by the Division of International Psychology (Division 52) and the Division of Measurement, Evaluation, and Statistics (Division 5). The purpose of the task force was to identify methodological aspects of cross-cultural research that were in need of improvement and to promote training in these aspects. In addition to training offered by the APA, other international professional organizations such as the International Test Commission, International Association of Applied Psychology, International Congress of Psychology, and the European Congresses of Psychology also offer training workshops on cross-cultural testing and measurement during their conventions.

At a more practical level, it is imperative that practitioners become familiarized with the literature on cross-cultural validity and applications of the instruments that they intend to use across cultures. It is insufficient to be only familiar with the original tests that they may be trained to administer. They should consult the test publishers on the language versions of the tests that are available in the cultures in which they intend to administer their assessment. They should be wary of cross-cultural biases and incorporate their knowledge of cross-cultural differences in their interpretation of test results. The MMPI-2 international conferences and workshops are examples of the venue where practitioners can gain such knowledge.

As psychology joins the global village, the discipline can no longer ignore the cultural contexts that inform our knowledge base. The cultural perspective is not a sideline to mainstream psychology. Cross-cultural training should become an integral part of graduate and professional training, not only for students interested in cross-cultural psychology, but also as a basic tenet of training in psychological assessment and research methodology.

Acknowledgments

The CPAI projects reported in this chapter were partially supported by the Hong Kong Government Research Grants Council Earmarked Grants CUHK4333/00H, CUHK4326/01H, CUHK4259/03H, CUHK4254/03H, and CUHK4715/06H, and by Direct Grants #89106, 91113, 2020662, 2020745, 2020717, and 2020871 of the Chinese University of Hong Kong.

References

Allwood, C. M., & Berry, J. W. (2006). Origins and development of indigenous psychologies: An international analysis. *International Journal of Psychology, 41,* 243–268.

American Psychological Association (2003). Guidelines on multicultural education, training, research, practice, and organizational change for psychologists. *American Psychologist, 58,* 377–402.

American Psychological Association Council of Representatives (2004). *Resolution on culture and gender awareness in international psychology.* Washington, DC: American Psychological Association.

Barnouw, V. (1963). *Culture and personality.* Homewood, IL: Dorsey Press.

Buss, D. M. (2001). Human nature and culture: An evolutionary psychological perspective. *Journal of Personality, 69,* 955–978.

Butcher, J. N. (2004). Personality assessment without borders: Adaptation of the MMPI-2 across cultures. *Journal of Personality Assessment, 83,* 90–104.

Butcher, J. N., & Cheung, F. M. (2006, May). *Discussion and Case Interpretation.* Presentation at the Workshop on MMPI-2 Jointly Organized by the Clinical Psychological Service Branch of Social Welfare Department and the Chinese University of Hong Kong, Hong Kong.

Butcher, J. N., Derksen, J., Sloore, H., & Sirigatti, S. (2003). Objective personality assessment of people in diverse cultures: European adaptations of the MMPI-2. *Behavior Research and Therapy, 41,* 819–840.

Butcher, J. N., & Han, K. (1996). Methods of establishing cross-cultural equivalence. In J. N. Butcher (Ed.), *International adaptations of the MMPI-2* (pp. 44–63). Minneapolis, MN: University of Minnesota Press.

Butcher, J. N., Mosch, S. C., Tsai, J., & Nezami, E. (2006). Cross cultural applications of the MMPI-2. In J. N. Butcher (Ed.), *MMPI-2: The practitioner's guide* (pp. 505–537). Washington, DC: American Psychological Association.

Butcher, J. N., Nezami, E., & Exner, J. (1998). Psychological assessment of people in diverse cultures. In S. Kazarian & D. R. Evans (Eds.), *Cross-cultural clinical psychology* (pp. 61–105). New York: Oxford University Press.

Butcher, J. N. & Pancheri, P. (1976). *Handbook of cross-national MMPI research.* Minneapolis, MN: University of Minnesota Press.

Cheung, F. M. (1985). Cross-cultural considerations for the translation and adaptation of the Chinese MMPI in Hong Kong. In J. N. Butcher & C. D. Spielberger (Eds.), *Advances in personality assessment* (Vol. 4, pp. 131–158). Hillsdale, NJ: Lawrence Erlbaum.

Cheung, F. M. (1995). *Administration manual of the Minnesota Multiphasic Personality Inventory (MMPI)* (Chinese ed.). Hong Kong: The Chinese University Press.

Cheung, F. M. (1998). Cross-cultural psychopathology. In A. S. Bellack & M. Hersen (Eds.), *Comprehensive clinical psychology,*

Vol. 10: Sociocultural and individual differences (pp. 35–51). Oxford: Pergamon.

Cheung, F. M. (2002). Universal and indigenous dimensions of Chinese personality. In K. S. Kurasaki, S. Okazaki, & S. Sue (Eds.), *Asian American mental health: Assessment theories and methods* (pp. 141–157). Dordrecht, The Netherlands: Kluwer Academic Press.

Cheung, F. M. (2004). Use of western and indigenously-developed personality tests in Asia. *Applied Psychology: An International Review, 53*, 173–191.

Cheung, F. M. (2007). Indigenous personality correlates from the CPAI-2 profiles of Chinese psychiatric patients. *World Cultural Psychiatry Research Review, 2*(4), 114–117.

Cheung, F. M., & Leung, K. (1998). Indigenous personality measures: Chinese examples. *Journal of Cross-Cultural Psychology, 29*, 233–248.

Cheung, F. M., Cheung, S. F., & Leung, F. (2008). Clinical utility of the Cross-Cultural (Chinese) Personality Assessment Inventory (CPAI-2) in the assessment of substance use disorders among Chinese men. *Psychological Assessment, 20*, 103–113.

Cheung, F. M., Cheung, S. F., Leung, K., Ward, C., & Leong, F. (2003). The English version of the Chinese Personality Assessment Inventory: Derived etics in a mirror position. *Journal of Cross-Cultural Psychology, 34*, 433–452.

Cheung, F. M., Cheung, S. F., Wada, S., & Zhang, J. X. (2003). Indigenous measures of personality assessment in Asian countries: A review. *Psychological Assessment, 15*, 280–289.

Cheung, F. M., Cheung, S. F., & Zhang, J. X. (2004). What is "Chinese personality"? Subgroup differences in the Chinese Personality Assessment Inventory (CPAI-2). *Acta Psychologica Sinica, 36*, 491–499.

Cheung, F. M., Cheung, S. F., Zhang, J. X., Leung, K., Leong, F. T. L., & Yeh, K. H. (2008). Relevance of openness as a personality dimension in Chinese culture. *Journal of Cross-Cultural Psychology, 39*, 81–108.

Cheung, F. M., Fan, W. Q., & To, C. W. W. (2008). The CPAI as a culturally relevant personality measure in applied settings. *Social and Personality Psychology Compass, 2*, 74–89.

Cheung, F. M., Gan, Y. Q., & Lo, P. M. (2005). Personality and psychopathology: Insight from Chinese studies. In W. S. Tseng, S. C. Chang, & M. Nishizono (Eds.), *Asian culture and psychotherapy: Implications for East and West* (pp. 21–39). Honolulu, HI: University of Hawaii Press.

Cheung, F. M., Kwong, J., & Zhang, J. X. (2003). Clinical validation of the Chinese Personality Assessment Inventory (CPAI). *Psychological Assessment, 15*, 89–100.

Cheung, F. M., Leung, K., Fan, R., Song, W. Z., Zhang, J. X., & Zhang, J. P. (1996). Development of the Chinese Personality Assessment Inventory (CPAI). *Journal of Cross-Cultural Psychology, 27*, 181–199.

Cheung, F. M., Leung, K., Zhang, J. X., Sun, H. F., Gan, Y. Q., Song, W. Z., et al. (2001). Indigenous Chinese personality constructs: Is the Five-Factor Model complete? *Journal of Cross-Cultural Psychology, 32*, 407–433.

Cheung, F. M., & Song, W. Z. (1989). A review on the clinical applications of the Chinese MMPI. *Psychological Assessment, 1*, 230–237.

Cheung, F. M., Song, W. Z., & Zhang, J. X. (1996). The Chinese MMPI-2: Research and applications in Hong Kong and the People's Republic of China. In J. N. Butcher (Ed.), *International adaptations of the MMPI-2: A handbook of research and applications* (pp. 137–161). Minneapolis, MN: University of Minnesota Press.

Cheung, F. M., Zhang, J. X., & Song, W. Z. (2003). *Manual of the Minnesota Multiphasic Personality Inventory-2 (MMPI-2)* (Chinese). Hong Kong: The Chinese University Press.

Cheung, M. W. L., Leung, K., & Au, K. (2006). Evaluating multilevel models in cross-cultural research: An illustration with social axioms. *Journal of Cross-Cultural Psychology, 37*, 522–541.

Cheung, S. F., Cheung, F. M., Howard, R., & Lin, Y. H. (2006). Personality across ethnic divide in Singapore: Are "Chinese traits" uniquely Chinese? *Personality and Individual Differences, 41*, 467–477.

Chiu, C. Y., & Hong, Y. Y. (2006). *Social psychology of culture.* New York: Psychology Press.

Church, A. T. (2001). Personality measurement in cross-cultural perspective. *Journal of Personality, 69*, 979–1006.

Costa, P. T., Jr., & McCrae, R. R. (1992). *Revised NEO Personality Inventory (NEO-PI-R) and NEO Five-Factor Inventory (NEO-FFI) professional manual.* Odessa, FL: Psychological Assessment Resources, Inc.

Digman, J. M. (1990). Personality structure: Emergence of the Five Factor Model. *Annual Review of Psychology, 41*, 417–440.

Enriquez, V. G. (1993). Developing a Filipino psychology. In U. Kim & J. W. Berry (Eds.), *Indigenous psychologies: Research and experience in cultural context* (pp. 152–169). Newbury Park, CA: Sage.

Gergen, K. J., Gulerce, A., Lock, A., & Misra, G. (1996). Psychological science in cultural context. *American Psychologist, 51*, 496–503.

Guanzon-Lapeña, M. A., Church, A. T., Carlota, A. J., & Katigbak, M. S. (1998). Indigenous personality measures: Philippine examples. *Journal of Cross-Cultural Psychology, 29*, 249–270.

Hambleton, R., Merenda, P., & Spielberger, C. (Eds.). (2005). *Adapting educational and psychological tests for cross-cultural assessment.* Mahwah, NJ: Erlbaum.

Hamid, P. N., Lai, J. C. L., & Cheng, S. T. (2001). Response bias and public and private self-consciousness in Chinese. *Social Behavior and Personality, 29*, 733–742.

Ho, D. (1998). Indigenous psychologies: Asian perspectives. *Journal of Cross-Cultural Psychology, 29*, 88–103.

Hofstede, G. (1991). *Culture and organizations.* London: McGraw-Hill.

Hofstede, G., & McCrae, R. R. (2004). Personality and culture revisited: Linking traits with dimensions of culture. *Cross-cultural Research, 38*, 52–88.

International Test Commission. *ITC guidelines for adapting tests.* Retrieved January 3, 2008 from http://www.intestcom.org/itc_projects.htm#ITC%20Guidelines%20on%20Adapting%20Tests

Isaka, H. (1990). Factor analysis of trait terms in everyday Japanese language. *Personality and Individual Differences, 11*, 115–124.

Kim, U., Park, Y. S., & Park, D. (1999). The Korean indigenous psychology approach: Theoretical considerations and empirical applications. *Applied Psychology: An International Review, 48*, 451–464.

Kwan, K. L. K. (1999). MMPI and MMPI-2 performance of the Chinese: Cross-cultural applicability. *Professional Psychology: Research and Practices, 30*, 260–268.

Kwong, J., & Cheung, F. M. (2003). Prediction of performance facets using specific personality traits in the Chinese context. *Journal of Vocational Behavior, 63*, 99–110.

Lewis-Fernandez, R., & Kleinman, A. (1994). Culture, personality, and psychopathology. *Journal of Abnormal Psychology, 103*, 67–71.

Lin, E. J., & Church, A. T. (2004). Are indigenous Chinese personality dimensions culture-specific? An investigation of the Chinese Personality Assessment Inventory in Chinese American and European American samples. *Journal of Cross-cultural Psychology, 35*, 586–605.

Markus, H. R., & Kitayama, S. (1991). Culture and self: Implications for cognition, emotion, and motivation. *Psychological Review, 98*, 224–253.

Marsella, A., & Leong, F. T. L. (1995). Cross-cultural issues in personality and career assessment. *Journal of Career Assessment, 3*, 202–218.

Marsella, A. J., Dubanoski, J., Hamada, W. C., & Morse, H. (2000). The measurement of personality across cultures: Historical, conceptual, and methodological issues and considerations. *American Behavioral Scientist, 44*, 41–62.

Matsumoto, D. (2007). Culture, context, and behavior. *Journal of Personality, 75*, 1285–1319.

McCrae, R. R., & Allik, J. (Eds.). (2002). *The Five-Factor Model across cultures.* New York: Kluwer Academic Press/Plenum.

McCrae, R. R., & Terracciano, A. (2006). National character and personality. *Current Directions in Psychological Science, 15*, 156–161.

McCrae, R. R., Terracciano, A., & 79 members of the Personality Profiles of Cultures Projects. (2005). Personality profiles of cultures: Aggregate personality traits. *Journal of Personality and Social Psychology, 89*, 407–425.

Meiring, D., van de Vijver, F., Rothmann, I., & de Bruin, D. (2008, July). Uncovering the Personality Structure of the 11 Language Groups in South Africa: SAPI Project. In F. M. Cheung (Chair), *Testing and assessment in emerging and developing countries. II: Challenges and recent advances.* Symposium conducted at the meeting of the 29th International Congress of Psychology, Berlin, Germany.

Ralston, D. A., Cunniff, M. K., & Gustafson, D. J. (1995). Cultural accommodation: The effect of language on the responses of bilingual Hong Kong Chinese managers. *Journal of Cross-Cultural Psychology, 26*, 714–727.

Russell, G. L., Fujino, D. C., Sue, S., Cheung, M., & Snowdon, L. R. (1996). The effects of therapist–client ethnic match in the assessment of mental health functioning. *Journal of Cross-cultural Psychology, 27*, 598–615.

Sue, S., Fujino, D. C., Hu, L., Takeuchi, D. T., & Zane, N. (1991). Community mental health services for ethnic minority groups: A test of the cultural responsiveness hypothesis. *Journal of Consulting and Clinical Psychology, 59*, 533–540.

Terracciano, A., Abdel-Khalek, A. M., Adam, N., Adamovova, L., Ahn, C. K., Ahn, H. N., et al. (2005). National character does not reflect mean personality trait levels in 49 cultures. *Science, 310*, 96–100.

Triandis, H. C. (2000). Dialectics between cultural and cross-cultural psychology. *Asian Journal of Social Psychology, 3*, 185–197.

Triandis, H. C. (2001). Individualism-collectivism and personality. *Journal of Personality, 69*, 907–924.

Van de Vijver, F., & Hambleton, R. (1996). Translating tests: Some practical guidelines. *European Psychologist, 1*, 89–99.

Van de Vijver, F., & Leung, K. (1997). *Methods and data analysis for cross-cultural research.* Thousand Oaks, CA: Sage.

Van de Vijver, F., & Leung, K. (2001). Personality in cultural context: Methodological issues. *Journal of Personality, 69*, 1007–1031.

Verma, J. (1999). Hinduism, Islam and Buddhism: The source of Asian values. In K. Leung, U. Kim, S. Yamaguchi, & U. Kashima (Eds.), *Progress in Asian social psychologies* (pp. 23–36). Singapore: John Wiley & Sons.

Yang, K. S. (1997). Theories and research in Chinese personality: An indigenous approach. In H. S. R. Kao & D. Sinha (Eds.), *Asian perspectives on psychology* (pp. 236–262). Thousand Oaks, CA: Sage.

Yang, K. S., & Bond, M. H. (1990). Exploring implicit personality theories with indigenous or imported constructs: The Chinese case. *Journal of Personality and Social Psychology, 58*, 1087–1095.

PART 3

Methodological and Conceptual Factors and Psychometric Considerations

4   Test Theory and Personality Measurement

Fritz Drasgow, Oleksandr S. Chernyshenko, *and* Stephen Stark

Abstract

This chapter reviews traditional approaches for the psychometric analysis of responses to personality inventories, including classical test theory item analysis, exploratory factor analysis, and item response theory. These methods, which can be called "dominance" models, work well for items assessing moderately positive or negative trait levels, but are unable to describe adequately items representing intermediate (or average) trait levels. This necessitates a shift to an alternative family of psychometric models, known as ideal point models, which stipulate that the likelihood of endorsement increases as respondents' trait levels get closer to an item's location. An ideal point model for personality measures using single statements as items is described, data are reanalyzed to show how the change of modeling framework improves fit, and the pairwise preference format is described for use in personality assessment. Two illustrative ideal point models for unidimensional and multidimensional pairwise preferences are discussed, which shows that, after correcting for unreliability, correlations of traits assessed with single statements, unidimensional pairs, and multidimensional pairs are very close to unity suggesting that the choice of format does not affect the trait being measured. Some exciting areas for future research are noted.

Keyword: personality test theory

Since Spearman's classic 1904 paper "General intelligence, objectively determined and measured," thousands of psychometrician-years have been devoted to the development and evaluation of test theories for the assessment of cognitive ability. Classical test theory (CTT; Gulliksen, 1950), item response theory (IRT; Lord, 1980), computerized adaptive testing (CAT; Sands, Waters, & McBride, 1997), and many other innovations have been developed to improve the measurement of cognitive ability. In addition to a great deal of research, ability testing is big business. The Educational Testing Service, for example, employed more than 2,400 people, administered more than 12 million exams, and had revenue in excess of $800 million in its fiscal year ending June 2007 (Hoovers, 2007).

So what are the implications of this massive research literature and business practice for personality measurement? Is it reasonable to simply adopt best models and practices from the cognitive ability domain or is there a need for different approaches and innovation? In this chapter, we will first review and illustrate the application of "tried and true" methods developed in the context of cognitive ability testing to personality assessment and contrast them with alternative ways of scaling personality items. We then focus on pairwise preference response formats, which are not commonly found in cognitive ability testing, but carry a number of advantages over the single-statement (SS) format for personality assessment. We present some methods for scoring both unidimensional and multidimensional pairwise preferences and relate these results to traditionally scored measures. In keeping with the cognitive ability tradition, we do not review methods for empirical keying; see Bergman, Drasgow, Donovan, Juraska, and Nejdlik (2006) for a review and illustration of several of these methods.

It is important to note that successful application of any method for modeling response data depends critically on assumptions about the underlying response process. At the most general level, for example, test theories for cognitive ability assume that individuals with greater ability have a higher probability of answering items correctly. Coombs (1964) used the term "dominance" to refer to models with this property.

Are dominance models appropriate for personality measurement? Consider, for example, an extraversion item that asks whether the respondent enjoys chatting quietly with a friend at a café. Are individuals with increasingly greater degrees of extroversion more and more likely to endorse this item? Or would individuals with moderate levels of extroversion have the greatest probability of endorsement? Coombs used the term "ideal point" in the context of models in which individuals are assumed to be more likely to endorse an item when it is *close* to them.

The idea for ideal point models can be traced back to a series of remarkable papers by Louis Thurstone (1927, 1928, 1929) that developed theory and methods for measuring attitudes. In one approach, a set of attitude statements is first compiled and then "two or three hundred subjects are asked to arrange the statements in eleven piles ranging from opinions most strongly affirmative to those most strongly negative" (1928, p. 545). These judgments are then used to compute scale values for the statements. Only after scaling the statements is it possible to assess an individual's attitude: In a second step, a respondent indicates which items he/she agrees with and then the mean of the scale values of the endorsed items is taken as his/her attitude value. For example, on a scale assessing attitude toward the church, two individuals might endorse three of ten items but receive very different attitude scale values because one person endorses items like "I think the church seeks to impose a lot of worn-out dogmas and medieval superstitions" (Thurstone, 1929, p. 232) and the other person endorses items such as "I feel the church services give me inspiration and help to live up to my best during the following week" (p. 232).

Certainly, Thurstone's methods are time-consuming and laborious. Likert (1932) introduced a technique that greatly simplified the analysis and yielded very similar results. Specifically, Likert suggested identifying one end of the attitude as positive, reverse-scoring items at the other end of the attitude continuum, and then computing a person's score as the sum of his or her item scores. For a five category

rating scale that ranged from "strongly approve" to "strongly disapprove," Likert found scoring response options with consecutive integers (e.g., 5 = "strongly approve" to 1 = "strongly disapprove") produced attitude scores that correlated in excess of .99 with scores computed following a more elaborate method of assigning values to rating scale categories. Likert also found that "using the method here described, a measure of a person's attitude as reliable as that obtained by the Thurstone method is secured by asking him to react to one-half as many items" (p. 33).

Likert (1932) used two methods for evaluating a scale and its items. First, Likert carefully examined the reliability of the scores produced by a given method. In addition, Likert used item–total correlations to assess the contribution of individual items. He noted, "If a zero or very low [item–total] correlation coefficient is obtained, it indicates that the statement fails to measure that which the rest of the statements measure.... Thus item analysis reveals the satisfactoriness of any statement so far as its inclusion in a given attitude scale is concerned" (pp. 48–49).

Likert (1932) found that "double-barreled items" such as "compulsory military training in all countries should be reduced but not eliminated" (p. 34) on an assessment of internationalism had low item–total correlations and thus he felt they should be eliminated. Thurstone, on the other hand, deliberately included such items. For example, his church attitude scale included "Sometimes I feel that the church and religion are necessary and sometimes I doubt it" (1929, p. 232). Thurstone found such items to have intermediate scale values, whereas the "worn-out dogmas" item had a very small scale value and the "church services give me inspiration" item had a very large scale value. Moreover, Thurstone devised methods to assess the discrepancy between a model and the data and found reasonably good fits for the intermediate items (e.g., see Table 6 in Thurstone, 1929).

The apparent contradiction between Likert and Thurstone's conclusions regarding intermediate items can be explained by the ideal point response process but not the dominance process. Specifically, if individuals endorse items whose scale values are close to the individuals' standings on the attitude being measured, then individuals who are low or high will not endorse intermediate items; only individuals who are intermediate will endorse such items. In contrast, only individuals who are high will endorse the most positive items. And only individuals who are low will endorse the most negative items so that after they are reverse-scored, only individuals who are high will be coded as endorsing the items. Thus, both of these latter types of items will have strong positive item–total correlations, but intermediate items will have near zero item–total correlations.

Why is this distinction between ideal point and dominance models important? First, for sophisticated measurement applications, such as computerized adaptive testing and analysis of differential item functioning across groups, it is important for one's psychometric model to provide a valid representation of the data. In such applications, a mis-specified model can easily lead to incorrect results and conclusions. Second, this distinction becomes very important for preferential choice items (i.e., pairwise preferences or tetrads or pentads), because one must explicitly specify how the choice for a given set of stimuli is made. Will individuals select stimuli that are most descriptive of them (i.e., an ideal point process) or those that they most dominate (i.e., a dominance process)? Third, important theoretical issues concerning the structure of personality hinge on psychometric analyses. For example, Ashton and Lee (2007) have argued for a six-dimensional (6-D) model of personality on the basis of results from a dominance model analysis (i.e., factor analysis). If the model is mis-specified, conclusions from such analyses should be drawn with less certainty. Finally, it is of basic scientific importance to know how people respond to personality instruments: How do people decide which option to select?

Classical Dominance Analyses

In this section, we describe and illustrate a set of analyses whose underlying theory is based on the assumption of a dominance process. Classical test theory (CTT), exploratory factor analysis (EFA), confirmatory factor analysis (CFA), and IRT analyses with the two-parameter logistic (2PL; Birnbaum, 1968) model and Samejima's (1969) graded response (SGR) model are all based on dominance assumptions. For example, an item–total correlation or a factor loading implicitly assumes that the relationship between trait level (either total score or factor score) and item score can be modeled by a monotonically increasing regression line (Chernyshenko, Stark, Drasgow, & Roberts, 2007).

To illustrate these analyses, we use a set of 20 items from the Tailored Adaptive Personality Assessment System (TAPAS) well-being scale, which is one of the facets of Emotional Stability in TAPAS (Chernyshenko, Stark, Drasgow, Hulin, &

Rivas, 2007). These items were administered to 502 army recruits, yielding a sample of 445 after list-wise deletion. The items were presented using a four-point response scale (1 = Strongly Disagree, 2 = Disagree, 3 = Agree, 4 = Strongly Agree).

Items were written to assess the full range of the trait continuum: five negative, six neutral, and nine positive. For example, a negative item, WELL04, is "I don't have as many happy moments in my life as others have," a neutral item, WELL17, is "My life has had about an equal share of ups and downs," and a positive item, WELL41, is "Most days I feel extremely good about myself." Table 4.1 lists ratings of item extremity made by subject matter experts (SMEs) for each item before any item responses were collected.

EFA and CTT Item Analysis

Prior to reverse-scoring, the item means ranged from about 2.1 to about 3.1 and all items had reasonably large standard deviations (see column 6 in Table 4.1). The correlations among the 20 items were computed and submitted to a principal components analysis. Factor loadings of the items (before reverse-scoring) are also shown in Table 4.1. The five negative items had large negative loadings, the nine positive items had large positive loadings, and the six neutral items had near-zero loadings. Note that this pattern is inconsistent with a dominance response process, because it assumes that all items measuring the same trait can be modeled by monotonically increasing regression lines. Yet, the pattern is perfectly consistent with what we expect when statistical procedures based on dominance assumptions are applied to responses actually made by an ideal point response process: flat regression lines are expected for items located in the middle of the trait continuum.

Figure 4.1, panel (a), shows the scree plot for all 20 items. The second eigenvalue in panel (a) is suggestive of a second factor; note that Davison (1977) found factor analysis of unidimensional ideal point data to yield an artifactual second factor. The scree plot obtained after deleting the six neutral items is shown in panel (b) of Figure 4.1. The elbow in this plot is remarkably sharp and clearly indicates a single factor, which should be the case as all items were written to measure well-being.

After reverse-scoring the five negative items, the corrected item–total correlations shown in Table 4.1 were obtained. Note that the correlations are large and positive for all five negative items as well as all nine positive items. However, the six neutral items have near-zero item–total correlations. Coefficient

Table 4.1. CTT item statistics for a 20-item well-being scale.

	Item_Name	Initial SME location	Reverse	Mean	SD	Factor Loading	CITC (alpha = 0.76)
1	WELL02	Negative	r	2.14	0.80	−0.40	0.35
2	WELL04	Negative	r	2.08	0.87	−0.45	0.40
3	WELL06	Negative	r	2.23	0.78	−0.55	0.45
4	WELL09	Negative	r	2.22	0.76	−0.53	0.42
5	WELL13	Negative	r	2.20	0.77	−0.54	0.45
6	WELL16	Neutral		2.48	0.85	0.08	0.08
7	WELL17	Neutral		2.82	0.73	0.13	0.15
8	WELL19	Neutral	r	2.85	0.65	−0.09	−0.05
9	WELL20	Neutral		3.00	0.89	0.04	0.06
10	WELL23	Neutral		3.03	0.64	0.07	0.11
11	WELL26	Neutral	r	2.80	0.78	−0.14	0.06
12	WELL29	Positive		2.89	0.74	0.36	0.48
13	WELL30	Positive		2.77	0.74	0.56	0.42
14	WELL34	Positive		3.13	0.70	0.46	0.35
15	WELL38	Positive		2.80	0.82	0.57	0.49
16	WELL40	Positive		2.53	0.75	0.56	0.48
17	WELL41	Positive		2.96	0.73	0.56	0.50
18	WELL43	Positive		3.13	0.66	0.63	0.55
19	WELL45	Positive		2.82	0.70	0.53	0.46
20	WELL46	Positive		2.89	0.72	0.47	0.41

Note: $N = 463$, SME = subject matter expert, Reverse = r (means that the item was reverse-scored when computing item–total correlations and coefficient alpha), SD = standard deviation, CITC = corrected item–total correlation.

alpha for the 20 item scale is .76, but can be increased to .83 by deleting the six neutral items. This is reminiscent of Likert's (1932) findings concerning Thurstone's intermediate items and highlights the importance of assessing the fit of a model to the data analyzed. More specifically, Thurstone's scaling methods provide assessments of model-data fit, whereas CTT analyses do not. In the present case, we see that coefficient alpha increases when the six neutral items are deleted, but we have no information about whether the underlying dominance model assumptions are satisfied.

IRT Dominance Analyses

Next, the data were analyzed by two dominance IRT models widely used in personality research. The first model, the 2PL, can be used to analyze dichotomous response data from assessment instruments such as the Minnesota Personality Questionnaire, the Hogan Personality Inventory, or the California Psychological Inventory (for an example, see Reise & Waller, 1990). The second model, the SGR, can be used to analyze polytomous data with ordered response categories such as NEO PI-R or Goldberg's Big Five markers (for an example, see Chernyshenko, Stark, Chan, Drasgow, &

Williams, 2001). Note also that the SGR model is a generalization of the 2PL to the case of ordered polytomous responses, so that the SGR simplifies to the 2PL when the data consist of only two response categories.

DICHOTOMOUS ANALYSIS

For the 2PL analysis, the well-being data (after reverse-scoring the negative items) were dichotomized (Strongly Disagree and Disagree were coded as negative responses and Agree and Strongly Agree were coded as positive responses) and submitted to the BILOG (Mislevy & Bock, 1991) computer program. BILOG estimates an item discrimination parameter, a_i, and an item extremity parameter, b_i, for each item i. The mathematical formula for the 2PL model relating the probability of a positive response ($U_i = 1$) to item i and person j's trait level on the continuum underlying responses, θ_j, is

$$P(U_i = 1 | \theta_j) = \frac{1}{1 + \exp[-1.7 a_i (\theta_j - b_i)]},$$

where a_i is the discrimination parameter for item i, b_i is the location parameter for item i, and 1.7 is a scaling constant used for historical reasons.

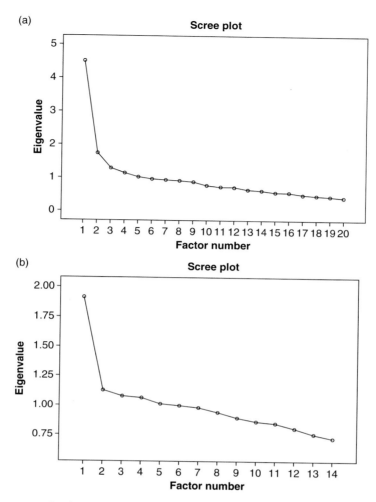

(a)

Scree plot

(b)

Scree plot

Fig. 4.1 Scree plots for well-being scale with and without neutral items.

Figure 4.2 illustrates the results for the item WELL41, which has an $a_{41} = 1.08$ and $b_{41} = -1.13$. The x-axis refers to the latent personality trait, well-being, that the item measures. For convenience, BILOG assumes that the latent trait assessed by the items is standardized to a mean of zero and a standard deviation of 1. The y-axis refers to the probability of endorsing the item, conditional on one's standing on well-being. For example, among individuals with well-being equal to -1, there is about a .5 probability of a positive response whereas for individual with well-being equal to 0.5, there is about a .95 probability of a positive response.

The smoothly rising probability curve in Figure 4.2 illustrates several characteristics of dominance items. First, Guttman perfect scale items notwithstanding, the probability of endorsing rises smoothly; there is no discontinuity in the curve. Second, individuals with low standings on well-being are virtually certain to *not* endorse the item, and individuals with high standings to endorse the item. Third, we have portrayed the item as measuring only a single latent characteristic of respondents. This "simple structure" (Thurstone, 1947) reflects the fact that we wish to avoid factorially complex items. Fourth, Figure 4.2 reflects the fact that individuals low in well-being cannot have a negative probability of endorsing the item and high well-being individuals cannot have a probability of endorsement greater than 1. Thus, the curve in monotonically, but not linearly, increasing. Finally, the probability curve in Figure 4.2 is the nonlinear regression of the dichotomously scored, 1 = endorsement and 0 = nonendorsement,

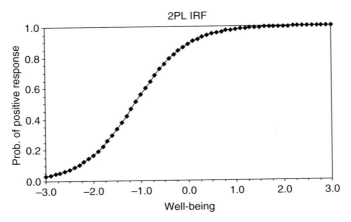

Fig. 4.2 Item response function for WELL41 with $a = 1.08$ and $b = -1.13$.

response to WELL41 on the latent trait. To see this, let the dichotomously scored response variable be denoted U_i and use θ to denote the latent well-being trait. Then the nonlinear regression of U_i on θ is

$$E(U_i|\theta) = 1 \cdot P(U_i = 1|\theta) + 0 \cdot P(U_i = 0|\theta)$$
$$= P(U_i = 1|\theta)$$

The 2PL results in Table 4.2 are consistent with the CTT and EFA results in Table 4.1 and again suggest that the neutral items fail to adequately assess well-being. For example, WELL17 has a very low discrimination parameter estimate (0.26) and would be normally deleted from further consideration during the scale construction process. Other items judged to have neutral content had even lower discrimination parameter estimates and all would have been eliminated, because most test developers would use a minimum cutoff of 0.50 for the 2PL discrimination parameter. Yet all these items should assess well-being as they tap into such content domains as self-esteem, depression, and overall life happiness.

An advantage of IRT is that the fit of the model can be tested. For example, let $f(\theta)$ denote the distribution of the latent trait, which we can assume to be the standard normal. Then the expected number of positive responses to item i is

$$E_i(U_i = 1) = N \int P(U_i = 1|\theta) \, f(\theta) \, d\theta,$$

where $P(U_i = 1|\theta)$ is the probability of a positive response to item i by individuals with standing θ

on the latent trait and N is the sample size. The expected number of negative responses, $U = 0$, can be computed as

$$E_i(U_i = 0) = N \int [1 - P(U_i = 1|\theta)] \, f(\theta) \, d\theta,$$

and then a chi-square statistic can be computed by the usual formula comparing observed O_i and expected E_i number of responses,

$$\chi_i^2 = \frac{[O_i(U_i = 1) - E_i(U_i = 1)]^2}{E_i(U_i = 1)}$$
$$+ \frac{[O_i(U_i = 0) - E_i(U_i = 0)]^2}{E_i(U_i = 0)}.$$

This analysis can be extended to assess the fit of the IRT model to more than one item at a time. For example, the expected number of positive responses to both item i and item m is

$$E_{i,m}(U_i = 1, U_m = 1)$$
$$= N \int P(U_i = 1|\theta) \, P(U_m = 1|\theta) \, f(\theta) \, d\theta.$$

When this analysis was conducted for two neutral items, WELL17 and WELL26, a chi-square of 18.8 with three degrees of freedom (df) was obtained. Because chi-square statistics are sensitive to sample size, we have found it useful to adjust observed values to that expected for a fixed sample size of 3,000 (Drasgow, Levine, Tsien, Williams, & Mead, 1995). This can be accomplished by noting that the expected value of a noncentral chi-square is equal to its degrees of freedom plus N times the noncentrality parameter δ,

$$E(\chi^2) = df + N\delta$$

where N is the size of the sample used in the analysis. So an estimate of the noncentrality parameter is

$$\hat{\delta} = (\chi^2 - df)/N.$$

To adjust to a sample size of, say, 3,000, use

Adjusted to a sample of 3,000 $\chi^2 = df + 3,000\hat{\delta}$.

Because 445 people answered both WELL17 and WELL26,

$$\hat{\delta} = (18.8 - 3)/445 = 0.0355,$$

and

Adjusted to a sample of 3,000 $\chi^2 = 3$
$+ 3,000(0.0355) = 109.5$

Consequently, the adjusted chi-square to df ratio is $109.5/3 = 36.5$, which is very poor indeed. This very large adjusted chi-square to df ratio results because many more people endorse both WELL17 and WELL26 (the people with intermediate standings on the well-being latent trait) or endorse neither

item (people with high or low standings on the latent trait) than the 2PL dominance model predicts. This is clear evidence of model mis-specification and the results we expect based on an ideal point response process.

Finally, examination of item location parameter estimates for the 2PL model in Table 4.2 clearly indicates that these values are not particularly informative for test developers or for those interested in issues related to content of personality statements. This is because the term "item location parameter" ordinarily refers to the location on the latent trait continuum where the item is informative about the trait being assessed. For example, the item WELL41 has a location parameter estimate of -1.13 and it effectively differentiates people with θ's somewhat lower than this value from people with θ's somewhat larger (e.g., people with $\theta = -2$ have less than a 20% chance of answering positively whereas people with $\theta = 0$ have more than an 80% chance of answering positively). The reason that calling b-parameters "item locations" is a misnomer in the context of personality assessment is that there is no clear relationship between the parameter values and item content. For example, WELL02 and WELL46 have nearly

Table 4.2. IRT parameters for the 20-item well-being scale.

Item_Name	Initial SME location	SGR parameters				2PL parameters		GGUM parameters		
		alpha	b1	b2	b3	a	b	alpha	delta	tau
WELL02	Negative	0.50	−3.52	−1.27	1.81	0.52	−1.19	0.87	−4.02	−2.72
WELL04	Negative	0.57	−3.01	−1.17	1.27	0.61	−1.09	0.96	−3.65	−2.44
WELL06	Negative	0.81	−2.64	−0.77	1.58	0.68	−0.79	1.09	−2.44	−1.46
WELL09	Negative	0.77	−2.74	−0.74	1.63	0.67	−0.77	1.22	−1.81	−0.95
WELL13	Negative	0.76	−2.91	−0.69	1.65	0.78	−0.67	1.30	−1.89	−1.11
WELL16	Neutral	0.12	−9.70	−0.43	9.89	0.23	−0.19	0.47	0.71	−0.71
WELL17	Neutral	0.14	−13.33	−3.96	7.36	0.26	−2.14	1.24	0.10	−1.45
WELL19	Neutral	0.04	−47.57	−15.02	27.24	0.14	−4.56	0.97	−0.46	−1.89
WELL20	Neutral	0.12	−11.93	−6.04	3.79	0.16	−4.59	0.55	−0.61	−2.82
WELL23	Neutral	0.13	−17.41	−8.57	6.61	0.32	−3.53	0.74	0.51	−3.19
WELL26	Neutral	0.16	−6.16	3.52	10.29	0.24	2.45	1.27	−0.26	−1.48
WELL29	Positive	0.81	−2.70	−0.70	1.75	0.79	−0.70	1.31	2.12	−2.82
WELL30	Positive	0.66	−3.88	−1.90	0.93	0.62	−2.01	1.03	2.18	−4.17
WELL34	Positive	0.50	−4.20	−1.51	1.95	0.46	−1.59	1.19	0.59	−1.85
WELL38	Positive	0.80	−2.57	−0.65	1.38	0.69	−0.70	1.08	1.92	−2.60
WELL40	Positive	0.81	−2.50	−0.08	2.17	0.74	−0.04	1.14	2.45	−2.45
WELL41	Positive	0.84	−2.87	−1.25	1.32	1.08	−1.13	1.94	2.40	−3.51
WELL43	Positive	1.09	−3.09	−1.57	0.79	0.92	−1.71	1.95	0.95	−2.53
WELL45	Positive	0.75	−3.23	−0.99	1.76	0.77	−0.98	1.27	1.64	−2.61
WELL46	Positive	0.65	−3.78	−1.13	1.65	0.61	−1.15	1.27	0.89	−1.92

Note: SGR = Samejima's graded response model, 2PL = two-parameter logistic model, GGUM = generalized graded unfolding model.

identical 2PL model parameters, despite being totally opposite in content. Moreover, the neutral items have extremely low b-parameter estimates, despite the fact that their content is intermediate. This paradoxical situation is in stark contrast to the cognitive ability domain, where b-parameters are indicative of how easy or difficult the item is and content experts can easily and accurately anticipate item properties prior to pretesting (a more detailed discussion of this issue is provided by Chernyshenko, Stark, Drasgow, & Roberts, 2007).

POLYTOMOUS ANALYSIS

Although models for dichotomously scored items have been used far more frequently than models for polytomously scored items, we can also analyze the original responses to the four-option well-being items with a polytomous model. The SGR model assumes that the response options refer to ordered categories, as is the case here, rather than nominal categories (e.g., response options on multiple-choice test items). According to the SGR model, the probability of selecting option k on item i is

$$P(U_i = k | \theta_j) = \frac{1}{1 + \exp\left[-1.7a_i(\theta_j - b_{i,k})\right]} - \frac{1}{1 + \exp\left[-1.7a_i(\theta_j - b_{i,k+1})\right]},$$

where U_i denotes the person's response to the polytomously scored item i; k is the particular option

selected by the respondent; a_i is the item discrimination parameter, which is assumed to be the same for each option within a particular item; b is the extremity parameter that varies from option to option given the constraints $b_{k-1} < b_k < b_{k+1}$, and b_0 is taken as $-\infty$ and b_K is taken as $+\infty$. The above equation and the software we used to estimate parameters assumes that the K options are coded $k = 0, \dots, K-1$; a slightly different range of subscripts would be needed if the responses were coded $k = 1, \dots, K$.

To illustrate the application of the SGR model, we analyzed the well-being scale with the MULTILOG 7.03 computer program (Thissen, 1991). Figure 4.3 depicts the option response functions, which give the probability of selecting the options as a function of the latent trait θ, for WELL41. The upper left panel depicts the probability of choosing the "Strongly Disagree" option as a function of well-being. Note that individuals very low in well-being are increasingly likely to select the Strongly Disagree response option for WELL41, which is logical because the stem of this item, "Most days I feel extremely good about myself," reflects strongly positive well-being. As well-being increases, however, individuals become less and less likely to endorse the Strongly Disagree option. Figure 4.3 shows that the majority of people with intermediate well-being (i.e., θ's near 0) select the third response option, Agree. The bottom right panel depicts the probability of endorsing the

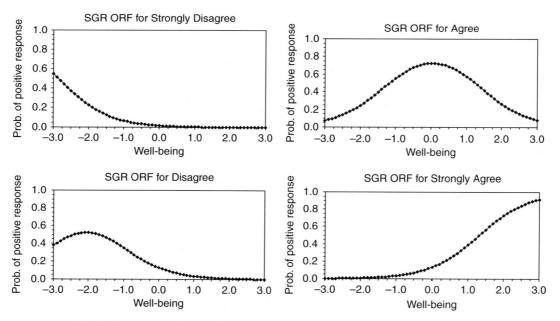

Fig. 4.3 Option response functions for WELL41 with $a = 0.84$, $b_1 = -2.87$, $b_2 = -1.25$, and $b_3 = 1.32$.

Strongly Agree category. This probability curve is very near zero for low values of well-being, but rises toward 1 at high levels of well-being.

Looking at the SGR parameter estimates in Table 4.2, it is apparent that low discrimination values for neutral items were also observed for the SGR model. Hence, switching to a polytomous dominance model made little difference and, if anything, made things worse. The discrimination parameter estimates for the neutral items were even lower than those observed for the 2PL. The fit was also worse: For example, the average adjusted chi-square to df ratio for pairs of well-being items was 4.05 versus 2.39 for the 2PL analysis. The consequences of the response process mis-specification should be more apparent in the polytomous case because the model makes more articulated predictions about the data (i.e., the model specifies that a respondent is most likely to choose one of four options, rather than one of two).

Summary of Dominance Analyses

Dominance models – CTT, factor analysis, the 2PL, and SGR – have been the principal data analysis tools for psychometric assessments of personality scales since the time of Likert. Obviously, these methods have provided useful answers to questions about personality measurement. However, their application is reminiscent of Spearman's (1904) two-factor theory of intelligence, which postulated that performance in any domain is a function of general intelligence or g and an ability that is specific to that domain. With a careful selection of tests, Spearman found a good fit of his model to the data. But when tests were not carefully preselected, Spearman's model proved inadequate; Carroll's (1993) three-stratum model provides a much better description of the structure of intelligence.

For dominance models to adequately fit responses to personality items, items must similarly be carefully preselected and, specifically, neutral items must be excluded. In analyses that do not provide assessments of fit (e.g., classical test theory) or use heuristic measures of fit (e.g., factor analysis), the inadequacy of dominance models can be glossed over or misattributed to "double-barreled" items. In IRT where the fit of a model to 2×2 contingency tables for dichotomously scored data or $K \times K$ contingency tables for polytomously scored data can be explicitly evaluated, misfit is more difficult to ignore. In fact, our concerns about the 2PL and SGR began when we noticed that these IRT models did not fit personality data nearly as well as the three-parameter logistic (3PL) model and

Bock's (1972) nominal model fit cognitive ability data (Chernyshenko et al., 2001). After repeated failures to find adequate fits, we were forced to think outside of the dominance model IRT box, which led us to ideal point models (Chernyshenko, Stark, Drasgow, & Roberts, 2007; Stark, Chernyshenko, Drasgow, & Williams, 2006).

Ideal Point Analyses

Far fewer psychometrician-years have been devoted to the development of psychometric models that assume an ideal point response process. Consequently, the number of models for responses to individual items is smaller here than with the dominance response process. However, there is an extensive literature on choice and preference, which is relevant when individuals are asked which of two (or more) statements better describes them. In this section we begin by describing one ideal point model for personality items consisting of an SS where the respondent makes an Agree or Disagree response. Then we discuss two models for two-alternative forced choice items.

As noted above, the Achilles heel of dominance models lies in their inability to fit neutral items. If ideal point models better represent the underlying psychological processes involved in responding to personality items, we should see larger discrimination parameter estimates for such items. Moreover, the fit of the model to neutral items should be improved. Consequently, in this section we pay careful attention to these issues.

Ideal Point Analysis of Single-Statement Items

With an SS format with two response options, respondents simply Agree or Disagree that the statement (i.e., usually a trait adjective) describes them. For unidimensional scales with dichotomously scored responses, several ideal point models are available (e.g., Andrich's 1988 squared simple logistic model and Andrich and Luo's 1993 hyperbolic cosine model). Although it was designed for polytomously scored items, we have found Roberts, Donoghue, and Laughlin's generalized graded unfolding model (GGUM) to work well with dichotomously scored items.

The GGUM uses four "latent" response categories to model two "observed" (i.e., Agree and Disagree) response categories. To understand the role of the latent response categories, the difference, $\theta - \delta_i$, between the person's standing θ on the underlying trait and item i's location parameter δ_i on the latent trait continuum must be considered. If the person's θ is far below the item's location, the person is said to "disagree from below." This would be illustrated by a very distressed person disagreeing with the item "My life has had about an equal share of ups and downs," from the TAPAS well-being scale. On the other hand, a person very high in well-being might also disagree with this item, which would constitute a "disagree from above" judgment. When a person's θ is close to item i's location parameter δ_i, but θ is slightly lower than δ_i, the respondent is likely to "agree from below." Similarly, When a person's θ is close to item i's location parameter δ_i, but θ is slightly larger than δ_i, the respondent is likely to "agree from above."

The GGUM equation for the probability of the agree from below latent response category is assumed to be

$$P(\text{agree from below}|\theta) = \exp\{\alpha_i[(\theta - \delta_i) - \tau_i]\}/\gamma,$$

where α_i is item i's discrimination parameter, τ_i is a response category threshold parameter, and γ is a scaling constant. The probability of the latent agree from above category is

$$P(\text{agree from above}|\theta) = \exp\{\alpha_i[2(\theta - \delta_i) - \tau_i]\}/\gamma.$$

These two probabilities are then added to compute the probability of an observed agree response:

$$P(\text{agree}|\theta) = [\exp\{\alpha_i(\theta - \delta_i) - \tau_i\} + \exp\{2\alpha_i(\theta - \delta_i) - \tau_i\}]/\gamma.$$

The probability of an observed disagree response is obtained similarly and equals

$$P(\text{disagree}|\theta) = [1 + \exp\{3\alpha_i(\theta - \delta_i)\}]/\gamma.$$

Incidentally, the scaling constant γ equals the sum of the numerators of the probability of the observed agree and disagree equations,

$$\gamma = 1 + \exp\{\alpha_i[(\theta - \delta_i) - \tau_i]\} + \exp\{\alpha_i[2(\theta - \delta_i) - \tau_i]\} + \exp\{3\alpha_i(\theta - \delta_i)\}.$$

To illustrate the ideal point analysis, we analyzed the dichotomously scored TAPAS well-being data with GGUM. Figure 4.4 shows the results for WELL17. In this figure, "Option 1" refers to the

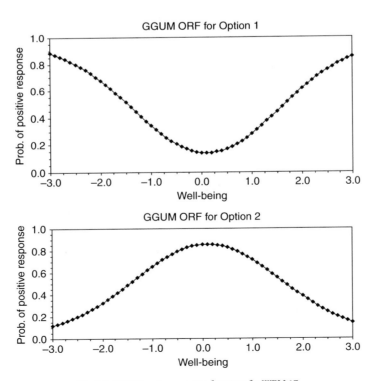

Fig. 4.4 GGUM option response functions for WELL17.

collapsed Strongly Disagree and Disagree response options from the original four category item and "Option 2" refers to the combined Agree and Strongly Agree response options. Option 2 clearly shows an ideal point option response function: individuals low and high in well-being do not agree or strongly agree with "My life has had about an equal share of ups and downs." But individuals with intermediate well-being have a high likelihood of agreeing or strongly agreeing: nearly .90 for individuals with standardized well-being scores near zero.

The GGUM item parameter estimates are shown in Table 4.2. The estimates of the location parameters δ_i are interesting. Note that the mean of the δ_i estimates for five items that the SMEs expected to have negative locations was −2.76, the mean of the six neutral items was 0.00, and the mean of the nine positive items was 1.68. In fact, the correlation of the estimated δ_i values with corresponding ratings of locations (coded as 1, 2, or 3) made by the SMEs was .923. In contrast, the correlation between 2PL location parameter estimates and expert ratings was −.003. Clearly, the SMEs accurately identified the portion of the latent well-being continuum where the items would be informative and there was a strong intuitive correspondence between what experts believed the locations of personality items to be and what the GGUM estimated locations actually were.

There is another way that the interpretation of the item location parameter changes from the 2PL to the ideal point model (Chernyshenko, Stark, Drasgow, & Roberts, 2007). For the 2PL, the item location parameter is the point on the latent trait continuum where the item endorsement rate is expected to be 50%. Specifically, when $\theta = b_i$,

$$P(U_i = 1 | \theta_j) = \frac{1}{1 + \exp[-1.7 a_i (b_i - b_i)]}$$
$$= \frac{1}{1 + \exp(0)} = \frac{1}{1 + 1} = .50.$$

In contrast, with the ideal point model, $\theta = b_i$ is the point on the latent trait continuum where item endorsement is most likely. To state it another way, the ideal point item location parameter can be interpreted as referring to the group of people (i.e., the people with θ's equal to the item difficulty) having the highest probability of endorsing that item, rather than by the group that has a 50% chance of answering affirmatively.

The GGUM fit the dichotomous well-being data much better than the 2PL: The mean of the adjusted chi-square to df ratios was 0.71 for the pairs of items. In contrast, the mean was 2.39 for the 2PL analysis of the same data. Moreover, the difference in fits was not just due to greater effects of random error for the dominance analysis. The 2PL failed to fit in systematic and predictable ways: For example, the 2PL was unable to model the responses to the neutral items whereas the GGUM fit them well and indicated an ideal point pattern of responding (see Option 2 in Figure 4.4).

The discrimination parameter estimates for the six neutral items were substantially larger for the GGUM model than the SGR or 2PL: 0.87 versus 0.12 and 0.22. Thus, for the ideal point model, the neutral items were found to discriminate among individuals with varying well-being. This is clearly illustrated by Figure 4.4, which shows that people very low in well-being (e.g., $\theta = -2$) had about a 30% chance of endorsing WELL17 and people very high (e.g., $\theta = +2$) had about a 40% change, but people intermediate in well-being (e.g., $\theta = 0$) had a nearly 90% chance.

Pairwise Preference Formats

The vast majority of personality testing research and applications to date have focused on scales consisted of individual statements requiring respondents to indicate their level of agreement using a dichotomous or polytomous response format. In the broader discipline of psychology, however, there has been a long interest in forced-choice formats, which require a respondent to choose between two or more alternatives. Rather than asking people to choose a response category on a rating scale, we instead ask people to simply select which of two statements more accurately describes them. To illustrate using the well-being items, respondents can be asked to check which of the following two items is more like them:

_____ I don't have as many happy moments in my life as others have
_____ My life has had about an equal share of ups and downs

If we assume that the respondent's current level of well-being is the only relevant trait guiding his/her choice of a particular statement in a pair, then, provided we have a mathematical model relating person locations to statement parameters, we can estimate that person's well-being level from the response data. Note that the item pair is not necessarily restricted to both statements being from the same dimension. When statements are from different dimensions, we could assume that the choice is guided by two traits and specify a multidimensional pairwise preference (MDPP) model.

Also note that, in principle, more than two statements can compose an item. For example, the Assessment of Individual Motivation inventory developed by White and Young (1998) consists of four statements. Here the respondent is asked to select two statements: the statement that best describes the respondent and the statement that is least like the respondent. This more complex format is of course more difficult to model psychometrically. As a result, we have limited our attention to unidimensional and multidimensional pairwise preference models.

Advantages of the Pairwise Preference Format

There are several reasons why the two-alternative format is attractive for measuring personality and other noncognitive constructs. First, this format appears to be more resistant to rater errors (central tendency, leniency, severity) than the traditional SS items (see Borman, Buck, Hanson, Motowidlo, Stark, & Drasgow, 2001) and idiosyncratic interpretations of rating scale categories such as Agree and Strongly Agree (Böckenholt, 2004). Because people may (and probably do) use rating scale categories differently, a response of "3" or "Agree" by one person does not necessarily mean the same thing as the same response by another person. As was shown by Brady (1989), when the assumption that respondents interpret category labels in similar ways is not met, factor analysis and related methods can produce spurious results. Brady provided a hypothetical example where half of a sample consisted of Pollyannas who saw good in everything and half consisted of cynics who were consistently negative. As a model of differential use of a rating scale, Brady shifted Pollyannas' ratings upward by a constant. A factor analysis of this data yielded one strong dimension that explained 70% of the variance and two weaker dimensions that explained 13% and 10% of the variance. Interestingly, the strong dimension was an artifact of the inconsistent use of the response scale and the two weak dimensions were the ones used to generate the data. Thus, idiosyncratic use of a response scale can create

artificial factors that appear much stronger than the real factors underlying people's judgments.

Industrial-organizational psychologists have devoted a great deal of effort to devise rating scales formats that minimize errors in the context of job performance ratings or to assure that category labels are consistently understood, but this line of research is generally regarded as a failure. In fact, the results are so dismal that Landy and Farr (1980) called for a "moratorium" on research in this area.

A second advantage of paired comparison judgments noted by Böckenholt (2004) is that respondents can make finer distinctions than are possible with rating scales. For example, with a Agree/Disagree format, respondents might see great differences in the extent to which a set of trait adjectives describe them, but would be forced to use only the Agree and Disagree response options. With the paired comparison format, respondents are always allowed to say which of the two statements is more like them.

Another important advantage of the two-alternative format is that test construction and adaptive testing become feasible even when only a small pool of statements is available. Because the one statement can be paired with many other statements, a pool of 20 statements results in many unique pairs. In fact, if there are no "item enemies" (i.e., pairs of items that cannot be allowed together in a statement, perhaps because their content is too similar), a set of 20 statements would generate $\binom{20}{2} = \frac{20 \cdot 19}{2} = 190$ pairs. Hence, a relatively large number of pairwise preference items can be created by allowing some statement repetition. This is particularly beneficial for CAT applications, creating alternate test forms, and measurement in domains where it is difficult to generate a large number of behavioral indicators.

Finally, forced choice formats may be more resistant to dissimulation by respondents. By pairing statements that are similar in social desirability, respondents in high-stakes settings should have a harder time discerning which is the better answer, thus making "faking good" more difficult. Note that thus far empirical results testing this hypothesis have been mixed, with some studies showing that multi-statement forced choice measures do reduce score inflation and maintain criterion-related validities in situations where examinees are motivated to fake (Bowen, Martin, & Hunt, 2002; Christiansen, Burns, & Montgomery, 2005; White & Young,

1998) and others showing substantial score inflation, particularly with regard to conscientiousness (Heggestad, Morrison, Reeve, & McCloy, 2006). Nevertheless, this format provides a fertile area for future research.

Law of Comparative Judgment

There is a long history of quantitative models for pairwise preferences. Perhaps the most famous is Thurstone's (1927) law of comparative judgment. This model assumes person j evaluates two stimuli, s and t, and chooses the one with the higher utility value. Let j's mean evaluation of s be denoted μ_{js} and the mean evaluation of t be μ_{jt}. In the evaluation of s and t the latent judgment variable is

$$y_{jst} = \mu_{js} - \mu_{jt} + \varepsilon_{jst},$$

where ε_{jst} is a random error term, assumed to be independent across pairs of stimuli, normally distribution with mean zero and variance σ_{st}^2. Thurstone's model then assumes that the probability of choosing s over t is

$$P(y_{jst} > 0) = \Phi\left(\frac{\mu_{js} - \mu_{jt}}{\sigma_{st}}\right)$$

where $\Phi(\cdot)$ denotes the cumulative standard normal distribution.

Coombs Unfolding Model

The law of comparative judgment does not address how person j forms the evaluations μ_{js} and μ_{jt}. Coombs (1950) unfolding model separated the person parameter (the person's "ideal point") from parameters for the stimuli and proposed that the evaluation of a stimulus is based on the absolute value of the difference between the ideal point and the stimulus. Let θ_j denote person j's ideal point and let μ_s denote the location parameter for stimulus s. Then person j's evaluation of stimulus s is simply $|\theta_j - \mu_s|$. Coombs assumed the person would prefer s to t if

$$|\theta_j - \mu_s| \leq |\theta_j - \mu_t|.$$

The Zinnes–Griggs Model

A limitation on Coombs model is that it is deterministic; it is written in terms of parameters and so there is no element of randomness in the judgment process. Zinnes and Griggs (1974) remedied this

shortcoming by devising a probabilistic version of Coombs unfolding model. They assumed that the parameters θ_j, μ_s, and μ_t are perceived with error, so that person j's judgment is based on the random variables q_j, m_s, and m_t, which are independently and normally distributed:

$$q_j \sim N(\theta_j, \sigma^2), \quad m_s \sim N(\mu_s, \sigma_s^2), \quad and$$
$$m_t \sim N(\mu_t, \sigma_t^2),$$

where "$\sim$" means "is distributed as" and $\sigma_s^2 = \sigma_t^2$ for all stimuli s and t. Then the Zinnes and Griggs (ZG) model states that the probability of preferring s to t is

$$P_{st} = P(|q_j - m_s| \leq |q_j - m_t|).$$

Dominance models could be formulated as alternatives to the ZG model but we believe the directions "Choose the statement that is more like you" imply closeness: Respondents should choose the statement that they perceive is closer to their standing on the trait being measured. This is exactly what the deterministic and probabilistic versions of Coombs unfolding model quantify.

In the context of personality assessment, the ZG model assumes that when presented with a personality item composed of a pair of statements representing, say, sociability, a respondent will probabilistically choose the statement in each pair that better describes him/her, based on the perceived distances of the statements on the trait continuum relative to his/her own location. In other words, the respondent will tend to choose the statement in each pair that is located nearer to him/her on the trait continuum, which is consistent with the ideal point response process assumptions.

The ZG model is appropriate for unidimensional two-alternative forced choice data. It is unidimensional in that only a single person parameter is used: θ_j. A variety of other IRT models have been developed for calibrating and scoring unidimensional pairwise preference (UPP) items (for a review, see Bossuyt, 1990), but the ZG model (Zinnes & Griggs, 1974) has received the most attention in the recent applied psychology literature. Borman et al. (2001), for example, applied the ZG model to the performance measurement domain. More recently, in the personality domain, U.S. Navy researchers used the ZG model as the basis for the Navy Computerized Adaptive Personality Scales (NCAPS; Houston, Borman, Farmer, & Bearden, 2005).

Zinnes and Griggs (1974) showed that the probability of choosing or preferring statement s to statement t could be simplified to

$$P_{st}(\theta_j) = 1 - \Phi(a_{st}) - \Phi(b_{st}) + 2\Phi(a_{st})\Phi(b_{st}),$$

where

$$a_{st} = (2\theta_j - \mu_s - \mu_t)/\sqrt{3}$$

and

$$b_{st} = \mu_s - \mu_t.$$

In the context of personality assessment, θ_j represents the respondent's standing on the trait being assessed, μ_s and μ_t represent the locations of the respective personality statements on the trait continuum, and $\Phi(a_{st})$ and $\Phi(b_{st})$ are cumulative standard normal distributions evaluated at a_{st} and b_{st}, respectively. Thus, each personality statement is characterized by a single parameter, μ, but to compute response probabilities, three parameters (μ_s, μ_t, and θ) are needed.

Figures 4.5(a) and 4.5(b) present two illustrative item response functions (IRFs) for the ZG model computed for θ values ranging from -3 to $+3$ using the equations given above. The item represented in Figure 4.5(a) involves statements having location parameters $\mu_s = 2.0$ and $\mu_t = -1.4$; consequently, the difference between the statements is 3.4. Figure 4.5(b) presents the item response function (IRF) for an item involving statements with location parameters $\mu_s = 0.6$ and $\mu_t = 2.2$; here the difference $\mu_s - \mu_t$ is -1.6. Examination of the curve for each item (i.e., pair of statements) reveals that the probability of preferring statement s to statement t, $P_{st}(\theta)$, ranges from near zero to 1 and, for the first pair, looks very much like the 2PL item response function presented in Figure 4.2. Note that the item response function in Figure 4.5(b) is monotonically decreasing, rather than increasing, because in Figure 4.5(b), $\mu_s < \mu_t$.

The slope of the ZG item response function becomes steeper as the distance between statements composing an item increases. The second pair of statements has a difference of -1.6 versus 3.4 for the first pair and consequently Figure 4.5(b) has a shallower slope than Figure 4.5(a). In this way the slopes of the item response functions vary even though the model has no explicit parameter for

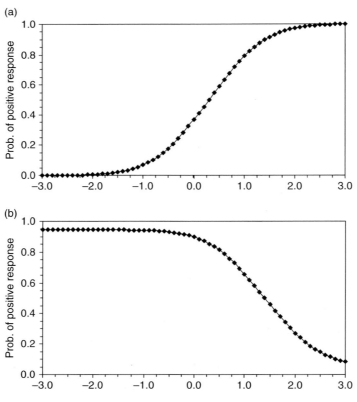

Fig. 4.5 ZG item response functions for two UPP items.

TEST THEORY AND PERSONALITY MEASUREMENT

item discrimination. If the two statements composing an item have identical locations, the probability of endorsing either statement is exactly .5 across the trait continuum, and the item response function is flat (nondiscriminating).

Stark and Drasgow (2002) developed a marginal maximum likelihood (MML) estimation procedure for estimating the ZG location parameters for personality statements and a Bayes modal procedure for estimating ZG trait scores. It was shown that accurate stimulus parameter estimates and standard errors could be achieved with samples of approximately 400 people and conventional tests (i.e., nonadaptive) as short as 10 items. Since then, we have replaced the iterative Bayes modal trait estimation procedure with expected a posteriori (EAP) scoring, which does not require iterative methods. We have also found that, when limited samples are available for test construction, SMEs' ratings of statement location can be used in place of estimated stimulus parameters without adversely affecting the accuracy of trait estimates. Specifically, a recent investigation revealed a correlation of .97 between trait scores based on average SME ratings of statement locations and those based on MML stimulus parameter estimates (Stark & Chernyshenko, 2006).

To illustrate the ZG model, we used SME ratings of statement locations to construct and score three 12-item unidimensional two-alternative scales: order, self-control, and sociability (a detailed description of this study can be found in Chernyshenko, Stark, Prewett, Gray, Stilson, & Tuttle, 2006, 2009). No statement was allowed to appear more than twice in a single scale. The average distance, $|\mu_s - \mu_t|$, between statement locations was 3.0 for the order scale, 2.83 for self-control, and 3.16 for sociability. These items were administered to a sample of 602 respondents, along with 12-item order, self-control, and sociability scales consisting of SSs scored dichotomously. MDPP measures of the same dimensions, described below, were also administered.

Summary statistics for the nine scales are presented in Table 4.3. The trait scores for the scales with SS items were computed using the GGUM model, scores for the scales with UPP items were computed using the ZG model, and scores for the MDPP scales were computed using methods described in the next section of this chapter. Bayesian estimation was used for all three types of scales, yielding scores that should have means of approximately zero and standard deviations slightly less than 1. Trait scores for UPP scales, for example, were obtained using Stark's (2006b) ZG_EAP program.

Of particular interest are the reliabilities of the alternative format scales. Reliability estimates for all three types of scales are reported in the last column of Table 4.3. The CTT reliability coefficient can be estimated using the results from an IRT analysis via the formula (Thissen & Wainer, 2001)

$$\bar{\rho} = \frac{\sigma_\theta^2 - \bar{\sigma}_e^2}{\sigma_\theta^2},$$

where σ_θ^2 is the variance of the estimated trait scores and $\bar{\sigma}_e^2$ is the average of the squared standard error

Table 4.3. Summary statistics for single-stimulus, unidimensional, and multidimensional pairwise preference order, self-control, and sociability scales.

Measures	Number of Items/pairs	N	Scale statistics				
			Mean	SD	Min.	Max.	Reliability
Order SS	12	602	0.00	0.89	−2.71	1.65	.74
Order UPP	12	602	0.85	0.80	−1.66	2.15	.75
Order MDPP	12	602	−0.27	0.74	−2.34	1.99	.75
Self-control SS	12	602	0.00	0.82	−2.94	2.07	.54
Self-control UPP	12	602	0.15	0.59	−1.59	1.74	.53
Self-control MDPP	12	602	−0.41	0.72	−2.24	1.97	.66
Sociability SS	12	602	0.00	0.85	−2.28	1.86	.62
Sociability UPP	12	602	0.02	0.89	−1.89	1.85	.78
Sociability MDPP	12	602	0.06	0.72	−1.97	1.94	.73

Note: SS = single statement, UPP = unidimensional pairwise preference, MDPP = multidimensional pairwise preference. Reliability estimates for personality measures are marginal reliabilities.

estimates for these trait scores. In this formula, the numerator is an estimate of true score variance and the denominator provides a measure of total variance.

As can be seen in Table 4.3, reliability estimates for the UPP personality measures ranged between .53 and .78, which is about what one would expect given that scales were relatively short and dichotomously scored. Because items with larger distances between pairs of statements have more discriminating slopes with the ZG model, and more discrimination translates into less error for trait estimates, it is not surprising that the sociability scale had the highest reliability of the three UPP scales, followed by order and self-control scales. Interestingly, the three SS scales of the same length had reliabilities of .74, .54, and .62. Clearly, using the paired comparison format did not lead to a large decrement in reliability.

Multidimensional Pairwise Preferences

Developing models for multidimensional IRT with effective parameter estimation software has proved to be very difficult. A number of such approaches have been proposed. For example, Bock, Gibbons, and Muraki (1988) developed full-information item factor analysis, which was subsequently implemented in the TESTFACT computer program (Bock et al., 2003) for dichotomously scored ability test items. Nonetheless, even this state-of-the-art program does not appear to be used routinely.

Rather than attempting to devise an explicit multidimensional model for pairwise preference data, we have taken a tack originally suggested by Andrich (1989, p. 197). Andrich proposed a model that assumes when person j encounters stimuli s and t (which, in our case, correspond to two personality statements), the person considers whether to endorse s and, independently, considers whether to endorse t. This leads to four possible outcomes: The person may wish to endorse both, neither, only s, or only t. But, when faced with a two-alternative forced choice judgment, the first two of these outcomes do not lead to a viable decision. Consequently, Andrich suggested that, in this case, the person independently reconsiders whether to endorse the two options. This process of independently considering the two stimuli continues until one and only one stimulus is endorsed. A preference judgment can then be represented by the joint outcome (Agree with s, Disagree with t) or (Disagree with s, Agree with t). Using a 1 to indicate agreement and a 0 to indicate disagreement, the outcome (1,0) indicates that statement s was endorsed but statement t was not, leading to the decision that s was preferred to statement t; an outcome of (0,1) similarly indicates that stimulus t was preferred to s. Thus, the probability of endorsing a stimulus s over a stimulus t can be formally written as

$$P_{(s>t)_i}(\theta_{d_s}, \theta_{d_t}) = \frac{P_{st}(1,0|\theta_{d_s}, \theta_{d_t})}{P_{st}(1,0|\theta_{d_s}, \theta_{d_t}) + P_{st}(0,1|\theta_{d_s}, \theta_{d_t})},$$

where

$P_{(s>t)_i}(\theta_{d_s}, \theta_{d_t})$ = probability of a respondent preferring statement s to statement t in pairing i;

i = index for items (pairs of statement), where $i = 1$ to I;

d = index for dimensions, where $d = 1, \ldots, D$, and d_s represents the dimension assessed by statement s;

s, t = indices for first and second stimuli, respectively, in a pairing;

$\theta_{d_s}, \theta_{d_t}$ = latent trait values for a respondent on dimensions d_s and d_t, respectively;

$P_{st}\{1,0|\theta_s, \theta_t\}$ = joint probability of endorsing stimulus s and not endorsing stimulus t given latent traits $(\theta_{d_s}, \theta_{d_t})$,

and

$P_{st}\{1,0|\theta_s, \theta_t\}$ = joint probability of not endorsing stimulus s and endorsing stimulus t given latent traits $(\theta_{d_s}, \theta_{d_t})$.

With the assumption that the two statements are evaluated independently, and with the usual IRT assumption that only θ_{d_s} influences responses to statements on dimension d_s and only θ_{d_t} influences responses to dimension d_t (i.e., local independence), we have

$$\begin{aligned} P_{(s>t)_i}(\theta_{d_s}, \theta_{d_t}) &= \frac{P_{st}(1,0|\theta_{d_s}, \theta_{d_t})}{P_{st}(1,0|\theta_{d_s}, \theta_{d_t}) + P_{st}(0,1|\theta_{d_s}, \theta_{d_t})} \\ &= \frac{P_s(1|\theta_{d_s})P_t(0|\theta_{d_t})}{P_s(1|\theta_{d_s})P_t(0|\theta_{d_t}) + P_s(0|\theta_{d_s})P_t(1|\theta_{d_t})} \end{aligned}$$

where

$P_s(1|\theta_{d_s})$, $P_s(0|\theta_{d_s})$ = probability of endorsing/not endorsing stimulus s given the latent trait value θ_{d_s},

and

$P_t(1|\theta_{d_t})$, $P_t(0|\theta_{d_t})$ = probability of endorsing/not endorsing stimulus t given latent trait θ_{d_t}.

The probability of endorsing a stimulus in a pair depends on θ_{d_s} and θ_{d_t} and also depends inherently on the model chosen to characterize the process of responding to single statements. To this end, Stark (2002) proposed using the dichotomous case of the GGUM (Roberts et al., 2000) and Stark (2006a) developed software for scoring MDPP data.

Traditional approaches to computing scores from pairwise preference items suffer from the problem of ipsativity (Cattell, 1944). A set of scales is said to be ipsative when the total score, computed as the sum of the scale scores, is a constant. In this case, the scale scores can be meaningfully compared for a given person but not across people. Thus, scale scores are relative in that a person may have a higher score on one scale than another, but we do not know if the respondent's standing on the trait assessed by that scale is high relative to other people. Böckenholt (2004) recently suggested three approaches to upgrading the measurement properties of paired comparison judgments so that they can be compared across people. Similarly, we have devised a technique for computing scores in a way that yields normative results. Specifically, we embed a small number of unidimensional pairing (usually 5% or 10% of the total scale length) in the set of MDPP statements. In this case, both statement s and t assess the same underlying dimension. This approach allows us to statistically identify the latent trait metric and calculate normative scores.

Because MDPP items may involve statements representing different personality dimensions, 3-D item response "surfaces" are possible. These are somewhat difficult to describe and interpret, because they exhibit a number of peaks and valleys. An example item response surface involving personality statements representing sociability ("My social skills are about average") and order ("Usually, my notes are so jumbled, even I have a hard time reading them") is shown in Figure 4.6. In the figure, values along the vertical axis indicate the probability of preferring the sociability statement (i.e., stimulus s) to the order statement (i.e., stimulus t) given a respondent's standing on the respective dimensions and each statement's GGUM parameters. Readers interested in details regarding MDPP IRFs are referred to Stark, Chernyshenko, and Drasgow (2005a).

Using simulation methodology, Stark (2002) and Stark et al. (2005a) examined the viability of MDPP test construction and scoring for 2-D scales of 20, 40, and 80 pairwise preference items. They found average correlations between estimated and known (generated) trait scores ranging from .80 in the most unfavorable condition (a 20-item scale with 10% unidimensional pairings) to .96 in the most favorable (80-item scale with 40% unidimensional pairings). The average correlation was about .90 for the 40-item scales, regardless of the percentage of unidimensional pairings. Moreover, in a recent study exploring the recovery of trait scores with tests of higher dimensionality, Stark, Chernyshenko, and

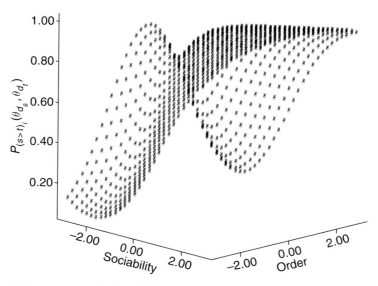

Fig. 4.6 Item response surface for an MDPP item measuring two dimensions (order and sociability).

Drasgow (2005b) found correlations of .88 and .94 for 5-D tests of 50 and 100 items, respectively.

The MDPP items used for the research reported in Tables 4.3 and 4.4 were developed as follows. First, SMEs rated the social desirability of each personality statement on a scale of 1 to 7. Next, statements similar in desirability (e.g., differing by less than 1.0 in their mean rating), but representing different dimensions, were paired to form 30 multidimensional items. Then six unidimensional items (two per trait) were created; they had no overlapping content with the UPP version of our questionnaire. GGUM parameters for each individual statement were available from a previous investigation (Chernyshenko, 2002). Each scale was scored using Stark's (2006a) MDPP-EAP program. Reliabilities were computed using the same approach as with UPP measures; as seen in Table 4.3 these were of similar magnitude compared to the other two formats.

RELATIONSHIPS BETWEEN TRAIT SCORES FOR
FORCED-CHOICE AND SINGLE-STIMULUS MEASURES

Table 4.4 presents the correlations among the nine scales obtained by Chernyshenko et al. (2006, 2009). The observed correlations appear below the diagonal and correlations corrected for unreliability appear above the diagonal. The monotrait/heteromethod (Campbell & Fiske, 1959) validities appear in bold and show that the scale format makes very little difference. The corrected monotrait/heteromethod validities above the diagonal are particularly informative: After correcting for the effects of unreliability, the measures of each of the three traits correlate almost perfectly. Consequently, it appears that the response format (SS, UPP, MDPP) had little or no effect and items measuring, say, order, measure order regardless of the format used. This result is very promising for personality assessment because it suggests that we can utilize alternative formats without concern that different traits are being measured.

The large monotrait–heteromethod correlations in Table 4.4 are not due simply to an overall response bias: The heterotrait–monomethod correlations shown in this table are small to moderate, even after correcting for unreliability. More importantly, the pattern of correlations is similar across response formats. For the SS format, the correlation between the order and self-control dimensions was .26, which is consistent with previous research (Roberts, Chernyshenko, Stark, & Goldberg, 2005). The correlations between order and self-control for the UPP

and MDPP formats were very similar to the SS correlation: .28 and .34, respectively. Note that these two traits are facets of conscientiousness and are therefore expected to have moderate, positive correlations.

On the other hand, correlations between facets of conscientiousness and facets of extraversion are expected to be negative. Therefore, the order and self-control scales should have negative correlations with the sociability scale. For the SS measures, these two correlations were −.09 and −.23, for the UPP scales the correlations were −.12 and −.30, and for the MDPP scales the correlations were −.14 and −.17. Again, the pattern of correlations was highly similar across response formats.

Returning to the results reported in Table 4.4, note that there were positive correlations between the order and self-control scale scores for all three formats. This is a very important finding because it is well known that traditional scoring of ipsative measures yields negative correlations among the scale scores (see Meade, 2004, for a recent empirical example). In our study, however, the UPP and MDPP scores correlated in about the same way as the traditional SS scores. Clearly, the scores do not have an important feature of ipsative measures.

Summary and Conclusions

In this chapter, we briefly reviewed psychometric models that have traditionally been used for evaluating assessments of personality (i.e., CTT, common factor theory, the 2PL IRT model, and the SGR IRT model). These approaches collectively can be called "dominance" analyses, because they all assume that endorsement probabilities increase with an increase in examinees' trait levels. However, using an empirical example of a 20-item scale measuring the well-being facet of emotional stability, we showed how these methods systematically fail in their descriptions of personality statements describing intermediate (or average) trait levels. In science, this type of observation is the hallmark of the beginning of progress from an old theory to a new, improved theory.

While perhaps not of the same importance as the transformation from Newtonian physics to Einstein's physics, this chapter has highlighted several exciting new methods for personality-scale development and analysis. For many years, psychometric methods for personality assessment have simply been adapted from the cognitive ability domain without explicit consideration of their appropriateness. Yet, we have argued here and in our earlier papers (Chernyshenko et al., 2001;

Table 4.4. Correlations between personality facet scores obtained using single-statement, unidimensional pairwise preference, and multidimensional pairwise preference formats.

Format	Facet	Response Format								
		SS			UPP			MDPP		
		Order	Self-control	Sociability	Order	Self-control	Sociability	Order	Self-control	Sociability
SS	Order	**.74**	.41	-.14	**1.00**	.38	-.08	**1.00**	.27	-.14
	Self-control	.26	**.54**	-.40	.47	**1.00**	-.43	.50	**.91**	-.21
	Sociability	-.09	-.23	**.62**	-.18	-.46	**1.00**	-.29	-.43	**1.00**
UPP	Order	.75	.30	-.12	**.75**	.45	-.15	**.99**	.36	-.17
	Self-control	.24	.55	-.27	.28	**.53**	-.47	.49	**1.00**	-.29
	Sociability	-.06	-.28	.76	-.12	-.30	**.78**	-.23	-.43	**.96**
MDPP	Order	.75	.32	-.20	.74	.31	-.18	**.75**	.48	-.19
	Self-control	.19	.54	-.27	.25	.62	-.31	.34	**.66**	-.24
	Sociability	-.10	-.13	.75	-.13	-.18	.73	-.14	-.17	**.73**

Note: $N = 602$, SS = single statement, UPP = unidimensional pairwise preference, MDPP = multidimensional pairwise preference. Reliability estimates appear in bold on the main diagonal, observed correlations are provided below the diagonal, and correlations corrected for unreliability are provided above the diagonal. Monotrait/heteromethod validities appear in bold.

Chernyshenko, Stark, Drasgow, & Roberts, 2007; Stark et al., 2006) that responding to personality questions is fundamentally different from responding to cognitive ability test items. Whereas dominance models provide excellent fits to the cognitive ability tests, they perform poorly in the personality domain unless items are preselected and responses are reverse-scored. If, however, the full range of statements is retained for pretesting, only ideal point models appear to provide better fit and yield parameters that are easily interpretable and intuitively understood. Moreover, the shift in response process assumptions from dominance to ideal point effectively paves the way for a variety of forced-choice formats in personality assessment, which are rapidly becoming popular in personnel selection settings due to their resistance to a variety of response biases (i.e., halo, social desirability). In this chapter, we discussed two ideal point IRT models for unidimensional and multidimensional pairwise preference formats (i.e., the ZG and MDPP models) and empirically showed them to produce scores comparable to those produced by the ideal point model with an SS format (i.e., the GGUM). Consequently, it appears ideal point methods, as a class of models, are well suited for personality assessment.

With suitable models, interesting and important innovations are feasible. For example, IRT differential item functioning analysis can provide insights about the effects of culture on responses to personality items. Highly efficient computer adaptive assessment should substantially reduce the numbers of items needed for accurate personality assessment. New measures like TAPAS or NCAPS are examples of this new generation of personality assessment tools. Perhaps most importantly, questions about the fundamental structure of personality can be examined without analytical artifacts possibly lurking in the background. We predict that these and other advances will be realized as more ideal point models and methods for evaluating quality of items are developed.

In conclusion, we believe that psychometric models for personality assessment data should reflect the unique characteristics of this domain. Even though it is convenient to use models and methods from the cognitive ability domain, we believe that such an approach short-changes the richness of personality. We hope this chapter has demonstrated that new models are needed and that, as a first attempt, ideal point methods provide a better characterization of personality assessment data. Clearly, measurement theory for personality assessment is an area offering a great opportunity for innovative new research.

Acknowledgments

The work described in this chapter was supported in part by a grant from the U.S. Army Research Institute, contract number W74V8H-06-C-006. We thank Dr. Len White for his extensive contributions to this research.

References

Andrich, D. (1988). The application of an unfolding model of the PIRT type to the measurement of attitude. *Applied Psychological Measurement, 12,* 33–51.

Andrich, D. (1989). A probabilistic IRT model for unfolding preference data. *Applied Psychological Measurement, 13,* 193–216.

Andrich, D., & Luo, G. (1993). A hyperbolic cosine latent trait model for unfolding dichotomous single-stimulus responses. *Applied Psychological Measurement, 17,* 253–276.

Ashton, M. C., & Lee, K. (2007). Empirical, theoretical, and practical advantages of the HEXACO model of personality structure. *Personality and Social Psychology Review, 11,* 150–166.

Bergman, M. E., Drasgow, F., Donovan, M. A., Juraska, S. E., & Nejdlik, J. B. (2006). Scoring situational judgment tests: Once you get the data, your troubles begin. *International Journal of Selection and Assessment, 14,* 223–235.

Birnbaum, A. (1968). Some latent trait models and their use in inferring an examinee's ability. In F. M. Lord & M. R. Novick, *Statistical theories of mental test scores* (pp. 395–479). Reading, MA: Addison-Wesley.

Bock, R. D. (1972). Estimating item parameters and latent ability when responses are scored in two or more nominal categories. *Psychometrika, 37,* 29–51.

Bock, R. D., Gibbons, R., & Muraki, E. (1988). Full-information item factor analysis. *Applied Psychological Measurement, 12,* 261–280.

Bock, R. D., Gibbons, R., Schilling, S. G., Muraki, E., Wilson, D. T., & Wood, R. (2003). *TESTFACT 4.0* (Computer software and manual). Lincolnwood, IL: Scientific Software International.

Böckenholt, U. (2004). Comparative judgments as an alternative to ratings: Identifying the scale origin. *Psychological Methods, 9,* 453–465.

Borman, W. C., Buck, D. E., Hanson, M. A., Motowidlo, S. J., Stark, S., & Drasgow, F. (2001). An examination of the comparative reliability, validity, and accuracy of performance ratings made using computerized adaptive rating scales. *Journal of Applied Psychology, 86,* 965–973.

Bossuyt, P. (1990). *A comparison of probabilistic unfolding theories for paired comparisons data.* Berlin: Springer-Verlag.

Bowen, C., Martin, B. A., & Hunt, S. T. (2002). A comparison of ipsative and normative approaches for ability to control faking in personality questionnaires. *International Journal of Organizational Analysis, 10,* 240–259.

Brady, H. E. (1989). Factor and ideal point analysis for interpersonally incomparable data. *Psychometrika, 54,* 181–202.

Campbell, D. T., & Fiske, D. W. (1959). Convergent and discriminant validation by the multitrait-multimethod matrix. *Psychological Bulletin, 56,* 81–105.

Carroll, J. B. (1993). *Human cognitive abilities: A survey of factor-analytic studies*. New York: Cambridge University Press.

Cattell, R. B. (1944). Psychological measurement: Normative, ipsative, interactive. *Psychological Review, 51*, 292–303.

Chernyshenko, O. S. (2002). Applications of ideal point approaches to scale construction and scoring in personality measurement: The development of a six-faceted measure of conscientiousness (Doctoral dissertation, University of Illinois at Urbana-Champaign, 2002). *Dissertation Abstracts International, 63*, 5556.

Chernyshenko, O. S., Stark, S., Chan, K.-Y., Drasgow, F., & Williams, B. (2001). Fitting item response theory models to personality inventories: Issues and insights. *Multivariate Behavioral Research, 36*, 523–562.

Chernyshenko, O. S., Stark, S. E., Drasgow, F., Hulin, C., & Rivas, G. (2007). *Behavioral domains assessed by TAPAS*. Technical Report No. 2007-009. Urbana, IL: Drasgow Consulting Group.

Chernyshenko, O. S., Stark, S., Drasgow, F., & Roberts, B. W. (2007). Constructing personality scales under the assumption of an ideal point response process: Toward increasing the flexibility of personality measures. *Psychological Assessment, 19*, 88–106.

Chernyshenko, O. S., Stark, S., Prewett, M., Gray, A., Stilson, R., & Tuttle, M. (2006). *Normative score comparisons from single stimulus, unidimensional forced choice, and multidimensional forced choice personality measures using item response theory*. Paper presented at the 21st annual conference for the Society of Industrial and Organizational Psychologists, Dallas, TX.

Chernyshenko, O. S., Stark, S., Prewett, M. S., Gray, A. A., Stilson, F. R., & Tuttle, M. D. (2009). Normative scoring of multidimensional pairwise preference personality scales using IRT: Empirical comparisons with other formats. *Human Performance, 22*, 1–23.

Christiansen, N. D., Burns, G. N., & Montgomery, G. E. (2005). Reconsidering forced-choice item formats for applicant personality assessment. *Human Performance, 18*, 267–307.

Coombs, C. H. (1950). Psychological scaling without a unit of measurement. *Psychological Review, 57*, 145–158.

Coombs, C. H. (1964). *A theory of data*. New York: John Wiley & Sons.

Davison, M. L. (1977). On a metric, unidimensional unfolding model for attitudinal and developmental data. *Psychometrika, 42*, 523–548.

Drasgow, F., Levine, M. V., Tsien, S., Williams, B., & Mead, A. D. (1995). Fitting polytomous item response theory models to multiple-choice tests. *Applied Psychological Measurement, 19*, 143–165.

Gulliksen, H. (1950). *Theory of mental tests*. New York: John Wiley & Sons.

Heggestad, E. D., Morrison, M., Reeve, C. L., & McCloy, R. A. (2006). Forced-choice assessments of personality for selection: Evaluating issues of normative assessment and faking resistance. *Journal of Applied Psychology, 91*, 9–24.

Hoovers (2007). *Educational Testing Service*. Retrieved 2007, from http://www.hoovers.com/educational-testing-service/–ID__54718–/free-co-factsheet.xhtml.

Houston, J. S., Borman, W. C., Farmer, W. L., & Bearden, R. M. (2005). *Development of the Enlisted Computer Adaptive Personality Scales (ENCAPS), renamed Navy Computer Adaptive Personality Scales (NCAPS)* (Technical Report No. 502). Navy Personnel Research, Studies, and Technology (NPRST), Navy Personnel Command.

Landy, F. J., & Farr, J. L. (1980). Performance rating. *Psychological Bulletin, 87*, 72–107.

Likert, R. (1932). A technique for the measurement of attitudes. *Archives of Psychology, 22*(140), 1–55.

Lord, F. M. (1980). *Applications of item response theory to practical testing problems*. Hillsdale, NJ: Erlbaum.

Meade, A. W. (2004). Psychometric problems and issues involved in creating and using ipsative measures for selection. *Journal of Occupational and Organizational Psychology, 77*, 531–551.

Mislevy, R. J., & Bock, R. D. (1991). *BILOG user's guide*. Chicago: Scientific Software International.

Reise, S. P., & Waller, N. G. (1990). Fitting the two-parameter model to personality data. *Applied Psychological Measurement, 14*, 45–58.

Roberts, B. W., Chernyshenko, O. S., Stark, S., & Goldberg, L. R. (2005). The structure of conscientiousness: An empirical investigation based on seven major personality questionnaires. *Personnel Psychology, 58*, 103–139.

Samejima, F. (1969). *Estimation of latent ability using a response pattern of graded scores* (Psychometric Monograph No. 18). Iowa City, IA: Psychometric Society.

Sands, W. A., Waters, B. K., & McBride, J. R. (Eds.) (1997). *Computerized adaptive testing: From inquiry to operation*. Washington, DC: American Psychological Association.

Spearman, C. (1904). "General intelligence," objectively determined and measured. *American Journal of Psychology, 15*, 201–293.

Stark, S. (2002). A new IRT approach to test construction and scoring designed to reduce the effects of faking in personality assessment. Doctoral dissertation, University of Illinois at Urbana-Champaign.

Stark, S. (2006a). *An Excel program for scoring MDPP items*. Unpublished manuscript, University of Illinois at Urbana-Champaign.

Stark, S. (2006b). *EAP scoring program for ZG model*. Unpublished manuscript, University of Illinois at Urbana-Champaign.

Stark, S., & Chernyshenko, O. S. (2006). *Streamlining the construction of unidimensional pairwise preference scales: Effects on scoring accuracy and test validity*. Paper submitted to the American Psychological Association conference, New Orleans, LA.

Stark, S., Chernyshenko, O. S., & Drasgow, F. (2005a). An IRT approach to constructing and scoring pairwise preference items involving stimuli on different dimensions: The multi–unidimensional pairwise preference model. *Applied Psychological Measurement, 29*, 184–203.

Stark, S., Chernyshenko, O. S., & Drasgow, F. (2005b). *Examining the recovery of normative scores with three- and five-dimensional nonadaptive multidimensional forced choice tests*. Paper presented at the 47th annual conference of the International Military Testing Association, Singapore.

Stark, S., Chernyshenko, O. S., Drasgow, F., & Williams, B. A. (2006). Examining assumptions about item responding in personality assessment: Should ideal point methods be considered for scale development and scoring? *Journal of Applied Psychology, 91*, 25–39.

Stark, S., & Drasgow, F. (2002). An EM approach to parameter estimation for the Zinnes and Griggs paired comparison IRT model. *Applied Psychological Measurement, 26*, 208–227.

Thissen, D. (1991). *MULTILOG user's guide* (Version 6). Mooresville, IN: Scientific Software International.

Thissen, D., & Wainer, H. (Eds.). (2001). *Test scoring*. Mahwah, NJ: Lawrence Erlbaum Associates.

Thurstone, L. L. (1927). A law of comparative judgment. *Psychological Review, 34*, 278–286.

Thurstone, L. L. (1928). Attitudes can be measured. *American Journal of Sociology, 33*, 529–554.

Thurstone, L. L. (1929). Theory of attitude measurement. *Psychological Review, 36*, 222–241.

Thurstone, L. L. (1947). *Multiple-factor analysis*. Chicago: University of Chicago Press.

White, L. A., & Young, M. C. (1998). *Development and validation of the Assessment of Individual Motivation (AIM)*. Paper presented at the Annual Meeting of the American Psychological Association, San Francisco, CA.

Zinnes, J. L., & Griggs, R. A. (1974). Probabilitic, multidimensional unfolding analysis. *Psychometrika, 39*, 327–350.

Construct Validation of Personality Measures

Gregory T. Smith *and* Tamika C. B. Zapolski

Abstract

Current construct validity theory emphasizes the following points. The process of validating measures of unobservable constructs is also the process of validating theories of psychological functioning. That process is ongoing for each measure and theory: construct validity is never fully established, but rather evidence for the validity of measures and theories accrues over time. To facilitate the process, researchers should conduct validation tests that are as informative as possible, that is, which directly address core components of one's theory. Measure and theory validation should be conducted on measures of homogeneous constructs: the use of single scores to represent multidimensional entities cannot be defended. An important new development is that it is now possible to validate the claims of personality theory by testing them in relation to daily, moment-to-moment reactions and behavior. Extraordinary progress has been made in the study of personality, and the further implementation of sound construct validation principles will lead to continued, improved, and successful measure and theory validation in the future.

Keywords: construct validity, homogeneous constructs, measurement validation, personality, theory validation, validation

Over the last century, both validation theory and personality theory have made enormous strides, and progress in the two domains has been closely linked. A great deal of the history of validation theory in psychology has been driven by the need to assess personality-based dysfunction; at the same time, progress in understanding how to validate measures of unobservable constructs has led to improvements in personality theory and assessment.

In this chapter, we begin with an overview of this history. We then discuss recent advances in construct validation theory in some depth. In doing so, we discuss the philosophical and theoretical basis for the recent advances, as well as ongoing difficulties in the implementation of construct validation methods. One important, recent advance is a growing appreciation of the need to make measures of unidimensional, rather than multidimensional, constructs the focus of both construct validation and theory validation. Although this need has been recognized since the modern beginning of validation efforts, researchers have not consistently focused their efforts on unidimensional measures. As a result, some important changes in the measurement and validation of personality constructs are necessary. We then provide examples of the kinds of advances in knowledge that have been realized in personality and psychopathology research following the introduction of construct validity and also following appreciation of the need to focus on homogeneous psychological entities. Finally, we discuss an important new challenge and opportunity for the validation of personality measures: to validate measures in relation to humans' day-to-day and moment-to-moment reactions and behaviors.

An Historical Overview of the Joint History of Construct Validation Theory and Personality Theory

Early Attempts to Validate Personality/ Psychopathology Measures

A good place to start a brief history of validation theory is with the Woodworth Personal Data Sheet (WPDS), a questionnaire developed in 1919 to help the U.S. Army screen out recruits who might be susceptible to "shell shock" or "war neurosis." It was thought to measure emotional stability (Garrett & Schneck, 1928; Morey, 2002). Although the failure of the WPDS is well known, it is nevertheless the case that in both the construction of the test and in subsequent attempts to use it, researchers did show real concerns with the scale's validity. We briefly consider this literature, because one can observe the presence of concerns that very much anticipate the ensuing development of methods for construct and theory validation.

In constructing the test, Woodworth developed its 116 dichotomous items on both rational and empirical grounds. He drew on the case histories of individuals identified as neurotic for item content, and then deleted items scored in the dysfunctional direction by 50% or more of his normal test group (Garrett & Schneck, 1928). In subsequent writing on the test, some researchers stressed the need to establish the scale's validity empirically. For example, Flemming and Flemming (1929) began their empirical investigation of the WPDS with this statement: "[Of the nine studies published using the WPDS], in only one . . . has any attempt been made to validate the test by the correlation technique" (p. 500). Similar statements decrying the lack of validity evidence for many current instruments are abundant in today's literature.

Total WPDS score (or, alternatively, a percentage of all items endorsed in the dysfunctional direction) did not well differentiate dysfunctional from normal individuals. Garrett and Schneck (1928) found that the WPDS did not differentiate between college freshmen (at that time, a more elite group than are freshmen today) and "avowed psychoneurotics." Flemming and Flemming (1929) found that WPDS scores did not correlate with teacher ratings of students' emotional stability. To investigate the basis for this failure, researchers considered the obvious diversity of item content (Garrett & Schneck, 1928; Laird, 1925). Sample WPDS items are: "Have you ever lost your memory for a time?," "Can you sit still without fidgeting?," "Does it make you uneasy to have to cross a wide street or an open

square?," and "Does some particular useless thought keep coming into your mind to bother you?" In noting the variety of items and the mixture of mental complaints that sparked them, Garrett and Schneck (1928) concluded:

> It is this fact, among others, which is causing the present-day trend away from the concept of mental disease as an entity. Instead of saying that a patient has this or that disease, the modern psychiatrist prefers to say that the patient exhibits such and such symptoms. (p. 465)

This thinking led them to investigate the performance of individual items, rather than the test as a whole; further, they sought to identify covariation between individual item responses and specific diagnoses, rather than membership in a global category of "mentally disturbed." In this early study, Garrett and Schneck recognized both the need to avoid combining items of different content and the need to avoid combining individuals with different symptom pictures. Their approach anticipated two important subsequent advances. First, their use of an empirical item–person classification produced very different results from prior rational classifications (Laird, 1925), thus implicating the importance of empirical validation and anticipating criterion-keying methods of test construction. Second, they anticipated the current appreciation for construct homogeneity, with its emphasis on unidimensional traits and unidimensional symptoms as the proper objects of theoretical study and measure validation (Edwards, 2001; McGrath, 2005, 2007; Smith, Fischer, & Fister, 2003; Smith, McCarthy, & Zapolski, 2007).

In the end, the WPDS rested on a far too incomplete understanding of personality and psychopathology to prove effective. Although efforts to validate the measure occurred in the absence of well-developed test and construct validation theory, this work undoubtedly paved the way for ensuing advances in both personality/psychopathology theory and validation theory.

The Centrality of Criterion-Related Validity in the Early and Middle Twentieth Century

In the following years, perhaps in part due to the failures of rationally based test construction, and perhaps in part due to suspicion of theories describing unobservable entities (Blumberg & Feigl, 1931), test validity came to be understood in terms of a test's ability to predict a practical criterion (Cureton, 1950; Kane, 2001). In fact, many validation theorists explicitly rejected the idea that scores on a test mean anything beyond their ability to predict an outcome. As Anastasi (1950) put it,

> It is only as a measure of a specifically defined criterion that a test can be objectively validated at all. . . .
> To claim that a test measures anything over and above its criterion is pure speculation.
> (p. 67)

This approach to test validation proved quite useful, both methodologically and substantively. Concerning method, it led to the criterion-keying test construction approach, in which one selects items entirely on the basis of whether the items predict the criterion. This method was used in the construction of two of the most prominent measures of personality and psychopathology, the Minnesota Multiphasic Personality Inventory (MMPI; see Chapter 14) and the California Psychological Inventory (CPI; see Chapter 17). As Kane (2001) noted, it also led to (a) very sophisticated treatments of the relationship between test scores and criteria and (b) the development of decision rules using considerations of utility (Cronbach & Gleser, 1965). Perhaps it is also true that the focus on prediction of criteria as the defining feature of validity contributed to another improvement in prediction: the finding that statistical combinations of test data are superior to clinical combinations, and that this is true across domains of inquiry (Grove, Zald, Lebow, Snitz, & Nelson, 2000; Swets, Dawes, & Monahan, 2000).

Substantively, personality/psychopathology scales constructed using criterion-keying methods have proven useful across a wide range of settings. For example, the MMPI-2 has provided valid distinctions among psychiatric inpatients and outpatients and has proven useful for treatment planning (Butcher, 1990; Greene, 2006; Nichols & Crowhurst, 2006; Perry, Miller, & Klump, 2006). It has been applied usefully to normal populations (e.g., in personnel assessment: Butcher, 2002; Derksen, Gerits, & Verbruggen, 2003), to head-injured populations (Gass, 2002), and in correctional facilities (Megargee, 2006). The CPI has also validly predicted a wide range of criteria (Gough, 1996), including, most recently, unprofessional performance in medical school (Hodgson, Teherani, Gough, Bradley, & Papadakis, 2007). The substantive success of criterion-keyed tests meant that clinical psychologists, and others, could make important predictions that affected people's lives with improved validity.

Nonetheless, there are two, crucial limitations to an exclusive focus on criterion-related validity. First, the validity tests were only as good as the criteria they predicted. As Bechtoldt (1951) put it, reliance on criterion-related validity "involves the *acceptance* of a set of operations as an adequate definition of whatever is to be measured [or predicted]" (p. 1245). The validity of the criterion is presumed, not evaluated. Because criteria are often based on some aspect of judgment, such as psychiatric diagnosis, supervisor ratings, or skill ratings by experts, one may well have reason to question their validity. And of course, to the degree there are limits to the validity of a criterion, there are limits to one's capacity to validate one's measure. Returning to the WPDS, it now seems clear that an enormous limitation to validating the measure was the relative absence of sound criteria, given the absence of a sound, well-validated model of psychopathology. The constructs to which scores on the WPDS were associated seem, by today's standards, vague, poorly defined, and inadequately measured.

The second problem is that, when tests are developed for the specific intent of predicting a circumscribed criterion, and when they are only validated with respect to that predictive task, the process adds little to basic theory. In the absence of developing theory, the clinician lacks a foundation for proposing new possible relationships among variables. Criterion-validated tests are not well suited for use in testing theories describing relationships among psychological processes. To test such theories, one often needs tests that represent psychological entities that cannot be captured by a single criterion (Cronbach & Meehl, 1955). From today's standpoint, it seems that an exclusive focus on predicting narrow criteria retarded theory development; thus, comprehensive theories of personality functioning (Costa & McCrae, 1992) or models identifying core dimensions of psychopathology (Krueger & Markon, 2006) were simply not available as objects of inquiry.

As important as this oft-mentioned limitation is, it needs to be understood within its historical context. In the early and middle parts of the twentieth century, the states of knowledge in personality and psychopathology simply did not permit the development of sound measures based on well-developed theory. The predictive failure of the WPDS is testament to that reality. It seems clear that the reliance on criterion-related validity methods at the time was necessary, and in fact led to a vast growth in knowledge that has made possible many of the theoretical advances that have taken place since then. Perhaps ironically, the success of the criterion-related validity method led to its ultimate replacement with construct validity theory. The criterion approach led to significant advances in knowledge, which made possible the development of integrative theories of personality and psychopathology. But such theories could not be validated using the criterion approach; there was thus a need for advances in validation theory to make possible the emerging advances in theories of personality and psychopathology. This need was addressed by several construct validity authors in the middle of the twentieth century (Campbell & Fiske, 1959; Cronbach & Meehl, 1955; Loevinger, 1957).

The sciences of personality and psychopathology have moved far beyond the need to rely on strict criterion prediction for validity, but that is true because of the strong insistence on empirical, criterion-based validation that characterized the best research during that period of history. Today, theory testing and the psychometric representation of unobservable processes is the norm. Even research using instruments originally developed through criterion-keying now emphasizes theory development and validation. Recent advances in research using the MMPI-2 have addressed precisely these topics; authors have developed and validated content scales thought to represent basic, homogeneous dimensions of both personality (Harkness & McNulty, 2006) and psychopathology (Butcher, 1995).

The Emergence of Construct Validity and of Theory Testing

To address the emerging need to validate theories, rather than simply predict criteria of importance, Meehl and Challman, working as part of the American Psychological Association Committee on Psychological Tests, introduced the concept of construct validity in the 1954 Technical Recommendations (American Psychological Association, 1954). Cronbach and Meehl (1955), of course, further developed the meaning of the concept, as did Loevinger (1957). The core idea of construct validity is as follows.

To develop theories of psychological functioning, it is typically necessary to refer to psychological attributes that, though presumably real, are not directly observable. For example, the theory that both low positive affect and high negative affect contribute to depression (Clark & Watson, 1991) is a theory that specifies three entities along which individuals vary: levels of positive affect, levels of negative affect, and levels of depression. None of these three entities is directly observable, so to test the theory, one needs a measure to represent each entity. The challenge, of course, is to determine whether individual differences on one's measure validly reflect individual differences in the unobservable target entity. This validation process is necessarily inferential. One must demonstrate that one's measure of a given construct relates to measures of other constructs in theoretically predictable ways. For measures of inferred constructs, the only way to build evidence that a measure reflects a construct validly is to test whether scores on the measure conform to a theory, of which the target construct is a part.

If I develop a measure of hypothetical construct A, I can only validate my measure if I have some theoretical argument that, for instance, A relates positively to B, but is unrelated to C. If I have such a theory, and if I have measures of constructs B and C, I can test whether my measure of A performs as predicted by my theory. Thus, the construct validation process requires the prior development of theories. And more than that, the process simultaneously involves testing the validity of a measure and the validity of the theory of which the measured construct is a part. Construct validation is also theory validation.

As one can readily see, the construct validation process is indeterminate. If my measure of A performs as expected by my theory, then I am likely to have increased confidence in both my theory and my measure of A. However, I cannot be certain that both my theory is correct and my measure is accurate. Suppose, instead, my new measure of A inadvertently overlaps with B (known not to correlate with C), and my supportive results are really due to the measures of A and B partly reflecting the same construct. Thus, positive results increase one's confidence in one's measure and in one's theory, but they do not constitute either proof of a theory or full validation of a measure.

Similarly, if my measure of A does not perform as expected by my theory, I must consider whether the measure, the theory, both, or neither, lack validity. Suppose A relates to both B and C. I have no certain basis for determining whether (a) my theory was accurate but my measure of A was inadequate; (b) my theory was incorrect and my measure of A was adequate; or (c) my theory was correct, my measure of A was adequate, but my measure of C was inadequate. There are other possibilities as well, including inadequate study design.

Clinical psychologists measure inferred constructs and the validity of any measure is part and parcel of the validity of the theory that led to the measure. One of the realities of this process is that it does not yield definitive, final results. As we discuss further below, there are always reasons to question either an underlying theory or a measure of an inferred psychological entity. This reality does not reflect a relative weakness in psychological science as compared to other scientific disciplines; on the contrary, this uncertainty is a normal part of the scientific process across disciplines. We return to this point below.

Problems with Construct Validation and Advances in the Concept

In their treatment of construct validity, Cronbach and Meehl (1955) relied on the concept of a "nomological network," which refers to a set of lawful relations among entities. The process of construct validation involved specifying the lawful relations between an inferred construct and other constructs, and then testing whether one's measure of the inferred construct produced the results specified in the nomological network. Today, validation theorists identify two problems with this perspective. We next discuss those problems in relation to recent advances in construct validity theory.

Strong versus Weak Construct Validation: Toward Informative Validation Tests

The first problem is this: the idea that one can define constructs by their place in a lawful network of relationships assumes a theoretical precision that is generally not present in the social sciences. Typically, personality and psychopathology researchers are faced with the task of validating their measures and theories despite the absence of a set of precisely definable, expected lawful relations among constructs and the measures that represent them. Under this circumstance, the meaning of construct validity, and what counts as construct validation, is ambiguous.

Cronbach (1988) addressed this issue by contrasting strong and weak programs of construct validity. Strong programs depend on precise theory that leads to specific predictions. They represent what appears to have been meant by construct validation using a nomological network of relationships. Given the typical lack of precision in psychological science, strong programs should perhaps be understood to represent an ideal to which researchers aspire. Weak programs, on the other hand, stem from less fully articulated

theories and construct definitions. With weak validation programs, there is less guidance as to what counts as validity evidence (Kane, 2001). One result can be approaches in which almost any statistically significant correlation between a target measure and another measure, of any magnitude, can be described as validation evidence (Cronbach, 1988). In the absence of a commitment to precise construct definitions and specific theories, validation research can have an ad hoc, opportunistic quality (Kane, 2001), in which sets of correlations with readily available measures are cobbled together as evidence of construct validity. The results of this kind of approach tend not to provide strong bases for confidence in the validity of measures.

If strong programs of construct validity tend to be aspirational rather than real, and if weak programs tend to provide little information, how should personality and psychopathology researchers approach the validation of their measures? Fortunately, researchers are not stuck between an unattainable ideal and ill-conceived, weak theory testing. Rather, there is an iterative process in which tests of partially developed theories provide information that leads to theory refinement and elaboration, which in turn provides a sounder basis for subsequent construct and theory validation research and more precise validation tests. Cronbach and Meehl (1955) referred to this bootstrapping process and to the inductive quality of construct definition and theory articulation. This process has proven effective; it is evident throughout this book that striking advances in clinical research have provided clear benefits to the consumers of clinical services.

We suggest a standard for evaluating validation research that acknowledges the iterative nature of theories and empirical tests of them. Personality and psychopathology researchers should consider whether their theoretical statements and validation tests are "informative," given the current state of knowledge (Smith, 2005). To what degree does a hypothesis involve direct criticism of a theory, or direct comparison between two, alternative theoretical explanations? To what degree does a hypothesis involve a direct response to a criticism of a theory? To what degree does a hypothesis involve a claim that, if supported, would undermine criticism of one's theory? To what degree does a hypothesis involve a claim that, if not supported, would cast real doubt on one's theory? Given the state of development of any one theory, tests of this kind may or may not constitute strong programs of construct validation, but they do not represent weak validation programs. They address questions that will clarify the validity of theories and the measures used to test them. Because of the iterative nature of the development and validation of theory and measurement, theoretical tests of this kind are likely to provide important information.

One characteristic of informative theory tests is that they evaluate, as directly as possible, specific claims made for a theory. In clinical risk factor research, to assert that trait A is a risk factor for syndrome B requires as direct a test of that specific claim as possible. Demonstration of a positive cross-sectional correlation between A and B does provide information (the absence of a correlation would pose serious problems for a risk theory), but its information value is limited because it is not a direct test of the risk factor hypothesis. In contrast, prospective designs in which trait A predicts onset of syndrome B, and other possible explanations for the onset of B have been controlled, are more informative. Such a design provides greater reason for confidence in both the theory and the measures of the constructs specified by the theory. Tests of mediation in which the putative cause predicts subsequent changes in the putative mediator, and the mediator then predicts still later changes in the putative consequence (e.g., Fried, Cyders, & Smith, 2008; Stice, 2001), are informative because they are more direct tests of a mediational risk process than are cross-sectional correlations, and so have ruled out several possible explanations that compete with the mediational theory. Tests comparing alternate theoretical explanations of the same data (Bartusch, Lynam, Moffitt, & Silva, 1997) can also be informative, because they hold multiple theories up to critical examination, both individually and in comparison to each other. Doing so is an effective way to provide information to researchers and clinicians.

Advances in Philosophy of Science: Nonjustificationism and Construct Validation

The second problem in Cronbach and Meehl's (1955) use of the nomological network concept has been illuminated by advances in both the philosophy of science and the study of the history of science; these advances have taken place since their seminal paper was published.

Earlier perspectives from the philosophy of science on theory validation have been described, by Bartley (1962) and others, as justificationist: theories could be fully justified or fully disproved based on observation or empirical evidence. The classic idea of a critical experiment, the results of which could demonstrate that a theory is false, is an example of justificationism (Duhem, 1914/1991; Lakatos, 1968). Logical positivism (Blumberg & Feigl, 1931), with its belief that theories are straightforward derivations from observed facts, is one example of justificationist philosophy of science. Under justificationism, one could imagine the validity of a theory and its accompanying measures being fully and unequivocally established following a series of critical experiments.

In recent decades, historians of science and philosophers of science have moved away from justificationism, endorsing, instead, what is referred to as nonjustificationism (Bartley, 1987; Campbell, 1987, 1990; Feyerabend, 1970; Kuhn, 1970; Lakatos, 1968; Rorer & Widiger, 1983; Weimer, 1979). Nonjustificationism refers to the concept that scientific theories are neither fully justified nor definitively disproven by individual, empirical studies. It is based on the following considerations. The test of any theory presupposes the validity of several other theories (often referred to as auxiliary theories), including theories of measurement, that also influence the empirical test (Lakatos, 1999; Meehl, 1978, 1990). Consider the brief example we presented above, in which we referred to measures of constructs A, B, and C. To test our theory of A, we must rely on the validity of the theory of how construct B operates, the validity of the theory that we have a valid measure of construct B, the validity of the theory of how construct C operates, the validity of the theory that we have a valid measure of construct C, and the validity of the theory that B is unrelated to C. Empirical results that are negative for A could thus reflect the failure of any number of theories other than the validity of our measure of construct A.

In part for this reason, no theory is ever fully proved or disproved, hence the term nonjustificationism. Instead, at any one time, evidence tends to favor some theories over others. Confirming evidence can be evaluated in terms of how informative the theory test was (Smith, 2005). To evaluate disconfirming evidence, one must make judgments as to whether the negative results likely stemmed from problems in the core theory under consideration, one of the auxiliary theories invoked to conduct the test, or another, more specific auxiliary hypothesis (Lakatos, 1968, 1999; Meehl, 1990). Obviously, researchers can and do disagree. Philosophers have proposed various means for evaluating the evidence: for example, Lakatos (1999) advocated judgments as to whether a research program is progressing (generating new knowledge and new ideas, along with new, successful theory tests) or degenerating (characterized by theory defenses that involve new, post hoc theory shifts, and unlikely to yield new knowledge or understanding).

From the nonjustificationist perspective, each component of theory derivation, each auxiliary theory, each hypothesis formation, and each empirical test is open to potential criticism. Weimer (1979) integrated these perspectives by arguing that what characterizes science is "comprehensively critical rationalism"; every aspect of the research enterprise is open to criticism, and hence to potential revision. The natural process of science involves some scientists strenuously criticizing theories and conducting critical tests of those theories, while others seek, at the same time, to adamantly defend and verify the same theories. In the end, each proposition, and each piece of theoretical evidence, is part of an argument for one theory or against another (Weimer, 1979).

What makes the effort science, rather than opinion debate, is this: good science embraces critical evaluation, both in the form of theoretical argument and empirical test. It involves informative validation tests. And clearly, the process of theory evaluation is an ongoing one: those advocating for a theory can defend it by arguing that an apparent disconfirmation reflected a problem with an auxiliary theory or hypothesis (such as measurement), and those criticizing the theory can lay the problem at the doors of the core theory under consideration. As the process continues, informative validation tests lead to one perspective being favored over another. Smith (2005) provides a sample of recent debates in clinical and psychological science, and the progress that resulted from them. It is important to appreciate that the ongoing nature of this process is not specific to psychological science, nor does it reflect a lack of maturity in psychological science. The ongoing, iterative process theorists describe characterizes science as a whole.

Certainly Cronbach and Meehl's original treatment of construct validity was noteworthy in its appreciation of the iterative nature of theory building and the need for bootstrapping to facilitate the development of measures that approximated real psychological phenomena. In many ways, they anticipated some of the advances in the philosophy of science that came later. Nevertheless, from today's perspective, their work was perhaps more heavily influenced by justificationism than now seems ideal. The idea that we can specify a lawful network of relations and confirm nomologicals appears to imply that empirical investigations provide more certainty than we now recognize to be the case. Indeed, decades later, Meehl (1990) referred to his earlier overemphasis on justificationism. The concept of construct validity has evolved since 1955: there is now a greater appreciation for the indeterminate, ongoing nature of theory building, theory revision, and scientific criticism.

Construct Homogeneity

Over the last 10–15 years, psychometric theory has evolved in a fundamental way that is crucial for personality researchers to appreciate. In the past, psychometrics writers argued for the importance of including items on scales that tap a broad range of content. Researchers were taught to avoid including items that were highly redundant with each other, because then the breadth of the scale would be diminished and the resulting high reliability would be associated with an attenuation of validity (Loevinger, 1954). To take the logic further, researchers were sometimes encouraged to choose items that were largely uncorrelated with each other, so that each new item could add the most possible incremental predictive validity over the other items (Meehl, 1992). Thus, in the end, scales should have items that are only modestly correlated with each other (Briggs & Cheek, 1986; Clark & Watson, 1995).

In recent years, a number of psychometricians have identified a core difficulty with this approach. If items are selected to be only moderately or weakly related to each other, it is likely that they do not represent the same underlying construct. As a result, the meaning of a score on such a test is unclear. Edwards (2001) noted that researchers have long appreciated the need to avoid heterogeneous items: if such an item predicts a criterion, one will not know which aspect of the item accounts for the covariance. The same reasoning extends to tests: a test comprising items that represent different constructs is, by definition, multidimensional. If one uses a single score from a test with multiple dimensions, one cannot know which dimensions account for the test's covariance with measures of other constructs.

There are two sources of uncertainty built into any validation test that uses a single score to reflect multiple dimensions. First, one cannot know the nature of the different dimensions' contributions to that score, and hence to correlations of the measure with measures of other constructs. The second source of uncertainty is perhaps more severe than the first. The same composite score is likely to reflect different combinations of constructs for different members of the sample.

McGrath (2005) clarified this point by drawing a useful distinction between psychological constructs that represent real psychological entities, on the one hand, and concepts designed to refer to covariations among more elemental psychological entities. Consider the NEO PI-R measure of the Five-Factor Model of personality (Costa & McCrae, 1992; Chapter 16). One of the five factors is neuroticism, which is understood to be composed of six elemental constructs. Two of those are angry hostility and anxiety. Measures of those two traits covary reliably; they consistently fall on a neuroticism factor in exploratory factor analyses conducted in different samples and across cultures (McCrae, Zonderman, Costa, Bond, & Paunonen, 1996). However, they are not the same construct. Their correlation was .47 in the standardization sample; they share only 22% of their variance.

Clearly, one person could be high in angry hostility and low in anxiety, and another could be low in angry hostility and high in anxiety. Those two different patterns could produce exactly the same score on neuroticism. It therefore makes sense to develop theories relating angry hostility, or anxiety, to other constructs, and tests of such theories are coherent. However, a theory relating overall neuroticism to other constructs is imprecise and unclear. If neuroticism correlates with another measure, one does not know which traits account for the covariation, or even whether the same traits account for the covariation for each member of the sample. Using McGrath's (2005) language, we should understand neuroticism as a social construction, designed to indicate the consistent covariation among identified psychological entities. We should not understand it as a coherent, psychological entity. Presuming continued evidence for the homogeneity of measures of angry hostility and anxiety, those two measures can be theorized to represent real psychological entities.

Hough and Schneider (1995), McGrath (2005, 2007), Paunonen and Ashton (2001), Schneider, Hough, and Dunnette (1996), and Smith et al. (2003), among others, have all noted that use of scores of broad measures often obscures predictive relationships. Paunonen (1998) and Paunonen and Ashton (2001) have shown that prediction of theoretically relevant criteria is improved when one uses facets of the big five personality scales, rather than the composite, big five dimensions themselves. Consider, for example, the occupational variable of service orientation to consumers (Hogan & Hogan, 1992). Although appealing, it would be imprecise to hypothesize that conscientiousness, as measured by the NEO PI-R, relates to service orientation. Using McGrath's language, such a hypothesis involves a social construction, conscientiousness, rather than presumably real, unidimensional psychological entities.

Instead, one should develop hypotheses concerning the putative entities themselves. Indeed, Costa and McCrae (1995) found that one trait within the conscientiousness domain, dutifulness, correlated .35 with service orientation; while another, achievement striving, correlated −.01 with the same criterion. Achievement striving did correlate highly with a different occupational variable, managerial potential ($r = .63$), but another facet of conscientiousness, order, accounted for comparatively little variance in that criterion ($r = .25$). These findings are typical: facets within domains of the NEO PI-R often have markedly different external correlates. This reality strongly supports the psychometric argument for focusing validation tests on homogeneous construct measures. If, instead, researchers conduct validation tests using single scores to reflect multidimensional measures, they risk averaging the different effects of different constructs. When researchers study homogeneous constructs, their tests are more precise and more coherent; as a result, they can be more informative.

A second example concerns the construct of impulsivity. Over the last several years, clinical researchers have recognized that the term "impulsivity" has been used in a variety of ways: various measures with that label can tap what appear to be different constructs, and many impulsivity measures appear to include items tapping multiple constructs (Bagby, Joffe, Parker, & Schuller, 1993; Depue & Collins, 1999; Evenden, 1999; Petry, 2001; Smith et al., 2007; Whiteside & Lynam, 2001, 2003; Whiteside, Lynam, Miller, & Reynolds, 2005; Zuckerman, 1994).

Efforts to disaggregate the set of constructs included within the impulsivity framework have proved quite useful. One current model involves identification of five, separate constructs that involve dispositions to rash action: sensation seeking, lack of planning, lack of perseverance, positive urgency (the tendency to engage in rash actions when in an extremely positive mood), and negative urgency (the tendency to engage in rash actions when in an extremely negative mood) (Cyders & Smith, 2007; Cyders et al., 2007; Smith et al., 2007; Whiteside & Lynam, 2001, 2003; Whiteside et al., 2005).

Measures of the five traits are only modestly correlated, the traits do not load on an overall, "impulsivity" factor, and the traits have different external correlates (Smith et al., 2007). The urgency traits appear to relate to problem levels of involvement in risky behaviors, sensation seeking appears to relate to the frequency of engaging in risky behaviors, lack of planning relates to some problem behaviors but not others, and lack of perseverance relates to school performance (Fischer & Smith, 2008; Fischer, Smith, Annus, & Hendricks, 2007; Miller, Flory, Lynam, & Leukefeld, 2003; Smith et al., 2007; Whiteside & Lynam, 2003; Whiteside et al., 2005). These different patterns of correlates are consistent with theory (Fischer, Smith, Spillane, & Cyders, 2005). In addition, different interventions are likely to be effective for different ones of the traits (perhaps distress tolerance for the urgency traits and safe, alternative ways to seek sensations for sensation seeking: Fischer & Smith, 2008; Palmgreen & Donohew, 2003). These advances could not have occurred had researchers continued to rely on a single score from what turned out to be multidimensional measures of "impulsivity."

In one sense, we are arguing that recent advances in construct validation theory require a significant departure from much current practice in personality research. Researchers should not propose or test hypotheses involving multidimensional variables. It lacks coherence to specify hypotheses concerning broad personality domains, such as neuroticism, conscientiousness, or agreeableness, because those terms do not reflect potentially real psychological entities. It lacks coherence to describe broader dimensions of personality, such as Digman's (1997) alpha and beta, as having effects on other variables, because those terms denote patterns of covariation among lower-level constructs; they do not denote constructs themselves.

In another sense, what we are advocating follows from a straightforward application of psychometric theory; it requires no new tools for personality researchers, and it is already well underway (as illustrated by the above examples). In our view, this is an especially exciting time for personality research, because researchers have the psychometric tools, the statistical tools, and the emerging theory to understand both the operation of real, homogeneous psychological entities and the ways in which such entities covary in humans.

In sum, for personality and psychopathology research to continue to advance, researchers must study coherent, cohesive entities. To use multifaceted, complex constructs as predictors or criteria in validity or theory studies cannot be defended. Researchers can generate theories that identify putatively homogenous, coherent constructs. There are many statistical tools that facilitate comparative dimensionality tests, such as confirmatory factor analysis and latent class analysis. Researchers can compare the theory that a putative attribute is homogeneous to the theory that it is a combination of separate attributes.

In the next section of this chapter, we briefly consider recent examples of progress in personality and psychopathology research. These examples involve significant theoretical advances in both areas; they were made possible by the emergence of the construct validity perspective, with its emphasis on theory testing. The examples we use also illustrate the importance of construct homogeneity.

Recent Advances in the Study of Personality and Psychopathology

One overarching, recent development in the study of personality and psychopathology concerns increasing differentiation among elemental psychological entities, together with a clearer understanding of the nature of hierarchical organizations of the elemental entities (Smith, 2005). This process has occurred extensively in personality theory and is now well underway in the study of psychopathology. We consider examples from each domain.

The most basic advances in hierarchical understanding have concerned the overall structure of personality. One measure of the Five-Factor Model of personality (the NEO PI-R; see Chapter 16) has identified 30 separate dimensions of personality functioning, which can be organized along five broad dimensions. This structure has proved remarkably stable in exploratory factor analyses (McCrae et al., 1996). The consistency of this structure of covariation among elemental personality traits is important; the structure may approximate real dimensions of individual differences in human functioning. And, personality can be organized at higher levels of abstraction as well. Recently, Markon, Krueger, and Watson (2005) presented evidence for covariation of the five broad factors; they described broader three-factor (negative emotionality, disinhibition, and positive emotionality) and two-factor (alpha and beta; see Digman, 1997) aggregate structures. As a result of this work, researchers and clinicians have a much clearer understanding of which sets of lower-level traits tend to covary. Theory testing should take place at the level of homogeneous constructs (here represented by the 30 facets of the NEO PI-R), but by understanding the structural relations among these 30 trait dimensions, researchers and clinicians have a growing understanding of typical patterns of individual differences in personality functioning.

Distinctions among putatively elemental psychological entities can alter researchers' understanding of the hierarchical structure of those entities. Consider the above example concerning impulsivity-like constructs, in which five, distinct pathways to rash action have been identified. Interestingly, there has been no evidence that those five constructs should be understood as facets of a broader, overall impulsivity domain. Instead, positive and negative urgency appear to be facets of an overall emotion-based disposition to rash action; lack of perseverance and lack of planning appear to be facets of an overall low conscientiousness disposition to rash action; and sensation seeking stands alone, loading on neither of those factors (Cyders & Smith, 2007). Thus, a higher-order integration of the five pathways suggests at least three different broad dispositions to rash action. The term "impulsivity" appears not to have a clear referent in the personality domain. Recognition of the structure of these traits clarifies understanding of the personality contribution to rash, ill-considered action.

Other distinctions among elemental traits suggest hierarchical organizations of dysfunction. Recognition that the dimensions of positive affect and negative affect were distinct helped researchers understand the difference between anxiety and depression (Clark & Watson, 1991; Diener, Larsen, Levine, & Emmons, 1985; Watson, Clark, & Carey, 1988). The two appear to share high, overall negative affect, but they differ in positive affect. Individuals high in negative affect but unremarkable in positive affect tend to be anxious, and those high in negative affect and also low in positive affect tend to be depressed. Thus, researchers and clinicians have available a hierarchical, tripartite structure for distress; it includes an overall affective distress factor (high negative affect) and differentiation among two expressions of distress: anxiety and depression (Clark & Watson, 1991).

In recent years, progress in differentiating among constructs and the resulting implications for hierarchical organization has begun to be applied to the study of psychopathology. A great deal of research uses DSM-IV diagnoses, or DSM-IV symptom counts, as predictors or criteria in validation studies. Using diagnoses and symptom counts in that way involves the presumption of the validity of the disorders, and recent advances suggest that presumption may not always be warranted. Researchers have noted that many currently defined disorders may not reflect coherent psychological constructs; instead, they appear to represent composites of multiple, separable constructs.

Applying our above discussion of construct homogeneity, if disorders are not unidimensional entities, then the use of disorder scores or symptom counts as variables in an analysis is problematic for at least two reasons. First, the scores represent the influence of multiple psychological constructs, so they lack clear theoretical meaning. Second, different individuals are likely attaining the same score through endorsement of different symptoms, so the relative degree of influence of the different constructs varies from person to person (McGrath, 2005, 2007). Thus, for at least some disorders, the meaning of scores may not be clear.

Clinical researchers have increasingly demonstrated the likely reality of this concern. In one striking example, Widiger and Trull (2007) noted that two individuals could both be diagnosed with obsessive compulsive personality disorder, and yet not share a single symptom in common. Clinical researchers have increasingly identified multiple dimensions, in some cases with different etiologies, within single mental disorders. We next briefly review relevant evidence pertaining to a sample of disorders.

THE DISAGGREGATION OF PSYCHOPATHY

The disaggregation of the many components of psychopathy has received considerable attention and constitutes a good, recent example of progress stemming from construct validation theory, including the need to study homogeneous constructs (Brinkley, Newman, Widiger, & Lynam, 2004; Cooke & Michie, 2001; Harpur, Hakistan, & Hare, 1988; Harpur, Hare, & Hakistan, 1989; Lynam & Widiger, 2007). See Chapter 29 for a more detailed consideration of psychopathy. Hare's (2003) Psychopathy Checklist Revised (PCL-R) identified two separate factors, one representing the callous and remorseless use of others and the other representing a deviant and antisocial lifestyle. In the PCL-R, the two factors share only 25% of their variance (Hare, 1990; Harpur et al., 1988), and they have numerous different correlates (Harpur et al., 1989). Cooke and Michie (2001) identified three factors, described as (a) arrogant and deceitful interpersonal style, (b) deficient affective experience, and (c) impulsive and irresponsible behavioral style. To complicate matters further, the PCL-R does not include all of the dimensions of the classic description of psychopathy provided by Cleckley (1941); for example, low anxiousness is not represented (Lynam & Widiger, 2007; Rogers, 1995). Brinkley et al. (2004) note that psychopathy, as measured by the PCL-R, is an etiologically heterogeneous entity. If psychopathy includes multiple dimensions that do not always covary, and if those dimensions have different etiologies, it follows that psychopathy is not a coherent, meaningful psychological construct (McGrath, 2005; Smith et al., 2007).

Most recently, Lynam and Widiger (2007) took advantage of the hierarchical disaggregation of personality to develop a comprehensive, consensus description of the psychopathy construct. For each of the 30 facets of the NEO PI-R, they identified whether (a) the trait related to psychopathy, and (b) whether high or low trait scores reflected the psychopathy construct. The result is a placement of psychopathy along each of the 30 homogeneous dimensions of personality; in this view, psychopathy is understood to represent a multidimensional combination of constructs, rather than a coherent theoretical entity in and of itself. Interestingly, Lynam and Widiger's (2007) consensus view of psychopathy made extensive use of distinctions between personality facets of the same broad personality domain. For example, psychopaths were understood to be high on impulsiveness and angry hostility and low on anxiety and self-consciousness; all four of those traits are placed on the neuroticism domain of the Five-Factor Model (Lynam & Widiger, 2007).

THE DISAGGREGATION OF DEPRESSION

Jang, Livesley, Taylor, Stein, and Moon (2004) studied the factor structure of several symptom lists of depression. They identified 14 subfactors. Examples of subfactors included high negative affect ("feeling blue and lonely"), low positive affect ("positive affect"), "insomnia," "loss of appetite," and "psychomotor retardation." Intercorrelations among the factors ranged from .00 to .34, and the factors were differentially heritable, with heritability coefficients ranging from 0.00 to 0.35. It appears to be the case that (a) some of the dimensions of depression do not covary substantially and (b) some have a heritable basis and others do not: their etiologies appear to differ. McGrath (2005, 2007) also provides interesting examples of the heterogeneity of depression symptom items.

Depression does not appear to be a coherent, homogeneous psychological construct; at best, it may be a hierarchical, social construction denoting shared variance among several, separable constructs (McGrath, 2005). These recent advances in the study of depression suggest that researchers should avoid use of overall depression scores as a criterion in construct validity/theory testing studies. For example, it makes sense to test whether stressful events are a risk factor for increased negative affect, or for reduced positive affect, but it may not make sense to test whether stressful events are a risk factor for depression. The latter hypothesis is imprecise, and a test of it necessarily yields imprecise results.

THE DISAGGREGATION OF OBSESSIVE COMPULSIVE DISORDER

Many authors have separated obsessive compulsive disorder into several dimensions. Watson and Wu (2005) identified obsessive checking, obsessive cleanliness, and compulsive rituals as separate and only moderately related constructs, and concluded that the disorder may be both phenotypically and genotypically heterogeneous. Leckman et al. (1997) found four dimensions within the criterion set that were intercorrelated between .50 and .56, and Mathews, Jang, Hami, and Stein (2004) did as well. If the putative disorder has four dimensions, which tend to share only 25–31% of their variance with each other, then, by definition, individuals can be high on one dimension without being high on another dimension: elevation in obsessive checking does not necessitate, for example, elevation in hoarding. The putative disorder is a combination of only moderately related constructs, and those constructs may have distinct genetic etiologies. Based on these findings, obsessive compulsive disorder appears not to be a homogeneous psychological construct. Recognizing this structure offers real potential for new advances: as researchers study the individual dimensions, rather than composites of those dimensions, progress in understanding both etiology and treatment will accelerate.

THE DISAGGREGATION OF POST-TRAUMATIC STRESS DISORDER

The symptoms of posttraumatic stress disorder have been shown to fall on four factors (intrusions, avoidance, dysphoria, and hyperarousal; see Simms, Watson, & Doebbeling, 2002). Intercorrelations among the four ranged from .43 to .61, indicating substantial unshared variance in each factor. King, Leskin, King, and Weathers (1998) also found that a four-factor model (re-experiencing, effortful avoidance, emotional numbing, and hyperarousal) fit their 17-symptom clinical interview better than did any other model, including a single-factor model or a hierarchical model, in which an overall factor was thought to underlie the four factors. Clearly, identical posttraumatic stress disorder symptom counts can refer to very different symptom pictures. It thus appears to be the case that the term "posttraumatic stress disorder" does not denote a real, unidimensional psychological entity; rather, it denotes the tendency of four dimensions of distress to covary. Again, this recognition can only accelerate the rate of acquisition of new knowledge about these dimensions of distress.

THE DISAGGREGATION OF SCHIZOTYPAL PERSONALITY DISORDER

The apparent heterogeneity of some DSM-IV disorders is not limited to Axis 1 disorders. Fossati et al. (2005) compared several different factor structures for the schizotypal personality disorder criteria, and found that a three-factor model (cognitive-perceptual, interpersonal, and disorganization) fit best. Intercorrelations among the three factors ranged from .14 to .63, again indicating substantial unshared variance in each factor. Here, too, individuals can be high on one factor but not on another. Again in this case, the same quantitative symptom count could reflect very different dysfunctional experiences.

IMPLICATIONS OF THIS DISAGGREGATION RESEARCH

It follows from these recent advances that, for many disorders, the use of diagnostic status or a disorder score as either a predictor or a criterion in theory-testing studies will tend to produce unclear results. A score on depression, or a depression diagnosis, reflects scores on several constructs. To test a theory that experience X is a risk factor for depression is to be imprecise. It may be the case that experience X is a risk factor for one factor within depression, but not for other factors. A validation test in which the criterion was overall depression scores could easily produce nonsignificant results. One would risk missing the association altogether.

Perhaps more problematically, in such a situation one has to assume that the symptom count score reflects the same variable for each person, but that may well not be true. Individuals could have very similar symptom counts, yet very different patterns of scores on individual constructs. When that is the case, the symptom count is not a coherent theoretical entity, and its correlation with measures of other constructs has unclear meaning. In 1928,

Garrett and Schneck argued that one should not validate the WPDS against overly broad criteria, such as disease status. Instead, they felt, researchers should use specific symptoms as criteria.

It is certainly true that our understanding of psychopathology has come a long way since 1928. For example, the DSM-IV committee conducted and published 175 qualitative literature reviews and 48 additional empirical studies to provide the scientific underpinnings of their efforts (Widiger & Clark, 2000). Each new version of the DSM has relied more heavily on the available science than previous versions, and each new version has benefited from an ever-increasing body of scientific knowledge.

At the same time, it appears to be the case that validation research still suffers from the use of overly broad, multidimensional criteria in the form of putative mental disorders. The recent success in disaggregating some of these disorders should perhaps be best understood as a continuation of the effort called for by Garrett and Schneck in 1928. Just as theories of psychopathology have advanced dramatically since 1928, we can expect them to continue to advance as researchers further sharpen their focus to study elemental, homogeneous psychological entities. Perhaps today, just as in 1928, one of the biggest obstacles to test validation is the imprecision present in many criterion variables.

It seems to us that one of the obvious implications of this disaggregation research may be that, in some cases, the diagnoses themselves need to be rethought. Just as some diagnostic categories may be best understood as social constructions denoting a set of moderately related constructs (McGrath, 2005), it is also true that certain constructs are represented in the diagnostic criteria for many different disorders. Psychological constructs cut across disorders, and disorders combine separate psychological constructs. Perhaps a system describing dysfunction in terms of homogeneous dimensions of functioning would accelerate research progress dramatically. It is also true that, in the case of some disorders, researchers may identify clear disease processes, where a single cause produces elevations on what are otherwise only moderately correlated dimensions of functioning. (Although achy muscles, nausea, and a fever are only moderately correlated, they can occur together as a result of a single cause, such as is the case with the flu.) However, that possibility cannot be confirmed until the specific, homogeneous dimensions are themselves identified, described, and measured.

The possibility of describing dysfunction along dimensions of functioning is not an abstract ideal for an imaginary future. It is happening right now.

There has been growing evidence that many forms of psychopathology can be understood to reflect extreme scores on various dimensions of normal personality functioning (Clark, 2007; Widiger & Samuel, 2005; Widiger & Trull, 2007). This recognition is enormously helpful, because it indicates the relevance of personality research to psychopathology and of psychopathology research to personality. It is also, as it turns out, quite practical.

Samuel and Widiger (2006) showed that descriptions of clinical cases using the 30 NEO PI-R facets of the Five-Factor Model were found to be significantly more useful to clinicians than were DSM-IV diagnoses. The detailed descriptions of patients along each of 30 unidimensional components of personality were rated as more useful in providing global personality descriptions of clients, in communicating information to clients, in describing clients' important personality difficulties, and in formulating effective treatment interventions (Samuel & Widiger, 2006). As those authors noted, the detailed information provided by the use of all 30 facets, rather than just the five broad personality scales, likely improved the model's clinical utility significantly. Clinical psychologists now have the capacity to describe clients' characteristic functioning using numerous detailed and coherent constructs, and doing so has proved quite useful. Widiger and Trull (2007) address this issue in depth, as do Widiger and Boyd (Chapter 18).

We believe that progress in psychopathology research will continue to involve identification of cohesive, homogeneous dimensions of dysfunction and the development of descriptive systems using those dimensions as a basis. The continued use of DSM categories as either predictors or criteria in psychopathology research requires the assumption that they are coherent entities. Many may not be. Instead, the diagnoses may point to important problems in living that might more fruitfully be described in terms of placement on unidimensional dimensions of functioning, such as are available in comprehensive models of personality.

We next briefly discuss an important new opportunity for the validation of personality constructs. Recent methodological advances appear to offer the prospect of facilitating further integration of trait theory and the assessment of everyday, even moment-to-moment, behavior. Indeed, a crucial, outstanding question in trait theory concerns the degree to which individual differences in traits actually covary with individual differences in reactions to daily events and daily behavioral choices. To address this question is to address one of the basic, outstanding challenges to the validity of trait concepts.

The Integration of Trait and Behavior Assessment

In recent years, technical advances have made possible the moment-to-moment assessment of individuals' moods, reactions, and behaviors. Terms such as "electronic diaries" (EDs) and "ecological momentary assessment" (EMA) have been used to denote a range of technical approaches to moment-specific assessment, such as handheld computers (Piasecki, Huford, Solham, & Trull, 2007; Stone & Shiffman, 2002). Researchers assess individuals at multiple times during the day, often over periods of 1 or 2 weeks, and can therefore profile relations between personal characteristics and behaviors of clinical interest.

One challenge facing the validation of personality theory and personality measures is that it turns out that EMAs can yield qualitatively different findings from those provided by traditional assessment methods, such as self-report questionnaires (Piasecki et al., 2007). Traditional assessments involve memories of past behaviors, moods, and reactions that may well not be fully accurate. The structure of human memory is such that individuals may not be able to recall and then count past experiences, in order to summarize their tendencies in response to questionnaire items (Schwarz & Oyserman, 2001). And current mood states, contextual cues, characteristics of rating scales, and time passed, all appear to influence self-reports of putatively stable personal tendencies (Piasecki et al., 2007). It is also possible that individuals' reports represent memories altered by self-perception and other factors.

Shiffman et al. (1997) compared smokers' retrospective reports of lapses and relapses to what they had earlier reported using an ED. They found that only 23% of participants retrospectively reported the correct day of their first lapse, and the average error in dating was 14.5 days. In addition, personal precursors to lapses were remembered differently after the fact. Retrospective reports described higher pre-lapse negative affect than did real-time reports. The difference in findings between the two reports is important: if one relied only on retrospective reports, one would risk overestimating the importance of negative affect as a precursor to a lapse by recovering smokers.

Findings such as these indicate the need for a new type of validation of personality constructs: it is important to demonstrate that individual differences in personality do in fact predict individual differences in daily reactions and behaviors. Recently, validation evidence of this kind has begun to emerge. To provide an example of this work, we briefly consider EMA as applied to the disorder bulimia nervosa.

One model of risk for the binge-eating characteristic of bulimia nervosa is that it is precipitated by the experience of negative mood (Agras & Telch, 1998; Sanftner & Crowther, 1998; Telch & Agras, 1996). With the emergence of ED technology, it has become possible to test this hypothesis "in the moment." A series of studies have recently begun to do so. Wonderlich et al. (2007) compared bulimic participants with three different personality profiles in their daily moods and their symptomatic behavior. They contrasted a cluster of individuals characterized by interpersonal-emotional distress (e.g., high scores on cognitive dysregulation, identity problems, anxiousness, suspiciousness, and self-harm) with individuals characterized by stimulus seeking-hostile behavior and individuals with a relative absence of personality pathology. Consistent with self-reported personality data, the interpersonal-emotional cluster reported more momentary negative mood and less momentary positive mood than did either of the other two clusters via ED assessment. And consistent with theory, those individuals also reported the highest rates of daily binge eating and vomiting.

Smyth et al. (2007) found that, among bulimia nervosa patients, days in which individuals engaged in binge eating or vomiting were characterized by lower levels of positive affect, higher levels of negative affect, higher levels of hostility, and more stress. They also analyzed within-day trends, and found that decreasing positive affect, increasing negative affect, and increasing anger/hostility preceded symptomatic events. And, consistent with the view that binge eating and purging provide negative reinforcement in the form of distress relief, they found that following symptomatic events, positive affect increased and both negative affect and anger/hostility decreased. Together, these findings provide important validation for the negative reinforcement theory of bulimia nervosa symptom expression. They also provide important validation for the personality measures contributing to the personality clusters (in this case, taken from the Dimensional Assessment of Personality Pathology: Livesley & Jackson, 2002); individual differences on the measures predicted individual differences in both mood and behavior.

These tests had a number of properties that we believe characterize sound validation tests. First, they were informative: they put both the personality measures and the negative reinforcement theory to direct tests. Failures of prediction would have cast doubt on the theory, the measures, or both. Second, the criteria were likely unidimensional constructs: negative mood, positive mood, hostility, binge eating, and vomiting. That the authors used specific symptoms as their predictive criteria satisfies the demand of Garrett and Schneck (1928) and the recent rerecognition of the importance of unidimensionality in theory tests. Third, they used what appear to be homogeneous personality constructs to create latent profiles: they identified groups of individuals with co-occurring personality traits, but they understood the groups to reflect probabilistic combinations of distinct traits.

ED methodology provides an opportunity for rigorous, informative tests of the validity of personality measures. We anticipate that research will show that traits do tend to predict individual differences in reactivity to the environment and in behavioral choices, as measured on a moment-to-moment basis (as was true in the examples we selected). If that turns out to be true, personality researchers will have come one step closer to describing individual differences in pathways from inherited disposition all the way to present behavior. Of course, failures to find expected relations between personality and daily experience will lead to re-examination of both theory and assessment method. In either case, these types of studies are likely to be highly informative, and therefore likely to advance our understanding of personality. They constitute useful validation tests for both theories and the measures used to embody them.

Summary

We wish to emphasize the following points from this chapter. First, the history of validity theory is characterized by rigorous efforts to determine the best ways to validate measures of psychological constructs, and, over time, to validate theories of psychological functioning. It is inaccurate to look at past efforts, such as the attempt to validate the WPDS and the use of criterion-related validity, as simply inadequate efforts. Rather, each step in validity theory can be understood to provide advances that made possible the next step. And, the advances in validity theory occurred hand-in-hand with advances in personality theory; each stimulated the development of the other.

Second, we urge researchers to consider whether the validation tests they are considering are informative, given the current state of knowledge. The relative absence of strong, precise psychological theories does not permit weak, ad hoc, opportunistic validation research. Instead, researchers should embrace the critical process of scientific inquiry and conduct the kinds of validation tests that involve direct challenges to existing theories or comparisons between competing theoretical perspectives.

Third, researchers should appreciate that the validation process is ongoing and indeterminate. Each finding pertains to the validity of one's theory and the measures one uses to test it. The construct validity of a measure is never fully established. One may have evidence one believes strongly supports the validity of one's measure, but one's validation evidence is always subject to critical scrutiny.

Fourth, construct validation tests and theory validation tests should be conducted on measures of homogeneous psychological entities. The use of single scores to represent multidimensional processes cannot be defended. Accordingly, researchers should focus their validation efforts on lower-level personality constructs and single-symptom dimensions, rather than composite personality measures and multifaceted disorders. Once homogeneous dimensions are identified, it is useful to investigate the degree to which they covary, enabling one to describe higher-order, abstract composites of psychological entities. There is good reason to believe that this approach will significantly advance personality and psychopathology research.

Fifth, a great deal of progress has been made in personality and psychopathology research. Vastly more is known now, than was known when Woodworth made his measurement effort. Researchers have developed much more sophisticated, valid models of personality. There is good reason to believe we are close to describing valid dimensional approaches to psychopathology as well. Early research using such approaches suggests that clinicians will find these advances helpful.

Sixth, researchers are engaged in the important new frontier of validating measures against daily, moment-to-moment accounts of reactions and behavior. The technological advances that make this research possible are facilitating far more comprehensive accounts of individual differences, i.e. from heritable disposition to daily behavior, than was once thought possible.

In sum, this is an exciting time for personality research. Researchers do face new challenges, but because of the availability of comprehensive personality models, the emphasis on elemental psychological constructs, and the ability to relate personality to daily behavior, we are likely to experience extraordinary advances in validity over the coming years.

Future Directions

The following topics are likely to receive more attention in the future:

1. One important, often unstated auxiliary theory employed in most personality validation research is this: test validation automatically extends to special populations, such as ethnic minorities, children, the elderly, or individuals with developmental or mental deficits. Although there has been important progress in testing this assumption, there is a need for more researchers to do so.

2. Models for the disaggregation and hierarchical integration of putative mental disorders are likely to continue to develop. Specific rules for determining when a set of related dimensions can and should be understood as facets of an overall disorder must be further articulated and tested.

3. Psychometrists' contentions concerning construct homogeneity are likely to elicit alternative proposals from researchers. For example, one argument might be that the five dimensions of the NEO PI-R represent core constructs, and the individual facets reflect variance in both the core construct and in variance unique to that facet. Researchers are likely to investigate the generative quality of the construct homogeneity perspective versus that of the core-unique variance perspective. It may also turn out that the two perspectives are not fundamentally different.

4. We discussed personality validation in relation to daily, moment-to-moment accounts of reactions and behavior. There are many other, fascinating new avenues for the validation of personality theory and measures. For example, the use of brain imaging techniques is likely to shed further light on the validity of personality theories and measures (see Chapter 19).

References

Agras, W. S., & Telch, C. F. (1998). Effects of caloric deprivation and negative affect on binge eating in obese binge eating disordered women. *Behavior Therapy, 29*, 491–503.

American Psychological Association. (1954). Technical recommendations for psychological tests and diagnostic techniques. *Psychological Bulletin Supplement, 51*, 1–38.

Anastasi, A. (1950). The concept of validity in the interpretation of test scores. *Educational and Psychological Measurement, 10*, 67–78.

Bagby, R. M., Joffe, R. T., Parker, J. D. A., & Schuller, D. R. (1993). Re-examination of the evidence for the DSM-III personality disorder clusters. *Journal of Personality Disorders, 7*, 320–328.

Bartley, W. W., III. (1962). *The retreat to commitment*. New York: A. A. Knopf.

Bartley, W. W., III. (1987). Philosophy of biology versus philosophy of physics. In G. Radnitzky & W. W. Bartley, III (Eds.), *Evolutionary epistemology, rationality, and the sociology of knowledge* (pp. 7–46). La Salle, IL: Open Court.

Bartusch, D. R. J., Lynam, D. R., Moffitt, T. E., & Silva, P. A. (1997). Is age important? Testing a general versus a developmental theory of antisocial behavior. *Criminology, 35*, 13–48.

Bechtoldt, H. P. (1951). Selection. In S. S. Stevens (Ed.), *Handbook of experimental psychology* (pp. 1237–1266). Oxford: John Wiley & Sons.

Blumberg, A. E., & Feigl, H. (1931). Logical positivism. *Journal of Philosophy, 28*, 281–296.

Briggs, S. R., & Cheek, J. M. (1986). The role of factor analysis in the development and evaluation of personality scales. *Journal of Personality, 54*, 107–147.

Brinkley, C. A., Newman, J. P., Widiger, T. A., & Lynam, D. R. (2004). Two approaches to parsing the heterogeneity of psychopathy. *Clinical Psychology: Science and Practice, 11*, 69–94.

Butcher, J. N. (1990). *Use of the MMPI-2 in treatment planning*. New York: Oxford University Press.

Butcher, J. N. (1995). *Clinical personality assessment: Practical approaches*. New York: Oxford University Press.

Butcher, J. N. (2002). Assessing pilots with "the wrong stuff": A call for research on emotional health factors in commercial aviators. *International Journal of Selection and Assessment, 10*, 1–17.

Campbell, D. T. (1987). Evolutionary epistemology. In G. Radnitzky & W. W. Bartley, III (Eds.), *Evolutionary epistemology, epistemology, rationality, and the sociology of knowledge* (pp. 47–89). La Salle, IL: Open Court.

Campbell, D. T. (1990). The Meehlian corroboration-verisimilitude theory of science. *Psychological Inquiry, 1*, 142–147.

Campbell, D. T., & Fiske, D. W. (1959). Convergent and discriminant validation by the multi-trait multi-method matrix. *Psychological Bulletin, 56*, 81–105.

Clark, L. A. (2007). Assessment and diagnosis of personality disorder: Perennial issues and an emerging reconceptualization. *Annual Review of Psychology, 58*, 227–257.

Clark, L. A., & Watson, D. (1991). Tripartite model of anxiety and depression: Psychometric evidence and taxonomic implications. *Journal of Abnormal Psychology, 100*, 316–336.

Clark, L. A., & Watson, D. (1995). Constructing validity: Basic issues in objective scale development. *Psychological Assessment, 7*, 309–319.

Cleckley, H. (1941). *The mask of sanity*. St Louis: Mosby.

Cooke, D. J., & Michie, C. (2001). Refining the construct of psychopathy: Towards a hierarchical model. *Psychological Assessment, 13*, 171–188.

Costa, P. T. & McCrae, R. R. (1992). *Revised NEO Personality Inventory manual*. Odessa, FL: Psychological Assessment Resources.

Costa, P. T., & McCrae, R. R. (1995). Domains and facets: Hierarchical personality assessment using the revised NEO Personality Inventory. *Journal of Personality Assessment, 64*, 21–50.

Cronbach, L. J. (1988). Five perspectives on validation argument. In H. Wainer & H. Braun (Eds.), *Test validity* (pp. 3–17). Hillsdale, NJ: Erlbaum.

Cronbach, L. J., & Gleser, G. C. (1965). *Psychological test and personnel decisions*. Urbana, IL: University of Illinois Press.

Cronbach, L. J., & Meehl, P. E. (1955). Construct validity in psychological tests. *Psychological Bulletin, 52*, 281–302.

Cureton, E. E. (1950). Validity. In E. F. Lingquist (Ed.), *Educational measurement*. Washington, DC: American Council of Education.

Cyders, M. A., & Smith, G. T. (2007). Mood-based rash action and its components: Positive and negative urgency and their relations with other impulsivity-like constructs. *Personality and Individual Differences, 43*, 839–850.

Cyders, M. A., Smith, G. T., Spillane, N. S., Fischer, S., Annus, A. M., & Peterson, C. (2007). Integration of impulsivity and positive mood to predict risky behavior: Development and validation of a measure of positive urgency. *Psychological Assessment, 19*, 107–118.

Depue, R. A., & Collins, P. F. (1999). Neurobiology of the structure of personality: Dopamine, facilitation of incentive motivation, and extraversion. *Behavioral and Brain Sciences, 22*, 491–569.

Derksen, J., Gerits, L., & Verbruggen, A. (2003). *MMPI-2 profiles of nurses caring for people with severe behavior problems*. Paper given at the 38th MMPI-2 Conference on Recent Developments in the Use of the MMPI-2 and MMPI-A, Minneapolis, MN.

Diener, E., Larsen, R. J., Levine, S., & Emmons, R. A. (1985). Intensity and frequency: Dimensions underlying positive and negative affect. *Journal of Personality and Social Psychology, 48*, 1253–1265.

Digman, J. M. (1997). Higher-order factors of the big five. *Journal of Personality and Social Psychology, 73*, 1246–1256.

Duhem, P. (1914/1991). *The Aim and Structure of Physical Theory* (P. Weiner, trans.). Princeton, NJ: Princeton University Press (First published in 1914 as *La Théorie physique: Son objet, sa structure*).

Edwards, J. R. (2001). Multidimensional constructs in organizational behavior research: An integrative analytical framework. *Organizational Research Methods, 4*, 144–192.

Evenden, J. (1999). Varieties of impulsivity. *Journal of Psychopharmacology, 146*, 348–361.

Feyerabend, P. (1970). Against method. In M. Radner & S. Winokur (Eds.), *Minnesota studies on the philosophy of science, Vol. IV: Analyses of theories and methods of physics and psychology* (pp. 17–130). Minneapolis, MN: University of Minnesota Press.

Flemming, E. G., & Flemming, C. W. (1929). The validity of the Matthews' revision of the Woodworth personal data questionnaire. *Journal of Abnormal and Social Psychology, 23*, 500–506.

Fischer, S., & Smith, G. T. (2008). Binge eating, problem drinking, and pathological gambling: Linking behavior to shared traits and social learning. *Personality and Individual Differences, 44*, 789–800.

Fischer, S., Smith, G., Annus, A., & Hendricks, M. (2007). The relationship of neuroticism and urgency to negative consequences of alcohol use in women with bulimic symptoms. *Personality and Individual Differences, 43*, 1199–1209.

Fischer, S., Smith, G. T., Spillane, N., & Cyders, M. A. (2005). Urgency: Individual differences in reaction to mood and implications for addictive behaviors. In A. V. Clark (Ed.), *The Psychology of Mood* (pp. 85–108). New York: Nova Science Publishers.

Fossati, A., Citterio, A., Grazioli, F., Borroni, S., Carretta, I., Maffei, C., et al. (2005). Taxonic structure of schizotypal personality disorder: A multiple-instrument, multi sample study based on mixture models. *Psychiatry Research, 137,* 71–85.

Fried, R. E., Cyders, M. A., & Smith, G. T. (2008, June). Longitudinal validation of the acquired preparedness model. Paper presented at the annual meeting of the Research Society on Alcoholism, Washington, DC.

Garrett, H. E., & Schneck, M. R. (1928). A study of the discriminate value of the Woodworth Personal Data Sheet. *Journal of General Psychology, 1,* 459–471.

Gass, C. S. (2002). Personality assessment of neurologically impaired patients. In J. Butcher (Ed.), *Clinical personality assessment: Practical approaches* (2nd ed., pp. 208–244). New York: Oxford University Press.

Gough, H. G. (1996). *CPI manual.* Palo Alto, CA: Consulting Psychologists Press.

Greene, R. L. (2006). Use of the MMPI-2 in outpatient mental health settings. In J. Butcher (Ed.), *MMPI-2: A practitioner's guide* (pp. 253–272). Washington, DC: American Psychological Association.

Grove, W. M., Zald, D. H., Lebow, B. S., Snitz, B. E., & Nelson, C. (2000). Clinical versus mechanical prediction: A meta-analysis. *Psychological Assessment, 12,* 19–30.

Hare, R. D. (1990). *The Hare Psychopathy Checklist revised manual.* Toronto: Multi-Health Systems.

Hare, R. D. (2003). *PCL-R technical manual.* Towanda, NY: Multi-Health Systems.

Harkness, A. R., & McNulty, J. L. (2006). An overview of personality: The MMPI-2 personality psychopathology five (PSY-5) scales. In J. Butcher (Ed.), *MMPI-2: A practitioner's guide* (pp. 73–98). Washington, DC: American Psychological Association.

Harpur, T. J., Hakistan, A. R., & Hare, R. D. (1988). Factor structure of the psychopathy checklist. *Journal of Consulting and Clinical Psychology, 56,* 741–747.

Harpur, T. J., Hare, R. D., & Hakistan, A. R. (1989). Two-factor conceptualization of psychopathy: Construct validity and assessment implications. *Psychological Assessment, 1,* 6–17.

Hodgson, C. S., Teherani, A., Gough, H. G., Bradley, P., & Papadakis, M. A. (2007). The relationship between measures of unprofessional behavior during medical school and indices of the California Psychological Inventory. *Academic Medicine, 82,* S4–S7.

Hogan, R., & Hogan, J. (1992). *Hogan Personality Inventory Manual* (2nd ed.). Tulsa, OK: Hogan Assessment Systems.

Hough, L. M., & Schneider, R. J. (1995). Personality traits, taxonomies, and applications in organizations. In K. R. Murphy (Ed.), *Individuals and behavior in organizations* (pp. 31–88). San Francisco, CA: Josey-Bass.

Jang, K., Livesley, W., Taylor, S., Stein, M., & Moon, E. (2004). Heritability of individual depressive symptoms. *Journal of Affective Disorders, 80,* 125–133.

Kane, M. T. (2001). Current concerns in validity theory. *Journal of Educational Measurement, 38,* 319–342.

King, D., Leskin, G., King, L., & Weathers, F. (1998). Confirmatory factor analysis of the clinical administered PTSD scale: Evidence for the dimensionality of posttraumatic stress disorder. *Psychological Assessment, 10,* 90–96.

Krueger, R., and Markon, K. (2006). Reinterpreting comorbidity: A model-based approach to understanding and classifying psychopathology. *Annual Review of Clinical Psychology, 2,* 111–133.

Kuhn, T. S. (1970). *The structure of scientific revolutions.* Chicago, IL: University of Chicago Press.

Laird, D. A. (1925). A mental hygiene and vocational test. *The Journal of Educational Psychology, 16,* 419–422.

Lakatos, I. (1968). Criticism and the methodology of scientific research programs. *Proceedings of the Aristotelian Society, 69,* 149–186.

Lakatos, I. (1999). Lectures on scientific method. In I. Lakatos & P. Feyerabend (Eds.), *For and Against Method* (pp. 19–112). Chicago, IL: The University of Chicago Press.

Leckman, J. F., Grice, D. E., Boardman, J., Zhang, H., Vitale, A., Bondi, C., et al. (1997). Symptoms of obsessive-compulsive disorder. *American Journal of Psychiatry, 154,* 911–917.

Livesley, W. J., & Jackson, D. N. (2002). *Manual for the Dimensional Assessment of Personality Pathology—basic questionnaire (DAPP).* London, ON: Research Psychologists' Press.

Loevinger, J. (1954). The attenuation paradox in test theory. *Psychological Bulletin, 51,* 493–504.

Loevinger, J. (1957). Objective tests as instruments of psychological theory. *Psychological Reports, Monograph Supplement, 3,* 635–694.

Lynam, D. R., & Widiger, T. A. (2007). Using a general model of personality to identify the basic elements of psychopathy. *Journal of Personality Disorders, 21,* 160–178.

Markon, K., Krueger, F., & Watson, D. (2005). Delineating the structure of normal and abnormal personality: An integrative hierarchical approach. *Journal of Personality and Social Psychology, 88,* 139–157.

Mathews, C. A., Jang, K. L., Hami, S., & Stein, M. B. (2004). The structure of obsessionality among young adults. *Depression and Anxiety, 20,* 77–85.

McCrae, R., Zonderman, A., Costa, P., Bond, M., and Paunonen, S. (1996). Evaluating replicability of factors in the revised NEO Personality Inventory: Confirmatory factor analysis versus Procrustes rotation. *Journal of Personality and Social Psychology, 70,* 552–566.

McGrath, R. E. (2005). Conceptual complexity and construct validity. *Journal of Personality Assessment, 85*(2), 112–124.

McGrath, R. E. (2007). Toward validity (Manuscript submitted for publication).

Meehl, P. E. (1978). Theoretical risks and tabular asterisks—Karl, Ronald, and slow progress of soft psychology. *Journal of Consulting and Clinical Psychology, 46,* 806–834.

Meehl, P. E. (1990). Appraising and amending theories: The strategy of Lakatosian defense and two principles that warrant it. *Psychological Inquiry, 1,* 108–141.

Meehl, P. E. (1992). Factors and taxa, traits and types, differences of degree and differences in kind. *Journal of Personality, 60,* 117–173.

Megargee, E. I. (2006). Use of the MMPI-2 in correctional settings. In J. Butcher (Ed.), *MMPI-2: A practitioner's guide* (pp. 327–360). Washington, DC: American Psychological Association.

Miller, J., Flory, K., Lynam, D., & Leukefeld, C. (2003). A test of the four factor model of impulsivity related traits. *Personality and Individual Differences, 34,* 1403–1418.

Morey, L. (2002). Measuring personality and psychopathology. In J. Schinka, W. Velicer, & I. Weiner (Eds.), *Handbook of psychology, Vol. 2: Research methods in psychology* (pp. 377–406). Hoboken, NJ: John Wiley & Sons.

Nichols, D. S., & Crowhurst, B. (2006). Use of the MMPI-2 in inpatient mental health settings. In J. Butcher (Ed.), *MMPI-2: A practitioner's guide* (pp. 195–252). Washington, DC: American Psychological Association.

Palmgreen, P. & Donohew, L. (2003). Handbook of drug abuse prevention: Theory, science, and practice. In Z. Sloboda &

W. Bukoski (Eds.), *Effective mass media strategies for drug abuse prevention campaigns* (pp. 27–43). New York: Springer.

Paunonen, S. V. (1998). Hierarchical organization of personality and prediction of behavior. *Journal of Personality and Social Psychology, 74*, 538–556.

Paunonen, S. V., & Ashton, M. C. (2001). Big five factors and facets and the prediction of behavior. *Journal of Personality and Social Psychology, 81*, 524–539.

Perry, J. N., Miller, K. B., & Klump, K. (2006). Treatment planning with the MMPI-2. In J. Butcher (Ed.), *MMPI-2: A practitioner's guide* (pp. 143–164). Washington, DC: American Psychological Association.

Petry, N. (2001). Substance abuse, pathological gambling, and impulsiveness. *Drug and Alcohol Dependence, 63*, 29–38.

Piasecki, T., Huford, M., Solham, M., & Trull, T. (2007). Assessing clients in their natural environments with electronic diaries: Rationale, benefits, limitations, and barriers. *Psychological Assessment, 19*, 25–43.

Rogers, R. (1995). *Diagnostic and structured interviewing.* Odessa, FL: Psychological Assessment Resources.

Rorer, L., & Widiger, T. (1983). Personality structure and assessment. *Annual Review of Psychology, 34*, 431–463.

Samuel, D., & Widiger, T. (2006). Clinicians' judgments of clinical utility: A comparison of the DSM-IV and Five-Factor models. *Journal of Abnormal Psychology, 115*, 298–308.

Sanftner, J. L., & Crowther, J. H. (1998). Variability in self-esteem, moods, shame, and guilt in women who binge. *International Journal of Eating Disorders, 23*, 391–397.

Schneider, R. J., Hough, L. M., & Dunnette, M. D. (1996). Broadsided by broad traits: How to sink science in five dimensions or less. *Journal of Organizational Behavior, 17*, 639–655.

Schwarz, N., & Oyserman, D. (2001). Asking questions about behavior: Cognition, communication, and questionnaire construction. *American Journal of Evaluation, 22*, 127–160.

Shiffman, S., Hufford, M., Hickcox, M., Paty, J. A., Gnys, M., & Kassel, J. D. (1997). Remember that? A comparison of real-time versus retrospective recall of smoking lapses. *Journal of Consulting and Clinical Psychology, 65*, 292–300.

Simms, L., Watson, D., & Doebbeling, B. (2002). Confirmatory factor analyses of posttraumatic stress symptoms in deployed and nondeployed veterans of the Gulf War. *Journal of Abnormal Psychology, 111*, 637–647.

Smith, G. T. (2005). On construct validity: Issues of method and measurement. *Psychological Assessment, 17*, 396–408.

Smith, G. T., Fischer, S., Cyders, M. A., Annus, A. M., Spillane, N. S., & McCarthy, D. M. (2007). On the validity and utility of discriminating among impulsivity-like traits. *Assessment, 14*, 155–170.

Smith, G. T., Fischer, S., & Fister, S. M. (2003). Incremental validity principles in test construction. *Psychological Assessment, 15*, 467–477.

Smith, G. T., McCarthy, D. M., & Zapolski, T. C. B. (2007). On the Value of Homogeneous Constructs for Construct Validation, Theory Testing, and the Description of Psychopathology (Invited manuscript submitted for publication).

Smyth, J. M., Wonderlich, S. A., Heron, K. E., Sliwinski, M. J., Crosby, R. D., Mitchell, J. E., et al. (2007). Daily and momentary mood and stress are associated with binge eating and vomiting in bulimia nervosa patients in the natural environment. *Journal of Consulting and Clinical Psychology, 75*, 629–638.

Stice, E. (2001). A prospective test of the dual-pathway model of bulimic pathology: Mediating effects of dieting and negative affect. *Journal of Abnormal Psychology, 110*, 124–135.

Stone, A. A., & Shiffman, S. (2002). Capturing momentary self-report data: A proposal for reporting guidelines. *Annals of Behavioral Medicine, 24*, 236–243.

Swets, J. A., Dawes, R. M., & Monahan, J. (2000). Psychological science can improve diagnostic decisions. *Psychological Science in the Public Interest, 1*, 1–26.

Telch, C. F., & Agras, W. S. (1996). Do emotional states influence binge eating in the obese? *International Journal of Eating Disorders, 20*, 271–290.

Watson, D., Clark, L. A., & Carey, G. (1988). Positive and negative affect and their relation to anxiety and depressive disorders. *Journal of Abnormal Psychology, 97*, 346–353.

Watson, D., & Wu, K. (2005). Development and validation of the Schedule of Compulsions, Obsessions, and Pathological Impulses (SCOPI). *Assessment, 12*, 50–65.

Weimer, W. B. (1979). *Notes on the methodology of scientific research.* Hillsdale, NJ: Lawrence Erlbaum.

Whiteside, S. P., & Lynam, D. R. (2001). The Five Factor Model and impulsivity: Using a structural model of personality to understand impulsivity. *Personality and Individual Differences, 30*, 669–689.

Whiteside, S. P., & Lynam, D. R. (2003). Understanding the role of impulsivity and externalizing psychopathology in alcohol abuse: Applications of the UPPS impulsive behavior scale. *Experimental and Clinical Psychopharmacology, 11*, 210–217.

Whiteside, S. P., Lynam, D. R., Miller, J. D., & Reynolds, S. K. (2005). Validation of the UPPS impulsive behavior scale: A four-factor model of impulsivity. *European Journal of Personality, 19*, 559–574.

Widiger, T. A., & Clark, L. A. (2000). Toward DSM V and the classification of psychopathology. *Psychological Bulletin, 126*, 946–963.

Widiger, T., & Samuel, D. (2005). Diagnostic categories or dimensions? A question for the *Diagnostic and statistical manual of mental disorders*—fifth edition. *Journal of Abnormal Psychology, 114*, 494–504.

Widiger, T. A., & Trull, T. J. (2007). Plate tectonics in the classification of personality disorder: Shifting to a dimensional model. *The American Psychologist, 62*, 71–83.

Wonderlich, S., Crosby, R., Engel, S., Mitchell, J., Smyth, J., & Miltenberger, R. (2007). Personality-based clusters in bulimia nervosa: Differences in clinical variables and ecological momentary assessment. *Journal of Personality Disorders, 21*, 340–357.

Zuckerman, M. (1994). *Behavioral expressions and biological bases of sensation seeking.* Cambridge: Cambridge University Press.

Standards and Standardization

Kurt F. Geisinger *and* Janet F. Carlson

Abstract

The meaningfulness of measures depends upon a number of factors: validity studies, score scales that are understood by test users, knowledge that the measure has been studied with members of a population to which an individual test taker or a group of test takers belongs, and so on. Fundamental to such considerations is that the measure has been administered under the same or comparable circumstances as it was when normed, validated, checked for appropriate types of reliability, and otherwise researched. This chapter addresses issues specific to testing individuals. In some cases, specialized validity studies are needed to document that a test can be adapted or accommodated to the needs of specific test takers and have its scores still carry the same or similar meaning as with the original population. Essentially, we need to perform generalizability studies to show that the meaningfulness and validity of tests generalizes across administrative changes, language variations, and cultural differences for varying groups of individuals. Truly, psychological testing needs to stay rooted into its very basis: the science of individual differences.

Keywords: disability, generalizability research, Hispanics, individual differences, norms, reliability

We would like to begin this chapter with a fictionalized court case that draws heavily upon reality—as experienced by many psychometricians and others concerned with assessment. The case is that of *Jenna C. v. Unified School District.*

Jenna C. v. Unified School District

It was a blustery day outside, but the temperature in the courtroom was at least 78 degrees. The various parties nervously adjusted their seats and looked around the courtroom as though trying to memorize the scene. The court clerk called, "All rise; this court is now in session." A formal-looking judge entered the room and was seated. Her hair was a variety of shades of gray and tied sternly in a bun at the back of her head. Papers were shuffled. The judge fixed her gaze on the attorney for the prosecution, who rose. "We call Dr. Glaubenweiss to the stand." The short but distinguished-looking psychologist rose slowly, leaning heavily on his cane. He wore a gray tweed jacket, and gray flannel slacks. He began a slow trek

to the front of the courtroom. The man reached the witness stand and turned slowly and stiffly. As he took the oath, his heavy German accent was evident. He settled into the witness chair and in response to questions from the attorney began tracing his background—his education among masters in Vienna and Zurich, his many years of practice in New York City, awards that he had received from various educational and civic groups, and the popular books that he had written on raising children with learning disabilities. He grunted and scowled in response to a query about *Newsweek* and other popular publications referring to him as "the Benjamin Spock of the learning disabled." The questioning attorney asked the court to qualify the witness as an expert. The judge shifted her line of vision toward the opposing attorney, who began to rise. This second attorney was silent for a moment after he stood; then he stated slowly, "The people are not convinced that Dr. Glaubenweiss meets current standards as an expert in this area." He paused momentarily, but before he was able to continue, the first attorney retorted, "Your Honor, he has already been qualified as an expert in this district and six other federal districts as well as in Canada and several European countries. He has given invited talks at the annual meetings of the American Bar Association on the legal nature of learning disabilities; if he is not an expert, who is?"

The judge shrugged slightly, frowned momentarily, and stated, "The court recognizes him as an expert. Objections to and limitations on that qualification can be discussed in cross-examination."

The first attorney returned to his questioning. "Are you familiar with a student in the Unified School District who is being referred to in these proceedings as Jenna C.?"

"I am," Dr. Glaubenweiss responded.

"Did you make an appraisal of her educational status at the request of her parents and her counsel?"

"I did." Dr. Glaubenweiss took off his thick glasses as he responded and peered at them as if they troubled him.

"So Dr. Glaubenweiss, please tell the court what measures you used to assess Jenna C."

Dr. Glaubenweiss commenced reciting his procedures as he began to clean his glasses against his sweater vest. "I first met with Jenna C. along with her parents. Her parents told me that Jenna had not been performing as well as school officials thought that she should. They told me that they had tried both working with her themselves and tutoring, but that nothing worked. Then I met Jenna on several occasions. During the first meeting, I conducted an interview with her to determine what activities she enjoyed and to establish rapport. On the second and third visits, I administered, of course," he paused for effect and then returned to his description, "I administered the Glaubenweiss Test of Learning Disabilities and the Glaubenweiss Survey of Instructional Deficits. Administration of these measures was quite straightforward and the results, as usual, were quite informative . . . definitive, really."

"And what were those results, Doctor?"

"That Jenna C. is experiencing significant learning disabilities of unknown origin and that her school district needs to provide additional instruction, one-on-one. They have been unwilling to do so, quite unwilling, and she is being harmed each and every day that they refuse. Indeed, the results show that she is learning disabled."

The attorney confirmed, "So your opinion is that she is learning disabled?"

"Indeed, correct," was the response.

"And how certain are you of your diagnosis, Doctor?"

"Oh. Quite certain, quite certain. I have never used the Glaubenweiss instruments and been incorrect. No, never. It's a certainty." After he finished speaking, he made a quiet "Humph" sound to no one in particular, as if he had been surprised by such a naive question. "And you're scientifically convinced of the remediation that is needed?" the attorney asked.

"Ja, yes, quite certain. I detailed what is needed in my report. You have that, no? You want me to discuss my report?"

"No, Doctor, we have already entered your report as evidence; that is not necessary. Thank you, Doctor, thank you." The attorney looked at the judge and said, "That concludes our direct testimony then, your Honor, but we reserve the right to redirect after cross."

The judge stated, "So noted," and shifted her gaze to the defense attorney, who rose slowly, still intently reviewing a thick, dog-eared, legal-sized pad of notes and questions.

"Doctor, you have never published an article in a refereed journal, now have you?"

"A journal? No, not a journal. It's the wrong place to reach the people. The wrong place."

"And you've never engaged in empirical research, is that correct?"

"Wrong," he retorted, "I have indeed. I do research all the time, all the time. Silly question, silly."

"Let me rephrase my question, then, Doctor. You have never validated either your Glaubenweiss Test of Learning Disabilities or the Glaubenweiss Survey of Instructional Deficits, is that not correct?"

"No need to validate. They are valid measures. I know it."

"But there's a difference, isn't there, Doctor, between validation and validity? Isn't it true that you believe that your measures are valid, but you have not validated them?"

"Ja. Validation is the process of proving that a measure is valid. These measures are valid, however, so there's no need to perform a validation study."

"Have there been any published studies by others documenting that your measures are valid, Doctor?"

"Not that I know of. Because only I use my measures, that would be difficult, no?"

"Have you developed norms for your measures, Doctor, norms against which to evaluate the meaning of scores?"

"No, there are no norms, but I know what scores mean."

The defense attorney managed to roll his eyes at the judge while informing the judge that he had completed his cross-examination. The prosecuting attorney had no additional questions and the judge called a recess in the trial.

A day later the prosecution rested and the defense, representing the Unified School District, began its case. Their first witness was Dr. Al Bookman. He was tall and lean and appeared only about 25 years old. His hair were blond and tidily cut. As he walked to the stand, his posture was athletic. He was wearing an expensive Italian suit, with a pin representing the American Psychological Association's centennial celebration on the lapel of his jacket.

As with Dr. Glaubenweiss, the initial questions to the defense witness concerned his background. He described his education at one of the large midwestern state universities; his seminal dissertation under the nationally prominent psychologist, Dr. Jack Baker, author of the Tennessee Three-Factor Personality Inventory or TTPI; his 10-year record at the local state university, where he had quickly been tenured and promoted to the rank of professor; his two books entitled *Statistics in Clinical and School Psychology* and *Measurement in Clinical and School Psychology: Theoretical Perspectives*; his several dozen publications in academic journals; and his service on the consulting boards of several journals in the field. He taught courses at the state university in assessment and statistics.

Once during the questioning, he was asked his age and responded 43. So young did he look that several people in the audience gasped and exchanged murmurs. The judge pounded her gavel but looked surprised herself. He was quickly recognized as an expert without reservation. Then the questioning related to his opinions and his basis for these opinions began.

"Dr. Bookman, have you reviewed the report prepared by Dr. Glaubenweiss regarding Jenna C.?"

"Yes, I have."

"And, Professor, do you have an opinion about this report?"

"Yes, I do." Unlike Glaubenweiss, whose voice rose and fell as he spoke, Bookman's voice was a monotone, without any discernible modulation.

"Please tell the court what your expert opinion is regarding Dr. Glaubenweiss' assessment of Jenna C."

"It is totally without foundation. The instruments that he used to make his assessments have never been validated and therefore are not useful in any manner. It is unacceptable for psychologists to make such baseless and utterly preposterous diagnoses. The numbers that his instruments yield are virtually random numbers."

"And, do you have problems with the manner in which Dr. Glaubenweiss administers his own tests, Professor Bookman?"

"Yes, indeed I do. In his deposition prior to the trial, Dr. Glaubenweiss stated that he administered the test differently to different children. In psychological testing, we work with standardized tests. Standardization means that tests are always administered under constant and precisely articulated conditions. Only then can the scores that emerge from them be meaningful. Standardization of test administration procedures is accomplished by the test developer. Before a test is published and used by other professionals, the test developer must make the test administration procedures uniform so that all administrators will give the test the same way. These test administration procedures are carefully described in the test manual. All psychologists know that one gives a test strictly in accordance with the procedures provided in the test manual. Dr. Glaubenweiss generated two instruments but he failed to develop constant methods for administering them. That is an unacceptable practice and would render the scores meaningless even if the measures were valid, which they are not."

The lawyer queried, "You don't like these tests much, do you, Professor Bookman?"

"I would not use the word, like. These instruments fail to meet the most minimal standards for use in a professional setting as provided in the Standards for Educational and Psychological Testing published by the American Educational Research Association, American Psychological Association, and the National Council for Measurement in Education in 1999."

"Let's move on to a different topic, Professor Bookman. Are you familiar with the assessment of learning disabilities?"

"I certainly hope so. That has been the primary area of my research."

"Can you define for the court what is meant by learning disabilities?" The lawyer nodded toward the judge.

The witness turned toward the judge and said, "The consensus among experts in the field is that learning disabilities are diagnosed when discrepancies emerge between what one expects a child to learn in school and what that child actually learns. When a child is consistently below the level expected of him or her, and no other condition such as visual, hearing, or motor handicaps, mental retardation, emotional disturbance, or environmental, cultural, or economic disadvantage is present, then the diagnosis of learning disability is made. So we must first rule out explanations such as visual, hearing, or motor handicaps, mental retardation, emotional disturbance, or environmental, cultural, or economic disadvantage. We do this through various psychometrically sound measures and through interviews with parents and teachers, observations of the children, and interviews with the children themselves. Then we look for the most common learning disabilities: perceptual handicaps, brain injuries, dyslexia, and developmental aphasia. Many psychologists have had good success with a variety of psychometrically sound measures. The Kaufman Assessment Battery for Children, second edition, the Stanford-Binet Intelligence Scales, fifth edition, and the fourth edition of the Wechsler Intelligence Scale for Children are all appropriate. The reason that I prefer using the formulas that I developed for identifying and assessing the extent of learning disabilities is that they recognize the underlying regression model that must be involved in assessing learning disabilities. In my research, I have established a multiple regression formula—essentially the formula for a straight line—that permits us to evaluate whether a child's academic performance is consistent with the levels expected for a child based on his or her tested intellectual ability. When a child is no more than 11/2 standard errors of estimate below the predicted achievement level, using the regression formula, then he or she is not learning disabled."

Bookman, who had been looking at the judge as he spoke, paused and looked at his attorney, who had been trying to get his attention while rolling his eyes perceptively. Dr. Bookman became still.

The lawyer asked, "So it is a discrepancy between expected performance and actual performance that indicates a learning disability; is that correct, Doctor?"

"Yes. There are some exceptions, as in the case with children with other disabilities. But, in general, yes."

"And psychologists estimate expected performance with the use of tests such as intelligence tests, is that correct, Professor?"

"Yes, it is."

"And having tested Jenna C., do you believe that she is learning disabled?"

"No, I do not."

"And on what basis do you make this judgment?" the lawyer asked.

"Her tested achievement is within the range expected given her level of tested intelligence. Perhaps her achievement level is slightly below that which I might have expected, but not by much, and she is certainly not in the learning-disabled range. Therefore, she is not learning disabled."

"And you stake your professional reputation on it?"

"I do."

"Your honor, the defense rests."

The defense attorney sat down and the attorney for Jenna C. rose. "Dr. Bookman, you are a professor, is that correct?"

"Yes."

"And do you have a private practice, Professor?"

"No."

"And isn't it also true that you do not practice at all? That is, that you do not see any patients therapeutically?"

"No, I supervise graduate students at the university clinic. These graduate students see clients, who are ultimately my clients, because I am the licensed psychologist who supervises these students and their clinical work," Bookman responded.

"But your graduate students actually meet with these patients, isn't that correct?"

"Yes, it is."

"And you do not see these patients yourself, isn't that also correct?"

"It's generally correct, although I listen to tapes of their therapy sessions and sometimes I have the occasion to meet some of these clients."

"How many assessments of learning disabilities have you made in your career, Professor Bookman?"

"Oh, I do not know. Dozens."

"Now, Professor, let's see if I understand your assertion. You have been working in the field of psychology for over 15 years and you consider yourself an expert in the assessment of learning disabilities, but you believe that you have made only a few dozen assessments?"

"That's not a fair statement. I am an expert because I have conducted research on assessments and have identified the ways in which we can make assessments of learning disabilities most effectively."

"Isn't it true, Professor, that you would not know a learning-disabled student if you saw one?" As the defense attorney rose, calling out, "Your Honor," the questioning attorney stated, "Withdrawn."

The attorney for Jenna C. asked again, "Professor, you stated that the standardization of tests is critical, did you not?"

"Yes," came the reply.

"And you stated that you disapproved of the fact that Dr. Glaubenweiss did not administer his instruments to Jenna C. in the same manner that he would to all other children, isn't that correct?"

"Yes, indeed." Bookman had a proud look about him, as if he believed that he had either stumped or actually educated the attorney for Jenna C.

"And you, who have assessed dozens of children, believe that Dr. Glaubenweiss should test every child the same way?" The attorney looked at Bookman quizzically.

"Yes, I do, with the possible exception of age differences. Of course, the administration of many tests differs depending on how old the child is when he or she is examined."

"So, age is the only variable that would lead you to administer a test differently, is that correct, Doctor?"

"Yes, I believe so," affirmed Dr. Bookman.

"Well then, Professor, what about children with handicaps, would you test them differently?"

"Yes . . . well, maybe, depending upon the nature of their disability."

"So now, Professor, you are saying that you would test children differently depending upon their age and upon whether or not they have a disability. All the others would be tested the same, is that now correct, Professor?"

"I don't think that your summarization is fair. All children would receive the same test. Just the administration would change. And of course if you administered the test in a manner that differed from the procedures provided in the test manual you may have to 'flag' the score to show that the test administration was not performed in the prescribed manner. It's called a 'nonstandard score'."

"But, Professor, you still appear to be saying that you would administer a test in the same manner to all children, but that you might administer it differently if a child were of a different age or had a disability. Is that now correct?"

"I guess that I could accept that, yes."

"Okay, Professor, let me try a different question. How would you test a young Hispanic child?"

The professor was silent for a few seconds, then, with one eyebrow beginning to twitch up and down somewhat nervously, in a quiet voice he asked, "Does he or she speak English?"

"Does it matter, Professor?"

"Well, yes. You see, Hispanics who speak English are included in the norm group of most major tests in relation to their proportion in the population. Therefore, one can use the standard tests with those Hispanics who speak English."

"What about Hispanics who do not speak any English, could you use the same test with them, Professor?"

"No, but I could make a referral to a Spanish-speaking psychologist who would be able to test the child using a test in Spanish. That would be the proper procedure." Bookman sat up straight and smiled wanly as though he hoped that others would see him as confident in his response.

"And what about a Hispanic child who has lived in this country for several years. His English is not perfect, but neither is his Spanish. What would you do then, Professor?"

"First, I would give the child a test of language dominance—a test that assesses language skills in both languages. Alternatively, I could give tests of language proficiency in both English and Spanish. In either case, first I would make a determination of whether the child should be tested in English or Spanish. Depending on that answer, I would either test him in English myself or refer him to a Spanish psychologist."

"So, Professor, you are saying that you now believe that you would test all children alike, except if they differed by age, by having a disability of some sort, or if they did not speak English very well. Is that now a complete and correct list?"

Bookman stared downward toward the front wall of the witness box. His voice was soft now and somewhat wavering. "Yes, I believe that is correct. But you have to remember, the vast majority of children are normal. They can be tested using standardized tests without a problem."

The questioning attorney looked at Bookman gleefully. "But why would you need to test a normal child?," he asked rhetorically to a flustered Dr. Bookman. "That will be all," he informed the court.

The judge looked sad and as though she had eaten something too spicy for lunch and it had not agreed with her.

How would you decide the case of Jenna C.? What factors would you consider in your opinion? Many cases, especially cases involving individual diagnosis or classification decisions, present real testing dilemmas. We can either test individuals using the procedures developed and refined carefully that were employed during the test's standardization or adapt testing procedures to meet the apparent needs of individual test takers.

Through Dr. Glaubenweiss's testimony, the foregoing case illustrates the importance of maintaining test administration in as uniform a manner as possible. And—courtesy of Dr. Bookman—it also highlights some of the problems inherent in retaining strict standards of test administration and scoring, problems that are especially apparent when one tests those who differ from the majority of the test-taking population. The litigious atmosphere surrounding cognitive assessment has been recognized for many years and has produced a rich legal history. It should be noted, however, that these same illustrative principles apply in the case of clinical personality assessment, family functioning, vocational assessment, or any form of assessment that depends on making score comparisons in order to evaluate an individual's standing. Projective techniques, for example, make similar comparisons, as scorers consider such things as whether a particular Rorschach percept constitutes a popular response and whether the response makes use of "common" or "rare" details of the blot. Clearly, such comparisons can be made only through the use of information from a reference group.

Intelligence measures and personality measures certainly are not unrelated. In particular, individually administered measures of cognitive ability have a notable impact on the assessment of personality. This is partly because a test administrator spends a fair amount of time with a test taker—upward of 3.5 hr according to one report (Camara, Nathan, & Puente, 2000)—and cannot avoid observing important characteristics of his or her functioning. Historically, clinical interpretations of intelligence test scores have been attempted (Glasser & Zimmerman, 1967; Zimmerman & Woo-Sam, 1973) although validation evidence for doing so is generally lacking. Kaufman's interpretive approach to the Wechsler Intelligence Scale for Children-Revised (WISC-R) and the Wechsler Intelligence Scale for Children, third edition (WISC-III) (Kaufman, 1979, 1994) offered guidance on translating test scores, subtest scores, and factor indices into meaningful clinical and educational intervention strategies. Thus, we believe that the history of legal challenges involving largely cognitive/ability testing has a direct bearing on standards and standardization of measures used to assess personality.

Consider the dilemma about adherence to standards versus adapting test administration to the needs of individuals by focusing on two of the examples provided in *Jenna C. v. Unified School District*: the assessment of minority, especially non-English-speaking, test takers, and of those with disabilities. Before taking up these issues, as well as that of testing internationally, however, we need to consider the relationship between test standardization and test administration procedures.

Test Standardization and Test Administration

"The standardization of a test is the establishment of uniform procedures for the (1) administration and (2) scoring of that instrument. . . . Without standardization, measurement is only an informal process that varies from examiner to examiner" (Geisinger,

2001, p. 1683). It appears that some changes in the flexibility with which tests are to be administered have occurred in recent years. The 1985 version of the Standards for Educational and Psychological Testing (American Educational Research Association, American Psychological Association, & National Council on Measurement in Education, 1985) stated that test administration procedures were to be controlled primarily through detailed instructions in test manuals. Standard 3.21 stated, for example, that in test manuals "the directions for test administration should be presented with sufficient clarity and emphasis so that it is possible to approximate for others the administrative conditions under which the norms and the data on reliability and validity were obtained" (p. 29). However, Standards 5.1 and 5.2 of the 1999 Standards for Educational and Psychological Testing (American Educational Research Association et al., 1999) report that "Test administrators should follow carefully the standardized procedures for administration and scoring specified by the test developer, unless the situation or a test taker's disability dictates an exception should be made" and "Modifications or disruptions of standardized test administration procedures or scoring should be documented" (p. 63).

Test authors must develop administration procedures including, for example, instructions to examinees, testing conditions, and scoring rubrics for their tests that clearly describe the administrative procedures that were followed when the norming, reliability, and validation data were collected as well as how the tests should be scored. In short, all information regarding both normal and atypical administration procedures must be provided by the test developer. Test administrators are expected under normal conditions to follow the standardized procedures carefully as described in the manual. Test norms—by which the meaning of individual test scores can be interpreted in conjunction with reliability and validity information—are developed by administering a test under standardized conditions to a large and representative group of test takers (Geisinger, 2001).

Although increased flexibility is provided to test users (including test administrators) under the 1999 *Test Standards*, the requirements on test developers are nevertheless high. Standard 4.10 (American Educational Research Association et al., 1999, p. 57) requires supporting evidence that scores are equivalent across different forms of a test. An accommodated form, hence, would need to be studied for its comparability to tests in use with the general population.

The test user too has responsibilities. Standard 11.19 (American Educational Research Association et al., 1999) requires that when a test administration does not follow the standard administration, the test user "should have a sound rationale for concluding that validity, reliability, and appropriateness of norms will not be compromised" (p. 117).

The Testing of Individuals from Minority Groups

The Larry P. case is a well-known class action suit that led to the banning of the use of intelligence tests for the placement of African American students into classes for the educable mentally retarded (EMR) in California (*Larry P. v. Riles*, 1972). It has been argued (Elliott, 1987; Lambert, 1981) that the amount of evidence provided at the trial was rather meager. Yet the evidence was sufficient to bring about a ban on the use of intelligence tests throughout the state of California. From across that state, five African-American children were chosen as individuals most likely to have been misplaced into EMR classes and these children were then retested by representatives of the Bay Area Association of Black Psychologists on behalf of the plaintiffs. These five children had been tested frequently in their years in the educational system. Four different psychologists tested these five children; three psychologists tested one child each, and one tested two of them. Two of these psychologists testified in court about their test administrations. They believed that they needed to modify the test administration procedures. One psychologist stated, "If the purpose of psychological testing is to tap psychological function and if by asking a child a question different from the way it is posed in the manual affords me to tap that function, then that appears to be much more important to me than to be somewhat compulsive and concretistic in mentioning every word that is listed in the manual" (line RT 1003; also cited in Elliott, 1987, p. 33). The second psychologist went a step further in openly criticizing psychologists who followed the standardized administration procedures for their "strict, almost pathological adherence to the manual" (RT 3102; also cited in Elliott, 1987, p. 33).

Some of the variations in test administration and scoring may help elucidate the nature of these adaptations. They accepted answers as correct that were not listed as such in the manual; they waived time limits; they rephrased questions; they went past discontinuation limits; and they even wrote new questions that were substituted for those actually on the test. One child responded to how scissors and a copper pan are alike with "they are both iron," which was accepted as correct. When one psychologist asked one of the children why criminals should be locked up, the psychologist also defined what criminals are so that the child could provide an answer. As a final example, when one of the children was asked "How are a yard and a pound alike?" the psychologist credited the following answer, "A yard has leaves, and a dog pound has dirt" (RT 3102; also cited in Elliott, 1987, p. 33).

On one hand, accommodations to the uniform administration procedures may provide useful information about a test taker to a clinician working with that individual. On the other hand, it is also clear that violations of the standardization procedures to this extent make the scores that result from this test administration of unknown meaning. Except with inexperienced or untrained test administrators, it is probable that departures from standardized testing procedures seldom follow from a willful disregard for test publishers' recommendations regarding test administration. Rather, failure to adhere strictly to these guidelines may result from what has been termed clinical intuition—a euphemism for common sense based on clinical experience. For example, if a test giver realizes that a test taker has misunderstood instructions even after the standard set of directions has been provided, he or she is likely to intervene rather than to end up with an invalid set of responses. Similarly, when an invalid Minnesota Multiphasic Personality Inventory-2 (MMPI-2) profile is obtained, test takers are sometimes retested with modified instructions, such as to respond quickly without over-deliberation or to be less literal in interpreting statements. Test givers who stretch the limits of standard procedures in these ways probably believe that they are retaining a considerable measure of standardization—considerable enough that interpretations based on the test results are valid. The problem is that in attempting to ameliorate one source of invalidity, they have probably introduced another.

It is important to realize that departing from standardized testing procedures is not an all-or-nothing phenomenon. Essentially the question that confronts us is how much is too much movement away from the established standards of test administration. It is likely that at the time a test is standardized, some minor variations in the administration procedures occur naturally. Thus, when the test is given later, departures from standard procedures that go beyond the magnitude of those that have occurred during the test standardization process make scores less meaningful. Similarly, when the administration of a test differs from that used in its validation, the information carried by a specific score is, at least in part, lost.

Wherever one positions oneself on the continuum of adherence to standardized test procedures there are important ramifications. On one extreme of the continuum are zealots who believe that departures from standardized procedures are not permissible under any circumstances. Dr. Bookman's position appears to be fairly close to this extreme. Individuals at this end of the spectrum may question the probity of procedural modifications as well as test interpretations that take into account educational, cultural, linguistic, sociologic, or physical factors. They might advocate computer-generated reports, such as those available for objective tests of personality, despite the dearth of evidence concerning their validity that has persisted in the face of early calls to action on this front (Matarazzo, 1986; Moreland, 1985b). Many experts continue to advise that computer-based test interpretations be used as adjuncts to, rather than replacements for, informed professional judgment (Butcher, Perry, & Atlis, 2000; Moreland, 1985a; Snyder, 2000) that approximates consultation from one professional to another. Thus, the psychologist who receives the report is the final gatekeeper of information so generated and bears the responsibility of evaluating the report, editing and integrating its content with other information about the individual case (Butcher, 1987; Eyde et al., 1993).

On the other end of the continuum are those who agree with Dr. Glaubenweiss and who have an abiding faith in the powers of clinical intuition. They would support Glaubenweiss's statements that he does not administer tests in the same manner to every test taker and that he knows what the scores mean without benefit of norms or validation research.

The Testing of Individuals with Disabilities

It is clear that disabilities of various types affect and in many cases hinder performance on tests of all types. These differences are clearest when we consider cognitive tests. Someone unable to move his or her hands and arms will have difficulty on nearly all of the performance-based subtests of the major tests of cognitive ability, such as the Stanford-Binet, Kaufman, and Wechsler series. In a related vein, such an individual will be unable to complete paper-and-pencil

inventories in the typical manner. The use of a scribe or oral administration as reasonable accommodations for test taking may compromise validity as these differences in administration may introduce new concerns, such as social desirability, that are not present in standard administrations. A disability, of course, may affect performance in many ways in addition to the inability to actually perform the task in question. A disability affects the experiences that shape and in part determine an individual's life history, which in turn influences both an individual's cognitive and personality development in myriad ways. Performance on many specific and widely used personality tests, too, may be affected by disabilities. Those with visual disabilities would have difficulty with many projective measures both directly (in their inability to view the stimuli themselves) and indirectly (in their differential and reduced history of dealing with visual stimuli). More generally, persons with disabilities may be more susceptible to fatigue than persons without disabilities. Certainly, visual, physical, and emotional handicaps might negatively affect one's tolerance for completing lengthy personality inventories, such as the MMPI-2.

Most large standardized testing programs have modifications of typical test administration procedures for those with disabilities. In fact, under the Americans with Disabilities Act (ADA; Equal Employment Opportunity Commission, 1991), tests and testing programs are required to make reasonable accommodations for test takers with disabilities. The testing literature has tended to address four types of disability: visual impairment, hearing impairment, learning disability, and physical handicap (Geisinger, 1994b; Willingham, 1988). In addition, other categories of disabilities, some of which are qualitatively different from the above and some of which might be subsumed into these four categories, can be listed: emotional disturbance, mental retardation, neurological impairment, autism spectrum disorders, speech disorders, and so on. Most paper-and-pencil cognitive testing programs, for example, offer a variety of modifications for different disabilities, depending on the particular needs of the individual test taker. For any of these groups, tests may be administered with normal time limits, extended time limits, or in an untimed fashion. For example, tests administered to persons with visual impairments may be the regular test, a large-type version of the test, or a Braille version, or the test may be provided on an audiocassette or with a reader. Time limits may be strictly applied, relaxed to a specified degree, or waived entirely. Test scores earned under any of the atypical test administrations may be "flagged" or marked so that someone viewing the score immediately knows that the score was earned under conditions of a nonstandard test administration, or the nature of the test administration may be described. The research on the validity of test scores earned on cognitive tests administered under accommodated test administrations (i.e., to help a user of test scores to know how comparable the meaning of nonstandard scores is to those earned under standard conditions) comes mostly from the largest testing programs (e.g., Willingham, 1988, on the SAT and the GRE; Ziomek & Andrews, 1996, on the ACT). The research needed to provide proper interpretability includes collection of normative data on the different test administration modifications, reliability data and validation studies of various types, and studies of how these test data are actually used by professionals in the field.

The 1985 version of the *Test Standards* (American Educational Research Association et al., 1985) for the first time devoted a chapter to the testing of those with disabilities. The more recent version of the test standards (American Educational Research Association et al., 1999) maintains a chapter on testing individuals with disabilities (and also a chapter on testing individuals of diverse language backgrounds). Standards 10.3 and 10.4 indicate that accommodations should be pilot-tested for appropriateness and feasibility and that "these modifications should be described in detail in the test manual" (p. 106) along with the rationale justifying the modification and evidence of validity for the modification. Standard 10.6 calls for the use of empirical procedures to establish revised time limits for modified versions of tests (p. 107). Fatigue also should be investigated as a potentially important factor when time limits are extended. Standard 10.5 states that technical materials that describe the test should "alert users to changes that are likely to alter the validity of inferences drawn from the test score" (p. 106). The standards further caution professionals against interpreting test scores that emerge from nonstandard testing as if they were from standard testing. As noted, only the largest testing programs have the resources to research the norms and validity of scores achieved under nonstandard administrations. Indeed, in even those cases, only the most common nonstandard test administrations will face scrutiny. There are not enough test takers earning scores with each kind of test modification to allow comprehensive empirical research. Moreover, the criteria that would be used in such validation research are not likely to be widely available across many of the individuals in the research sample, given that they are likely to come from different institutions. If any such criteria do exist, they are generally likely to lack meaningfulness.

As a profession, we need to begin training testing professionals who also are experts in various kinds of disabilities so that we can best modify our tests and interpret the scores that result from them to meet the needs of those individuals with disabilities. A good starting point would be lists of recommended testing accommodations and test-score interpretive rules of thumb written by those expert in both standardized testing and a particular disability. (See Geisinger and Carlson, 1998, for a more advanced treatment of training implications.)

Legal issues in the treatment of ethnic minorities and individuals with disabilities has been unfolding during the past 50 years. Those affecting ethnic minorities typically occurred first and followed the passage of the Civil Rights Act of 1964. The recent past, since the enactment of ADA in 1991, has been replete with cases related to the rights of individuals with disabilities. The consideration of the testing and assessment of individuals with disabilities was specifically addressed in the ADA, but the legislation lacked the specificity needed for making various operational decisions and the courts have, of necessity, intervened. Among the topics that have been litigated in recent years include the competencies and needed experiences of those individuals who makes test accommodation decisions for individuals with disabilities to enable them to take cognitive tests validly and how much extended time is appropriate for timed, cognitive tests for individuals who require extra time for a valid score to be achieved. (In a California state court, for example, it was found in 2006 that a testing organization needed to use individuals with specialized training and experience with individuals with learning disabilities to make accommodation decisions, although in the time it has taken for this book to be published it was successfully appealed and that reversal is also likely to be appealed; Turner v. Association of American Medical Colleges, 2008.) In high-stakes testing situations, perhaps the groups which have led to the most controversies are those with learning and reading disabilities including those with other cognitive disabilities, such as attention deficit/hyperactivity disorder (ADHD). Such individuals often receive extra time for tests used in making admissions decisions and may receive another, comparable test for those state educational achievement tests mandated by legislation such as "No Child Left Behind."

One particularly thorny issue relates to the actual "flagging" of test scores that emerge from nonstandard testing. The technical standards for testing professionals (American Educational Research Association et al., 1999) acknowledge the controversy of flagging. On one hand, test scores may be flagged so that test users can easily identify the fact that the score emerged from an atypical administration. In some cases, all nonstandard testings are flagged. In other cases, this flagging occurs only under some of the conditions, for example, when the time one has to respond to the test questions is extended, whereas for other accommodated test administrations, the flag is not imposed. Advocates for persons with disabilities, on the other hand, argue that identifying scores in this way invades the privacy of those with disabilities by identifying them as having a disability without their prior authorization. In general, in the authors' opinion, the use of flagging generally is declining. The fact that ADA provides the requirement that disabilities not be disclosed prior to decisions related to employment or acceptance into educational institutions is the primary justification for removing the flag. By and large, the current *Test Standards* call for empirical information to help make this decision.

International Testing Issues

As the global society continues to shrink psychologically due to the ease of communication across linguistic, cultural, and political boundaries, psychological testing too is becoming more of an international enterprise than it ever has been. It has long been believed that psychological tests should not simply be translated and used in a new culture as they have been in the original culture and country. Because culture so often impacts test content, the content of test items must often be adjusted when a test is translated; thus, the preference for the term "adaptation" in lieu of "translation." The ideas contained in perhaps the most informative book on adapting psychological tests for cross-cultural use (Hambleton, Merenda, & Spielberger, 2005) suggest in numerous places the need to evaluate carefully the linguistic, cultural, and psychometric equivalence of tests when adapted from one cultural-linguistic setting to another. A number of the 1999 testing standards apply to and govern this process, but the International Testing Commission also has promulgated guidelines for this task (International Test Commission, 2001; also available in Hambleton, 2005). Clearly, considerable research is generally needed before one can use appropriately a measure that has been translated and culturally adapted from one language where it has been validated and appropriately used to a new target language and culture. Yet research is emerging that some central constructs (e.g., the Big Five, intelligence) and some oft-used measures (e.g., MMPI-2, MMPI-A, and NEO PI-R) are being adapted and used validly across a wide number of countries, langues, and cultures (Butcher, Cabiya, Lucio, & Garrido, 2007; Carlson & Geisinger, 2008).

Of course, international testing issues are very similar to the concerns faced when testing newcomers to the United States (or any country), as individuals need to acculturate to their new society, a process that often includes learning a new language, as well as learning all of the other customs of the new culture (Comas-Diaz & Grenier, 1998). The ability to cross international borders and immigrate has been made far easier in the modern world as well. The psychological impact of language and cultural issues affects both cognitive and noncognitive constructs. Butcher et al. (2007) have introduced the testing of Hispanics using the MMPI-2 and the MMPI-A with an overriding conclusion that the various Spanish and cultural adaptations work with Hispanic clients very comparably to how the standard English version works in the United States. They identified four qualities that are critical to establish test equivalence for adapted (translated) measures: linguistic equivalence, construct equivalence, psychometric equivalence, and psychological equivalence. Increasingly, all practitioners must be aware of these issues, which are both theoretical and very applied, as they may affect testing results and one's interpretation in what are often high-stakes, life-changing decisions. When using tests with populations that are not from the West, clinicians must be especially concerned with what has been called Eurocentric biases in our measures. Geisinger (1998) enumerated most of the matters that must be considered as one is making the determination of whether the test is appropriate for differing populations. As noted, however, early evidence on several of our most significant constructs and measures as used in psychodiagnosis have provided strong evidence of equivalence across cultural groups (Butcher et al., 2007). The adaptation of tests from one language where they have been used successfully is likely to continue increasing given the many successful efforts to date.

Concluding Thoughts

"No assessment of clinical status is independent of the reliability and validity of the methods used to determine the presence of a diagnosis—be it by an unstructured clinical interview, a structured clinical assessment, or a highly structured instrument" (Regier et al., 1998, p. 114). If we want meaning to be conveyed with the test scores that we use—and there is no greater reason to use test scores other than as a shortcut communication device among and between professionals—then we hope to administer our tests in accordance with the standard testing procedures that are called for in a test manual and that were used in conjunction with the norm, reliability, and validation research studies. Simply put, we must follow the directions under normal circumstances.

There are situations, however, where it is apparent that following set procedures makes little or no sense. Imagine administering the Block Design subtest from a Wechsler test or a Picture Absurdities subtest from the Stanford-Binet to a person who is blind. Is it possible for such results to be meaningful? Of course not. To give other examples, test takers from varied cultures or subcultures, who use or prefer languages other than English—such as Limited English Proficient (LEP) students—or who have experienced deprivations of various types, may require somewhat different tests, test administrations, and test interpretations. At present, we are not able to answer what appear to be many of the most basic of questions.

If psychology does not take steps to remedy these deficiencies in our knowledge base, others will take them. Worse, however, is that individuals will take steps that are based on impressions rather than relevant knowledge. Judge Grady was the judge who tried the *PASE v. Hannon* (1980) case in Chicago, a case that reached a decision opposite that in *Larry P. v. Riles* (1972). Intelligence tests were permitted for making educational decisions about minority group children in the Chicago city schools. Judge Grady, exasperated over the diversity of opinions offered by expert-witness psychologists, took the matter into his own hands. He read every item of both the Stanford-Binet Intelligence Scale and the Wechsler Intelligence Scale for Children into the court record for all readers to see and decided that the vast majority of these questions were not biased test items. He expressed his disappointment with psychologists in general and especially the expert witnesses in the case. The following two quotations on the court record reveal his opinion:

First, he said:

> None of the witnesses in this case has so impressed me with his or her credibility or expertise that I would feel secure in basing a decision simply on his or her opinion. In some instances, I am satisfied that the opinions expressed are more the result of doctrinaire commitment to a preconceived idea than they are the result of scientific inquiry. I need something more than the conclusions of witnesses in order to arrive at my own conclusions. . . . I have not disregarded the expert testimony in this case but neither do I feel bound by it.
>
> (p. 836; also cited in part by Bersoff, 1984, p. 104, and in part by Elliott, 1987, p. 193)

Furthermore, at one point in the trial, plaintiffs' attorney objected to a defense witness answering a question about the cultural bias of intelligence tests, on the ground that the witness, a school official, was not a qualified psychologist. Judge Grady overruled, saying, "The fact that someone wears a hat that says 'psychologist' should not overly impress anyone who has sat through two weeks of this trial" (Elliott, 1987, p. 193).

With all due respect for Drs. Glaubenweiss and Bookman, it is time to move beyond both purely judgmental, speculative interpretations of test results and extrapolations from the general population to specific cases that do not much resemble the remainder of the population. Especially in the personality assessment of individuals from a clinical population, validity issues loom large. Many personality inventories standardized on normal volunteer subjects are used regularly in clinical settings. Validation evidence for such uses of these instruments typically follows—rather than precedes—their publication. In this spirit, Ben-Porath and Waller (1992) cautioned against using "normal" personality tests to substitute for "clinical" ones and suggested that the former be used only to augment, rather than to replace, the latter. We agree, and we would add that this caveat is more poignant when the test taker belongs to a clinical population that itself is demographically distinct, because of language dominance, ethnicity, handicapping condition, cultural differences, immigrant status, and so on. In these areas there is a striking paucity of research. "A ubiquitous issue in psychological testing is the questionable practice of assessing ethnic, socioeconomic, or linguistic minorities with instruments that have been conceived, standardized, and validated from a non-minority, middle-class, English-speaking perspective" (Malgady, Rogler, &

Costantino, 1987, p. 229). Decades ago, Padilla and Ruiz (1973) "maintained that psychometric research had yet to offer valid testing procedures (particularly projective techniques) for personality assessment of Hispanics, and it is safe to say that neglect of this topic persists today" (Malgady et al., 1987, p. 230), but there is certainly more research on Hispanics than any other linguistic minority group. Some reliable Spanish translations of paper-and-pencil tests are available, but evidence of the scales' validities for Hispanic test takers have lagged behind English-language versions, although in the recent decades, substantial advancement has occurred both in terms of procedures to follow (Butcher et al., 2007; Geisinger, 1994a) and of the tests that have been evaluated in this manner. Too many translated tests are perhaps better suited for research purposes than for use in clinical assessments and test publishers have sometimes offered adapted/translated instruments without performing the critically needed research (e.g., Maldonaldo & Geisinger, 2005). Often, English-language instruments are translated and used in a few research studies. In such cases, data needed for careful clinical assessments are not available. Along similar lines, Vélasquez and Callahan (1992) noted that between 1949 and 1992 the numbers of studies on Hispanics in clinical settings using the Rorschach and the Thematic Apperception Test were three and one, respectively. Only the MMPI was used in a sizable number of studies (i.e., 61). According to these authors, several other personality measures, including the California Personality Inventory, Sixteen Personality Factors (16-PF), Beck Depression Inventory, and Comrey Personality Scales, apparently were not used at all in research assessing personality among Hispanic clinical populations.

We are faced with a significant dilemma in all forms of assessment. Psychology holds the promise of answering such questions, but to date, these questions have been raised all too infrequently. When they are raised, perfunctory, "canned" responses—like those of Dr. Bookman—commonly are given. These questions need to be raised; they need to be thoroughly discussed; and they need to be answered. At present, we have only fragments of answers, and our answers will undoubtedly evolve and change over time. With regard to special administration of tests for individuals with disabilities, we need to validate the scores that emerge from these assessments (American Psychological Association Division of Evaluation, Measurement, and Statistics, 1993). As further interpretive guides, norm studies and reliability checks are needed as well as similar validation research for members of linguistic minorities. The time for answers to these questions is now, the process must be ongoing, and the answers must come from research.

References

American Educational Research Association, American Psychological Association, & National Council on Measurement in Education. (1985). *Standards for educational and psychological testing.* Washington, DC: American Psychological Association.

American Educational Research Association, American Psychological Association, & National Council on Measurement in Education. (1999). *Standards for educational and psychological testing.* Washington, DC: American Educational Research Association.

American Psychological Association, Division of Evaluation, Measurement, and Statistics. (1993). Psychometric and assessment issues raised by the Americans with Disabilities Act (ADA). *The Score, 15,* 1–2, 7–15.

Ben-Porath, Y. S., & Waller, N. G. (1992). "Normal" personality inventories in clinical assessment: General requirements and the potential for using the NEO Personality Inventory. *Psychological Assessment, 4,* 14–19.

Bersoff, D. N. (1984). Social and legal influences on test development and usage. In B. S. Plake (Ed.), *Social and technical issues in testing: Implications for test construction and use* (pp. 87–109). Hillsdale, NJ: Erlbaum.

Butcher, J. N. (1987). The use of computers and psychological assessment: An overview of practices and issues. In J. N. Butcher (Ed.), *Computerized psychological assessment: A practitioner's guide* (pp. 3–14). New York: Basic Books.

Butcher, J. N., Cabiya, J., Lucio, E., & Garrido, M. (2007). *Assessing Hispanic clients using the MMPI-2 and MMPI-A.* Washington, DC: American Psychological Association.

Butcher, J. N., Perry, J. N., & Atlis, M. M. (2000). Validity and utility of computer-based test interpretation. *Psychological Assessment, 12,* 6–18.

Camara, W. J., Nathan, J. S., & Puente, A. E. (2000). Psychological test usage: Implications in professional psychology. *Professional Psychology: Research and Practice, 31,* 141–154.

Carlson, J. F., & Geisinger, K. F. (2008). Psychological diagnostic testing. In R. Phelps (Ed.), *Correcting fallacies about educational and psychological testing* (pp. 67–88). Washington, DC: American Psychological Association.

Comas-Diaz, L., & Grenier, J. R. (1998). Migration and acculturation. In J. Sandoval, C. L. Frisby, K. F. Geisinger, J. D. Scheuneman, & J. R. Grenier (Eds.), *Test interpretation and diversity: Achieving equity in assessment* (pp. 213–240). Washington, DC: American Psychological Association.

Elliott, R. (1987). *Litigating intelligence: IQ tests, special education, and social sciences in the courtroom.* Dover, MA: Auburn House.

Equal Employment Opportunity Commission. (1991). *Americans with Disabilities Act: A technical assistance manual on the employment provisions* (Title I). Washington, DC: Author.

Eyde, L. D., Robertson, G. J., Krug, S. E., Moreland, K. L., Robertson, A. G., Shewan, C. M., et al. (1993). *Responsible test use: Case studies for assessing human behavior.* Washington, DC: American Psychological Association.

Geisinger, K. F. (1994a). Cross-cultural normative assessment: Translation and adaptation issues influencing the normative interpretation of assessment instruments. *Psychological Assessment, 6,* 304–312.

Geisinger, K. F. (1994b). Psychometric issues in testing students with disabilities. *Applied Measurement in Education, 7,* 121–140.

Geisinger, K. F. (1998). Psychometric issues in test interpretation. In J. Sandoval, C. L. Frisby, K. F. Geisinger, J. D. Scheuneman, & J. R. Grenier (Eds.), *Test interpretation and diversity: Achieving equity in assessment* (pp. 17–30). Washington, DC: American Psychological Association.

Geisinger, K. F. (2001). Test standardization. In W. E. Craighead & C. B. Nemeroff (Eds.), *The Corsini encyclopedia of psychology and behavioral science* (3rd ed., Vol. 4, pp. 1683–1684). New York: John Wiley & Sons.

Geisinger, K. F., & Carlson, J. F. (1998). Training psychologists to assess members of a diverse society. In J. Sandoval, C. L. Frisby, K. F. Geisinger, J. D. Scheuneman, & J. Ramos Grenier (Eds.), *Test interpretation and diversity* (pp. 375–386). Washington, DC: American Psychological Association.

Glasser, A. I., & Zimmerman, I. L. (1967). *Clinical interpretation of the Wechsler Intelligence Scale for Children.* New York: Grune & Stratton.

Hambleton, R. K. (2005). Issues, designs, and technical guidelines for adapting tests into multiple languages and cultures. In R. K. Hambleton, P. F. Merenda, & C. D. Spielberger (Eds.), *Adapting educational and psychological tests for cross-cultural assessment* (pp. 3–38). Mahwah, NJ: Erlbaum.

Hambleton, R. K., Merenda, P. F., & Spielberger, C. D. (Eds.) (2005). *Adapting educational and psychological tests for cross-cultural assessment.* Mahwah, NJ: Erlbaum.

International Test Commission. (2001). *International Test Commission guidelines for test adaptation.* London: Author.

Kaufman, A. S. (1979). *Intelligent testing with the WISC-R.* New York: John Wiley & Sons.

Kaufman, A. S. (1994). *Intelligent testing with the WISC-III.* New York: John Wiley & Sons.

Lambert, N. M. (1981). Psychological evidence in *Larry P. v. Wilson Riles*: An evaluation by a witness for the defense. *American Psychologist, 36,* 937–952.

Larry P. v. Riles. 343 F. Supp. 306 (N.D. Cal. 1972), aff'd. 502 F. 2d (9th Cir. 1974); 495 F. Supp. 926 (N.D. Cal. 1979), aff'd. in part and rev'd in part, 793 F. 2d 969 (9th Cir. 1984).

Maldonaldo, C. Y., & Geisinger, K. F. (2005). Conversion of the Wechsler Adult Intelligence Scale into Spanish: An early test adaptation effort. In R. K. Hambleton, P. F. Merenda, & C. D. Spielberger (Eds.), *Adapting educational and psychological tests for cross-cultural assessment* (pp. 213–234). Mahwah, NJ: Erlbaum.

Malgady, R. G., Rogler, L. H., & Costantino, G. (1987). Ethnocultural and linguistic bias in mental health evaluation of Hispanics. *American Psychologist, 42,* 228–234.

Matarazzo, J. D. (1986). Computerized clinical psychological interpretations: Unvalidated plus all mean and no sigma. *American Psychologist, 41,* 14–24.

Moreland, K. L. (1985a). Computer-assisted psychological assessment in 1986: A practical guide. *Computers in Human Behavior, 1,* 221–233.

Moreland, K. L. (1985b). Validation of computer-based test interpretations: Problems and prospects. *Journal of Consulting and Clinical Psychology, 53,* 816–825.

Padilla, A. M., & Ruiz, R. A. (1973). *Latino mental health: A review of the literature* (DHEW Publication No. HSM 73-9143). Washington, DC: U.S. Government Printing Office.

PASE v. Hannon, 506 F. Supp. 931 (N.D. Ill. 1980).

Regier, D. A., Kaelber, C. T., Rae, D. S., Farmer, M. E., Knauper, B., Kessler, R. C., et al. (1998). Limitations of diagnostic criteria and assessment instruments for mental disorders. *Archives of General Psychiatry, 55,* 109–115.

Snyder, D. K. (2000). Computer-assisted judgment: Defining strengths and liabilities. *Psychological Assessment, 12,* 52–60.

Turner v. American Association of Medical Colleges. (2008). WL 4741737 (Cal.App. 1 Dist.), 08 Cal. Daily Op. Serv. 13,706.

Vélasquez, R. J., & Callahan, W. L. (1992). Psychological testing of Hispanic Americans in clinical settings: Overview and issues. In K. F. Geisinger (Ed.), *Psychological testing of Hispanics* (pp. 253–265). Washington, DC: American Psychological Association.

Willingham, W. W. (1988). Testing handicapped people—the validity issue. In H. Wainer & H. I. Braun (Eds.), *Test validity* (pp. 89–103). Hillsdale, NJ: Erlbaum.

Zimmerman, I. L., & Woo-Sam, J. M. (1973). *Clinical interpretation of the Wechsler Adult Intelligence Scale.* New York: Grune & Stratton.

Ziomek, R. I., & Andrews, K. M. (1996). *Predicting the college grade point averages of special-tested students from their ACT assessment scores and high school grades.* ACT Research Report Series Nos. 96–97. Iowa City, IA: ACT, Inc.

Changing or Replacing an Established Psychological Assessment Standard: Issues, Goals, and Problems with Special Reference to Recent Developments in the MMPI-2

Michelle B. Ranson, David S. Nichols, Steven V. Rouse, *and* Jennifer L. Harrington

Abstract

The question of whether to revise a psychological test often emerges during the test development phase rather than after the publication of the test because there are always unanswered questions or alternative strategies one could have taken. For an assessment "standard" that has found broad acceptance among practitioners and researchers the considerations that bear on its change or revision can be especially complex and demanding. This chapter provides an overview of some of these considerations, including how changes in a test are to be occasioned and warranted; the motives that may become involved in driving changes; issues pertaining to the differing and at times conflicting interests of the various constituencies (designers, advisors, consultants, publishers, distributors, practitioners, consumers) that may be involved in the preparation, decisions, and processes entailed in change and revision; and the various ethical expectations, implications, and responsibilities that have a role to play in guiding and influencing all of these. We have included a case study to illustrate some of the recent issues that have emerged with proposed changes to one standard personality measure, the Minnesota Multiphasic Personality Inventory-2 (MMPI-2).

Keywords: test revision, personality, testing standards, Watson and Tellegen model, MMPI-2, RC Scales, MMPI-2-RF, ethical issues in test development

Many articles, book chapters, and books have been written on the process of test development. By contrast, the literature on the topic of test revision is relatively undeveloped; this is unfortunate because, as Adams (2000) wrote, test revision is a continuous process, where consideration of the need for revision begins at the time of the release of any edition of a test. This chapter reviews literature relevant to the process of test revision and draws examples from recent developments in the Minnesota Multiphasic Personality Inventory (MMPI-2), and in view of these issues, offers a critique of the wisdom, conceptualization, methodology, and marketing issues associated with a recent and significant scale revision effort.

Reasons for Revision

Several valid reasons for test revision have been mentioned in the literature, but they generally fall into two categories. On one hand, there are changes that can be made to reduce flaws of the current form of the test. We might refer to these as "deficiency changes." In fact, several authors (Adams, 2000; Butcher, 2000; Campbell, 2002) have noted that a revision is a healthy process, allowing the test developers to identify and correct imperfections in the test. On the other hand, there are changes that are not designed to correct flaws but to allow the test to develop in new ways. We might refer to these as "growth changes."

Deficiency Changes

When considering changes to a self-report personality test, the motivations that come to mind most quickly (and are most often discussed in the professional literature) are those changes that will repair or reduce the flaws that have been discovered since the publication of the current version. For example, several years before formal work began on the revision of the MMPI in the 1980s, Dahlstrom (1972) noted that the revision process should be guided by critiques in the published literature. Several changes of this type were integral to the revision of the MMPI as well as to those of other measures.

First, items may be outdated or even antiquated (Butcher, 2000). An item that had clear relevance to a personality construct when the test was created may, with the passage of time, become irrelevant or tap an entirely different construct. For example, Campbell (1972) noted that, at the time of revision, one version of the Strong Vocational Interest Blank included references to interest in magazines which had not even been published during the lifetimes of college-aged test takers. Similarly, prior to its revision, the MMPI possessed items that were clearly outdated by today's standards. Examples of outdated MMPI items included such statements as "I used to like drop-the-handkerchief" and "Horses that don't pull should be beaten or kicked." Even when the items are not antiquated, cultural trends gradually change to the point where some items seem old-fashioned to the modern test taker (Adams, 2000). In these cases, a test revision provides the opportunity to remove or rephrase items that are no longer adequate.

Second, test revisions are necessary when the norms are no longer adequate for the current purpose of test use (Adams, 2000). Because a raw score on a self-report test generally only gains meaning by being compared against scores obtained by a normative sample, it is essential for the normative sample to be representative of the population of test takers who are currently assessed with that test. For example, Butcher (2000) voiced concern that the norms of the Millon Clinical Multiaxial Inventory—third edition (MCMI-III; Millon, 1994) were based upon a psychiatric sample. While this would be appropriate if the test was used exclusively in a psychiatric context, as the test's use grew beyond the realm of clinical assessment (such as into the area of personnel selection), the norms were no longer sufficient for that expanded range of applications.

Third, and especially relevant to the area of forensic assessment, is the necessity to revise an instrument when the items or test stimuli have leaked into the public domain (Adams, 2000). For example, if copyright laws have been violated by placing items on Internet sites, or when a large number of individuals have been coached on test-taking practices that are likely to lead to desired scores on the test, the integrity of the test may be compromised to the point where confidence in its scores is undermined.

Fourth, a test revision may be motivated by the goal to improve flawed psychometric properties of the original instrument. Reise, Waller, and Comrey (2000) noted that factor analytic studies sometimes demonstrate that a scale's factor structure published in the test manual does not replicate across divergent samples. Similarly, factor analytic studies might suggest that a scale is not providing an adequate representation of a construct of interest. If a component of the construct is not present in the factor structure of that scale, the validity of the scale will be severely compromised. It is even possible, according to Reise et al., that factor analytic research might show that the scale is actually more highly loaded on a related construct than it is on the intended construct. While all of these concerns were likely considered before the publication of the first form of the test, the gradual accumulation of data might point to psychometric flaws that were not apparent with the initial research samples. An example of the way factor analytic research can guide test development and revision is illustrated in the most recent revision of the Job Description Index (JDI), as recounted by Stanton, Bachiochi, Robie, Perez, and Smith (2002). The original scale was developed in 1969 as a measure of job satisfaction, but when it was revised in 1985 a small number of new items were added. As research accumulated, however, it became clear that some of the new items did not measure job satisfaction specifically. Instead these items measured job stress. They asked questions about whether work was too tiring or frustrating and whether respondents felt they had too much work to complete. Although job satisfaction and job stress are negatively correlated, they represent two distinctly different constructs. Therefore, when the scale was revised again in 1997, the job stress items were replaced with additional items, more directly related to job satisfaction. Although research on the factor structure showed that stress and satisfaction are intertwined, the resulting scale is more unidimensional in nature.

Finally, a test that once provided a valid assessment of a construct might need revision when the professional understanding of that construct changes. For example, if a test provides a valid assessment of posttraumatic stress disorder, in accordance with the DSM-IV-TR (American Psychiatric Association, 2000), this scale may need revision if the diagnostic criteria for the disorder changes in the development of the DSM-V (Adams, 2000). This is, as Dahlstrom (1972) noted, even a challenge in the area of normal-range personality, where diagnostic criteria do not provide a strong standard against which constructs are defined. The abstract conceptualizations of personality constructs fluctuate, and as greater understanding of a construct accumulates in the literature, scales may need to adapt to remain consistent with the empirical conceptualization of that construct.

The first three reasons for revising a test are clear and indisputable; where items are clearly outdated, test security has been irreparably compromised, or the norms are inconsistent with a test's application, the process of revision is generally widely supported as necessary and, arguably, urgent. The latter two reasons for revision, however, tend to invoke more controversy within the community, as researchers are rarely in agreement about the correct boundaries of a given construct, or the most effective strategy for psychometrically triangulating upon it. As a consequence of the fluidity of these interrelated concerns, those responsible for undertaking a revision effort find themselves in the position of needing to persuasively establish that an inadequacy exists, defending the veracity of their target modification, justifying the efficacy and parsimony of their intended strategy, and satisfactorily addressing the challenges rightfully raised as the community struggles to accept or reject the purported solution.

DEFICIENCY CHANGES PURSUED THROUGH THE DEVELOPMENT OF THE RC SCALES

In contrast to the 1989 revision of the MMPI, which sought to address the types of widely acknowledged inadequacies enumerated by the first three reasons offered for test revision, the recently introduced MMPI-2 Restructured Clinical (RC) Scales (Tellegen, Ben-Porath, McNulty, Arbisi, Graham, & Kaemmer, 2003) and, by extension, the recently announced alternative form of the MMPI-2, the MMPI-2-RF (Restructured Form), provide an illustrative example of a revision effort motivated by the last two reasons described above. The example is salient to explore in a chapter describing the issues associated with test revision because it allows us to examine, in a case study format, the

above-referenced responsibilities that are incumbent upon those that advocate for and pursue revision. Because the MMPI-2-RF remains unpublished at the time of this writing, we will focus our examination on the RC Scales. These scales replace the MMPI-2 Clinical Scales in the MMPI-2-RF.

BACKGROUND FOR THE DEVELOPMENT OF THE RC SCALES

The RC Scales were developed over several years and were added to one of the products distributed by Pearson Assessments, the "Extended Score Report," in January 2003, several months prior to the publication of the RC Scales monograph, *MMPI-2 Restructured Clinical (RC) Scales: Development, validation, and interpretation* (Tellegen et al., 2003), in March of that year (Pearson Assessments, 2003). This new set of scales recently came under substantial critical scrutiny (Butcher, Hamilton, Rouse, & Cumella, 2006; Caldwell, 2006; Gordon, 2006; Nichols, 2006a, 2006b; Rogers, Sewell, Harrison, & Jordan, 2006; Rouse, Greene, Butcher, Nichols, & Williams 2008), and was subsequently defended by the RC Scale authors (Tellegen, Ben-Porath, Sellbom, Arbisi, McNulty, & Graham, 2006).

In several ways, the material presented in this chapter will extend these earlier critical analyses, particularly as they exemplify issues associated with test revision and their handling. We will show that the authors of the RC Scales do not sufficiently compel the acceptance of their goals or methods in their revision of the Clinical Scales, particularly with respect to the growth-oriented aspects of their agenda. More generally and importantly, we will also present data and analyses that raise doubts regarding the extent to which any of the authors' primary aims for scale revision were realized in the construction of the RC Scales. Taken together, the purpose of evaluating the case of the RC Scales, as an exemplar of scale revision, is to demonstrate how carefully researchers must attend to issues such as parsimony and proof when advancing a major scale revision, and how questionably efficacious the resultant solution may be, vis-à-vis its stated aims, when these issues are not exhaustively attended to.

Overview of the Development of the RC Scales

"The RC Scales were designed to preserve the important descriptive properties of the existing Clinical Scales while enhancing their distinctiveness" (Tellegen et al., 2003, p. 1). This statement nicely captures the two primary aims of the RC Scales project, the first addressing a deficiency change, the second a growth change.

With respect to pursuing the deficiency change, Tellegen et al. sought to substantially reduce the covariation that compromises the discriminant validity of the MMPI-2 Clinical Scales. On this point, the authors' justification was hardly required; the Clinical Scales have long been recognized as having lower discriminant validity than desired, and previous attempts at resolving the issue have been numerous, each with varying degrees of success and acceptance.

With respect to pursuing a growth change, the authors sought to identify and build upon what they described as "the distinctive substantive core" (p. 15) of each Clinical Scale in order to produce a new set of scales intended to represent each Clinical Scale's core construct. Further evidencing a growth aspiration, modified definitions of the core construct in question were identified for at least two of those new scales, in order to, the authors reasoned, allow the MMPI-2 to keep pace with "contemporary conceptions of psychopathology" (Tellegen et al., 2006, p. 158, et passim). On this point, the pursuit of growth change, the authors take on significant burdens: to establish that their selected core constructs truly represent the most distinctive features of the Clinical Scales, to justify the efficiency and parsimony of their intended strategy, to defend the integrity of their target modifications, and to satisfactorily address legitimate challenges raised by their peers in the best spirit of ongoing scientific inquiry.

Before evaluating the choices invoked by Tellegen et al. (2003) in their mission to revise the Clinical Scales, it is helpful to understand, in general terms, the procedures they followed. (For a more detailed account of the steps they undertook and why, the interested reader is referred to the RC Scales monograph [Tellegen et al., 2003]. For a more detailed critical analysis of the steps they undertook, and of the content of the monograph more generally, the interested reader is referred to Nichols, 2006a.) The development of the RC Scales proceeded in four steps:

Step 1: Capturing Demoralization. Having embraced a factor analytic scale construction strategy, Tellegen et al. (2003) sought to construct a marker to measure the "broad, emotionally colored dimension, captured, for example, by Welsh's well-known A scale (2000, 1956), sometimes referred to as the 'MMPI-2 first factor' " (p. 11), for the purpose

of enabling the extraction of the dimension they believed to be most responsible for inflating the correlations among the Clinical Scales. Desiring to ground their scale modification efforts in an applicable theoretical context, they construed this dimension as equivalent to the Pleasantness versus Unpleasantness axis of Watson and Tellegen's (1985) hierarchical model of Positive Affect and Negative Affect, and labeled it Demoralization. An initial set of Demoralization items were identified from a series of factor analyses performed on Scales 2 and 7, to which additional items were added from the remainder of the item pool, to comprise an initial 23-item Demoralization scale (Dem).

Step 2: Identifying the "Core" Components of the Clinical Scales. The next step in the development of the RC Scales sought to identify "the distinctive substantive core" (Tellegen et al., 2003, p. 15) of each of the Clinical Scales. First, the Dem items were appended to each[1] of the Clinical Scales, in turn, and the combined item set was factored using principal components analysis with Varimax rotation (PCA/V) to yield two to five principal components, one of which was considered a replicate of the Dem marker. One of the remaining factors was then designated the distinctive core component of the Clinical Scale in question.

Step 3: Deriving the Restructured Clinical Seed Scales. In Step 3, 158 items were selected as candidates for inclusion in a "seed" scale intended to represent the core construct chosen for each Clinical Scale at Step 2. Items were selected if they did not achieve "salient" loadings on their Demoralization-marked factors and did obtain loadings of $>|.26|$ on the residual factors in at least two of their development samples. The authors applied to these items an iterative set of procedures designed to maximize their relationship to their respective core constructs, and to minimize their relationship to the core constructs chosen for the other RC scales. The items surviving these procedures became the seeds for each of the final nine RC Scales.

Step 4: Deriving the final Restructured Clinical Scales. In the final step, the seed scales derived in Step 3 were augmented by gathering those items from the total MMPI-2 item pool that most highly correlated with them, provided that they were not concurrently correlated with another seed scale. At the conclusion of these steps the final versions of the RC Scales were complete (see Table 7.1). Some subsequent adjustments were made to Dem to create its final version, RCd.

Table 7.1. MMPI-2 RC Scales and corresponding Clinical Scales.

RC Scale	Clinical Scale
RCd—Demoralization	
RC1—Somatic Complaints	Scale 1—Hypochondriasis
RC2—Low Positive Emotions	Scale 2—Deprestsion
RC3—Cynicism	Scale 3—Hysteria
RC4—Antisocial Behavior	Scale 4—Psychopathic Deviate
RC6—Ideas of Persecution	Scale 6—Paranoia
RC7—Dysfunctional Negative Emotions	Scale 7—Psychasthenia
RC8—Aberrant Experiences	Scale 8—Schizophrenia
RC9—Hypomanic Activation	Scale 9—Hypomania

REDUCTION OF CLINICAL SCALE COVARIATION

The problems represented by the extensive covariation among the Clinical Scales, as well as straightforward approaches to reducing it, have been recognized for more than half a century. Although multiple approaches are available for reducing such covariation, by far the most obvious is to simply eliminate the items that are shared among two or more of the Clinical Scales. Helmes and Reddon (1993) identified item overlap as among the major structural deficiencies of the MMPI/MMPI-2 (pp. 457–459). Eliminating the overlapping items addresses the RC authors' stated aims simultaneously because such items are both the most obvious contributors to clinical scale covariation (CSC) and because they are, by definition, nondistinctive.

Although not mentioned by Tellegen et al. (2003), this was precisely the approach taken by Welsh (1952) and later by Adams and Horn (1965) to address the CSC problem. In commenting on "the source of high correlations between measures of presumably very distinctive personality attributes," Tellegen et al. (2003) recognized the problem of item overlap but appear to minimize it: "the high scale intercorrelations reflect only in part the spurious correlations between measurement errors that occur when the scales in question contain overlapping items" (p. 6). Among the possible competitors with overlapping items in accounting for CSC, Tellegen et al. (2003) include "response-style variance" (p. 6) (which they tend to dismiss), "unanticipated 'comorbidity' " (p. 6), and "invalid" (p. 5) subtle items[2] (although the latter items, relative to the so-called obvious items, show a much lower rate of overlap). If one is to judge from the information provided in the RC Scales monograph, however, no effort was made to explore the relative strength of these competing factors, nor to evaluate the extent of

the role played by item overlap itself, either within their own samples or generally.

It should be noted that our criticism, here, is not that the strategy used in the development of the RC Scales (i.e., reducing CSC and increasing Clinical Scale purification by eliminating or reducing item overlap) was abandoned after being tried and found wanting. Rather, we are concerned that this strategy was ignored, despite historical precedent, and despite its representing a more straightforward means of achieving the authors' stated goals.

As a demonstration of the achievements in scale independence that could be had from more parsimonious methods, Nichols (2006a) explored three different alternate solutions to the problem of Clinical Scale covariation using a data set of 26,118 male and 26,425 female MMPI-2 protocols (Caldwell, 1997a). In one test, Nichols simply eliminated from each Clinical Scale the 35 items that overlap at least three of the basic Clinical Scales (1–4 and 6–9). As a result, the average intercorrelation among these scales dropped from .59 to .39, a decrease in shared variance of 20% $(1 - [(.59 \times .59) - (.39 \times .39)])$, while the average correlation between the altered scale and the intact parent scale remained high at .94, a loss of only 12% $[1 - (.94 \times .94)]$ in shared variance. In the second test, Nichols identified 37 items from the Clinical Scales that loaded on the First Factor in two independent factor analyses (Johnson, Butcher, Null, & Johnson, 1984; Waller, 1999); he then removed the variance of this set of 37 items from each of the Clinical Scales. Using this strategy, Nichols achieved an increase in scale independence of 13% (with average intercorrelations dropping from .59 to .47), while maintaining an average correlation with their parent scales of .97, a loss of only 6% in shared variance. In the third test, Nichols combined the two strategies by removing from the Clinical Scales those items that appeared on both markers and achieved a gain in Clinical Scale independence of 25% (with average intercorrelations dropping from .59 to .32), while maintaining an average correlation between the altered scale and the parent scale of .88, a loss of 23% in shared variance. These simple tests, all showing how straightforward adjustments to the Clinical Scales can achieve increases in independence without even greater losses for the fidelity of their modified versions to their parent scales, demonstrate how readily the expressed aims of the RC Scales authors could be achieved, without a need to resort to the radical procedures that resulted in a set of revised clinical scales with "concordances [to their parent scales] too low to extrapolate any meaningful interpretations for the RC Scales" (Rogers et al., 2006, p. 146; also Butcher et al., 2006).

A NEW ANALYSIS OF CLINICAL SCALE COVARIATION

The authors of the RC Scales dismissed Nichols' (2006a) analyses on two grounds: (a) their judgment of the inadequacy of internal analyses of the MMPI/MMPI-2 relative to analyses involving external criteria (Tellegen et al., 2006, pp. 149, 156), and (b) their conclusion that the data set used by Nichols (and also by Rogers et al., 2006, whose findings were similarly dismissed) is problematic. With respect to their first point, we agree that analyses involving external criteria are invaluable in the establishment of construct validity, criterion validity, and other demonstrations of import to newly developed or revised scales. The value of external analyses, however, in no way diminishes the importance of findings resulting from internal analyses; in fact, the method and procedures followed in the construction of the RC Scales depended overwhelmingly on such internal analyses. When, therefore, Tellegen et al. (2006) denigrate the internal analyses employed by their critics as "blind empiricism" (pp. 149, 157), they invoke a double standard.

With respect to their second point, Tellegen et al. (2006) concluded, on the basis of their comparisons of the skewness and kurtosis of the Caldwell sample with their own samples, along with similar comparisons involving various measures of response style, "that the Caldwell dataset is not representative of any specific clinical or other meaningfully defined population and is more appropriately described as a composite sample, an amalgam, than as a well-defined clinical sample" (p. 152). It is notable, however, that despite their availability, the authors chose not to replicate, using their own samples, *any* of the analyses Nichols reported. Such replications, had they

been presented, could have provided direct evidence of the putative inadequacies of the Caldwell sample. Given the size of the Caldwell data set (N > 52,000), it seems unlikely that the values reported for Nichols' analyses are misleading. Nevertheless, in deference to these authors' concerns, all analyses reported in this chapter are based upon 24 of the 25 diverse research samples, excluding the Caldwell data set, obtained from clinical, forensic, college, medical, personnel, military, and community settings. These samples, reflecting the wide variety of settings in which the MMPI-2 is used, were collected by Rouse et al. ([2008]; total $N = 29,983$), are presented in Table 7.2. For each sample, the exclusion criteria proposed by Butcher, Graham, and Ben-Porath (1995) were applied; that is, respondents were eliminated from the research samples if they had 30 or more omitted items, raw scores less than 6 or greater than 12 on TRIN, raw scores greater than 30 on F, or T-scores greater than 80 on VRIN, L, K, or S.

The findings of this reanalysis largely replicated Nichols' earlier (2006a) findings: The mean correlation among the Clinical Scales for the aggregate sample was .546. For the first analysis, dropping the 35 items that overlap at least three of the basic Clinical Scales reduced the scales' average intercorrelation to .395, a reduction in shared variance of 14%. The average correlation between each altered scale and its parent scale was .941, a decrease of 11% in the shared variance of the modified scale with its original version. In the second analysis, in which the 37 replicated First Factor items were dropped, we achieved an increase in scale independence of 9% (with average intercorrelations dropping from .546 to .455), while maintaining an average correlation with their parent scales of .961, a reduction of 8% in shared variance. In the third test, in which these two sets of items (35 + 37 items, less the 10 items common to both sets = 62 items) were combined and dropped from any Clinical Scale on which they appeared, we achieved a gain in Clinical Scale independence of 20% (with average intercorrelations dropping from .546 to .321), while maintaining an average correlation between the altered scale and the parent scale of .876, a reduction of 23% in shared variance.

Contrast these findings with identical analyses comparing the Clinical Scales with the RC Scales. The mean intercorrelation among the RC Scales in the aggregate sample is .497, a decrease of 5% in independence as compared with the shared variance

Table 7.2. Description of samples.

Samples	Men (n)	Women (n)	Inpatient or Incarcerated	Source
Clinical				
Alcohol/Drug 1	510	349	Yes	Greene et al. (1996)
Alcohol/Drug 2	799	369	Yes	McKenna & Butcher (1987)
Psychotherapy	176	252	No	Butcher (1998)
State Hospital	234	268	Yes	Greene (1992)
VA Inpatient	1,161	87	Yes	Schinka (2004)
College Students				
Sample 1	57	80	No	Butcher (1998)
Sample 2	510	762	No	Butcher, Graham et al. (1990)
Forensic				
Child Custody 1	844	863	No	Butcher (1997)
Child Custody 2	952	950	No	Caldwell (2004)
Child Custody 3	534	514	No	Hoppe et al. (2004)
Corrections	263	33	Yes	Butcher (1997)
Criminal Psych.	780	122	Yes	Davis (2001)
Death Row	74	0	Yes	Gelbort (2002)
Personal Injury 1	49	95	No	Butcher (1997)
Personal Injury 2	74	67	No	Greenberg, Lees-Haley, & Otto (2005)
Medical Chronic Pain	104	316	No	Caldwell (1998)
Neuropsych. 1	97	71	No	Cripe (2000)
Neuropsych. 2	41	41	No	Solomon (2004)
Military, Active Duty	1,354	174	No	Butcher, Jeffrey, Cayton, Colligan, DeVore, & Minnegawa (1990)
MMPI-2 Normative	1,108	1,421	No	Butcher et al. (1989)
Native American	264	361	No	Robin et al. (2003)
Personnel Screening				
Clergy	234	276	No	Friedman & Damsteegt (2002)
General	3,630	1,569	No	Caldwell (1997b)
Police	6,168	926	No	Christiansen & Cohen (2003)

among the Clinical Scales. The average correlation between each RC Scale and its Clinical Scale parent is .724, a loss of 48% in the variance shared between the RC Scales and their parent Clinical Scales. Even after eliminating the weakest correlation from inclusion (that between Scale 3 and RC3), the average correlation achieved between the RC Scales and their respective parent scales is .808, a loss of 35% in the average shared variance between the RC Scale and its corresponding Clinical Scale. Thus the small gain in the independence achieved in the RC Scales is swamped by a loss in the variance that they share with their Clinical Scale counterparts.

In summary, improved Clinical Scale independence can be achieved by simply eliminating from the scales those nondistinctive items that overlap three or more Clinical Scales, or mark the major source of nonspecific variance on the Clinical Scales, or both. In the present investigation, we achieved reductions in CSC of between 9% and 20%, with decreases in fidelity to their unaltered versions of from 8% to 23%. This finding largely replicates Nichols' previous demonstration (2006a), wherein, using the same methods, he achieved reductions in CSC of between 13% and 25%, with decreases in fidelity of from 6% to 23%. In contrast, the correlations among the RC Scales in our aggregate sample show only nominal reductions in covariation (5%), but at a cost of a roughly 10-fold loss in fidelity (48%) to their parent Clinical Scales. By this standard, the first of the RC authors' goals, that of substantially reducing the covariation that compromises the discriminant validity of the MMPI-2 Clinical Scales, appears to have been met only marginally, and by methods both substantially more questionable and complicated than could be achieved by more straightforward means.

Growth Changes

In the previous section, we discussed the first of two primary motivations often invoked in the revision of a test or a scale: to address known areas of deficiency. In this section, we discuss the second motivation to revise a test or scale; to address changes that would better position the instrument for present and future use in clinical and research applications, given current and cutting-edge knowledge in the domains measured by the instrument. Norman (1972) exemplified this consideration in asking whether, and how, changes should be made to the original MMPI:

> [H]ow may we best incorporate what we have learned from the past thirty years, or more, of research with this and other techniques in order to generate the quantum jump in personality theory and methods of assessment and diagnosis which is, I believe, potentially attainable? (p. 60)

Through the process of incorporating growth changes, the revised scale may develop new strengths. Occasionally, the process of addressing deficiencies in the instrument simultaneously incorporates growth changes, particularly when addressing a deficiency necessitates revisiting and reconsidering the assumptions and goals guiding the development of the original version (Adams, 2000). More often, however, growth changes target domains of measurement not known or relevant at the time of the measure's original development, and the revision process seeks to incorporate those changes while leaving intact the goals and assumptions underlying the development of the original measure.

Returning to the perspective expressed in Norman's (1972) quotation, above, the process leading to a successful personality test revision will often include consideration of constructs that were available but were either bypassed in the previous test version, or were unavailable or lacked sufficient currency to be included. If an instrument is to remain current, its revision must consider embracing new constructs relevant to its range of application. Advances in personality and psychopathology periodically are accompanied by conceptual innovations that revision committees can usefully heed, provided that the means for their accurate measurement are at hand, and that there is sufficient demand for them. For the MMPI-2, one or more scales related to the Five-Factor Model (FFM; Digman, 1990) of personality, one of the more influential developments in personality assessment in the past quarter-century

(Goldberg, 1993), might be considered. Similarly, in the arena of psychopathology, constructs related to, for example, attention deficit disorder (ADD), attention deficit/hyperactivity disorder (ADHD), dissociative identity disorder (DID), and body dysmorphic disorder would seem to command interest.

It should be remembered, however, that appeals to contemporary fashions and terminology can be overstated. Hathaway (1972a) noted, for example, that

> Perhaps conversion hysteria has gone out of style . . . but even an amateur reader of MMPI profiles who sees a code '13' . . . can for a moment feel professional identity in giving a little interpretive statement about the modal person who produces such a profile. He can usually enrich this description with some insightful item. He is, for example, rather safe if he asks what disablement the person developed when he encountered a period of psychological stress. (p. xiv)

Several possible growth changes have been noted (Adams, 2000), and are described below. Some allow for the reconsideration of the assumptions and goals that guided development of the original version, and some seek to preserve those assumptions and goals while expanding the current utility of the instrument.

First, the revision of a test allows for the inclusion of constructs not tapped by the first version (Dahlstrom, 1972). For example, one of the guiding principles in the MMPI-2 restandardization process was to replace the outdated and unused items with items that could address contemporary clinical problems not included in the original edition of the MMPI, in order to broaden the test's utility (Butcher, 2000). This new item content was then employed to build scales measuring constructs unavailable in the original MMPI, such as Type A Behavior (TPA), Negative Treatment Indicators (TRT), and the admission of problems related to addictions (Addiction Admission Scale, AAS).

Second, during a revision, the test developers can use new scale construction methods that were not available at the time of the original test's development. Item response theory (IRT) provides a test developer with a set of scale development tools that allows for greater flexibility in tailoring the test question to the needs of the test. When the goal is to create a scale that effectively differentiates between people above and below a specific cutoff level, for example, IRT methods allow for the identification of items that are maximally informative at that precise criterion level, but when the goal is to create a scale that effectively differentiates across the whole continuum, more diverse items can be included.

Third, the revision of a test allows for the consideration of new test administration methods. For example, computerized administration procedures, including computerized adaptive testing, can be incorporated into the test revision. More discussion of the comparability of computerized and paper-and-pencil administration follows below.

Fourth, the revision of a test allows for the assessment of new population groups that had not been adequately assessed in the past. Okazaki and Sue (2000) provided an example of this point by arguing that a test revision provides an opportunity to gain greater understanding of under-served populations. For example, Asian American communities have been generally ignored in assessment research, as seen in the way that Asian-Americans were included in a meaninglessly heterogeneous "Other" category (along with Native Americans, Alaskan Natives, Pacific Islanders, and multiracial individuals) for the WAIS-III (*Wechsler Adult Intelligence Scale* – Third edition, Wechsler, 1997) standardization sample. The inclusion of previously underrepresented populations is not merely a deficiency change, correcting a previous flaw, but can be seen as a growth change, because (as Okazaki and Sue, 2000, noted), the test development procedure often includes provisions for gathering data from large representative samples of different populations; when properly funded by a test development company—this would not only allow for a representative normative sample, but would allow the researchers to gain data about the characteristics and mental health needs of those under-served populations.

Although a test revision does allow for new growth and development when guided by empirical literature, Campbell (1972) admonished test developers not to merely chase after current trends, but to be discerning in considering whether a change is truly a new development or merely reaction to a short-term fad. In the context of whether or not the original MMPI should be revised, he wrote

[F]ads tend to dominate the field; the MMPI reviser will be under tremendous pressure to incorporate whatever is faddish at the moment. For example, response sets, acquiescence and social desirability, are currently popular, and the reviser will have to pay attention to those concepts even though the data in support of them are will-o'-the-wispy, at best, and, at worst, probably simply superstitious. Except possibly

for factor analysis, no other psychometric issue has channeled so much high-powered wisdom into such trivial matters. (p. 119)

This admonition remains valid today, and modern test developers should continue to follow his advice, conscientiously considering whether a planned change would represent a long-term improvement in the test or merely a short-term response to momentary topics of interest.

GROWTH AIMS PURSUED IN THE DEVELOPMENT OF THE RC SCALES

As discussed earlier, the RC Scales were developed primarily to address the deficiencies long known to plague the Clinical Scales of the MMPI/MMPI-2, reducing Clinical Scale covariation the most prominent among them. Additionally, though, the authors of the RC Scales positioned their revision effort within a growth framework, and argued that their resultant scales were developed with two particular growth opportunities in view.

The most important growth domain shaping their revision, in their estimation, was the incorporation of an explicit theoretical foundation to shape the new scales and subsequently ground their interpretation. In their monograph describing the development of the RC Scales, Tellegen et al. (2003) cite authors who disparage the wisdom of the empirical keying approach used to develop the original scales and insist that "no psychologically significant test construction is possible without the guidance of explicit substantive theory" (p. 5). Underscoring this point, Tellegen et al. (2006) state in a subsequent article,

The [RC] scales do represent a move away from the "blind empiricism" that has long been associated with the MMPI-2 toward a more theoretically grounded . . . approach. The RC Scales are linked in meaningful ways to contemporary models of personality and psychopathology. This allows MMPI-2 users to draw for their interpretations on not only the empirical correlates of the RC Scales but also the nomological framework embedding these correlates. (p. 149)

Others have commented on the benefit of a substantive theory–based reconceptualization of the main scales of the MMPI-2, using a contemporary theory of personality and/or psychopathology, in order to increase the MMPI-2's applicability in research and its usefulness to today's clinician (Finn & Kamphuis, 2006; Sellbom & Ben-Porath,

2005; Simms, 2006). Tellegen et al. (2003) appear to have satisfied this growth aim with the theoretically grounded RC Scales, and offer up their revision as the MMPI's defense against impending obsolescence. We will review the merits of their scale revision strategy, vis-à-vis this growth opportunity, below.

The second area of growth focused on by the authors of the RC Scales emanates from their use of theory and results in scales that incorporate substantially modified definitions of the mood-disordered constructs measured by the MMPI-2 and accepted, more generally, by the psychological community at large. Specifically, Tellegen et al. (2006) assert that the constructs measured by their scales RC2, RC7, and RCd better reflect current developments in mood assessment (than the original scales), follow in predicted ways from the theory shaping their development, diverge in important ways from the constructs represented by the original scales, and "link the MMPI-2 directly to contemporary conceptions of psychopathology" (p. 158).

In view of admonitions against revising a test in order to keep pace with contemporary trends that may or may not be upheld across time, it is important that we consider in more detail the growth-oriented claims offered by the authors of the RC Scales in support of their methods. The first involved the need to revise the main scales of the test in order to locate those scales within a current theory of personality and/or psychopathology that will facilitate their clinical interpretation and increase the instrument's contemporary relevance. The second involved the revision of several scales, bringing them into conformity with significant, theory-based modifications to the current conceptualization of given mood disorder constructs.

PRIMARY GROWTH AIM: A THEORETICAL CONTEXT

Despite Tellegen et al.'s (2003) claim that their scale revision "methods are pervasively empirical" (p. 11), the RC Scales provide an example of a scale revision methodology that departed in important ways from the empirical methods traditionally invoked in the development of the scales it set out to revise. In this case, the methodological departure involved a flight from the empirical methods of scale construction long associated with the MMPI to a strategy that was framed as being more substantively and structurally directed (p. 12). The authors explained their departure by addressing the purported liabilities associated with the more traditional empirical methods and suggesting, alternatively, the

benefits of a strategy that is more theoretically informed. Generally speaking, we agree that a theoretical foundation provides an advantageous context for shaping scale constructs and contextualizing interpretation; however, such benefits require that the identified theory is both relevant and appropriately applied to the intent and range of the instrument. In the case of the RC Scales, the authors' allegiance to the senior author's previously developed model of affect, the Watson and Tellegen model of affect (Watson & Tellegen, 1985), may be understood as having compromised the growth opportunity with which they were presented.

From the outset, the authors' allegiance to their theory appears to have stifled their curiosity about such apparently parsimonious resolutions for high Clinical Scale intercorrelation as reducing item overlap and/or extracting First Factor covariance using empirically validated markers. The decision to confine themselves to their theoretical model, without considering other applicable models or alternate strategies appears to have biased their methods in favor of an unnecessarily radical approach and one that excluded the exploration of empirically based methods that maintain the tradition of MMPI-2 scale development, as well as the recognizability of the resultant scales. Moreover, their allegiance to the Watson and Tellegen model appears to have exerted undue, and unfortunate, influence in the shaping of their own marker for First Factor variance (i.e., Demoralization, eventually their RCd scale), rendering the entire theoretical basis of their revision effort vulnerable to critique.

In the next section, we examine the Watson and Tellegen model of affect with respect to its general character, its position among competing models, and its applicability to the MMPI-2.

The Watson and Tellegen Model of Affect: A Brief Examination

The Watson and Tellegen model of Positive Affect (PA) and Negative Affect (NA) (1985, 1999) is a factor analytically based dimensional model of affective structure, as applied to self-rated mood. The model is represented by a three-level hierarchy that purports to describe the structure of felt affect. At the apex of the hierarchy is a single, bipolar dimension reflecting variations in hedonic valence (i.e., pleasant versus unpleasant; PU). At the intermediate level of the hierarchy are two independent, "truly unipolar constructs" (Watson, Weise, Vaidya, & Tellegen, 1999, p. 827): one representing positive activation (or its absence), and the other representing negative activation (or its absence). At the base of the hierarchy are specific, discrete affects, such as fear, anger, sadness, guilt, and so forth. Relative to other models of affective structure, the defining features of the Watson and Tellegen model can be summarized as its being composed of hierarchical structure, as comprising one bipolar valence dimension (PU) and two unipolar affect/activation dimensions (NA and PA), and by the independence of the latter two dimensions.

Tellegen et al. (2003) used the framework of the Watson and Tellegen model to shape and clarify the Demoralization construct intended to target problematic covariation on the Clinical Scales. Importantly, they asserted that Demoralization is the MMPI-2 equivalent of the affect model's PU dimension. As a general factor of affect that is broader than the intermediate level factors (i.e., the activation dimensions), the PU dimension is thought, by the authors of the model, to be "pervasive in clinical inventories such as the MMPI" (Tellegen et al., 2003, p. 13). Thus, according to the theoretical tenets of the model, the broad hedonic nature and pervasive presence of the PU dimension, manifest on the MMPI-2 as Demoralization, explains the high intercorrelations seen across Clinical Scales that should otherwise be more independent. Informed by these assumptions, Tellegen et al. (2003) extracted the Demoralization dimension from the Clinical Scales and isolated it to its own scale in an effort to create a set of restructured clinical scales that are more conceptually distinct.

The Watson and Tellegen model also informs and clarifies other aspects of the development and interpretation of the RC Scales, not just the Demoralization construct. Importantly, RC Scales 2 and 7 are directly related to the intermediate level of the hierarchical model, with RC2 (Low Positive Emotionality) understood to be measuring primarily a low level of "positive [and activated] emotional content" (Tellegen et al., 2003, p. 15), and RC7 (Dysfunctional Negative Emotions) understood to be measuring primarily affective content that is characterized by negative activation. Because RC Scales 2 and 7 closely mirror the theoretical constructs of PA (reversed) and NA, respectively, the affective constructs measured by these scales should result in scales that are independent of one another, just as PA and NA are understood to be independent.

Given the absence of any explanation in the RC Scales monograph for the selection of the Watson and Tellegen model for the purpose of informing Tellegen et al.'s MMPI-2 restructuring effort, the uninformed reader might assume that the Watson and Tellegen model is universally accepted and ubiquitously applied where a model of affect structure is needed. In fact, there are a number of competing models (Larsen & Diener, 1992; Russell, 1980; Thayer, 1996) describing the structure of affect, and the Watson and Tellegen model articulates notable differences that set it apart from other widely validated, and arguably more prominent, models. On the basis of the differences that uniquely define it, the Watson and Tellegen model has been vigorously challenged and, in the wake of numerous studies and a published debate occurring in the late 1990s, "some people . . . came to see serious flaws in the Watson and Tellegen affect model once the issues were laid out in various articles" (J. A. Russell, personal communication, March 12, 2007; see also, e.g., Carroll, Yik, Russell, & Feldman Barrett, 1999, and Green & Salovey, 1999).

The differences between the Watson and Tellegen model and other competing models have been detailed elsewhere (Huelsman, Furr, & Nemanick, 2003; Ranson, 2008), along with a summary of the serious flaws referred to by Russell (Ranson, 2008). For our purposes, it is important to understand that affect researchers have debated the veracity of the Watson and Tellegen model vis-à-vis competing models on four critical areas of difference. In each instance, the tenets of the Watson and Tellegen model were found lacking.

The first debate pertains to whether the structure of affect is best delineated by the more prominent circumplex structure or by Watson and Tellegen's hierarchical structure. Russell's (1980) circumplex model is characterized by a circular ordering of a limitless number of affect terms, each of which has a theoretical bipolar opposite. The circumplex is ordered by two orthogonal bipolar dimensions: degree of pleasantness and degree of activation. The two bipolar dimensions combine in an integral fashion, so that, subjectively, a person experiences a single feeling, as opposed to separate awareness of each component. According to Russell and Feldman Barrett (1999), a circumplex structure is delineated because factor analyses of affect data (e.g., self-rated emotions, multidimensional scaling of words, facial expressions of emotion) consistently yield the two broad dimensions identified, and the resulting emotion categories spread themselves more or less predictably around the circle defined by the axes, rather than clustering at the axes. Moreover, the data fall in such a way that the variables are equidistant from the center of the circle.

In Russell's model, any given affect is thus identified by the intersection of the "pleasantness" dimension and the "activation" dimension, which sit at a 90-degree angle to one another. Every emotion term—each a blend of some degree of pleasure and some degree of arousal—can be located around the perimeter of the circumplex space, according to its standing on each of the two dimensions. Russell (2003) claims that a person's present feeling state is always located at a single point on the circumplex, that it moves about in response to external and internal prompts, and that affect is always present somewhere on the circumplex, though individuals may be more or less consciously aware of their affective status, depending on the intensity of the affect.

Importantly, in numerous studies comparing the fit of the respective models to the data, the circumplex model has been shown repeatedly to be a good fit. The relative superiority of the circumplex model to the hierarchical model has been established using meta-analyses of affect data (Remington, Fabrigar, & Visser, 2000); actual affect data (Carroll et al., 1999; Fabrigar, Visser, & Browne, 1997; Green & Salovey, 1999); affect data drawn from numerous cross-cultural contexts (Yik & Russell, 2003; Yik, Russell, Ahn, Dols, & Suzuki, 2002; Yik, Russell, Oceja, & Dols, 2000); and in evaluations of the predictions made by the circumplex model in relation to other theoretical domains of relevance, such as theories of psychopathology (Heller, Schmidtke, Nitschke, Koven, & Miller, 2002; Kring, Feldman Barrett, & Gard, 2003), and the structure of personality (Gurtman, 1994; Soldz, Budman, Demby, & Merry, 1993; Widiger & Hagemoser, 1997; Wiggins, Steiger, & Gaelick, 1981).

The second debate pertains to whether the two widely acknowledged orthogonal dimensions are independent (and thus uncorrelated) and unipolar, as Watson and Tellegen assert; or whether they are bipolar (and thus positively to negatively correlated). One of the implications of endorsing one set of dimensions (e.g., Watson's independent dimensions of NA and PA) versus another set of dimensions (other models' bipolar dimensions of pleasure and activation) pertains to where a given affect might be found vis-à-vis each model. Returning to the revision of the MMPI-2 scales, the problem of where a given affect is correctly located relates directly to the predicted performance of the scales informed by that determination (RC Scales 2, 7, and RCd, for example). It is the varying "placement" of affect terms, which is a function of the difference in the structural dimensions across models, that represents one of the tests of "fit to the available data" (Watson et al., 1999). Importantly, in the "fit to the available data" investigations cited earlier, the data supported the circumplex structure and its placement of affect terms, over Watson and Tellegen's hierarchical structure.

The third debate pertains to whether affect is, by definition, limited to only those states that are characterized by high levels of activation, as Watson and Tellegen's model requires, or whether affect is more correctly represented in any combination of activation (or lack thereof) and valence. Note that, in order for support to be found for Watson and Tellegen's claim that PA and NA are independent (the topic of the second debate), the definition of affect must be limited to activated states only. Russell and Carroll (1999) summarized the implications of the more limited definition:

> Restricting the definition of affect [to valence accompanied by high arousal, only] leaves out a large number of states, such as happiness, serenity, misery, sadness, and depression that other researchers might want included. Psychology must surely examine [these] states. Arbitrary definitions can exclude them from the domain of affect, but cannot exclude them from the human condition. (p. 21)

The relevance to the MMPI-2 of a model that primarily focuses on highly activated affect states to the relative exclusion of moderately activated or chronic affect states can be seen as limiting and otherwise problematical.

A fourth area of debate focuses on the influence of "time" upon the measurement of affect. Russell (2003) explicitly characterizes his model as one describing "momentary affect," and argues that models such as his, and the Watson and Tellegen model, are defining the structure of affect at given moments in time. Berkowitz (2000) concurs, with direct reference to the Watson and Tellegen model. In fact, in clarifying this point, Berkowitz paraphrases Watson et al. (1999) in writing, "their findings seem to be clearest, they noted, when the feelings have to do with one's current, momentary experience rather than with one's mood over, say, an entire day" (p. 16).

Watson and Tellegen have taken an exceptional position among the competing models, however, in asserting that their model also can be applied to define the structure of extended, or trait, affect. They substantiate their claim by reporting the high stability coefficients obtained of their Positive and Negative Affect Schedule (PANAS; Watson, Clark, & Tellegen, 1988) under the "how have you felt generally" instruction set. Moreover, they cite evidence of the high correlation coefficients obtained for extended affect ratings across differing retrospective recollection conditions when using their PANAS scales (Watson, 1988; Watson & Tellegen, 1999; Watson & Walker, 1996).

Several independent lines of research call into question, however, the validity of the claims that the Watson and Tellegen model can be reliably generalized to extended, or trait, affect. The most salient of these arguments focuses on the reliability of the PANAS scales. Schmidt, Le, and Ilies (2003) evaluated the effects of transient measurement error on the reliability estimates for measures of affect, including the PANAS scales, and found that the PANAS scales suffered the highest level of reliability overestimation of all the measures they assessed. Schmidt et al. (2003) explained this finding by the fact that the PANAS scales use mood descriptors to assess trait affect, resulting in potentially high levels of transient error. This finding is consistent with the results of other studies that have identified various biases that contaminate the accuracy of retrospective ratings of mood. Taken together, the research suggests that the Watson and Tellegen model is most validly and reliably applied as a model of momentary affect, and not as a model of extended affect. The brief, highly unstable, momentary mood states that are reliably assessed by measures of momentary affect and thus understood by the models that shape their predictions, are not shifts that are of particular relevance to, or meaningful for, MMPI-2 measurement of enduring clinical conditions.

The latter conclusion suggests that none of the affect structure models is appropriately applied in the service of restructuring the Clinical Scales of the MMPI-2, because these models most validly and reliably describe momentary, rather than extended affect. However, even if a model of momentary affect could be seen as appropriately applied, there is little reason to consider that the hierarchically structured Watson and Tellegen model represents a better fit to the data than the circumplex model, or is for any other reason more compelling in its application to the MMPI-2. Therefore, for the purpose of guiding the identification and extraction of First Factor covariance or, more generally, of restructuring the Clinical Scales, the use of the Watson and Tellegen model appears to be an arbitrary choice, and its use can be

identified as all the more arbitrary by the authors' failure to account for its selection from among competing, and arguably superior, models.

Returning to the growth-motivated revisions advanced by the authors of the RC Scales, one can see that their first goal, to embed the revised scales within a theoretical model that shaped their development and guides their interpretation, has not been achieved in a way that leaves the resultant scales theoretically trustworthy. That any model best described as characterizing momentary affect could be reliably used to shape and inform scales intended to measure chronic states of distress is doubtful.

Moreover, the use of the Watson and Tellegen model, in particular, is problematic and leaves the resultant scales untrustworthy in practical ways. Multiple investigations have established that other conceptualizations of the structure of affect are at least equal, and arguably superior, to that advanced by Watson and Tellegen. Particularly problematic is the model's assertion that PA (on which RC2 is modeled) and NA (on which RC7 is modeled) are independent dimensions, a claim that is both theoretically debatable and empirically upheld only under the single condition wherein affect is intensely activated. Under conditions in which positive or negative valence occurs with moderate to no activation, the independence otherwise predicted by the model vanishes. The variability of the activation condition poses problems for the construct validity of RC2 and RC7, and complicates the theoretical basis of their interpretation. Importantly, the dubiousness of the model's independence claims may help to explain why RC2 and RC7 are so routinely found to achieve medium to large intercorrelations, despite the theoretical prediction of their distinction. Simms, Casillas, Clark, Watson, and Doebbeling (2005), for example, found the correlation between RC2 and RC7 to be .55 in one sample, and .47 in another. Similarly, Sellbom, Graham, and Schenk (2006) found the correlation between the two scales to be .47 in their sample, while Sellbom, Ben-Porath, and Graham (2006) reported the correlation at .44 in their investigation, and Wallace and Liljequist (2005) reported it at .42 in theirs. Indeed, in the authors' own data (Tellegen et al. (2003)) the reported correlations obtained between RC2 and RC7 in their clinical samples ranged from .40 to .54, averaging .48.

Demoralization: A Theory-Driven Marker for Clinical Scale Covariation

In the previous section, we considered the general theoretical applicability of the Watson and Tellegen model to the task of guiding the revision of the MMPI-2 Clinical Scales, and examined its standing among competing models. In each case, we found that the authors' loyalty to this model may have blinded their consideration of more appropriately applied theories, and appears to have distorted at least a few of the resulting scales in ways that reflect the limitations of theory.

Similarly, the authors' commitment to the Watson and Tellegen model resulted in what appears to have been an unwillingness to explore other, perhaps better, markers for First Factor variance. As described above, in Step 1, Tellegen et al. (2003) chose to develop a Demoralization scale, a scale reflecting the PU dimension of the Watson and Tellegen model, which they also believe to be analogous to what is conventionally referred to as the MMPI-2 First Factor, the general or nonspecific source of variance deemed most responsible for the covariation among the clinical scales. This marker was then appended to each clinical scale in turn to identify those items with a greater affinity for the marker than for the remaining clinical scale items. It is unknown whether any empirically derived First Factor markers were considered as alternatives to their Demoralization scale; however, if such an alternative marker had been considered, there were several candidates from which to choose:

1. As the oldest, most traditional marker for the First Factor, Welsh's (1956) Anxiety scale (A) would seem an obvious choice for the authors' purposes. Although the RC authors do not address A as a potential marker, it could be viewed as less than suitable on at least three grounds: First, having been developed in the early 1950s, it may have been considered dated. Second, A was constructed using two samples ($n = 150$ and 137, respectively) of male VA patients and may not fairly represent the First Factor among women. Finally, the A dimension lacks specificity. Developed as a dimension within the original MMPI environment, and based upon the total MMPI item pool, A could and perhaps should be considered insufficiently local to the specific domain of interest, the Clinical Scales. One indication of this lack of specific locality is that, of the 39 items scored on A, more than half, 22/39, are scored on none of the Clinical Scales in the same

direction as they are on A and, of these, 21 do not overlap with the Clinical Scales in either direction.

Given the goals of the RC authors, the latter objection is especially salient. The eight basic Clinical Scales are the domain of interest explicitly invoked by Tellegen et al. (2003, pp. 1, 11–12, et passim), and reiterated by Tellegen et al. (2006): "we needed to focus our effort on the Clinical Scales" (p. 158).

2. More contemporary options could have emerged from an examination of the literature involving factor analyses of the MMPI/MMPI-2 item pool. One of these is the principal component (JB1) identified in the replicated item-level factor analysis of the total MMPI item pool of Johnson et al. (1984) in a large (11,138) sample of inpatients and outpatients served by the Missouri Department of Mental Health. In this research, principal components analysis with Varimax rotation (PCA/V) was used in a cross-validation design with an initial sample of 5,506 Missouri inpatients and outpatients, and a replication sample of 5,632 similar patients. Eighty-seven items emerged on the First Factor. Of these, 83 survive in the MMPI-2 item pool and 42 (JB1C) are scored on one or more of the Clinical Scales.

3. A similarly attractive third choice is the first factor (W1) found in Waller's (1999) iterated item factor analysis of tetrachoric correlations in a sample of 28,390 medical and psychiatric patients treated at the University of Minnesota Hospitals. The first factor in this analysis comprised 143 items of which 135 survive in the MMPI-2 item pool; 76 (W1C) of these items are scored on one or more of the Clinical Scales.

4. Still another option, not so obvious, but proposed by Nichols (2006a), could have emerged from an examination of the pattern of item overlap between the primary factors, JB1 and W1, found by Johnson et al. (1984) and Waller (1999). Seventy-two (87%) of the replicated items of JB1 were again replicated in W1, despite the differences in their two samples and in the factor methods applied to them. Fortunately, of these 72 items (JBW72), slightly more than half, 37 (hereafter JBW37), are scored on one or more of the basic Clinical Scales of the MMPI-2. These 37 items, from an aggregate of 39,528 clinical patients in separate geographic locales and twice cross-validated, would appear to be a marker ideally suited for targeting and extracting, precisely, the source of variance that is most responsible for the major source of covariation among the MMPI-2 Clinical Scales.

5. Finally, an obvious option available to the RC authors would have been to factor their own data sets. The items scored on the Clinical Scales for each of the seven samples reported in their monograph (Tellegen et al., 2003), or some combination thereof, could have been used to replicate and select items for a suitable marker for their First Factor. The aggregate N of 6,072 (2,270 men, 3,802 women) would appear to be sufficient for relatively stable subsequent findings.

Despite the varying but substantial appeal of most of these empirically based options, including a sufficient number of suitable data sets from which to develop a satisfactory alternative empirical marker and the availability of an apparently near-ideal marker for the First Factor (JBW37) focused on the Clinical Scales, the RC Scale authors' acknowledged domain of interest, none appears to have been considered. The reason for this omission appears to rest, again, in Tellegen et al.'s (2003) allegiance to the Watson and Tellegen (1985) model of affect.

In an outcome analogous to the problematic influence of an inappropriately applied theory upon the resultant scales, the influence of the Watson and Tellegen model upon the fashioning of the RC Demoralization marker and the method adopted for its construction imposed a bias away from both of the authors' initial aims, as described above. In the first place, the procedures followed in constructing the preliminary Demoralization scale (Dem) recruited and retained items that are found on none of the Clinical Scales. Indeed, such offscale items amount to almost half of the scale's length. With the creation of Dem, therefore, the aspiration to target the most relevant source of CSC, items actually contained within the Clinical Scales, was, in effect, abandoned. Consequently, the adoption of Dem entailed a shift away from the Clinical Scales, the RC authors' explicitly stated domain of interest, to the MMPI-2 item pool as a whole. In this sense, Dem is similar to A in that it is a roughly equal mix of offscale items and items scored on one or more of the Clinical Scales (Dem: 10:13, 10/ 23 = 43%; A: 21:18; 21/39 = 54%). In contrast, the number of items confined to the Clinical Scales from the Johnson et al. and Waller first factors, and from JBW37, are 42, 76, and 37, respectively. Coincidentally, having significantly fewer items than the latter item sets, Dem would appear to be less reliable as well.

In the second place, the decision to adopt the theoretically derived Demoralization construct required (a) a departure from the empirical tradition of the MMPI/MMPI-2 and (b) the adoption of a search procedure for the Demoralization construct that would ultimately exert a biasing influence on what could emerge as "the distinctive substantive core" of each Clinical Scale as restructuring procedures went forward.

The examination of RC7, the RC counterpart of Scale 7 (Psychasthenia, Pt), provides a particularly telling example of one of the consequences of adopting a theory-driven rather than an empirically driven strategy for the determination of the latter scale's core construct. Each of the seven seed items selected to represent Scale 7's core construct overlaps with at least one of the empirically derived First Factor markers: four items overlapped with A (289, 301, 310, and 328), five items with JB1 (289, 301, 302, 320, and 328), and six with W1 (301, 302, 310, 320, 327, and 328). Seed items 301 and 328 overlapped with all three markers. Given this pattern of overlap, it is difficult to see how these seven core items could recruit items with distinctive, as opposed to general First Factor, variances in Step 4 of RC scale development.

In a preliminary analysis, we factored the combination of Scale 7 items and those of JBW37 in our aggregate sample using PCA/V, to two factors. Three of the seven seed items, #s 301, 310, and 327, fell on the JBW37-marked factor; the other four fell on the residual Scale 7 factor with relatively high but nondistinctive loadings, suggesting a fragile and unstable core.

Nichols (2006a, p. 133) pointed out that the restructuring procedures used to develop RC7 resulted in the importation of four anger (ANG) items, or 17% of the content of RC7, raising the question of construct drift (Scale 7 includes only one ANG item, 2% of its content). In response, Tellegen et al. (2006) assert that RC7's "stronger association . . . with measures of anger reflects evidence of the improved convergent validity of this measure of dysfunctional negative emotions" (p. 162). To investigate this matter further, we factored RC7 using PCA/V to two factors and found that although three of the four anger items appeared on the first factor, only two of the seed items selected by Tellegen et al. (2003) did so. Conversely, the five remaining seed items appeared on the second, or residual, factor. Additionally, 12 of the 16 offscale items, those added to the seed items in Step 4, appear on the first factor. This pattern of findings suggests that RC7 may not only have drifted from the construct of its parent Scale 7, but also from the authors' conception of their core construct as embodied in their own seed items.

That the majority of the offscale items in RC7 fell on the dominant factor in this analysis reinforces Nichols' (2006a) conclusion that "in the process of augmenting the seed scales, some of the First Factor variance that was removed from the Clinical Scales in Step 2 was reintroduced to the seeds in Step 4" (p. 126). Indeed, Nichols found that, with the exception of RC1, the nonseed portions of the RC scales were more highly correlated with each of the seven markers, including Dem and RCd, for the First Factor than were the seed items (p. 127).

To explore this effect further, we examined the pattern of item overlap between RC7 and each of the three empirically derived markers for the First Factor and two of their combinations, A, JB1, W1, JBW72, and AJBW, on the one hand, and that between Scale 7 and the same markers, on the other. The results are presented in Table 7.3.

Every one of the 21 eligible RC7 items overlapped with one or more of the First Factor markers. Sixteen overlapped with two or more, and eight overlapped with all three. Hence, despite the procedures used in its development, there are more empirically derived and thrice-replicated First Factor items on RC7 than there are RC7 seed items. Moreover, RC7 contains nearly twice as many items overlapping JBW72 as is it does items overlapping Scale 7 (14 versus 8).

These findings provide dramatic support for Nichols' (2006a) contention that Step 4 of the RC authors' restructuring process reintroduced First Factor variance to RC7, and to the other RC scales as well, save RC1, leaving it not appreciably less saturated with the First Factor than was its Scale 7 parent, if at all. Recall that it was just such variance that the authors' restructuring

procedures were designed to remove. That these procedures manifestly failed to achieve the authors' aims in the case of RC7 raises disturbing questions about their selection of the theoretically derived Demoralization marker.

Additionally, the apparent reintroduction of unanticipated variances in Step 4 of the restructuring process appears to have caused RC7, as well as other scales, particularly RC4 and RC9, to "drift" (Nichols, 2006a) away from the "distinctive substantive core" of their parent Clinical Scales. Consequently, these RC Scales measure somewhat different constructs than those in view when the authors "designed [the RC Scales] to preserve the important descriptive properties of the existing MMPI-2 Clinical Scales" (Tellegen et al., 2003, p. 1). A more comprehensive account of Nichols' identification of "construct drift" in the RC Scales is beyond the scope of this chapter; the interested reader is referred to Nichols (2006a).

SECONDARY GROWTH AIM: KEEPING CURRENT WITH DEVELOPMENTS IN PERSONALITY AND PSYCHOPATHOLOGY

Tellegen et al. (2003) pursued a second growth-related goal through their development of the RC Scales: to link the MMPI-2 directly to contemporary conceptions of psychopathology. Although the RC Scales monograph makes no particular claim to an updating of terminology or of given diagnostic constructs in order to tie the MMPI-2 to more contemporary models of personality and psychopathology, its authors have stressed this virtue in subsequent presentations. For example, in response to the critical analyses of Nichols (2006a) and Rogers et al. (2006), Tellegen et al. (2006) seek to frame their endeavors as efforts to "modernize" (p. 149) the MMPI-2 by bringing it into accord with contemporary models/conceptions/knowledge of personality and psychopathology (cf. pp. 149, 157–158, 161, 169), and warn,

Table 7.3. The proportion of RC7 and Scale 7 items that overlap with empirically derived markers for the First Factor.

	A	JB1	W1	JBW72	AJBW
RC7	48	76	90	67	38
Scale 7	27	52	79	50	17

Note: Decimals omitted. RC7 = Dysfunctional Negative Emotions. (The divisor for RC7 was 21 because three of the RC7 items do not appear on the First Factor markers, all of which were developed within the MMPI-1 environment.) Scale 7 = Psychasthenia. A = Anxiety (Welsh, 1956). JB1 = Johnson–Butcher first factor (Johnson et al., 1984). W1 = Waller first factor (Waller, 1999). JBW72 = Items overlapping both JB1 and W1. AJBW = Items overlapping all three First Factor markers.

If interpretive guidelines focus almost exclusively on lists of empirical correlates and do not provide organizing conceptual principles, the MMPI-2 will be left out of the mainstream of current thinking about personality and psychopathology and be increasingly disconnected from important conceptual developments in the field.

(p. 157)

Their argument appears to be that the MMPI-2 has not kept pace with modern developments in personality and psychopathology, and that the RC Scales are in some sense a remedy for this failure.

However, when one examines these implications more objectively, it can be seen that neither will bear much weight. In the first place, if one looks in their 2006 rebuttal of criticism for examples of "contemporary conceptions of personality and psychopathology," that do not figure in the Watson and Tellegen model of affect, there are none. Moreover, to take one example, the implication that the MMPI-2 has failed to keep pace with current developments in personality and psychopathology does not conveniently square with the incorporation of the Personality Psychopathology Five (PSY-5) Scales more than a decade ago, and on which there has accumulated a wealth of favorable psychometric research. This group of scales bears notable similarities (albeit with important differences; see McNulty & Harkness, 2002) to a contemporary theory of personality, the Five Factor Model (FFM; Digman, 1990), globally regarded as a current standard. However, even if the indictment against the declining significance of the MMPI-2 were accurate, in order to be persuaded that the RC Scales serve as bulwark to the MMPI-2's obsolescence one would have to accept that the Watson and Tellegen model of affect is either a widely accepted model, which it is not; or that it held certain promise in launching leading-edge developments, which seems unlikely. Without the tenets of the Watson and Tellegen model to which they are conceptually tied, the RC Scales are just another set of unidimensional content scales that offer little in the way of unique contemporary relevance.

In the second place, for those two concepts on which these authors lay particular stress as conceptual innovations—demoralization and low positive emotions/anhedonia—the situation they describe is misleading. Let us take these two concepts in turn.

Demoralization

The first construct framed as modeling current advancements in personality or psychopathology is Demoralization. In the RC authors' usage, Demoralization is essentially an alternate label for the Unpleasantness pole of the Pleasantness–Unpleasantness (PU) dimension that stands at the apex of the Watson and Tellegen model of self-rated affect. The construct is thus both embedded in a single theoretical model of mood, one of several competing models as described above, and highly specific. The authors underscored its theoretical and conceptual specificity when explaining, "the construct of Demoralization played a crucial role in their approach to restructuring and was based on a well-confirmed and *well-embedded* (italics added) model of affect" (Tellegen et al., 2003, p. 12). Its application to the field of personality and general psychopathology is both uncertain and in dispute. In their defense of the Demoralization construct, however, Tellegen et al. (2006) cite and quote a number of authors (Dohrenwend, Shrout, Egri, & Mendelsohn, 1980; Frank, 1974a, 1974b; Joiner, Walker, Pettit, Perez, & Cukrowicz, 2005), who have employed the same *word*, demoralization. Yet, Tellegen et al. make no corresponding effort to link either the Watson and Tellegen model of affect, or the demoralization construct emanating from it, to the notion of demoralization as it has figured in the writings of those they cite with approval (pp. 156–158).

Similarly, the reference lists of Frank and Frank (1991) and Joiner et al. (2005) provide no indication that the latter are even aware of the Watson and Tellegen model of affect, much less that their own usage of the term, demoralization, is in accord with the specific Demoralization/Unpleasantness construct employed by Watson and Tellegen (1985).

To take only a single example, the RC authors seek to link their Demoralization construct to the writings of Jerome Frank who, until his recent death, was a revered opinion leader in psychiatry. In his influential book, *Persuasion and Healing* (Frank & Frank, 1991 [original publication, 1961]), Frank invoked the concept of demoralization to denote "the psychological state that responds to the elements shared by all psychotherapies" (p. 14). Demoralization, in Frank's usage, is, in essence, that which brings the patient to seek psychotherapy, regardless of his or her emotional state, whether from a failure to fulfill others' expectations, or their own, feelings of helplessness, hopelessness, stress, inability to cope, confusion, subjective incompetence, powerlessness, fearfulness, alienation, isolation, despair, or "related feelings" (p. 14). Demoralization may be either cause or consequence, or both (p. 35). One could hardly imagine a broader psychopathological construct, yet it applies, in Frank's usage, only secondarily, if at all, to the person who chooses *not* to seek psychotherapy.

In essence, then, in their attempt to justify and emphasize the importance and currency of their highly specific demoralization construct, Tellegen et al. (2006) inappropriately tie the latter to the far broader construct used by a respected commentator on psychotherapy, Frank, in the apparent hope that the reader will view the broader construct as either in accord with, or as in some other sense legitimizing, their own far narrower construct.

While it may be true that there may be some incidental semantic union of the terms as they are used by their respective authors, Tellegen et al.'s (2003) Demoralization construct is limited in the scope of its reference by the shared boundaries of two factors (PU and First Factor) that define it, at least if it is to be properly anchored within a theoretical context. On the other hand, if the scope of its usage is allowed to shift to a more colloquial meaning when convenient, then the construct is not theoretically embedded; the authors of the RC Scales cannot have it both ways.

In summary, what the RC authors fail to accomplish in the defense of their Demoralization construct is to establish its equivalence to the concept of demoralization as this term is used by others. In this they lose sight of Bateson's maxim, "the name is not the thing named, and the name of the name is not the name" (in Bateson, 1977, p. 243). Bateson is here drawing on a point made more vividly by Alice in her conversation with the White Knight. Recall the White Knight and Alice. Alice is rather tired of listening to songs and, offered yet another, she asks its name.

"The name of the song is called '*Haddocks' Eyes*'," says the White Knight.

"That's the name of the song, is it?" says Alice.

"No, you don't understand," says the White Knight, "that's not the name of the song, that's what the name is *called*."

(*Carroll*, 1960 [original publication, 1872], p. 212)

Anhedonia

The second construct that the RC Scale authors emphasize for its importance in contemporary thinking in psychopathology is anhedonia. They apparently view this construct as interchangeable with the Positive Activation (reversed) pole of the Watson and Tellegen model's affect/activation dimension, and equivalent to their low positive emotions scale (RC2). In their article written in response to criticism of the RC Scales, Tellegen et al. (2006) mention low positive emotions once; anhedonia, seven times.

The term anhedonia was coined by Ribot (1897), but did not gain significant entree into American clinical psychology until the APA presidential address of Paul Meehl (1962), who inspired Chapman, Chapman, and Raulin (1976) to develop their physical and social anhedonia scales for its measurement, and use in much of their subsequent research program.

Contrary to the impression that might be drawn from the emphasis of Tellegen et al. (2006) on the importance of having the MMPI-2 keep pace with contemporary developments in personality and psychopathology, Watson, Klett, and Lorei (1970) developed an MMPI scale for the measurement of anhedonia (Anhed) that predated the Chapman et al. scales by more than 5 years. A second, related, MMPI scale for the measurement of hedonic capacity (HedCap) was published by Dworkin and Saczynski in 1984.

To these anhedonia scales may be added another developed within the MMPI-2 environment, the introversion/low positive emotionality scale (INTR; Harkness, McNulty, & Ben-Porath, 1995), one of the set of five PSY-5 scales mentioned earlier for their collective link to important contemporary theory. Thus, given the availability of two MMPI-based measures of anhedonia for more than 20 years (neither of which has so far received mention by the RC authors), plus the recent addition of a third, it is hardly the case that the MMPI/MMPI-2 has lagged contemporary developments in personality and psychopathology, at least so far as the anhedonia construct is concerned.

With the availability of existing anhedonia scales in view, the RC Scales' purported rectification of this putative gap fails to justify the development of a scale on growth grounds. On the other hand, the importance of the scale's development on deficiency grounds could be supported where existing measures are regarded as inadequate. The availability of Tellegen et al.'s (2003) low positive emotions

Table 7.4. Correlations among the Chapman Physical and Social Anhedonia Scales and MMPI/MMPI-2 anhedonia measures.

	RC2	Anhedonia	Hedonic Capacity	INTR	Si
Study 1					
Physical Anhedonia	.21	.26	.24	.26	.20
Social Anhedonia	.25	.36	.34	.37	.29
Study 2					
Physical Anhedonia	.26	.23	.27	.39	.25
Social Anhedonia	.42	.42	.54	.51	.45

Note: RC2 = Low Positive Emotions, Anhed = Anhedonia, HedCap = Hedonic Capacity (reversed keyed), INTR = Introversion/Low Positive Emotionality, Si = Social Introversion.

Scale, RC2, makes possible the comparison of its performance against other MMPI/MMPI-2 measures of anhedonia.

Study 1. The sample for our first study consisted of 450 male and 438 female Midwestern University undergraduates between the ages of 18 and 25 years, inclusive, who served as participants in earlier research reported by Merritt, Balogh, and DeVinney (1993). All subjects completed both the original MMPI and the Physical and Social Anhedonia Scales (Chapman et al., 1976).

Study 2. Participants in the second study were drawn from a sample of 120 male and 200 female Midwestern undergraduates between the ages of 18 and 24 years, inclusive, who participated in the study in order to receive course credit. In order to be considered for inclusion in the final sample, participants' responses had to meet several validity criteria for the MMPI-2 and the Wisconsin schizotypy scales (WSS; Kwapil, Chapman, & Chapman, 1999). Respondents were eliminated if they had more than 20 omitted items; raw scores greater than 13 on VRIN, less than 5 or greater than 13 on TRIN, greater than 30 on F, greater than 20 on Fb; T-scores greater than 120 on Fp, or greater 83 on L; 38 participants were dropped from the sample after application of these validity criteria. The remaining validity criteria consisted of endorsement of less than three items on the WSS infrequency scale and omission of no more than 10 items. The application of both sets of validity criteria resulted in a final sample of 89 males and 189 females.

For both samples, Pearson product moment correlations were computed between the Wisconsin anhedonia scales, and each of five MMPI/MMPI-2-based anhedonia scales: RC2, anhedonia, hedonic capacity

(reversed), INTR, and the MMPI-2 social introversion scale (Si).

The correlations between all of the MMPI/MMPI-2 anhedonia measures and each of the Wisconsin anhedonia scales were significant at $p < .0001$. The results from both samples, presented in Table 7.4, indicate that RC2 predicts no better than, and in most cases less well than, the MMPI/MMPI-2 measures of anhedonia that were already available at the time that RC Scales were developed. Scale 0 also predicted scores on the social anhedonia scale somewhat better than RC2, and predicted physical anhedonia scores only slightly less well, in both samples. INTR performed best among the MMPI/MMPI-2 scale for both of the Wisconsin anhedonia scales, in both samples.

Invalid Motivations for Change

Although there are several valid motivations for test revision, a test need not be revised simply because of the passage of time. Hathaway (1972b), for example, when considering the possibility of the revision of the original MMPI, noted that there were flaws in the measure and hoped that the future would bring an improvement (either in the form of a revised version of the MMPI or a new similar test), but he argued that test revision should only be attempted with unconventional thinking about the constructs or unconventional methods of test development. A test need not be revised due to age unless there is a compelling reason to change or a compelling strategy for improvement.

Adams (2000) noted that although the ethical standards of the American Psychological Association do prohibit psychologists from using outdated tests, there are no ethical codes driving the timing of test revision. However, one could still argue that an unnecessary change to an established standard still raises serious ethical implications. After all, when a test is revised, the psychologists who use that test have the ethical responsibility to switch to the new version within a reasonable amount of time; however, if that revision is unnecessary, this may be an onerous burden, both in terms of the time spent to learn the intricacies of the new test and in terms of the monetary cost of replacing one's testing materials. Johnson (1973) lamented this type of situation:

> While test revisions are necessary and desirable, they produce problems for both the practitioner and the researcher. The practitioner must gain familiarity with a new version of the test, thus forsaking much of the clinical acumen he has acquired with the old version. The researcher may be caught midstream in a longitudinal project which forces him either to change test forms or use an obsolete test form.
> (p. 44)

Johnson was not merely making a rhetorical point, but referred to his own frustrations in conducting a long-term study which was severely hindered by a test revision. Similarly, Schaie (1996) encountered this issue in his work with the Seattle longitudinal study:

> One of the limitations (of longitudinal designs) is the fact that outmoded measurement instruments must usually continue to be employed, even though newer (and possibly better) instruments may become available, in order to allow orderly comparisons of the measurement variables over time.
> (p. 205)

Although, as Nelson (2000) noted, there are unresolved issues regarding the continued use of older versions of a test, there may be a need for a discussion of the ethical inappropriateness of unneeded revisions of psychological tests, especially during a time period witnessing a trend toward a shorter lag time between test revisions, as discussed below. Moreover, test developers should consider ideas (such as a test buyback, as proposed by Butcher [2000]) to help offset the costs that the revision imposes on test users.

Scale Redundancy

Adding to the point, made earlier, that a test ought not to be revised unless there is a compelling reason to change, or a compelling strategy for improvement, we would also add that the acceptance of a set of revised scales into standard scoring practice should not be advocated unless their inclusion is supported by compelling evidence of their uniqueness. Several researchers (Butcher & Williams, 2000; Butcher et al., 2006; Sellbom et al., 2006) have indicated the importance of comparing new MMPI-2 scales to all existing widely accepted scales already serving as standards, citing the recommendation of Butcher et al. (1995) on new scale development and validation. Only those new scales that produce scores of greater reliability and validity, or those assessing constructs not measured by existing scales, meet the criteria for new scale inclusion suggested by Butcher and Tellegen (1978).

To the extent that a test revision expands the number of overlapping constructs, the burden is increased both on the test user and on students seeking to learn effective use of the test. Further, the addition of scales measuring constructs adequately covered by scales available in the previous edition of the test compromises the psychometric efficiency of the instrument due to the construct overlap among scales. By such means what might be promoted as an enhancement by those responsible for the revision may actually be a structural deficiency. The literature on test revision appears to overlook the possibility that modification may result in an inferior version of the test; however, it does seem likely that a revised or alternate version of a "standard" that was deemed inferior, whether on psychometric or clinical utility grounds, could subject the test to judgments of deficiency and possibly accelerate movement toward competing instruments.

Returning to the idea of adding scales to a measure where sufficient coverage appears to exist, in the case of the MMPI-2, there are already 111 scales listed in the most recent edition of the MMPI-2 manual (Butcher et al., 2001), a number sufficient to tax the clinician and daunt the student. Indeed, the sheer number of scales, especially when there are substantial redundancies among them, as in the case of the MMPI-2, will, sooner or later, risk placing the test at a competitive disadvantage. The RC Scales have already been added to the Extended Score Report sold by the test's distributor, Pearson Assessments, but were developed too late to be included in the manual. Among the several shortcomings of the RC Scales monograph was the complete omission of comparisons between the RC Scales and other, better known scales that had already accumulated substantial research evidence for their validity and clinical utility such as the MMPI-2 Content, Supplementary, and PSY-5 scales. Despite denials of their redundancy by the RC authors (Sellbom & Ben-Porath, 2005, p. 186), research following the publication of the RC monograph by others (Nichols, 2006a; Rouse et al., 2008), and by the RC authors themselves (Ben-Porath, 2003; Forbey, Ben-Porath, & Tellegen, 2004), has demonstrated that the RC Scales are indeed highly redundant with many of these older, better known scales. The consequence of this omission in the monograph caused the RC Scales to appear more novel than they are. One might contrast this scope of presentation with that of the authors of the monograph describing the MMPI-2 Content Scales (Butcher, Graham, Williams, & Ben-Porath, 1990). In the latter monograph, unlike Tellegen et al., the authors enabled their readers to compare the new content scales to their conceptually and empirically related Wiggins content scale predecessors, and scales measuring the major known sources of variance in the MMPI/MMPI-2 item pool.

Stakeholders in the Test Revision Process

A recent trend in the test revision process has been the growing involvement of corporate owners. Today, Adams (2000) noted, test publishers are often part of large corporations for whom the economic return of the test may prevail over the scientific need as an incentive for revision; the focus having shifted to the test being profitable and expanding the markets into which it can be sold. This "may pit psychologists attempting to honor test standards or ethical standards against nonpsychologists whose appreciation of or allegiance to these standards is entirely elective" (p. 283). For example, Campbell (2002) provided an account of his frustrations and legal complications when the management of the Strong Campbell Interest Inventory was taken on by a commercial organization instead of the university press that had managed it for several years.

Because test revision is a commercial enterprise, Campbell (1972) advised that one of the first steps of the test revision process should be to form a clear agreement among all collaborators and sponsoring organizations regarding royalties, authorship, research funding, and work responsibilities. Ideally, these processes should be open and transparent if consumer confidence in the revision is to be maximized. With any multiauthor work in psychology, he noted, if one were to ask all contributors to estimate their percentage of involvement, the sum would be close to 200%; therefore, it is essential to

broach the uncomfortable discussion topic early in the test development stage. In some cases, the issue of royalties has been sidestepped simply by the authors' declining any personal profit. For example, early in the MMPI-2 development process, the revision committee agreed to forgo royalties from the revision, focusing on the development of a stronger assessment instrument instead of personal gain in the form of financial profit from the revision (Butcher, 2000).

Relatedly, in order to avoid the appearance of conflicts of interest, matters related to grants for research and development in support of the revision, such as advertising grant availability, the integrity and consistency of procedures for reviewing and criteria for funding research proposals, and the preparation and filing of progress reports, should be explicit and documented. Conflicts of interest may be especially in question when consultant reviewers, some of whom may have a financial interest in the revision, fail to recuse themselves from decisions regarding grant proposals that they may themselves submit.

Preparation for Revision

Another recent trend relating to test revisions (and perhaps influenced by the recent trend toward greater corporate involvement in revisions) is the shortening of time intervals between revisions of the same test; as Silverstein and Nelson (2000) noted, revisions of scales are "sophisticated, frequent, and expectable" (p. 303). Although Adams (2000) did not consider this trend to be reversible, he recognized some negative implications of the short "shelf-life" of psychological tests. When there was a longer period of time between revisions, more opportunity existed for the test developers to conscientiously consider the revision, incorporating evidence from independent scientific investigators to inform the revision process. This permitted deliberate planning. In fact, Butcher (2000) considered the amount of time spent on the MMPI-2 restandardization to be one of the reasons for the success of the revised instrument. Discussion and debate about the possibility of revision was initiated in 1969, a full 20 years before the release of the MMPI-2, when a special conference was called to contemplate revising the MMPI. Butcher invited a wide range of contemporary luminaries in the field of personality assessment, David Campbell, Jane Loevinger, and Warren Norman among them, to encourage and consider the broadest variety of expert opinion available at the time (Butcher, 1972). Formal work on the revision was responsive to the previous discussions and spanned the 1980s, with a self-study running concurrently with the formal test revision. It seems unlikely, however, that such deliberate and restrained test revisions will be common as test revisions become more frequent.

Despite pressures to produce a rapid revision, it is important for test developers to solicit feedback from test users and invite constructive comments from those test users early in the revision stage; this would promote a greater level of professional acceptance after the new measure has been developed (Adams, 2000). Likewise, it is important to make intentions for revisions well known in advance so researchers and clinicians are given the opportunity to voice opinions on proposed changes, although the opinions of a few focus-group members should not drastically sway the revision process. For example, Butcher (2000) recounted a difference of opinion that arose during the MMPI-2 restandardization. A few researchers expressed disappointment about the proposal to drop 16 repeated items, noting that these repeated items allowed for the calculation of the Test–Retest (TR) index, an early response consistency measure. However, this view was countered by the view of others, who pointed out the infrequency of use of the TR index and who noted that some test takers complained that the duplication of some items seemed like tricks to trap the respondent. In the end, the decision was made to drop the duplicated items, and confidence in this decision was bolstered by responses to surveys of test users and focus group members.

One of the greatest values of the solicitation of test user feedback is the opportunity to become aware of practical considerations that might not be apparent to the test developer. For example, Campbell (1972) recounted the value of this type of insight in the development of the Strong Vocational Interest Blank. When it was announced that the new version would have 405 items (instead of 400 items on the original form), one of the surveyed test users expressed concern that the new longer form would not be able to be scored using the standard hardware used for scoring the other test, and there did not appear to be any way to reconfigure the answer sheet or the hardware to accommodate the larger number of items. Fortunately, this information was provided early enough in the revision process for a slight modification to be made—the elimination of a handful of items to bring the test to a total of 399. Had the information been not received early enough, it would have been likely to undermine the success of the revision.

In contrast, the development of the recently, and extravagantly, announced MMPI-2-RF (APA Annual Convention, August, 2007), for example, was initiated no earlier than 2002 and appears to have been undertaken with far less review and consultation, including consumer feedback, than that characterizing the MMPI-2. It was released in July, 2008.

Structural Changes
Test Format Changes

In most cases, the test format stays consistent during a test revision. One common format change, however, is the development of computerized administration. Strauss, Spreen, and Hunter (2000) noted that computerized formats cannot be assumed to operate in the same way as the original. For some tests, research does show comparability of the computer-administered and standard-format versions of the test. For example, scores on Raven's Progressive Matrices are very comparable across the computerized and standard formats (Strauss et al., 2000), and a preponderance of research supports the equivalence of MMPI-2 paper-and-pencil and computerized formats (Atlis, Hahn, & Butcher, 2006). For other tests, however, the computerized format changes the nature of the test. For example, scores on the Wisconsin Card Sorting Test are comparable across computerized and face-to-face formats for normal subjects, but autistic children make significantly fewer errors on the computerized form (Strauss et al., 2000). Therefore, test developers who produce computerized revisions of a standard test must provide data to indicate the extent to which scores are or are not comparable across formats.

Item Format Changes

A test developer considering a change in item formats is likely to encounter many personal opinions about the superiority of different formats, but empirical research seems to suggest a comparability of formats. For example, Emons, Sijtsma, and Meijer (2007) did not observe a meaningful difference in the classification accuracy rates between dichotomous formats (in which only two response options are available, such as a "True/False" format) and polytomous formats (in which there is a limited number of response options, but more than two are available, such as a Likert format). Reise et al. (2000), however, pointed to the strengths and weaknesses of each. For example, dichotomous formats can weaken factor analytic research on a scale; for this type of format, it is likely for non-content-based factors to emerge, but polytomous formats are more likely to result in content-based factors. On the other hand, polytomous item formats are likely to introduce the response set of the willingness to endorse extreme or moderate responses, and tests with a large number of response points may be asking the test taker to make fine distinctions in attitudes and self-beliefs that are, frankly speaking, unrealistic. In the end, when faced with a lack of evidence for clear superiority of one format over another, Campbell (2002) chose to use a format that simply had the greatest level of test-taker acceptance.

Changes in the Length of Scales

The length of the revised test must be considered, balancing the desire for a shorter test that may be preferred by the test taker and a longer test that has greater psychometric strength and can measure more clinically relevant constructs. Although it is a truism that scores on longer scales are more psychometrically reliable than those on shorter scales (assuming item equivalence across the different lengths of scales), Emons et al. (2007) demonstrated this empirically. When used for classification purposes, 12-item scales produced dichotomous classifications that were less reliable than scores on 20-item and 40-item versions of the same scale. While there will always be an interval of scores around the cut-point where classifications are prone to error, that interval is smaller (resulting in a greater number of accurate classifications) when the scale is longer. Short scales—15 or fewer items—are often used in clinical psychology, health psychology, medicine, and psychiatry. Emons et al. (2007) acknowledged that sometimes the brevity is preferred because of realistic benefits (e.g., concentration or attention problems resulting from dementia or brain injury). However, in many cases there is no compelling need for a short scale; for example, there is no compelling need for a five-item test anxiety scale or a seven-item scale on alcohol use patterns since most test takers are able to complete longer and more reliable scales. "[E]ven if items have high quality, short tests must be used only for making decisions about people who are located outside the unreliability interval for that test," (p. 117) and with shorter scales there is a greater probability that a large number of people will receive unreliable scores. Both Campbell (1972) and Johnson (1973) recommended ensuring

that the two forms of a test have different numbers, merely to allow easy differentiation of the forms, but a substantial reduction in items might have the negative effect of resulting in a psychometrically weaker scale.

An increased role for financial considerations in decision making around test revision may disturb the inevitable tension between length and coverage to favor the introduction of briefer test products that test takers may view as more "user-friendly." However, such products may entail a significant sacrifice in the number and clinical relevance of the constructs available to the assessor and, in particular, to the potentially informative configural relationships among them. An abbreviated instrument may well compromise the means to a more comprehensive assessment, one based on a greater number of constructs, with many, perhaps most, being measured more reliably, than is possible in an instrument having substantially reduced coverage. When revisions or alternate forms emphasize scale constructs based largely upon item content, reductions in the accuracy of assessments using such test versions can be anticipated. It is well known, for example, that scores on the MMPI-2 Content Scales are readily suppressed (or inflated) when examinees feel motivated to under- or overreport psychopathology; the face validity of the items on content scales makes them vulnerable to response-style distortion. The MMPI-2-RF, published in 2008, would appear to be a case in point for potential reductions in accuracy. Having 40% fewer items than the MMPI-2, the MMPI-2-RF consists of 8 consistency and response-style scales and 42 substantive scales, including the RC Scales. Because all the substantive scales of this form's reduced item pool measure content dimensions, it is likely to prove more vulnerable to response-style distortions than the MMPI-2—which is based upon empirically derived scales with a greater variety of items, including subtle—content (Sellbom, Ben-Porath, Graham, Arbisi, & Bagby, 2005).

Psychometric Data at Time of Release

During the process of gathering normative and psychometric data for the revision of the test, data from the previous version of the test can be used to generate predictions and expectations. Although it is important to ensure that the normative sample is representative of the populations who will be taking the test (Butcher, 2000), data that has accumulated with the previous edition can show the extent to which different subpopulations are expected to differ from each other. For example, Reliability Generalization (RG; Vacha-Haase, 1998) is a meta-analytic procedure that allows for the systematic examination of variability in reliability estimates across different characteristics of research samples. By collecting reliability estimates obtained for diverse samples of test takers, the test reviser is able to determine whether, and by how much, measurement error is affected by such characteristics as gender, ethnicity, education level, and assessment setting. Similarly, a comparison of mean score levels across diverse samples for the original version can lead to some predictions for how the actual scores might be affected by these characteristics. These data can guide the test developer in conscientiously collecting a normative sample that is reflective of the salient characteristics that might influence responses on the test.

Ultimately, however, it is important for psychometric data to be presented using the final form of the test, not merely a provisional form. An item's performance is affected by the context of that item within the test; although test developers and test users often assume that responses to individual items are independent, Knowles and Condon (2000) argued that the test taker reads each item in relation to the items that he or she has already answered—assuming, for example, that a specific item may relate to answers given on a previous item. Similarly, Knowles and Condon (2000) reviewed literature that showed test takers adapt to the test as they are in the process of taking it, becoming more or less situation-specific, and better skilled at attending to the relevant information in a test question while disregarding irrelevant information. Since responses to an item can even be affected by their proximity to items that assess similar or different constructs, final normative data should ideally be collected using the final form of the test.

Professional Acceptance

Although Silverstein and Nelson (2000) were confident about a test revision's likelihood of replacing its predecessor, other writers have argued that the test revision process is a risky endeavor. For example, Adams (2000) noted that psychologists are like other people in their preferences for things that are familiar, and therefore a psychologist is unlikely to embrace a new form of the test if that new form lacks the specific scores and indices that are familiar to him or her. Campbell (1972) offered an even greater note of caution—that the average

test user will be unlikely to tolerate as much change as the reviser will be inclined to make on the test. The test reviser, then, is faced with a difficult dilemma—changing the test enough so that the test users are willing to expend the time and money needed to embrace the new version while not changing it so much that the loyal test users are alienated by too much novelty. Moreover, a second dilemma relates specifically to the timing of acceptance of the new test. According to Butcher (2000), time is required for the typical test user to accept the new form. Although the Strong Campbell Interest Inventory enjoyed a 90% acceptance during its first year after release (Campbell, 2002), this reflected a rare situation, and most revisions are unlikely to be embraced so quickly. However, if the shelf life of a test is shrinking, with new revisions coming more quickly on the heels of previous revisions (Adams, 2000), the test reviser is placed in the dilemma of determining an appropriate way to encourage user acceptance in the shortest possible amount of time. This may be the reason that the last few years have seen a growth in the use of catchy marketing campaigns in professional periodicals and at professional conferences to herald the arrival of a new test edition.

Summary

A decision to revise a test or scale must be made carefully, and only after evaluating the net effect of the gains and losses likely to result from its introduction. Gains are often easy to identify; they organize around resolving known deficiencies and/or converging upon growth opportunities that better position the test for ongoing acceptance. Losses can be harder to anticipate but must be considered in order to determine the most responsible course of action. Once a decision has been made to revise a test or scale, other considerations become prominent, such as researcher preparedness; decisions about format, construct, or item modification; stakeholder concerns; and issues pertaining to professional acceptance.

The recently developed RC Scales for the MMPI-2 (Tellegen et al., 2003) offer an example of a scale revision effort that can be evaluated for its attention to the domains of responsible decision making reviewed in this chapter. In this way, the example set by this significant revision effort serves as a case study from which future scale developers might learn.

The authors of the RC Scales sought to redress a believed deficiency seen to compromise the utility of the Clinical Scales, and to advance the modernization of the instrument by incorporating into their revision paradigm contemporary diagnostic constructs and a theoretical model of affect. We conclude that neither the deficiency goal nor the growth goal driving the scale revision process was accomplished in a way that establishes the RC Scales as unique or deserving of wide-ranging acceptance. We view this outcome to be, at least in part, a reflection of the authors' inadequate attention to the kinds of test revision considerations outlined here.

Notes

1. In the case of Scale 2, the eight correction items, those that Hathaway and McKinley (1942) found to discriminate non-depressed patients who obtained high scores on a preliminary version of Scale 2 from their criterion depressives, were omitted from this analysis as "not . . . relevant to our concerns" (p. 15).
2. It is worth noting that the RC authors do not take the view that all subtle items are created equal, that is, are equally invalid. In the case of RC3, for example, all five of its initial seed items overlap with Hy-S (Weiner, 1948), and three additional items were added from the subtle items of Scale 6 (Pa-S). Thus the final RC3 scale contains more subtle items than obvious ones (8/15). The view taken by the authors is consistent with the view of Dannenbaum and Lanyon (1993) that at least some of the "invalid subtle items" become valid when the direction of their scoring is reversed.

References

Adams, D. K., & Horn, J. L. (1965). Nonoverlapping keys for the MMPI scales. *Journal of Consulting Psychology, 29,* 284.

Adams, K. M. (2000). Practical and ethical issues pertaining to test revisions. *Psychological Assessment, 12,* 281–286.

American Psychiatric Association (2000). *Diagnostic and statistical manual of mental disorders* (4th ed., Text rev.). Washington, DC: American Psychiatric Press, Inc.

Atlis, M. M., Hahn, J., & Butcher, J. N. (2006). Computer-based assessment with the MMPI-2. In J. N. Butcher (Ed.), *MMPI-2: A practitioner's guide* (pp. 445–476). Washington, DC: American Psychological Association.

Bateson, G. (1977). Afterward. In J. Brockman (Ed.), *About Bateson* (p. 243). New York: E. P. Dutton.

Ben-Porath (2003, October). *Psychometric characteristics of the RC Scales.* Paper presented at MMPI-2/MMPI-A Workshops and Symposia, Cleveland, OH.

Berkowitz, L. (2000). *Causes and consequences of feelings.* Studies in emotion and social interaction, Second series. New York: Cambridge University Press.

Butcher, J. N. (1972). Personality assessment: Problems and perspectives. In J. N. Butcher (Ed.), *Objective personality assessment: Changing perspectives* (pp. 1–20). New York: Academic Press.

Butcher, J. N. (1997) *MMPI-2 User's Guide. The Minnesota Report: Reports for Forensic Settings.* Pearson Assessments, Minneapolis, MN.

Butcher, J. N. (1998) *The Butcher Treatment Planning Inventory: Manual.* The Psychological Corporation, San Antonio, TX.

Butcher, J. N. (2000). Revising psychological tests: Lessons learned from the revision of the MMPI. *Psychological Assessment, 12,* 263–271.

Butcher, J. N., Dahlstrom, W. G., Graham, J. R., Tellegen, A., & Kaemmer, B. (1989). *Manual for the Minnesota Multiphasic Personality Inventory-2: MMPI-2. Manual for administration and scoring.* Minneapolis, MN: University of Minnesota Press.

Butcher, J. N., Graham, J. R., & Ben-Porath, Y. S. (1995). Methodological problems and issues in MMPI/MMPI-2/MMPI-A research. *Psychological Assessment, 7,* 320–329.

Butcher, J. N., Graham, J. R., Ben-Porath, Y. S., Tellegen, A., Dahlstrom, W. G., & Kaemmer, B. (2001). *Minnesota Multiphasic Personality Inventory-2: Manual for administration and scoring* (Rev. ed.). Minneapolis, MN: University of Minnesota Press.

Butcher, J. N., Graham, J. R., Dahlstrom, W. G., & Bowman, E. (1990). The MMPI-2 with college students. *Journal of Personality Assessment, 54,* 1–15.

Butcher, J. N., Graham, J. R., Williams, C. L., & Ben-Porath, Y. S. (1990). *Development and use of the MMPI-2 Content Scales.* Minneapolis, MN: University of Minnesota Press.

Butcher, J. N., Hamilton, C. K., Rouse, S. V., & Cumella, E. J. (2006). The deconstruction of the Hy scale of MMPI-2: Failure of RC3 in measuring somatic symptom expression. *Journal of Personality Assessment, 87,* 186–192.

Butcher, J. N., Jeffrey, T., Cayton, T. G., Colligan, S., DeVore, J., & Minnegawa, R. (1990). A study of active duty military personnel with the MMPI-2. *Military Psychology, 2,* 47–61.

Butcher, J. N., & Tellegen, A. (1978). *Essentials of the MMPI-2 and MMPI-A clinical interpretation* (2nd ed.). Minneapolis, MN: University of Minnesota Press.

Butcher, J. N., & Williams, C. L. (2000). *Essentials of MMPI-2 and MMPI-A interpretation* (2nd ed.). Minneapolis, MN: University of Minnesota Press.

Caldwell, A. B. (1997a). [MMPI-2 data research file for clinical patients]. Unpublished raw data.

Caldwell, A. B. (1997b). [MMPI-2 data research file for personnel applicants]. Unpublished raw data.

Caldwell, A. B. (1998). [MMPI-2 data research file for pain patients]. Unpublished raw data.

Caldwell, A. B. (2004). [MMPI-2 data research file for child-custody litigants]. Unpublished raw data.

Caldwell, A. B. (2006). Maximal measurement or meaningful measurement: The interpretive challenges of the MMPI-2 Restructured Clinical (RC) Scales. *Journal of Personality Assessment, 87,* 193–201.

Campbell, D. P. (1972). The practical problems of revising an established psychological test. In J. N. Butcher (Ed.), *Objective personality assessment: Changing perspectives* (pp. 117–130). New York: Academic Press.

Campbell, D. P. (2002). The history and development of the Campbell Interest and Skills Survey. *Journal of Career Assessment, 10,* 150–168.

Carroll, J. M., Yik, M. S. M., Russell, J. M., & Feldman Barrett L. (1999). On the psychometric principles of affect. *Review of General Psychology, 3,* 14–22.

Carroll, L. (1960). *Alice through the looking glass.* New York: New American Library.

Chapman, L. J., Chapman, J. P., & Raulin, M. L. (1976). Scales for physical and social anhedonia. *Journal of Abnormal Psychology, 85,* 374–382.

Christiansen, E., & Cohen, M. L. (2003). [MMPI-2 data research file for police officer applicants]. Unpublished raw data.

Cripe, L. (2000). [MMPI-2 data research file for neuropsychology outpatients]. Unpublished raw data.

Dahlstrom, W. G. (1972). Whither the MMPI? In J. N. Butcher (Ed.), *Objective personality assessment: Changing perspectives* (pp. 85–115). New York: Academic Press.

Dannenbaum, S. E., & Lanyon, R. I. (1993). The use of subtle items in detecting deception. *Journal of Personality Assessment, 61*, 501–510.

Davis, J. (2001). [MMPI-2 data research file for criminal psychiatric inpatients]. Unpublished raw data.

Digman, J. M. (1990). Personality structure: Emergence of the Five-Factor Model. *Annual Review of Psychology, 41*, 417–440.

Dohrenwend, B. P., Shrout, P. E., Egri, G., & Mendelsohn, F. S. (1980). Non-specific psychological distress and other dimensions of psychopathology. *Archives of General Psychiatry, 37*, 1229–1236.

Dworkin, R. H., & Saczynski, K. (1984). Individual differences in hedonic capacity. *Journal of Personality Assessment, 48*, 620–626.

Emons, W. H. M., Sijtsma, K., & Meijer, R. R. (2007). On the consistency of individual classification using short scales. *Psychological Methods, 12*, 105–120.

Fabrigar, L. R., Visser, P. S., & Browne, M. W. (1997). Conceptual and methodological issues in testing the circumplex structure of data in personality and social psychology. *Personality and Social Psychology Review, 1*, 184–203.

Finn, S. E., & Kamphuis, J. H. (2006). The MMPI-2 Restructured Clinical (RC) Scales and restraints to innovation, or "What have they done to my song?" *Journal of Personality Assessment, 87*, 202–210.

Forbey, J. D., Ben-Porath, Y. S., & Tellegen, A. (2004, March). *Associations between and the relative contributions of the MMPI-2 Restructured Clinical (RC) scales and content scales.* Paper presented at the Society for Personality Assessment Meeting, Miami, FL.

Frank, J. D. (1974a). Common features of psychotherapies and their patients. *Psychotherapy and Psychosomatics, 24*, 368–371.

Frank, J. D. (1974b). Psychotherapy: The restoration of morale. *American Journal of Psychiatry, 131*, 271–274.

Frank, J. D., & Frank, J. B. (1991). *Persuasion and healing: A comparative study of psychotherapy* (3rd ed.). Baltimore, MD: Johns Hopkins University Press.

Friedman, A., & Damsteegt, D. (2002). [MMPI-2 data research file for clergy applicants]. Unpublished raw data.

Gelbort, M. (2002). [MMPI-2 data research file for death row inmates]. Unpublished raw data.

Goldberg, L. R. (1993). The structure of phenotypic personality traits. *American Psychologist, 48*, 26–34.

Gordon, R. M. (2006). False assumptions about psychopathology, hysteria and the MMPI-2 Restructured Clinical Scales. *Psychological Reports, 98*, 870–872.

Green, D. P., & Salovey, P. (1999). In what sense are positive and negative affect independent? A reply to Tellegen, Watson, and Clark. *Psychological Science, 10*, 304–306.

Greenberg, S. A., Lees-Haley, P., & Otto, R. (2005). [MMPI-2 data research file for personal-injury claimants]. Unpublished raw data.

Greene, R. L. (1992). [MMPI-2 data research file for state hospital psychiatric inpatients]. Unpublished raw data.

Greene, R. L., Banken, J., & Arrendondo, R. (1996). [MMPI-2 data research file for alcoholic inpatients]. Unpublished raw data.

Gurtman, M. B. (1994). The circumplex as a tool for studying normal and abnormal personality: A methodological primer. In S. Strack & M. Lorr (Eds.), *Differentiating normal and abnormal personality* (pp. 243–263). New York: Springer.

Harkness, A. R., McNulty, J. L., & Ben-Porath, Y. S. (1995). The Personality Psychopathology Five (PSY-5): Constructs and MMPI-2 scales. *Psychological Assessment, 7*, 104–114.

Hathaway, S. R. (1972a). Forward to the new edition. In W. G. Dahlstrom, G. S. Welsh, & L. E. Dahlstrom (Eds.), *An MMPI Handbook, Vol. 1.* Minneapolis, MN: University of Minnesota Press.

Hathaway, S. R. (1972b). Where have we gone wrong? The mystery of the missing progress. In J. N. Butcher (Ed.), *Objective personality assessment: Changing perspectives* (pp. 21–43). New York: Academic Press.

Hathaway, S. R., & McKinley, J. C. (1942). A mutiphasic personality schedule (Minnesota): III. The measurement of symptomatic depression. *Journal of Psychology: Interdisciplinary and Applied, 14*, 73–84.

Heller, W., Schmidtke, J. I., Nitschke, J. B., Koven, N. S., & Miller, G. A. (2002). States, traits, and symptoms: Investigating the neural correlates of emotion, personality, and psychopathology. In D. Cervone & W. Mischel (Eds.), *Advances in personality science* (pp. 106–126). New York: Guilford.

Helmes, E., & Reddon, J. R. (1993). A perspective on developments in assessing psychopathology: A critical review of the MMPI and MMPI-2. *Psychological Bulletin, 113*, 453–471.

Hoppe, C., Lee, M., Olesen, N., Singer, J., & Walters, M. G. (2004). [MMPI-2 data research file for child-custody litigants]. Unpublished raw data.

Huelsman, T. J., Furr, R. M., & Nemanick, R. C., Jr. (2003). Measurement of dispositional affect: Construct validity and convergence with a circumplex model of affect. *Educational and Psychological Measurement, 63*, 655–673.

Johnson, J. H., Null, C., Butcher, J. N., & Johnson, K. N. (1984). Replicated item level factor analysis of the full MMPI. *Journal of Personality and Social Psychology, 47*, 105–114.

Johnson, R. W. (1973). Recommendations for test revisions. *Measurement and evaluation in guidance, 6*, 44–46.

Joiner, T. E., Jr., Walker, R. L., Pettit, J. W., Perez, M., & Cukrowicz, K. C. (2005). Evidence-based assessment of depression in adults. *Psychological Assessment, 17*, 267–277.

Knowles, E. S., & Condon, C. A. (2000). Does the rose still smell as sweet? Item variability across forms and revisions. *Psychological Assessment, 12*, 245–252.

Kring, A. M., Feldman Barrett, L., & Gard, D. E. (2003). On the broad applicability of the affective circumplex: Representations of affective knowledge among schizophrenia patients. *Psychological Science, 14*, 207–214.

Kwapil, T. R., Chapman, L. J., & Chapman, J. (1999). Validity and usefulness of the Wisconsin manual for assessing psychotic-like experiences. *Schizophrenia Bulletin, 25*, 363–375.

Larsen, R. J., & Diener, E. (1992). Promises and problems with the circumplex model of emotion. In M. S. Clark (Ed.), *Review of personality and social psychology: Emotion* (Vol. 13, pp. 25–29). Newbury Park, CA: Sage.

McKenna, T., & Butcher, J. (April, 1987). *Continuity of the MMPI with alcoholics.* Paper given at the 22nd Annual Symposium on Recent Developments in the Use of the MMPI, Seattle, Washington.

McNulty, J. L., & Harkness, A. R. (2002). The MMPI-2 Personality Psychopathology-Five (PSY-5) scales and the Five Factor Model. In B. de Raad & M. Perugini (Eds.), *Big Five assessment* (pp. 436–452). Ashland, OH: Hogrefe & Huber.

Meehl, P. E. (1962). Schizotaxia, schizotypy, schizophrenia. *American Psychologist, 17,* 827–838.

Merritt, R. D., Balogh, D. W., & DeVinney, S. E. (1993). Use of the MMPI to assess the construct validity of the revised social anhedonia scale as an index of schizotypy. *Journal of Personality Assessment, 60,* 227–238.

Millon, T. (1994). *MCMI-III: Manual.* Minneapolis, MN: National Computer Systems.

Nelson, L. D. (2000). Introduction to the special section on methods and implications of revising assessment instruments. *Psychological Assessment, 12,* 235–236.

Nichols, D. S. (2006a). The trials of separating bath water from baby: A review and critique of the MMPI-2 Restructured Clinical Scales. *Journal of Personality Assessment, 87,* 121–138.

Nichols, D. S. (2006b). Commentary on Rogers, Sewell, Harrison, and Jordan. *Journal of Personality Assessment, 87,* 172–174.

Norman, W. T. (1972). Psychometric considerations for a revision of the MMPI. In J. N. Butcher (Ed.), *Objective personality assessment: Changing perspectives* (pp. 59–83). New York: Academic Press.

Okazaki, S., & Sue, S. (2000). Implications of test revisions for assessment with Asian Americans. *Psychological Assessment, 12,* 272–280.

Pearson Assessments, News Release. Retrieved on January 29, 2003, www.pearsonassessments.com/news/pr012203.htm

Ranson, M. B. (2008). *The MMPI-2 Restructured Clinical (RC) Scales: A critique of the existing RC Scales and an alternate proposal for reconstruction.* Unpublished doctoral dissertation, Fielding Graduate University, Santa Barbara, CA.

Reise, S. P., Waller, N. G., & Comrey, A. L. (2000). Factor analysis and scale revision. *Psychological Assessment, 12,* 287–297.

Remington, N. A., Fabrigar, L. R., & Visser, P. S. (2000). Reexamining the circumplex model of affect. *Journal of Personality and Social Psychology, 79,* 286–300.

Ribot, T.-A. (1897). *The psychology of the emotions.* New York: Charles Scribner's Sons.

Robin, R. W., Greene, R. L., Albaugh, B., Caldwell, A., & Goldman, D. (2003). Use of the MMPI-2 in American Indians: I. Comparability of the MMPI-2 between two tribes and with the MMPI-2 normative group. *Psychological Assessment, 15,* 351–359.

Rogers, R., Sewell, K. W., Harrison, K. S., & Jordan, M. J. (2006). The MMPI–2 restructured clinical scales: A paradigmatic shift in scale development. *Journal of Personality Assessment, 87,* 139–147.

Rouse, S. V., Greene, R. L., Butcher, J. N., Nichols, D. S., & Williams, C. L. (2008). What do the MMPI-2 restructured clinical scales reliably measure? *Journal of Personality Assessment, 90,* 435–442.

Russell, J. A. (1980). A circumplex model of affect. *Journal of Personality and Social Psychology, 39,* 1161–1178.

Russell, J. A. (2003). Core affect and the psychological construction of emotion. *Psychological Review, 110,* 145–172.

Russell, J. A., & Feldman Barrett, L. (1999). Core affect, prototypical emotion episodes, and other things called *emotion:* Dissecting the elephant. *Journal of Personality and Social Psychology, 76,* 805–819.

Russell, J. A., & Carroll, J. M. (1999). On the bipolarity of positive and negative affect. *Psychological Bulletin, 125,* 3–30.

Schaie, K. W. (1996). *Intellectual development in adulthood: The Seattle longitudinal study.* New York: Cambridge University Press.

Schinka, J. A. (2004). [MMPI-2 data research file for VA psychiatric inpatients]. Unpublished raw data.

Schmidt, F. L., Le, H., & Ilies, R. (2003). Beyond alpha: An empirical examination of the effects of different sources of measurement error on reliability estimates for measures of individual differences constructs. *Psychological Methods, 8,* 206–224.

Sellbom, M., & Ben-Porath, Y. S. (2005). Mapping the MMPI-2 Restructured Clinical Scales onto normal personality traits: Evidence of construct validity. *Journal of Personality Assessment, 85,* 179–187.

Sellbom, M., Ben-Porath, Y. S., & Graham, J. R. (2006). Correlates of the MMPI-2 Restructured Clinical (RC) Scales in a college counseling setting. *Journal of Personality Assessment, 86,* 89–99.

Sellbom, M., Ben-Porath, Y. S., Graham, J. R., Arbisi, P. A., & Bagby, R. M. (2005). Susceptibility of the MMPI-2 Clinical, Restructured Clinical (RC), and Content scales to overreporting and underreporting. *Assessment, 12,* 79–85.

Sellbom, M., Graham, J. R., & Schenk, P. W. (2005). Symptom correlates of MMPI-2 scales and codes types in a private practice setting. *Journal of Personality Assessment, 84,* 163–171.

Sellbom, M., Graham, J. R., & Schenk, P. W. (2006). Incremental validity of the MMPI-2 restructured clinical (RC) scales in a private practice sample. *Journal of Personality Assessment, 86,* 196–205.

Silverstein, M. L., & Nelson, L. D. (2000). Clinical and research implications of revising psychological tests. *Psychological Assessment, 12,* 298–303.

Simms, L. J. (2006). Bridging the divide: Comments on the Restructured Clinical Scales of the MMPI-2. *Journal of Personality Assessment, 87,* 211–216.

Simms, L. J., Casillas, A., Clark, L. A., Watson, D., & Doebbeling, B. N. (2005). Psychometric evaluation of the Restructured Clinical Scales of the MMPI-2. *Psychological Assessment, 17,* 345–358.

Soldz, S., Budman, S., Demby, A., & Merry, J. (1993). Representation of personality disorders in circumplex and Five Factor space: Explorations with a clinical sample. *Psychological Assessment, 5,* 41–52.

Solomon, G. (2004). [MMPI-2 data research file for neuropsychology outpatients]. Unpublished raw data.

Stanton, J. M., Bachiochi, P. D., Robie, C., Perez, L. M., & Smith, P. C. (2002). Revising the JDI Work Satisfaction subscale: Insights into stress and control. *Educational and Psychological Measurement, 62,* 877–895.

Strauss, E., Spreen, O., & Hunter, M. (2000). Implications of test revisions for research. *Psychological Assessment, 12,* 237–244.

Tellegen, A., Ben-Porath, Y. S., McNulty, J. L., Arbisi, P. A., Graham, J. R., & Kaemmer, B. (2003). *The MMPI-2 Restructured Clinical (RC) Scales: Development, validation, and interpretation*. Minneapolis, MN: University of Minnesota Press.

Tellegen, A., Ben-Porath, Y. S., Sellbom, M., Arbisi, P. A., McNulty, J. L., & Graham, J. R. (2006). Further evidence on the validity of the MMPI-2 Restructured Clinical (RC) scales: Addressing questions raised by Rogers, Sewell, Harrison and Jordan and Nichols. *Journal of Personality Assessment, 87,* 148–171.

Thayer, R. E. (1996). *The origin of everyday moods: Managing energy, tension, and stress.* New York: Oxford University Press.

Vacha-Haase, T. (1998). Reliability generalization: Exploring variance in measurement error affecting score reliability across studies. *Educational and Psychological Measurement, 58,* 6–20.

Wallace, A., & Liljequist, L. (2005). A comparison of the correlational structures and elevation patterns of the MMPI-2 Restructured Clinical (RC) and Clinical Scales. *Assessment, 12,* 290–294.

Waller, N. G. (1999). Searching for structure in the MMPI. In S. E. Embretson & S. L. Hershberger (Eds.), *The new rules of measurement: What every psychologist and educator should know* (pp. 185–217). Mahwah, NJ: Lawrence Erlbaum.

Watson, C. G., Klett, W. G., & Lorei, T. W. (1970). Toward an operational definition of anhedonia. *Psychological Reports, 26,* 371–376.

Watson, D. (1988). The vicissitudes of mood measurement: Effects of varying descriptors, time frames, and response formats of measures of positive and negative affect. *Journal of Personality and Social Psychology, 55,* 128–141.

Watson, D., Clark, L. A., & Tellegen, A. (1988). Development and validation of brief measures of positive and negative affect: The PANAS scales. *Journal of Personality and Social Psychology, 54,* 1063–1070.

Watson, D., & Tellegen, A. (1985). Toward a consensual structure of mood. *Psychological Bulletin, 98,* 219–235.

Watson, D., & Tellegen, A. (1999). Issues in the dimensional structure of affect B effects of descriptors, measurement error, and response formats: Comment on Russell and Carroll (1999). *Psychological Bulletin, 125,* 601–610.

Watson, D., & Walker, L. M. (1996). The long-term stability and predictive validity of trait measures of affect. *Journal of Personality and Social Psychology, 70,* 567–577.

Watson, D., Wiese, D., Vaidya, J., & Tellegen, A. (1999). The two general activation systems of affect: Structural findings, evolutionary considerations, and psychobiological evidence. *Journal of Personality and Social Psychology, 76,* 820–838.

Wechsler, D. (1997). *Wechsler Adult Intelligence Scale* (3rd ed.). San Antonio, TX: Psychological Corporation.

Weiner, D. N. (1948). Subtle and obvious keys for the Minnesota Multiphasic Personality Inventory. *Journal of Consulting Psychology, 12,* 164–170.

Welsh, G. S. (1952). A factor study of the MMPI using scales with item overlap eliminated. *American Psychologist, 7,* 341.

Welsh, G. S. (1956). Factor dimensions A and R. In G. S. Welsh & W. G. Dahlstrom (Eds.), *Basic readings on the MMPI in psychology and medicine* (pp. 264–281). Minneapolis, MN: University of Minnesota Press.

Widiger, T. A. & Hagemoser, S. (1977). Personality disorders and the interpersonal circumplex. In R. Plutchik & H. R. Conte (Eds.), *Circumplex models of personality and emotions* (pp. 299–325). Washington, DC: American Psychological Association.

Wiggins. J. S., Steiger, J. H., & Gaelick, L. (1981). Evaluating circumplexity in personality data. *Multivariate Behavioral Research, 16,* 263–289.

Yik, M. S. M., & Russell, J. A. (2003). Chinese affect circumplex: 1. Structure of recalled momentary affect. *Asian Journal of Social Psychology, 6,* 185–200.

Yik, M. S. M., Russell, J. A., Ahn, C. K., Dols, J. M. F., & Suzuki, N. (2002). Relating the Five-Factor Model of personality to a circumplex model of affect: A five-language study. In R. R. McCrae & J. Allik (Eds.), *The Five-Factor Model of personality across cultures. International and cultural psychology series* (pp. 79–104). New York: Kluwer Academic/Plenum.

Yik, M. S. M., Russell, J. A., Oceja, L. V., & Dols, J. M. F. (2000). Momentary affect in Spanish: Scales, structure, and relationship to personality. *European Journal of Psychological Assessment, 16,* 160–176.

Incorporating Base Rate Information in Daily Clinical Decision Making

Stephen E. Finn

Abstract

This chapter discusses the need for practitioners to consider the relative frequency of phenomena (base rates) in particular clinical settings in order to make diagnoses and interpret psychological test scores appropriately. Topics discussed include what are base rates, base rates and predictive power, implications of base rates for clinical practice and test use, and how to use base rates to benefit you and your clients.

Keywords: base rates, clinical decision making, clinical judgment, clinical prediction, confirmatory bias, cutting scores, diagnosis

What Are Base Rates?

What are your chances of being hit by lightning? Of winning the lottery? Of developing schizophrenia? The probabilities of these events, usually expressed in a percentage, are called base rates. Base rates are often calculated in clinical settings. Thus, if 5 out of every 100 of your clients try to commit suicide, the base rate of suicide attempts in your practice is 5%. If you work in an inpatient hospital where three out of every five clients have schizophrenia, the base rate of schizophrenia is 60%. Base rates are defined for specified populations and are restricted to them. For example, the base rate of schizophrenia in some inpatient settings may be 60%, but the base rate of schizophrenia in the general population is about 1%. Thus, if we know nothing else about a group of 100 people than that they are alive, we would predict that one person in that group has schizophrenia. However, if we consider people who have one biological parent with schizophrenia, we would predict a much higher probability of schizophrenia, for the base rate of schizophrenia in this group of individuals is 5.6% (Gottesman & Shields, 1982). To give another example, the base rate of suicide attempts for inpatients with major depression may be as high as 25%, but it's generally much lower in outpatient settings

(e.g., in my outpatient practice, it is around 3%). Thus, a base rate is the a priori chance or prior odds that a member of a specified population will have a certain characteristic, if we know nothing else about this person other than that he or she is a member of the population we are examining.

Base rates have important implications for a wide variety of issues in clinical practice. Although sometimes overlooked, base rates affect the prediction of behaviors (e.g., suicide), the interpretation of test data (e.g., Minnesota Multiphasic Personality Inventory-2 [MMPI-2] scores), and the making of diagnostic decisions.

Base Rates and Predictive Power

Suppose that from previous records you know that 5% of the inpatient population of your hospital will assault a staff person at some point in time. You could randomly predict that 1 of every 20 clients will commit assault and that all others will not. This would lead to the estimates depicted in Table 8.1. The column percentages show the base rates of actual assault and no assault (5% and 95%, respectively). In making your predictions you would match these base rates, as the row percentages indicate. To calculate the probability of the different cells in the table, cross-multiply the column and

Table 8.1. Predicting assault by base rates alone.

	Assault	No assault	Row %
Predicted assault	0.25% True positive *Cell A*	4.75% False positive *Cell B*	5%
Predicted no assault	4.75% False negative *Cell C*	90.25% True negative *Cell D*	95%
Column %	5%	95%	100%

Notes: True positive = cases for which assault was predicted and occurred, False positive = cases for which assault was predicted and none occurred, True negative = cases for which no assault was predicted and no assault occurred, False negative = cases for which no assault was predicted and assault did occur.

row percentages, since your predictions will be made randomly and are consistent with the axiom of independent probabilities.[1] Cell A shows the probability of your predicting assault for a client who will actually assault a staff person (0.25%). Cell D shows the probability of your predicting no assault for a client who will not make an assault (90.25%). Thus, your predictions of assault, made with base rates alone, would be right 90.5% of the time (Cell A + Cell D = total accuracy).

Now suppose a colleague, unfamiliar with the concept of base rates, claims that he can identify future assaulters by having a 5-min conversation with each patient. Suppose further that he is able to successfully identify all (100%) assaulters (Cell A is 100% of 5%), but that he incorrectly classifies one out of every eight (12.5%) of the nonassaulters as assaulters (Cell B is 12.5% of 95%). As can be seen in Table 8.2, his overall predictive accuracy, despite hours of interviews, will be lower than yours (88.1%, obtained by summing true positives or Cell A, and true negatives, or Cell D).

This is a counterintuitive point: Decisions derived from more information may actually be less

accurate than those derived from less information. A procedure that has predictive power beyond the base rate accuracy is called "efficient." Clearly, in the above example, the colleague's interview would not be considered efficient relative to the base rates. However, if we were exclusively interested in predicting true positives (Cell A), he would be considered efficient, for by his method 100% of the assaulters were successfully identified versus only 5% of the assaulters successfully identified by base rates alone. In other words, efficiency depends on the purpose of the test or procedure; we will return to this issue when we discuss utilities. Let us assume for now that we are interested in the overall accuracy of our classifications: When is it useful (efficient) to use a test? When does it increase the number of correct decisions?[2]

Implications of Base Rates for Clinical Practice
Predicting Phenomena with Low Base Rates Is Difficult

In general, it is easier to increase predictive accuracy when the events to be predicted are moderately

Table 8.2. Using interview data to predict assault.

	Assault	No assault	Row %
Predicted assault	5% True positive *Cell A*	11.9% False positive *Cell B*	16.9%
Predicted no assault	0% False negative *Cell C*	83.1% True negative *Cell D*	83.1%
Column %	5%	95%	100%

Notes: True positive = cases for which assault was predicted and occurred, False positive = cases for which assault was predicted and none occurred, True negative = cases for which no assault was predicted and no assault occurred, False negative = cases for which no assault was predicted and assault did occur.

likely to occur (i.e., occur with a probability close to 50%) than when the events are unlikely to occur (i.e., occur with a probability closer to 0%). This is easy to see from the example in the previous section. It is very difficult to design a test that will improve upon the overall accuracy of base rate predictions (such as those in Table 8.1) when the base rate is very low. As shown in the table, simply predicting "no assault" all the time will result in 95% predictive accuracy.

Meehl and Rosen (1955), in their paper on antecedent probabilities, derived a helpful rule from Bayes' theorem to help decide whether a test adds to predictive accuracy. In statistical terms, a test or procedure increases the overall number of correct decisions when

$$\frac{\text{Base rate of event}}{\text{Base rate of}} > \frac{\text{false positives using}}{\text{true positives using}} \quad (1)$$
$$\frac{}{\text{no event}} \qquad \frac{}{\text{the procedure}}$$

In other words, a test or procedure predicts better than the base rate when the fraction of the base rate of occurrence to the base rate of nonoccurrence exceeds the fraction of the rates of false positives to the rates of true positives. In our example we would like to know whether

$$\frac{\text{Base rate of assault}}{\text{Base rate of}} > \frac{\text{false positives using}}{\text{the interview}} \quad (2)$$
$$\frac{}{\text{no assault}} \qquad \frac{}{\text{true positives using}}$$

This would mean that the fraction of false positives (i.e., erroneously predicted assaulters) to true positives (i.e., successfully predicted assaulters) should be lower than 5%/95% = 0.05%. Let us verify this for the colleague. His false-positive rate (Cell B) is 11.9%, his true-positive rate is 5% (Cell A), which when divided results in 2.4%. This is greater than 0.05%; thus, the colleague's predictions are not consistent with the rule for efficient tests. It is again demonstrated that his interviews lead to fewer correct decisions than merely following base rate predictions.

One way of dealing with the problem of predicting rare events is to increase the base rate—closer to a probability of 50%—by formulating a more restrictive definition of the population for which you are trying to predict the behavior. In our example, the colleague might get better results if he limits his predictions to patients who

already have a history of assault. By thus making the definition more restrictive, he is likely to find more positive cases in his population, that is, to obtain a higher base rate. There would be a cost to this restriction—his interview could only be used with a subset of the entire psychiatric population—but it most likely would result in greater predictive accuracy.

Optimal Test Cutting Scores Vary by Base Rates

Very commonly, psychological tests that produce a range of numerical scores are used to classify patients into dichotomous categories. When this is done, one must set a "cutting score" and place people who obtain a score equal to or higher than the cutting score in one category and all other people in the other category. For example, in one school in my area, students are eligible for classes for the "gifted" only if their IQ test scores are equal to or above 130.

For reasons similar to those outlined earlier, optimal cutting scores for psychological tests depend on the base rate of occurrence of the behavior or trait you are trying to predict with the test. To explain this, we will examine what happens when one overlooks the effects of base rates upon making predictions. Exner and Wylie (1977) attempted to predict suicide using multiple indicators from the Rorschach. They compared Rorschach protocols of successful suicides ($n1 = 59$) with the protocols of patients who made suicide attempts that failed ($n2 = 31$), the protocols of depressed patients ($n3 = 50$), the protocols of schizophrenic patients ($n4 = 50$), and the protocols of normals ($n5 = 50$) to identify an optimal set of predictors of suicide (which later came to be known as the suicide constellation, or S-CON).

On the basis of the above groups, Exner and Wylie proposed a cutting score of 8 on the S-CON for identifying a person as being at risk for a serious suicide attempt. Their sample had a base rate of 24.6% of suicide (59 out of 240). How can we determine overall predictive accuracy, taking base rates into account? First, let's make a table that crosses prediction of suicide with actual suicide, just as we did with assault in Tables 8.1 and 8.2. The overall accuracy can be calculated by multiplying the correctly predicted percentage of suicide cases with the base rate of suicide and adding to this the product of the percentage of correct "no suicide" predictions with the base rate of "no suicide." Table 8.3 shows the results for three different base rates.

Table 8.3. Exner and Wylie's predictive accuracy for different base rates.

Score on S-CON	Base rate = 24.6%			Base rate = 5%			Base rate = 1%		
	%True positives	%True negatives	%Total accuracy	%True positives	%True negatives	%Total accuracy	%True positives	%True negatives	%Total accuracy
6	23	35	58	05	44	48	01	45	46
7	20	48	68	04	60	64	01	63	64 ·
8	18	63	81	04	79	83	01	83	83
9	16	69	85*	03	87	90	01	90	91
10	13	72	85*	03	90	93	01	95	95
11	06	73	79	01	92	94*	00	96	96*

Note: The total percentages are not always equal to the sum of the true positives and true negatives because of rounding errors.
* Denotes highest overall accuracy (hit rate).

As you can see in the table, a cutting score of 9 or 10 appears to maximize the overall hit rate in Exner and Wylie's sample, but at the cost of fewer true-positive predictions than their proposed cutting score of 8.[3] More important, for settings in which the base rate of suicide is lower than 24.6%—and I assume that there (fortunately) are many such settings—a different cutting score should be used. For example, in a setting with a base rate of 5% or 1%, a cutting score of 11 signs maximizes the overall predictive accuracy. Clearly, base rates are essential in deciding on optimal cutting scores for test predictions. Awareness of this issue can greatly improve our clinical decision making.

Where do we encounter base rate effects in clinical practice? As clinicians, we are often faced with situations in which the same numbers have different meanings in different settings (because different settings are likely to have different base rates). Two everyday examples will suffice: MMPI-2 scores and clinical diagnoses. It has long been known that MMPI-2 elevations should be interpreted differently across settings. This is reflected in statements in MMPI-2 code books like "in inpatient settings, it is likely that the patient has . . ." or "in women, this score tends to be associated with . . ." Why this type of qualification? Because the claims made are only valid for the patient population under study; with different base rates, different cutting scores or interpretations are necessary.

Another illustration was provided in a study on the Rorschach trauma content index (TCI; Kamphuis, Kugeares, & Finn, 2000): Predictive accuracy of the TCI in detecting sexual abuse greatly depends on the local base rate (and even at best, is insufficient for definitively identifying clients who have been sexually abused).

Although it is not yet widely recognized, the DSM-IV-TR (American Psychiatric Association, 2000) diagnostic rules are also (in the best of cases) dependent on minimizing error for a certain base rate. For example, a client must meet five or more of nine criteria to be given the diagnosis of borderline personality disorder (BPD). It is unclear from the DSM-IV-TR for what setting or base rate this cutting score was chosen. However, as is clear from the S-CON example, this decision rule may not apply equally well across clinical settings if they have significantly different base rates of BPD (Finn, 1982; Widiger, Hurt, Frances, Clarkin, & Gilmore, 1984). In a clinical setting that sees very few clients with BPD, the best diagnostic rule may be eight or more criteria. In a setting that sees a great number of clients with BPD, a cutting score of four or three criteria may maximize diagnostic accuracy.

Utilities Can Also Affect Cutting Scores

Back to the Exner and Wylie (1977) study: The earlier discussion assumed that we strive to optimize the overall rate of correct diagnostic decisions. However, overall predictive accuracy may not be the appropriate criterion for evaluating the usefulness of a psychological test. Surely, failing to predict a suicide is of much more consequence than overpredicting suicide. Conversely, some might argue that underdiagnosing schizophrenia is less of a problem than overdiagnosing the disorder, in view of the societal "labeling costs" of being diagnosed schizophrenic. Hence, the usefulness of a certain test or procedure depends not only on base rates but also on the relative seriousness of the types of error it produces. If a researcher designs a test to rule out a certain disorder, he or she should pay more attention to the rate of false negatives than to the rate of false positives.

The issues outlined above refer to the asymmetry of utilities (i.e., costs and benefits) of Type I (false-negative) and Type II (false-positive) errors. If you do not specify a decision about the weights that you attach to the two types of error, a default decision of equal weighting will result: the so-called utility-balanced diagnostic rule (Finn, 1983).

Salient Personal Experience Tends to Be Weighed More Than Base Rates

A great deal of research now shows that human decision makers are quite poor in using base rates to reach informed decisions. For example, in one of a series of classic studies, Kahneman and Tversky (1972, 1973) asked subjects to estimate the base rate of students in various graduate school programs, such as law, social work, computer science, and engineering. Subjects then read the following short biography:

> Tom W. is of high intelligence, although lacking in true creativity. He has a need for order and clarity, and for neat and tidy systems in which every detail finds its appropriate place. His writing is rather dull and mechanical, occasionally enlivened by somewhat corny puns and by flashes of imagination of the sci-fi type.
> (*Kahneman & Tversky*, 1973, p. 283)

After this, subjects made two ratings: (1) the degree to which Tom W. was similar to their experience of students in the different graduate programs; and (2) the likelihood that Tom W. was a graduate student in law, social work, computer science, and so on. As you might anticipate, subjects weighed their personal experience more heavily than the estimated base rates in judging the likelihood of Tom W. pursuing various areas of study. For example, Tom W. was given the highest likelihood of studying computer science, although subjects estimated that only 7% of graduate students were in that area. Subjects considered him least likely to be studying social work or humanities, although they judged the base rates in these areas to be 17% and 20%, respectively. The overall correlation between base rates and likelihood ratings was $r = -.65$, while the correlation between similarity and likelihood ratings was $r = .97$.

The implications of this type of error for clinical practice are clear and have been expounded upon by others (Arkes, 1981; Garb, 1998). Let us return to the Exner and Wylie suicide constellation index for an example. You may tell fellow clinicians that in their outpatient setting (with a base rate of suicide of 5%) only 4% of clients with an S-CON score of 8 are likely to make serious suicide attempts (see Table 8.3). However, clinicians who have dealt with a suicide attempt from a past client with an S-CON score of 8 may still claim that the suicide risk with such clients is extremely high and urge that they

be hospitalized immediately. Past suicide attempts are very salient for clinicians and tend to override any information about base rates.[4]

Subjective Base Rate Estimates Are Difficult to Shift

Subjective base rates are probability estimates we develop and hold internally, based on our experience with a certain population. Thus, a clinician will probably have a subjective estimate of the base rate of psychosis in his or her clinical setting from accumulated experience working with clients. One well-known problem in clinical decision making occurs when practitioners develop relatively accurate subjective base rates in one setting but fail to shift their base rate estimates when making decisions in a different setting.

As an example, imagine that two different clinicians, Dr. Smith and Dr. Jones, are shown a videotape of diagnostic interviews of five clients who have mixed symptomatology of psychosis and severe dissociation. Dr. Smith specializes in the treatment of psychosis and primarily has seen psychotic clients for the last 10 years of her professional life. Dr. Jones heads an inpatient program for the treatment of dissociative disorders, and most patients referred to the program have been previously diagnosed as having a dissociative disorder. Research has shown that Dr. Smith is more likely to diagnose the five clients as psychotic and Dr. Jones is more likely to diagnose them as dissociative (Katz, Cole, & Lowery, 1969). These biases probably do not reflect Dr. Smith's or Dr. Jones' salient experience with one or two clients, nor do they indicate that Dr. Jones and Dr. Smith are ignoring base rate information altogether. Rather, the two clinicians' diagnoses are likely to reflect their tendency to use their subjective base rate estimates from their own settings when making diagnostic decisions in a new setting. To make the most accurate diagnoses, each clinician would have to inquire about the relative frequency of psychotic and dissociative clients in the population from which the research sample was drawn, and then hold this information in mind when making a diagnosis. Although we tend to think of diagnoses as real and immutable, in fact their accuracy is influenced by base rates just as much as the Exner and Wylie (1977) S-CON index.

Base Rates Can Influence Perceptions and Information Collection Strategies

An even more disturbing bias exists than subjective base rates influencing diagnoses: subjective base rates also influence clinicians' information collection strategies and their perception of signs and symptoms. The familiar adage needs to be modified only slightly to capture this problem, which is called "confirmatory bias": "We see what we expect to see."

To illustrate, let us return to the previous example. We already know that Drs. Smith and Jones are likely to differ on their diagnostic decisions. What is less evident is that Dr. Smith and Dr. Jones are likely to base their different diagnoses on different symptom ratings; Dr. Smith will actually "observe" more psychotic symptoms and fewer dissociative symptoms, while Dr. Jones is likely to perceive the opposite (Arkes & Harkness, 1980; Garb, 1998; Katz et al., 1969).

These biases are further complicated by another well-demonstrated factor: If Dr. Jones and Dr. Smith are allowed to interview these same patients independently (rather than viewing taped diagnostic interviews), their internalized base rates are likely to guide their symptom search. That is, Drs. Smith and Jones may further buttress their diagnostic biases by asking about symptoms that fit their internal expectations and failing to inquire about symptoms that are inconsistent with their diagnoses (Gauron & Dickinson, 1969). Thus, our original adage can be extended again: "We expect to see what we're used to seeing, we see what we expect to see, and we inquire about what we expect to see rather than about what we don't expect to see."

Davis (1976) used the phenomenon of subjective base rate bias to ingeniously explain the events of the controversial Rosenhan (1973) pseudopatient study. To review, Rosenhan and seven of his colleagues presented themselves at the admissions offices of 12 mental hospitals complaining of hearing a voice that said "empty," "hollow," and "thud." Apart from describing this symptom and falsifying their name, vocation, and employment, no other symptoms or history were simulated. Rosenhan reported that he and the other pseudopatients were hospitalized at all 12 hospitals and in 11 cases were given a diagnosis of schizophrenia.

Davis (1976) argued that the diagnosis and treatment of the pseudopatients was largely determined by the hospital psychiatrists' (perhaps subconscious) knowledge of the base rates of disorder and symptomatology in their settings. Given the low probability of normal persons presenting themselves at mental hospitals and asking for admission and the high base rate of auditory hallucinations among schizophrenics, Davis showed mathematically that psychiatrists' diagnoses may have been statistically

justifiable. Furthermore, these base rates—and the diagnoses they subsequently engendered—seemed to keep the hospital staff from accurately perceiving features of patients that were inconsistent with schizophrenia or from inquiring about symptoms that would have pointed toward other diagnoses. Hospital records suggested that nonschizophrenic features were either ignored, inaccurately perceived, or not properly weighted when diagnoses were assigned and patients were observed in the hospitals. For example, a behavior that would have been perceived as innocuous in another setting (writing notes) was described in the nursing notes as pathologic ("Patient engaged in writing behavior").

High Co-occurring Base Rates Can Lead to the Erroneous Perception of Correlations and Causal Relationships

Suppose you are doing intakes in an inpatient hospital where for geographic or other reasons most of the clients are Latino, with a base rate of .90. Let us also imagine that because of the way different hospitals in the area share resources, your setting handles most of the severe psychoses, giving a base rate of .90 in your hospital for schizophrenia. We know from the clinical research literature that there is no association in the general psychiatric population between being schizophrenic and being Latino. Therefore, the fourfold table between Latino heritage and schizophrenia for 100 random admissions in your setting would probably look like that shown in Table 8.4. As shown in the table, there is no significant association between Latino heritage and schizophrenia. Although there are a large number of cases in Cell A (Latino and schizophrenic), this is due simply to the co-occurrence of the two high base rates for Latino heritage and for schizophrenia. If a significant association existed, there would also be an overrepresentation of cases in Cell D, non-Latino, not schizophrenic.

Table 8.4. Co-occurrence of schizophrenia and Latino heritage in one inpatient setting.

		Diagnosis of schizophrenia		Row %
		Yes	No	
Latino heritage	Yes	81%	9%	90%
		Cell A	Cell B	
	No	9%	1%	10%
		Cell C	Cell D	
Column %		90%	10%	100%

Note: $\chi^2 = 0$, $\Phi = 0$.

These figures and the resulting lack of association are exactly as expected given our previously mentioned knowledge about schizophrenia.

What most clinicians may not know is that if they were intake workers in such an inpatient setting, it would be very easy to perceive a correlation between Latino heritage and schizophrenia, even though none exists. Smedslund (1963), Nisbett and Ross (1980), Arkes (1981), Kayne and Alloy (1988), and others have shown that high co-occurring base rates give observers the impression of a substantial association, because of the high number of cases in Cell A. Apparently, most of us have difficulty realizing that Cells B, C, and D are as important for estimating an association as is Cell A. You, as an intake worker, might be protected from overestimating an association if you already knew that the large number of clients you saw in Cell A was due to the peculiarities of geography and how your hospital shares resources with others. You might also be helped if you knew the research literature on schizophrenia and the general lack of association between schizophrenia and Latino heritage. Suppose, however, that you were faced with variables that were not as well researched or understood?

This is the situation that I faced some years ago as part of the Eating Disorders Research Group at the University of Minnesota. The research group was contacted over several years by a number of clinicians in Minneapolis who said they noted a strong association between a history of sexual abuse and eating disorders in women they were treating in psychotherapy. These clinicians were intrigued by the association they perceived and had begun musing about a causal relationship between sexual abuse of women and subsequent eating disorders. When the eating disorders research team assessed abnormal eating patterns and sexual abuse in the very clinical settings from which the reports came, the results were as follows. There was a high base rate of past sexual abuse among the 85 women in the sample (70%) as well as a high rate of abnormal eating patterns (82%). There was no significant statistical association at all between eating disorders and sexual abuse ($\chi^2 = 0$, $\Phi = .50$), and the cell frequencies of the fourfold table were exactly equal to those that would be derived from the cross-multiplication of cell and column frequencies: Cell A = 57%, Cell B = 25%, Cell C = 13%, and Cell D = 5% (Finn, Hartman, Leon, & Lawson, 1986). Although post hoc hypotheses must be considered tentatively, it seems likely that the clinicians who gave the initial reports of an association between eating disorders and sexual abuse had

been influenced by the large number of women in their settings who had both of these problems (i.e., the large number of cases in Cell A). In effect, the clinicians had no "control group" (women without sexual abuse or eating disorders) to help shape their perceptions.

How to Use Base Rates to Benefit You and Your Clients

Should we clinicians give up entirely the task of making diagnostic and treatment decisions or use Ouija boards to guide our actions? We don't think so. A few simple guidelines can greatly help all of us to incorporate base rates intelligently in clinical decision making.

Investigate the Base Rates in Your Setting

If you want base rates to work for you, use the tests and decision rules that minimize overall error for your particular clients. This will require you to have at least some knowledge of the base rates of certain client characteristics in your setting. Pertinent information can be collected through examination of previous records or perhaps through comparison with data from related settings. If you collect information about the base rates of phenomena of interest in your setting, you are likely to improve your clinical decision making in the long run.

Be Suspicious of Simple Interpretations of Test Scores

ERROR IS A FACT

Especially with low base rate phenomena, errors in prediction are a given. Be aware of this and avoid claiming more than you can substantiate, especially if you work in the area of forensic psychology. For example, clinicians are often asked to make predictions of dangerousness, suicide potential, and other low base rate characteristics in court. Consistent with the current ethical code of psychologists, you should appropriately qualify any opinions you express about a particular client showing such characteristics (American Psychological Association, 2002; Principles 5.01 and 9.06).

Tests are most useful if the base rate is close to 50%. We have seen in the hypothetical example of predicting assault in your clinic that it is difficult for a test to improve upon the base rate predictions if the base rates are extreme, that is, are close to 0%. It follows from Meehl and Rosen's (1955) optimizing rule that tests are more likely to contribute positively to the quality of decision making when the base rate of the behavior or condition to be predicted is closer to

50%. Two other corrolaries are that: (1) when the base rate of a condition is low, a test is best used to rule out the condition, but not rule it in, and (2) when the base rate of a condition is high, a test is best used to rule it in, but not to rule it out (Streiner, 2003).

DO NOT USE FIXED CUTTING SCORES

As shown earlier, statements like "an MMPI-2 T-score equal to or above 65 means . . ." should be critically examined. Adopting simple rules of thumb such as the above may well lead to false decisions that can be avoided if base rates are respected. Remember, cutting scores for tests are based on minimizing errors given certain base rates. Therefore, a T-score of 65 may not be the optimal cutting score in your setting. It depends on whether the base rate in your setting equals the base rate on which the test cutting score was normed.

LOOK FOR CROSS-VALIDATED TESTS

As mentioned, cutting scores for tests are based on minimizing errors given certain base rates. Thus, limited trust is appropriate when cutting scores were based on one sample alone. More confidence can be placed on test predictions when the same results have been generated from multiple samples, especially if those samples have different base rates of the characteristic being predicted. In other words, look for tests that have been cross-validated in different settings and samples.

USE TESTS THAT WERE DESIGNED FOR YOUR SETTING

There is a related recommendation: Investigate the base rates in samples that were used to derive and standardize tests, in order to assess whether the test is appropriate in your setting. By studying the test manual you can determine what the base rates were in the standardization sample. You can then compare these base rates with those in your own setting. If base rate information is not explicitly given in the manual, you may still be on firm ground with the test if it was developed in a setting similar to yours.

IF NECESSARY, INTELLIGENTLY MODIFY THE RECOMMENDED CUTTING SCORE

You can intelligently modify your use of a test that was not designed for your setting by adjusting decision rules according to your own base rates. For example, as shown in Table 8.3, if the base rate of suicide in your setting is 5% or less, you should probably use a cutoff score on the S-CON that is higher than 8. To their credit, Exner and Wylie provided the figures that make such calculations possible. When no such data are available and you still want to use a test, you can at least specify the direction in which the cutoff score must be changed and moderate your confidence in the test findings. As shown in Table 8.3, lower base rates generally go with more restrictive cutoff scores.

Ask Yourself: What Are the Alternatives?

Much improvement in clinical decision making could be accomplished if each of us remembered to think about base rates every time we made a clinical hypothesis. Unfortunately, research has resoundingly shown that simply resolving to think about base rates and the particular biases they produce rarely aids decision making (Fischoff, 1977; Hamm, 1994; Kurtz & Garfield, 1978; Wood, 1978).

One debiasing strategy that does seem to produce improvement (Ross, Lepper, Strack, & Steinmutz, 1977) is to make yourself think about alternatives (test interpretations, diagnoses, hypotheses, etc.) after you have generated an initial impression. In my clinical work, I have found this strategy to be especially easy to implement with extreme base rate phenomena. For example, some years ago I saw a 5-year-old girl in outpatient practice who appeared to be psychotically depressed. Part of this initial impression was based on a salient personal experience: the client strongly resembled a client I had worked with closely in an inpatient setting during my training. I stopped to question my initial impression, however, because I had never before run across a psychotic child in this particular outpatient setting. (My estimate of the local base rate of childhood psychosis was 0%.) Thinking about alternatives led to consultations with other colleagues, which later revealed that the child's psychotic symptoms were due to the overdose and interaction of certain allergy medications.

As a general rule, when faced with what appear to be low base rate phenomena, we should all probably pause, take a second look, and carefully ask, "What are the alternatives?" If we find ourselves unable to generate alternatives, it is time to seek the consultation of colleagues who work in different settings with different base rates. In the end, we may still decide to make a low base rate prediction or diagnosis; however, when going against the base rates, we should require more facts to support our conclusion.

Hunt for Disconfirming Information

Because base rates tend to influence both our information-gathering procedures and what we actually perceive, another good strategy is to hunt for information that will disprove our initial impressions. This goes against our natural tendency to look for information that confirms our internalized base rates. Thus, in the previous example, I should have rigorously sought all information that might prove my client was psychotically depressed, as well as information that was in accord with my internalized base rates. This would have helped me make an accurate diagnosis.

Delay Clinical Decisions while Information Is Collected

Consistent with the above strategies, research has generally shown that the most accurate clinical decision makers tend to arrive at their conclusions later than do less accurate clinicians (Elstein, Shulman, & Sprafka, 1978; Sandifer, Hordern, & Green, 1970). We may all be tempted to impress students and colleagues by showing how quickly we can diagnose a client or how few responses we need to interpret a Rorschach protocol. In such instances, however, we appear to be most susceptible to bias from internalized base rates.

When You Think There Is an Association, Look for the Control Group

The Minneapolis clinicians who thought they perceived an association between eating disorders and sexual abuse are to be commended; they asked researchers to test this hypothesis among the women the clinicians were treating. Unfortunately, many of us in clinical practice do not have research teams at our immediate disposal. In such a situation, a good strategy is to look for the control group that will test the association we think we perceive (i.e., clients who do not possess the characteristic of interest). To return to our example in Table 8.4, should clinicians perceive an association between Latino heritage and schizophrenia (because of the large number of cases in Cell A) they need only ask themselves, "Are non-Latino clients more likely than Latino clients to receive a diagnosis other than schizophrenia?" (a comparison of Cell B with Cell D). As one quickly sees, they are not, which shows that there is no association between Latino heritage and schizophrenia.

Do Not Confuse Statistically Based Decisions with a Lack of Caring for Clients

When I urge clinicians to incorporate base rates into their clinical decision making, I find that many are reluctant to do so because they feel it involves "treating clients like numbers" or "not caring about the individual." Meehl (1977) bemoaned this same phenomenon in his classic paper, "Why I Do Not Attend Case Conferences," reporting that when he spoke about base rates in case conferences some clinicians would respond, "We aren't dealing with groups, we are dealing with an individual case." Meehl responded pointedly in his paper to this reasoning: "If you depart in your clinical decision making from a well-established (or even moderately well-supported) empirical frequency . . . [this] will result in the misclassifying of other cases that would have been correctly classified had such nonactuarial departures been forbidden" (p. 234). As clinicians, we may believe that we are caring more about clients when we avoid using statistics to make decisions that affect them. In fact, however, the costs of such decisions are likely to far outweigh their benefits. We show our greatest caring when we use all the information available to make the most accurate decisions possible about our clients.

Notes

1. The probability of two independent events co-occurring is equal to the probability of one event times the probability of the other event.
2. Many indices assess the psychometric quality of tests used for clinical decision making. "Sensitivity" is the probability of a person with a certain trait or condition being picked up by a test [$a/(a + c)$]; "specificity" is the probability that a person without a certain trait or condition being identified by the test as not having that trait or condition [$d/(b + d)$]. "Positive predictive power" is the likelihood of a person identified by the test as having a certain trait or condition actually possessing that characteristic [$a/(a + b)$]; "negative predictive power" indicates the probability of a person identified by the test as not having a certain trait or condition actually not having that characteristic [$d/(c + d)$]. All of these indices, including the rate of correct decisions we use in Tables 8.1–8.3, are helpful in clinical decision making, depending on the specific goal of the clinician. See Baldessarini, Finklestein, and Arana (1983), Kraemer (1992), and Streiner (2003) for in-depth discussions of these various indicators.
3. Exner and Wylie's (1977) cutting score of 8 is entirely reasonable; apparently they opted to increase the number of true-positive decisions at the cost of a slight decrease in the overall number of accurate decisions.
4. Hospitalization of such clients could be based on clinicians' decision to weigh false-negative errors much more than false-positive errors. However, if this is true, the clinicians should appropriately argue that even though their clients appear to have only a 4% probability of a serious suicide attempt, the negative utilities of not intervening are so high that some steps must be taken.

References

American Psychiatric Association. (2000). *Diagnostic and statistical manual of mental disorders* (4th ed., Text rev.) (DSM-IV-TR). Washington, DC: American Psychiatric Association.

American Psychological Association. (2002). *Ethical principles of psychologists and code of conduct*. Washington, DC: American Psychological Association.

Arkes, H. R. (1981). Impediments to accurate clinical judgment and possible ways to minimize their impact. *Journal of Consulting and Clinical Psychology, 49*, 323–330.

Arkes, H. R., & Harkness, A. R. (1980). Effect of making a diagnosis on subsequent recognition of symptoms. *Journal of Experimental Psychology: Human Learning and Memory, 6*, 568–575.

Baldessarini, R. J., Finklestein, S., & Arana, G. W. (1983). The predictive power of diagnostic tests and the effect of prevalence of illness. *Archives of General Psychiatry, 40*, 569–573.

Davis, D. A. (1976). On being detectably sane in insane places: Base rates and psychodiagnosis. *Journal of Abnormal Psychology, 85*, 416–422.

Elstein, A. S., Shulman, A. S., & Sprafka, S. A. (1978). *Medical problem solving: An analysis of clinical reasoning*. Cambridge, MA: Harvard University Press.

Exner, J. E., Jr., & Wylie, J. (1977). Some Rorschach data concerning suicide. *Journal of Personality Assessment, 41*, 339–348.

Finn, S. (1982). Base rates, utilities, and DSM-III: Shortcomings of fixed-rule systems of psychodiagnosis. *Journal of Abnormal Psychology, 91*, 294–302.

Finn, S. E. (1983). Utility-balanced and utility-imbalanced rules: Reply to Widiger. *Journal of Abnormal Psychology, 92*, 499–501.

Finn, S. E., Hartman, M., Leon, G. R., & Lawson, L. (1986). Eating disorders and sexual abuse: Lack of confirmation for a clinical hypothesis. *International Journal of Eating Disorders, 5*, 1051–1060.

Fischoff, B. (1977). Perceived informativeness of facts. *Journal of Experimental Psychology: Human Perception and Performance, 3*, 349–358.

Garb, H. N. (1998). *Studying the clinician: Judgment research and psychological assessment*. Washington, DC: American Psychological Association.

Gauron, E. F., & Dickinson, J. K. (1969). The influence of seeing the patient first on diagnostic decision making in psychiatry. *American Journal of Psychiatry, 126*, 199–205.

Gottesman, I. I., & Shields, J. (1982). *Schizophrenia: The epigenetic puzzle*. Cambridge: Cambridge University Press.

Hamm, R. M. (1994). Underweighting of base-rate information reflects important difficulties people have with probabilistic inference (Electronic version). *Psycoloquy, 5*.

Kahneman, D., & Tversky, A. (1972). Subjective probability: A judgment of representativeness. *Cognitive Psychology, 3*, 430–454.

Kahneman, D., & Tversky, A. (1973). On the psychology of prediction. *Psychological Review, 80*, 237–251.

Kamphuis, J. H., Kugeares, S. L., & Finn, S. E. (2000). Rorschach correlates of sexual abuse: Trauma content and aggression indices. *Journal of Personality Assessment, 75*, 212–225.

Katz, M. M., Cole, J. O., & Lowery, H. A. (1969). Studies of the diagnostic process: The influence of symptom perception, past experience, and ethnic background on diagnostic decisions. *American Journal of Psychiatry, 125*, 937–947.

Kayne, N. T., & Alloy, L. B. (1988). Clinician and patient as aberrant actuaries: Expectation based distortions in estimation of covariation. In L. Y. Abramson (Ed.), *Social cognition and clinical psychology: A synthesis* (pp. 365–395). New York: Guilford Press.

Kraemer, H. C. (1992). *Evaluating medical testis: Objective and quantitative guidelines*. Newbury Park, CA: Sage.

Kurtz, R. M., & Garfield, S. L. (1978). Illusory correlation: A further explanation of Chapman's paradigm. *Journal of Consulting and Clinical Psychology, 46*, 1009–1015.

Meehl, P. E. (1977). Why I do not attend case conferences. In *Psychodiagnosis: Selected papers* (pp. 225–302). New York: Norton.

Meehl, P. E., & Rosen, A. (1955). Antecedent probability and the efficiency of psychometric signs, patterns, or cutting scores. *Psychological Bulletin, 52*, 194–216.

Nisbett, R. E., & Ross, L. (1980). *Human inference: Strategies and shortcomings of social judgment*. Englewood Cliffs, NJ: Prentice-Hall.

Rosenhan, D. L. (1973). On being sane in insane places. *Science, 179*, 250–258.

Ross, L., Lepper, M. R., Strack, F., & Steinmutz, J. (1977). Social explanation and social expectation: Effects of real and hypothetical explanations on subjective likelihood. *Journal of Personality and Social Psychology, 35*, 817–829.

Sandifer, M. G., Hordern, A., & Green, L. M. (1970). The psychiatric interview: The impact of the first three minutes. *American Journal of Psychiatry, 126*, 968–973.

Smedslund, J. (1963). The concept of correlation in adults. *Scandinavian Journal of Psychology, 4*, 165–173.

Streiner, D. L. (2003). Diagnosing tests: Using and misusing diagnostic and screening tests. *Journal of Personality Assessment, 81*, 209–219.

Widiger, T. A., Hurt, S. W., Frances, A., Clarkin, J. F., & Gilmore, M. (1984). Diagnostic efficiency and the DSM-III. *Archives of General Psychiatry, 41*, 1005–1012.

Wood, G. (1978). The knew it all effect. *Journal of Experimental Psychology: Human Perception and Performance, 4*, 345–353.

Theory and Measurement of Personality Traits

Allan R. Harkness

Abstract

This chapter describes the connections between basic emotion systems and personality traits. The fear, anger (or rage), interest (or seeking), and joy emotion systems are described and linked to personality traits. The case is argued that modern psychological findings from behavior genetic, longitudinal, and clinical studies cannot be interpreted without including stable individuating personality traits as causes in psychological theories. Using personality sketches to illustrate behavioral features, the chapter provides an introduction to trait concepts that can enrich clinical case conception. The highly available Minnesota Multiphasic Personality Inventory-2 (MMPI-2) personality trait scales, called the Personality Psychopathology-Five (PSY-5) scales, are described. The chapter provides a brief review of key PSY-5 research and clinical literature.

Keywords: emotion, personality, personality assessment, personality traits, MMPI-2, PSY-5

What is a personality trait? Permit me to narrate the inner experience of a hypothetical patient:

Jane thought her coffee tasted a bit off, perhaps a taste of pencil eraser. She thought "cryptosporidium." This germ just popped into her mind. She remembered it was an infectious agent that survives water treatment. She had seen a picture of them; they had ugly microscopic capsules that protected their innards from chlorine. She thought, "That stuff is run-off from pig farms or chicken farms, right?" Jane tried to use humor to calm herself. She thought of funny chickens, funny pigs. She hoped the coffee maker would kill those things. But worry—readiness to think of creepy cryptosporidium—was stronger than humor or faith in coffee makers.

Jane started her car. She caught a new sound. Subtle, but new. It could be expensive. Expensive like the last time. That sound. That subtle sound meant giving up control. That sound meant being at the mercy of people she did not trust. It meant another month with no savings. No savings. "These are the years when I SHOULD be saving for retirement," she scolded

herself. The thoughts fluidly associated to other dangers. She turned on the radio to tune herself out.

The first purpose of this chapter is to describe what is meant by the term personality trait. I will use the case of hypothetical Jane to make trait theory concrete and understandable for the reader. A second purpose of this chapter is to introduce a convenient measure of personality traits for clinical work: the Minnesota Multiphasic Personality Inventory-2 (MMPI-2) Personality Psychopathology-Five (PSY-5) scales (Harkness, McNulty, Ben-Porath, & Graham, 2002).

Personality Trait Theory: At the Core of Psychology

Personality traits connect emotions, thinking, learning, attention, the patterning of behavioral outputs, and clinical problems. *They are indispensable* because no psychological theory can cope with the data available today without them. The data of behavioral genetics, which allows us to compare people of different degrees of relatedness and environment sharing, cannot be interpreted without personality traits. The interpretation of longitudinal studies, for example, work described by Caspi (2000) or Saudino, Pedersen, Lichtenstein, McClearn, and Plomin (1997), would be incomprehensible without traits acting as causal agents. The facts of the "comorbidity" of psychiatric disorders, and the longitudinal patterns that persist over time require an ingredient in psychological theories: powerful individual differences that persist over time, are real, causal, and can be studied.

What is a personality trait? Tellegen (1988) defined a trait as ". . . a psychological (therefore organismic) structure underlying a relatively enduring behavioral disposition, i.e., a tendency to respond in certain ways under certain circumstances. In the case of a personality trait some of the behaviors expressing the disposition have substantial adaptational implications" (p. 622).

Think back to Jane. Think of her reaction to the odd taste of the coffee, to the new sound from her car. There could be many different causes for her mental contents and behaviors. Perhaps her brother had just had a horrible cryptosporidium infection. Perhaps she had had several very bad nights' sleep because of a sore back. Perhaps she was just in an unexplained mood or a hormonal flux. But none of those explanations are personality traits.

For Jane to have a personality trait, she must have an "organismic structure that underlies a disposition." Trait theorists believe that traits are real psychobiological structures that cause things to happen. Currently some of the evidence for the existence of structures is indirect: behavior genetic evidence shows consistent heritabilities for traits, psychopharmacologic interventions can change the operating properties of naturally occurring systems, and so on. Other evidence for these psychobiological structures is more direct. For example, LeDoux (1996) has elegantly synthesized anatomical studies and psychobiological studies to make the case for a high-speed danger analysis system with the amygdala as its hub. If our Jane were to have some enduring property of this system—say a readiness to detect danger—this would yield a behavioral disposition.

Take a moment to distinguish between underlying structures and dispositions. As an analogy, the underlying atomic structure of a piece of glass (great irregularity compared to the regular structure of crystal) gives rise to the disposition of "fracture upon breakage." The underlying atomic structure is always there in the glass, but the disposition of fracture upon breakage is a potential that is only observed under special circumstances. Given a baseball bat,

the disposition can be demonstrated. In the case of Jane, if a personality trait were at work, then some underlying structure, such as enduring properties of cell networks in her nervous system, would generate behavioral dispositions. Jane might be chronically disposed to treat relatively neutral but novel stimuli as newly detected dangers.

Traits Are Individuating

Much of psychology is concerned with general laws—psychological principles that apply to all vertebrates, or all mammals, or all human beings. In contrast, the personality traits described in this chapter are part of individual differences science (Harkness & Lilienfeld, 1997). These traits display naturally occurring variation in the systems that underlie important adaptive behaviors. Individual differences in the levels of the trait, across a group showing variation, create what Tellegen (1988) has called a "trait dimension." Think back to Jane. If her inner experience were replicated across a variety of occasions and events, it would suggest that she has a readiness to treat novel information as clues to danger. Perhaps she is at a high trait level of negative emotionality. But the dimension of negative emotionality does not exist in any single person. The dimension exists only in a population of Janes, Kaylas, Toms, and Maxwells, each of whom has a real threat analysis system that endures across time, and that is set at an individuating trait level.

Traits versus States

Traits last a long time. States last a short time. Systems displaying stable parameters over months, years, or decades show the endurance required of a trait. Structures that create dynamic parameters lasting instants, seconds, minutes, hours, or perhaps even weeks have the endurance of states. Yes, Jane's danger analysis system does vary from moment to moment, day to day. However, if there are fundamental parameters that endure, then she has a trait level around which state variation occurs.

So is Jane at a high trait level of readiness to detect danger? Or was she just in a bad mood? Had she been a recent victim of distressing events? For the clinician, her history would be critical. We would be very interested in information like this:

> From early childhood, Jane has had a talent for imagining how things could go wrong. Always on alert, she prides herself on not being surprised by bad events. The emotion of tense worry, of anxiety, is a frequent

visitor. Jane experiences more negative emotions than most people do.

Is It Plausible that Real Organismic Structural Differences Underlie Traits?

When traits are studied by behavior genetic methods, the evidence is overwhelming that a substantial portion of the variance in those traits arise from genetic variation, consistent with Tellegen's concept of trait as an organismic structure underlying a relatively enduring behavioral disposition.

For example, Loehlin and Rowe (1992) conducted an exemplary early study of the behavior genetics of personality traits using structural equations modeling. This allowed the simultaneous examination of data from large twin studies, adoption studies, and studies of the relatives of twins. They reported findings that have held up well in light of subsequent research:

> Somewhere between 40 and 50 percent of the Big Five Traits is genetic, according to this analysis, and between 50 percent and 60 percent is due to environment, plus error and interaction. The environmental effects are mostly non-familial, but there is a small component due to shared environment.
>
> (*Loehlin & Rowe*, 1992, p. 358).

The above quotation contains a finding that I believe will eventually come to be regarded as one of the great surprises and achievements of twentieth-century social science. Environment is powerful in shaping personality, but Loehlin and Rowe found that it does not work the way we assumed. In contrast to our expectations, environmental forces on personality sculpt in a way that does *not* create similarity among family members. David Rowe (1994) developed this theme in a book entitled, *The Limits of Family Influence: Genes, Experience, and Behavior*. Rowe (1994) contrasted well-replicated findings from behavior genetics with the core assumptions of socialization theories. When we usually consider the power of the environment, we instinctively think in social learning terms. We think of parents as powerful role models shaping personalities of their young. The general picture that has emerged from a vast literature of behavior genetic examinations of the source of population variance in personality trait dimensions indicates that the resemblance between family members comes mostly from shared genetics. When the environment shapes personality, for the most part, it does not produce similarity between people who share the same family.

The extremely informative German Observational Study of Adult Twins (GOSAT; Borkenau, Riemann, Angleitner, & Spinath, 2001) included not only self-reported personality, but also observations of behavior made by multiple independent judges. The work was methodologically rigorous, with predominantly molecular methods used to assess type of twinning and some 1.26 million ratings collected on videotapes of individual twins in 15 behavior challenges. Reliable variance in self-reported and peer-rated personality was estimated to be about 67% genetic in origin and 33% due to environment, with little or no evidence that sharing family life makes people more similar in personality. Analyses of the behavioral observations suggested 40% of the variance was genetic in origin, 35% was environmental variance that does not tend to produce family similarity, and 25% of the variance arose from environmental influence that does produce similarity among those sharing a family environment. Behavior is, of course, determined by many causes, not just traits. Certainly family styles and habits may be among those influences on individual behavioral observations. However when self-reporters and observers reflect on the major enduring and individuating dispositions that characterize a personality, both individuating genetics and individuating environment seem to be predominant shaping forces.

If it is personality we are seeing in Jane, then we would expect to see similarities between Jane and a genetically identical twin of Jane, even if they were raised in different families. But we would not expect Jane's family life to strongly shape those structures, the traits that shape her major enduring dispositions. Nevertheless, in looking at any particular stream of behavior, we might see the signatures of Jane's family habits, beliefs, and values.

Some Personality Traits Are Stable Individuating Properties of Emotion Systems

Meehl (1975) and Tellegen (1982, 1985) both suggested that some personality traits might best be understood as the dispositions of emotion systems. All mammals share a number of basic emotion systems (Panksepp, 1998). Some of the emotion systems that are particularly relevant to personality traits are enumerated in Table 9.1. The major emotion theorists who developed the understanding of these systems are listed in Table 9.1. Most of these theorists describe seven or more systems, and generally agreement across theorists is quite good with a few areas of disagreement. When the list of emotion systems is pared down to a few

Table 9.1. Basic emotion systems particularly relevant to personality, as described by major emotion theorists.

Fear	Anger/rage	Interest/seeking	Joy
Ekman[*]	Ekman	—	Ekman
Izard[**]	Izard	Izard	Izard
Panksepp[†]	Panksepp	Panksepp	Panksepp
Tomkins[‡]	Tomkins[‡]	Tomkins[§]	Tomkins[§]

[*]Ekman (2007).
[**]Izard (1991).
[†]Panksepp (1998).
[‡]Tomkins (1991).
[§]Tomkins (1962).

that are particularly relevant to personality traits, as shown in Table 9.1, the agreement between theorists is excellent.

Each of the basic emotion systems referenced in Table 9.1 can rapidly detect a distinct class of stimulus events (Ekman, 2007). Starting with the left column of Table 9.1, the fear system detects signals of impending danger. As each emotion system is activated by its own relevant class of stimuli, the system organizes adaptive behaviors, structures thought, and creates powerful motivations (Izard, 1991). The systems in Table 9.1 have reasonably distinct and well-characterized underlying neural systems, and some have distinct biochemical signaling systems (Depue & Lenzenweger, 2006; Panksepp, 1998; Patrick & Bernat, 2006).

The fear system is explored further in Figure 9.1. The system is represented by an elongated oval. The left side of the oval represents the input side of the system, and the right side represents the output side. The fear system allows the organism to respond quickly to major adaptive challenges even before consciousness becomes engaged (LeDoux, 1996). For example, very rudimentary analyses of rapidly looming objects (predator signature) or loss of support (falling) can activate the fear system at the same time the cortex is receiving the information for deeper analysis, for the assignment of meaning, and for providing representations of the event in consciousness. The fear system can be potentiated by factors such as being alone, being in the dark, novel stimulation such as odd tastes, sounds, sights, skin sensations, and so on. Some set of releasing stimuli and potentiators are thought to be species-typical givens, the unlearned primitives of the fear system. This is shown on the left end of the oval in Figure 9.1.

Ekman (2007) offers the term "autoappraisers" for the cognitive elements of an emotion system that are charged with a continual screening of information from the external senses. They are screening for any stimuli that are releasers of the system. In the fear system, autoappraisers search for signals of "potential for bodily injury or death." Through learning mechanisms, new stimuli can become rapid releasers of the outputs of the fear system. Ekman has called the set of rapid releasers for a system the "triggers" of the system. Figure 9.1 raises the interesting possibility that some of the emotion systems have their own onboard learning subunit, a learning system that operates in parallel with the more general learning systems of the organism.

On the right side in Figure 9.1, we see that the fear system coordinates a range of behavioral and cognitive outputs such as a characteristic facial expression. Ekman (2007) describes the facial output of a falling man: "his upper eyelids are raised as high as they can go, ... eyebrows are raised and drawn together, ... lips are stretched horizontally toward his ears ... his chin is pulled back" (p. 162). Cognition is structured by the system. The ability to think creatively is lost: thinking focuses on the threat. There are changes in blood pressure. Heart rate changes, and blood flow is directed toward the legs. Depending on the behavior and proximity of the threat, there may be total behavioral inhibition (freezing) or escape behavior. And after much of this behavior is well under way, only then does the person possibly begin to sense a feeling—perhaps there is the feeling of fear. Thus it is critical to understand that what is being discussed here is an evolved emotion system—Panksepp calls them mammalian homologies—which are much more than a feeling: they are complete adaptive dynamic systems that deal with classes of stimuli that are far too important to the organism to be left to slower thought and reflection.

It is critical to be aware that the emotion system may be strongly controlling cognition even before the person becomes cognitively aware that they are

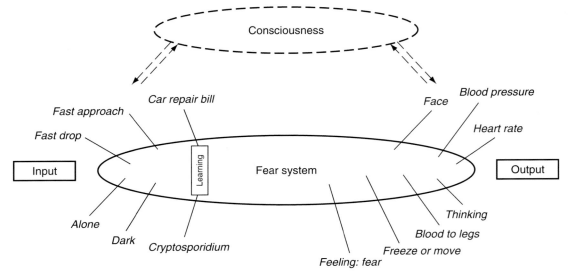

Fig. 9.1 The fear system.

having an emotion. On December 29, 1972, as Eastern Airlines Flight 401, a Lockheed L-1011, was approaching for Miami International for landing, the crew became aware that one of the landing gear indicator lights had not come on. The pilot, the copilot, and the flight engineer, each under the command of their own emotion systems, began to focus on the threat. First someone tapped on the light. Then they began to take apart the light display. The flight engineer was sent below to visually verify the position of the nose gear, as the rest of the crew worked on the light. As they all diligently focused on the threat cue, the airliner crashed into the Florida Everglades and 101 of 176 aboard died. Range of thought was narrowed by the fear system: all focus was on the threat.

Note that in Figure 9.1, the systems involved in consciousness are just sketched in, but they are separated from the fear system. Conscious awareness of the various inputs and outputs of the system may be strongly controlled by the system. Each flight crew member was focusing on a threat cue—the landing gear display. Thinking was strongly directed toward that cue, and away from an even more important danger—terrain contact. Even though the fear system was commanding cognition, it is possible that none of the flight crew was even conscious of fear when working on the light display. Ekman (2007), Izard and Ackerman (2004), and LeDoux's (1996) work is particularly recommended for fascinating accounts of the interaction of emotion systems and consciousness.

Again, consider Jane. Like all of us, Jane has a fear system. Perhaps her system, like a jumpy car alarm, has a low threshold of activation. An odd taste, which might simply potentiate the system for most people, actually activates Jane's system. She regards the taste as a signal of a dangerous threat, a germ, and she has difficulty letting go of it. Another potential threat, an unusual sound, then sets off thoughts about a potential automotive repair bill. When the emotion system controls on her cognitions are slightly loosened, she can still think only of associated dangers, costs, financial problems, and future poverty. Jane has the same fear system that is homologous in all mammals. But there are enduring, individuating parameters of that system that are at the core of Jane's personality, and will remain with Jane throughout her life.

All mammals share a number of these systems. Returning to Table 9.1, the second column refers to the anger/rage system. This system detects frustration of one's goals and agendas. The primitive triggers relate to frustration of one's basic needs at the lower levels of a Maslowian hierarchy. Physical restraint sets off the system in a 2-year-old. The system then organizes the topography of behavioral responses with characteristic facial expression, sympathetic preparation for energy expenditure, an agonistic orientation to the agent of frustration, and strong motivation to overcome obstacles. Even pain is dampened as the rage system is activated.

Feelings of different qualities result from the emotion systems on the right-hand side of Table 9.1.

The interest/seeking system and the joy system have benefited from both psychological and biological characterization (Berridge & Robinson, 1998; Depue & Lenzenweger, 2006; Panksepp, 1998; Patrick & Bernat, 2006). The interest/seeking system can be conceptually tied to wanting, to incentive motivation. This system is subserved in part by dopamine tracts originating in the midbrain and terminating in the *nucleus accumbens.* Opportunities—potential resources—are triggers for this system. Think of a child seeing a toy catalog. Wanting is activated.

On the other hand, the enjoyment of culmination and consummation is the province of the joy system, based on biochemical signaling by endogenous opiates. The psychological distinction between interest/seeking and joy is clear in the phenomenon of buyer's remorse, when one finds that the degree of wanting had far overpredicted the eventual joy of consumption.

How do emotion systems interact? Figure 9.2 shows several basic emotion systems operating in parallel. Izard (2004) has argued that mutual interactions between the emotion systems—amplifications or inhibitions—contribute importantly to the observed dynamics of emotion. This section has introduced a few of the emotion systems that are particularly relevant to major personality traits. Which personality traits are the major ones?

Which Are the Major Personality Traits? Don't Personality Theorists All Disagree?

Markon, Krueger, and Watson (2005) performed an exemplary meta-factor analysis. First, they identified 44 scales from five widely used personality instruments. Then they scoured the literature for correlations between these 44 scales, and found 77 different samples ranging in size from $n = 158$ to $n = 52,879$. Using the published correlations, they generated weighted averages for each value in the 44×44 matrix, and then performed several exploratory factor analyses, extracting two-, three-, four-, and five-factor solutions, rotated to Varimax criteria.

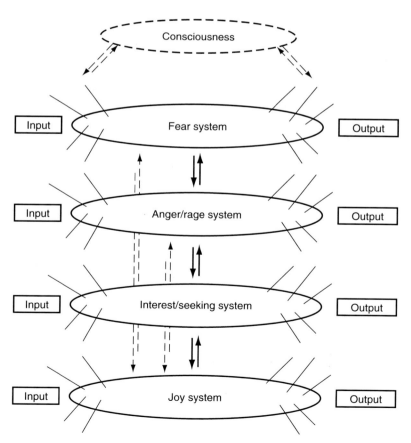

Fig. 9.2 Multiple parallel emotion systems with dynamic interactions.

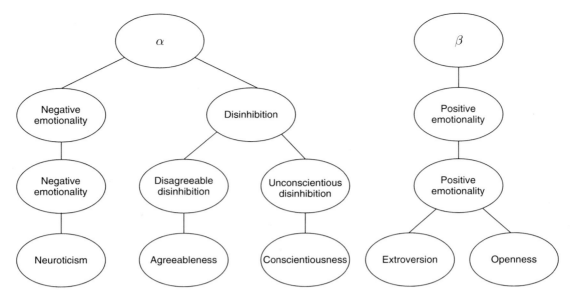

Fig. 9.3 Heirarchical structure of personality. Adapted from Markon, Krueger, and Watson (2005), p. 148; Copyright American Psychological Association.

Figure 9.3, adapted from their article, presents the factors they found underlying these 44 popular scales. At the top of Figure 9.3 are two ovals bearing the labels α and β. This is the result of extracting two factors. The three-factor extraction is the next row of three ovals, and so on down to the last row showing the five-factor level. There are very broad bandwidth traits at the two-factor level, and more differentiated, narrow traits at each subsequent level of extraction. The authors argued that taken together, the factor solutions comprise a single coherent hierarchical structure.

At the two-factor level, Markon et al. (2005) found that the α factor has loadings from scales tapping worry, anxiety, the experience of negative emotions, emotional instability, aggressiveness, negative distortion of thinking, lack of conscientiousness, oppositionality, identity disturbance, and poor self-control. Jane, the hypothetical patient at the beginning of this chapter, might be well characterized with descriptors like worry, anxiety, the experience of negative emotions, and negative distortions of thinking. However, we do not know if Jane would be well characterized by general emotional instability, aggressiveness, oppositionality, identity disturbance, and poor self-control. The high-level α factor appears to be too coarse for a good description of Jane. As you look at how α is decomposed at lower levels of the figure, you see how more narrow traits offer further opportunities to refine the description.

Markon et al. reported that the β factor had high loadings on scales measuring extraversion, a sense of well-being, and social ease. Note that this factor remains relatively stable at subsequent three-, and four-factor extraction levels. From the brief description of Jane's inner experience we cannot estimate her status on this dimension.

Markon et al. next extracted three factors. The three factors are coherently related to the earlier two factors. The big negative α factor split into two more narrow factors. They found a split between worry, anxiety, and being easily stressed and a split-off factor relating to being aggressive and poorly self-controlled. The third factor remained extraversion, social interest, and well-being.

At this three-factor level, we can better capture Jane. From the brief narration of inner experience, we would guess that she is characterized by elevated negative emotionality, but that we do not have strong evidence on her status on disinhibition or, again, on positive emotionality.

At the four-factor level, Markon et al. (2005) found that aggressiveness split off from poor self-control. Aggressiveness separated from what Watson and Clark (1993) referred to as behavioral disinhibition. Tellegen (1982) referred to this trait dimension as Constraint. In work with my collaborators, I used Tellegen's trait construct and labeled the same trait dimension from the reverse end as disconstraint (Harkness et al., 2002). Markon et al.'s four factors converge neatly with the four constructs Trull and Durrett (2005) arrived at by literature review. Trull and Durrett suggested that there is converging support for dimensional systems that tap four broad domains of personality: "neuroticism/negative affectivity/emotional dysregulation; extraversion/positive emotionality; dissocial/antagonistic behavior; and constraint/compulsivity/conscientiousness" (p. 131). Widiger (1998) and Watson, Clark, and Harkness (1994) also singled out these four trait dimensions as particularly relevant to clinical issues related to personality. At the five-factor level, Markon et al. identified the model that underlies the NEO PI-R, with openness splitting off from positive emotionality. This yields the five-factor model of neuroticism, agreeableless, conscientiousness, extraversion, and openness.

Markon et al. (2005) produced a picture of the hierarchy by starting with large factors and decomposing them into more and more narrow factors. This could be called the top-down approach. Harkness (1992) and Harkness and McNulty (1994) produced bottom-up studies of hierarchical structure, starting with very narrow markers of personality features. We used psychological distance measures rather than correlations, and yet we arrived at a very similar solution: aggressiveness, disconstraint, negative emotionality/neuroticism, introversion/low positive emotionality. However, for our fifth dimension, we identified the degree of reality contact, a trait dimension we called psychoticism. This dimension arose from the presence of psychotic phenomena descriptors in personality disorder criteria. This model is the Personality Psychopathology-Five or PSY-5 (Harkness & McNulty, 1994; Harkness et al., 2002).

Links between Emotion Systems and Major Personality Traits

Links between some of the particularly relevant emotion systems and major personality traits found at the four-factor level of Markon et al. (2005)

meta-analysis, and four of the PSY-5 traits, are shown in Table 9.2. The fear system's enduring parameters of threshold for activation are a predominant element in negative emotionality. The potentiation of that system can be called anxiety, which involves state-like variation in the dynamic threshold. But the long-run average thresholds, arising from the cellular networks comprising the system, are the focus of negative emotionality down at the four-factor level of the personality models shown in Table 9.2.

Similarly, long-term enduring parameters of the anger/rage system comprise the individual differences variables called disagreeable disinhibition and PSY-5 aggressiveness. Both the interest/seeking system and joy system are related to positive emotionality (or its reflected labels, introversion/low positive emotionality). Depue and Lenzenweger (2006) argue convincingly that the interest/seeking System, involved in incentive motivation, relates more to drive and surgent aspects of positive emotionality, whereas the opiate-driven positive states following consummatory behavior are more linked with the positive joyful hedonic reactions to affiliation.

Unconscientious disinhibition and disconstraint have a more complex link to basic emotion systems. For these individual differences variables, the focus is not on the here and now; rather, it is on the capacity of the person to readily, spontaneously build models of the future that incorporate potential dangers. Thus a constrained individual is constrained because he or she projects into the future and is guided by constructions of the bad things that may happen down the road. This is risk assessment, and risk assessment is always about the future. This interesting connection between emotion and time perspective is discussed further in the subsequent section on disconstraint.

This section has detailed the connection between the emotion systems that we each have, and the individuating parameters of those systems, called personality traits. This connection between the

Table 9.2 A few links between emotion systems and major personality traits

Emotion system	MKW-4	PSY-5
Fear	Negative emotionality	Negative emotionality
Anger/rage	Disagreeable disinhibition	Aggressiveness
Interest/seeking	Positive emotionality	Introversion/low PE
Joy	Positive emotionality	Introversion/low PE
Fear × time perspective	Unconscientious disinhibition	Disconstraint

Notes: MKW-4 is the four-factor solution of Markon et al. (2005). "Fear × time perspective," described in more detail later in the chapter, indicates that spontaneously mapping emotional tags onto models of the future is central to the personality traits called unconscientious disinhibition or disconstraint.

emotion systems and the personality traits lies at the connection of the two branches of psychological science. Much of psychology is the psychology of general laws—principles like habituation or operant conditioning, the power and log laws relating stimulus magnitudes to sensory neuron firng rates; these are general laws that may apply across all vertebrates, all mammals, or all people. The basic emotion systems we have considered are, as Jaak Panksepp (1998) noted, mammalian homologies. All mammals—all mice, all cats, goats, whales, lemurs, and humans—have these basic emotion systems. But every mouse, cat, goat, and human has enduring parameters—long-lasting characteristics of those shared systems. This is what Allport (1937) meant by a nomothetic trait—individual variation in a system that is shared by a population. Those long-lasting individuating properties—those are personality traits. Traits belong to the other side of the scientific psychology—the individual differences. Personality traits can guide the clinician to properly apply the general laws to the case of the individual patient.

From an evolutionary perspective, why would individual differences remain in a critical adaptive system? If the systems deal with important problems, should not selection have wrung out all the variation between individuals? No. Selection can never remove individual differences when the selection cannot be unidirectional. Too much fear is bad, but so is too little. And fear is a particularly interesting example for the preservation of variance in that fear of predators may act in exactly the opposite way to fear of sexual competitors in terms of contributions to reproductive fitness. With a fear system set point controlled by many genes, a single gene promoting a highly reactive fear system can at times act like a protective factor, useful in a population because it prevents, on average, having a fear system set too low. This action as a protective factor balances its cost as a risk factor in promoting too strong a fear system. And you can see on the other side, that genes promoting low fear set points can serve as protective factors against overly reactive fear systems, balancing their cost as promoters of inadequate fear systems. Individual differences can be quite prominent and stable in major adaptive systems with polygenic control when there can be no unidirectional selection. Nike shoe company may tout "No Fear," but nature does not.

The MMPI-2 PSY-5 Scales

A convenient overview of personality traits can be scored from an administration of the MMPI-2: The Personality Psychopathology Five (PSY-5) scales

(Harkness, McNulty, & Ben-Porath, 1995). Because the PSY-5 Scales are scored from the MMPI-2, it is highly available to practitioners. Pope, Butcher, and Seelen (2006) suggest that the MMPI-2 remains the most widely used psychopathology and personality assessment instrument.

The psychometric properties of the PSY-5 scales, and guidelines for interpretation are reported in a University of Minnesota Press test report (Harkness et al., 2002). The PSY-5 model has been described by Butcher and Rouse (1996), Millon and Davis (2000), Widiger and Trull (1997), and by Widiger and Simonsen (2005). Pearson Assessments provides PSY-5 scores with three MMPI-2 reports: the Extended Score Report, The Minnesota Reports, and the Criminal Justice and Correctional Report. A number of textbooks offer instruction on interpretation of the PSY-5 scores: Butcher and Williams (2000) and Friedman, Lewak, Nichols, Webb (2000), and Graham (2006).

The PSY-5 measurement model (Harkness & McNulty, 1994) is connected to current models of personality and psychopathology (Watson, Clark, and Harkness, 1994), for example, it measures the four-factor level in the meta-analysis of Markon et al. (2005), described in a preceding section, with its Aggressiveness, Disconstraint, Negative Emotionality/Neuroticism, and Introversion/Low Positive Emotionality Scales. Further, the PSY-5 taps clinically relevant disconnection from reality with its Psychoticism scale. The relationship of the PSY-5 model to normal sample-based five factor models has been well established and described (McNulty & Harkness, 2002; Trull, Useda, Costa, & McCrae, 1995), evidencing robustness across translation and culture (Egger, De Mey, Derksen, & van der Staak, 2003).

Brief Introduction to PSY-5 Scale Interpretations

In this section, I provide a brief introduction to PSY-5 interpretation based on a test report (Harkness et al., 2002). The clinician interested in a more detailed description of the MMPI-2 PSY-5 scales can consult the test report and also Harkness and McNulty (2006).

AGGRESSIVENESS (AGGR)

Aggression can be used to try to get things and to try to dominate others. The underlying psychological system detects connections between one's agenda and the potential threats to that agenda. Energy is organized and motivation is directed to agonistically remove obstacles. Thus it is hypothesized that AGGR is an individual differences variable involving enduring parameters of the rage system. Panksepp (1998) noted that dominance involves interactions between the seeking system and the rage system. The seeking system is involved in incentive motivation and thus agenda setting; the rage system detects threats to the agendas directed by incentive motivation.

If a patient has an MMPI-2 AGGR uniform T-score of 65 or greater, he or she may attempt to intimidate others and use aggression to achieve ends. Outpatients with high AGGR scores were found to be more likely to have a history of being physically abusive. High-AGGR men were more likely to have been domestically violent. High-AGGR women were more likely to have been arrested. It is now recommended that low scores (uniform T-score of 40 or less) should be interpreted as reflecting passivity, and an inability to assert or defend one's agenda (Weisenburger, Harkness, McNulty, Graham, & Ben-Porath, 2008).

The PSY-5 AGGR scale has shown some utility in forensic settings (Petroskey, Ben-Porath, & Stafford, 2003). When AGGR was included in a multiple regression along with the other PSY-5 scales, PSY-5 produced larger R^2 values than the NEO PI battery in predicting a targeted aggression scale (Sharpe & Desai, 2001).

PSYCHOTICISM (PSYC)

How connected to reality is the patient? Does the patient depart from the reality seen by a consensus of his or her peers? PSY-5 PSYC assesses disconnection from reality. No single system is detailed because so many varied sensory, perceptual, and cognitive systems underlie a person's net connection to reality. Human mental mechanisms did not evolve to directly appreciate reality; rather, they evolved to maximize reproductive and inclusive fitness. Thus mental mechanisms put a spin on reality from the first milliseconds of information processing—the sharpening of contrast in the visual system, for example. Commitment to truth and connection to reality require thought, evidence, logic, and willingness to sacrifice our wishes for truth, and they certainly require effort. And they create an amazingly potent individual difference.

Patients with MMPI-2 PSYC uniform T-scores greater than 65 have a higher probability of delusions of reference, thinking that is disorganized, bizarre, disoriented, circumstantial, or tangential. Harkness, McNulty, Finger, Arbisi, and Ben-Porath (1999) found that in an inpatient setting: high-PSYC patients were found to have had admission chart notations indicating psychosis, paranoid suspiciousness, ideas of reference, loosening of associations, hallucinations, or flight of ideas. Low scores on PSYC should not be interpreted.

DISCONSTRAINT (DISC)

DISC involves the capacity to spontaneously model the future in a way that allows the anticipation of negative consequences. High-DISC people tend not to model the future in a way that allows them to anticipate danger. Constrained people seem to naturally anticipate future danger, and thus they model risk quite differently. DISC thus involves both taking a future time perspective, and also the mapping of emotionally valenced risks (and perhaps opportunities) onto spontaneously generated representations of the future. This individual difference follows one of the great divides in human history: the farmer versus the hunter-gatherer. A farmer considering the next season needs to be much more constrained than the hunter-gatherer. The hunter-gatherer probably needs to be more disconstrained and risk taking. In fact, an entire suite of psychological traits involving risk assessment, rule following, traditionalism, spontaneity, and the enjoyment of the gamble aligns with each major human strategy.

A similar difference applies to child-bearing strategy. In order to succeed by rearing a small number of offspring with great investment in each, anticipation of danger is critical. To instead parent many children, with little investment in each, one must be more risk taking. DISC is one personality variable with a reliable gender difference: men tend to be higher on DISC. Thus women may simply tend to do a better job of taking the long view. Having a future viewing model of the world might serve a reproductive strategy of concentrating parental effort on a few offspring.

The DISC construct grew out of Tellegen's (1982) exploratory Multidimensional Personality Questionnaire (MPQ) construction program. DISC is a version of Tellegen's constraint, but its name is "reflected." Constraint was one of the three superfactors of the original MPQ. Tellegen's (1982) primary factors of traditionalism, harm avoidance, and control were heavily weighted in forming the superfactor of constraint.

The history of Tellegen's (1982) harm avoidance scale points to the importance of anticipating the future negative consequences. Lykken (1955) had developed an item format in his doctoral dissertation that forced a choice between a future physical risk versus a boring task. A collaboration between David

Lykken and Auke Tellegen produced a precursor to the MPQ harm avoidance scale (Lykken, Tellegen, & Katzenmeyer, 1973). A major feature of Lykken's (1957) dissertation had involved the performance of psychopaths in a mental maze that required anticipation of future punishment.

PSY-5 DISC correlates solidly with MPQ constraint (reversed). Persons with scores on PSY-5 DISC greater than 65 tend to be more risk taking, impulsive, and less traditional. Since an alternative future does not readily appear for them, they are more susceptible to boredom when faced with a routine task in the here and now. High-DISC outpatients tend to have a history of being arrested and abusing alcohol, cocaine, and marijuana. They show a slight tendency to prefer romantic partners with elevated DISC.

In contrast, low scores on DISC (uniform T-scores of less than 40) suggest a constrained personality pattern. Constrained individuals tend to take less risk, and exhibit greater self-control and boredom tolerance. They show more tendency to be rule followers, and evidence a slight tendency to prefer romantic partners with similarly constrained personality patterns. Some people are just more likely than others to consider what that eagle tattoo will look like in 50 years!

DISC predicts which back pain patients will be unwilling to try potentially painful but effective treatment regimes (Vendrig, Derksen, & De Mey, 2000). DISC appears to be unusally effective in predicting alcohol and drug use (Rouse, Butcher, & Miller, 1999). DISC also appears to be effective in isolating an externalizing subtype of PTSD patient (Miller, Kaloupek, Dillon, & Keane, 2004).

NEGATIVE EMOTIONALITY/NEUROTICISM (NEGE)

This chapter began with a description of Jane, who thought "cryptosporidium" when her coffee tasted odd. The danger analysis system hypothesized by Tellegen (1985) and elucidated by LeDoux (1996) is thought to underlie individual differences in NEGE. Jane, and others at a high trait level of NEGE, would tend to focus on the signals of danger in incoming information. Watson and Clark (1984) noted such persons tend to worry, to be self-critical, to feel guilty, and to concoct worst-case scenarios. Outpatients with NEGE scores greater than 65 were found to have higher rates of depression and dysthymia, were more socially isolated, and tended to have lower levels of functioning. Their therapists rated them higher on anxiety, depression, and sad mood state. Low NEGE scores should not be interpreted.

INTROVERSION/LOW POSITIVE EMOTIONALITY (INTR)

Both lower levels of incentive motivation and lower responses to positive consummatory events are the hallmarks of high INTR. Meehl (1975) drew attention to the joy side of the individual differences in his work on "hedonic capacity." When a warm fire on a cold night, a giggly baby, and chocolates fail to produce the experience of joy and positive engagement, the person is hedonically impaired. The PSY-5 INTR scale elevations also imply reduced levels of incentive motivation, or lower urgency or drive. Outpatient men with INTR scores greater than 65 showed increased rates of dysthymia and depression diagnoses, were depressed and sad during completion of a mental status exam, and were rated by their therapists as having low achievement orientation. Outpatient women with INTR scores greater than 65 were more likely to have been prescribed antidepressant medication, and to have few or no friends.

Persons with low INTR scores (MMPI-2 uniform T-scores of 40 or less) tend to exhibit an extroverted/high positive emotionality pattern, having a greater capacity to experience pleasure and joy, and be more social and energetic. Extremely low scores may be associated with hypomanic features.

Two Futures for Jane

Traits are enduring; but traits are not destiny. Given that Jane is at a high trait level of negative emotionality, that she has a low-threshold danger analysis system, what kind of life will she have? Let me briefly sketch two alternative Janes. "Clinical Jane" finds that her frequent sense of tension is reduced, for brief time, by inhaled nicotine. Her fingers and lungs become stained by a heavy addiction to cigarettes. Clinical Jane finds that it is more comfortable to focus her talented danger detector on the TV set rather than on her real life. Yes, she worries about the characters on TV, but that is less upsetting than worrying about her job, taxes, retirement, and relationship problems. Unfortunately, this means she spends little time actively solving her problems. Clinical Jane's frequent experience of tension and worry is fertile soil for the negative reinforcement of quick-acting tension reducers. In addition to cigarettes, Clinical Jane finds that candy, fatty foods, and alcohol all bring respite. As she assesses her acquaintances, their faults and failings are foremost in her thoughts: they are danger signals, and her fear system commands that she focus on them. She isolates herself, reducing opportunities for social support and warmth. Clinical Jane clearly sees the problems and limitations of each job she holds. So she never holds them for long, creating a lack of seniority and experience that increases her financial problems.

"Nonclinical Jane" finds a partner who is not disturbed by her worries. Nonclinical Jane finds that exercise is a good way to get relief from tension. Nonclinical Jane finds a job in the occupational safety field; her uncanny ability to spot potential problems is richly rewarded. To be safe, nonclinical Jane gets a guard dog that turns out to be a fine companion to Jane and her partner. Nonclinical Jane may be jumpy, ready to interpret the new as the dangerous. But she can also develop a sense of herself as a normal human being with an especially sensitive danger-detection system—something she must always factor into her decisions and self-assessment, and evaluations of her achievements. Learning to live well while accepting and appreciating what makes you an individual—that is a deep life achievement.

A clinician cannot understand a patient using only a Diagnostics and Statistics Manual (DSM). The clinician needs a complete psychology that links emotion systems, sensation, perception, learning, thinking, and motivation to life history. Personality traits are an indispensable link holding together this complete psychology. In 1997, Harkness and Lilienfeld suggested that assessment of personality traits offers a rapid route to helping a person understand the fundamental parameters that distinguish him or her from others and provide major adaptive challenges in life. A skilled clinician can help provide Jane with a specific owner's manual, helping her to learn to live effectively with the enduring characteristics that are her personality traits. For the reader more interested in therapeutics, Harkness and McNulty (2002) outlined a strategy to bring personality trait assessment to bear on clinical problems and human growth.

Acknowledgment

The author greatly appreciates that Claire Harkness read the earlier versions of this chapter.

References

Allport, G. W. (1937). *Personality: A psychological interpretation*. New York: Holt.

Berridge, K. C., & Robinson, T. E. (1998). What is the role of dopamine in reward: Hedonic impact, reward learning, or incentive salience? *Brain Research Reviews, 28*, 309–369.

Borkenau, P., Riemann, R., Angleitner, A., & Spinath, F. M. (2001). Genetic and environmental influences on observed personality: Evidence from the German observational study of adult twins. *Journal of Personality and Social Psychology, 80*, 655–668.

Butcher, J. N., & Rouse, S. V. (1996). Personality: Individual differences and clinical assessment. *Annual Review of Psychology, 47*, 87–111.

Butcher, J. N., & Williams, C. L. (2000). *Essentials of MMPI-2 and MMPI-A interpretation* (2nd ed.). Minneapolis, MN: University of Minnesota Press.

Caspi, A. (2000). The child is the father of the man: Personality continuities from childhood to adulthood. *Journal of Personality and Social Psychology, 78*, 158–172.

Depue, R. A., & Lenzenweger, M. F. (2006). A multidimensional neurobehavioral model of personality disturbance. In R. F. Krueger & J. L. Tackett (Eds.), *Personality and psychopathology* (pp. 210–261). New York: Guilford.

Egger, J. I. M., De Mey, H. R. A., Derksen, J. J. L., & van der Staak, C. P. F. (2003). Cross-cultural replication of the Five-Factor Model and comparison of the NEO PI-R and the MMPI-2 PSY-5 scales in a Dutch psychiatric sample. *Psychological Assessment, 15*, 81–88.

Ekman, P. (2007). *Emotions revealed: Recognizing faces and feelings to improve communication and emotional life* (2nd ed.). New York: Owl.

Friedman, A. F., Lewak, R., Nichols, D. S., & Webb, J. T. (2000). *Psychological assessment with the MMPI-2*. Mahwah, NJ: Lawrence Erlbaum Associates.

Graham, J. R. (2006). *MMPI-2: Assessing personality and psychopathology* (4th ed.). New York: Oxford University Press.

Harkness, A. R. (1992). Fundamental topics in the personality disorders: Candidate trait dimensions from lower regions of the hierarchy. *Psychological Assessment, 4*, 251–259.

Harkness, A. R., & Lilienfeld, S. O. (1997). Individual differences science for treatment planning: Personality traits. *Psychological Assessment, 9*, 349–360.

Harkness, A. R., & McNulty, J. L. (1994). The Personality Psychopathology Five (PSY-5): Issue from the pages of a diagnostic manual instead of a dictionary. In S. Strack & M. Lorr (Eds.), *Differentiating normal and abnormal personality*. New York: Springer.

Harkness, A. R., & McNulty, J. L. (2002). Implications of personality individual differences science for clinical work on personality disorders. In P. T. Costa, Jr. & T. A. Widiger (Eds.), *Personality disorders and the Five-Factor Model of personality* (2nd ed., pp. 391–403). Washington, DC: American Psychological Association.

Harkness, A. R., & McNulty, J. L. (2006). An overview of personality: The MMPI-2 Personality Psychopathology-Five Scales (PSY-5). In J. N. Butcher (Ed.), *MMPI-2: A practitioner's guide* (pp. 73–97). Washington, DC: American Psychological Association.

Harkness, A. R., McNulty, J. L., & Ben-Porath, Y. S. (1995). The Personality Psychopathology Five (PSY-5): Constructs and MMPI-2 scales. *Psychological Assessment, 7*, 104–114.

Harkness, A. R., McNulty, J. L., Ben-Porath, Y. S., & Graham, J. R. (2002). *The Personality Psychopathology Five (PSY-5) scales: Gaining an overview for case conceptualization and treatment planning*. Minneapolis, MN: University of Minnesota Press.

Harkness, A. R., McNulty, J. L., Finger, M. S., Arbisi, P. A., & Ben-Porath, Y. S. (1999). *The pleiometric nature of psychoticism items, or why the Big-5 does not measure psychoticism*. Paper presented at the 34th Annual MMPI-2 Symposium, Huntington Beach, CA, April 1999.

Izard, C. E. (1991). *The psychology of emotions*. New York: Plenum.

Izard, C. E., & Ackerman, B. P. (2004). Motivational, organizational, and regulatory functions of discrete emotions. In M. Lewis & J. M. Haviland-Jones (Eds.), *Handbook of emotions* (2nd ed., pp. 253–264). New York: Guilford.

LeDoux, J. (1996). *The emotional brain: The mysterious underpinnings of emotional life*. New York: Touchstone.

Loehlin, J. C., & Rowe, D. C. (1992). Genes, environment, and personality. In G. Capara & G. L. Van Heck (Eds.), *Modern personality psychology: Critical reviews and new directions* (pp. 352–370). New York: Harvester Wheatsheaf.

Lykken, D. T. (1955). *A study of anxiety in the sociopathic personality*. Unpublished doctoral dissertation, University of Minnesota.

Lykken, D. T. (1957). A study of anxiety in the sociopathic personality. *Journal of Abnormal and Social Psychology, 55*, 6–10.

Lykken, D. T., Tellegen, A., & Katzenmeyer, C. (1973). *Manual for the activity perference questionnaire*. Unpublished manuscript, Department of Psychiatry, University of Minnesota.

Markon, K. E., Krueger, R. F., & Watson, D. (2005). Delineating the structure of normal and abnormal personality: An integrative hierarchical approach. *Journal of Personality and Social Psychology, 88*, 139–157.

McNulty, J. L., & Harkness, A. R. (2002). The MMPI-2 PSY-5 Scales and the Five-Factor Model. In B. De Raad & M. Perugini (Eds.), *Big Five assessment* (pp. 435–456). Seattle: Hogrefe & Huber.

Meehl, P. E. (1975). Hedonic capacity: Some conjectures. *Bulletin of the Menninger Clinic, 39*, 295–307.

Meehl, P. E. (1986). Trait language and behaviorese. In T. Thompson & M. D. Zeiler (Eds.), *Analysis and integration of behavioral units* (pp. 315–334). Hillsdale, NJ: Erlbaum.

Miller, M. W., Kaloupek, D. G., Dillon, A. L., & Keane, T. M. (2004). Externalizing and internalizing subtypes of combat-related PTSD: A replication and extension using the PSY-5 Scales. *Journal of Abnormal Psychology, 113*, 636–645.

Millon, T., & Davis, R. (2000). *Personality disorders in modern life*. New York: John Wiley & Sons.

Panksepp, J. (1998). *Affective neuroscience: The foundations of human and animal emotions*. New York: Oxford University Press.

Patrick, C. J., & Bernat, E. M. (2006). The construct of emotion as a bridge between personality and psychopathology. In R. F. Krueger & J. L. Tackett (Eds.). *Personality and psychopathology* (pp. 174–209). New York: Guilford.

Petroskey, L. J., Ben-Porath, Y. S., & Stafford, K. P. (2003). Correlates of the Minnesota Multiphasic Personality Inventory-2 (MMPI-2) Personality Psychopathology Five (PSY-5) Scales in a Forensic Assessment Setting. *Assessment, 10*, 393–399.

Pope, K. S., Butcher, J. N., & Seelen, J. (2006). The MMPI, MMPI-2, and MMPI-A in court testimony. In K. S. Pope, J. N. Butcher, & J. Seelen (Eds.), *The MMPI, MMPI-2, & MMPI-A in court: A practical guide for expert witnesses and attorneys* (3rd ed., pp. 7–36). Washington, DC: American Psychological Association.

Rouse, S. B., Butcher, J. N., & Miller, K. B. (1999). Assessment of substance abuse in psychotherapy clients: The effectiveness of the MMPI-2 substance abuse scales. *Psychological Assessment, 11*, 101–107.

Rowe, D. C. (1994). *The limits of family influence: Genes, experience, and behavior*. New York: Guilford.

Saudino, K. J., Pedersen, N. L., Lichtenstein, P., McClearn, G. E., & Plomin, R. (1997). Can personality explain genetic influences on life events? *Journal of Personality and Social Psychology, 72*, 196–206.

Sharpe, J. E., & Desai, S. (2001). The revised NEO Personality Inventory and the MMPI-2 Psychopathology Five in the prediction of aggression. *Personality and Individual Differences, 31*, 505–518.

Tellegen, A. (1982). *Brief manual for the Differential Personality Questionnaire*. Unpublished manuscript, University of Minnesota, Minneapolis, MN (since renamed Multidimensional Personality Questionnaire).

Tellegen, A. (1985). Structures of mood and personality and their relevance to assessing anxiety, with an emphasis on self-report. In A. H. Tuma & J. D. Maser (Eds.), *Anxiety and the anxiety disorders*. Hillsdale, NJ: Lawrence Erlbaum.

Tellegen, A. (1988). The analysis of consistency in personality assessment. *Journal of Personality, 56*, 621–663.

Tomkins, S. (1962). *Affect-imagery-consciousness, Vol. I: The positive affects*. New York: Springer.

Tomkins, S. (1991). *Affect-imagery-consciousness, Vol. III: The negative affects, anger and fear*. New York: Springer.

Trull, T. J., & Durrett, C. A. (2005). Categorical and dimensional models of personality disorder. *Annual Reviews of Clinical Psychology, 1*, 355–380.

Trull, T. J., Useda, J. D., Costa, P. T., & McCrae, R. R. (1995). Comparison of the MMPI-2 Personality Psychopathology Five (PSY-5), the NEO PI, and NEO PI-R. *Psychological Assessment, 7*, 508–516.

Vendrig, A. A., Derksen, J. J. L., & De Mey, H. R. (2000). MMPI-2 Personality Psychopathology Five (PSY-5) and prediction of treatment outcome for patients with chronic back pain. *Journal of Personality Assessment, 74*, 423–438.

Watson, D., & Clark, L. A. (1984). Negative affectivity: The disposition to experience aversive emotional states. *Psychological Bulletin, 96*, 465–490.

Watson, D., & Clark, L. A. (1993). Behavioral disinhibition versus constraint: A dispositional perspective. In D. M. Wegner & J. W. Pennebaker (Eds.), *Handbook of mental control* (pp. 506–527). New York: Prentice Hall.

Watson, D., Clark, L. A., & Harkness, A. R. (1994). Structures of personality and their relevance to psychopathology. *Journal of Abnormal Psychology, 103*, 18–31.

Weisenburger, S. M., Harkness, A. R., McNulty, J. L., Graham, J. R., & Ben-Porath, Y. S. (2008). Interpreting low PSY-5 aggressiveness scores on the MMPI-2: Use of graphical, robust, and resistant data analysis. *Psychological Assessment, 20*, 403–408.

Widiger, T. A. (1998). Four out of five ain't bad. *Archives of General Psychiatry, 55*, 865–866.

Widiger, T. A., & Simonsen, E. (2005). Alternative dimensional models of personality disorders: Finding a common ground. *Journal of Personality Disorders, 19*, 110–130.

Widiger, T. A., & Trull, T. J. (1997). Assessment of the Five-Factor Model of personality. *Journal of Personality Assessment, 68*, 228–250.

Computer-Based Assessment

James N. Butcher, Julia N. Perry, *and* Brooke L. Dean

Abstract

Practitioners are increasingly using computer-administered and computer-interpreted personality assessments in their practice to gain a broader and quicker evaluation of their client's problems. Although psychologists have made great strides in developing computer-based test interpretation reports of traditional measures, the available technology has not been fully utilized in several areas such as development of virtual reality (lifelike) test stimuli, maximal data processing methods, and complex interpretation strategies that account for the complexities of the real world. Also, adaptive versions are likely to have limited utility since most practitioners (particularly forensic psychologists) need thorough evaluations, not just to save a few minutes of client time. Internet-based assessment is faced with problems as well as opportunities. The development and validation of Internet-based assessment resources has not kept pace with the technological developments and there has been relatively limited research on the equivalence in testing conditions, equivalence of normative databases, etc., important to reliable and valid test use.

Keywords: computer adaptive testing, Internet-based assessment, computerized interviews, CBTI, BTPI, MMPI/MMPI-2

Psychological assessment emerged during the early twentieth century with the development of tests for assessing characteristics such as intelligence, personality, and suitability for employment (Butcher, 2006; Weiner & Greene, 2008). Psychological testing has become integral to clinical and forensic practice in contemporary psychology today, and numerous psychological assessments exist for use by clinicians and researchers alike. These assessments and tests provide evaluation for various areas of functioning, such as neuropsychology, personality, career interests and values, and psychopathology.

There are generally two sources of information available for computer-based personality tests: the published psychological literature and the publisher's catalogs of commercially available tests. For the most part, this chapter will address the published psychological literature. The goals are as follows:

(a) to provide a contemporary overview of computer-based personality assessment; (2) to examine the extent of current computer-based assessment; (3) to provide a historical context for computerized psychological assessment; and (4) to illustrate computer-based personality assessment with a clinical case example. In addition, later in the chapter, we will address some contemporary issues in computer-based assessment, including computer-adapted test administration strategies and the use of the Internet to conduct psychological assessments.

In a survey of psychologists (Camara, Nathan, & Puente, 2000), the eleven most commonly used assessments by clinicians were the Wechsler Adult Intelligence Scale-Revised (WAIS-R), the Minnesota Multiphasic Personality Inventory (MMPI), the Wechsler Intelligence Scale for Children (WISC), the Rorschach Inkblot Test, the Bender Visual Motor Gestalt Test, the

Thematic Apperception Test (TAT), the Wide Range Achievement Test (WRAT), the House-Tree-Person Projective Technique, the Wechsler Memory Scale-Revised (WMS-R), the Millon Clinical Multiaxial Inventory (MCMI), and (tied with the MCMI for 10th position) the Beck Depression Inventory. Strikingly, only 12% of the clinical psychologists from this survey reported that they engage in assessment-related practice (i.e., administration, scoring, and interpretation/report writing) for more than 10 hr per week. Underscoring the perceived value of these select few instruments in guiding psychological services is the fact that there has been little change over the last 30 years with regard to the assessments endorsed as being most frequently used by clinicians. In addition, it is interesting to note that they still include a mix of objective and projective assessments (Cashel, 2002; Lubin, Larsen, Matarazzo, & Seever, 1985; Watkins, Campbell, Nieberding, & Hallmark, 1995).

Not only do clinicians have a multitude of assessment instruments from which to choose, but there are also numerous settings in which these assessments can be utilized. For instance, assessments are commonly used in college counseling centers, community clinics, hospitals, law enforcement, businesses and organizations, and forensic settings. Data show that the amount of time spent using assessments may depend on the psychologist's work setting. For instance, Camara and colleagues' (2000) study suggests that most clinical psychologists spend less than 10 hr per week in assessment-related practice, but also shows that one-third of neuropsychologists spend an average of 20 hr or more per week in assessment-related practice; thus they would have more opportunity to incorporate computerized assessments into their work. However, there has been a recent trend toward limiting compensation or assessment benefits for insurance holders on the part of managed care policies. This is apt to have a negative impact on psychologists utilizing particular assessments, such as the Wechsler scales and the MMPI-2, in their clinical work due to lack of reimbursement (Camara et al., 2000; Cashel, 2002).

Utilization of Computerized Assessments

Recent technological advances have propelled all of society into a new generation of computer usage, and psychological professionals are no exception (Bartram & Hambleton, 2006). Psychological assessment has not gone untouched during this recent fervor to use computers more and paper-and-pencil tasks less. In general, approximately 75% of clinicians report using computers as part of their daily work, albeit primarily for word processing purposes (Rosen & Weil, 1996). Moreover, approximately 25% of clinicians indicated they had Internet access at their practice location (Rosen & Weil, 1996). Nonetheless, even though computer interactive strategies have been shown to engage clients in tasks effectively (Hake, 1998), survey results suggest that clinicians are not using computer-based assessments at the rates that we might expect in light of the increasing popularity of computer technology in the general population. As a means of communication related to service delivery, only 2% of clinicians sampled in one recent study reported utilization of Internet or satellite-based video connection technology, whereas nearly every clinician endorsed use of the telephone for practice-related communication (VandenBos & Williams, 2000). These findings beg the question of how computer technology has affected the use of computerized assessments specifically, as it has been suggested that there are few common behaviors among clinicians regarding computer-related technology (McMinn, Buchanan, Ellens, & Ryan, 1999).

Almost 20 years ago, Farrell (1989) surveyed 227 practicing psychologists and determined that 41% frequently used computers for test scoring, and 29% used them for test interpretation. More recent surveys of computer assessment utilization actually report a decrease in rates, such that approximately 26% of clinicians frequently use computers for test scoring, and 20% use them for test interpretation (McMinn et al., 1999; see also Rosen & Weil, 1996). Although clinicians may not frequently use computers in their daily practice activities, at least two-thirds of them do report using computers for testing purposes or assisting with psychological testing (Ball, Archer, & Imhof, 1994). Another recent survey found that the most common service utilized by both neuropsychologists and clinical psychologists is scoring with computer-based assessments, which comprises about 10% of all testing services conducted. On the other hand, administration and interpretation applications each accounted for only 3% of testing services (Camara et al., 2000). Moreover, clinicians reported using computer-based assessment most often for personality and/or psychopathology assessment (Camara et al., 2000), suggesting considerable potential when one considers the range of areas in which computers are seemingly underutilized.

Additional Computer Applications in Clinical Assessment

Psychological testing is not the only application for using computers, as opportunities exist for computers to aid in other areas of clinical work. In reviewing articles that illustrate the various computer applications in clinical assessment, the examples fell roughly into one of two groups: The first was composed of applications within traditional clinical work in which a computer application served as an aid to the clinician; the second consisted of applications available online, via the Internet, some of them replacing the clinician. Applications in the former group include aids to clinical interviews, diagnosis, psychopathology screening, and psychotherapy treatment interventions. Applications in the latter group place greater emphasis on psycho-educational tools and provision of services. For example, Barak (1999) lists several Internet psychological applications that include information resources and self-help guides, help in seeking counseling services, actual psychological advice through e-mail or messages posted on e-bulletin boards, and ongoing personal psychotherapy and support groups.

The following section addresses additional computer applications for use in clinical assessment in three areas: clinical interview and diagnosis, psychopathology screening, and psychotherapy treatment intervention.

Clinical Interviews, Screening, and Diagnosis

One of the most basic and routine aspects of clinical work is the initial interview with a client, which subsequently provides information leading to a diagnosis. During the initial interview, clinicians are faced with the difficult task of obtaining a large amount of information about a client in a short amount of time. If a computer program could ascertain most of this client information without the presence of a clinician, then during the actual face-to-face interview, the clinician could obtain a greater amount of pertinent information highlighted from the basic data gathered by the computer program. Carr, Ghosh, and Ancill (1983) attempted this strategy over 20 years ago using a computer program to obtain personal histories from patients in a psychiatric unit. The results were compared with the information recorded by clinicians to judge whether the computer was able to gather similar information as a clinician would in a face-to-face situation. The researchers suggested that a computer program was indeed helpful and allowed clinicians to focus on areas most relevant during the face-to-face interview.

Over 20 years later, use of computer-based applications for screening purposes may not yet be common, but there seems to be high potential for them to aid with clinical assessment, whether computers serve as adjuncts or alternatives to clinicians as data gatherers. Some current computer programs interview the client and detect particular symptoms through voice recognition software or analyzing content of speech.

Computer applications have shown promise with regard to detecting multiple types of psychopathology and problems (Berger, 2006), including depressive symptomatology and suicidal ideation (Gonzalez & Shriver, 2004; Levine, Ancill, & Roberts, 1989), substance misuse (Ames et al., 2007; Freeman, Lester, McNamara, Melby, & Schumacher, 2006; Hester & Miller, 2006; Koski-Jannes, Cunningham, Tolonen, & Bothas, 2007), anxiety (Chen, 2007), and eating disorders (Roy & Forest, 2006). Levine, Ancill, and Roberts (1989) actually suggest that computers predict suicidality better than clinicians, in that participants confided more readily to the computer than to the clinician. Other recent literature is positive with regard to the promise of computerized methods. Reips (2006) has noted several advantages of web-based assessment methods, and Richard and Gloster (2006) have put forth a discussion of how technology could assist clinicians with behavioral assessment, based on clinicians' attitudes toward technology integration.

Garb's 2007 review highlights the potential for time savings with computerized evaluations and also notes their promise with regard to improving the comprehensiveness of evaluations, specifically with regard to overshadowing, or the tendency for clinicians to make selected diagnoses but overlook others. He cites data suggesting anywhere from "poor" to "fair" concordance with clinician diagnoses, depending on the type of interview, clinicians, and diagnostic category in question. He also notes that computer-based interviews tend to result in more diagnoses than clinician-based interviews.

There is room to debate whether Garb's last finding is a positive, negative, or neutral one. Moreover, whether diagnoses are made in greater or lesser numbers, it is important of course to consider their accuracy and helpfulness. A recent review of clinical decision support systems (CDSSs), in which patient-specific recommendations are generated by software through matching patient qualities to a computerized knowledge base, examined whether practitioner performance in determining diagnosis and creating treatment plans or patient outcome was improved by using this computer aid (Garg et al., 2005). Of the 100 studies included in this particular review, only four were studies assessing CDSS for mental health use. Only one of those four mental health trials led to improvement in practitioner performance. Two of the four studies also measured patient outcomes, but neither was successful in improving patient outcomes (Garg et al., 2005; Lewis, Sharp, Bartholomew, & Pelosi, 1996; Rollman et al., 2002). Thus, all told, there is mixed evidence with regard to potential "best practices" in utilizing computer-based applications in clinical interviews and diagnosis.

Psychotherapy Interventions

The existing computer applications for psychotherapy treatment interventions involve those in which the computer aids the clinician in a traditional work setting and those in which the clinician offers the intervention online, via the Internet. Kelly, Kay-Lambkin, and Kavanagh (2007) recently noted the potential benefit of computers for providing access to interventions to those people located in remote areas, which could help to remove a significant barrier to service for such individuals.

However, this literature is not new. Marin and Splete's older (1991) study examined career counseling interventions with two research conditions: computer-only and computer-plus-counselor interventions. Using a computer-based career counseling program was found to increase participants' career decidedness, and the computer-plus-counselor intervention was more effective, overall, than the computer-only intervention. Research similar to this study may help elucidate which computer applications (i.e., those accompanying clinicians or those replacing them) are most beneficial to clients.

The more recent publication regarding Internet psychotherapy interventions (which often incorporate an assessment component) tend to cluster into three subgroupings of those addressing general counseling services, those focused on online support groups, and those examining career counseling. Among the articles addressing general counseling services, the primary content focuses on the ethical nature of psychotherapy via the Internet (Alleman, 2002; McCrickard & Butler, 2005; Rochlen, Zack, & Speyer, 2004; Tate & Zabinski, 2004). Internet counseling, whether in the form of either a one-time session or multiple sessions, is easily available. However, caution is advised to both potential clients and therapists (McCrickard & Butler, 2005). The identity and credentials of the therapists may be difficult to verify by the potential client, and the identity and emergency contact information of the client may be similarly difficult to verify by the therapist, which would significantly interfere with the clinicians' ability to take needed action in the event that they must act to prevent clients from harming themselves or others (McCrickard & Butler, 2005; Robson & Robson, 2000; Rochlen et al., 2004).

Nevertheless, Alleman (2002) suggests that online counseling can certainly be done ethically and offers strategies for how this might best be conducted by the therapist. In support of one of Kelly and colleagues' (2007) observations, McCrickard and Butler (2005) list such benefits to online counseling as greater accessibility, cost-effectiveness, relatively immediate service, and access to a large amount of information. Moreover, Tate and Zabinski (2004) suggest capitalizing on computer technology by having clients complete assignments online and submit them electronically to the clinician, encouraging client support from peers, and obtaining feedback of an educational nature rather than typical therapeutic dialogue.

A key area in which Internet interventions are expanding is in career counseling. Many career-related assessments are available online to clients but access is given for this service by the clinician working with the client. This service allows a client to complete the assessment at a time and location convenient for them and then the completed assessment can be quickly received and scored by the clinician. However, this online assessment service is a computer-based application falling within traditional clinical work and not a replacement for face-to-face psychotherapy services. Other interventions for career counseling via the Internet are beginning to appear in the psychological literature. A recent review examined multiple Internet career counseling programs (Clark, Horan, Tompkins-Bjorkman, Kovalski, & Hackett, 2000). The programs reviewed by Clark and colleagues ranged in content from focusing on women's irrational career beliefs and stereotypes about occupations for women to child-rearing beliefs for parents that may influence their child's career choice to targeting at-risk youth's academic motivation and performance. These three examples of using the Internet for career counseling interventions demonstrate the variety of problems and issues that can be addressed, as well as the type of clients (e.g., youth, women, parents). Further discussion of Internet-based assessment will be addressed later in this chapter.

Computer-based interventions for various forms of mental health problems are varied as well. Hochlehnert et al. (2006) have researched the potential advantages of using computerized systems in a somewhat straightforward way, to provide education about chronic pain. On the other end of the spectrum, Anderson, Jacobs, and Rothbaum's (2004) review examined how clinicians can employ computer technology as an adjunctive tool in treating anxiety disorders. For example, palmtop computers can be used to assess the client's anxiety symptoms (e.g., frequency of obsessive thoughts or amount of time spent worrying) at designated intervals and provide feedback to the client in the form of coping statements. They also noted the potential for using virtual reality technology to aid in exposure-based treatments of fearful situations or memories.

Another example of computer-based interventions used in traditional clinical work is in aiding outcome measurement. Although Ware, Gandek, Sinclair, and Bjorner (2005) evaluated the measurement of a computer adaptive testing (CAT) program, the implications of using similar computer programs in assessing treatment outcomes make this study worth mentioning here (CAT will be discussed more fully later in the chapter). The researchers used a CAT software program to measure rehabilitation patients' levels of movement and physical activity. Using CAT, traditional pencil-and-paper assessments can be shortened in item number and amount of time needed to complete the assessment, while maintaining comparable reliability and validity to the original versions.

Treatment planning is a critical step in any mental health intervention, and computerized methods are being employed to assist therapists and clients in undertaking this process as well (Garb, 2007). For example, the Computer Assisted System for Psychotherapy Evaluation and Research (CASPER; Farrel & McCollough-Vaillant, 1996; Kinnaman, Farrell, & Bisconer, 2006) is one program that can identify treatment problems, help track progress toward goals, and examine treatment outcomes in a standard way that promotes objectivity. Multiple other systems can monitor progress as well (see Garb, 2007, for a comprehensive review). Chinman et al. (2007) have shown that computer-gathered data about treatment can improve communication between clients and providers, which would argue in favor of its use.

The History of Computers in Personality Assessment

Computer technology has long played a key role in psychological assessment, keeping in step with an increase in demands on mental health providers (Drasgow & Chuah, 2006). Fowler's (1985) account provides a helpful encapsulation of the history of its application to the field, outlining the influence of the growth in popularity of community mental health services during the mid-twentieth century and the consequent increase in the public's acceptance of mental health services. Coinciding with these developments was an increased need for psychological assessment in the face of limits to the available resources. Thus, psychology professionals came to recognize the desirability of procedures that enhanced their efficiency. See Butcher (2003), Butcher, Perry, and Atlis (2000), Butcher, Perry, and Hahn (2004), and Garb (2007) for recent reviews of computer-based assessment.

There is a long history of using mechanical means to score psychological tests. The first data-scoring computer applications were developed in the 1950s, accompanying the call for more objective clinical decision making and the advocacy of actuarial prediction methods, especially by Meehl (1954, 1956). In the 1960s, practitioners began to capitalize on computers' capabilities to assist with data interpretation as well. Optical scanners that "read" answer sheets and tabulated responses were connected with programs written to analyze the scores and report the results in a clinically meaningful way (Fowler, 1967). Today, scoring is made even easier through the use of online testing, which can provide for the nearly instant computerized tabulation of results (Baker, 2007).

An initial concern to psychologists wanting to use a computer version of an assessment rather than a paper-and-pencil version was whether the two forms are psychometrically equivalent to each other. Finger and Ones (1999) conducted a meta-analysis of 14 studies to investigate this exact question about whether the MMPI computer and booklet versions are equivalent. Their findings suggest that the two MMPI forms are psychometrically equivalent and that differences found in previous individual studies can be explained by sampling error. The majority of evidence provided by psychologists is that computer and paper-and-pencil versions of assessments are generally equivalent and any differences are typically small and inconsequential (Atlis, Hahn, & Butcher, 2006; Gershon, 2005; Pinsoneault, 1996; Simms & Clark, 2005). However, authors continue to point to the need to consider carefully the instrument and the circumstances in question (Garb, 2007).

Some 30 years after the first programs were developed, Butcher (1987) outlined perceived advantages of using prevailing computer systems, including objectivity, rapid turnaround, cost effectiveness, and reliability. He also specified possible disadvantages, such as potential for misuse, questions about form equivalence, and excessive clinician startup time. Additionally highlighted were such considerations as who would have access to reports and how acceptable validity criteria would be established. With regard specifically to expert computer interpretation systems, Vale and Keller (1987) outlined such additional advantages as standardization, currency of incorporated knowledge, ease of validation, and permanence.

Since its inception, the technology has been applied within a range of fields of psychology, including the neuropsychological and industrial/organizational domains (Butcher, 2003; Butcher Perry & Atlis, 2000, 2004). Baker's (2007) review noted the vast range of psychological tests, including single-use scales at one end of the continuum and fully validated and normed instruments at the other end. However, the literature is richest in the area of personality assessment. From the start, personality inventories have been regarded as natural targets for computer technology, especially because they are structured and involve an empirical approach to interpretation (Fowler, 1967). Thus, personality tests were the early focus of computer-based test interpretation (CBTI) systems (Fowler, 1985). Among the personality assessment instruments, the most investigative attention has been paid to the MMPI and its revised version, the MMPI-2 (Butcher, Dahlstrom, Graham, Tellegen, & Kaemmer, 1989; Butcher, Graham, Ben-Porath, Tellegen, Dahlstrom, & Kaemmer, 2001).

MMPI and MMPI-2

The first computer-assisted interpretative system, which originated at the Mayo Clinic (Rome et al., 1962; Swenson & Pearson, 1964; Swenson, Rome, Pearson, & Brannick, 1965), used the original MMPI. It was a somewhat rudimentary method (compared to today's standards) of pairing clinical scale elevations with descriptive statements in a manner suggestive of the interpretive strategies employed today. The early technology enabled large numbers of patients to be screened quickly and economically, which helped to compensate for the small staff of psychology personnel and facilitated the psychological screening of individuals who otherwise might never have received it (Fowler, 1985).

The next wave of programs expanded the capabilities of the existing technology and focused on creating clinically useful narrative reports, with the continuing goal of helping psychiatrists and psychologists arrive at diagnoses. The first of these to receive widespread attention was developed by Fowler (1964, 1965, 1967, & 1969). His program was created to evaluate the test taker's attitude toward the testing and the validity of the protocol as well as to provide interpretive statements based on clinical scale elevations, which were considered both singly and configurally. Decision rules accounted for elevations on "special scales" as well. The final product was a three-page printout, complete with narrative paragraphs, T-score values, and a list of "critical items" intended to alert clinicians to potential avenues for further follow-up.

Fowler (1985) has described other early MMPI narrative reports that were developed by Finney (1965, 1966), Caldwell (1971), and Lachar (1974). Butcher (1987) outlined several limitations associated with the early programs, including their inclusion of scales and indices that had not been well validated and their use of rationally developed (as opposed to the empirically validated) lists of critical items.

The system, known as the Minnesota report, was first published in 1982 by National Computer Systems and remains the most widely used among clinicians today. Since its development, it has been geared toward clinical relevance and ease of use, with information based on empirical test correlates (Butcher, 1987). It includes scores for validity, clinical, content, and widely researched supplementary scales. As Graham (2006) describes, the full report also contains several narrative sections. They describe the validity of the profile and the stability of the profile, and they also include hypotheses about interpersonal relationships, diagnoses, and treatment considerations.

Deskovitz (2006) examined the reliability of multiple commercially available computer-based interpretation programs, making between-program comparisons as well as between-interpreter comparisons. This dissertation research showed mostly similarities, though it also noted slight variability for certain code types.

Psychological testing has long transcended cultural boundaries, and the MMPI/MMPI-2 in particular has steadily broadened its reach internationally. There are now over 33 translations of the MMPI-2 (over 150 translations of the original instrument were completed) that are in use in dozens of countries. Psychologists in many of those countries have investigated the utility of computer-driven assessment procedures. Butcher and his colleagues (1998) summarized empirical data regarding computer-based MMPI-2 reports in Australia, France, and Norway, and they concluded that the computerized interpretations generalized appropriately to patients in those settings, with 66% of computer-based reports being judged as 80–100% accurate and 87% of reports being judged as 60% accurate or more. They concluded that, because many disorders show common patterns of symptoms across cultural lines, the breadth of problems sampled by the MMPI-2 items, coupled with a well-translated set of items, could produce familiar profile patterns. Moreover, they pointed to the potential for computer-based interpretations to reduce the "subjectivity in interpretation in cross-cultural psychopathology comparisons" (p. 311). Nonetheless, they did caution that cultural factors not be dismissed as irrelevant or trivial. In addition, it bears considering that their investigations were of Westernized cultures. The generalizability of computer-based interpretations of the MMPI-A was also shown in an international study of clinical cases (Butcher, Ellertsen et al., 2000).

Other Personality Assessment Instruments

Personality measures other than the MMPI have been the subjects of CBTI systems as well. The origins of some of the associated programs coincided with the development of the early MMPI computer technology. Soon after the Mayo Clinic's MMPI system, for example, a scoring program was developed for another inventory, the Sixteen Personality Factor, or 16-PF (Eber, 1964). That program evolved over time, incorporating additional personality measures as well as intelligence and achievement testing, so that combined reports could be generated for use in correctional and public safety settings (Fowler, 1985). In the 1970s, the Karson Clinical Report was created in order to "emulate the workings of one clinician's mind" (Karson & O'Dell, 1987, p. 199) as such an individual went about interpreting a profile.

The Rorschach Inkblot Test had its first computer-based interpretation system in the 1960s as well, as developed by Piotrowski (1964). Exner (1987) has described the subsequent attempts to ease Rorschach protocol interpretation (though not through providing full interpretation data) by using the Rorschach Interpretation Assistance Program. Exner went on to develop a better known, empirically based interpretive system in 1974. However, he has also argued against the notion that computer technology can truly replicate the complex process of integrating protocol data in a manner that replicates the thought process of an experienced clinician (Exner, 1986).

The initial CBTI systems for the MCMI and the Personality Inventory for Children (PIC), two other personality inventories, provided evidence of the heights to which computer-based technology had risen by the 1980s. As Fowler's historical review (1985) notes, the interpretation systems for some tests were developed by their respective authors along with the tests themselves, for example, the MCMI (Millon, 1977). The interpretive system for the PIC was modeled after that for the original MMPI, with information interpretation on a scale-by-scale basis and correlates connected with specific T-score ranges in an effort to maximize the accuracy of predictions (Lachar, 1987).

The BTPI

The Butcher Treatment Planning Inventory (BTPI) is a relative new comer to the field (Butcher, 2004). The BTPI is an objective, fundamentally atheoretical personality and symptom questionnaire specifically intended to aid with psychological treatment planning. It bridges psychotherapeutic intervention and objective personality assessment, allowing therapists to assess the therapeutic climate and also identify possible impediments to treatment, particularly those related to personality and symptoms.

The instrument's 210 true-or-false items comprise 14 scales and are organized into three clusters. The validity indicators assess irregularities in test takers' report of symptoms (Inconsistent Responding, INC), their efforts to portray themselves as unrealistically moral (Overly Virtuous Self-Views, VIR), their endorsement of unusual numbers of symptoms (Exaggerated Problem Presentation, EXA), and their tendency to resist self-disclosure and change (Closed-Mindedness, CLM). The Treatment Issues Scales measure vulnerability to relationship problems (Problems in Relationship Formation, REL), tendency to channel psychological problems into bodily symptoms (Somatization of Conflict, SOM), skepticism about the value of psychotherapy (Low Expectation of

Therapeutic Benefit, EXP), self-indulgent interpersonal styles (Self-Oriented/Narcissism, NAR), and feelings of emotional distance from others (Perceived Lack of Environmental Support, ENV). Finally, the Current Symptoms Scales assess depression (Low Mood, DEP), anxiety (Anxiety, ANX), tendency to express anger outwardly (Anger-Out, A-O), tendency to internalize anger (Anger-In, A-I), and extreme behaviors and possibly delusional beliefs (Unusual Thinking, PSY). For additional information about the BTPI, see Perry and Butcher (2004).

Caveats and Limitations

From the start, the practical considerations of using CBTI have been at the forefront in discussions of their usefulness, their applicability, and the ethics of their implementation. Fowler (1985) noted that the American Psychological Association (APA) created official guidelines for CBTI as early as 1966, setting standards for mail-in assessment services. In summarizing the CBTI-related ethical limitations and considerations of the time, he highlighted such key matters as who is qualified to use the reports and how the validity of the reports will be established. In his description of the early version of the MMPI Minnesota report, Butcher (1987) cautioned that it was designed for use only by professionals knowledgeable about MMPI interpretation. He further advocated for the report to be adjunctive and an augment to clinical data obtained via other means, rather than its serving as a replacement for them. He additionally outlined the importance of ensuring that computerized narratives be internally consistent and focused on empirical data, such that they factor in specific demographic and other characteristics as appropriate.

The creators and users of CBTI technology have also long cautioned against the notion that computer-based methods ultimately could replace clinicians (Fowler, 1967). The question of whether computers counterproductively "dehumanize" the assessment process has been posed from the start and has been answered in part by noting that the paper-and-pencil administration method is no less impersonal (Fowler, 1985). However, not all users of the technology express trepidation, especially in recent years. Over time, there has been a call for computers to provide more assistance with personality assessment, not less. This has been the case particularly as clinicians and resources become increasingly stretched and also, presumably, as the technology improves. Greene recently went so far as to state that "computer scoring and computer interpretation

of all psychological assessment techniques should become the basis for the psychological report" and that "psychological assessment should become a computer-based field" (2005, p. 6). Some degree of debate is likely to persist among practitioners approaching this debate from different perspectives.

Case Example

BACKGROUND

Mr. R was a 40-year-old, male, divorced, Caucasian, who presented for treatment at an outpatient mental health clinic. His chief complaint was distress about a recent on-the-job back injury. The injury had left him unable to work at packaging company and had resulted in a layoff. When he had been denied disability compensation for the injury, Mr. R suspected that there was a conspiracy between his employer and his disability attorney. This notion was highly upsetting to him.

During an intake interview with a psychologist (who went on to serve as his psychotherapist), he endorsed long-standing symptoms of depression and anxiety, as well as chronic back pain. The resulting "working diagnosis" was dysthymic disorder, and it was unclear whether his conspiracy claims warranted additional diagnosis. Therefore, the psychologist recommended psychological assessment with the MMPI-2 and the Butcher Treatment Planning Inventory (BTPI; Butcher, 2004; Butcher & Perry, 2008), for the purposes of diagnostic clarification and treatment planning.

INITIAL ASSESSMENT

Figure 10.1 shows the BTPI profile. His MMPI-2 profile was notable for paranoid ideation and persecutory thinking, possibly consistent with a thought disorder. For the purposes of treatment planning, the psychologist noted that he was likely to have a great deal of difficulty in forming trusting relationships, including those with mental health providers. See the computer-based report for the MMPI-2 and the BTPI in Figure 10.2.

Mr. R produced an essentially valid BTPI protocol, though the validity scales did suggest some over-endorsement of symptoms and problems on his part. This profile showed that he was prone to develop new or worsening physical symptoms when facing conflict and distress. It also identified potentially delusional thinking patterns, in addition to such problems as anxiety symptoms and a tendency to express anger in the form of hostility.

In conjunction with the initial evaluation, the psychologist assigned Mr. R a psychotic disorder

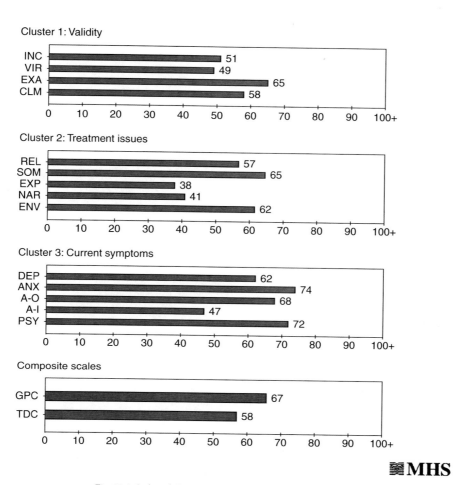

Cluster 1: Validity

Cluster 2: Treatment issues

Cluster 3: Current symptoms

Composite scales

≋MHS

Fig. 10.1 Scale and Composite T-scores. Reproduced with permission.

BTPI Interpretive Report

VALIDITY OF THE REPORT

The BTPI™ scales are likely to be a valid indication of Raymond's treatment-related attitudes because he approached the item content in an open, consistent manner. The therapist is likely to find the present symptom review a credible picture of the client's current functioning.

Raymond has reported a number of symptoms and problems, more than most people do. This high degree of symptom expression could result from a felt need to have the therapist pay immediate attention to his problems. The potential sources of his high number of problems should be carefully evaluated to determine whether they are the appropriate focus of therapy.

High symptom endorsement, as shown by his elevated EXA score, is relatively common among clients engaged in psychotherapy. About 22% of clients in the Minnesota Psychotherapy Assessment Project had EXA as their highest validity scale score, with T-score > 64. There is a tendency for women in therapy to report significantly more problems than men in therapy do.

TREATMENT ISSUES

Individuals who score high on the Somatization of Conflict (SOM) scale are reporting a considerable amount of physical distress at this time. They seem to feel their problems are, for the most part, physical, and they do not like to deal with emotional conflict. They have a tendency to channel conflict into physical symptoms such as headache, pain, or stomach distress. They tend to worry about their health and seem to be reducing their life activities substantially as a result of their physical concerns. They view themselves as tired and worried that their health is not better.

Fig. 10.2 BTPI report for Mr.R.Reproduced with permission of MHS.

The use of somatic defenses and the development of physical problems under psychological conflict are prominent mechanisms in outpatient therapy. Over a quarter (28%) of the clients in the Minnesota Psychotherapy Assessment Project produced high scores ($T > 64$) on the SOM scale. In addition, SOM led other Cluster 2 scales as the most frequent peak score (with 19% of the clients having a peak SOM T-score > 64).

CURRENT SYMPTOMS

Raymond appears to be extremely anxious at this time. He is reporting great difficulty as a result of this tension, fearfulness, and inability to concentrate effectively. He seems to worry a great deal and feels that he can't seem to sit still at times. His daily functioning is severely impaired because of his worries and an inability to make decisions. The elevation he obtained on the Anxiety (ANX) scale is relatively common among psychotherapy clients. The ANX scale was the second most frequent peak score in the Minnesota Psychotherapy Assessment Project, with 28% of the cases having T-scores > 64 (6% of these with ANX as the peak Current Symptom scale score). However, peak ANX elevations were more prominent for women (9%) than for men (2%).

In addition, he has presented a number of other serious problems through the BTPI items that require careful evaluation at this time. He has also obtained a high score on the PSY scale. Scores in this range reflect very unusual thinking. Individuals with extreme scores, such as his, are reporting that their minds are not working well and that they are having difficulty with their thought processes. Unusual and magical thoughts are characteristic of their belief systems. He also appears to be extremely mistrustful and suspicious of others. There is some possibility that his unusual thoughts are delusional in nature.

Along with the problems described above, there are other symptoms reflected in his BTPI response pattern that need to be considered in assessing his current symptomatic picture. His responses to the BTPI items suggest that he is likely to be somewhat aggressive and irritable toward other people. He feels as though he lives in a world full of antagonism and reports feeling so these and irritable that he thinks he is "going to explode." He reports behavior that suggests he has temper control problems and may feel angry and resentful of other people.

TREATMENT PLANNING

His symptom description suggests some concerns that could become the focus of psychological treatment if the client can be engaged in the treatment if the client can be engaged in the treatment process. The provision of test feedback about his problem description might prove valuable in promoting accessibility to therapy.

His reliance upon somatic defense mechanisms and his need to view conflicts in medical terms need to be the dealt with in therapy if he is going to be able to effectively resolve conflicts that occur in his interpersonal relations.

Treatment planning should proceed with the understanding that the client maintains the view that he lives in a very unsupportive environment. This perceived lack of a supportive context for change, whether real or imagined, can prove frustrating to the client's efforts at self-improvement.

His intense anxiety and high tension would likely be good target symptoms to address in therapy. He appears to be experiencing some disabling cognitions and may need to explore these vulnerabilities in some detail to alleviate the sources of this anxious states. Directing treatment toward tension reduction and focusing upon more effective stress management strategies would likely serve to improve his life adjustment.

His rigid beliefs and opinionated interaction style are likely to challenge the therapist as treatment proceeds.

PROGRESS MONITORING

Raymond obtained a general pathology composite (GPC) T-score of 67. His GPC index score indicates that he has endorsed a number of mental health symptoms that may require consideration in psychological treatment planning. For a statistically significant change, based on a 90% confidence interval, a subsequent GPC T-score must be above 73 or below 71.

Raymond obtained a treatment difficulty composite (TDC) T-score of 58. Overall, his TDC index score is well within the normal range, indicating that he has not acknowledged many of the personality-based symptoms addressed by the BTPI to assess difficult treatment relationships. For a statistically significant change, based on a 90% confidence interval, a subsequent TDC T-score must be above 65 or below 51.

SPECIAL ISSUES TO ADDRESS IN THERAPY

The client has endorsed item content that likely bears some critical importance to his progress in psychological treatment. The Special Problem items are printed out if the client responded in the critical direction. The item endorsement frequencies for the item are also provided for the Normative Sample (N) and the Clinical Sample. These issues noted below should be followed up in an early treatment session.

He has endorsed item content indicating that he has concerns over his anger to the point of openly expressing aggression toward another person. The potential that he might act out in an aggressive or violent manner should be explored in early treatment sessions.205. (T) My temper sometimes flares up to the point that I cannot control what I do or say. (N% = 27.3) (C% = 31.7).

Fig. 10.2 *continued.*

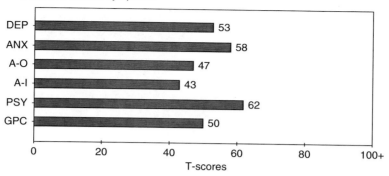

Fig. 10.3 Follow-up BTPI for Mr. R. Reproduced with permission of MHS.

diagnoses and arranged for additional psychiatric evaluation of his suitability for antipsychotic medication. The patient and psychologist decided to expand his psychotherapy plan by adding group therapies to his individual psychotherapy regimen.

REASSESSMENT

After 3 months, Mr. R's psychologist requested that he complete the MMPI-2 and BTPI again, in order to monitor his treatment progress. He repeated the full MMPI-2 battery and was administered an abbreviated version of the BTPI that included only the Current Symptoms Scales. His new MMPI-2 profile was similar to his previous one in its indication of ruminative thinking; however, the second MMPI-2 did not evidence the degree of paranoid ideation, persecutory thinking, and cynicism toward others that was suggested by the initial one. Figure 10.3 shows his second BTPI profile. He did not produce elevated scores on any of the BTPI symptom scales, supporting the notion of improvement in his thinking problems. See Figure 10.4 for the follow-up narrative reports of the BTPI.

CONCLUSIONS ABOUT THE ASSESSMENT

The computer-based test interpretations in this case served multiple purposes. First, they provided objective baseline data against which to measure changes in Mr. R's problems and symptoms over time. Second, they provided extensive, objective input regarding diagnoses and treatment considerations. The computerized interpretations afforded the psychotherapist and the patient scientifically rigorous data. The psychologist found that having such information facilitated the feedback process by helping to reduce Mr. R's skepticism about the information in his profiles and his general defensiveness about his

symptoms. He was accepting of the feedback because he could appreciate it as an objective distillation of his own answers to a large number of specific items. Mr. R's demeanor in the feedback sessions suggested that the profiles had helped him to get some distance from his problems. The resulting discussions, which were about highly sensitive subjects, thereby seemed to be more collaborative. Finally, the computer-based summaries eased some of the burden on the psychologist with regard to interpreting the test data. In addition to facilitating and truncating the interpretation process, they reduced the likelihood of biased interpretative statements and human error. Nonetheless, as was discussed with Mr. R, the interpretations did need to be individualized so as to ensure that they applied specifically to him.

Developments in Computer-Based Assessment

In this section we will examine in more detail two issues concerning computer-based assessment that are gaining increasing attention today: CAT and Internet-based test administration and interpretation.

Computerized Adaptive Testing

People differ greatly in terms of the number and range of problems and characteristics they experience. Why then would it not be desirable, in a mental health assessment, to use a varied symptom review strategy that is tailored to the person's problems rather than using a fixed questionnaire that asks the same questions of all persons in a standard order as the majority of personality questionnaires do? In most standard psychological tests, everyone is administered the same items in a fixed sequence even though some

BTPI Interpretive Report

CURRENT SYMPTOMS

His moderate elevation on the Unusual Thinking (PSY) scale needs to be evaluated further. There is some possibility that his unusual beliefs reflect unusual thought content. He appears to be somewhat mistrustful and suspicious of others. There is some possibility that his unusual thoughts reflect intractable beliefs.

PROGRESS MONITORING

The general pathology composite (GPC) T-score of 50 places Raymond in the 62nd percentile when compared to the normative sample. Overall, his GPC index score is well within the normal range suggesting that he has not acknowledged many mental health symptoms. For a statistically significant change, based on a 90% confidence interval, a subsequent GPC T-score must be above 56 or below 44.

Fig. 10.4 Follow-up BTPI report for Mr. R. Reproduced with permission.

might not be appropriate for some clients. An "adaptive" test, on the other hand, is an individualized procedure that aims to provide the same information as the full test but with fewer items. A computer adaptive instrument can be programmed to determine when sufficient information has been collected from the client to estimate the traits or characteristics being assessed. The primary goal of an adaptive test is to acquire the necessary information by administering a reduced number of items. Studies have shown that an adaptive administration can result in reduced item administration (Forbey & Ben-Porath, 2007).

During the adaptive test administration procedure, the first administered item is scored immediately to assess the difficulty and discrimination levels to determine the next item to be administered. For example, in a computer adapted ability test, if the examinee answers the item in a particular direction, the next item to be administered will be a more difficult one or the one designed to assess the content area more thoroughly. If the examinee fails to respond in a predetermined direction then the next item will be an easier one or the one that is aimed at sampling a slightly different aspect of the same domain. The third item is administered and scored in the same manner and is chosen based on the responses from the previous two items. The adaptive administration is discontinued when the procedure determines that a sufficient number of items have been answered to assess the characteristic in question.

Most adaptive testing strategies have been based on a testing procedure referred to as item response theory or IRT (Weiss, 1985). In this procedure, the conditional probability of the response to an item for different levels of underlying latent trait or ability is estimated. For example, if an individual has a high latent trait, the probability of that person responding to an item in the keyed direction is considered to be greater. This relationship between the probability of the item endorsement and the latent trait characteristic can be graphically expressed in an S-shaped curve, called item characteristic curve (ICC). The major goal of the IRT procedure is to determine the most accurate ICC for each test taker (Weiss & Yoes, 1988).

An extensive program of research by Weiss and his colleagues (Brown & Weiss, 1977; Kiely, Zara, & Weiss, 1983; Weiss & Yoes, 1988) has demonstrated the effectiveness of IRT and CAT procedures over traditional methods in ability testing. In their approach, computers administer items, score the responses, and select the next items based on the responses to the previous items, and determine if the optimal amount of information has been obtained and thus terminate the test. Their procedure starts with an item of predetermined difficulty; then the preprogrammed computer decides if an examinee answered in the keyed or nonkeyed direction, based on which it selects the next item that can provide maximal information about the person's latent trait. The computer program then automatically discontinues this process if the termination criterion is met.

The major advantage of CAT over conventional testing is that participants are provided with only the items that are necessary to measure the assessment questions, and they do not have to take the redundant or inappropriate items. As a result, test length and time can be significantly reduced.

COMPUTERIZED ADAPTIVE TESTING WITH THE MMPI-2

Can personality characteristics be evaluated by computer adaptive strategies such as IRT? Some researchers have found that the IRT assumption of an underlying unidimensional latent trait is problematic when applied in personality scales because some measures contain heterogeneous content (Butcher, Keller, & Bacon, 1985; Weiss & Suhdolnik, 1985). The two underlying assumptions of IRT are that the model used for parameter estimation must adequately fit the data, and that all the test items assess a single underlying latent trait (Hulin et al., 1983). Many personality and clinical tests are designed to measure multiple personality traits, frequently overlapping domains. For example, the MMPI-2 clinical scales with their empirically derived structure are generally heterogeneous in content. Thus, some researchers have suggested that CAT only be applied to homogeneous scales. Waller and Reise (1989) and Ben-Porath, Waller, Slutske, and Butcher (1988) showed that application of CAT to the unidimensional tests or to individual scales from a multi-dimensional measure can be successful. However, Simms and Clark (2005) recently reported that even with homogeneous content scales psychometric differences can emerge between computer adaptive and paper-and-pencil tests.

Countdown Method

Butcher, Keller, and Bacon (1985) proposed a somewhat different strategy to adaptive testing than IRT because of the requirement for homogeneity in the scales—the countdown method. This approach "involves" two strategies (Ben-Porath, Slutske, & Butcher, 1989; Butcher et al., 1985). The first is referred to as a "classification procedure" (CP); it is most useful when the assessment question is simply to know whether the responses of the test takers fall below or beyond the cutoff scores. In this approach, if a psychiatric screening instrument consists of 30 items and a score of 20 is a cutoff value to classify clinically meaningful elevation, then a person who does not endorse the first 11 items cannot be classified within the extreme response group. But if a participant endorses 20 items, then they are positively classified into the extreme response group, and no additional items will be administered. In a parallel strategy referred to as the "full scores on elevated scales" (FSES) strategy, the computer is programmed to terminate item administration when scale elevation is "ruled out," in other words, when the responses exceed the established cutoff scores for the scale. If an individual reaches clinical elevation, all items in that scale are then administered in order

to obtain the full score on that scale. Ben-Porath et al. (1989) found that cost minimization in the countdown method can be achieved by administering items in the order of the endorsement rate. For example, the main purpose of the FSES strategy is to rule out scale elevation. Consequently, one can first administer the items that are less likely to be endorsed in the keyed direction (e.g., depression). If an examinee endorses the items that are less likely to be endorsed by depressed individuals, one can more quickly rule out the possibility of scale elevation for that examinee.

Ben-Porath et al. (1989) tested both the CP and the FSES strategies using two personnel-selection sample ($n = 470$) and two clinical samples ($n = 232$) from four different settings in Minnesota and Ohio. The results were promising with an item administration saving of up to 31.3% of the items in the CP strategy, and up to 31.1% using the FSES strategy. In another study, Roper, Ben-Porath, and Butcher (1995) compared the computerized adaptive MMPI-2 based on the countdown method to the conventional booklet version of the MMPI-2 in a sample of 571 undergraduate college students. In this study, three versions of the MMPI-2 were administered: a booklet version, an adaptive computerized version, and a conventional computerized version. The same format was administered twice: each participant took the booklet and adaptive computerized versions (in counterbalanced order), or took the conventional and adaptive computerized versions (in counterbalanced order).

Roper et al. (1995) reported few statistically significant differences between the mean scale scores of the computerized adaptive and conventional MMPI-2, suggesting that the two administration methods were equivalent. Mean item savings of computerized adaptive version produced item savings of 30–34%. In addition to comparing the two versions of the MMPI-2, this study evaluated the external validity of the different forms against external criteria. Correlations between the MMPI-2 scores and the criterion measures Beck Depression Inventory (BDI; Beck, War, Mendelson, Mock, & Erbaugh, 1961), the anxiety and anger scales from the State-Trait Personality Inventory (STPI; Spielberger, 1979), and the Symptom Checklist Revised (SCL-90-R; Derogatis, 1983) were comparable for the computerized adaptive and conventional MMPI-2. Handel, Ben-Porath, and Watt (1999) also explored the validity of the countdown method in an empirical study of a group of VA hospital patients who were entering an addictions program. Each participant was administered the MMPI-2 twice after being randomly assigned one of the two conditions: computerized conventional test-retest or computerized conventional-computerized adaptive. They compared the correlations between conventional and adaptive MMPI-2 scales with scores on criterion measures including NEO PI-R scales (Costa & McCrae, 1992), the BDI (Beck et al., 1961), the Self-Report Personality Questionnaire (SCID-Q; First, Spitzer, Gibbson, & Williams, 1995), Aggression Questionnaire (AQ; Buss & Perry, 1992), and the fifth edition of the Addiction Severity Index (ASI; McLellan et al., 1992). Similar to the Roper et al. (1995) study described earlier, the results showed comparability of the computerized adaptive MMPI-2 based on the countdown method. However, some statistically significant differences between computerized adaptive and conventional versions on certain clinical and content scales were found. Most of these differences were not clinically meaningful. In terms of external validity, none of the correlations between MMPI-2 and the criterion measures were significantly different between the computerized adaptive and conventional booklet versions.

Limitations of Adaptive MMPI-2 Testing

The only advantage of using an adapted administration of a test is that it allows the client to finish the test administration in a shorter time; it is not a more valid or effective assessment procedure. An adapted version of the MMPI-2 is an extracted version of some scales on the test, not a full form of the instrument. It provides only one or two most elevated clinical scale scores, not a full form on which the substantial research literature serves as an interpretive base. Therefore, the adaptive version of the MMPI-2 is, in many respects, similar to other short forms of the test and shares some of the disadvantages of short forms of the MMPI-2 that have been noted (Butcher & Hostetler, 1990).

An important factor to keep sight of is what the primary goal of a psychological assessment is—getting a thorough, reliable, and valid perspective on a client's personality and problems. The primary goal is not simply to save the client a few minutes' time. For example, in a personal injury forensic examination where the main goal is evaluating the cooperativeness of the client and obtaining an accurate description of the personality characteristics and

symptoms one would want to use the most comprehensive and validated form of the test, and not simply a quick glimpse at the problem through a brief exam. In most psychological assessments, time saving is less important than thorough and comprehensive understanding of the client. In these settings, an abbreviation of the test through an adaptive version becomes a liability rather than a desired goal.

Personality Assessment via the Internet

The growth of the Internet and the availability of technology and resources for remotely conducting psychological evaluations have created some interesting prospects as well as problems in contemporary psychology. The availability of psychological tests on the Internet has been extensively discussed by a committee of the American Psychological Association and a number of cautions about their use provided (Naglieri et al., 2004).

A number of novel data collection strategies have emerged through Internet-based efforts (Koski-Jannes et al., 2007; Mackay, Schulz, Rubinelli, & Pithers, 2007; Williamson, Mislevy, & Bejar, 2006). There is increasing interest and pressure for test publishers to make available online test administration, scoring, and interpretation of psychological tests.

As noted earlier in this chapter, in recent years, the Internet has emerged as a possible medium for the provision of psychological services such as assessment or counseling in the context of providing mental health services. This mode of information gathering and dissemination is different from traditional assessment and treatment and raises issues that require consideration (Buchanan, 2002; Buchanan & Smith, 1999; Cernich, Brennana, Barker, & Bleiberg, 2007; Harris, 2006; Reips, 2006; VandenBos & Williams, 2000). See Bartram and Hambleton (2006) for a discussion on international test guidelines for Internet test applications.

The development and validation of Internet-based assessment resources has not kept pace with the technological developments. For example, there has been limited research on the equivalence in testing conditions and equivalence of normative databases, and similarity in test-taking attitudes are lagging behind the technological expansion. For example, an earlier hope of using virtual reality stimuli for personality assessment has not materialized. Although, there has been some use of Internet-based testing for the MMPI-2, this application has been limited and for the most part unauthorized test users and unvetted assessment programs. The only existing published study with the MMPI-2 on the Internet involved the norming of the Flemish-Dutch MMPI-2, which was standardized using an Internet-based data collection (Sloore, Derksen, de Mey, & Hellenbosch, 1996). These investigators collected Flemish-Dutch standardization norms using a representative sample of the population of Holland. The questionnaires were administered through the University of Amsterdam Telepanel—a computer-guided data gathering system that loaned a computer and a modem to 1,630 households throughout Holland in exchange for their weekly participation in various surveys. A total of 1,244 people participated in the study. Although the standardization sample may not have been fully representative of the Flemish-Dutch population because they were quite familiar with the use of computers, their demographic characteristics closely resembled the general population in Holland. A number of similarities were found between the U.S. normative and Flemish-Dutch MMPI-2 administrations, suggesting that the two versions are generally equivalent (Sloore et al., 1996). In spite of this successful test adaptation program that resulted in a highly efficient data collection program, the Internet does not appear to be the answer to an effective, acceptable medium for assessment of clinical measure at this time for a number of reasons. Several problems with administering clinical tests like the MMPI-2 on the Internet have been described by Butcher et al. (2004).

The comparability of Internet-administered personality scales has been questioned (Meade, Michels, & Lautenschlager, 2007). In order for psychological tests to provide reliable and usable test information, the test taker must be fully cooperative with the evaluation—neither too defensive nor exaggerating problems. One possibility is that response patterns would differ between test administrations in a monitored office environment and an uncontrolled response approach on the computer from one's home. Although some research has shown equivalence between Internet and other administrative formats (Chuah, Drasgow, & Roberts, 2006), such extremely different test administration procedures cannot be assumed to produce equivalent test results. In one study, Pasveer and Ellard (1998) reported that administering tests online resulted in problems worth serious consideration such as multiple submission of records by the same test taker. Other studies have also found that different test-taking situations might produce different test results.

For instance, Buchanan and Smith (1999) pointed out that the equivalence between the two administration procedures cannot be assured. Further research needs to be conducted on Internet-based test administration to assure that online test administration strategies would not produce results different from results obtained through standard administration procedures.

Many psychological tests, such as the MMPI-2, are interpreted by comparing the test scores of a particular client to those of a known standardization group or normative sample collected under controlled conditions. Some available evidence suggests that tests administered on the Internet produce somewhat different results than those administered under standard conditions (Buchanan & Smith, 1999). The use of available test norms requires that persons being compared on the test norms be tested under similar conditions. Most test norms for standard tests, like the MMPI-2, were developed using paper-and-pencil tests under closely monitored conditions. (One exception was noted above: the Dutch language version of the MMPI-2 noted earlier which was standardized through an Internet normative program; Sloore et al., 1996.) Therefore, widely used clinical tests like the MMPI-2 do not have appropriate online test administration norms. The deviation from standard testing practices by using norms that have not been verified for the particular application is not an appropriate test use.

Another psychometric variable that needs to be considered in evaluating the utility of Internet-based psychological tests is the matter of test validity. The use of any psychological test for making pragmatic decisions about people requires that the instrument has demonstrated reliability and validity for the application in question. Although some research has reported that Internet-administered tests have construct validity when compared to traditional administration procedures (Buchanan & Smith, 1999), there needs to be more extensive test validation research with this application to support its use in clinical decision making. Harris (2006) cautions that in order for Internet testing to be acceptable it is important that procedural fairness be assured.

It is also important to assure that the security of test items is not jeopardized by being publicly available on the Internet. Unfortunately, this requirement is difficult to assure with information placed online, given the general lack of security of the Internet. Moreover, most commercially available psychological tests are copyrighted, and test publishers protect copyright by either refusing permission to use or by allowing only limited use of test items. Some test publishers have actually increased their security over test items by refusing to allow psychologists to cite them even in scientific publications with a more restricted audience range.

Summary

This chapter addressed how clinicians use assessments, which assessments are the most widely used by clinicians, and in what various settings do clinicians use and incorporate assessments into their practice. Moreover, this section examined some reported rates of computer and computerized assessment usage by clinicians. Another interesting area explored was how clinicians use computers in other ways as part of their clinical assessment practices. For instance, clinicians use computers as part of clinical interviews/diagnoses, screening for psychopathology, and other interventions such as aiding the clinician within his/her work setting or online via the Internet.

The twenty-first century with its extensive unfolding of computer-based technology offers both challenge and opportunity for assessment-oriented psychologists. Although psychologists have made great strides in developing computer-based test interpretation reports of traditional measures, the available technology has not been fully utilized in several areas such as development of virtual reality (lifelike) test stimuli, maximal data processing methods, and complex interpretation strategies that account for the complexities of the real world. A number of problems surrounding Internet-based assessment procedures using established, valid, and widely used psychological tests have limited Internet-based test availability.

Some studies suggest that computerized adaptive versions of the MMPI-2 show a potential of producing time savings in items administered with a minimal loss of test validity for the peak clinical scale scores. Adaptive versions of the more homogeneous MMPI-2 content scales based on both the IRT and countdown methods have been found to be valid and generally equivalent to the traditional paper-and-pencil and computer-administered versions. Although these procedures save administration time, they only provide limited information about the client. Thus, adaptive versions are likely to have limited utility since most practitioners (particularly forensic psychologists) need thorough evaluations, not just to save a few minutes of client time.

The wide availability of the Internet today has created new prospects for providing broadly accessible psychological assessment. Internet-based assessment, however, is faced with problems as well as opportunities. The development and validation of Internet-based assessment resources has not kept pace with the technological developments and there has been relatively limited research on the equivalence in testing conditions, equivalence of normative databases, etc., important to reliable and valid test use. Moreover, more research needs to be conducted on the similarity in test-taking attitudes for Internet-based tests compared with traditional testing approaches.

References

Alleman, J. R. (2002). Online counseling: The Internet and mental health treatment. *Psychotherapy: Theory, Research, Practice, Training, 39*, 199–209.

Ames, S. L., Grenard, J. L., Thrush, C., Sussman, S., Wiers, R. W., & Stacy, A. W. (2007). Comparison of indirect assessments of association as predictors of marijuana use among at-risk adolescents. *Experimental and Clinical Psychopharmacology, 15*, 204–218.

Anderson, P., Jacobs, C., & Rothbaum, B. O. (2004). Computer-supported cognitive behavioral treatment of anxiety disorders. *Journal of Clinical Psychology, 60*, 253–267.

Atlis, M. M., Hahn, J., & Butcher, J. N. (2006). Computer-based assessment with the MMPI-2. In J. N. Butcher (Ed.), *MMPI-2: A practitioner's guide* (pp. 445–476). Washington, DC: American Psychological Association.

Baker, J. D. (2007). Queendom Online Test Repository. In R. A. Reynolds, R. Woods, & J. D. Baker (Eds.), *Handbook of research on electronic surveys and measurements* (pp. 352–354). Hershey, PA: Iea group Reference/IGI Global.

Ball, J. D., Archer, R. P., & Imhof, E. A. (1994). Time requirements of psychological testing: A survey of practitioners. *Journal of Personality Assessment, 63*, 239–249.

Barak, A. (1999). Psychological applications on the Internet: A discipline on the threshold of a new millennium. *Applied and Preventive Psychology, 8*, 231–245.

Bartram, D., & Hambleton, R. K. (2006). *Computer-based testing and the Internet.* New York: John Wiley & Sons.

Beck, A. T., Ward, C. H., Mendelson, M., Mock, J., & Erbaugh, J. (1961). An inventory for measuring depression. *Archives of General Psychiatry, 12*, 57–62.

Ben-Porath, Y. S., Slutske, W. S., & Butcher, J. N. (1989). A real-data simulation of computerized administration of the MMPI. *Psychological Assessment: A Journal of Consulting and Clinical Psychology, 1*, 18–22.

Ben-Porath, Y. S., Waller, N. G., Slutske, W. S., & Butcher, J. N. (1988). *A comparison of two methods for adaptive administration of MMPI-2 content scales.* Paper presented at the 96th annual meeting of the American Psychological Association, Atlanta, GA, August 1988.

Berger, M. (2006). Computer assisted clinical assessment. *Child and Adolescent Mental Health, 11*, 64–75.

Brown, J. M., & Weiss, D. J. (1977). *An adaptive testing strategy for achievement test batteries* (Research Rep. No. 77-6).

Minneapolis, MN: University of Minnesota, Department of Psychology, Psychometrics Method Program.

Buchanan, T. (2002). Online assessment: Desirable or dangerous? *Professional Psychology: Research and Practice, 33*(2), 148–154.

Buchanan, T., & Smith, J. L. (1999). Using the Internet for psychological research: Personality testing on the World Wide Web. *British Journal of Psychology, 90*, 125–144.

Buss, A. H., & Perry, M. (1992). The Aggression Questionnaire. *Journal of Personality and Social Psychology, 63*, 452–459.

Butcher, J. N. (Ed.). (1987). *Computerized psychological assessment: A practitioner's guide.* New York: Basic Books.

Butcher, J. N. (2003). Computer-based psychological assessment. In J. R. Graham & J. Naglieri (Eds.), *Comprehensive handbook of psychology, Vol 10: Assessment psychology* (pp. 141–164). New York: John Wiley & Sons.

Butcher, J. N. (2004). *Butcher Treatment Planning Inventory (BTPI): Technical manual.* North Tonawanda, NY: Multi-Health Systems.

Butcher, J. N. (2006). Assessment in clinical psychology: A perspective on the past, present challenges, and future prospects. *Clinical Psychology: Science and Practice, 13*(3), 205–209.

Butcher, J. N., Berah, E., Ellertsen, B., Miach, P., Lim, J., Nezami, E., et al. (1998). Objective personality assessment: Computer-based Minnesota Multiphasic Personality Inventory-2 interpretation in international clinical settings. In C. Belar (Ed.), *Comprehensive clinical psychology: Sociocultural and individual differences* (pp. 277–312). New York: Elsevier.

Butcher, J. N., Dahlstrom, W. G., Graham, J. R., Tellegen, A., & Kaemmer, B. (1989). *Minnesota Multiphasic Personality Inventory-2 (MMPI-2): Manual for administration and scoring.* Minneapolis, MN: University of Minnesota Press.

Butcher, J. N., Ellertsen, B., Ubostad, B., Bubb, E., Lucio, E., Lim, J., et al. (2000). *International case studies on the MMPI-A: An objective approach.* Minneapolis, MN: MMPI-2 Workshops (see http://www1.umn.edu/mmpi to download monograph).

Butcher, J. N., Graham, J. R., Ben-Porath, Y. S., Tellegen, A., Dahlstrom, W. G., & Kaemmer, B. (2001). *Minnesota Multiphasic Personality Inventory-2 (MMPI-2): Manual for administration and scoring* (Rev. ed.). Minneapolis, MN: University of Minnesota Press.

Butcher, J. N., & Hostetler, K. (1990). Abbreviating MMPI item administration: Past problems and prospects for the MMPI-2. *Psychological Assessment: A Journal of Consulting and Clinical Psychology, 2*, 12–22.

Butcher, J. N., Keller, L. S., & Bacon, S. F. (1985). Current developments and future directions in computerized personality assessment. *Journal of Consulting and Clinical Psychology, 53*, 803–815.

Butcher, J. N., & Perry, J. L. (2008). *Personality assessment in treatment planning.* New York: Oxford University Press.

Butcher, J. N., Perry, J. N., & Atlis, M. (2000). Validity and utility of computer-based test interpretation. *Psychological Assessment, 12*, 6–18.

Butcher, J. N., Perry, J. N., & Hahn, J. (2004). Computers in clinical assessment: Historical developments, present status, and future challenges. *Journal of Clinical Psychology, 60*, 331–345.

Caldwell, A. B. (1971). *Recent advances in automated interpretation of the MMPI.* Paper presented at the 6th Annual MMPI Symposium, Minneapolis, MN, April 1971.

Camara, W. J., Nathan, J. S., & Puente, A. E. (2000). Psychological test usage: Implications in professional psychology. *Professional Psychology: Research & Practice, 31*, 141–154.

Carr, A. C., Ghosh, A., & Ancill, R. J. (1983). Can a computer take a psychiatric history? *Psychological Medicine, 13*, 151–158.

Cashel, M. L. (2002). Child and adolescent psychological assessment: Current clinical practices and the impact of managed care. *Professional Psychology: Research and Practice, 33*, 446–453.

Cernich, A. N., Brennana, D. M., Barker, L. M., & Bleiberg, J. (2007). Sources of error in computerized neuropsychological assessment. *Archives of Clinical Neuropsychology, 22*, S39–S48.

Chen, Y. (2007). Development of a computer-administered analog assessment to evaluate PTSD symptoms in college students who have experienced a motor vehicle crash (MVC). *Dissertation Abstracts International, Section B: The Sciences and Engineering, 67*, 4098.

Chinman, M., Hassell, J., Magnabosco, J., Nowlin-Finch, N., Marusak, S., & Young, A. S. (2007). The feasibility of computerized patient self-assessment at mental health clinics. *Adminstration and Policy in Mental Health and Mental Health Services Research, 34*, 401–409.

Chuah, S. C., Drasgow, F., & Roberts, B. W. (2006). Personality assessment: Does the medium matter? No. *Journal of Research in Personality, 40*, 359–376.

Clark, G., Horan, J. J., Tompkins-Bjorkman, A., Kovalski, T., & Hackett, G. (2000). Interactive career counseling on the Internet. *Journal of Career Assessment, 8*, 85–93.

Costa, P. T., & McCrae, R. R. (1992). *Revised NEO Personality Inventory (NEO PI-R) and NEO Five-Factor Inventory (NEO FFI).* Odessa, FL: Psychological Assessment Resources.

Derogatis, L. J. (1983). *SCL-90-R administration, scoring, and procedure manual-II.* Towson, MD: Clinical Psychometric Research.

Deskovitz, M. (2006). Interpretive reliability of six computer-based test interpretation programs for the Minnesota Multiphasic Personality Inventory-2. *Dissertation Abstracts International, Section B: The Sciences and Engineering, 66*, 3944.

Drasgow, F., & Chuah, S. C. (2006). Computer-based testing. In M. Eid & E. D. Diener (Eds.), *Handbook of multimethod measurement in psychology* (pp. 87–100). Washington, DC: American Psychological Association.

Eber, H. W. (1964). *Automated personality description with 16-PF data.* Paper presented at the meeting of the American Psychological Association, Los Angeles, September 1964.

Exner, J. E., Jr. (1974). *The Rorschach: A comprehensive system (Vol. 1).* New York: John Wiley & Sons.

Exner, J. E., Jr. (1986). *The Rorschach: A comprehensive system, Vol. 1: Basic Foundations* (2nd ed.). New York: John Wiley & Sons.

Exner, J. E., Jr. (1987). Computer assistance in Rorschach interpretation. In J. N. Butcher (Ed.), *Computerized psychological assessment: A practitioner's guide* (pp. 218–235). New York: Basic Books.

Farrell, A. D. (1989). Impact of computers on professional practice: A survey of current practices and attitudes. *Professional Psychology: Research and Practice, 20*, 172–178.

Farrell, A. D., & McCollough-Vaillant, L. (1996). Computerized Assessment System for Psychotherapy Evaluation and Research (CASPER): Development and current status. In M. J. Miller, K. W. Hammond, & M. G. Hile (Eds.), *Mental health computing* (pp. 34–53). New York: Springer.

Finger, M. S., & Ones, D. S. (1999). Psychometric equivalence of the computer and booklet forms of the MMPI: A meta-analysis. *Psychological Assessment, 11*, 58–66.

Finney, J. C. (1965). *Purposes and usefulness of the Kentucky program for the automatic interpretation of the MMPI.* Paper presented at the meeting of the American Psychological Association, Chicago, September 1965.

Finney, J. C. (1966). Programmed interpretation of the MMPI and CPI. *Archives of General Psychiatry, 15,* 75–81.

First, M. B., Spitzer, R. L., Gibbson, M., & Williams, J. B. (1995). The Structured Clinical Interview for DSM-III-R Personality Disorders (SCID-II): Description. *Journal of Personality Disorders, 9,* 93–91.

Forbey, J. D., & Ben-Porath, Y. S. (2007). Adaptive personality testing: A review and illustration with the MMPI-2 computerized adaptive version. *Psychological Assessment, 19,* 14–24.

Fowler, R. D. (1964). *Computer processing and reporting of personality test data.* Paper presented at the meeting of the American Psychological Association, Los Angeles, September 1964.

Fowler, R. D. (1965). *Purposes and usefulness of the Alabama program for the automatic interpretation of the MMPI.* Paper presented at the meeting of the American Psychological Association, Chicago, September 1965.

Fowler, R. D. (1967). Computer interpretation of personality tests: The automated psychologist. *Comprehensive Psychiatry, 8,* 455–467.

Fowler, R. D. (1969). Automated interpretation of personality test data. In J. N. Butcher (Ed.), *MMPI: Research developments and clinical applications* (pp. 105–126). New York: McGraw-Hill.

Fowler, R. D. (1985). Landmarks in computer-assisted psychological assessment. *Journal of Consulting and Clinical Psychology, 53,* 748–759.

Freeman, M. J., Lester, K. M., McNamara, C., Meilby, J. B., & Schumacher, J. E. (2006). Cell phones for ecological momentary assessment with cocaine-addicted homeless patients in treatment. *Journal of Substance Abuse Treatment, 30,* 105–111.

Garb, H. N. (2007). Computer-administered interviews and rating scales. *Psychological Assessment, 19,* 4–13.

Garg, A. X., Adhikari, N. K. J., McDonald, H., Rosas-Arellano, M. P., Devereaux, P. J., Beyene, J., et al. (2005). Effects of computerized clinical decision support systems on practitioner performance and patient outcomes: A systematic review. *Journal of the American Medical Association, 293,* 1223–1238.

Gershon, R. C. (2005). Computer adaptive testing. *Journal of Applied Measurement, 6,* 109–127.

Gonzalez, G. M., & Shriver, C. (2004). A bilingual computerized voice-interactive system for screening depression symptoms. *Journal of Technology in Human Services, 22,* 1–20.

Graham, J. R. (2006). *MMPI-2: Assessing personality and psychopathology* (4th ed.). New York: Oxford.

Greene, R. L. (2005). Computer scoring and interpretation in psychological report writing. *SPA Exchange, 17,* 6.

Hake, R. R. (1998). Interactive-engagement versus traditional methods: A six thousand student survey of mechanics test data for introductory physics courses. *American Journal of Physics Teachers, 66,* 64–74.

Handel, R. W., Ben-Porath, Y. S., and Watt, M. (1999). Computerized adaptive assessment with the MMPI-2 in a clinical setting. *Psychological Assessment, 11,* 369–380.

Harris, M. M. (2006). Internet testing: the examinee perspective. In D. Bartram & R. K. Hambleton (Eds.), *Computer-based testing and the Internet* (pp. 115–133). New York: John Wiley & Sons.

Hester, R. K., & Miller, J. H. (2006). Economic perspectives: Screening and intervention: Computer-based tools for diagnosis and treatment of alcohol problems. *Alcohol Research and Health, 29,* 36–40.

Hochlehnert, A., Richter, A., Bludau, H., Blumenstiel, K., Mueller, K., Wilke, S., et al. (2006). A computer-based information tool for chronic pain patients: Computerized information to support the process of shared decision-making. *Patient Education and Counseling, 61,* 92–98.

Hulin, C. L., Drasgow, F., & Parsons, C. K. (1983). *Item response theory: Applications to psychological measurement.* Homewood, IL: Dow Jones Irwin.

Karson, S., & O'Dell, J. W. (1987). Computer-based interpretation of the 16PF: The Karson Clinical Report in contemporary practice. In J. N. Butcher (Ed.), *Computerized psychological assessment: A practitioner's guide* (pp. 198–217). New York: Basic Books.

Kelly, B., Kay-Lambkin, F. J., & Kavanagh, D. J. (2007). Rurally isolated populations and co-existing mental health and drug and alcohol problems. In A. Baker & R. Vellerman (Eds.), *Clinical handbook of co-existing mental health and drug and alcohol programs* (pp. 159–176). New York: Routledge/Taylor & Francis Group.

Kiely, G. L., Zara, A. R., & Weiss, D. J. (1983, January). *Alternate forms reliability and concurrent validity of adaptive and convergent tests with military recruits.* Drafts report submitted to Navy Personnel Research and Development Center, San Diego, CA.

Kinnaman, J. E. S., Farrell, A. D., & Bisconer, S. W. (2006). Evaluation of the Computerized Assessment System for Psychotherapy Evaluation and Research (CASPER) as a measure of treatment effectiveness with psychiatric inpatients. *Assessment, 13,* 154–167.

Koski-Jannes, A., Cunningham, J. A., Tolonen, K., & Bothas, H. (2007). Internet-based self-assessment of drinking—3-month follow-up data. *Addictive Behaviors, 32,* 533–542.

Lachar, D. (1974). *The MMPI: Clinical assessment and automated interpretation.* Los Angeles: Western Psychological Services.

Lachar, D. (1987). Automated assessment of child and adolescent personality: The Personality Inventory for Children (PIC). In J. N. Butcher (Ed.), *Computerized psychological assessment: A practitioner's guide* (pp. 262–292). New York: Basic Books, Inc.

Levine, S., Ancill, R. J., & Roberts, A. P. (1989). Assessment of suicide risk by computer delivered self-rating questionnaire: Preliminary findings. *Acta Psychiatrica Scandinavica, 80,* 216–220.

Lewis, G., Sharp, D., Bartholomew, J., & Pelosi, A. J. (1996). Computerized assessment of common mental disorders in primary care: Effect on clinical outcome. *Family Practice, 13,* 120–126.

Lubin, B., Larsen, R. M., Matarazzo, J. D., & Seever, M. (1985). Psychological test usage patterns in five professional settings. *American Psychologist, 40,* 857–861.

Mackay, J., Schulz, P., Rubinelli, S., & Pithers, A. (2007). Online Patient Education and Risk Assessment: Project OPERA from Cancerbackup: Putting inherited breast cancer risk information into context using augmentation theory. *Patient Education and Counseling, 67,* 261–266.

Marin, P. A., & Splete, H. (1991). A comparison of the effect of two computer-based counseling interventions on the career decidedness of adults. *The Career Development Quarter, 39*, 360–371.

McCrickard, M. P., & Butler, L. T. (2005). Cybercounseling: A new modality for counselor training and practice. *International Journal for the Advancement of Counselling, 27*, 101–110.

McKenna, T., & Butcher, J. (1987, April). *Continuity of the MMPI with alcoholics.* Paper given at the 22nd Annual Symposium on Recent Developments in the Use of the MMPI. Seattle, Washington.

McLellan, A. T., Kushner, H., Metzger, D., & Peters, R. (1992). The fifth edition of the Addiction Severity Index. *Journal of Substance Abuse Treatment, 9*, 199–213.

McMinn, M. R., Buchanan, T., Ellens, B. M., & Ryan, M. K. (1999). Technology, professional practice, and ethics survey findings and implications. *Professional Practice: Research and Practice, 30*, 165–172.

Meade, A. W., Michels, L. C., & Lautenschlager, G. J. (2007). Are internet and paper-and-pencil personality tests truly comparable?: An experimental design measurement invariance study. *Organizational Research Methods, 10*, 322–345.

Meehl, P. E. (1954). *Clinical versus statistical prediction: A theoretical analysis and a review of the evidence.* Minneapolis, MN: University of Minnesota Press.

Meehl, P. E. (1956). Wanted: A good cookbook. *American Psychologist, 11*, 263–272.

Millon, T. (1977). *Millon Clinical Multiaxial Inventory.* Minneapolis, MN: National Computer Systems.

Naglieri, J. A., Drasgow, F., Schmit, M., Handler, L., Prifitera, A., Margolis, A., et al. (2004). Psychological testing on the Internet: New problems, old issues. *American Psychologist, 59*(3), 150–162.

Pasveer, K. A., & Ellard, J. H. (1998). The making of a personality inventory: Help from the WWW. *Behavior Research Methods, Instruments, & Computers, 30*, 309–313.

Perry, J. N., & Butcher, J. N. (2004). The Butcher Treatment Planning Inventory (BTPI): An objective guide to treatment planning. In M. E. Maruish (Ed.), *The use of psychological testing for treatment planning and outcomes assessment: Instruments for adults* (3rd ed., pp. 589–601). Mahwah, NJ: Lawrence Erlbaum.

Pinsoneault, T. B. (1996). Equivalency of computer-assisted and paper-and-pencil administered versions of the Minnesota Multiphasic Personality Inventory-2. *Computers in Human Behavior, 12*, 291–300.

Piotrowski, Z. A. (1964). A digital computer administration of inkblot test data. *Psychiatric Quarterly, 38*, 1–26.

Reips, U. (2006). Web-based methods: In M. Eid & E. D. Diener (Eds.), *Handbook of multimethod measurement in psychology* (pp. 73–85). Washington, DC: American Psychological Association.

Richard, D. C. S., & Gloster, A. (2006). Technology integration and behavioral assessment. In M. Hersen (Ed.), *Clinician's handbook of adult behavioral assessment* (pp. 461–495). San Diego, CA: Academic Press.

Robson, D., & Robson, M. (2000). Ethical issues in Internet counseling. *Counselling Psychology Quarterly, 13*, 249–257.

Rochlen, A. B., Zack, J. S., & Speyer, C. (2004). Online therapy: Review of relevant definitions, debates, and current empirical support. *Journal of Clinical Psychology, 60*, 269–283.

Rollman, B. L., Hanusa, B. H., Lowe, H. J., et al. (2002). A randomized trial using computerized decision support to improve treatment of major depression in primary care. *Journal of General Internal Medicine, 17*, 493–503.

Rome, H. P., Swenson, W. M., Mataya, P., McCarthy, C. E., Pearson, J. S., Keating, F. R., et al. (1962). Symposium on automation techniques in personality assessment. *Proceedings of the Staff Meeting of the Mayo Clinic, 37*, 61–82.

Roper, B. L., Ben-Porath, Y. S., & Butcher, J. N. (1995). Comparability and validity of computerized adaptive testing with the MMPI-2. *Journal of Personality Assessment, 65*, 358–371.

Rosen, L. D., & Weil, M. M. (1996). Psychologists and technology: A look at the future. *Professional Psychology: Research and Practice, 27*, 635–638.

Roy, M., & Forest, F. (2006) Assessment of body image distortion in eating and weight disorders: the validation of a computer-based tool (Q-BID). *Eating and Weight Disorders, 12*, 1–11.

Simms, L. J., & Clark, L. A. (2005). Validation of a computerized adaptive version of the Schedule for Nonadaptive and Adaptive Personality (SNAP). *Psychological Assessment, 17*, 28–43.

Sloore, H., Derksen, J., de Mey, H., & Hellenbosch, G. (1996). The Flemish/Dutch version of the MMPI-2: Development and adaptation of the inventory for Belgium and the Netherlands. In J. N. Butcher (Ed.), *International adaptations of the MMPI-2: Research and clinical applications* (pp. 329–460). Minneapolis, MN: University of Minnesota Press.

Spielberger, C. D. (1979). *Preliminary manual for the State-Trait Personality Inventory (STPI).* Tampa, FL: University of South Florida.

Swenson, W. M., & Pearson, J. S. (1964). Automation techniques in personality assessment—a frontier in behavioral science and medicine. *Methods of Information in Medicine, 3*, 34–36.

Swenson, W. M., Rome, H. P., Pearson, J. S., & Brannick, T. L. (1965). A totally automated psychological test: Experience in a medical center. *Journal of the American Medical Association, 191*, 925–937.

Tate, D. F., & Zabinski, M. F. (2004). Computer and Internet applications for psychological treatment: Update for clinicians. *Journal of Clinical Psychology, 60*, 209–220.

Vale, C. D., & Keller, L. S. (1987). Developing expert computer systems to interpret psychological tests. In J. N. Butcher (Ed.), *Computerized psychological assessment: A practitioner's guide* (pp. 64–83). New York: Basic Books.

VandenBos, G. R., & Williams, S. (2000). The Internet versus the telephone: What is telehealth, anyway? *Professional Psychology: Research and Practice, 31*, 490–492.

Waller, N. G., & Reise, S. P. (1989). Computerized adaptive personality assessment: An illustration with the absorption scale. *Journal of Personality and Social Psychology, 57*, 1051–1058.

Ware, J. E., Gandek, B., Sinclair, S. J., & Bjorner, J. B. (2005). Item response theory and computerized adaptive testing implications for outcomes measurement in rehabilitation. *Rehabilitation Psychology, 50*, 71–78.

Watkins, C. E., Campbell, V. L., Nieberding, R., & Hallmark, R. (1995). Contemporary practice of psychological assessment by clinical psychologists. *Professional Psychology: Research & Practice, 26*, 54–60.

Weiner, I. B., & Greene, R. L. (2008). *Handbook of personality assessment.* New York: John Wiley & Sons.

Weiss, D., & Suhdolnik, D. (1985). Robustness of adaptive testing to multidimensionality. In D. J. Weiss (Ed.), *Proceedings of the 1982 Item Response Theory and Computerized Adaptive Testing Conference* (pp. 248–280). Minneapolis, MN: University of Minnesota, Department of Psychology, Computerized Adaptive Testing Laboratory.

Weiss, D. J. (1985). Adaptive testing by computer. *Journal of Consulting and Clinical Psychology, 53,* 774–789.

Weiss, D. J., & Yoes, M. E. (1988). Item response theory. In R. K. Hambleton & J. N. Zaal (Eds.), *New developments in testing: Theory and applications. Evaluation in education and human services series* (pp. 69–95). New York, NY: Kluwer Academic/Plenum Publishers.

Williamson, D. M., Mislevy, R. J., & Bejar, I. (2006). *Automated scoring of complex tasks in computer-based testing.* Mahwah, NJ: LEA Press, Inc.

Personality Assessment in Clinical Settings

PART 4

Personality Assessment Procedures and Instruments

Behavioral Observations

Martin Leichtman

Abstract

Introductory sections of test reports devoted to "Behavioral Observations" are among the most neglected and poorly handled aspects of psychological evaluations. To highlight the contributions these paragraphs can make to reports and provide a framework for presenting them, this chapter examines (1) ways of conceptualizing the behavior in test situations to which they are devoted; (2) the role of behavior observations in the inference process through which psychologists can seek answers to diagnostic questions; and (3) the function these paragraphs serve in reports.

Keywords: behavioral observations, planning, psychological testing, report writing, treatment

The TSAT

The Test Situation Apperception Test (TSAT) is a new instrument that, by conservative estimates, is among the most potent assessment tools created in the last half century (Leichtman, 1995). Qualities that recommend the test to experienced clinicians include the remarkable ease with which it can be administered, the rapidity with which it can be mastered, the range of subjects with whom it can be used, and the fact that it can be employed by psychologists of widely differing theoretical persuasions. Moreover, when used in conjunction with other instruments, it does not lengthen standard test batteries.

Similar to but more powerful than its namesake, the TSAT is based on two dramatic alterations in Thematic Apperception Test (TAT) procedures. First, in place of dated 1930s illustrations, stimulus material consists of clients playing themselves in real-life situations. Second, instead of subjects making up stories, psychologists are required to do so.

Test procedures are simple. First, psychologists enlist the aid of a confederate, preferably a respected mental health professional, whose function is to send clients with the instruction that testing is needed because they may suffer from psychological problems requiring diagnosis and treatment. Second, after

beginning sessions with a few minutes of discussion about why clients have come and the procedures to be used, psychologists administer a number of tests in a pleasant, businesslike manner that does not interfere with subjects' ordinary propensities to act as they wish. The choice of tests is unimportant, although ideally they should contain both items subjects can do easily and ones on which they may experience failure; tasks whose purpose seems clear and others that are a bit odd; and some activities that are potentially interesting and others that are likely to be experienced as boring. Third, at the conclusion of the evaluation, psychologists write a paragraph they believe best describes the clients and their behavior during the test process. As with the TAT, authors are free to use their imagination if they choose, but with the stipulation that stories must be rooted in the actions they have observed. Finally, psychologists can then consider where the main characters described in these stories fit within the classificatory scheme of their choice. If they have no preference in the matter, they may wish to consider a system developed for the TSAT by the American Psychiatric Association (2000).

The operation of the test can be illustrated by its use with a 15-year-old troubled by morbid thoughts that so interfered with his schoolwork he was unable to finish the 10th grade. Asked by the referring psychiatrist whether the boy exhibited severe character pathology as well as an obsessive-compulsive disorder, a psychologist wrote the following paragraph on the basis of the TSAT:

A tall, slender, effeminate adolescent whose nervous mannerisms are reminiscent of the actor Anthony Perkins, Don approached the tests with considerable anxiety and a strong desire to be ingratiating. Yet he had little idea of how to interact in socially appropriate ways and, from the first, treated the examiner as an admirer who would be fascinated by his every thought, no matter how strange. Thus, he began the first session by launching into a detailed lecture on his odd obsessions as if he were a case in a medical text. On the tests, he tried to be precise and meticulous, but had increasing difficulty doing so. So eager was he to impress that he was loath to give one answer to a question when three would do, but often was unable to decide which of the three were good and which poor. He had particular difficulty with mathematical tasks because he had forbidden himself the use of certain numbers and he clutched his left side when they were mentioned. He worried constantly about making mistakes and, when encountering test items he could not do, he would begin to shake, noting nonchalantly that he often had such "violent spasms" when upset. As the testing progressed, his thinking became looser. Occasionally he used odd words of his own creation or spoke in Russian to demonstrate his proficiency in a language he had taught himself. Toward the end of the tests, tangential associations to a question led him to give an elaborate description of an imaginary kingdom he had invented and about which he spent many hours each day fantasizing over the last several years.

Classifying his TSAT story according to the DSM-IV scheme favored by his colleague, the psychologist suggested that, while there was evidence of the obsessive-compulsive problems noted by the psychiatrist, they were present in a boy with prominent schizotypal personality characteristics who was at high risk for decompensation.

In addition to the standard TSAT task, an optional variation may be undertaken as well. After completing the initial story, psychologists are encouraged to imagine that their clients will soon enter situations that bear some similarity to testing. For example, they may assume that a child who has just taken intelligence and achievement tests is about to enter a remediation program or an adult who has taken the Rorschach is soon to begin psychotherapy.

A second story may then be written about how subjects are likely to behave in such situations and how teachers or therapists might most effectively respond to them.

Field tests of the TSAT indicate that it possesses some extraordinary characteristics. For example, the scope of its application extends far beyond that of any established assessment instrument. It may be utilized in unmodified form with subjects who range in age from neonates to the elderly and who display every known form of psychopathology. It is equally appropriate for the severely retarded and the gifted, and neither physical disabilities nor neurological impairments pose any restrictions on its use. Indeed, the TSAT can even be employed with other species, although how far down the phylogenetic scale we may proceed before it ceases to be fruitful is still a matter of contention.

As a means of studying character and predicting behavior, the TSAT has been found to have greater content validity than other projective tests. Early investigations suggest that concurrent validity is high. For example, there is an impressive correlation between diagnostic impressions formed by experienced psychologists on the basis of the TSAT and those advanced by experienced clinicians on the basis of interviews. In addition, studies of predictive validity have established that subjects described as reflective on the TSAT do well in expressive psychotherapy; subjects who are depicted as distractible, hyperactive, and emotionally labile frequently display these characteristics at home and at school; and subjects who are described as assaulting the examiner on the TSAT not only have histories of violent behavior but are at high risk for aggressive acting out in the future.

As anticipated at the time of the test's introduction, only three problems have been encountered. First, reliability is a bit lower than that of many objective instruments, though higher than that of most projective tests. Second, the TSAT is subject to misinterpretation. Misunderstanding the nature of the task, supervisors and colleagues at times do not focus on the subjects of the stories but instead analyze protocols from the standpoint of what they reveal about their authors. On occasion, this has exposed psychologists to rude comments about their clinical judgment, their literary style, and even their grammar and punctuation. Third, and most important, because the test does not require so much as a modestly priced manual or inexpensive scoring form, let alone a costly kit, it has been of little interest to major publishers. In the absence of advertising and vigorous marketing, the TSAT may well be destined for oblivion.

Behavioral Observations and Their Neglect

There is, of course, no TSAT. What has been described is a thinly disguised version of a section of test reports that typically follows an initial paragraph devoted to reasons for referral, background information, and questions the evaluation seeks to answer and precedes the body of the report in which findings are presented in one form or another (Aiken, 1999; Groth-Marnat, 1997: Huber, 1961; Kellerman & Burry, 1981: Klopfer, 1960: Ownby, 1987: Seagull, 1979; Tallent, 1988; Wolber & Carne, 2002). These paragraphs may be labeled "Behavioral Observations," "General Observations," "Clinical Observations," or "Test Behavior"; included in the report with no designation at all; or simply incorporated into the introduction or later sections of the report.

That a chapter on the topic in a handbook on assessment should begin in so curious a manner might be attributed simply to the immaturity of the author and a lapse in judgment on the part of the editors were it not for a more curious fact. "Behavioral Observations" possess all of the qualities ascribed to our hypothetical test instrument, yet are among the most neglected and poorly handled aspects of psychological evaluations (Tallent, 1988).

Reasons for this neglect are not hard to find. To begin with, there is little that is unique about such observations. They are similar to those made by psychiatrists as part of a consultation and, for that matter, by teachers, nurses, family members, and, indeed, anyone having contact with clients. In evaluations involving a variety of disciplines, the psychologist's "Behavioral Observations" may well seem redundant (Tallent, 1988).

More important, such observations appear mundane and plebeian to professionals whose identity, livelihood, and self-esteem rest on claims to a command of rigorous scientific techniques or an artistry with esoteric projective methods that enables them to penetrate surface appearances and reveal aspects of personality and behavior hidden from other disciplines and the lay public. If we must deal with observations of behavior, we would prefer to do it in our own way, using state-of-the-art recording equipment, coding systems and rating scales, and trained observers whose reliability can be monitored (Woody & Robertson, 1988).

A third strike against "Behavioral Observations" lies in their "subjectivity." As our hypothetical test suggests, reports of test behavior do resemble TAT stories. Given differences in personalities, skills, and theoretical orientations among psychologists and the selectivity necessary to describe hours of test behavior in a single paragraph, it is to be expected that a variety of accounts can be generated about the same situation, accounts that may reveal as much about their authors as about their subjects. And it is to be expected that this fact alone renders these sections suspect in a discipline in which subjectivity is identified with a lack of reliability, undisciplined speculation, and unrecognized bias—and in which striking anecdotes and empirical studies can be offered to justify this view (Fogel & Nelson, 1983).

Given these attitudes, it is hardly surprising that, with a few notable exceptions (e.g., Knoff, 1986; Sattler, 1988; Tallent, 1988; Wolber & Carne, 2002), the topic is touched upon only in a perfunctory manner in most of the literature on report writing and is often addressed haphazardly, if at all, in the teaching and supervision of assessment. Nor is it is surprising to find that "Behavioral Observations" are often among the most poorly written and least useful aspects of evaluations. Tallent (1988, p. 87), for example, observes: "It should be a matter of concern that there is no rationale or consensual basis for what should appear in this section; this becomes obvious when we consider how much irrelevant and unoriginal data are found here." Because of these problems, some psychologists suggest that this paragraph can often be omitted altogether (Ownby, 1987) or treated in specialized ways in the body of the report (Appelbaum, 1972).

Yet most practicing clinicians are reluctant to dispense with "Behavioral Observations" in their traditional form because of a conviction that these observations can make important contributions to test reports. To clarify the nature of those contributions and provide a framework for presenting them, this chapter will examine the ways in which they are grounded in assumptions governing common clinical practice. In particular, it will consider three sets of issues: (1) ways of conceptualizing the behavior in the test situation to which this section of the report is devoted; (2) the role of behavioral observations in the inference process through which psychologists answer diagnostic questions; and (3) the function these paragraphs serve in the reports through which this information is conveyed.

The "Behavior" Observed
"Behavioral Observations" and Their Rationale

Of the problems encountered in "Behavioral Observations" paragraphs, two types are especially worthy of note because of what they reveal about how these accounts are conceived. Undoubtedly the most exasperating is the long, banal description of behavior that has little bearing on the psychological issues the report is intended to address (Tallent, 1988). For example, clinicians who have extensive contact with a child may be informed he has blue eyes and blond hair, wore jeans and a T-shirt emblazoned with the word "Cougars" to the initial test session, smiled when meeting the examiner in the waiting room, but glanced apprehensively at his mother, walked down the hall holding the psychologist's hand, looked in the toy closet upon entering the office, but came to the desk when asked, and so forth. At the other extreme are "Behavioral Observations" that consist of little more than a terse statement such as: "The patient is a white, female Caucasian, age 36, who exhibited constriction, dysphoric affect, and psychomotor retardation in the course of testing." In contrast to rambling, unfocused accounts of subjects' behavior, such paragraphs are blessedly brief and move readers on quickly to the main test findings. At the same time, their impersonal, technical tone typically heralds a report written in the same fashion that will afford little sense of what subjects are like as people.

What is most significant about the first example is that it may be seen as a conscientious effort to act on a central tenet of the catechism that all psychologists, regardless of sect, learn at the beginning of their training: Everything a person thinks, feels, and does is behavior and merits careful observation. This tenet is hard to dispute. In fact, so much can be gleaned from careful observation of test behavior that psychologists can give remarkably good diagnostic pictures of profoundly disturbed children on the basis of how they act in the process of being "untestable" (Kaplan, 1975; Leichtman & Nathan, 1983). Yet the principle is difficult to translate into practice. Acting on it, inexperienced clinicians may produce long, meandering narratives of test behavior that have the unintended consequence of suggesting that no test behavior is of particular significance. Skilled clinicians can use test behavior to gain insights into every aspect of psychological functioning, but the value of their observations does not derive chiefly from the assumption that all behavior is important. Hours of testing yield an enormous volume of material, and the precept provides no basis for deciding how observations are to be selected and organized into a paragraph of presumably moderate length.

The second example may be seen as an outgrowth of assumptions rooted in a purely psychometric approach to testing that takes laboratory procedures as its model (Cronbach, 1960, pp. 59–60). Though willing to concede that everything that occurs in the test situation is behavior, adherents of such a perspective presuppose that there are two classes of behavior and a "class system" based on qualitative differences between them. On one hand, there are test data, data gathered in standardized, delimited conditions, subject to rigorous observation and precise measurement, and analyzed in terms of established norms. On the other, there are those additional observations psychologists make while gathering this information, observations that center on more obvious, superficial behavior, that are less systematic and more subject to bias, and that are, in any case, only a limited sample of the kind of behavior that can be explored more fully in diagnostic interviews. The former data are viewed as the source of the unique, invaluable contributions psychologists make to diagnostic evaluations. The latter are relatively unimportant, and hence are best stated in as brief and objective a manner as possible.

For "Behavioral Observations" to play an effective role in test reports, a rationale is required that involves greater specificity than the view that all behavior is important and that recognizes that these accounts have a legitimate and even indispensable role to play in the report.

The Nature of the Test Process

The basis for such a rationale can be appreciated if we examine how test data are gathered. Consider, for example, this process with John, a 5-year-old referred for an evaluation 18 months after he suffered organic damage that resulted in a variety of cognitive impairments, hyperactivity, problems with attention and concentration, and aggressive behavior. As would be anticipated, referral questions center on assessment of his intellectual abilities and the impact of his injury on his psychological development. As would also be anticipated with the referral, the psychologist receives fair warning that the boy will not be easy to test.

This warning is repeated by the receptionist, who makes it clear that the rambunctious child needs to leave the waiting room quickly. Upon meeting John, the psychologist encounters a feisty youngster who, like his father, is dressed in cowboy boots, western attire, and a belt with a large silver buckle and who walks with a swagger. Initially frightened, the boy alternates between hiding behind his parents and challenging the examiner with a large jackknife that was a gift from his father. When the examiner shows an interest in the knife, John is able to leave his parents and come to the office. There, after a few minutes of talk about his knife, his boots, and his interests, all occasions to boast about how masculine and daring he is, John agrees to take the tests.

Not surprisingly, testing is an arduous undertaking for both parties. John is highly impulsive, distractible, and labile. Though eager to show off what he can do, he has no tolerance for tasks at which he might fail or that prove mildly frustrating. Consequently, he races though many items carelessly and tries to avoid or refuse others; he changes tasks he thinks are too hard into ones he can do easily; he reverses roles, giving the examiner the tests instead of taking them himself; and, when all else fails, he attacks the test equipment, banging it angrily on the table or threatening to cut it with his knife. Working with John requires the examiner to make a number of decisions: when and how to provide the boy with support and reassurance and when and how to be firm and keep him at tasks he is ready to slough off; whether to accept an answer as a genuine response or repeat the item now or later; when to tolerate defensive efforts to avoid or change tasks and when and how to confront John about them; and so forth. Such decisions are seldom conscious or deliberate; rather, they are usually intuitive and only half-recognized. Indeed, much of what the examiner does to enable the testing to flow smoothly consists of an expression, a posture, a tone of voice, or a way of establishing the rhythm of testing that is not recognized at all.

Yet even if such tactics are not consciously planned, as the testing progresses, the psychologist does develop a sense of particular patterns that govern his interaction with John and allow the evaluation to be conducted with a minimum of disruption. Sensing that John fatigues easily, the examiner quickly learns that a more accurate picture of his abilities can be obtained when breaks are allowed and test sessions shortened. Intuitively recognizing the youngster's attention problems, the psychologist engages in a variety of actions to help him register tasks. For example, in giving a vocabulary test, the examiner finds himself lifting the book of pictures, turning the page, and replacing it with a flourish every few items, actions that he realizes on later

reflection are efforts to refocus the boy's attention and offset his concentration problems. Aware of John's hypersensitivity to failure, the examiner finds subtle ways of being reassuring, is more tolerant of defensive strategies than he is with many other youngsters, reorders some test items, returns to easy items on occasion, and finds other opportunities for the boy to display skills.

Above all, almost from the first, the examiner senses the importance of maintaining a specific relationship. John works best when he experiences the psychologist as a mentor who is tough enough to control him, ready to help him master the tasks before him, and an appreciative audience for the skills he displays and his tales of masculine prowess. In contrast, when he feels the examiner exposes his incompetence or when he feels threatened by anxieties stirred by projective materials, John either experiences the examiner as dangerous and responds by acting in a reckless, challenging manner or suddenly regresses, converses in baby talk, and acts like a 2-year-old.

As John is tested in ways that make allowance for his problems and his need for a particular kind of working relationship, data are obtained that have an important bearing on planning treatment. John's level of intellectual functioning, although obscured by his behavioral problems, is substantially higher than a year earlier, but a marked discrepancy between verbal skills and difficulties in visual-motor areas is now apparent. Both his behavior and the test results underline the centrality of a number of conflictual issues—those bearing on competence, maintenance of masculine identity, and dealing with trauma around the injury he has sustained. They also suggest that his high activity level and impulsivity are not simply consequences of his brain injury, but also serve defensive functions as they enable him to deny, avoid, or escape threatening situations. Finally, not only the tests, but even more the interactions that make testing possible, offer a basis for recommendations about how teachers can help John with his learning problems and about transference themes that subsequently prove to be central to his therapy (Leichtman, 1992a, 1992b).

Though perhaps disagreeing with some decisions the examiner makes in handling this testing, most psychologists will recognize the test process as a familiar one that illustrates the two critical components of test administration stressed in almost every manual and text on the subject. First, the examiner strives to "establish rapport," and second, within the context of this relationship, tests are administered in a standardized form or at least as close to a standardized form as seems possible. Yet the case also illustrates a point of particular importance that is typically acknowledged in manuals and texts only to be quickly glossed over in the interest of emphasizing the standardization of test conditions: *Depending on differences in clients and examiners, there are, in fact, marked variations in how "rapport" is established and even what constitutes "standardized administration."*

Rapport, for example, is usually described in general, abstract ways as if it consists of little more than adopting a "positive, nonthreatening tone," "putting the child at ease," and "conveying interest and enthusiasm" to create a positive, relaxed atmosphere (Wechsler, 1991). However, in emphasizing the "importance of rapport" in the administration of the Stanford-Binet, Terman and Merrill (1960) wrote:

> To elicit the subject's best efforts and maintain both high motivation and optimal performance level throughout the test session are the *sine qua non* of good testing, but the means by which these ends are accomplished are so varied as to defy specific formulation. The address which puts one child at least with a strange adult may belittle or even antagonize another. The competent examiner, like the good clinician, must be able to sense the needs of the subject so that he can help him accept and adjust to the testing situation. Sympathetic, understanding relationships with children are achieved in the most diverse ways and no armory of technical skills is a satisfactory substitute for this kind of interpersonal know-how. (pp. 50–51)

Stylistic and personality differences among examiners also affect this process. As Phares and Tull (1997, p. 257) observed, "There are many ways to achieve good rapport—perhaps as many as there are clinicians."

Similarly, there is considerable diversity in "standardized" test administration. Sattler (1988, p. 87) noted, "Countless variations preclude giving an examination that is always the same." Even with relatively simple evaluations, the pace of testing differs because some children react quickly and others slowly, and the number and types of follow-up questions vary with the ambiguity of responses and examiners' judgments of them. Moreover, with individuals referred because of serious emotional problems, evaluations are anything but simple. Clients come struggling desperately to hide their psychoses, fearful of failure, angry, frightened, elated, depressed, or oppositional. Obtaining

an accurate diagnostic picture requires giving tests in ways that address clients' concerns and cope with the defensive maneuvers through which they seek to escape serious engagement with the tests (Palmer, 1983). While at times this necessitates explicit interpretations and modification of test procedures, in most cases it is done without going beyond the parameters of standard test administration. As with John, examiners may handle these problems in subtle, often nonverbal ways though their posture, expression, or tone of voice, through the timing of the tests, or through judgments about whether to accept responses, repeat them, or inquire further. In a sense, test instructions are like a play. Examiners are bound by the script, but there is wide latitude in how they and their clients interpret their roles. This latitude is, in fact, the subject of an extensive literature on examiner effects on test performance and their implications for the validity of particular tests such as intelligence scales (see Jensen, 1980; Sattler, 1988) or the Rorschach (Exner, 2003).

These influences, it should be stressed, are not unfortunate intrusions of extraneous variables into the test process that can be minimized or fully controlled, but rather are inescapable consequences of the fact that tests are given by one human being to another. If tests were administered to each subject in exactly the same way, the result would be less useful information rather than more. For example, were John tested in this manner, rather than seeing his capacities we might learn little more than that the boy's hyperactivity, distractibility, and defensiveness interfered with his performance on tests and with every other aspect of his life, a point already clear to the receptionist after a few minutes' contact with him.

Even more important, it is essential to realize that what are referred to as "rapport" and appropriate test administration are processes that are a great deal more complex than the often cursory discussions of them in textbooks and manuals would lead one to believe. Rapport involves more than developing a positive, accepting relationship in order to "arouse the test takers' interest in the test, elicit their cooperation, and encourage them to respond in a manner appropriate to the objectives of the test" (Anastasi & Urbina, 1997, p. 17). It requires sensing roles clients strive to enact that are central to their identities, and in natural, intuitive, often unrecognized ways enacting reciprocal roles (Leichtman, 1996). Similarly, administering tests effectively involves far more than adhering to their instructions in rigid, unbending ways. It also requires attending to and helping compensate for the specific manner in which clients' problems may interfere with their responding to those instructions appropriately. As has been seen, with young and markedly disturbed clients, examiners function as what psychoanalysts describe as "auxiliary egos." Each testing has its own unique form determined by the relationships that make it possible.

To consider the nature of psychological testing, then, is to appreciate that it occurs within and is shaped by its interpersonal context. As Cronbach (1960) noted:

> The tester has been accustomed to think of himself as an unemotional, impartial task-setter. His traditions encourage the idea that he, like the physical scientist or engineer, is "measuring an object" with a technical tool. But the "object" before him is a person, and the testing involves a complex psychological relationship. (p. 602)

"Behavioral Observations" may be viewed as ways of conceptualizing the test process that seek to do justice to these "real social-psychological complexities" and to report them in ways that not only allow for an assessment of the validity of test data, but also make use of valuable information learned in administering the tests.

Testing as a Standardized Interview

Historically, the group that has given the greatest attention to these complexities has been psychoanalytically oriented psychologists, many of whom have been followers of Rapaport (Berg, 1986; Leichtman, 1996; Lerner, 1991, 1998; Schachtel, 1966: Schafer, 1954; Schlesinger, 1973; Shevrin & Schectman, 1973; Sugarman, 1978, 1981). Like Rapaport (Rapaport, Gill and Schafer, 1945–1946), they view testing as similar to a standardized clinical interview. In contrast to open-ended interviews, tests provide a common, invariant framework that confronts clients and examiners with distinct challenges. Yet, as is the case with clinical interviews, the interpersonal context of the test situation or "the patient–examiner relationship" is seen to have a significant bearing on how those challenges are handled and the information derived from them. Schafer (1954), for example, noted:

> The clinical testing situation has a complex psychological structure. It is not an impersonal getting-together of two people in order that one, with the help of a little "rapport" may obtain some "objective" test responses from the other. The psychiatric patient is in some acute or chronic life crisis. He cannot but bring many hopes, fears, assumptions, demands and expectations into the test situation. He cannot but respond intensely to certain real as well as fantasied attributes of that situation. Being human and having to make a living—facts often ignored—the tester too bring[s] hopes, fears, assumptions, demands and expectations into the test situation. He too responds personally and often intensely to what goes on—in reality and in fantasy—in that situation, however well he may conceal his personal response from the patient, from himself, and from his colleagues. (p. 6)

Assimilating the test situation to a psychoanalytic model, these theorists argue that test productions and their interpretation need to be understood in the light of potent forces of transference and countertransference (Schafer, 1956; Sugarman, 1981).

Although many psychologists may question the specific psychoanalytic interpretations these theorists offer of the test situation, most accept their general assumptions. They accept that the test situation has three basic components—the client, the examiner, and the tests; that each of these components has certain more or less invariant features—the social prescriptions governing the roles of tester and test taker and the structure of the tests themselves; and that as a result of what both participants bring to the situation and their interaction, each of these components is given a distinctive form. "Behavioral Observations" may be viewed as descriptions of these forms in each individual case.

From this perspective, these sections of reports should answer three sets of questions. First, how do clients present themselves? What roles are they trying to enact, and what concerns do they bring to the test situation? Second, what is the nature of the relationship that emerges as examiners try to engage them in the test process in ways that balance the need to maintain rapport with the need to administer tests in appropriate ways? And third, what are the clients' attitudes toward the tests, their general modes of approaching them, and their reactions toward their productions? Psychologists may also wish to include observations of a host of other matters, but answers to these questions are germane in every case and a core around which to organize these paragraphs.

Conceiving of "Behavioral Observations" in this way has important implications for how they may be written. Insofar as they are understood as answers to a delimited set of questions, they need not be long. Although a psychologist has enough material to write pages on a client's dress, appearance, and manner during the testing, a few lines may be sufficient to give a reasonable view of the overriding impression the client creates. Indeed, the term "Behavioral Observations" is a misnomer in the sense that what is sought are generalizations. For example, a multitude of observations may go into formulating an impression of a youngster's attitude toward and modes of approaching the tests, but only a good example or two are necessary to illustrate it.

Behavioral Observations and the Inference Process
Attitudes toward Clinical Impressions

Psychologists typically are most comfortable with those questions about the test situation concerned with the client's modes of handling the tests because answers can be based on observable behavior that lends itself to quantification (Sattler, 1988). In contrast, many are uneasy with questions about the roles clients play, and even more about relationships with examiners, because these require greater reliance on subjective impressions and clinical judgment. Consequently, there are significant differences of opinion about how these answers should be given and what role they should play in the inference process through which diagnostic formulations are developed.

Articulating a position shared by many psychologists with psychometric and behavioral orientations, Knoff (1986) advocated caution in the use of observations and behavior. He asserted: "To date, there is no empirically sound observational system available for completion by the practitioner during or immediately after the individual assessment section; nor are there procedures to control the potential bias when data (observed or recalled) are generalized into diagnostic hypotheses" (p. 552). Accordingly, he recommended: (1) recognizing that "assessment observations are based on a narrow, artificial situation and may not represent the child's behavior in 'real life' situations"; (2) emphasizing "observed and documented behavior over recollections and inferences"; (3) "utiliz[ing] observers behind one-way mirrors and determining interrater reliabilities for observations and interpretation"; and (4) stressing "consistencies across the entire assessment process" and "discounting inconsistencies that may be situation-specific and 'chance fluctuations'" (p. 552).

Most clinicians, however, are likely to find these recommendations excessively cautious and impractical. Though useful in training, one-way mirrors and checks on inter-rater reliability can play little role in a busy clinical practice. Too heavy an emphasis on documented behavior and a reluctance to generalize, while admirable from a scientific standpoint, may diminish the usefulness of reports to referral sources and leave the task of generalizing to others who are probably less skilled and certainly less familiar with the data. In addition, as Aiken (1999) suggests, such attitudes may underestimate the accuracy with which human beings can read kinesic, proximic, and paralinguistic cues they have spent a lifetime mastering. Although acknowledging that mistakes can be made, he observes: ". . . most people probably succeed more often than not in interpreting nonverbal messages in their own culture correctly" (p. 134). Most important, this approach underestimates the value of what Polanyi (1958) described as "personal knowledge," the judgment and expertise that constitute the art of a profession.

The Interplay of Inferences from Different Sources of Data

An alternate approach to the problem is one that encourages the use of a disciplined subjectivity in the inference process. A useful exercise in teaching this kind of clinical skill consists of having trainees rate the degree of pathology exhibited by clients they have just tested on a 5-point scale ranging from normality to psychosis and categorize the client's character style and type of pathology according to DSM-IV (Diagnostic and Statistical Manual, 4th edition) or whatever nosological scheme is preferred in their setting. In approaching these tasks, they are asked to imagine that they will not be allowed to score and analyze tests or make use of individual test responses, but must rely solely on their impressions of clients in the test situation and articulate the bases for those impressions. Then they are asked to repeat the task assuming answers to the diagnostic questions must be based only on information gathered from each of the tests they have administered. Finally, they compare the answers they have offered.

The exercise has a number of benefits. First, subjective impressions are brought into the open and examined rather than driven underground where they are less likely to disappear than to influence diagnoses in unacknowledged ways. Second, insisting that distinct sets of inferences can be made from different sources of data helps wean novice psychologists away from a covert overreliance on their behavioral observations and teaches them how to use test data. Third, the exercise sharpens skills in forming clinical impressions, since these impressions can be compared with those of supervisors, other members of clinical teams, teachers, and family. Finally, by encouraging comparison of inferences from a variety of sources of data, it teaches an approach to formulating diagnostic pictures that is invaluable in clinical work.

As clinicians gain experience, there is a substantial degree of convergence in the diagnostic opinions they form on a basis of behavioral observations and test data. They find that the young woman who appears for testing in a tight skirt, behaves seductively with the examiner, and approaches tests in a flighty, impressionistic manner often produces test results that point to a histrionic character. The adolescent who wears a Harley-Davidson T-shirt and a surly expression and who makes it clear that he doesn't give a damn about the examiner and his "friggin' tests" often displays antisocial signs on many tests. The sad, lethargic man with the self-critical attitude usually scores high on depressive indices of the Rorschach and MMPI. This correspondence of inferences made from behavior in the test situation and particular tests contributes substantially to clinicians' convictions about the correctness of their formulations.

Even more can be learned when impressions based on observations diverge from those based on other sources of data. A youngster who seems bright may score poorly on intelligence tests; a man who appears well attuned to reality may exhibit thought disorder signs on the Rorschach; a seemingly cheerful, carefree woman may give TAT stories that suggest a significant suicide potential. In such cases, it is essential not to discount the behavioral presentation or dismiss it as a "chance fluctuation." Rather, inquiring into the discrepancies is essential in understanding clients and growing as a clinician.

One explanation of these differences is, of course, that one set of inferences is wrong. Discovering that their opinions based on behavioral observations consistently fail to jibe with what tests reveal can be a powerful impetus for young clinicians to hone their clinical skills. In individual cases, even experienced clinicians find that analysis of tests helps them recognize mistaken impressions of a client. At the same time, tests are not infallible. If a child seems intelligent, yet does poorly on the Wechsler Intelligence Scale for Children-IV (WISC-IV), a careful review of the test is in order. As Groth-Marnat (1997) observes, a description of clients' behaviors can not only confirm, but also lead to modification and questioning of test interpretations.

The most interesting situations are those in which there are differences between behavioral impressions and test data, and the examiner trusts both. Making sense of these discrepancies yields insights into individuals' personalities that can be critical in treatment planning because the ways in which skilled clinicians experience clients are seldom, in fact, idiosyncratic and purely subjective. Typically, these experiences are similar to the experiences of family, teachers, therapists, and others who enter into intimate relationships with clients. The boy with low scores on intelligence tests who looks much smarter is often a youngster who works hard to create that impression. He may come for help precisely because of the problems caused by the gulf between his abilities and the expectations he and the others have for him. Similarly, the contrast between a client's seemingly normal self-presentation and a vulnerability to decompensation seen on the Rorschach or between a cheerful exterior and suicidal themes on projective tests are issues that should be highlighted in case formulations to ensure that disastrous mistakes are avoided as treatment is undertaken.

The Value of Subjectivity

Behavioral Observations offer more than simply an additional source of data; they provide a unique type of information that is rooted in the process of testing itself. As Brooks (1989, p. 21) observes, establishing rapport is based on "the ability to enter someone else's model of the world and let them know that we truly understand their model." Doing so and conducting tests effectively with human beings with significant psychological problems requires drawing upon what Peebles-Kleiger (2002, p. 99) describes as a "disciplined subjectivity" as examiners intuitively sense and respond to their clients' emotional states, defensive styles, and modes of relating to others. In reflecting on their experience of the testing—on why they make the decisions they do in the course of assessments, on the roles they assume, and on the feelings the encounter stirs in them—psychologists not only learn a great deal about clients but can also better understand the struggles of families, therapists, teachers, and hospital staff who live with and care for them.

By its very nature, much of this type of data is personal and private. Yet its value lies in this subjectivity, which accords access to insights to which dispassionate, objective observers will be blind (Sugarman, 1981). For example, in testing a youngster with attention deficit/hyperactivity disorder (ADHD), the examiner may experience not only the usual fatigue and frustration that arise in coping with marked impulsivity and distractibility, but also a disconcerting aversion to the child. When, with some reluctance, he shares these feelings in his report, the child's psychiatrist and teachers are relieved and reveal that they have similar reactions that have been hard to acknowledge. The family therapist adds that she suspects that the parents feel the same way and that their anger and guilt interfere with accepting the child and setting appropriate limits. Clearly, dealing with the youngster's attention problems, hyperactivity, and learning disability will not be enough. Effective treatment will require understanding and addressing why the child is disliked and why the child creates this feeling.

The value of subjective data is not confined to those cases in which unanticipated information about clients is uncovered. In every testing, the psychologists' personal experience of clients provides a means of translating objective, quantitative, often impersonal data from tests into full-bodied pictures of human beings. This experience also allows psychologists to empathize with families and clinicians to whom their reports are addressed. It is this integration of objective and subjective data that enables psychologists to reconcile the "scientific" and "humanistic" aspects of the assessment process (Sugarman, 1978).

Perhaps the most significant contributions the examiner's experience of clients can make in formulating cases are to treatment recommendations. Although clinicians at times act as if diagnosis and treatment are separate processes, clients do not. For them, diagnosis is the first step in the treatment process. Even proponents of objective instruments recognize that when conducted properly, testing can have important therapeutic benefits (Butcher & Perry, 2008; Finn & Kamphuis, 2006). Psychodynamic psychologists who view testing as a clinical interview go further. Treating the test situation as paradigmatic of the therapy process, they argue that transference–countertransference patterns established in the former can predict those that will arise in the latter (Schlesinger, 1973; Sugarman, 1981). For example, Lerner (1998) asserts: "Because of the similarities between the assessment and treatment frames, the examiner who explicitly sets the assessment frame and then observes patient responses to it is in a unique position to predict patient reactions to the treatment frame" (p. 68).

With John, the neurologically impaired youngster described above, the relationship established with the psychologist during the testing afforded a remarkably good basis for anticipating the ways in which the boy was to use his therapist and the issues that would disrupt the therapeutic relationship in the years that followed (Leichtman, 1992b). Appelbaum (1972) attached such importance to this aspect of the testing that he advocated devoting a major section of the report to "How the Patient Responds to Various Interpersonal Approaches."

Although many psychologists would dispute so close an identification of testing and therapy, they would acknowledge important common features. Therapists, like testers, need to establish rapport and engage in explorations in which they seek to learn what clients are like, including secrets and vulnerabilities wished hidden. Also, as psychologists help children take intelligence or achievement tests, they grapple with many of the same problems with which teachers and tutors struggle in educational settings. Because of these similarities, examiners can draw on their experiences of what facilitates and disrupts testing to make the kinds of specific, individualized recommendations that are of particular help to those who will treat clients.

Appreciating the potential benefits of the use of subjective data helps place concerns about their liabilities in a proper perspective. Though drawing on private, emotion-laden experience, psychologists can check their impressions against those of others and against test data. Though we can never be sure that our impressions are not biased or idiosyncratic, confining reports to objective data because of concerns about bias and unreliability will not keep our virtue unsullied. There are sins of omission as well as commission, Type I as well as Type II errors. To ignore subjective data may be to neglect vital information about clients, miss opportunities to offer richer pictures of them in reports, and diminish the utility of treatment recommendations. Clients may be better served when psychologists risk mistakes, trust their capacities to make emphatic contact, and work to develop the kinds of skills that warrant such trust.

The Function of "Behavioral Observations" Sections in Reports

The importance of the phenomena about which "Behavioral Observations" are made and their significance in inference process are not sufficient to justify devoting a separate introductory section of test reports to them. Such information, after all, can be included in a variety of places. In fact, contending that the formats in which these observations are treated separately creates an artificial distinction between internal and external aspects of personality, Sugarman (1981) argued that these data should be integrated throughout the body of the report. However, there are a number of reasons for accepting the traditional approach to report writing in which "Behavioral Observations" follow an introductory statement of presenting problems and questions to be answered and precede discussion of test findings and their implications.

Consumer Rights

One reason for this format is "truth in packaging." Because reports are based on information gathered in circumstances that may influence the nature of the data and their analysis, readers have a right to know about test conditions at their outset. These observations are especially important when clients' resistances or idiosyncratic approaches to testing raise questions about the validity of findings (Wolber & Carne, 2002). Psychologists may be concerned that such revelations will undermine faith in their reports, but readers are entitled to this information and usually give greater credence to interpretations in which problematic aspects of testing are considered carefully.

A description of test conditions early in a report may be of particular help to psychologists who evaluate the individual later. Differences in findings, such as a sharp drop in IQ scores, can be understood quickly when it is clear that the belligerent youngster just tested was compliant and cooperative several years ago.

Humanizing Reports

Some authorities have implied that, by focusing on how clients look, behave, and interact in social relationships, "Behavioral Observations" deal with more superficial aspects of personality than those revealed by tests. However, far from constituting a criticism of these sections, this point provides a second reason for opening reports with them. Beginning reports with vivid descriptions of how clients present themselves helps ensure that readers will approach subsequent information and interpretations with images of recognizable human beings in mind.

Although it can be argued that "Behavioral Observations" are unnecessary because every paragraph of a report should serve this function, translating such a principle into practice is difficult. Much of what we pride ourselves on as psychologists—our ability to quantify behavior, our analytic skills that enable us to attempt to isolate aspects of behavior, our technical language and often esoteric theories, our talents at fitting individuals into diagnostic categories—may interfere with readers' maintaining an image of the subjects of our reports as real people. Most of us have had occasion to complain that other psychologists' reports are too riddled with jargon, too preoccupied with numbers, too mechanistic in their description of seemingly discrete functions, or too filled with convoluted theoretical formulations, whether they are about psychosexual development or central processing dysfunctions. Yet all but the most talented or obtuse of us recognize that such problems are not easily avoided in our own reports.

It could hardly be otherwise. What distinguishes jargon from precise communication, useless tables from rigorous quantification, and empty abstractions from refined theories is often how much the reader shares the language, sophistication, or theoretical framework of the writer. What may seem mechanical or confusing to one reader in one context may be quite useful to another in a different context. Even outright vices in report writing that cannot be rationalized in this manner, like other vices, are ones from which few of us are free. Writing reports is difficult, demanding work; the volume of this work is often heavy and time is limited; and our skills and training as psychologists, not to mention as writers, are frequently less than we, and even more our readers, wish.

When reports start with "Behavioral Observations," the failings of later sections in this regard are minimized. As in person perception experiments in which information presented first has a potent effect on how later information is organized and understood (Asch, 1946; Luchins, 1957), these paragraphs increase the likelihood that readers will view technical discussions of test findings, jargon, and even abstruse theorizing later in reports as efforts to describe attributes of human beings rather than ignore them or think of clients as collections of functions, traits, or psychic structures.

Persuasion

Appelbaum (1970) stressed that reports must not only be "right," but also convincing to those responsible for implementing recommendations. Besides being scientists and experts, he suggested, psychologists should also be salesmen. "Behavioral Observations" have a good deal to contribute to the task of persuasion.

Referral sources have ambivalent attitudes toward psychologists (Schectman, 1979). For both realistic and unrealistic reasons, those with less clinical sophistication may defer to psychologists' authority too readily, accepting recommendations uncritically and applying them too rigidly. Yet these same individuals may suspect that our complex methodologies and seemingly arcane theories are pseudoscientific and blind us to what is obvious and practical in assisting clients. Such suspicions are likely to be especially high when conclusions about clients from testing differ from what their overt behavior or presenting symptoms lead others to believe. Similar problems occur even when there is a difference of opinion with sophisticated clinicians who share the same theoretical perspective, as for example when test findings suggest a markedly different view of a client than does a psychiatric interview.

Although it has been suggested that readers are put off by reports that tell them what they already know about clients (Tallent, 1988), the opposite may be the case. Well-observed accounts of how clients present themselves in the testing situation can reassure others that psychologists are seeing the same individuals they are. When reports start by establishing a common ground, readers are more inclined to accept test results that differ from surface impressions and to see differences of opinion as a product of the perspectives afforded by particular methods rather than of a misdiagnosis on someone's part.

Art and Style

Appelbaum (1970) also suggested that writing effective test reports involves art as well as science and salesmanship. He noted: "Just as advertising people do, the writer of psychological reports may use techniques of art (again, with different motives as well as technical differences). As does the artist, the writer of a test report may arouse expectations, build, sustain and relieve tension, integrate and recapitulate" (p. 351). By providing a transition from statements of symptoms and referral questions to the body of reports, "Behavioral Observations" can make important contributions in these respects as well.

Because behavioral and characterological problems manifest themselves so readily in the test situation, a description of how patients present themselves and act often provides readers with an experience of the clients' difficulties that goes far beyond what is often a generic list of symptoms in the introduction. What is meant by "hyperactivity," for example, can be brought home to the reader by a vignette describing trying to test this particular child while he is sitting on, under, and through his chair. Similarly, readers gain an appreciation of a referral problem stated as "problems managing aggression" when an examiner recounts walking on eggshells as she tries to cope with a client's simmering rage and subtle—and at times none-too-subtle—intimidation.

"Behavioral Observations" can stimulate an interest in learning more about clients by drawing attention to incongruous phenomena. For example, when an examiner experiences an adolescent as dependent and surprisingly cooperative in spite of the child's effort to maintain a tough, antisocial facade, readers are likely to be curious about why. Or the contrast between presenting problems and the psychologist's observations may highlight central issues that reports need to address. Why is a child who is impulsive, hyperactive, and distractible at school capable of working diligently for extended periods of time in the test situation? Why does a client others describe as psychologically minded and insightful leave the examiner feeling frustrated and annoyed as she tries to use the testing to explore and clarify the man's problems? What is one to make of the cheerful, relentlessly upbeat woman whose history has been one of repeated trauma and loss? Such questions capture the reader's attention and prepare the way for answers that may be critical in recommending particular forms of treatment.

Even where "Behavioral Observations" are consistent with both presenting symptoms and test findings, they can provide an initial statement of a theme that subsequent sections of reports will develop with increasing richness. For example, with Don, the adolescent described in the introduction, "Behavioral Observations" give readers a sense of his obsessional and schizotypal characteristics. Subsequent sections of his report use data from the tests to amplify the particular qualities of his thinking, his relationships with others, and his central conflicts and defensive structure.

The stylistic contributions of "Behavioral Observations" to reports can be as varied as the individuals tested, the goals of reports, and the talents and ingenuity of their writers. What is important for present purposes is a recognition of the diverse opportunities these sections afford for making their subjects come alive and transforming reports into something more than dry inventories of test findings.

Conclusion: The Test Situation as a Test

Although there is no TSAT, the test situation in fact resembles a projective test. Like a TAT card, it has a structure to which all clients must respond in some way. Tester and test taker play more or less objective roles according to prescribed social conventions, and the tests are standardized tasks to which all subjects must respond. Yet as with a TAT story, the meaning clients and examiners attribute to each aspect of the test situation may be extraordinarily varied, allowing for an appreciation of individual differences (Leichtman, 1996).

Just as clients will ascribe a wide range of psychological characteristics to the boy looking at a violin in a TAT card, so too will they seek to define themselves in a multitude of ways in the test situation through how they dress, carry themselves, and interact. Just as the boy may have a host of attitudes toward the violin—an eagerness to learn, a desire to show off, a sense of inadequacy and helplessness, resentful compliance or open defiance with parental demands, or utter indifference—so too will clients exhibit a multiplicity of attitudes and behaviors toward the tests. And just as diverse relationships may be ascribed to two figures in a TAT card, so too will the interactions between client and examiner assume innumerable forms. Children, for example, may assimilate tests to their concept of school tests and treat examiners as teachers. Yet one will play the role of a good, compliant student eager to win praise and approval from a benign mentor; a second will feel like a hopeless failure forced to confront her inadequacies by a stern taskmaster; and a third will act like a truant kept after school, working halfheartedly on assignments while watched but ready to abandon the lesson altogether the moment the teacher's back is turned. Others experience the relationship like that of a delinquent before a judge or parole officer—one defiant and rebellious, another hiding such feelings to run a con game. Still others treat the relationship as a search for care and nurturance, a seduction, a performance before an audience, or a desperate attempt to conceal their craziness.

No additional tests need be administered to obtain such rich data. It is there for the taking, and there to be used to improve diagnoses and enliven the reports through which they are communicated.

References

Aiken, L. R. (1999). *Personality assessment: Methods and practices.* Seattle: Hogrefe & Huber.

Anastasi, S., & Urbina, S. (1997). *Psychological testing.* Upper Saddle River, NJ: Prentice Hall.

American Psychiatric Association. (2000). *Diagnostic and Statistical Manual, Mental Disorders* (4th ed., Text rev.) (DSM-IV-TR). Washington, DC: American Psychiatric Association.

Appelbaum, S. A. (1970). Science and persuasion in the psychological test report. *Journal of Consulting and Clinical Psychology, 35,* 349–355.

Appelbaum, S. A. (1972). A method of reporting psychological test findings. *Bulletin of the Menninger Clinic, 36,* 535–545.

Asch, S. E. (1946). Forming impressions of personality. *Journal of Abnormal and Social Psychology, 41,* 258–290.

Berg, M. (1986). Diagnostic use of the Rorschach with adolescents. In A. I. Rabin (Ed.), *Projective techniques for adolescents and children* (pp. 111–141). New York: Springer.

Brooks, M. (1989). *Instant rapport.* New York: Warner Books.

Butcher, J. N., & Perry, J. L. (2008). *Personality assessment in treatment planning.* New York: Oxford University Press.

Cronbach, L. J. (1960). *Essentials of psychological testing* (2nd ed.). New York: Harper.

Exner, J. E., Jr. (2003). *The Rorschach: A comprehensive system, Vol. 1: Basic foundations and principles of interpretation* (4th ed.). Hoboken, NJ: John Wiley & Sons.

Finn, S. E., & Kamphuis, J. H. (2006). Therapeutic assessment with the MMPI-2. In J. N. Butcher (Ed.), *MMPI-2: The practitioner's handbook* (pp. 165–191). Washington, DC: American Psychological Association.

Fogel, L. S., & Nelson, R. O. (1983). The effects of special education labels on teachers' behavioral observations, checklist scores, and grading of academic work. *Journal of School Psychology, 21,* 241–252.

Groth-Marnat, G. (1997). *Handbook of psychological assessment* (3rd ed.). New York: John Wiley & Sons.

Huber, J. T. (1961). *Report writing in psychology and psychiatry.* New York: Harper & Row.

Jensen, A. R. (1980). *Bias in mental testing.* New York: Free Press.

Kaplan, L. J. (1975). Testing nontestable children. *Bulletin of the Menninger Clinic, 39,* 420–435.

Kellerman, H., & Burry, A. (1981). *Handbook of psychodiagnostic testing: Personality analysis and report writing.* New York: Grune & Stratton.

Klopfer, W. G. (1960). *The psychological report: Use and communication of psychological findings.* New York: Grune & Stratton.

Knoff, H. M. (1986). The personality assessment report and the feedback and planning conference. In H. M. Knoff (Ed.), *The assessment of child and adolescent personality* (pp. 547–582). New York: Guilford Press.

Leichtman, M. (1992a). Psychotherapeutic interventions with brain-injured children and their families: I. Diagnosis and treatment planning. *Bulletin of the Menninger Clinic, 56,* 321–337.

Leichtman, M. (1992b). Psychotherapeutic interventions with brain-injured children and their families: II. Psychotherapy. *Bulletin of the Menninger Clinic, 56,* 338–360.

Leichtman, M. (1995). Behavioral Observations. In J. N. Butcher (Ed.), *Clinical personality assessment: Practical approaches* (pp. 251–266). New York: Oxford University Press.

Leichtman, M. (1996) *The Rorschach: A developmental perspective.* Hillsdale, NJ: Analytic Press.

Leichtman, M., & Nathan, S. (1983). A clinical approach to the psychological testing of borderline children. In K. Robson (Ed.), *The borderline child: Approaches to etiology, diagnosis, and treatment* (pp. 121–170). New York: McGraw-Hill.

Lerner, P. (1991). *Psychoanalytic theory and the Rorschach.* Hillsdale, NJ: Analytic Press.

Lerner, P. (1998). *Psychoanalytic perspectives in the Rorschach.* Hillsdale, NJ: Analytic Press.

Luchins, A. S. (1957). Primacy-recency in impression formation. In C. I. Hovland, L. Mandell, E. H. Campbell, T. Brock, A. S. Luchins, A. R. Cohen, et al. (Eds.), *The order of presentation in persuasion* (pp. 33–61). New Haven, CT: Yale University Press.

Ownby, R. L. (1987). *Psychological reports: A guide to report writing in professional psychology.* Brandon, VT: Clinical Psychology.

Palmer, J. O. (1983). *The psychological assessment of children* (2nd ed.). New York: John Wiley & Sons.

Peebles-Kleiger, M. J. (2002). *The art and science of planning psychotherapy*. Hillsdale, NJ: Analytic Press.

Phares, E. J., & Tull, T. J. (1997). *Clinical psychology: Concepts, methods, and profession* (5th ed.). Pacific Grove, CA: Brooks/Cole.

Polanyi, M. (1958). *Personal knowledge: Towards a post-critical philosophy*. Chicago: University of Chicago Press.

Rapaport, D., Gill, M. M., & Schafer, R. (1945–1946). *Diagnostic psychological testing* (2 Vols). Chicago: Year Book.

Sattler, J. M. (1988). *Assessment of children's intelligence and special abilities* (3rd ed.). San Diego: Jerome M. Sattler.

Schachtel, E. (1966). *Experiential foundations of Rorschach's test.* New York: Basic Books.

Schafer, R. (1954). *Psychoanalytic interpretation in Rorschach testing.* New York: International Universities Press.

Schafer, R. (1956). Transference in the patient's reaction to the tester. *Journal of Projective Techniques, 20,* 26–32.

Schechtman, F. (1979). Problems in communicating psychological understanding: Why won't they listen to me?! *American Psychologist, 34*(9), 781–790.

Schlesinger, H. (1973). Interaction of dynamic and reality factors in the diagnostic testing interview. *Bulletin of the Menninger Clinic, 37,* 495–517.

Seagull, E. A. W. (1979). Writing the report of a psychological assessment of a child. *Journal of Clinical Child Psychology, 8,* 39–42.

Shevrin, H., & Schectman, F. (1973). The diagnostic process in psychiatric evaluations. *Bulletin of the Menninger Clinic, 37,* 451–494.

Sugarman, A. (1978). Is psychodiagnostic assessment humanistic? *Journal of Personality Assessment, 42,* 11–21.

Sugarman, A. (1981). The diagnostic use of countertransference reactions in psychological testing. *Bulletin of the Menninger Clinic, 45,* 473–490.

Tallent, N. (1988). *Psychological report writing* (3rd ed.). Englewood Cliffs, NJ: Prentice-Hall.

Terman, L., & Merrill, M. (1960). *Stanford-Binet Intelligence Scale.* Boston: Houghton-Mifflin.

Wechsler, D. (1991). *Weschler Intelligence Scale for Children—third edition: Manual.* San Antonio, TX: Psychological Corporation.

Wolber, G. J., & Carne, W. F. (2002). *Writing psychological reports: A guide for clinicians* (2nd ed.). Sarasota, FL: Professional Resource Press.

Woody, R. H., & Robertson, M. (1988). *Becoming a clinical psychologist.* Madison, CT: International Universities Press.

The Clinical Interview

Robert J. Craig

Abstract

This chapter presents the anatomy of the basic clinical interview. We discuss its structure, content, factors affecting the clinical interview, interviewing techniques, types of clinical interviews, patient and psychologists' expectations, interview reliability, and computer-assisted clinical interviews.

Keywords: clinical interview, assessment, reliability, computer-based testing

In this chapter, I use the term "clinical interview" to mean the assessment of personality, personality disorders, and psychopathology using the clinical interview. There are other (supplemental) means of performing this clinical function, such as collateral information, record reviews, behavioral observations, psychological testing, and other sources of anamnestic data. Indeed, when these supplemental sources are consulted, the accuracy of clinical diagnoses and assessment conclusions are often enhanced. I lament the fact that too often clinicians rely primarily on the clinical interview as their major tool for assessment and diagnosis. This is often never the case among forensic psychologists who routinely consult these sources as part of their exploration to determine fact. However, in this chapter, the focus is exclusively on using the clinical interview devoid of these other sources, even though, in clinical practice, such overreliance is frowned upon.

Also, in this chapter, I use the term "client" and "patient" interchangeably. Psychologists continue to argue which is the preferred term to use. Clinicians operating in psychiatric outpatient clinics and hospitals generally use the term "patient," while clinicians working in private practice or in university mental health clinics often use the term "client." Both terms are used in this chapter with no value pinned on one or the other.

Finally, this chapter focuses exclusively on clinical interviews with adults. There are other sources on interviewing children (Hersen & Thomas, 2007a; Logan, 2005) and the reader is urged to consult these authoritative sources.

Matarazzo (1965, 1978) was among the first psychologists to study the anatomy of the clinical interview, reporting on its reliability and validity in a plethora of clinical usages. Matarazzo was able to take a unilateral perspective of the clinical interview because special focus interviews had not yet been developed. Contemporary usage of the clinical interview has evolved into more standardized and semistandardized structured and semistructured clinical interviews, such that it is no longer appropriate to discuss the reliability and validity of a clinical interview. Rather, we must now study the reliability and validity of a specific (kind of) interview under consideration (Craig, 2003). Indeed, there are now a substantial number of clinical interviews that have been published designed to aid in the diagnosis of major psychiatric syndromes and clinical personality patterns/disorders.

Anatomy of a Clinical interview

The elements of a clinical interview include its structure, theoretical orientation of the clinical interviewer, the expectations of both client and clinician, as well as the content and process of the interview.

Clinician's Theoretical Orientation

Patients come to an interview with certain expectations; clinicians also approach a clinical interview with their own set of predispositions. They do not enter the room with a blank slate. Rather they approach the patient with a philosophical orientation that influences the structure, process, and content of the interview. This theoretical framework influences the areas and methods of inquiry, how they conduct the evaluation, and how they understand the meaning of elicited client information.

Let us take a closer look at how one's theoretical information influences the interview process. We will briefly discuss the interview process from the prospective of the psychodynamic, phenomenological-existential-nondirective, behavioral and family systems orientations.

PSYCHODYNAMIC

Clinicians operating from a psychodynamic philosophical orientation emphasize the role of early developmental history, trauma, vulnerability to self-esteem injury, and unconscious conflict in the development of psychological maladjustment (Yalof & Abraham, 2005). Drive theory, self-psychology, and object relations theories may be the philosophical substrate that guides the clinician's thinking. However, it is not unusual to find both the models of intrapsychic structure and interpersonal relations in a psychodynamic interview.

Given this background, psychodynamic clinicians pay particular attention to the way the patient is relating to the clinician and are continually observing for the development of transference, even in the initial session. They view the resolution of this transference as the *sine qua non* of treatment. Interpretations are the main source of interventions and may be attempted within the first session, if the clinician deems this appropriate. Both supportive and exploratory interventions may occur here.

CLIENT-CENTERED/PHENOMENOLOGICAL/ EXISTENTIAL

Client-centered therapy was developed by Carl Rogers (1942, 1951) who argued that empathy, genuineness and congruence, and unconditional positive regard practiced by the clinician toward the client (Rogers did not believe in calling the person a "patient") are the necessary and sufficient conditions that allowed for client self-actualization and personal growth (Rogers, 1957). A client-centered approach anchors itself in phenomenological theory. Phenomenology believes that the object of study is people's perceptions and life experiences. The therapist's goal is to understand these in terms of the patient's intentions, purposes, and personal meaning and to come to a clear understanding of the patient's underlying assumptions and presuppositions (Gruba-McCallister, 2005). A patient's behavior is totally determined by their beliefs and life experiences. The focus is on the here-and-now and how the self develops and grows amid these personal beliefs.

Existential theory is closely allied with these two humanistic approaches. Existential theory posits that the search for meaning is the basic motivation underlying behavior (Husserl, 1962). The goal of therapy is to help the person discover their true meaning. The clinician is a participant-observer in the phenomenological world of the client.

COGNITIVE BEHAVIOR

Cognitive-behavior theory anchors itself within a behaviorist epistemology, where behavior is a function of antecedents and consequences (i.e., rewards and punishments) within a specific environmental context. It relies on classical and operant conditioning models as well as the role of modeling in shaping human behavior. All behavior is learned and there are no mediating variables (i.e., traits) to explain behavior. The clinical interview is the start of a "functional analysis of behavior" which helps the client identify the antecedent conditions to the problem, the cognitions that related to the problem, and the consequences of problematic behavior. Interventions may begin within the initial interview. For example, the family of an enuretic might be asked to begin to self-monitor and record the extent and frequency of bedwetting, knowing that the act of self-monitoring may also reduce the behavior being monitored. An alcoholic man might be told to vary his route home in an effort to break the chain of behaviors that leads him into the bar after work.

Cognitive behavior therapists have offered suggestions as to the content of the initial interview. Lazarus (1976) suggested that the comprehensive assessment of the patient includes (the pneumonic) device of BASIC ID, where

B = behavior, especially those that are
   problematic;
A = affective responses, especially those
   requiring modification;
S = sensory deficits (e.g., emotional pain);
I = imagery (such as fantasies);
C = cognitions, especially those that are illogical
   (Ellis, 1962);

- I = interpersonal relationships; and
- D = drugs, a category that includes not only those prescribed and those taken illicitly, but also a person's well-being, health, and exercise.

Wolpe (1973) recommends that data be obtained in five areas: early family history, education, employment, sexual history, and current relationships. Kanfer and Scheft (1988) recommend an analysis of the presenting problem, the cause of the abnormal behavior, a motivation and developmental analysis, a review of self-control skills and social relationships, and an analysis of the person's social, cultural, and physical environment.

FAMILY SYSTEMS PERSPECTIVE

A family systems perspective relies on general systems theory, where the orientation is on the interaction of parts rather than on the individual parts themselves, and on cybernetics, which focuses on communication, feedback, and control. There are a number of family therapy theories, but all share the belief that the identified patient is a manifestation of a dysfunctional family. From this perspective, it is possible to do "family therapy" even when working with an individual patient. Van dyke (2005) has suggested that the initial family therapy interview deal with the presenting problem (especially how the family reacts to the problem), the family structure subsystems, communication patterns within the family, power structures (i.e., who has the final say), family roles, family lifestyle changes, and various contextual issues, such as culture, gender, and religion.

Personal Beliefs and Values

An additional factor that will influence the nature of the clinical interview is the psychologist's personal values and beliefs. Of course, these are somewhat influenced by their theoretical orientation as well. First, while the patient may discuss a myriad of issues within a session, the clinician will select that which s/he believes is most important (i.e., valued from their perspective). For example, one psychologist may value a patient's inner mental life and therefore focus on introspection. Another may emphasize expressions of feelings and catharsis, while still a third may value humor whereas yet another eschew it. Some clinicians use a directed approach while others prefer a nondirective style. Certain kinds of content are also more highly esteemed than others. Some focus on behavior and their antecedents and consequences, while others focus on stream of consciousness and free associations. Finally,

psychologists have a set of assumptions about behavior change and then intervene based on those assumptions. Other areas of difference could be elucidated, but the point here is that clinicians operate from a set of beliefs, values, and frameworks that guide their interventions. While client-centered clinicians rely primarily on the use of reflection to advance the interview, psychologists from the existential theoretical framework act as a participant observer. They try to develop a receptive, open relationship, employing active listening (see section on interviewing techniques) and strive to share the person's worldview as a way to promote mutual understanding. In this regard, existential clinicians are not passive and may even confront issues of meaninglessness, boredom, ennui, and isolation (Maddi, 2005).

To see more clearly how a theoretical orientation influences how the clinician views behavior, let us take the following example. A heroin addict is brought for treatment by his wife, who has threatened to leave him on multiple occasions but has never done so. She alleges that psychotherapy is his last chance, or else "she will leave."

A psychodynamically oriented clinician might view this problem as an oral fixation in the patient and a masochistic need to suffer in his wife. A family systems clinician might see this problem in terms of a dominant–submissive relationship with the wife controlling the power and desiring to maintain her husband in a dependent relationship as the patient fears independence and also fears changing the family roles, thereby maintaining a homeostatic relationship within this dyad. A client-centered clinician would focus on the perceptions of both parties, how the "self" continues to evolve or be arrested within this relationship, and the role of heroin in forestalling self-actualization and personal growth. A behaviorally oriented clinician would focus on the antecedents of his using heroin as well as the consequences, identifying via behavioral analysis the rewards that maintain the heroin-using behavior.

Structure and Process

Clinical interviews may be structured, semistructured, and unstructured. Some standardized clinical interviews, designed to establish psychiatric diagnoses, are rigidly structured. The clinician reads from a prepared list of questions and records the patient's responses. Others are semistructured where the clinician is allowed more probative lines of inquiry depending on the response of the client. Some clinical interviewers prefer that the client take the lead in the interview and value a rather unstructured approach within the interview process so as to not interfere with the cognitive and emotional flow of the client. These types of interviews will be elaborated on later in this chapter.

With the introduction of DSM-III (APA, 1980), and continuing through DSM-III-R (APA, 1987) and DSM-IV (APA, 1994), a large number of structured and semistructured clinical interviews began to be published in the professional literature. Initially they were comprehensively focused on surveying major Axis I syndromes, such as the Schedule for Affective Disorders and Schizophrenia (SADS) (Endicott & Spitzer, 1978), the Diagnostic Interview Schedule (DIS) (Robins, Helzer, Croughan, & Ratcliff, 1981), and the Structured Clinical Interview for DSM-III (SCID) (Spitzer & Williams, 1984). Then structured clinical interviews began to appear for the assessment of personality disorders for assessing Axis II conditions, such as the Structured Clinical Interview for DSM-III-R (SCID-II) (Spitzer, Williams, Gibbon, & First, 1992), the Personality Disorder Diagnostic Interview (Widiger, Mangine, Corbitt, Ellis, & Thomas, 1995), and the Diagnostic Interview for DSM-IV Personality Disorders (Zanarini, Frankenburg, Sickel, & Yong, 1995). Thereafter followed the development of structured and semistructured clinical interviews for specific psychiatric syndromes, including anxiety disorders (Spitzer & Williams, 1988), depression (Jamison & Scogin, 1992), and posttraumatic stress disorder (Watson, Juba, Manifold, Kucala, & Anderson, 1991). Today, structured clinical interviews have been published for most major psychiatric disorders. (For a more detailed presentation of these instruments, see Craig, 2003, and Rogers, 2001.)

The SADS is a semistructured diagnostic interview consisting of two main sections. The instrument is designed to reduce the need for clinical judgment. The first section asks questions to ascertain a patient's symptoms and their severity. The level of impairment is determined by comparing the patient's responses to standard descriptions. The second section queries mental disorders clustered within each main section of the DSM. This section addresses history of current episode, mood, symptoms, and impairment. The instrument takes 1–2 hrs to administer.

The DIS is a structured clinical interview. The clinician reads the questions exactly as they appear in the interview booklet without subsequent probing. There are 32 different diagnoses assessed with the DIS. Current symptoms are assessed for the past 2 weeks, 4 weeks, 6 months, and 12 months. It takes 45–90 min to administer.

The SCID is semistructured clinical interview with an administration time of 60–90 min. The patient initially describes the problem and the clinician responds with open-ended questions guided by the interview booklet. After each section, the examiner rates the severity level of the disorder in terms of mild, moderate, or severe. DSM provides a hierarchical structure to its organization (i.e., substance use disorders, psychotic disorders, affective disorders, anxiety disorders, etc.), and the SCID follows this hierarchical structure in its questioning. The SCID-II was then developed to assess DSM personality disorders.

Within psychiatry the SCID/SCID-II has become the most frequently used (semistructured) clinical interview and is the standard to diagnose Axis I and Axis II disorders in psychiatric research.

Table 12.1 presents an illustration of how these structured clinical interviews appear in actual text. Screening for antisocial personality disorder is highlighted.

Structure of the Initial Clinical Interview

Even an apparent unstructured clinical interview may be actually having a structure. The social psychiatrist Harry Stack Sullivan believed that interpersonal and social relationships were more important in the derivation of psychological disorders than unconscious conflicts and arrested psychosexual development. Sullivan published no material on his seminal ideas, but his psychiatric residents recorded his notes and subsequently published them under his name in a critical book entitled *The Psychiatric Interview* (Sullivan, 1954).

Sullivan argued that the structure of the clinical interview consisted of four parts: (a) formal inception, (b) reconnaissance, (c) detailed inquiry, and (d) termination.

In the first phase of the interview, or formal inception, the clinician learns why the client is seeking assistance. Sullivan believed this should take no more than 5 min. In the reconnaissance, the clinician should take not more than 20 min to get an overview of the patient, and ascertain history, strengths, defenses, and associated concurrent comorbidities. In the detailed inquiry, the clinician develops ideas as to the cause of the problem as well as a working plan to assist in problem resolution. The last phase (termination) should take 5–10 min and provide the patient with an action plan as well as address basic issues such as frequency of future sessions, fees, confidentiality, and the like.

Table 12.1. Sample structured clinical interview format (for antisocial personality disorder).

Screening questions	Yes	No
Conduct disorder		
1. Prior to the age of 15, have you ever done things for which you could have been arrested.	—	—
If yes, ask: What were some of those things?		
Have you ever been arrested?		
Have you ever spent time in jail? How Long?		
Deceitfulness, manipulations & conning		
2. Would you say that you are especially good at fooling people?	—	—
If yes, say "Give me some examples"		
Impulsivity		
3. Do you prefer to (a) think about things before you act or (b) jump right in?	—	—
If "a" ask "Give me two examples"		
Aggressiveness and fighting		
4. Have you ever engaged in physical fighting?	—	—
If yes, ask "What were the circumstances of these fights?"		
Recklessness		
5. Do you take chances that others might consider reckless?	—	—
If yes, ask "Give me some examples"		
Irresponsibility		
6. Have you ever lost, been fired, or walked off a job?	—	—
If yes, ask "What were the reasons you lost these jobs?"		
7. Are you in debt?	—	—
If yes, ask "What for and how much do you owe?"		
Lack of guilt or remorse		
8. Do you feel that people have abused you, hurt you, or in other ways mistreated you?	—	—
If yes, ask "Give me some examples"		
9. In general do you feel guilty when you physically or emotionally hurt someone?	—	—
If yes, ask "Why not?" (look for justifications and rationalizations)		
Criminality		
10. As an adult have you been in trouble with the law?	—	—
If yes, ask "Why were you arrested?		
"What did they charge you with?		
"How much time have you spent in jail?		
Maintenance of independence		
11. Do you maintain your independence at all costs?	—	—
If yes, ask "Why is that?"		
12. Do you think that others try to control you?	—	—
If yes, ask "Give me some examples"		
13. Record here any additional question(s) you may have asked and the patient's response(s) to them.		
14. Record below the patient's (a) way of relating to you, (b) degree of cooperativeness, and (c) manner of dress.		
15. Rate the overall truthfulness of the patient's responses.		
(A) Probably truthful — (B) Mostly truthful —		
(C) Somewhat truthful — (D) Unlikely to be truthful — (E) Uncertain —		

Other clinicians have sought to provide a structural model of a clinical interview from a different theoretical perspective. For example, Sullivan took a perspective in creating his structural model, whereas Benjamin (1981) took a psychosocial perspective to the clinical interview and divided it into three main stages called initiation (i.e., statement of the problem), development (where client and clinician mutually agree on the nature of the problem), and closing.

From a behavioral perspective, the clinical interview has been divided into role structuring, creating a therapeutic alliance, developing a commitment for change, analyzing behavior, negotiating treatment, and planning and implementation (Kanfer & Scheft, 1988). More recently, Beach (2005) argued that a behavioral clinical interview should consist of the identification of problematic behaviors, a determination of the variables causally related in a behavioral chain to the development of the problem, identification of patient characteristics that will facilitate or retard treatment, the assessment of environmental variables that will positively or negatively reward behavior, and finally selecting a behavioral treatment method.

Beach (2005) has recommended that the initial interview begin with a definition of the presenting problem, invoking one of the assessment models previously discussed (i.e., Wolpe, Lazarus, and Kanfer & Scheft), developing a preliminary hypothesis for variables affecting the patient's behavior, testing this hypothesis through detailed questioning of variables controlling the patient's behavior, and then designing a treatment approach that will lead to problem resolution and behavior change.

From a client-centered perspective, Carl Rogers characterized the clinical interview in the following manner: the client comes for help, the situation is defined through therapist acceptance, clarification, and the expression of positive feelings, and finally there is the development of insight (Rogers, 1942).

I have adapted Sullivan's model of the structure of a clinical interview both in my clinical practice and when leading seminars in clinical interviewing among graduate students in clinical psychology. I conceive of the interview as consisting of an "introduction," which roughly corresponds to Sullivan's formal inception phase. Here we learn why the patient is seeking mental health services. It is also the phase where we begin to establish both trust and rapport. This can be facilitated by discussing privacy and confidentiality issues, addressing the clients by their preferred name, arranging seating to promote observation, avoiding unnecessary interruptions, using language that is appropriate to the client, being nonjudgmental, and displaying empathy.

I call the next phase "exploration." This phase corresponds to Sullivan's reconnaissance and detailed inquiry. In this phase, the clinician ascertains a clinical diagnosis and associated comorbidities, and develops an initial hypothesis based on one's theoretical orientation. You may characterize the nature of the problem as an unbalanced family hierarchy with triangulated communications (a family theory perspective), problematic negative reinforcements (a behavioral perspective), distorted object relations, and arrested psychological development (a psychoanalytic perspective). The important point here is to develop a working hypothesis that is tested within subsequent moments of the interview. Eliciting this kind of information can best be accomplished by asking open-ended questions (see below), intervening at critical points of client elaborations, clarifying any inconsistencies, and interrupting in ways that suggest clinician competence.

I need to diverge somewhat here to comment on the importance of "assessing the syndrome" in this phase of the interview. By that I mean that the clinician demonstrates his or her knowledge of the problem by inquiring on symptoms, problems, and disorders known to be associated with the primary problem or diagnosis. For example, suppose that you are a diabetic and experience a job relocation that requires you to find another physician to help manage your diabetes. You receive the names of two physicians and contact them to make an appointment, stating that you are looking for someone to treat your elevated glucose levels. Both of them give you an appointment and instruct you to go to a local lab for a blood test. When you see Dr. A, s/he reviews your test results, takes your medical history, and prescribes 500 mg of Glucophage (metformin) BID. Next you visit Dr. B, who reviews your blood test results, takes a medical history, examines your heart, checks your extremities for peripheral neuropathy, orders a 24-hr kidney functioning test, recommends that you see an ophthalmologist annually to check for diabetic retinopathy, and also suggests you take a cardiac stress test. S/he also prescribes 500 mg of Glucophage (metformin) BID. Other things being equal, which physician will you select? I believe you will choose Doctor B, who, based on the actions within the interview, has demonstrated thorough knowledge of the syndrome being treated. Dr. A may be just as knowledgeable and just as competent as Dr. A, but you would not know that by the actions within the examination.

In the same manner, clinicians need to demonstrate their knowledge and competence of the syndrome or problem by inquiring into all known parameters of the disorder. By so doing, you convey this sense of competence to the client who will then most likely return for the next session.

I call the third phase "hypothesis testing." Here the clinician engages in additional inquiries to test the hypothesis by exploring further into additional areas of the patient's life. To the extent that one's personality is integrated, the material uncovered within this inquiry should be consistent with your earlier hypothesis, thereby validating it. If subsequent information is inconsistent with your hypothesis, then your understanding of the cause of the patient's behavior is probably inaccurate and you need to revise your explanation. These two phases—the exploration and the hypothesis testing—are the most difficult ones for novice clinicians because of their lack of experience and the depth of analysis required.

The last phase I refer to as "feedback," which loosely corresponds to Sullivan's termination phase. Here the psychologist offers the client, in a language that is clearly understood, what the therapist thinks is the source of the problem. This should be easily done if the second and third phases of the interview are conducted properly. For example, when a patient goes to a physician, they tell the doctor what their symptoms and problems are, the doctor may conduct a physical examination, and at the end of the appointment, the patient knows the diagnosis and the treatment plan—the doctor writes medication orders. Or the doctor may suggest the probable diagnosis and order confirmatory tests. On the other hand, the symptoms may be due to several causes and the physician orders several kinds of tests to rule out various diseases. Eventually, however, the patient is told the diagnosis and the plan of care.

Note that this model rarely occurs in most mental health interviews. Traditionally, a patient comes to a mental health clinician, engages in catharsis, is questioned by the clinician, and then, at the end of the session, leaves the office with no more understanding than when s/he arrived, because the clinician never tells a patient anything. It is no wonder why many patients fail to return to the second session.

Once I had a contract with a psychiatric HMO. My responsibility was to interview the patient, render a diagnosis, determine what type of psychotherapy was recommended to treat the problem, what kind of provider would best serve the patient,

and how many sessions would be needed to resolve the problem. As part of the contract, I was required to go to a central location and submit to a role-played, video-taped "psychiatric interview" with a hired actor. Since there were some 20 similar clinicians hired for this role, they were also required to see this actor for a role-played interview. The head of the firm was using this as a demonstration that these therapists were competent at the initial hiring. The actor portrayed a probable real-life issue he was having with his father and had done so during the other role-played sessions with the other therapists. At the end of the interview, I asked the "patient" if he had any questions and when he responded "no," the tape was turned off. I then asked him what he thought of this interview and he told me that of all the clinicians he had done this with, I was "the best." When I asked him why he felt I did the best job, he said it was because I was the only one who suggested a course of immediate and future actions that might help to alleviate the situation. I truly believe that patients are looking for more than reflection, empathy, and positive regard. They are looking for help and if they perceive that the clinician is helpful, then they will return for subsequent sessions.

I have taught this model, highlighted in Table 12.2, to graduate students in clinical psychology and require them to give the patient feedback on their thinking and to do so in plain language. For example, you probably would not tell the patient that he has a dependent personality disorder. Rather, you would probably say that he has certain personality characteristics that result in him being easily taken advantage of, due to his lack of assertiveness and tendency to rely on others to make major decisions. This model has also been incorporated into a recommended training model to teach clinical and diagnostic interviewing (Rudolph, 2005).

Content of the Clinical Interview

The content of a clinical interview will depend on the "kind of interview" being conducted. Table 12.3 presents an overview of content areas that may be included in clinical interviews. These content areas need not be included in every initial interview, depending on the nature of the interview itself.

Kinds of Clinical Interviews

This section reviews the major kinds of clinical interviews that have appeared in the literature and the type of content mostly likely to appear in them. The interviews are presented separately for didactic

Table 12.2. Overview of the structure of a clinical interview.

Phase	Requirements
Introduction	Learn the reason for seeking mental health services
Exploration	Elicit signs, symptoms, and problematic behaviors
	Establish a clinical diagnosis for both psychiatric disorders and personality pathology
	Assess for comorbidities and risk factors associated with the primary and secondary diagnoses
	Develop a working hypothesis as to how and why these problems developed
Hypothesis testing	Ask questions that result in confirming or revising your etiological hypothesis
Feedback	Give the patient feedback on what you see as the cause of the problem and make suggestions as to how they can be alleviated
	Establish the parameters of subsequent sessions, such as length, frequency, time, fees, and policies

Table 12.3. Common content area in an assessment interview.

History of the problem	Presenting complaint
	Onset of the problem with intensity and duration
	Antecedents and consequences
	Prior treatment episodes
Personal history	Relevant developmental milestones
	Education
	History of childhood problems (including physical and/or sexual abuse)
	Medical problems
	Legal problems
	Work history/vocational problems
	Marital/partner history
	Use of illegal substances and alcohol
	Current and former significant relationships
	Emotional stability
	History of psychological treatment
Family background	Family constellation
	Relationship with parents/care-givers
	Socioeconomic level
	Cultural/ethnic factors
	Family atmosphere/relationships
	Occupational level
	Medical problems
	Familial support

purposes, but in reality, their boundaries are permeable and clinicians often engage in several of these activities within a single session.

BRIEF SCREENING INTERVIEWS

The brief screening interview is distinguished by its time-limited and focused structure designed to address a specific question. Is the patient suicidal? Is the patient dangerous to others? Is the client psychologically fit to stand trial? Does the patient need to be hospitalized? Is medical referral needed? Does the patient have an adequate relapse prevention plan?

Does the patient have acceptable aftercare plans? Does the patient understand the consequences should s/he test positive for HIV? In most cases, a referral for some other mental health intervention usually follows the brief clinical interview.

CASE HISTORY EXAMS

Case histories often comprise the richest part of a clinical interview. Occasionally they are conducted separately, but more often than not they are part of a routine clinical interview. In some cases a more detailed sketch of the patient's background is required, focusing on specific instances of behavior, their antecedents and consequences. Case histories may also be obtained from the patient's family or friends.

CRISIS INTERVIEW

While most students are taught how to conduct in-depth clinical interviews, psychologists are often called upon to conduct a brief, specific interview in a crisis situation. The site where this most often occurs is the ER, or a psychiatric outpatient clinic—perhaps attached to a general hospital, where psychologists might be on call to determine whether the patient is a danger to himself (i.e., suicidal) or to others (i.e., homicidal) and therefore needs inpatient hospitalization. Under these circumstances, diagnostic and interview questions are direct, focused, and specific (Somers-Flanagan & Somers-Flanagan, 1995). The relationship is not designed to be therapeutic and hence oriented toward long-term behavior change. Rather it seeks to answer a specific and immediate question. A prototype of this kind of interview is the suicide hotline, staffed by paraprofessionals trained and supervised often by clinical psychologists.

DIAGNOSTIC INTERVIEW

Whether the patient is interviewed solely to establish a formal diagnosis, or, more often, a psychiatric diagnosis is part a clinical interview, some form of diagnosis ensues by the completion of most initial clinical interviews. Within mental health, there are two official diagnostic systems in widespread use. The first is the *International Classification of Disease*, 10th edition of the World Health Organization (ICD-10; WHO, 1992). The second, which is more popular in the United States and increasingly so among Western countries, is the *Diagnostic and Statistical Manual of Mental Disorders*, fourth edition of the American Psychiatric Association (1994). Both diagnostic systems are acceptable to insurance companies, though most mental health clinicians use the DSM-IV.

All medical subspecialties have a diagnostic manual that lists an array of diagnoses that the medical subspecialty believe are under the purview of their physicians to diagnose and/or treat. Coding clerks at hospitals as well as medical and psychological billing services rely on these diagnostic manuals since they use the diagnostic codes associated with the disorders within the manuals to bill insurance companies for reimbursement.

The diagnoses in DSM-IV, and in all its previous renditions, were derived by forming committees of experts within a certain classification of disorders (i.e., affective disorders, anxiety disorders, substance-induced disorders, etc.). These committees met and conducted literature reviews on research associated with each of the disorders within these broad categories. After inspecting this research, judgments were made as to whether or not the criteria sets within each disorder required revision, deletion, or further behavioral anchoring. Then field tests were conducted to establish the reliability of these criteria sets. The final version was then submitted to the DSM revision committee who eventually submitted their final recommendations to the APA board of directors and then for a consensus vote of the membership at their annual convention.

Here I point to an interesting development that occurred within the substance use disorders committee. This group wanted to include a diagnosis called "familial alcoholism," which they believed has a genetic base. This committee had initially relied upon animal studies, concordance rates of identical twins with and without a history of alcoholism in their family, and adoption studies, primarily from Scandinavia. Their initial diagnostic criteria was to include (a) early age of onset; (b) a severe form of the disorder sufficient to require hospitalization; (c) a family history positive for alcoholism, and (d) absence of major psychiatric syndromes other than depression (in women) and anti-social disorder (in men). However, when reviewing the latest research, they concluded that other factors (family environment, psychological trauma, poverty, poor parenting, other psychological disorders) could not be clearly be ruled out as possibly related to the development of alcoholism. Hence, they decided to refrain from including this as a diagnosis, even though the working subgroup continues to believe this to be a real diagnosis.

Several concerns have been raised concerning each publication of DSM revisions. For psychologists, there was a concern that, while officially the developers of DSM-IV took an atheoretical approach to psychiatric diagnosis, there were subtle inclusions within various diagnoses that suggested otherwise. For example, if schizophrenic-like symptoms appear, but have not been extant for at least 6 months, then the diagnosis is schizophreniform disorder. This assumes a kind of biological destiny which some object to. Similarly, they have included schizotypal personality disorder within the spectrum of personality disorders as a kind of biological substrate for the subsequent development of schizophrenia.

There was an earlier attempt to include premenstrual disorder, under the rubric of "late-luteal phase dysphoria." Of course only a physician would be able to diagnose the phase of the menstrual cycle. Women's advocacy groups also objected to the implication that they would be deemed normal for 3 weeks out of every month, but would have a psychiatric disorder 1 week out of every month. These groups also objected to the possible inclusion of a sadistic and a masochistic personality disorder. They argued that women in abusive relationships might be diagnosed with a masochistic personality disorder, whereas other explanatory models might also explain why they remain in these situations (i.e., the psychology of victimization, women socialized into care-taking roles, lack of independent economic viability, etc.). They also feared that rapists might receive attenuated prison sentences because they would be diagnosed with a sadistic personality disorder.

There were other complaints about the DSM, but the important point here is to recognize that the DSM is both a scientific and a sociopolitical document.

ETIOLOGIC INTERVIEWS

Despite one's theoretical orientation, all clinicians want to understand why the patient is behaving the way s/he is behaving. This requires some formulation as to motivation. This motivation may be unconscious, such as in psychodynamic or family theory formulations, or it may be semiconscious as in client-centered, or simply a matter of failing to consider the various environmental influences and conditionings, as explicated by the behaviorists. At the end of the first interview, the clinician should have a working hypothesis as to the cause of the problematic behavior. This will lead toward goals of treatment.

FORENSIC INTERVIEWS

Forensic interviews address such issues as competency to stand trial, the question of legal insanity, psychological damage following industrial accidents, assessment of sexual predators, and child custody evaluations. Many times the interviewee is referred to as a defendant rather than client or patient.

A forensic interview differs in a number of ways from a traditional clinical interview. First, contrary to clinical interviews, forensic interviews are not confidential. In fact, the clinician must inform the defendant that any and all material uncovered in this process can and will be reported to the court. Second, while clinical interviews take a supportive, accepting, and empathic stance toward the patient, the forensic interview adopts a more investigative and probative role in seeking the truth. Third, the goal of the clinician interviewer is to help the client,

whereas the goal of the forensic interviewer is to help the court. Fourth, while a psychotherapist will see the client over multiple sessions, the forensic clinician may see the client only once or twice. Fifth, the forensic clinician spends more time examining records and historical material, compared to the usual clinical work. Finally, the referred patient may not be the "patient" to the forensic clinician. Rather, the court or the referring attorney may be the actual client here (Craig, 2005a).

FOLLOW-UP INTERVIEWS

These are generally special-focus evaluations to determine the status or outcome of previously delivered services. The most frequent example of this kind on interview is a researcher who contacts a patient 1 year after termination of treatment to determine the effectiveness of an intervention. I once had a contract with an HMO to screen the patient, determine the diagnosis and the kind of treatment required, and authorize the number of sessions to resolve the problem. The contract required me to interview the patient at the midpoint of treatment and at the end of treatment to determine outcome and patient satisfaction with the services.

INTAKE INTERVIEWS

Intake interviews generally occur within agencies that need to determine if the client is eligible for services or whether a referral to more specialized treatment is warranted. They are also used to communicate agency policies and procedures, or to gain enough clinical material to present the case at a clinical case conference, where treatment goals and perhaps therapist assignment occurs.

MENTAL STATUS EXAMS

Mental status exams may be conducted to determine the amount of mental impairment and cognitive deficit associated with the given clinical disorder. These exams are routinely conducted for major psychiatric disorders and substance-induced disorders or when neurological complications are suspected for a given disorder. Several mental status exams have been published (e.g., Folstein, Folstein, & McHugh, 2005), but most only provide content areas that should be addressed during these exams and provide only qualitative rather than quantitative findings. Furthermore, these standard-type measures are more typically used in neurological rather than in psychiatric settings.

Mental status exams may be conducted using standardized instruments or, more generally, they are given while discussing other content areas. For example, when you ask a patient to "tell me a time when you feel less than adequate," you will be able to follow the patient's train of thought, directed associations, organization of thoughts, and so on. Similarly, traditional content areas of a mental status exam may be ascertained trough traditional questions of relevant content areas of a routine clinical interview. Table 12.4 highlights the content areas that may be addressed in mental status exams along with subcategories associated with these major content areas.

Generally we start with a patient's basic appearance, which is the most obvious to us. For example, I once conducted a disability evaluation for a male who was using a woman's first name. When I went to greet him in the reception room, I saw that he was gaudily made up with powder, rouge, and lipstick, but had male stubble on his cheeks and chin, was

Table 12.4. Common content areas in a mental status exam.

Appearance		
	Level of consciousness	Eye contact
	Grooming	Hygiene
	Position of body	Physical appearance
	Dress/clothing	Gait
	Distant	Sensory impairments
Attention	Distractibility	
Attitude	Cooperative	Uncooperative
	Guarded	Defensive
	Candid	Subdued
	Indifferent/lethargic	Seductive
Insight	Intact comprehension	Impaired
Language	Audible	Clear
	Appropriate	Expressive/receptive
Memory	Immediate	Remote
	Short term	Long term
	Recent	Dissociative
	Amnestic	Confabulation
Mood (affect)	Euphoric	Dysphoric
	Anxious	Flat
	Apathetic	Appropriate
	Hostile	Manic
	Alexithymic	Euthymic
	Bland	Restricted
	Labile	Blunted
	Exaggerated	Irritable
Movements	Tics	Spasms
	Compulsions	Automatic; spontaneous
	Voluntary	Involuntary
Perception	Hallucinations	Delusions
	Depersonalization	Derealization
	Superstitions	Deja vu
Orientation	Time	Place
	Person	Space
Speech	Articulation	Aphasic
	Stream of consciousness	Stuttering
	Volume	Rate
	Loquacious	Fluency
	Poverty (minimal speech)	Mute
	Pressured	Slow
	Impoverished	
Thought content	Blocked	Overinclusive thinking
	Clanging	Perseverations

continued

Table 12.4. (*continued*).

	Violent thoughts	Neologisms
	Phobias	Compulsions
	Ruminations	Preoccupations
	Suicidal ideation	Homicidal ideations
	Delusions	Grandiose
	Magical thinking	Nihilistic
	Paranoid	Thought broadcasting
	Thought insertions	Obsessions
Thought processes		
Associations	Goal-directed	Loose
	Concrete	Logical
	Neologisms	Clang associations
	Rambling	Word salad
	Circumstantial	Detailed
	Flight of ideas	Blocking
	Preservations	Tangential
Intellectual	Abstract thinking	Concrete thinking
Judgment	Intact	Impaired

This is an expanded version from a chapter by this author entitled "Assessing Personality and Psychopathology with Interviews" originally appearing in J. R. Graham & J. A. Neglieri (Eds.). "Assessment Psychology" published by Wiley & Sons, 2003, and is used with permission.

dressed in women's clothing that lacked coordination, and stumbled awkwardly in high heels as he entered my office. Upon speaking, he had a normal male bass tone. These observations suggested that, if he was a transsexual or transgendered, this was very early in his new open identity, because he had not yet learned how to dress or walk as a woman, nor had he learned how to apply makeup. If he was on hormones, they had not yet taken effect as he retained the secondary male characteristics.

Next, we address content areas most appropriate to the circumstances of the evaluation. While in standard and formal mental status exams we may be required to assess every area, in routine clinical evaluations we assess only those areas that are relevant to the clinical disorder. For example, if the patient is in a manic state, then we would observe their stream of speech, rambling and grandiose associations, rapidity of verbiage, difficulty in maintaining control of their speech, and perhaps difficulty in remaining still. On the other hand, if the patient is in a clinical depression, we would observe their poverty of speech, depressive mood, affect and thought content, possible suicidal ideation, general lethargy, and slow thought processes.

Thus we see that we can ascertain a significant amount of information concerning a patient's mental status merely by observing and questioning them in key areas.

MOTIVATIONAL INTERVIEWS

A special type of interview, termed "motivational interviewing," has been developed by Miller and Rollnick (2002), as a means of helping patients change their behavior. Consistent with modern theories of behavior change (Prochaska, DiClemente, & Norcross, 1992), originally developed to understand smoking behavior (Prochaska & DiClemente, 1983), but which have now been applied to a myriad of health behaviors (Prochaska et al., 1994), Miller initially applied his interviewing model to alcoholics. He argued that the therapist style is a main determiner of treatment success. Clients come to treatment at various degrees of readiness to change and it is the clinician's responsibility to influence the client's decision to change. Miller identified the main ingredients to the motivational interview using the acronym FRAMES. This consisted of giving the client feedback, placing the responsibility of change on the client, giving advice when needed, providing the client with a menu of choices as to interventions, demonstrating accurate empathy, and promoting self-efficacy. Motivational interviewing also requires the clinician to avoid argumentation, roll with rather than confront resistance, and remove barriers to getting help. Motivational interviewing techniques have now been applied to many other problematic behaviors in addition to alcoholism.

ORIENTATION INTERVIEWS

Here the clinician orients the client to some treatment protocol, or research standard or requirements. A clinician in private practice may use this time to discuss administrative policies, such as fees, cancellation procedures, insurance claims, and billing, or perhaps what to expect from treatment. This is a good time to clarify any misunderstandings the patient may have about the entire process of counseling. Some clinicians prefer to have the client sign a document that highlights or elaborates all major administrative issues while others prefer a verbal understanding.

PRE- AND POST-TESTING INTERVIEWS

These types of interviews are most often given during the testing process, where the clinician interviews the patient, conducts a more thorough psychological evaluation, and then discusses the results with the patient. A psychiatrist may conduct this type of interview before and after medication induction or before and after shock therapy.

SCREENING INTERVIEWS

Screening interviews are designed to elicit information on a specific topic, such as dangerousness to self or others. In this context they may also serve as a crisis interview. They may also be conducted to determine if a patient meets the specific requirements for a given medication, if the patient is eligible for services at an agency, or if they can be discharged.

SPECIALIZED INTERVIEWS

Sometimes a special interview is needed for a specific purpose. The question of competency and ability to stand trial is a good example of this kind of interview. Another example is interviewing a patient to see if s/he can be taken off suicide precautions. A plethora of specialized diagnostic interviews for various psychiatric conditions have been published for this purpose and books on clinical interviewing now routinely include examples of these kinds of interviews for special populations and for specialized types of assessments (Craig, 2005b; Hersen & Thomas, 2007b).

TERMINATION INTERVIEWS

Clinicians will often use a termination interview to discuss client progress and review treatment goals and future plans. Clinicians in psychiatric hospitals use these kinds of interviews to review aftercare plans with the patient.

Expectations of the Clinical Interviewer

Clinicians expect to develop a working alliance with a client. In this alliance with patient, the interviewer will explore their problematic behavior and their relationships and the clinician will impute some psychological meaning to these matters as well as act in ways to redress the problem. How they engage in this process will differ, depending on their theoretical orientation, but all will act in ways consistent with their beliefs about behavior change.

Expectations of the Client

Clients do not come to the interview with a blank slate, and many factors will influence how a patient behaves within a session. The first matter of importance is whether or not the patient came there voluntarily. Many patients come to treatment involuntarily. Examples of this would be adolescents brought to counseling by a parent, or a defendant sent to counseling by the court. Even apparent voluntary clients may actually not want counseling. Examples of this would be a drug addict who enters a detoxification program, but in actuality is hiding from the police, or a husband who comes for therapy with his wife who has threatened to leave him. In general, treatment outcome will be better when the patient is self-referred and motivated to change, though there are exceptions.

Second, a patient may have hidden agendas for coming to a session, and this may never be revealed. Lawyers in civil litigation frequently suggest to their clients that they go for counseling in order to establish psychological damage, which would then be helpful at trial. In such circumstances, it is unlikely that the client will reveal their true motivation for counseling.

Third, clients have some idea as to how they will be helped. If the clinician acts in ways contrary to these expectations, the patient may not return to the next session. It is good practice to ask clients what they think will happen in counseling and what they expect to get out of it.

Fourth, clients develop perceptions of the clinician. Social psychologists have recorded the often long-lasting effects of first impressions. Analytic clinicians have discussed the effects of object relations and subsequent transferences. Adolescents often will view the clinician as yet another authority figure. These processes can influence the ongoing client–clinician relationship that is often outside the awareness of the client.

Interviewing Techniques

Most clinicians rely on a set of interviewing techniques, irrespective of their theoretical orientation. Some orientations (i.e., Rogerian/nondirective) may only utilize a few of these techniques (i.e., reflection, silence), while others (i.e., psychodynamic) may place emphasis on a particular technique (i.e., interpretation). Still, the eclectic clinician will tend to use most if not all of the techniques listed below.

QUESTIONING

We begin this section with the use of questioning, which is the heart of most clinical interviews—especially the initial clinical interview, and which is generally replete with the use of questioning as a predominant interviewing tool. In general, questioning is the fastest way to generate information and so this technique is frequently employed in most clinical interviews.

There are two basic kinds of questions: open and closed. The latter often begins with words, such as who, where, when, and why. These are direct questions that elicit a closed response, especially when they are framed to elicit a "yes" or "no" response. The client will then wait for the interviewer to ask the next question. Excessive use of this method is regressive and stifles true communication. They should be used sparingly. An example of a direct or closed question is "How many times have you been fired from a job?"

An open-ended question allows for a fuller range of client response and elaboration, and facilitates the interviewing process. Open-ended questions do not evoke a "yes" or "no" response nor a specific reply. An example of an open-ended question is "How do you feel the next morning after you wake up with yet another hangover?"

Students learning how to interview tend to over-rely on the method of direct questioning and generally have trouble framing their questions so that they elicit an open-ended response. It actually requires clinical acumen to frame a question so that it elicits a maximum return while promoting the free-floating communication required for a good interview. To demonstrate the awkwardness of an overreliance in direct questions, role-play a clinical interview and ask only direct questions for 5 min. At the end of this time, ask your partner how s/he felt when being asked these questions in this way. Reverse roles now: the counselor becomes the client and is required to answer only closed-ended questions from the examiner. At the end of this time, process how you felt while being asked questions in this format.

Both open- and closed-ended questions will be necessary to conduct a competent clinical interview. Try to avoid too many closed-ended questions because they inhibit the flow of the session.

ACCURATE EMPATHY

Empathy is defined as the ability of the clinician to understand the client from the perspective of the client. Most people want to be understood, and demonstrating accurate empathy (along with active listening) communicates to clients that you understand them. Accurate empathy is not feeling what the client is feeling. Rather it is understanding what the client is feeling. Sometimes this is not really expressed directly, but can be palpably felt within the session.

Example:

> *Client*: You know, doc, I want to stop using drugs and actually stopped for three weeks. Then I went into this bar and picked up a girl and we got a room at a hotel and she pulled some cocaine out of her purse and so I used because I didn't want her to think I wasn't a man. Afterwards I felt awful and thought to myself, "How could I do that?" You know the same thing happened when my mom found drugs in my room. She yelled at me and I just sat there and took it.
>
> *Therapist*: You know the common thread to both of these situations is your guilt over your drug-using behavior. When you're in a situation where you might be criticized, you begin to feel less than a man.
>
> *Client*: You know, I think you're right.

Along with active listening, expressing accurate empathy are techniques that should be used throughout the clinical interview. A long history of psychological research has demonstrated that these techniques (along with unconditional positive regard and acceptance) are related to positive outcomes in mental health. They actually are more of an attitude than a technique.

ACTIVE LISTENING

Active listening is defined as the ability of the clinician to accurately state the content, feeling, and/or meaning of what the patient has just communicated to you. It actually is one of the most important tools in the clinician's armamentarium. It requires you to "listen" to what the client says, "restate" their words using "reflective" statements, and then "observe" the patient's response to your reflection. The client's reaction to your intervention will tell you whether or not you have accurately understood the client.

In order to promote active listening, you must position yourself vis-à-vis the patient so you can directly observe verbal and nonverbal communication, and reduce potential distractions such as interruptions (phone calls, etc.), because these may convey to clients that you really don't care about them or that you don't have time for them. Even with your full attention, you may not able to communicate that you are actively listening to the client because this technique takes time to learn until it becomes automatic.

In order to practice this technique, role-play a clinical interview with a partner and issue only active listening responses to the client. Have the "client" advise you whether you have accurately captured the meaning of the statement in your response. If not, have the "client" restate his true meaning. The following is an example of an active listening response (using the technique of reflection, discussed later).

Client: I'm here to talk about my early problems with my father and how he physically abused me when I was younger. Now I know that sooner or later you're going to find out that I'm an alcoholic, but I'm not here to talk about my drinking nor do I plan to stop drinking. I'm here to work on my relationship with my father, OK?

Therapist: You feel you only want to address your history of physical abuse and are not ready to address your problematic drinking.

ADVICE

Sometimes it is necessary for a clinician to give advice to a client. The difficulty with this technique is the client may begin to rely on the clinician to make recommendations for subsequent behaviors and problems and the advice given may prove to be unhelpful. The client may then blame the clinician and it may inhibit them from making their own decisions. Still there are times when giving advice is warranted.

Example:

Client: I couldn't believe what I did just prior to making a suicide attempt. I went down to main street and started giving passers-by all my money. I made some appointments to give away my CDs, DVDs, TV, even my furniture. It was Christmas time and I thought I was in the holiday spirit.

Clinician: You weren't in the holiday spirit. You were experiencing clinical depression. If you begin to feel that way again, it is important for you to get professional help. What you did is often a sign of someone who is planning to kill themselves.

CLARIFICATION

Sometimes the client's statements are confusing or even contradictory. At those times, the clinician needs to elicit more elaboration through the use of questions that result in clarification. Asking clarifying questions will rarely produce defensiveness because most clients want to be understood (from their perspective) and hence this gives them the opportunity to provide additional details so that they are understood. An example of clarification is noted below.

Client: Sometimes my husband calls and says he'll be late coming home. Sometimes he doesn't come home at all. Sometimes he doesn't call and doesn't come home. When I confront him about it, he gets mad and says he has to work.

Therapist: What do you suspect he's doing during these times?

CONFRONTATION

In using confrontation, the psychologist points out the discrepancy between what the client states and what the clinician observes. Inconsistencies between attitudes and behaviors may also require the use of confrontation. Addiction and substance abuse counselors often use confrontation to try and break through the denial that is so often observed in these patients. Patients with character disorders, such as rapists, child abusers, and kleptomaniacs, are also confronted about their behavior by well-meaning clinicians, who find it easier to confront these behaviors rather than to try and understand them. However, Miller and Rollnick (2002) have demonstrated that the use of confrontation, even within a substance-abusing clientele, is counterproductive, breeds defensiveness, results in argumentation and in psychological reactance, thereby instilling in the client the psychological state that the counselor was trying to negate. They further argued that there is no real evidence that the use of confrontation leads to an effective or desirable outcome.

Confrontation has, in some circles, become a pejorative term, since it had become the predominating technique in therapeutic communities, which are long-term residential treatment programs for drug addicts, staffed by recovering addicts. Too often it is done in a hostile and in an anxiety-producing manner that seems to disrespect a patient's humanity and creates psychological reactance. It need not be so. When done in a thoughtful, considerate and empathic manner, it can have a positive effect. Still, students in counseling should not use this without first discussing it with their clinical supervisor. Even seasoned counselors should only use confrontation sparingly, if at all.

Example:

Client: I think my problem drinking is behind me.
Therapist: Your wife told me you came home drunk last night!

EDUCATION

It has been said that education is the answer when ignorance is the problem. Sometimes it is necessary to educate a client as part of the interview process. Psycho-immunology is a term used to describe efforts by a psychologist to educate a patient in order to prevent problematic behaviors. Education is a technique frequently used by substance abuse counselors to help clients learn about their alcoholism. It deserves a place in our interviewing technique repertoire.

Example:

Client: After I'm discharged from this program, I plan to go back to my musical career. However, I assure you I'm through using drugs. Besides I have learned that using drugs the way I did puts me at risk for getting AIDS and believe me I don't want to get that.
Therapist: That's good news! However, you also have a history of picking up women and the women you picked up were having sex with guys who were also using drugs so you could get AIDS from them too.

EXPLORATION

Rarely does a patient provide information in sufficient detail such that no further questions are warranted. Furthermore, some areas require a more in-depth inquiry than others so that most clinicians will be required to engage in additional questioning in order to get a fuller picture of the issue at hand. Most clients expect to be questioned and generally do not resent a clinician's further inquiry. They may even wonder (to themselves) why certain areas were not addressed further. The mental health interviewer should not be reluctant to explore areas that many consider sensitive.

Example:

Client: When I was in Vietnam, my unit was overrun by the Viet Cong, so I had to lay there and pretend to be dead.
Therapist (sample exploration questions): How long did you lie there? What about your bodily functions? How were you rescued? And so on.

HUMOR

Originally, clinical interviewing was viewed as a distinctly professional interaction between client and clinician and one where humor played no role in the process. Freud believed that humor was the highest defense mechanism, but thought that the use of humor by the psychoanalyst was evidence of countertransference. We are now beginning to realize the value of humor in mental health interventions. In fact, there are conferences devoted exclusively to the role of humor in psychotherapy.

As with any technique, it should be used in moderation and only to benefit the client. Such benefits may include the reduction of anxiety in the patient, facilitating the clinical interviewing process and enhancing the flow of the interview. However, there is the danger that the client may not take you seriously so one has to be careful and judicious when injecting humor into the session.

Example:

Client: Sometimes, Doc, I do so many strange things that I don't even recognize myself. Maybe I have a split personality.
Clinician: In that case, the fee will be $100 each.

INTERPRETATION

One area that separates psychologists and psychiatrists from many other mental health professions is the use of interpretation—particularly psychodynamic interpretation. Freud considered interpretation of the unconscious as the *sine qua non* of psychoanalysis, but felt that the analyst had to wait until transference became obvious before the analyst should begin to use this technique. Freud believed that human motivation was largely outside the conscious awareness of the analysand and that one of the goals of therapy was to make the unconscious conscious.

Interpretation is essentially exploring a client's motivating factors in their life so that they are understood and altered when necessary. Interpretation tries to link two or more streams of consciousness (i.e., free association), events, or behaviors so that this linkage reveals a common source. Interpreting a client's behavior and motivation should always be done carefully. It is a difficult technique to master and requires comprehensive knowledge of a patient's history, motivation, and dynamics. It requires expertise in personality theory and should rarely be done by clinicians in training unless they first discuss this with their clinical supervisor.

Furthermore, interpretations may be inaccurate but, because of the professional standing and authority of the clinician, the client may come to accept them as true when they are not. Also, patients with a dependent personality disorder are likely to submit to clinician-generated pronouncements since, unconsciously, they do not want to upset an authority figure because they rely on it for support. They may agree with the interpretation merely to avoid conflict. Patients with an aggressive personality disorder or an antisocial personality disorder may disagree with an interpretation because they tend to be oppositional with authority figures, though the interpretation may be accurate.

Despite these dangers, most therapeutic orientations, except for nondirective, client-centered therapies, will use this technique at some point in the sessions. Whether the use of interpretation should be reserved for later therapeutic sessions or whether it can be appropriately used within the initial clinical interview is a judgment that needs to be made by the clinician.

Example:

Client: I get myself in so many fights with teachers, cops, bosses, and supervisors just because they think they know everything. It just makes me so angry, and then I go off. I can't help it.

Counselor: These people are substitute authority figures for you. Unconsciously, they remind you of your father and you are really angry at your father for abandoning you as a child. But your father isn't around for you to express your angry feelings so you take it out on those that are here.

REFLECTION

In this technique, the clinician restates what the client has just said, capturing its essence and feelings. The psychologist skillfully includes the cognitive and emotional material, thereby demonstrating that the client's statements have been accurately understood. Clinicians from a nondirective, client-centered theoretical orientation use reflection almost exclusively, for they believe that this is the heart of behavior change. They have produced seminal research showing that reflection is often associated with therapeutic change. This technique also requires training before it can be fully mastered. Occasional use of reflection can be accomplished easily, but unless you have the proper training, exclusive reliance on this technique will be counterproductive. Although Rogerian counselors would probably disagree, the overuse of reflection in the initial interview results in important material omitted from discussion. For example, a patient with a bipolar disorder will probably focus on his symptoms and relations, but may be unlikely to talk about possible problem drinking, which can be part of the symptom cluster for many patients with this disorder. A treatment plan may therefore fail because alcohol abuse was not included in the planned interventions.

Example:

Client: I try so hard to get ahead but I don't seem to be getting anywhere.

Clinician: Your lack of progress frustrates you.

REFRAMING

Sometimes this technique is termed "paraphrasing" or "cognitive restructuring." In this technique, the clinician simply rephrases client statements, attitudes, beliefs, opinions, or feelings so the client more accurately understands them. It may be done using reflection, but differs from reflection in purpose and design. Reframing is often used to facilitate understanding, whereas reflection is often used as a therapeutic intervention. Using reframing can help a client reduce negative self-statements, can provide a different perspective or a new way of thinking, and may enable the client to stop irrational and maladaptive thoughts.

Example:

Client: My wife had a tubal ligation after our son was born because she didn't want any more kids. However the boy was born with a deformity and died within a few hours of my wife's ligation. Now she believes that God has punished her because she was planning to practice birth control which is against our religion. She's really depressed and now under psychiatric care.

Clinician: But I believe your religion also teaches you that God is merciful and forgiving.

SELF-DISCLOSURE

By self-disclosure we mean the clinician conveys personal information about himself/herself to the client. The psychoanalytic tradition held that the analyst was to behave as a blank slate, never revealing any aspect of the analyst to allow the phenomenon of transference to develop naturally. This led clinicians to believe that discussing personal information to a client was unprofessional, stemming from countertransference. However, early research found that use of self-disclosure by therapists actually facilitates self-disclosure in patients (Cozby, 1973). Today we realize that telling the patient personal information about ourselves can be therapeutic, if used in a judicious manner.

Conveying personal information can be counterproductive, however, and should always be done to facilitate the therapeutic process. Clinicians should ask themselves, "Why am I telling this patient this information?" Usually it is done to reduce an emotional blockage in a client, to promote elaboration, or to reduce resistance. Substance abuse counselors with a personal history of addiction who are now in recovery often tell alcoholics that they, too, are in recovery. For many such patients, it seems to promote understanding between these two parties.

Example:

> *Client*: How would you know what I'm going through?
> *Clinician*: Because I'm an alcoholic and have been in recovery for over 15 years now.

SILENCE

Sometimes the best response is no response. Carl Rogers (1951), in fact, argued that silence can and does have many beneficial effects and discussed a case wherein he had said nothing during the entire sessions. The next session the client came in and thanked Rogers for how much he had helped him in the previous session. Rogers began to reflect on what had occurred during this process and came to the conclusion that silence allows the client to process his thoughts and feelings in a safe, nonjudgmental environment.

Silence allows clients to recompose themselves after an emotional expression, and helps promote introspection. It can help clients consolidate and integrate session material and move the therapeutic process. Again, it must be done in a timely and appropriate manner. The important point here is that clinicians do not always have to say something in response to a client's statements. Sometimes a clinician's too rapid response can actually interfere with the clinical interview.

Counselors in training often feel silence on the part of a client as a dreadful experience. They feel somewhat inadequate and tend to believe that interviews must always proceed with continuous verbiage. Silence may occur because of clinician inadequacy as an interviewer, but it may also occur as part of the clinician's intervention as a clinical tool.

Example:

> *Client*: This guy at work keeps harassing me. He never agrees with anything I say, he continuously interrupts me, says bad things about me behind my back and recently told people that he thinks I'm gay. I swear one of these days I'm going to meet him after work in the parking lot and make sure that he never has children, if you know what I mean.
> *Clinician*: (no response).

CLINICIAN ATTITUDES

These interviewing techniques are also used in conducting psychotherapy. A few other "attitudes" deserve mention, even though they are not specific interviewing techniques. I am referring to the qualities of acceptance, positive regard, and a nonjudgmental frame of reference.

Students have frequently discussed the difficulty they have in accepting a client's behavior, which often is heinous and incorrigible. The same students talk about the reprehensible behaviors they hear of in counseling sessions and feel quite judgmental about them. They report difficulty in having any feelings of positive regard for such clients.

Carl Rogers and his students have argued that acceptance, unconditional positive regard, and empathy are the necessary and sufficient conditions of behavior change and have produced a prodigious amount of research to back up their claims. The essential thing to remember is that we are accepting the person and not the person's behavior.

SUMMARIZING

Briefly summarizing what a client has conveyed to you in the interview may be a useful tool because it can convey to the client that you understand the problem or issue at hand and allows the client to correct any clinician misunderstandings.

Example:

> *Clinician*: OK. So the main issue as I understand it is that you feel stuck in an abusive relationship. You feel guilty for thinking about leaving him because your religion teaches you to stay in a marriage and try to work things out, and you don't have the economic means to live independently. One solution you have thought about is suicide but, again, your religion teaches you that this is a serious sin and you are afraid to see a psychiatrist for medication because this will upset your husband, who might beat you again for spending money unnecessarily.

A Practice Exercise

Using the example below, practice each interviewing technique listed above. Record your answers and discuss them with other students who should do the same.

Client: Doc, I'm afraid I have to tell you that I have started using heroin again and my depression has returned. I think I started using heroin because I wanted to block out all that has happened in my life and all that is going on now. But, you know, Doc, it really doesn't help because even when I'm under the influence, I still think of all the things that have happened to me and that are happening to me and that might happen to me.

I went for an HIV test, and I'm afraid of finding out what those results show. If the results were serious, they would have called me by now and I think they might have called me because someone called and asked for me by name, but I told them he wasn't home. They left no message. I don't want to know the results. And I think that if I tested negative then they would have just told me that over the phone. So now I'm really scared.

Table 12.5 summarizes these interviewing techniques.

Clinical Interview Report

Often the last step in the interviewing process is to prepare a professional report. This report may be sent to the referring agent, be made part of the clinical file and used in the clinical case conference review for purposes of treatment planning, or remain in the records of clinicians in private practice. A sample report based on a clinical interview appears at the end of the chapter.

Computer-Administered Interviews

Computers continue to make an impact in mental health, including initial assessments, delivery of services, electronic recording of interventions, progress and outcomes, delivering research items and program evaluation activities, such as patient satisfaction with mental health services. Much of the early research on the use of computer-assisted questionnaires in mental health concentrated on its feasibility, reliability, and concordance with similar measures delivered in a more conventional manner. This kind of research continues up to the present, thought there is a slight shift toward the need to incorporate this kind of methodology in routine clinical practice.

There are a number of advantages in using computer-assisted technology. Computers can easily record basic client information, such as demographics and reported symptoms that can be made available when the psychologist initially screens the patient. Interviews administered via computers tend to be more comprehensive and more reliable than are interviews conducted by clinicians (Garb, 2007). Administering structured clinical interviews can be time consuming. This factor is essentially eliminated when the items are computer administered. Incidental advantages are also extant with computer-administered questionnaires. For example, the results from these evaluations can be entered directly into an electronic database. This reduces the clerical tasks of the clinician.

Clinical interviews are replete with interpersonal processes between examiner/clinician and patient that are absent when that same question is asked via computer. For example, if the interviewer asks "Was you father a good man?", the client may wonder what the clinician may think should be the answer be "no." This is not of the same immediate concern when that same question is asked via computer.

While there had been concerns that patients would consider computer-administered measures as impersonal, this fear proved to be unfounded. Research has demonstrated that clients actually disclose more sensitive information to a computer than they will when a clinician asks that same question (Turner et al., 1998). Patients also prefer computer-assisted "interviews" (Sweeny, McGrath, Leigh, & Costa, 2001; Wijndaele et al., 2007). Computer-assisted interviews are also useful for patients residing in rural areas or in areas where access is difficult (Kelly, Kay-Lambkin, & Kavanagh, 2007).

There appears to be few disadvantages to using computer-administered clinical interviewing measures. One major disadvantage is that the psychologist cannot see the body language of the patient as s/he responds to a given question. This can be a significant aspect to a clinician-administered evaluation.

One concern is that the diagnostic concordance between clinician and computer-generated diagnoses via structured interview is generally low (Komiti et al., 2001), though some studies show moderate concordance in the areas of general health, symptom expression, perceived stress, and coping skills (Wijndaele et al., 2007). This is probably because the computer-generated instrument systematically reviews the major diagnostic categories, whereas an individual psychologist tends to focus only on the major presenting symptoms that need immediate intervention. Also, computer-generated interview measures tend to generate more false-positive diagnoses compared to clinician-administered interviews (Garb, 2007). This means that computer-assisted interviews need to be

Table 12.5. Basic clinical interviewing techniques.

Techniques	Client statement	Clinician response
Questioning: Closed	I got arrested again for a DUI	How many DUI arrests do you have?
Open	I got arrested again for a DUI	What were the circumstances?
Active listening	For once I have been able to do something without the interference of my parents. It feels good to know that I can do it.	You can feel good to know that you can be independent.
Accurate empathy	Whenever I see these good looking women in their skimpy outfits I get so aroused I want to jump them then and there.	It's difficult for you to control your feelings and behavior when you get so aroused.
Advising	I was fired from my job because I failed a drug test. I used marijuana at a party and they let me go.	They can't do that. The law states they have to allow you to get help. Mention this to your boss or see an EEO counselor at work.
Clarification	I got arrested but it wasn't my fault. I was with some people and just got caught up in the action.	What were you doing and what were you charged with?
Confrontation	My wife over-reacts. I can handle my liquor	You go out every night and get drunk. You come home and argue with your wife. And you were recently arrested for a DUI. Help me understand how this shows you can handle liquor.
Education	The doctor said the medication I'm on will control my bipolar disease.	Yes it will but you also have stop drinking because people with your disease also tend to develop a problem with drinking.
Exploration	I came home and found my wife in bed with the post man.	How did that make you feel? What was your reaction? What did you say to her?
Humor	My shoulders having really been hurting me.	Maybe it's rust
Interpretation	It's so easy for me to pick up women. I take them home, screw them and then don't ask them out again. I don't know why. They want to keep seeing me.	Your wife "screwed" you in a sense when she left you. So now, to get back at her you screw other women and then leave them just like your wife did to you.
Reflection	I came home last night and my wife told me she was leaving me for my best Friend. I didn't know any-thing was wrong with our marriage.	You are both perplexed and upset to learn that your wife is leaving when things were going so well.
Reframing	My girl friend dumped me and gave me no reason. She said she just didn't want to go out with me any more.	While her leaving upsets you now, this will give you the chance to go out with other girls and perhaps find a better match.
Self disclosure	I just can't learn. No matter how hard I try I don't get good grades.	I had a problem with dyslexia, too, but it can be overcome with special education.
Silence	Some day I'm going to tell my boss "take this job and shove it"	(no response)
Summarizing	(Client has finished talking)	Your plans are to go to AA, avoid your high risk situations and relapse triggers, attend outpatient counseling and agree to random alcohol breath tests.

integrated with routine clinical activities rather than using them as a definitive source of diagnosis.

Furthermore, the availability of computer-administered interviews allows researchers to study the reliability and validity of diagnostic interviews without the clinicians ever seeing the patient. For example, researchers can preload answers to expected questions and ask participants to ask the computer diagnostic questions, after they have been given some basic information about the "patient." The researcher can then examine the nature and kinds of questions asked by the clinicians as well as ascertain their diagnostic accuracy. This was the paradigm used by Brammer (2002), who compared psychologists and psychology graduate students in a simulated clinical interview administered by computer. Brammer was interested in learning whether the level of experience was associated with improved diagnostic accuracy. It was. He found that psychologists asked the kinds of questions that were more relevant to a clinical diagnosis and tended to omit questions that were not needed to answer the basic diagnostic question.

It had been rather safely predicted that computers would continue to show great promise in diagnostic work (Craig, 2003). The subsequent years have proven this prediction to be accurate. Computer-generated symptom surveys and diagnostic interviews have proven valuable and beneficial in the areas of general mental health (Chipman et al., 2007), alcohol-related problems (Hester & Miller, 2006; Koski-Jannes, Cunningham, Tolonen, & Bothas, 2007), and sexuality (Morrison-Beedy, Carey, & Tu, 2006). We can expect to see more of this kind of research in the future.

The research to date indicates that computer-assisted diagnostic questionnaires and symptom measures are both feasible and practical. However, they have not been integrated into mainstream practice. The Department of Veterans Affairs (DVA) has mandated the use of the computer-generated version of the Addiction Severity Index (McLellan et al., 1992) for all newly admitted patients in its alcohol and drug abuse treatment programs. The DVA also requires that this measure be readministered every 6 months for as long as the patient remains in treatment. This could then be used as a measure of patient progress in treatment (Craig, & Olson, 2004). This is one of the few examples of the routine utilization of computer-assisted screening measures in mental health. No doubt the future will reflect greater utilization of this technology.

Sample Clinical Interview Report
Reason for Admission

The patient is a 41-year-old, separated, unemployed black male who was voluntarily admitted to an inpatient psychiatric treatment unit following a suicide attempt. He was placed on short-term antidepressant therapy (Imipramine) and then transferred to a 21-day inpatient drug rehab program within that same facility.

His drug history reflects alcohol use with onset in the early high-school years, marijuana use beginning in his senior year of high school, with use of both drugs continuing practically up to the present time. He tried injectable Darvon with some "acid" while in service but discontinued these drugs because he did not like the way they made him feel and also because he does not like to use needles. The patient reported continued use of alcohol and marijuana for the past 20 years, claiming no adverse consequences of their use. He began to free-base cocaine about 1½ years ago and experienced incipient psychosocial deterioration, resulting in two inpatient treatment episodes for alcohol abuse and one treatment for drug abuse prior to the most recent admission. He has a history of noncompliance with aftercare plans.

The stressors surrounding the most recent suicide attempt leading up to the present admission were financial and housing problems, causing the patient to become homeless and living in abandoned buildings for the past month, cognitions telling himself that he was a failure, drug and alcohol abuse that lowered his inhibitions and reduced his judgment, and a personality prone toward depression when he experiences frustration and/or object loss.

More specifically, he had lost his leatherwork business due to a flood, had some problems with the landlord of a one-room apartment where he lived, had to work day labor to survive and became angry at the amount of money taken out for taxes, and owed his sister some money but was unable to pay her. He had recently been discharged from a substance abuse program as well. While in this frame of mind, he was riding on a bus when he spotted a female walking along the sidewalk, who looked like a cocaine user to him. Although he did not know her, he jumped off the bus, asked her if she used drugs, and then paid her $50 to buy cocaine. She took him to her apartment, but only bought $10 worth of drugs. She later brought her boyfriend back to the apartment where the patient decided to leave rather than provoke an argument. He journeyed to a dope house, where he paid more money for cocaine, but, while in the bathroom, other addicts there used up much of what he had bought. He left there and drank alcohol to help him come down from the cocaine. He was riding on a bus when he passed a lagoon. Feeling depressed and a failure, he took off his jacket and swam out to the middle of the lagoon with the intention of drowning. However, he became quite cold and returned to shore, putting on his jacket and then went to his mother's house, where he told her he had just tried to kill himself. She convinced him to apply for public aid and gave him some clothes. He was still depressed, withdrawn, and felt that life was hopeless. He found the odor and the people in the abandoned buildings to be offensive. In the interim he had gotten high, he went to his mother's house, stole her watch and threatened her—something he said he had never done before. He bought some rat poison and once again went to his mother, telling her that he was thinking of committing suicide. His mother, now fearful of him, threw him out of the house.

The patient reasoned that he would rather be dead or in jail than living this way so he approached a White policeman stating that he was a drug abuser, stole from his mother, and was considering suicide. He felt sure that a White cop would arrest him and put him in jail. However, the officer recognized the patient as a trumpet player from one of the local nightclubs and convinced the patient to seek hospitalization and drug treatment. He was taken to a neighborhood treatment program and then transferred here.

History

The patient's history shows dysfunctional parenting, a chaotic environment, and an absence of positive role models. His mother was an alcoholic and has only been in recovery for the past 4 years. He was born out of wedlock and his biological father was married to someone else and was not involved in his rearing. The patient's mother had a series of boyfriends, many of whom were also alcoholic and some of whom physically abused him. His uncle often came to the house, beat him once, but ridiculed him often. The patient also reports fearing for his life while in grammar school, often running home to avoid the gangs, and reports that, on one occasion, gang members tried to recruit him and chased him up the stairs trying to kill him when he refused to join them. He used music and athletics as social interests that helped him avoid the gangs.

He entered service following graduation from high school and spent most of the last two decades as a professional musician, traveling around the country, drinking, using marijuana, and womanizing. He shows a repeated pattern of moving in with a female and then escalating his alcohol use and/or sleeping with other women, thereby causing that woman to kick him out. He was married once, to a White female who he said was an opera singer. They have one child, but this union lasted only 2 years. He was caught in bed with another woman, leading to the separation. Divorce is pending. He admits to hitting his wife "once" and professes guilt over this behavior. He says he doesn't seem to be able to maintain a commitment to one female and never thought he would marry. He also reported one prior suicide attempt precipitated by a woman leaving him for another man. He withdrew into his room for 2 weeks, lost his appetite, and was anergic. He tried to overdose by taking a bottle of sleeping pills. His tolerance for depressant drugs, caused by repeated alcohol and marijuana use, probably saved his life.

He reports no medical problems nor any sexual dysfunction. Legal history reflects only minor charges for possession and for disorderly conduct. He has never been in jail.

Mental Status

A mental status exam revealed no signs of psychosis, no homicidal nor current suicidal ideation, but there did remain some mild depression or dysphoria with cognitive but not vegetative symptoms. He was oriented in time, place, and person, and his degree of reality contact was good. He was neatly dressed in color-coordinated clothes and hygiene seemed good. There were no signs of hallucinations or obvious delusions. He did evince some mild errors in judgment, believing that the music industry is controlled by the Jewish and Italian mafia who might kill you if you do not obey them. He related in a rather open manner. His speech was audible but somewhat circumlocutious in relating his story, though he tolerated interruptions and direct questioning without apparent resentment. He seemed desirous to please the examiner. History does show some impulsivity.

Case Formulation

This patient is an orally fixated personality with many unresolved dependency needs that have left him unable to successfully cope with stress, frustrations, and setbacks, and perhaps prone toward depression and substance abuse as well. His family history is positive for alcoholism, which further increases his risk in these areas as well. Mother, an alcoholic herself, probably did not meet his basic psychological needs in infancy, leaving the patient to feel rejected, unloved, and emotionally abandoned (unconscious). His pattern of moving in with women and then acting in ways to get rejected is seen as a repetition compulsion to master this original conflict. He is a dependent personality who is seeking nurturing relationships from females, yet he feels inadequate, inferior, and undeserving (as he unconsciously felt with his mother as an infant) and hence he acts in ways to get rejected (which is similar to mother's early response to him). His hedonistic lifestyle of alcohol, drugs, and sex can be seen as both reinforcing his pleasure drives but also as ways of coping with his unconscious depression. (His belief that he might get killed in the music world if he is not obedient demonstrates the pervasiveness of his dependency needs.)

Significant also may be his ultimate choice of drugs. He did not like "acid" or Darvon but got hooked onto cocaine, perhaps because, in addition to the drug's powerful CNS reinforcing effects on the brain, it also self-medicates the affect of depression, thereby showing a pharmacodynamic interaction between his choice of drugs and his underlying personality. His need for nurturing can be seen in his response to the two most recent suicide attempts (one an actual attempt and the other probably a suicidal gesture). On both occasions he went to his mother's house reporting that he had tried to commit suicide or was thinking of committing suicide. We can speculate that he was desperately trying once again to behave in ways that would force his mother to take care of him. However, the mother did not, which increased his depression. Perhaps his seeking jail or hospitalization can also be seen as looking for a nurturing object that would care for his basic needs.

The patient's early object loss has left him prone toward depression, suicide, and substance abuse. It is noteworthy that, in almost every incident reported by the patient, a frustrating event, often in relations to a female, resulted in either drug use or a suicide attempt.

Despite these dynamics, despite being raised in a dysfunctional family and an impoverished environment, the patient does show some ego resources. He is outwardly independent. He was able to resist gang involvement as a child. He has no significant legal history and is neither stealing nor selling drugs. He had to be convinced to apply for public aid and he has an entrepreneurial spirit, with talents in music and in leather crafts and design. He is not antisocial. He is able to form a working therapeutic alliance that suggests some possible effective use of psychotherapy as part of his rehabilitation plan.

Treatment Recommendations

The patient shows little ability to remain free from alcohol or drugs while in the community and a long-term therapeutic community is the treatment of choice at this time. Also, despite his reports of earlier Black militancy, he does show an unexplained affinity toward Caucasians. He chose a White policeman (thinking consciously he would get arrested) when seeking help, his best friend in service was white, his only marriage was to a White female, and he opened up to a White psychologist while in treatment for drug abuse and to a White psychiatrist while under psychiatric care. He did not open up to a Black male counselor while in drug rehab. It is suggested that a White therapist may achieve more rapid beneficial results in psychotherapy with this particular patient.

Long-term psychotherapy with this client, concurrent with drug abuse treatment in a therapeutic community, can be expected to be quite arduous. Initially he will be acquiescent, obliging, cooperative, and perhaps even docile and self-effacing. To seek the therapist's approval, he may provide the therapist with content he thinks the therapist wants to hear. The patient's unconscious behavior is also likely to elicit strong countertransference feelings in the therapist to begin to nurture and in other ways take care of the patient. However, the patient also has strong unconscious beliefs that he is undeserving of love. He also has much anger and resentment toward the very person who attempts to nurture him, and therefore can be expected to act in ways to get the therapist to reject or abandon him or be critical of him. Insight into this pattern will need to be established so that it can be worked through in a mature fashion.

Finally, this patient has been noncompliant with aftercare. The importance of continued support and attention, once he leaves residential treatment, must be accepted by him to help him prevent relapse. He also needs to develop coping skills to resist his high-risk situations and relapse triggers, which, for him, are the music world, where drugs are frequent, and his present need to pick up women who often use drugs themselves.

DSM-IV Dx

I. (304.20) Cocaine dependence, without physiological dependence

(305.00) Alcohol abuse

(296.33) Major depression, recurrent, without psychotic features, and with inter-episode recovery

II. (301.60) Dependent personality disorder

III. None, by patient self-report

IV. Problems related to the social environment: General psychosocial deterioration induced by free-basing cocaine

    V. 45

References

American Psychiatric Association (1980). *Diagnostic and statistical manual of mental disorders* (3rd ed.). Washington, DC: American Psychiatric Association.

American Psychiatric Association (1987). *Diagnostic and statistical manual of mental disorders* (3rd ed. –Rev.). Washington, DC: American Psychiatric Association.

American Psychiatric Association (1994). *Diagnostic and statistical manual of mental disorders* (4th ed.). Washington, DC: American Psychiatric Association.

Beach, D. A. (2005). The behavioral interview. In R. J. Craig (Ed.), *Clinical and diagnostic interviewing* (2nd ed., pp. 91–105). Lanham, MD: Jason Aronson.

Benjamin, A. (1981). *The helping interview* (3rd ed.). Boston: Houghton Mifflin.

Brammer, R. (2002). Effects of experience and training on diagnostic accuracy. *Psychological Assessment, 14*, 110–113.

Chipman, M., Hassell, J., Magnabosco, J., Nowlin-Finch, N., Marusak, S., & Young, A. S. (2007). The feasibility of computerized patient self-assessment at mental health clinics. *Administration and Policy in Mental Health Services Research, 34*, 401–409.

Cozby, P. C. (1973). Self-disclosure: A literature review. *Psychological Bulletin, 79*, 73–91.

Craig, R. J. (2003). Assessing personality and psychopathology with interviews. In J. Graham & J. Naglieri (Eds. *Handbook of psychology. Vol. 10: Assessment psychology* (pp. 487–508). New York: John Wiley & Sons.

Craig, R. J. (2005a) *Personality-guided forensic psychology.* Washington, DC: American Psychological Association.

Craig, R. J. (Ed.). (2005b). *Clinical and diagnostic interviewing* (2nd ed.). Lanham, MD: Jason Aronson.

Craig, R. J., & Olson, R. E. (2004). Predicting methadone maintenance treatment outcomes using the Addiction Severity Index and the MMPI-2 Content Scales (Negative Treatment Indicators and Cynicism Scales). *American Journal of Drug and Alcohol abuse, 30*, 823–839.

Ellis, A. (1962). *Reason and emotional in psychotherapy.* New York: Lyle Stuart.

Endicott, J., & Spitzer, R. L. (1978). A diagnostic interview: The schedule for affective disorders and schizophrenia. *Archives of General Psychiatry, 35*, 837–844.

Folstein, M. F., Folstein, S. E., & McHugh, P. R. (2005). *The mini-mental state examination.* Odessa, FL: Psychological Assessment Resources.

Garb, H. N. (2007). Computer-administered interviews and rating scales. *Psychological Assessment, 19*, 4–13.

Gruba-McCallister, F. (2005). Phenomenological orientation to the interview. In R. J. Craig (Ed.), *Clinical and diagnostic interviewing* (2nd ed., pp. 42–53). Lanham, MD: Jason Aronson.

Hersen, M., & Thomas, J. C. (2007a). *Handbook of clinical interviewing with children.* Thousand Oaks, CA: Sage Publications.

Hersen, M., & Thomas, J. C. (2007b). *Handbook of clinical interviewing with adults.* Thousand Oaks, CA: Sage Publications.

Hester, R. K., & Miller, J. H. (2006). Economic perspectives: Screening and intervention: Computer-tools for diagnosis and treatment of alcohol problems. *Alcohol Research and Health, 29*, 36–40.

Husserl, E. (1962). *Ideas* (W. R. Boyce Gibson, Trans.). New York: Collier.

Jamison, C., & Scogin, F. (1992). Development of an interview-based geriatric depression rating scale. *International Journal of Aging and Human Development, 35*, 193–204.

Kanfer, F. H., & Scheft, B. K. (1988). *Guiding the process of therapeutic change.* Champaign, IL: Research Press.

Kelly, B., Kay-Lambkin, F. J., & Kavanagh, D. J. (2007). Rurally isolated populations and co-existing mental health and drug and alcohol problems. In A. Baker & R. Velleman (Eds.), *Clinical handbook of co-existing mental health and drug and alcohol problems* (pp. 159–176). New York: Routledge/Taylor & Francis.

Komiti, A. A., Jackson, H. J., Judd, F. K., Cockram, A. M., Kyrios, M., & Yeatman, R. (2001). A comparison of the Composite International Diagnostic Interview (CIDI-Auto) with clinical assessment in diagnosing mood and anxiety disorders. *Australian and New Zealand Journal of Psychiatry, 35*, 224–230.

Koski-Jannes, A., Cunningham, J. A., Tolonen, K., & Bothas, H. (2007). Internet-based self-assessment of drinking: 3-month follow-up data. *Addictive Behaviors, 32*, 533–542.

Lazarus, A. (1976). *Multimodal behavior therapy.* New York: Springer.

Logan, N. (2005). Diagnostic assessment of children. In R. J. Craig (Ed.), *Clinical and diagnostic interviewing* (2nd ed., pp. 303–322). Lanham, MD: Jason Aronson.

Maddi, S. (2005). The existential/humanistic interview. In R. J. Craig (Ed.), *Clinical and diagnostic interviewing* (2nd ed., pp. 106–130). Lanham, MD: Jason Aronson.

Matarazzo, J. D. (1965). The interview. In B. Wolman (Ed.), *Handbook of clinical Psychology* (pp. 403–452). New York: McGraw-Hill.

Matarazzo, J. D. (1978). The interview: Its reliability and validity in psychiatric diagnosis. In B. Wolman (Ed.), *Clinical diagnosis of medical disorders* (pp. 47–96). New York: Plenum.

McLellan, A. T., Kushner, H., Metzger, D. S., Peters, R., Smith, I., Grissom, G., et al. (1992). The fifth edition of the Addiction Severity Index. *Journal of Substance Abuse Treatment, 9*, 199–213.

Miller, W. R., & Rollnick, S. (2002). *Motivational interviewing: Preparing people to change addictive behavior.* New York: Guilford Press.

Morrison-Beedy, D., Carey, M. P., & Tu, X. (2006). Accuracy of audio computer-assisted self-interviewing (ACASI) and self-administered questionnaires for the assessment of sexual behavior. *Aids and Behavior, 10*, 541–552.

Prochaska, J., & DiClemente, C. C. (1983). Stages and processes of self-change of smoking: toward an integrated model of change. *Journal of Consulting and Clinical Psychology, 51*, 390–395.

Prochaska, J. O., DiClemente, C. C., & Norcross, J. C. (1992). In search of how people change: Applications to the addictive behaviors. *American Psychologist, 47*, 1102–1114.

Prochaska, J. O., Velicer, W. F., Rossi, J. S., Goldstein, M. G., Marcus, B. H., Rakowski, W., et al. (1994). Stages of change and decisional balance for twelve problem behaviors. *Health Psychology, 13*, 39–46.

Robins, L. N., Helzer, J. E., Croughan, J., & Ratcliff, K. S. (1981). National Institute of Mental Health Diagnostic Interview Schedule. *Archives of General Psychiatry, 38*, 381–389.

Rogers, C. (1942). *Counseling and psychotherapy.* Cambridge: Houghton Mifflin.

Rogers, C. (1951). *Client-centered therapy: Its current practice, implications and theory.* Boston, MA: Houghton Mifflin.

Rogers, C. (1957). The necessary and sufficient conditions of therapeutic personal change. *Journal of Consulting Psychology, 21*, 95–103.

Rogers, R. (2001). *Handbook of diagnostic and structured interviews.* New York: Guilford Pub.

Rudolph, B. A. (2005). Teaching diagnostic and clinical interviewing. In R. J. Craig (Ed.), *Clinical and diagnostic interviewing* (2nd ed., pp. 3–20). Lanham, MD: Jason Aronson.

Somers-Flanagan, J., & Somers-Flanagan, R. (1995). Intake interviewing with suicidal patients: A systematic approach. *Professional Psychology: Research and Practice, 26*, 41–47.

Spitzer, R., & Williams, J. B. (1984). *Structured clinical interview for DSM-III disorders.* New York: Biometrics Research Development, New York State Psychiatric Institute.

Spitzer, R., & Williams, J. B. (1988). Revised diagnostic criteria and a new structured interview for diagnosing anxiety disorders. *Journal of Psychiatric Research, 22*(Suppl. l), 55–85.

Spitzer, R., Williams, J. B., Gibbon, M., & First, M. B. (1992). *Structured Clinical Interview for DSM-III-R (SCID-II).* Washington, DC: American Psychiatric Association.

Sullivan, H. S. (1954). *The psychiatric interview.* New York: W. W. Norton.

Sweeny, M., McGrath, R. E., Leigh, E., & Costa, G. (2001). *Computer-assisted interviews: A meta-analysis of patient acceptance.* Paper presented at the annual meeting of the Society for Personality Assessment, New Orleans, LA.

Turner, C. F., Ku, L., Rogers, S. M., Lindberg, L. D., Pleck, J. H., & Sonnenstein, F. L. (1998). Adolescent sexual behavior, drug use and violence: Increased reporting with computer survey technology. *Science, 280*, 5365.

Van Dyke, D. (2005). The family therapy interview. In R. J. Craig (Ed.), *Clinical and diagnostic interviewing* (2nd ed., pp. 131–142). Lanham, MD: Jason Aronson.

Watson, C. G., Juba, M. P., Manifold, V., Kucala, T., & Anderson, P. E. (1991). The PTSD interview: Rationale, description, reliability and concurrent validity of a DSM-III-based technique. *Journal of Clinical Psychology, 47*, 179–188.

Widiger, T., Mangine, S., Corbitt, E. M., Ellis, C. G., & Thomas, G. V. (1995). *Personality disorder interview-IV: A semi-structured interview for the assessment of personality disorders.* Odessa, FL: Psychological Assessment Resources.

Wijndaele, K., Matton, L., Duvigneaud, N., Lefevre, J., Duquet, W., Thomis, M., et al. (2007). Reliability, equivalence and respondent preference of computerized versus paper-and-pencil mental health questionnaires. *Computers in Human Behavior, 23*, 1958–1970.

Wolpe, J. (1973). *The practice of behavior therapy.* New York: Pergamon.

World Health Organization (1992). *The ICD-10 classification of mental and behavioral disorders.* Geneva: World Health Organization.

Yalof, J., & Abraham, P. P. (2005). Psychoanalytic interviewing. In R. J. Craig (Ed.), *Clinical and diagnostic interviewing* (2nd ed., pp. 57–90). Lanham, MD: Jason Aronson.

Zanorini, M., Frankenburg, F. R., Sickel, A. E., & Yong, L. (1995). *Diagnostic interview for DSM-IV personality disorders.* Laboratory for the Study of Adult Development, McLean Hospital, and the Department of Psychiatry, Harvard University, Boston, MA.

Clinical Applications of Behavioral Assessment

Stephen N. Haynes, Dawn T. Yoshioka, Karen Kloezeman, *and* Iruma Bello

Abstract

This chapter uses a case study of a family with marital, substance use, mood, external stressors, and parent–child difficulties to illustrate the principles and methods of pretreatment behavioral assessment. Several guiding principles are discussed: (a) an emphasis on identifying functional relations relevant to behavior problems and treatment goals, especially those that help us explain behavior problems; (b) a multimodal focus during assessment, attending to overt behavior, thoughts, emotions, and physiology; (c) the importance of the conditional and contextual nature of behavior; (d) an emphasis on temporally contiguous and environmental events, thoughts, and emotions in triggering and maintaining behavior problems; (e) the dynamic nature of behavior problems and causal variables; (f) an emphasis on specificity and precision of measurement; and (g) individual differences in the elements, correlates, and causes of behavior problems. A diverse set of methods is congruent with the principles of behavioral assessment and include behavioral interviews and questionnaires, observation in natural and analog environments, and self- and instrument-aided monitoring of behavior and events in natural and analog environments.

Keywords: functional relation, idiographic, self-monitoring, self-report, time sampling, treatment goals

Introduction to Behavioral Assessment

Advances in a science-based discipline depend on the measurement technology available to that discipline. Our ability to describe and explain the behavior of planets, protons, parrots, and people depends on measurement "accuracy"—the degree to which our measures reflect the true state of light, particle motion, sound, and human actions.[1] As the fundamental technology of a science, "measurement" is the process of assigning a numerical value to an attribute dimension (e.g., rate, intensity, and duration of planetary motion or of a person's behavior). The accuracy of a measure is the degree to which the assigned numbers truly reflect the attribute being measured. Advances in clinical applications of psychological science, which is the focus of this chapter, are also contingent on measurement accuracy. "Behavioral assessment" is a conceptual and methodological approach to clinical assessment that emphasizes accuracy and precision of measurement

and validity of the clinical judgments that are derived from measurements.

The ultimate goals of clinical assessment are to describe, predict, and especially to explain human behavior. "Descriptions" of human behavior include formal diagnoses of behavior problems, such as the diagnostic system described in the *Diagnostic and statistical manual of mental disorders,* fourth edition, text revision (DSM-IV-TR; American Psychiatric Association, 2000), the identification of a person's behavior problems and strengths (e.g., through interviews or problem checklists), the specification of treatment effects, and the classification of social and physical environments and events (e.g., classification of different life stressors or social environments). "Predictions" of human behavior include estimates of a person's likely response to a treatment, the likelihood that a person will relapse following successful therapy, or the degree to which he or she is vulnerable to the adverse effects of future traumatic life events. "Explanations" of human behavior include the identification of the factors that can trigger or maintain a person's behavior problems, the mediating variables that account for a relationship between distal events and a person's current behavior problem (e.g., variables that account for the likelihood that early trauma will affect later social functioning), and the mechanisms that underlie treatment effects.

The degree to which these goals of clinical science can be achieved depends on the accuracy with which behavioral, cognitive, physiological, emotional, and environmental events can be measured. Ultimately, our judgments about treatment outcome and other ultimate goals in clinical science depend on the degree that they are based on the best available science-based measures of persons and events. A principle of behavioral assessment is that clinical inferences are most likely to be valid when they are based on measures that are empirically supported, precise, accurate, comprehensive, and sensitive to change.

Behavioral assessment is also a conceptual as well as a methodological paradigm. It emphasizes that the description, prediction, and explanation of behavior and behavior problems are strengthened by examining the contexts for behavior; that is, the identification of functional relations among motor, behavioral, cognitive, physiological, and environmental events. We presume that these goals are most likely to be achieved with the use of multiple assessment methods and sources of information; the use of lower-level, less inferential, and more specific variables; and time-sampling measurement strategies to capture the dynamic nature of behavior.

This chapter outlines the concepts and methods of behavioral assessment that are applicable to clinical assessment. Although our focus is on pretreatment clinical assessment for case formulation and treatment design, behavioral assessment is a useful paradigm for treatment outcome evaluation and research (Haynes, Kaholokula, & Yoshioka, 2008), clinical research (Haynes, Pinson, Yoshioka, & Kloezeman, 2008), and psychopathology research (Haynes, 1992). Our presentation is necessarily limited but in-depth presentations of behavioral assessment are available in Haynes and O'Brien (2000), Haynes and Heiby (2004), and Hersen (2006). We begin the chapter with a case study to illustrate the conceptual foundations and diversity of behavioral assessment that are discussed in subsequent sections.

To prime the reader for major points emphasized in this chapter, we list several distinguishing attributes of behavioral assessment:

1. Behavioral assessment emphasizes the "functional relations"[2] relevant to behavior problems and treatment goals. In addition to specifying problems and goals, behavioral assessment attempts to explain behavior by identifying controlling variables, such as antecedent and consequent environmental events, physiological events, social interactions, and cognitions that affect behavior. For example, we are not only interested in specifying deficits and excesses associated with depressed mood—we also are interested in the factors that affect mood.

2. Consistent with an emphasis on functional relations, behavioral assessment emphasizes the "conditional" and "contextual" nature of behavior. That is, we presume that behavior problems are often conditional: their rate, duration, and intensity can vary across contexts. For example, we are interested in the degree to which a child's aggressive behavior (e.g., its rate, form, and target) varies across classroom settings, between home and school, across social settings, as a function of sleep quality, or depending on medication state.

3. Although historical events are often informative, behavioral assessment emphasizes the role of temporally contiguous behaviors, environmental events, thoughts, and emotions in triggering and maintaining behavior problems. While not ignoring the importance of historical factors in the development of behavior problems, the methods of behavioral assessment (see "Methods of Behavioral Assessment" section) are congruent with this focus on contemporaneous events.

4. Behavioral assessment emphasizes the "dynamic nature of behavior problems" and "causal variables." That is, behavior problems, such as mood, sleep, and social interactions, and causal variables, such as triggering stimuli or response contingencies, can change in intensity, frequency, or duration across time. To capture these important changes across time, we often use "time-sampling assessment strategies" in which important variables are repeatedly sampled across time.

5. Behavioral assessment emphasizes "specificity" and "precision" of measurement. Because of the high degree of error variance associated with the use of heterogeneous higher-order personality constructs, the accuracy and utility of clinical inferences can often be increased by using more specific, lower-level constructs. Thus, for example, we are more likely to emphasize measures of specific thoughts, social behaviors, and sleep behaviors of a client with depressed mood rather than measure the higher-order construct of "depressed mood."

6. Behavioral assessment emphasizes "individual differences" in the elements, correlates, and causes of behavior problems and allows for "idiographic assessment" strategies. Consequently, case formulations, optimal treatment designs, and the most sensitive assessment strategy are likely to differ across types of behavior problems and across persons with the same behavior problems.

7. Because it is a conceptually and empirically based assessment paradigm, behavioral assessment includes a diverse set of methods including behavioral interviews and questionnaires, observation in natural and analog environments, and self- and instrument-aided monitoring in natural and analog environments.

Mrs. Kalani: A Case Study to Illustrate Behavioral Assessment Methods and Underlying Concepts

Referral and Initial Assessment Session

Referral and initial assessment goals. Mrs. Lynda Kalani, a married 38-year-old native Hawaiian female, was referred to an outpatient mental health clinic for a behavioral assessment after a lack of significant progress in outpatient therapy and following a 10-day psychiatric hospitalization. She had been seeing a therapist weekly for 6 months and was admitted to the hospital after she expressed suicidal ideation to her husband and therapist on a number of occasions. The primary goals of the first assessment session were to identify and specify Mrs. Kalani's behavior problems and personal treatment goals and to explore possible functional relations among her behavior problems (i.e., how particular behavior problems may affect others) in order to select a valid and useful assessment strategy and to design an effective intervention program.[3]

A major goal of all assessment sessions is to establish and maintain rapport with the client. We do this by clearly discussing with clients the methods and purpose of all assessment strategies, by using client-centered interview methods such as open-ended questions, behavioral reflections, empathic and supportive comments, and by addressing barriers to adherence with the assessment process.

Self-reported behavior problems. During the initial semistructured interview, Mrs. Kalani reported increasing feelings of sadness, excessive fatigue and sleepiness, increased appetite, and lack of energy during the previous 10 months. Mrs. Kalani stated that her symptoms of depression had recently worsened because she was experiencing increased marital problems. After marital conflicts with her husband, Peter Kalani, which were occurring several times a week, Mrs. Kalani would

often feel severely depressed and isolate herself in her bedroom, frequently for days at a time.

Mrs. Kalani's depressed mood was characterized by feelings of guilt about her role as mother and wife, disturbances in her sleep, worry about impending failure and stressors, and a decrease in physical activity. During her depressive episodes, she reported difficulty getting out of bed and would sometimes spend the entire day watching television, eating, and sleeping in her bedroom. On days when Mrs. Kalani was able to leave the house and take care of her parental and household duties, she experienced a lessening in her depressive symptoms and feelings of guilt. Mrs. Kalani also mentioned that she often felt more depressed in the evenings.

Four months prior to the initial visit, she had quit her job as an administrative assistant in an accounting firm due to an increase in her depressive symptoms (e.g., feelings of fatigue, difficulty concentrating, and increased absenteeism). Mrs. Kalani also reported difficulties attending to and caring for Frank, her 6-year-old son. Frank had missed a number of days at school (1 or 2 days every week) in the last several months because Mrs. Kalani had been unable to get him ready for school in the mornings and he was becoming increasingly disobedient and oppositional at home.

In addition, she reported being increasingly concerned with Mr. Kalani's drinking. Many of their marital conflicts and disagreements focused on the amount of money that Mr. Kalani was spending on alcohol and how alcohol affected his behavior toward Mrs. Kalani and Frank. After these conflicts, Mrs. Kalani would often feel guilty and ruminate about her inability to be a good mother and wife. These ruminations and feelings of guilt became so severe that several weeks prior to the initial assessment Mrs. Kalani began to have thoughts of suicide. She was subsequently admitted to an inpatient psychiatric facility and was discharged 1 week prior to the intake interview. Since her discharge from the hospital, Mrs. Kalani had not experienced suicidal thoughts, but her depressive symptoms had remained severe enough to significantly impair her functioning.

Personal treatment goals. Mrs. Kalani's goals for therapy included feeling less depressed, having a better relationship with her husband, improving the quality of her sleep, experiencing more enjoyment in her daily activities (e.g., a more positive relationship with Frank, less dread of household chores, more recreation and time with friends, and more positive time with husband), and being able to resume work outside the home. She also wanted to be more physically active by returning to her routine of jogging several times a week.

Questionnaires. Information obtained from the initial interview is often used to plan additional assessment strategies. Clinical judgments from assessment information are most likely to be valid when derived from multiple assessment methods (e.g., structured and semistructured interviews, self-report questionnaires, diaries, and behavioral observations), multiple instruments (e.g., more than one self-report questionnaire on depression), and multiple response modes (e.g., behavior, thoughts, and emotions). Therefore, Mrs. Kalani was asked to complete a number of self-report questionnaires after the interview. The Beck Depression Inventory-II (BDI-II; Beck, Steer, & Brown, 1996) and Scale of Suicide Ideation (SSI; Beck, Kovacs, & Weissman, 1979) were administered to Mrs. Kalani because she reported frequent and severe depressed mood and past suicidal behaviors. She also filled out the Marital Satisfaction Inventory-Revised (MSI-R; Snyder, 1997) and the Dyadic Adjustment Scale (DAS; Hunsley, Best, Lefebvre, & Vito 2001) to assess her marital satisfaction and the Communications Patterns Questionnaire (CPQ; Christensen, 1987) to identify the communication styles that were utilized during conflicts with her husband.

Self-monitoring. We know that people can behave differently in different settings, and the assessment process can have strong "reactive effects." For example, the process of observing their discussion can affect the way a couple discusses a problem. We are also often unsure of the degree to which data obtained in a clinic are representative of the behavior of clients in their natural environments. Therefore, we often use assessment methods designed to acquire data in their natural environments. In addition to the naturalistic observation process, discussed later in this chapter, we can use self-monitoring diaries and other ambulatory assessment methods.

"Self-monitoring diaries and ambulatory assessment methods" have been used in a number of studies to provide real-time data on diurnal mood (Stone, Smyth, Pickering, & Schwartz, 1996), marital processes (Laurenceau, Barrett, & Rovine, 2005), and family processes (Cummings, Goeke-Morey, Pap, & Dukewich, 2002). "Electronic diaries" utilize personal digital assistants (PDAs; Piasecki, Hufford, Solhan, & Trull, 2007), which are hand-held computers used to monitor specific behaviors such as mood, marital conflicts, and drinking. In our case study, Mrs. Kalani was given a PDA to record her moods several times throughout the day, as well as her sleep patterns and physical activity daily, over a period of 1 week.

"Event-contingent recording" can provide measures of an individual's behavior, thoughts, and feelings every time a specific event occurs. Since Mrs. Kalani reported a number of conflicts in her marriage, she was asked to answer a series of questions on the PDA about events, experiences, and feelings preceding and following these conflicts. In addition, the assessor asked Mrs. Kalani to wear an "actigraph" at night to measure nocturnal movement, which is correlated with sleep stages (Haynes & Yoshioka, 2007; Tryon, 2006), in order to supplement the self-report measures of her sleep patterns.

Initiating couple assessment and inspecting records. Because Mrs. Kalani was concerned about her marital relationship, and marital conflict seemed to trigger or exacerbate some of her problems, the assessor suggested that Mrs. Kalani ask her husband to accompany her to the second session. After the initial session with Mrs. Kalani and with her written permission, the assessor obtained copies of her medical records from the psychiatric facility where she had recently received inpatient care and from her former outpatient psychiatrist. These records were obtained to gather information about Mrs. Kalani from additional sources. Information from these records indicated a history of depression and suicide in her family.

Second Assessment Session

Couple assessment. In the second session the following week, the assessor conducted interviews with Mr. and Mrs. Kalani together and then separately. The goals of the second assessment session were to (a) identify the couple's marital problems and their causes, (b) establish treatment goals for their marriage, (c) assess Mr. Kalani's behavior problems, and (d) continue to explore functional relations among Mrs. Kalani's depression and the couple's individual behavior and marital problems. Individual interviews were conducted in addition to the couple's conjoint interview because past research has suggested that conjoint interviews can reduce the validity of self-reports of "sensitive" issues such as sexual problems or domestic violence (see reviews of couple assessment strategies in Snyder, Heyman, & Haynes, 2005). In the conjoint interview, the couple was queried about the problems in their relationship, goals for their marriage, and commitment to maintain the marriage. Additionally, the data obtained from Mrs. Kalani's PDA were downloaded and the information collected on the couple's marital conflicts and Mrs. Kalani's mood was reviewed.

The interview with the couple revealed that Mr. Kalani had recently been consuming large quantities of alcohol (e.g., six to eight 12-oz. beers) every night. When drinking, Mr. Kalani often (three to five times a week) became loudly critical of Mrs. Kalani's role as mother and wife and her lack of income. A review of Mrs. Kalani's diary of marital interactions revealed that the couple had experienced five marital conflicts over the previous week and that these marital conflicts often preceded a worsening in Mrs. Kalani's mood and depressive behaviors. The conflicts were either related to Mr. Kalani's drinking or his complaints about Mrs. Kalani's inability to maintain a clean house, prepare meals, and supervise their son.

Mr. Kalani had also begun shouting at Frank on numerous occasions when Frank was disobedient or playing roughly around the house. Mrs. Kalani feared that her husband's behavior toward Frank was becoming increasingly abusive although he had never hit Frank. The couple also mentioned that Frank had been displaying aggressive, inattentive, and oppositional behaviors at his elementary school and at home. His teachers had threatened to hold Frank back a grade due to his "lack of readiness" and inability to attend to and complete his schoolwork.

Analogue behavioral observation of couple interaction. Behavioral assessment strongly emphasizes the direct "observation" of behavior by the assessor and researchers and clinicians have often used observation methods to assess marital interaction (see Gottman & Notarius, 2000, for a review). Since Mr. and Mrs. Kalani reported having frequent disagreements about problems in their relationship, the assessor conducted two 10-min analog observations of Mr. and Mrs. Kalani attempting to solve their marital problems in order to identify communication strengths and problems (Heyman & Slep, 2004; Snyder et al., 2005). The couple was first asked to role-play a situation when Mr. Kalani had stayed out late at night drinking. In the second analog observation, the couple was asked to discuss how best to handle Frank's behavior problems at school. The couple's interactions were coded using the Marital Interaction Coding System (MICS; Weiss & Summers, 1983). As indicated by Heyman, Eddy, Weiss, and Vivian (1995), the observation codes were collapsed into the following four categories: hostility, constructive problem discussion, humor, and responsibility discussion. During the analog observations, Mr. and Mrs. Kalani displayed high levels of hostility and low levels of constructive problem discussion, humor, and responsibility discussion.

Marital and child behavior problem questionnaires. While the individual interview sessions with one partner were conducted, the other partner completed written questionnaires. Since studies have found alcohol abuse to be related to the perpetration of marital violence (Murphy & O'Farrell, 1994; Pan, Neidig, & O'Leary, 1994), Mr. and Mrs. Kalani were asked to independently complete the Conflict Tactics Scale 2 (CTS2; Straus, Hamby, Boney-McCoy, & Sugarman, 1996) to measure events that may occur during their disagreements. Mr. Kalani also completed the DAS, MSI-R, and CPQ to gather more information about the couple's relationship. In addition, Mr. and Mrs. Kalani each completed a Child Behavior Checklist (CBCL; Achenbach, 1991) to provide their evaluation of Frank's behavior problems and a measure of social support (the Perceived Social Support Scale-Revised, PSSS-R; Blumenthal et al., 1987).

Interview with Mrs. Kalani. The assessor met with Mrs. Kalani individually and interviewed her about her mood and feelings of guilt during the previous week. Since Mrs. Kalani scored in the severe range on the BDI-II and the mild–moderate range on the SSI, the assessor focused the interview on Mrs. Kalani's depressive symptoms, antecedents and consequents of her symptoms, and possible mediators and moderators of changes in her mood.[4]

The data obtained from the PDA revealed that Mrs. Kalani had experienced some diurnal variability in her moods over the previous week. It showed that her mood ratings were significantly lower after 5:00 p.m. compared to the morning. Mrs. Kalani was also queried about her sleeping patterns and physical activity. The sleep data obtained from the actigraph revealed that Mrs. Kalani had an average sleep-onset latency of 68 min and an average total time in bed of 10.3 hr a night (a measure of sleep "efficiency"). The actigraph also revealed a distinct 2-hr period each afternoon (i.e., 2:00–4:00 p.m.), during which time Mrs. Kalani stayed in bed and her activity level was very low. Mrs. Kalani participated in very little physical activity over the previous week. Her diary data showed that there were 3 days of the week during which she did not leave the house and she reported no participation in aerobic activity during the week. Mrs. Kalani was instructed to continue using the PDA diary and the actigraph.

Interview with Mr. Kalani. During his individual interview, Peter Kalani, a 40-year-old native Hawaiian male, stated that he was recently under a great deal of stress and worked long hours managing the family's restaurant. A number of the restaurant's employees had been failing to show up for their work shifts. In response to these stressors, Mr. Kalani had started staying out late after work and drinking with his friends. Mr. Kalani's drinking had been the source of a number of recent marital conflicts between the couple. Mr. Kalani was given the Short Michigan Alcohol Screening Test (SMAST; Selzer, Vinokur, & van Rooijen, 1975) to assess the severity of his drinking. To obtain a measure of his daily drinking in his natural environment, Mr. Kalani was given a PDA and instructed to record the number and type of alcoholic beverages that he consumed every day, his daily workload, and stress level, and to identify the settings and triggers associated with his drinking and marital conflicts.

Information about Frank. An important behavioral assessment strategy is to obtain information about an individual's behavior across *multiple settings and sources.* Thus, in addition to obtaining information about Mr. and Mrs. Kalani's son, Frank, through their questionnaires and interviews, the assessor contacted Frank's teacher between the second and third sessions to obtain information about Frank's behavior in his school setting. During the telephone interview, Frank's teacher mentioned that over the past few months, Frank had been engaging in more aggressive, oppositional, and inattentive behaviors, which were having a negative effect on his performance at school and impairing his social relationships with other students. She stated that Frank would often (once or twice a day) push other children or try to take objects away from them. In addition, Frank frequently failed to complete his schoolwork and often did not follow classroom rules. As a result, Frank was often placed in "time-out," which had little effect on his behavior. Frank's teacher also pointed out that Frank had missed an excessive number (i.e., 13) of school days over the past few months. His absences were having a negative effect on his schoolwork and she was considering making him repeat the first grade. The teacher agreed to ask her assistant to record Frank's aggressive behavior, on-task behavior, and social interactions with peers every 2 hr for 1 week.[5] Frank's teacher also completed a CBCL regarding Frank's behavior at school.

On a weekly basis, beginning with Assessment Session 2, Mr. and Mrs. Kalani each completed short-form questionnaires that were idiographically constructed using the most salient items from the previously administered questionnaires (marital satisfaction questionnaire for both, depression questionnaire for Mrs. Kalani, and alcohol use questionnaire for Mr. Kalani). They were also asked to bring Frank with them to the next session.

Third Assessment Session

Goals and review of data. The goals of the third assessment session were to (a) continue to identify the form, sequences, and contexts of Mr. and Mrs. Kalani's marital problems; (b) gather data on Mr. and Mrs. Kalani's individual behavior problems and goals; and (c) specify the form and functional relations relevant to Frank's behavior problems.

The results from the marital questionnaires that Mr. and Mrs. Kalani completed during the previous sessions were reviewed with them. On the MSI-R, the couple scored high in global distress, disagreement about finances, role orientation, and conflict over child rearing. The couple scored low on the affective communication, problem-solving communication, and time-together scales. The information obtained from the CPQs indicated high levels on the couples' perceptions of demanding, withdrawal, and avoidance communication patterns. The couples' perceptions of constructive communication and woman demand/man withdraw were low. Results of the CT2 showed that both Mr. and Mrs. Kalani demonstrated high levels of psychological aggression. In contrast, both spouses endorsed a zero or low score on the physical aggression, injury, sexual coercion, and negotiation subscales of the CT2. Mr. and Mrs. Kalani both scored in the distressed range on the four subscales of the DAS (cohesion, satisfaction, consensus, and affectional expression).

A review of Mr. and Mrs. Kalani's diaries of marital interactions showed that the couple had experienced four marital conflicts during the previous week, all associated with Mr. Kalani's coming home after drinking and a worsening in Mrs. Kalani's mood. After these conflicts, Mrs. Kalani would usually become depressed and go to bed, while Mr. Kalani remained angry and would stay up late drinking beer and watching television. The couple did not discuss these conflicts in the morning and were uncommunicative the following day. On the PSSS-R, Mrs. Kalani scored very low on measures of social support from family, friends, and significant others.

Frank's behavior problems and parent–child interactions. As requested, Mr. and Mrs. Kalani brought Frank to the third session with them. Studies have found significant relations between the number of types of children's behavior problems and marital conflict (e.g., Grych & Fincham, 1990). Additional research has found that parents' negative emotionality and negative conflict tactics are related to children's insecure emotional and behavioral responses (Cummings, Goeke-Morey, Pap, & Dukewich, 2002). The assessor reviewed the results of the CBCLs that

Mr. Kalani, Mrs. Kalani, and Frank's teacher had completed to provide an estimate of the frequency and severity of Frank's behavior problems at home and at school. Mr. and Mrs. Kalani both rated Frank in the clinical range on the attention problems subscale of the CBCL. Frank's teacher reported that Frank's behavior at school was in the clinical range on the attention problems, social problems, delinquency, and aggression subscales of the CBCL.

The couple was then queried about the functional relations between Mr. Kalani's drinking and Mrs. Kalani's depression, the couple's marital problems, and Frank's behavior problems. The assessor inquired about the situations and contexts in which Frank was more and less likely to exhibit his behavior problems (i.e., the assessor gathered data on the "conditional probabilities" of behavior problems, which provides important information about possible causal factors), how they responded to his behavior problems, how they responded to his positive behaviors, and their attributions about his oppositional and inattention behaviors. Mrs. Kalani attributed Frank's behavior problems at school to Mr. Kalani's drinking and the family's financial instability, while Mr. Kalani perceived Frank's problems to be a reaction to Mrs. Kalani's lack of attention and discipline during her depressive episodes. The couple also stated that Frank would often lock himself in his room or throw his toys after being yelled at by Mr. Kalani. The couple would usually leave Frank alone after these episodes, which often occurred in the middle of their own marital conflicts.

Analog behavior observations of parent–child interactions. Analog observations have been used as a method to assess child behavior problems (Mori & Armendariz, 2001) and parent–child interaction (Roberts, 2001) in clinic settings. Given the concerns about Frank's behavior problems, the assessor wanted to observe Frank's behavior and his interactions with his parents. Therefore, during the third session the assessor conducted analog observations of Frank's attention to academic tasks and aggressive behavior during interactions with his parents. The first clinic analog observation involved placing Frank in a simulated academic setting (i.e., desk, workbook materials) and asking him to complete schoolwork for 10 min. Frank's behavior was coded for on-task and off-task behavior. Results from the first analog observation indicated that Frank was on task for 25% of the observation session.

The second analog observation was a parent-directed play and a "chore" situation in which Mr. and Mrs. Kalani were asked to first play a game of Frank's

choice for 10 min and then to instruct Frank to put the toys away in a toy box. The assessor gathered qualitative data on Frank and parent–child interactions (e.g., how Frank's parents responded to his positive and noncompliant behaviors). Frank's behavior was coded for compliance and aggressive behavior. Frank was compliant with 45% of his parents' requests and demonstrated one act of aggressive behavior in which he threw a toy across the room (the parents did not respond when he threw the toy). During the "play" situation, the parents made no positive comments to and engaged in no positive physical contact with Frank.

Additional assessments and feedback. The assessor again met individually with Mr. and Mrs. Kalani. Self-monitoring logs and ambulatory assessment data were downloaded and independently reviewed with Mr. and Mrs. Kalani. The sleep data obtained from the actigraph and self-monitoring revealed that during the previous week Mrs. Kalani had an average sleep-onset latency of 65 min and an average total "in bed" time of 10.1 hr a night, with frequent (e.g., 6–15) awakenings during the night (i.e., a low "sleep efficiency" score). These sleep patterns were not significantly different than her sleep patterns during the previous week. Also, there were no significant changes in Mrs. Kalani's activity level from the previous week.

Since Mr. Kalani had scored in the high range on the SMAST, during this session the assessor focused the interview on Mr. Kalani's drinking and perceived stress at work. According to the data obtained from Mr. Kalani's PDA, he had consumed 6–12 beers per night during the previous week. Review of his daily workload and stress level recorded on the PDA indicated that Mr. Kalani drank less (i.e., an average of 6 beers) on days when his stress levels were lower than on days when his stress levels were higher. All of the nights when the couple experienced marital conflicts were nights when Mr. Kalani had been under a great deal of stress at work and consumed a large quantity (>10 beers) of alcohol prior to returning home from work.

The couple was instructed to continue PDA diary recordings of their marital conflicts, Mrs. Kalani's mood, and Mr. Kalani's drinking; and Mrs. Kalani was instructed to continue to wear the actigraph. Mr. and Mrs. Kalani were also asked to provide a daily behavior rating on their PDAs of Frank's aggressive and noncompliant behaviors during the upcoming week.

At the end of the third session, the assessor presented a preliminary case formulation (in the form of an FACCM, Functional Analytic Clinical Case Model [see below]). The goals of this presentation were to get feedback about the hypothesized behavior problems and functional relations, to assess commitment for therapy, and to secure informed consent about the focus and methods of treatment. An additional session with the family would have been preferable, but it was not possible to conduct another session given the time constraints.

Brief Case Formulation

The case formulation for Mrs. Kalani, in the form of a FACCM, is illustrated in Figure 13.1 (with Figure 13.2 as the legend for Figure 13.1).

The FACCM in Figure 13.1 depicts a "higher-order case formulation" based on information obtained from multiple methods and sources. It is "higher-order" in that each causal variable, behavior problem, and functional relation can be broken down to more specific elements for the purpose of

developing more focused treatment strategies. Figure 13.2 identifies the symbols of the FACCM.

To summarize some elements of the functional analysis, Mrs. Kalani was experiencing depressed mood, decreased levels of physical activity, worry, feelings of guilt, and impairment in many of her normal activities. In addition, her depressed mood affected, and was affected by, distressing interactions with her husband and son. The frequent arguments with Mr. Kalani often led to a worsening of Mrs. Kalani's depressed mood, which then led to increased conflicts among her, her husband, and their son. Deficits in marital problem-solving skills, financial stressors, and her husband's work stress and alcohol intake were also contributing factors to Mrs. Kalani's depressed mood.

During periods when Mr. Kalani was consuming large amounts of alcohol, partially in response to work and family stressors, the financial status of the family further eroded, leading to increases in

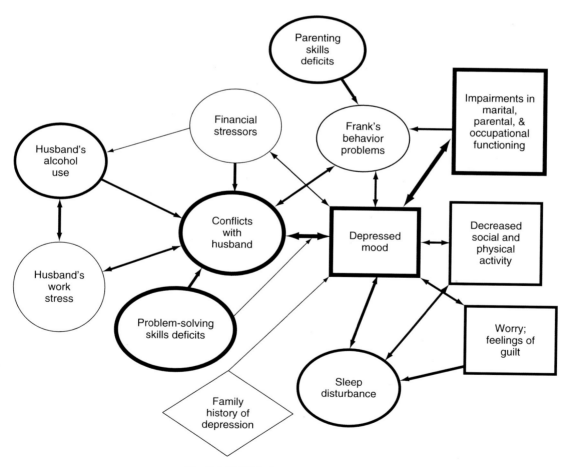

Fig. 13.1 FACCM of Mrs. Kalani and her family.

Importance/modifiability of variables
(using width of variable boundary and coefficients)

| X1 .2 | Low importance/ modifiability | | X1 .8 | High importance/ modifiability |

Type and direction of relationship between variables

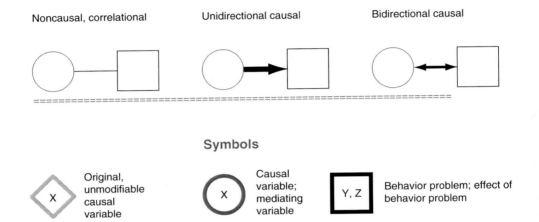

Noncausal, correlational   Unidirectional causal   Bidirectional causal

Symbols

◇ X — Original, unmodifiable causal variable

◯ X — Causal variable; mediating variable

☐ Y, Z — Behavior problem; effect of behavior problem

Strength of relationship between variables

Indicated by arrow thickness; more precisely by coefficients

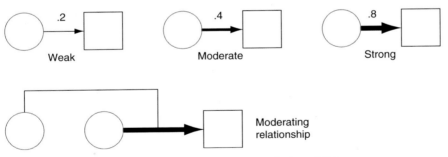

.2 — Weak

.4 — Moderate

.8 — Strong

Moderating relationship

Fig. 13.2 Legend for the FACCM.

the frequency of the couple's arguments and level of marital distress. Frank's increasing levels of aggressive and oppositional behaviors were a function of behavior management skills by his parents (e.g., less attention to and inconsistent responses to his positive and negative behaviors).

Increased levels of marital discord have been found to have a negative effect on a child's adjustment (see Cummings & Davies, 2002, for a review), which is consistent with the assessor's hypothesis that the couple's relationship distress might be contributing to their son's behavior problems. Additionally, one study on mediators and moderators in the relationship between parent problem drinking and their child's adjustment found that maternal depressive symptoms partially accounted for the relationship between paternal parental drinking and child social problems (El-Sheikh &

Flanagan, 2001). Alcohol abuse has also been found to be associated with severe marital distress and higher levels of male aggression (Halford & Osgarby, 1993). These studies demonstrate the bidirectional relationships among paternal problem drinking, marital conflict, maternal depressive symptoms, and child behavior problems and highlight the need for behavioral marital and family therapy.

Based on the preliminary case formulation, the assessor, Mr. Kalani, and Mrs. Kalani agreed on individual and family behavioral treatment plans. Mrs. Kalani agreed to continue with her individual treatment for depression. After discussion and review of the treatment options available for him, Mr. Kalani resolved to join a substance abuse program to reduce his alcohol consumption. Mr. and Mrs. Kalani agreed to continue with their daily self-monitoring logs. The couple decided to begin attending behavioral marriage counseling to address the problems in their relationship. The couple also agreed to find a family psychologist to help them reduce Frank's behavior problems and enhance the positive aspects of their family relationships.

Limitations of the Functional Analysis

All models of case formulation, including the functional analysis, are limited in their stability over time, domain in which they are valid, internal validity, and clinical utility. Several of these limitations are summarized below.

1. Case formulations are always "incomplete and imperfect." An assessor should be modest about his or her case formulation, be open to new findings and hypotheses about a client, and acknowledge potential limitations in the component clinical judgments. This conceptual humbleness derives from several sources: (a) all measures used to construct the case formulation have intrinsic error; (b) it is difficult to measure some variables (e.g., clients sometimes cannot or will not report their thoughts or behaviors; there is no well validated measures of manic states), and they must be hypothesized or subjectively estimated; (c) the assessor may have drawn erroneous inferences from the assessment data; (d) the assessor may have overlooked important causal variables, behavior problems, and functional relations; and (e) assessment data can be conflicting and difficult to integrate.

2. Given the multiple sources of error in clinical assessments and the clinical judgments that are involved, case formulations are always "subjective estimates," even when based on comprehensive and valid data.

3. Case formulations are "not exclusive." A valid functional analysis does not preclude other valid functional analyses of the same client. For example, a valid cognitively based case formulation of a depressed client does not preclude valid behavioral- or neurotransmitter-based models of the client. Often, there are multiple possible causal pathways (e.g., multiple causal paths from early childhood abuse to intimate partner violence that can involve modeling, peer selection, social skills deficits, deficits in emotional regulation, and attitude toward members of the other sex, along with other causal paths).

4. Functional analyses are "dynamic and unstable." Elements of the functional analysis (e.g., behavior problems, causal relations) are likely to change over time. Changes in a functional analysis are likely because: (a) causal variables can disappear (e.g., a hostile supervisor, violent partner, or ineffective teacher may no longer be present); (b) new causal variables can appear (e.g., new supportive friends, medications, or new stressors); (c) the client can be increasingly sensitized or desensitized to stressors, response contingencies, and triggering events; (d) the assessor may acquire new data about the client; and (e) there may be changes (e.g., "reactive effects") associated with assessment and treatment.

5. Case formulations have a "limited domain of validity." Functional analyses are always conditional. Behavior problems and functional relations can be different across environmental settings, states of the client, or time. For example, the rates, triggers and consequences for a child's aggressive behavior, or a psychiatric inpatient's delusions, can differ between home, school, and psychiatric unit.

6. Case formulations can be "pseudo-precise." The specificity of the judgments (e.g., estimated strength of relations, modifiability of causal variables) can suggest a degree of precision unwarranted by the validity and precision of available assessment technology.

7. Case formulations are "difficult to validate." Validation involves convergent validation of elements of the case formulation through multiple measures, predictive validation (e.g., time-series studies to validate hypothesized functional relations; see Mumma, 2004 for an example), or treatment validity—the degree to which treatment outcome is enhanced if it is guided by a functional analysis.

Conceptual and Empirical Foundations of Behavioral Assessment

Why did we use self-monitoring and analog observation with Mrs. Kalani and her family? Why did we attend to marital conflict, sleep quality, and parenting skills? Why did we not administer standardized personality assessment questionnaires? Our assessment strategy with Mrs. Kalani's family, and with all assessment contexts, are guided by research findings and empirically supported postulates about the nature of behavior problems, client goals, the causal relations associated with behavior problems, principles of measurement, and the clinical judgment process. A table outlining these postulates and their implications for behavioral assessment strategies has been presented in Haynes, Kaholokula, and Yoshioka (2008). Because it is a science-based assessment paradigm, behavioral assessment is an evolving, dynamic paradigm. It assimilates new methods of assessment, such as ecological momentary sampling (see "Methods of Behavioral Assessment" section), and reflects new concepts of behavior disorders (e.g., new findings on sensitization to stressors in posttraumatic stress disorder). Haynes and O'Brien (2000) and Haynes and Heiby (2004) have articulated these postulates in greater detail and we briefly discuss a subset of them below.

Many Clients Have Multiple Functionally Related Behavior Problems

The assessment strategy used with Mrs. Kalani and her family and the resulting functional analysis are guided by the findings from many studies indicating that persons who request behavioral health services often present with multiple behavior problems and that these problems can interact in complex ways (see Krueger & Markon, 2006, for a discussion of comorbidity in clinical samples). The assumption that a new client may have multiple behavior problems guides the methods, focus, and ultimate case formulation of behavioral assessment. Assessment methods, such as behavioral interviews and questionnaires, probe for multiple behavior problems, which are then reflected in the subsequent case formulation.

Behavioral assessment focuses on the identification and specification of behavior problems, but, more importantly, emphasizes their functional interrelationships. We are particularly interested in chains of events that trigger, maintain, or strengthen behavior problems. Based on multiple sources of information, the FACCM illustrates our hypothesis that Mrs. Kalani's depressed mood had strong bidirectional causal relations with marital conflicts. She was more likely to feel depressed after an argument with her husband and when depressed, she was less likely to behave positively and more likely to be irritable with her husband.

Behavioral assessment interviews, questionnaires, observations, and self-monitoring differ from nonbehavioral assessment methods in their emphasis on identifying functional relations. For example, openended questions in behavioral interviews would not only attempt to characterize Mrs. Kalani's sleep difficulties and marital conflicts, they would be directed at the functional relations between them: "About how often after you and your husband have had an argument do you have trouble falling asleep?" Also, because of the focus on functional relations when observing couple interactions we also look for sequences of behaviors, such as patterns of anger escalation, in addition to how disagreements and emotions are expressed.

There are two additional implications from this set of postulates: (a) the validity of judgments about behavior problems and their functional relations depends on the validity of the measures obtained during the clinical assessment—invalid measures are likely to lead to invalid clinical judgments and less-than-optimal treatment decisions; and (b) small changes in clinical assessment judgments can lead to large changes in the design of intervention programs. For example, if we failed to identify marital conflict and problem-solving skills as important causal variables, or if we underestimated the strength of relations between marital conflict and depressed mood, treatment would more likely emphasize cognitive, parent–child, and sleep factors. This treatment focus could still be beneficial to Mrs. Kalani and her family because several causal variables for her depressed mood would be addressed. However, the "relative magnitude of effect" of the treatment would be decreased because more important causal variables would not be addressed in the treatment.

If important variables or functional relations are overlooked, the functional analysis will have insufficient "content validity." In this case, all of the causal variables in the functional analysis would be relevant, but the array of causal variables would not be representative of the array of causal variables that truly affected Mrs. Kalani's depressed mood. Content validity would also be compromised if unimportant variables were included (i.e., if the case formulation included variables, such as early childhood experiences or birth order, that were not important for understanding the targeted problems).

Behavior Problems, Causal Variables, and Functional Relations Can Change over Time

Many studies have shown that clients' behavior problems, goals, life stressors, moderator variables, and the contexts for behavior problems change over time. In Mrs. Kalani's case, it is likely that the sources of marital conflict, she and her husband's behavior during conflict, the characteristics of parent–child conflict, Frank's aggressive behavior, her sleeping difficulties, and the external stressors impinging on the family have changed over time and will continue to change.

Behavior problems and their causes tend to be dynamic for several reasons. First, conditioning or extinction can occur with repeated exposure to causal variables, such as trauma-related or conditional aversive stimuli, leading to changes in the intensity, rate, or duration of behavior problems. Second, as Bandura (1982) noted, people's lives are often affected by chance encounters with new sources of support or new sources of stress; sometimes the stressors in one's life disappear. One can meet new friends, a more effective teacher can take over a classroom with noncompliant children, or other mediating or moderating variables can change. Also, a behavior problem can give rise to other problems if it persists, as when persistent depressive episodes or long-term excessive alcohol intake can lead to social isolation and family conflict.

The dynamic nature of behavior and environmental events has several implications for clinical assessment. First, time-series assessment strategies are necessary to capture changes in persons' behaviors and their environments. Measurement should be an ongoing process from the initial assessment and throughout treatment. Note that we continued to monitor Mrs. Kalani's depressed mood, sleep, and marital interactions across assessment sessions.

Second, we are often interested in the "phase" of a behavior problem, whether it is increasing or decreasing, as well as its "state" (i.e., the level or rate of a variable at the time of measurement). That is, the time-course context of a behavior can help us predict future behavior and identify the factors associated with behavior change (see Haynes, Blaine, & Meyer, 1995, for a discussion of "state-phase functions").

Third, because of their specificity and efficiency, some assessment methods are more amenable to applications in time-series measurement strategies than others. Examples include self-monitoring, ecological momentary sampling, measurement with ambulatory biosensors, and brief questionnaires. Data from these methods are likely to yield specific indices of important variables, be "sensitive to change," and prove clinically useful.

Behavior Problems Are Conditional and Vary across Contemporaneous Contexts and Settings

The conditional nature of most behavior problems is well documented. A client's aggressive behaviors, delusional statements, self-injurious behaviors, social anxieties, negative and positive mood states, marital conflicts, or sleep-onset latencies can vary in severity, duration, and rate, as a function of his or her immediate social environment, the presence of conditioned fear stimuli, recent history of social exchange, level of fatigue, medication state, and recent history of environmental stressors (see review in Haynes, 1992).

The identification of covariances involving behavior problems and contexts is important in behavioral assessment because such relations point to the differential operation of causal variables and treatments often attempt to modify causal variables. If a child is more likely to be inattentive, aggressive, or prosocial in one classroom than in another, or in the presence of one adult more than in the presence of another, there are differences between those environments or people that serve to trigger or maintain the behaviors. Perhaps one adult uses more reliable response contingencies than another, or one classroom includes more hyperactive classmates, or one teacher arranges for a more structured environment.

Because of this emphasis on the conditional nature of behavior problems, behavioral interviews often focus on how behavior varies across contexts, settings, and as a function of antecedent conditions, as illustrated in the case of the Kalani family. Nonbehavioral interviews and questionnaires often limit their foci to "descriptions" of behavior (e.g., history, their current level, associated symptoms). The conditional nature of behavior problems also strengthens the use of self-monitoring, analog observation, and data collected from the natural environment that measures behavior within particular contexts.

An Emphasis on Contemporaneous Functional Relations

Although historical events, learning experiences, neurophysiologically based variables, and generalized behavior patterns can strongly affect many behavior problems, behavior is also strongly affected by contemporaneous behavior–environment interactions. For example, thousands of studies have documented the impact of immediate response "contingencies," how behavior is "selected" by its effects, and how behavior can be affected by immediate environmental discriminative stimuli (see *Journal of Applied Behavior Analysis* for examples).

The role of response contingencies, and other conditional elements of behavior, draws our assessment attention to variance in behavior across time and settings within persons. Of course, our assessment is aimed at describing and specifying a client's behavior problems and goals and to understand the origins and historical determinants of behavior problems. But in a behavioral assessment paradigm we are also likely to address questions such as "Under what conditions is the client more likely to have trouble going to sleep, experience depressed feelings, feel anxious, be reinforced for inappropriate behavior, or hit a classmate?"

The effects on assessment methods and strategies with emphases on temporally contiguous events, settings, and contexts were illustrated with the Kalani family: (a) we focused interviews on contemporaneous more than on historical factors, (b) we focused on the contemporaneous functional nature of behavior, (c) we paid particular attention to the contingencies for behavior problems and their positive alternatives, and (d) we used observation methods that were particularly suited for a contemporaneous focus.

Methods of Behavioral Assessment

Earlier in this chapter we discussed how the theoretical framework of an assessment paradigm, along with research on a targeted population and behavior problems, dictate the methods used in the assessment paradigm. The methods of assessment subsequently guide the ultimate clinical judgments made about clients and the recommended treatment foci. As an assessment paradigm based on empirically based concepts of behavior, causality, and measurement, behavioral assessment is distinguished from other forms of assessment by its diversity of assessment methods. Direct observation is the method most often associated with behavioral assessment, but, as we discuss below, many self-report questionnaires, biomeasurements, self-monitoring methods, psychophysiological laboratory procedures, and interviews are congruent with the behavioral assessment paradigm.

An assessment method and strategy are congruent with a behavioral assessment paradigm to the degree that they provide valid information on: (a) "specific" behaviors and events (rather than aggregated variables, molar traits, highly inferential constructs, or variables considered as "signs" of higher order constructs); (b) the "dynamic" aspects of behavior (rather than "snapshot" measures of a client's current state); (c) the proximal and distal "contexts and conditional nature" of events (rather than providing an unconditional measure of behavior or events, such as aggregated trait measures); and (d) "functional relations" relevant to the client's target behaviors (e.g., related antecedent stimuli, and maintaining contingencies).

Note that the theoretical framework within which behavior problems and their causes are viewed guide the inclusion and exclusion criteria for behavioral assessment methods. Note also that the assessment methods provide a template for the kinds of clinical judgments that will result. As illustrated in the functional analysis of Mrs. Kalani, clinical judgments will emphasize the identification of functional relations involving important, modifiable, and contemporaneous causal variables associated with specified behavior problems.

In this section, we review several behavioral assessment methods, as well as their conceptual basis, clinical utility, and limitations. More detailed presentations can be found in Haynes and Heiby (2004), Hersen (2006), and Shapiro and Kratochwil (2000).

A Note on Behavioral Assessment: Strategies versus Methods

We focus on assessment "methods" in this section but we also consider assessment "strategies." An "assessment method" refers to a class of procedures (e.g., self-report questionnaires, behavioral observations in the natural environment, interviews) for deriving data about a person's behavior. An "assessment strategy" refers to the overall plan for applying those methods. It involves a particular set of assessment methods, instruments, instructions to the client, time-sampling parameters, and the context of assessment (e.g., in the home, at the office, for different goals of assessment).

Good assessment methods and instruments, applied at the wrong time or place, or within the wrong context, can lead to invalid judgments. Consider the impact on our case formulation if we had selected valid but inappropriate questionnaires, failed to evaluate parent–child interactions, or failed to examine marital communication patterns: Many of our clinical judgments could still be accurate but the overall content validity of the case formulation would be diminished because important problems and causal factors would be missing.

Assessment strategies are also derived from underlying postulates of the behavioral assessment paradigm and emphasize the use of (a) multiple informants (rather than depending only on data from the client); (b) multiple methods of assessment (rather than only, for example, self-report methods); (c) multiple samples of targeted events across time (rather than a single time sample); (d) methods that are consistent with the goals of assessment and the characteristics of the client (i.e., a "functional approach" to assessment); (e) measures that have been shown to be valid for the assessment context (such as the goals of the assessment and the characteristics of the client); and (f) strategies that attend to behavior–environment functional relations. Table 13.1 provides examples of several behavioral assessment methods across a variety of settings and populations.

Behavioral Questionnaires, Interviews, and Checklists

Behavioral interviews, questionnaires, and checklists are commonly used in behavioral assessments because they are cost-beneficial (i.e., they efficiently provide useful information; Fernandez-Ballesteros, 2004). Note that self-report and other-report questionnaires on marital distress and satisfaction, marital communication and conflict resolution, child behavior problems, alcohol use, and depression were used in the assessment of Mrs. Kalani and her family. Questionnaires and checklists can cover a wide range of behaviors, can help the assessor efficiently identify multiple behavior problems and goals, and can help to specify a client's most significant behavior problems. Furthermore, they are useful in gathering data from multiple informants and about the different "dimensions of behaviors" (i.e., their rate, intensity, and duration; Barbour & Davison, 2004). Because behavioral (compared to nonbehavioral) questionnaires are often more narrowly focused, they are also more amenable to time-series assessment strategies, such as monitoring treatment outcome.

As we noted earlier in this chapter, and illustrated with the case of Mrs. Kalani, an important difference between behavioral and traditional interviews is the focus on functional relations. Queries in behavioral interviews focus on the context and proximal and distal factors associated with a behavior, in addition to the description of the behavior. For example, following a discussion about the meaning of "feeling depressed," queries might also include the following: "About how often after an argument with your husband do you begin to feel depressed?" "Can you walk me through, step by step, what happened last night when your husband came home late after drinking with friends?" "Tell me about what happened, what were you thinking, and how you felt?"

The emphasis on functional relations was illustrated in the interviews with Mrs. Kalani and her family, which focused on "explaining" her depression and marital distress: for example, identifying the variables that affected the onset, duration, or severity of her depressed mood and "why" she and her husband are having conflicts. Furthermore, the "explanations" tend to be specific. That is, we are interested in specific thoughts she may be having after an argument with her husband, in the specific events that precede or trigger an argument, and in what she says to her son Frank when he complies with one of her requests.

Some advantages of interviews, questionnaires, and checklists are that they can be used in diverse settings, with most populations, and with most behavior problems. However, it is important to note that a questionnaire or interview format may not provide equally valid information across "dimensions of individual difference"—that is, across clients who differ in age, ethnicity, or level of severity of the behavior (Tanaka-Matsumi, 2004). Furthermore, accuracy of the information provided may be reduced because of perceptual biases, cognitive deficits (e.g., distortions or memory limitations), state-dependent memory, purposeful omission, and/or social desirability. Interviewer characteristics, such as age, sex, ethnicity, training, and experience, can also affect the validity of data (see Fernandez-Ballesteros, 2004, for an extended discussion on questionnaires).

Behavioral Observation in Natural Environments

The assessment of persons in their natural settings (e.g., home, school, institution) is the iconic method of behavioral observation because it can provide valuable information about the characteristics, contexts, and immediate antecedent and consequent factors that might be maintaining behavior problems. Furthermore, information from natural environments often has "incremental clinical utility"—often, clinically significant interactions that

Table 13.1. Behavioral Assessment Method: Interviews, Checklists, Questionnaires, Naturalistic Observation, Analogue Observation, Ambulatory Self-Monitoring, Ambulatory Psychophysiological Assessment, and Functional Interviews.

	Reference	Disorder/Focus	Target Population	Assessment Instrument/ Measures	Clinical Applicability/Utility	Reliability	Validity	Sources of Error/ Limitations in Clinical Assessment
Interviews, checklists, and questionnaires	Nock, Holmberg, Photos, & Michel (2007)	Self-Injurious behaviors	Adolescents and young adults	Self-Injurious Thoughts and Behaviors Interview (SITBI)	• Assesses the presence, frequency, and characteristics of self-injurious behaviors including suicidal ideation, plans, gestures, and attempts as well as non-suicidal self-injurious behaviors. • Broad screening measures that provide basic information	• Good inter-rater reliability: kappas ranged from .90 to 1.0 • Test–retest reliability: kappas ranged from .25 to 1.0	• Construct validity (using other measures of self-injury): kappas ranged from .48 to 1.0 • Statistically significant correlations ranging from .64 to .73 found between the SITBI and another measure of nonsuicidal self-injurious behaviors	• Small sample consisting only of adolescents • Fails to ask about other self-destructive behaviors that may not directly be self-injurious
	Barton et al. (2005)	Depression	Adult out-patients with depression	Sentence Completion Test for Depression (SCD)	• Idiographic assessment of depressive thinking • Can be used to complement other depression questionnaires • May help identify hypotheses of target problems and dysfunctional beliefs within a cognitive-behavioral case formulation	• Internal consistency: Kuder-Richardson 20 = .882 • Sensitivity varied from 92% to 100% • Specificity varied from 96% to 100%	• Good construct, content, and discriminant validity • Pearson correlation between SCD negative statements and BDI scores: $r = .43$ • SCD negative statements were significantly greater in the depressed group, $p < .001$	• Further study is necessary to ensure generalizability to other depressed populations such as adolescents, older adults, non-Western cultures, etc.

	Citation	Construct	Sample	Measure	Description	Reliability	Validity	Limitations
	Fromme, Stroot, & Kaplan (1993)	Positive and negative expected effects of alcohol	Undergraduate students in psychology classes	Comprehensive Effects of Alcohol Questionnaire (CEOA)	• Provides information about the effects (physiological, psychological, and behavioral) that people associate with different amounts of drinking • By measuring subjective evaluations of drinking clinicians can track client's appraisal of drinking and predict future involvement	• Test–retest reliability: correlations ranged between .53 and .81, $p < .01$	• Construct validity: confirmatory factor analysis revealed a good four factor structure; loadings ranged from .15 to .84 • Criterion-related validity: positive and negative expectancy were significantly related to alcohol use measures	• May not be generalizable outside of college students • May fail to capture important variables identified using an idiographic approach
Naturalistic observation	Buckley, Klein, Durbin, Hayden, & Moerk (2002)	Child temperament	Preschool-aged children	Child Temperament and Behavior Q-Set	• May be a good measure of observer-rated preschooler's behavior in their natural home environment • May help with the identification of externalizing problems in children • May be too time consuming for practitioners but others could be trained to use it to gather data on temperament and behavior for the clinician's use	• Inter-rater reliability: ranged from 0.58 to 0.80. • Test–retest stability: median ranged from 0.14 to 0.51 • Reliability of four observers: ranged from 0.66 to 0.86	• Construct validity: High correlations on maternal ratings for externalizing problems with the Child Behavior Checklist ($r = .55, p < .01$) • High correlations with several subscales of the Child Behavior Questionnaire (−.30–.49)	• Necessary to cross-validate results with a different sample • Make constructs relevant to developmental stages
Analog behavioral observation	Johnson (2002)	Marital satisfaction	Newly wed couples	Behavioral Affective Rating System (BARS)	• Couples are asked to come to a resolution about an important marital complaint including sex, in-laws, or money • Discussions are videotaped and then coded for affect • Helps predict marital satisfaction (dyadic expressions of positive emotions have been associated with marital happiness while expressions of negative emotions have been associated with marital distress)	• Reliability of behavioral observations ranged from .41 to .85	• Correlations with other measures of marital satisfaction (e.g., MAT and QMI) ranged from .72 to .89, $p < .01$	• Results may not be generalizable to more established couples • Possibility of observer bias • Did not compute inter-rater reliability

continued

Table 13.1. (*continued*)

	Reference	Disorder/Focus	Target Population	Assessment Instrument/ Measures	Clinical Applicability/Utility	Reliability	Validity	Sources of Error/ Limitations in Clinical Assessment
Ambulatory self-monitoring	Johnston, Beedie, & Jones (2006)	Work-related stress	Stressed workers	• Palm IIIe, personal digital assistant (PDA) • Diary software program written for the study	• Ambulatory diary for ecological momentary assessment (EMA) • Diaries entered on small hand-held computers (PDAs) in which recordings are made in real time in the working environment • PDA is user friendly with entries made via tapping the stylus on the screen • Behavioral diaries that measure effort–demand, control, reward, and stress throughout nurse's shift at approx. 90-min intervals (±5, 10, 15 min determined randomly) over 3 or 4 shifts • Format for diary questions based on the Diary of Ambulatory Behavioural States[1]	• Self-reported stress across 3 nursing shifts covaried reliably with both demand–control and effort–reward imbalance ($p < .001$)	• Slope of EMA measures on questionnaire measures (Job Content Questionnaire, Karasek, 1985; Effort–Reward Imbalance Questionnaire, Siegrist, 1996) significant for demand–control ($p < .01$) and effort–reward imbalance ($p < .001$)	• May be more time consuming and costly compared with paper-and-pencil questionnaires • May have technical problems • May have response burden on subjects • May lack stringent control over stimuli and responses found in lab setting
Ambulatory psychophysiological	Paul, Wai, Jewell, Shaffer, & Varadan (2006)	Cough, including psychogenic coughing	Children and adults of all ages	• Cough monitoring system; monitor w/ accelerometer, electronic package, cable to connect accelerometer to package, compact-flash memory card	• Objective, non-invasive, self-contained, ambulatory cough monitoring system that measures vibration and transmits output data through cable to package • Typically worn on belt or in a pocket; stores data on memory card; stores up to 24 hr of data	• Agreement between 2 investigators (1 w/ prior experience in cough research and 1 w/o prior experience; experience not found to impact findings): • For audio counts = 0.998 ($p < 0.001$)	• Used gold-standard of video recording; comparison of investigators' video counts to corresponding audio counts: • For investigator 1 = 0.968 ($p = 0.026$)	• Findings limited in that each did not match video recorded cough to the device recorded cough

Method	Population	Target behaviors	Description	Reliability	Validity	Limitations
			• Accelerometer attached to skin at suprasternal notch; advantages: below larynx so speech that causes vibrations is unintelligible on audio recording, maintains privacy for subject in ambulatory setting, eliminates interference from swallowing, relatively comfortable location does not interfere w/ daily activities, eliminates movement artifact or distance from externally located microphone	• For video counts = 0.997 ($p < 0.001$)	• For investigator 2 = 0.973 ($p = 0.015$)	
Functional interview Kearney, Cook, Chapman, & Bensaheb (2006)	Children through adults	Maladaptive/ problem behaviors (functional relations: attention, tangible, escape, sensory)	Motivation Assessment Scale (MAS) • 16-item, 7-point Likert-type rating scale (ranging from *Never* to *Always*) that assesses the functions or motivations of behavior problems • May be completed independently or through an interview (parents, teachers, careproviders) • Questions about the likelihood of a behavior problem occurring in a variety of situations	• Depending on the severity of the behavior problem • Inter-rater reliability varies from −.24 to .92 • Test–retest reliability varies from .39 to .98	• Predictive validity between MAS and observational data (for developmentally disabled children w/ frequent self-injurious behaviors): $r = .99$, $p < .001$	• May be less effective in cases of very low or very high frequency behavior • Reliability may be lower because of possible unstable factor structure • May be best used in combination with various methods of functional analysis

were not reported during interviews can be observed in the natural environment. Direct observation of parent–child, couple, teacher–child, patient–patient, and staff–patient interactions can also compensate for some of the errors and imprecision associated with self-report methods.

Naturalistic observations are often designed to maximize the chance that clinically relevant patterns of behavior are observed. This is often accomplished by imposing minimal constraints on the environment. For example, during an observation, a family might be requested to remain in two rooms, keep the television off, not engage in long phone conversations, and not receive visitors. These constraints can not only increase the cost benefits of naturalistic observations but also compromise the ecological validity of the obtained data.

Interactions are often video- and tape-recorded and later quantified through the systematic use of definitions and codes (see Kahng & Iwata, 1998, for a discussion of computerized data collection from observation videotapes). Furthermore, participant observers (e.g., teachers, nurses, and parents) who are part of the setting can gather data (see discussions in Dishion & Granic, 2004).

A study by Buckley et al. (2002) illustrates the role of external observers in measuring preschoolers' behavior and temperament. Trained graduate and undergraduate students observed the children during two home visits lasting 2–3 hr. Researchers scheduled each visit at different times of the day and arranged for different observers to attend each one. This strategy was designed to minimize observer bias by rotating observers to increase the setting generalizability of the data.

Mehl, Gosling, and Pennebaker (2006) tried to reduce the reactive effects of observation by using an electronically activated recorder (EAR) rather than a live observer. The EAR is a digital voice recorder that periodically records snippets of ambient sounds. Participants wore the device for 2 days and were unaware of when it was recording. The recordings were later collected, coded, and rated for depressive talk. Judges' ratings were significantly correlated with BDI ($r = .55$) scores but only for those participants who had higher levels of depressive symptoms. An important limitation of this assessment strategy, given the emphasis on functional relations in behavioral assessment, is that the snippets of data provided very little information about the contexts in which the recorded behaviors occurred.

Both of these studies, and the sources previously cited, highlight the utility and limitations of behavioral observation in natural environments: (a) it can be a rich source of data and hypotheses about functional relations; (b) it can be often be conducted by observers who are normally part of the setting; (c) it can be expensive; (d) the presence of an observer can evoke atypical behaviors from the participants; (e) observers can make consistent assessment errors, fabricate data, or decline in consistency and accuracy over time; and (f) careful construction of the observation strategy is necessary to strengthen its ecological validity and cost benefits.

Behavioral Observations in Analog Environments

In analog behavioral observations (ABOs), the assessment context is arranged to efficiently observe important behaviors and interactions (see Haynes & O'Brien, 2000; Heyman & Slep, 2004; and the special section on analogue behavioral observation in *Psychological Assessment*, March 2001, Vol. 13, No. 1). In ABOs, the physical setting, presence of confederates, and cues and instructions to the client are arranged to increase the likelihood that important behaviors and functional relations will occur. Examples include the observation in a clinic setting of couples attempting to resolve a problem in their relationship, role plays with a psychiatric patient to assess social skills and social anxiety, behavioral avoidance tests with clients experiencing fears and phobias, and "experimental functional analysis" involving the systematic manipulation of presumed antecedent and consequent variables (e.g., testing the effect of response contingent attention on the self-injurious behaviors of a child).

ABOs are designed to be more cost-beneficial, compared to naturalistic observations, and can be used to collect data across response modes. Not only can important behaviors and social interactions be observed, but assessors can also gather data on clients' emotions, affect, feelings, thoughts, and psychophysiological reactions during the ABO (see Hawkins, Carrère, & Gottman, 2002, for an example of measuring affect during couple interactions).

A study by Johnson (2002) evaluated marital satisfaction in newly wed couples using an ABO. Couples were asked to discuss and reach a resolution about an important marital complaint (e.g., sex, in-laws, money). The discussions were videotaped and then coded for affect using the Behavioral Affective Rating Scale (BARS). This method is useful for assessing marital satisfaction since expressions of positive emotions have been found to be associated with marital happiness while expressions of negative emotions have been found to be associated with marital distress.

Another study by Sheeber, Davis, Leve, Hops, and Tildesley (2007) used ABOs to explore the nature of mother–adolescent and father–adolescent interactions in adolescents with and without symptoms of depression. During two 10-min problem-solving interactions, adolescents and their parents were asked to discuss problems they had rated as highly problematic on a self-report instrument. Parental behaviors categorized as facilitative or aggressive were coded during these interactions using The Living in Family Environments coding system. Results indicated that adolescents with sub-diagnosed and diagnosed depression experienced less supportive and facilitative and more conflictual and aggressive interactions with each parent than healthy adolescents.

The limitations for ABOs are similar to those of naturalistic observations. In addition, the contrived assessment setting may increase reactive effects and limit the ecological validity of some inferences. The psychometric characteristics of ABOs have been discussed in Haynes (2001).

Ambulatory Monitoring

Ambulatory monitoring is an assessment method used to collect time-series data on clients' physiological, emotional, cognitive, and motor activities, most often in the natural environment (Haynes & Yoshioka, 2007). The foci of ambulatory monitoring include multiple domains and can include such variables as duration of physical exercise, heart rate, thoughts, cortisol and glucose levels, physical movement and activity, blood pressure, social interactions, and anxiety and stress. Ambulatory monitoring allows for repeated measurement during specific time periods and is often instrument-aided, thus requiring little effort from the client. Measurement can occur at preset or random times throughout a day. For example, ambulatory blood pressure and heart rate can periodically and automatically be monitored throughout the day. Combined with self-monitoring information on settings, contexts, and conditions in which the data are acquired, ambulatory monitoring can be useful in identifying functional relations.

Ambulatory monitoring is useful because it (a) allows for the measurement of multiple dimensions of behavior within multiple domains; (b) is amenable to time sampling and sequential analysis across a range of settings; (c) can be used in within-subject, interrupted time-series designs; (d) allows for unconstrained collection of data in natural settings to maximize ecological validity; (e) allows for the collection of real-time data to reduce the errors associated with retrospective reports; (f) reduces the likelihood of falsification of data with self-monitoring diary methods; and (g) has been found to be as easy to use as paper diaries and to have higher compliance rates (Hufford, Stone, Shiffman, Schwartz, & Broderick, 2002).

Ambulatory assessment also has limitations: (a) it can be more time consuming and costly to recover the data and compare with data from other assessment methods (e.g., Buse & Pawlik, 2001); (b) technical problems can disrupt data collection; (c) variability in natural settings can render data difficult to interpret; and (d) some methods and strategies can burden subjects.

Ambulatory monitoring in a clinically controlled setting. Continuous psychophysiological monitoring can be a useful method in analog environments, such as a clinic or laboratory. This was illustrated in a study by Oosterman and Schuengel (2007) that assessed physiological activity in the emotional responses of children. Their study was designed to produce accumulating stress in 3–6-year-old children through 10 episodes of a separation–reunion procedure based on the strange situation test (Ainsworth & Wittig, 1969) and extended by using guidelines for coding preschool attachment (Cassidy & Marvin, 1992) for parallel episodes with the parent and a stranger. To collect data on autonomic nervous system (ANS) activity (e.g., heart rate, respiratory sinus arrhythmia), the subjects wore surface electrodes that were connected to the Vrige Universiteit-Ambulatory Monitoring System 46 (VU-AMS), a small and lightweight device placed in the pocket of a jacket the child wears. The child was seated at a table with toys during the procedure. Results showed elevated ANS responses in young children during separation and reunion with their parents, indicative of ANS arousal.

Continuous psychophysiological ambulatory monitoring in natural environments. Continuous ambulatory monitoring of autonomic and other events can also be conducted in a subject's natural environment. For example, Chee, Han, Youn, and Park (2005) developed a method of measuring heart rate, respiration, and physical movement during sleep with an air mattress sensing system. This system helps to eliminate the need for subjects to be fitted with cumbersome biosensors in order to collect data on these variables.

McGarvey, Warke, McNiff, Heaney, and MacMahon (2003) used an ambulatory cough monitoring system to evaluate medically unexplained coughing by a 13-year-old boy. A monitor that included a mini-microphone attached to the boy's chest identified conditions associated with his high and low rates of coughing. High rates of coughing were associated with bullying at school and behavioral intervention focused on this social stressor resulted in his gradual reintegration into the school and cessation of coughing.[6]

Ecological momentary assessment using PDAs. Ambulatory monitoring can also involve the collection of data on a client's momentary states, behaviors, and contexts in real time and in the subject's natural environment. This approach, termed "ecological momentary assessment" (EMA) by Shiffman and Hufford (2001), enhances ecological validity, enables momentary assessment, and allows representation of the client's experiences across settings. PDAs are small, hand-held, user-friendly computers in which diary entries are made in real time. The client can be prompted, randomly or at preset times, to enter data on variables such as mood, anxiety, hunger, sleep, pain, recent social exchanges, and thoughts, as well as the contexts within which they occur.

Johnston et al. (2006) tested the feasibility of using EMA to study work-related stress in nurses by using self-report PDA diaries. During the nurses' working shifts, the PDA alarm sounded at approximately 90-min intervals, which prompted the nurses to answer questions by tapping a stylus on the PDA screen. Results showed that measures of nurses' work-related stress from PDA diaries and traditional self-report questionnaires were significantly correlated. Electronic diaries have been found to be as easy to use as paper-style diaries. More importantly, PDA diaries were found to enhance compliance rates (Hufford et al., 2002).

Summary

A clinical case was used to illustrate the underlying principles and methods of behavioral assessment and the functional analysis approach to behavioral case formulation. Behavioral assessment emphasizes the identification of functional relations relevant to behavior problems and treatment goals. We are interested not only in the description of a client's behavior excesses and deficits, but also in the variables that affect their occurrence and other dimensions. Consequently, we often measure antecedent stimuli, social environments, contexts, and response contingencies concurrently with measures of client behaviors.

Although we focus on contemporaneous variables and immediate behavior–environment interactions, a consideration of contextual variables affecting behavior problems often leads us to examine extended causal systems. That is, we may also consider the factors that affect "why" a staff member uses inconsistent contingencies with a patient. These extended systems factors might include training, supervision, staff communication, contingencies in the institution that affect the behavior of the staff person (e.g., union rules, consequences if problem behaviors are recorded), or state of the staff member (e.g., depressed mood).

The methods and strategies of behavioral assessment are also designed to be sensitive to changes across time in behavior and environmental events. The emphasis on the dynamic aspects of behavior results in an emphasis on the use of lower-level, more specific, and less aggregated measures. For example, we are more likely to measure specific aspects of depression, such as sleep, causal attributions, and specific automatic negative thoughts, rather than, or in addition to, the aggregated construct of "depression."

Behavioral measurement is also likely to occur within a time-series assessment strategy. Repeated measurements with highly focused instruments are more likely to capture the dynamic aspects of behavior and to identify the variables that affect variance across time. Furthermore, the characteristics of a behavior problem and their controlling variables are likely to differ across persons with the same disorder. Consequently, idiographic assessment strategies are congruent with a behavioral assessment paradigm.

These principles, and others noted in this chapter, provide the clinician with the data necessary to construct a functional analysis—the identification of important, controllable variables associated with a client's behavior problems. The functional analysis, and other models of behavioral case formulation, is essential for idiographic treatment planning because it identifies the causal variables that are the target of behavioral intervention strategies. Thus, treatment for a client's depression, for example, might differentially emphasize augmenting social support, reducing social anxiety, enhancing sleep quality, reducing automatic negative thoughts, strengthening positive outcome expectancies, or promoting "behavioral activation," depending on the outcome of pretreatment behavioral assessment.

The validity of treatment decisions depends on the validity of the clinical case formulation, which depends in turn on the validity of data acquired during the pretreatment clinical assessment. Clinical inferences and the data upon which they are based are more likely to be valid when based on multiple methods, multiple instruments, and measures that are precise, specific, and appropriate and valid for the person and context.

Given the validity of the assessment data and the clinical judgments based on them, clinical case formulations are limited in several ways: (a) case formulations are always imperfect in that measurement error is unavoidable and important variables may have been missed; (b) with current technological limitations, case formulations remain mainly subjective estimates of functional relations; (c) there can be multiple, equally valid case formulations for a particular client; (d) behavior problems, client strengths, and causal variables change over time and, therefore, the validity of a functional analysis decays; (e) a case formulation may be more valid in some contexts than in others; and (f) the functional analysis can be pseudo-precise, in that the specificity of clinical judgments may surpass the specificity and precision of the measures upon which they are based.

The principles underlying the behavioral assessment paradigm affect which assessment methods are most congruent. Self- and other-report questionnaires are frequently used but tend to be more narrowly focused than are traditional personality or projective instruments. Behavior observation is the set of methods most frequently associated with behavioral assessment. Observation can occur in natural or analog environments and can be used to gather data on client's thoughts, beliefs, emotions, and behavior. Several methods of self-monitoring, many instrument aided, can also be useful in obtaining data on behavior, cognitions, psychophysiological reactions, and relevant functional relations.

Notes

1. Definitions of terms are derived from the behavioral assessment web site http://www2.hawaii.edu/~sneil/ba/:

    "Accuracy" is the degree to which a measure of an attribute reflects the true state of that attribute.

    "Precision," in assessment, is estimated by the degree to which replicated measures of an attribute agree with one another or the standard error of measurement. Measures can be precise yet inaccurate.

    A "measure" is a number that represents the variable being measured. In psychological assessment, it is usually a number derived from an assessment instrument.

2. A "functional relation" is any relation that can be expressed as an equation. Of most interest in behavioral assessment are functional relations that are causal, that is, variables that can explain variance in another variable and satisfy other criteria for inferring causality.

3. For an overview of the many goals of behavioral assessment (e.g., informed consent for the assessment process, establishing a trusting relationship between the assessor and client, selecting additional assessment strategies, establishing expectations for the assessment sessions), see Haynes and O'Brien (2000, chap. 4).

4. A "mediating variable" ("intervening variable") explains the relations between other variables. It provides a causal link between other variables.

    A "moderating variable" affects the relation between two or more other variables. (see http://www2.hawaii.edu/~sneil/ba/).

5. "Momentary time sampling" (Hartmann, Barrios, & Wood, 2004) is an observation procedure in which the observer notes the status of the target behavior at the end of preset intervals (e.g., once every 2 hr).

6. A more reliable and validated ambulatory self-contained cough monitoring system designed to be noninvasive and inexpensive has recently been developed by Paul et al. (2006).

References

Achenbach, T. M. (1991). *Manual for the child behavior checklist 4-18 and 1991 profile.* Burlington, VT: University of Vermont, Department of Psychiatry.

Ainsworth, M. D. S., & Wittig, B. A. (1969). Attachment and exploratory behavior of one-year-olds in a strange situation. In B. M. Foss (Ed.), *Determinants of infant behavior* (Vol. 4, pp. 113–136). London: Methuen.

American Psychiatric Association. (2000). *Diagnostic and statistical manual of mental disorders* (4th ed., Text rev.). Washington, DC: Author.

Bandura, A. (1982). The psychology of chance encounters and life paths. *American Psychologist, 37,* 747–755.

Barbour, K. A., & Davison, G. C. (2004). Clinical interviewing. In S. N. Haynes & E. M. Heiby (Eds.), *Comprehensive handbook of psychological assessment* (Vol. 3, pp. 181–193). Hoboken, NJ: John Wiley & Sons.

Barton, S., Morely, S., Bloxham, G., Kitson, C., & Platts, S. (2005). Sentence completion test for depression (SCD): An idiographic measure of depressive thinking. *British Journal of Clinical Psychology, 44,* 29–46.

Beck, A. T., Kovacs, M., & Weissman, A. (1979). Assessment of suicidal ideation: The scale for suicide ideation. *Journal of Consulting and Clinical Psychology, 47,* 343–352.

Beck, A. T., Steer, R. A., & Brown, G. K. (1996). *Beck Depression Inventory manual* (2nd ed.). San Antonio, TX: Psychological Corporation.

Blumenthal, J. A., Burg, M. M., Barefoot, J., Williams, R. B., Haney, T., & Zimet, G. (1987). Social support, type A behavior, and coronary artery disease. *Psychosomatic Medicine, 49,* 331–340.

Buckley, M. E., Klein, D. N., Durbin, C. E., Hayden, E. P., & Moerk, K. C. (2002). Development and validation of a q-sort procedure to assess temperament and behavior in preschool-age children. *Journal of Child Clinical and Adolescent Psychology, 31,* 525–539.

Buse, L., & Pawlik, K. (2001). Computer-assisted ambulatory performance tests in everyday situations: Construction, evaluation, and psychometric properties of a test battery measuring mental activation. In J. Fahrenberg & M. Myrtek (Eds.), *Progress in ambulatory assessment: Computer-assisted psychological and psychophysiological methods in monitoring and field studies* (pp. 3–23). Seattle, WA: Hogrefe & Huber.

Cassidy, J., & Marvin, R. S. (1992). *Attachment organization in preschool children: Procedures and coding manual*. Seattle, WA: John D. and Catherine T. MacArthur Network on the transition from infancy to early childhood. (Unpublished manuscript).

Chee, Y., Han, J., Youn, J., & Park, K. (2005). Air mattress sensor system with balancing tube for unconstrained measurement of respiration and heart beat movements. *Physiological Measurement, 26*, 413–422.

Christensen, A. (1987). Detection of conflict patterns in couples. In K. Hahlweg & M. J. Goldstein (Eds.), *Understanding major mental disorder: The contribution of family interaction research* (pp. 250–265). New York: Family Process Press.

Cummings, E. M., & Davies, P. T. (2002). Effects of marital conflict on children: Recent advances and emerging these in process-oriented research. *Journal of Child Psychology and Psychiatry, 43*, 33–63.

Cummings, E. M., Goeke-Morey, M. C., Pap, L. M., & Dukewich, T. L. (2002). Children's responses to mothers' and fathers' emotionality and tactics in marital conflict in the home. *Journal of Family Psychology, 16*, 478–492.

Dishion, T. J., & Granic, I. (2004). Naturalistic observation of relationship process. In S. N. Haynes & E. M. Heiby (Eds.), *Comprehensive handbook of psychological assessment* (Vol. 3, pp. 143–161). Hoboken, NJ: John Wiley & Sons.

El-Sheikh, M., & Flanagan, E. (2001). Parental problem drinking and children's adjustment: Family conflict and parental depression as mediator and moderators of risk. *Journal of Abnormal Child Psychology, 29*, 417–432.

Fernandez-Ballesteros, R. (2004). Self-report questionnaires. In S. N. Haynes & E. M. Heiby (Eds.), *Comprehensive handbook of psychological assessment* (Vol. 3, pp. 194–221). Hoboken, NJ: John Wiley & Sons.

Fromme, K., Stroot, E., & Kaplan, D. (1993). Comprehensive effects of alcohol: Development and psychometric assessment of a new expectancy questionnaire. *Psychological Assessment, 5*, 19–26.

Gottman, J. M., & Notarius, C. I. (2000). Decade review: Observing marital interaction. *Journal of Marriage and Family, 62*, 927–947.

Grych, J. H., & Fincham, F. D. (1990). Marital conflict and children's adjustment: A cognitive-contextual framework. *Psychological Bulletin, 108*, 267–290.

Halford, W. K., & Osgarby, S. M. (1993). Alcohol abuse in clients presenting with marital problems. *Journal of Family Psychology, 6*, 245–254.

Hartmann, D. P., Barrios, B. A., & Wood, D. D. (2004). Principles of behavioral observation. In S. N. Haynes & E. H. Heiby (Eds.), *Behavioral Assessment* (pp. 108–127). Hoboken, NJ: John Wiley & Sons.

Hawkins, M. W., Carrère, S., & Gottman, J. M. (2002). Marital sentiment override: Does it influence couples' perceptions? *Journal of Marriage and Family, 64*, 193–201.

Haynes, S. N. (1992). *Models of causality in psychopathology: Toward synthetic, dynamic and nonlinear models of causality in psychopathology*. Des Moines, IA: Allyn & Bacon.

Haynes, S. N. (2001). Clinical applications of analogue observation: Dimensions of psychometric evaluation. *Psychological Assessment, 13*, 73–85.

Haynes, S. N., Blaine, D., & Meyer, K. (1995). Dynamical models for psychological assessment: Phase-space functions. *Psychological Assessment, 7*, 17–24.

Haynes, S. N., & Heiby, E. M. (2004). *Behavioral assessment*. Hoboken, NJ: John Wiley & Sons.

Haynes, S. N., Kaholokula, K., & Yoshioka, D. (2008). Behavioral assessment in treatment research. In A. M. Nezu & C. Nezu (Eds.), *Evidenced-based outcome research: A practical guide to conducting randomized control trials for psychosocial interventions* (pp. 67–94). New York: Oxford University Press.

Haynes, S. N., & O'Brien, W. O. (2000). *Principles of behavioral assessment: A functional approach to psychological assessment*. New York: Plenum/Kluwer.

Haynes, S. N., Pinson, C., Yoshioka, D., & Kloezeman, K. (2008). Behavioral assessment in clinical psychology research. In D. McKay (Ed.), *Handbook of research methods in abnormal and clinical psychology* (pp. 125–140). Los Angeles, Sage.

Haynes, S. N., & Yoshioka, D. T. (2007). Clinical assessment applications of ambulatory biosensors. *Psychological Assessment, 19*, 44–57.

Hersen, M. (Ed.) (2006). *Clinician's handbook of child behavioral assessment*. San Diego, CA: Academic Press.

Heyman, R. E., Eddy, J. M., Weiss, R. L., & Vivian, D. (1995). Factor analysis of the Marital Interaction Coding System (MICS). *Journal of Family Psychology, 9*, 209–215.

Heyman, R. E., & Slep, A. M. S. (2004). Analogue behavioral observation. In S. N. Haynes & E. M. Heiby (Eds.), *Comprehensive handbook of psychological assessment* (Vol. 3, pp. 162–180). Hoboken, NJ: John Wiley & Sons.

Hufford, M. R., Stone, A. A., Shiffman, S., Schwartz, J. E., & Broderick, J. E. (2002). Paper vs. electronic diaries. *Applied Clinical Trials, 11*, 38–43.

Hunsley, J., Best, M., Lefebvre, M., & Vito, D. (2001). The seven-item short form of the Dyadic Adjustment Scale: Further evidence for construct validity. *American Journal of Family Therapy, 29*, 325–335.

Johnson, M. D. (2002). The observation of specific affect in marital interactions: Psychometric properties of a coding system and a rating system. *Psychological Assessment, 14*, 423–438.

Johnston, D. W., Beedie, A., & Jones, M. C. (2006). Using computerized ambulatory diaries for the assessment of job characteristics and work-related stress in nurses. *Work and Stress, 20*, 163–172.

Kahng, S. W., & Iwata, B. A. (1998). Computerized systems for collecting real-time observational data. *Journal of Applied Behavior Analysis, 31*, 253–261.

Kearney, C. A., Cook, L. C., Chapman, G., & Bensaheb, A. (2006). Exploratory and confirmatory factor analyses of the motivation assessment scale and resident choice assessment scale. *Journal of Developmental and Physical Disabilities, 18*, 1–11.

Krueger, R. F., & Markon, K. E. (2006). A model-based approach to understanding and classifying psychopathology. *Annual Review of Clinical Psychology, 2*, 111–133.

Laurenceau, J.-P., Barrett, L. F., & Rovine, M. J. (2005). The interpersonal process model of intimacy in marriage: A daily-diary and multi-level modeling approach. *Journal of Family Psychology, 19*, 314–323.

McGarvey, L. P. A., Warke, T. J., McNiff, C., Heaney, L. G., & MacMahon, J. (2003). Psychogenic cough in a schoolboy: Evaluation using an ambulatory cough recorder. *Pediatric Pulmonology, 36*, 73–75.

Mehl, M. R., Gosling, S. D., & Pennebaker, J. W. (2006). Personality in its natural habitat: Manifestations and implicit folk theories of personality in daily life. *Journal of Personality and Social Psychology, 90*, 862–877.

Mori, L. T., & Armendariz, G. M. (2001). Observational assessment of child behavior problems. *Psychological Assessment, 13*, 36–45.

Mumma, G. H. (2004). Validation of idiosyncratic cognitive schema in cognitive case formulations: An intra-individual idiographic approach. *Psychological Assessment, 16*, 211–230.

Murphy, C. M., & O'Farrell, T. J. (1994). Factors associated with marital aggression in male alcoholics. *Journal of Family Psychology, 8*, 321–335.

Nock, M. K., Holmberg, E. B., Photos, V. I., & Michel, B. D. (2007). Self-injurious thoughts and behaviors interview: Development, reliability, and validity in an adolescent sample. *Psychological Assessment, 19*, 309–317.

Oosterman, M., & Schuengel, C. (2007). Physiological effects of separation and reunion in relation to attachment and temperament in young children. *Developmental Psychobiology, 49*, 119–128.

Pan, H. S., Neidig, P. H., & O'Leary, K. D. (1994). Predicting mild and severe husband-to-wife physical aggression. *Journal of Consulting and Clinical Psychology, 62*, 975–981.

Paul, I. M., Wai, K., Jewell, S. J., Shaffer, M. L., & Varadan, V. V. (2006). Evaluation of a new self-contained, ambulatory, objective cough monitor. *Cough, 2*, 7.

Piasecki, T. M., Hufford, M. R., Solhan, M., & Trull, T. J. (2007). Assessing clients in their natural environments with electronic diaries: Rationale, benefits, limitations, and barriers. *Psychological Assessment, 19*, 25–43.

Roberts, M. W. (2001). Clinic observations of structured parent–child interaction designed to evaluate externalizing disorders. *Psychological Assessment, 13*, 46–58.

Selzer, M. L., Vinokur, A., & van Rooijen, L. (1975). A self-administered Short Michigan Alcoholism Screening Test (SMAST). *Journal of Studies on Alcohol, 36*, 117–126.

Shapiro, E. S., & Kratochwil, T. R. (2000). *Behavioral assessment in schools, second edition: Theory research and clinical foundations.* New York: Guilford Press.

Sheeber, L. B., Davis, B., Leve, C., Hops, H., & Tildesley, E. (2007). Adolescents' relationships with their mothers and fathers: Associations with depressive disorder and subdiagnostic symptomatology. *Journal of Abnormal Psychology, 116*, 144–154.

Shiffman, S., & Hufford, M. R. (2001). Ecological momentary assessment. *Applied Clinical Trials, 10*, 42–45.

Snyder, D. K. (1997). *Manual for the Marital Satisfaction Inventory-Revised.* Los Angeles: Western Psychological Association.

Snyder, D. K., Heyman, R. E., & Haynes, S. N. (2005). Evidence-based approaches to assessing couple distress. *Psychological Assessment, 17*, 288–307.

Stone, A. A., Smyth, J. M., Pickering, T., & Schwartz, J. (1996). Daily mood variability: For of diurnal patterns and determinants of diurnal patterns. *Journal of Applied Social Psychology, 26*, 1286–1305.

Straus, M. A., Hamby, S. L., Boney-McCoy, S., & Sugarman, D. B. (1996). The Revised Conflict Tactics Scale (CTS2): Development and preliminary psychometric data. *Journal of Family Issues, 17*, 283–316.

Tanaka-Matsumi, J. (2004). Individual differences and behavioral assessment. In S. N. Haynes & E. M. Heiby (Eds.), *Comprehensive handbook of psychological assessment, Vol. 3: Behavioral assessment* (pp. 128–139). Hoboken, NJ: John Wiley & Sons.

Tryon, W. W. (2006). Activity measurement. In M. Hersen (Ed.) *Clinician's handbook of adult behavioral assessment* (pp. 85–120). New York: Academic Press.

Weiss, R. L., & Summers, K. J. (1983). Marital Interaction Coding System-III. In E. Filsinger (Ed.), *Marriage and family assessment* (pp. 85–116). Newbury Park, CA: Sage.

The MMPI-2: History, Interpretation, and Clinical Issues

Andrew C. Cox, Nathan C. Weed, *and* James N. Butcher

Abstract

The Minnesota Multiphasic Personality Inventory-2nd edition (MMPI-2; Butcher, Dahlstrom, Graham, Tellegen, & Kaemmer, 1989) is the most widely used personality assessment instrument in research and clinical practice. The goals of this chapter are to orient new users to the test and to highlight a number of current issues with the test that may also be of interest to experienced users. The chapter begins by briefly illustrating the development of MMPI-2, from its origins in the University of Minnesota Hospitals to its current form. The sections that follow describe some of its key features and the contributions they make to assessing personality and psychopathology: Validity Scales, Clinical Scales, Content Scales, Supplementary Scales, Personality Psychopathology Five Scales, and Restructured Clinical Scales. The chapter concludes with discussions of specific clinical issues related to using the MMPI-2 and of new developments involving the MMPI-2: assessment of ethnic minority clients, international adaptation of the MMPI-2, short forms, and computer applications. Although basic test interpretive information is provided, this chapter should not be considered a comprehensive interpretive guide. An annotated bibliography is included for those interested in further reading on the MMPI-2.

Keywords: Clinical Scales, content interpretation, international test adaptation, MMPI-2, short forms of the MMPI-2, Validity Scales

Brief History of the MMPI-2
Development of the Original MMPI

The first Minnesota Multiphasic Personality Inventory (MMPI) was published by Starke Hathaway, PhD, and J. Charnley McKinley, MD, in 1943. Diagnostic assessment at that time typically entailed subjecting each patient to an interview, mental status exam, and individually administered psychological testing. Prior to the MMPI's publication the test authors worked in the University of Minnesota Hospitals system, and they found this process quite time consuming and demanding of hospital resources. Hathaway and McKinley believed that a paper-and-pencil survey, which could be administered in a group format, would allow clinicians to gather a large amount of information in a relatively short period of time. This instrument could be designed to detect features of the most common diagnostic categories of the day in a

relatively objective way. It was hoped that clinicians would be able to use test results to arrive at one or more conclusive diagnoses, making the assessment process quicker and more reliable.

Hathaway and McKinley began constructing this new instrument by creating an item pool of approximately 1,000 statements. These statements were assembled from a review of case histories, textbooks, and a variety of other trait scales that were in use at the time. About half of the statements were eliminated based on redundant content, leaving a total of 504 items keyed true or false. These items were then administered to approximately 1,500 adults not hospitalized for a psychiatric condition, the majority of which were visitors of patients at the University of Minnesota Hospitals, and to a group of 221 psychiatric inpatients in the same hospital system. These inpatients were selected based on the presence of one of eight common psychiatric diagnoses. Patients with multiple diagnoses, or a diagnosis that was questionable, were excluded from the sample.

Items were assigned to scales using the empirical keying method. This method involves the selection of items for scale membership that maximally distinguish between two criterion groups, in this case Minnesota normals and inpatients assigned a particular diagnosis. Responses to each item were compared between the relatively nonpathological Minnesota sample and each inpatient diagnostic sample. Items that were statistically meaningful predictors of group membership were assigned to a scale. No attempt was made to avoid item overlap between scales, so many items were scored on multiple scales.

Eight separate measures emerged from this empirical keying process. They were known collectively as the Clinical Scales, and they were named for their original diagnostic criterion groups—Hypochondriasis (Hs), Depression (D), Hysteria (Hy), Psychopathic Deviate (Pd), Paranoia (Pa), Psychasthenia (Pt), Schizophrenia (Sc), and Hypomania (Ma). After the MMPI's publication, two more Clinical Scales were added. The Masculinity–Femininity (Mf) scale (Hathaway, 1956) was designed to identify features of "male sexual inversion," (homosexuality). Drake (1946) developed the Social Introversion (Si) scale to measure pathological variations of shyness. Together, these 10 Clinical Scales formed the cornerstone of the original MMPI.

In addition to the Clinical Scales, the MMPI also contained a set of Validity Scales designed to detect problematic response biases. Extreme scores on any of these scales suggested that the test taker had responded in an atypical manner, and that the profile should be interpreted with caution or not at all. The Cannot Say (?) scale was simply a count of the total number of unscorable items (either not answered or marked both true and false). The Lie (L) scale measured naive attempts to fake good or present oneself as unrealistically virtuous. Attempts to malinger, on the other hand, were detected with the Infrequency (F) scale, composed of items only rarely endorsed in the normal sample. Test takers tended to obtain high scores on this scale if they were severely disturbed, pretending to be severely disturbed, or responding randomly. The final Validity Scale on the original MMPI was the Correction scale (K). High scores on K indicated reluctance to disclose psychological problems, and portions of scores on this scale were typically added to scores on some of the Clinical Scales to correct for defensiveness.

Many other important scales, including subscales of the Clinical Scales, face-valid Content Scales, and Supplementary Scales, were added to the MMPI throughout the years using the items available in its copious item pool. Scoring keys for scales found to be useful were published and made part of the standard test. Many of these original scales are still in use on the MMPI-2, in updated versions, and will be discussed in greater depth in later sections.

Within a short time, the MMPI became the most widely used personality assessment instrument in the United States in both inpatient and outpatient settings (Lubin, Larsen, & Matarazzo, 1984). Even though it was designed to be used only with adults, it also became the most popular inventory for assessing adolescents (Archer, Maruish, Imhof, & Piotrowski, 1991). By the late 1980s, over 10,000 studies had been published using the MMPI.

Reasons for Restandardization

Despite its unparalleled success in the field of objective personality assessment, the MMPI eventually began to show its age. By the 1970s, a substantial number of researchers and practitioners were calling for a revision. Two key criticisms of the original test formed the basis of these arguments.

First, much of the item content was inappropriate given contemporary standards. Some items included antiquated terms that would not resonate with modern examinees, such as streetcars, sleeping powders, and playing "drop the handkerchief." Others used language that could be considered sexist, pathologized certain religious beliefs, or contained crude references to bodily functions. Some items that were neither archaic nor offensive were simply poorly worded or suffered from grammatical errors. In addition, over time it became apparent that the original item pool was inadequate for measuring some important aspects of psychopathology, such as suicidality and illicit drug use.

Serious criticisms were also leveled against the normative sample. The norms still used to score the test were generated in the early 1940s, and American society had changed meaningfully since then. The norms were also decidedly unrepresentative of the U.S. population at the time. All of the original respondents lived in Minnesota, the vast majority were Caucasian, and most were married, living in low-population areas, and had only about 8 years of education.

The Restandardization Project and the Birth of the MMPI-2

After years of debate and controversy, the University of Minnesota Press formed a restandardization committee in 1982 that consisted of

James N. Butcher, W. Grant Dahlstrom, and John R. Graham. Auke Tellegen also joined at a later date. The goals of this committee were to address the two primary criticisms discussed above. First, item content was to be altered to make the test more easily understandable and less offensive to modern examinees, and new items would be added that would tap into additional domains of pathology. Once this objective had been completed, this new form was to be administered to a large sample representative of the current U.S. population in order to establish a sounder normative base.

Although the need to update the item content of the test was clear, the committee did not wish to alter it so much that the enormous research base that supported the test would no longer be useful. As a result, these revisions were fairly innocuous. A total of 82 items underwent minor linguistic tweaks (the word "cross" became "irritable," for example) in order to improve clarity and eliminate bias, offensive language, and poor grammar. Great pains were taken to maintain continuity with the meaning of the original items, and endorsement patterns of these items did not change significantly between their old and new versions (Ben-Porath & Butcher, 1989). Several items were also deleted. The most substantial portion of these was a set of 16 exact duplicates of other items already found in the test. They were originally included in order to assist in an early version of machine scoring that is now obsolete. Many examinees did not understand their purpose, however, and were bothered by their presence, so they were eliminated from the new form. A total of 154 items measuring a variety of content domains were added to the experimental version of the test booklet (Form AX) that was administered to the normative sample, although many of these were deleted due to a desire to keep the test to a reasonable length.

The normative sample was designed to approximate proportions of demographic characteristics found in the 1980 U.S. census. Data were collected from a variety of geographic regions, including Minnesota, Ohio, North Carolina, Washington, Pennsylvania, Virginia, and California. Efforts were made to include a substantial number of ethnic minority participants as well. Profiles were obtained from almost 3,000 individuals. Once they had been screened for incomplete forms and invalid responding, a total normative sample of 2,600 people remained, ages 18–85, and about equal in proportion with respect to gender.

The finalized form of the Minnesota Multiphasic Personality Inventory-2nd edition (MMPI-2) was published in 1989 by Butcher, Dahlstrom, Graham, Tellegen, and Kaemmer. It contains 567 statements that the examinee is asked to endorse as either true or false. The test quickly gained widespread acceptance among users of the original MMPI, and in 1999 the University of Minnesota Press stopped publishing the older version. Since its adoption, over 2,800 studies using the MMPI-2 have been published. Empirical support for its validity and utility for clinical personality assessment is overwhelming, and its research base continues to grow. A timeline of major developments in the history of the MMPI and MMPI-2 is provided in Table 14.1; a broader historical context for these developments is provided in Chapter 1. The remainder of the chapter will describe the essential features of the MMPI-2, as well as some of the critical developments that have taken place in recent years.

Validity Scales

In order for self-report data to be useful, examinees must comply with the instructions they are given and respond candidly. If adequate rapport is established and the importance of testing is properly explained, these conditions are usually met. It should not be assumed, however, that all examinees will provide accurate data. Some test takers may be unable or unwilling to sufficiently engage the test material, as may be the case with clients suffering from severe cognitive disturbances. Still others may deliberately attempt to falsify their answers. This practice is common in certain contexts, such as forensic, preemployment, and custody evaluations. Chapters 19 and 32 deal at length with the difficulties involved in the assessment of malingering and defensiveness. The MMPI-2 has several scales designed to detect inadequate effort and attempts to distort test results. The most frequently used measures, summarized in Table 14.2, are discussed below.

Cannot Say (?)

The Cannot Say scale from the original MMPI was retained for the MMPI-2. It is simply the total number of unscorable items, those that were either not marked or were marked both true and false. High scores may indicate a lack of cooperation on the part of the examinee or ambivalence about the nature of his or her functioning. The revised MMPI-2 manual (Butcher et al., 2001) suggests that tests containing 30 or more unscoreable items should not be interpreted, as scale scores will be artificially lowered. More conservative cutoffs, however, should be used if it is discovered that several unscorable items

Table 14.1. Timeline of major developments in the history of the MMPI-2.

Year	Development and citation
1940	First journal publication on the Multiphasic Schedule (Hathaway & McKinley)
1943	*Time* magazine announcement of the broad use of the MMPI
	Applications of the MMPI in medical assessment (Schiele, Baker, & Hathaway)
1945	Value of the MMPI in personnel selection established (Abramson)
	Meehl's empiricist manifesto
	First use of the MMPI with adolescents (Capwell)
1946	Development of the Social Introversion scale (Drake)
1947	Simulated patterns on the MMPI (Gough)
1948	First international translations of the MMPI
1951	Successful analysis and prediction of delinquency (Hathaway & Monachesi)
1952	First factor analysis of the test establishing the factor structure of the MMPI scales (Welsh)
1954	Meehl's article on clinical vs. statistical prediction, establishing the actuarial prediction approach in psychology
1955	Work by Reitan contributed to the inclusion of the MMPI in neuropsychological assessment
	Empirical validation of code types (Halbower)
	Development of the Harris–Lingoes Subscales (Harris & Lingoes)
1956	Factors in test translation (Sundberg)
1960	First comprehensive interpretative text for the MMPI (Dahlstrom & Welsh)
1962	Development of the first computer interpretation system at the Mayo Clinic (Rome, Swenson, Mataya, McCarthy, Pearson, Keating, & Hathaway)
1963	Marks & Seeman's interpretive cookbook for MMPI codes with outpatients based on actuarial prediction methods
1965	Gilberstadt & Duker's MMPI cookbook for inpatients
	Block's book dispelling the power of response sets
	Establishment of the Symposium on Recent Developments in the Use of the MMPI, which has brought new research and clinical interpretation strategies to psychologists for over 40 years
	Craig MacAndrew's development of the MacAndrew Alcoholism Scale
1966	Wiggins's content interpretation approach
	Gottesman & Shields's MMPI study on the genetics of schizophrenia and personality
	Strength of actuarial methods in psychological assessment (Sines)
1967	Development of the first narrative MMPI interpretive program with Roche Laboratories (Fowler)
1969	First public discussion of the need for an MMPI revision by a panel of MMPI experts at the 5th MMPI Symposium on Recent Developments in the Use of the MMPI at Minneapolis, MN
1970	First International Symposium on Recent Developments in the MMPI in Mexico, highlighting international use of the MMPI
1972	Changing perspectives in objective personality assessment; detailed discussion on the need for and factors in the revision of the MMPI (Butcher)
1976	Development of rigorous methodology for MMPI translation (Butcher & Pancheri)
1977	Established a system for the classification of profiles of criminal offenders (Megargee)
	Publication of John Graham's long-running and widely used interpretive MMPI textbook, *The MMPI: A Practical Guide*
1978	Innovative clinical programming that integrated the MMPI into chronic pain treatment programs (Fordyce)
1982	The MMPI-2 Restandardization Committee is formed consisting of James Butcher, John Graham, W. Grant Dahlstom, & Auke Tellegen
1985	Predicting behavior with the MMPI in job applicants (Beutler)
1988	Malingering assessment in psychological tests (Schretlen)
1989	MMPI-2 is published (Butcher et al., 1989)
	Criteria for assessing inconsistent patterns of item endorsement (Nichols, Greene, & Schmolck)
1990	Development of the MMPI-2 content scales (Butcher, Graham, Williams, & Ben-Porath)
1991	Research verified the utility of the MMPI-2 Validity Scales (Berry, Baer, & Harris; Graham, Watts, & Timbrook)
1992	MMPI-A was published (Butcher, Williams, Graham, Archer, Tellegen, Ben-Porath, & Kaemmer)
	Therapeutic assessment (test feedback in therapy) demonstrated to be an effective treatment strategy (Finn & Tonsager).

continued

Table 14.1. (*continued*)

Year	Development and citation
	Derivation of uniform T-scores for MMPI-2 (Tellegen & Ben-Porath)
	Development of new measures for assessing substance abuse (Weed, Butcher, Ben-Porath, & McKenna)
1993	Content Component Scales developed (Ben-Porath & Sherwood)
1995	Development of the Infrequency-Psychopathology scale (Arbisi & Ben-Porath)
	Development of the Superlative Self-Presentation scale (Butcher & Han)
	Importance of validity indicators in MMPI-2 evaluation (Bagby)
	Established the continuity of MMPI code-type correlates in the MMPI-2 (Archer, Griffin, & Aiduk)
	Publication of the Personality Psychopathology Five (PSY-5) Scales (Harkness, McNulty, & Ben-Porath)
2003	Publication of the Restructured Clinical (RC) Scales (Tellegen, Ben-Porath, McNulty, Arbisi, Graham, & Kaemmer) as supplemental measures
2005	PSY-5 Facet Scales identified (Arnau, Handel, & Archer)
2006	Special issue of *Journal of Personality Assessment* devoted to RC Scales (Meyer, 2006)

Source: Adapted from Butcher (2005).

Table 14.2. Summary of validity scales.

Scale	Brief Interpretation
Cannot Say (?)	Number of unscorable responses
Variable Response Inconsistency (VRIN)	Inconsistent or random responding
True Response Inconsistency (TRIN)	Inconsistent and true/false response bias
Infrequency (F)	Random responding or fake-bad response bias
Back Infrequency (Fb)	F scale for the latter part of the test
Infrequency-Psychopathology (Fp)	F particularly useful with psychiatric inpatients
Lie (L)	Naive fake-good responding
Correction (K)	Fake-good responding and denial of problems
Superlative Self-Presentation (S)	Fake-good responding and denial of problems

appear on a single scale. If an examinee fails to properly answer a large number of items, it is standard practice to request that the person reconsider his or her responses to those items so that a valid profile may be obtained.

Variable Response Inconsistency (VRIN)

The Variable Response Inconsistency (VRIN) scale was added to the MMPI-2 during the restructuring process. It is scored by comparing the examinees' responses to various items pairs judged to be related in their content. Contradictory responding to these items increases scores on this scale. Examinees who respond randomly or those who do not adequately evaluate item content before responding tend to return elevated scores on this measure.

True Response Inconsistency (TRIN)

True Response Inconsistency (TRIN) was also created by the restructuring committee for the MMPI-2. Scores are generated by contrasting pairs

of items that are opposite in their content. Inconsistent true or false responding increases the score. Both acquiescence (the tendency to answer in the affirmative regardless of content) and nonacquiescence (the tendency to answer in the negative regardless of content) produce elevated scores on this scale. Wetter and Tharpe (1995) conducted a simulation study to test the effects of randomly inserting true or false item responses on TRIN scores. They concluded that TRIN is sensitive to both kinds of response styles, and that it demonstrates utility beyond the other Validity Scales in detecting them.

Infrequency (F)

The F scale of the original MMPI was largely retained in the MMPI-2, only some items having been deleted in the restructuring process. The scale is composed of items answered in the scored direction by fewer than 10% of the MMPI normative sample. Although it was originally designed to detect failure on the part of the examinee to properly attend to the meaning of items, scores on the F scale can have a variety of interpretations. Because the content of these items generally reflects manifestations of severe psychopathology, examinees suffering from psychotic symptoms may obtain elevated scores even when approaching the test in an earnest manner.

Very high scores likely indicate an invalid response style. Random responding, acquiescence, extreme nonacquiescence, malingering, and exaggeration all tend to produce scores in this range. Examination of the VRIN and TRIN scales can be useful for clarifying the meaning of F scale elevations. If VRIN is elevated along with F, then random responding is indicated. Examinees' scores on TRIN indicate whether a true or false response bias may have contributed to F scale elevations. If neither VRIN nor TRIN is elevated, then it can be inferred that the examinee purposefully and consistently reported a number of severe symptoms. The profile should not necessarily be considered invalid, though. One of the newer Validity Scales, Infrequency Psychopathology, should be evaluated in order to assess malingering and exaggeration. More information on making these determinations will be discussed below in the section describing that scale.

Back Infrequency (Fb)

Because the items in the F scale all appear toward the beginning of the test, it does not assess deviant response styles that develop toward the end. The Fb scale was created by the restructuring committee (Butcher et al., 1989) in order to address this concern. Its development mirrored that of the F scale. Items in the second half of the test booklet that were endorsed by less than 10% of the normative sample (generally reflecting severe psychopathology) compose the scale. Fb is interpreted similarly to F, and the same procedures discussed above should be used to understand its meaning if both scales are elevated. If Fb is substantially higher than F, however, it is likely that the examinee's response style became less valid toward the end of the test. The most obvious reasons for such a change are waning interest or attention, although little research has focused on clarifying this issue. If Fb is elevated, then only the original Validity Scales (F, L, and K) and the Clinical Scales can be interpreted.

Infrequency Psychopathology (Fp)

As discussed earlier, the F and Fb scales may be elevated by people truthfully admitting to severe symptoms. Fp was designed in order to disentangle actual maladjustment from a deviant response style.

It was developed by Arbisi and Ben-Porath (1995) by identifying items rarely endorsed by both clinical and nonclinical populations. High scores on this scale provide strong evidence of invalid responding across settings, helping to clarify the meaning of the F and Fb scales. If these scales are elevated, and Fp is not, then it is likely that the examinee responded in a valid manner if severe disturbance is evident, or exaggerated her or his symptoms in an effort to obtain help or be taken seriously. High scores on Fp may also be obtained from examinees responding randomly or those not attending to item content, in which case VRIN and TRIN would be elevated as well. If Fp is elevated, and VRIN and TRIN are not, then the possibility of malingering should be seriously considered.

Lie (L)

The L scale was a part of the original MMPI and was constructed rationally of items indicating the presence of very minor flaws that most people would be willing to admit. It was designed to detect naive attempts by examinees to present as unrealistically virtuous and without defect. The full L scale was preserved for the MMPI-2.

Although very high scores are strongly indicative of a defensive style that invalidates the profile, more moderate scores may allow for cautious interpretation. Scores in this range are frequently seen in contexts in which examinees are highly motivated to appear healthy and competent, such as child custody evaluations and pre-employment screenings, and do not necessarily indicate a deliberate attempt at dissimulation. The L scale may also be elevated due to a nonacquiescent response style, which can be determined by examining the TRIN scale.

Correction (K)

The K scale was a part of the original MMPI, and is fully preserved on the MMPI-2. It was derived empirically by comparing the item responses of obviously disturbed psychiatric patients who produced normal profiles with those from individuals in the normative sample who also produced normal profiles. It was hoped that K scale scores would be able to differentiate between mentally ill people who are trying to deny problems and people who are legitimately well, doing so in a manner less obvious than the L scale. The K scale is indeed useful for this purpose, and its interpretation is similar to that of the L scale. High K scale scores indicate an overly defensive response style, and these profiles should not be interpreted. In nonclinical settings, however, moderately elevated K scale scores are quite common if examinees are motivated to appear well, such as in personnel screenings. These scores do not indicate deception, but rather an attempt to make a favorable impression, and the profiles of these individuals should be interpreted with only slight caution. Mild elevations on K can actually indicate better than average psychological adjustment and resilience (McGrath, Sweeney, O'Malley, & Carlton, 1998). A nonacquiescent response bias can contribute to K scale elevations, which can be evaluated through examination of the TRIN scale.

K scale scores have also been used to mathematically "correct" some Clinical Scales for defensiveness, essentially increasing scores on these scales. Subsequent research, however, indicates that this practice does not strengthen their external validity (Clopton, Shanks, & Preng, 1987; Silver & Sines, 1962; Weed & Han, 1992; Wooten, 1984).

Superlative Self-Presentation (S)

Butcher and Han (1995) developed the S scale empirically by contrasting the responses of airline pilot applicants with those of men from the MMPI-2 normative sample. High scores on S indicate that the test has been completed in an overly defensive manner and should not be interpreted. The S scale tends to correlate highly with K. Although S is a newer addition to the Validity Scales and does not have as much research behind it as the others, a recent meta-analytic review (Baer & Miller, 2002) confirmed that S is useful for measuring a fake-good response style.

The MMPI-2 Clinical Scales

The Clinical Scales were the centerpiece of the original MMPI, and they were retained for the MMPI-2 with only minor alterations. They cover the domains of Hypochondriasis, Depression, Hysteria, Psychopathic Deviate, Paranoia, Psychesthenia, Schizophrenia, and Hypomania. Two other scales designed to measure Masculinity–Femininity and Social Introversion are also included in the Clinical Scale profile, although they are now thought of as interest scales, as they do not measure inherently pathological phenomena.

Although these scales were initially created as a diagnostic shortcut in the hope of eliminating the need for lengthy intake procedures, it quickly became apparent that they were insufficient to perform this task. One of the primary problems observed with this approach was that these scales do not adequately discriminate between diagnostic syndromes. Due in large part to item overlap, the Clinical Scales are highly intercorrelated. Furthermore, these scales do not posess the convergent validity with their respective diagnoses necessary for use as stand alone diagnostic instruments. It is likely that the unreliability of the procedures used to establish the diagnoses in the scale construction sample (unstructured interview, projective testing, and an unstandardized mental status exam) contributed to this shortcoming, as did the lack of rigorous refinement through cross-validation. One of the largest problems with the psychodiagnostic approach to using the Clinical Scales alone is the fact that the syndromes they were designed to detect either no longer exist in modern nosology (e.g., psychasthenia) or their meanings have been altered drastically (e.g., hysteria has been separated roughly into conversion disorder and histrionic personality disorder).

Through years of research, however, the construct validity of the Clinical Scales has grown, pushing their utility beyond their original purpose. Most users of the MMPI-2 do not view these scales as necessarily good indicators of modern psychiatric syndromes. Instead, these scales are interpreted in terms of the empirical correlates that have been established for them. As such, a variety of meanings are attached to each scale. To avoid confusion with their original diagnostic labels, the Clinical Scales are often referred to by number instead of name: 1 for Hypochondriasis, 2 for Depression, 3 for Hysteria, 4 for Psychopathic Deviate, 5 for Masculinity–Femininity, 6 for Paranoia, 7 for Psychasthenia, 8 for Schizophrenia, 9 for Hypomania, and 0 for Social Introversion (see Table 14.3).

In addition to basic investigations conducted on single scales, a great deal of research has focused on profile code types. A profile is assessed for its code type by examining the one, two, or three highest Clinical Scale elevations, and is usually referred to by

Table 14.3. Summary of clinical scales.

Scale	Original Label
Scale 1 (Hs)	Hypochondriasis
Scale 2 (D)	Depression
Scale 3 (Hy)	Hysteria
Scale 4 (Pd)	Psychopathic Deviate
Scale 5 (Mf)	Masculinity/Femininity
Scale 6 (Pa)	Paranoia
Scale 7 (Pt)	Psychasthenia
Scale 8 (Sc)	Schizophrenia
Scale 9 (Ma)	Hypomania
Scale 0 (Si)	Social Introversion

number for shorthand. A person whose two highest Clinical Scale elevations occur on the Depression and Psychasthenia scales would be said to have a 2–7 code type, for example. A variety of code types have been examined for their empirical correlates. A responsible review of this research is necessarily lengthy and complex, and thus beyond the scope of this chapter. Instead, an overview of each of the Clinical Scales, and the interest scales 5 and 0, will be presented. All of the information concerning scale reliability references the MMPI-2 normative sample, the breakdown of which can be found in greater detail in the test's manual (Butcher et al., 2001). Readers desiring a more comprehensive understanding of interpetive strategies for these scales are referred to the books *MMPI-2: A practitioner's guide* (Butcher, 2006) and *MMPI-2: Assessing Personality and Psychopathology*, 4th edition (Graham, 2006).

Scale 1: Hypochondriasis (Hs)

This scale was initially designed to detect symptoms of pathological preoccupation with bodily function and illness. It is the most homogeneous of the Clinical Scales, both factorally and in terms of item content. Its internal consistency and 1-week retest reliability in the MMPI-2 normative sample are both adequate. Items represent complaints of physical symptoms that may be either vague or specific, as well as denial of good health. High scores are usually obtained by examinees diagnosed with somatization disorder or conversion disorder. Caution should be exercised when interpreting this scale, however, as medical patients with legitimate physiological problems, those having suffered a mild traumatic brain injury, chronic pain patients, and older people may also obtain slightly elevated scores that do not reflect psychological maladjustment.

Scale 1 has been associated with a number of personality traits. The thinking of individuals with high scores tends to be colored by pessimism. High scorers are viewed by others as lethargic, whiny, and interested primarily in their own problems. These problems are typically long-standing, and they may see no hope of resolving them. As such, they are prone to negative affect, and if they present for psychological treatment it is usually for this reason. They are, however, poor candidates for traditional psychotherapy. Their negativism tends to make them critical and dismissive of advice, even though they are very demanding of sympathy, and they may terminate therapy prematurely if it is suggested that their physical symptoms might have a psychological basis.

Scale 2: Depression (D)

Scale 2 measures a variety of traits and symptoms associated with depression. These include sadness, anhedonia, fatigue, difficulty concentrating, psychomotor retardation, physical discomfort, and suicidality. High scorers may also suffer from symptoms of anxiety, such as guilt, agitation, muscle tension, and fearfulness. These people experience a great deal of distress. Scale 2 displayed moderately low internal consistency in the MMPI-2 normative sample, although its 1-week retest reliability was good.

One of the most prominent features of high scorers is hopelessness. These people give up easily when they encounter difficulties, and are prone to feeling overwhelmed. High scorers are disengaged from important domains of living, and are typically withdrawn from others. Because of the intensity of their emotional discomfort, they are generally motivated for treatment, and tend to achieve positive results.

Scale 3: Hysteria (Hy)

This scale was originally meant to detect the presence of classical conversion symptoms, which are characterized by the disruption or loss of bodily function as the result of a psychological cause. It is factorally complex. Most of the items deal with vague physical complaints, while others represent naivete and denial of psychological problems. The internal consistency of Scale 3 is low, and its retest reliability is moderately low. Cautions similar to those advised for interpreting Scale 1 should be observed for this scale, as patients with legitimate medical problems may obtain slightly elevated scores in the absence of clinically significant psychopathology.

Those who score high on Scale 3 tend to react to stress with physical symptoms. These symptoms are often associated with secondary gain, such that they are reinforced by the avoidance of responsibility and the sympathy and attention of others. High scorers have a strong need for attention, and typically have an active social life. Their relationships, however, tend to be one-sided and immature. They may use their symptoms to manipulate others, but seem to have little awareness of doing so. Although high scorers are easily disappointed if their needs for attention go unfulfilled, they tend to either suppress their resentment or express it passively. Their excessive use of somatization is usually sufficient to avoid severe psychological discomfort, so they tend not to report much subjective distress, aside from possibly feeling tired. The prognosis for psychotherapy with these patients is similar to that of those scoring high on Scale 1. They respond positively to sympathy and attention, although any sort of psychological interpretation of their symptoms is likely to be met with resistance. Lasting gains in traditional short-term therapy are unlikely.

Scale 4: Psychopathic Deviate (Pd)

Scale 4 was created by contrasting the item responses of individuals with histories of delinquent behavior (lying, petty theft, excessive use of alcohol, etc.) with those of the MMPI normative sample. No effort was made to include those who had committed serious legal offenses. Items reflect a variety of problems, including dissatisfaction with life, a difficult home environment, youth conduct offenses, resentment of authority, and lack of social anxiety. The internal consistency of Scale 4 was low in the MMPI-2 normative sample, and its retest reliability ranged from good (for men) to low (for women). It should also be noted that certain minority groups, particularly African-Americans and Hispanics, tend to score slightly higher on this scale than do Caucasians, even though there is no external evidence of differences in antisocial personality traits.

High scorers exhibit chronic social maladjustment. Although they may appear confident and tend to make good first impressions, their relationships lack depth. Many seem unable to establish close bonds with others, and, in fact, frequently manipulate people consciously for their own gain. They tend not to experience much guilt for this behavior, and they externalize blame excessively. High scores on this scale are also associated with difficulty profiting from negative or punishing experiences. As such, patterns of irresponsible behavior tend to continue regardless of their personally harmful consequences. Dissatisfaction with this lifestyle may be expressed, but its effect on future behavior tends to be minimal. Due to their impulsivity and remorseless manipuation of others, conflict with authority and family members is common. Substance abuse is also frequent within this population. As scores increase, aggression and criminality become more likely. The prognosis for psychotherapy with these individuals is poor. The negative affect they experience tends to be associated with situational stressors, the sources of which are externalized to other people or situations beyond their control. As a result, their motivation for change is generally low.

Scale 5: Masculinity–Femininity (Mf)

The development of Scale 5 began with the intent of differentiating homosexual men from heterosexual men. Only a handful of items, however, were found to be useful for this purpose. The focus of the scale's construction was then shifted to differentiating men from women, and it became a scale of masculine and feminine interests. Items mostly deal with activities and preferences stereotypically associated with one gender or the other. Its internal consistency is low for men, and quite low for women, although retest reliability is adequate for both. In addition, higher scores for men are moderately associated with educational attainment, as are lower scores for women, though only modestly so.

High scores on Scale 5 indicate a preference for activities and attitudes typically associated with the opposite gender. Men scoring high on this scale tend to eschew more masculine interests in favor of aesthetic values, and are more willing to participate in child-rearing and domestic activities. Women who score high on this scale, on the other hand, reject the stereotypically feminine gender role, and prefer sports and other hobbies usually associated with men. They are also seen as more competitive and assertive than most women. Low scores on this scale are meaningful as well. For both genders, they indicate adherence to traditional sex roles. There is little evidence that Scale 5 measures any aspect of psychopathology or response to treatment.

Scale 6: Paranoia (Pa)

Given that the initial criterion sample for this scale was experiencing paranoid symptoms so severe that they necessitated hospitalization, many of the items on this scale are frankly psychotic in nature. They cover such topics as delusions of persecution and grandeur, as well as ideas of reference. It is possible, however, to obtain an elevated score without endorsing any of these items. More neurotic range content includes emotional sensitivity, suspicion of the motives of others, dissatisfaction with life, and idealistic denial of cynical attitudes. Given the broad range of item content, it is not surprising that the internal consistency of Scale 6 is quite poor, and its retest reliability is low as well. Although it is relatively insensitive to more moderate range symptoms, it is a highly specific indicator of paranoia when it is elevated (Graham, 2006). At severe elevations, diagnoses of schizophrenia and paranoid disorders are common.

Moderately high scores are more indicative of a paranoid relational schema than they are of a psychotic disturbance. Examinees scoring in this range tend to interpret innocuous interpersonal stimuli as threatening or personally insulting. These people tend to react with anger to perceived slights and to harbor grudges. Chronic social maladjustment is to be expected. Others view them as guarded and suspicious. High scorers rigidly cling to moralistic opinions about themselves and others, and may look at those around them with contempt. Examinees with elevated Scale 6 scores may seek treatment for depression or anxiety, but their prognosis is poor. Such clients are extremely defended, intellectualizing and blaming others for their problems, and they may be unable to establish an effective therapeutic relationship.

Scale 7: Psychasthenia (Pt)

Psychasthenia is most closely related to the modern diagnosis of obsessive compulsive disorder. Patients diagnosed with psychasthenia expressed anxious preoccupation with multiple fears and insecurities, and often engaged in ritualized acts designed to alleviate anxiety. The item content of this scale revolves around emotional turmoil and self-doubt. The internal consistency of Scale 7 is good, although its retest reliability is slightly low, perhaps as a result of fluctuating anxiety levels over time.

As scores on this scale increase, examinees experience greater degrees of emotional discomfort. Anxiety is prominent, and may manifest in agitation, worry, fear, difficulty concentrating, fatigue, insomnia, and tearfulness. Physical symptoms are also common, and include tachycardia, sweating, trembling, stomach aches, headaches, and dizziness. High scorers may engage in compulsive rituals in order to relieve anxiety. The thinking of these people tends to be rigid, obsessively ruminative, and colored by catastrophizing. They hold themselves to very high standards, and are intropunitive when they inevitably fail to meet them. Although moderately high scorers are methodical, organized, and reliable, they may be highly reactive to stress. These people are typically socially anxious and shy around others. Those around them are likely to view them with sympathy, but the rigidity of their interpersonal style hinders their ability to establish long-term, reciprocal relationships. Those who obtain elevated Scale 7 scores should be expected to make gains in therapy due to their strong motivation to relieve their symptoms, but these gains tend to be slow. They fear change, and have difficulty tolerating ambiguity.

Scale 8: Schizophrenia (Sc)

Scale 8 measures a variety of symptoms associated with schizophrenia. These include hallucinations, delusions, alienation from self and others, disturbed thinking, fearfulness, and dissatisfaction with life.

Very high scores on this scale are strongly suggestive of the presence of a psychotic disorder. Examinees obtaining such scores are typically confused, have difficulty thinking clearly, and may be displaying both positive and negative symptoms of schizophrenia. The internal consistency of Scale 8 is good, although its retest reliability is slightly low for men and particularly poor for women. Caution should be exercised when interpeting this scale for college students and for some ethnic minorities, as these groups tend to score slightly higher than average. Also, due to the presence of items reflecting aberrant sensory experiences and cognitive deficits, some patients with neurological impairments may return elevated scores that do not indicate a psychotic disturbance. Examinees who are experiencing severe emotional turmoil at the time of the evaluation may also obtain elevated scores.

Moderately high scores may be obtained by individuals who are not actively psychotic, although they may have odd beliefs that are not necessarily delusional in nature. These people tend to report feeling alienated and different from others, and they usually have poor social skills. Their judgment is also generally poor, and they may act impulsively with little planning or logical forethought. The thinking of some high scorers may be dominated by rumination over perceived failings, insecurities, and issues related to their sexuality. Retreat into fantasy is a common defense. The prognosis for traditional psychotherapy for these people is not good. Problems tend to be long-standing and intractable. In addition, their difficulties in social relations and communication interfere with the therapeutic process. In such cases, psychotropic medication may be prescribed to help control severe symptoms.

Scale 9: Hypomania (Ma)

Scale 9 was designed to differentiate patients who were experiencing a pathologically elevated mood state from Minnesota normals. As scores increase, it is more likely that the examinee is experiencing a manic or hypomanic episode. At extremely high scores, psychotic symptoms, including hallucinations and delusions, may be present. A few of this scale's items are face-valid representations of hypomania (psychomotor acceleration, grandiosity, rapidity of thought and speech, etc.), but most of them appear to be only tangentially related to the construct. Some of these items reflect acceptance of antisocial values, symptoms of dissociation, and attitudes related to the family. Given the heterogeneity of its item composition, it is not surprising that Scale

9 has low internal consistency. Its retest reliability is acceptable for men, although it is low for women. Similar to Scale 8, younger people and some ethnic minorities tend to score slightly higher than average.

Individuals with moderate elevations may not meet full criteria for a mood disturbance, although several traits are notable. These people are filled with energy, so much so that they may find it difficult to contain. As a result, their actions tend to be impulsive and erratic. They may pursue several goals simultaneously and with gusto, but they rarely bring any long-term project to fruition. Social relations are pursued with equal fervor, and high scorers tend to make good first impressions with their spontaneity and creativity. Their involvement in these relationships, however, tends to be as superficial and transient as their investment in anything else. Some of these individuals may also manipulate others for their own ends. In addition, the mood of high scorers can be very reactive, shifting unpredictably from joy to nervous aggitation to explosive anger. Difficulties with family members, substance abuse, and the legal system are common. They do not make good candidates for psychotherapy, as their impulsivity prevents them from focusing consistently on productive therapeutic activities and tends to make their attendance to sessions irregular.

Scale 0: Social Introversion (Si)

This scale was originally added to the MMPI by Drake in 1946. It was constructed by contrasting the responses of women who scored high on the Minnesota T-S-E Social Introversion–Extroversion scale with women who scored low. Because introversion is not a pathological syndrome, Scale 0 is not technically considered a Clinical Scale, although it appears in the Clinical Scale profile. It has good internal consistency and excellent retest reliability for both men and women.

High scorers tend to be shy and reserved in social situations. They may be excessively self-conscious and feel nervous in the presence of others. These people are generally responsible, but their cautiousness and indecisiveness lead them to limit the number of novel experiences to which they are willing to expose themselves. Periodic episodes of anxiety or depression may cause them to seek treatment. Their reticence, however, makes it difficult to establish a therapeutic relationship with them. Low scorers, on the other hand, display an opposite cluster of traits. They feel at ease in social situations and may be well liked by others. These people are generally articulate, energetic, and competitive.

Content Interpetation of the MMPI-2

Objective personality assessment with the MMPI-2 is often viewed as process of direct communication between the person being assessed and the assessing clinician (Butcher et al., 2001). Examinees' responses can be interpreted as a face-valid report of how they view their problems. In order for the interpretation of item content to be useful, however, the examinee must have access to the information being requested and be able to report it accurately. Thus content scales typically cover a range of concrete matters related to examinees' direct experience, such as their subjective distress and history of legal infractions. Provided that clients are motivated to share this information, they can be excellent reporters of their own mental health problems.

Limitations of Content Interpretation

Despite the elegance and relative simplicity of content interpretation, such a perspective was initially shunned by the creators of the original MMPI (Hathaway & McKinley, 1940). When the test emerged and began to gain acceptance during the early 1940s, there was a clear admonition against considering item responses as personal communication. The traditional position developed by Hathaway and Meehl held that self-report of symptoms could not be trusted or accepted at face value (Meehl, 1945). These authors believed that the content of the items endorsed was irrelevant. All that mattered, they maintained, were the empirical correlates associated with patterns of item endorsement. Although a thorough analysis of Hathaway and Meehl's perspective on empirical versus rational scale interpretation is beyond the scope of this chapter, two of their points are particularly important and remain relevant to practitioners using the MMPI-2.

First, it should be understood that scores on personality inventories can be distorted by clients who are motivated to deceive the examiner or otherwise influence the outcome of the assessment. In order for personality inventories to be interpreted, it must be assumed that the examinee responded candidly. This assumption is particularly violable when interpreting face-valid content. Because items are assumed to measure what they appear to measure, this transparency in the assessment process may be used by some clients to manipulate the results. Lack of cooperation, therefore, is an important source of error to consider when interpreting scale content. Attempts to influence test results in this manner should be anticipated in some settings, such as forensic evaluations or personnel screening, in which individuals are highly motivated to present themselves in a certain manner. Even in help-seeking situations, clients may distort their responses. They may fear the consequences of divulging too much about themselves or may exaggerate their difficulties as a cry for help. Thus it is important for the practitioner to ensure that the examinee has responded to the test in a forthright manner. Validity indicators should be evaluated carefully to determine the extent of the client's cooperation with the evaluation.

Second, the information obtained from personality inventories is limited to what the client is able to provide. Clients may not know or have the capacity to recall accurately all of the information needed for the assessment. Thus error may be introduced not only due to lack of cooperation, but also through lack of awareness. Examinees' opinions about their functioning may not accurately reflect their actual functioning. For example, lack of insight is a defining characteristic of personality disorders (DSM-IV-TR; American Psychiatric Association, 2000). Given this potential for error, scores on content scales, as with all test data, must be interpreted in the context of the entire evaluation, including outside sources of information. If a client fails to obtain an elevated score on a content scale, it should not be taken for granted that the client does not have problems related to that content dimension.

Advantages of Content Interpretation

As research in objective personality assessment has continued to grow, content interpretation has come to be embraced. There are clear advantages to using homogeneous content scales in clinical assessment. One of the most important advantages is that these rationally constructed scales tend to have stronger psychometric properties than their empirically derived counterparts. The empirical keying process used to create the Clinical Scale of the MMPI, for example, led to the inclusion of items that seem to be unrelated to the construct in question, but that were useful for differentiating between populations in the scale construction sample. These items, however, actually tend to dilute the psychometric efficiency of the scales when applied to other samples. Scales constructed rationally based on their content do not suffer from this weakness. Second, by virtue of their homogeneity, content-based scales are easier to interpret. Interpretation of broad, multifaceted scales is necessarily more complex due to the variety of distinct patterns of item endorsement that may lead to scale elevations.

The advantages of content interpretation also extend to some of the more practical aspects related to working with clients. Examinees' responses to such scales can be viewed as a means of direct communication by clients to the examiner. In that sense, clinicians are able to assess not only their clients' functioning, but also their insight regarding their functioning. Behavioral data from outside sources may be synthesized with the score report in order to compare clients' history of recent problems with their perceptions of these problems. Finally, a related advantage is that scores on a particular content scale represent the extent to which the clients have shared concerns about particular difficulties with the practitioner. This information may be valuable in settings in which test feedback will be provided to clients and can be used to facilitate empathy (see Butcher, 1990; Finn & Butcher, 1990; and Finn & Tonsager, 1992).

Although certain limitations do exist to this approach, the consensus among users of the MMPI-2 seems to be that the benefits of content interpretation outweigh its risks. Several approaches are used with the MMPI-2 to assess the content of client responses, including the Harris–Lingoes Subscales, the MMPI-2 content scales, and critical items lists.

Harris–Lingoes Subscales

The traditional empirical approach used to construct the MMPI Clinical Scales assumed that answers to test items represent signs of problems, as opposed to symptoms in and of themselves. The scales' creators believed that the way in which an item is endorsed, not its content, is the most important factor in the prediction of behavior. An empirically derived scale, so they believed, has meaning only with respect to the empirical relationships that have been established for it, regardless of its makeup.

The empirical keying process used to create the Clinical Scales resulted in scales composed of a variety of heterogeneous items. Because of this heterogeneity, the same elevation on a particular Clinical Scale can be obtained by clients endorsing markedly different patterns of symptoms. For example, a client who is reporting a large number of physical complaints without depressed mood can obtain a similar score on Scale 2 to a different client who is reporting depressed mood without any physical complaints. In an effort to disambiguate this interpretive quandary related to the Clinical Scales, Harris and Lingoes (1955) developed sets of content-homogeneous subscales composed of the items from several of the Clinical Scales. They reasoned that MMPI

Clinical Scale elevations could be better understood if they could be evaluated in terms of their constituent components. The authors rationally divided the items of several of the factorially complex Clinical Scales (Depression, Hysteria, Psychopathic Deviate, Paranoia, Schizophrenia, and Mania) into subgroups. They did not consider it necessary to construct subscales for the Hypochondriasis and Psychasthenia scales, which were considered to have more homogeneous item content.

The Harris–Lingoes Subscales can provide a very useful means of understanding elevations on the Clinical Scales. For example, a clinically significant elevation on the Psychopathic Deviate scale would be interpreted by simply applying the personality descriptors for that scale that have been established as empirical correlates. Of course, not all of the descriptors would apply for any given person. Such descriptors are simply the correlates that have been established for groups of individuals with prominent Scale 4 elevations. Reporting all of them for a given person would lead to a rather vague analysis at best, and a misleading analysis at worst. The person could be described as callous, antisocial, resentful of authority, underachieving, selfish, and manipulative, as well as having poor impulse control, a chronically conflictual interpersonal style, and a possible substance abuse problem (Graham, 2006). If, however, the subscales of Scale 4 are examined, and it is found that the individual returned a very high score on the Familial Discord (Pd1) subscale, with relatively low scores on the other subscales, the interpretation of this person's profile would be quite different. The person could be described as extremely dissatisfied with her or his home life, but other more pejorative descriptions, such as the ones listed above, would not be reported.

Although the Harris–Lingoes Subscales can be a useful tool for refining interpretation of the Clinical Scales, it is important to remember that they only have meaning in the context of their parent scale. That is, Pd1 should not be considered an index of family problems independent of its contribution to the Psychopathic Deviate construct. Other family problems, and indeed other items on the MMPI-2 tapping into these kinds of problems, exist independent of what is measured on this scale. Thus a high score on this scale does not indicate global impairment in family functioning, any more than a low score would indicate good family functioning. Consequently, many practitioners do not interpret subscale elevations unless the parent scale is elevated in the clinically significant range.

In addition, some of the Harris–Lingoes scales are quite short (some as small as six items) and thus are not considered sufficiently reliable for psychometric prediction by themselves. Table 14.4 contains a list of the Harris–Lingoes Subscales, classified under each of their parent scales.

MMPI-2 Content Scales

The MMPI-2 content scales (Butcher et al., 1990) were designed to assess the major content dimensions found within the MMPI-2 item pool. The process of their construction was largely based on strategies used by Wiggins (1966) in developing the content scales of the original MMPI. The item pools for the scales were derived by rationally selecting and categorizing items from the experimental version of the MMPI-2, MMPI form AX. These item groups were then refined statistically within several normal and clinical

Table 14.4. Summary of Harris–Lingoes Subscales.

Clinical Scale	Subscales
Scale 2	Subjective Depression (D1) Psychomotor Retardation (D2) Physical Malfunctioning (D3) Mental Dullness (D4) Brooding (D5)
Scale 3	Denial of Social Anxiety (Hy1) Need for Affection (Hy2) Lassitude-Malaise (Hy3) Somatic Complaints (Hy 4) Inhibition of Aggression (Hy5)
Scale 4	Familial Discord (Pd1) Authority Problems (Pd2) Social Imperturbability (Pd3) Social Alienation (Pd4) Self-Alienation (Pd5)
Scale 6	Persecutory Ideas (Pa1) Poignancy (Pa2) Naiveté (Pa3)
Scale 8	Social Alienation (Sc1) Emotional Alienation (Sc2) Lack of Ego Mastery, Cognitive (Sc3) Lack of Ego Mastery, Conative (Sc4) Lack of Ego Mastery, Defective Inhibition (Sc5) Bizarre Sensory Experiences (Sc6)
Scale 9	Amorality (Ma1) Psychomotor Acceleration (Ma2) Imperturbability (Ma3) Ego Inflation (Ma4)

samples. This process yielded 15 distinct scales possessing good internal consistency and test–retest reliability.

A variety of empirical investigations have demonstrated the validity of the content scales beyond the Clinical Scales. The MMPI-2 content scales of Depression, Antisocial Practices, Anxiety, and Negative Treatment Indicators, for example, appear to be better predictors of treatment outcome than the original Clinical Scales (Chisolm, Crowther, & Ben-Porath, 1997). Ben-Porath, Butcher, and Graham (1991) also found that the content scales outperform the Clinical Scales in discriminating schizophrenics from depressed inpatients. Munley, Busby, and Jaynes (1997) obtained similar results, reporting that the Depression and Bizarre Mentation content scales more effectively distinguished depressed inpatients from schizophrenic inpatients in their sample than did Clinical Scales 2 and 8.

An exhaustive discussion of the incremental validity of the content scales over the Clinical Scales is beyond the scope of this chapter, but some of the research on the Depression content scale can serve as an example. Faull and Meyer (1993) found that this content scale outperformed Clinical Scale 2 in the assessment of subjective depression in a group of primary medical patients. The Depression scale has also been shown to have higher internal consistency and greater convergent validity with respect to other measures of depression than Clinical Scale 2 (Faull & Meyer, 1993). The Depression content scale is also more strongly related to specifc measures of depressive symptoms, such as hopelessness, low self-esteem, and suicidal ideation, than is Clinical Scale 2 (Boone, 1994).

Although the content scales were originally developed to be unidimensional, Ben-Porath and Sherwood (1996) were able to further divide some of these scales into meaningful content component scales. They suggested that the relative elevations on these component scales could provide the clinician with additional information regarding content scale elevations, similar to the way the Harris–Lingoes Subscales serve to clarify elevations on the Clinical Scales. Each of the content scales (summarized in Table 14.5) is briefly described below, in addition to any component scales when present, following the interpretive strategies of Butcher et al. (1990). Readers interested in a more detailed description of the content scales and their use are referred to Butcher's (2006) MMPI-2 interpretive text.

Table 14.5. Summary of content scales.

Content Scale	Subscales
Anxiety (ANX)	None
Fears (FRS)	FRS1: Generalized Fears
	FRS2: Multiple Fears
Obsessiveness (OBS)	None
Depression (DEP)	DEP1: Lack of Drive
	DEP2: Dysphoria
	DEP3: Self-Depreciation
	DEP4: Suicidal Ideation
Health Concerns (HEA)	HEA1: Gastrointestinal Symptoms
	HEA2: Neurological Symptoms
Bizarre Mentation (BIZ):	BIZ1: Psychotic Symptomology
	BIZ2: Schizotypal Characteristics
Anger (ANG)	ANG1: Explosive Behavior
	ANG2: Irritability
Cynicism (CYN)	CYN1: Misanthropic Beliefs
	CYN2: Interpersonal Suspiciousness
Antisocial Practices (ASP)	ASP1: Antisocial Attitudes
	ASP2: Antisocial Behavior
Type A Behavior (TPA)	TPA1: Impatience
	TPA2: Competitive Drive
Low Self-Esteem (LSE)	LSE1: Self-Doubt
	LSE2: Submissiveness
Social Discomfort (SOD)	SOD1: Introversion
	SOD2: Shyness
Family Problems (FAM)	FAM1: Family Discord
	FAM2: Familial Alienation
Work Interference (WRK)	None
Negative Treatment Indicators (TRT)	TRT1: Low Motivation
	TRT2: Inability to Disclose

ANXIETY (ANX)

The ANX scale contains 23 items assessing symptoms of generalized anxiety. Individuals who score high on ANX are those experiencing symptoms of anxiety that include bodily sensations, such as tension, heart palpitations, and shortness of breath, as well as excessive worry, difficulty concentrating, and insomnia. Extremely high scorers may feel overwhelmed, think of committing suicide, fear that they are losing their mind, and have difficulty making even minor decisions. ANX does not have any component scales.

FEARS (FRS)

The FRS scale contains 23 items assessing very specific fears or phobic behaviors. High scorers report being afraid of a variety of objects and situations. These fears range from those that are common, such as being afraid of certain animals or high places, to those that are more rare or unusual, such as being indoors. FRS has two component scales: Generalized Fearfulness (FRS1) and Multiple Fears (FRS2).

OBSESSIVENESS (OBS)

The OBS scale contains 16 items focusing on maladaptive rumination and obsessive thinking. Clients who score high on OBS have extreme difficulty making decisions and report that they worry excessively, which may cause others to become impatient with them. They tend to fear change, and their attitudes are rigid. Extremely high scorers also report engaging in compulsive behaviors such as counting or hoarding, and these behaviors may interfere with daily functioning. OBS has no component scales.

DEPRESSION (DEP)

The DEP scale contains 33 items that measure symptoms of depression. These symptoms include low mood, anhedonia, fatigue, hopelessness, guilt, insomnia, loneliness, lack of confidence, and tearfulness. High scorers feel empty and may experience suicidal ideation. They may believe that they are condemned or have committed unpardonable sins, and view their family and friends as unsupportive. DEP has four component scales that measure Lack of Drive (DEP1), Dysphoria (DEP2), Self-Depreciation (DEP3), and Suicidal Ideation (DEP4).

HEALTH CONCERNS (HEA)

The HEA scale contains 36 items that measure worry about one's physical health and bodily dysfunction. Individuals with high scores on HEA report numerous physical symptoms across multiple body systems. They worry about their health a great deal and tend to feel unwell more often than do most people. These clients also have poor coping skills and typically present as somewhat dysphoric. They are frequently diagnosed with depressive disorders. Keller and Butcher (1991) found the HEA scale to be one of the most powerful discriminators between chronic pain patients and clients with other problems. The component scales of HEA include Gastrointestinal Symptoms (HEA1), Neurological Symptoms (HEA2), and General Health Concerns (HEA3).

BIZARRE MENTATION (BIZ)

The BIZ scale is made up of 24 items that reflect severe symptoms of formal thought disorder. Individuals who score high on this scale report symptoms of psychosis, such as auditory, visual, or olfactory hallucinations. They feel that their own thoughts are strange and peculiar. Delusions of persecution or grandeur may also be present, and these individuals may have a history of suicide attempts or substance abuse as well. They are frequently assigned diagnoses of psychotic disorders. The two component scales of BIZ are Psychotic Symptomology (BIZ1) and Schizotypal Characteristics (BIZ2).

ANGER (ANG)

The ANG scale is made up of 16 items. High scorers feel angry more frequently than do most people, and experience it in an extreme and poorly modulated fashion. Their difficulty maintaining their composure, combined with a high sensitivity to criticism, can sometimes lead to verbal outbursts, destruction of property, or physical assault. Clark (1993) found that patients in a Veterans Administration chronic pain program who had high scores on ANG showed frequent and intense anger, felt unfairly treated by others, felt frustrated, were hypersensitive to criticism, were quick-tempered, tended to externalize their problems, had tenuous anger control, and were impulsive. ANG has two component scales: Explosive Behavior (ANG1) and Irritability (ANG2).

CYNICISM (CYN)

The CYN scale contains 23 items related to the basic untrustworthiness of others. High scorers report that other people generally use one another and are only friendly for selfish reasons. Although they may be hostile and demanding of others, they resent even the slightest demands placed on them. The two component scales of CYN are Misanthropic Beliefs (CYN1) and Interpersonal Suspiciousness (CYN2).

ANTISOCIAL PRACTICES (ASP)

The 22-item ASP scale measures psychopathic attitudes and behaviors. High scorers hold misanthropic beliefs similar to those measured by CYN, but are also more likely to act in ways consistent with those beliefs, manipulating others for their own ends. A history of legal problems, absence of close interpersonal relationships, and substance abuse are common. These clients tend to be self-centered, aggressive, and resentful of authority. Egeland, Erickson, Butcher, and Ben-Porath (1991) reported that ASP scores were also associated with women who had been identified as potential child abusers. The ASP scale is significantly related to antisocial personality and behavior (Lilienfeld, 1996) as defined in DSM-III-R. ASP's two component scales, Antisocial Attitudes (ASP1) and Antisocial Behaviors (ASP2), make an important distinction between clients who merely approve of the above actions and beliefs, and those who actually engage in them.

TYPE A (TPA)

The TPA scale contains 19 items that reflect a combination of driven, competitive, and hostile personality traits. High scorers view themselves as fast-moving, work-oriented, and perfectionistic. They indicate that there is never enough time in the day for them to complete their tasks, even though they may work very efficiently. Others, however, view them as high-strung, aggressive, overbearing, and petty over minor details. They have little frustration tolerance, are easily annoyed, and may lash out verbally at others. This constellation of personality traits is associated with increased risk for cardiovascular disease. TPA has two component scales: Impatience (TPA1) and Competitive Drive (TPA2).

LOW SELF-ESTEEM (LSE)

The LSE scale contains 24 items that address negative self-referential beliefs. High scorers believe that they are not liked by other people and feel unimportant. They appraise themselves as unattractive, awkward, useless, and a burden to others. They lack self-confidence, have difficulty making decisions, and find it hard to accept compliments. Others tend to see these people as passive and lacking in initiative. LSE tends to have high internal consistency and is strongly related to external measures of self-esteem (Brems & Lloyd, 1995). It is composed of the Self-Doubt (LSE1) and Submissiveness (LSE2) component scales.

SOCIAL DISCOMFORT (SOD)

The SOD scale includes 24 items that indicate uneasiness in social situations. Individuals who score high on this scale tend to be very uncomfortable around others and express a preference for being alone. They may have poor social skills, suffer from social anxiety, and be especially sensitive to shame and embarrassment. In clinical settings, they are frequently diagnosed with a depressive disorder. The component scales of SOD are Introversion (SOD1) and Shyness (SOD2). Although seemingly similar, SOD1 measures the examinee's preference for spending time alone, whereas SOD2 measures his or her feelings of discomfort in the presence of others.

FAMILY PROBLEMS (FAM)

The FAM scale contains 25 items that focus on family relationship problems. High scorers report considerable discord in their home life. They describe their families as lacking in love and support, quarrelsome, and generally unpleasant. Some may report hating members of their family. They indicate that their childhood was marked by abusive relationships, that their past intimate relationships were troubled, and that their relationships have generally been unhappy and lacking in affection. In clinical settings, they are often assigned diagnoses of depressive disorders. Hjemboe and Butcher (1991) found that the FAM scale significantly discriminated couples who were experiencing marital distress from non-distressed couples. The component scales of FAM are broken down into Familial Discord (FAM1), indicating the presence of active hostility within the family, and Familial Alienation (FAM2), a perceived lack of love and support from one's family.

WORK INTERFERENCE (WRK)

The WRK scale contains 33 items that address problems that may impair school or job performance. High WRK scorers are likely to report negative attitudes toward their profession, lack of family support for their career choice, questioning their career choice, and negative attitudes toward coworkers. Some items reflect the presence of personal problems that hinder their ability to work effectively, including feelings of failure, concentration difficulties, lack of drive, tension, and indecision. High scorers are frequently given depressive disorder diagnoses. Ben-Porath and Stafford (1993) reported that prison inmates who scored high on this scale had difficulty maintaining employment and had sporadic and unstable work histories. The WRK scale is also associated with poor performance as assessed by a measure of productive persistence (Quereshi & Kleman, 1996). WRK contains no component scales.

NEGATIVE TREATMENT INDICATORS (TRT)

The TRT scale contains 26 items that reflect examinees' doubts about their ability to accept help or to changing their behavior. Individuals who score high on TRT possess negative attitudes toward doctors and mental health treatment. They do not feel that others can understand them or help them with their difficulties, and they are not comfortable discussing personal problems. They may not want to change their behavior, or they feel that they are unable to do so. High scorers may be experiencing a great deal of emotional distress, as well as suicidal ideation. If they do participate in treatment, they are likely to terminate services prematurely. This scale contains two components, Low Motivation (TRT1) and Inability to Disclose (TRT2).

Critical Items

Several sets of critical items have been developed out of the MMPI item pool for use as indicators of specific problems. The first set was introduced by Grayson (1951), who published a list of rationally developed critical items designed to screen for serious psychopathology. Although this set of items failed to adequately distinguish between examinees in crisis and those who were not (Koss, Butcher, & Hoffman, 1976), their use nevertheless became popular. In order to improve on the early work of Grayson, two other sets of critical items were developed for the original MMPI using more empirically based procedures: the Koss–Butcher Critical Items (Koss & Butcher, 1973) and the Lachar–Wrobel Critical Items (Lachar & Wrobel, 1979).

Koss and Butcher's (1973) critical items were selected rationally, and were intended to distinguish between the presenting problems of examinees seeking admission to an inpatient psychiatric facility. It was found that these items were able to differentiate between six different patient groups, which were labeled Acute Anxiety State, Depressed Suicidal Ideation, Threatened Assault, Situational Stress Due to Alcoholism, Mental Confusion, and Persecutory Ideation. Lachar and Wrobel's (1979) investigation of critical items cross-validated several of the Koss–Butcher items and extended the number of content categories by adding items related to Antisocial Attitudes, Family Conflict, Somatic Symptoms, and Sexual Concern and Deviation. Both sets of critical items are currently used with the MMPI-2, although only the Koss–Butcher set was updated after the revision of the original MMPI in 1989.

Critical item responses are best viewed as "red flags" of potentially serious problems that should be discussed with examinees. They are not absolute indicators of severe psychological disturbance. Single true/false items do not possess the reliability necessary to draw such conclusions responsibly. Carelessness, misreading, or mismarking by examinees can result in items being endorsed inadvertently. Critical items, therefore, should be used to help build hypotheses regarding a client's functioning. These hypotheses

should then be tested by gathering data from other sources and by following up critical item responses with clients.

Supplementary and PSY-5 Scales
Supplementary Scales

Throughout the history of the original MMPI, researchers have augmented its traditional scales with newer measures composed of various configurations of existing items. Over 450 of these scales had been created 30 years after its publication (Dahlstrom, Welsh, & Dahlstrom, 1975). The methods used to construct them, and the degrees of success they achieved, varied as much as their purposes. While most of these Supplementary Scales did not make the transition to the MMPI-2, a few were retained for their popularity and utility. The standard score report issued by Pearson Assessments provides scores for 15 of these scales (summarized in Table 14.6). For ease of discussion, they will be grouped in terms of factor scales, scales of personal resources, scales of adjustment, scales of anger, scales of substance abuse, and scales of gender role identification.

FACTOR SCALES

In 1956, Welsh conducted an item-level factor analysis of the Clinical and Validity Scales of the MMPI. The results of his analysis yielded several distinct factors. The first factor was labeled Anxiety (A), and the second factor was labeled Repression (R).

Both A and R were retained for the MMPI-2, with R absent only a few items. In the MMPI-2 normative sample, the internal consistency for A was excellent, while it was low for R. Both have good retest reliability over short time intervals. A is most closely associated with Clinical Scales 7 and 8. As such, high scorers tend to present as anxious, disorganized, and insecure. They appear to be highly attuned to their emotional state, which is generally chaotic. R, however, correlates most strongly with Clinical Scales 1, 2, and 3, as well as Scale 9 negatively. High-scoring examinees may seem dull or lethargic, and they tend to deny experiencing psychological symptoms. Somatization and withdrawal are common defenses, and these people tend to behave passively in social relationships.

SCALES OF PERSONAL RESOURCES

The Ego Strength scale (Es) was created by Barron in 1953, and Dominance (Do) and Social Responsibility (Re) were created by Gough, McClosky, and Meehl in 1951 and 1952, respectively. Es was originally developed to predict positive

Table 14.6. Summary of supplementary scales.

Scale	Brief interpretation
Anxiety (A)	MMPI-2 first factor
Repression (R)	MMPI-2 second factor
Ego Strength (Es)	Good psychological adjustment and resilience
Dominance (Do)	Social facility
Social Responsibility (Re)	Moral conscience and dependability
College Maladjustment (Mt)	Distress among college students
Posttraumatic Stress Disorder (Pk)	Symptoms of traumatic adjustment
Marital Distress (MDS)	Distress among couples
Hostility (Ho)	Angry cynicism
Overcontrolled Hostility (O-H)	Reluctance to express anger
MacAndrew Alcoholism Scale-Revised (MAC-R)	Possible substance abuse
Addiction Acknowledgement Scale (AAS)	Admission of substance abuse
Addiction Potential Scale (APS)	Possible substance abuse
Masculine Gender Role (GM)	Stereotypical masculinity
Feminine Gender Role (GF)	Stereotypical femininity

outcome in psychotherapy. It was created empirically by contrasting the responses of patients judged to have improved in treatment, compared with those who did not. Do and Re were also empirically derived. Research participants were given definitions of the constructs and asked to nominate peers either high or low in each. Item responses from each group were contrasted in order to create the scales.

The internal consistency of Es and Re were both low in the MMPI-2 normative sample, while the internal consistency for Do was good. Retest reliability over a 1-week interval was acceptable for all of these scales. High scores on Es are suggestive of good psychological adjustment. If examinees who obtain elevated scores on this scale are experiencing problems, they are likely to be transient and easily ameliorated. Those who score high on Do exhibit greater than average mastery of social situations. They appear confident, do not suffer from debilitating psychological problems, and may possess other attributes that contribute to good leadership skills. Re scores are associated with examinees' dependability and reliability. High scorers have a strong sense of justice and strive to maintain moral values.

SCALES OF ADJUSTMENT

These scales include College Maladjustment (Mt), Posttraumatic Stress Disorder (PK), and Marital Distress (MDS). Each is designed to measure pathological adjustment to potentially stressful situations. Mt and PK were derived empirically, using methods similar to those discussed above. For Mt, Kleinmuntz (1961) identified a group of maladjusted college students seeking counseling at a university clinic, and contrasted their responses to the MMPI with those of a group of well-adjusted students. PK was constructed by contrasting the responses of Vietnam veterans diagnosed with posttraumatic stress disorder (PTSD) with those who had some other diagnosis (Keane, Malloy, & Fairbank, 1984). The creation of MDS (Hjemboe, Almagor, & Butcher, 1992) was substantially different from the other two. Items were selected for the scale based on their correlation with the Dyadic Adjustment Scale (Spanier, 1976) in a mixed group of distressed and non-distressed couples. Once the initial scale was formed, items were then either removed or added based on both rational and empirical considerations.

The internal consistency for Mt and PK is excellent, whereas it is low for MDS. Short interval retest reliability is also excellent for Mt and PK, and acceptable for MDS. Mt is best viewed as a scale of internalizing symptoms among college students. Little is known about its validity with other populations. PK scores are strongly related to symptoms of PTSD, although this scale is related to general distress as well. High scorers report mixed internalizing symptoms, emotional turmoil, and fear of losing control. MDS appears to be sensitive to marital distress, and is only interpreted in this context. Those who score high on this scale may feel hurt, rejected, angry, or depressed regarding their situation with their partner.

SCALES OF ANGER

Two scales are included in this cluster: Hostility (Ho) and Overcontrolled-Hostility (O-H). Ho was designed by Cook and Medley (1954) to predict the quality of student–teacher interactions based on the personality traits of teachers. The MMPI responses of teachers who scored either high or low on the Minnesota Teacher Aptitude Inventory were compared, and those items endorsed differently that reflected hostility were selected for the scale. The scale does indeed predict difficulty interacting with students. Since its initial publication, its construct validity has been expanded to encompass a broader domain of traits beyond classroom behavior. O-H was developed by Megargee, Cook, and Mendelsohn (1967). The authors believed that especially violent crimes may be committed by those whose anger is overcontrolled—bottled up instead of expressed appropriately. These individuals, while usually passive and meek, may essentially snap under too much provocation and strike out against perceived wrongs in a manner grossly disproportionate to what is actually warranted. With this theory in mind, the authors contrasted the MMPI responses of individuals convicted of violent crimes who displayed a passive interpersonal style with those who did not, creating the O-H scale.

Both the internal consistency and retest reliability of Ho are good. O-H, on the other hand, has exceptionally poor internal consistency, and low retest reliability. Neither of these scales is a good predictor of overt aggression. Instead, they are better thought of as attitude scales. Those who score high on Ho are cynical, tend to look on others with contempt, and are hypersensitive to personal slights. They may also be at an elevated risk for heart disease due to the strain under which they live. Interpretations of O-H should be made with caution due to its low internal consistency, especially when used outside of the population of violent offenders. High scorers may be reluctant to express their anger directly, and may display passive or dependent personality traits.

SCALES OF SUBSTANCE ABUSE

The MMPI-2 has three scales designed to measure drug and alcohol problems—the MacAndrew Alcoholism Scale-Revised (MAC-R), the Addition Acknowledgement Scale (AAS), and the Addiction Potential Scale (APS). The original MacAndrew Alcoholism Scale (MacAndrew, 1965) was derived by contrasting the MMPI responses of people seeking treatment for alcohol dependence with those who were seeking treatment for other psychological conditions. After the deletion and addition of a few items during the restandardization process of the MMPI-2, it was relabled MAC-R. AAS and APS were created by Weed, Butcher, McKenna, and Ben-Porath (1992). AAS was constructed using largely rational procedures, and is composed of only face-valid items that indicate a substance abuse problem. APS was designed to be a more subtle counterpart to AAS. It was derived empirically by contrasting the responses of those with an acknowledged substance abuse problem with the responses of psychiatric inpatients and normals who did not have such problems. Items containing obvious substance abuse content were intentionally removed from the scale.

MAC-R and APS both have poor internal consistency, whereas the internal consistency of AAS is excellent. The retest reliability of MAC-R is slightly low, although it is good for AAS and APS. MAC-R and APS both measure personality traits associated with substance abuse in general, not just alcoholism. Some of these traits include extraversion, risk-taking, cognitive impairment, and aggression. AAS, on the other hand, is a more direct measure of admission of substance abuse problems. It is also associated with antisocial traits and poor judgment. High scores on any of these scales suggest that the examinee may be having difficulty managing his or her use of drugs or alcohol. Chapter 30 deals at length with issues related to assessment of substance abuse with objective inventories.

SCALES OF GENDER ROLE IDENTITIFICATION

This final group of Supplementary Scales contains the Masculine Gender Role (GM) and Feminine Gender Role (GF) scales created by Peterson and Dahlstrom (1992). These scales were developed by contrasting the responses of men and women in the MMPI-2 normative sample. GM items were endorsed by most men and relatively few women, whereas GF items were endorsed by most women and relatively few men.

The internal consistency of GM is adequate, and it is low for GF. Retest reliability ranges from adequate to good (depending on the scale and the gender) for both measures. Research on these scales suggests that, regardless of the gender of the examinee, higher GM scores are associated with better overall psychological adjustment, and higher GF scores are marginally related to anger control problems and substance abuse (Peterson & Dahlstrom, 1992).

Personality Psychopathology Five (PSY-5) Scales

The PSY-5 Scales, discussed more thoroughly in Chapter 9, were introduced by Harkness, McNulty, and Ben-Porath (1995). The authors wished to develop a series of scales that would be useful for characterizing personality pathology dimensionally, instead of categorically. To this end, they assembled a variety of descriptors based on both pathological and normal range personality traits, and asked volunteers to sort them based on their similarity. These data were subjected to statistical analyses, which yielded five major factors. The factors, listed in Table 14.7, were labeled Aggressiveness (AGGR), Psychoticism (PSYC), Disconstraint (DISC), Negative Emotionality/Neuroticism (NEGE), and Low Positive Emotionality/Introversion (INTR).

In order to measure these traits with the MMPI-2 item pool, Harkness et al. used an item selection procedure they referred to as replicated rational selection. The constructs of the PSY-5 were explained to a large number of research participants, and they were asked to nominate MMPI-2 items for each scale. Those that were selected by the majority of participants were combined to form a preliminary scale for each of the constructs. This procedure led to a PSY-5 item pool of nearly half of the items contained within the MMPI-2. Items were then deleted based on both rational and empirical grounds, and the scales were refined using standard scale construction procedures.

In general, the internal consistency of the PSY-5 Scales is good with respect to the MMPI-2 normative sample, and the scales tend to be stable over time (Graham, 2006). They are also moderately intercorrelated, especially Psychoticism and Negative Emotionality. The traits measured by the PSY-5 are similar, but by no means identical, to the traits of the Five-Factor Model of personality (agreeableness, openness to experience, conscientiousness, neuroticism, and extraversion). Instead, they represent aspects of these traits that are exaggerated to a pathological extent. Aggresiveness measures the propensity of examinees to attempt to dominate and to exercise power over others. High scores on Psychoticism reflect the presence of schizotypal traits such as unusual thinking and perception,

alienation, and paranoia. Disconstraint may be interpreted in terms of both high and low scores. High scores indicate impulsivity and a strong need for stimulation, whereas low scores indicate self-control and the ability to modulate frustration. Negative Emotionality and Low Positive Emotionality are conceptually two sides of the same coin. The former indicates the presence of unpleasant affect, and the latter the absence of pleasant affect.

Arnau, Handel, and Archer (2005) have published facet scales for the PSY-5. These scales generally have few items and low internal consistency, however, so it is not recommended that they be used as stand-alone measures. Instead, they may be interpreted in the same fashion as the Harris–Lingoes Subscales are used to clarify the meanings of Clinical Scale scores. Examination of the PSY-5 Facet Scales may help clinicians to understand the reasons for PSY-5 Scale elevations.

Restructured Clinical (RC) Scales

In the past, efforts have been made to alter or supplant the original MMPI Clinical Scales using different construction strategies as a means of improving discrimination in clinical cases or to provide a neater psychometric measure, such as lowering interscale correlations. For example, Rosen (1962) attempted to develop better diagnostic scales than the Clinical Scales by contrasting MMPIs of clearly defined patient groups to other psychiatric cases, rather than to normals as Hathaway and McKinley had originally done. Welsh (1952) attempted to develop more differentiating scales than the clinical scales using factor analysis to obtain more homogeneous item groupings: Scales A and R were the result. In both of these research programs the resulting scales did not improve upon or replace the existing Clinical Scales in assessing psychopathology. In their revision of the MMPI and development of MMPI-2, the MMPI Restandardization Committee (see Butcher et al.,

Table 14.7. Summary of Personality Psychopathology Five Scales.

Scale	Brief interpretation
Aggressiveness (AGGR)	Hostile dominance of others
Psychoticism (PSYC)	Schizotypal traits
Disconstraint (DISC)	Impulsivity and thrill-seeking
Negative Emotionality (NEGE)	Dysphoric affect
Low Positive Emotionality/Introversion (INTR)	Lack of pleasant affect and slow tempo

2001) chose not to alter the original Clinical Scales (except the removal of a few objectionable items) in order to maintain continuity of the MMPI-2 with the original MMPI instrument to preserve the extensive data-based constructs.

In 2003, the Restructured Clinical Scales or RC Scales (Tellegen et al., 2003) were developed to serve as supplemental measures to the original MMPI Clinical Scales. The RC Scales were developed by Tellegen et al. (2003) in order to assess the basic constructs underlying the Clinical Scales but without the item overlap in the Clinical Scales. In addition, the authors wanted to eliminate the so-called subtle items from the scales, that is, items on the Clinical Scales that contained content not obviously related to the constructs. They also hoped to improve convergent and discriminant validity for the revised scales by removing items from each scale that were associated with a construct termed "demoralization," a scale property thought to be inherent in the MMPI-2 symptom scales (resulting from the empirical scale development approach) that resulted in unnecessary overlap of constructs.

The RC Scales were developed as follows: First, the authors constructed a "Demoralization scale" to isolate items that were contained on the eight clinical scales that tended to be influenced by general mal-adjustment. Next, they developed a set of small "seed" scales for the eight clinical scales by removing the demoralization items. Then, the RC core constructs were expanded through obtaining items from the item pool by examining the core's correlation with them. Finally, internal and external validity analyses were conducted on several existing data-bases to further explore the RC Scales' psychometric functioning. The manual published to introduce the scales included analyses of the RC Scales' internal validity and predictive validity with mental health patients from the Portage Path Outpatient Sample (Graham, Ben-Porath, & McNulty, 1999) and two inpatient samples (Arbisi, Ben-Porath, & McNulty, 2003). The RC Scales are listed in Table 14.8.

Despite their recent advent, the RC Scales have already been hotly debated. A special section of the *Journal of Personality Assessment* (Meyer, 2006) was devoted to reviews and commentary on these scales. Critics argue that the RC Scales do not faithfully represent the core of the original Clinical Scales (Butcher, Hamilton, Rouse, & Cumella, 2006; Nichols, 2006), contend that RC constructs are redundant with existing MMPI-2 measures (see Rouse, Greene, Butcher, Nichols, & Williams, 2008, and replies), and express concern that they may be less

Table 14.8. Summary of restructured clinical scales.

Scale	Label
RCd (dem)	Demoralization
RC1 (som)	Somatic Complaints
RC2 (lpe)	Low Positive Emotions
RC3 (cyn)	Cynicism
RC4 (asb)	Antisocial Behavior
RC6 (per)	Ideas of Persecution
RC7 (dne)	Dysfunctional Negative Emotions
RC8 (abx)	Aberrant Experiences
RC9 (hpm)	Hypomanic Activation

sensitive to psychopathology than the Clinical Scales (see Megargee, 2006; Rogers, Sewell, Harrison, & Jordan, 2006; Wallace & Liljequist, 2005). Proponents point to the efficiency and the accumu-lating empirical research on these scales. Fueling the debate is the recent release of an abbreviated form of the MMPI-2, the MMPI-2-RF (Restructured Form), along with a computer interpretation system with the RC Scales at its center. The RC Scales are supple-mented by restructured versions of the Validity and PSY-5 Scales, and a variety of new scales. Clearly, these developments will and should stimulate a great deal of research attention in the coming years.

Other Issues Related to Use of the MMPI-2

Throughout the long history of the MMPI-2, a number of important developments have taken place. A large amount of research has been focused on better understanding personality assessment with ethnic minority and international popula-tions. In addition, a variety of shorter forms have been created in order to maximize the efficiency of administration. This section will highlight some of these developments.

Assessment of Ethnic Minority Clients in the United States

The United States is a multicultural society composed of people from a variety of backgrounds. American psychologists, therefore, should be prepared to provide services to individuals from different cultural backgrounds in a competent manner. With respect to psychological assessment, practitioners must ensure that the instruments they use are reliable and valid for those whose backgrounds differ from the dominant culture (American Psychological Association, 2002; Hays, 2001). A variety of researchers have provided evidence that the MMPI-2 meets this standard, producing scores that are free of cultural bias for a variety of populations (Arbisi, Ben-Porath, & McNulty, 2002; Garrido & Velasquez, 2006; Greene, Robin, Albaugh, Caldwell, & Goldman, 2003; Hall, Bansal, & Lopez, 1999; McNulty, Graham, Ben-Porath, & Stein, 1997). An exhaustive discussion of these efforts is beyond the scope of this chapter; fuller discussion of these issues can be found in Chapters 3 and 20–22. Evidence of the effectiveness of the MMPI-2 in assessing Hispanic populations is provided here as an example of its overall utility for cross-cultural assessment.

In general, the MMPI-2 produces similar findings when comparing Hispanic and Caucasian populations. There are several approaches to providing an appropriate reference population for Hispanics in the United States. The American English-language norms have been shown to be relevant and appropriate for many Hispanic clients (Garrido & Velasquez, 2006), as these norms contain a substantial subpopulation of Hispanic individuals. A meta-analysis by Hall, Bansal, and Lopez (1999) found differences between the MMPI-2 profiles of Hispanics, Caucasians, and African-Americans to be trivial. These norms, therefore, are widely used with Hispanics whether they took the test in English or in Spanish. There are also Hispanic norms for the adolescent population in the United States (Butcher et al., 1998). Well-established Mexican norms (Lucio & Reyes-Lagunes, 1996) are available as well, and can be used to interpret the scores of Mexican-Americans who only speak Spanish.

A recent volume by Butcher, Cabiya, Lucio, and Garrido (2007) provides pertinent background and discussion of these issues in greater depth, as well as practical strategies for assessing Hispanic clients with the MMPI-2 and MMPI-A. This book also provides an extensive bibliography of most of the existing MMPI/MMPI-2/MMPI-A studies that have been published with Spanish-speaking clients, containing nearly 500 citations. It is recommended to readers desiring a more extensive treatment of this subject.

International Adaptations of the MMPI-2

In order for any psychological test to have broad cultural generalizability, its international adaptation must be functionally equivalent to its original form. The constructs underlying the test need to be comparable and describe the same behavioral factors in both cultures. The items must be meticulously translated and verified through back-translation, a process that requires a great deal of time and effort to assure item equivalency (see Butcher & Han, 1996, for a discussion of test adaptation procedures).

With its objective format and vast empirical database, the MMPI-2 has proven to be a valuable means of objectively comparing mental health problems across cultures. The original MMPI underwent approximately 150 different translations beginning in the 1940s, and at present there are 32 available translations of the MMPI-2. International research has shown the original version of the test (Butcher & Pancheri, 1976; Quevedo & Butcher, 2005) and the updated MMPI-2 (Butcher, 1996; Butcher, Cheung, & Lim, 2003; Butcher, Derksen, Sloore, & Sirigatti, 2003; Butcher, Tsai, Coelho, & Nezami, 2006), to have both validity and utility across a variety of cultures.

Abbreviated Versions and Short Forms of the MMPI-2

The MMPI-2 is a comparatively long test, containing 567 items and taking most clients about an hour to an hour and a half to finish. Most clinical, forensic, and personnel psychologists using the test believe that the time spent is justified. They generally want all of the information possible when evaluating examinees, not merely a brief sketch of their personality; thus the full form is typically administered. Several shortened versions of the test, however, have been published. These versions have achieved varying degrees of success in reproducing the data obtained from original MMPI-2 in a more efficient manner.

Abbreviated Administration

The items on the MMPI-2 are arranged so that scores on the traditional validity scales (L, F, and K) and the 10 basic (Clinical) scales can be obtained from administration of only the first 370 items. Doing so is referred to as an abbreviated administration. This type of administration does not, however, allow for the scoring of the MMPI-2 content scales, Restructured Clinical Scales, PSY-5 Scales, and many of the Supplementary Scales, as these scales contain items that appear later in the test. An abbreviated administration also does not allow for a thorough assessment of protocol validity as measured by the newer Validity Scales, VRIN, TRIN, S, Fb, and Fp, which add considerably to the assessment of the client's response style.

MMPI and MMPI-2 Short Forms

A number of past efforts to obtain effective shortened versions of the MMPI and MMPI-2 have been attempted but none have produced the desired results—that is, to shorten the administration time while providing valid estimates of the MMPI constructs. During the 1970s and 1980s, there were a number of shortened versions of the original MMPI developed, such as the Mini-Mult (Kincannon, 1968), the Faschingbauer (FAM; Faschingbauer, 1974), and the MMPI 168 (Overall & Gomez-Mont, 1974). Each of these instruments was evaluated through a number of studies. These short forms, however, did not completely capture the meanings of the full MMPI scale scores (see reviews by Butcher & Hostetler, 1990, and Dahlstrom, 1980). As a result, they gained little professional acceptance.

The revision of the MMPI in 1989 reduced the interest in developing a short form of the MMPI-2, because virtually all of the 567 MMPI-2 items were contained in at least one of the widely used validity, clinical, content, or supplemental scales. Over the past few years, some researchers have attempted to reduce the number of items administered while hoping to obtain the same information contained in the long form. Dahlstrom and Archer (2000), for example, published a shortened form of the MMPI-2 that comprised the first 180 items in the booklet. This approach to abbreviating the test failed to produce an effective measure of the existing scales, because the Clinical Scales are not found in equal proportions within the first 180 items—some scales are more extensively represented in this item group than others. Gass and Luis (2001), similar to previous short-form research on the original MMPI, found that this form was unreliable for predicting clinical code types, identifying the high-point scale, and predicting the scores on most of the basic scales. Another shortened version by McGrath, Terranova, Pogge, and Kravic (2003), the MMPI-297, proved more successful than the Dahlstrom and Archer version. This form, however, tends to produce T-scores that are substantially different (discrepancies of $T > 5$) from those derived from the full form of the MMPI-2, and its converget validity is also weaker across a number of domains (McGrath et al., 2003). It does not give estimates of Fp, one of the more useful Validity Scales, or the supplemental, Psychopathology Five, or Restructured Clinical Scales.

Computer Adaptive Testing

With the wide availability of computers, efforts have been made to develop computer adaptive tests (CATs) of personality measures like the MMPI-2. The goal of CAT is to make test administration more efficient by reducing the number of items that are presented. Once examinees have answered a certain number of items in the unscored direction, such that it would be impossible to obtain an elevated score on a particular scale, the computer stops administering items for that scale. One of the initial motivations for developing adaptive versions of personality tests was that this approach would provide an efficient way of assessing a wide range of personality variables from an extensive collection of items, literally thousands, in a timely manner. Most personality measures, though, are not that lengthy. Current tests, the longest of which can be administered in 1–2 hr, contain only a few hundred items.

Researchers have instead created computer programs for administering the MMPI-2 in order to save time. These programs, for example, can produce the most elevated one or two scores on the clinical profile using only about half of the items on the original MMPI (Butcher, Keller, & Bacon, 1985). To do so, the adaptive version only administers the items necessary to understand the particular client's problems rather than having a fixed format for administering all of the items. That is, the computerized approach tailors the test to the client by only administering items that are needed to assess her or his major symptom patterns. Two strategies have been studied for adaptive administration: the item response theory approach (Roper, Ben-Porath, & Butcher, 1995) and the "countdown" method (Butcher et al., 1985). Research participants appear to respond to both of these formats in a manner that does not hinder the psychometric performance of the test.

Although MMPI-2 CAT saves time, it does not display scores for any scale below $T = 65$. These subclinical scores may be useful in understanding examinees' problems, even though they are not technically considered "elevated." Clinicians considering using CAT should weigh this drawback carefully against the potential time savings that might be gained.

Computer-Based Test Interpretation

Computers also have a long and continuing history of use in facilitating interpretation of the MMPI-2 (Butcher, 1987; Fowler, 1967). Williams and Weed (2004) recently reviewed six commerically available computer-based test interpretation (CBTI) software programs for use with the MMPI-2. These programs varied considerably in terms of their software features (e.g., the ability to export reports into a word processor file), their report features (e.g., length, MMPI-2 scales interpreted), and their ease of use. Some CBTI reports were authored by prominent MMPI-2 researchers; for one of the CBTI reports, authorship was unclear. Research on the validity of CBTI reports is generally supportive, but there are many important considerations in their use. Extensive treatment of this topic can be found in Chapter 13; Chapter 37 describes appropriate use of CBTI reports.

Concluding Comments

Although many features of the MMPI-2 were unique to the instrument at the time of their innovation, other personality assessment instruments have since been constructed to perform functions similar to those of this measure. Why, then, does the MMPI-2 maintain its dominant place in the assessment arsenal of researchers and clinicians? Perhaps the answer goes beyond the matchless research base underlying MMPI-2 interpretation. Although published by the University of Minnesota Press, the scientific community has come to embrace the MMPI-2 as its own. One might compare the MMPI-2 to an open source computer program that can be adapted and enhanced depending on the needs of its users, the improvements shared with any who desire them. Although originally developed by a pair of visionaries, today's MMPI-2 is not the product of one or two authors with a single vision. Numerous individuals seeking to improve the quality of psychological assessment have added to it throughout the years, each leaving a distinct mark. Further, it is the ongoing creation of the psychometric community. As long as that community maintains its interest in pursuing greater depth and clarity of knowledge, it will continue to flourish.

References

Abramson, H. A. (1945). The Minnesota personality test in relation to selection of specialized military personnel. *Psychosomatic Medicine, 7*, 178–184.

American Psychiatric Association. (2000). *Diagnostic and statistical manual of mental disorders* (4th ed., Text rev.). Washington, DC: Author.

American Psychological Association. (2002). Ethical principles of psychologists and code of conduct. *American Psychologist, 57*, 1060–1073.

Arbisi, P. A., & Ben-Porath, Y. S. (1995). An MMPI-2 infrequency scale for use with psychopathological populations: The Infrequency-Psychopathology Scale, F(p). *Psychological Assessment, 7*, 424–431.

Arbisi, P. A., Ben-Porath, Y., & McNulty, J. (2002). A comparison of MMPI-2 validity in African American and Caucasian psychiatric inpatients. *Psychological Assessment, 14*, 3–15.

Arbisi, P. A., Ben-Porath, Y., & McNulty, J. (2003). Empirical correlates of common MMPI-2 two-point codes in male psychiatric inpatients. *Assessment, 10*, 237–247.

Archer, R. P. (2005). *MMPI-A: Assessing Adolescent Psychopathology* (3rd ed.). Mahwah, NJ: Lawrence Erlbaum.

Archer, R. P., Griffin, R., & Aiduk, R. (1995). Clinical correlates for ten common code types. *Journal of Personality Assessment, 65*, 391–408.

Archer, R. P., Maruish, M., Imhof, E. A., & Piotrowski, C. (1991). Psychological test usage with adolescent clients: 1990 survey findings. *Professional Psychology: Research and Practice, 22*, 247–252.

Arnau, R. C., Handel, R. W., & Archer, R. P. (2005). Principal components analyses of the MMPI-2 PSY-5 Scales: Identification of facet subscales. *Assessment, 12*, 186–198.

Baer, R. A., & Miller, J. (2002). Underreporting of psychopathology on the MMPI-2: A meta-analytic review. *Psychological Assessment, 14*, 16–26.

Bagby, R. M. (1995). Relative effectiveness of the standard validity scales in detecting fake-bad and fake-good responding: Replication and extension. *Psychological Assessment, 7*, 84–92.

Barron, F. (1953). An ego strength scale which predicts responses to psychotherapy. *Journal of Consulting Psychology, 17*, 327–333.

Ben-Porath, Y. S., & Butcher, J. N. (1989). Psychometric stability of rewritten MMPI items. *Journal of Personality Assessment, 53*, 645–653.

Ben-Porath, Y. S., Butcher, J. N., & Graham, J. R. (1991). Contribution of the MMPI-2 content scales to the differential diagnosis of psychpathology. *Psychological Assessment, 3*, 634–640.

Ben-Porath, Y. S., & Sherwood, N. (1996). *The MMPI-2 content component scales*. Minneapolis, MN: University of Minnesota Press.

Ben-Porath, Y. S., & Stafford, K. P. (1993). *Empirical correlates of MMPI-2 scales in a forensic diagnostic sample: An interim report.* Paper presented at the 101st Annual Meeting of the American Psychological Association, Toronto, ON, August 1993.

Berry, D. T., Baer, R. A., & Harris, M. J. (1991). Detection of malingering on the MMPI: A meta-analysis. *Clinical Psychology Review, 11*, 585–591.

Beutler, L. E. (1985). Parameters in the prediction of police officer performance. *Professional Psychology: Research and Practice, 16*, 324–335.

Block, J. (1965). *The challenge of response sets*. New York: Appleton-Century Crofts.

Boone, D. E. (1994). Validity of the MMPI-2 Depression content scale with psychiatric inpatients. *Psychological Reports, 74*(1), 159–162.

Brems, C., & Lloyd, P. (1995). Validation of the MMPI-2 Low Self-Esteem Scale. *Journal of Personality Assessment, 65*(3), 550–556.

Butcher, J. N. (Ed.). (1972). *Objective personality assessment: Changing perspectives*. New York: Academic Press.

Butcher, J. N. (1987). Computerized clinical and personality assessment using the MMPI. In J. N. Butcher (Ed.), *Computerized psychological assessment* (pp. 161–197). New York: Basic Books.

Butcher, J. N. (1990). *Use of the MMPI-2 in treatment planning*. New York: Oxford University Press.

Butcher, J. N. (Ed.). (1996). *International adaptations of the MMPI-2: Research and clinical applications*. Minneapolis, MN: University of Minnesota Press.

Butcher, J. N. (2005). *Highlights from MMPI history: A timeline perspective*. Paper presented at 9th Annual Conference on Contemporary Applications of Psychological Testing, Boston.

Butcher, J. N. (Ed.). (2006). *MMPI-2: A practitioner's guide.* Washington, DC: American Psychological Association.

Butcher, J. N., Cabiya, J., Lucio, E., & Garrido, M. (2007). *Assessing Hispanic clients using the MMPI-2 and MMPI-A.* Washington, DC: American Psychological Association Books.

Butcher, J. N., Cabiya, J., Lucio, E. M., Pena, L., Scott, R., & Ruben, D. (1998). *Hispanic version of the MMPI-A manual supplement.* Minneapolis, MN: University of Minnesota Press.

Butcher, J. N., Cheung, F. M., & Lim, J. (2003). Use of the MMPI-2 with Asian populations. *Psychological Assessment, 15,* 248–256.

Butcher, J. N., Dahlstrom, W. G., Graham, J. R., Tellegen, A. M., & Kaemmer, B. (1989). *Minnesota Multiphasic Personality Inventory-2 (MMPI-2): Manual for administration and scoring.* Minneapolis, MN: University of Minnesota Press.

Butcher, J. N., Derksen, J., Sloore, H., & Sirigatti, S. (2003). Objective personality assessment of people in diverse cultures: European adaptations of the MMPI-2. *Behavior Research and Therapy, 41,* 819–840.

Butcher, J. N., Graham, J. R., Ben-Porath, Y. S., Tellegen, A., Dahlstrom, W. G., & Kaemmer, B. (2001). *Minnesota Multiphasic Personality Inventory-2: Manual for administration and scoring* (Rev. ed.). Minneapolis, MN: University of Minnesota Press.

Butcher, J. N., Graham, J. R., Williams, C. L., & Ben-Porath, Y. (1990). *Development and use of the MMPI-2 content scales.* Minneapolis, MN: University of Minnesota Press.

Butcher, J. N., Hamilton, C. K., Rouse, S. V., & Cumella, E. J. (2006). The deconstruction of the Hy scale of MMPI-2: Failure of RC3 in measuring somatic symptom expression. *Journal of Personality Assessment, 87,* 199–205.

Butcher, J. N., & Han, K. (1995). Development of an MMPI-2 scale to assess the presentation of self in a superlative manner: The S scale. In J. N. Butcher & C. D. Spielberger (Eds.), *Advances in personality assessment* (Vol. 10, pp. 25–50). Hillsdale, NJ: Lawrence Erlbaum.

Butcher, J. N., & Han, K. (1996). Methods of establishing cross-cultural equivalence. In J. N. Butcher (Ed.), *International Adaptations of the MMPI-2* (pp. 44–66). Minneapolis, MN: University of Minnesota Press.

Butcher, J. N., & Hostetler, K. (1990). Abbreviating MMPI item administration: Past problems and prospects for the MMPI-2. *Psychological Assessment: A Journal of Consulting and Clinical Psychology, 2,* 12–22.

Butcher, J. N., Keller, L. S., & Bacon, S. F. (1985). Current developments and future directions in computerized personality assessment. *Journal of Consulting and Clinical Psychology, 53,* 803–815.

Butcher, J. N., & Pancheri, P. (1976). *Handbook of cross-national MMPI research.* Minneapolis, MN: University of Minnesota Press.

Butcher, J. N., Tsai, J., Coelho, S., & Nezami, E. (2006). Cross cultural applications of the MMPI-2. In J. N. Butcher (Ed.), *MMPI-2: The practioner's handbook* (pp. 505–537). Washington, DC: American Psychological Association.

Butcher, J. N., Williams, C. L., Graham, J. R., Archer, R., Tellegen, A., Ben-Porath, Y. S., et al. (1992). *MMPI-A manual for administration, scoring, and interpretation.* Minneapolis, MN: University of Minnesota Press.

Capwell, D. (1945). Personality patterns of adolescent girls: II. Delinquents and non-delinquents. *Journal of Applied Psychology, 29,* 289–297.

Chisolm, S. M., Crowther, J. H., & Ben-Porath, Y. S. (1997). Selected MMPI-2 scales' ability to predict premature termination and outcome from psychotherapy. *Journal of Personality Assessment, 69*(1), 127–144.

Clark, M. E. (1993). *MMPI-2 anger and cynicism scales: Interpretive cautions.* Paper presented at the 28th Annual Symposium on Recent Developments in the Use of the MMPI/MMPI-2, St. Petersburg, FL, March 1993.

Clopton, J. R., Shanks, D. A., & Preng, K. W. (1987). Classification accuracy of the MacAndrew scale with and without K corrections. *The International Journal of the Addictions, 22,* 1049–1051.

Cook, W. N., & Medley, D. M. (1954). Proposed hostility and pharisaic-virtue scales for the MMPI. *Journal of Applied Psychology, 38,* 414–418.

Dahlstrom, W. G. (1980). Altered forms of the MMPI. In W. G. Dahlstrom & L. E. Dahlstrom (Eds.), *Basic readings on the MMPI* (pp. 386–393). Minneapolis, MN: University of Minnesota Press.

Dahlstrom, W. G., & Archer, R. P. (2000). A shortened version of the MMPI-2. *Assessment, 7,* 131–137.

Dahlstrom, W. G., & Welsh, G. S. (1960). *An MMPI handbook: A guide to use in clinical practice and research.* Minneapolis, MN: University of Minnesota Press.

Dahlstrom, W. G., Welsh, G. S., & Dahlstrom, L. E. (1975). *An MMPI handbook: Vol. II. Research applications.* Minneapolis, MN: University of Minnesota Press.

Drake, L. E. (1946). A social I. E. scale for the Minnesota Multiphasic Personality Inventory. *Journal of Applied Psychology, 30,* 51–54.

Egeland, B., Erickson, M., Butcher, J. N., & Ben-Porath, Y. S. (1991). MMPI-2 profiles of women at risk for child abuse. *Journal of Personality Assessment, 57,* 254–263.

Faschingbauer, T. R. (1974). A 166 item short form for the group MMPI: The FAM. *Journal of Consulting and Clinical Psychology, 42,* 645–655.

Faull, R., & Meyer, G. J. (1993). *Assessment of depression with the MMPI-2: Distinctions between Scale 2 and the DEP.* Paper presented at the Midwinter Meeting of the Society for Personality Assessment, San Francisco, March 1993.

Finn, S. E., & Butcher, J. N. (1990). Clinical objective personality assessment. In M. Hersen, A. E. Kazdin, & A. S. Bellack (Eds.), *The clinical psychology handbook* (2nd ed.). New York: Pergamon Press.

Finn, S. E., & Tonsager, M. E. (1992). Therapeutic effects of providing MMPI-2 test feedback to college students awaiting therapy. *Psychological Assessment, 4,* 278–286.

Fordyce, W. E. (1978). Relationship of patient semantic pain descriptions to physician diagnostic judgments, activity level measures and MMPI. *Pain, 5,* 293–303.

Fowler, R. D., Jr. (1967). Computer interpretation of personality tests: The automated psychologist. *Comprehensive Psychiatry, 8*(6), 455–467.

Garrido, M., & Velasquez, R. (2006). Interpretation of Latino/Latina MMPI-2 profiles: Review and application of empirical findings and cultural-linguistic considerations. In J. N. Butcher (Ed.), *MMPI-2: The practioner's handbook* (pp. 477–504). Washington, DC: American Psychological Association.

Gass, C. S., & Luis, C. A. (2001). MMPI-2 short form: Psychometric characteristics in a neuropsychological setting. *Assessment, 8,* 425–429.

Gilberstadt, H., & Duker, J. (1965). *A handbook for clinical and actuarial MMPI interpretation*. Philadelphia: W. B. Saunders.

Gottesman, I. I., & Shields, J. (1966). Schizophrenia in twins: 16 years' consecutive admissions to a psychiatric clinic. *British Journal of Psychiatry, 112*, 809–818.

Gough, H. G. (1947). Simulated patterns on the Minnesota Multiphasic Personality Inventory. *Journal of Abnormal and Social Psychology, 42*, 215–225.

Gough, H. G., McClosky, H., & Meehl, P. E. (1951). A personality scale for dominance. *Journal of Abnormal and Social Psychology, 46*, 360–366.

Gough, H. G., McClosky, H., & Meehl, P. E. (1952). A personality scale for social responsibility. *Journal of Abnormal and Social Psychology, 47*, 73–80.

Graham, J. R. (1977). *The MMPI: A practical guide*. New York: Oxford University Press.

Graham, J. R. (2006). *MMPI-2: Assessing personality and psychopathology* (4th ed.). New York: Oxford University Press.

Graham, J. R., Ben-Porath, Y. S., & McNulty, J. L. (1999). *MMPI-2 correlates for outpatient mental health settings*. Minneapolis, MN: University of Minnesota Press.

Graham, J. R., Watts, D., & Timbrook, R. (1991). Detecting fake-good and fake-bad MMPI-2 profiles. *Journal of Personality Assessment, 57*, 264–277.

Grayson, H. M. (1951). *Psychological admission testing program and manual*. Los Angeles: Veterans Administration Center, Neuropsychiatric Hospital.

Greene, R. L., Robin, R. W., Albaugh, B., Caldwell, A., & Goldman, D. (2003). Use of the MMPI-2 in American Indians: II. Empirical correlates. *Psychological Assessment, 15*(3), 360–369.

Halbower, C. C. (1955). A comparison of actuarial versus clinical prediction to classes discriminated by the Minnesota Multiphasic Personality Inventory. *Dissertation Abstracts International, 15*, 1115.

Hall, G. C., Bansal, A., & Lopez, I. R. (1999). Ethnicity and psychopathology: A meta-analytic review of 31 years of comparative MMPI/MMPI-2 research. *Psychological Assessment, 11*(2), 186–197.

Harkness, A. R., McNulty, J. L., & Ben-Porath, Y. S. (1995). The Personality Psychopathology Five (PSY-5): Constructs and MMPI-2 scales. *Psychological Assessment, 7*, 104–114.

Harris, R. E., & Lingoes, J. C. (1955). *Subscales for the MMPI: An aid to profile interpretation* (Mimeographed materials). Langley Porter Clinic, Department of Psychiatry, University of California, San Francisco.

Hathaway, S. R. (1956). Scales 5 (masculinity–femininity), 6 (paranoia), and 8 (schizophrenia). In W. G. Dahlstrom & L. E. Dahlstrom (Eds.), *Basic readings on the MMPI*. Minneapolis, MN: University of Minnesota Press.

Hathaway, S. R., & McKinley, J. C. (1940). A multiphasic personality schedule (Minnesota): I. Construction of the schedule. *Journal of Psychology: Interdisciplinary and Applied, 10*, 249–254.

Hathaway, S. R., & Monachesi, E. D. (1951). The prediction of juvenile delinquency using the Minnesota Multiphasic Personality Inventory. *American Journal of Psychiatry, 108*, 469–473.

Hays, P. (2001). *Addressing cultural complexities in practice: A framework for clinicians and counselors*. Washington, DC: American Psychological Association.

Hjemboe, S., Almagor, M., & Butcher, J. N. (1992). Empirical assessment of marital distress: The marital distress scale (MDS) for the MMPI-2. In J. N. Butcher & C. D. Spielberger (Eds.), *Advances in personality assessment: Vol. 9* (pp. 141–152). Hillsdale, NJ: Lawrence Erlbaum.

Hjemboe, S., & Butcher, J. N. (1991). Couples in marital distress: A study of demographic and personality factors as measured by the MMPI-2. *Journal of Personality Assessment, 57*, 216–237.

Keane, T. M., Malloy, P. F., & Fairbank, J. A. (1984). Empirical development of an MMPI subscale for the assessment of combat-related post-traumatic stress disorder. *Journal of Consulting and Clinical Psychology, 52*, 888–891.

Keller, L. S., & Butcher, J. N. (1991). *Use of the MMPI-2 with chronic pain patients*. Minneapolis, MN: University of Minnesota Press.

Kincannon, J. C. (1968). Prediction of the standard MMPI scale scores from 71 items. *Journal of Consulting and Clinical Psychology, 32*, 319–325.

Kleinmuntz, B. (1961). The College Maladjustment scale (Mt): Norms and predictive validity. *Educational and Psychological Measurement, 21*, 1029–1033.

Koss, M. P., & Butcher, J. N. (1973). A comparison of psychiatric patients' self-report with other sources of clinical information. *Journal of Research in Personality, 7*, 225–236.

Koss, M. P., Butcher, J. N., & Hoffman, N. G. (1976). The MMPI critical items: How well do they work? *Journal of Consulting and Clinical Psychology, 44*, 921–928.

Lachar, D., & Wrobel, T. A. (1979). Validating clinicians' hunches: Construction of a new MMPI critical item set. *Journal of Consulting and Clinical Psychology, 47*, 277–284.

Lilienfeld, S. O. (1996). The MMPI-2 Antisocial Practices Content Scale: Construct validity and comparison with the Psychopathic Deviate Scale. *Psychological Assessment, 8*, 281–293.

Lubin, B., Larsen, R. M., & Matarazzo, J. D. (1984). Patterns of psychological test usage in the United States: 1932–1982. *American Psychologist, 39*, 451–454.

Lucio, G. M. E., & Reyes-Lagunes, I. (1996). The Mexican version of the MMPI-2 in Mexico and Nicaragua: Translation, adaptation, and demonstrated equivalency. In J. N. Butcher (Ed.), *International adaptations of the MMPI-2* (pp. 265–283). Minneapolis, MN: University of Minnesota Press.

MacAndrew, C. (1965). The differentiation of male alcoholic outpatients from nonalcoholic psychiatric outpatients by means of the MMPI. *Quarterly Journal of Studies on Alcohol, 26*, 238–246.

Marks, P. A., & Seeman, W. (1963). *The actuarial description of personality: An atlas for use with the MMPI*. Baltimore, MD: Williams and Wilkins.

McGrath, R. E., Sweeney, M., O'Malley, W. B., & Carlton, T. K. (1998). Identifying psychological contributions to chronic pain complaints with the MMPI-2: The role of the K scale. *Journal of Personality Assessment, 70*, 448–459.

McGrath, R. E., Terranova, R., Pogge, D. L., & Kravic, C. (2003). Development of a short form for the MMPI-2 based on scale elevation congruence. *Assessment, 10*(1), 13–28.

McNulty, J. L., Graham, J. R., Ben-Porath, Y. S., & Stein, L. A. R. (1997). Comparative validity of MMPI-2 scores of African American and Caucasian health center clients. *Psychological Assessment, 9*(4), 464–470.

Meehl, P. E. (1945). The dynamics of "structured" personality tests. *Journal of Clinical Psychology, 1*, 296–303.

Meehl, P. E. (1954). *Clinical versus statistical prediction: A theoretical analysis and a review of the evidence.* Minneapolis, MN: University of Minnesota Press.

Megargee, E. I. (Ed.) (1977). A new classification system for criminal offenders [Special issue]. *Criminal Justice and Behavior, 4*(2).

Megargee, E. I. (2006). *Using the MMPI-2 in criminal justice and correctional settings.* Minneapolis, MN: University of Minnesota Press.

Megargee, E. I., Cook, P. E., & Mendelsohn, G. A. (1967). The development and validation of an MMPI scale of assaultiveness in overcontrolled individuals. *Journal of Abnormal Psychology, 72*, 519–528.

Meyer, G. J. (2006). MMPI-2 Restructured Clinical Scales [Special issue]. *Journal of Personality Assessment, 87*(2).

Munley, P. H., Busby, R. M., & Jaynes, G. (1997). MMPI-2 findings in schizophrenia and depression. *Psychological Assessment, 9*, 508–511.

Nichols, D. S. (2006). The trials of separating bath water from baby: A review and critique of the MMPI-2 Restructured Clinical Scales. *Journal of Personality Assessment, 87*, 121–138.

Nichols, D. S., Greene, R. L., & Schmolck, P. (1989). Criteria for assessing inconsistent patterns of item endorsement on the MMPI: Rationale, development, and empirical trials. *Journal of Clinical Psychology, 45*, 239–250.

Overall, J. E., & Gomez-Mont, F. (1974). The MMPI-168 for psychiatric screening. *Educational and Psychological Measurement, 34*, 315–319.

Peterson, C. D., & Dahlstrom, W. G. (1992). The derivation of gender role scale GM and GF for the MMPI-2 and their relationship to Scale 5 (Mf). *Journal of Personality Assessment, 59*, 486–499.

Quereshi, M. Y., & Kleman, R. (1996). Validation of selected MMPI-2 basic and content scales. *Current Psychology: Developmental, Learning, Personality, Social-Psychology, 15*(3), 249–253.

Quevedo, K. M., & Butcher, J. N. (2005). The use of MMPI and MMPI-2 in Cuba: A historical overview from 1950 to the present. *International Journal of Clinical and Health Psychology, 5*(2), 335–347.

Reitan, R. M. (1955). Affective disturbances in brain-damaged patients; measurements with the Minnesota Multiphasic Personality Inventory. *Archives of Neurology and Psychiatry, 73*, 530–532.

Rogers, R., Sewell, K. W., Harrison, K. W., & Jordan, M. J. (2006). The MMPI-2 Restructured Clinical Scales: A paradigmatic shift to scale development. *Journal of Personality Assessment, 87*, 139–147.

Rome, H. P., Swenson, W. M., Mataya, P., McCarthy, C. E., Pearson, J. S., Keating, F. R., et al. (1962). Symposium on automation techniques in personality assessment. *Proceedings of the Staff Meetings of the Mayo Clinic, 37*, 61–82.

Roper, B., Ben-Porath, Y. S., & Butcher, J. N. (1995). Comparability and validity of computerized adaptive testing with the MMPI-2. *Journal of Personality Assessment, 65*, 358–371.

Rosen, A. (1962). Development of MMPI scales based on a reference group of psychiatric patients. *Psychological Monographs, 76* (8, Whole No. 527).

Rouse, S. V., Greene, R. L., Butcher, J. N., Nichols, D. S., & Williams, C. L. (2008). What do the MMPI-2 Restructured Clinical Scales reliably measure? *Journal of Personality Assessment, 90*, 435–422.

Schiele, B. C., Baker, A. B., & Hathaway, S. R. (1943). The Minnesota Multiphasic Personality Inventory. *Lancet, 63*, 292–297.

Schretlen, D. J. (1988). The use of psychological tests to identify malingered symptoms of mental disorder. *Clinical Psychology Review, 8*, 451–476.

Silver, R. J., & Sines, L. K. (1962). Diagnostic efficiency of the MMPI with and without K correction. *Journal of Clinical Psychology, 18*, 312–314.

Sines, J. O. (1966). Actuarial methods as appropriate strategy for the validation of diagnostic tests. *Psychological Review, 71*, 517–523.

Spanier, G. B. (1976). Measuring dyadic adjustment: New scales for assessing the quality of marriage and similar dyads. *Journal of Marriage and the Family, 38*, 15–28.

Sundberg, N. D. (1956). The use of the MMPI for cross-cultural personality study: A preliminary report on the German translation. *Journal of Abnormal and Social Psychology, 58*, 281–283.

Tellegen, A., & Ben-Porath, Y. S. (1992). The new uniform T-scores for the MMPI-2: Rationale, derivation, and appraisal. *Psychological Assessment, 4*, 145–155.

Tellegen, A., Ben-Porath, Y. S., McNulty, J., Arbisi, P., Graham, J. R., & Kaemmer, B. (2003). *The MMPI-2 Restructured Clinical (RC) Scales: Development, validation, and interpretation.* Minneapolis, MN: University of Minnesota Press.

Wallace, A., & Liljequist, L. (2005). A comparison of the correlational structures and elevation patterns of the MMPI-2 Restructured Clinical (RC) and Clinical Scales. *Assessment, 12*, 290–294.

Weed, N. C., Butcher, J. N., McKenna, T., & Ben-Porath, Y. S. (1992). New measures for assessing alcohol and drug abuse with the MMPI-2: The APS and AAS. *Journal of Personality Assessment, 58*, 389–404.

Weed, N. C., & Han, K. (1992). *Is K correct?* Paper presented at the 27th Annual Symposium on Recent Developments in the Use of the MMPI (MMPI-2 and MMPI-A), Minneapolis, MN, May 1992.

Welsh, G. S. (1952). Factor dimensions A and R. In G. S. Welsh & W. G. Dahlstrom (Eds.), *Basic readings on the MMPI.* Minneapolis, MN: University of Minnesota Press.

Welsh, G. S. (1956). Factor dimensions A and R. In G. S. Welsh & W. G. Dahlstrom (Eds.), *Basic readings on the MMPI* (pp. 264–281). Minneapolis, MN: University of Minnesota Press.

Wetter, M. W., & Tharpe, B. (1995). *Sensitivity of the TRIN scale on the MMPI-2.* Paper presented at the 30th Annual Symposium on Recent Developments in the Use of the MMPI-2 and MMPI-A, St. Petersburg, FL, March 1995.

Wiggins, J. S. (1966). Substantive dimensions of self-report in the MMPI item pool. *Psychological Monographs, 80* (22, Whole No. 630).

Williams, J. E., & Weed, N. C. (2004). Review of computer-based test interpretation software for the MMPI-2. *Journal of Personality Assessment, 83*, 78–83.

Woodworth, R. S. (1920). *The Personal Data Sheet.* Chicago: Stoelting.

Wooten, A. J. (1984). Effectiveness of the K correction in the detection of psychopathology and its impact on profile height and configuration among young adult men. *Journal of Consulting and Clinical Psychology, 52*, 468–473.

Personality Assessment with the Rorschach Inkblot Method

Irving B. Weiner *and* Gregory J. Meyer

Abstract

This chapter reviews the development of the Rorschach Inkblot Method (RIM) and delineates its value in identifying a broad range of personality characteristics. Attention is paid to particularly useful purposes served by Rorschach assessment in clinical and forensic evaluations when it is integrated with self-report measures. Available evidence indicates that Rorschach assessment is a psychometrically sound procedure that is being actively practiced and studied, both in the United States and in many other parts of the world, and that can be meaningfully applied in diverse countries and cultures. Some concern is raised, however, about the adequacy of education and training in Rorschach assessment currently provided in graduate programs.

Keywords: Rorschach, self-report measures

Rorschach assessment became public in 1921, when Hermann Rorschach published the results of his inkblot studies with 117 non-patients and 288 mental hospital patients with various types of disorder (Rorschach, 1921/1942). Interest in the inkblot method as an instrument for assessing personality functioning spread to many parts of the world during the 1920s and reached the United States near the end of that decade. The first English-language articles on Rorschach's method were published by Samuel Beck in 1930 (Beck, 1930a, 1930b), and several years later the first English-language textbooks on Rorschach assessment were authored by Beck (1937) and by Bruno Klopfer and Douglas Kelley (1942). Since that time, this personality assessment measure, now often referred to as the Rorschach Inkblot Method (RIM; Weiner, 1994), has become widely known to professional psychologists and among the lay public as well.

During the first 50 years of its history, a proliferation of methods of administering and scoring the RIM impeded systematic accumulation of information about its psychometric characteristics and

practical utility. This situation began to change with the 1974 publication of Exner's *The Rorschach: A Comprehensive System*, which integrated various aspects of previous Rorschach methods into a standardized and research-based set of administration and coding guidelines (Exner, 1974). Over the course of four editions of this text (see Exner, 2003), the Comprehensive System (CS) became by far the most widely used Rorschach method in the United States and in many other countries as well, and its standardization contributed to substantial advances in Rorschach research and international communication about Rorschach assessment issues.

By virtue of being a performance-based method and providing a broad range of information about personality characteristics, the RIM is frequently valuable to include in a psychological test battery. Rorschach assessment serves particularly useful purposes in clinical and forensic evaluations, which are the two contexts in which it is most often applied. This chapter reviews the value of the RIM in a test battery and how Rorschach assessment can be applied. Following these reviews, the chapter takes up four questions that frequently have been asked about the RIM: (1) Is Rorschach assessment a psychometrically sound procedure? (2) Is Rorschach assessment actively practiced and studied? (3) Can Rorschach assessment be applied in diverse countries and cultures? (4) Is Rorschach assessment being widely and adequately taught? Although of long standing, these questions define ongoing contemporary issues, and the discussion presents current information on the psychometric foundations, usage frequency, and cross-cultural applicability of Rorschach assessment and the status of Rorschach education and training.

Value of Rorschach Assessment in a Test Battery

Following the suggestion of the Psychological Assessment Work Group (PAWG), a task force appointed by the American Psychological Association Board of Professional Affairs, it has become common practice to refer to two different types of personality assessment instruments as "self-report" or "performance-based" (Meyer et al., 2001). The data in self-report measures consist of what people say about themselves when asked; the data in performance-based measures consist of how people go about performing a task. Self-report assessment is thus a direct, explicit procedure based on acceptance of what examinees say, whereas performance-based assessment is an indirect, implicit procedure based on inferences from what examinees do.

As elaborated elsewhere, self-report and performance-based methods have some potential advantage and limitations relative to each other (Meyer, 1997; Weiner, 2005c). Usually the best way to learn something about people is to ask them about it. How people answer direct questions about themselves is more likely to provide definitive information about what they think, feel, plan, and have experienced than indirect impressions based on how they perform some task. On the other hand, what people self-report is limited to what they are able and willing to say about themselves—which depends on how fully they are aware of their own characteristics and how inclined they are to be open and truthful. Limited self-awareness or reluctance to disclose can detract from the dependability of the answers people give on a self-report inventory (Dunning, Heath, & Suls, 2004; Wilson & Dunn, 2004).

Performance-based measures can often circumvent this limitation of self-report inventories. Although indirect methods generate fewer definite conclusions than a direct inquiry, they are often more likely than self-reports to reveal personality characteristics that people do not fully recognize in themselves or are hesitant to admit when asked about them directly (Bornstein, 1999; Schmulke & Egloff, 2005). They also are more adept at providing a clinician with a glimpse of the clients' internal representations and behavioral or problem-solving predilections. As a performance-based measure in which inferences about people are derived not from what they say about themselves but from what they actually do (i.e., say about inkblots), the RIM provides valuable balance to the self-report data obtained in a personality assessment. In recognition of the fact that self-report and performance-based methods measure personality characteristics at different levels of a person's ability to recognize and willingness to acknowledge these characteristics, and in light of the relative advantages and limitations of these methods, contemporary authors commonly recommend an integrative approach to personality assessment that combines both kinds of measures. According to the PAWG report, for example, conjoint testing with both self-report and performance-based measures is a procedure "by which practitioners have historically used the most efficient means at their disposal to maximize the validity of their judgments about individual clients" (Meyer et al., 2001, p. 150; see also Beutler & Groth-Marnat, 2003; Weiner & Greene, 2008).

Purposes Served by Rorschach Assessment

As a personality assessment instrument, the RIM provides information about an individual's adaptive capacities, coping style, underlying attitudes and concerns, and dispositions to think, feel, and act in certain ways. These indications of a person's states, traits, and inner life frequently facilitate decisions in which personality characteristics are a relevant consideration. Rorschach assessment thereby serves useful purposes in clinical and forensic psychology, which commonly call for personality-based decisions and, as noted, the two contexts in which Rorschach findings are most often applied.

Clinical Purposes

Rorschach assessment contributes to decision making in clinical cases by virtue of the relevance of personality characteristics to the manner in which various types of psychological disturbance are manifest and experienced (see American Psychiatric Association, 2000; PDM Task Force, 2006). In addition to assisting in differential diagnosis, personality characteristics identified or suggested by Rorschach data are often useful in treatment planning and outcome evaluation.

DIFFERENTIAL DIAGNOSIS

Many of the states and traits identified by Rorschach variables are associated with particular forms of psychopathology. For example, schizophrenia is characterized by disordered thinking and impaired reality testing, and Rorschach indices of incoherent associations, illogical reasoning, and perceptual distortion (e.g., high X-%, elevated WSum6) accordingly increase the likelihood that a person has a schizophrenia spectrum disorder. Similarly, because paranoia involves suspiciousness and heightened alertness to environmental sources of danger or threat, a Rorschach index of hypervigilance (HVI) suggests a paranoid stance in how a person looks at the world. Depressive disorder is suggested by Rorschach indices of dysphoria (elevated C', color-shading blends) and negative self-attitudes (elevated vista, morbid responses). For additional information concerning these and other applications of Rorschach findings in differential diagnosis, readers are referred to an article by Hartmann, Nørbech, and Grønnerød (2006) and books by Huprich (2006), Kleiger (1999), and Weiner (2003).

While recognizing how Rorschach assessment of personality characteristics can contribute to differential diagnosis, however, practitioners must also be aware of its limitations in this regard. With respect to descriptive psychopathology, for example, Rorschach data seldom identify the particular symptoms a person is likely to show. An individual with Rorschach indications of an obsessive compulsive personality style could be a compulsive handwasher, an obsessive prognosticator, or neither. Someone with depressive affect and ideation could be having crying spells, disturbed sleep, episodes of agitation and irritability, none of these, or active denial of dysphoric and distressing affect. The presence of specific symptoms that might lead to a diagnosed condition is better determined from observing or asking directly about them than by attempting to infer them from Rorschach indications of personality characteristics.

Similarly in the case of venturing opinions about whether a person has had certain life experiences (e.g., been sexually abused) or behaved in certain ways (e.g., abused alcohol or drugs), Rorschach data rarely provide dependable information. Only when there is a substantial known correlation between particular personality characteristics and the likelihood of certain experiences or behavior patterns can Rorschach findings indicate the probability of their having occurred. In common with most personality assessment instruments, moreover, the RIM works best in identifying true positives and less well in avoiding false negative findings. That is, a condition strongly suggested by a person's Rorschach responses is likely to be present, whereas the absence of Rorschach indications of a condition hardly ever provides sufficient basis for ruling it out.[1]

TREATMENT PLANNING

Rorschach assessment measures numerous personality characteristics that are relevant to decisions made prior to and during an intervention process. Initially, the degree of disturbance or coping incapacity shown in a person's Rorschach responses has implications for whether the individual requires inpatient care or is functioning sufficiently well to be treated in an outpatient basis. The personality style and severity of distress or disorganization reflected in Rorschach findings can help determine whether an individual's treatment needs will best be met by a supportive approach aimed at relieving distress, a cognitive-behavioral approach designed to modify symptoms or behavior, or an exploratory approach intended to enhance self-understanding. Whichever of these approaches is implemented, maladaptive traits and underlying concerns suggested by Rorschach responses can help therapists decide, in consultation with their patients, what the goals for the treatment should be and in what order these treatment targets should be addressed (see Weiner, 2005a).

Certain personality characteristics measured by Rorschach variables can also help therapists anticipate the course of psychotherapy.[2] Being open to experience (average or low Lambda), cognitively flexible (number of responses per card, or perhaps a balanced *active:passive* ratio), emotionally responsive (adequate WSumC and Affective Ratio), interpersonally receptive (presence of Texture, adequate SumH and GHR), and personally introspective (presence of Form Dimensional responses) are usually associated with being able to participate in and benefit from psychological treatment. Contrariwise, having an avoidant or guarded approach to experience, being set in one's ways, having difficulty recognizing and expressing one's feelings, being interpersonally aversive or withdrawn, and lacking psychological mindedness are often obstacles to engagement and progress in psychotherapy (Clarkin & Levy, 2004; Weiner, 1998, chap. 2). Awareness of such potential obstacles to engagement and progress can stave off therapist impatience or discouragement in the face of initially slow going in treatment, while also directing attention to the importance of overcoming or circumventing these obstacles in order for progress to be made.

OUTCOME EVALUATION

Along with providing guidance in planning and conducting psychotherapy, Rorschach assessment can assist in monitoring treatment progress and outcome. As an illustration, suppose a pretreatment assessment identifies some treatment targets that can be expressed in Rorschach terms, like the following: reducing subjectively felt distress, as in changing a $D < 0$ to a $D = 0$; increasing receptivity to emotional arousal, as in bringing up a low Affective Ratio; promoting more careful problem solving, as in reducing a $Zd < -3.5$. With such test data as a baseline, retesting after some period of time can provide quantitative indications of how much progress has been made toward achieving these goals. Rorschach markers of the extent to which treatment goals have been achieved can provide guidance in deciding when termination is indicated and evaluating whether a course of therapy has been effective.

The utility of Rorschach assessment in monitoring treatment progress and outcome has been demonstrated in both research studies and case reports. In studies by Weiner and Exner (1991) and Exner and Sanglade (1992), patients in long-term, short-term, and brief psychotherapy were examined at several points during and after their treatment. The data analysis focused on 27 Rorschach structural variables considered to have implications for a person's overall level of adjustment. The patients in these studies showed significant positive changes in these Rorschach variables over the course of their therapy, and their amount of improvement was directly related to the length of their therapy. These findings would appear to demonstrate both the effectiveness of psychotherapy in promoting positive personality change and the validity of the RIM in measuring such change.

In a study with similar implications, Fowler et al. (2004) monitored the progress of a group of previously treatment-refractory patients who entered a residential treatment center and were engaged in psychodynamically oriented psychotherapy. After a treatment duration averaging 16 months, these patients showed significant improvement in their average behavior ratings on scales related to social and occupational functioning, and these improvements were mirrored by significant changes for the better in their scores on three Rorschach content scales. With respect to its content as well as its structural variables, then, Rorschach assessment has been shown to provide valid measurement of treatment progress. For additional research, commentary, and a case illustration concerning Rorschach

monitoring of psychotherapy, readers are referred to contributions by Blatt and Ford (1994), Grønnerød (2004), and Weiner (2004, 2005a).

Forensic Purposes

Personality characteristics have implications for the resolution of a variety of legal issues. Rorschach assessment accordingly proves useful in forensic cases by identifying features of personality that are relevant to the types of issues commonly raised in criminal, personal injury, and family law cases. Psychologists using the RIM in forensic consultation need also to be informed with respect to the admissibility into evidence of Rorschach-based testimony.

CRIMINAL CASES

The most common issues addressed by psychologists consulting in criminal cases concern an accused person's competence to stand trial and the person's responsibility for his or her alleged criminal behavior. Competence to stand trial consists in legal terms of having a rational and factual understanding of the legal proceedings in which one is involved and being capable of participating effectively in one's defense. Courts typically operationalize these general criteria of competence by determining whether defendants (a) appreciate the nature of the charges against them and the possible penalties they are facing, (b) understand the adversarial process and the roles of the key people in it, (c) can disclose pertinent facts in their case to their attorney, and (d) will be able to behave appropriately in the courtroom and testify relevantly in their own behalf (Stafford, 2003; Zapf & Roesch, 2006).

The dimensions of personality functioning most closely related to these aspects of competence involve being able to think logically and coherently and to perceive people and events accurately. Disordered thinking and impaired reality testing, together with the poor judgment and inappropriate behavior that often result from them, are likely to interfere with a person's being able to demonstrate competence. For this reason, the previously mentioned Rorschach indices of disordered thinking and impaired reality testing (high $X-\%$, elevated WSum6), although not by themselves evidence of incompetence, can help psychologists account for and explain to the court why a person is having difficulty satisfying legal criteria for competence.

Criminal responsibility refers to whether an accused person was legally insane at the time of committing an alleged offense. Insanity is defined in most jurisdictions as a cognitive incapacity that interferes with a person's being able to recognize the criminality of his or her actions or appreciate the wrongfulness of this conduct. In some jurisdictions, insanity consists of either this type of cognitive incapacity or a loss of behavioral control that rendered the person unable to alter or refrain from the alleged criminal conduct (Goldstein, Morse, & Shapiro, 2003; Zapf, Golding, & Roesch, 2006).

Both cognitive incapacity and behavioral dyscontrol are personality characteristics that can be and often are reflected in Rorschach responses. Cognitive incapacity is identified on the RIM by the previously mentioned indices of disordered thinking and poor reality testing. Behavioral dyscontrol is suggested by Rorschach indices of acute and chronic stress overload (minus D-score, minus AdjD-score), which are commonly associated with limited frustration tolerance and episodes of impulsive behavior and outbursts of intemperate affect. However, diminished criminal responsibility due to insanity is defined by a person's state of mind at the time of an alleged offense, not at the time when the person is being examined psychologically. Hence, to provide a relevant basis for inferences about criminal responsibility, Rorschach findings identifying cognitive impairment or suggesting susceptibility to loss of control must be supplemented by information about a defendant's mental health history and observed behavior just prior to and during the alleged offense.

PERSONAL INJURY CASES

As prescribed by tort law, personal injury cases involve accusations that an individual or organization, by acting in ways that constituted a dereliction of its duty, has caused a plaintiff to suffer mental or physical damage (see Greenberg, 2003). Personality assessment in such cases can help the court establish if and to what extent a complainant has become emotionally distressed or incapacitated subsequent to a defendant's allegedly irresponsible behavior. Rorschach indications of posttraumatic stress disorder (PTSD), depressive affect and cognitions, and psychotic loss of touch with reality are particularly likely to be relevant in identifying such psychic injury.

Individuals with PTSD tend to produce either flooded or constricted Rorschach protocols. The Rorschach responses of those whose stress disorder is characterized mainly by the reexperiencing of distressing events and a state of mental and physical hyperarousal commonly reflect the pronounced interference of anxiety with their personal comfort and functioning effectiveness. Such flooded records usually feature a large minus D-score and minus Adj D-score suggesting severe stress overload, together with a high percentage of response contents suggesting concern about bodily harm (e.g., Aggression, Anatomy, Blood, Morbid, Sex; see Armstrong & Kaser-Boyd, 2004; Kelly, 1999; Luxenberg & Levin, 2004).

Some persons with PTSD display instead of reexperiencing and hyperarousal a pattern of withdrawal in which they strive to avoid thoughts, feelings, or situations that might cause them psychological distress. Individuals showing such defensive avoidance are likely to give constricted rather than flooded Rorschach records, marked by a low response total, a narrow range of response content, a high percentage of F (pure form) responses, and other indications of guardedness.

However, neither flooded nor constricted Rorschach protocols are specific to stress disorders, and neither constitutes conclusive evidence that a person has such a disorder. Considered in tandem with other clinical, historical, or test data consistent with PTSD, these types of Rorschach records serve only to increase the likely presence of this condition. Moreover, as in the case of evaluating sanity, the results of a present personal injury examination must be interpreted in the context of past events. Forensic consultants in personal injury cases must give adequate attention to whether any currently observed stress overload or withdrawal predated the allegedly improper conduct by the defendant and whether the plaintiff's psychological difficulties represents a decline from some previously higher level of functioning capacity prior to when the misconduct occurred.

Similar considerations apply in the assessment of depressive or psychotic features in plaintiffs seeking personal injury damages. As noted in discussing differential diagnosis of depression, unusually high or low scores on several Rorschach variables are helpful in identifying the presence of dysphoric affect and negative cognitions, but normal range scores on these variables are not sufficient basis for ruling out these features of depression. As also mentioned, psychotic impairment of reality testing is usually indicated by an abundance of inaccurate perceptions, as measured by a high X-%. However, present indications of psychosis seldom support a plaintiff's claim to have suffered psychic injury unless other reliable data (e.g., previous testing, historical indications of sound mental health) leave little doubt that this person was not psychotic prior to the allegedly damaging conduct by the defendant.

FAMILY LAW CASES

Legal determination of child custody and visitation rights is commonly based in part on the personality characteristics of separated or divorced parents and their children. Judges in these family disputes are particularly likely to value information from psychological tests about the personality strengths and weaknesses of a child's parents. There are few if any precise indicators of suitability to parent or which of two persons would be the better parent for a particular child. Nevertheless, certain personality characteristics that can be measured by the RIM are generally considered to enhance or detract from parents' abilities to meet the needs of their children. These characteristics include the severity of any psychological disturbance, the adequacy of the person's coping skills, and the extent of his or her interpersonal accessibility.

With respect to psychological disturbance, having mental or emotional problems does not necessarily prevent a person from being a good parent. However, being seriously disturbed or psychologically incapacitated is likely to interfere with a person's having sufficient judgment, impulse control, energy, and peace of mind to function effectively in a parental capacity. Previously mentioned Rorschach variables that help to identify such serious disturbance include indices of significantly disordered thinking, substantially impaired reality testing, pervasive dysphoria and negative cognitions, and overwhelming anxiety.

As for coping skills, effective parenting is facilitated by capacities for good judgment, careful and timely decision making, flexibility in solving problems, and adequate stress management. Conversely, poor judgment, careless or delayed decisions, inflexible problem-solving, and inability to manage stress without becoming distraught are likely to interfere with effective parenting. Rorschach findings can in many instances reflect a person's skills in these respects. A low X-% and WSum6 is usually associated with good judgment; a high Zf or DQ+ with problem-solving ability; relatively more GHR to PHR indicating a positive and enhancing representation of interpersonal relations as opposed to destructive or distorted representations; and a zero or positive D-score with average or above-average stress tolerance. These illustrations do not comprise a definitive list of coping skills relevant to effective parenting or an exhaustive list of Rorschach variables that can prove helpful in estimating parental effectiveness, but they do sample useful applications of Rorschach assessment in family law consultation.

In regard to interpersonal accessibility, the quality of child care that parents are able to provide is usually enhanced by their being interested in people and comfortable in their presence, nurturing and caring in their relationships with others, and sufficiently empathic to recognize the needs and feeling of other people and appreciate their concerns. Conversely, interpersonal disinterest and discomfort are likely to detract from parental effectiveness, as is being a detached, self-absorbed, or insensitive person. Accordingly, the likelihood of a person's being a good parent is measured in part by a cluster of Rorschach findings usually associated with good interpersonal adjustment, including their relative standing on SumH, H:Hd + (H) + (Hd), p:a, Texture, Cooperative Movement, accurate versus inaccurate M, and Good Human Representation versus Poor Human Representation (see Weiner, 2003, chap. 5).

In common with Rorschach-based inferences about parents' adjustment level and coping capacities, inferences concerning their interpersonal accessibility are suggestive of how they are likely to interact with their children, but never conclusive. Only by observing and obtaining reports of how parents are functioning can examiners determine how their personality strengths and limitations as shown by the RIM are affecting their care of their children. Integration of Rorschach findings with behavioral observations and collateral reports, as well as other test data, should always precede conclusions about a person's parental effectiveness. These and other substantive guidelines for forensic Rorschach evaluations in criminal, personal injury, and family law cases are elaborated by Erard (2005), Gacono, Evans, Kaser-Boyd, and Gacono (2008), Johnston, Walters, and Olesen (2005), and Weiner (2005b, 2006, 2007).

ADMISSIBILITY INTO EVIDENCE

Forensic applications of Rorschach assessment depend not only on the implications of the test findings in particular kinds of cases, but also on whether testimony based on these findings will be admissible into evidence in courtroom proceedings. Federal and state jurisdictions vary in their criteria for admissibility, and judges have considerable leeway in determining what testimony they will allow. Nevertheless, pursuant to published guidelines and case law, the criteria for admissibility applied in individual cases typically involve some combination of three considerations: (a) whether the testimony is relevant to the issues in the case and will help the judge or jury arrive at their decision, which comes from the Federal Rules of Evidence; (b) whether the testimony is based on generally accepted methods and procedures in the expert's field, which is known as the Frye standard; and (c) whether the testimony is derived from scientifically sound methods and procedures, which is referred to as the Daubert standard (see Ewing, 2003; Hess, 2006).

The RIM satisfies criteria for admissibility in all three of these respects. The potential relevance of Rorschach findings to issues in forensic cases and the assistance they can provide in resolving these issues are delineated in the preceding discussion of psychological consultation in criminal, personal injury, and family law cases. The general acceptance of the Rorschach method is attested by its long history and the frequency with which it continues to be used and studied, as documented in the next section. The sound psychometric foundations of Rorschach assessment were reviewed in the opening section of this chapter.

The expectations concerning the forensic utility of Rorschach assessment and the admissibility into evidence of Rorschach-based testimony have been confirmed empirically by the frequency with which Rorschach assessment and testimony are in fact welcomed in the courtroom. In a survey of almost 8,000 cases in which psychologists appeared in court to provide Rorschach-based testimony, Weiner, Exner, and Sciara (1996) found only six instances in which the appropriateness of the RIM was challenged, and in only one of these cases was the testimony ruled inadmissible. Reviewing the full set of 247 cases in which Rorschach evidence was presented to a federal, state, or military court of appeals during the half-century from 1945 to 1995, Meloy, Hansen, and Weiner (1997) found that the admissibility and import of the Rorschach findings were questioned in only 10.5% of the hearings. Most of these questions were directed at the interpretation of the test data, not the Rorschach method itself, and in only two of these appellate cases was the relevance and utility of Rorschach assessment challenged.

In a follow-up to the Meloy et al. (1997) study, Meloy (2008) examined the full set of 150 published cases in which Rorschach findings were cited in federal, state, and military appellate court proceedings between 1996 and 2005. These 150 cases over a 10-year span indicate an average of 15 Rorschach citations per year in appellate cases, which is 3 times the annual rate of citation found by Meloy et al. (1997) during the preceding 50 years. In addition to finding this greatly increased use of the RIM in appellate courts, Meloy noted a substantial decrease

in the percentage of cases in which these court records included criticisms of Rorschach testimony, from the 10.5% during 1945–1995 to just 2% during 1996–2005. To quote Meloy, "There has been no Daubert challenge to the scientific status of the Rorschach in any state, federal, or military court of appeal since the U.S. Supreme Court decision in 1993 set the federal standard for admissibility of scientific evidence" (p. 85).

Despite widespread dissemination of this information, some contributors to the literature have asserted that Rorschach assessment does not satisfy criteria for admissibility into evidence and have discouraged forensic examiners from using the RIM, even to the point of calling for a moratorium on its use in forensic settings (Garb, 1999; Grove & Barden, 1999). These Rorschach critics have not presented any data to refute the available surveys of actual practice in this regard, which clearly indicate otherwise. This does not mean that forensic psychologists using the RIM, or any other assessment method for that matter, will be spared rigorous cross-examination on the witness stand. What it does mean is that adequately informed examiners will not be hard-pressed to defend the relevance, acceptance, and psychometric soundness of Rorschach assessment. For further discussion of the value and propriety of Rorschach-based testimony in courtroom proceedings, readers are referred to contributions by McCann (1998, 2004), McCann and Evans (2008), Ritzler, Erard, and Pettigrew (2002), and Hilsenroth and Stricker (2004).

Psychometric Foundations of Rorschach Assessment

The psychometric foundations for Rorschach-based assessment can be considered from three increasingly stringent standards: reliability, validity, and utility. Reliability is the extent to which a construct is assessed consistently. Once assessed consistently, it is necessary to establish that what is being measured is actually what is supposed to be measured (validity) and that the measured information is helpful in some applied manner (utility). We will consider each topic in turn.

Reliability

There are four main types of reliability: internal consistency, split half or alternate forms, test–retest, and inter-rater. Internal consistency reliability examines item-by-item uniformity in content to determine whether the items of a scale all measure the same thing (Streiner, 2003a, 2003b). Split-half and alternate forms reliability are more global; they examine consistency in total scores across parallel halves of a test or parallel versions of a full-length test. They allow for some item-by-item heterogeneity because they evaluate whether the composite of information on each form of the test produces a consistent and equivalent score. Although there are exceptions (e.g., Bornstein, Hill, Robinson, Calabreses, & Bowers, 1996; Dao & Prevatt, 2006), researchers typically do not investigate split-half and alternate forms reliability with the Rorschach because each Rorschach card—and even each location within a card—has its own distinct stimulus properties that pull for particular kinds of variables (Exner, 1996). For instance, the cards vary in the extent to which they are unified versus fragmented, shaded, colored, and so on. As a result, each "item" on the test, whether an item is defined as each response or as the responses to each card, is not equivalent and internal consistency analyses are generally considered inapplicable. The same factors make it impossible to split the inkblots into truly parallel halves or to produce an alternative set of inkblots that have stimulus properties that are equivalent to the original set.

Somewhat different issues affect internal consistency analyses of the six CS Constellation Indices (e.g., Dao & Prevatt, 2006), which were created as heterogeneous composite measures to maximize validity, not as homogeneous scales of a single construct. This process of scale construction makes internal consistency reliability largely immaterial (Streiner, 2003a). Psychometrically, predictive validity is maximized by combining unique and nonredundant sources of information, so strong validity can occur despite weak internal consistency reliability, even with a short and simple measure.

Test–retest reliability evaluates the stability of scores over time to repeated administrations of the same instrument. This has been studied fairly often with the Rorschach, and Grønnerød (2003) provided a systematic meta-analysis of the literature. The results showed acceptable to good stability for Rorschach scores, including for the CS (also see Meyer & Archer, 2001; Viglione & Hilsenroth, 2001). For the CS and other systems, scores thought to measure more trait-like aspects of personality produced relatively high retest coefficients, even over extended time periods, whereas scores thought to reflect state-like emotional process produced relatively low retest coefficients even over short time intervals. Grønnerød found that across all types of Rorschach scores and over an average retest interval

of slightly more than 3 years, the average reliability was $r = .65$ using data from 26 samples ($N = 904$).

Meyer (2004) organized results from all the meta-analyses of test–retest reliability in psychology, psychiatry, and medicine that had been published through 2001. Grønnerød's results compare favorably to the stability of other characteristics included in that review, including personality disorder diagnoses (kappa = .44 over 7.1 months); self-reported Big Five personality traits ($r = .73$ over 1.6 years); or disorganized parent–child attachment patterns ($r = .34$ over 2.1 years). The Rorschach findings also compare favorably to the extent to which the same professionals in medicine, psychology, business, meteorology, and human resources show "intra-rater" reliability by making consistent judgments when presented with the same information at two different times ($r = .76$ over 2.9 months).

Although these meta-analytic results indicate Rorschach stability compares favorably to other variables, Sultan, Andronikof, Réveillère, and Lemmel (2006) recently published a well-designed study of CS stability that was methodologically and financially supported by Exner's Rorschach Workshops. Sultan et al. found lower than anticipated consistency over a 3-month retest period. Stability across a range of CS scores is affected by the extent to which protocol complexity is aligned on both testing occasions. The two variables that index the overall richness or complexity of a protocol are R, the number of responses, and Lambda (or PureForm%), the proportion of responses prompted by simple form features. In the Sultan et al. study, stability coefficients for these variables were .75 and .72, respectively. Because these variables are excellent markers of the CS's first factor (i.e., the primary source of variance in CS scores), when they are unstable, most other scores also will be unstable. And this is what Sultan et al. observed; the median 3-month stability coefficient across 87 ratios, percentages, and derived scores that are emphasized in interpretation was just .55.

Although lower than desirable, this level of stability is similar to that observed with memory tests and job performance measures (Viglione & Meyer, 2008). Perhaps not surprisingly, Sultan et al. found that stability was moderated by R and Lambda; it was higher when people had values that did not change much over time and lower among those with values that did change. More research on Rorschach stability is needed, and Sultan et al.'s (2006) findings need to be replicated. However, it would be prudent for clinicians and researchers to carefully attend to this study, which indicates that generally healthy people who volunteer for a study can provide noticeably different protocols when tested by one reasonably trained examiner at baseline and by another reasonably trained examiner 3 months later.

The final type of reliability is inter-rater reliability, which assesses the consistency of judgments across raters. For the Rorschach, this type of reliability concerns scoring reliability as well as the reliability of interpretation across clinicians. The reliability of Rorschach scoring has been studied regularly and there are six meta-analyses summarizing this literature. Two of the meta-analyses examined CS reliability (Meyer, 1997; Meyer et al., 2002). Two others addressed the Rorschach Prognostic Rating Scale and the Rorschach Oral Dependency Scale (see Meyer, 2004). A fifth meta-analysis examined Elizur's Hostility Scale and Holt's aggression variables (Katko, Meyer, Mihura, & Bombel, in press), and the sixth addressed the Rorschach Mutuality of Autonomy (MOA) Scale (Bombel, Mihura, Meyer, & Katko, 2005). All the meta-analyses indicated that reasonably trained raters achieve good reliability. Across studies, the average Pearson or intraclass correlations (ICCs) for summary scores were above .85 and average kappa values for scores assigned to each response were above .80. The exception was for the Holt scales, where the values were .84 and .73, respectively.[3]

Meyer (2004) compared Rorschach inter-rater reliability data to all the other published meta-analyses of inter-rater reliability in psychology, psychiatry, and medicine available at that time. The data showed Rorschach scoring compared favorably to a wide range of other applied judgments. For instance, Rorschach raters agreed more than supervisors evaluating the job performance of employees ($r = .57$), surgeons or nurses diagnosing breast abnormalities on a clinical exam (kappa = .52), and physicians evaluating the quality of medical care provided by their peers (kappa = .31). For many Rorschach variables, scoring showed the same degree of reliability as when physicians estimated the size of the spinal canal and spinal cord from magnetic resonance imaging (MRI), computed tomography (CT), or X-ray scans ($r = .90$); dentists and dental personnel counted decayed, filled, or missing teeth in early childhood (kappa = .79); or when physicians or nurses rated the degree of drug sedation for patients who were in intensive care ($r = .91$, ICC = .84). These comparisons show that Rorschach coding for reasonably trained examiners

is typically a fairly straightforward activity, and good agreement can be obtained across raters.

At the same time, there are lingering difficulties associated with Rorschach scoring. Several studies have shown that low-base-rate variables have erratic reliability coefficients (e.g., Acklin, McDowell, & Verschell, 2000; McGrath et al., 2005; Meyer et al., 2002; Viglione & Taylor, 2003). Low-base-rate variables can be considered those that occur on average one time or less in each record (i.e., in $<5\%$ of responses; e.g., sex, reflections, color projection). For these kinds of variables, very large samples are needed to accurately estimate their reliability.

There also are some more common codes that often have lower reliability and thus appear to be more challenging to code accurately. These include the differentiation of unusual form quality from ordinary or minus; differentiating the various types of shading; the extent to which form is primary, secondary, or absent when coded in conjunction with color or shading responses; the differentiation between botany, landscape, and nature contents; and, perhaps most importantly, classifying specific types of cognitive disorganization. Meyer, Erdberg, and Shaffer (2007) examined reliability findings across 27 sets of normative reference data for the CS collected from various countries around the world ($n = 997$ protocols). Using kappa-equivalent iota coefficients (Janson & Olsson, 2004) computed at the response level, the average reliability for coding complete responses was .84, which indicates excellent agreement. However, iota differed by segment of the response. From lowest to highest chance-corrected agreement, the findings were: special scores = .67, form quality = .72, determinants = .82, developmental quality = .83, contents = .85, Z-scores = .87, popular = .90, pairs = .91, location and space = .92. Although having adequate reliability, special scores and form quality clearly are the most challenging variables to code.

Rorschach assessors also need to know that inter-rater reliability is not a fixed property of the score or test instrument. Rather, it is entirely dependent on the training, skill, and conscientiousness of the examiner. Thus, repeated practice and calibration with criterion ratings are essential for good practice.

Most reliability research (for the Rorschach and for other instruments) relies on raters who work or train in the same setting. To the extent that site-specific guidelines develop to contend with scoring ambiguity, those who work or train together will have greater agreement with each other than with different sites or work groups. As a result, the reliability literature, which quantifies agreement among two fallible coders, may give an overly positive view of the extent to which scoring is consistent or accurate across settings around the world.

In a preliminary report, Meyer, Viglione, Erdberg, Exner, and Shaffer (2004) studied this issue for the CS. They examined 40 randomly selected protocols from Exner's new CS non-patient reference sample (Exner, 2007) and 40 protocols from Shaffer, Erdberg, and Haroian's (2007) non-patient sample from Fresno, California. These 80 protocols were then blindly recoded by a third group of advanced graduate students who were trained at a site in San Diego. To determine the degree of cross-site reliability, the original scores assigned by Exner or Shaffer et al. were compared to the second set of scores assigned by the San Diego group. The median across-site ICC for protocol-level CS summary scores was .72. Although this would be considered "good" reliability according to standard benchmarks, it is lower than typical reliability found for trained coders working together in the same setting, which is generally $\geq$.85.

These findings suggest that there are coding complexities that are not fully clarified in standard CS training materials (Exner, 2001, 2003). It appears that in response to this, training sites develop local standards to help resolve these residual complexities, even though these standards are not uniform and may not generalize from one training site to another. To reduce these kinds of problems, researchers and clinicians should thoroughly practice their scoring against the across-site "gold standard" scores, which are the 300 practice responses in Exner's (2001) workbook and the 25 cases with complete responses in the basic CS texts (Exner, 2003; Exner & Erdberg, 2005). In addition, Viglione's (2002) advanced coding text should prove helpful.

In addition to scoring agreement, a significant issue concerns the extent to which clinicians interpret Rorschach results in a consistent manner. In the 1950s and 1960s it was fairly common for researchers to study the agreement among clinicians interpreting personality tests (not just the Rorschach), though since then this topic has rarely been addressed (Meyer, Mihura, & Smith, 2005). It is particularly important to study this issue with the Rorschach, as some have suggested that the inferences clinicians generate from the test may say more about them than about the client being assessed. Meyer, Mihura, and Smith examined agreement on CS interpretations in four data sets using protocols from 55 patients, each of which were interpreted by 3–8 clinicians. A total of 20 different clinicians participated in the research. Consistency was assessed across a representative set of 29 personality characteristics (e.g., "This person experiences himself as damaged, flawed, or hurt by life."). Substantial reliability was observed across all the data sets, with aggregated judgments having higher agreement (M r = .84) than judgments to individual interpretive statements (M r = .71). Meyer et al. also showed that these findings compared favorably to meta-analytic summaries of inter-rater agreement for other types of applied judgments in psychology, psychiatry, and medicine. For instance, therapists or observers ratings the quality of the therapeutic alliance in psychotherapy produce an average agreement of r = .78, while neurologists classifying strokes produce an average agreement of kappa = .51.

Meyer et al. (2005) also discovered that some clinicians were more reliable than others. For instance, the average reliability for aggregated judgments among the three most consistent judges was r = .90, but among the three least consistent judges it was r = .73. Thus, even though the overall findings indicated that experienced clinicians could reliably interpret CS data, some clinicians were clearly more consistent than others. These findings highlight how one needs to conscientiously learn principles of interpretation and then carefully and systematically consider all relevant testing data when conducting an idiographic clinical assessment.

Validity

Construct validity refers to evidence that a test scale is measuring the construct it is supposed to measure. It is determined by the full array of research findings on a scale and addresses both convergent and discriminant validity. Convergent validity refers to expected associations with criteria that theoretically should be related to the target construct, while discriminant validity refers to an expected lack of association with criteria that theoretically should be independent of the target construct. It is difficult to evaluate the construct validity of a multidimensional instrument like the Rorschach because of the complexity associated with systematically reviewing the full historical pattern of evidence attesting to convergent and discriminant validity for every test score. An easier, though less desirable, task is to evaluate the global evidence for the validity of Rorschach scales. We review meta-analyses addressing global validity, as well as a handful of meta-analyses addressing the validity of individual scales for assessing particular constructs.

Thousands of studies from around the world have provided evidence for Rorschach validity (e.g., for narrative summaries of specific variables, see Bornstein & Masling, 2005; Exner & Erdberg, 2005; Viglione, 1999). Meyer and Archer (2001) summarized the available evidence from Rorschach meta-analyses, including four that examined the global validity of the test and seven that examined the validity of specific scales in relation to particular criteria. The scales included CS and non-CS variables. For comparison, they also summarized the meta-analytic evidence available on the validity of the MMPI and IQ measures. Subsequently, Meyer (2004) compared the validity evidence for these psychological tests to meta-analytic findings for the medical assessments reported in Meyer et al. (2001).

Although the use of different types of research designs and validation tasks makes it risky to compare findings across meta-analyses, the broad review of evidence indicated three primary conclusions. First, psychological and medical tests have varying degrees of validity, ranging from scores that are essentially unrelated to a particular criterion to scores that are strongly associated with relevant criteria. Second, it was difficult to distinguish between medical tests and psychological tests in terms of their average validity; both types of tests produced a wide range of effect sizes and had similar averages. Third, test validity is conditional and dependent on the criteria used to evaluate the instrument. For a given scale, validity is greater against some criteria and weaker against others.

Within these findings, validity for the Rorschach was much the same as it was for other instruments; effect sizes varied depending on the variables considered but, on average, validity was similar to other instruments. Thus, Meyer and Archer (2001) concluded that the systematically collected data showed the Rorschach produced good validity coefficients that were on par with other tests:

> Across journal outlets, decades of research, aggregation procedures, predictor scales, criterion measures, and types of participants, reasonable hypotheses for the vast array of Rorschach . . . scales that have been empirically tested produce convincing evidence for their construct validity.
>
> (*Meyer & Archer*, 2001, p. 491)

Like others before them who conducted meta-analytic reviews of the Rorschach literature (e.g., Parker, Hanson, & Hunsley, 1988), Meyer and Archer concluded that a dispassionate review of the evidence would not warrant singling out the Rorschach for particular criticism. However, they also noted that the same evidence would not warrant singling out the Rorschach for particular praise. Its broadband validity appears both as good as and also as limited as that for other psychological tests.

Robert Rosenthal, a highly regarded meta-analytic expert, was commissioned to conduct an impartial comparative analysis of Rorschach and MMPI validity for a special issue of the journal *Psychological Assessment*. He and his coauthors (Hiller, Rosenthal, Bornstein, Berry, & Brunell-Neuleib, 1999; Rosenthal, Hiller, Bornstein, Berry, & Brunell-Neuleib, 2001) found the Rorschach and MMPI were equally valid on average. At the same time, they identified moderators to validity for each instrument. The Rorschach demonstrated greater validity against criteria that they classified as objective, while the MMPI demonstrated greater validity against criteria consisting of other self-report scales or psychiatric diagnoses.[4] Their objective criteria included a range of variables that were largely behavioral events, medical conditions, behavioral interactions with the environment, or classifications that required minimal observer judgment, such as dropping out of treatment, history of abuse, number of driving accidents, history of criminal offenses, having a medical disorder, cognitive test performance, performance on a behavioral test of ability to delay gratification, or response to medication. Viglione (1999) conducted a systematic descriptive review of the Rorschach literature and similarly concluded that the Rorschach was validly associated with behavioral events or life outcomes involving person–environment interactions that emerge over time. In general, these findings are consistent with the types of spontaneous behavioral trends and longitudinally determined life outcomes that McClelland, Koestner, and Weinberger (1989) showed were best predicted by tests measuring implicit characteristics, as opposed to the conscious and deliberately chosen near-term actions that were best predicted by explicit self-report tests (also see Bornstein, 1998).

Grønnerød (2004) conducted the most recent meta-analysis of Rorschach validity, and it was not considered in the previous reviews. Grønnerød systematically reviewed research on Rorschach scales as measures of personality change from psychological treatment. He found the Rorschach produced a level of validity that was equivalent to alternative instruments based on self-report or clinician-ratings. Grønnerød also examined moderators to validity. As expected, Rorschach scores changed more with longer treatment, suggesting that more therapy produced more healthy change in personality. Also, effect sizes were smaller when it was more certain that researchers were blind to whether the protocols being scored were obtained before or after treatment. Effect sizes were larger in studies where researchers clearly described their scoring reliability procedures and obtained good reliability results using conservative statistics.

Overall, the meta-analytic evidence supports the general validity of the Rorschach. Globally, the test appears to function as well as other clinical assessment instruments. To date, only a few meta-analyses have systematically examined the validity of specific scales in relation to particular criteria. The evidence has been positive and supportive for the Rorschach Oral Dependency (ROD) scale, the Rorschach Prognostic Rating Scale (RPRS), and the precursor to the PTI, the Schizophrenia Index (SCZI), though the evidence does not support the Depression Index (DEPI) as a diagnostic indicator (see Meyer & Archer, 2001). As is true for other commonly used tests, such as the MMPI-2, Personality Assessment Inventory (PAI; Morey, 1991), Millon Clinical Multiaxial Inventory-III (MCMI-III; Millon, 1994), or Wechsler scales (e.g., Wechsler, 1997), additional focused meta-analytic reviews that systematically catalog the validity evidence of particular Rorschach variables relative to specific types of criteria will continue to refine and enhance clinical practice.

Utility

In general, the utility of a test refers to the value of the information it provides relative to its costs. The Rorschach takes time to administer, score, and interpret. To make up for these costs, it needs to provide useful information that cannot be obtained from other measures or methods that are readily available and less time consuming. One way to evaluate this issue is through incremental validity analyses (see Hunsley & Meyer, 2003), where the Rorschach and a less time intensive source of information are compared statistically. To demonstrate incremental validity and statistically document the Rorschach was providing unique information, a Rorschach scale would need to predict a criterion over and above what could be predicted by the simpler or less costly data source.

Although utility and cost–benefit considerations go beyond incremental validity analyses, the latter is one type of evidence that can attest to utility. Utility also can be demonstrated when a test predicts important real-world behaviors, life outcomes, and the kind of ecologically valid criteria that are important in the context of applied practice. Research reviews and meta-analyses show that the Rorschach possesses utility in all of these forms, such that Rorschach variables predict clinically relevant behaviors and outcomes and have demonstrated incremental validity over other tests, demographic data, and other types of information (Bornstein & Masling, 2005; Exner & Erdberg, 2005; Hiller et al., 1999; Meyer, 2000a; Meyer & Archer, 2001; Viglione, 1999; Viglione & Hilsenroth, 2001; Weiner, 2001).

Here we just briefly review a sample of recent utility findings. Studies from the United States and Europe show the Rorschach provided incremental validity when predicting subsequent success in Norwegian naval special forces training (Hartmann, Sunde, Kristensen, & Martinussen, 2003), future delinquency in Swedish adolescents and adults (Janson & Stattin, 2003), subsequent psychiatric relapse among previously hospitalized U.S. children (Stokes et al., 2003), future improvement across a range of interventions in U.S. adults (Meyer, 2000a; Meyer & Handler, 1997), subsequent benefit from antidepressant medication in adult U.S. inpatients (Perry & Viglione, 1991), recent glucose stability levels in diabetic French children (Sultan, Jebrane, & Heurtier-Hartemann, 2002), and future emergency medical transfers and drug overdoses in U.S. inpatients (Fowler, Piers, Hilsenroth, Holdwick, & Padawer, 2001). In these studies, the Rorschach had incremental validity over various alternative data sources, including self-report scales, psychiatric diagnoses, reports from others, and intelligence tests.

Studies have repeatedly shown that Rorschach and self-report scales have minimal correlations even when they purportedly measure similar constructs (Bornstein, 2002; Krishnamurthy, Archer, & House, 1996; Meyer & Archer, 2001; Viglione, 1996). Although this lack of association was unexpected, to the extent that both types of measures are related to a criterion but not to each other, the Rorschach should display incremental validity over self-report scales (and vice versa). At this point, there are more studies documenting the limited associations between these two data sources than their combined value. However, studies have shown that the combination of Rorschach-assessed and self-reported dependency provides the optimal ability to predict certain kinds of dependent behavior (Bornstein, 1998). In addition, the CS scales of psychotic symptoms (i.e., PTI or SCZI) have regularly demonstrated incremental validity over

MMPI-2 scales for predicting psychotic disorders (e.g., Meyer, 2000b; Ritsher, 2004).

A series of studies with obese patients in Sweden demonstrated the Rorschach had utility for predicting practical behaviors and life outcome criteria. Rorschach scores predicted how quickly patients consumed an experimental meal, their propensity to atypically accelerate their rate of eating during that meal, their eventual weight loss, and their response to weight loss medication (Elfhag, Barkeling, Carlsson, Lindgren, & Rössner, 2004; Elfhag, Barkeling, Carlsson, & Rössner, 2003; Elfhag, Carlsson, & Rössner, 2003; Elfhag, Rossner, & Carlsson, 2004).

Two recent theory-driven studies examined the relation of Rorschach CS scores to therapy processes. Bihlar and Carlsson (2001) showed pretreatment CS scores predicted whether therapists would need to modify their initial treatment plans during the course of therapy. These results indicated that Rorschach scores were identifying characteristics that were not otherwise obvious from the baseline information that had been obtained from interviews, behavioral observation, and history. Nygren (2004) found CS scores were associated with clinician ratings of ego strength and the capacity to engage in dynamic therapy. She also found CS scores discriminated patients who were selected for intensive, long-term psychoanalytic therapy from those who were not.

Lundbäck et al. (2006) studied Swedish patients who had recently attempted suicide. Previous research indicated low cerebrospinal fluid (CSF) concentrations of the serotonin metabolite 5-hydroxyindoleacetic acid (5-HIAA) were associated with more violent and severe suicide attempts. As expected, the CS Suicide Constellation (S-CON) was negatively correlated with 5-HIAA levels ($r_S = -.39$). Post hoc analyses showed that vista responses and the color dominance index (CF + C > FC) were the two strongest predictor variables from the S-CON. Lundbäck et al. also found 5-HIAA was unrelated to the DEPI ($r_S = -.21$) and Coping Deficit Index (CDI; $r_S = .26$). These results are similar to Fowler et al.'s (2001) US findings, where the S-CON predicted subsequent suicidal behavior but the DEPI and CDI did not. Both studies provide evidence for the convergent and discriminant validity of the S-CON.

As a final example, many studies have examined the ROD as an index of dependency. Bornstein (1996, 1999) conducted a systematic meta-analysis of the literature and documented how ROD scores predict help-seeking behavior, conformity, compliance, suggestibility, and interpersonal yielding in laboratory and clinical settings. ROD scores have

discriminant validity in that they are unrelated or minimally related to scales of alternative constructs like social desirability, IQ, and locus of control.

This brief summary of studies related to utility is limited in several ways. First, some of the samples were small and so the initial findings need to be replicated. Second, even though all the researchers provided carefully considered a priori hypotheses, the results did not always support the hypothesized variables. For instance, Elfhag, Carlsson, and Rossner did not find support for the ROD in relation to eating behavior and Nygren did not find support for several variables she thought would predict who would be selected for intensive psychotherapy (e.g., inanimate movement, distorted or arbitrary form quality, dimensionality based on form).

Nonetheless, based largely on the kinds of findings reviewed in this section, the Board of Trustees of the Society for Personality Assessment synthesized the available evidence and issued an official statement on the scientific foundation for using the Rorschach in clinical and forensic practice. They concluded "the Rorschach possesses reliability and validity similar to that of other generally accepted personality assessment instruments and its responsible use in personality assessment is appropriate and justified" (p. 219; Society for Personality Assessment, 2005).

Usage Frequency of Rorschach Assessment

Surveys over the past 40 years have regularly shown substantial endorsement of Rorschach assessment as a valuable method to learn, study, and practice. As reported by Hogan (2005), the RIM has over this span of time consistently been the fourth most frequently used test among clinical psychologists, exceeded only by the Wechsler Adult Intelligence Scale (WAIS), the Minnesota Multiphasic Personality Inventory (MMPI), and the Wechsler Intelligence Scale for Children (WISC), in that order. Survey data have further indicated that over 80% of clinical psychologists engaged in providing assessment services use the RIM in their work and believe that clinical students should be competent in Rorschach assessment (Camara, Nathan, & Puente, 2000). In a survey by Mihura and Weinle (2002) of American Psychological Association graduate student affiliates, 87% of 254 respondents indicated having had an introductory course that included Rorschach assessment. Of the students who had had some Rorschach training, 78% reported that they would like to increase their knowledge of the RIM. Most of these respondents with some Rorschach training had found Rorschach assessment helpful in understanding people they were evaluating, and 83% stated that they expected to use the RIM in their professional practice.

Rorschach assessment has a prominent place in clinical evaluations of young people as well as adults. In a survey by Cashel (2002) of child and adolescent practitioners, 162 respondents indicated that the RIM was their third most frequently used personality assessment measure, following sentence completion and figure drawing methods. Among 346 psychologists working with adolescents in a variety of clinical and academic settings, Archer and Newsom (2000) found that the RIM was their most frequently used personality test and second among all tests only to a Wechsler intelligence scale (WAIS or WISC).

Psychology internship training directors responding to surveys have similarly identified the RIM as among the three measures most frequently included in test batteries in their setting, following the WAIS/WISC and the MMPI-2/MMPI-A. As testimony to their endorsement of the value of Rorschach assessment, surveyed training directors have commonly expressed a preference for their incoming interns to have had a Rorschach course or at least a good working knowledge of the instrument (Clemence & Handler, 2001; Stedman, Hatch, & Schoenfeld, 2000).

Survey data document an established place for Rorschach assessment in forensic as well as clinical practice. Among responding forensic psychologists in several different studies, 30% reported using the RIM in evaluations of competency to stand trial, 32% in evaluations of criminal responsibility, 41% in evaluations of personal injury, 44–48% in evaluations of adults involved in custody disputes, and 23% in evaluations of children in custody cases (Ackerman & Ackerman, 1997; Boccaccini & Brodsky, 1999; Borum & Grisso, 1995; Quinell & Bow, 2001). In a recent study, Archer, Buffington-Vollum, Stredny, and Handel (2006) found a 36% frequency of Rorschach usage for all purposes combined among forensic psychologists they surveyed. At the same time, there are some forensic questions (e.g., risk for sexual violence, competency to waive Miranda rights) that are better answered by focused forensic assessment instruments than multifaceted, broad-band measures of personality like the Rorschach (e.g., Lally, 2003).

With respect to the Rorschach assessment as a subject for scientific study, the professional literature has for many years included a steady and substantial volume of published research concerning RIM

characteristics and utility. Buros (1974) *Tests in Print II* identified 4,580 Rorschach references from its 1921 inception through 1971, which averages to a rate of 92 publications annually during this 50-year period. In the 1990s, Butcher and Rouse (1996) found an almost identical trend continuing from 1974 to 1994, with an average of 96 Rorschach research articles appearing annually in journals published in the United States during this 20-year period. In the Butcher and Rouse data, the RIM was second only to the MMPI among personality assessment instruments in the volume of research it generated. For the 3-year period 2004–2006, PsycINFO lists 350 scientific articles, books, book chapters, and dissertations worldwide concerning Rorschach assessment.

In this last regard, the application and scientific study of Rorschach assessment extends far beyond American borders to a large international community of Rorschach scholars and practitioners whose research published abroad has for many years made important contributions to the literature (see Weiner, 1999). As testimony to the international utilization of Rorschach assessment, a survey of test use in Spain, Portugal, and Latin American countries by Muniz, Prieto, Almeida, and Bartram (1999) showed the RIM as the third most widely used psychological assessment instrument, following the Wechsler scales and versions of the MMPI. On the other side of the world, surveys in Japan have indicated that about 60% of Japanese clinical psychologists use the RIM in their practice (Ogawa, 2004).

Cross-Cultural Applicability of Rorschach Assessment

The cross-cultural applicability of Rorschach assessment involves considering (a) whether the RIM is appropriate for use with minority populations within the United States and (b) whether it can be used to good effect in other countries around the world. The first of these considerations can be addressed in terms of available research data, and the second consideration touches on conceptual perspectives in cross-cultural personality research as well as on extensive international research findings concerning the normative characteristics of Rorschach variables.

Rorschach Assessment with Minority Groups

Some critics of Rorschach assessment have alleged that "Blacks, Hispanics, Native Americans, and non-Americans score differently on important Rorschach variables" and have concluded, without reporting or referencing any supportive data, that "because there are important cross-cultural differences, and because appropriate norms have not been developed, it is doubtful whether the Comprehensive System should be used to evaluate members of American minority groups" (Wood & Lilienfeld, 1999, pp. 341 & 342). Although the U.S. normative reference data for the Rorschach CS include almost 20% of non-Caucasian participants, it is the case that there are no separate Rorschach norms for these groups. However, the lack of separate minority group norms for the RIM or any other personality measure warrants concern only if there is evidence that minority persons respond differently to them. To the contrary, Rorschach research studies with American minority groups have in fact identified few CS differences among them.

Presley, Smith, Hilsenroth, and Exner (2001) found a clinically significant difference on only 1 of 23 core Rorschach variables between 44 African-Americans and 44 demographically matched Caucasian Americans in the CS non-patient reference sample. Meyer (2002), examining the protocols of 432 persons consecutively evaluated in a hospital-based psychological testing program, found no association between ethnicity and 188 Rorschach summary scores among demographically matched European-American, African-American, Hispanic-American, Asian-American, and Native American individuals. Meyer concluded his research report by noting that "the available data clearly support the cross-ethnic use of the Comprehensive system" (p. 127).

Rorschach Assessment with Multinational Groups

The RIM is a relatively culture-free measuring instrument that can be and has been successfully administered and scored in many diverse cultures in numerous Eastern and Western Hemisphere countries. Provided that the examiner and the person being examined can communicate in a language in which they are both fluent, the test can be expected to provide dependable and interpretable data. With respect to interpreting the obtained data, however, cross-cultural Rorschach assessment could become problematic if the normative response patterns of persons from particular backgrounds and locales differ in clinically significant ways. The extent to which this potential problem does in fact impede cross-cultural applications must be judged on the basis of some conceptual considerations and on empirical findings collected in appropriately designed normative studies.

From a conceptual perspective, there are two alternatives to consider. On one hand, clinically significant differences in patterns of Rorschach responses across different cultures and countries might mandate developing separate norms for these groups, especially as a basis for inferring deviant or maladaptive personality characteristics. On the other hand, group differences in Rorschach or other test patterns may be an accurate reflection of actual personality differences between the groups, especially with respect to whether certain personality characteristics are relatively common and adaptive in their society or relatively uncommon and maladaptive (see Ephraim, 2000). In this latter case, cultural differences in personality characteristics would not militate against using a test to identify personality characteristics in the same way with diverse groups. What would be needed instead of culture-specific norms would be cultural sensitivity to the differential import of these personality characteristics in an individual examinee's sociocultural context.

With respect to appropriate research design, cross-cultural studies of normative Rorschach patterns should meet four criteria for ensuring comparability of the obtained data. First, the participant groups should be demographically similar, especially with respect to their level of education. Second, if one's goal is to have a normal functioning standard rather than a broad representative sample of the whole population, the participants should be screened for mental health problems, to exclude persons who are psychologically disturbed. Third, the RIM should be administered by experienced examiners who are familiar with the requirements for doing an adequate inquiry. Fourth, adequate steps should be taken to promote involvement in the testing process, as a way of minimizing deviant responses by participants who do not take their task seriously (see Allen & Dana, 2004; Ritzler, 2004; Weiner, 2001).

Over the past decade researchers from various countries around the world have compiled normative CS data for adults, adolescents, and children. Almost all of these findings were recently published in a special supplement to the *Journal of Personality Assessment* (Shaffer, Erdberg, & Meyer, 2007). Meyer et al. (2007) summarized the results from these studies. Using 21 samples of adult data from 17 countries ($N = 4,704$ protocols) they pooled the results and created a composite set of internationally based reference norms (i.e., means and standard deviations) from which they then computed

T-scores for each sample. They found that the adult samples from around the world were generally quite similar, with average T-scores across structural summary variables generally falling in a narrow range between 45 and 55 (i.e., within a half an SD of the international mean). Thus, the authors concluded, "by-and-large, adults look pretty much the same on the CS no matter what language they speak, what country they reside in, and what cultural background influences them." Although it was not clear whether the relatively minimal residual variation between countries was due to differences in culture, language, participant selection criteria, administration standards, coding benchmarks, and/or examiner skill, the impact of all these potential influences was modest, supporting the international use of the Rorschach.

At the same time, Exner's current reference sample of 450 U.S. non-patients (Exner, 2007; Exner & Erdberg, 2005) was notable in a number of respects. It defined the high end of the sample average values on a number of variables, with T-scores in the 55–57 range on D, DQ+, EA, FC, CF, Popular, and GHR, and it defined the low end of the samples on other variables, with T-scores in the 44–47 range on Lambda, Dd, DQv, M−, Pure C, Xu%, PHR, and the PTI. Furthermore, this sample was a relative outlier on certain variables. It had low total scores on the DEPI, CDI, and S-CON, with T-scores between 38 and 42. For form quality variables, it had low scores on X−% (T = 42), and high scores on X+%, WDA%, and XA% (T-range: 58–62). Exner's protocols also had relative outlier values on WSumC, COP, and HRV scores (T-range: 57–59).

These differences do not appear to reflect differences in the underlying health of the samples, as most of the other researchers used selection criteria that equaled or exceeded the criteria used by Exner. However, based on data that compared a sample of Exner's protocols to the adult sample collected by Shaffer, Erdberg, and Haroian (2007), Meyer et al. concluded the observed differences were probably due to artifacts associated with site-specific conventions in administration, inquiry, and scoring. Because the Composite International Reference Values showed a basic consistency that transcended cultures, languages, levels of examiner training, site-specific conventions in administration, inquiry, and scoring, non-patient exclusion criteria, and participant recruitment strategies, Meyer et al. (2007) encouraged clinicians to integrate these normative values into their interpretation of protocols.

They indicate what can be expected from reasonably functioning adults across countries and cultures, while taking into account the limits of our current administration, inquiry, and scoring guidelines. Not only do they incorporate the seemingly small variability that may result from cultural differences, but more importantly they incorporate the kind of variability that can be expected within a country or region from different examiners administering, inquiring, and scoring the test. Using these values in clinical practice should help ensure that inferences about functioning generalize across examiners, levels of skill in administration and scoring, testing context, language, and culture. Inferences drawn from them also should help ensure that patients are being evaluated relative to a contemporary and broadly generalizable reference standard.

The adult findings indicated the CS can be used confidently by clinicians and researchers around the world. Unfortunately, the findings were quite different for children and adolescents. The available CS norms for children and adolescents were first published by Exner and Weiner in 1982. Even then, the authors doubted that their samples were representative and feared they probably reflected an overly healthy and well-functioning standard. To evaluate this issue, Meyer et al. (2007) plotted the 19 child and adolescent samples published in the *Journal of Personality Assessment* supplement as well as Exner's (2003) 12 samples for ages 5–16 on the Adult Composite International Norms. Unlike the adult samples, the 31 child and adolescent samples (total N = 2,647) produced erratic and often quite extreme values on many scores.

For instance, Lambda values were quite elevated in many of the samples (e.g., Japanese and Portuguese children had raw means from 3.1 to 8.5 and 2.9 to 4.0, respectively) and they diverged substantially both from the adult international norms and from Exner's reference values for children (which had Lambda values that ranged from .49 to .86). Similarly, form quality scores often looked quite unhealthy. For example, Japanese children had raw means on X−% that ranged from .47 to .66; for U.S. children the raw means ranged from .28 to .44. These scores again deviated from the adult international norms and differed markedly from Exner's child reference values, which had X−% values that ranged from .03 to .10. Within a country (but not so clearly across countries) Lambda and form quality also showed the greatest degree of developmental changes in the newer samples, with

Lambda decreasing and form quality becoming more conventional as children age. Based on this, Meyer et al. (2007) inferred:

> Lambda and FQ may be the most sensitive to the style or manner in which the test administration is conducted, the administration and inquiry skill of the examiner, across-site differences in administration and scoring conventions, developmental processes, and, perhaps most importantly, the interaction of all the forgoing factors with culture-specific conventions that may be present when a cue-sensitive child completes a rather unstructured and open-ended task with an unfamiliar adult.

Given the above, Meyer et al. (2007) discouraged clinicians from using many CS scores to make nomothetic, score-based inferences about psychopathology in children and adolescents until the developmental, cultural, and administrative/inquiry factors that contribute to the variability across samples becomes clearer. Instead, they encouraged clinicians to use much of the Rorschach data collected from children and adolescents in an idiographic and exploratory manner. There were two exceptions to this recommendation. First, when a child produces healthy looking scores, with relatively high R, low Lambda, high DQ+, healthy form quality, and low WSum6, a clinician could reasonably infer strengths and assets in functioning. Second, to the extent that a child obtains scores that are unhealthier than the most extreme mean from any of the supplement samples, one could begin to infer difficulties in adaptation and functioning.

The *JPA* supplement is an important milestone in CS research. However, it provides clinicians and researchers with a mixed picture of the CS. To the extent that others, like us, wish to have normative reference values that transcend countries, cultures, languages, recruitment strategies, types of normative target populations, examiner training, and age, the adult findings revealed a reasonable degree of similarity across samples and countries. Relative to a composite international standard, adults from various countries around the world generally look similar. These findings are consistent with the largest and most systematically organized effort to study personality around the world. McCrae and his colleagues have obtained self- and observer-rating data from 50 cultures on the Revised NEO Personality Inventory (NEO PI-R; see McCrae & Terracciano, 2006; McCrae et al., 2005a, b; Terracciano et al., 2005). They documented both the transcultural similarity in adult personality and that perceptions of so-called "national character" are based upon unfounded stereotypes that are not reflected in actual personality characteristics (McCrae & Terracciano, 2006; Terracciano et al., 2005). The adult data in the *JPA* supplement are consistent with these conclusions, even though they are based on a very different method of assessment.

However, the child and adolescent findings in the supplement were quite different and they challenge the use of the CS in these populations. The data for children and adolescents were certainly less comprehensive and complete than for adults. Consequently, it is imperative to collect additional results from carefully designed studies that examine developmental processes expressed on the Rorschach across cultures.

Status of Education and Training in Rorschach Assessment

As illustrated by the preceding responses to the first three of the four questions raised in introducing this discussion of contemporary issues in Rorschach assessment, these are not bad times for the RIM. Although reservations have been raised by some critics about the scientific status of Rorschach assessment, research findings have established that the instrument rests on a solid psychometric foundation. The RIM has been identified as serving valuable clinical and forensic purposes, and survey findings have indicated its continued popularity as the second most frequently used and studied personality assessment instrument. An international community of Rorschach scholars and practitioners is thriving and a large-scale, multinational collaborative project for collecting cross-cultural normative data reveals that the CS is quite transportable across cultures for adults, though challenges and uncertainties are present for using the CS with children.

In response to the fourth question about the status of education and training in Rorschach assessment, there is some reason for concern about the current preparation of the next generation of Rorschach researchers and practitioners. In the previously mentioned survey of internship directors, the value placed on Rorschach assessment and the preference for interns to have had prior Rorschach coursework were commonly accompanied by expressed dissatisfaction with the amount and quality of assessment training that students are receiving in their graduate programs (Clemence & Handler, 2001; Stedman et al., 2000; see also Childs & Eyde, 2002). In the Mihura and Weinle (2002) survey mentioned previously, 87% of students reported having some Rorschach coursework, and

Viglione and Hilsenroth (2001) refer to survey data indicating that 80% of graduate psychology programs teach the RIM.

Nevertheless, times change, and in the present authors' experience in 2007, there appear to be increasingly frequent anecdotal reports of Rorschach assessment being given short shrift in clinical psychology curricula, or omitted from them entirely. In some graduate departments, we have heard, Rorschach assessment is not only not taught, but actively demeaned, despite the abundant evidence of its practical utility and psychometric sturdiness. This position is curious, as it is not based on a balanced review of the scientific evidence, even though that is the justification given.

Like any other measuring instrument, on the other hand, the RIM has limitations that must be recognized. On the positive side, the general validity of Rorschach assessment, as determined by meta-analyses, matches that of other commonly used multidimensional personality instruments. The RIM provides clinicians with an *in vivo* sample of behavior that, when examinees are open and spontaneous, sheds considerable light on their approach to problem solving, their resources and cognitive flexibility, the imagery that occupies their mind, and conflicts and concerns dynamics they may have that are not otherwise readily accessible in initial interviews. In addition, non-patient adults around the world generally look pretty similar to each other in their Rorschach responses.

On the other hand, there is still much research to be done and much to be learned about how, why, and when the RIM works. Future investigations need in particular to clarify and specify the Rorschach's "locus of effectiveness" as an assessment instrument, in order to document what unique information it provides and when it is likely to be of greatest value in a clinical assessment. The recently reported data on children and adolescents call for special attention to unraveling the developmental progression of young people as reflected in their Rorschach responses. Rather than discouraging further research or applications of Rorschach assessment, current gaps in knowledge provide a compelling blueprint for potentially productive efforts to continue expanding our grasp how Rorschach findings can contribute to understanding people and being of help to them.

Notes

1. This conclusion is moderated, however, by the complexity of an individual's protocol. Long and complex records are generally prone to false-positive errors (i.e., there are elevations across a range of indicators that may have more to do with psychological complexity or overengagement with the task than any specific disturbance), while short and simplistic records are prone to generate false-negative errors (i.e., the absence of elevations across CS scores is more the result of psychological simplicity or lack of engagement with the task than the absence of any particular difficulty).

2. Although we focus here on the CS, other approaches to scoring the RIM have also documented impressive validity for predicting treatment response (Meyer, 2000; Meyer & Handler, 1997).

3. For ICC or kappa values, findings above .74 are considered excellent, above .59 are considered good, and above .39 are considered fair (Cicchetti, 1994).

4. Note that despite this finding the literature shows that Rorschach scales validly identify psychotic diagnoses and validly measure psychotic symptoms (Lilienfeld, Wood, & Garb, 2000; Meyer & Archer, 2001; Perry, Minassian, Cadenhead, Sprock, & Braff, 2003; Viglione, 1999, Viglione & Hilsenroth, 2001; Wood, Lilienfeld, Garb, & Nezworski, 2000). Unlike most other diagnostic conditions, which are heavily dependent on the patient's self-reported symptoms, psychotic disorders are often diagnosed on the basis of the patient's observed behavior rather than on their specific reported complaints. This may account for the differential validity that the Rorschach has shown relative to diagnostic criteria, where evidence is much more consistent and strong for assessing psychotic disorders compared to other disorders, such as depression.

References

Ackerman, M. J., & Ackerman, M. C. (1997). Custody evaluations in practice: A survey of experienced professionals (revisited). *Professional Psychology, 28*, 137–145.

Acklin, M. W., McDowell, C. J., & Verschell, M. S. (2000). Interobserver agreement, intraobserver reliability, and the Rorschach Comprehensive System. *Journal of Personality Assessment, 74*, 15–47.

Allen, J., & Dana, R. H. (2004). Methodological issues in cross-cultural and multicultural Rorschach research. *Journal of Personality Assessment, 82*, 189–206.

American Psychiatric Association (2000). *Diagnostic and statistical manual of mental disorders* (4th ed., Text rev.). Washington, DC: Author.

Archer, R. P., Buffington-Vollum, J. K., Stredny, R. V., & Handel, R. W. (2006). A survey of psychological test use patterns among forensic psychologists. *Journal of Personality Assessment, 87*, 84–94.

Archer, R. P., & Newsom, C. R. (2000). Psychological test usage with adolescent clients: Survey update. *Assessment, 7*, 227–235.

Armstrong, J., & Kaser-Boyd, N. (2004). Projective assessment of psychological trauma. In M. J. Hilsenroth & D. L. Segal (Eds.), *Comprehensive handbook of psychological assessment, Vol. 2: Personality assessment* (pp. 500–512). New York: John Wiley & Sons.

Beck, S. J. (1930a). Personality diagnosis by means of the Rorschach test. *American Journal of Orthopsychiatry, 1*, 81–88.

Beck, S. J. (1930b). The Rorschach test and personality diagnosis. *American Journal of Psychiatry, 10*, 19–52.

Beutler, L. E., & Groth-Marnat, G. (2003). *Integrative assessment of adult personality* (3rd ed.). New York: Guilford.

Beck, S. J. (1937). Introduction to the Rorschach method. *American Orthopsychiatric Association Monograph I.* New York: American Orthopsychiatric Association.

Bihlar, B., & Carlsson, A. M. (2001). Planned and actual goals in psychodynamic psychotherapies: Do patients' personality characteristics relate to agreement? *Psychotherapy Research, 11*, 383–400.

Blatt, S. J., & Ford, R. Q. (1994). *Therapeutic change.* New York: Plenum.

Boccaccini, M. T., & Brodsky, S. L. (1999). Diagnostic test usage by forensic psychologists in emotional injury cases. *Professional Psychology, 30*, 253–259.

Bombel, G., Mihura, J. L., Meyer, G. J., & Katko, N. J. (2005). *A meta-analysis of Mutuality of Autonomy (MOA) scale reliability.* Paper presented at the annual meeting of the Society for Personality Assessment, Chicago, on March 5, 2005.

Bornstein, R. F. (1996). Construct validity of the Rorschach Oral Dependency Scale: 1967–1995. *Psychological Assessment, 8*, 200–505.

Bornstein, R. F. (1998). Implicit and self-attributed dependency strivings: Differential relationships to laboratory and field measures of help-seeking. *Journal of Personality and Social Psychology, 75*, 779–787.

Bornstein, R. F. (1999). Criterion validity of objective and projective dependency tests: A meta-analytic assessment of behavioral prediction. *Psychological Assessment, 11*, 48–57.

Bornstein, R. F. (2002). A process dissociation approach to objective-projective test score interrelationships. *Journal of Personality Assessment, 78*, 47–68.

Bornstein, R. F., Hill, E. L., Robinson, K. J., Calabreses, C., & Bowers, K. S. (1996). Internal reliability of Rorschach Oral Dependency Scale scores. *Educational and Psychological Measurement, 56*, 130–138.

Bornstein, R. F., & Masling, J. M. (Eds.) (2005). *Scoring the Rorschach: Seven validated systems.* Mahwah, NJ: Lawrence Erlbaum.

Borum, R., & Grisso, T. (1995). Psychological test use in criminal forensic evaluations. *Professional Psychology, 26*, 465–473.

Buros, O. K. (Ed.). (1974). *Tests in print II.* Highland Park, NJ: Gryphon.

Butcher, J. N., & Rouse, S. V. (1996). Personality: Individual differences and clinical assessment. *Annual Review of Psychology, 47*, 87–111.

Camara, W., Nathan, J., & Puente, A. (2000). Psychological test usage: Implications in professional use. *Professional Psychology, 31*, 141–154.

Cashel, M. L. (2002). Child and adolescent psychological assessment: Current clinical practices and the impact of managed care. *Professional Psychology: Research and Practice, 33*, 446–453.

Childs, R. A., & Eyde, L. D. (2002). Assessment training in clinical psychology doctoral programs: What should we teach? What do we teach? *Journal of Personality Assessment, 78*, 139–144.

Cicchetti, D. V. (1994). Guidelines, criteria, and rules of thumb for evaluating normed and standardized assessment instruments in psychology. *Psychological Assessment, 6*, 284–290.

Clarkin, J. F., & Levy, K. N. (2004). The influence of client variables on psychotherapy. In M. J. Lambert (Ed.), *Bergin and Garfield's handbook of psychotherapy and behavior change* (5th ed., pp. 194–226). Hoboken, NJ: John Wiley & Sons.

Clemence, A. J., & Handler, L. (2001). Psychological assessment on internship: A survey of training directors and their expectations for students, *Journal of Personality Assessment, 76*, 18–47.

Dao, T. K., & Prevatt, F. (2006). A psychometric evaluation of the Rorschach Comprehensive System's Perceptual Thinking Index. *Journal of Personality Assessment, 86*, 180–189.

Dunning, D., Heath, C., & Suls, J. M. (2004). Flawed self-assessment implications for health, education, and the workplace. *Psychological Science in the Public Interest, 5*, 69–106.

Elfhag, K., Barkeling, B., Carlsson, A. M., Lindgren, T., & Rössner, S. (2004). Food intake with an antiobesity drug (sibutramine) versus placebo and Rorschach data: A crossover within-subjects study. *Journal of Personality Assessment, 82*, 158–168.

Elfhag, K., Barkeling, B., Carlsson, A. M., & Rössner, S. (2003). Microstructure of eating behavior associated with Rorschach characteristics in obesity. *Journal of Personality Assessment, 81*, 40–50.

Elfhag, K., Carlsson, A. M., & Rössner, S. (2003). Subgrouping in obesity based on Rorschach personality characteristics. *Scandinavian Journal of Psychology, 44*, 399–407.

Elghag, K., Rossner, S., & Carlsson, A. M. (2004). Degree of body weight in obesity and Rorschach personality aspects of mental distress. *Eating & Weight Disorders, 9*, 35–43.

Ephraim, D. (2000). Culturally relevant research and practice with the Rorschach Comprehensive System. In R. H. Dana (Ed.), *Handbook of cross-cultural and multicultural personality assessment* (pp. 303–328). Mahwah, NJ: Lawrence Erlbaum.

Erard, R. E. (2005). What the Rorschach can contribute to child custody and parenting time evaluations. *Journal of Child Custody, 2*, 119–142.

Ewing, C. P. (2003). Expert testimony: Law and practice. In I. B. Weiner (Ed.), *Handbook of psychology, Vol. 11: Forensic psychology* (pp. 55–66). Hoboken, NJ: John Wiley & Sons.

Exner, J. E. (1996). Critical bits and the Rorschach response process. *Journal of Personality Assessment, 67*, 464–477.

Exner, J. E., Jr. (1974). *The Rorschach: A comprehensive system.* New York: John Wiley & Sons.

Exner, J. E., Jr. (2001). *A Rorschach Workbook for the Comprehensive System* (5th ed.). Asheville, NC: Rorschach Workshops.

Exner, J. E., Jr. (2003). *The Rorschach: A comprehensive system, Vol. 1: Basic foundations and principles of interpretation* (4th ed.). Hoboken, NJ: John Wiley & Sons.

Exner, J. E., Jr. (2007). A new US adult nonpatient sample. *Journal of Personality Assessment, 89*, S154–S158.

Exner, J. E., Jr., & Andronikof-Sanglade, A. (1992). Rorschach changes following brief and short-term therapy. *Journal of Personality Assessment, 59*, 59–71.

Exner, J. E., Jr., & Erdberg, P. (2005). *The Rorschach: A comprehensive system, Vol. 2: Interpretation* (3rd ed.). Oxford: John Wiley & Sons.

Exner, J. E., Jr., & Weiner, I. B. (1982). *The Rorschach: A comprehensive system, Vol. 3: Assessment of children and adolescents.* New York: John Wiley & Sons.

Fowler, J. C., Ackerman, S. J., Speanberg, S., Bailey, A., Blagys, M., & Conklin, A. C. (2004). Personality and symptom change in treatment-refractory inpatients: Evaluation of the phase model of change using Rorschach, TAT and DSM-IV Axis V. *Journal of Personality Assessment, 83*, 306–322.

Fowler, J. C., Piers, C., Hilsenroth, M. J., Holdwick, D. J., & Padawer, J. R. (2001). The Rorschach Suicide Constellation: Assessing various degrees of lethality. *Journal of Personality Assessment, 76*, 333–351.

Gacono, C. B., Evans, F. B., Kaser-Boyd, N., & Gacono, L. (Eds.). (2008). *Handbook of forensic Rorschach psychology.* Mahwah, NJ: Lawrence Erlbaum.

Garb, H. N. (1999). Call for a moratorium on the use of the Rorschach Inkblot Test in clinical and forensic settings. *Assessment, 6,* 311–318.

Goldstein, A. M., Morse, S. J., & Shapiro, D. L. (2003). Evaluation of criminal responsibility. In I. B. Weiner (Ed.), *Handbook of psychology, Vol. 11: Forensic psychology* (pp. 381–406). Hoboken, NJ: John Wiley & Sons.

Greenberg, S. A. (2003). Personal injury examinations in torts for emotional distress. In I. B. Weiner (Ed.), *Handbook of psychology, Vol. 11: Forensic psychology* (pp. 233–257). Hoboken, NJ: John Wiley & Sons.

Grønnerød, C. (2003). Temporal stability in the Rorschach method: A meta-analytic review. *Journal of Personality Assessment, 80,* 272–293.

Grønnerød, C. (2004). Rorschach assessment of changes following psychotherapy: A meta-analytic review. *Journal of Personality Assessment, 83,* 256–276.

Grove, W. M., & Barden, R. C. (1999). Protecting the integrity of the legal system: The admissibility of testimony from mental health experts under Daubert/Kumho analyses. *Psychology, Public Policy, and Law, 5,* 224–242.

Hartmann, E., Nørbech, P. B., & Grønnerød, C. (2006). Psychopathic and nonpsychopathic violent offenders on the Rorschach: Discriminative features and comparisons with schizophrenic inpatient and university student samples. *Journal of Personality Assessment, 86,* 291–305.

Hartmann, E., Sunde, T., Kristensen, W., & Martinussen, M. (2003). Psychological measures as predictors of military training performance. *Journal of Personality Assessment, 80,* 88–99.

Hess, A. K. (2006). Serving as an expert witness. In I. B. Weiner & A. K. Hess (Eds.), *Handbook of forensic psychology* (3rd ed., pp. 652–700). Hoboken, NJ: John Wiley & Sons.

Hiller, J. B., Rosenthal, R., Bornstein, R. F., Berry, D. T. R., & Brunell-Neuleib, S. (1999). A comparative meta-analysis of Rorschach and MMPI validity. *Psychological Assessment, 11,* 278–296.

Hilsenroth, M. J., & Stricker, G. (2004). A consideration of attacks upon psychological assessment instruments used in forensic settings: Rorschach as exemplar. *Journal of Personality Assessment, 83,* 141–152.

Hogan, T. P. (2005). 50 widely used psychological tests. In G. P. Koocher, J. C. Norcross, & S. S. Hill, III, *Psychologists' desk reference* (2nd ed., pp. 101–104). New York: Oxford.

Hunsley, J., & Meyer, G. J. (2003). The incremental validity of psychological testing and assessment: Conceptual, methodological, and statistical issues. *Psychological Assessment, 15,* 446–455.

Huprich, S. K. (Ed.) (2006). *Rorschach assessment of the personality disorders.* Mahwah, NJ: Lawrence Erlbaum.

Janson, H., & Olsson, U. (2004). A measure of agreement for interval or nominal multivariate observations by different sets of judges. *Educational and Psychological Measurement, 64,* 62–70.

Janson, H., & Stattin, H. (2003). Prediction of adolescent and adult antisociality from childhood Rorschach ratings. *Journal of Personality Assessment, 81,* 51–63.

Johnston, J. R., Walters, M. G., & Olesen, N. W. (2005). Clinical ratings of parenting capacity and Rorschach protocols of custody-disputing parents: An exploratory study. *Journal of Child Custody, 2,* 159–178.

Katko, N. J., Meyer, G. J., Mihura, J. L., & Bombel, G. (in press). The interrater reliability of Elizur's hostility systems and Holt's aggression variables: A meta-analytic review *Journal of Personality Assessment.*

Kelly, F. D. (1999). *The psychological assessment of abused and traumatized children.* Mahwah, NJ: Lawrence Erlbaum.

Kleiger, J. H. (1999). *Disordered thinking and the Rorschach.* Hillsdale, NJ: Analytic Press.

Klopfer, B., & Kelley, D. M. (1942). *The Rorschach technique.* Yonkers, NY: World Book Company.

Krishnamurthy, R., Archer, R. P., & House, J. J. (1996). The MMPI-A and Rorschach: A failure to establish convergent validity. *Assessment, 3,* 179–191.

Lally, S. (2003). What tests are acceptable for use in forensic evaluations? A survey of experts. *Professional Psychology: Research and Practice, 34,* 491–498.

Lilienfeld, S. O., Wood, J. M., & Garb, H. N. (2000). The scientific status of projective techniques. *Psychological Science in the Public Interest, 1,* 27–66.

Lundbäck, E., Forslund, K., Rylander, G., Jokinen, J., Nordström, P., Nordström, A.-L., et al. (2006). CSF 5-HIAA and the Rorschach test in patients who have attempted suicide. *Archives of Suicide Research, 10,* 339–345.

Luxenberg, T., & Levin, P. (2004). The role of the Rorschach in the assessment and treatment of trauma. In J. P. Wilson & T. M. Keane (Eds.), *Assessing psychological trauma and PTSD* (2nd ed., pp. 190–225). New York: Guilford.

McCann, J. T. (1998). Defending the Rorschach in court: An analysis of admissibility using legal and professional standards. *Journal of Personality Assessment, 70,* 125–144.

McCann, J. T. (2004). Projective assessment of personality in forensic settings. In M. Hersen (Ed.), *Comprehensive handbook of psychological assessment, Vol. 2: Personality assessment* (pp. 562–572). Hoboken, NJ: John Wiley & Sons.

McCann, J. T., & Evans, F. B. (2008). Admissibility of the Rorschach. In C. B. Gacono, F. B. Evans, N. Kaser-Boyd, & L. Gacono (Eds.), *Handbook of forensic Rorschach psychology* (pp. 55–78). Mahwah, NJ: Lawrence Erlbaum.

McClelland, D. C., Koestner, R., & Weinberger, J. (1989). How do self-attributed and implicit motives differ? *Psychological Review, 96,* 690–702.

McCrae, R. R., & Terracciano, A. (2006). National character and personality. *Current Directions in Psychological Science, 15,* 156–161.

McCrae, R. R., & Terracciano, A., & 78 members of the Personality Profiles of Cultures Project. (2005a). Universal features of personality traits from the observer's perspective: Data from 50 cultures. *Journal of Personality and Social Psychology, 88,* 547–561.

McCrae, R. R., & Terracciano, A., & 79 members of the Personality Profiles of Cultures Project. (2005b). Personality profiles of cultures: Aggregate personality traits. *Journal of Personality and Social Psychology, 89,* 407–425.

McGrath, R. E., Pogge, D. L., Stokes, J. M., Cragnolino, A., Zaccario, M., Hayman, J., et al. (2005). Field reliability of Comprehensive System scoring in an adolescent inpatient sample. *Assessment, 12,* 199–209.

Meloy, J. R. (2008). The authority of the Rorschach: An update. In C. B. Gacono, F. B. Evans, N. Kaser-Boyd, & L. Gacono (Eds.), *Handbook of forensic Rorschach psychology* (pp. 79–88). Mahwah, NJ: Lawrence Erlbaum.

Meloy, J. R., Hansen, T., & Weiner, I. B. (1997). Authority of the Rorschach: Legal citations in the past 50 years. *Journal of Personality Assessment, 69,* 53–62.

Meyer, G. J. (1997). On the integration of personality assessment methods: The Rorschach and MMPI-2. *Journal of Personality Assessment, 68,* 297–330.

Meyer, G. J. (2000a). Incremental validity of the Rorschach prognostic rating scale over the MMPI ego strength scale and IQ. *Journal of Personality Assessment, 74,* 356–370.

Meyer, G. J. (2000b). On the science of Rorschach research. *Journal of Personality Assessment, 75,* 46–81.

Meyer, G. J. (2002). Exploring possible ethnic differences and bias in the Rorschach Comprehensive System. *Journal of Personality Assessment, 78,* 104–129.

Meyer, G. J. (2004). The reliability and validity of the Rorschach and TAT compared to other psychological and medical procedures: An analysis of systematically gathered evidence. In M. Hersen (Ed.), *Comprehensive handbook of psychological assessment, Vol. 2: Personality assessment* (pp. 315–342). Hoboken, NJ: John Wiley & Sons.

Meyer, G. J., & Archer, R. P. (2001). The hard science of Rorschach research: What do we know and where do we go? *Psychological Assessment, 13,* 486–502.

Meyer, G. J., & Handler, L. (1997). The ability of the Rorschach to predict subsequent outcome: A meta-analysis of the Rorschach prognostic rating scale. *Journal of Personality Assessment, 69,* 1–38. (Revised analyses published in *Journal of Personality Assessment, 74,* 504–506.)

Meyer, G. J., Erdberg, P., & Shaffer, T. W. (2007). Towards international normative reference data for the Comprehensive System. *Journal of Personality Assessment, 89,* S201–S216.

Meyer, G. J., Finn, S. E., Eyde, L. D., Kay, G. G., Moreland, K. L., Dies, R. R., et al. (2001). Psychological testing and psychological assessment: A review of evidence and issues. *American Psychologist, 56,* 128–165.

Meyer, G. J., Hilsenroth, M. J., Baxter, D., Exner, J. E., Jr., Fowler, J. C., Piers, C. C., et al. (2002). An examination of interrater reliability for scoring the Rorschach Comprehensive System in eight data sets. *Journal of Personality Assessment, 78,* 219–274.

Meyer, G. J., Mihura, J. L., & Smith, B. L. (2005). The interclinician reliability of Rorschach interpretation in four data sets. *Journal of Personality Assessment, 84,* 296–314.

Meyer, G. J., Viglione, D. J., Erdberg, P., Exner, J. E., Jr., & Shaffer, T. (2004). *CS scoring differences in the Rorschach Workshop and Fresno nonpatient samples.* Paper presented at the annual meeting of the Society for Personality Assessment, Miami, FL, March 11, 2004.

Mihura, J. L., & Weinle, C. A. (2002). Rorschach training: Graduate students' experiences and preferences. *Journal of Personality Assessment, 79,* 39–52.

Millon, T. (1994). *Manual for the MCMI-III.* Minneapolis, MN: National Computer Systems.

Morey, L. C. (1991). *Personality assessment inventory: Professional manual.* Odessa, FL: Psychological Assessment Resources.

Muniz, J., Prieto, G., Almeida, L., & Bartram, D. (1999). Test use in Spain, Portugal, and Latin American countries. *European Journal of Psychological Assessment, 15,* 151–157.

Nygren, M. (2004). Rorschach Comprehensive System variables in relation to assessing dynamic capacity and ego strength for psychodynamic psychotherapy. *Journal of Personality Assessment, 83,* 277–292.

Ogawa, T. (2004). Developments of the Rorschach in Japan: A brief introduction. *South African Rorschach Journal, 1,* 40–45.

Parker, K. C. H., Hanson, R. K., & Hunsley, J. (1988). MMPI, Rorschach, and WAIS: A meta-analytic comparison of reliability, stability, and validity. *Psychological Bulletin, 103,* 367–373.

PDM Task Force (2006). *Psychodynamic diagnostic manual.* Silver Spring, MD: Alliance of Psychoanalytic Organizations.

Perry, W., & Viglione, D. J. (1991). The Ego Impairment Index as a predictor of outcome in melancholic depressed patients treated with tricyclic antidepressants. *Journal of Personality Assessment, 56,* 487–501.

Perry, W., Minassian, A., Cadenhead, K., Sprock, J., & Braff, D. (2003). The use of the Ego Impairment Index across the schizophrenia spectrum. *Journal of Personality Assessment, 80,* 50–57.

Presley, G., Smith, C., Hilsenroth, M., & Exner, J. (2001). Clinical utility of the Rorschach with African Americans. *Journal of Personality Assessment, 78,* 104–129.

Quinell, F. A., & Bow, J. N. (2001). Psychological tests used in child custody evaluations. *Behavioral Sciences & the Law, 19,* 491–501.

Ritsher, J. B. (2004). Association of Rorschach and MMPI psychosis indicators and schizophrenia spectrum diagnoses in a Russian clinical sample. *Journal of Personality Assessment, 83,* 46–63.

Ritzler, B. (2004). Cultural applications of the Rorschach, apperception tests, and figure drawings. In M. Hersen (Ed.), *Comprehensive handbook of psychological assessment, Vol. 2: Personality assessment* (pp. 573–585). Hoboken, NJ: John Wiley & Sons.

Ritzler, B., Erard, R., & Pettigrew, T. (2002). Protecting the integrity of Rorschach expert witnesses: A reply to Grove and Barden (1999) re: The admissibility of testimony under Daubert/Kumho analysis. *Psychology, Public Policy, and the Law, 8,* 201–215.

Rorschach, H. (1942). *Psychodiagnostics: A diagnostic test based on perception.* Bern, Switzerland: Hans Huber (Originally published in 1921).

Rosenthal, R., Hiller, J. B., Bornstein, R. F., Berry, D. T. R., & Brunell-Neuleib, S. (2001). Meta-analytic methods, the Rorschach, and the MMPI. *Psychological Assessment, 13,* 449–451.

Schmulke, S. C., & Egloff, B. (2005). A latent state-trait analysis of implicit and explicit personality measures. *European Journal of Psychological Assessment, 21,* 100–107.

Shaffer, T. W., Erdberg, P., & Haroian, J. (2007). Rorschach Comprehensive System data for a sample of 283 adult nonpatients from the United States. *Journal of Personality Assessment, 89,* S159–S165.

Shaffer, T. W., Erdberg, P., & Meyer, G. J. (Eds.) (2007). International reference samples for the Rorschach Comprehensive System [Special issue]. *Journal of Personality Assessment, 89* (Suppl. 1).

Society for Personality Assessment (2005). The status of the Rorschach in clinical and forensic practice: An official statement by the Board of Trustees of the Society for Personality Assessment. *Journal of Personality Assessment, 85,* 219–237.

Stafford, K. P. (2003). Assessment of competence to stand trial. In I. B. Weiner (Ed.), *Handbook of psychology, Vol. 11: Forensic psychology* (pp. 359–380). Hoboken, NJ: John Wiley & Sons.

Stedman, J. M., Hatch, J. P., & Schoenfeld, L. S. (2000). Preinternship preparation in psychological testing and psychotherapy: What internship directors say they expect. *Professional Psychology: Research and Practice, 31,* 321–326.

Stokes, J. M., Pogge, D. L., Powell-Lunder, J., Ward, A. W., Bilginer, L., DeLuca, V. A. (2003). The Rorschach Ego Impairment Index: Prediction of treatment outcome in a child psychiatric population. *Journal of Personality Assessment, 81,* 11–19.

Streiner, D. L. (2003a). Being inconsistent about consistency: When coefficient alpha does and doesn't matter. *Journal of Personality Assessment, 80*, 217–222.

Streiner, D. L. (2003b). Starting at the beginning: An introduction to coefficient Alpha and internal consistency. *Journal of Personality Assessment, 80*, 99–103.

Sultan, S., Andronikof, A., Réveillère, C., & Lemmel, G. (2006). A Rorschach stability study in a nonpatient adult sample. *Journal of Personality Assessment, 87*, 330–348.

Sultan, S., Jebrane, A., & Heurtier-Hartemann, A. (2002). Rorschach variables related to blood glucose control in insulin-dependent diabetes patients. *Journal of Personality Assessment, 79*, 122–141.

Terracciano, A., Abdel-Khalek, A. M., Ádám, N., Adamovová, L., Ahn, C.-K., et al. (2005). National character does not reflect mean personality trait levels in 49 cultures. *Science, 310*, 96–100.

Viglione, D. J. (1999). A review of recent research addressing the utility of the Rorschach. *Psychological Assessment, 11*, 251–265.

Viglione, D. J. (2002). *Rorschach coding solutions: A reference guide for the Comprehensive System*. San Diego: Donald J. Viglione.

Viglione, D. J., & Hilsenroth, M. J. (2001). The Rorschach: Facts, fictions, and future. *Psychological Assessment, 11*, 251–265.

Viglione, D. J., & Meyer, G. J. (2008). An overview of Rorschach psychometrics for forensic practice. In C. B. Gacono & F. B. Evans (Eds.), *The handbook of forensic Rorschach assessment* (pp. 21–54). New York: Routledge.

Viglione, D. J., & Taylor, N. (2003). Empirical support for interrater reliability of the Rorschach Comprehensive System coding. *Journal of Clinical Psychology, 59*, 111–121.

Viglione, D. J. (1996). Data and issues to consider in reconciling self report and the Rorschach. *Journal of Personality Assessment, 67*, 579–587.

Wechsler, D. (1997). *WAIS–III manual: Wechsler Adult Intelligence Scale* (3rd ed.). San Antonio, TX: Psychological Corporation.

Weiner, I. B. (1994). The Rorschach Inkblot Method (RIM) is not a test: Implications for theory and practice. *Journal of Personality Assessment, 62*, 498–504.

Weiner, I. B. (1998). *Principles of psychotherapy* (2nd ed.). New York: John Wiley & Sons.

Weiner, I. B. (1999). Contemporary perspectives on Rorschach assessment. *European Journal of Psychological Assessment, 15*, 78–86.

Weiner, I. B. (2001). Considerations in collecting Rorschach reference data. *Journal of Personality Assessment, 77*, 122–127.

Weiner, I. B. (2003). Assessment psychology. In I. B. Weiner (Ed.), *Handbook of psychology, Vol. 1: History of psychology* (pp. 29–302). Hoboken, NJ: John Wiley & Sons.

Weiner, I. B. (2003). *Principles of Rorschach interpretation* (2nd ed.). Mahwah, NJ: Lawrence Erlbaum.

Weiner, I. B. (2004). Monitoring psychotherapy with performance-based measures of personality functioning. *Journal of Personality Assessment, 83*, 323–331.

Weiner, I. B. (2005a). Rorschach Inkblot method. In M. Maruish (Ed.), *The use of psychological testing in treatment planning and outcome evaluation* (3rd ed., Vol. 3, pp. 553–588). Mahwah, NJ: Lawrence Erlbaum.

Weiner, I. B. (2005b). Rorschach assessment in child custody cases. *Journal of Child Custody, 2*, 99–120.

Weiner, I. B. (2005c). Integrative personality assessment with self-report and performance-based measures. In S. Strack (Ed.), *Handbook of personality and psychopathology* (pp. 317–331). Hoboken, NJ: John Wiley & Sons.

Weiner, I. B. (2006). The Rorschach Inkblot method. In R. P. Archer (Ed.), *Forensic uses of clinical assessment instruments* (pp. 181–207). Mahwah, NJ: Lawrence Erlbaum.

Weiner, I. B. (2007). Rorschach assessment in forensic cases. In A. M. Goldstein (Ed.), *Forensic psychology: Emerging topics and expanding roles* (pp. 127–153). Hoboken, NJ: John Wiley & Sons.

Weiner, I. B., & Exner, J. E., Jr. (1991). Rorschach changes in long-term and short-term psychotherapy. *Journal of Personality Assessment, 56*, 453–465.

Weiner, I. B., & Greene, R. L. (2008). *Handbook of personality assessment*. Hoboken, NJ: John Wiley & Sons.

Weiner, I. B., Exner, J. E., Jr., & Sciara, A. (1996). Is the Rorschach welcome in the courtroom? *Journal of Personality Assessment, 67*, 422–424.

Weiner, I. B., & Greene, R. L. (2008). *Handbook of personality assessment*. Hoboken, NJ: John Wiley & Sons.

Wilson, T. D., & Dunn, E. W. (2004). Self-knowledge: Its limits, value, and potential for improvement. *Annual Review of Psychology, 55*, 493–518.

Wood, J. M., & Lilienfeld, S. O. (1999). The Rorschach Inkblot Tests: A case of overstatement? *Assessment, 6*, 341–349.

Wood, J. M., Lilienfeld, S. O., Garb, H. N., & Nezworski, M. T. (2000). The Rorschach test in clinical diagnosis: A critical review, with a backward look at Garfield (1947). *Journal of Clinical Psychology, 56*, 395–430.

Zapf, P. A., & Roesch, R. (2006). Competency to stand trial. In I. B. Weiner & A. K. Hess (Eds.), *Handbook of forensic psychology* (3rd ed., pp. 305–331). Hoboken, NJ: John Wiley & Sons.

Zapf, P. A., Golding, S. L., & Roesch, R. (2006). Criminal responsibility and the insanity defense. In I. B. Weiner & A. K. Hess (Eds.), *Handbook of forensic psychology* (3rd ed., pp. 332–364). Hoboken, NJ: John Wiley & Sons.

The Five-Factor Model
and the NEO Inventories

Paul T. Costa, Jr. *and* Robert R. McCrae

Abstract

Personality traits provide distal explanations for behavior and are compatible with personality development, useful in clinical applications, and intrinsically interesting. They must, however, be understood in the context of a broader system of personality functioning. For decades factor analysts offered competing models of trait structure. By the 1980s the Five-Factor Model (FFM) emerged, and studies comparing its dimensions to alternative models led to a growing consensus that the FFM is comprehensive. The model is also universal, applicable to psychiatric as well as normal samples. To assess the FFM we developed the NEO Inventories, which offer computer administration and interpretation, are available in a number of languages, and adopt a novel approach to protocol validity. Research using the NEO Inventories has led to a reconceptualization of the importance of the person in the social sciences, and may be the basis for a revolutionary new approach to the diagnosis of personality disorders.

Keywords: domains, facets, Five-Factor Model, human nature, NEO, traits

The NEO Inventories are operationalizations of the Five-Factor Model (FFM) of personality traits (Digman, 1990; McCrae & John, 1992). The FFM is currently the most widely accepted model of personality trait structure, and the NEO Inventories have been used around the world in clinical, research, and applied contexts (Costa & McCrae, 2008). In this chapter we provide an overview of the FFM and its place in personality psychology; we then give a detailed account of the development, validation, and applications of the NEO Inventories. First, however, we must address some hurdles to an appreciation of the contribution of traits themselves to an understanding of people.

Overcoming the Prejudice against Trait Psychology

Despite the fact that trait measures have been used for decades and continue to be a central feature in psychological research, there is no doubt that the trait approach is stigmatized by many psychologists and defended by few. Even some of the major

contributors to contemporary trait models seem eager to distance themselves from the topic. Jerry Wiggins (1997), in a classic defense of the trait construct, backed away from the simple dispositional view that laypersons (and some of us psychologists) have of traits, claiming only that they represented regularities in behavior that called for explanation by other mechanisms. Saucier and Goldberg (1996) declared that trait theory was "a rubric that may have no meaning outside introductory personality texts" (p. 25). Historically, the major schools of psychology were taken to be psychoanalysis, behaviorism, and humanism; a recent analysis (Robins, Gosling, & Craik, 1999) replaced humanism with cognitive psychology and neuroscience. Trait psychology continues to be marginalized.

Other psychologists are openly hostile or frankly indifferent to traits. Among the objections voiced are that (a) traits are mere cognitive fictions; (b) even if they are real, they offer only descriptions, not explanations for behavior; (c) the trait construct is incompatible with human growth and development;

(d) because traits cannot be changed, they are irrelevant to clinical practice; (e) trait accounts of personality are dry and uninteresting; and (f) traits offer an incomplete account of human psychology or even personality psychology. Contemporary trait theory and research can address each of these objections.

Cognitive Fictions?

Critiques of trait psychology by Mischel (1968), Shweder (1975), and others led many researchers (especially social psychologists) to the view that traits were mere attributions that did not refer to any real psychological mechanism. The chief basis for this inference was the fact that people could easily attribute personality traits to strangers based on little or no information, and that these ratings mimicked the structure of real trait ratings. It is surely the case that people can and do make false attributions about traits, but studies of consensual validation (McCrae et al., 2004), behavior genetics (Yamagata et al., 2006), and the prediction of behaviors (Funder & Sneed, 1993) and life outcomes (Ozer & Benet-Martínez, 2006) have by now produced "uncontroversial and overwhelming evidence" (Perugini & Richetin, 2007, p. 980) of the existence of traits and the validity of their assessments from knowledgeable raters (including, of course, self-reports). Like them or not, personality traits are a fact of life.

Trait Explanations

From Lamiell (1987) to Cervone (2004), some critics have argued that traits at best provide a description of patterns of behavior; they cannot provide a causal explanation of it. A full response to this charge cannot be made here; the interested reader can see McCrae and Costa (1995, 2008a). But in brief, we argue that social-cognitive explanations are proximal, whereas trait explanations are distal. Both forms of explanation are legitimate, and both are useful in some contexts. If one is trying to prevent quarrels between two lab partners who must cooperate to pass a required course, proximal explanations grounded in the situational context are probably more useful than distal ones. But if one is trying to understand why an individual quarrels with her lab partner, is prone to fits of jealousy, regards herself as better than others, and alienates her roommate, then a distal, trait explanation (one suspects disagreeableness) is more useful.

Trait Immutability?

The philosopher Ralph Waldo Emerson was perhaps the first to raise the objection that "temperament puts all divinity to rout" (Emerson, 1844/1990). Instead of the freedom and spontaneity that we think we see in people's behavior, long-term observation shows that actions simply reflect underlying and enduring traits. In Dweck's (2000) terminology, Emerson was by preference an "incremental theorist" who wanted to believe in the malleability of traits but was forced by long experience to become an "entity theorist," seeing traits as fixed. Dweck and other researchers have shown that these implicit views of personality have powerful effects on personal motivation and on attributions about others. Some of the harshest views of trait psychology come from researchers who seem to be incremental theorists and who believe that trait psychology is only compatible with entity theories. Lifespan developmentalist Orville Brim, for example, was quoted as saying "Properties like gregariousness don't interest me.... You want to look at how a person grows and changes, not at how a person stays the same" (Rubin, 1981, p. 24).

Curiously, even some trait psychologists seem to regard others as entity theorists, attributing to them a belief in the immutability of traits (Costa & McCrae, 2006). But the data do not support any claim of immutability. Individuals change in rank order (Terracciano, Costa, & McCrae, 2006), and people as a whole show predictable developmental changes in the mean levels of traits. For example, conscientiousness increases from adolescence through age 70, whereas extraversion declines—albeit very gradually (Terracciano, McCrae, Brant, & Costa, 2005). Trait levels rise or fall in response to clinical depression and its remission (Costa, Bagby, Herbst, & McCrae, 2005), and neurological conditions such as Alzheimer's disease profoundly affect personality traits (Siegler et al., 1991).

McCrae and colleagues (2000) are perhaps singled out as entity theorists who conceptualize traits as "inherent and immutable internal dispositions" (Johnson, Hicks, McGue, & Iacono, 2007, p. 266) because their Five-Factor Theory (FFT; McCrae & Costa, in 2008b) postulates that traits are biologically based, largely uninfluenced by life experience. A study of essentialism by Haslam, Rothschild, and Ernst (2000) showed that laypersons have a conception of "natural kinds" of categories characterized by discreteness, naturalness, immutability, historical stability, and necessary features. The categories "men" and "women," for example, are distinct types, biologically based, fixed (at least until the advent of sex-change surgery), seen throughout history, and quintessentially defined by the number of X-chromosomes they have. Perhaps the claim that personality traits are natural and based in biology invites the inference that they are also immutable. But these covarying features of lay theories are not necessarily reflected in the real world, or in scientific theories that rely on observations of the real world. The FFT postulate that personality traits are solely biologically based is by no means an established fact, and is in fact almost certain to prove an oversimplification. But even if it were true, it would not imply that traits are immutable; they are not.

Traits are, however, highly stable over periods of years and decades, especially after age 30 (Roberts & DelVecchio, 2000). Does this destroy human spontaneity? Not at all. In the first place, any given instance of behavior is determined by a range of influences, of which traits are only one. People can and do act out of character routinely (Fleeson, 2001), although they feel most authentic when they act in character (Sheldon, Ryan, Rawsthorne, & Ilardi, 1997). Second, spontaneity of behavior is itself an individual difference variable, likely related to openness to experience and extraversion. Open extraverts act spontaneously all their lives; closed introverts rarely do. But both are true to their enduring traits. Third, stability of traits is consistent with change and growth in many other psychological attributes, called "characteristic adaptations" in FFT. Over the course of years, an individual might learn to speak Gaelic, take up the trombone, switch political parties, and acquire a taste for Thai food, all without altering his personality traits.

Clinical Relevance

Many clinicians have found trait assessments to be valuable components of psychotherapy (Miller, 1991; Singer, 2005). But other clinicians, counselors, and interventionists argue that assessment of traits is fruitless, because traits are immutable—or at least very difficult to change—and that interventions are better aimed at modifying specific behaviors or habits of thought (a view consistent with FFT; see Harkness & McNulty, 2002). But there is some evidence for trait change as a result of psychotherapy (Piedmont, 2001), and even small changes in personality trait levels might make the difference in saving a marriage or keeping a job or preventing a suicide. Attempts to optimize adaptation (Sheldon, 2004) should not be abandoned because stability is the natural history of traits.

However, even if no change in traits were possible, trait assessment can be valuable to clinicians because of what it tells them about the client. Clients are more likely to trust and cooperate with their therapist if they believe the therapist understands them, and personality inventories succinctly and systematically draw out information about the client. As Singer (2005) remarked, "Whenever I dive into a personality analysis based on the NEO-PI-R, I am stunned by the depth and complexity of information that a 30–40 minute questionnaire can provide" (p. 43). This information can help the clinician interpret the presenting problem and anticipate other problems that have not yet been presented. Scores on agreeableness can suggest how easy or difficult it will be to create a therapeutic alliance, and scores on conscientiousness can inform the clinician about how motivated the client is likely to be to perform the work of therapy. Extraversion and openness to experience are particularly relevant to the choice of therapies: talk therapies are more congenial to extraverts (Shea, 1988); dream interpretation appeals to open individuals (Hill, Diemer, & Heaton, 1997).

Dryness?

McCrae and Sutin (2007) argued that literary criticism should go beyond psychoanalysis, and that "it is now time for serious students of literature and drama to begin to view characters in terms of current knowledge about personality" (p. 13). An anonymous reviewer scoffed at this idea, writing, "I just can't see how the FFM can compete with the Oedipal drama, death instinct, etc. Freud's incorporation of the tragic and ironic in life into psychoanalysis makes it very attractive to writers and dramatists . . . . The FFM, for all of its appeal to academics, would have a hard time, I think, maintaining intuitive appeal among our literary colleagues."

A similar sentiment is sometimes encountered among psychologists, who regard trait psychology as the enterprise of reducing a living human being to a series of *T*-scores. This view is bolstered by the fact that most trait psychologists deal with groups rather than individuals, canceling out the individuating details in a statistical average. But what has been learned from groups can illuminate the individual case. A psychologist who understands the conceptions and correlates of openness to experience (McCrae & Costa, 1997a) can appreciate why the philosopher Jean-Jacques Rousseau, prototypically open, "could have spent whole months with my crayons and pencils, without ever going out" (Rousseau, 1781/1953, p. 174). The construct of extraversion can help explain how and why Heitor Villa-Lobos composed music while listening to the radio, smoking cigars, and chatting with friends (McCrae, 2006).

Because of the rich network of associations surrounding traits, a T-score of 25 (extremely low) on agreeableness in itself is as interesting to the experienced interpreter of personality profiles as an inheritance of $14 million is to a gold digger. Combinations of traits, such as low openness to values and high openness to ideas, can stimulate many ideas, and a complete personality profile can sometimes be as fascinating as the first specimen of a new species. But normally the interest of a case study lies in the interplay between trait profile and life history. Horatio, Lord Nelson was a paragon of dutifulness who rigidly eschewed the common practice of enriching himself on navy procurements and lost an arm and the sight of one eye in intrepid fighting. But he also flagrantly disregarded orders of battle whenever he saw a tactical opportunity, and once released a captured Spanish captain who was of noble English descent, explaining that "I always act as I feel right, without regard to custom" (Southey, 1813/1922, p. 94). Nelson's dutifulness must be understood in the context of his independent thinking and his complete absence of modesty; his brilliant military career can be seen as the outcome of both devotion to duty and extraordinary personal ambition (Costa & McCrae, 1998).

Incompleteness

The casual use of the term "Big Five" as a label for the FFM can be misleading: Critics sometimes see the FFM as assessing nothing more than five broad personality factors that offer only a superficial portrait of the individual (Kagan, 2007). But a factor model is by definition composed of both factors and variables, where the variables are specific traits or facets that define the factors. Analysis of facets gives a far more detailed description of the person. Kagan lists a number of individual difference variables that he believes are "serious omissions" from the FFM, including honesty; the capacities for empathy, love, shame, and guilt; identification with conventional roles; energy level; need for power and status; and hostility toward authority. Yet these are all closely related to facet scales of the NEO-PI-R—namely, Straightforwardness, Openness to Feelings, Warmth, Self-Consciousness, Depression, (low) Openness to Values, Activity, Achievement Striving, and (low) Compliance. Kagan also notes sexual orientation, which is surely an important individual difference variable, but not usually considered a personality trait.

It is perhaps an unfortunate tradition that trait measures are often called "personality inventories" (e.g., Bernreuter, 1933; Costa & McCrae, 1992b;

Hathaway & McKinley, 1943), because this phrase seems to suggest that they inventory the totality of personality. Many writers have pointed out that this is not so (McAdams, 1992; McCrae & Costa, 1984). Trait models, for example, do not explain how behavior is organized and ordered, and, as abstract and general tendencies, traits cannot explain contextualized features of personality such as personal projects (Little, Lecci, & Watkinson, 1992). When people are asked to answer the question "Who am I?" about a quarter of their responses could be interpreted as trait responses ("I am methodical")—but three-quarters could not (McCrae & Costa, 1988). The critics are right: There is more to personality than traits.

What is needed is a broader theory that can not only incorporate traits but also accommodate other aspects of personality and, ideally, explain how they all interact. Maddi (1980) distinguished between core and peripheral components of personality, and assigned traits to the periphery, usually to be explained as an outcome of core processes. For example, psychosexual development is a core component of psychoanalysis, and traits like neatness and frugality are considered to be the outcome of particular paths of development. More recently, theorists have upgraded the status of traits, placing them at the foundation of the personality system. McAdams (1996), for example, interpreted personality in terms of three levels, of which traits were the first, followed by personal concerns and then life stories. Singer (2005) added an interpersonal level to this structure.

FFT (McCrae & Costa, 1996, 2008b) represents an attempt to interpret and summarize the body of findings that research on the FFM has generated. Those findings will be described in a later section, but they can be anticipated by Figure 16.1, which depicts personality as an open dynamic system. Here "Basic tendencies" (including McAdams's Level 1 variables) and "Characteristic adaptations" (McAdams's Level 2 and 3 variables) are the central elements of personality; they interact with biology and with the environment to shape the experience and behaviors and, cumulatively, the life history (or "Objective biography") of the individual.

Critics of trait approaches often complain that traits are decontextualized; they "fail to specify the settings in which a person is presumed to behave in accord with their assigned trait and, therefore, are incomplete descriptions" (Kagan, 2007, p. 368). But as Tellegen (1991) pointed out, all trait operations presuppose a situational context and explicitly or

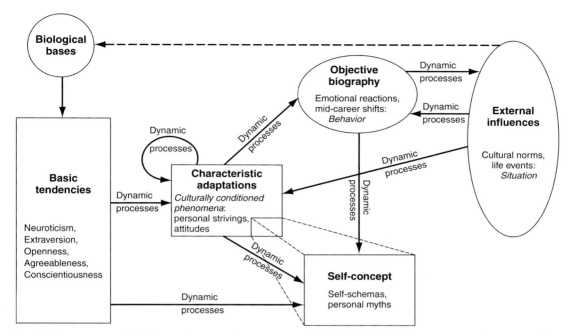

Fig. 16.1 A representation of the FFT personality system. Core components are in rectangles; interfacing components are in ellipses. Adapted from McCrae & Costa, 2008b.

implicitly "delineate the particular circumstances in which the behavioral trait manifestations are likely to take place" (p. 17). If we assert that extraverts like to laugh, sing, and dance, it is understood by any competent English speaker that we mean "when the circumstances permit it," not, say, at a funeral or in a hostage situation. FFT goes farther than this by making explicit that characteristic adaptations are formed when traits operate in the context of the social environment, and that behavior emerges from the contextualized expression of characteristic adaptations.

In FFT the elements of the personality system are connected by arrows that represent dynamic processes; these are the causal pathways that specify the operation of the system. The distinctive feature of FFT, in contrast to most other personality theories (e.g., Rentfrow, Gosling, & Potter, 2008), is the lack of any direct arrow from "External influences" to "Basic tendencies." This is a highly controversial feature of the theory, but it is supported by surprisingly strong data, and, even if it ultimately turns out to be incorrect, seems well chosen to inspire revealing research.

The Structure of Personality Traits
The Problem of Structure

People are routinely characterized by a vast number of more or less distinct traits. They may be called "arrogant," "bawdy," "complicated," "dense,"

"ebullient," and so on. Psychologists and psychiatrists have created hundreds of technical terms to refer to trait-like characteristics, such as psychological mindedness, intolerance of ambiguity, and ego strength. An indefinitely long list of traits poses a host of problems for the science of personality psychology: How do we know that any particular selection adequately covers the range of relevant traits? If we are interested in personality development, what traits ought we to select for a longitudinal study? How can a clinician be confident that she has assessed those aspects of personality that explain a client's problems in living? How can we compare the results of two studies when different traits are chosen by different investigators? The possibilities for systematic and cumulative research and assessment are distinctly limited.

Fortunately, psychologists long ago realized that traits are not independent, but almost always covary with other traits. People who are "arrogant" are also "haughty"—in fact, it is not clear that these are any more than different words for the same trait. But beyond mere synonyms, it is clear that traits show empirical relations. People who are energetic are also likely to be cheerful, and every clinician knows that clients who are prone to anxiety are also likely to experience feelings of depression. These observations long ago led personality psychologists to seek clusters of traits that could provide a framework for organizing trait information. This is known as "personality structure," although it refers to the structure of covariation of traits in a population, not the structure within the individual (which might be more along the lines of Figure 16.1).

J. P. Guilford (e.g., Guilford & Guilford, 1934) was among the first to use factor analysis to examine trait structure. Fundamentally, factor analysis is a procedure for sorting variables into independent groups of related traits. Although there are many variations in the specific statistical techniques, the results of a factor analysis are chiefly determined by the choice of the variables factored and the number of factors extracted. Some researchers preferred a few very broad factors; others preferred many specific factors. Among the more influential schemes were the early 2-factor system of neuroticism and extraversion (Eysenck, 1947), Cattell's far more elaborate 16-factor structure (Cattell, Eber, & Tatsuoka, 1970), and Guilford's 10-factor model (Guilford, Zimmerman, & Guilford, 1976).

Even more problematic than the number of factors was the choice of variables. In the absence of a well-established theory of personality, variables tended to be assembled because they seemed important to a particular investigator. One problem with this method is that variables related to psychopathology were overrepresented, because psychologists were keenly interested in clinical assessment, and personality theories tended to be focused on abnormal variants of personality traits. Other variables were omitted. For example, it is presumably because Eysenck (1991) considered intellectual curiosity to be a function of intelligence, not personality, that he failed to include it in his personality analyses.

Discovery and Rediscovery

Historically, what we have come to consider the resolution to the problem of personality structure was based on the lexical hypothesis (John, Angleitner, & Ostendorf, 1988). This was the view that traits are so significant in human interactions that every language should have developed words for all traits. An unabridged dictionary would, therefore, yield a comprehensive list of traits, and a factor analysis of those traits would reveal the structure of personality. Allport and Odbert (1936) had already scoured the dictionary for trait names, but the yield—some 18,000 words—was far too large to factor. Cattell, however, combined synonyms into scales and factored these scales, which formed the basis of his own 16-factor system. Other researchers had difficulty replicating his intricate structure

(Howarth, 1976), and in the late 1950s two U.S. Air Force psychologists reanalyzed observer rating data using Cattell's scales (or closely related variables) in eight different samples (Tupes & Christal, 1961/1992). To their surprise, results consistently supported five factors, which they labeled surgency, agreeableness, dependability, emotional stability, and culture.

Tupes and Christal reported their results in a technical report that was not published in a mainstream journal for 30 years. Norman (1963) replicated their findings in college student samples and published his work in the major personality journal of the day, but almost no one noticed. Established personality researchers like Eysenck and Cattell continued to promote their own systems, and trait psychology itself came under attack from social cognitive psychologists like Mischel. Researchers like Jackson (1974) and Block (1961), who were willing to consider dispositional constructs and who were not already committed to another system, were skeptical that the terms used by laypersons could provide a scientific map of personality. Surely we would not consider lay terms for body parts as an adequate guide to human anatomy; why should the case be different for personality structure (cf. McCrae & Costa, 1985; Kagan, 2007)?

In the early 1980s we had proposed a three-factor model, adding openness to experience to the broad factors of neuroticism and extraversion (Costa & McCrae, 1980). Our model was based on a synthesis of trait research drawing most directly on the work of Cattell, Coan (1974), and Buss and Plomin (1975). At the same time, Goldberg (1983) was renewing lexical studies and rediscovering that five factors seemed to work. We administered his adjective scales (with additional items of our own) to members of the Augmented Baltimore Longitudinal Study of Aging (BLSA; Shock et al., 1984), who had already completed our instrument, the NEO Inventory (McCrae & Costa, 1983). In this study, a model summarizing the questionnaire tradition, grounded in psychological theorizing, met a model based solely on lay conceptions of personality. Results were clear (McCrae & Costa, 1985). NEO neuroticism was the polar opposite of lexical emotional stability, NEO extraversion was essentially equivalent to lexical surgency, and NEO openness was strongly related to lexical culture. Agreeableness and dependability (or conscientiousness) were missing in our three-factor model.

One reason for that was that we had avoided highly evaluative traits, such as niceness, manipulativeness, sloppiness, and willpower. We did not know if self-reports on such traits would reflect real attributes of the person or merely attempts to make oneself look good (or perhaps bad). But it was easy to find out. We wrote questionnaire measures of agreeableness and conscientiousness and administered them along with the NEO Inventory and lexical measures to both Augmented BLSA participants and the friends and neighbors they had nominated to provide ratings of them. For all five factors there was substantial agreement across both instruments and observers (McCrae & Costa, 1987), yielding what Ozer (1989, p. 229) later called a "virtually picture-perfect" multitrait, multimethod matrix. All five factors were legitimate and necessary aspects of personality.

Creating Consensus

The advantage of a comprehensive taxonomy of traits is that it allows researchers to conduct systematic research. Important phenomena can go unnoticed if variables are chosen haphazardly, or if they are carefully selected on the basis of theories that happen to be wrong or incomplete. Before 1991 there were hundreds of studies examining Alzheimer's disease and depression, but none linking it to conscientiousness. Systematic research with a measure of the FFM led to the discovery that Alzheimer's disease leads to dramatic declines in conscientiousness (Siegler et al., 1991), and later suggestions that levels of conscientiousness may themselves predict the development of Alzheimer's disease (Wilson, Schneider, Arnold, Bienias, & Bennett, 2007).

Clearly, the benefits of systematic research would be multiplied manyfold if most researchers used the same comprehensive model. But for that to happen, the field had to be convinced that the FFM was both comprehensive and scientifically respectable, covering the full range of traits known to be useful in personality prediction and assessment. The lexical hypothesis led to the discovery of the FFM, but it remained a hypothesis that had to be tested. To investigate its claim of comprehensiveness we relied on the generous assistance of members of the Augmented BLSA, who, in the course of a few years, completed a wide range of standard personality instruments, including the Minnesota Multiphasic Personality Inventory (MMPI; Costa, Busch, Zonderman, & McCrae, 1986), the Myers–Briggs Type Indicator (MBTI; McCrae & Costa, 1989a), the Personality Research Form (Costa & McCrae, 1988), the California Psychological Inventory (McCrae, Costa, & Piedmont, 1993), the Personality Assessment Inventory (PAI; Costa & McCrae, 1992a), and the

California Adult Q-Set (McCrae, Costa, & Busch, 1986). With a few minor and understandable exceptions (such as the Thinking Disorder scale of the PAI) the scales of all these instruments were meaningfully and substantially related to one or more of the five factors. Other researchers, with other samples, have reported similar results (Markon, Krueger, & Watson, 2005; O'Connor, 2002).

Collectively, these studies provided the fundamental evidence that the FFM covers the full range of personality traits—even when these traits are conceptualized as needs (Jackson, 1974), preferences (Myers & McCaulley, 1985), folk concepts (Gough, 1987), or personality disorder symptoms (Clark & Livesley, 2002). Although the FFM originated in analyses of natural language, it has been validated against the best scientific constructs and measures psychologists have been able to devise—a fact sometimes forgotten by those who focus on its origin (e.g., Kagan, 2007). Table 16.1 summarizes some notable associations between the five factors and scales from a variety of measures of normal and abnormal personality.

These straightforward correlational studies were initially seen as a way to test the pervasiveness and comprehensiveness of the FFM, but they had two other consequences. The first was that they helped illuminate the constructs of personality. Showing the substantial overlap between the needs identified by Henry Murray and the traits of the FFM made it clear that traits are not superficial habits, but rather have deep motivational implications (Costa & McCrae, 1988). Analyses of the MBTI in terms of the FFM led to the conclusion that personality is better construed in terms of continuous dimensions than discrete types (McCrae & Costa, 1989a). Correlations between measures of psychopathology and the FFM showed that the old distinction between normal and abnormal psychology had been greatly exaggerated: General personality traits affect both adaptations and maladaptations (Costa & McCrae, 1992a). As a careful reading of Table 16.1 suggests, each correlate also helps extend and illuminate the nature of the five factors. Openness, for example, is seen not only in a need for cognitive understanding, but also in a willingness to face uncomfortable truths (low Denial), and in the propensity to see the world in unusual ways (Eccentric Perceptions). Agreeableness is related to cooperation, but is also a part of what we mean by femininity and dependency (low Independence).

The second bonus from these studies was an empirically based way of mapping traits from a

Table 16.1. Examples of scales associated with the five factors.

Instrument	Study	Factor				
		Neuroticism	Extraversion	Openness	Agreeableness	Conscientiousness
CPI	McCrae et al., 1993	Well-Being (R)	Sociability	Flexibility	Femininity	Achievement via conformance
MBTI	McCrae & Costa, 1989		Extraversion	Intuition	Feeling	Judging
PAI	Costa & McCrae, 1992a	Borderline features			Paranoia (R)	
PRF	Costa & McCrae, 1988	Defendence	Play	Understanding	Aggression (R)	Order
BPI	Costa & McCrae, 1992a	Anxiety	Self-depreciation (R)	Denial (R)	Interpersonal problems (R)	
DAPP	Markon et al., 2005	Identity disturbance	Restricted expression (R)	Stimulus seeking	Callousness (R)	Compulsivity
SNAP	Markon et al., 2005	Dependency	Exhibitionism	Eccentric perceptions	Manipulativeness (R)	Workaholism
MMPI-2	Quirk et al., 2003	Psychasthenia	Social introversion (R)			Psychopathic deviance (R)
MCMI-II	Costa & McCrae, 1990	Passive–aggressive	Schizoid (R)		Antisocial (R)	Compulsive
MIPS	Millon, 1994	Hesitating	Outgoing	Intuiting	Agreeing	Systematizing
TCI	De Fruyt, Van de Wiele, & Van Heeringen, 2000	Self-directedness (R)	Harm avoidance (R)	Self-transcendence	Cooperativeness	Persistence
16PF	Conn & Rieke, 1994	Anxiety	Extraversion	Tough-mindedness (R)	Independence (R)	Self-control

Notes: All factor loadings or correlations between the factors and associated scales are greater than .40 in absolute magnitude. "(R)" indicates a reversed scale. CPI = California Psychological Inventory (Gough, 1987), MBTI = Myers-Briggs type indicator (Myers & McCaulley, 1985), PAI = Personality Assessment Inventory (Morey, 1991), PRF = Personality Research Form (Jackson, 1974), BPI = Basic Personality Inventory (Jackson, 1989); DAPP = Dimensional Assessment of Personality Pathology (Livesley & Jackson, 2008), SNAP = Schedule for Nonadaptive and Adaptive Personality (Clark, 1993), MMPI-2 = Minnesota Multiphasic Personality Inventory-2 (Butcher, Dahlstrom, Graham, Tellegen, & Kaemmer, 1989), MCMI-II = Millon Clinical Multiaxial Inventory (Millon, 1994), MIPS = Millon Inventory of Personality Styles (Millon, 1994), TCI = Temperament and Character Inventory (Cloninger, Przybeck, Svrakic, & Wetzel, 1994), 16PF = Sixteen Personality Factor Questionnaire (Conn & Rieke, 1994).

variety of instruments onto a common framework. This is of particular importance in meta-analyses, where a variety of different personality measures have been used to study the same phenomenon. It has now become routine to use the FFM as the framework for meta-analyses (e.g., DeNeve & Cooper, 1998; Feingold, 1994; Roberts, Walton, & Viechtbauer, 2006).

The FFM as a Theory of Everyone

Research conducted in the Augmented BLSA showed that the FFM can be generalized across a wide range of personality constructs and measures, but the BLSA is a very select sample of healthy and generally well-educated volunteers. It was not clear when we began our research whether the structure we saw could be replicated in different populations. Indeed, our earlier work on the three-factor model had been conducted in a population of men (Costa & McCrae, 1980), so its replication in women was an important step. Because we had worked only with adult samples from longitudinal studies, we did not know for some time whether the FFM could be found in college samples. A large and diverse sample of employees from a national organization allowed us to compare personality structure in younger versus older groups, in men versus women, and in White versus non-White subsamples. The FFM was found in all groups (Costa, McCrae, & Dye, 1991). The structure was later replicated in a sample of older African-Americans (Savla, Davey, Costa, & Whitfield, 2007). Recently, using a version with slightly simplified language, we found the same structure in middle school children (Costa, McCrae, & Martin, 2008).

All of these studies, however, were conducted in North American samples using the original English-language version of the test. Beginning around 1990, investigators around the world began to approach us and ask if they could translate the NEO-PI-R. At that time it was an open question whether the FFM could be found in other cultures, and whether the items of the NEO-PI-R could be meaningfully translated. One reviewer doubted it: "The simplistic (a posteriori) basis of the Five-Factor Model, as it is derived from colloquial usage of language, makes the model and its tools intrinsically bound to the culture and language that spawned it. Different cultures and different languages should give rise to other models that have little chance of being five in number nor of having any of the factors resemble those derived from the linguistic/social network of middle-class Americans" (Juni, 1996, p. 864).

That was a testable hypothesis, and as translators began to gather data the results soon became clear: Neuroticism and conscientiousness were invariably found, and openness was always suggested, although some of its facets occasionally failed to show substantial loadings (McCrae & Costa, 1997b). Extraversion and agreeableness emerged in most cultures, but in a minority of cultures, varimax rotation instead produced love and dominance factors (Rolland, 2002). Readers familiar with the interpersonal circumplex will recognize these as two of its axes, about 45° away from the positions of extraversion and agreeableness (McCrae & Costa, 1989b). Because the axes chosen to define a circumplex are always more or less arbitrary, we eventually learned to compare factor structures after rotating them to maximum similarity. This is a form of confirmatory factor analysis that seems better suited to the analysis of personality instruments than the maximum likelihood methods that are sometimes used (McCrae, Zonderman, Costa, Bond, & Paunonen, 1996). The procedure we now recommend uses targeted rotation and evaluates the degree of replication by computing congruence coefficients for both factors and variables; factor congruence coefficients above .85 are considered replications (Lorenzo-Seva & ten Berge, 2006).

The cross-cultural generalizability of the FFM was tested again in a study of 50 cultures (McCrae et al., 2005). Unlike previous studies, which had examined self-reports of personality, this study asked college students to rate someone they knew well on the third-person version of the NEO-PI-R (Costa & McCrae, 1992b), which had been translated into 26 different languages. Assigned targets were either college age or adults over age 40. A factor analysis of the full sample ($N = 11,985$) was compared to the adult American self-report normative structure; factor congruence coefficients were .98, .97, .97, .97, and .97 for neuroticism, extraversion, openness to experience, agreeableness, and conscientiousness, respectively, suggesting almost perfect replication. The structure was also clearly replicated in college-age males, college-age females, adult males, and adult females, with congruence coefficients ranging from .96 to .98.

When analyses were conducted on the 50 individual cultures, the smaller sample sizes introduced more error. Even so, the total congruence coefficient was greater than .90 in 46 (92%) of the cultures. The lowest factor congruences (as low as .53) were found in five Black African nations (Burkina Faso, Nigeria, Uganda, Ethiopia, and Botswana), which might suggest a different personality structure among these cultures. However, respondents in these cultures used English or French versions of the NEO-PI-R, which was not generally their first language, and other indicators of poor data quality, such as missing data and patterns of acquiescent responding, suggested that random error, rather than a real difference in personality structure, might account for the poor replications. We tested that hypothesis by pooling the data from the five cultures; in this larger sample ($N = 940$) the FFM was clearly replicated, with factor congruence coefficients ranging from .88 for openness to .96 for neuroticism and conscientiousness.

Several researchers have proposed that the structure of personality may depend on the cognitive style (Toomela, 2003) or ability (Brand, Egan, & Deary, 1992) of the respondent. But when proper analyses are used, this does not seem to be the case. The familiar FFM structure of the NEO-PI-R has been found in the self-reports of concrete thinkers and abstract thinkers, of older subjects with less than a high school education, and in patients with traumatic brain injury (Allik & McCrae, 2004). Austin, Deary, and Gibson (1997) failed to find evidence of a predicted fusing of extraversion with conscientiousness among less intelligent farmers. What the data do show is that internal consistencies and scale variances are lower among less intelligent (Austin et al., 1997; Allik, Laidra, Realo, & Pullmann, 2004) and younger (Costa et al., 2008) respondents. These rather subtle effects may be due to the fact that individuals with lower intelligence do not understand themselves as well as more intelligent respondents do, or it may simply reflect greater difficulty in understanding the items. A better test of real structural differences in different intelligence groups would utilize observer ratings by intelligent and well-informed raters.

One last but crucial issue of generalization concerns the applicability of the FFM to psychiatrically impaired individuals. Based on decades of use of normal personality inventories in clinical populations, the NEO-PI was offered from the beginning as a tool for clinical assessment, and its use was soon endorsed by clinicians (e.g., Miller, 1991; Mutén, 1991) and supported by clinical research (e.g., Bagby, Joffe, Parker, Kalemba, & Harkness, 1995; Brooner, Schmidt, & Herbst, 1994). But clinicians rarely compile sufficient numbers of cases to conduct factor analyses, and the first replications of the FFM in psychiatric samples were not published until 1999 (Bagby et al., 1999; Yang et al., 1999).

In that year, Bagby and colleagues reported a clear replication (factor congruence coefficients ranged from .95 to .97) in a sample of 176 psychiatric patients with schizophrenia, bipolar disorder, or major depression.

Yang et al. (1999) gathered data from a large ($N = 1,980$) sample of psychiatric patients at 13 sites in the People's Republic of China. After targeted rotation, congruence coefficients for all factors exceeded .85 for patients with neurosis ($n = 715$) and major depression ($n = 360$). In the substance abuse ($n = 174$) and schizophrenia ($n = 329$) subsamples, the openness factor barely missed the cutoff for replication (both factor congruence coefficients = .83), and in the bipolar mood disorder subsample ($n = 228$) both extraversion and openness showed marginal replication (.79 and .78); but the other factors were plainly reproduced in all subsamples. These small variations in structure might suggest that psychiatric disorders can distort personality structure. Alternatively, as in data from Africa, simple error of measurement might also be responsible. When error was minimized by pooling data from all diagnostic groups, all factor congruences exceeded .90. When the FFM was first announced as a useful tool for clinicians (McCrae & Costa, 1986), few would have guessed that a structure "derived from the linguistic/social network of middle-class Americans" would so aptly describe the personalities of psychiatric patients in China.

Perhaps the most surprising of these findings is the applicability of the FFM and NEO-PI-R to patients with schizophrenia, who are characterized by "a range of cognitive and emotional dysfunctions that include perception, inferential thinking, language and communication, behavioral monitoring, affect, fluency and production of thought and speech, hedonic capacity, volition and drive, and attention" (American Psychiatric Association, 1994, p. 274). Yet enough research has now been conducted on patients with schizophrenia that a literature review has been published. Dinzeo and Docherty (2007) first addressed the question of whether valid self-report data can be obtained from psychotic patients, and concluded that "self-report measures have adequate reliability and validity in patients who are relatively stable" (p. 422). They summarized their review by stating that "there is evidence suggesting that the personality characteristics of N[euroticism], E[xtraversion], A[greeableness], C[onscientiousness], and O[penness] are each related in unique ways to phenomena relevant to schizophrenia" (p. 426).

To our knowledge, there have been no studies of the FFM in preliterate cultures, or in individuals with profound mental retardation, or in Zen monks who have attained enlightenment. But the data available so far suggest that the FFM is a "theory of everyone."

Assessing the FFM: The NEO Inventories
History of the Instruments

Today there are many instruments to assess the FFM, at least at the level of the five factors (De Raad & Perugini, 2002). However, the first instrument designed specifically as a questionnaire measure of the FFM was the NEO-PI (Costa & McCrae, 1985), and that was an adaptation of an earlier instrument. A brief history of the development of the NEO Inventories can also serve as a history of progress in understanding personality structure.

We began our research using archival data collected during the 1960s at the Veterans Administration's Normative Aging Study, a multidisciplinary longitudinal study of male veterans located in Boston (Bell, Rose, & Damon, 1972). Our predecessors had administered the 1962 edition of the Sixteen Personality Factors Questionnaire (16PF; Cattell et al., 1970) in the 1960s; in the 1970s we administered a 1967 revision of the 16PF along with several other questionnaires. These data formed the basis of two of our most important ideas: First, we found that the scales of the 16PF could be grouped into three clusters, which we identified as neuroticism, extraversion, and openness to experience (Costa & McCrae, 1976); and second, we found that all three dimensions were remarkably stable across age groups and over the decade retest interval (Costa & McCrae, 1977). Neuroticism and extraversion were well-known personality factors, so we were particularly interested in openness. Important work on that factor had been done by Fitzgerald (1966) and extended by Coan (1974), whose Experience Inventory was a model for the development of our own Experience Inventory (Costa & McCrae, 1978). Three of its facets (then spelled Phantasy, Esthetics, and Ideas) were adapted from Coan's instrument; we added scales to measure Openness to Feelings, Actions, and Values. Results of research with this instrument lead us to adopt the same strategy for assessing neuroticism and extraversion (Costa & McCrae, 1980).

Our approach was based on our experience with other inventories. We had found that the greatest agreement across the many competing personality structure systems was found at the broad factor level, so we began at the top with the neuroticism, extraversion, and openness domains. We thought of domains as sets of trait indicators, in terms of which specific traits could be viewed as subsets. The ideal instrument would carve each domain into a group of facets that were mutually exclusive and jointly exhaustive of the domain, and that would correspond to constructs (such as anxiety or activity) that were known to be useful from the psychological literature. This conceptualization led us to identify a set of facets for each domain and to write items for each. Item factor analyses within domain were then used to select items that loaded on the general factor but that also showed maximal convergent and discriminant validity as indicators of their intended facet. For example, when the 48 openness items are factored and six factors are extracted, they ought to correspond to the six a priori openness facet scales; recent research confirms that they do (McCrae & Costa, 2008a).

We chose to assess six facets for each domain, in part because Gorsuch (1974) had recommended six markers to define a factor, and in part because it seemed a manageable number of relatively specific traits (Costa & McCrae, 1995). We tried to write simple and straightforward items that conveyed the tone of the trait as well as its content; many translators have remarked that the result is somewhat idiomatic language. We used a five-point Likert response format to allow more differentiation than true–false formats; the result seems to have been scales that work relatively well across the full range of trait levels (see Reise & Henson, 2000). We made special efforts to approximate balanced item keying, to avoid serious problems that can arise because of acquiescent responding (McCrae, Herbst, & Costa, 2001). We determined from the beginning that we would try out both self-report (Form S) and observer rating (Form R) versions of the inventory, although we did not know at the time if these two would converge—indeed, the prevailing wisdom was that they would not (Fiske, 1978).

We took the NEO Inventory with us when we moved to the National Institute on Aging in Baltimore and administered it to a population of BLSA volunteers and their spouses; 6 months later we asked them to provide ratings of their spouses on third-person versions of the inventory. The self-report data (plus a small number of cases from a clinical sample) provided the basis for final item selection, and the addition of spouse rating data demonstrated that the three hypothesized factors could be found not only in self-reports and in spouse ratings, but also in a joint analysis of self-reports with spouse ratings (McCrae & Costa, 1983).

In 1983 we began to collect adjective scale data on all five factors, and quickly became convinced that our three-factor model was incomplete. We therefore wrote new items to assess agreeableness and conscientiousness, first in self-reports and later, with an expanded item pool, in peer ratings provided by friends and neighbors whom BLSA participants had nominated. From these peer rating data we selected 18-item global scales to assess agreeableness and conscientiousness, and published them, along with the 144 items of the NEO Inventory, as the NEO-PI (Costa & McCrae, 1985).

The NEO-PI was soon used by academic colleagues who administered it to college student samples. Although the factor structure was unchanged, it soon became clear that adult norms were misleading when applied to college students, and that students from a variety of different colleges showed very similar patterns. These data provided our first evidence of age differences in the mean level of personality traits, and necessitated new, college-age norms. These were based on data generously provided by colleagues, and were published in a manual supplement (Costa & McCrae, 1989). That supplement also introduced the NEO Five-Factor Inventory (NEO-FFI), a 60-item brief version that assesses only the five factors, and *Your NEO Summary*, a widely used feedback sheet.

The lack of facet scales for agreeableness and conscientiousness was clearly the next task to be addressed. We wrote more items and administered them to BLSA participants and their peer raters; David Dye collected data on a large sample ($N=1,539$) of employees from a national organization. Item analyses in these samples (Costa, McCrae, & Dye, 1991) led to the creation of 12 new facet scales and the publication of the Revised NEO Personality Inventory (NEO-PI-R; Costa & McCrae, 1992b). This instrument has been used in most subsequent research.

Table 16.2 provides a list of NEO-PI-R facets and an example of its factor structure. The 30 facets are grouped by domain. The data are observer ratings of college age and adult men and women made by Slovenian students administered a Slovene translation of the instrument. Each facet loads above .40 on its intended factor, and for 28 of the scales, this is the largest loading. (The agreeableness and conscientiousness factors are larger in observer rating data than in self-reports, so it is not surprising that the loadings of N2: Angry Hostility and E3: Assertiveness on the agreeableness factor are slightly larger than their loadings on their assigned factor. Both scales have strong secondary loadings on agreeableness in self-report data.)

The original sets-and-subsets model of domains and facets might lead to the expectation that each facet should load only on a single factor, but human nature does not appear to be that tidy. Traits like Angry Hostility are affected by more than one factor: People are more likely to experience frequent anger if they are prone to negative emotions in general or if they are highly antagonistic toward others. Simple structure could only be achieved by discarding personality traits that are indispensable to a complete personality profile, so we abandoned the goal of simple structure long ago. The relatively complex structure seen in Table 16.2 is both meaningful and, as the congruence coefficients with the American normative self-report structure show, highly replicable.

The NEO-FFI had been chosen from the items of the earlier NEO-PI, where only a limited number of agreeableness and conscientiousness items had been available. An examination of published NEO-FFI item factor analyses showed nine items had relatively poor factor loadings, and five more items were considered difficult to understand by a sample of adolescents. We therefore conducted new analyses and chose 14 different NEO-PI-R items to replace them. The resulting (unpublished) Revised NEO-FFI (McCrae & Costa, 2004) had slightly improved psychometric properties and should be applicable to a wider range of respondents. Subsequently, one more item was replaced, yielding the NEO-FFI-3 that will eventually replace the NEO-FFI (McCrae & Costa, 2007).

Research on students aged 12–17 showed that the NEO-PI-R worked well in that age range, but that some words and thus items were not understandable to a significant minority of respondents (McCrae et al., 2002). On the basis of readability ratings and item-total correlations we identified 48 items as candidates for replacement in a new, simplified version of the instrument. We wrote two new items for each candidate, and administered the NEO-PI-R and the 96 trial items to 500 respondents aged 14–20. We also obtained observer rating data, some of it from siblings who rated each other. Good replacements were found for 37 items, yielding the NEO-PI-3 (McCrae, Costa, & Martin, 2005). This instrument worked as well or better than the NEO-PI-R in adult (McCrae, Martin, & Costa, 2005) and middle school–age (Costa et al., 2008) samples. We anticipate the NEO-PI-3 will be published shortly, and recommend its use in younger-age samples and in those where literacy is limited.

Table 16.2. Factor loadings for observer-rated NEO-PI-R facet scales in a Slovenian sample.

NEO-PI-R Facet	Factor					VCC[†]
	N	E	O	A	C	
N1: Anxiety	**.81**	−.14	−.02	.14	.05	.95**
N2: Angry hostility	**.56**	.16	−.04	**−.58**	−.11	.96**
N3: Depression	**.75**	−.27	.00	−.01	−.30	.98**
N4: Self-consciousness	**.68**	−.27	−.08	.19	−.12	.97**
N5: Impulsiveness	**.53**	.33	−.12	**−.40**	−.32	.96**
N6: Vulnerability	**.70**	−.16	−.06	−.11	**−.46**	.98**
E1: Warmth	−.10	**.76**	.18	.34	.18	.99**
E2: Gregariousness	−.22	**.73**	.05	.10	−.08	.99**
E3: Assertiveness	−.32	**.44**	.05	**−.47**	**.41**	.95**
E4: Activity	−.17	**.61**	.20	−.06	**.41**	.92*
E5: Excitement seeking	−.09	**.53**	.31	−.36	−.25	.92*
E6: Positive emotions	−.20	**.74**	.31	.12	−.01	.96**
O1: Fantasy	.27	.18	**.67**	.05	−.33	.96**
O2: Aesthetics	.14	.09	**.81**	.15	.05	.99**
O3: Feelings	.28	**.55**	**.55**	.18	.19	.96**
O4: Actions	−.21	.15	**.58**	−.02	−.24	.95**
O5: Ideas	−.07	−.13	**.74**	−.06	.34	.96**
O6: Values	−.18	.29	**.48**	.20	.07	.76
A1: Trust	−.31	**.41**	.11	**.59**	.09	.97**
A2: Straightforwardness	−.12	−.09	.08	**.77**	.24	.96**
A3: Altruism	−.05	**.47**	.08	**.68**	.32	.98**
A4: Compliance	−.18	−.02	.01	**.81**	−.07	.99**
A5: Modesty	.08	−.13	−.11	**.79**	.07	.95**
A6: Tender-mindedness	.07	.33	.15	**.65**	.23	.95**
C1: Competence	**−.41**	.14	.16	.06	**.70**	.99**
C2: Order	−.02	−.05	−.18	−.08	**.68**	.98**
C3: Dutifulness	−.04	.03	−.09	.36	**.79**	.97**
C4: Achievement striving	−.17	.17	.13	−.02	**.81**	.98**
C5: Self-Discipline	−.26	.11	−.05	.14	**.80**	.99**
C6: Deliberation	−.31	−.30	.08	.33	**.65**	.98**
Congruence[§]	.98**	.97**	.96**	.95**	.96**	.96**

Note: N = 209. These are principal components rotated to the American normative target (Costa & McCrae, 1992a). Loadings greater than .40 in absolute magnitude are given in boldface. N = Neuroticism, E = Extraversion, O = Openness, A = Agreeableness, C = Conscientiousness.
[†]Variable congruence coefficient. [§]Factor/total congruence coefficient. *Congruence higher than that of 95% of rotations from random data. **Congruence higher than that of 99% of rotations from random data. Data from McCrae et al., 2005a.

Special Features of the NEO Inventories

COMPUTER INTERPRETATION

Like most published personality instruments, the NEO Inventories lead a double life: They are widely used in research on groups, which accounts for their familiarity in scientific journals, but they are also intended for the assessment of individuals, where research findings can help psychologists and psychiatrists understand real human beings and their problems and promise. Profile sheets are available on which clinicians or counselors can plot raw scores and obtain normed profiles; these can be interpreted by reference to the manual, the literature, and training materials provided at occasional workshops.

But a simpler method relies on computer technology. Since its original publication, the NEO Inventories have included the option of computer administration, scoring, and interpretation. Computer interpretation of personality inventories was relatively new in 1985, and our major concern was that the interpretations offered were scientifically based. In the first manual we gave illustrations of cases and the reports that the computer would generate for them, and provided references to document each inference we made. The interpretive report has been upgraded several times since then, but attention to the empirical evidence has always been our foremost consideration.

The current software system gives a general interpretation that includes a description of the respondent's standing on the five factors, a detailed report of the 30 facets, and descriptions of likely coping mechanisms, somatic complaints, and needs and motives for the respondent based on known personality correlates. An optional clinical hypotheses section compares the profile to prototypes for Axis II personality disorders, indicating which disorders are likely or unlikely for the respondent.

The interpretations can be based on either self-reports or observer ratings, and a combined report can give a weighted average score based on one self-report and one rating of the same individual. Profile agreement statistics (McCrae, 1993) are used to identify areas where the two sources disagree. These interpretations are particularly valuable in dealing with couples, because they may point out areas of different perceptions of the target that may be a continuing source of misunderstanding (Singer, 2005).

The software can also generate a client report that provides detailed but nontechnical feedback to the respondent. Normally, this would be reviewed by the clinician and client together, and may be a useful source of insight for the client. Client feedback as part of therapeutic assessment has been advocated for some years, but we initially limited feedback to very broad and nonthreatening statements about the five factors presented as *Your NEO Summary* (Costa & McCrae, 1989). Clinicians (e.g., Mutén, 1991), however, argued that clients could benefit from more frank and detailed information, and the Client Report was developed in response.

TRANSLATIONS

The NEO Inventories have been translated into over 40 languages and used extensively in cross-cultural research (e.g., Terracciano, Abdel-Khalak et al., 2005). Many of these translations are at present useful only for research, but published versions, suitable for use in clinical practice and industrial/organizational applications, are available in Brazilian Portuguese, British English, Bulgarian, Canadian French, Croatian, Czech, Danish, Dutch, French, German, Hebrew, Japanese, Korean, Lithuanian, Norwegian, Polish, Portuguese, Russian, Slovak, Slovene, Spanish, Swedish, and Turkish.

Unpublished translations are available by license from the publisher, Psychological Assessment Resources. These versions rarely have local norms, but there is a growing body of evidence (McCrae, 2002; McCrae et al., 2005b) that translations of the NEO Inventories show at least rough scalar equivalence—that is, that a given raw score has the same interpretation in every language. To the extent that this is true, NEO scores can all be interpreted in terms of American norms, provided that one recalls that the individual is being compared to Americans. For example, a Japanese respondent with an American-normed T-score of 56 on neuroticism would be high compared to Americans, and inclined to suffer the same worries, somatic complaints, and diminished psychological well-being as an anxious American. As a group, Japanese score higher than Americans on measures of neuroticism (Matsumoto, 2006), so the same respondent might be considered average using Japanese norms—but he or she would still have worries, somatic complaints, and diminished well-being.

PROTOCOL VALIDITY

The most distinctive feature of the NEO Inventories as clinical instruments is their approach to protocol validity. Most clinical instruments, such as the MMPI and the PAI, include a variety of validity scales intended to detect random responding, defensive distortion, socially desirable responding, and so on. These indicators are first examined to see if the substantive scales are to be trusted, and some computer programs will not score protocols deemed invalid.

Although they include some indicators of data quality, the NEO Inventories do not include the usual validity scales and do not automatically discard data because there are indications of problems. Instead, administrators are advised to interpret scores with caution and to discuss possible invalidity with respondents.

These somewhat unorthodox procedures are based on both clinical practice and empirical research. Although there are some instances in which respondents are strongly motivated to misrepresent themselves (e.g., child custody evaluations), clients who voluntarily enter psychotherapy or counseling are usually ready to cooperate and provide reasonably honest information about themselves. We recommend that assessors attempt to establish rapport and elicit cooperation by explaining the nature and purpose of the assessment, and perhaps by offering feedback. The results must be interpreted carefully, taking into account other knowledge the assessor has, observation of the respondent's behavior, and perhaps discussion of the results with the respondent. Surely such a procedure is more likely to assist in the development of a therapeutic alliance than an assessment designed to catch the client in a lie.

If validity scales could detect invalid protocols with reasonably high sensitivity and specificity, their use might be justified in routine practice, and surely would be desirable in cases where cooperation cannot be assumed. But the empirical evidence on the value of validity scales is at best mixed. On the one hand, there are hundreds of studies in which experimental subjects are instructed to fake their responses (e.g., Paulhus, Bruce, & Trapnell, 1995; Schinka, Kinder, & Kremer, 1997); such studies typically show that faking can be detected with validity scales. On the other hand, there are dozens of studies in which the validity of real-life assessments are compared to external criteria (e.g., Lonnqvist, Paunonen, Tuulio-Henriksson, Lonnqvist, & Verkasalo, 2007; Piedmont, McCrae, Riemann, & Angleitner, 2000), and these typically show little utility for the validity scales.

Consider validity scales proposed by Schinka et al. (1997), which used NEO-PI-R items to assess negative presentation management (NPM) and positive presentation management (PPM). These scales admirably discriminated groups instructed to fake good or fake bad from groups given standard instructions. However, Yang, Bagby, and Ryder (2000) tested them in a sample of Chinese psychiatric patients: They used NPM and PPM scores to assign patients to valid and invalid protocol groups, and then examined the validity of the NEO-PI-R scores by correlating them with spouse ratings of the patients. Across the five factors, the median cross-observer correlation for the valid protocols was .40; for the allegedly invalid protocols it was .42. Schinka and colleagues also created an inconsistency scale that worked well in computer simulations, but we found that agreement between NEO-PI-R domains and adjective measures of the FFM were as high among the least consistent responders ($Mdn\ r = .63$) as among the most consistent responders ($Mdn\ r = .65$; Costa & McCrae, 1997).

The NEO-PI-R does include validity checks, but they are either transparent or unobtrusive. At the end of the answer sheet, three items ask if the respondents "tried to answer all of these questions honestly and accurately," if they "responded to all of the statements," and if they "entered your responses

in the correct areas." A response of *disagree* or *strongly disagree* to the first of these, or *no* to the last suggests invalidity. More than 40 missing items (one-sixth of the test) is considered grounds for distrusting results. Finally, the computer version includes a check for repetitive strings of responses that are statistically unusual. For example, saying *strongly disagree* to more than six consecutive items was never observed in a large volunteer sample, and it is taken as an indication of random responding that normally invalidates a test. Counts for acquiescence or nay saying are also made by the computer, but they do not invalidate the test.

Do these simple checks identify invalid protocols? Yes and no. In one study of opioid-dependent outpatients (a group in which cooperation might be expected to be minimal), almost one-quarter of the sample had invalid protocols by these rules. The median 4-month retest correlation across the five domains was .72 in the valid group, whereas it was only .48 in the invalid group, suggesting that the validity checks differentiated more from less valid protocols. However, retest correlations for the invalid group were still statistically significant for all five domains ($rs = .38–.57$, $n = 71$, $ps < .001$). Results were more pronounced at the facet level, where scales are much shorter. Here the median retest correlations across the 30 facets were .57 in the valid group but only .34 in the invalid group, and only 22 of the 30 facets showed a significant correlation. If validity is in doubt, it may be wise to interpret only the factors. Similar results were found in a study of adolescents, where 36 of 536 protocols were deemed invalid. Nevertheless, coefficient alphas for the five domains ranged from .80 to .88, and NEO-PI-R scores were still significant predictors of subjective well-being and self-reported grades in these "invalid" protocols (McCrae, Costa et al., 2005). Such findings suggest that validity is best regarded as a matter of degree.

For researchers, we recommend analyzing the data with and without the inclusion of invalid cases; a footnote usually suffices to report the differences, if any. Certainly there are instances when a clinician should disregard a protocol—for example, if all the items are marked "neutral." But for marginal cases, our recommendation is that the clinician consider the information, but with more than the usual caution. Even getting the gist of a client's personality may make it easier to understand why there was so little cooperation in the assessment process, and that may make future assessments more fruitful.

There are, of course, some circumstances in which self-reports are inherently untrustworthy, a situation often faced in forensic psychology. Validity scales or statistical corrections are unlikely to be able to salvage useful information from a truly tainted source. In such cases, we recommend the substitution of observer ratings from those who know the target but do not share his or her motivation to distort.

Research Findings, Applications, and Future Directions
Findings
The availability of a comprehensive model of personality and validated instruments to assess it have made rapid advances in personality psychology possible, and the past two decades have seen solid achievements. In 1980, most psychologists would likely have believed that (a) the historical experiences of each generation will give it a distinctive cast, and cross-sectional studies will be powerfully affected by these cohort effects; (b) personality, and especially character, is shaped largely by the interaction of parents with their children; (c) because patterns of child-rearing differ across cultures, personality should also differ; and (d) gender differences in personality are the result of patterns of socialization that reflect the more or less patriarchal customs of each culture. All of these beliefs have been called into question by research using the NEO Inventories.

Consider the issue of cohort effects. The rings of a tree reflect the growing conditions of each successive season, with wider rings during periods of high rainfall. In the same way, it was widely believed that each generation was imprinted by its early life experience, and thus that a cross-sectional study of personality traits would show age differences that reflected each cohort's "growing conditions," although maturational changes might also account for some age differences. It is impossible to separate cohort effects from maturational effects in the usual cross-sectional study, because everyone of a given age grew up in the same environment. But different nations have different histories; 60-year-olds in the People's Republic of China lived through the imposition of a communist state during the 1950s, when Americans of the same age were watching Mickey Mouse and playing with hula-hoops. In the 1980s, Reagan turned America to the Right, while Deng led the Chinese into capitalism. If the events of history shape personality, cross-sectional findings in China should differ radically from those in America—but in fact they are very similar (Yang, McCrae, &

Costa, 1998). A series of cross-cultural comparisons of cross-sectional age differences confirmed this finding: Everywhere in the world older adults are lower in neuroticism, extraversion, and openness, and higher in agreeableness and conscientiousness than younger adults (McCrae et al., 1999; McCrae et al., 2005a)—although the differences are rather small. A direct comparison of cross-sectional age differences with longitudinal changes in the BLSA showed very similar patterns (Terracciano, McCrae et al., 2005), suggesting that age differences are more a result of maturation than a reflection of early life experience.

History has surprisingly little effect on personality; more surprising still is the lack of effect attributable to parenting. Behavior genetic studies consistently fail to find effects for the shared environment—for example, monozygotic twins raised in different households are just as similar as those raised together (Tellegen et al., 1988). Adoption studies show that, as adults, children do not resemble their adopted siblings any more than a person taken at random (Bouchard & Loehlin, 2001). We know that culture does not affect the structure of personality, because the FFM is found everywhere (McCrae et al., 2005a), although it is still an open question whether culture influences the mean level of traits. The fact that Japanese score higher than Americans on neuroticism might be due to their culture or to their ethnicity; only acculturation studies are likely to resolve that issue.

In the 1980s, gender differences in personality were routinely interpreted as the result of socialization, as boys and girls internalized the roles assigned to them. Such a view would lead to two hypotheses: First, the pattern of gender differences would be expected to vary across cultures, where sex roles presumably differed. Second, the magnitude of gender differences would be largest in traditional cultures with clearly demarcated sex roles, and smallest in modern, egalitarian cultures that emphasize individuality rather than conformity to traditional roles. Cross-cultural studies using self-reports (Costa, Terracciano, & McCrae, 2001) and observer ratings (McCrae et al., 2005a) on the NEO-PI-R provided little support for these assumptions. The patterns of gender differences found around the world closely resembled those found in Americans, and the differences were largest in modern countries. That surprising finding might be explained by arguing that in traditional cultures respondents compare themselves (or their targets) only to people of the same sex, whereas respondents in modern cultures compare themselves to all others. Guimond and colleagues (2007) provided some evidence of this by manipulating the frame of reference: When specifically asked to compare themselves to both men and women, the usual gender differences appeared in traditional samples. Gender differences, once properly assessed, seem very much the same everywhere, and may be the result of evolution: Men are more aggressive than women because, freed from the duties of child-bearing, men took on the roles of hunters and warriors.

The relative imperviousness of personality traits to environmental influences is incorporated in FFT and illustrated in Figure 16.1 by the lack of an arrow directly from "External influences" to "Basic tendencies." Instead, FFT explains traits in terms of "Biological bases." A striking confirmation of that hypothesis was provided by Yamagata et al. (2006), who used twin studies to estimate the genetic cross-correlations between NEO-PI-R facets. These genetic correlations are based on the associations between different facets (say, E1: Warmth and E6: Positive Emotions) in monozygotic versus dizygotic twins. In Japanese, German, and Canadian samples, factoring the matrix of genetic correlations replicated the FFM seen in phenotypic analyses.

These findings were replicated in a fourth culture using an entirely different design. An Italian translation of the NEO-PI-R was administered to over 5,000 people from four small villages in Sardinia (Pilia et al., 2006). They included siblings, parents and children, cousins, uncles and aunts, and so on. To the extent that traits are heritable, correlations and cross-correlations ought to be higher among those more closely related than among those who are less closely related or unrelated. The expected genetic similarity between, say, second cousins, is very small indeed, but researchers were able to identify over 30,000 relative pairs (each subject might have several relatives in the sample), and from these data were able to calculate additive genetic correlations. Table 16.3 presents a factor analysis of these correlations. The large size of the factor loadings is due to the fact that genetic correlations are estimated as they would be if measured without error, but the pattern of loadings is very similar to the pattern of loadings from uncorrected phenotypic correlations among American adults. This is powerful corroboration of the findings of Yamagata and colleagues (2006), and strongly suggests that the phenotypic structure of the FFM is universal because it arises from the universal human genome.

The overall effect of research on personality traits in the past quarter century has been to return the person to the center of psychology. In the short run, the situation often determines behavior and experience; in the long run, enduring dispositions in the individual are powerful forces in shaping life as a whole. Indeed, it can be argued that, over time, culture itself is heavily influenced by collective personality traits (McCrae, 2004). Trait psychology and the FFM may find themselves at the core of all the social sciences.

Applications and Future Directions

In the 1970s and 1980s, personality assessment had fallen into disfavor among industrial/organizational psychologists. That changed dramatically when Barrick and Mount (1991) published a meta-analysis of personality and job performance, using the FFM as a framework. That article has now been cited almost 1,000 times and led the way to a revival of studies of personality not only as a predictor of job performance, but of occupational safety (Cellar, Nelson, York, & Bauer, 2001), job satisfaction (Judge, Heller, & Mount, 2002), transformational leadership (De Hoogh, Den Hartog, & Koopman, 2005), team performance (LePine, 2003), lifetime earnings (Soldz & Vaillant, 1999), career counseling (Hammond, 2001), white-collar crime (Blickle, Schlegel, Fassbender, & Klein, 2006), shopping preferences (Mooradian & Olver, 1996), burnout (Rodgerson & Piedmont, 1998), and on-the-job training (Herold, David, Fedor, & Parsons, 2002).

All five factors are relevant to aspects of vocational behavior. Conscientiousness has been the focus of most attention because it predicts job performance across all types of jobs. Openness is particularly relevant to learning and to performance in jobs that require creativity or adaptation to change. Extraversion is associated with leadership, successful job interviews, and higher earnings. Neuroticism is inversely related to job satisfaction and directly related to burnout, whereas agreeableness is related to cooperation in work settings.

As in clinical psychology, there is currently considerable controversy over the role of socially desirable responding in I/O settings, particularly among job applicants (Peterson & Griffith, 2008). It appears to be the case that scores are distorted in the favorable direction, but that this happens more or less uniformly across applicants. As a result, scores are valid as long as they are interpreted in terms of applicant norms (Lonnqvist et al., 2007; Ones, Viswesvaran, & Reiss, 1996).

Table 16.3. Factor loadings for genetic correlations in a Sardinian sample.

NEO-PI R Facet	N	E	O	A	C	VCC[†]
N1: Anxiety	**.87**	−.02	−.22	.09	.08	.94**
N2: Angry hostility	**.79**	−.19	−.25	−.35	−.01	.91**
N3: Depression	**.81**	−.16	−.32	−.01	−.32	.93**
N4: Self-consciousness	**.71**	−.25	−.35	.00	−.34	.93**
N5: Impulsiveness	**.45**	.18	.36	−.31	−.41	.86**
N6: Vulnerability	**.82**	−.07	−.27	.20	−.48	.97**
E1: Warmth	−.20	**.72**	.21	.45	.28	.99**
E2: Gregariousness	−.35	**.71**	−.21	.17	−.03	.93**
E3: Assertiveness	−.33	**.51**	.44	−.21	.42	.96**
E4: Activity	.13	.47	.18	−.23	**.65**	.96**
E5: Excitement seeking	−.01	**.67**	.04	−.43	−.11	.99**
E6: Positive emotions	−.40	**.67**	.39	.10	.21	.88**
O1: Fantasy	−.03	.44	**.78**	−.02	−.18	.89**
O2: Aesthetics	.06	.42	**.70**	.14	.02	.87**
O3: Feelings	.10	.41	**.81**	.07	.19	.90**
O4: Actions	−.24	.31	**.51**	−.01	−.23	.94**
O5: Ideas	−.15	.25	**.80**	.02	−.03	.91**
O6: Values	−.28	−.14	**.70**	−.01	−.16	.93**
A1: Trust	−.41	.36	.19	**.55**	.00	.98**
A2: Straightforwardness	.08	−.17	.10	**.82**	.28	.96**
A3: Altruism	.11	.37	.03	**.71**	.39	.94**
A4: Compliance	−.20	.17	−.28	**.69**	−.01	.88**
A5: Modesty	.20	−.41	−.19	**.76**	.04	.95**
A6: Tender-Mindedness	.28	.23	.53	**.73**	−.09	.88**
C1: Competence	−.41	.36	.05	.15	**.62**	.96**
C2: Order	−.08	.12	−.35	−.02	**.69**	.98**
C3: Dutifulness	−.05	.04	.02	.35	**.80**	.97**
C4: Achievement striving	−.25	.25	−.01	−.36	**.78**	.94**
C5: Self-discipline	−.35	−.05	.01	.18	**.86**	.95**
C6: Deliberation	−.39	.07	−.43	.22	**.64**	.79
Congruence[§]	.94**	.89**	.87**	.96**	.97**	.93**

Note: N = 5,657. These are Procrustes-rotated principal components from the genetic correlations among the 30 facets of the NEO-PI-R, targeted to the American normative factor structure. The largest loading for each facet is given in boldface. N = Neuroticism, E = Extraversion, O = Openness, A = Agreeableness, C = Conscientiousness.
[†]Variable congruence coefficient. [§]Factor/total congruence coefficient. *Congruence higher than that of 95% of rotations from random data. **Congruence higher than that of 99% of rotations from random data.
Source: Adapted from Pilia et al., 2006.

The NEO-PI-R is widely used in clinical practice as a basic tool for understanding the client and establishing rapport, anticipating the course of therapy, and selecting appropriate forms of therapy (Piedmont, 1998; Singer, 2005). Although the clinical value of the FFM was pointed out some time ago (Costa, 1991), much research remains to be done to demonstrate the most effective ways to utilize information from the NEO-PI-R in clinical practice (McCrae & Sutin, 2007). In contrast, there have been hundreds of studies on the diagnostic relevance

of FFM traits, especially in relation to depression (Bagby et al., 1998), psychopathy (J. D. Miller, Lynam, Widiger, & Leukefeld, 2001), and the personality disorders (Costa & Widiger, 2002). These studies make it clear that, as T. A. Widiger has remarked, the NEO Inventories do not measure "normal" personality traits; they measure "general" personality traits, applicable to everyone and relevant to many forms of psychopathology.

Perhaps the most exciting potential application of the FFM is in the revision of *DSM-V*'s Axis II, which classifies personality disorders. The existing personality disorder categories have been widely criticized as being arbitrary, redundant, and without empirical foundation (McCrae, Löckenhoff, & Costa, 2005). Widiger and Trull (2007) have recently proposed a revolutionary revision of Axis II that embodies a four-step process. The first is assessment of personality at the level of the FFM and its facets; the second queries the client about problems that are likely to be associated with his or her personality traits, using a list of personality-related problems that would be provided in *DSM-V*; the third is a clinical judgment of whether the problems cause sufficient distress or social or occupational impairment to merit the designation of a disorder; and the fourth, optional, step is a summary of the personality profile and associated problems in terms of a specific personality disorder pattern, based on prototype matching (Miller, Bagby, Pilkonis, Reynolds, & Lynam, 2005) or through the use of NEO-PI-R personality disorder scales that attempt to operationalize *DSM-IV* definitions (Costa & McCrae, 2005). For example, a woman might be assessed in the first step and found to be very high in extraversion and openness and very low in agreeableness (Costa & Piedmont, 2003). Individuals low in agreeableness may have difficulties in working with others and in intimate interpersonal relationships. If so, and if the difficulties are pronounced and prolonged, the judgment at Step 3 would be that she has a low agreeableness-related personality disorder; together with the high E and O scores, she might be described in Step 4 as having an antisocial or narcissistic personality disorder pattern.

This alternative to categorical personality disorder diagnosis has many advantages. There are validated instruments for assessing personality in the first step; the second step proceeds directly to the problems in living that are likely to be the focus of clinical treatment after the assessment phase; the third step is optional, and could be omitted in counseling and other settings where the therapist wishes to avoid the label of mental disorder. Because the factors are orthogonal, comorbidity is minimized. Although problems in living may vary across cultures, the dimensions of personality, and thus the relevant diagnostic classifications, are universal. Of greatest importance, however, is the fact that there is a very large and solid body of data on the origins, developmental course, and operation of the traits of the FFM. An Axis II built on this foundation would provide a sound basis for effective treatment.

Conclusion

One of the recurring challenges to personality psychology has been the classification of personality traits into a meaningful system. After decades of research, the FFM has emerged as the most successful candidate to date. Alternatives are still being proposed (e.g., Ashton et al., 2004), but most psychologists have come to regard the FFM as the "adequate taxonomy" that Norman (1963) envisioned. The NEO Inventories, developed to assess the FFM, have been used by clinicians and researchers around the world and have been instrumental in revealing a new picture of human nature, in which personality traits are seen to have a central role in human life.

Acknowledgments

Preparation of this chapter was supported by the Intramural Research Program of the NIH, National Institute on Aging. We thank Velko S. Rus, Nuska Podobnik, and Agata Zupancic for providing Slovene data. Paul T. Costa, Jr., and Robert R. McCrae receive royalties from the NEO Inventories.

References

Allik, J., Laidra, K., Realo, A., & Pullmann, H. (2004). Personality development from 12 to 18 years of age: Changes in mean levels and structures of traits. *European Journal of Personality, 18*, 445–462.

Allik, J., & McCrae, R. R. (2004). Escapable conclusions: Toomela (2003) and the universality of trait structure. *Journal of Personality and Social Psychology, 87*, 261–265.

Allport, G. W., & Odbert, H. S. (1936). Trait names: A psycholexical study. *Psychological Monographs, 47*, (1, Whole No. 211).

American Psychiatric Association. (1994). *Diagnostic and statistical manual of mental disorders* (4th ed.). Washington, DC: Author.

Ashton, M. C., Lee, K., Perugini, M., Szarota, P., De Vries, R. E., Di Blass, L., et al. (2004). A six-factor structure of personality descriptive adjectives: Solutions from psycholexical studies in seven languages. *Journal of Personality and Social Psychology, 86*, 356–366.

Austin, E. J., Deary, I. J., & Gibson, G. J. (1997). Relationships between ability and personality: Three hypotheses tested. *Intelligence, 25*, 49–70.

Bagby, R. M., Costa, P. T., Jr., McCrae, R. R., Livesley, W. J., Kennedy, S. H., Levitan, R. D., et al. (1999). Replicating the Five-Factor Model of personality in a psychiatric sample. *Personality and Individual Differences, 27*, 1135–1139.

Bagby, R. M., Joffe, R. T., Parker, J. D. A., Kalemba, V., & Harkness, K. L. (1995). Major depression and the Five-Factor Model of personality. *Journal of Personality Disorders, 9*, 224–234.

Bagby, R. M., Rector, N. A., Bindseil, K., Dickens, S. E., Levitan, R. D., & Kennedy, S. H. (1998). Self-report ratings and informant ratings of personalities of depressed outpatients. *American Journal of Psychiatry, 155*, 437–438.

Barrick, M. R., & Mount, M. K. (1991). The Big Five personality dimensions and job performance: A meta-analysis. *Personnel Psychology, 44*, 1–26.

Bell, B., Rose, C. L., & Damon, A. (1972). The Normative Aging Study: An interdisciplinary and longitudinal study of health and aging. *International Journal of Aging and Human Development, 3*, 5–17.

Bernreuter, R. G. (1933). The theory and construction of the Personality Inventory. *Journal of Social Psychology, 4*, 387–405.

Blickle, G., Schlegel, A., Fassbender, P., & Klein, U. (2006). Some personality correlates of business white-collar crime. *Applied Psychology: An International Review, 55*, 220–233.

Block, J. (1961). *The Q-sort method in personality assessment and psychiatric research*. Springfield, IL: Charles C Thomas.

Bouchard, T. J., & Loehlin, J. C. (2001). Genes, evolution, and personality. *Behavior Genetics, 31*, 243–273.

Brand, C., Egan, V., & Deary, I. (1992). Personality and general intelligence. In G. L. VanHeck, P. Bonainto, I. Deary, & W. Nowack (Eds.), *Personality psychology in Europe* (Vol. 4, pp. 203–228). Lisse, The Netherlands: Swets & Zeitlinger.

Brooner, R. K., Schmidt, C. W., & Herbst, J. H. (1994). Personality trait characteristics of opioid abusers with and without comorbid personality disorders. In P. T. Costa, Jr., & T. A. Widiger (Eds.), *Personality disorders and the Five-Factor Model of personality* (pp. 131–148). Washington, DC: American Psychological Association.

Buss, A. H., & Plomin, R. (1975). *A temperament theory of personality development*. New York: John Wiley & Sons.

Butcher, J. N., Dahlstrom, W. G., Graham, J. R., Tellegen, A., & Kaemmer, B. (1989). *MMPI-2: Manual for administering and scoring*. Minneapolis, MN: University of Minnesota Press.

Cattell, R. B., Eber, H. W., & Tatsuoka, M. M. (1970). *The handbook for the Sixteen Personality Factor Questionnaire*. Champaign, IL: Institute for Personality and Ability Testing.

Cellar, D. F., Nelson, Z. C., York, C. M., & Bauer, C. (2001). The Five-Factor Model and safety in the workplace: Investigating the relationships between personality and accident involvement. *Journal of Prevention and Intervention in the Community, 22*, 43–52.

Cervone, D. (2004). Personality assessment: Tapping the social-cognitive architecture of personality. *Behavior Therapy, 35*, 113–129.

Clark, L. A. (1993). *Manual for the Schedule for Nonadaptive and Adaptive Personality*. Minneapolis, MN: University of Minnesota Press.

Clark, L. A., & Livesley, W. J. (2002). Two approaches to identifying dimensions of personality disorder: Convergence on the Five-Factor Model. In P. T. Costa, Jr., & T. A. Widiger (Eds.), *Personality disorders and the Five-Factor Model of personality* (2nd ed., pp. 161–176). Washington, DC: American Psychological Association.

Cloninger, C. R., Przybeck, T. R., Svrakic, D. M., & Wetzel, R. D. (1994). *The Temperament and Character Inventory (TCI): A guide to its development and use*. St. Louis, MO: Author.

Coan, R. W. (1974). *The optimal personality: An empirical and theoretical analysis*. New York: Columbia University Press.

Conn, S. R., & Rieke, M. L. (Eds.). (1994). *16PF fifth edition technical manual*. Champaign, IL: Institute for Personality and Ability Testing.

Costa, P. T., Jr. (1991). Clinical use of the Five-Factor Model: An introduction. *Journal of Personality Assessment, 57*, 393–398.

Costa, P. T., Jr., Bagby, R. M., Herbst, J. H., & McCrae, R. R. (2005). Personality self-reports are concurrently reliable and valid during acute depressive episodes. *Journal of Affective Disorders, 89*, 45–55.

Costa, P. T., Jr., Busch, C. M., Zonderman, A. B., & McCrae, R. R. (1986). Correlations of MMPI factor scales with measures of the Five-Factor Model of personality. *Journal of Personality Assessment, 50*, 640–650.

Costa, P. T., Jr., & McCrae, R. R. (1976). Age differences in personality structure: A cluster analytic approach. *Journal of Gerontology, 31*, 564–570.

Costa, P. T., Jr., & McCrae, R. R. (1977). Age differences in personality structure revisited: Studies in validity, stability, and change. *International Journal of Aging and Human Development, 8*, 261–275.

Costa, P. T., Jr., & McCrae, R. R. (1978). Objective personality assessment. In M. Storandt, I. C. Siegler, & M. F. Elias (Eds.), *The clinical psychology of aging* (pp. 119–143). New York: Plenum.

Costa, P. T., Jr., & McCrae, R. R. (1980). Still stable after all these years: Personality as a key to some issues in adulthood and old age. In P. B. Baltes & O. G. Brim, Jr. (Eds.), *Life span development and behavior* (Vol. 3, pp. 65–102). New York: Academic Press.

Costa, P. T., Jr., & McCrae, R. R. (1985). *The NEO Personality Inventory manual*. Odessa, FL: Psychological Assessment Resources.

Costa, P. T., Jr., & McCrae, R. R. (1988). From catalog to classification: Murray's needs and the Five-Factor Model. *Journal of Personality and Social Psychology, 55*, 258–265.

Costa, P. T., Jr., & McCrae, R. R. (1989). *The NEO-PI/NEO-FFI manual supplement*. Odessa, FL: Psychological Assessment Resources.

Costa, P. T., Jr., & McCrae, R. R. (1990). Personality disorders and the Five-Factor Model of personality. *Journal of Personality Disorders, 4*, 362–371.

Costa, P. T., Jr., & McCrae, R. R. (1992a). Normal personality assessment in clinical practice: The NEO Personality Inventory. *Psychological Assessment, 4*, 5–13.

Costa, P. T., Jr., & McCrae, R. R. (1992b). *Revised NEO Personality Inventory (NEO-PI-R) and NEO Five-Factor Inventory (NEO-FFI) professional manual*. Odessa, FL: Psychological Assessment Resources.

Costa, P. T., Jr., & McCrae, R. R. (1995). Domains and facets: Hierarchical personality assessment using the Revised NEO Personality Inventory. *Journal of Personality Assessment, 64*, 21–50.

Costa, P. T., Jr., & McCrae, R. R. (1997). Stability and change in personality assessment: The Revised NEO Personality Inventory in the year 2000. *Journal of Personality Assessment, 68*, 86–94.

Costa, P. T., Jr., & McCrae, R. R. (1998). Six approaches to the explication of facet-level traits: Examples from conscientiousness. *European Journal of Personality, 12*, 117–134.

Costa, P. T., Jr., & McCrae, R. R. (2005). A Five-Factor Model perspective on personality disorders. In S. Strack (Ed.), *Handbook of personology and psychopathology* (pp. 257–270). Hoboken, NJ: John Wiley & Sons.

Costa, P. T., Jr., & McCrae, R. R. (2006). Age changes in personality and their origins: Comment on Roberts, Walton, & Viechtbauer (2006). *Psychological Bulletin, 132*, 26–28.

Costa, P. T., Jr., & McCrae, R. R. (2008). The Revised NEO Personality Inventory (NEO-PI-R). In G. Boyle, G. Matthews, & D. Saklofske (Eds.), *Sage handbook of personality theory and assessment* (Vol. 2, pp. 179–198). Los Angeles: Sage.

Costa, P. T., Jr., McCrae, R. R., & Dye, D. A. (1991). Facet scales for agreeableness and conscientiousness: A revision of the NEO Personality Inventory. *Personality and Individual Differences, 12,* 887–898.

Costa, P. T., Jr., McCrae, R. R., & Martin, T. A. (2008). Incipient adult personality: The NEO-PI-3 in middle-school-aged children. *British Journal of Developmental Psychology, 26,* 71–89.

Costa, P. T., Jr., & Piedmont, R. L. (2003). Multivariate assessment: NEO-PI-R profiles of Madeline G. In J. S. Wiggins (Ed.), *Paradigms of personality assessment* (pp. 262–280). New York: Guilford.

Costa, P. T., Jr., Terracciano, A., & McCrae, R. R. (2001). Gender differences in personality traits across cultures: Robust and surprising findings. *Journal of Personality and Social Psychology, 81,* 322–331.

Costa, P. T., Jr., & Widiger, T. A. (Eds.). (2002). *Personality disorders and the Five-Factor Model of personality* (2nd ed.). Washington, DC: American Psychological Association.

De Fruyt, F., Van de Wiele, L., & Van Heeringen, C. (2000). Cloninger's psychobiological model of temperament and character and the Five-Factor Model of personality. *Personality and Individual Differences, 29,* 441–452.

De Hoogh, A. H. B., Den Hartog, D. N., & Koopman, P. L. (2005). Linking the Big Five factors of personality to charismatic and transactional leadership: Perceived dynamic work environment as a moderator. *Journal of Organizational Behavior, 26,* 839–865.

De Raad, B., & Perugini, M. (Eds.). (2002). *Big Five assessment.* Göttingen, Germany: Hogrefe & Huber.

DeNeve, K. M., & Cooper, H. (1998). The happy personality: A meta-analysis of 137 personality traits and subjective well-being. *Psychological Bulletin, 124,* 197–229.

Digman, J. M. (1990). Personality structure: Emergence of the Five-Factor Model. *Annual Review of Psychology, 41,* 417–440.

Dinzeo, T. J., & Docherty, N. M. (2007). Normal personality characteristics in schizophrenia: A review of the literature involving the FFM. *Journal of Nervous and Mental Disease, 195,* 421–429.

Dweck, C. S. (2000). *Self-theories: Their roles in motivation, personality, and development.* Philadelphia: Psychology Press.

Emerson, R. W. (1990). Experience. In *Essays: First and second series.* New York: Vintage. (Original work published in 1844)

Eysenck, H. J. (1947). *Dimensions of personality.* London: Routledge & Kegan Paul.

Eysenck, H. J. (1991). Dimensions of personality: 16, 5, or 3?—Criteria for a taxonomic paradigm. *Personality and Individual Differences, 12,* 773–790.

Feingold, A. (1994). Gender differences in personality: A meta-analysis. *Psychological Bulletin, 116,* 429–456.

Fiske, D. W. (1978). *Strategies for personality research.* San Francisco: Jossy-Bass.

Fitzgerald, E. T. (1966). Measurement of openness to experience: A study of regression in the service of the ego. *Journal of Personality and Social Psychology, 4,* 655–663.

Fleeson, W. (2001). Toward a structure- and process-integrated view of personality; Traits as density distributions of states. *Journal of Personality and Social Psychology, 80,* 1011–1027.

Funder, D. C., & Sneed, C. D. (1993). Behavioral manifestations of personality: An ecological approach to judgmental accuracy. *Journal of Personality and Social Psychology, 64,* 479–490.

Goldberg, L. R. (1983, June). *The magical number five, plus or minus two: Some considerations on the dimensionality of personality descriptors.* Paper presented at a research seminar, Gerontology Research Center, Baltimore, MD.

Gorsuch, R. L. (1974). *Factor analysis.* Philadelphia: W. B. Saunders.

Gough, H. G. (1987). *California Psychological Inventory administrator's guide.* Palo Alto, CA: Consulting Psychologists Press.

Guilford, J. P., & Guilford, R. B. (1934). An analysis of the factors in a typical test of introversion–extroversion. *Journal of Abnormal and Social Psychology, 28,* 377–399.

Guilford, J. S., Zimmerman, W. S., & Guilford, J. P. (1976). *The Guilford–Zimmerman Temperament Survey handbook: Twenty-five years of research and application.* San Diego, CA: EdITS.

Guimond, S., Brunot, S., Chatard, A., Garcia, D. M., Martinot, D., Branscombe, N. R., et al. (2007). Culture, gender, and the self: Variations and impact of social comparison processes. *Journal of Personality and Social Psychology, 92,* 1118–1134.

Hammond, M. S. (2001). The use of the Five-Factor Model of personality as a therapeutic tool in career counseling. *Journal of Career Development, 27,* 153–165.

Harkness, A. R., & McNulty, J. L. (2002). Implications of personality individual differences science for clinical work on personality disorders. In P. T. Costa, Jr., & T. A. Widiger (Eds.), *Personality disorders and the Five-Factor Model of personality* (2nd ed., pp. 391–403). Washington, DC: American Psychological Association.

Haslam, N., Rothschild, L., & Ernst, D. (2000). Essentialist beliefs about social categories. *British Journal of Social Psychology, 39,* 113–127.

Hathaway, S. R., & McKinley, J. C. (1943). *The Minnesota Multiphasic Personality Inventory* (Rev. ed.). Minneapolis, MN: University of Minnesota Press.

Herold, D. M., Davis, W., Fedor, D. B., & Parsons, C. K. (2002). Dispositional influences on transfer of learning in multistage training programs. *Personnel Psychology, 55,* 851–869.

Hill, C. E., Diemer, R. A., & Heaton, K. J. (1997). Dream interpretation sessions: Who volunteers, who benefits, and what volunteer clients view as most and least helpful. *Journal of Counseling Psychology, 44,* 53–62.

Howarth, E. (1976). Were Cattell's "personality sphere" factors correctly identified in the first instance? *British Journal of Psychology, 67,* 213–236.

Hřebíčková, McCrae, R. R., Costa, P. T., Jr., Terracciano, A., Parker, W. D., Mills, C. J., De Fruyt, F., et al. (2002). Personality trait development from 12 to 18: Longitudinal, cross-sectional, and cross-cultural analyses. *Journal of Personality and Social Psychology, 83,* 1456–1468.

Jackson, D. N. (1974). *Personality Research Form manual* (Rev. ed.). Port Huron, MI: Research Psychologists Press.

Jackson, D. N. (1989). *Basic Personality Inventory manual.* Port Huron, MI: Sigma Assessment Systems.

John, O. P., Angleitner, A., & Ostendorf, F. (1988). The lexical approach to personality: A historical review of trait taxonomic research. *European Journal of Personality, 2,* 171–203.

Johnson, W., Hicks, B. M., McGue, M., & Iacono, W. G. (2007). Most of the girls are alright, but some aren't: Personality trajectory groups from ages 14 to 24 and some associations with outcomes. *Journal of Personality and Social Psychology, 93*, 266–284.

Judge, T. A., Heller, D., & Mount, M. K. (2002). Five-Factor Model of personality and job satisfaction: A meta-analysis. *Journal of Applied Psychology, 87*, 530–541.

Juni, S. (1996). Review of the Revised NEO Personality Inventory. In J. C. Conoley & J. C. Impara (Eds.), *12th Mental Measurements Yearbook* (pp. 863–868). Lincoln: University of Nebraska Press.

Kagan, J. (2007). A trio of concerns. *Perspectives on Psychological Science, 2*, 361–376.

Lamiell, J. T. (1987). *The psychology of personality: An epistemological inquiry.* New York: Columbia University Press.

LePine, J. A. (2003). Team adaptation and postchange performance: Effects of team composition in terms of members' cognitive ability and personality. *Journal of Applied Psychology, 88*, 27–39.

Little, B. R., Lecci, L., & Watkinson, B. (1992). Personality and personal projects: Linking Big Five and PAC units of analysis. *Journal of Personality, 60*, 501–525.

Livesley, W. J., & Jackson, D. N. (2008). *Manual for the Dimensional Assessment of Personality Pathology.* Port Huron, MI: Sigma Press.

Lonnqvist, J.-E., Paunonen, S. V., Tuulio-Henriksson, A., Lonnqvist, J., & Verkasalo, M. (2007). Substance and style in socially desirable responding. *Journal of Personality, 75*, 291–322.

Lorenzo-Seva, U., & ten Berge, J. M. F. (2006). Tucker's congruence coefficient as a meaningful index of factor similarity. *Methodology, 2*, 57–64.

Maddi, S. R. (1980). *Personality theories: A comparative analysis* (4th ed.). Homewood, IL: Dorsey Press.

Markon, K. E., Krueger, R. F., & Watson, D. (2005). Delineating the structure of normal and abnormal personality: An integrative hierarchical approach. *Journal of Personality and Social Psychology, 88*, 139–157.

Matsumoto, D. (2006). Are cultural differences in emotion regulation mediated by personality traits? *Journal of Cross-Cultural Psychology, 37*, 421–437.

McAdams, D. P. (1992). The Five-Factor Model *in* personality: A critical appraisal. *Journal of Personality, 60*, 329–361.

McAdams, D. P. (1996). Personality, modernity, and the storied self: A contemporary framework for studying persons. *Psychological Inquiry, 7*, 295–321.

McCrae, R. R. (1993). Agreement of personality profiles across observers. *Multivariate Behavioral Research, 28*, 13–28.

McCrae, R. R. (2002). NEO-PI-R data from 36 cultures: Further intercultural comparisons. In R. R. McCrae & J. Allik (Eds.), *The Five-Factor Model of personality across cultures* (pp. 105–125). New York: Kluwer Academic/Plenum.

McCrae, R. R. (2004). Human nature and culture: A trait perspective. *Journal of Research in Personality, 38*, 3–14.

McCrae, R. R. (2006). O que é a personalidade? [What is personality?]. In C. Flores-Mendoza & R. Colom (Eds.), *Introdução à psicologia das diferenças individuals [Introduction to the psychology of individual differences; in Portuguese]* (pp. 203–218). Porto Alegre, Brazil: ArtMed.

McCrae, R. R., & Costa, P. T., Jr. (1983). Joint factors in self-reports and ratings: Neuroticism, extraversion, and openness to experience. *Personality and Individual Differences, 4*, 245–255.

McCrae, R. R., & Costa, P. T., Jr. (1984). *Emerging lives, enduring dispositions: Personality in adulthood.* Boston: Little, Brown.

McCrae, R. R., & Costa, P. T., Jr. (1985). Updating Norman's "adequate taxonomy": Intelligence and personality dimensions in natural language and in questionnaires. *Journal of Personality and Social Psychology, 49*, 710–721.

McCrae, R. R., & Costa, P. T., Jr. (1986). Clinical assessment can benefit from recent advances in personality psychology. *American Psychologist, 41*, 1001–1003.

McCrae, R. R., & Costa, P. T., Jr. (1987). Validation of the Five-Factor Model of personality across instruments and observers. *Journal of Personality and Social Psychology, 52*, 81–90.

McCrae, R. R., & Costa, P. T., Jr. (1988). Age, personality, and the spontaneous self-concept. *Journal of Gerontology: Social Sciences, 43*, S177–S185.

McCrae, R. R., & Costa, P. T., Jr. (1989a). Reinterpreting the Myers–Briggs type indicator from the perspective of the Five-Factor Model of personality. *Journal of Personality, 57*, 17–40.

McCrae, R. R., & Costa, P. T., Jr. (1989b). The structure of interpersonal traits: Wiggins's circumplex and the Five-Factor Model. *Journal of Personality and Social Psychology, 56*, 586–595.

McCrae, R. R., & Costa, P. T., Jr. (1995). Trait explanations in personality psychology. *European Journal of Personality, 9*, 231–252.

McCrae, R. R., & Costa, P. T., Jr. (1996). Toward a new generation of personality theories: Theoretical contexts for the Five-Factor Model. In J. S. Wiggins (Ed.), *The Five-Factor Model of personality: Theoretical perspectives* (pp. 51–87). New York: Guilford.

McCrae, R. R., & Costa, P. T., Jr. (1997a). Conceptions and correlates of openness to experience. In R. Hogan, J. A. Johnson, & S. R. Briggs (Eds.), *Handbook of personality psychology* (pp. 825–847). Orlando, FL: Academic Press.

McCrae, R. R., & Costa, P. T., Jr. (1997b). Personality trait structure as a human universal. *American Psychologist, 52*, 509–516.

McCrae, R. R., & Costa, P. T., Jr. (2004). A contemplated revision of the NEO Five-Factor Inventory. *Personality and Individual Differences, 36*, 587–596.

McCrae, R. R., & Costa, P. T., Jr. (2007). Brief versions of the NEO-PI-3. *Journal of Individual Differences, 28*, 116–128.

McCrae, R. R., & Costa, P. T., Jr. (2008a). Empirical and theoretical status of the Five-Factor Model of personality traits. In G. Boyle, G. Matthews, & D. Saklofske (Eds.), *Sage handbook of personality theory and assessment* (Vol. 1, pp. 273–294). Los Angeles: Sage.

McCrae, R. R., & Costa, P. T., Jr. (2008b). The Five-Factor Theory of personality. In O. P. John, R. W. Robins, & L. A. Pervin (Eds.), *Handbook of personality: Theory and research* (3rd ed., pp. 157–180). New York: Guilford.

McCrae, R. R., Costa, P. T., Jr., & Busch, C. M. (1986). Evaluating comprehensiveness in personality systems: The California Q-Set and the Five-Factor Model. *Journal of Personality, 54*, 430–446.

McCrae, R. R., Costa, P. T., Jr., Lima, M. P., Simões, A., Ostendorf, F., Angleitner, A., et al. (1999). Age differences in personality across the adult life span: Parallels in five cultures. *Developmental Psychology, 35*, 466–477.

McCrae, R. R., Costa, P. T., Jr., & Martin, T. A. (2005). The NEO-PI-3: A more readable Revised NEO Personality Inventory. *Journal of Personality Assessment, 84*, 261–270.

McCrae, R. R., Costa, P. T., Jr., Martin, T. A., Oryol, V. E., Rukavishnikov, A. A., Senin, I. G., et al. (2004). Consensual validation of personality traits across cultures. *Journal of Research in Personality, 38*, 179–201.

McCrae, R. R., Costa, P. T., Jr., Ostendorf, F., Angleitner, A., Hřebíčková, M., Avia, M. D., et al. (2000). Nature over nurture: Temperament, personality, and lifespan development. *Journal of Personality and Social Psychology, 78*, 173–186.

McCrae, R. R., Costa, P. T., Jr., & Piedmont, R. L. (1993). Folk concepts, natural language, and psychological constructs: The California psychological inventory and the Five-Factor Model. *Journal of Personality, 61*, 1–26.

McCrae, R. R., Herbst, J. H., & Costa, P. T., Jr. (2001). Effects of acquiescence on personality factor structures. In R. Riemann, F. Ostendorf, & F. Spinath (Eds.), *Personality and temperament: Genetics, evolution, and structure* (pp. 217–231). Berlin: Pabst Science Publishers.

McCrae, R. R., & John, O. P. (1992). An introduction to the Five-Factor Model and its applications. *Journal of Personality, 60*, 175–215.

McCrae, R. R., Löckenhoff, C. E., & Costa, P. T., Jr. (2005). A step towards *DSM-V*: Cataloging personality-related problems in living. *European Journal of Personality, 19*, 269–270.

McCrae, R. R., Martin, T. A., & Costa, P. T., Jr. (2005). Age trends and age norms for the NEO Personality Inventory-3 in adolescents and adults. *Assessment, 12*, 363–373.

McCrae, R. R., & Sutin, A. (2007). New frontiers for the Five-Factor Model: A preview of the literature. *Social and Personality Psychology Compass, 1*, 10.1111/j.1751-9004.2007.00021.x.

McCrae, R. R., Terracciano, A., & 78 Members of the Personality Profiles of Cultures Project. (2005a). Universal features of personality traits from the observer's perspective: Data from 50 cultures. *Journal of Personality and Social Psychology, 88*, 547–561.

McCrae, R. R., Terracciano, A., & 79 Members of the Personality Profiles of Cultures Project. (2005b). Personality profiles of cultures: Aggregate personality traits. *Journal of Personality and Social Psychology, 89*, 407–425.

McCrae, R. R., Zonderman, A. B., Costa, P. T., Jr., Bond, M. H., & Paunonen, S. V. (1996). Evaluating replicability of factors in the Revised NEO Personality Inventory: Confirmatory factor analysis versus Procrustes rotation. *Journal of Personality and Social Psychology, 70*, 552–566.

Miller, J. D., Bagby, R. M., Pilkonis, P. A., Reynolds, S. K., & Lynam, D. R. (2005). A simplified technique for scoring *DSM-IV* personality disorders with the Five-Factor Model. *Assessment, 12*, 404–415.

Miller, J. D., Lynam, D. R., Widiger, T. A., & Leukefeld, C. (2001). Personality disorders as extreme variants of common personality dimensions: Can the Five-Factor Model adequately represent psychopathy? *Journal of Personality, 69*, 253–276.

Miller, T. (1991). The psychotherapeutic utility of the Five-Factor Model of personality: A clinician's experience. *Journal of Personality Assessment, 57*, 415–433.

Millon, T. (1983). *Millon Clinical Multiaxial Inventory manual* (3rd ed.). Minneapolis: Interpretive Scoring Systems.

Millon, T. (1994). *Millon Index of Personality Styles manual.* San Antonio, TX: Psychological Corporation.

Mischel, W. (1968). *Personality and assessment.* New York: John Wiley & Sons.

Mooradian, T. A., & Olver, J. M. (1996). Shopping motives and the Five-Factor Model: An integration and preliminary study. *Psychological Reports, 78*, 579–592.

Morey, L. (1991). *Personality Assessment Inventory: Professional manual.* Odessa, FL: Psychological Assessment Resources.

Mutén, E. (1991). Self-reports, spouse ratings, and psychophysiological assessment in a behavioral medicine program: An application of the Five-Factor Model. *Journal of Personality Assessment, 57*, 449–464.

Myers, I. B., & McCaulley, M. H. (1985). *Manual: A guide to the development and use of the Myers–Briggs type indicator.* Palo Alto, CA: Consulting Psychologists Press.

Norman, W. T. (1963). Toward an adequate taxonomy of personality attributes: Replicated factor structure in peer nomination personality ratings. *Journal of Abnormal and Social Psychology, 66*, 574–583.

O'Connor, B. P. (2002). A quantitative review of the comprehensiveness of the Five-Factor Model in relation to popular personality inventories. *Assessment, 9*, 188–203.

Ones, D. S., Viswesvaran, C., & Reiss, A. D. (1996). Role of social desirability in personality testing for personnel selection: The red herring. *Journal of Applied Psychology, 81*, 660–679.

Ozer, D. J. (1989). Construct validity in personality assessment. In D. M. Buss & N. Cantor (Eds.), *Personality psychology: Recent trends and emerging directions* (pp. 224–234). New York: Springer-Verlag.

Ozer, D. J., & Benet-Martínez, V. (2006). Personality and the prediction of consequential outcomes. *Annual Review of Psychology, 57*, 401–421.

Paulhus, D. L., Bruce, M. N., & Trapnell, P. D. (1995). Effects of self-presentation strategies on personality profiles and their structure. *Personality and Social Psychology Bulletin, 21*, 100–108.

Perugini, M., & Richetin, J. (2007). In the land of the blind, the one-eyed man is king. *European Journal of Personality, 21*, 977–981.

Peterson, M. H., & Griffith, R. L. (Eds.). (2008). *A closer examination of applicant faking behavior.* Charlotte, NC: Information Age Publishing.

Piedmont, R. L. (1998). *The Revised NEO Personality Inventory: Clinical and research applications.* New York: Plenum.

Piedmont, R. L. (2001). Cracking the plaster cast: Big Five personality change during intensive outpatient counseling. *Journal of Research in Personality, 35*, 500–520.

Piedmont, R. L., McCrae, R. R., Riemann, R., & Angleitner, A. (2000). On the invalidity of validity scales in volunteer samples: Evidence from self-reports and observer ratings in volunteer samples. *Journal of Personality and Social Psychology, 78*, 582–593.

Pilia, G., Chen, W.-M., Scuteri, A., Orrú, M., Albai, G., Deo, M., et al. (2006). Heritability of cardiovascular and personality traits in 6,148 Sardinians. *PLoS Genetics, 2*, 1207–1223.

Quirk, S. W., Christiansen, N. D., Wagner, S. H., & McNulty, J. L. (2003). On the usefulness of measures of normal personality for clinical assessment: Evidence of the incremental validity of the Revised NEO Personality Inventory. *Psychological Assessment, 15*, 311–325.

Reise, S. P., & Henson, J. M. (2000). Computerization and adaptive administration of the NEO-PI-R. *Assessment, 7*, 347–364.

Rentfrow, P. J., Gosling, S. D., & Potter, J. (2008). The geography of personality: A theory of the emergence, persistence, and expression of geographic variation in psychological characteristics. *Perspectives on Psychological Science, 3*, 339–369.

Roberts, B. W., & DelVecchio, W. F. (2000). The rank-order consistency of personality traits from childhood to old age: A quantitative review of longitudinal studies. *Psychological Bulletin, 126*, 3–25.

Roberts, B. W., Walton, K. E., & Viechtbauer, W. (2006). Patterns of mean-level change in personality traits across the life course: A meta-analysis of longitudinal studies. *Psychological Bulletin, 132,* 3–25.

Robins, R. W., Gosling, S. E., & Craik, K. H. (1999). An empirical analysis of trends in psychology. *American Psychologist, 54,* 117–128.

Rodgerson, T. E., & Piedmont, R. L. (1998). Assessing the incremental validity of the Religious Problem-Solving Scale in the prediction of clergy burnout. *Journal for the Scientific Study of Religion, 37,* 517–527.

Rolland, J.-P. (2002). Cross-cultural generalizability of the Five-Factor Model of personality. In R. R. McCrae & J. Allik (Eds.), *The Five-Factor Model of personality across cultures* (pp. 7–28). New York: Kluwer Academic/Plenum.

Rousseau, J.-J. (1953). *The confessions* (J. M. Cohen [Trans.]). London: Penguin Books. (Original work published 1781)

Rubin, Z. (1981). Does personality really change after 20? *Psychology Today, 15,* 18–27.

Saucier, G., & Goldberg, L. R. (1996). The language of personality: Lexical perspectives on the Five-Factor Model. In J. S. Wiggins (Ed.), *The Five-Factor Model of personality: Theoretical perspectives* (pp. 21–50). New York: Guilford.

Savla, J., Davey, A., Costa, P. T., Jr., & Whitfield, K. E. (2007). Replicating the NEO-PI-R factor structure in African-American older adults. *Personality and Individual Differences, 43,* 1279–1288.

Schinka, J., Kinder, B., & Kremer, T. (1997). Research validity scales for the NEO-PI-R: Development and initial validation. *Journal of Personality Assessment, 68,* 127–138.

Shea, M. T. (1988, August). *Interpersonal styles and short-term psychotherapy for depression.* Paper presented at the American Psychological Association Annual Convention, Atlanta, GA.

Sheldon, K. M. (2004). *Optimal human being: An integrated multi-level perspective.* Mahwah, NJ: Erlbaum.

Sheldon, K. M., Ryan, R. M., Rawsthorne, L. J., & Ilardi, B. (1997). Trait self and true self: Cross-role variation in the Big Five personality traits and its relations with psychological authenticity and subjective well-being. *Journal of Personality and Social Psychology, 73,* 1380–1393.

Shock, N. W., Greulich, R. C., Andres, R., Arenberg, D., Costa, P. T., Jr., Lakatta, E. G., et al. (1984). *Normal human aging: The Baltimore Longitudinal Study of Aging* (NIH Publication No. 84–2450). Bethesda, MD: National Institutes of Health.

Shweder, R. A. (1975). How relevant is an individual difference theory of personality? *Journal of Personality, 43,* 455–484.

Siegler, I. C., Welsh, K. A., Dawson, D. V., Fillenbaum, G. G., Earl, N. L., Kaplan, E. B., et al. (1991). Ratings of personality change in patients being evaluated for memory disorders. *Alzheimer Disease and Associated Disorders, 5,* 240–250.

Singer, J. A. (2005). *Personality and psychotherapy: Treating the whole person.* New York: Guilford.

Soldz, S., & Vaillant, G. E. (1999). The Big Five personality traits and the life course: A 45-year longitudinal study. *Journal of Research in Personality, 33,* 208–232.

Southey, R. (1922). *Life of Nelson.* New York: Dutton. (Original work published 1813)

Tellegen, A. (1991). Personality traits: Issues of definition, evidence and assessment. In W. Grove & D. Cicchetti (Eds.), *Thinking clearly about psychology: Essays in honor of Paul Everett Meehl* (Vol. 2, pp. 10–35). Minneapolis: University of Minnesota Press.

Tellegen, A., Lykken, D. T., Bouchard, T. J., Jr., Wilcox, K. J., Segal, N. L., & Rich, S. (1988). Personality similarity in twins reared apart and together. *Journal of Personality and Social Psychology, 54,* 1031–1039.

Terracciano, A., Abdel-Khalak, A. M., Ádám, N., Adamovová, L., Ahn, C.-k., Ahn, H.-n., et al. (2005). National character does not reflect mean personality trait levels in 49 cultures. *Science, 310,* 96–100.

Terracciano, A., Costa, P. T., Jr., & McCrae, R. R. (2006). Personality plasticity after age 30. *Personality and Social Psychology Bulletin, 32,* 999–1009.

Terracciano, A., McCrae, R. R., Brant, L. J., & Costa, P. T., Jr. (2005). Hierarchical linear modeling analyses of NEO-PI-R scales in the Baltimore Longitudinal Study of Aging. *Psychology and Aging, 20,* 493–506.

Toomela, A. (2003). Relationships between personality structure, structure of word meaning, and cognitive ability: A study of cultural mechanisms of personality. *Journal of Personality and Social Psychology, 85,* 723–735.

Tupes, E. C., & Christal, R. E. (1992). Recurrent personality factors based on trait ratings. *Journal of Personality, 60,* 225–251. (Original work published 1961).

Widiger, T. A., & Trull, T. J. (2007). Plate tectonics in the classification of personality disorder: Shifting to a dimensional model. *American Psychologist, 62,* 71–83.

Wiggins, J. S. (1997). In defense of traits. In R. Hogan, J. A. Johnson, & S. R. Briggs (Eds.), *Handbook of personality psychology* (pp. 95–115). San Diego, CA: Academic Press.

Wilson, R. S., Schneider, J. A., Arnold, S. E., Bienias, J. L., & Bennett, D. A. (2007). Conscientiousness and the incidence of Alzheimer disease and mild cognitive impairment. *Archives of General Psychiatry, 64,* 1204–1212.

Yamagata, S., Suzuki, A., Ando, J., Ono, Y., Kijima, N., Yoshimura, K., et al. (2006). Is the genetic structure of human personality universal? A cross-cultural twin study from North America, Europe, and Asia. *Journal of Personality and Social Psychology, 90,* 987–998.

Yang, J., Bagby, R. M., & Ryder, A. G. (2000). Response style and the Revised NEO Personality Inventory: Validity scales and spousal ratings in a Chinese psychiatric sample. *Assessment, 7,* 389–402.

Yang, J., McCrae, R. R., & Costa, P. T., Jr. (1998). Adult age differences in personality traits in the United States and the People's Republic of China. *Journal of Gerontology: Psychological Sciences, 53B,* P375–P383.

Yang, J., McCrae, R. R., Costa, P. T., Jr., Dai, X., Yao, S., Cai, T., et al. (1999). Cross-cultural personality assessment in psychiatric populations: The NEO-PI-R in the People's Republic of China. *Psychological Assessment, 11,* 359–368.

The California Psychological Inventory

Edwin I. Megargee

Abstract

This chapter first describes the California Psychological Inventory (CPI) and presents a brief overview of how it has been used (Gough, 1957, 1987; Gough & Bradley, 1996). Next, it discusses Harrison Gough's philosophy of test construction and how it guided the development and evolution of the CPI. The third section provides a brief description of the 20 current CPI folk construct scales, focusing on their construction and the correlates of high and low scores. This is followed by a brief account of the CPI's factor structure. The next section discusses the CPI's three vector scales assessing the dimensions of person orientation, values orientation, and level of realization and describes how they are used to define four personality types. The concluding section offers a brief overview of CPI interpretation.

Keywords: California Psychological Inventory, test construction, personality types

Scientists and theologians continue to debate whether life as we know it was created all at once or whether it evolved gradually through a process of trial and error. There can be no doubt, however, regarding the origins of the California Psychological Inventory (CPI; Gough, 1957, 1987; Gough & Bradley, 1996). The CPI as we know it definitely evolved over a period of six decades.

The CPI's immediate ancestor was the original Minnesota Multiphasic Personality Inventory (MMPI; Hathaway & McKinley, 1943), from which its author, Harrison Gough, borrowed items and empirical scale construction techniques as he sought to measure constructs that were relevant to everyday social interactions such as academic achievement (Gough, 1953a, c), social status (Gough, 1948), and prejudice (Gough, 1951). Other forebears were scales developed to assess behaviors relevant to research in sociology and political science, such as delinquency, dominance, and responsibility (Gough, McClosky, & Meehl, 1951, 1952; Gough & Peterson, 1952).

Although the DNA for the CPI originated on the snowy campus of the University of Minnesota where Gough, a native Minnesotan, obtained his BA in sociology (1942) and his MA (1947) and PhD (1949) in psychology, it developed, matured, and eventually flourished on the fog-shrouded hillsides of the University of California at Berkeley, specifically at the Institute of Personality Assessment and Research (IPAR), which specialized in broad but in-depth assessments of well-functioning and creative individuals. There additional CPI scales were developed and there Gough was able to relate these measures to wide arrays of collateral information collected in the course of IPAR evaluations.

The first copyrighted edition of the CPI contained 548 true–false items and included 15 scales. Five years later, an 18-scale, 480-item version was issued by Consulting Psychologists Press, along with a series of administrator's manuals (Gough, 1957, 1960, 1969). In 1972, the author's *California Psychological Inventory Handbook*, which attempted to integrate the fast-burgeoning CPI literature, was published (Megargee, 1972). During the 1960s and 1970s, the conceptual validity of the "CPI 480," as it later came to be called, was strengthened as the 18 scales were related to other measures and to behavioral observations in the course of IPAR evaluations and independent personality research.

The next generation in the evolution of the CPI was a 462-item version (the "CPI 462") which added two new scales, a revised profile sheet that was more consistent with the CPI's factor structure, and a new approach to interpretation based on three new "vector scales" utilizing a "cuboid theoretical model" (Gough, 1987). And, in less than a decade, a third revision, the "CPI 434," was brought forth with revised items designed to be compatible with the 1990 Americans With Disabilities Act (ADA), along with a new 419-page administrator's manual (Gough & Bradley, 1996) that was substantially more detailed and comprehensive than any of its predecessors.

In the pages that follow, I will first describe the CPI and then present a brief overview of how it has been used. Next, I will discuss Harrison Gough's philosophy of test construction and how it guided the evolution of the CPI. The third section will provide a brief description of the 20 current CPI folk construct scales, focusing on their construction and the correlates of high and low scores. This will be followed by a brief account of the CPI's factor structure. The next section will discuss the three vector scales, the four CPI personality types, and the cuboid model. This will be followed by a list of special purpose and research scales that may be scored at the examiner's discretion. The concluding section will offer a brief overview of CPI interpretation.

Description

The current version of the CPI is a 434-item, true–false, self-administering personality inventory that is scored on 20 scales reflecting "folk culture" constructs drawn from everyday life and social discourse in cultures around the world. It can be taken on a computer or in paper and pencil format with a reusable test booklet. The raw scores are converted to T-scores and displayed on a profile sheet on which high scores reflect the positive aspect of the various dimensions.

The profile sheet groups the scales into four clusters or sectors. Sector I consists of seven scales assessing various aspects of interpersonal effectiveness, social poise, and self-assurance. Sector II is comprised of seven scales measuring adjustment, socialization, and normative values. Three of these measures also serve as validity scales. Sector III contains three scales assessing cognitive and intellectual functioning and achievement motivation. Sector IV includes three scales assessing roles and personal styles.

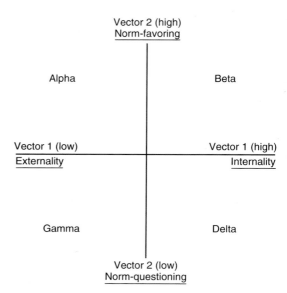

Fig. 17.1 Grid classifying the four CPI types on the basis of their scores on Vector Scales 1 and 2. Adapted from Gough (1989, Fig. 4-1).

Recorded separately are the scores on three orthogonal "vector" or "structural" scales assessing dimensions underlying the 20 folk culture scales. Vector 1 assesses interpersonal orientation, ranging from extraversion to introversion, while Vector 2 assesses incorporation of social values, ranging from norm-favoring to norm-questioning. Plotted together in a classificatory grid, the four possible combinations of high and low scores on these two vectors define four different personality types. Type Alpha is extraverted and norm accepting, Type Beta is introverted and norm accepting, Type Gamma is extroverted and norm questioning, and Type Delta is introverted and norm questioning (see Figure 17.1).

Vector 3 defines seven levels of psychological integration and fulfillment that indicate how effectively people of each personality type realize its potential. They range from ineffectiveness, maladjustment, and poor integration at the lowest levels, through average realization and coping ability in the mid-range, to superior integration, and self-actualization at the highest levels (Gough, 1989; Gough & Bradley, 1996).

Use

Over the years, the CPI has been widely used by practitioners and researchers in the fields of education, counseling, and industrial/organizational psychology. Some of the most frequently studied areas are the following:

- Academic achievement at various levels ranging from secondary school, through college and various professional schools and among various groups such as academically gifted students and different ethnic and minority groups
- Characteristics, achievement, and performance in various occupational groups including accountants, air traffic controllers, architects, clergymen, dentists, engineers, mathematicians, managers, military personnel, nurses, physicians, police officers, psychologists, research scientists, teachers, and telephone counselors
- Creativity in fields as diverse as architecture, cinematography, engineering, mathematics, and science
- Personal and social problems among alcoholics, criminals, delinquents, drug and substance abusers, pathological gamblers, rape victims, and Type A coronary-prone individuals (Gough, 1989; Groth-Marnat, 1997; Megargee, 1972)

Other topics that have been widely studied using the CPI are athletic interests and performance, behavioral genetics, behavioral medicine and health psychology, leadership, life span development, marital relationships, and mate selection (Gough, 1989, pp. 67–69; Gough & Bradley, 1996; Megargee, 1972).

An especially noteworthy aspect of the CPI literature is the prevalence of cross-cultural and cross-national studies performed in dozens of countries around the world.

Development

The original CPI 480 evolved as a no-nonsense tool to solve practical assessment problems. Its goal was "to predict what people will say and do in specific contexts" and "to identify individuals who will be evaluated and described in differentiating and interpersonally significant ways" (Gough & Bradley, 1996, p. 8). It was conceived as being an open system, with the eventual number of scales being dictated by their ability, alone or, more often, in combination, to forecast all the various sorts of interpersonal behavior that might interest practitioners and researchers (Gough, 1989).

This emphasis on pragmatism differentiates the CPI from instruments whose nature and structure are dictated by psychometric elegance. Scales that are designed to measure traits, as opposed to merely predicting behavior, should have maximal internal consistency and minimal correlations with each other (Gough & Bradley, 1996). However, since

the regular CPI scales are not viewed as trait measures, internal consistency and homogeneity are not considered essential unless they contribute to the practical prediction of relevant behaviors. If certain behaviors, such as leadership and achievement, are associated in most people, then CPI scales predicting these behaviors should also be positively correlated.[1]

Gough also believes that the scales on a personality inventory should reflect the context in which it will be utilized. Because the original MMPI was designed to be used in neuropsychiatric facilities, its scales were designed to assess various types of psychopathology, just as the scales on the Strong Vocational Interest Blank (Strong, 1943) reflected the world of work.

Because the CPI was designed to predict the interpersonal behavior of ordinary people, Gough drew on what he termed the "folk culture" for behaviors to assess. By the folk culture, he means the concepts that people around the world have used throughout history to describe and understand one another. These folk constructs are to be found in the natural language (Gough, 1968; Megargee, 1972). The CPI thus differs from inventories that were designed to define unitary traits derived from psychological theory, such as the Myers–Briggs Type Indicator (MBTI; Myers & Briggs, 1943/1962) or identified through factor analytic research, like the Revised NEO Personality Inventory (NEO PI-R; Costa & McRae, 1992).

True to its Minnesota ancestry, most of the CPI folk scales were constructed empirically through external criterion analyses. Based on peer nominations, scores on other tests, academic performance, demographic factors, or life events, groups who were high or low on the targeted behavior were selected. These groups, who were often comprised of high school and/or college students, were typically administered a pool of potential items, some of which may have been drawn from the original MMPI, as well as others that were specially written to assess the behavior being scaled. Items differentiating the two groups would be selected for a preliminary scale, which was then cross-validated by being correlated with other criterion measures. As a result, CPI scales are typically bimodal, with both high and low scores being interpretable for men and women alike.

On other scales, a bootstrap technique called "internal consistency analysis" was used. A group of items thought to reflect the behavior in question was written and administered to various samples. Those items with the highest correlations with the total scores on this preliminary measure were then chosen for further validation.

When the various scales were first gathered together, profiled, and published as the CPI, it was decided that high scores on all scales (except for F/M) would reflect the more culturally approved or socially valued pole. This resulted in changing the direction and renaming some scales such as Delinquency (De), which became Socialization (So), and Prejudice (Pr), which became Tolerance (To). Over the years, as the CPI was used in IPAR assessments, the empirical correlates of these scales were further explored as they were correlated with a wide array of other measures used in these evaluations.

The Twenty Folk Culture Scales
Sector I Scales: Measures of Poise, Self-Assurance, and Patterns of Interpersonal Behavior

Gough's first sector consists of seven scales which measure ascendancy, social skills, and self-confidence: Dominance (Do), Capacity for Status (Cs), Sociability (Sy), Social Presence (Sp), Self-Acceptance (Sa), Independence (In), and Empathy (Em). Gough regards these seven scales as reflecting different "facets or themes within the domain of interpersonal effectiveness" (Gough & Bradley, 1996, p. 86).

DOMINANCE (DO; 36 ITEMS)

The Dominance scale was originally derived in connection with research on political participation (Gough et al., 1951). The goal was to identify strong, dominant, influential, and ascendant individuals who are able to take the initiative and exercise leadership. It was constructed by contrasting the responses of male and female high school and college students who had been nominated by their peers as being exceptionally high or low in social influence, self-confidence, and leadership ability in face-to-face interactions (Megargee, 1972). Many validity studies have shown that individuals with high Do scale scores are described as self-confident, verbally fluent, assertive, enterprising, and able to influence others in a socially positive manner, while those with low Do scores are seen as socially awkward, reticent, submissive, ineffective, and lacking ambition.[2]

CAPACITY FOR STATUS (CS; 28 ITEMS)

Cs was developed to provide a personality scale that would correlate significantly with external

criteria of socioeconomic status (SES) such as the relative levels of income, education, prestige, and power attained in one's sociocultural milieu (Gough, 1968). However, over time it came to be regarded as a measure of the personal attributes such as ambition and self-assurance that led to the attainment of social status rather than SES per se (Gough & Bradley, 1996). It was initially derived by comparing the MMPI responses of small-town Minnesota high school students who were one standard deviation above or below the group's mean on a measure of SES. In addition to differing in SES, the initial criterion groups also differed significantly in IQ and grade point average (Gough, 1948).

High scorers on Cs are typically described as being ambitious, optimistic, socially effective, verbally fluent, and having wide-ranging interests. Low scorers are seen as being inadequate, socially ineffective, inarticulate, and low in achievement motivation.

SOCIABILITY (SY; 32 ITEMS)

Originally designated the Sp or "Social Participation" scale, the Sy scale was devised to differentiate people with an outgoing, sociable, participative temperament from those who shun involvement and avoid social visibility (Gough, 1952c, 1968, 1969). The CPI item pool was administered to three samples of high school seniors who ranked in the top and bottom quartiles of their classes in the number of extracurricular activities in which they participated. Those items that significantly differentiated the groups in all three samples were selected. Although it was originally designed to predict participation in social activities, subsequent research with the measure convinced Gough that it assessed sociability more than social participation, and he renamed the scale accordingly.

People with high Sy scale scores enjoy going out, meeting, and interacting with people. They make favorable impressions on others and are described as being outgoing, extraverted, self-confident, and talkative. Low scorers prefer more solitary pursuits, such as reading or watching TV. They hang back, speak only when spoken to, and are seen as being awkward, inept, reticent, and inhibited.

SOCIAL PRESENCE (SP; 38 ITEMS)

The Sp scale was constructed by means of internal consistency analyses to assess poise, self-confidence, verve, and spontaneity in social interactions (Gough, 1968, 1969). A pool of items that appeared to reflect these behaviors was assembled and administered to unspecified samples. The correlation of each item with the total scores for men and women was computed. Those items with low or marginal correlations were deleted and the process was repeated until a 56-item scale remained in CPI 480. When Form 462 was devised, the correlations of the Sp items with external criteria, such as IPAR staff assessment ratings, were also considered, leading to the deletion of 18 more items.

Sp is closely related to Sy, but, whereas the high scorer on Sy simply enjoys the company of others, high scorers on Sp are more hedonistic and self-centered people who may use or manipulate others and be verbally aggressive or sarcastic (Megargee, 1972). They are seen as spontaneous, clever, self-assured, and pleasure seeking. Low scorers are more inhibited and ill at ease in social situations. Self-doubting and submissive, they are more prone to feelings of inferiority and inadequacy.

SELF-ACCEPTANCE (SA; **28** ITEMS)

Sa was developed to assess secure feelings of personal worth, self-confidence, and self-assurance with regard to social functioning. The scale was rationally constructed through internal consistency analyses. As with Sp, the intercorrelations among a pool of items judged likely to assess self-acceptance were examined, with those having the highest item-total correlations being selected for the initial Sa scale. As the CPI was revised, the items with the lowest correlations with the total Sa score and with external criterion measures were dropped.

People scoring high on Sa are described as being optimistic, self-confident, articulate, and outgoing. They are apt to be oriented toward high status, well-paying occupations. Likeable, they make favorable impressions on others, although extremely high scorers may be seen as somewhat self-centered and demanding. Low scorers strike others as being timid, self-doubting, insecure, and lacking self-esteem. They keep in the background and let others make decisions.

INDEPENDENCE (IN; **30** ITEMS)

The In scale was introduced in CPI 462. Independence was thought to consist of competence combined with disengagement. Seventeen adjectives embodying this construct (7 positive and 10 negative) were selected from the 300 adjectives on the Gough–Heilbrun (1983) Adjective Check List (ACL). The ACLs of 236 couples who had described each other were scored on this provisional scale and the resulting scores were correlated with their CPI responses. Thirty CPI items correlating significantly with this provisional ACL independence scale in both the male and female samples were chosen for the In scale,

which was subsequently cross-validated on various external criteria (Gough & Bradley, 1996).

Scale In assesses competence and self-sufficiency. High scorers are seen as self-assured, assertive, intelligent, and able to function capably on their own. Low scorers are described as being dependent, indecisive, and awkward in social situations. Lacking self-confidence, they are seen as submissive, preferring to take directions from others.

EMPATHY (EM; **38** ITEMS)

Hogan (1969) adopted a mixed rational and empirical approach to devise an Empathy Scale. The Q-sort descriptions of 211 men who had been assessed by IPAR staff members were scored on a provisional empathy scale consisting of five indicative and five contraindicative items. Item analyses were then conducted by contrasting the MMPI and CPI responses of the men in the highest and lowest 27% on this provisional scale. Other items that intuitively appeared related to the construct were also included. In subsequent research, the MMPI items were dropped, the Em scale was extended to women, and its external correlates were determined (Hogan, 1969; Megargee, 1972).

High scorers on Em have proved to be outgoing, versatile, verbal, and friendly people who are sensitive to the feelings and needs of others. They are socially effective, liberal, enterprising, and self-confident without having any of the exploitative tendencies sometimes found in high scorers on Do or Sa. Low scorers are seen as being constrained, inhibited, awkward, and self-defeating. They strike others as being conventional, moralistic, and narrow-minded.

Sector II Scales: Measures of Adjustment, Maturity, and Social Values

Sector II includes seven scales that Gough felt assessed aspects of socialization, maturity, responsibility, and intrapersonal structuring of values. They are Responsibility (Re), Socialization (So), Self-control (Sc), Good Impression (Gi), Communality (Cm), Well-being (Wb), and Tolerance (To).Three of these scales, Gi, Cm, and Wb, also serve as validity scales.

RESPONSIBILITY (RE; **36** ITEMS)

Like Do, Re was developed as part of a study on political behavior by Gough et al. (1952) to identify people who are conscientious, responsible, dependable, and considerate, complying with rules and believing that life should be governed by reason (Gough, 1968, 1969). Like Do, Re was derived by comparing the responses to MMPI and specially written items of high school and college students who were nominated as being high or low in responsibility by fellow students or by teachers.

Re differs from the related So and Sc scales in that Re emphasizes the degree to which values and controls are conceptualized and understood (Gough, 1965a). High scorers are described as being conscientious, reliable, trustworthy, and attentive to their duties and obligations. Low scorers are seen as irresponsible, undisciplined, hedonistic, unpredictable, and unethical. Rebellious and self-indulgent, they are apt to break the rules and may have records of delinquent or even criminal behavior. Early Sunday morning, a high scorer is apt to be dressing for church while a low scorer is lurching home from a night on the town.

SOCIALIZATION (SO; 46 ITEMS)

So was originally was published independently as the Delinquency (De) scale (Gough & Peterson, 1952). De was constructed through external criterion analyses by comparing the responses of several samples of delinquent and nondelinquent adolescents to items reflecting Gough's role-taking theory of sociopathy (Gough, 1948; Gough & Peterson, 1952). When the De scale was included on the CPI, its keying was reversed and it was renamed Socialization. Subsequent research demonstrated that So actually ordered people throughout the full range of socialization, with low scores indicating antisocial and even criminal behavior, mid-range scores representing ordinary adherence to social norms, and high scores identifying people of unusual honesty and integrity such as high school "best citizens" (Gough, 1960, 1994; Megargee, 1972). Therefore, the present So scale reflects the degree of social maturity, integrity, and rectitude the individual has attained (Gough, 1965b).

Moderately high scorers are described as being conscientious, honest, reliable, and well-organized, with strong, internalized values. Those with extremely high scores may be overly righteous and moralistic. Low scorers are seen as unconventional, independent, and undependable, with poorly developed values. As a result, they are apt to flout society's rules and get into trouble with the law.

SELF-CONTROL (SC; 38 ITEMS)

Initially termed "Impulsivity," the Sc scale was designed to assess nondelinquent freedom from restraints "aimed at impetuosity, high spirits, caprice, and a taste for deviltry" (Gough, 1987, p. 45). Later, the Impulsivity scale was reversed and renamed

Self-control in accordance with the decision to have high scores on all CPI scales reflect positive attributes.

The Sc scale was constructed through internal consistency analyses in which a small cluster of CPI items that appeared to reflect impetuous behavior was rationally devised. Scores on this cluster were then correlated with the total CPI item pool; those having the highest correlations for both genders in various unspecified research samples were selected (Gough, 1987). When the revised CPI 462 was published, the scale was shortened by deleting a number of items that overlapped with other scales.

Individuals with elevated Sc scale scores are described as disciplined, self-denying, judgmental, and conscientious. Indeed Groth-Marnat (1997) suggests that extremely high scores may be indicative of my syndrome of overcontrol of hostile impulses (Megargee, 1966). Low scorers are seen as impulsive, willful, uninhibited, and pleasure seeking.

GOOD IMPRESSION (GI; 40 ITEMS)

Gi is one of three validity scales on the CPI, the others being Communality (Cm) and Well-being (Wb). The original purpose of the scale was to identify dissimulated records for which the normative data did not apply (Gough, 1952b, 1968). It is also used to assess the degree to which test-takers engage in impression management in their responses to the CPI items and their concern about how others react to them (Gough, 1969).

Gi was constructed through external criterion analyses of the responses of high school students to 150 specially devised items. The questionnaire was first administered using standard instructions and later with instructions to respond as if one were applying for a very important job or trying to make an especially favorable impression. Those items which changed significantly from the first to the second administration were selected (Gough, 1952b). Gi was thus one of the first scales constructed to assess what came to be called "social desirability."

Gi raw scores ≥ 30 suggest positive dissimulation, especially if the case history suggests that the client's overall adjustment is less than perfect. Moderately elevated scores are obtained by people who are tactful, obliging, helpful, and concerned with making a favorable impression on others, especially superiors. However, they may be less considerate of subordinates. Low-scoring individuals have an arrogant disregard for the feelings or opinions of others. They are seen as cynical, dissatisfied, complaining nonconformists who want to have things their own way and do not mind stepping on others' toes to do so. Extremely low scores ≤10 are consistent with exaggeration of symptoms or faking bad, especially if Wb is also quite low (Groth-Marnat, 1997).

COMMUNALITY (CM; 38 ITEMS)

The second validity scale, Cm, was designed to detect nonresponsive protocols on which the respondent answered without due regard to the content of the items in the question booklet. Originally designated as the Infrequency (In) scale, its items were chosen by surveying the response frequencies obtained in a number of samples. The items answered in a particular direction by no more than 5% of the respondents were selected for the scale. When the CPI was published and the decision made that high scores would reflect positive traits, the keying was reversed and the scale was designated as Communality. Thus in its present form, Cm consists of items answered in the keyed direction by 95% or more participants in normative samples.

Cm raw scores ≤24 indicate atypical responding that could result from random, fixed pattern, or other types of nonresponsive answering which can result from reading or language problems, failure to understand instructions, or unwillingness to cooperate with the assessment. Less extreme low scores are also obtained by people who are unstable or alienated, as well as those who are independent, unconventional, or somewhat bohemian. High scorers, on the other hand, are described as seen as being conventional, conscientious, and rather bourgeois.

WELL-BEING (WB; 38 ITEMS)

Originally called the Dissimulation (Ds) scale, Wb was derived to identify individuals feigning psychiatric disorders. It was derived through three external criterion analyses contrasting the MMPI responses of actual psychiatric patients with those of normal individual asked to feign neurosis (Gough, 1954). Items showing similar and significant differences in all three analyses were retained for the Ds scale, which was widely used on the original MMPI. The CPI Wb scale was created by eliminating the MMPI items not included on the CPI and reversing the scoring, so high scores reflected positive functioning.

Considerable research has been carried out testing the Wb scale's ability to detect feigned protocols. According the CPI manual, raw scores ≤20 "raise the possibility of exaggerated or unwarranted emphasis on personal problems, and even of a deliberate attempt to fake bad" (Gough & Bradley, 1996, p. 121).

Gough (1968, 1969) states, that in addition to its implications for validity, interpretation of Wb is also feasible. High scores indicate psychological health, energy, verve, and self-confidence. They characterize people who are effective and able to cope successfully with life's demands. Low scores, on the other hand, characterize ineffective, tense, anxious people who have difficulty dealing with everyday problems.

TOLERANCE (TO: 32 ITEMS)

To, originally dubbed Pr (for prejudice), was devised in the course of Gough's early research on social intolerance (Gough, 1951). The MMPI was administered to students who had high and low scores on the California F Scale (Adorno, Frenkel-Brunswik, Levinson, & Sanford, 1950) and the Levinson–Sanford Anti-Semitism scale (Levinson & Sanford, 1944) and items that significantly differentiated them were selected. The Pr scale was later rekeyed and renamed Tolerance for inclusion on the CPI, with four CPI items replacing those that appeared only on the original MMPI. The purpose of this revised scale was the identification of permissive, accepting, and nonjudgmental social beliefs and attitudes (Gough & Bradley, 1996).

High scorers on To are, in fact, described as being tolerant, intelligent, broad minded, and nonjudgmental. Low scorers are described as being dissatisfied, narrow minded, rigid, and authoritarian.

Sector III Scales: Measures of Cognitive and Intellectual Functioning and Achievement Orientation

The third cluster of scales assesses achievement potential and intellectual ability. They include Achievement via Conformance (Ac), Achievement via Independence (Ai), and Intellectual Efficiency (Ie). The overall level of these scales indicates whether an individual has the personality traits associated with academic success; differences between the scales can be interpreted configurally to predict different types or patterns of achievement.

ACHIEVEMENT VIA CONFORMANCE (AC; 38 ITEMS)

The original goal of the Ac scale was to assess the motivational and personality factors associated with academic achievement in high school settings (Gough, 1953c). It was originally named Achievement, but, "Gradually, through working with the scale and through individual acquaintance with high scorers, it became clear that the basic theme of the measure was one of a strong need for achievement coupled with a deeply internalized appreciation of structure and organization" (Gough, 1968, p. 69).

The Ac scale was constructed by the external criterion method. After reviewing the literature on academic achievement, Gough (1953c) made up a pool of items that appeared to be related to high school achievement. They were administered to samples of students matched for IQ but differing in grade point average. Items discriminating the higher- and lower-achieving students in all the samples were retained. The scale was initially cross-validated by correlating scores with grade point averages in new samples. Ac proved to be effective in predicting high school achievement, but did not correlate well with college grades.

High scorers are described as being ambitious, well-organized, and effective in structured settings. They are seen as hard-working, well-adjusted, conscientious and diligent, with traditional social and family values. Low scorers are described as nonconformists who feel confined by regulations and structure. If they have high ability, as indicated by Ai and Ie, they may be inventive or creative. If not they are likely to be low achievers who are more interested in having fun than they are in following the rules or attaining academic success. Such rebellious behavior can lead to authority conflicts and delinquency.

ACHIEVEMENT VIA INDEPENDENCE (AI; 38 ITEMS)

Ai was initially developed to forecast college-level academic success, especially in undergraduate courses in psychology (Gough, 1953a). The derivation method closely paralleled that used with Ac, with a specially formulated pool of items being administered to samples of higher- and lower-achieving college students, except that with Ai the samples were not matched for intelligence. As data on the scale accumulated, it appeared that Ai predicted achievement in settings where independence of thought, creativity, and self-actualization were rewarded. Hence, Ai, which had initially been dubbed Honor Point Ratio (Hr), was renamed Achievement via Independence.

High scorers on Ai are described as being bright, independent, and clear thinking, with a high tolerance for ambiguity. They have wide-ranging interests and do well dealing with complexity and abstractions. However, they may be somewhat egotistic and cool toward others. Low scorers are lacking in ambition and do not do well in high school or college, especially on ambiguous or unstructured tasks. Interpersonally, they are warmer and more comfortable and conventional than their high-Ai peers.

INTELLECTUAL EFFICIENCY (IE; 42 ITEMS)

Originally referred to as a "nonintellectual intelligence test," the Ie scale was constructed to provide a set of personality items that would correlate significantly with accepted measures of intelligence. Ie was constructed empirically by contrasting the responses of senior high school students scoring in the top and bottom quartiles on conventional IQ tests to a pool of MMPI items supplemented by specially written items (Gough, 1953b). The scale was cross-validated and refined by correlating it with measures of intelligence in various samples of high school and college students.

Those scoring high on Ie are described as being intelligent, effective, persevering, capable people who are successful and achievement-oriented. Low scorers are seen as dull, uncertain, and ineffective people who are uninterested in intellectual activities.

Sector IV Scales: Measures of Role and Personal Style

Sector IV includes three scales assessing intellectual and interest modes and personal style: Psychological-mindedness (Py), Flexibility (Fx), and Femininity/Masculinity (F/M).

PSYCHOLOGICAL-MINDEDNESS (PY; 28 ITEMS)

The purpose of the Py scale was to identify people interested in and capable of outstanding achievement in academic psychology (as opposed to other fields). During the late 1940s and early 1950s, a pool of 300 experimental items was given to 25 outstanding young psychologists who, in their later careers, rose to positions of eminence in the field, being elected to office in state, regional, and national professional organizations, winning numerous awards for professional and research contributions to psychology, and producing a vast array of publications. Their responses were contrasted with those of people in other fields and training programs. The 75 items that distinguished these groups were then correlated with instructors' ratings of the competence and potential of graduate students in psychology. Those items that correlated significantly with this second criterion were retained (Gough, 1968).

High scorers are described as being bright, fluent, individualistic, perceptive, and creative, with wide-ranging interests and an openness to new experiences. They excel at research, but are somewhat distant and cool in their interpersonal relations. Low scorers are seen as conventional, practical, down to earth, and wedded to routine. Somewhat lacking in self-confidence, they are less ambitious and less interested in new experiences.

FLEXIBILITY (FX; **28** ITEMS)

The scale that became Fx was first devised as a measure of rigidity. Gough and Nevitt Sanford wrote items they felt embodied inflexibility of thought and manner and resistance to change. These items were then administered to various research samples including undergraduates and individuals assessed at IPAR. Those items having the highest correlations with the overall total scores were selected. In subsequent analyses, this "Gough–Sanford Rigidity" scale was correlated with various other measures of this dimension such as the California Ethnocentrism and F scales. When it was included on the CPI, the Rigidity scale was renamed Flexibility, and the direction of the keying was changed accordingly (Megargee, 1972).

According to Gough (1968, 1969), the Fx scale was designed to identify people who are flexible, adaptable, and even somewhat changeable in their thinking, behavior, and temperament. Moderately high scorers are described as imaginative, spontaneous, clever, and original individuals who are open to new experiences. Extremely high scores, however, suggest someone who is flighty, careless, undependable, and volatile. Moderately low scorers are seen as serious, conventional, deliberate, and well-organized, but extremely low scorers may be rigid, intolerant, and stubborn.

FEMININITY/MASCULINITY (F/M; **32** ITEMS)

The concepts of masculine and feminine are well embedded in folk cultures and languages around the world. The F/M scale should not only "differentiate between men and women everywhere, in all cultures," but also "array respondents along a dimension that is consonant with folk notions of femininity and masculinity" (Gough & Bradley, 1996, pp. 146–147).[3]

F/M was derived by external criterion analyses in which the responses of men and women were compared on a specially constructed item pool. Items that significantly differentiated between male and female high school and college students were selected (Gough, 1952a). F/M has been found to differentiate between women and men in numerous countries and cultures around the world. It has also been found to order occupations in a manner consistent with their stereotypical femininity (Gough & Bradley, 1996).

There are some characteristics associated with high and low F/M scale scores that apply to everyone regardless of gender. High scorers are described as being sensitive, solicitous, and inhibited. They tend to avoid conflict or confrontations. Low scorers are seen as being stronger, more assertive, more self-confident, and more open in their expressions of anger or hostility.

On other measures, women and men with high and low F/M scale scores are described differently. High-scoring women are seen as being sensitive, gentle, warm and sympathetic, but also as weak and dependent, while low-scoring women are described as being strong, independent, assertive, and self-reliant but also somewhat cynical. High-scoring men are described as being feminine, delicate, and, as we have seen, sensitive, but also as imaginative and creative. In addition to being assertive and self-assured, low-scoring men are seen as being strong, robust, and adventurous.

Structure of the CPI

The 20 folk culture scales of the CPI all assess aspects of interpersonal functioning and, with the exception of Scale F/M, they are all keyed so that high scores reflect more socially desirable behavior patterns. Therefore, it is not surprising that most of the scales correlate positively with one another, with rs ranging from -0.15 to $+0.83$ and a median of 0.44 for both men and women (Gough, 1987). The structure of the CPI has been investigated through factor analyses (Gough, 1987; Megargee, 1972) and smallest space analysis (SSA; Karni & Levin, 1972).

Factor Analyses

Factor analysis of the 20-scale CPI 462 and, presumably, the CPI 434, yields four factors; 19 of the 20 scales have loadings ≥ 0.50 on one or more of these four factors (Gough, 1987). The exception is Scale F/M, which is independent of the other 19 scales and which often forms its own residual factor. This factor structure is consistent with the overall findings of 20 factor analyses involving the 18-scale CPI 480 as summarized by Megargee (1972).

Factor 1 is defined by high loadings on Scales Do, Cs, Sy, Sp, Sa, In, and Em, all of which deal with various aspects of effective interpersonal relations. Gough (1987) labeled this factor, "extraversion." This factor appeared as Factor 2 in earlier analyses of Form 480, where it was referred to as "social poise," "interpersonal effectiveness," and "extraversion" (Megargee, 1972).

Factor 2 is defined by high loadings from Scales Re, Sc, Gi, Wb, To, and Ac, all of which deal with social values, conformity to social norms, and achievement orientation. Gough (1987) calls this factor "control." This factor appeared as Factor 1 in analyses of the CPI 480, where it was variously described as "positive adjustment," "conformity and value orientation," or "mental health and personal efficiency" (Megargee, 1972).

Factor 3 on all forms of the CPI is defined by large loadings from Scales To, Ai, and Fx, as well as by smaller loadings from Py and Ie. These scales all deal with independent thinking and openness to new experiences. Gough (1987) calls this factor "flexibility." Previous analysts have referred to it as "capacity for independent thought and action" and "adaptive autonomy" (Megargee, 1972).

Factor 4 has its primary loadings from Scale Cm along with Scales Re, So, and Wb, which reflect conventional social values and conformity. Gough (1987) terms this factor, "consensuality." Other analysts have described it as "conventionality," "social conformity," and "super-ego strength" (Megargee, 1972).

Smallest Space Analysis

SSA is a technique for geometrically representing the relationships among data points such as correlation coefficients. Karni and Levin's (1972) SSA of the CPI identified three dimensions: a "person orientation," a "values orientation," and a "self-orientation." This SSA analysis, which is compatible with the factor analytic findings, influenced the next major advance in the evolution of the CPI, namely the development of orthogonal "vector" scales assessing these three dimensions.

Vector Scales and the Cuboid Model
The Three Vector Scales

Approximately three decades after the publication of the CPI 480, the second generation of CPIs, Forms 462 (Gough, 1987) and 434 (Gough and Bradley, 1996) were introduced. In addition to two new folk culture scales, In and Em, these two new forms of the CPI had evolved to include three new "vector" scales assessing the dimensions identified in Karni and Levin's (1972) SSA analysis. These three measures were used to define four CPI-based personality types, each with seven different levels of realization.

Each vector scale was designed to be bipolar and unrelated or orthogonal to the other two. Gough (1987) constructed them by means of internal analyses in which he sought items that had high correlations with the CPI scales that marked each SSA cluster along with negligible correlations with the scales marking the other clusters, a process he described as a, "long and arduous task, involving a great deal of trial and error, and taking a number of years to complete" (Gough & Bradley, 1996, p. 14).

VECTOR 1 (V. 1; 34 ITEMS)

Vector 1 measures the "external/internal" or "involved/detached" dimension associated with the SSA "person orientation." Scales Sa, Sy, Do, and Sp were used as markers for the extraversion pole while F/M, Sc, and Gi were the markers for introversion (Gough, 1987). According to Gough (1989, p. 78), "Lower scores on v. 1 are associated with a more outgoing, involved, interpersonally responsive orientation, and high scores with a more inwardly directed, private, and interpersonally focused inclination."

VECTOR 2 (V. 2; 36 ITEMS)

Vector 2 assesses the norm-questioning/norm-favoring dimension associated with the SSA "value orientation." The norm-favoring pole was marked by scales Cm and So, while the norm-questioning dimension was marked by Scale Fx. Gough (1989, p. 78) wrote, "Lower scores on v. 2 are associated with rule-questioning, rule-resisting, and even rule-violating dispositions. Higher scores are associated with rule-accepting, rule-observing, and even rule-cathecting tendencies."

VECTOR 3 (V. 3; 58 ITEMS)

The third vector scale was designed to define seven levels of self-realization or competence. Items were selected that had minimal correlations with the v. 1 and v. 2 scales and maximal correlations with the 19 CPI folk scales exclusive of Scale F/M. The sum of the T-scores on Scales Wb, To, and Ie served as a marker for Scale v. 3. According to Gough (1989, p. 80), "Persons with high scores on v. 3 tend to be described by others as intelligent, resourceful, and insightful. Persons with low scores tend to be described as complaining, narrow in interests, and self-defeating."

The Cuboid Model

When scores on the first two orthogonal vector scales, v. 1 and v. 2, are plotted at right angles on the reverse side of the CPI profile sheet, they form a grid with four equal quadrants (see Figure 17.1). Each quadrant, labeled Alpha, Beta, Gamma, or Delta, is thought to define "four lifestyles or ways of living . . . each having its own potentiality and particular type of fulfillment, and each having its own pitfalls and dangers to be avoided" (Gough, 1989, p. 79).

The scores on v. 3 indicate the degree to which the positive or negative implications of each type are realized. Since the scores on v. 3 are normally distributed, more people fall in the mid-range levels 3, 4, and 5 than at the extreme levels 1 and 2 or 6 and 7. Gough's "cuboid model" graphically represents the interactions of the three vector scales as a series of seven four-quadrant grids stacked upon one another like tiers in a parking garage according to their levels as defined by v. 3, with level 1 at the bottom and level 7 at the top.

GROUP ALPHA

On each 2 × 2 grid, Alphas, defined by below-average scores on v. 1 and above-average scores on v. 2, are norm-favoring extroverts who are engaged with others and who accept society's rules and behave accordingly. They are likely to be ambitious, goal-oriented, and strong in social skills and leadership potential. They often are joiners who are involved in many extracurricular, social service, or church-based groups. At high levels of integration, as indicated by v. 3, Alphas can be well-organized charismatic leaders in the military, politics, or business. At low levels of integration, however, Alphas may be opportunistic or authoritarian (Gough, 1989; Gough & Bradley, 1996).

GROUP BETA

Betas, defined by above-average scores on both v. 1 and v. 2, are norm-favoring introverts. They prefer to work for the public good out of the public eye. At high levels, Gough (1987, p. 28) thinks of them as the elders who preserve the wisdom and traditions of their tribes, such as judges, philosophers, or theologians. At low levels of realization, however, they may be cautious, conventional, or constricted (Gough, 1989; Gough & Bradley, 1996).

GROUP GAMMA

Gammas, defined by below-average scores on both v. 1 and v. 2, are norm-questioning extroverts. Socially involved doubters and skeptics, they engage others while questioning the status quo, trusting their personal values more than conventional mores. At high levels of integration, they may be adventurers or innovators who found progressive social movements. At a low level of integration, a Gamma might be a rabble-rousing malcontent or insurgent (Gough, 1989; Gough & Bradley, 1996).

GROUP DELTA

Deltas, defined by above-average scores on v. 1 and below-average scores on v. 2, are norm-questioning introverts. More solitary and internal than Gammas, Deltas march to a different drummer and question society's values. Idiosyncratic and detached, they may be creative and visionary at high levels of integration. At lower levels, they may be eccentric, withdrawn, and prone to psychopathology (Gough, 1989; Gough & Bradley, 1996).

Special Purpose and Research Scales

In addition to the folk culture and vector scales and the cuboid typology, the CPI manual (Gough & Bradley, 1996; pp. 175–179) provides item lists for 13 special purpose scales that may be scored at the examiner's discretion. They include

1. Managerial Potential (Mp)
2. Work Orientation (Wo)
3. Creative Temperament (CT)
4. Leadership (Lp)
5. Amicability (Ami)
6. Law Enforcement Orientation (Leo)
7. Tough-mindedness (Tm)
8. Baucom scale for masculinity (B-MS)
9. Baucom scale for femininity (B-FM)
10. Anxiety (Anx)
11. Narcissism (Nar)
12. Dicken Social Desirability (D-SD)
13. Dicken Acquiescence (D-AC)

Brief descriptions of these scales and references to sources for additional information are contained in appendix A of the manual.

Interpreting the CPI

There are six basic steps in interpreting a CPI. They are (a) establishing profile validity, (b) considering the cuboid type and level of integration, (c) interpreting the elevation of the overall profile and individual folk scales, (d) examining scale configurations, (e) scoring and interpreting any special or research scales, and (f) considering the implications of situational or environmental factors and data from other tests on the interpretation.

Establishing Profile Validity

Establishing profile validity begins with checking the answer sheet to identify any omitted or double-checked items; 30 or more such items may invalidate the profile. If the answer sheet is checked when it is turned in, the examinee can be instructed to make the necessary corrections.

For most purposes, validity can be determined by inspecting the raw scores on the three validity scales.

As noted earlier, Cm raw scores ≤24 indicate atypical or nonresponsive, such as fixed pattern or random, responding. Raw scores ≥30 on Gi suggest positive dissimulation or faking good, while Wb raw scores ≤20 imply faking bad (malingering) or serious personal problems. A set of three more precise equations involving weighted combinations of raw scores on several scales which are applied sequentially in a decision tree approach have been devised for CPI 462 and CPI 434 (Lanning, 1989). These equations and their cutting scores along with relevant normative and validity data can be found in the manual (Gough & Bradley, 1996, pp. 67–73).

Interpreting the Profile

CPI interpretation begins with ascertaining the cuboid type—Alpha, Beta, Gamma, or Delta—and its level of realization. The type and the level establish the overall context for the interpretation.

Once the profile is classified, the interpreter should consider its overall elevation, paying particular attention to those scales that are above T60 and below T40, and considering the differences in elevation within and between the four clusters or sectors. A wealth of information can be found in the CPI interpretive literature (Gough, 1968, 1989; Gough & Bradley, 1996; Groth-Marnat, 1997; McAllister, 1996; Megargee, 1972). In general the higher the elevation, the more favorable the behavioral implications. This examination of the individual scales should sharpen and refine the broader implications of the cuboid type and level.

The next step is to examine the configuration of selected sets of scales. For example, the relative elevations of Scales Ac and Ai have important implications for patterns of achievement-oriented behavior, Re, So, and Sc for honesty versus misbehavior, and Do, Re, and Gi for the manner in which leadership is exercised (Groth-Marnat, 1997; McAllister, 1996; Megargee, 1972).

After extracting as much information as possible from the CPI profile, the examiner should consider relevant situational and environmental factors before making behavioral assessments and predictions. For example, in a series of experiments, my colleagues and I discovered that whether or not men and women with high scores on the Dominance scale (High Do) assumed leadership positions when paired with low-Do partners was strongly influenced by situational variables such as the demands of the task, social mores, and gender role expectations (Megargee, 1969; Megargee, Bogart, & Anderson, 1966). In these studies, only by considering situational as well as personality factors could accurate predictions be made.

Conclusion

In the six decades since its first scales were developed, the CPI has evolved significantly. The initial scales assessing a few selected aspects of social functioning grew into an interrelated array of measures designed to assess, singly or in combination, all relevant aspects of effective interpersonal functioning. Later, orthogonal vector scales defining four different personality types and assessing their level of effectiveness were added.

The CPI was designed to be an open system, and new applications and uses continue to be added. While I have focused on the concepts and the structure of the CPI, as with other personality inventories there have also been important technological advances as hand scoring has given way to computerized administration, scoring, and interpretation. If the past is a guide to the future, it seems certain that the CPI will continue to evolve in the years to come.

Notes

1. When critics frown on the fact that most of the CPI's folk culture scales are positively correlated with one another, Gough points to the Strong Vocational Interest Blank (SVIB), a collateral ancestor of the CPI, and notes that no one disapproves of the fact that the SVIB's scales for physicist and mathematician are positively correlated because, in the real world, most physicists have mathematical talents, and many mathematicians have an interest in physics. Therefore, valid measures of these interests should be associated with one another (Gough & Bradley, 1996, p. 8).

2. These descriptors for Do and the other 19 folk culture scales are drawn from Gough (1989), Gough and Bradley (1996), Groth-Marnat (1997), and Megargee (1972).

3. Gough notes that some have difficulty with the notion of a bipolar Femininity/Masculinity scale (Gough & Bradley, 1996). Regardless of the conceptual difficulties, the fact remains that F/M scores correlate reliably with how people describe one another. Those who prefer unipolar scales on which people can obtain high or low scores on both masculinity and femininity can use the Baucom scales for Masculinity (B-MS) and Femininity (B-FM) (Baucom, 1976).

References

Adorno, T. W., Frenkel-Brunswik, E., Levinson, D., & Sanford, R. (1950). *The authoritarian personality.* New York: Harper.

Baucom, D. H. (1976). Independent masculinity and femininity scales on the California Psychological Inventory. *Journal of Consulting and Clinical Psychology, 44,* 876.

Costa, P. T., Jr., & McRae, R. R. (1992). *Revised NEO Personality Inventory (NEO PI-R) and NEO Five-Factor Inventory (NEO-FFI)) professional manual.* Odessa, FL.: Psychological Assessment resources.

Gough, H. G. (1948). A new dimension of status: I. Development of a personality scale. *American Sociological Review, 13,* 401–409.

Gough, H. G. (1951) Studies of social intolerance: II. A personality scale for anti-Semitism. *Journal of Social Psychology, 33,* 247–255.

Gough, H. G. (1952a). Identifying psychological femininity. *Educational and Psychological Measurement, 12,* 427–439.

Gough, H. G. (1952b). On making a good impression. *Journal of Educational Research, 46,* 33–42.

Gough, H. G. (1952c). Predicting social participation. *The Journal of Social Psychology, 35,* 227–233.

Gough, H. G. (1953a). The construction of a scale to predict scholastic achievement. *Journal of Applied Psychology, 37,* 361–366.

Gough, H. G. (1953b). A non-intellectual intelligence test. *Journal of Consulting Psychology, 42,* 242–246.

Gough, H. G. (1953c). What determines the academic achievement of high school students? *Journal of Educational Research, 46,* 321–331.

Gough, H. G. (1954). Some common misconceptions about neuroticism. *Journal of Consulting Psychology, 18,* 287–292.

Gough, H. G. (1957). *Manual for the California Psychological Inventory* (1st ed.). Palo Alto, CA: Consulting Psychologists Press.

Gough, H. G. (1960). *Manual for the California Psychological Inventory* (Rev. ed.). Palo Alto, CA: Consulting Psychologists Press.

Gough, H. G. (1965a). Conceptual analysis of psychological test scores and other diagnostic variables. *Journal of Abnormal Psychology, 70,* 294–302.

Gough, H. G. (1965b). Cross-cultural validation of a measure of asocial behavior. *Psychological Reports, 17,* 379–387.

Gough, H. G. (1968). An interpreter's syllabus for the California Psychological Inventory. In P. McReynolds (Ed.), *Advances in psychological assessment* (Vol. 1, pp. 55–79). Palo Alto, CA: Science and Behavior Books.

Gough, H. G. (1969). *Manual for the California Psychological Inventory* (Rev. ed.). Palo Alto, CA: Consulting Psychologists Press.

Gough, H. G. (1987). *Administrator's guide for the California Psychological Inventory.* Palo Alto, CA: Consulting Psychologists Press.

Gough, H. G. (1989). The California Psychological Inventory. In C. S. Newmark (Ed.), *Major psychological instruments* (Vol. 2., pp. 67–98). Boston: Allyn & Bacon.

Gough, H. G. (1994). Theory, development, and interpretation of the CPI socialization scale. *Psychological Reports, 75,* 651–700.

Gough, H. G., & Bradley, P. (1996). *Manual for the California psychological inventory* (3rd ed.). Palo Alto, CA: Consulting Psychologists Press.

Gough, H. G., & Heilbrun, A. P. (1983). *The Adjective Checklist manual—1983 edition.* Palo Alto, CA: Consulting Psychologists Press.

Gough, H. G., McClosky, P., & Meehl, P. E., (1951). A personality scale for dominance. *Journal of Abnormal and Social Psychology, 46,* 360–366.

Gough, H. G., McClosky, P., & Meehl, P. E., (1952). A personality scale for responsibility. *Journal of Abnormal and Social Psychology, 47,* 73–80.

Gough, H. G., & Peterson, D. R. (1952). The identification and measurement of predispositional factors in crime and delinquency. *Journal of Consulting Psychology, 16,* 207–212.

Groth-Marnat, G. (1997). *Handbook of psychological assessment* (3rd ed.). New York: John Wiley & Sons.

Hathaway, S. R., & McKinley, J. C. (1943). *The Minnesota Multiphasic Personality schedule.* Minneapolis, MN: University of Minnesota Press.

Hogan, R. (1969). Development of an empathy scale. *Journal of Consulting and Clinical Psychology, 33,* 307–316.

Karni, E. S., & Levin, J. (1972). The use of smallest space analysis in studying scale structure: An application to the California Psychological Inventory. *Journal of Applied Psychology, 56,* 341–346.

Lanning, K. (1989) Detection of invalid response patterns on the California Psychological Inventory. *Applied Psychological Measurement, 13,* 45–56.

Levinson, D., & Sanford, R. N. (1944). A scale for the measurement of anti-Semitism. *Journal of Psychology, 17,* 339–370.

McAllister, L. W. (1996). *A practical guide to CPI interpretation.* Palo Alto, CA: Consulting Psychologists Press.

Megargee, E. I. (1966). Undercontrolled and overcontrolled personality types in extreme antisocial aggression. *Psychological Monographs, 80* (3, Whole No. 611).

Megargee, E. I. (1969). The influence of sex roles on the manifestation of leadership. *Journal of Applied Psychology, 53,* 377–382.

Megargee, E. I. (1972). *The California Psychological Inventory handbook.* San Francisco: Jossey-Bass.

Megargee, E. I., Bogart, P., & Anderson, B. J. (1966). The prediction of leadership in a simulated industrial task. *Journal of Applied Psychology, 50,* 292–295.

Myers, I. B., & Briggs, K. C. (1943/1962). *The Myers–Briggs type indicator.* Palo Alto, CA: Consulting Psychologists Press.

Strong, E. K., Jr. (1943). *The vocational interests of men and women.* Stanford, CA: Stanford University Press.

Personality Disorders Assessment Instruments

Thomas A. Widiger *and* Sara E. Boyd

Abstract

This chapter provides an overview of the assessment of personality disorder, focusing in particular on self-report inventories and semistructured interviews. The convergent validity reported in 68 studies among five semistructured interviews, one rating form, and 10 self-report inventories are summarized and discussed. Discussed as well are discriminant validity, the boundaries with Axis I disorders, the boundaries with normal personality functioning, the boundaries among the personality disorders, and gender, culture, and ethnicity bias.

Keywords: personality disorders, self-report inventories, semistructured interviews, convergent validity, discriminant validity, gender bias, culture, ethnicity

Personality disorders were placed on a separate diagnostic axis (Axis II) in the influential third edition of the American Psychiatric Association's (APA) *Diagnostic and statistical manual of mental disorders* (DSM; APA, 1980). Most other mental disorders were and continue to be placed on Axis I (APA, 2000). This unique distinction for the personality disorders is to encourage the recognition of maladaptive personality traits in virtually every patient because personality traits will affect the occurrence, expression, course, and/or treatment of most Axis I disorders (Frances, 1980). In addition, a significant proportion of patients will be in treatment primarily because of a personality disorder. Personality disorders are among the most difficult of the mental disorders to treat, but they are not untreatable (Perry, Banon, & Ianni, 1999). Clinically significant and meaningful improvements to personality functioning are often obtained.

The assessment of personality disorders should then be of substantial importance to clinicians (Widiger, 2002). Clinicians who are concerned primarily with the treatment of an Axis I mental disorder should include a measure of maladaptive personality functioning if they intend to account

fully for the variation in their patients' treatment responsivity, and clinicians who are concerned primarily with the treatment of a personality disorder are advised to include objective measures of personality disorder symptomatology to document empirically the effectiveness of their intervention.

Personality disorders, however, can be difficult to assess. One of the major innovations of DSM-III (APA, 1980) was the provision of relatively more specific and explicit diagnostic criterion sets that facilitated substantially the obtainment of more reliable clinical diagnoses. This innovation, however, has been problematic for the personality disorders. It is difficult, perhaps even impossible, to provide a brief list of specific diagnostic criteria for the broad and complex behavior patterns that constitute a personality disorder (Westen, 1997). As acknowledged in DSM-III-R, "for some disorders . . . , particularly the Personality Disorders, the criteria require much more inference on the part of the observer" (APA, 1987, p. xxiii).

An additional difficulty is that many of the personality disorders affect self-description. Antisocial persons will be dishonest, dependent persons can be overly self-denigrating, paranoid persons will be reluctant to provide personal information, histrionic persons would be expected to be melodramatic, and narcissistic persons might deny the existence of faults and inadequacies. The self-description of persons with personality disorders should not be taken at face value (Widiger & Samuel, 2005). Most self-report inventories include validity scales to detect denial, exaggeration, or other forms of dissimulation. These scales are typically used to identify invalid or questionable test results but they could also be detecting personality disorder symptomatology.

One approach for addressing distortions in self-image is to request that one or more persons who know the patient well to provide their perspective on his or her personality. Spouses, friends, and close colleagues will not provide an entirely accurate description of an identified patient, as they will not be familiar with all aspects of the person's functioning and they may have their own axes to grind. Nevertheless, they do provide a useful source of additional information, and they would lack the distortions, denials, and exaggerations that characterize the patient's personality disorder. Agreement between self-descriptions and informant descriptions of personality disorders has been only adequate to poor (Klein, 2003; Klonsky, Oltmanns, & Turkheimer, 2002; Ready & Clark, 2002). The reasons for the poor agreement are many (e.g., distortion of self-descriptions secondary to personality and mood disorder, or biased and inadequate bases for informant descriptions), but the disagreement does at least indicate the importance of obtaining multiple sources of input for a diagnostic assessment and for conducting additional research into the bases for this disagreement. Oltmanns and Turkheimer (2006) have been conducting a particularly creative and intriguing investigation of the agreement and disagreement between self-descriptions and peer nominations of personality disorder. They indicated, for example, that there is considerable agreement among peers within a particular social circle regarding who is narcissistic but, perhaps not surprisingly, the persons identified as being narcissistic do not necessarily describe themselves that way. They described themselves as being outgoing, gregarious, and likeable.

A further difficulty is the amount of time it takes to provide a systematic and comprehensive assessment of all of the personality disorders included within DSM-IV-TR (APA, 2000). The DSM-IV-TR personality disorders include 80 diagnostic criteria, not counting the 14 diagnostic criteria for the two disorders (negativistic and depressive) included within an appendix for disorders not yet receiving official approval. Even if one spent "only" 2 hr assessing the personality disorders, that would still allow (on average) only 90 s to assess borderline identity disturbance or narcissistic lack of empathy. As a result, clinicians often fail to assess adequately the full range of personality disorder symptomatology that is in fact present in their clients (Garb, 2005; Zimmerman & Mattia, 1999a, b).

Instruments for the Assessment of Personality Disorders

Fortunately, there are a number of instruments available that improve considerably the reliability and validity of personality disorder assessments. This chapter will be confined to interviews and self-report inventories. There is currently only limited research on the use of projective tests for the assessment of most of the DSM-IV-TR personality disorders (Huprich, 2005) and some controversy over the validity of these assessments (Wood, Garb, Lilienfeld, & Nezworski, 2002). In any case, this additional literature is beyond the scope of this chapter. Huprich (2005) provides a thorough coverage of the literature on the use of the Rorschach in the assessment of personality disorders and Gacano and Meloy (Chapter 29) review the literature on the use of projective techniques for the assessment of the antisocial personality disorder.

Semistructured Interviews

The preferred method for the assessment of personality disorders in general clinical practice is an unstructured clinical interview (Watkins, Campbell, Nieberding, & Hallmark, 1995; Westen, 1997), whereas the preferred method in research is the semistructured interview (Segal & Coolidge, 2007; Widiger & Samuel, 2005; Zimmerman, 2003). Semistructured interviews have several advantages over unstructured interviews (McDermut & Zimmernan, 2008; Rogers, 2003). Semistructured interviews ensure and document that a systematic and comprehensive assessment of each personality disorder diagnostic criterion has been made. This documentation can be particularly helpful in situations in which the credibility or validity of the assessment might be questioned, such as forensic or disability evaluations. Semistructured interviews also increase the likelihood of reliable and replicable assessments (Farmer, 2000; Rogers, 2003; Segal & Coolidge, 2007; Wood et al., 2002).

Semistructured interviews provide specific, carefully selected questions for the assessment of each diagnostic criterion, the application of which increases the likelihood that assessments will be consistent across interviewers. In addition, the manuals that accompany a semistructured interview frequently provide a considerable amount of helpful information for understanding the rationale of each diagnostic criterion, for interpreting vague or inconsistent symptoms, and for resolving diagnostic ambiguities (e.g., Loranger, 1999; Widiger, Mangine, Corbitt, Ellis, & Thomas, 1995).

Semistructured interviews have been described as superficial and mindless symptom counting (Westen & Shedler, 1999a). However, it is not the case that semistructured interviews are simply a series of direct questions as to the presence of each DSM-IV-TR diagnostic criterion (Widiger, 2007a). Semistructured interviews are "semi"-structured because they include many open-ended questions, indirect inquiries, and observations of the respondents' manner of relating to the interviewer, in addition to the relatively more direct questions. Furthermore, interviewers administering a semistructured interview do not simply record respondents' answers to queries. They use their clinical expertise to rate each diagnostic criterion based on the substantial amount of information that is generated by the interview.

Semistructured interviews allow interviewers to conduct their own follow-up queries when confronted with an ambiguous response to the questions provided by the interview schedule. Nevertheless, clinicians will still find semistructured interviews to be constraining. Many naturally prefer to rely on their own unique, personalized manner for obtaining information and developing rapport (Westen, 1997). However, a major strength of a semistructured interview is the assurance through an explicit structure that each relevant diagnostic criterion is being adequately and systematically assessed (Rogers, 2003). Idiosyncratic and subjective interviewing techniques are also more likely to result in gender and cultural biases (Garb, 2005). Studies have indicated that assessments based on unstructured clinical interviews do not consider all of the necessary or important diagnostic criteria (Blashfield & Herkov, 1996; Garb, 2005; Zimmerman & Mattia, 1999b). For example, Zimmerman and Mattia (1999a) reported that clinicians diagnosed less than 1% of patients with borderline personality disorder; whereas 14.4% were diagnosed with this

disorder when a semistructured interview was used. They subsequently provided the clinicians with the additional information obtained from the semistructured interview. The rate of diagnosis increased from 0.4% to 9.2%. "This is inconsistent with the notion that personality disorder diagnoses based on semistructured interviews are not viewed as valid by clinicians" (Zimmerman & Mattia, 1999a, p. 1570). If clinicians are provided with systematic and comprehensive assessments of personality disorder symptomatology, they do recognize the value of this information.

Studies have also indicated that personality disorder assessments in the absence of structured clinical interviews tend to be unreliable (Garb, 2005; Mellsop, Varghese, Joshua, & Hicks, 1982; Spitzer, Forman, & Nee, 1979). Clinicians tend to diagnose personality disorders hierarchically, failing to assess additional symptoms once they reach a conclusion that a particular personality disorder is present (Adler, Drake, & Teague, 1990; Herkov & Blashfield, 1995). The identified personality disorder may even be based on idiosyncratic interests (Mellsop et al., 1982).

Few clinicians would attempt to diagnose mental retardation on the basis of an unstructured clinical interview, yet structured assessments are rarely used for the diagnosis of most other mental disorders. A proposal for DSM-V (unlikely, however, to be implemented) is to make comparable requirements for the diagnosis of the anxiety, mood, personality, and other mental disorders (Widiger & Clark, 2000). The APA and the National Institute of Mental Health DSM-V Nomenclature Work Group recommended that the DSM-V Task Force consider incorporating more structured assessments into criterion sets in order to assure that they are being assessed systematically. "At present, results of psychological testing are not included in DSM-IV diagnostic criteria, with the exception of IQ testing and academic skills . . . [and] this exception points the way for research that could lead to incorporation of psychological test results as diagnostic criteria for other disorders" (Rounsaville et al., 2002, p. 24).

DSM-IV-TR PERSONALITY DISORDER INTERVIEWS

There are currently five semistructured interviews coordinated explicitly with the diagnostic criteria provided within DSM-IV-TR (APA, 1994, 2000): (1) Diagnostic Interview for Personality Disorders (DIPD; Zanarini, Frankenburg, Chauncey, & Gunderson, 1987); (2) International

Personality Disorder Examination (IPDE; Loranger, 1999); (3) Personality Disorder Interview-IV (PDI-IV; Widiger et al., 1995); (4) Structured Clinical Interview for DSM-IV Axis II Personality Disorders (SCID-II; First & Gibbon, 2004); and (5) Structured Interview for DSM-IV Personality Disorders (SIDP-IV; Pfohl, Blum, & Zimmerman, 1997). There are also personality disorder rating forms that can be completed by a clinician who is already very familiar with the patient: the Personality Assessment Form (PAF; Pilkonis, Heape, Ruddy, & Serrao, 1991), and the Shedler–Westen Assessment Procedure (SWAP-200; Shedler, 2002).

Each of the semistructured interviews has particular advantages and disadvantages relative to one another (Widiger, Costa, & Samuel, 2006; McDermut & Zimmerman, 2008). The SIDP-IV, SCID-II, and IPDE have more empirical support than either the DIPD or PDI-IV. The PDI-IV has been used in the least number of studies. The manuals for the SIDP-IV and SCID-II are relatively limited in the amount of information and guidance provided for scoring, whereas the manual for the PDI-IV is the most thorough and detailed, providing the history, rationale, and major assessment issues for each of the 94 DSM-IV-TR personality disorder diagnostic criteria. Some researchers have administered one interview (e.g., SIDP-IV), yet used the manual for another (e.g., PDI-IV) for the training of the interviewers (e.g., Jane, Oltmanns, South, & Turkheimer, 2007).

The SCID-II includes a self-report screening questionnaires that can save time by allowing the interviewer to cover only those personality disorders that obtain elevated scores on the screening measure (First & Gibbon, 2004). However, if a self-report inventory is administered, clinicians and researchers might as well use one of the heavily researched and validated self-report measures discussed later in this chapter. The IPDE takes the most time to administer, as it includes the largest number of required and recommended inquiries per diagnostic criterion. The IPDE is the only semistructured interview to include an assessment of the diagnostic criteria for the personality disorders included within the World Health Organization's (1992) International Classification of Diseases (ICD-10; WHO, 1992), although it should be noted that the IPDE does not actually provide separate questions for the assessment of these two alternative nomenclatures. The IPDE simply indicates which questions developed for the assessment of the DSM-IV-TR personality disorders could also be used for the assessment of

each ICD-10 diagnostic criterion. One could not then actually use the IPDE to compare the DSM-IV-TR and ICD-10 nomenclatures, as the scoring for the ICD-10 is derived from the assessment of the DSM-IV-TR criterion sets.

The SWAP-200 is a 200-item Q-sort of personality disorder symptomatology. SWAP-200 items are not rated on the basis of a semistructured interview; instead, the SWAP-200 relies on "the empathically attuned and dynamically sophisticated clinician given free rein to practice his or her craft" (Shedler, 2002, p. 433). Approximately half of the SWAP-200 items are reproductions of the DSM-IV-TR personality disorder diagnostic criteria (at times with a more psychodynamic orientation); most of the other items are additional traits, symptoms, or defense mechanisms hypothesized to be diagnostic of personality dysfunction (e.g., "Tends to create relationships that repeat or reenact problematic aspects of his or her relationship with a parent"); the few remaining items refer to healthy personality functioning.

The SWAP-200 is also unique in its use of a Q-sort format (Westen & Shedler, 1999a), which is essentially a requirement that respondents provide scores that are consistent with a desired distribution. To describe an individual using the SWAP-200, a rater arranges the items into eight categories from those that are not descriptive of the individual (assigned a value of 0) to those that are highly descriptive (assigned a value of 7). The typical distribution used is to require that half (100) of the items be provided with a ranking of 0, 22 scored 1, 18 scored 2, 16 scored 3, 14 scored 4, 12 scored 5, 10 scored 6, and 8 scored 7 (e.g., Westen & Shedler, 1999b).

OTHER PERSONALITY DISORDER INTERVIEWS

There are also interviews for the assessment of individual personality disorders, such as (but not limited to) the Revised Diagnostic Interview for Borderlines (DIB-R; Zanarini, Gunderson, Frankenburg, & Chauncey, 1989), the Diagnostic Interview for Narcissism (DIN; Gunderson, Ronningstam, & Bodkin, 1990), and the Hare Psychopathy Checklist-Revised (PCL-R; Hare, 2003). There is currently only one interview for the assessment of a dimensional model of personality disorder: the Structured Interview for the Five-Factor Model (SIFFM; Trull & Widiger, 1997).

The DIB-R, DIN, and PCL-R are very useful when the clinician's or researcher's interest is confined to the borderline, narcissistic, or psychopathic personality disorder, respectively (McDermut & Zimmerman, 2008). However, each of these interviews can require as much time to assess an individual personality disorder as the SIDP-IV, SCID-II, or PDI-IV would use to assess all 10 of them. The individual personality disorder interviews provide more fidelity (specificity, detail); the DSM-IV-TR interviews provide more bandwidth (coverage). For example, the DIB-R will provide a more thorough assessment of borderline symptomatology than is provided by the SIDP-IV (e.g., it provides substantially more coverage of disturbances in cognition) but the DIB-R will fail to assess for the presence of other personality disorder symptomatology that might also be of substantial clinical or scientific importance, given the substantial rate of diagnostic co-occurrence (Bornstein, 1998; Clark, 2007; Trull & Durrett, 2005).

Psychopathy is a personality disorder that is of particular importance to clinicians and researchers working within forensic settings. Psychopathy, as assessed by the PCL-R, overlaps substantially with DSM-IV-TR antisocial personality disorder. The primary distinctions are that the PCL-R includes four personality traits not included within the DSM-IV-TR criterion set (i.e., arrogance, glib charm, lacking in empathy, and shallow affect; Widiger, 2005) and the DSM-IV-R criterion set places relatively more emphasis on behaviorally specific acts (Hare, 2003). The PCL-R is a well-validated checklist and is the preferred instrument for the assessment of antisocial personality disorder (or psychopathy) within prison and forensic settings (APA, 2000; Hare, 2003). However, as suggested by its title, the PCL-R is better described as a checklist than as a semistructured interview. Many of its items are scored primarily (if not solely) on the basis of a person's criminal record rather than on the basis of interview questions (e.g., a history of murders or rapes is used to indicate the presence of a lack of empathy; Hare, 2003). This is somewhat ironic since the purported advantage of PCL-R psychopathy relative to DSM-IV-TR antisocial has been its emphasis on personality traits rather than specific acts of criminality (Hare, 2003). In fact, it has been suggested that the PCL-R may place too heavy of a reliance on criminal history and that a more valid assessment of psychopathy would be obtained if all references to criminal behavior were excluded from the assessment (Skeem & Cooke, in press). In any case, clinicians will have some difficulty administering the PCL-R outside of prison and forensic settings due to its reliance on a criminal record to score many of its items.

Self-Report Inventories

The complete administration of a semistructured personality disorder interview generally requires 1–2 hr, with some as long as 4 hr (e.g., IPDE; Loranger, 1999). Hence it is understandable that clinicians are reluctant, if not unable, to administer an entire semistructured interview. We therefore recommend that one first administer a self-report inventory to identify the principle areas of normal and abnormal personality functioning that warrant additional consideration followed by the administration of a semistructured interview confined to the scales that elevated on the respective self-report inventory (Widiger & Samuel, 2005).

Self-report inventories are useful in alerting clinicians to maladaptive personality functioning that might otherwise be missed due to false expectations or assumptions, such as failing to notice antisocial personality traits in female patients (Garb, 2005; Widiger, 1998). A further advantage of a well-validated self-report inventory is the presence of normative data to facilitate interpretation. A substantial amount of normative data have been obtained and reported for some of the self-report inventories (e.g., Colligan, Morey, & Offord, 1994; Costa & McCrae, 1992; Millon, Millon, & Davis, 1997). These normative data facilitate validation as well as interpretation. The specific and explicit nature of self-report inventories has also been very useful in researching the psychometric properties of the instruments. Much more is known about the effects of different item formats, scale length, demographic variables, base rates, response sets, and other moderating variables from self-report inventories than from research using semistructured interviews.

The high degree of structure of self-report inventories will also contribute to much better inter-site reliability than would be obtained by semistructured or unstructured interviews. The correlation between two self-report inventories is much more likely to be replicated across time and across research sites than the correlation between two semistructured interviews. The findings of self-report inventories are more sensitive to the anxious, depressed, or angry mood states of respondents, contributing at times to poor test–retest reliability (an issue that is discussed further below), but this susceptibility may itself be more reliably observed across different studies than the lack of susceptibility of semistructured interviews.

DSM-IV-TR SELF-REPORT PERSONALITY DISORDER INVENTORIES

There are currently at least 10 self-report inventories used for the assessment of the DSM-IV-TR personality disorders: (1) the personality disorder scales of the Minnesota Multiphasic Personality Inventory-2 (MMPI-2; Hathaway et al., 1989) developed originally by Morey, Waugh, and Blashfield (1985) but revised for the MMPI-2 by Colligan et al. (1994) and for the DSM-IV by Somwaru and Ben-Porath (1995); (2) Millon Clinical Multiaxial Inventory-III (MCMI-III, Millon et al., 1997); (3) Personality Diagnostic Questionnaire-4 (PDQ-4; Bagby & Farvolden, 2004; Hyler, 1994); (4) Personality Assessment Inventory (PAI; Morey & Hopwood, 2006); (5) Wisconsin Personality Disorders Inventory (WISPI; Klein et al., 1993); (6) Coolidge Axis II Inventory (CATI; Coolidge & Merwin, 1992); (7) Schedule for Nonadaptive and Adaptive Personality (SNAP; Simms & Clark, 2006); (8) OMNI Personality Inventory (Loranger, 2001); (9) Multi-Source Assessment of Personality Pathology (MAPP; Oltmanns & Turkheimer, 2006); and (10) Assessment of DSM-IV Personality Disorders (ADP-IV; Schotte, De Doncker, Vankerckhoven, Vertommen, & Cosyns, 1998).

Regrettably, none of them is without some significant disadvantages. The MMPI-2, MCMI-III, and PDQ-4 are the most commonly used in clinical research. In contrast, there does not yet appear to be a study on the validity of the OMNI published within a scientific journal (Guess, 2006). The OMNI, ADP-IV, SNAP, MAPP, MCMI-III, PDQ-4, WISPI, and Somwaru and Ben-Porath (1995) MMPI-2 scales are coordinated with DSM-IV-TR, whereas the CATI and PAI were constructed for the DSM-III-R criterion sets (APA, 1987) and the Morey et al. (1985) MMPI-2 scales were constructed in reference to DSM-III (APA, 1980). Clark, Livesley, and Morey (1997) suggested that "poorer convergence is obtained when two instruments target different versions of the DSM Axis II disorders" (p. 207). Morey (1988), for example, indicated that the changes made to the criterion sets for DSM-III-R resulted in an 800% increase in the prevalence of schizoid personality disorder. These findings were subsequently replicated by Blashfield, Blum, and Pfohl (1992), who suggested that "small, apparently minor changes in diagnostic criteria can sometimes have major effects" (p. 251). As noted by Widiger et al. (1995), only 10 of the 93 DSM-III-R personality disorder criteria (11%)

remained unchanged for DSM-IV-TR, 10 were deleted, 9 were added, and 52 (56%) received a significant revision (21 were judged to have received only a minor revision to wording).

The MMPI-2 is a 567-item, true–false inventory for the general assessment of psychopathology (Butcher, 2006). A potential disadvantage of the Morey et al. (1985) scales is that the item pool was confined to those items available within the MMPI, an instrument not written specifically for the assessment of the 10 personality disorders of DSM-IV-TR. Most of the items selected by Morey et al. were retained in the MMPI-2 (i.e., 157 of the 164). However, Somwaru and Ben-Porath (1995) had expert clinicians select items from the MMPI-2 that would be optimal for the assessment of the DSM-IV-TR personality disorders, including the 107 new MMPI-2 items. They selected 292 items, only 42% of which had been included within the original Morey et al. scales (in fact, 49% of the items selected by Morey et al. and still included in the MMPI-2 were not selected by Somwaru and Ben-Porath). Three independent studies have since demonstrated that the Somwaru and Ben-Porath scales (particularly the borderline) do appear to be superior to the original Morey et al. scales (Hicklin & Widiger, 2000; Jones, 2005; Rossi, Van den Brande, Tobac, Sloore, & Hauben, 2003).

An advantage of the Somwaru and Ben-Porath (1995) scales is their inclusion within the most frequently used self-report measure of psychopathology, the MMPI-2 (Butcher, 2006; Watkins et al., 1995). Many clinicians and researchers will be administering the MMPI-2 for reasons other than their interest in the assessment of personality disorders. Scoring the MMPI-2 for personality disorder symptomatology using the scales of Somwaru and Ben-Porath may not require much additional effort or cost. However, neither the Morey et al. (1985) nor the Somwaru and Ben-Porath personality disorder scales have typically been included within routine MMPI-2 scoring systems, and they are generally mentioned only in passing within the predominant MMPI-2 texts (e.g., Ben-Porath, 2006; Derksen, 2006).

The MCMI-III includes 175 items, a subset of which is used to assess the DSM-IV-TR personality disorders (Millon et al., 1997). The MCMI-III is the most heavily researched inventory but this research has often raised critical concerns (Boyle & Le Dean, 2000; Hsu, 2002; Lampel, 1999; Rogers, Salekin, & Sewell, 1999). Potential advantages of the MCMI-III are the inclusion of scales for Axis I disorders, the inclusion of validity scales, the availability of a computerized scoring system and hand-scoring templates, and the coordination of many of the personality disorder scales with the theoretical model of Millon et al. (1996). The coordination with the theory of Millon et al., however, will be a disadvantage to the extent that this theoretical model is flawed (Mullins-Sweatt & Widiger, 2007). The MCMI-III computerized scoring system is also expensive and the hand-scoring templates require a substantial amount of time and effort.

The PDQ-4 is a relatively brief, 99-item self-report inventory (Bagby & Farvolden, 2004; Hyler, 1994). The brevity of the PDQ-4 and its coordination with DSM-IV-TR are probably the primary reason that it is the most frequently used self-report measure. However, the PDQ-4 may also be the least psychometrically sophisticated. Most of the DSM-IV-TR diagnostic criteria are assessed by just one PDQ-4 item, leaving little room for error. The CATI is somewhat preferable in this regard, including two items per criterion (total of 200 items), although its items were written in regards to the DSM-III-R criterion sets (Coolidge & Merwin, 1992). Further compounding the brevity of the PDQ-4 is that many of its items are simply direct queries as to the presence of a diagnostic criterion under the questionable assumption that persons with personality disorders will be adequately aware of and willing to acknowledge their maladaptive personality traits (e.g., #59: "Lying comes easily to me and I often do it" for antisocial deceitfulness; and #44: "I need very much for other people to take notice of me or compliment me" for narcissistic need for admiration).

The WISPI is comparable in length to the CATI (i.e., 204 items) and has been updated for DSM-IV (Smith, Klein, & Benjamin, 2003). A unique feature of the WISPI is that many of its items were written from an object-relational, interpersonal perspective. This might provide a particular advantage for clinicians and researchers who wish to assess personality disorders from this particular theoretical perspective (Benjamin, Conrad, & Critchfield, 2006). A potential disadvantage of the WISPI though is that many of its items appear to require considerable insight and forthrightness on the part of respondents. The items not only assume an ability and willingness to acknowledge socially undesirable behaviors but also an understanding of a particular motivation for their occurrence (e.g., antisocial item: "Before I was 15 years old, I tortured animals to show how tough and cool I was;" histrionic item: "I have gotten so frustrated in an argument that I have made a suicidal scene in order to get the attention I need"). The MAPP, in stark contrast, translates the DSM-IV-TR criteria into a lay language (103 items), avoiding all clinical jargon, in order to facilitate its administration within general population samples and informant, peer assessments (Oltmanns & Turkheimer, 2006).

The PAI personality disorder scales, like the MCMI-III and MMPI-2, are included within a larger inventory (344 items) that provides assessments of many clinically relevant Axis I disorders (Morey & Hopwood, 2006). The PAI also includes validity scales to detect symptom exaggeration and denial. Perhaps the greatest advantage of the PAI is that it is the only self-report inventory to include subscales to differentiate among various facets of a respective personality disorder. For example, the PAI borderline scale includes subscales for the assessment of affective instability, identity problems, negative relationships, and self-harm; the PAI antisocial scale includes subscales for antisocial behaviors, egocentricity, and stimulus seeking (Morey & Hopwood, 2006). These subscales could provide information of more specific and precise importance to treatment, outcome, and other clinical decisions than the broad clinical diagnoses (Morey & Hopwood, 2006; Widiger, 2008). However, a substantial disadvantage of the PAI is that it includes only two personality disorders scales: borderline and antisocial. Other PAI scales can be used to diagnose the remaining personality disorders (e.g., a diagnosis of dependent personality disorder is said to be indicated by high scores on the PAI warmth scale and low scores on the dominance, verbal aggression, and grandiosity scales), but no data are provided for the validity of these suggested algorithms. There has not in fact been a published study on the validity of the PAI to assess personality disorders other than borderline or antisocial.

A significant limitation of all of the self-report inventories is that they are unlikely to provide compelling assessments for the presence of a respective personality disorder or estimates of prevalence. The SNAP does not have cutoff points for interpretation. Items of the WISPI, CATI, MAPP, ADP-IV, and PDQ-4 were written to assess each diagnostic criterion of a respective personality disorder. Therefore, one could, in theory, obtain a diagnosis by simply counting the number of respective items that were endorsed (e.g., Brinded, Simpson, Laidlaw, Fairley, & Malcolm, 2001). However, existing research suggests that this typically yields considerably higher prevalence rates than would be provided by a semistructured interview (Bagby & Farvolden, 2004; Schotte, 2000; Widiger & Samuel, 2005). The ADP-IV attempts to provide a more accurate estimate by having a two-stage scoring procedure. Respondents first indicate whether the criterion is present. If yes, they are then asked to indicate whether it has "caused you or others distress or problems" (Schotte et al., 1998, p. 1180).

"An important feature that distinguishes the MCMI from other inventories is its use of actuarial base rate data rather than normalized standard score transformations" (Millon et al., 1997, p. 5). Most self-report measures determine cutoff points for scale interpretation on the basis of deviation from a population norm (e.g., OMNI, PAI, and MMPI-2). A potential limitation of using normative distributions to set cutoff points is the problematic assumption that diagnostic decisions should be governed primarily by statistical deviance (Widiger & Sankis, 2000). The 10 DSM-IV-TR personality disorders do not all have the same prevalence rate (i.e., normative scoring uses the same cutoff point for all 10 personality disorders), nor is this prevalence likely to be coincidentally equivalent to, for instance, 1.5 standard deviations from the mean. Cutoff scores that are coordinated with the actual base rate of a disorder will provide more accurate diagnoses (Meehl & Rosen, 1955). On the other hand, the advantages of using base rates to set cutoff points are lost if they are not adjusted for changes in the prevalence rates across different settings. As indicated by the authors of the MCMI-III, "local base rates and cutting lines must still be developed for special settings" (Millon et al., 1997, p. 5). Millon et al. (1997) suggest that "the MCMI can be used on a routine basis in outpatient clinics, community agencies, mental health centers, college counseling programs, general and mental hospitals, independent and group practice offices, and in court" (p. 5) but clinicians working within settings in which substantial clinical symptomatology is not commonplace (e.g., college counseling, divorce mediation, or child custody evaluations) will likely find that MCMI-III cutoff points overestimate substantially the extent and breadth of psychopathology. This appears to be particularly true for the MCMI-III histrionic, narcissistic, and obsessive compulsive scales (Boyle & Le Dean, 2000; King, 1994; Lampel, 1999).

OTHER PERSONALITY DISORDER INVENTORIES

There are a number of other inventories that could be of considerable use to clinicians and researchers. There are self-report inventories for the assessment of dimensional models of personality disorder, such as the MMPI-2 Personality Psychopathology Five (PSY-5; Ben-Porath, 2006), the NEO Personality Inventory-Revised (NEO PI-R; Costa & McCrae, 1992), the maladaptive personality scales from the SNAP (Simms & Clark, 2006), the general personality scales from the OMNI (Loranger, 2001), the Dimensional Assessment of Personality Disorder Pathology-Basic Questionnaire (DAPP-BQ; Livesley, 2006), the Inventory of Interpersonal Problems (IIP; Horowitz, Alden, Wiggins, & Pincus, 2000), the Intrex Structural Assessment of Social Behavior (SASB; Benjamin et al., 2006; Pincus & Gurtman, 2006), and the Temperament and Character Inventory (TCI; Cloninger, 2006). An advantage of these inventories relative to DSM-IV-TR inventories is that they provide assessments of domains of personality functioning that might be more fundamental than the diagnostic categories within DSM-IV-TR (Widiger, 2008; Widiger et al., 2006). The DSM-IV-TR personality disorders are unlikely to have specific etiologies or pathologies, representing instead diverse but overlapping constellations of maladaptive personality traits (Clark, 2007; Widiger & Trull, 2007). Obtaining an assessment of the individual traits that together constitute a particular personality disorder (e.g., the angry hostility, vulnerability, impulsivity, depressiveness, and anxiousness evident in a borderline personality disorder) might be more useful to understanding etiology, pathology, and treatment than the more global diagnostic category. Dimensional models of personality disorder provide more specific and reliable descriptions of each individual's particular constellation of maladaptive personality traits, avoid arbitrary distinctions between normal and abnormal personality functioning, and do not result in the confusion generated by the provision of multiple personality disorder diagnostic categories (Widiger & Trull, 2007).

Lynam and Widiger (2001) obtained descriptions of prototypic cases of each of the 10 DSM-IV-TR personality disorders in terms of the 30 facets of the Five-Factor Model (FFM) of general personality structure. These descriptions agreed well with subsequent descriptions provided by clinicians (Samuel & Widiger, 2004) and with an FFM coding of the DSM-IV-TR criterion sets (Widiger, Trull, Clarkin, Sanderson, & Costa, 2002). An advantage of these FFM descriptions is that they go well beyond the limited criterion sets of DSM-IV-TR. Westen and Shedler (1999b) have decried the narrow range of coverage provided by DSM-IV-TR criterion sets, suggesting, for instance, that the DSM-IV-TR paranoid PD criterion set is "essentially seven indices of a single trait" (p. 274). The FFM description of this criterion set suggests that it is more than just suspiciousness and mistrust, including as well references to angry hostility, deception, and oppositionalism (Widiger et al., 2002), but, more importantly, "the clinicians' FFM descriptions of paranoid personality disorder [also] went beyond the DSM-IV description to include [as well] low positive emotionality, low openness to values, high anxiousness, low warmth, low gregariousness, low altruism, and low tender mindedness" (Samuel & Widiger, 2004, pp. 298–300).

Subsequent research has also demonstrated that, in some instances, the correlation of an individual's FFM personality profile with the profile of a prototypic case of a respective personality disorder will correlate as highly with explicit measures of this personality disorder as they correlate with one another. This has been well demonstrated for the antisocial and psychopathic personality disorders (Miller & Lynam, 2003) and for the borderline personality disorder (Trull, Widiger, Lynam, & Costa, 2003). However, a comparable degree of success in using a measure confined largely to normal, adaptive personality traits to assess maladaptive personality functioning might not occur for some of the other personality disorders (Saulsman & Page, 2003). Miller et al. (2008) report predictive power statistics for many of the NEO PI-R prototypal matching scores that were generally quite low (although still above the base rates for respective personality disorders). A limitation of the NEO PI-R as a measure of maladaptive personality functioning is that some of its scales fail to include a sufficient representation of maladaptive variants of FFM domains and facets, particularly maladaptive agreeableness (necessary for the assessment of dependent personality traits), maladaptive conscientiousness (necessary for the assessment of obsessive compulsive personality traits), and maladaptive openness (necessary for the assessment of schizotypal personality traits).

Haigler and Widiger (2001), for example, reported correlations of only .04, .17, and .04 with NEO PI-R agreeableness for the SNAP, MMPI-2, and PDQ-4 dependent PD scales (respectively). However, they had also constructed an experimental version of NEO PI-R agreeableness by converting each item to its maladaptive variant (e.g., "I try to be courteous to everyone I meet" was revised to "I am overly courteous to everyone I meet," and "I would rather cooperate with others than compete with them" became "I cooperate with others even when it would be better to compete"). The correlations of SNAP, MMPI-2, and PDQ-4 dependent PD with this maladaptive version of NEO PI-R agreeableness were .57, .66, and .45, respectively. Similar findings were reported for the relationship of NEO PI-R openness with schizotypal symptomatology and conscientiousness with obsessive compulsive symptomatology.

Widiger, Costa, and McCrae (2002) proposed a four-step procedure for the diagnosis of a personality disorder from the perspective of the FFM. The first step is to assess the person in terms of the domains and facets of the FFM using, for instance, the NEO PI-R. The second step is to determine whether the person has any impairments or problems in living associated with his or her personality traits. The second step is provided because the existing measures of the FFM may not systematically or comprehensively assess for impairments associated with each personality trait (Widiger & Lowe, 2007). For example, persons with elevations on NEO PI-R conscientiousness will be high in order, dutifulness, and achievement striving, but they may not be engaging in the maladaptive variants of these traits.

The PSY-5, DAPP-BQ, SNAP, and IIP self-report inventories place substantially more emphasis on the assessment of maladaptive personality functioning than the NEO PI-R. If the test administrator's interests are confined to maladaptive personality functioning, the PSY-5, DAPP-BQ, SNAP, and IIP might provide a more precise and relevant assessment than the NEO PI-R (Haigler & Widiger, 2001). The IIP and Intrex SASB will be of particular value if one's interests are confined to maladaptive interpersonal functioning, as they provide reasonably comprehensive assessments of the different ways in which a person can be interpersonally dysfunctional (Benjamin et al., 2006; Locke, 2006; Pincus & Gurtman, 2006).

The OMNI and the SNAP are unique as they include separate scales for the assessment of normal and abnormal personality functioning. The OMNI includes 25 scales to assess normal personality traits (e.g., aestheticism, dutifulness, and assertiveness), 10 scales to assess the DSM-IV personality disorders, and 7 higher-order scales derived from joint factor analyses of the normal and abnormal scales. The 7 higher-order factors are empirically derived higher-order constructs (i.e., agreeableness, conscientiousness, extraversion, narcissism, neuroticism, openness, and sensation-seeking) that integrate the normal and abnormal scales within a common hierarchical model. The SNAP, in a similar fashion, also includes 12 scales to assess maladaptive personality traits (e.g., mistrust, detachment, self-harm) and 3 additional scales that assess three broad personality domains of negative temperament, positive temperament, and disinhibition. However, unlike the OMNI, the 3 broad personality scales of the SNAP are not higher-order factors of the abnormal personality scales and it is unclear if a factor analysis of the 12 SNAP scales would yield a three-factor structure commensurate with negative temperament, positive temperament, and disinhibition.

Livesley's (2006) DAPP-BQ was developed in a manner comparable to the development of the 12 SNAP maladaptive personality trait scales. Livesley first obtained personality disorder symptoms and features from a thorough content analysis of the literature. An initial list of criteria was then coded by clinicians with respect to their prototypicality for respective personality disorders. One hundred scales (each with 16 items) were submitted to a series of factor analyses to derive a set of 18 fundamental dimensions of personality disorder that cut across the existing diagnostic categories (e.g., anxiousness, self-harm, intimacy problems, social avoidance, passive opposition, and interpersonal disesteem). Additional analyses indicate that these 18 dimensions can be subsumed within four higher-order dimensions: emotional dysregulation, dissocial, inhibitedness, and compulsivity. Joint factor analyses of the DAPP-BQ and the SNAP personality disorder symptom scales typically yield this four-factor solution (Clark & Livesley, 2002; Clark, Livesley, Schroeder, & Irish, 1996).

The PSY-5 has only the five broad scales of positive emotionality, negative emotionality, constraint, aggressiveness, and psychoticism, but it does have an advantage of being embedded within the commonly used MMPI-2 (Ben-Porath, 2006). All of the other MMPI-2 clinical, validity, and supplemental scales are available to the clinician or researcher who uses the PSY-5. An advantage of the PSY-5 and SNAP relative to the DAPP-BQ, IIP, Intrex SASB, TCI, and NEO PI-R is the availability of a variety of validity scales. On the other hand, the PSY-5 and DAPP-BQ are comparably weak in the assessment of both normal and adaptive personality functioning. The NEO PI-R, OMNI, and TCI can provide a more comprehensive

description of an individual's personality functioning, identifying personality traits that might facilitate treatment responsivity (e.g., openness to change and conscientiousness) as well as identifying maladaptive personality traits.

There are also many self-report inventories for the assessment of individual personality disorders, such as (but not limited to) the Narcissistic Personality Inventory (NPI; Raskin & Terry, 1988), the Revised Personality Style Inventory (Bagby et al., 2001), and the Psychopathic Personality Inventory (PPI; Lilienfeld & Andrews, 1996). Comparable to interview schedules devoted to individual personality disorders, these inventories will usually provide a more thorough and precise assessment of the respective personality disorder than would be provided by an inventory that covers all of the DSM-IV-TR personality disorders. Some also include subscales for the assessment of various components or facets of a respective disorder (e.g., the NPI & PPI) which will, most likely, provide a more differentiated and nuanced description.

Convergent and Discriminant Validity Research

As just indicated, there are quite a few differences among the many alternative instruments for the assessment of DSM-IV-TR personality disorders. It is difficult, however, to identify which instruments have the strongest empirical support as there have been few comparative validity studies. The existing validity data are confined largely to studies in which one instrument is correlated with another. There are in fact quite a few such studies, although even in this respect there is a limited amount of validity data for some of the instruments (e.g., ADP-IV, DIPD, OMNI, PAI, & SWAP-200).

Convergent Validity

We have identified 68 studies reporting on the convergent validity of the assessment of the DSM-III, DSM-III-R, or DSM-IV-TR personality disorders. Twenty-four of these studies provided information concerning the convergence among two or more self-report inventories. Table 18.1 presents their findings. Excluded from this list are studies that involved screening measures (constructed to err in the direction of false positive assessments; Morse & Pilkonis, 2007) and studies that did not provide data on at least half of the personality disorders. Table 18.1 includes no data concerning the ADP-IV, OMNI, or PAI as we could find no

Table 18.1. Convergence among self-report inventories.

Instruments	PRN	SZD	SZT	ATS	BDL	HST	NCS	AVD	DPD	OBC	PAG
MCMI/PDQ[1]	.30	.28	.38	.15	.47	.15	.47	.68	.53	−.47	.59
MCMI/MMPI[2]	.33	.64	.41	.30	.55	.61	.66	.62	.52	−.38	.51
MCMI/MMPI[3]	.44	.35	.51	.14	.28	.66	.55	.65	.68	−.42	.50
MCMI/MMPI[4]	.69	.68	.78	.25	.54	.71	.55	.76	.68	−.31	.48
MCMI/MMPI[5]	.45	.61	.55	.14	.49	.71	.70	.77	.60	−.49	.70
MCMI/MMPI[5]	.19	.22	.57	.13	.49	.44	.49	.69	.59	−.50	.65
MCMI/MMPI[6]	.08	.67	.74	.15	.42	.68	.78	.82	.50	−.30	.57
MCMI/MMPI[7]	.32	.74	.53	.25	.37	.69	.73	.79	.67	−.27	.46
MCMI/MMPI[7]	.26	.71	.44	.20	.52	.64	.61	.67	.67	−.24	.46
MCMI/MMPI[8]	.27	.62	.48	.09	.46	.63	.66	.76	.53	−.13	.50
MCMI-II/MMPI[9]	.50	.73	.86	.57	.68	.74	.65	.87	.56.	−.04	.70
MCMI-II/MMPI2-SB[10]	.70	.79	.77	.76	.88	.64	.29	.82	.50	−.11	—
MCMI-II/MMPI2[10]	.68	.71	.85	.71	.70	.65	.49	.83	.49	−.08	.75
MCMI-II/MMPI2[11]	.65	.61	.70	.53	.65	.64	.60	.69	.56	.13	.65
MCMI-II/MMPI2[12]	.48	.54	.70	.61	.66	.61	.54	.50	.31	−.02	.65
MCMI-II/PDQ-4[13]	.73	.60	.70	.67	.70	.52	.57	.73	.36	.15	—
MCMI-II/MMPI[14]	.52	.66	.68	.46	.68	.57	.68	.76	.63	−.10	.70
MCMI-III/MMPI2[15]	.79	.71	.84	.57	.57	.73	.65	.84	.75	−.26	—
MCMI-III/MMPI2-SB[15]	.81	.79	.84	.72	.82	.77	.58	.83	.80	−.30	—
MCMI-III/MMPI2-SB[16]	.69	.61	.66	.65	.75	.68	.56	.73	.72	−.12	—
MCMI-III/MMPI2[16]	.65	.54	.67	.66	.60	.61	.62	.74	.68	−.07	—
MCMI-III/MMPI2[16]	.66	.60	.63	.65	.73	.67	.56	.72	.70	−.15	—
MCMI-II/CATI[17]	.58	.22	.65	.57	.87	.72	.38	.80	.43	.10	.86
MCMI-II/CATI[18]	.55	−.13	.57	.70	.88	.10	.40	.55	.20	−.11	.77
MCMI-II/CATI[11]	.56	.30	.62	.63	.72	.64	.52	.66	.54	.40	.65
MCMI/WISPI[19]	.38	.48	.43	.32	.14	.10	.57	.79	.68	−.26	.50
MMPI-PD/CATI[11]	.59	.40	.65	.60	.63	.47	.28	.75	.74	.35	.62
MMPI/PDQ-R[20]	.61	.23	—	.63	—	−.04	.24	.73	.58	.47	.57
MMPI/PDQ-R[21]	.42	.26	.46	.51	.75	.32	−.04	.57	.60	.36	.62
MMPI/PDQ-R[22]	.38	.31	.50	.50	.53	.09	−.12	.56	.35	.19	.20
MMPI2/PDQ-4[23]	.59	.59	.56	.60	.62	.29	.21	.80	.68	.44	—
MMPI2/PDQ-4[15]	.73	.64	.69	.53	.62	.21	.14	.72	.53	.62	—
MMPI2-SB/PDQ-4[15]	.66	.70	.72	.60	.71	.10	−.11	.69	.55	.70	—
WISPI/PDQ[19]	.66	.37	.72	.68	.54	.79	.67	.75	.79	.57	.67
SNAP/PDQ-4[23]	.78	.70	.77	.78	.76	.66	.67	.76	.82	.60	—
SNAP/MMPI2[23]	.76	.72	.76	.79	.69	.59	.42	.81	.77	.51	—
SNAP/MAPP[24]	.55	.48	.53	.49	.50	.38	.40	.44	.42	.31	—
SNAP/MAPP[24]	.49	.51	.51	.51	.52	.39	.40	.49	.46	.43	—
Median	*0.57*	*0.60*	*0.65*	*0.57*	*0.62*	*0.62*	*0.55*	*0.73*	*0.59*	*−0.07*	*0.62*

Notes: PRN = paranoid, SZD = schizoid, SZT = schizotypal, ATS = antisocial, BDL = borderline, HST = histrionic, NCS = narcissistic, AVD = avoidant, DPD = dependent, OBC = obsessive compulsive, PAG = passive–aggressive, MCMI = Millon Clinical Multiaxial Inventory (Millon et al., 1997), PDQ = Personality Diagnostic Questionnaire (Hyler, 1994), MMPI = Minnesota Multiphasic Personality Inventory (Morey et al., 1985), MMPI-SB = MMPI-II (Somwaru & Ben-Porath, 1995) scales, CATI = Coolidge Axis II Inventory (Coolidge & Merwin, 1992), WISPI = Wisconsin Personality Disorder Inventory (Klein et al., 1993), SNAP = Schedule for Nonadaptive and Adaptive Personality (Clark et al., in press), MAPP = Multisource Assessment of Personality Pathology (Oltmanns & Turkheimer, 2006).

[1] Reich, Noyes, & Troughton (1987), [2] Streiner & Miller (1988), [3] Dubro & Wetzler (1989), [4] Morey & LeVine (1988), [5] Zarrella, Schuerger, & Ritz (1990), [6] McCann (1989), [7] Schuler, Snibbe, & Buckwalter (1994), [8] Wise (1994), [9] McCann (1991), [10] Jones (2005), [11] Sinha & Watson (2001), [12] Wise (2001), [13] Blackburn, Donnelly, Logan, & Renswick (2004), [14] Wise (1996), [15] Hicklin & Widiger (2000), [16] Rossi, vanden Brande, et al. (2003), [17] Coolidge & Merwin (1992), [18] Silberman, Roth, Segal, & Burns (1997), [19] Klein et al. (1993), [20] Trull, Goodwin, Schopp, Hillenbrand, & Schuster (1993), [21] Trull (1993), [22] O'Maille & Fine (1995), [23] Haigler & Widiger (2001), [24] Oltmanns & Turkheimer (2006).

published data on their convergence with another self-report inventory for at least half of the personality disorders.

It is evident from Table 18.1 that good to excellent convergent validity is generally obtained for the seven self-report inventories for which published data are available, although in many instances poor to weak convergent validity is obtained for one or more of the scales within any one particular study. The median convergent validity of .57 for the assessment of antisocial personality disorder does underestimate the true value somewhat as it includes results involving the first edition of the MCMI-III, which obtained a median convergent validity coefficient of only .15 with other self-report inventories (11 correlations reported in seven studies). The MCMI-II and MCMI-III obtained a median convergent validity of .65 (15 correlations with other self-report inventories). If one excludes the results obtained with the first edition of the MCMI-III, the median convergent validity across all instruments is .62.

It is perhaps also apparent that none of the instruments stands out as obtaining consistently better or worse convergent validity than any other self-report measure, with perhaps one exception. It is evident from Table 18.1 that the assessment of obsessive compulsive personality disorder (OCPD) with the current and earlier versions of the MCMI-III is quite different from the assessment of this disorder provided by virtually every other instrument. The median convergent validity of an MCMI(-III) dimensional assessment of OCPD with any other instrument is −.14 (26 correlations) whereas the median convergent validity of any two other instruments' dimensional assessment of OCPD is .45 (12 correlations). It is problematic to fail to obtain a significant positive convergent validity coefficient; it is striking to obtain negative convergent validity coefficients. Persons who obtain elevated scores on the MCMI-III assessment of OCPD are likely to obtain lower (rather than higher) scores on the PDQ-4, MMPI-2, WISPI, or CATI OCPD scales (the correlation of .40 reported in Sinha and Watson, 2001, is a clear outlier that may represent a miscoding within their report).

Table 18.2 provides the correlations of self-report inventories with semistructured interviews as reported in 27 studies. A self-report inventory is essentially equivalent to a fully structured interview that is being self-administered. The correlations of the dimensional ratings provided in Table 18.2,

when compared to Table 18.1, suggest that personality disorder semistructured interviews fall well short of being fully structured, as the median convergent validity coefficients decrease appreciably when these two different methods of assessment are correlated to one another. Self-report inventories and semistructured interviews both rely substantially on the reporting of symptoms by the respondent, but semistructured interviews do tend to be relatively more open-ended and rely more heavily on the professional judgments of the interviewer rather than the opinions and beliefs of the interviewee (Widiger, 2007a). The appreciable decrease in convergent validity with the self-report inventories suggests that the open-ended questions and clinical judgments of the interviewers are having a significant impact on the results.

It is not really clear which method obtains the most valid results. Semistructured interviews are generally preferred over self-report inventories in clinical research (Rogers, 2003; Segal & Coolidge, 2007) and they are often used as the criterion measure with which the validity of a self-report inventory is tested (Zimmerman, 2003). Rarely are self-report inventories used as criterion measures to assess the validity of a semistructured interview (although there are exceptions; e.g., Trull et al., 1998). The preference of researchers for semistructured interviews, however, could be analogous to the preference of clinicians for unstructured interviews. One reason that semistructured interviews are preferred over self-report inventories is that they provide the researcher the opportunity to have a direct, personal impact on the assessment; follow-up queries can be provided and inadequacies in self-insight and awareness can be addressed (McDermut & Zimmerman, 2008; Rogers, 2003; Segal & Coolidge, 2007). However, the opportunity of the interviewer to personally impact the assessment might also contribute to less reliable and ultimately less valid assessments (comparable to the lower reliability obtained with unstructured interviews relative to semistructured interviews). The findings obtained with self-report inventories are more likely to replicate across research sites than the findings obtained with semistructured interviews simply because there is little to no room for inter-rater disagreement in the administration and scoring of a self-report inventory. There are data to suggest that semistructured interviews might be more successful than self-report inventories in differentiating maladaptive personality traits from other mental disorders (an issue discussed further below) but given the considerable expense of administering semistructured interviews, additional research on the relative validity of these two methods of assessment is perhaps warranted. What is sorely needed are studies that compare directly the validity of a self-report inventory with a semistructured interview.

It is also evident from Table 18.2 that the convergent validity for categorical diagnoses is appreciably lower than for dimensional ratings across all of the personality disorders. Median convergent validity across all studies for a categorical diagnosis ranged from a low of .09 for the schizoid to a high of only .34 for the borderline and avoidant diagnoses.

Table 18.2. Convergence of self-report with semistructured interviews.

Instruments	PRN	SZD	SZT	ATS	BDL	HST	NCS	AVD	DPD	OBC	PAG
Categorical											
PDQ/SIDP[1]	.00	.00	.27	.14	.30	.38	.00	.20	.08	.13	.00
PDQ-R/SIDP[2]	.27	.25	.28	.32	.54	.49	.14	.37	.40	.34	.21
PDQ-R/SIDP-R[3]	.18	—	.17	.46	.17	.09	.08	.20	.30	.16	.28
PDQ-R/IPDE[4]	.12	−.02	.54	.36	.46	.18	.42	.53	.52	.38	.21
PDQ-R/IPDE[5]	.10	.26	.00	—	.42	.22	.10	.37	.14	.37	.33
PDQ-R/SIDP[6]	.00	.11	.24	.24	.20	.02	−.04	—	.15	.04	.14
PDQ-R/SCID-II[4]	.27	.43	.48	.42	.53	.24	.34	.63	.57	.30	.23
PDQ-R/SCID-II[5]	.25	.00	−.03	—	.37	.32	.23	.46	.53	.42	.46
PDQ-R/SCID-II[7]	.25	.13	.05	—	.15	.33	.24	.30	.07	.34	.16
PDQ-4/SCID-II[8]	.16	.09	.09	.28	.19	.12	.28	.15	.24	.09	.09
PDQ-4/IPDE[9]	.13	.21	.11	.28	.16	.10	.09	.19	−.02	.16	—
PDQ-4/PDI-IV[10]	.11	.08	.02	.33	.11	.03	.11	.21	.24	.08	.11
PDQ-4/SCID-II[11]	.35	.05	.11	.49	.57	—	.14	.40	—	.20	.18
PDQ-4/PAS[12]	.24	.03	.21	.30	.15	.12	.18	.14	.48	.05	—
MMPI2/SCID-II[13]	.05	.21	.22	.20	.28	−.05	.19	.42	.37	—	.18
MMPI/SIDP-R[3]	.08	—	—	.20	.26	−.03	—	—	−.10	—	.18
MCMI/SIDP[14]	.38	.06	.07	—	.51	.22	—	.14	.22	−.06	.29
MCMI/SIDP[15]	.19	−.03	.18	.06	.53	.12	.25	.36	.15	.00	.38
MCMI-II/SCID-II[13]	.05	.21	.24	.10	.53	.12	.37	.28	.13	−.05	.22
MCMI-II/SCID-II[16]	.21	—	—	—	.25	.14	.16	.51	.28	.38	.30
MCMI-II/MMPI[13]	.30	.31	.48	.19	.34	.25	.37	.44	.27	—	.25
MCMI-II/IPDE[17]	.00	.00	−.02	.00	.41	.29	−.04	.30	.26	−.07	−.05
MCMI-II/IPDE[9]	.20	.30	.05	.36	.30	−.04	.08	.17	.04	.13	—
ADP-IV/SCID-II[18]	.34	.07	.14	.29	.65	.45	.19	.77	.50	.33	—
WISPI-IV/SCID-II[19]	.48	—	—	—	.38	—	—	.34	.19	.08	.14
Median	*0.19*	*0.09*	*0.15*	*0.28*	*0.34*	*0.14*	*0.17*	*0.34*	*0.24*	*0.14*	*0.21*
Dimensional											
MCMI/SIDP[20]	.29	.40	.31	.23	.32	.05	.04	.53	.51	−.29	.28
MCMI/SIDP[21]	.22	.39	.37	—	.32	.20	.18	.42	.38	−.05	.14
MCMI/SIDP[14]	.28	.20	.15	.30	.80	.22	.14	.31	.38	.15	.50
MCMI/SIDP[15]	.20	.31	.23	.14	.63	.07	.26	.56	.31	.02	.41
MCMI/SIDP[22]	.03	.47	.39	.23	.33	.26	.34	.60	.21	−.04	.17
MCMI/PDI-I[23]	.08	.02	.33	.28	.51	.01	.21	.53	.64	−.32	.15
MCMI-II/SCID-II[24]	.39	.31	.17	.47	.51	.32	.34	.55	.40	.08	.38
MCMI-II/PDI-II[23]	.30	.52	.21	.32	.63	.24	.32	.64	.36	.11	.64
MCMI-II/PDI-III[25]	.44	.53	.61	.58	.63	.30	.42	.58	.50	−.04	.44
MCMI-II/IPDE[17]	.38	.48	.39	.37	.60	.56	.41	.51	.38	−.05	.41
MCMI-II/IPDE[9]	.33	.52	.50	.49	.41	.13	.10	.64	.30	.20	—
PDQ/SIDP[20]	.56	.33	.49	.78	.64	.47	.53	.51	.59	.52	.46
PDQ/SIDP[1]	.43	.24	.34	.55	.39	.42	.26	.30	.35	.47	.37

continued

Table 18.2. (continued)

Instruments	PRN	SZD	SZT	ATS	BDL	HST	NCS	AVD	DPD	OBC	PAG
PDQ-R/SIDP[6]	.22	.32	.31	.20	.39	.38	.15	.21	.36	.29	.26
PDQ-R/SIDP[2]	.32	.44	.45	.60	.50	.43	.30	.49	.44	.26	.39
PDQ-R/SIDP[3]	.31	.60	.32	.44	.48	.40	.38	.35	.55	.47	.43
PDQ-4/SCID-II[8]	.36	.19	.20	.37	.40	.29	.42	.36	.39	.28	.30
PDQ-4/IPDE[9]	.36	.45	.50	.57	.46	.18	.21	.66	.48	.36	—
PDQ-4/PDI-IV[10]	.34	.19	.23	.47	.39	.29	.31	.43	.35	.32	.34
OMNI/IPDE[26]	.52	.67	.61	.57	.81	.66	.52	.67	.71	.65	—
MMPI/SIDP[3]	.33	.47	.35	.53	.66	.31	.10	.47	.40	.24	.47
WISPI/SCID-II[27]	.43	.40	.51	.24	.61	.29	.15	.65	.49	.59	.46
WISPI/IPDE[27]	.11	.36	.18	.39	.47	.22	.38	.58	.51	.40	.54
WISPI-4/SCID-II[19]	.60	.36	.32	.40	.60	.43	.54	.60	.53	.44	.38
ADP-IV/SCID-II[18]	.58	.49	.34	.38	.65	.53	.49	.67	.51	.52	—
Median	*0.33*	*0.40*	*0.34*	*0.39*	*0.51*	*0.29*	*0.31*	*0.53*	*0.40*	*0.26*	*0.39*

Notes: PRN = paranoid, SZD = schizoid, SZT = schizotypal, ATS = antisocial, BDL = borderline, HST = histrionic, NCS = narcissistic, AVD = avoidant, DPD = dependent, OBC = obsessive compulsive, PAG = passive–aggressive. PDQ = Personality Diagnostic Questionnaire (Hyler, 1994), SIDP = Structured Interview for Personality Disorders (Pfohl et al., 1997), IPDE = International Personality Disorder Examination (Loranger, 1999), SCID-II = Structured Clinical Interview for Personality Disorders (First & Gibbon, 2004), PDI = Personality Disorder Interview-IV (Widiger et al., 1995), PAS = Personality Assessment Schedule (Tyrer & Alexander, 1979), MMPI = Minnesota Multiphasic Personality Inventory; Morey et al., 1985), MCMI = Millon Clinical Multiaxial Inventory (Millon et al., 1997); ADP-IV = Assessment of DSM-IV Personality Disorders (Schotte et al., 1998), WISPI = Wisconsin Personality Disorder Inventory (Klein et al., 1993), OMNI = OMNI Personality Inventory (Loranger, 2001).
[1] Zimmerman & Coryell (1990), [2] DeRuiter & Greeven (2000), [3] Trull & Larson (1994), [4] Hyler et al. (1990), [5] Hyler, Skodol, Oldham, Kellman, & Doidge (1992), [6] Yeung, Lyons, Waternaux, Faraone, & Tsuang (1993), [7] van Velzen, Luteijn, Scholing, van Hout, & Emmelkamp (1999), [8] Fossati et al. (1998), [9] Blackburn, Donnelly, Logan, & Renwick (2004), [10] Yang et al. (2000), [11] Davison, Leese, & Taylor (2001), [12] Whyte, Fox, & Coxell (2006), [13] Hills (1995), [14] Nazikian, Rudd, Edwards, & Jackson (1990), [15] Jackson, Gazis, Rudd, & Edwards (1991), [16] Renneberg, Chambless, Dowdall, Fauerbach, & Gracely (1992), [17] Soldz, Budman, Demby, & Merry (1993), [18] Schotte et al. (2004), [19] Smith, Klein, & Benjamin (2003), [20] Reich et al. (1987), [21] Torgensen & Alneas (1990), [22] Hogg, Jackson, Rudd, & Edwards (1990), [23] Widiger & Freiman (1988), [24] Marlowe, Husband, Bonieskie, Kirby, & Platt (1997), [25] Corbitt (1995), [26] Loranger (2001), [27] Barber & Morse (1994).

The improvement in convergent validity for a dimensional rating is not simply a statistical artifact of the increase in power provided by more quantitative ratings. The results indicate that reliable and valid information is being lost by the use of categorical distinctions. The results also indicate little to no confidence in the agreement between a self-report inventory and a semistructured interview with respect to a categorical diagnosis.

Table 18.3 provides the convergent validity coefficients for clinical interviews, whether semistructured or unstructured, as reported in 21 studies. The extent of convergence among the existing semistructured interviews is difficult to judge because only three studies have even attempted to provide this information (i.e., O'Boyle & Self, 1990; Pilkonis et al., 1995; Skodol et al., 1991). All three studies were confined to just two of the five semistructured interviews. Only two of the studies administered the interview schedules to the same patients (i.e., O'Boyle & Self, 1990; Skodol et al., 1991), and only one reported findings for at least half of the personality disorders (Skodol et al., 1991). Skodol et al. administered the IPDE and SCID-II to 100 inpatients of a personality disorders treatment unit. Both interviews were administered blind to one another on the same day (one in the morning, the other in the afternoon). Order of administration was staggered. Kappa for individual diagnoses ranged from a low of .14 (schizoid) to a high of .66 (dependent), with a median kappa of .50 (obsessive compulsive). This convergence is better than the consistently poor agreement between a self-report inventory with a semistructured interview but the authors acknowledged that the agreement for some of the categorical diagnoses was discouraging. "It is fair to say that, for a number of disorders (i.e., paranoid, schizoid, schizotypal, narcissistic, and passive–aggressive) the two [interviews] studied do not operationalize the diagnoses similarly and thus yield disparate results" (Skodol et al., 1991, p. 22). They also indicated that, in general, the SCID-II yielded appreciably more personality disorder diagnoses than the IPDE (35 versus 15 diagnoses). On the other hand, agreement with respect to the extent to which each personality disorder was present (i.e., dimensional rating) was considerably better, with correlations ranging from a low of .58 (schizoid) to

Table 18.3. Convergence of clinical interviews.

Instruments	PRN	SZD	SZT	ATS	BDL	HST	NCS	AVD	DPD	OBC	PAG
Convergence of Semistructured Interviews											
Categorical											
IPDE/SCID-II[1]	.29	.14	.44	.59	.53	.58	.44	.56	.66	.50	.21
Dimensional											
IPDE/SCID-II[1]	.68	.58	.72	.87	.76	.77	.80	.78	.81	.77	.74
Convergence with Unstructured Clinical Interviews											
Categorical											
Clinician/Clinician[2]	.35	.01	.19	.49	.29	.23	—	.23	.40	.20	—
IDCL-P/IPDE[3]	.63	-.03	-.03	—	.55	-.07	.54	.71	.27	.30	.66
Clinician/PDQ[4]	.40	-.16	.01	.07	.46	.15	.10	.10	.08	.08	-.02
Conf/SIDP-R[5]	.04	—	—	.25	.40	.46	.39	.51	.52	.40	.47
Conf/IPDE[5]	—	—	—	—	-.06	.24	.20	.37	.09	.51	.11
Conf/IPDE[1]	.25	—	.34	—	.01	.31	.04	.29	.41	.06	-.01
Conf/SCID-II[1]	.54	—	.53	—	.22	.25	.03	.23	.60	.30	.03
SWAP-200/SCID-II[6]	.13	.30	-.06	.49	.27	—	.54	—	—	.65	.10
Clinician/SCID-II[7]	.26	.13	.32	.49	.77	.34	.20	-.04	-.04	.31	.10
Conf/PDQ-4[8]	.05	—	—	—	.20	—	—	.26	.13	.08	—
Clinician/PDQ-R[9]	.12	-.03	.12	-.03	.27	.25	.11	.31	.52	.13	.07
Median	0.19	0.13	0.32	0.49	0.24	0.28	0.11	0.26	0.41	0.21	0.07
Dimensional											
Clinician/Clinician[10]	.58	.14	.52	.49	.51	.41	.45	.34	.39	.16	—
Clinician/MCMI[11]	-.08	.12	.33	.04	.13	.00	.09	.06	.05	.05	.03
Clinician/MCMI-III[12]	.13	.11	.09	.29	.47	.13	.32	.31	.34	.13	—
SWAP-200/SCID-II[13]	-.06	.33	—	.70	.20	.49	.47	.37	.30	.23	—
SWAP-200/SCID-II[6]	.48	.52	-.07	.73	.37	.43	.33	.44	.41	.49	.39
PAF/WISPI[14]	.23	.21	.40	.41	.27	.36	.49	.28	.37	.26	.40
SWAP-200/SWAP-SR[15]	.07	.22	—	.11	.24	.27	.43	.63	.46	-.06	—
Clinician/SWAP-200[16]	.55	.68	.62	.86	.82	.80	.67	.82	.67	.82	—
Clinician/SWAP-200[17]	—	.46	.55	.71	.48	—	.59	—	—	.57	—
Clinician/SWAP-200[18]	.53	.68	—	.70	—	.58	.51	—	—	.32	—
Clinician/SWAP-200A[19]	—	.51	—	.72	.47	.69	.55	—	—	—	—
Clinician/SWAP-200A[20]	—	—	.62	.69	.68	.72	.75	.67	—	.57	—
Clinician/SWAP-200A[21]	.71	.66	.56	.78	.60	.65	.68	.77	.54	.75	—
Median	0.53	0.52	0.58	0.71	0.48	0.69	0.57	0.67	0.54	0.57	0.39

Notes: PRN = paranoid, SZD = schizoid, SZT = schizotypal, ATS = antisocial, BDL = borderline, HST = histrionic, NCS = narcissistic, AVD = avoidant, DPD = dependent, OBC = obsessive compulsive, PAG = passive–aggressive. IPDE = International Personality Disorder Examination (Loranger, 1999), SCID-II = Structured Clinical Interview for Personality Disorders (First & Gibbon, 2004), Clinician = rating for each personality disorder provided by a clinician based on unstructured interview, IDCL-P= International Diagnostic Checklist for Assessment of DSM-III-R & ICD-10 Personality Disorders; Conf = Consensus conference ratings using all available information other than the other instrument (Pilkonis et al., 1995), MCMI = Millon Clinical Multiaxial Inventory (Millon et al., 1997), WISPI = Wisconsin Personality Disorder Inventory (Klein et al., 1993), PAF = Personality Assessment Form (Klein et al., 1993), SWAP-200 = Shedler Westen Assessment Procedure (Westen & Shedler, 1999a, 1999b), SWAP-200A = SWAP-200 Adolescent Version (Westen, Dutra, & Shedler, 2005), SWAPSR = SWAP-200 Self-Report Version.

[1] Skodol, Oldham, Rosnick, & Hyler (1991), [2] Mellsop et al. (1982), [3] Bronisch & Mombour (1994), [4] Hyler et al. (1989), [5] Pilkonis, Heape, Proietti, Clark, McDavid, & Pitts (1995), [6] Marin-Avellan, McGauley, Campbell, & Fonagy (2005), [7] Fridell & Hesse (2006), [8] Wilberg, Dammen, Friis (2000), [9] Bronisch, Flett, Garcia-Borreguero, & Wolf (1993), [10] Hesse (2005), [11] Chick, Sheaffer, Goggin, & Sison (1993), [12] Rossi, Hauben, Van Den Brande, & Sloore (2003), [13] Loffler-Stastka et al. (2007), [14] Klein et al. (1993), [15] Davison, Obonsawin, Sells, & Patience (2003), [16] Westen & Muderrisoglu (2003), [17] Shedler & Westen (2004), [18] Westen & Shedler (1999a, 1999b), [19] Westen, Shedler, Durrett, Glass, & Martens (2003), [20] Westen et al. (2005), [21] Durrett & Westen (2005).

a high of .87 (antisocial), surpassing even the median convergence across two self-report inventories (see Table 18.1). Nevertheless, perhaps the most important point here is that these are the results from just one study, conducted over 15 years ago.

Not surprisingly, the convergent validity coefficients decrease when at least one of the two methods is an unstructured clinical interview (see Table 18.3). In addition, most of the positive findings for unstructured interviews should be tempered by significant methodological limitations, most notably that in many instances the assessments were not in fact blind to one another. For example, the two clinicians in Hesse (2005) "regularly discussed [the] patients at meetings" (p. 1245). In Durrett and Westen (2005), Shedler and Westen (2004), Westen and Shedler (1999a, b), Westen, Dutra, and Shedler (2005), and Westen et al. (2003), the same person actually provided both ratings. In the Marin-Avellan et al. (2005) comparison of SWAP-200 (unstructured) and SCID-II assessments, two of the three interviewers provided both ratings. This method of test validation is comparable to having semistructured interviewers provide their own criterion diagnoses. No such semistructured interview study has ever been published because the criterion contamination is so very problematic. Median convergent validity coefficients for (dimensional) studies that kept the two assessments blind to one another ranged from .07 (paranoid) to .43 (narcissistic), with an overall median value of .27. Median convergent validity coefficients for (dimensional) studies in which the interview assessments were not blind to one another ranged from .39 (passive–aggressive) to .71 (antisocial), with an overall median value of .55.

There is one SWAP-200 study in which the predictor and criterion ratings were blind to one another. Westen and Muderrisoglu (2003) obtained SWAP-200 ratings of 16 persons in outpatient treatment on the basis of a 3-hr, mostly unstructured, clinical interview, as well as additional SWAP-200 ratings from clinicians who were treating the respective patients (Westen and Muderrisoglu, 2006, report additional findings from this same data collection). These ratings were blind to one another. As indicated in Table 18.1, the median convergent validity of these DSM-IV-TR personality disorder assessments was .74, with half of them above .80. These values are substantially better than those obtained when semistructured interviews are correlated with clinicians' ratings (e.g., Pilkonis et al., 1995), and they are better than the convergent validity of SWAP-200 assessments with semistructured interview assessments (i.e., Loffler-Stastka et al., 2007; Marin-Avellan et al., 2005). Such results are certainly encouraging but it would be useful if additional investigators replicated the findings with a larger sample of participants.

Discriminant Validity

Only a small minority of the 68 studies listed in Tables 18.1–18.3 provided discriminant validity data. The absence of much attention to discriminant validity is partly a recognition that the diagnostic constructs assessed by these measures do not themselves have compelling discriminant validity. For example, Skodol et al. (1991) reported the convergent validity of the IPDE and SCID-II semistructured interviews but did not discuss nor provide any data on their discriminant validity. Instead, Oldham et al. (1992) subsequently used the same data to report an excessive co-occurrence among the personality disorder diagnostic categories and concluded that most of this co-occurrence was due to overlap among the disorders' criterion sets rather than flaws or inadequacies within the IPDE or SCID-II. Because the DSM-IV-TR personality disorders overlap extensively (Clark, 2007; Trull & Durrett, 2005; Widiger & Samuel, 2005), perhaps a valid assessment should obtain weak discriminant validity with respect to near neighbor diagnostic constructs. For example, a valid measure of antisocial personality disorder probably should correlate significantly with a valid measure of narcissistic personality disorder. These may not in fact be qualitatively distinct conditions (Widiger, 2005). The personality disorder scales of the MMPI-2 and MCMI-III in fact overlap substantially in order to compel the obtainment of a co-occurrence considered to be consistent with theoretical expectations (Millon et al., 1997; Morey et al., 1985; Somwaru & Ben-Porath, 1995).

Morey, Gunderson, Quigley, and Lyons (2000) administered the NEO Five-Factor Inventory (NEO FFI; Costa & McCrae, 1992), an abbreviated measure of the FFM, to 144 patients sampled for the pilot phase of the Collaborative Longitudinal Study of Personality Disorders. They reported very little differentiation among the personality disorders using the NEO FFI and concluded that the FFM could not adequately differentiate among them. However, they also acknowledged the presence of substantial co-occurrence among the personality disorder criterion diagnoses, as assessed by the DIPD

(Zanarini et al., 1987). For example, the least amount of overlap occurred for borderline personality disorder, which still obtained an average co-occurrence rate of three other personality disorder diagnoses! Morey et al. (2002) subsequently replicated their earlier findings but this time repeated the analyses after removing diagnostic co-occurrence among the four categories that were the particular focus of their investigation. "The elimination of patients with comorbid study diagnoses did appear to sharpen the distinction between the personality disorder groups, whereas only 18 facets [of the FFM] revealed substantive differences (i.e., effect sizes larger than .50), among the cell-assigned personality disorder diagnoses, 31 facets achieved this threshold using the noncomorbid groups" (Morey et al., 2002, pp. 224–225). Discrimination would probably increase further if the diagnostic co-occurrence with the six other personality disorders was also excluded.

In sum, the failure of the FFM to adequately differentiate among the personality disorders may speak more to the lack of the diagnoses' discriminant validity than to a limitation of the FFM. Quite a bit of research has documented the excessive diagnostic co-occurrence among these diagnostic categories (Bornstein, 1998; Clark, 2007; Trull & Durrett, 2005). Lynam and Widiger (2001) and O'Connor (2005) demonstrated that the diagnostic co-occurrence among the personality disorders is itself readily explained if the personality disorders are understood as maladaptive variants of the traits included within the FFM. The DSM-IV-TR personality disorders appear to overlap to the extent that they share FFM personality traits.

SWAP-200 assessments have obtained better differentiation among the personality disorders than is obtained by other instruments (Westen, Gabbard, & Blagov, 2006). However, this success is probably due in large part to the requirement that test respondents report as absent half of the SWAP-200 items, and they are allowed to provide high ratings for only a very small number of items. Co-occurrence is artifactually decreased if test respondents are not allowed to record as present items that would produce diagnostic co-occurrence. As suggested by Sheets and Craighead (2007), "because of the SWAP-200's fixed distribution of personality features, these findings are not as relevant to discussion of the true structure of personality pathology" (p. 91). Of interest for future research would be the administration of the SWAP-200 without any constraints on respondents' descriptions of their patients.

Issues to Consider in the Assessment of Personality Disorders

The assessment of personality disorders can be exceedingly difficult (Clark, 2007; Farmer, 2000; Westen, 1997; Widiger & Samuel, 2005). It is not simply a matter of mindlessly administering a semi-structured interview or a self-report inventory. Four issues that are worth considering in particular are (1) boundaries with Axis I disorders; (2) boundaries with normal personality functioning; (3) boundaries among the personality disorders, and (4) gender, culture, and ethnicity bias.

Boundaries with Axis I Mental Disorders

Diagnostic assessments are needed most at the beginning of treatment, yet it is precisely at this time that it can be most difficult to differentiate between a personality and an Axis I disorder. Most persons with a personality disorder probably seek treatment when they are in crisis or at least experiencing acute levels of distress, anxiety, or depression, and persons who are significantly anxious, depressed, angry, or distraught will often fail to provide an accurate description of their usual way of thinking, feeling, behaving, and relating to others. Hopelessness, low self-esteem, and negativism are common during the occurrence of a depressive mood disorder, and it is to be expected that depressed persons will provide inaccurate and distorted self-descriptions. One of the well-replicated findings in personality disorder assessment research are distortions in self-image due to mood states (Farmer, 2000).

Piersma (1987), for example, reported in an early but still quite informative study substantial changes in MCMI scale elevations across a brief inpatient hospitalization. Twenty-five percent of his 151 patients were diagnosed by the MCMI with borderline personality disorder at admission, only 7.3 percent at discharge; 12 percent were diagnosed with schizotypal personality disorder at admission, only 4 percent at discharge. Test–retest kappa was only .11 for the borderline diagnosis, .09 for compulsive, .01 for passive–aggressive, and .27 for schizotypal. Comparable results were subsequently reported for the MCMI-II (Piersma, 1989) and the MCMI-III (Piersma & Boes, 1997). It is likely that some of this change in scores reflected true changes in personality functioning. However, contrary to this hypothesis is that the hospitalizations were quite brief and were not focused on personality functioning. In fact, in Piersma and Boes (1997), hospitalization lasted no longer than 10 days. In addition, Piersma (1989) and Piersma and Boes (1997) reported significant increases in histrionic and narcissistic scale scores across the brief hospitalization, due in large part to the inclusion of items within these scales assessing normal self-confidence, assertion, self-esteem, and gregariousness. If the change scores on the MCMI-III did reflect true changes in personality, then perhaps the hospital should take responsibility for having created narcissistic and histrionic personality disorders within a subset of the patients. Piersma (1989) concluded instead that "quite clearly . . . the MCMI-II is not able to measure long-term personality characteristics ('trait' characteristics) independent of symptomatology ('state' characteristics)" (p. 91).

Semistructured interviews have the potential of being relatively more resilient to the effects of mood state distortions (Loranger et al., 1991) but they are not immune (Widiger & Samuel, 2005). An interviewer can easily fail to appreciate the extent to which patients' self-descriptions are being distorted by an Axis I disorder. In fact, results equivalent to those reported for the MCMI and MCMI-II by Piersma (1987, 1989) were obtained in the one study that argued for the resilience of semistructured interviews. Loranger et al. (1991) compared IPDE assessments obtained at the beginning of an inpatient admission to those obtained 1 week to 6 months later and reported that "there was a significant reduction in the mean number of criteria met on all of the personality disorders except schizoid and antisocial" (p. 726). Loranger et al. argued that the reduction was not due to an inflation of scores secondary to depressed or anxious mood because changes in personality disorder scores were not correlated with changes in anxiety or depression. However, an alternative perspective is that the study simply lacked sufficiently sensitive or accurate measures to explain why there was a substantial decrease on all but a few of the personality disorder scales. It is unlikely that 1 week to 6 months of treatment resulted in the extent of changes to personality that were indicated by the IPDE (the change scores also failed to correlate with length of treatment). In fact, four of the patients were diagnosed with a histrionic personality disorder by the IPDE at admission whereas eight patients were diagnosed with this disorder at discharge, comparable to the increase in histrionic scores obained by Piersma (1989) and Piersma and Boes (1997).

Adequate differentiation of a personality disorder from most Axis I disorders will require that the clinician assess whether the maladaptive behavior pattern has been evident since late childhood or early adulthood. Personality disorders must have an age of onset that "can be traced back at least to adolescence or early adulthood" (APA, 2000, p. 689). Self-report inventories fail to make adequate distinctions between Axis I and personality disorders in part because they typically fail to even make any reference to age of onset. The MMPI-2 makes no reference to age of onset in its instructions to respondents (Hathaway et al., 1989); the PDQ-4 indicates that respondents should describe themselves in reference to how they have been over the past several years (Hyler, 1994); and the MCMI-III instructs respondents to answer the questions in reference to their current problem(s) (Millon et al., 1997). Semistructured interviews make a more concerted effort to determine whether the behavior pattern has been characteristic of much of the adult life but the interviews vary substantially in how they operationalize the age of onset requirement. The PDI-IV only encourages the interviewer to document that each diagnostic criterion was evident in young adulthood and has remained evident throughout much of the person's adult life. The IPDE is more explicit in its requirements but also more liberal, as it requires that only one of the diagnostic criteria for a respective personality disorder be present since the age of 25; all of the others can be evident only within the past few years. The SCID-II generally requires that each diagnostic criterion be evident over a 5-year period, whereas the DIPD focuses its assessment on just the prior 2 years.

The DIPD is being used in the widely published Collaborative Longitudinal Personality Disorders Study (CLPS; Gunderson et al., 2000). One of the more intriguing findings of this research program has been the extent to which persons fail to maintain personality disorder symptomatology. For example, 23 of 160 persons (14%) diagnosed with borderline personality disorder at the study's baseline assessment met criteria for two or fewer of the nine diagnostic criteria 6 months later (Gunderson et al., 2003). Eighteen sustained this reduction from 6 months to 1 year. Gunderson et al. (2003) concluded that only one of these 18 persons had been inaccurately diagnosed at baseline; the rest were considered to be valid instances of "dramatic" and "unexpected sudden improvements" (p. 113).

However, it is difficult to imagine so many persons meeting the diagnostic criteria for borderline personality disorder since late childhood and continuing to manifest these symptoms throughout their adult life, suddenly changing personality functioning soon after the onset of the study. Few, if any, were in treatment for their personality disorder.

The purportedly valid diagnoses include one person whose original symptoms were determined to be secondary to the use of a stimulant for weight reduction: "the most dramatic improvement following a treatment intervention occurred when a subject discontinued a psychostimulant she had used the year prior to baseline for purposes of weight loss. . . . Discontinuation was followed by a dramatic reduction of her depression, panic, abandonment fears, and self-destructiveness" (p. 116). It is perhaps reasonable to suggest that borderline symptoms that were secondary to the use of a weight loss medication during the year prior to her assessment do not represent a valid diagnosis. Five of the remaining 18 remissions "had the dramatic reduction of borderline personality disorder criteria at the same time as the remission of a coexisting Axis I disorder" (p. 114). "In these five cases, the remission of the Axis I disorder was judged to be the most likely cause for the sudden improvement" (p. 114). For eight cases, "the changes involved gaining relief from severely stressful situations they were in, at or before the baseline assessment" (p. 115). "For example, one subject (case 16) reported that the stress of an unexpected divorce and custody struggle led to anger, substance abuse, and the revival of early abandonment trauma" (p. 115). With the resolution of the temporary stress of the divorce, the "borderline" symptoms abated. Four additional participants experienced sudden, dramatic improvements "after relocating from very intense, conflicted, and tight cohabiting situations" (p. 115). In sum, the "borderline" symptoms in many of these cases were probably not in fact evident since late childhood or adolescence. They were mistaken to be borderline symptoms because the DIPD assessment was confined largely to the prior 2 years in which (for instance) particularly stressful life events were occurring or new medications were being ingested.

The CLPS project is providing findings that are increasing our understanding of the course of personality disorders, but it may also be helpful in alerting clinicians and researchers to additional complications and difficulties in obtaining valid assessments. It appears to be clear that the personality disorder field has not yet developed or applied adequate instruments for the distinction between personality and Axis I disorders. Some personality and Axis I disorders may not in fact be distinguishable (e.g., generalized social phobia and avoidant personality disorder), but if progress is to be made in studying the relationship between the other personality and Axis I disorders, further effort probably needs to be given to obtaining valid distinctions.

Boundaries with Normal Personality Functioning

Existing research has failed to support the existence of a qualitative distinction between normal and abnormal personality functioning, with perhaps the exception of the schizotypal (Lenzenweger, McLachlan, & Rubin, 2007), but even here the findings may not in fact be entirely compelling (Widiger, 2001). DSM-IV-TR provides specific and explicit rules for the distinction between normal and abnormal personality functioning for each of the 10 personality disorders (e.g., five of eight specified criteria are necessary for the diagnosis of histrionic personality disorder). However, no rationale or explanation has ever been provided for the diagnostic thresholds for the avoidant, schizoid, paranoid, histrionic, narcissistic, dependent, or obsessive compulsive personality disorders. The schizotypal and borderline are the only two for which a published rationale has been provided and it is evident that the justification for these thresholds no longer applies (Samuel & Widiger, 2006). Their cutoff points were selected on the basis of maximizing agreement with diagnoses provided by a large sample of clinicians (Spitzer, Endicott, & Gibbon, 1979). There have since been so many revisions, deletions, and additions to the criterion sets that the current diagnostic thresholds no longer relate well to the original thresholds (Blashfield et al., 1992).

Rather than perpetuate the apparent myth that personality disorders are qualitatively distinct from normal personality functioning, it might be preferable to integrate the psychiatric nomenclature with research within psychology on general personality structure (Widiger & Trull, 2007). This would transfer to the psychiatric nomenclature a wealth of knowledge concerning the origins, development, mechanisms, and stability of the dispositions that underlie personality disorder, it would bring with it well-validated and researched instruments and methods of assessment, and it would allow the clinician to identify normal, adaptive personality traits that would facilitate treatment responsivity as well the maladaptive personality traits (Widiger & Lowe, 2007). Widiger et al. (2002) suggest in their four-step procedure for an FFM diagnosis of personality disorder that the diagnosis should be provided at a consistent level of impairment; more specifically, when global assessment of functioning (GAF; APA, 2000) is estimated to be at 60 or below. A score of 71 or above on the GAF indicates a normal range of functioning (e.g., problems are transient and expectable reactions to stressors); a score of 60 or below represents a clinically significant level of impairment (moderate difficulty in social or occupational functioning, such as having few friends or significant conflicts with coworkers). This point of demarcation does not carve nature at a discrete joint, but it does at least provide a cutoff point that would be consistent across all personality disorder diagnoses. Further explication of this scale is provided by the Global Assessment of Relational Functioning (GARF) and the Social and Occupational Functioning scales (SOF; APA, 2000; Hilsenroth et al., 2000).

Boundaries among the Personality Disorders

Many patients will meet DSM-IV-TR diagnostic criteria for more than one personality disorder (Bornstein, 1998; Clark, 2007; Farmer, 2000; Livesley, 2003; Trull & Durrett, 2005), yet clinicians typically provide only one diagnosis to each patient. As noted earlier, clinicians tend to diagnose personality disorders hierarchically. Once a patient is identified as having a particular personality disorder (e.g., borderline), they fail to assess whether additional personality traits are present (Herkov & Blashfield, 1995). For example, Adler et al. (1990) provided 46 clinicians with case histories of a patient that met the DSM-III criteria for four personality disorders (i.e., histrionic, narcissistic, borderline, and dependent). "Despite the directive to consider each category separately . . . most clinicians assigned just one [personality disorder] diagnosis" (p. 127). Sixty-five percent of the clinicians provided only one diagnosis, 28 percent provided two, and none provided all four. Similar results have been reported by Zimmerman and Mattia (1999b).

Westen and Shedler (2000) suggest that their alternative prototypal matching procedure addresses the problem of diagnostic co-occurrence. They propose that the diagnostic manual provide a narrative description of a prototypic case of each personality disorder (half to full page, containing 18–20 features), rather than diagnostic criterion sets. The clinician can then indicate on a 5-point scale the extent to which a patient matches this description (i.e., 1 = little to no match; 2 = slight match, only minor features; 3 = significant match; 4 = good match, patient has the disorder; and 5 = very good match, exemplifies the disorder, prototypic case).

"To make a diagnosis, diagnosticians rate the overall similarity or 'match' between a patient and the prototype using a 5-point rating scale, considering the prototype as a whole rather than counting individual symptoms" (Westen, Shedler, & Bradley, 2006, p. 847). The absence of diagnostic criterion sets is also advantageous in saving a considerable amount of time, as "clinicians could make a complete Axis II diagnosis in 1 or 2 minutes" (Westen, Shedler and Bradley, 2006, p. 855).

Empirical support for their prototypal matching procedure was provided by Westen, Shedler, and Bradley (2006). They compared empirically the extent of diagnostic co-occurrence that is obtained with their prototypal matching with the extent of diagnostic co-occurrence that is obtained if the same clinicians systematically considered each DSM-IV-TR diagnostic criterion. They reported considerably less diagnostic co-occurrence with their prototypal matching. However, it is also quite possible that their findings are simply indicating that the prototypal matching procedure is addressing the problem of diagnostic co-occurrence by simply neglecting to provide an adequate recognition of its existence. The fact that diagnostic co-occurrence increases when clinicians are encouraged to consider specific features of other personality disorders suggests that the diagnostic co-occurrence is actually present but it is not being recognized when clinicians are allowed to base their diagnoses on whatever feature or feature(s) they wish to consider (Zimmerman & Mattia, 1999a, b).

A much less radical proposal for DSM-V is to have clinicians provide a dimensional profile of a patient in terms of the 10 personality disorders (Oldham & Skodol, 2000). A personality disorder could be characterized as prototypic if all of the diagnostic criteria are met, moderately present if one or two criteria beyond the threshold for a categorical diagnosis are present, threshold if the patient just barely meets diagnostic threshold, subthreshold if symptoms are present but are just below diagnostic threshold, traits if no more than one to three symptoms are present, and absent if no diagnostic criteria are present (Oldham & Skodol, 2000). This proposal was in fact made for DSM-IV (Widiger & Sanderson, 1995) but it was rejected at that time as being too radical of a shift in classification, as it would discourage differential diagnosis and undermine categorical distinctions. It is now, perhaps, one of the more conservative of proposals (Widiger & Trull, 2007) and likely to be implemented in DSM-V.

A limitation of the proposal of Oldham and Skodol (2000) is that clinicians would continue to be describing patients in terms of markedly heterogeneous and overlapping constructs. A profile description of a patient in terms the antisocial, borderline, dependent, histrionic, and other DSM-IV-TR constructs is essentially solving the problem of excessive diagnostic co-occurrence by simply accepting it. This is comparable to the decision made by the authors of DSM-III-R (APA, 1987) to address the problematic heterogeneity of the diagnostic categories by abandoning monothetic criterion sets that required homogeneity and converting to polythetic criterion sets that accepted the existence of the problematic heterogeneity (Widiger, Frances, Spitzer, & Williams, 1988).

Gender, Culture, and Ethnic Bias

Many of the personality disorders have a differential sex prevalence rate (APA, 2000). The suggestion that these differential sex prevalence rates reflect gender biases has been among the more difficult and heated diagnostic issues (Widiger, 2007b). Gender bias concerns have been raised with respect to the conceptualization of personality disorders, the wording of diagnostic criteria, the application of diagnostic criteria, thresholds for diagnosis, clinical presentation, research sampling, the self-awareness and openness of patients, and the items included within self-report inventories (Morey, Warner, & Boggs, 2002; Widiger, 1998).

Studies though have not demonstrated significant gender bias within the DSM-IV-TR diagnostic criterion sets (Boggs et al., 2005; Jane et al., 2007). Much of the gender differences of the DSM-IV-TR personality disorders do appear to be consistent with normative differences in general personality structure (Lynam & Widiger, 2007). However, research has consistently reported gender biases in clinical judgments (e.g., Crosby & Sprock, 2004; Flanagan & Blashfield, 2005) and in self-report inventories (e.g., Lindsay, Sankis, & Widiger, 2000).

For example, some self-report inventories include gender-related items that are keyed in the direction of adaptive rather than maladaptive functioning. An item need not assess for dysfunction to contribute to a valid assessment of personality disorders. Items assessing gregariousness can identify histrionic persons, items assessing self-confidence can identify narcissistic persons, and items assessing conscientiousness can identify obsessive compulsive persons (Millon et al., 1997). Items keyed in the direction of adaptive rather than maladaptive functioning can also be helpful in countering the tendency of some respondents to deny or minimize personality disorder symptomatology. However, these items will not be useful in differentiating abnormal from normal personality functioning and are likely to contribute to the overdiagnosis of personality disorders in normal or minimally dysfunctional populations, such as student counseling centers, child custody disputes, or personnel selection (Boyle & Le Dean, 2000). When these items are related to the sex or gender of respondents, as many are in the case of the histrionic, dependent, narcissistic, and obsessive compulsive personality disorder scales of the MCMI-III (Millon et al., 1997) and the MMPI-2 (Colligan et al., 1994), they may contribute to gender-biased assessments (Lampel, 1999; Lindsay et al., 2000).

One might also expect considerable variation in the diagnosis and assessment of personality disorders across different cultural and ethnic groups (Millon & Grossman, 2005). One of the more curious findings is the tendency of forensic clinicians to at times underdiagnose antisocial personality pathology in Blacks (Mikton & Grounds, 2007). This could reflect a tendency to normalize criminal behavior within a minority group or concerns about being perceived as prejudicial.

Ethnic biases may also be present within self-report inventories. Items within self-report inventories are generally written from the perspective of a member of the predominant ethnic, cultural group, and such items may not have the same meaning or implications when read by members of a minority ethnic group (Okazaki & Sue, 2003). Studies report higher scores by African-Americans (compared to Caucasian Americans) on the paranoid personality disorder scale of the MCMI-III (e.g., Munley, Vacha-Haase, Busby, & Paul, 1998). One possible social-cultural explanation for the different elevations obtained with African-Americans on paranoid personality scales could simply be a history of experiencing racial discrimination and prejudice (Widiger & Samuel, 2005). Membership within a minority ethnic group that has historically been severely mistreated and exploited, and continues to experience prejudicial, discriminatory, or antagonistic behaviors from members of the majority ethnic group, would understandably contribute to feelings of mistrust, skepticism, and suspicion that would not be shared by members of the majority ethnic group. African-Americans who have experienced a history of racial discrimination might respond differently than Caucasian Americans to such paranoid personality disorder items as "I am sure I get a raw deal from life," or "The people I work with are not sympathetic with my problems" (Colligan et al., 1994; Millon et al., 1997). Similar hypotheses might be generated for the interpretation of personality disorder test items by members of other ethnic, cultural groups but little to no research has in fact been conducted on potential ethnic or cultural biases within personality disorder self-report inventories.

Conclusions

We favor the use of semistructured interviews for the assessment of personality disorders, particularly when the patient is appreciably depressed or anxious, or suffering from any other Axis I disorder that might affect his or her self-description. The many advantages of semistructured interviews outweigh their limitations, and some are now being used routinely in general clinical practice when the results of the clinical assessment might be subsequently questioned or reviewed (e.g., custody, disability, and forensic assessments).

We do not recommend one particular semistructured interview over another, nor would we recommend that clinicians become familiar with only one of them. We would recommend instead that a clinician obtain a copy of at least a few of them, gleaning from each useful questions, suggestions, and ideas. What is important is to have an explicit set of informative interview questions that are systematic and comprehensive in their coverage and that are used consistently across patients.

We also advise an initial or joint administration of a self-report inventory. Self-report inventories can be particularly useful as initial screening devices, alerting the clinician to domains of personality disorder symptomatology that might otherwise have been missed (Morse & Pilkonis, 2007). The tendency of self-report inventories to err in the direction of false positives rather than false negatives is advantageous for a screening measure, and the amount of time that is required for the complete administration of a semistructured interview can be reduced substantially when the interview is confined to the disorders that were elevated on the self-report inventory.

Administering an inventory or an interview to a close friend or relative of the patient can also be useful in addressing self-image distortions that are secondary to an Axis I disorder or the personality disorder, or simply missed for various other reasons during the interview with the patient (Klonsky et al.,

2002). Given the complexity of a personality disorder assessment, multiple methods of assessment that provide a cross-validation of diagnostic impressions should be the norm rather than the exception.

However, what is also evident in a review of the existing literature on the assessment of personality disorders is the lack of adequate research on the significant problems and issues that undermine the obtainment of a valid assessment. There is a considerable amount of research whose purpose is to assess the convergent validity of a respective instrument (e.g., see Tables 18.1–18.3), but little research on issues and problems that impair validity. For example, there is essentially no research on the impact of adhering to, or ignoring, age of onset when assessing personality disorder yet age of onset does appear to be fundamental to the concept of a personality disorder and a central point of distinction with Axis I disorders. There is considerable literature on the impact of gender on the assessment of personality disorders, but almost no research on the impact of ethnicity or culture, despite the social and theoretical significance of this area of research. There are now at least 10 different self-report inventories and 5 semistructured interviews, yet only limited research that attempts to directly compare or contrast them with respect to validity. There have been only two studies directly comparing alternative semistructured interviews. There is little attention being given to the question of whether a semistructured interview or a self-report inventory provides a more valid assessment. In sum, the assessment of personality disorder continues to be ripe for investigation.

References

Adler, D. A., Drake, R. E., & Teague, G. B. (1990). Clinicians' practices in personality assessment: Does gender influence the use of DSM-III Axis II? *Comprehensive Psychiatry, 31*, 125–133.

American Psychiatric Association. (1980). *Diagnostic and statistical manual of mental disorders* (3rd ed.). Washington, DC: Author.

American Psychiatric Association. (1987). *Diagnostic and statistical manual of mental disorders* (3rd ed., Rev.). Washington, DC: Author.

American Psychiatric Association. (1994). *Diagnostic and statistical manual of mental disorders* (4th ed.). Washington, DC: Author.

American Psychiatric Association. (2000). *Diagnostic and statistical manual of mental disorders. Text revision* (4th ed., Rev.). Washington, DC: Author.

Bagby, R. M., & Farvolden, P. (2004). The Personality Diagnostic Questionnaire-4 (PDQ-4). In M. J. Hilsenroth, D. L. Segal, & M. Hersen (Eds.), *Comprehensive handbook of psychological assessment, Vol. 2: Personality assessment* (pp. 122–133). New York: John Wiley & Sons.

Bagby, R. M., Gilchrist, E. J., Rector, N. A., Dickens, S. E., Joffe, R., Levitt, A., et al. (2001). The stability and validity of the sociotropy and autonomy personality dimensions as measured by the Revised Personal Style Inventory. *Cognitive Therapy and Research, 25*, 765–779.

Barber, J. P., & Morse, J. Q. (1994). Validation of the Wisconsin Personality Disorders Inventory with the SCID-II and PDE. *Journal of Personality Disorders, 8*, 307–319.

Benjamin, L. S., Conrad, J., & Critchfield, K. L. (2006). The use of Structural Analysis of Social Behavior (SASB) as an assessment tool. *Annual Review of Clinical Psychology, 2*, 83–110.

Ben-Porath, Y. S. (2006). Differentiating normal from abnormal personality with the MMPI-2. In S. Strack (Ed.), *Differentiating normal and abnormal personality* (2nd ed., pp. 337–381). New York: Springer.

Blackburn, R., Donnelly, J. P., Logan, C., & Renwick, S. J. D. (2004). Convergent and discriiminant validity of interview and questionnaire measures of personality disorder in mentally disordered offenders: A multitrait-multimethod analysis using confirmatory factor analysis. *Journal of Personality Disorders, 18*, 129–150.

Blashfield, R. K., & Herkov, M. J. (1996). Investigating clinician adherence to diagnosis by criteria: A replication of Morey and Ochoa (1989). *Journal of Personality Disorders, 10*, 219–228.

Blashfield, R. K., Blum, N., & Pfohl, B. (1992). The effects of changing Axis II diagnostic criteria. *Comprehensive Psychiatry, 33*, 245–252.

Boggs, C. D., Morey, L. C., Skodol, A. E., Shea, M. T., Sanislow, C. A., Grilo, C. M., et al. (2005). Differential impairment as an indicator of sex bias in DSM-IV criteria for four personality disorders. *Psychological Assessment, 17*, 492–496.

Bornstein, R. F. (1998). Reconceptualizing personality disorder diagnosis in the DSM-V: The discriminant validity challenge. *Clinical Psychology: Science and Practice, 5*, 333–343.

Boyle, G. J., & Le Dean, L. (2000). Discriminant validity of the illness behavior questionnaire and Millon Clinical Multiaxial Inventory-III in a heterogeneous sample of psychiatric outpatients. *Journal of Clinical Psychology, 56*, 779–791.

Brinded, P. M. J., Simpson, A. F., Laidlaw, T. M., Fairley, N., & Malcolm, F. (2001). Prevalence of psychiatric disorders in New Zealand prisons: A national study. *Australian and New Zealand Journal of Psychiatry, 35*, 166–173.

Bronisch, T., Flett, S., Garcia-Borreguero, D., & Wolf, R. (1993). Comparison of self-rating questionnaire with a diagnostic checklist for the assessment of DSM-III-R personality disorders. *Psychopathology, 26*, 102–107.

Bronisch, T., & Mombour, W. (1994). Comparison of a diagnostic checklist with a structured interview for the assessment of DSM-III-R and ICD-10 personality disorders. *Psychopathology, 27*, 312–320.

Butcher, J. N. (Ed.). (2006). *MMPI-2: A practitioner's guide.* Washington, DC: American Psychological Association.

Chick, D., Sheaffer, C. I., Goggin, W. C., & Sison, G. F. (1993). The relationship between MCMI personality scales and clinician-generated DSM-III-R personality disorder diagnoses. *Journal of Personality Assessment, 61*, 264–276.

Clark, L. A. (2007). Assessment and diagnosis of personality disorder: Perennial issues and an emerging reconceptualization. *Annual Review of Psychology, 58*, 227–257.

Clark, L. A., & Livesley, W. J. (2002). Two approaches to identifying the dimensions of personality disorder:

Convergence on the Five-Factor Model. In P. T. Costa & T. A. Widiger (Eds.), *Personality disorders and the Five-Factor Model of personality* (2nd ed., pp. 161–176). Washington, DC: American Psychological Association.

Clark, L. A., Livesley, W. J., & Morey, L. (1997). Personality disorder assessment: The challenge of construct validity. *Journal of Personality Disorders, 11*, 205–231.

Clark, L. A., Livesley, W. J., Schroeder, M. L., & Irish, S. L. (1996). Convergence of two systems for assessing personality disorder. *Psychological Assessment, 8*, 294–303.

Clark, L. A., Simms, L. J., Wu, K. D., Casillas, A. (in press). *Manual for the Schedule for Nonadaptive and Adaptive Personality.* Minneapolis, MN: University of Minnesota Press.

Cloninger, C. R. (2006). Differentiating personality deviance, normality, and well-being by the seven-factor psychobiological model. In S. Strack (Ed.), *Differentiating normal and abnormal personality* (2nd ed., pp. 65–81). New York: Springer.

Colligan, R. C., Morey, L. C., & Offord, K. P. (1994). MMPI/MMPI-2 personality disorder scales. Contemporary norms for adults and adolescents. *Journal of Clinical Psychology, 50*, 168–200.

Coolidge, F. L., & Merwin, M. M. (1992). Reliability and validity of the Coolidge Axis II Inventory: A new inventory for the assessment of personality disorders. *Journal of Personality Assessment, 59*, 223–238.

Corbitt, E. (1995). *Sex bias and the personality disorders.* Unpublished manuscript.

Costa, P. T., & McCrae, R. R. (1992). *Revised NEO Personality Inventory (NEO PI-R) and NEO Five-Factor Inventory (NEO-FFI) professional manual.* Odessa, FL: Psychological Assessment Resources.

Crosby, J. P., & Sprock, J. (2004). Effect of patient sex, clinician sex, and sex role on the diagnosis of antisocial personality disorder: Models of underpathologizing and overpathologizing biases. *Journal of Clinical Psychology, 60*, 583–604.

Davidson, K. M., Obonsawin, M. C., Seils, M., & Patience, L. (2003). Patient and clinician agreement on personality using the SWAP-200. *Journal of Personality Disorders, 17*, 208–218.

Davison, S., Leese, M., & Taylor, P. J. (2001). Examination of the screening properties of the Personality Diagnostic Questionnaire 4+ (PDQ-4+) in a prison population. *Journal of Personality Disorders, 15*, 180–194.

De Ruiter, C., & Greeven, P. G. J. (2000). Personality disorders in a Dutch forensic psychiatric sample: Convergence of interview and self-report measures. *Journal of Personality Disorders, 14*, 162–170.

Derksen, J. J. (2006). The contribution of the MMPI-2 to the diagnosis of personality disorder. In J. N. Butcher (Ed.), *MMPI-2: A practitioner's guide* (pp. 99–120). Washington, DC: American Psychological Association.

Dubro, A. F., & Wetzler, S. (1989). An external validity study of the MMPI personality disorder scales. *Journal of Clinical Psychology, 45*, 570–575.

Durrett, C., & Westen, D. (2005). The structure of Axis II disorders in adolescents: A cluster- and factor-analytic investigation of DSM-IV categories and criteria. *Journal of Personality Disorders, 19*, 440–461.

Farmer, R. F. (2000). Issues in the assessment and conceptualization of personality disorders. *Clinical Psychology Review, 20*, 823–852.

First, M. B., & Gibbon, M. (2004). The Structured Clinical Interview for DSM-IV Axis I disorders (SCID-I) and the Structured Clinical Interview for DSM-IV Axis II disorders

(SCID-II). In M. J. Hilsenroth, D. L. Segal, & M. Hersen (Eds.), *Comprehensive handbook of psychological assessment, Vol. 2: Personality assessment* (pp. 134–143). New York: John Wiley & Sons.

Flanagan, E. H., & Blashfield, R. K. (2005) Gender acts as a context for interpreting diagnostic criteria. *Journal of Clinical Psychology, 61,* 1485–1498.

Fossati, A., Maffei, C., Bagnato, M., Donati, D., Donini, M., Fiorilli, M., et al. (1998). Brief communication: Criterion validity of the Personality Diagnostic Questionnaire-4+ (PDQ-4+) in a mixed psychiatric sample. *Journal of Personality Disorders, 12,* 172–178.

Frances, A. J. (1980). The DSM-III personality disorders section: A commentary. *American Journal of Psychiatry, 137,* 1050–1054.

Fridell, M., & Hesse, M. (2006). Clinical diagnosis and SCID-II assessment of DSM-III-R personality disorders. *European Journal of Psychological Assessment, 22,* 104–108.

Garb, H. (2005). Clinical judgment and decision making. *Annual Review of Clinical Psychology, 1,* 67–89.

Guess, P. (2006). OMNI personality inventory. *Journal of Psychoeducational Assessment, 24,* 160–166.

Gunderson, J. G., Bender, D., Sanislow, C., Yen, S., Rettew, J. B., Dolan-Sewell, R., et al. (2003). Plausibility and possible determinants of sudden "remissions" in borderline patients. *Psychiatry, 66,* 111–119.

Gunderson, J. G., Ronningstam, E., & Bodkin, A. (1990). The diagnostic interview for narcissistic patients. *American Journal of Psychiatry, 47,* 676–680.

Gunderson, J. G., Shea, M. T., Skodol, A. E., McGlashan, T. H., Morey, L. C., Stout, R. L., et al. (2000). The collaborative longitudinal personality disorders study: I. Development, aims, design, and sample characteristics. *Journal of Personality Disorders, 14,* 300–315.

Haigler, E. D., & Widiger, T. A. (2001). Experimental manipulation of NEO PI-R items. *Journal of Personality Assessment, 77,* 339–358.

Hare, R. D. (2003). *Hare Psychopathy Checklist Revised (PCL-R).* Technical manual. North Tonawanda, NY: Multi-Health Systems.

Hathaway, S. R., McKinley, J. C., Butcher, J. N., Dahlstrom, W. G., Graham, J. R., & Tellegen, A. (1989). *Minnesota Multiphasic Personality Inventory test booklet.* Minneapolis, MN: Regents of the University of Minnesota.

Herkov, M. J., & Blashfield, R. K. (1995). Clinicians' diagnoses of personality disorder: Evidence of a hierarchical structure. *Journal of Personality Assessment, 65,* 313–321.

Hesse, M. (2005). Social workers' ratings of comorbid personality disorders in substance abusers. *Addictive Behaviors, 30,* 1241–1246.

Hicklin, J., & Widiger, T.A. (2000). Convergent validity of alternative MMPI-2 personality disorder measures. *Journal of Personality Assessment, 75,* 502–518.

Hills, H. A. (1995). Diagnosing personality disorders: An examination of the MMPI-2 and MCMI-II. *Journal of Personality Assessment, 65,* 21–34.

Hilsenroth, M. J., Ackerman, S. J., Blagys, M. D., Baumann, B. D., Baity, M. R., Smith, S. R., et al. (2000). Reliability and validity of DSM-IV Axis V. *American Journal of Psychiatry, 157,* 1858–1863.

Hogg, B., Jackson, H. J., Rudd, R. P., & Edwards, J. (1990). Diagnosing personality disorders in recent-onset schizophrenia. *Journal of Nervous and Mental Disease, 178,* 194–199.

Horowitz, L. M., Alden, L. E., Wiggins, J. S., & Pincus, A. L. (2000). *Inventory of Interpersonal Problems.* Odessa, FL: The Psychological Corporation.

Hsu, L. M. (2002). Diagnostic validity statistics and the MCMI-III. *Psychological Assessment, 14,* 410–422.

Huprich, J. (Ed.) (2005). *Rorschach assessment of the personality disorders.* Mahwah, NJ: Lawrence Erlbaum.

Hyler, S. E. (1994). Personality Diagnostic Questionnaire-4 (PDQ-4) (Unpublished test). New York: New York State Psychiatric Institute.

Hyler, S. E., Rieder, R. O., Williams, J. B. W., Spitzer, R. L., Lyons, M., & Hendler, J. (1989). A comparison of clinical and self-report diagnoses of DSM-III personality disorders in 552 patients. *Comprehensive Psychiatry, 30,* 170–178.

Hyler, S. E., Skodol, A. E., Kellman, H. D., Oldham, J. M., & Rosnick, L. (1990). Validity of the Personality Diagnostic Questionnaire-Revised: Comparison with two structured interviews. *American Journal of Psychiatry, 147,* 1043–1048.

Hyler, S. E., Skodol, A. E., Oldham, J. M., Kellman, H. D., & Doidge, N. (1992). Validity of the Personality Diagnostic Questionnaire-Revised: A replication in an outpatient sample. *Comprehensive Psychiatry, 33,* 73–77.

Jackson, H. J., Gazis, J., Rudd, R. P., & Edwards, J. (1991). Concordance between two personality disorder instruments with psychiatric inpatients. *Comprehensive Psychiatry, 32,* 252–260.

Jane, J. S., Oltmanns, T. F., South, S. C., & Turkheimer, E. (2007). Gender bias in diagnostic criteria for personality disorders: An item response theory analysis. *Journal of Abnormal Psychology, 116,* 166–175.

Jones, A. (2005). An examination of three sets of MMPI-2 personality disorder scales. *Journal of Personality Disorders, 19,* 370–385.

King, R. E. (1994). Assessing aviators for personality pathology with the Millon Clinical Multiaxial Inventory (MCMI). *Aviation, Space, and Environmental Medicine, 65,* 227–231.

Klein, D. N. (2003). Patients' versus informants' reports of personality disorders in predicting 7.5 year outcome in outpatients with depressive disorders. *Psychological Assessment, 15,* 216–222.

Klein, M. H., Benjamin, L. S., Rosenfeld, R., Treece, C., Husted, J., & Greist, J. H. (1993). The Wisconsin Personality Disorders Inventory: I. Development, reliability, and validity. *Journal of Personality Disorders, 7,* 285–303.

Klonsky, E. D., Oltmanns, T. F., & Turkheimer, E. (2002). Informant-reports of personality disorder: Relation to self-reports and future research directions. *Clinical Psychology: Science and Practice, 9,* 399–411.

Lampel, A. K. (1999). Use of the Millon Clinical Multiaxial Inventory-III in evaluating child custody litigants. *American Journal of Forensic Psychology, 17,* 19–31.

Lenzenweger, M. F., McLachlan, G., & Rubin, D. B. (2007). Resolving the latent structure of schizophrenia endophenotypes using expectation-maximization-based finite mixture modeling. *Journal of Abnormal Psychology, 116,* 16–29.

Lilienfeld, S. O., & Andrews, B. P. (1996). Development and preliminary validation of a self-report measure of psychopathic personality traits in noncriminal populations. *Journal of Personality Assessment, 66,* 488–524.

Lindsay, K. A., Sankis, L. M., & Widiger, T. A. (2000). Gender bias in self-report personality disorder inventories. *Journal of Personality Disorders, 14,* 218–232.

Livesley, W. J. (2003). Diagnostic dilemmas in classifying personality disorder. In K. A. Phillips, M. B. First, & H. A. Pincus (Eds.), *Advancing DSM: Dilemmas in psychiatric diagnosis* (pp. 153–190). Washington, DC: American Psychiatric Association.

Livesley, W. J. (2006). The Dimensional Assessment of Personality Pathology (DAPP) approach to personality disorder. In S. Strack (Ed.), *Differentiating normal and abnormal personality* (2nd ed., pp. 401–430). New York: Springer.

Locke, K. D. (2006). Interpersonal circumplex measures. In S. Strack (Ed.), *Differentiating normal and abnormal personality* (2nd ed., pp. 383–400). New York: Springer.

Loffler-Stastka, H., Ponocny-Seliger, E., Fischer-Kern, M., Rossler-Schulein, H., Leithner-Dzlubas, K., & Schuster, P. (2007). Validation of the SWAP-200 for diagnosing psychostructural organization in personality disorders. *Psychopathology, 40,* 35–46.

Loranger, A. W. (1999). *International Personality Disorder Examination (IPDE).* Odessa, FL: Psychological Assessment Resources.

Loranger, A. W. (2001). *OMNI Personality Inventories: Professional manual.* Odessa, FL: Psychological Assessment Resources.

Loranger, A. W., Lenzenweger, M. F., Gartner, A. F., Susman, V. L., Herzig, J., Zammit, G. K., et al. (1991). Trait-state artifacts and the diagnosis of personality disorders. *Archives of General Psychiatry, 48,* 720–729.

Lynam, D. R., & Widiger, T. A. (2001). Using the Five-Factor Model to represent the DSM-IV personality disorders: An expert consensus approach. *Journal of Abnormal Psychology, 110,* 401–412.

Lynam, D. R., & Widiger, T. A. (2007). Using a general model of personality to understand sex differences in the personality disorders. *Journal of Personality Disorders, 21,* 583–602.

Marin-Avellan, L. E., McGauley, G., Campbell, C. & Fonagy, P. (2005). Using the SWAP-200 in a personality-disordered forensic population: Is it valid, reliable, and useful? *Criminal Behaviour and Mental Health, 15,* 28–45.

Marlowe, D. B., Husband, S. D., Bonieskie, L. M., Kirby, K. C., & Platt, J. J. (1997). Structured interview versus self-report test vantages for the assessment of personality pathology in cocaine dependence. *Journal of Personality Disorders, 11,* 177–190.

McCann, J. T. (1989). MMPI personality disorder scales and the MCMI: Concurreng validity. *Journal of Clinical Psychology, 45,* 365–369.

McCann, J. T. (1991). Convergent and discriminant validity of the MCMI-II and MMPI personality disorder scales. *Psychological Assessment, 3,* 9–18.

McDermut, W., & Zimmerman, M. (2008). Personality disorders, personality traits, and defense mechanisms measures. In A. J. Rush, M. B. First, & D. Blacker (Eds.), *Handbook of psychiatric measures* (2nd ed. pp. 687–729). Washington, DC: American Psychiatric Publishing.

Meehl, P. E., & Rosen, A. (1955). Antecedent probability and the efficiency of psychometric signs, patterns, or cutting scores. *Psychological Bulletin, 52,* 194–216.

Mellsop, G., Varghese, F. T. N., Joshua, S., & Hicks, A. (1982). The reliability of Axis II of DSM-III. *American Journal of Psychiatry, 139,* 1360–1361.

Mikton, C., & Grounds, A. (2007). Cross-cultural clinical judgment bias in personality disorder diagnosis by forensic psychiatrists in the UK: A case-vignette study. *Journal of Personality Disorders, 21,* 400–417.

Miller, J. D., & Lynam, D. R. (2003). Psychopathy and the five-factor model of personality: A replication and extension. *Journal of Personality Assessment, 81,* 168–178.

Miller, J. D., Lynam, D. R., Rolland, J.-P., De Fruyt, F., Reynolds, S. K., Pham-Scottez, A., et al. (2008). Scoring the DSM-IV personality disorders using the Five-Factor Model: Development and validation of normative scores for North American, French and Dutch-Flemish samples. *Journal of Personality Disorders, 22,* 433–450.

Millon, T., Davis, R. D., Millon, C. M., Wenger, A. W., Van Zuilen, M. H., Fuchs, M., et al. (1996). *Disorders of personality: DSM-IV and beyond.* New York: John Wiley & Sons.

Millon, T., & Grossman, S. D. (2005). Sociocultural factors. In J. M. Oldham, A. E. Skodol, & D. S. Bender (Eds.), *Textbook of personality disorders* (pp. 223–235). Washington, DC: American Psychiatric Publishing.

Millon, T., Millon, C., & Davis, R. (1997). *MCMI-III manual* (2nd ed.). Minneapolis, MN: National Computer Systems.

Morey, L. C. (1988). Personality disorders under DSM-III and DSM-III-R: An examination of convergence, coverage, and internal consistency. *American Journal of Psychiatry, 145,* 573–577.

Morey, L. C., Gunderson, J., Quigley, B. D., & Lyons, M. (2000). Dimensions and categories: The "Big Five" factors and the DSM personality disorders. *Assessment, 7,* 203–216.

Morey, L. C., Gunderson, J. G., Quigley, B. D., Shea, M. T., Skodol, A. E., McGlashan, T. H., et al. (2002). The representation of borderline, avoidant, obsessive-compulsive, and schizotypal personality disorders by the Five-Factor Model. *Journal of Personality Disorders, 16,* 215–234.

Morey, L. C., & Hopwood, C. J. (2006). The Personality Assessment Inventory and the measurement of normal and abnormal personality constructs. In S. Strack (Ed.), *Differentiating normal and abnormal personality* (2nd ed., pp. 451–471). New York: Springer.

Morey, L. C., & Le Vine, D. J. (1988). A multitrait-multimethod examination of Minnesota Multiphasic Personality Inventory (MMPI) and Millon Clinical Multiaxial Inventory (MCMI). *Journal of Psychopathology and Behavioral Assessment, 10,* 333–344.

Morey, L. C., Waugh, M. H., & Blashfield, R. K. (1985). MMPI scales for DSM-III personality disorders: Their derivation and correlates. *Journal of Personality Assessment, 49,* 245–251.

Morey, L. C., Warner, M., & Boggs, C. (2002). Gender bias in the personality disorders criteria. An investigation of five bias indicators. *Journal of Psychopathology and Behavioral Assessment, 24,* 55–65.

Morse, J. Q., & Pilkonis, P. A. (2007). Screening for personality disorders. *Journal of Personality Disorders, 21,* 179–198.

Mullins-Sweatt, S. N., & Widiger, T. A. (2007). Millon's dimensional model of personality disorder: A comparative study. *Journal of Personality Disorders, 21,* 42–57.

Munley, P. H., Vacha-Haase, T., Busby, R. M., & Paul, B. D. (1998). The MCMI-II and race. *Journal of Personality Assessment, 70,* 183–189.

Nazikian, H., Rudd, R. P., Edwards, J., & Jackson, H. J. (1990). Personality disorder assessments for psychiatric inpatients. *Australian and New Zealand Journal of Psychiatry, 24,* 37–46.

O'Boyle, M., & Self, D. (1990). A comparison of two interviews for DSM-III-R personality disorders. *Psychiatry Research, 32,* 85–92.

O'Connor, B. P. (2005). A search for consensus on the dimensional structure of personality disorders. *Journal of Clinical Psychology, 61*, 323–345.

Okazaki, S., & Sue, S. (2003). Methodological issues in assessment research with ethnic minorities. In A. Kazdin (Ed.), *Methodological issues and strategies in clinical research* (3rd ed., pp. 349–367). Washington, DC: American Psychological Association.

Oldham, J. M., & Skodol, A. E. (2000). Charting the future of Axis II. *Journal of Personality Disorders, 14*, 17–29.

Oldham, J. M., Skodol, A. E., Kellman, H. D., Hyler, S. E., Rosnick, L., & Davies, M. (1992). Diagnosis of DSM-III-R personality disorders by two semistructured interviews: Patterns of comorbidity. *American Journal of Psychiatry, 149*, 213–220.

Oltmanns, T. F., & Turkheimer, E. (2006). Perceptions of self and others regarding pathological personality traits. In R. F. Krueger & J. L. Tackett (Eds.), *Personality and psychopathology* (pp. 71–111). New York: Guilford.

O'Maille, P. S., & Fine, M. A. (1995). Personality disorder scales for the MMPI-2: An assessment of psychometric properties in a correctional populations. *Journal of Personality Disorders, 9*, 235–246.

Perry, J. C., Banon, E., Ianni, F. (1999). Effectiveness of psychotherapy for personality disorders. *American Journal of Psychiatry, 156*, 1312–1321.

Pfohl, B., Blum, N., & Zimmerman, M. (1997). *Structured Interview for DSM-IV personality*. Washington, DC: American Psychiatric Press.

Piersma, H. L. (1987). The MCMI as a measure of DSM-III Axis II diagnoses: An empirical comparison. *Journal of Clinical Psychology, 43*, 478–483.

Piersma, H. L. (1989). The MCMI-II as a treatment outcome measure for psychiatric inpatients. *Journal of Clinical Psychology, 45*, 87–93.

Piersma, H. L., & Boes, J. L. (1997). MCMI-III as a treatment outcome measure for psychiatric impatients. *Journal of Clinical Psychology, 53*, 825–831.

Pilkonis, P. A., Heape, C. L., Proietti, J. M., Clark, S. W., McDavid, J. D., & Pitts, T. E. (1995). The reliability and validity of two structured diagnostic interviews for personality disorders. *Archives of General Psychiatry, 52*, 1025–1033.

Pilkonis, P. A., Heape, C. L., Ruddy, J., & Serrao, P. (1991). Validity in the diagnosis of personality disorders: The use of the lead standard. *Journal of Consulting and Clinical Psychology, 3*, 46–54.

Pincus, A. L., & Gurtman, M. B. (2006). Interpersonal theory and the interpersonal circumplex: Evolving perspectives on normal and abnormal persoanlity. In S. Strack (Ed.), *Differentiating normal and abnormal personality* (2nd ed., pp. 83–111). New York: Springer.

Raskin, R., & Terry, H. (1988). A principal-components analysis of the Narcissistic Personality Inventory and further evidence of its construct validity. *Journal of Personality and Social Psychology, 54*, 890–902.

Ready, R. E., & Clark, L. A. (2002). Correspondence of psychiatric patient and informant ratings of personality traits, temperament, and interpersonal problems. *Psychological Assessment, 14*, 39–49.

Reich, J., Noyes, R., & Troughton, E. (1987). Lack of agreement between instruments assessing DSM III personality disorders. In C. Green (Ed.), *Conference on the Millon Clinical Inventories* (pp. 223–234). Minnetonka, MN: National Computer Systems.

Renneberg, B., Chambless, D. L., Dowdall, D. J., Fauerbach, J. A., & Gracely, E. J. (1992). The Structured Clinical Interview for DSM-III-R, Axis II and the Millon Clinical Multiaxial Inventory: A concurrent validity study of personality disorders among anxious outpatients. *Journal of Personality Disorders, 6*, 117–124.

Rogers, R. (2003). Standardizing DSM-IV diagnoses: The clinical applications of structured interviews. *Journal of Personality Assessment, 81*, 220–225.

Rogers, R., Salekin, R. T., & Sewell, K. W. (1999). Validation of the Millon Clinical Multiaxial Inventory for Axis II disorders: Does it meet the Daubert standard? *Law and Human Behavior, 23*, 425–443.

Rossi, G., Hauben, C., Van den Brande, I., & Sloore, H. (2003). Empirical evaluation of the MCMCI-III personality disorder scales. *Psychological Reports, 92*, 627–642.

Rossi, G., Van den Brande, I., Tobac, A., Sloore, H., & Hauben, C. (2003). Convergent validity of the MCMI-III personality disorder scales and the MMPI-2 scales. *Journal of Personality Disorders, 17*, 330–340.

Rounsaville, B. J., Alarcon, R. D., Andrews, G., Jackson, J. S., Kendell, R. E., & Kendler, K. (2002). Basic nomenclature issues for DSM-V. In D. J. Kupfer, M. B. First, & D. E. Regier (Eds.), *A research agenda for DSM-V* (pp. 1–29). Washington, DC: American Psychiatric Association.

Samuel, D. B., & Widiger, T. A. (2004). Clinicians' descriptions of prototypic personality disorders. *Journal of Personality Disorders, 18*, 286–308.

Samuel, D. B., & Widiger, T. A. (2006). Differentiating normal and abnormal personality from the perspective of the DSM. In S. Strack (Ed.), *Differentiating normal and abnormal personality* (2nd ed., pp. 165–183). New York: Springer.

Saulsman, L. M., & Page, A. C. (2003). Can trait measures diagnose personality disorders? *Current Opinion in Psychiatry, 16*, 83–88.

Schotte, C. K. W. (2000). New instruments for diagnosing personality disorders. *Current Opinion in Psychiatry, 13*, 605–609.

Schotte, C. K. W., De Doncker, D., Dmitruk, D., van Mulders, I., D'Haenen, H., & Cosyns, P. (2004). The ADP-IV questionnaire: Differential validity and concordance with the semistructured interview. *Journal of Personality Disorders, 18*, 405–419.

Schotte, C. K. W., De Doncker, D., Vankerckhoven, C., Vertommen, H., & Cosyns, P. (1998). Self-report assessment of the DSM-IV personality disorders. Measurement of trait and distress characteristics: The ADP-IV. *Psychological Medicine, 28*, 1179–1188.

Schuler, C. E., Snibbe, J. R., & Buckwalter, J. G. (1994). Validity of the MMPI personality disorder scales (MMPI-PI). *Journal of Clinical Psychology, 50*, 220–227.

Segal, D. L., & Coolidge, F. L. (2007). Structured and semistructured interviews for differential diagnosis: Issues and application. In M. Hersen, S. M. Turner, & D. C. Beidel (Eds.), *Adult psychopathology and diagnosis* (5th ed., pp. 72–103). New York: John Wiley & Sons.

Shedler, J. (2002). A new language for psychoanalytic diagnosis. *Journal of the American Psychoanalytic Association, 50*, 429–456.

Shedler, J., & Westen, D. (2004). Dimensions of personality pathology: An alternative to the Five-Factor Model. *American Journal of Psychiatry, 161*, 1743–1754.

Sheets, E., & Craighead, W. E. (2007). Toward an empirically based classification of personality pathology. *Clinical Psychology: Science and Practice, 14*, 77–93.

Silberman, C. S., Roth, L., Segal, D. L., & Burns, W. J. (1997). Relationship between the Millon Clinical Multiaxial Inventory-II and Coolidge Axis II Inventory in chronically mentally ill older adults: A pilot study. *Journal of Clinical Psychology, 53*, 559–566.

Simms, L. J., & Clark, L. A. (2006). The Schedule for Nonadaptive and Adaptive Personality (SNAP): A dimensional measure of traits relevant to personality and personality pathology. In S. Strack (Ed.), *Differentiating normal and abnormal personality* (2nd ed., pp. 431–449). New York: Springer.

Sinha, B. K., & Watson, D. C. (2001). Personality disorder in university students: A multitrait-multimethod study. *Journal of Personality Disorders, 15*, 235–244.

Skeem, J., & Cooke, D. J. (in press). Is criminal behavior a central component of psychopathy? Conceptual directions for resolving the debate. *Psychological Assessment.*

Skodol, A. E., Oldham, J. M., Rosnick, L., Kellman, H. D., & Hyler, S. E. (1991). Diagnosis of DSM-III-R personality disorders: A comparison of two structured interviews. *International Journal of Methods in Psychiatric Research, 1*, 13–26.

Smith, T. L., Klein, M. H., & Benjamin, L. S. (2003). Validation of the Wisconsin Personality Disorders Inventory-IV with the SCID-II. *Journal of Personality Disorders, 17*, 173–187.

Soldz, S., Budman, S., Demby, A., & Merry, J. (1993). Diagnostic agreement between the Personality Disorder Examination and the MCMI-II. *Journal of Personality Assessment, 60*, 486–499.

Somwaru, D. P., & Ben-Porath, Y. S. (1995). *Development and reliability of MMPI-2 based personality disorder scales.* Paper presented at the 30th Annual Workshop and Symposium on Recent Developments in Use of the MMPI-2 & MMPI-A, St. Petersburg Beach, FL.

Spitzer, R. L., Endicott, J., & Gibbon, M. (1979). Crossing the border into borderline personality and borderline schizophrenia. *Archives of General Psychiatry, 36*, 17–24.

Spitzer, R. L., Forman, J. B. W., & Nee, J. (1979). DSM-III field trials: I. Initial interrater diagnostic reliability. *American Journal of Psychiatry, 136*, 815–817.

Streiner, D. L., & Miller, H. R. (1988). Validity of the MMPI scales for DSM-III personality disorders: What are they measuring? *Journal of Personality Disorders, 2*, 238–242.

Torgensen, S., & Alnaes, R. (1990). The relationship between the MCMI personality scales and DSM-III, Axis II. *Journal of Personality Assessment, 55*, 698–707.

Trull, T. J. (1993). Temporal stability and validity of two personality disorder inventories. *Psychological Assessment, 5*, 11–18.

Trull, T., Goodwin, A. H., Schopp, L. H., Hillenbrand, T. L., & Schuster, T. (1993). Psychometric properties of a cognitive measure of personality disorders. *Journal of Personality Assessment, 61*, 536–546.

Trull, T. J., & Durrett, C. A. (2005). Categorical and dimensional models of personality disorder. *Annual Review of Clinical Psychology, 1*, 355–380.

Trull, T. J., & Larsen, S. L. (1994). External validity of two personality disorder inventories. *Journal of Personality Disorders, 8*, 96–103.

Trull, T. J., & Widiger, T. A. (1997). *Structured Interview for the Five-Factor Model of personality.* Odessa, FL: Psychological Assessment Resources.

Trull, T. J., Widiger, T. A., Lynam, D. R., & Costa, P. T. (2003). Borderline personality disorder from the perspective of general personality functioning. *Journal of Abnormal Psychology, 112*, 193–202.

Trull, T. J., Widiger, T. A., Useda, J. D., Holcomb, J., Doan, D.-T., Axelrod, S. R., et al. (1998). A structured interview for the assessment of the Five-Factor Model of personality. *Psychological Assessment, 10*, 229–240.

Tyrer, P., & Alexander, J. (1979). Classification of personality disorder. *British Journal of Psychiatry, 122*, 531–540.

van Velzen, C. J. M., Luteijn, F., Scholing, A., van Hout, W. J. P. J., & Emmelkamp, P. M. G. (1999). The efficacy of the Personalty Diagnostic Questionnaire-Revised as a diagnostic screening instrument in an anxiety disorder group. *Clinical Psychology and Psychotherapy, 6*, 395–403.

Watkins, C. E., Campbell, V. L., Nieberding, R., & Hallmark, R. (1995). Contemporary practice of psychological assessment by clinical psychologists. *Professional Psychology: Research and Practice, 26*, 54–60.

Westen, D. (1997). Divergences between clinical and research methods for assessing personality disorders: Implications for research and the evolution of Axis II. *American Journal of Psychiatry, 154*, 895–903.

Westen, D., Dutra, L., & Shedler, J. (2005). Assessing adolescent personality pathology. *British Journal of Psychiatry, 186*, 227–238.

Westen, D., Gabbard, G. O., & Blagov, P. (2006). Back to the future: Personality structure as a context for psychopathology. In R. F. Krueger & J. L. Tackett (Eds.), *Personality and psychopathology* (pp. 335–384). New York: Guilford.

Westen, D., & Muderrisoglu, S. (2003). Assessing personality disorders using a systematic clinical interview: Evaluation of an alternative to structured interviews. *Journal of Personality Disorders, 17*, 351–369.

Westen, D., & Muderrisoglu, S. (2006). Clinical assessment of pathological personality traits. *American Journal of Psychiatry, 163*, 1285–1287.

Westen, D., & Shedler, J. (1999a). Revising and assessing Axis II: I. Developing a clinically and empirically valid assessment method. *American Journal of Psychiatry, 156*, 258–272.

Westen, D., & Shedler, J. (1999b). Revising and assessing Axis II: II. Toward an empirically based and clinically useful classification of personality disorders. *American Journal of Psychiatry, 156*, 273–285.

Westen, D., & Shedler, J. (2000). A prototype matching approach to diagnosing personality disorders: Toward DSM-V. *Journal of Personality Disorders, 14*, 109–126.

Westen, D., Shedler, J., & Bradley, R. (2006). A prototype approach to personality disorder diagnosis. *American Journal of Psychiatry, 163*, 846–856.

Westen, D., Shedler, J., Durrett, C., Glass, S., & Martens, A. (2003). Personality diagnoses in adolescence: DSM-IV Axis II diagnoses and an empirically derived alternative. *American Journal of Psychiatry, 160*, 952–966.

Whyte, S., Fox, S., & Coxell, A. (2006). Reporting of personality disorder symptoms in a forensic inpatient sample: Effects of mode of assessment and response style. The *Journal of Forensic Psychiatry & Psychology, 17*, 431–441.

Widiger, T. A. (1998). Sex biases in the diagnosis of personality disorders. *Journal of Personality Disorders, 12*, 95–118.

Widiger, T. A. (2001). What can we learn from taxometric analyses? *Clinical Psychology: Science and Practice, 8*, 528–533.

Widiger, T. A. (2002). Personality disorders. In M. M. Antony & D. H. Barlow (Eds.), *Handbook of assessment,* treatment planning, and outcome for psychological disorders (pp. 453–480). New York: Guilford.

Widiger, T. A. (2005). Psychopathy and DSM-IV psychopathology. In C. Patrick (Ed.), *Handbook of psychopathy* (pp. 156–171). New York: Guilford.

Widiger, T. A. (2007a). Clinical interviews. In A. M. Nezu & C. M. Nezu (Eds.), *Evidence-based outcome research: A practical guide to conducting randomized clinical trials for psychosocial interventions* (pp. 47–65). New York: Oxford University Press.

Widiger, T. A. (2007b). DSM's approach to gender: history and controversies. In W. E. Narrow, M. B. First, P. J. Sirovatka, & D. A. Regier (Eds.), *Age and gender considerations in psychiatric diagnosis. A research agenda for DSM-V* (pp. 19–29). Washington, DC: American Psychiatric Association.

Widiger, T. A. (2008). Personality disorder. In J. Hunsley & E. J. Mash (Eds.), *A guide to assessments that work* (pp. 413–435). New York: Oxford University Press.

Widiger, T. A., & Clark, L. A. (2000). Toward DSM-V and the classification of psychopathology. *Psychological Bulletin, 126,* 946–963.

Widiger, T. A., Costa, P. T., & McCrae, R. R. (2002). A proposal for Axis II: Diagnosing personality disorders using the Five Factor Model. In P. T. Costa & T. A. Widiger (Eds.), *Personality disorders and the Five Factor Model of personality* (2nd ed., pp. 431–456). Washington, DC: American Psychological Association.

Widiger, T. A., Costa, P. T., & Samuel, D. (2006). Assessment of maladaptive personality traits. In S. Strack & M. Lorr (Eds.), *Differentiating normal and abnormal personality* (2nd ed., pp. 311–335). New York: Springer.

Widiger, T., Frances, A., Spitzer, R., & Williams, J. (1988). The DSM-III-R personality disorders: An overview. *American Journal of Psychiatry, 145,* 786–795.

Widiger, T. A., & Freiman, K. (1988). *Personality Interview Questions-II: Reliability, validity, and methodological issues.* Paper presented at the National Institute of Mental Health Workshop on Assessment of Personality Disorders, Bethesda, MD.

Widiger, T. A., & Lowe, J. (2007). Five Factor Model assessment of personality disorder. *Journal of Personality Assessment, 89,* 16–29.

Widiger, T. A., Mangine, S., Corbitt, E. M., Ellis, C. G., & Thomas, G. V. (1995). *Personality Disorder Interview-IV: A semistructured interview for the assessment of personality disorders. Professional manual.* Odessa, FL: Psychological Assessment Resources.

Widiger, T. A., & Samuel, D. B. (2005). Evidence based assessment of personality disorders. *Psychological Assessment, 17,* 278–287.

Widiger, T. A., & Sanderson, C. J. (1995). Towards a dimensional model of personality disorders in DSM-IV and DSM-V. In W. J. Livesley (Ed.), *The DSM-IV personality disorders* (pp. 433–458). New York: Guilford.

Widiger, T. A., & Sankis, L. (2000). Adult psychopathology: issues and controversies. *Annual Review of Psychology, 51,* 377–404.

Widiger, T. A., & Trull, T. J. (2007). Plate tectonics in the classification of personality disorder: Shifting to a dimensional model. *American Psychologist, 62,* 71–83.

Widiger, T. A., Trull, T. J., Clarkin, J. F., Sanderson, C. J., & Costa, P. T., Jr. (2002). A description of the DSM-IV personality disorders with the Five-Factor Model of personality. In P. T. Costa, Jr., & T. A. Widiger (Eds.), *Personality disorders and the Five-Factor Model of personality* (2nd ed., pp. 89–99). Washington, DC: American Psychological Association.

Wilburg, T., Dammen, T., & Friis, S. (2000). Comparing Personality Diagnostic Questionnaire-4 with longitudinal, all data (LEAD) standard diagnoses in a sample with a high prevalence of Axis I and Axis II disorders. *Comprehensive Psychiatry, 41,* 295–302.

Wise, E. A. (1994). Managed care and the psychometric validity of the MMPI and MCMI personality disorder scales. *Psychotherapy in Private Practice, 13,* 81–97.

Wise, E. A. (1996). Comparative validity of MMPI-2 and MCMI-II personality disorder classifications. *Journal of Personality Assessment, 66,* 569–582.

Wise, E. A. (2001). The comparative validity of MCMI-II and MMPI-2 personality disorder scales with forensic examinees. *Journal of Personality Disorders, 15,* 275–279.

Wood, J. M., Garb, H. N., Lilienfeld, S. O., & Nezworski, M. T. (2002). Clinical assessment. *Annual Review of Psychology, 53,* 519–543.

World Health Organization. (1992). *The ICD-10 classification of mental and behavioural disorders: Clinical descriptions and diagnostic guidelines.* Geneva, Switzerland: Author.

Yang, J., McCrae, R. R., Costa, P. T., Yao, S., Dai, X., Cai, T., et al. (2000). The cross-cultural generalizability of Axis II constructs: An evaluation of two personality disorder assessment instruments in the People's Republic of China. *Journal of Personality Disorders, 14,* 249–263.

Yeung, A. S., Lyons, M. J., Waternaux, C. M., Faraone, S. V., & Tsuang, M. T. (1993). Empirical determination of thresholds for case identification. Validation of the Personality Diagnostic Questionnaire-Revised. *Comprehensive Psychiatry, 34,* 384–391.

Zanarini, M. C., Frankenburg, F. R., Chauncey, D. L., & Gunderson, J. G. (1987). The Diagnostic Interview for Personality Disorders: Interrater and test–retest reliability. *Comprehensive Psychiatry, 28,* 467–480.

Zanarini, M. C., Gunderson, J. G., Frankenburg, F. R., & Chauncey, D. L. (1989). The Revised Diagnostic Interview for Borderlines: Discriminating BPD from other Axis II disorders. *Journal of Personality Disorders, 3,* 10–18.

Zarrella, K. L., Schuerger, J. M., & Ritz, G. H. (1990). Estimation of MCMI DSM-III Axis II constructs from MMPI scales and subscales. *Journal of Personality Assessment, 55,* 195–201.

Zimmerman, M. (2003). What should the standard of care for psychiatric diagnostic evaluations be? *Journal of Nervous and Mental Disease, 191,* 281–286.

Zimmerman, M., & Coryell, W. (1990). Diagnosing personality disorders in the community. A comparison of self-report and interview measures. *Archives of General Psychiatry, 47,* 527–531.

Zimmerman, M., & Mattia, J. I. (1999a). Differences between clinical and research practices in diagnosing borderline personality disorder. *American Journal of Psychiatry, 156,* 1570–1574.

Zimmerman, M., & Mattia, J. I. (1999b). Psychiatric diagnosis in clinical practice: Is comorbidity being missed? *Comprehensive Psychiatry, 40,* 182–191.

Functional Imaging in Clinical Assessment?
The Rise of Neurodiagnostics with fMRI

Angus W. MacDonald, III *and* Jessica A. H. Jones

Abstract

This chapter provides an update on progress in the use of neuroimaging for predicting clinical states, with particular attention to diagnosis. The chapter discusses the underpinnings of the blood oxygenation level–dependent (BOLD) response used in functional magnetic resonance imaging (fMRI), and issues involved in measuring this signal reliably. It then examines the logic underpinning the development of models based on brain data to examine latent states, such as deception, and latent traits, such as the diagnosis of schizophrenia. It concludes that neuroimaging, while not currently a practical tool for clinical assessment, is likely to provide an important avenue of new ideas. Biomarkers, such as those derived from neuroimaging, are likely to have a role in understanding dimensionality and the common origins of certain disorders (e.g., depression and anxiety) by providing biological principles around which to organize thinking in these areas.

Keywords: diagnosis, fMRI, independent components analysis, lie detection, pattern recognition, reliability, schizophrenia

The science fiction scenario that has provoked you into reading this chapter is this: Your client sits down across from you looking quite nervous, and reluctantly asks, "How bad is it, Doc?"

You mouse through a brief file sent over yesterday from radiology featuring brain images with colourful circles and lines. Soon you arrive at a familiar table at the bottom of the computer-generated readout.

"The good news is that your brain scan rules out a schizophrenia spectrum disorder, as well as any indication of pathological appetitive processes." Then, after a pause, "The bad news is that your default network and primary sensory components suggest very dominant avoidance processes ... here and here," you add, circling on the screen the highlighted pictures of the amygdala and medial orbitofrontal cortex.

She looks back, bewildered, "But, Doc, what does it all mean?"

You shuffle in your seat. You have hardly met the woman and yet you know the tests have placed her well within the confidence intervals of three different internalizing disorders. How can you tell her that if she's not depressed already she soon will be? Or, that the scan shows she is unlikely to be a good candidate for medication? "Well, it means that we know what to work on."

Imagining such a scenario is easy. We have had tests that function in this manner long before there were electronic medical records in which to record them. What takes a little more work is imagining *how* such a scenario might come about. What are all the little pieces that need to be in place to probe the brain's psychological and psychopathological states in a manner useful for clinical assessment? In this chapter, we will check in with current efforts to evaluate the little pieces that underpin the logic of clinical assessment, including personality assessment, with functional imaging. We will first describe the increasingly well-understood physiological basis of functional magnetic resonance imaging (fMRI). Next, we will address a topic close to the hearts of psychometrists, which is the reliability of functional imaging. We will then explore current efforts to understand implicit brain states, using studies of lie detection as an illustration. Finally, we will examine recent efforts to diagnose schizophrenia and other psychiatric illnesses using neuroimaging, and reflect on their relevance for the future of clinical assessment, including personality assessment.

For many, the prospect of viewing states of the brain directly, and from this inferring some latent truth about a person's internal state, is as mysterious as it is awe-inspiring. Neuroimaging technology is indeed awe-inspiring, but throughout this chapter seasoned clinical scientists will recognize familiar statistical problems refracted through this new lens. In addition to test–retest reliability, issues such as sensitivity, and specificity, and generalizability must be addressed. We have not escaped from these familiar testing criteria simply because we are dealing with images of biological phenomena rather than behaviors. Despite their promise, imaging approaches still have a long way to go to catch up with established interview and paper-and-pencil assessment practices.

Neural Basis of the BOLD Response

The BOLD response is the "blood oxygenation level–dependent" response that is measured in 99% of fMRI studies. (The other 1% measures the actual level of blood flow itself, but this is tricky business indeed, and no more will be said of it in this chapter.) Since very few people actually care whether the blood in the brain is oxygenated or deoxygenated, it is instructive to unpack this signal further to understand why this is a useful way to understand regional brain function. However, the following discussion is not for everyone. Readers interested in the practicalities of fMRI for clinical assessment with no interest in its theoretical basis should feel welcomed to jump to the next section.

Now, it is a misunderstanding to think of an MR scanner as just a big magnet. It is in fact a number of magnets working in tandem. The biggest magnet, B_o, is a supercooled monstrosity that produces a magnetic field many thousand times greater than the strength of the Earth's magnetic field and whose strength is measured in T, or tesla. Most functional neuroimaging today occurs on magnets whose B_o strength is 1.5–3 T. Such fields are strong enough to accelerate a hammer through a block of concrete. For non-ferromagnetic people, MRI scanners are harmless and are found by many to be very soothing. B_o needs to be this strong because it aligns all the protons within its magnetic field in more or less the same orientation. Why "more or less"?

Because protons in a magnetic field cannot help but wobble as they spin, which is known more elegantly as their precession. Luckily, the extent to which protons wobble depends on the strength of the magnetic field. This is where a collection of other magnets, known as gradients, comes in to play. The gradient magnets alter the main B_o field ever so slightly. As a result, all those protons process at an ever so slightly different frequency across space. This is the necessary setup for obtaining pretty pictures.

It is not enough to simply have a number of magnets working in tandem. MRI scanners must also have the capacity to transmit and receive radio signals. (Scanner rooms are surrounded with thick shielding to prevent outside radio signals from interfering with these local broadcasts.) The transmission and reception of signals is carefully orchestrated by a pulse sequence. A pulse sequence begins with a radio frequency (RF) pulse sent from a coil close to a person's head. This RF pulse knocks the protons from their alignment with B_o into some other, predetermined alignment. This also synchronizes their precessions, which is like setting the hands of a clock to 12:00. As each proton finds its way back into it own precession, a very slight signal is emitted which can be picked up with a very sensitive antenna if it is close to the source. By no coincidence at all (remember those gradients?), each location in space broadcasts at a slightly different frequency so by listening for a particular frequency, one can learn something about the proton's journey back to its original precession in that location. The broadcasts that are heard most readily are those from the hydrogen protons in H_2O.

Yes, this is a simplification of a number of complicated equations and technical marvels that have consumed physicists and engineers for more than half a century. It is not so gross a simplification to obscure the following insight: a proton's journey back to its own precession reveals important information about its immediate environment. One aspect of that environment is a useful magnetic property of the nearby hemoglobin. Dispatched from the lungs, and propelled by the heart, hemoglobin carries oxygen to all tissue in the body. When hemoglobin is on its outward, oxygenated path, it is diamagnetic like most tissue. That is, it has no magnetic properties to speak of. After the hemoglobin has made its oxygen delivery, it becomes paramagnetic. That means that within a larger magnetic field deoxygenated hemoglobin has the capacity to generate its own small magnetic field. This small magnetic field then affects the local protons as they desynchronize in the milliseconds after the RF pulse. Voila. Just by going about its business, hemoglobin provides a remote means for measuring where blood in the body is oxygenated and where is it not.

While the contrast between oxygenated and deoxygenated hemoglobin was seized upon in the early 1990s as a marker of cognitive functioning, it took a decade before experimental evidence provided a more thorough account of the relationship between the BOLD response and neuronal activity. This account, by Logothetis, Pauls, Augath, Trinath, and Oeltermann (2001), utilized simultaneous BOLD response imaging and electrophysiological recording from neurons in visual cortex. These electrodes were capable of recording action potentials in single neurons, across multiple neurons, and the local field potentials. Local field potentials are thought to reflect an average of inputs to dendrites and the propagation of signals from dendrites down to the soma. The researchers' principal discovery was that whereas spiking activity returned to baseline regardless of how long a visual stimulus lasted, both the BOLD response and the local field potentials were sensitive to stimulus duration. This suggested that what the BOLD response was tied to was the input and local processing within that brain region, rather than its output or spiking activity. Although at first a surprise, these findings are easily reconciled with what is known about glucose metabolism in the brain. Excitatory pyramidal glutamate neurons use 80–90% of the brain's energy, and by implication, a similar proportion of oxygen. While axonal firing does account for some portion of this, the majority of this energy is expended on the propagation of excitatory potentials from the dendrites to the soma. Given these considerations, Logothetis's observation of the relationship between local processing and the MR signal is an intuitive way to think about the link between the BOLD response and cognitive functioning. Readers further interested in this linkage are referred to several helpful sources (Heeger & Ress, 2002; Mintun et al., 2001).

Even though the BOLD response is not a direct measure of neural activity, it is demonstrably linked to activity in localizable populations of neurons. Thus, to the extent that brain functioning underlies psychopathology and functional imaging can measure something about brain functioning, it is at least principled to ask whether such imaging modalities can assist in clinical assessment. However, there are many sources of noise when making measurements using fMRI. Thus, the next question we will turn to is whether these imaging modalities provide a consistent answer. That is, how reliable is fMRI?

Reliability

A large number of factors affect the repeatability of BOLD measurements. One of the most common sources that may disrupt this fMRI signal is physiological "noise"; this often includes movement and individual differences such as cardiac variability (Liston et al., 2006; Shmueli et al., 2007) and rate of breathing (Thomason, Burrows, Gabrieli, & Glover, 2005). But noise is not limited to the basic functions to maintain life; it is also sensitive to what else is coursing through the blood stream. Substances such as caffeine (Laurienti et al., 2002); Liu et al., 2004), nicotine (Thiel & Fink, 2007), ethanol (Seifritz et al., 2000), and glucose (Anderson et al., 2006) change signal from session to session. Especially for single subject clinical assessments, it will be imperative to understand how these factors reduce the precision of fMRI measurement.

Given the potential for changes in noise, how do these affect the overall level of reliability? McGonigle et al. (2000) investigated the extent to which one session for a single subject "typifies" that subject's response across multiple sessions, using three different paradigms. In each paradigm, the context of the various sessions was found to have a significant effect on the subject's activation. The authors concluded that assessment of subjects with a single session should be interpreted with a great deal of caution. This finding was controversial, even outright depressing, as many of the hopes for fMRI lay in the realm of using single-session scans for both assessment and treatment aims. But the story soon became more nuanced. Upon conducting secondary analyses, Smith et al. (2005) concluded that while intersession variability played a significant role in a subject's activation, this variability was not significantly larger than within-session variability. That is, the tools (and power) necessary to cope with within-session variability—which the field has had to deal with since the outset—were likely going to be those needed to deal with between-session variability. This conclusion deflected much of the skepticism of the reliability of fMRI methods that had been cast with McGonigle et al. (2000) and restored belief that the activation of a subject from a single session might be a reasonable representation of subjects' brain activity over multiple time points.

Following the publication of McGonigle et al. (2000), but before the reanalysis by Smith et al. (2005), a second study investigated the test–retest reliability of fMRI activation using a checkerboard visual task with three conditions of varied attentional load (Specht, Willmes, Shah, & Jancke, 2003). Both individual and group contrast analyses of the intraclass correlation coefficient (ICC) were conducted. For all three conditions, the range of intraclass correlation coefficients observed was .4–1, with each condition showing a significant number of voxels in primary visual areas with ICC's above .8. Thus it would appear that primary visual areas can be reliability activated across testing sessions. As well, significantly more voxels were consistently activated in the two conditions that required greater attentional load.

Unfortunately, many of the brain regions of interest for clinical assessment are farther forward in the brain than primary visual areas and are only remotely linked to any given stimulus. Work by Manoach and colleagues (2001) have addressed this directly. They investigated test–retest reliability of fMRI activation using a working memory task known to activate prefrontal cortex. In addition, the researchers separately examined reliability in healthy controls and patients with schizophrenia. In regions associated with working memory function, such as dorsolateral prefrontal cortex, retest reliability among controls was ICC = .81, which was even stronger than the retest reliability in the primary motor areas associated with responding, which was ICC = .50. In contrast to the high level of reliability in controls, patients showed very low reliability in activating dorsolateral prefrontal cortex (ICC = .20), whereas primary motor cortex activation was similar to that of controls (ICC = .46). There are many factors that may play a role in this decreased reliability, including greater within-subject variability in behavioral performance or more motion. It is also possible that some aspect of the disorder itself conveys a higher level of variability. Overall the data suggested that, in controls anyway, regions outside of visual cortex might be reliably measured in single subjects.

These studies have all used fMRI in a rather "traditional" manner. That is, they have manipulated an independent variable (the stimulus) and evaluated the reliability of its effect on the dependent variable (the BOLD signal). Another approach to fMRI analysis that, as we shall see, is gaining currency is the use of independent components analysis (ICA). In this case, there is no independent variable, per se, but instead the relationships over time between different voxels are subject to analysis. Thus, brain maps can be calculated that reflect the extent to which different regions are linked through activity or inactivity at the same times. To anticipate the uses of ICA in neurodiagnostics, it is useful to consider the reliability of ICA brain maps at this time. In the only test–retest study of ICA to our knowledge, Lim et al. (2007) evaluated the resting state networks of seven healthy participants tested 6 weeks apart. The resting state networks identified included the posterior cingulate, ventral anterior cingulate, medial prefrontal, superior and inferior parietal cortices. The mean cross-correlation of the network identified at times 1 and 2 was $r = .49$, suggesting that while a consistent signal may be present there is much room for improvement.

Functional MRI has undergone some skepticism about its reliability. Many factors do impact the precision of fMRI both during and between sessions. However, the studies previously described illustrate that adequate levels of reliability can be found. At the same time, it is increasingly clear that MRI researchers have not been adept in translating the highly dimensional data they are obtaining into reliability coefficients that are either consistent within the field, or interpretable to interested observers. The field has yet a long way to develop before the definitive answer about the reliability of fMRI is known.

Inferring Latent States: The Case of Lie Detection

Assuming reliability will in time be demonstrated in a consistent and interpretable manner, one can turn to validity. In this regard, one of the great challenges in assessment, which is generally not present in fMRI research, is the use of measured variables to infer the presence of a latent factor—a personality profile, or a diagnosis. In fMRI research, the independent variables are generally known—the task condition, the patient groups—and the pattern of brain activity is the topic of investigation. But in the case of clinical assessment, that approach is off the board. That is, the brain activity is thrust into the role of the independent variable and is used to infer something that could not be otherwise measured. As we shall see in the next section, the capacity to infer a latent trait, such as a diagnosis, involves building a model to study the differences between people. Before we take that leap, it is informative to examine an intermediate case, which is the use of models to study state changes within the same person. In this case, the state in question is whether the person is telling the truth or not.

While the study of deception in our fellow citizens goes back to time immemorial, the capacity for using fMRI to do this began only recently. The first study of deception used a traditional approach in which periods of deception were established as a behavioral variable and the pattern of brain activity was the dependent variable and subjects were studied as a group (Lee et al., 2002). Subjects were instructed "to fake well, do it with skill, and avoid detection" (p. 159). When the investigators compared brain activity during a recall condition from cerebral activity during the deception condition, they found large regions of the brain including bilateral prefrontal, frontal, parietal, temporal, and subcortical regions were associated with the cognitive demands of lying. This study showed that, on average, people use particular parts of their brain more when lying, but it did not detect which events were lies per se.

Subsequent work has argued that deception events themselves can be measured in individual subjects (Langleben et al., 2005). This study used a forced-choice paradigm in which healthy undergraduate males were given two cards and were instructed to acknowledge possession of one card and deny possession of the other. At the beginning of the study, participants were given $20 and were instructed they could keep the money at the end of the study only if they successfully concealed their deception. In addition to the two cards given to the participant, distracter cards were presented to measure the activation associated with varying stimulus salience. The investigators found, on a group level, activation during the truth condition was increased in prefrontal and parietal areas compared to the lie condition. Most importantly, the authors examined the accuracy of using activation to distinguish truth from deception on a single-event level. The probability of their computational model correctly separating a pair of trials, with one trial as truth and one trial as deception, was 85%. While these results are impressive, and a necessary step in determining whether lie detection is feasible using fMRI, the presence or absence of a lie remained a measured rather than an inferred variable. Thus, the next step was to use brain activation alone to determine whether a subject was being deceitful.

To test the possibility of using fMRI as a lie detector in a manner analogous to, but hopefully better than, the polygraph, Kozel and colleagues (2005) asked subjects to take part in a mock "crime." This crime was to take a ring or watch from a specific room to the locker where the subject's personal belongings were kept, while being watched by an investigator. Money was used as an incentive to encourage skillful lying; the participants were instructed they would be given an additional $50

at the end of the experiment if a blind investigator could not tell when they were lying. The investigators started by collecting data on 30 participants and using the data to build a model for detecting deception. In building the model, deception events were known to the algorithm. The deception detection model then focused on three clusters of activation: right anterior cingulate, right orbitofrontal and inferior frontal areas, and right middle frontal areas. It was observed that relative increases in activity in these regions were positively correlated with the likelihood of lying. The researchers then tested their model on an independent group of 31 participants run through the same protocol. Using a combination of the regions associated with deception, the investigators were able to infer when the participants were being deceptive with a 90% accuracy rate.

There are a number of questions that this body of work raises specific to the problem of lie detection— does the model of Kozel and colleagues generalize to other crimes or just this one? Is 85–90% accuracy high enough to take action or convict? But beyond this work's capacity to increase the sale of MRI technology to law enforcement, such efforts suggest that the technique of building models based on fMRI data to predict unknown aspects of subsequently scanned subjects may be possible. In this case, the model was built to detect a change in state, from that of telling the truth to lying, within individuals. The challenge for the clinical assessment of personality or diagnosis is to build models that can distinguish between individuals.

Neurodiagnostics

Is there a pattern of activity in the brain that is so closely associated with, for example, an impulse control disorder that simply by knowing someone has that pattern of activity one can be reasonably certain they have the behavioral features of an impulse control disorder? A strictly theoretical approach to such a question might involve determining brain regions associated with reward-related activity, perhaps the ventral striatum, and brain regions associated with executive control, perhaps orbital and dorsolateral prefrontal cortices. One might then examine brain activity in these regions while performing a task that has been shown to be related to individual differences in impulse control. One could calculate the extent to which activity in these regions of interest predicts some external measure of impulse control. Indeed, a growing number of studies do indeed show correlations between brain activity and symptoms (e.g., MacDonald et al., 2005). However, very few of these studies have conceptualized this as a question of prediction, and therefore we have almost no knowledge of how good such approaches are for classification or prediction.

The most advanced efforts in using brain measurements to provide clinical information are theory-poor and data-driven. That is, as opposed to building up a clinical presentation based on an understanding of basic mechanisms, neurodiagnostics have used sophisticated statistical approaches applied to a lot of data. Machine learning tools are then used to sort through the data to pick out the data points that might be most relevant to differentiating between groups. The process would be recognizable to dust-bowl empiricists like Starke Hathaway who selected items for the Minnesota Multiphasic Personality Inventory (MMPI) based on their ability to discriminate groups. In this case, though, the data reflect patterns of brain activity rather than overt responses.

Apostolos Georgopoulos and colleagues have published the strongest proof of principle to date for the potential of brain data combined with modern computational algorithms to make differential diagnoses (Georgopoulos et al., 2007). In this case, their study used magnetoencephalography, or MEG, rather than fMRI. Like fMRI, MEG is a "noninvasive" method for detecting brain activity that measures changes in the local magnetic field. But there the comparisons end. Whereas fMRI measures blood oxygenation as discussed above, MEG measures the magnetic field disturbances associated with the electrical activity of neurons. To do this, MEG relies on a number of sensors placed around the skull. Like electroencephalography, or EEG, MEG has very fast temporal resolution. Thus investigators are able to measure 1,000 data points every second from each sensor (in contrast, fMRI acquires a whole brain image every 1.5–3 s). MEG is most sensitive to the activity of neurons in a particular orientation that are close to the sensors. Therefore, its strength lies not in producing uniform data about the brain, nor in measuring activity deep in the brain. Finally, the number of MEG machines in the world numbers in the tens, so it is currently an uncommon technology.

As many investigators had suggested before, Georgopoulos recognized that neurological and psychiatric disorders might occur when neurons stop communicating normally. For him, all those MEG sensors measuring activity on a millisecond timescale were ideal for measuring such communication problems. To this, Georgopoulos added two insights. First, he intuited that communication problems might be visible in the background chatter of neurons when staring at a point of light for 45 s. This solved the problems that come of asking participants with different ability levels to perform a task. The second insight addressed the problem that no one knew which signal would indicate the presence or absence of a disorder. Georgopoulos realized that he and his colleagues did not need to know the answer: computational algorithms can answer just this kind of question. "You know there is gold in America, but all you have is a map of the United States. The computer algorithm is there to show you where the gold is" (Georgopoulos, personal communication, October 2007).

To demonstrate the usefulness of this new formula, the investigators measured 52 participants with five different diagnoses—schizophrenia, alcoholism, Alzheimer's disease, multiple sclerosis, and Sjogren's syndrome, which is an autoimmune disorder that affects the glands that produce tears and saliva. They also included healthy control participants. After preprocessing the data, they computed correlations between the neural activity at each of the 271 sensors, and then identified sensor pairs that had the highest correlations. These steps served to reduce the data from about 271 (sensors) × 45 (s) × 1,000 (measurements per second) raw data points to a still very large, but somewhat more manageable, number of cross-correlations. About 18% or 5,500 of these cross-correlations differed significantly across the six groups. To sift through this still very large corpus of information, the investigators employed an evolutionary, or genetic, algorithm. Thus their algorithm for distinguishing diagnostic groups started with a random, and therefore nonoptimal, formula for separation. The algorithm then mutated and improved over many, many "generations" to better discriminate between groups. While the procedure employed was computationally intensive and the details somewhat arcane, the crucial point is this: a river of MEG information was available; through a series of principled decisions, this river was sifted for a small quantity of gold.

The discriminant function classification that emerged from these procedures has a number of properties of great interest to readers. First, there were many combinations of sensor pair correlations that correctly classified all of the 52 subjects, and far more than would be expected by chance. An example of such a combination is illustrated in Figure 19.1. But the true test came when they used

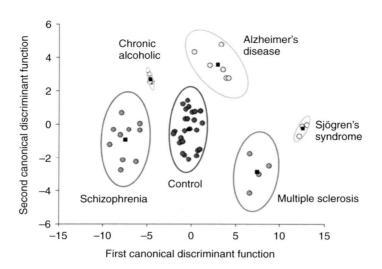

Fig. 19.1 Classification results from 52 participants from six different groups included in Georgopoulos et al. (2007) using the correlations between MEG sensors. The six groups are plotted on two out of five canonical discriminant functions to illustrate the separation between them that occurred for this particular iteration of their analysis path. Reprinted with kind permission of the author and publisher.

the algorithm derived on the initial sample in an independent sample of 46 subjects. Of the classification schemes that had given 100% correct classification in the first sample, many provided excellent classification in the new sample (hundreds provided better than 95% correct classification, and thousands more provided better than 90% correct classifications). The cross-validation approach used in these analyses is quite powerful; however the relative scarcity of MEG devices around the world and an unproven ability to repeat the results at another location will slow the adoption of this approach in clinical practice. Thus, the question can well be asked whether the data available from functional MRI is capable of a similar trick.

The use of fMRI to distinguish between diagnostic categories remains in its early stages, but a growing body of work suggests explosive growth in this area may be just around the corner. The work of Calhoun and colleagues (Calhoun, 2005; Calhoun, Maciejewski, Pearlson, & Kiehl, 2007) has made the greatest contributions we know of using this kind of data. Calhoun shares with Georgopoulous a theory-poor, machine-driven approach to data analysis and classification. It also utilizes the incidental correlations that arise across the brain. Whereas Georgopoulos used the very high temporal resolution of MEG to observe correlations as they occurred in time, Calhoun's method relies on ICA, described above.

To study whether such ICA brain maps were indicative of psychopathology, Calhoun evaluated two components that emerged when 21 chronic schizophrenia patients, 14 bipolar patients, and 26 healthy controls were asked to perform an auditory

oddball task during fMRI. The oddball task is simply a series of stimuli (one every 2 s) that establish a dominant pattern. Occasionally (25% of the time) something different from the dominant tone occurs, an oddball, and participants responded with a button press. Many studies of the oddball task have been conducted, and these have focused on brain regions associated with detecting and responding to the oddball stimuli. Analyzing the independent components that could be found within brains engaged in this task, however, was something quite different from these more traditional analyses. In this case, the researchers calculated maps of the default mode and temporal lobe networks from all of the participants. These networks are so named because they represent two different canonical sets of regions: the first is typified by activity in the posterior anterior cingulate, precuneus, and frontopolar cortex; the temporal lobe network was characterized by activity in the inferior temporal lobe and temporal poles. The researchers then left out one participant from each group during the training of an algorithm to distinguish people in each group. That is, they allowed the algorithm to learn the important differences between the different diagnoses in their default and temporal networks. (And conversely, the algorithm learned to ignore between-individual differences that were irrelevant to classification.) To test the resulting classification algorithm, he calculated how frequently it correctly identified the participants left out of that training. As illustrated in Figure 19.2, the average sensitivity of the models was 90%, whereas the average specificity was 95%. Among the different diagnostic groups, controls were classified correctly 95% of the time and bipolar patients were classified

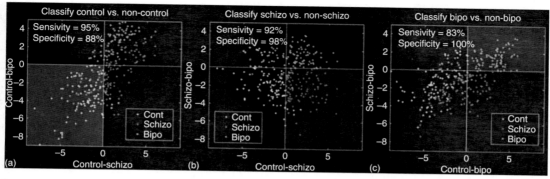

Fig. 19.2 Classification results from 21 chronic schizophrenia patients, 14 bipolar patients, and 26 healthy controls included in Calhoun et al. (2007). Each case is represented with a dot, with the gray scale indicating diagnosis. (a) Lower left shaded region shows the a priori decision region for controls versus noncontrols; (b) lower right shaded region shows the a priori decision region for schizophrenia versus nonschizophrenia patients; (c) upper right shaded region shows the decision region for bipolar disorder versus nonbipolar patients. Reprinted with the kind permission of the author and publisher.

correctly 83% of the time, with schizophrenia patients in between. Interestingly, the inclusion of more ICA networks did not appreciably increase sensitivity or specificity and indeed risked overfitting the data and thereby losing the ability to generalize to the untrained cases, much less cases from other scanners.

It is useful to remind readers before going on that this level of sensitivity and specificity is at least on a par with clinical ratings. For example, Jakobsen and colleagues (2005) reported the agreement between the hospital record–based OPCRIT (operationalized criteria) diagnosis of schizophrenia and that of an experienced psychiatrist was 85%, with 93% sensitivity and 62% specificity. Comparing DSM-IV emergency room diagnoses to inpatient discharge diagnoses from Woo, Sevilla, and Obrocea (2006), there was 86% agreement for all patients eventually diagnosed with either schizophrenia or bipolar disorder, with 88% sensitivity and 85% specificity for the diagnosis of schizophrenia or schizoaffective disorder. Compared to these efforts to apply the same phenotypic framework across different settings, the classification algorithm based on brain activity alone appears to be rather promising.

It is also useful to reflect on the importance of the tasks used in these two studies: they were largely irrelevant. That is, the cognitive demands of the tasks were not the basis of the diagnostic information. While Calhoun's participants were doing an oddball task, it would seem in principle that they may as well have been counting monkeys in the jungle. This is quite surprising for someone stepped in clinical cognitive neuroscience. One might think that tasks that tapped the deficits associated with schizophrenia would be those most useful in making diagnosis. But the implicit or explicit premise that the investigators began with is that schizophrenia is largely a disorder of connectivity; given enough machine power, functional data will reveal the nature of that disconnectivity in the absence of any particular task demand. This is important for many reasons, but two appear to be most directly relevant to the future of clinical assessment: first, the problems and questions associated with matching performance of patients and controls and the confounds that arise from individual differences in performance are ameliorated by using this kind of approach; second, schizophrenia may be an unusual disorder in this regard. Clinical assessment in domains other than psychosis, such as internalizing or externalizing pathology, may still require task-related activity rather than resting state activity to observe clinically relevant brain activity. That is, there are no basal patterns of activity or connectivity that distinguish someone with generalized anxiety disorder or a gambling addiction from controls. Thus, simply because in this case task demands and performance were not discussed at length, these may be important considerations for understanding some forms of psychopathology.

Conclusions

What are we to make of these developments at the edge of science fiction? On the one hand, the evidence for reliability as traditionally understood is poor. Test–retest of the reliability of voxels within an independent component, for example, is an unimpressive .49, on average. On the other hand, there is something of the feel of a large locomotive coming through a tunnel. At this point we can only feel the rumble and the wind being pushed in front of it; but soon, perhaps, it may change the landscape of clinical assessment. There are many questions that the preliminary steps in this domain give rise to. We will address four: the necessary next steps for neurodiagnosis to be validated; the potential role for neurodiagnosis in the clinic; the role of neurodiagnostic biomarkers in refining models of personality and diagnoses; and the shift toward theory-poor dust-bowl empiricism that this approach embraces.

First, there are a number of practical next steps that neurodiagnostics researchers need to address. The body of work to date is limited in scope, both to studies that take place on individual scanners, and to medicated patients, and to a limited number of diagnoses. Watch for developments in this domain in the near future, with increasing numbers of medication-naive patients being compared to other psychiatric groups. The importance of task demands and performance will also have to be evaluated to determine whether some tasks provide activation or correlation maps that provide better or worse classifications. Task performance and the issue of medication will also play into concerns about the repeatability of classification of the same individuals over time. In this chapter we examined test–retest reliability on a voxel-wise basis. It remains to be seen how important individual voxels are compared to the larger patterns of activity and correlations that have so far proved successful in neurodiagnostics. Furthermore, the use of neurodiagnostics will be limited to a few locations in major university medical centers until researchers develop classification algorithms that perform well on any scanner, not just the one on which they were developed. Finally, the cost effectiveness of neurodiagnostics will have to be addressed. How much incremental information can neurodiagnostics provide over and above traditional, less resource intensive (and less intimidating) practices such as interviews and self-report scales?

The issue of cost effectiveness is closely tied to questions one might ask about whether a neurodiagnostics assessment will help in treatment planning. Knowing that the patient sitting in your office has abnormal brain connectivity may come as a great relief to both the patient and his or her family. But it is only a variant of the current "chemical imbalances" explanation. Here the hope for neurodiagnostics, with fMRI or any other modality, is to go beyond brain maps and what is currently available within the assessment armamentarium. That is, these data will be most helpful in providing predictive information, such as the likelihood of future (comorbid) diagnoses that might be prevented, the likelihood of responding to different medications, or other ancillary risk factors

such as activation patterns linked to the likelihood of suicide. This remains pure science fiction at this point, beyond the grasp of the current body of work. However, such value-added information is likely to be necessary before neuroimaging becomes a common aspect of clinical assessment.

If the impact of neurodiagnostics and other forms of imaging assessment on day-to-day clinical practice is still some ways away, the impact of imaging on how we conceptualize personality, and psychiatric diagnosis in particular, is likely to be much closer to hand. Since time immemorial, the distinction between neurology and psychiatry has been the putative likelihood of a biological explanation of the former and a psychological explanation of the later. While biological explanations for psychiatric phenomena have been growing since the introduction of chlorpromazine in the 1950s for the treatment of schizophrenia, there have never been definitive biomarkers indicating the presence or absence of a diagnosable condition. The power of biomarkers over the psyche cannot be underestimated. While much of this excitement about biomarkers may be spurious to the actual treatment of mental disorders, such markers may be very helpful in the process of refining diagnostic categories which may eventually have treatment implications. While the DSM-V criteria already under development are unlikely to include imaging findings as any component of diagnosis, future editions may feature more meaningful subtypes, algorithms for dealing with intermediate cases, or a means for understanding the dimensionality of psychopathology (perhaps collapsing Axis 1 and Axis 2) based on neurodiagnostic information. That is, biomarkers may have a role in understanding dimensionality and the common origins of certain disorders (e.g., depression and anxiety) by providing biological principles around which to organize thinking in these areas.

Finally, it is instructive to reflect on the machine-driven approach to classification as a variant of the dust-bowl empiricism of the mid-twentieth-century psychology. Like much item-driven personality assessment of the past, the watchword is again "Let the algorithms sort it out." So, whereas much of clinical cognitive neuroscience is struggling to forge links between basic cognitive and affective sciences and how individual differences in these mechanisms translate into psychopathology, this algorithm-based work represents something of a step back to the future. In this respect, the work of basic psychologists and neuroscientists is not as important as the work of signal-processing scholars and statisticians.

This is doubtless overstating the dichotomy between empirical and theory-driven science for dramatic effect. While the emphasis at this phase in the development of assessment and neurodiagnostics is definitely on the empirical side of the balance, this is an iterative process that will give rise in turn to understanding the meaning of the differences detected. This is because the data derived from neuroimaging has biological meaning beyond that used for the purpose of the diagnosis itself (in contrast, for instance, with some questions on the MMPI, which have no real purpose beyond obtaining a scaled score). There is a great reservoir of knowledge about the brain regions that will differentiate cases and controls. This reservoir can be tapped to further understand the illness itself, which may, in turn, have the potential to suggest new interventions.

It is still too early to say whether neurodiagnostics will revolutionize clinical assessment or be an atrocious waste of time and treasure. As we have shown, there are now the first buds of promise in this neglected approach to neuroimaging data. The development of the field has been slow because it required the marriage of modern marvels of physics—MRI, or in one case MEG—to computationally intensive algorithms with the capacity to sift through immense amount of data such machines produce. As with any newly weds, there remains a great deal of work to do while this tech-heavy couple get their house in order. But there is reason to pay attention. This may be the avenue from which comes the next generation of big ideas in personality and clinical assessment.

References

Anderson, A. W., Heptulla, R. A., Driesen, N., Flanagan, D., Goldberg, P. A., Jones, T. W., et al. (2006). Effects of hypoglycemia on human brain activation measured with fMRI. *Magnetic Resonance Imaging, 24,* 693–697.

Calhoun, V. D., Adali, T., Giuliani, N. R., Pekar, J. J., Kiehl, K. A., & Pearlson, G. D. (2005). Method for multimodal analysis of independent source differences in schizophrenia: Combining gray matter structural and auditory oddball functional data. *Human Brain Mapping, 27*(1), 47–62.

Calhoun, V. D., Maciejewski, P. K., Pearlson, G. D., & Kiehl, K. A. (2007). Temporal lobe and "default" hemodynamic brain modes discriminate between schizophrenia and bipolar disorder. *Human Brain Mapping, 29*(11), 1265–1275.

Georgopoulos, A. P., Elissaios, K., Arthur, C. L., Scott, M. L., Joshua, K. L., Aurelio, A. A., et al. (2007). Synchronous neural interactions assessed by magnetoencephalography: A functional biomarker for brain disorders. *Journal of Neural Engineering, 4,* 349.

Heeger, D. J., & Ress, D. (2002). What does fMRI tell us about neuronal activity. *Nature Reviews Neuroscience, 3,* 142–151.

Jakobsen, K. D., Frederiksen, J. N., Hansen, T., Jansson, L. B., Parnas, J., & Werge, T. (2005). Reliability of clinical ICD-10 schizophrenia diagnoses. *Nordic Journal of Psychiatry, 59,* 209–212.

Kozel, F. A., Johnson, K. A., Mu, Q., Grenesko, E. L., Laken, S. J., & George, M. S. (2005). Detecting deception using functional magnetic resonance imaging. *Biological Psychiatry, 58,* 605–613.

Langleben, D. D., Loughead, J. W., Bilker, W. B., Ruparel, K., Childress, A. R., Busch, S. I., et al. (2005). Telling truth from lie in individual subects with fast event-related fMRI. *Human Brain Mapping, 26,* 262–272.

Laurienti, P. J., Field, A. S., Burdette, J. H., Maldjian, J. A., Yen, Y.-F., & Moody, D. M. (2002). Dietary caffeine consumption modulates fMRI measures. *Nueroimage, 17,* 751–757.

Lee, T. M. C., Liu, H.-L., Tan, L.-H., Chan, C. C. H., Mahankali, S., Feng, C.-M., et al. (2002). Lie detection by functional magnetic resonance imaging. *Human Brain Mapping, 15,* 157–164.

Lim, K. O., Chamchong, J., Bell, C. J., Fried, P., Mueller, B. A., & MacDonald, A. W., III. (2007). *Consistency of the resting state network within individual healthy participants across time.* Paper presented at the 46th Annual Meeting of the American College of Neuropsychopharmacology. Retrieved.

Liston, A. D., Lund, T. E., Salek-Haddadi, A., Hamandi, K., Friston, K. J., & Lemieux, L. (2006). Modelling cardiac signal as a confound in EEG–fMRI and its application in focal epilepsy studies. *NeuroImage, 30,* 827–834.

Liu, T. T., Behzadi, Y., Restom, K., Uludag, K., Lu, K., Buracas, G. T., et al. (2004). Caffeine alters the temporal dynamics of the visual bold response. *NeuroImage, 23,* 1402–1413.

Logothetis, N. K., Pauls, J., Augath, M., Trinath, T., & Oeltermann, A. (2001). Neurophysiological investigation of the basis of the fMRI signal. *Nature, 412*(6843), 150–157.

MacDonald, A. W., III, Carter, C. S., Kerns, J. G., Ursu, S., Barch, D. M., Holmes, A., et al. (2005). Specificity of prefrontal dysfunction and context processing deficits to schizophrenia in a never-medicated first-episode sample. *American Journal of Psychiatry, 162,* 475–484.

Manoach, D. S., Halpern, E. F., Kramer, T. S., Chang, Y., Goff, D. C., Rauch, S. L., et al. (2001). Test–retest reliability of a functional MRI working memory paradigm in normal and schizophrenic subjects. *American Journal of Psychiatry, 158,* 955–958.

McGonigle, D. J., Howseman, A. M., Athwal, B. S., Friston, K.J., Frackowiak, R. S. J., & Holmes, A. P. (2000). Variability in fMRI: An examination of intersession differences. *NeuroImage, 11,* 708–734.

Mintun, M., Lundstrom, B., Snyder, A. Z., Vlessenko, A. G., Shulman, G. L., & Raichle, M. E. (2001). Blood flow and oxygen deliver to human brain during functional activity: Theoretical modeling and experimental data. *Proceedings of the National Academy of Sciences of the United States of America, 98,* 6859–6864.

Seifritz, E., Bilecen, D., Hanggi, D., Haselhorst, R., Radu, E. W., Wetzel, S., et al. (2000). Effect of ethanol on bold response to acoustic stimulation: Implications for neuropharmacological fMRI. *Psychiatry Research Neuroimaging, 99,* 1–13.

Smith, S. M., Beckmann, C. F., Ramnani, N., Woolrich, M. W., Bannister, P. R., Jenkinson, M., et al. (2005). Variability in fMRI: A re-examination of inter-session differences. *Human Brain Mapping, 24,* 248–257.

Shmueli, K., van Gelderen, P., de Zwart, J. A., Horovitz, S. G., Fukunaga, M., Jansma, J. M., et al. (2007). Low-frequency fluctuations in the cardiac rate as a source of variance in the resting-state fMRI bold signal. *NeuroImage, 38,* 306–320.

Specht, K., Willmes, K., Shah, N. J., & Jancke, L. (2003). Assessment of reliability in functional imaging studies. *Journal of Magnetic Resonance Imaging, 17,* 463–471.

Thiel, C. M. F., & Fink, G. R. (2007). Visual and auditory altertness: Modality-specific and supramodel neural mechanisms and their modulation by nicotine. *Journal of Neurophysiology, 97,* 2758–2768.

Thomason, M. E., Burrows, B. E., Gabrieli, J. D. E., & Glover, G. H. (2005). Breath holding reveals differences in fMRI bold signal in children and adults. *Neuroimage, 25,* 824–837.

Woo, K. P., Sevilla, C. C., & Obrocea, G. V. (2006). Factors influencing the stability of psychiatric diagnoses in the emergency setting: Review of 934 consecutively inpatient admissions. *General Hospital Psychiatry, 28,* 434–436.

PART 5

Specific Populations

Clinical Personality Assessment with Asian Americans

Sumie Okazaki, Mimi Okazaki, *and* Stanley Sue

Abstract

Asian American population is a fast-growing population with enormous within-group heterogeneity. Although the past decade has seen significant gains in psychological research on this population, there continues to be notable paucity of research in some areas of clinical personality assessment with Asian American clients. This chapter's goal is to provide guidelines for practical considerations in conducting clinical personality assessment with Asian Americans. The chapter reviews recent research on the use of clinical assessment measures with Asian Americans and presents general guidelines for clinical assessment, followed by the case example of an Asian American client in a forensic assessment case. The chapter concludes with a discussion of remaining challenges and future directions.

Keywords: Asian American, clinical assessment, Asians, MMPI-2, cultural competence

Clinicians and researchers conducting personality assessment of a culturally different client are faced with the formidable task of evaluating the contribution of cultural factors to an individual's personality structure and functioning. With Asian Americans, the difficulty of the task is magnified due to a number of factors. First, there is an enormous degree of heterogeneity within this population on a number of important dimensions including culture of origin, languages, history in Asia, immigration and settlement history, and so forth. Second, there are no existing norms for this population even for the most extensively used assessment tools such as the Minnesota Multiphasic Personality Inventory (MMPI; Greene, 1987; Hall, Bansal, & Lopez, 1999), and many current versions of widely used instruments are not available in Asian languages. Finally, there is no consensus on how to conceptualize individual and group differences on measures of personality.

In the United States, the term Asian is used to designate persons from more than 20 culturally and linguistically distinct ethnic groups from East Asia, Southeast Asia, and the Indian subcontinent. Asian population in the United States has continued to grow in numbers in the past few decades. For example, the 1990 census (U.S. Bureau of the Census, 1993) showed the Asian and Pacific Islander population to number 7.3 million, or 2.9% of the U.S. population. The 2000[1] census showed that the population had reached 11.9 million, thus comprising 4.2% of the U.S. population (U.S. Bureau of the Census, 2004). The census bureau estimated Asian population in July 2005 to be at 14.4 million or 5% of the U.S. population. Between 2004 and 2005, Asian population grew at 3%—highest of any race group in the same period (U.S. Bureau of the Census, 2000). Chinese was the largest ethnic group at 3.3 million, followed by Filipinos (2.8 million), Asian Indians (2.5 million), Koreans (1.4 million), Japanese (1.2 million), and Vietnamese (1.2 million). Other Asian ethnic groups that compose at least 1% of the U.S. Asian population include Cambodian, Hmong, Laotian, Pakistani, and Thai. Other Asian groups include those who trace their ancestry to Bangladesh, Malaysia, Sri Lanka, Indonesia, and Nepal. With the exception of Japanese Americans, the majority

(60%) of Asian Americans in 1997 were born in foreign countries (U.S. Bureau of the Census, 1999). According to the 2000 census (U.S. Bureau of the Census, 2004), nearly one-third of Asian Americans were born in the U.S. (31.1%), another third were foreign-born naturalized U.S. citizens (34.4%), and the final third were foreign-born noncitizens (34.5%). Asian Americans also tend to be geographically concentrated and many are also linguistically isolated. The 2000 census indicated that over half (or 51%) of the Asian Americans lived in just three states: New York, California, and Hawaii. And of the 9.5 million Asians aged 5 and over, 79% spoke a language other than English at home and about 40% spoke English less than "very well."

Given such a diverse population, the purpose of this chapter is to provide guidelines for practical considerations in conducting a personality assessment of persons of Asian descent. To this end, the chapter is organized into two main sections: (1) a review of existing research on the use of clinical assessment measures with Asian Americans; and (2) practical considerations and guidelines for assessment. Due to gaps in research on personality assessment of Asian Americans, some of our discussion will be based on the literature from ethnic minority research and personality research on the Asians overseas.

A Review

Although psychological research on Asian Americans has grown in volume and in scope within the past decade (Leong, Okazaki, & David, 2006), there appears to be relatively little research on clinical personality assessment instruments and their uses.[2] However, across the Pacific, personality scales such as the MMPI-2 are enjoying increasing usage in various Asian nations (Butcher, Cheung, & Lim, 2003), and there is an active program of research in the cross-cultural adaptation of the Chinese Personality Assessment Inventory across Asia (F. M. Cheung, S. F. Cheung, Wada, & Zhang, 2003). In Asian American psychology, the more active area of research in personality assessment surrounds the development and validation of scales designed to assess cultural identity and values that characterize this population. In addition there have been some new findings from a nation-wide psychiatric epidemiological assessment of Asian Americans (e.g., Takeuchi et al., 2007). In the practical considerations section of this chapter, we discuss the implications and applications of these various developments to the practice of clinical personality assessment with Asian Americans.

MMPI Studies

MMPI STUDIES WITH ASIAN AMERICAN POPULATIONS

The MMPI is perhaps the most extensively studied personality instrument across cultures (Butcher, 1985) with available translated versions estimated to be in 125 languages (Lonner, 1990). Earlier, there was a concern about its use with ethnic minorities in the United States because of the lack of norms among minority populations (Colligan, Osborne, Swenson, & Offord, 1983) or because of interpretive bias (Dana, 1988). However, a review by Greene (1987) found no consistent main effects of majority or minority ethnic group status on the MMPI scales. Another meta-analytic review of MMPI and MMPI-2 research (Hall, Bansal, & Lopez, 1999) had also found that these instruments on the whole did not portray African American and Latino populations as more pathological than the White American population. Although these studies may have allayed some of the reservations regarding its use with ethnic minorities, the meta-analyses did not include Asian Americans because of lack of data. To this day, there continue to be very few studies on the use of the MMPI-2 with Asian Americans (in the United States).[3]

The two early studies with the original MMPI had found that scores on various clinical and validity scales among Asian Americans tended to be significantly more elevated (Marsella, Sanborn, Kameoka, Shizuru, & Brennan, 1975; S. Sue & D. W. Sue, 1974), especially among men. However, when Tsushima and Onorato (1982) compared the MMPI scores of White and Japanese American medical and neurological patients in Hawaii, they found no significant ethnic differences in the T-scores of validity or clinical scales when diagnoses were matched across ethnic groups. Significant gender effect was found across the two ethnic groups such that males scored higher than females on some of the scales (1, 2, 3, 4, 5, 7, 8, and 9) and females scored higher than males on Scale 0. The researchers suggested that their results, in contrast to those of the earlier study by Sue and Sue (1974), might be due to their matching the ethnic groups on diagnostic classifications.

Limited data on Asian Americans' performance on the MMPI-2 are available. Sue, Keefe, Enomoto, Durvasula, and Chao (1996) administered the MMPI-2 to a group of 133 English-speaking Asian American and 91 White American university students. Comparable internal consistency estimates (alpha coefficients) for the validity and clinical scales were reported for the two ethnic groups. Less acculturated

Asian Americans scored significantly higher than either the acculturated Asian Americans or White Americans on some of the clinical scales (F, 1, 2, 4, 6, 7, 8, 0). The mean profiles of the groups showed that acculturated Asian Americans and White Americans had similar profiles, whereas less acculturated Asian Americans scored in the more pathological direction. Tsai and Pike (2000) also investigated the effects of acculturation on the MMPI-2 scores among 90 Asian American university students. The Asian American sample was divided into three acculturation groups on the basis of an acculturation scale: low acculturated (foreign-born, mean number of years in the United States 5.0), bicultural (97% foreign-born, mean of 14.8 years in States), and high acculturated (46% foreign-born, mean of 15.7 years in States). Compared with a matched sample of White American students, low acculturated Asian Americans scored significantly higher on 9 of the 13 validity and clinical scales, whereas bicultural Asian Americans were elevated on 6 scales. Highly acculturated Asian Americans did not differ in their profile from the White Americans. Even with the limited range of acculturation among Asian American university students compared with the general Asian American population, the results from the S. Sue and colleagues and the Tsai and Pike studies point to the enormous influence of acculturation on the MMPI-2 response patterns in this population.[4]

Several studies have been conducted on the response patterns of Asian international students in the United States to the English version of the MMPI-2. Stevens, Kwan, and Graybill (1993) compared the MMPI-2 scores of 25 Chinese international students with those of a matched sample of 21 White American university students. Although the scores for both groups were within normal limits, Chinese men had a significantly higher T-score on Scale 0 and Chinese women had a significantly higher T-score on L scale than their White counterparts. In another study (Kwan, 2000), 35 Chinese international students responded to all the MMPI-2 items and also indicated which items were difficult to understand. On average, 7.5 items were rated as "difficult to understand" by the respondents with a range from 0 to 41 (out of 567 items). The number of items reported as difficult to understand was negatively correlated with their English proficiency test score. However, the overall MMPI-2 profile of the sample was within normal range, and their difficulty comprehending a small number of the items on the MMPI-2 scale did not appear to have a significant effect on their profile. Finally, Gong and Kwan (2000)

examined the MMPI-2 responses among 57 Korean international students studying in the United States. The respondents also rated 67 items that have shown at least 25% endorsement differences between Korean and U.S. normative samples (Han, 1996) on three cultural dimensions (response frequency, item desirability, and perceived shamefulness). Korean international students' mean MMPI-2 scale scores were generally more elevated than those of the U.S. normative sample or the Chinese international student sample. Perceived response frequency (i.e., "How frequently would Koreans give this response?") and perceived item desirability were related to the endorsement of items on some of the MMPI-2 scales. It should be kept in mind with this collection of MMPI-2 data on Asian international students that the small sample size in each study may had severely limited the studies' ability to detect cultural differences.

The MMPI and MMPI-2 studies with Asian Americans reviewed thus far are limited by the selective nature of the populations studied (either college students or medical patients), and sample sizes tend to be small. Consequently, the generalizability of these results to the Asian American population is not known. In addition, the MMPI or the MMPI-2 was administered in English and no translations were performed. However, the question of translation equivalence still remains, as it is not clear whether Asian American participants in the studies were as proficient in the English language as the non-Asian comparison subjects. There is some evidence to suggest that Asian Americans who have lived in the United States for several generations still experience some difficulty with English language mastery (Watanabe, 1973). Kwon (2002) had also called for caution in interpreting the MMPI-2 profiles, especially among those who are relatively less acculturated to mainstream American culture, as they may be reticent to request clarification for unclear idiomatic expressions. Because of this, the results should be interpreted as preliminary, with a need for further validation with larger and more representative samples of English-speaking Asian American populations.

An exception to the MMPI research with Asian Americans is the case of Southeast Asian refugee population. The MMPI-2 has been translated into several Asian languages.[5] In contrast to the MMPI translation efforts into East Asian languages that have been carried out primarily in Asia, the Vietnamese and the Hmong versions were developed primarily for use with Vietnamese and Hmong refugees residing in the United States

(Dienard, Butcher, Thao, Vang, & Hang, 1996; Tran, 1996). Of note, the Hmong translation of the MMPI-2 is also available on an audiocassette so that it can be administered aurally to illiterate monolingual Hmong individuals (Dienard et al., 1996). Preliminary validation studies of the Vietnamese and Hmong versions have been conducted with bilingual participants. Tran (1996) found that the test–retest reliability for a 2–8-day interval between the Vietnamese and English versions ranged from .51 to .87 with 35 bilingual Vietnamese Americans. Dienard and colleagues (1996) reported the 7-day test–retest reliability between the Hmong and English versions as .38 to .80 with 32 bilingual Hmong Americans.

In an effort to validate the Vietnamese MMPI-2, Tran (1996) administered the instrument to 193 Vietnamese American adults (94 males) in the St. Paul and Minneapolis area. The sample consisted largely of unemployed adults (63%) who were attending college or vocational or technical training. Over half of the sample had lived in the United States for 2 years or less. The mean profiles of the Vietnamese male and female samples plotted against the American norms were within the normal range, although Scales F and 8 were slightly higher than the American norms. Factor analysis of the Vietnamese MMPI-2 revealed a factor structure similar to that of the American normative sample. Similar to the conclusions reached by Tsai and Pike (2000) regarding the acculturation effect on the MMPI-2 scores, Tran (1996) also reported that the greatest differences from the American normative profile were seen in the Vietnamese American individuals who had immigrated most recently and were least acculturated to the United States.

In a more recent study, Dong and Church (2003) administered the Vietnamese MMPI-2 to 143 Vietnamese refugee adults in California. Compared to the U.S. norm, the mean scores in this population were moderately elevated (T above 60) on F and 8, replicating Tran's (1996) findings. There were also elevations on L, 1, 2, and 7 scales. In addition, Dong and Church found that the older age and lower levels of acculturation were associated with prior exposure to trauma, which in turn was associated with scale elevations on MMPI-2. These findings are likely the reflection of the patterns of Vietnamese refugee migration, in which those who were older tended to be exposed to more pre- and post-migration trauma and also migrated as older adults (and thus remained least acculturated). It is possible that there is more MMPI-2 research with Southeast Asian

refugees because of the higher rates of posttraumatic stress disorder (PTSD) and other significant trauma-related psychopathology in this population than in the East Asian or South Asian immigrant populations. Nonetheless, MMPI-2 (or other objective personality instrument) research with Asian American population is an understudied area in need of more research investment.

MMPI-2 STUDIES WITH OVERSEAS ASIAN POPULATIONS

Of the studies performed on Asians, most systematic investigations of the MMPI-2 with Asian populations overseas have been carried out in Hong Kong and China. Cheung and Song (1989) reviewed 26 studies of the Chinese-language version of the original MMPI on Chinese psychiatric populations. They found that the translation equivalence of the Chinese MMPI had been established through numerous back-translations and modification of items (Song, 1991). Thus, questions about the cross-cultural validity of the instrument were directed to its conceptual and metric equivalence. The cumulative results of the studies demonstrated that the Chinese version adequately differentiated between Chinese psychiatric patients and normal controls. Three scales (F, 2, and 8) were elevated among the normal Chinese subjects, yet Chinese psychiatric patients were elevated even higher than the baseline norm, often in the range of 3 standard deviations above the American norm for normal subjects. The patterns of profile elevations on the Chinese MMPI for major mental disorders (e.g., schizophrenia, mania, depression, and neurotic disorders) were comparable to the profile patterns of American subjects. On the basis of the review, Cheung and Song recommended the clinical applications of the Chinese version of the MMPI to Chinese, with a cautionary note on interpreting moderate elevations on Scales F, 2, and 8. Because of the significant sample size of the Chinese MMPI studies, metric equivalence could be addressed. Specifically, Cheung and Song suggested allowing for an adjustment of 1 additional standard deviation on Scales F, 2, and 8 when predicting psychopathology among Chinese.

Cheung and Ho (1997) administered the Chinese translation of the MMPI for Adolescents (MMPI-A) to 565 male and 664 female Chinese adolescents in Hong Kong. The Chinese adolescents' MMPI-A T-scores plotted against the American adolescent norms were elevated by more than 1 standard deviation on Scale 2 for both genders, on the L scale for female students, and on the A-lse scale (Adolescent Low Self-esteem) for male students. On Scale 2, most of the questions that differentiated Chinese adolescents from American teens were related to modesty, preference for inactivity, admittance of strange behaviors, and social avoidance. Cheung and Ho suggested that there is difficulty in establishing whether these scores reflect a higher level of psychopathology in Chinese adolescents or cultural differences in item interpretation, but they believe that previous studies on the Chinese MMPI (Cheung, Song, & Zhang, 1996) support the latter view. They proposed that it would be misleading to understand the elevations as evidence of psychopathology without first considering the cultural context surrounding those elevations. The joint use of Chinese and U.S. norms, as well as more studies with clinical samples, was recommended.

Extending their work on the Chinese MMPI, Cheung, Song, and Zhang (1996) reported on the validation of the Chinese MMPI-2, which was developed collaboratively between the researchers in Hong Kong and in the People's Republic of China (PRC). The pattern of scores for the Hong Kong and PRC normal samples were very similar, and the T-scores (plotted against the U.S. norms) fell within 1 standard deviation of the American norms, with none of the clinical or validity scales exceeding a T-score of 70. However, given the new MMPI-2 cutoff score of 65, T-scores of several scales (e.g., F, 1, 2, 7, 8) remained high. This pattern was consistent with the patterns of elevations on the original Chinese MMPI, although the T-scores tended to be lower in the MMPI-2. MMPI-2 studies with Chinese clinical populations reported by Cheung, Song, and Zhang (1996) suggested clinical validity of the Chinese MMPI-2.

The MMPI-2 has also been translated into Japanese (Shiota, Krauss, & Clark, 1996), Korean (Han, 1996), and Thai (Pongpanich, 1996). For the most part, there appears to be preliminary evidence that these translated versions have adequate psychometric characteristics. Shiota et al. (1996) found that 1,356 Japanese college students' mean profiles, plotted against the American norms, produced scores within the normative T-score range for both men and women. A study in Thailand (Pongpanich, 1996) with candidates for the Thai army revealed that responses to the Thai MMPI-2 strongly resembled U.S. norms. However, preliminary validation of the MMPI-2 with 726 college students in Korea (Han, 1996) indicated that the mean profiles of Korean men and women were elevated compared

with the American standardization norm, with significant elevations on Scales F and 8. The Korean MMPI-2 appeared to have adequate internal reliability and external validity, at least in this sample of college students. In a more recent effort toward establishing the cross-cultural equivalence of the Korean MMPI-2 with the U.S. version, Chung, Weed, and Han (2006) administered the MMPI-2 in Korean and English to 53 bilingual Korean Americans within a 1-week interval. For both versions, there were mean elevations (above T-score of 60) on F, 2, and 8 scales. The mean profiles of the Korean and English versions were similar to each other and to those found in an earlier study in Korea (Han, 1996). In a study with 169 college students and 50 hospitalized psychiatric patients in South Korea, Hahn (2005) used a simulation design (with instructions to fake good or to fake bad) to show that the Korean MMPI-2 validity scales were successful in classifying faking good and faking bad profiles. It appears then that culture-specific norms may be necessary for the use of the MMPI-2 with Korean population. Of note, Roberts, Han, and Weed (2006) recently expanded the potential use of Korean MMPI-2 for assessing culture-bound syndromes by developing a subscale for *Hwa-Byung*, a Korean illness pattern involving somatic and psychiatric symptoms. Interested readers are referred to the excellent review of the use of the MMPI-2 in Asia by Butcher, Cheung, and Lim (2003).

Measures of Asian Personality

One criticism of the imposed-etic approach to the assessment of Asians and Asian Americans, such as the use of the MMPI-2, is that Western personality theories underlying assessment measures may not be consistent with the culture or cultural explanations of Asians and Asian Americans. To counter such critique, there have been various efforts by researchers in Asian nations to construct culture-specific measures of personality. A comprehensive coverage of such efforts is beyond the scope of this present chapter. However, Cheung (2004) provides an excellent review of cross-cultural research involving use of Western personality instruments with Asian populations, the development of indigenous personality measures from an emic (or culture-specific) approach, and the trend toward the combined emic–etic (culture-specific and culture-universal) approach. Cheung, Cheung, Wada, and Zhang (2003) also provide a thorough review of the efforts to develop indigenous measures of personality assessment in India, Korea, Japan, the Philippines, Taiwan, Hong Kong, and mainland China. Here, we feature some of the notable recent developments on the Chinese Personality Assessment Inventory that may be relevant to the clinical assessment of Asian Americans.

Prior to the development of the Chinese Personality Assessment Inventory (CPAI; Cheung et al., 1996), there had been earlier efforts to implement the combined emic–etic approach toward identifying and constructing instruments to assess Chinese personality. For example, Yang and Bond (1990) identified five bipolar factors that may be regarded as the basic emic dimensions of Chinese personality perception: social orientation–self-centeredness; competence–impotence; expressiveness–conservatism; self-control–impulsiveness; and optimism–neuroticism. The researchers then examined the degree of overlap between these indigenous Chinese big five factors with the American big five. They concluded that overall, the American factors can be combined to reasonably identify four of the five indigenous Chinese factors (all but the optimism factor), even though there was one-to-one correspondence for only two factors, social orientation (with agreeableness) and optimism (with emotional stability).

Given that indigenous Chinese personality factors did not correspond well with the Western personality factors (Yang & Bond, 1990), the Multi-trait Personality Inventory (MTPI) was developed by Chinese scholars (Cheung, Conger, Hau, Lew, & Lau, 1992) specifically to address the inadequacy of the imposed-etic approach in dealing with functional and conceptual equivalence in personality assessment. The MTPI was developed from Chinese cultural perspective to identify which of the indigenous Chinese personality dimensions are constant across four major Chinese populations (mainland China, Taiwan, Hong Kong, and the United States). The MTPI consists of 122 items that represent attitudes, beliefs, typical behaviors, and affective reactions rated on 6-point bipolar scales. Cheung et al. (1992) found that all Chinese perceived themselves as trusting, principled, tolerant, responsible, self-controlled, and opposed to permissive sex. Such personality traits appear consistent with the Confucian values indigenous to Chinese culture.

In their efforts to examine the relationship between personality and values in a Hong Kong Chinese sample, Yik and Tang (1996) criticized a similar earlier effort by Luk and Bond (1993) that

had used the NEO PI-R (Costa & McCrae, 1992). Yik and Tang used the Sino-American Person Perception Scale (SAPPS; Luk & Bond, 1992), which was developed using the lexical approach in culling trait adjectives from the American and indigenous Chinese written materials. The Chinese SAPPS consists of 51 bipolar adjective scales that tap eight personality dimensions (emotional stability, sociability, application, openness to experience, assertiveness, restraint, helpfulness, and intellect). It had previously been documented that four SAPPS dimensions (application, restraint, intellect, and assertiveness) load onto NEO PI-R conscientiousness factor. Yik and Tang noted that the subdivision of conscientiousness into these four distinct dimensions enhanced the predictive utility of this important construct for their study of value endorsement in Chinese culture that would have not been uncovered with the use of an imposed-etic instrument such as the NEO PI-R.

The CPAI (F. M. Cheung et al., 1996) is a multiphasic personality inventory developed to assess personality characteristics for normal and clinical populations. The CPAI was developed in the early 1990s through the collaboration of Hong Kong and mainland Chinese psychologists so as to maximize its applicability to different Chinese societies. Of all the personality assessment instruments developed in Asia, this instrument appears to have enjoyed the most sustained effort toward validation and application. Care was taken to assess personality constructs relevant to the daily lives of Chinese people by sampling personality descriptions from contemporary Chinese novels, Chinese proverbs, psychological literature, professional opinions, and data collected on self-descriptors to arrive at 21 normal personality scales, 12 clinical scales, and 2 validity scales. Constructs that were considered of particular relevance to Chinese culture included harmony, *ren qin* (relationship orientation), modernization, thrift, "Ah-Q mentality" (defensiveness), graciousness, veraciousness–slickness, face, family orientation, and somatization. The CPAI has undergone preliminary psychometric validation and standardization with Hong Kong and PRC samples (Yung et al., 2000). Of note, the interpersonal relatedness factor that is unique to the CPAI was noted for its potential utility to examine an aspect of Chinese personality that would not have been assessed by Western personality measures (Cheung, 2004).

A joint factor analysis of the CPAI and the NEO PI-R (Cheung et al., 2001) found that the interpersonal relatedness factor comprised of mainly indigenous scales that assess Chinese cultural relationship values (e.g., maintaining harmony, avoiding conflict, saving face, adhering to norms and reciprocity, exchanging favors and affection according to implicit codes) was unique to CPAI and did not load onto any of the big five factors. However, none of the CPAI scales loaded onto the openness factor of the NEO PI-R. Consequently, additional items were written to assess the openness factor for the revised version of the CPAI. Other changes were also made to the original CPAI such as reducing the number of personality scale items and increasing the number of items in the clinical scales. The revised version was restandardized with 1,911 adults from different regions of mainland China as well as from Hong Kong (Cheung, Cheung, & Zhang, 2004a).

The CPAI has been translated into English, which is useful to note for its potential application with Asian American clients. Cheung, Cheung, Leung, Ward, and Leong (2003) showed that the English version of the original CPAI administered to Singaporeans as well as White Americans replicated the four-factor structure of dependability, interpersonal relatedness, social potency, and individualism. A recent study in Singapore with the English version of the CPAI-2 replicated the four-factor structure (Cheung, Cheung, Howard, & Lim, 2006). The CPAI-2 has also been translated into Japanese and Korean, and preliminary research in Japan and Korea, as well as in Singapore, suggest its potential beyond Chinese individuals (Cheung, Cheung, Howard, & Lim, 2006).

Cheung, Kwong, and Zhang (2003) offered clinical validation of CPAI by comparing the profiles of psychiatric patients with those of normative population in Beijing as well as with those of nonpsychiatric inmates and normative sample in Hong Kong. Results indicated personality profile differences among patients diagnosed with bipolar disorder, neurotic disorder, and schizophrenia. Bipolar patients when compared with neurotic patients scored higher on harmony, face, thrift, leadership, self- versus social orientation, logical versus affective orientation, and Ah-Q mentality (defensiveness); bipolar patients scored lower on flexibility, modernization, and introversion versus extraversion. Bipolar patients compared with schizophrenic patients scored higher on leadership, adventurousness, and introversion versus extraversion. Neurotic patients compared with schizophrenic patients scored higher on emotionality, flexibility, and introversion versus extraversion; they scored lower on

responsibility, optimism versus pessimism, meticulousness, harmony, *ren qing* (relationship) orientation, face, thrift versus extravagance, self- versus social orientation, logical versus affective orientation, and Ah-Q mentality. Six scales were able to differentiate patients from controls 70.4%: pathological dependence, distortion of reality, depression, sexual maladjustment, antisocial behavior, and somatization. Eleven personality scales were able to differentiate patients from controls 70.2%: modernization, external versus internal locus of control, inferiority versus self-acceptance, *ren qing* (relationship) orientation, introversion versus extraversion, family orientation, adventurousness, self- versus social orientation, thrift versus extravagance, face, and logical and affective orientation. Four clinical scales were able to differentiate inmates from control 79.9% (pathological dependence, antisocial behavior, somatization, sexual malajustment); seven personality scales were able to correctly classify inmates 75.5% of cases (thrift vs. extravagance, optimism vs. pessimism, veraciousness vs. slickness, *ren qing* [relationship] orientation modernization, flexibility, and adventurousness). Cheung, Cheung, and Zhang (2004b) compared the results of Chinese MMPI-2 and the CPAI among Hong Kong and mainland Chinese university students. The results showed that many of the CPAI clinical scales correlated significantly with the relevant MMPI-2 scales, providing further support for the clinical validity of the CPAI.

These ongoing efforts to develop and to utilize culture-specific Asian personality measures bode well for the assessment of immigrant Asian Americans. The indigenous personality constructs identified for Chinese in Hong Kong and PRC are likely to share cultural roots with Chinese American personality. Once some of the new Asian measures are validated and standardized on the overseas Asian samples, their applicability to Asian Americans may be determined for their possible use in conjunction with the Western-constructed instruments such as the MMPI-2 or the NEO PI-R.

Measures of Asian American Psychological Experiences

Two main factors that distinguish Asian Americans from many overseas Asian populations are their experience of being socialized to various degrees in two cultures and their racial minority status in North America. Researchers have developed various measures to assess a number of culture-related constructs (e.g., acculturation, cultural values, and cultural conflicts) that will be reviewed here. Although many of the measures are relatively new or in stages of development and have not been used extensively with clinical population, they illustrate important issues regarding the assessment of cultural and race-related experiences of Asian American clients. Clinicians may wish to consider administering some of these measures or incorporating key questions from these measures into clinical interviews to gain more culture-specific information about Asian American clients.

ACCULTURATION

Recent research has produced a number of measures designed specifically to assess various levels of acculturation and cultural identification among Asian Americans rather than to measure the Asian American personality per se. Acculturation is a multifaceted process that occurs when individuals from two or more cultures have continuous first-hand contact, resulting in changes in the original cultural patterns. Enculturation refers to the process of socialization to, and maintenance of, the norms of one's indigenous or heritage culture. Acculturation and enculturation are central constructs of interest in Asian American psychology, as they have been linked to psychological and vocational functioning, attitudes toward seeking mental health services, and therapy processes (Kim, 2006). However, there is no one standard way to assess acculturation or acculturative stress in Asian American populations (Dana, 1993; Paniagua, 1994), and various concerns have been raised regarding the conceptualization and psychometric properties of existing measures of acculturation in Asian Americans (Nagata, 1994; Ponterotto, Baluch, & Carielli, 1998).

Although Suinn–Lew Asian Self-Identity and Acculturation Scale (SL-ASIA; Suinn, Ahuna, & Khoo, 1992; Suinn, Rickard-Figueroa, Lew, & Vigil, 1987), a 21-item pan-Asian measure of acculturation and identity, used to be the most widely used measure in Asian American research. The measure was modeled after the Acculturation Rating Scale for Mexican Americans (ARSMA; Cuellar, Harris, & Jasso, 1980) and was based on a unilinear measurement model in which acculturation and enculturation were conceptualized as a process that takes place along a single or unilinear continuum. The total score is interpreted as the respondent's level of acculturation, from low acculturation (high Asian identity) to high acculturation (high Western identity or assimilation). A review of published studies that used SL-ASIA (Ponterotto et al., 1998)

noted the lack of conceptual clarity behind this instrument. The original SL-ASIA classified individuals on a unidimensional index from low to high acculturation, and those individuals scoring in the mid-range were labeled as "bicultural." However, it is possible for an individual to identify highly with both the minority and the majority culture (Oetting & Beauvais, 1990). In response to these critiques, Suinn (1998) added five additional items to the SL-ASIA to allow for the assessment of acculturation as reflecting Asian and Western values, behavioral competence (i.e., how well one fits in with Asian or Western social contexts), and self-identity as a bicultural person. However, the use of this instrument has become less common in the past decade due to researchers' and clinicians' shift toward bidimensional conceptualization and measurement of acculturation and enculturation.

There are newer acculturation scales that were devised with bidimensional model in mind. Tsai, Ying, and Lee (2000) developed the General Ethnicity Questionnaire (GEQ) to test both the unidimensional and bidimensional models of acculturation. To assess the meanings of "being Chinese" and "being American," these investigators compared three Chinese American groups: American-born Chinese, immigrants who had come to the United States after age 12, and immigrants who arrived before age 12. The relationship between the two identities, Chinese and American, was assessed, as was the participants' specific engagement in cultural domains such as activities and language proficiency. The results indicated that for American-born Chinese, the domains of being American or Chinese were unrelated, but they were negatively related for immigrant Chinese. Internal validity was high for the GEQ (both American and Chinese; alpha .92) and retest reliability was .62 (SD 5.22). Although not developed specifically for Asian Americans, Vancouver Index of Acculturation (Ryder, Alden, & Paulhus, 2000) assesses acculturation to mainstream culture (10 items) and enculturation of heritage culture (10 items) and may be a shorter alternative to the GEQ. Lee, Yoon, & Liu-Tom (2006) have also tested the bidimensional model of acculturation using ARSMA-II (Cuellar, Arnold, & Maldonado, 1995) and found that this measure appears to have reliability and validity for use with Asian Americans.

CULTURAL VALUES

One criticism that has been leveled against various existing measures of acculturation and cultural orientation such as the SL-ASIA, which would also apply to the GEQ, is that they measure only the behavioral aspects of acculturation (e.g., language usage, food and entertainment preferences). To close this gap, Kim, Atkinson, and Yang (1999) developed the Asian Values Scale (AVS), which contains 36 items regarding Asian cultural values (e.g., conformity to norms, family recognition through achievement, emotional self-control, collectivism, humility, and filial piety) rated on a 7-point Likert scale. Psychometric results indicated that the AVS has adequate internal and 2-week retest reliability. Further, AVS scores were compared with those on Individualism–Collectivism (Triandis, 1995) and the SL-ASIA and there was evidence of convergent and divergent validity for the AVS. Of note, Kim et al. (1999) found that Asian Americans are quicker to adopt behavioral aspects of acculturation but slower to do so with value orientation, such that Asian values were not found to differ significantly across generations since immigration. Since the publication of the initial AVS, Kim and colleagues have offered a 25-item Asian Values Scales-Revised (AVS-R; Kim & Hong, 2004) that improved on the psychometric properties of the original version, as well as the 42-item Asian American Values Scale-Multidimensional (AAVS-M; Kim, Li, & Ng, 2005) that assesses various dimensions of Asian cultural values (e.g., conformity to norms, emotional self-control, humility) separately. Wolfe, Yang, Wong, and Atkinson (2001) developed the 18-item European American Values Scale for Asian Americans (EAVS-AA), which measures values acculturation to mainstream American values (e.g., self-confidence, autonomy). This measure has also undergone revision, and the most updated version (EAVS-AA-R; Hong, Kim, & Wolfe, 2005) contains 25 items with improved psychometric properties.

CULTURAL CONFLICTS

There has been some research to assess the intrapersonal and interpersonal effects of cultural differences. Two such constructs are loss of face and family conflict. Loss of face is defined as the threat to or loss of one's social integrity, and it has been identified as a salient interpersonal dynamic factor in Asian social relations (Zane & Yeh, 2002). The construct is conceptualized as involving face-threatening behavior in the domains of social status, ethical behavior, social propriety, and self-discipline. Sensitivity to loss of face is considered as a personality or dispositional variable unrelated to psychological maladjustment. The Loss of Face scale

(LOF; Zane & Yeh, 2002) is a 21-item self-report scale designed to assess the degree to which one is sensitive to loss of face. Each item is measured on a 7-point scale of degree of agreement with each statement. Psychometric studies show good internal consistency and show concurrent and discriminant validity with measures of other-directedness, private and public self-consciousness, social anxiety, extraversion, and acting. In a preliminary study, Zane and Yeh (2002) found a significant ethnic difference between Asian American and White American college students, even when controlled for ethnic differences on social anxiety, acting, other-directedness, social desirability, and acculturation. The LOF has been used in several studies with Asian Americans. Concerns about the loss of face was a significant predictor of acculturative distress among Chinese American immigrants (Kwan & Sodowsky, 1997) and a protective factor against Asian American men's sexual aggression (Hall, DeGarmo, Eap, Teten, & Sue, 2006; Hall, Sue, Narang, & Lilly, 2000; Hall, Teten, DeGarmo, Sue, & Stephens, 2005). These findings point to the potential role that concerns with loss of face play in Asian Americans' interpersonal behavior. The LOF may be a useful instrument to include in assessment and treatment planning with Asian American clients.

Varying levels of acculturation between children and parents have been linked to family conflicts within immigrant families, and levels of family conflict in turn have been documented to predict delinquent behavior in Chinese American adolescents (Chen, Greenberger, Lester, Dong, & Guo, 1998). Thus, assessing the level of family conflict could have enormous clinical implications for Asian Americans. Lee, Choe, Kim, and Ngo (2000) described the construction and validation of their Asian American Family Conflicts Scale (FCS), a self-report measure containing 10 typical Asian American family conflicts that are rated for likelihood of occurrence and seriousness of conflict. Typical conflict areas include making one's own decision, importance of social life, sacrifice for the family, and so on. The likelihood scale correlated with socioeconomic and cultural variables and with measures of family cohesion, adaptability, and parent–child communication. A recent study (Lee & Liu, 2001) found that Asian American college students reported higher likelihood of intergenerational family conflicts than their Hispanic and White American counterparts. A greater use of indirect coping mechanisms was found to mediate the effect of family conflicts on psychological effects for Asian Americans and White Americans. This scale has also been used successfully with Hmong American college students (Su, Lee, & Vang, 2005). The results thus far suggest that the FCS is also a useful measure that can characterize ethnic-specific dynamics of Asian American individuals.

In addition to Lee et al.'s (2000) FCS, there is another scale of cultural conflict that is specific to South Asian–American women. Inman, Ladany, Constantine, and Morano (2001) created a 24-item Cultural Values Conflict Scale that assesses the extent to which a South Asian–American woman feels distressed over cultural conflicts between South Asian values and mainstream American values. Sample items include: "I feel conflicted about my behaviors and options as a woman within the South Asian and in the American culture" (sex-role expectations subscale item), and "I feel guilty when my personal actions and decisions go against my family's expectations" (intimate relations subscale item). Inman et al. reported that the scale has adequate internal consistency, test–retest reliability, and validity.

Summary

Taken together, the measures that have been developed to capture the specific aspects of the Asian American psychological experience demonstrate promising efforts to understand what may underlie cultural influences on the personality of Asian Americans. However, a critical shortcoming of these newer Asian American measures is that because they were developed primarily in university settings with English-speaking, highly acculturated Asian American college students, their reliability and validity with other Asian Americans are uncertain. Moreover, most measures—with few exceptions that have been noted—are available only in English, which limits their utility in clinical personality assessments with non-English-speaking Asian American clients. Further research on the relation between these measures and those commonly used in personality assessment may be helpful in examining the gaps in cultural equivalence of personality assessment.

Practical Considerations in Conducting Culturally Responsive Assessment
Locating the Client in a Cultural-Ecological Context

Cross-cultural and ethnic minority assessment scholars have long argued that ethnic minorities cannot easily be compared with members of the dominant cultural group using established assessment measures and techniques (e.g., Helms, 1992; Jones & Thorne, 1987). Generally speaking, the various guidelines for culturally responsive assessment agree that one must go beyond just noting the client's ethnicity or nationality in the assessment. Helms (1992), for example, asserted that "knowledge of a person's racial group membership reveals nothing about the amount or type of culture the person has absorbed" (p. 1091). Nevertheless, there are different opinions as to how to best incorporate culture into the actual assessment process. Following the "culturalist" perspective advocated by Helms (1992) called for specification and measurement of race-related psychological characteristics (e.g., behavior, beliefs, values, identification) that are hypothesized to describe and differentiate racial groups, many clinical guidelines (including the previous edition of this chapter) had recommended an administration of brief paper-and-pencil measures of acculturation and racial identity to ethnic minorities in clinical assessment. However, Helms's recommendation to measure race-related factors was made in a research context. Hays (2001) cautioned against the automatic administration of a measure of acculturation in clinical assessment, as the notion that "their culture needs assessing" may offend some ethnic minority individuals. Instead, Hays asserted that it would be more respectful to assess the client's cultural identity more directly through interviews.

Further, it should be noted that many available measures of acculturation and cultural or ethnic identity for Asian Americans were developed primarily with Asian American college population for research (rather than clinical) purposes. Consequently, most measures are available only in English and are appropriate for highly educated, English-fluent, college-age individuals. Nevertheless, measures specifically designed to assess behavioral acculturation (e.g., GEQ: Tsai et al., 2000) or value acculturation (e.g., AVS: Kim et al., 1999) among Asian Americans may be useful as preliminary measures for highly educated Asian American adults.

Extensive and detailed intake of the client's history is a critical step in placing the client's personality assessment responses within his or her culture or sociocultural context. For Asian Americans, it is especially important to obtain information regarding the client's nativity (i.e., U.S.-born vs. foreign-born), generational status, and their English proficiency as early in the assessment process as possible. Data from a recently conducted national psychiatric epidemiological study of Asian Americans suggested that the generational status (including nativity and age at immigration) in conjunction with gender is associated with mental health patterns in complex ways. For instance, Takeuchi, Hong, Gile, and Alegria (2007) found that among Asian American women, immigrant women had lower rates of lifetime and 12-month prevalence of most mental disorders than U.S.-born women. However, among Asian American men, those who spoke English proficiently had much lower lifetime and 12-month prevalence rates of mental disorders compared to men who were not proficient in English.

It is customary to designate individuals who were born overseas and immigrated to the United States as "first-generation," individuals born in the U.S. and raised by first-generation immigrant parents as "second-generation," and so forth. However, recent developments in immigration studies have suggested that making finer distinctions among the first-generation immigrants is important because there are different developmental challenges and opportunities for immigrants who arrive as children, adolescents, young adults, or midlife adults. For example, by distinguishing among immigrants who arrived at age 12 or before ("1.5 generation"), who arrived between ages of 13 and 17 ("1.25 generation"), who arrived between the ages of 18 and 40 ("1.0a generation"), and those who arrived after age 40 ("1.0b generation"), Takeuchi et al. (2007) found that immigrants who arrive earlier in life were more likely to have greater lifetime and 12-month rates of mental disorders. Overall, 1.5 generation immigrant Asian Americans and U.S.-born Asian Americans had higher prevalence compared to other first-generation immigrants. The data also showed that the period during and shortly after immigration (e.g., childhood for 1.5 generation, adolescence for 1.25 generation, and young adulthood for 1.0a generation) was associated with heightened risk for onset of major mental disorders among immigrant Asian Americans. The sole exception were those who arrived as midlife or older adults (1.0b generation), who were more likely to have had the onset of mental disorder prior to immigration. These recent epidemiological data not only support the long-held notion of acculturative stress (Berry & Annis, 1974) but also suggest that immigration confers differential challenges and stressors to immigrant Asian American men and women, which point to the vital importance of gathering life-history data including nativity, age at immigration, and the adjustment process following immigration.

Lee (1982) suggested four general indicators that assess a client's acculturation and adaptation: years in the United States, country of origin, professional affiliation, and age at the time of immigration. Further, Lee stated that a useful way to understand Chinese American clients is to understand the client system in three domains: (1) physical and manifest features; (2) psychological features, dynamics, and structures; and (3) social, cultural, and ecological features. Under physical and manifest features, it is important to inquire about language(s) and dialect(s) spoken and degree of fluency, physical health status and medical history, medications used (including herbs and Chinese medicines), work and job roles, help-seeking behaviors and patterns, and other significant demographic data (e.g., immigration status, age, sex, birth order, male and female siblings, educational background in the United States and elsewhere, marital status, income, years in the States, country of origin). Psychological features that must be assessed include rate and process of adaptation and acculturation, perceived problems and solutions, attitudes toward Western medicine and help, degree and kind of interruptions to the individual's life cycle, and perception of past successes and failures in problem solving and coping. Finally, under social, culture, and ecological features, Lee suggested assessing the individual's migration and relocation process and history, work hours and work environment, and extent of contact with the social and human services network. Although these suggestions originally targeted Chinese American clients, they are applicable to other Asian American clients as well. Lee's (1997) guidelines for the use of interpreters also contained detailed information regarding other important areas to assess with Asian American families (e.g., migration stress, impact of migration on individual and family life cycle, community influence, and stress caused by legal problems or racism).

Testing Procedures

Linguistic diversity poses a particular difficulty in clinical assessment with Asian American clients. If the client is non-English-speaking, interviews and measures must be translated appropriately by qualified translators and interpreters (who speak the client's dialect, not just their language). Excellent guidelines for working with interpreters can be found in book chapters by Lee (1997) and Hays (2001). However, it is important not to assume that linguistics is not an issue for English-speaking Asian American clients. Bilingual clients may be limited in the range of their vocabulary or their ability to express internal psychological experience in one or both languages, and they may require assistance from a translator or the assessing clinician in responding to various standardized measures if English is not their native language.

Ideally, a testing clinician would like to be able to select appropriate measures depending on the level of acculturation of the Asian American client. However, there is a notable lack of normative data for Asian Americans on most personality assessment tools (Okazaki & Sue, 2000). Some of the measures on which some Asian American data exist (e.g., NEO PI-R) are not widely used in clinical evalua- tions, and efforts to develop measures of indigenous psychological characteristics of Asian cultures have only begun. Jones and Thorne (1987) suggested that the established measures that are widely used in personality testing may be more valid for those who have achieved middle-class status, and such a principle appears to be applicable to Asian Americans who are acculturated and have had exten- sive exposure to the American educational system. The best course of action, then, is not to rely on any single measure of personality but to use multiple sources of information. In the absence of widely used measures with established norms for different Asian groups, it is wise to use assessment data to generate hypotheses that can be supported or not supported by other measures or information. The use of translated measures may be needed. An important aspect of the testing procedure is the client's nonverbal behavior. Foo and Kaser-Boyd (1993) suggested that a traditional Chinese client who is not familiar with psychology or testing may bring a certain "mental set" to testing. The mental set may include skepticism about psychology and Western medicine, a fatalistic world view (i.e., suf- fering is part of fate), and a reluctance to disclose one's troubles to strangers. Further, such a mental set may result in the client's being polite and overly cooperative, not openly confronting or challenging the clinician, yet minimally self-disclosing. The test material may look overly constricted, and the com- munication may be highly indirect.

Interpreting the Results

When the testing clinician is not familiar with the client's culture, it is imperative to contact an ethnic consultant about the assessment results regarding the conceptual equivalence of the measure and the client's responses. For some instruments (e.g., the MMPI-2), research has suggested using different interpretive norms for Asians living in Asia (see Cheung & Song, 1989). However, for Asian Americans who

are somewhat acculturated, it is not clear which norm (Asian or American) should be used. In using instruments with no Asian norm, the clinician must be more conservative and cautious in interpreting the results of less acculturated individuals whose scores deviate from the American norm. However, one must also be aware of the danger of potentially underesti- mating the level of pathology for a culturally different client by overattributing bizarre or atypical behavior, thought patterns, and test responses to that client's "culture" (Lopez, 1989). Westermeyer (1987) pro- vided a list of criteria that may be useful in distin- guishing between pathological beliefs and behavior from those that are normative within the client's cultural context, which the readers may wish to consult.

It is also important for the testing clinician to be aware of possible biases in making clinical observa- tions and judgments of those who are culturally dif- ferent. Li-Repac (1980) conducted a study with a small number of white and Chinese American thera- pists who were asked to rate the psychological func- tioning of Chinese and White clients interviewed on videotapes. The study found that there were signifi- cant differences between the two therapist groups on ratings of the same clients. The white therapists tended to rate the Chinese American clients as more depressed and inhibited and having less capacity for meaningful interpersonal relationships. The Chinese American therapists judged the White clients to be more severely disturbed and to have more psycho- pathology than did the White therapists. In a different study, Chang and Sue (2003) presented school tea- chers (the majority of who were White American female) with vignettes of overcontrolled, undercon- trolled, and normal school behavior of a hypothetical fourth-grader boy, and each vignette was paired with a photograph of an African American, Asian American, or a White American child. The teacher perceptions and ratings revealed that they tended to see overcon- trolled behavior (e.g., worrying, being anxious to please, afraid of making mistakes, clinging to adults, being shy and timid) in an Asian American child as more typical of Asian American children, and such behavior were not seen as serious or in need of refer- rals. Thus, cultural stereotyping may have a subtle but important role in the clinical evaluation of a client who is culturally different.

In some cases, it may be possible for the clinician to obtain clinical personality assessment instruments and symptom inventories that had been translated into various Asian languages (e.g., the MMPI-2, the Beck Depression Inventory-2). However, the quality of the translation as well as the availability of reliability, validity, and norm data for such instruments varies widely. In other cases, the client may have enough English fluency to proceed cautiously with the test administration with the English-language version of the instrument. Cheung (2004) offered an excellent set of questions to ask regarding the use and interpretation of the results with Western personality assessment instruments across culture.

Finally, as Chin (1983) asserted, personality assessment should emphasize the uniqueness of the individual and the diversity of Asian American groups, which differ in cultural views and values, as well as the sociocultural milieu. One must be careful not to adhere rigidly to Western standards of mental health (e.g., independence and autonomy, emotional expressiveness, open communication styles) or assume that acculturation to American culture is the sole definition of adaptive personal functioning, but instead consider what is socially and culturally functional for the given individual.

Case Example

The following is a case study of an Asian American client[6] who presented to an inpatient setting for psychiatric treatment and forensic evaluation. We chose a forensic assessment example because of the increasing role that clinical personality assessment is playing in legal and other applied settings (Butcher, 2006), including with Asian American clients.

V.T. was a 42-year-old Vietnamese American male who was born in Vietnam and immigrated to the United States as an adult refugee. He is the 10th-born with five brothers and seven sisters. Unlike many Vietnamese men his age, V.T. did not serve in the military. He fled Vietnam with his family in 1980 following the Chinese invasion of Vietnam; he was separated from family members while seeking asylum and resided in a temporary refugee camp in Malaysia until he was granted entry into the United States in 1983 under the Orderly Departure Program overseen by the United Nations High Commissioner for Refugees. Subsequent to settling in Florida and reuniting with his family, he worked for friends of the family in a food-processing plant. In 1985, he suffered a severe injury to his right hand resulting in severance of three digits and extensive burns while working; V.T. received a considerable amount of settlement money from workman's compensation. Given V.T.'s limited education and fluency in English combined with limited employable skills, he relied on disability income and the workman's compensation settlement as sources of income. His family became concerned regarding V.T.'s apparently reckless

management of disability income and settlement funds, and one of V.T.'s elder brothers became the "unofficial keeper" of his funds.

In 1993, during a confrontation with his brother regarding use of his disability income and settlement funds, V.T. grabbed a kitchen knife and threatened to stab his niece. Law enforcement officers responded to the 911 call and V.T. was shot by the police officers during the confrontation. A bullet severed his spinal cord, resulting in V.T.'s paraplegia. Following receipt of medical treatment, V.T. was released to the custody of county jail to await criminal proceedings on charges of aggravated assault with a deadly weapon. Though V.T. was not exhibiting grossly overt symptoms of psychosis, he frequently discussed being "controlled by spirits" in interviews with his attorneys while developing a defense strategy. V.T. was referred to Dr. S., a psychologist without a particular background in assessing culturally diverse individuals, to determine whether V.T. had any mental illness or emotional disturbance that might be relevant to his defense in the case. MMPI-2 was administered orally in English; results indicated elevations for Scales F, 1, 2, 3, and 8. He was committed to a state psychiatric facility following adjudication as Incompetent to Proceed, given his lack of knowledge and confusion regarding the American legal system as well as the diagnosis of Psychotic Disorder, Not Otherwise Specified given by Dr. S. based on the MMPI-2 results.

Upon arrival at the psychiatric facility for restoration of competence, V.T. was observed laughing and mumbling alone as if he were engaged in a conversation with unseen beings; staff members were unable to comprehend his verbalizations but noted "it didn't sound like English." In an interview with the assigned psychiatrist that was conducted in English, V.T. reported that he was being controlled by spirits, which was interpreted by the psychiatrist as evidence of psychosis and a small dose of antipsychotic medication was initiated.

Dr. M., an Asian American female psychologist assigned to assess V.T.'s mental status and legal issues, enlisted the service of a licensed Vietnamese/English interpreter (a male Vietnamese American man in his forties, previously unknown to V.T.) who was certified in medical and legal interpretation. As recommended by Hays (2001), sequential interpretation was utilized in the clinical interview. A preassessment meeting with the interpreter included a discussion regarding the need to assess whether V.T.'s verbalizations in his native language suggested any disorganized thought processes, such as irrelevant responses or tangential and circumstantial reasoning.

With the assistance of the interpreter, Dr. M. conducted a more culturally responsive assessment of V.T., including the client's history in relation to historical events. V.T. had migrated during what had been termed the "second wave" of Vietnamese refugees being admitted to the United States. The "first wave" of Vietnamese refugees had begun to arrive in 1975; majority of such refugees were professionals, government officials, and military personnel. They were predominantly young, relatively healthy, well educated, urban dwellers; majority of family members had immigrated to the United States in family groups. The "second wave" of Vietnamese refugees, in comparison, was less educated, separated from family, and encountered more health problems as result of fleeing from Vietnam and encountering sparse resources while displaced in temporary refuge camps in Southeast Asia (Muecke, 1983). V.T.'s personal history of his family's exodus out of Vietnam via the refugee camp was consistent with those of the "second wave" refugee contemporaries. Although V.T. did not serve in the military and thus may have been exposed to less traumatizing events as compared with Vietnamese veteran refugees, V.T.'s migration history still contained periods of considerable stress such as separation from members of his large family and time spent in Malaysian refugee camps under inhospitable conditions.

Although Dr. S., the previous psychologist, had assumed that V.T. was acculturated given his length of stay of more than 10 years in the United States, V.T. had resided within an established Vietnamese community in central Florida where many immigrants do not need to speak English in order to survive on a daily basis. It became evident in this evaluation that V.T. had a limited range of expression in the English language and low level of acculturation and identification with American culture, and he held a strong identification as a Vietnamese. He was much more comfortable and articulate expressing his thoughts and feelings in his native Vietnamese language than in English. Although V.T. continued to report to Dr. M. that he has been "controlled by spirits" ever since being shot by law enforcement officers, the interpreter explained that such assertions are not unusual in the Vietnamese culture following unforeseen accidents, as some Vietnamese believe that spirits have ability to bring good fortune and misfortune. The interpreter was able to confirm from V.T. that his sense of being "controlled by spirits" reflected his daily struggles with his physical limitations; V.T. expressed a belief that his paraplegia was a result of his disrespecting the ancestors by quarrelling with his elder brother regarding money. An additional interview with V.T.'s two elder brothers, with the aid of the

interpreter, also supported the cultural interpretation. The family interview revealed that V.T.'s family network was close-knit and generally supportive, although the family members also appeared to be contributing to V.T.'s belief that his current physical condition was a spiritual retribution for his behavior within the family.

The assessment suggested that V.T. did not show grossly overt signs of psychotic thought processes. Although he spoke in heavily accented English in brief and rudimentary sentences (e.g., "I want soup," "I'm wet," etc.), his requests and verbalizations were consistently coherent, relevant, and goal-directed. The interpreter reported that V.T. did not provide any irrelevant responses and that his thought processes were firmly associated. Behavioral observations of V.T. by Dr. M confirmed that he did not engage in overtly disorganized behavior, and staff members assigned to assist V.T.'s completion of activities of daily living due to his paraplegia (bathing, exchange of clothing, etc.) reported that V.T. has been cooperative with such activities. His emotional reactions have been broad and flexible in range and he actively participated in supervised social events (movie viewings, holiday parties, co-ed dances, etc.) without any need for encouragement. As result of the information obtained by Dr. M with the assistance of the interpreter, Axis I diagnosis was changed to Adjustment Disorder and his regimen of psychotropic medications were slowly tapered and discontinued. There was no observable change in V.T.'s mental status without the antipsychotic medication in his system.

In light of the cultural assessment by Dr. M. that V.T.'s symptomatology would be best understood within the Vietnamese spiritual belief system, V.T.'s English MMPI-2 results were reevaluated. It is debatable whether it was appropriate to administer the English version, given his 10-year residency in the United States. As noted by Butcher (2004), use of foreign-language versions of the MMPI-2 once the foreign-born individual learns the English language and acculturated to the American culture may not be appropriate. V.T.'s acculturation level had not been formally measured. The elevated scales were F, 1, 2, 3, and 8. Elevation in the infrequency (F) scale could be viewed from several perspectives: (1) cultural variance; (2) extenuating stressful circumstances (paraplegia as result of gunshot wound, incarceration, being away from Vietnamese community, etc.); (3) severe psychological disturbance; or (4) faking mental health problems. As discussed in Tran (1996), Vietnamese Americans tend to show elevations on Scale F, depending on their level of acculturation.

Assuming that the elevations on Scale F on the English version may have been due to lack of acculturation and stress, elevations on Scales 1, 2, 3, and 8 required further examination. Clinical interview conducted with the assistance of the interpreter revealed that V.T.'s physical disabilities had negatively affected his self-esteem and efficacy, as he was no longer able to complete basic activities of daily living without assistance. Elevations in the Harris–Lingoes Subscales D2, D3, Hy3, Hy4, and SC3, in addition to the elevations of the supplementary DEP, HEA, and PK scales, supported the elevations on Scales 1, 2, and 3. It was also important to consider the physical effects of his disabilities. V.T. endorsed items pertaining to fatigue, poor appetite, sleep problems, gastrointestinal complaints, and difficulties in concentrating. Examination of his medication regimen revealed that V.T. was prescribed muscle relaxant to counter spasms and narcotic to manage pain. Side effects of his medication regimen (nausea, constipation, etc.) would also account for elevation on these scales. Moreover, V.T. had relied heavily on family members and friends in making his most important life decisions prior to his current legal predicaments, thus being detained away from such close-knit Vietnamese community may have contributed to his sense of alienation. Elevations in the Harris–Lingoes Subscales Pd4, Pd5, and Sc1 as well as the lack of elevations in Scale 6, Pa1, Sc6, and BIZ supported endorsement of such items, which can be attributed to increased situational distress.

Dr. M. located the Vietnamese version of the MMPI-2 and administered it to V.T. for comparison with the English MMPI-2 results. Elevations of Scales F, 1, 2, 3, and 8 remained, though slightly lower T-scores as compared with results from the English version of MMPI-2. This result was not unexpected, as Tran (1996) found that Vietnamese refugees scored higher on Scales F and 8 using the Vietnamese version of MMPI-2. Results were also consistent with Dong and Church's (2003) findings that mean T-scores for Scales F, 1, and 8 for Vietnamese refugees were moderately elevated but below clinical threshold.

The importance of using a licensed translator is highlighted in this case. V.T.'s complaints of being controlled by spirits were originally viewed as a symptom of mental illness, in combination with MMPI-2 results indicating elevations in Scales F, 1, 2, 3, and 8. However, close examination of V.T.'s physical disabilities, combined with culturally responsive assessment at the psychiatric facility, showed that V.T. was not suffering from abnormalities in perception or depression. Understanding of his particular cultural beliefs was critical in this assessment.

Though variances in customs and practices within a country of origin (e.g., regions and ethnic groups) exist, use of translators native to the client's culture assists greatly in placing the individual client's behavior within a cultural context.

Conclusion

The case of V.T. illustrates the problems in making valid assessments and diagnosis of many Asian American clients. Clinicians may lack knowledge of the cultural backgrounds and environmental context of the client, fail to speak the client's primary language, be unable to find assessment instruments that are normed and validated on the client's ethnic population, and not have available ethnic consultants. Under such circumstances, valid assessment is difficult. We have pointed to the fact that few measures of personality are available for Asian Americans, so that established norms simply do not exist for most personality measures. Even with popular inventories such as the MMPI, which has been used and validated in various Asian countries, most of the work concerning Asian Americans has focused on student rather than non-student samples. What is encouraging is that progress is being made in the construction and validation of measures that examine acculturation, cultural values, acculturation conflict, and racial identity of Asian Americans.

In view of the difficulties in making valid assessments of Asian Americans, what steps can be taken to improve assessment procedures? Obviously, the field is in need of more research on the reliability, validity, and utility of personality and clinical instruments for Asian Americans. New measures that can tap into the cultural and contextual sensibilities of Asian Americans must also be developed. In the meantime, we have tried to outline some steps that clinicians can use in assessing Asian Americans. Clinicians should take special effort to find linguistically appropriate instruments and determine the cultural/ecological background of Asian American clients. Level of acculturation and immigrant/ minority group experiences are essential contextual information that should be assessed before deciding on the assessment instrument to use and before making interpretations of test performance. We have also suggested that multiple sources of data be gathered on clients in order to test the consistency of findings from these different sources. Finally, involving an ethnic consultant or interpreter who is knowledgeable about the client's cultural background is important. These steps, combined with the continued development of validated measures and assessment tools, are vitally needed.

Future Directions

Clinical personality assessment with Asian Americans is a field that faces many challenging problems that must be solved. One of the challenges is the continued paucity of active and programmatic research on clinical personality instruments with Asian American population. Because Asian American mental health is generally a blossoming and vibrant research area, the dearth of clinical assessment research on this population is somewhat puzzling. It is possible that clinical personality assessment research with Asian Americans lags behind other topical areas in Asian American mental health because most of the currently active researchers are situated at research universities with relatively easy access to the college population but not necessarily to clinical populations. However, as the field continues to grow and mature, it is critical to encourage more research with clinical population of Asian Americans at psychiatric, medical, and forensic settings.

Another challenge in this field is the relative emphasis of cultural over racial variables in mental health research. Much of the discussion about Asian Americans in the mental health literature is still predominated by "cultural" factors, with the potential cost of overlooking another critical aspect of Asian Americans' psychological experience. Because of their success in educational and occupational endeavors, Asian Americans are widely perceived as being insulated from racial discrimination and prejudice. Recent studies, however, point to the need to develop race-related measures for Asian Americans. For example, Alvarez, Juang, and Liang (2006) have found that among Asian American college students, fully 98% reported at least one experience with negative racial situations during the past year. Furthermore, racial experiences were related to racial identity. Sue, Bucceri, Lin, Nadal, and Torino (2007) documented eight main types of racial microaggressions (or small acts of everyday discriminations) that were directed toward Asian Americans, including being made to feel like an alien in one's own land, being assumed to be intelligent, being exoticized (for Asian women), feeling invalidated on inter-Asian differences, feeling that their racial reality is denied, feeling pathologized for Asian cultural values and communication styles, feelings of second-class citizenship, and feelings of invisibility. Perceived racial discrimination has also been found to predict lower self-esteem and greater depression for Asian American youth (Greene, Way, & Pahl, 2006). A recent study with a nationally representative sample of 2,095 Asian Americans found that perception of everyday discrimination was associated with many chronic health conditions, above and beyond the effects of age, gender, region, per capita income, education, employment, and social desirability bias (Gee, Spencer, Chen, & Takeuchi, 2007).

Although there is ongoing research on the relationship between race-related measures and psychopathology, there is no consistent effort to develop and validate a clinical assessment measure that can tap into this critical aspect of many Asian Americans' experience. To be sure, something as complex, dynamic, and historically situated as racial discrimination and its effect on Asian American individuals may not be possible to be assessed using simple instruments. However, there is much need for a clearer articulation of how a clinician might consider race- and racism-related factors in clinical personality assessment of Asian Americans.

Notes

1. In 2000, the census bureau separated "Asian" and "Native Hawaiian or other Pacific Islander" into two separate race groups. The 2000 census also allowed, for the first time, for respondents to mark more than one race category; thus the census data may be reported for those who reported "Asian" race alone (i.e., single-race individuals) and/or those who reported "Asian" race in combination with other races (i.e., mixed-race individuals). For the purpose of simplicity, this chapter uses the inclusive figures for "Asians alone or in combination."

2. Because there appeared to be only one or two new published study on the use of projective tests with Asian-American population since the publication of the previous edition of this chapter (Okazaki, Kallivayalil, & Sue, 2002), this chapter does not include the review of projective tests. Those interested in the uses of projective tests with Asian-Americans may consult Okazaki, Kallivayalil, and Sue (2002).

3. This review is limited to published studies. For a comprehensive review of MMPI and MMPI-2 studies with Asian-Americans, including unpublished studies, see Kwan (1999).

4. Note, however, that Kwon (2002) raised some methodological concerns (namely, not controlling for socioeconomic status, profile invalidity, and English fluency) in Tsai and Pike's (2000) study to suggest alternative explanations for the findings.

5. Butcher's (1996) compendium volume on the international adaptation of the MMPI-2 provides a list of the names and addresses of the translators and international researchers in an appendix to facilitate access to the Asian-language versions of the MMPI-2.

6. This hypothetical case is based on a composite of several different clients of similar cultural heritage who presented for evaluations in a forensic setting.

References

Alvarez, A. N., Juang, L., & Liang, C. T. (2006). Asian Americans and racism: When bad things happen to "model minorities." *Cultural Diversity and Ethnic Minority Psychology, 12,* 477–492.

Berry, J. W., & Annis, R. C. (1974). Acculturative stress: The role of ecology, culture and differentiation. *Journal of Cross-cultural Psychology, 5,* 382–406.

Butcher, J. N. (1985). Current developments in MMPI use: An international perspective. In C. D. Speilberger & J. N. Butcher (Eds.), *Advances in personality assessment* (Vol. 4, pp. 83–94). Hillsdale, NJ: Erlbaum.

Butcher, J. N. (Ed.). (1996). *International adaptations of the MMPI-2.* Minneapolis, MN: University of Minnesota Press.

Butcher, J. N. (2004). Personality assessment without borders: Adaptation of the MMPI-2 across cultures. *Journal of Personality Assessment, 83,* 90–104.

Butcher, J. N. (2006). Assessment in clinical psychology: A perspective on the past, present challenges, and future prospects. *Clinical Psychology: Science & Practice, 13,* 205–209.

Butcher, J. N., Cheung, F. M., & Lim, J. (2003). Use of the MMPI-2 with Asian populations. *Psychological Assessment, 15,* 248–256.

Chang, D. F., & Sue, S. (2003). The effects of race and problem type on teachers' assessment of school behavior. *Journal of Consulting and Clinical Psychology, 71,* 235–242.

Chen, C., Greenberger, E., Lester, J., Dong, Q., & Guo, M. (1998). A cross-cultural study of family and peer correlates of adolescent misconduct. *Developmental Psychology, 34,* 1770–1781.

Cheung, F. M. (2004). Use of Western and indigenously developed personality tests in Asia. *Applied Psychology: An International Review, 53,* 173–191.

Cheung, F. M., & Ho, R. M. (1997). Standardization of the Chinese MMPI-A in Hong Kong: A preliminary study. *Psychological Assessment, 9,* 499–502.

Cheung, F. M., & Song. W. (1989). A review on the clinical applications of the Chinese MMPI. *Psychological Assessment, 1,* 230–237.

Cheung, F. M., Cheung, S. F., Leung, K., Ward, C., & Leong, F. T. L. (2003). The English version of the Chinese Personality Assessment Inventory. *Journal of Cross-cultural Psychology, 34,* 433–452.

Cheung, F. M., Cheung, S. F., & Zhang, J. (2004a). What is "Chinese" personality? Subgroup differences in the Chinese Personality Assessment Inventory (CPAI-2). *Acta Psychologica Sinica, 36,* 491–499.

Cheung, F. M., Cheung, S. F., & Zhang, J. (2004b). Convergent validity of the Chinese Personality Assessment Inventory and the Minnesota Multiphasic Personality Inventory-2: Preliminary findings with a normative sample. *Journal of Personality Assessment, 83,* 92–103.

Cheung, F. M., Kwong, J. Y., & Zhang, J. (2003). Clinical validation of the Chinese Personality Assessment Inventory. *Psychological Assessment, 15,* 89–100.

Cheung, F. M., Song, W., & Zhang, J. (1996). The Chinese MMPI-2: Research and application in Hong Kong and the People's Republic of China. In J. N. Butcher (Ed.), *International adaptations of the MMPI-2* (pp. 137–161). Minneapolis, MN: University of Minnesota Press.

Cheung, F. M., Cheung, S. F., Wada, S., & Zhang, J. (2003). Indigenous measures of personality assessment in Asian countries: A review. *Psychological Assessment, 15,* 280–289.

Cheung, F. M., Leung, K., Fan, R. M., Song, W., Zhang, J., & Zhang, J. (1996). Development of the Chinese Personality Assessment Inventory. *Journal of Cross-cultural Psychology, 27,* 181–199.

Cheung, F. M., Leung, K., Zhang, J. X., Sun, H. F, Gan, Y. Q., Song, W. Z, et al. (2001). Indigenous Chinese personality constructs: Is the Five Factor Model complete? *Journal of Cross-cultural Psychology, 32,* 407–433.

Cheung, P. C., Conger, A. J., Hau, K., Lew, W. J. F., & Lau, S. (1992). Development of the Multi-trait Personality Inventory (MTPI): Comparison among four Chinese populations. *Journal of Personality Assessment, 59,* 528–551.

Cheung, S. F., Cheung, F. M., Howard, R., & Lim, Y-H. (2006). Personality across the ethnic divide in Singapore: Are "Chinese Traits" uniquely Chinese? *Personality & Individual Differences, 41,* 467–477.

Chin, J. L. (1983). Diagnostic considerations in working with Asian-Americans. *American Journal of Orthopsychiatry, 53,* 100–109.

Chung, J. J., Weed, N. C., & Han, K. (2006). Evaluating cross-cultural equivalence of the Korean MMPI-2 via bilingual test–retest. *International Journal of Intercultural Relations, 30,* 531–543.

Colligan, R. C., Osborne, D., Swenson, W. M., & Offord, K. P. (1983). *The MMPI: A contemporary normative study.* New York: Praeger.

Costa, P. T., Jr., & McCrae, R. R. (1992). *Revised NEO Personality Inventory (NEO PI-R) and NEO Five Factor Inventory (NEO-FFI) professional manual.* Odessa, FL: Psychological Assessment Resources, Inc.

Cuellar, I., Arnold, B., & Maldonado, R. (1995). Acculturation Rating Scale for Mexican Americans-II: A revision of the original ARSMA scale. *Hispanic Journal of Behavioral Sciences, 17,* 275–304.

Cuellar, I., Harris, L., & Jasso, R. (1980). An acculturation scale for Mexican American normal and clinical populations. *Hispanic Journal of Behavioral Sciences, 2,* 199–217.

Dana, R. H. (1988). Culturally diverse groups and MMPI interpretation. *Professional Psychology—Research and Practice, 19,* 490–495.

Dana, R. H. (1993). *Multicultural assessment perspectives for professional psychology.* Boston, MA: Allyn & Bacon.

Dienard, A., Butcher, J. N., Thao, U. D., Vang, S. H. M., & Hang, K. (1996). Development of a Hmong translation of the MMPI-2. In J. N. Butcher (Ed.), *International adaptations of the MMPI-2* (pp. 194–205). Minneapolis, MN: University of Minnesota Press.

Dong, Y. T., & Church, A. T. (2003). Cross-cultural equivalence and validity of the Vietnamese MMPI-2: Assessing psychological adjustment of Vietnamese refugees. *Psychological Assessment, 15,* 370–377.

Foo, L., & Kaser-Boyd, N. (1993, March). *Psychological assessment with ethnic Chinese: Variables in the testing process.* Paper presented at the annual meeting of the Society for Personality Assessment, San Francisco.

Gee, G. C., Spencer, M. S., Chen, J., & Takeuchi, D. (2007). A nationwide study of discrimination and chronic health conditions among Asian Americans. *American Journal of Public Health, 97,* 1275–1282.

Gong, Y., & Kwan, K. K. (2000). Effects of response frequency, item desirability, and perceived shamefulness on the MMPI-2 patterns of Korean students in the U.S. (Unpublished manuscript).

Greene, M. L., Way, N., & Pahl, K. (2006). Trajectories of perceived adult and peer discrimination among Black,

Latino, and Asian American adolescents. *Developmental Psychology, 42,* 218–238.

Greene, R. L. (1987). Ethnicity and MMPI performance: A review. *Journal of Consulting and Clinical Psychology, 55,* 497–512.

Hahn, J. (2005). Faking bad and faking good by college students on the Korean MMPI-2. *Journal of Personality Assessment, 85,* 65–73.

Hall, G. C. N., Bansal, A., & Lopez, I. R. (1999). Ethnicity and psychopathology: A meta-analytic review of 31 years of comparative MMPI/MMPI-2 research. *Psychological Assessment, 11,* 186–197.

Hall, G. C. N., DeGarmo, D. S., Eap, S., Teten, A. L., & Sue, S. (2006). Initiation, desistance, and persistence of men's sexual coercion. *Journal of Consulting and Clinical Psychology, 74,* 732–742.

Hall, G. C. N., Sue, S., Narang, D. S., & Lilly, R. S. (2000). Culture-specific models of men's sexual aggression: Intra- and interpersonal determinants. *Cultural Diversity and Ethnic Minority Psychology, 6,* 252–267.

Hall, G. C. N., Teten, A. L., DeGarmo, D. S., Sue, S., & Stephens, K. A. (2005). Ethnicity, culture, and sexual aggression: Risk and protective factors. *Journal of Consulting and Clinical Psychology, 73,* 830–840.

Han, K. (1996). The Korean MMPI-2. In J. N. Butcher (Ed.), *International adaptations of the MMPI-2* (pp. 88–136). Minneapolis, MN: University of Minnesota Press.

Hays, P. (2001). *Addressing cultural complexities in practice: A framework for clinicians and counselors.* Washington, DC: American Psychological Association.

Helms, J. E. (1992). Why is there no study of cultural equivalence in standardized cognitive ability testing? *American Psychologist, 47,* 1083–1101.

Hong, S., Kim, B. S. K., & Wolfe, M. M. (2005). A psychometric revision of the European American Values Scale for Asian Americans using the Rasch model. *Measurement and Evaluation in Counseling and Development, 37,* 194–207.

Inman, A. G., Ladany, N., Constantine, M. G., Morano, C. K. (2001). Development and preliminary validation of the Cultural Values Conflict Scale for South Asian women. *Journal of Counseling Psychology, 48,* 17–27.

Jones, E. E., & Thorne, A. (1987). Rediscovery of the subject: Intercultural approaches to clinical assessment. *Journal of Consulting and Clinical Psychology, 55,* 488–495.

Kim, B. S. K. (2006). Acculturation and enculturation. In F. T. L. Leong, A. G. Inman, A. Ebreo, L. H. Yang, L. Kinoshita, & M. Fu (Eds.) *Handbook of Asian American Psychology* (2nd ed., pp. 141–158). Thousand Oaks, CA: Sage.

Kim, B. S. K., Atkinson, D. R., & Yang, P. H. (1999). The Asian Values Scale: Development, factor analysis, validation, and reliability. *Journal of Counseling Psychology, 46,* 342–352.

Kim, B. S. K., & Hong, S. (2004). A psychometric revision of the Asian Values Scale using the Rasch model. *Measurement and Evaluation in Counseling and Development, 37,* 15–27.

Kim, B. S. K., Li, L. C., & Ng, G. F. (2005). The Asian American Values Scale-Multidimensional: Development, reliability, and validity. *Cultural Diversity and Ethnic Minority Psychology, 11,* 187–201.

Kwan, K.-L. K. (1999). MMPI and MMPI-2 performance of the Chinese: Cross-cultural applicability. *Professional Psychology: Research and Practice, 30,* 260–268.

Kwan, K.-L. K. (2000). The effect of language proficiency on item endorsement: Examining the cultural applicability of the English MMPI-2 to Chinese-speaking people in the United States (Unpublished manuscript).

Kwan, K.-L. K., & Sodowsky, G. R. (1997). Internal and external ethnic identity and their correlates: A study of Chinese American immigrants. *Journal of Multicultural Counseling and Development, 25,* 51–67.

Kwon, P. (2002). Comment on "Effects of acculturation on the MMPI-2 scores of Asian American students." *Journal of Personality Assessment, 78,* 187–189.

Lee, E. (1982). A social systems approach to assessment and treatment for Chinese Americans families. In M. McGoldrick, J. K. Pearce, & J. Giordano (Eds.), *Ethnicity and family therapy.* New York: Guilford.

Lee, E. (1997). Overview: The assessment and treatment of Asian American families. In E. Lee (Ed.), *Working with Asian Americans: A guide for clinicians* (pp. 3–36). New York: Guilford.

Lee, R. M., Choe, J., Kim, G., & Ngo, V. (2000). Construction of the Asian American family conflicts scale. *Journal of Counseling Psychology, 47,* 211–222.

Lee, R. M., & Liu, H. T. (2001). Coping with inter-generational family conflict: Comparison of Asian American, Hispanic, and European American college students. *Journal of Counseling Psychology, 48,* 410–419.

Lee, R. M., Yoon, Y., Liu-Tom, H.-T. T. (2006). Structure and measurement of acculturation/enculturation for Asian Americans using the ARSMA-II. *Measurement and Evaluation in Counseling and Development, 39,* 42–55.

Leong, F. T. L., Okazaki, S., & David, E. J. R. (2006). History and future of Asian American psychology. In F. T. L Leong, A. Inman, A. Ebreo, L. Yang, L. Kinoshita, & M. Fu (Eds.), *Handbook of Asian American Psychology* (2nd ed., pp. 11–28). Thousand Oaks, CA: Sage.

Li-Repac, D. (1980). Cultural influences on clinical perception: A comparison between Caucasian and Chinese-American therapists. *Journal of Cross-cultural Psychology, 11,* 327–342.

Lonner, W. J. (1990). An overview of cross-cultural testing and assessment. In R. W. Brislin (Ed.), *Applied cross-cultural psychology. Cross-cultural research and methodology series* (Vol. 14, pp. 56–76). Newbury Park, CA: Sage.

Lopez, S. R. (1989). Patient variable biases in clinical judgment: Conceptual overview and methodological considerations. *Psychological Bulletin, 106,* 184–203.

Luk, C. L., & Bond, M. H. (1992). Lexical and questionnaire approaches to Chinese personality (Unpublished manuscript, Chinese University of Hong Kong).

Luk, C. L., & Bond, M. H. (1993). Personality variation and values endorsement in Chinese university students. *Personality and Individual Differences, 14,* 429–437.

Marsella, A., Sanborn, K., Kameoka, V., Shizuru, L., & Brennan, J. (1975). Cross-validation of self-report measures of depression among normal populations of Japanese, Chinese, and Caucasian ancestry. *Journal of Clinical Psychology, 31,* 281–287.

Muecke, M.A. (1983). In search of healers—Southeast Asian refugees in the American health care system. *Cross-cultural Medicine, 139,* 835–840.

Nagata, D. K. (1994). Assessing Asian American acculturation and ethnic identity: The need for a multidimensional framework. *Asian American and Pacific Islander Journal of Health, 2,* 108–124.

Oetting, G. R., & Beauvais, F. (1990). Orthogonal cultural identification theory: The cultural identification of minority adolescents. *International Journal of the Addictions, 25,* 655–685.

Okazaki, S., & Sue, S. (2000). Implications of test revisions for assessment with Asian Americans. *Psychological Assessment, 12,* 272–280.

Okazaki, S., Kallivayalil, D., & Sue, S. (2002). Clinical personality assessment with Asian Americans. In J. N. Butcher (Ed.), *Clinical personality assessment: Practical approaches* (2nd ed., pp. 135–153). New York: Oxford University Press.

Paniagua, F. A. (1994). *Assessing and treating culturally diverse clients: A practical guide.* Thousand Oaks, CA: Sage.

Pongpanich, L. (1996). Use of the MMPI-2 in Thailand. In J. N. Butcher (Ed.), *International adaptations of the MMPI-2* (pp. 162–174). Minneapolis, MN: University of Minnesota Press.

Ponterotto, J. G., Baluch, S., & Carielli, D. (1998). The Suinn–Lew Asian Self-Identity Acculturation Scale (SL-ASIA): Critique and research recommendations. *Measurement and Evaluation in Counseling & Development, 31,* 109–124.

Roberts, M., Han, K., & Weed, N. C. (2006). Development of a scale to assess Hwa-Byung, a Korean culture-bound syndrome, using the Korean MMPI-2. *Transcultural Psychiatry, 43,* 383–400.

Ryder, A. G., Alden, L. E., & Paulhus, D. L. (2000). Is acculturation unidimensional or bidimensional? A head-to-head comparison in the prediction of personality, self-identity, and adjustment. *Journal of Personality and Social Psychology, 79,* 49–65.

Shiota, N. K., Krauss, S. S., & Clark, L. A. (1996). Adaptations and validation of the Japanese MMPI-2. In J. N. Butcher (Ed.), *International applications of the MMPI-2* (pp. 67–87). Minneapolis, MN: University of Minnesota Press.

Song, W. (1991). Use and evaluation of a modified MMPI in China. *International Journal of Mental Health, 20,* 81–93.

Stevens, M. J., Kwan, K. K., & Graybill, D. F. (1993). Comparison of MMPI-2 scores of foreign Chinese and Caucasian-American students. *Journal of Clinical Psychology, 49,* 23–27.

Su, J., Lee, R. M., & Vang, S. (2005). Intergenerational family conflict and coping among Hmong American college students. *Journal of Counseling Psychology, 52,* 482–489.

Sue, D. W., Bucceri, J., Lin, A. I., Nadal, K. L., & Torino, G. C. (2007). Racial microaggressions and the Asian American experience. *Cultural Diversity and Ethnic Minority Psychology, 13,* 72–81.

Sue, S., & Sue, D. W. (1974). MMPI comparisons between Asian-American and non-Asian students utilizing a student health psychiatric clinic. *Journal of Counseling Psychology, 21,* 423–427.

Sue, S., Keefe, K., Enomoto, K., Durvasula, R. S., & Chao, R. (1996). Asian American and White college students' performance on the MMPI-2. In J. N. Butcher (Ed.), *International adaptations of the MMPI-2* (pp. 206–218). Minneapolis, MN: University of Minnesota Press.

Suinn, R. M. (1998). Measurement of acculturation of Asian Americans. *Asian American and Pacific Islander Journal of Health, 6,* 7–12.

Suinn, R. M., Ahuna, C., & Khoo, G. (1992). The Suinn–Lew Asian Self-Identity Acculturation Scale: Concurrent and factorial validation. *Educational & Psychological Measurement, 52,* 1041–1046.

Suinn, R. M., Rickard-Figueroa, K., Lew, S., & Vigil, P. (1987). The Suinn–Lew Asian Self-Identity Acculturation Scale: An initial report. *Educational & Psychological Measurement, 47,* 401–407.

Takeuchi, D. T., Hong, S., Gile, K., & Alegria, M. (2007). Developmental contexts and mental disorders among Asian Americans. *Research on Human Development, 4,* 49–69.

Takeuchi, D. T., Zane, N. W. S., Hong, S., Chae, D. H., Gong, F., Gee, G., et al. (2007). Immigration-related factors and mental disorders among Asian Americans. *American Journal of Public Health, 97,* 84–90.

Tran, B. N. (1996). Vietnamese translation and adaptation of the MMPI-2. In J. N. Butcher (Ed.), *International adaptations of the MMPI-2* (pp. 175–193). Minneapolis, MN: University of Minnesota Press.

Triandis, H. C. (1995). *Individualism and collectivism.* Boulder, CO: Westview.

Tsai, D. C., & Pike, P. L. (2000). Effects of acculturation on the MMPI-2 scores of Asian American students. *Journal of Personality Assessment, 74,* 216–230.

Tsai, J. L., Ying, Y., & Lee, P. A. (2000). The meaning of "being Chinese" and "being American": Variation among Chinese American young adults. *Journal of Cross-cultural Psychology, 31,* 302–322.

Tsushima, W. T., & Onorato, V. A. (1982). Comparison of MMPI scores of White and Japanese-American medical patients. *Journal of Consulting and Clinical Psychology, 50,* 150–151.

U.S. Bureau of the Census. (1993). *We the Americans: Asians.* Washington, DC: U.S. Government Printing Office.

U.S. Bureau of the Census. (1999). Region of birth a key indicator of well-being for America's foreign-born population, Census bureau reports. Retrieved on December 15, 2008 at http://www.census.gov/Press-Release/www/1999/cb99-195.html

U.S. Bureau of the Census. (2000). Resident population estimates of the United States by sex, race, and Hispanic origin: April 1, 1990 to July 1, 1999, with short-term projection to September 1, 2000. Retrieved on December 15, 2008 at http://www.census.gov/population/estimates/nation/intfile3-1.txt.

U.S. Bureau of the Census. (2004). *We the people: Asians in the United States* (CENSR-17). Washington, DC: U.S. Department of Commerce.

Watanabe, C. (1973). Self-expressions and the Asian American experience. *Personnel and Guidance Journal, 51,* 390–396.

Westermeyer, J. (1987). Cultural factors in clinical assessment. *Journal of Consulting and Clinical Psychology, 55,* 471–478.

Wolfe, M. M., Yang, P. H., Wong, E. C., & Atkinson, D. R. (2001). Design and development of the European American values scale for Asian Americans. *Cultural Diversity and Ethnic Minority Psychology, 7,* 274–283.

Yang, K., & Bond, M. H. (1990). Exploring implicit personality theories with indigenous or imported constructs: The Chinese case. *Journal of Personality and Social Psychology, 58,* 1087–1095.

Yik, M. S. M., & Tang, C. S. (1996). Linking personality and values: The importance of a culturally relevant personality scale. *Personality and Individual Differences, 21,* 1767–1774.

Yung, Y., Chan, W., Cheung, F. M., Leung, K., Law, J. S., & Zhang, J. X. (2000). Standardization of the Chinese Personality Assessment Inventory: The prototype standardization method and its rationale. *Asian Journal of Social Psychology, 3,* 133–152.

Zane, N. W. S., & Yeh, M. (2002). The use of culturally-based variables in assessment: Studies on loss of face. In K. Kurasaki, S. Okazaki, & S. Sue (Eds.), *Asian American mental health: Assessment theories and methods.* New York, NY: Kluwer Academic/Plenum Publishers.

The Assessment of Psychopathology in Racial and Ethnic Minorities

Bernadette Gray-Little

Abstract

As accurate assessment is critical to diagnosis and treatment, understanding the association between race or ethnicity and the assessment of psychopathology has important practical significance. However, detecting and mitigating racial bias in assessment is a profoundly complex challenge. This chapter considers several conceptual issues germane to assessing U.S. minority groups and reviews efforts to address ethnic and racial bias in frequently used adult assessment instruments.

Keywords: acculturation, bias, clinical interview, ethnicity, minority, race, picture-story test, projective test, Rorschach, socioeconomic status, test

During the past 40 years considerable effort has been devoted to understanding how race and ethnicity might be associated with the assessment of psychopathology. Although knowledge of this association would benefit our theoretical understanding of the way culture influences personality and psychopathology, its practical value stems from the assumptions that accurate assessment is necessary for appropriate diagnosis, and that misdiagnosis leads to disparate treatment and poorer outcomes for minority group members. Moreover, because stigma is associated with severe mental disorders, findings of more severe or frequent psychopathology in minority groups foster negative stereotypes that may, in turn, be the basis for further discrimination. Investigations of this topic fall into two broad overlapping categories: attempts to negate or affirm the presence of bias in assessment instruments and efforts to develop modifications that eliminate presumed bias. Attempted modifications include both adjustments to the scoring and interpretation of existing instruments and the development of new instruments for particular ethnic groups. Despite such efforts, however, concerns persist that accurate assessment of psychopathology in minority groups lags that of majority group members, leading to poorer treatment outcomes. Detecting and mitigating ethnic and racial bias in psychological tests is a deeply complicated undertaking with numerous conceptual conundrums and methodological challenges. For example, what constitutes membership in a minority group? How do we identify the distinctive psychological profile of a particular minority group and then determine to which members of the group the profile is applicable? Perhaps more important, how do we define bias? Are group mean differences in test scores irrelevant, with claims of bias warranted only by evidence of a differential relationship between test scores and a criterion (slope bias) and by an over- or underprediction of the criterion (intercept bias) (Urbina, 2004)? This chapter will consider several conceptual issues germane to assessing U.S. minority groups and review efforts to address ethnic and racial bias in frequently used adult assessment instruments.

Race, Ethnicity, and Minority Status

For reasons that are primarily historical rather than logical, comparisons of Caucasians with African-Americans have traditionally been referred to as studies of racial difference, whereas those involving Asian-, Hispanic-, or Native Americans are referred to as ethnic or cultural comparisons. The terms race, ethnicity, and culture often are used interchangeably and may refer to the same characteristics. The primary distinction is that race more often refers to a major biological subgroup of interbreeding persons with similar physical characteristics, whereas ethnicity refers to primarily cultural features, the nonmaterial aspects or conceptual structures that determine patterns of living, such as language, customs, religion, and values. However, even race, as a category, can be viewed as primarily socially constructed because within-group genetic variability often exceeds that between any two racial groups (Williams, Lavizzo-Mourey, & Warren, 1994; see Rutter & Tienda, 2005, for a discussion of the genetic construction of ethnicity).

Although the study of ethnic groups requires attention to cultural features, it is also important to consider the status of the group within the socioeconomic system. Socioeconomic status (SES), which ranks individuals with regard to the distribution of resources, may set in motion some of the same features as ethnicity. For example, it is common in sociological literature to refer to the culture of the lower class or to middle-class values. Past and current research suggests that SES is reliably related to psychopathology (Bruce & Phelan, 2006; Johnson, Cohen, Dohrenwend, Link, & Brook, 1999) and may have a more profound effect than ethnicity in such areas as child-rearing, academic achievement, the outcome of child behavior disorders, and psychiatric symptomatology (Dohrenwend et al., 1998; Eaton, 1980). Moreover, identifiable ethnic groups may be economically and educationally disadvantaged, and as a result, both distinctions—race/ethnicity and recognizable class—may be applied to one group. African-Americans, for example, constitute a group with loosely clustered cultural elements whose members are disproportionately represented among lower SES classes.

When members of a racial or ethnic group are differentiated from others in the same society and occupy a subordinate position, they are also considered minorities. Minority status may also contribute to distinctive experiences that are similar to ethnicity. Fernando (2002) described ethnicity as a shared sense of belonging-together arising from similarities among persons within a group; he also suggested that a sense of ethnicity may arise when external pressures lead to the formation of an alliance against a common enemy or threat. Thus, disadvantaged-minority status can lead to effects similar to

culturally based ethnic features. As minority-group membership is a basis for differentiation in power, prestige, and resources, it might reasonably be seen as contributing to distress and psychopathology in much the same way as low SES (Eaton, 1980). However, research with both Native Americans (Davis, Hoffman, & Nelson, 1990) and African-Americans (Kessler & Neighbors, 1986) suggests that minority status makes an independent contribution to the understanding of psychopathology. Accordingly, the effects of SES and minority status are also pertinent and contribute to the complexity of understanding the assessment of pathology in ethnic minority groups.

Ethnic Identity and Acculturation

Ethnic groups share elements of the national culture, and each has distinctive cultural features. In the content of their beliefs and values, and in particular behavior patterns, members of minority groups may be more similar to the majority culture than to one another. Thus, there is little justification for automatically equating differences that might be found between Caucasians and Native Americans, for example, to differences between Caucasians and Hispanic-Americans. Because assignment to an ethnic group typically is derived from self-declared membership, it reveals neither biological race nor strength of ethnic identification. In an effort to better define the meaning of ethnicity, numerous investigators have attempted to develop scales to assess the strength and correlates of racial and ethnic group identification (e.g., Cross, 1978; Cuellar, Harris, & Jasso, 1980; Helms & Parhams, 1996; Kwan & Sodowsky, 1997; Phinney, 1992; Sellers & Nicole, 2003). However, ethnic identity scales have not found widespread use in clinical practice; perhaps because they address an issue—strength of identity with one's ethnic group—that many view as tangential to the use of traditional assessment instruments.

A more direct gauge of whether standardized tests provide useful information may lie in the level of "acculturation" of the group to the American mainstream. Like many constructs, acculturation, or the adoption of the beliefs, behaviors, and language of the majority, is more readily conceptualized than measured (Kang, 2006). Numerous acculturation scales have been developed. Matsudaira (2006) identified more than 50 acculturation scales, which vary widely in their conceptualization and structure. Although research investigators occasionally use acculturation as a control variable (Roesch, Wee, & Vaughn, 2006), acculturation scales have not yet achieved widespread use in clinical practice (see reviews by Burlew, Bellow, & Lovett, 2000 and Roysircar-Sodowsky & Maestas, 2000).

Culture- or ethnic-specific instruments also have been proposed as a way to ensure appropriate assessment of members of ethnic minority groups. Because the development of valid group-specific instruments would be at least as challenging as the development of existing instruments has been, there are significant practical obstacles to this approach. The few ethnic-specific instruments developed thus far have met mixed psychometric success and limited use (Cervantes, Padilla, & de Snyder, 1991; Costello, 1977; Dahlstrom, Lachar, and Dahlstrom, 1986; Jones, 1996). For example, Cervantes and colleagues developed the Hispanic Stress Inventory (HSI) as a clinical and research measure of stress-related psychopathology. Factor analyses showed that the HSI was not conceptually equivalent for American-born Latinos and Mexican-American immigrants, and that it was necessary to develop different versions of the inventory for the two groups. As new immigrations create additional ethnic minority groups, the challenge of appropriate assessment will grow, further straining attempts to create ethnic-specific instruments. Though promising, neither the concepts of ethnic identity and acculturation, nor the development of ethnic-specific tests has yet to be comprehensively incorporated into general assessment practice.

Assessment of Psychopathology
The Clinical Interview

The clinical interview remains the most common diagnostic strategy and often is used in conjunction with psychological testing. Because the clinical interview is ubiquitous in clinical settings, embodies many of the interpersonal features germane to the testing situation, and is often the criterion against which psychological tests are validated, a brief discussion of the clinical interview precedes the discussion of psychological testing. Numerous studies conducted during the past several decades have shown that clinical interviews can result in excess diagnosis of severe pathology or recommendations of more restrictive treatment for African-, Hispanic-, and Native American patients than for Whites (Blake, 1973; Flaherty & Meagher, 1980; Lawson, Yesavage, & Werner, 1984; Lu, 2004; Soloff & Turner, 1981; Mukherjee, Shukla, Woodle, Rosen, & Olarte, 1983; Neighbors, Trierweiler, Ford, & Muroff, 2003; Pavkov, Lewis, & Lyons, 1989;

Raskin, Crook, & Herman, 1975; Simon, Fleiss, Gurland, Stiller, & Sharpe, 1973; Strawkowski et al., 1995). A few have reported opposite results: Kunen, Niederhauser, Smith, Morris, and Mark (2005), for example, found an underdiagnosis of psychosis but still a relative overdiagnosis of schizophrenia in African-Americans, based on an examination of hospital charts. Investigators have reported both overdiagnosis (Aldwin & Greenberger, 1987) and underdiagnosis of psychopathology (Lu, 2004) of Asian-Americans relative to Caucasians. In a study that underscores the complexity of this issue, Zhang and Snowden (1999) showed that the magnitude and direction of ethnic differences varied with the geographic region of the sample and the type of disorder studied.

Ethnic differences in diagnosis may be attributable to one or a combination of factors: true differences in the rate of psychopathology, the presence of culturally meaningful differences that are misinterpreted as psychopathology, or bias in the clinician. As establishing true differences would necessitate prior elimination of the second and third explanations, most attention has centered on ethnic-specific manifestations of behavior and clinician bias.

Ethnic-specific Manifestations of Behavior

The cultural expression perspective assumes that racial and ethnic minorities may conduct themselves in distinctive ways that can lead to misdiagnosis during the clinical interview. Mental health and mental illness concern emotions, such as depression, happiness, or anger experienced by the individual; and the manner of expression is influenced by cultural and social factors (Barry, 2007; Mesquita & Frijda, 1992; Snowden, 1999; Whaley, 1997). In situations where the interviewer and client share a similar understanding of idioms of expression, communication is eased and idioms natural to both can be used. In the absence of shared understanding there is potentially a gulf, akin to that between a diagnostician and patient who speak different languages. This gulf might result in mislabeling "normal" behavior as problematic or to miscategorization of problematic behavior. The existence of ethnic variations in the expression of disorder, as well as the occurrence of culture-specific syndromes, is documented in psychiatric literature and recognized in recent diagnostic manuals (American Psychiatric Association, 2000; Westermeyer, 1987). For example, empirical studies have at times revealed more frequent somatic symptoms in depression for Hispanics (Beltran, 2006; Fabrega,

Rubel, & Wallace, 1967; Maduro, 1983; Weaver & Sklar, 1980), Asian-Americans (Marsella, Kinzie, & Gordon, 1973; Sue & Morishima, 1982), and Native Americans than in Caucasians (Manson, 1994).[1] Liss, Welner, Robins, and Richardson's (1973) review of psychiatric records of 256 patients revealed a better fit between symptoms and diagnosis for Caucasian than for African-Americans. They also observed a more frequent occurrence in Blacks than Whites of hallucinations and delusions that are unrelated to a diagnosis of schizophrenia, a finding that was replicated by Trierweiler et al. (2000). Apparently, both Hispanics and African-Americans with bipolar disorder report hallucinations more often than Whites with the same disorder (Lawson, 1986).

At stake here is the theoretically and practically important question of whether symptoms that express pathology, and which are canonized in our diagnostic categories, are invariant across racial and ethnic groups. Although further systematic study is needed, research spanning 40 years suggests greater congruence between symptoms and diagnostic categories for Caucasian than for ethnic minority patients. Thus, diagnostic categories may not be an equally "good fit" for all groups, a circumstance that can contribute to less accurate diagnosis of members of ethnic minority groups. Such inaccuracies are consequential for psychological tests, when clinical diagnosis is used as the criterion for predicting test validity.

Clinician Bias

Bias, which represents a directional response tendency, can arrive from many sources, including the interrelated effects of social distance, several types of cognitive and perceptual errors, as well as from personal and political beliefs. A social distance explanation posits that bias occurs when the patient and diagnostician hold very different locations in society. Ideally, the diagnostician will be able to take the role or perspective of the other, but different social positions make that difficult to do. If the behavior of the other seems unintelligible or foreign, even when it is not pathological, it is more likely to be labeled insane or abnormal (Rosenberg, 1984). With mental health professionals who are themselves members of a minority group there may be less social distance; however, social class differences may exist relative to their minority clients, and training may lead practitioners to view patients of their own ethnic or racial group as "the other." Actor-observer attribution bias may underlie the social distance phenomenon in that

when practitioners assume similarity between themselves and the patient, they are more prone to emphasize situational factors rather than inner causes, resulting in less severe diagnosis (Poland & Caplan, 2004; Trierweiler, Muroff, Jackson, Neighbors, & Munday, 2005). In an analogue investigation, whose results were consistent with both social-distance and other cognitive biases, Loring and Powell (1988) found that male and female, White and non-White psychiatrists were more accurate in diagnosing a case of their own gender and race than when either gender or race was different. Social distance does not adequately explain all their findings insofar as the psychiatrists were most accurate when neither race nor gender of the case was identified, suggesting that these bits of information led them to entertain faulty hypotheses associated with race and gender. A review of the pattern of errors is instructive. Consistent with a racial bias hypothesis, there was overestimation of pathology in the Black male patient, but less by Black than by White diagnostician. The authors speculated that psychiatrists and other mental health professional internalize standards provided in their training, for example, that Black male psychiatric patients are dangerous, violent, and suspicious. When gender and race information accompany a case, the stage is set for a confirmatory bias, which may be stimulated by symptoms, but is also derived from stereotypes about the patient's gender and ethnicity. The effects of bias can be far-reaching, affecting not only ongoing assessment, but also other cognitive processes such as memory. Memory structures are more complex for in-group than for out-group members, and we form more categories for storage of information regarding in-group members (Park & Rothbart, 1982; Poland & Caplan, 2004). It is conceivable that when recalling information about an ethnic minority patient, diagnosticians are prone to fill in with the available stereotypical information due to impoverished information storage, leading to diagnoses that confirm stereotypes and ultimately to the development of false statistical data on rates of psychopathology, which, in turn, lead to further error.

A related cognitive processing perspective suggests that errors can occur because of differential weighting of symptoms, that is, clinicians may note the same symptoms, but assign different weights depending on characteristics of the client. Trierweiler et al. (2000) found that clinicians weighted hallucinatory and paranoid symptoms more strongly in the diagnosis of African-American patients, but elevated and dysphoric mood symptoms more in the diagnosis of other patients, a bias which helps to explain the frequent "overdiagnosis" of schizophrenia in African-American patients. Neighbors et al. (2003) suggest that clinicians use a different process to link observed symptoms to diagnosis for African-American than Caucasian patients, especially in reference to schizophrenia diagnosis. Trierweiler et al. (2006) underscored the complexity of this literature by showing that clinician ethnicity may also be a factor in the way symptoms are weighted in the diagnostic process. The work of Trierweiler and associates along with studies by Malgady and Constantino (1998) and Iwamasa, Larrabee, and Merritt (2000) shows that rather than being ignored, race, ethnic, and cultural factors are used in a way that influences diagnostic decisions. Ethnic variations in symptoms present a challenge for the practitioner when they result in a poorer fit between symptoms and diagnostic category. This challenge is compounded by social distance, differential symptom attribution, and other cognitive processing errors. Whereas the traditional clinical interview seems maximally susceptible to such influences, structured diagnostic interviews were developed to overcome these sources of error (Kashner et al., 2003; Lyketsos, Aritzi, & Lyketsos, 1994).

Structured Clinical Interviews

Structured diagnostic interviews are more commonly used in research, especially epidemiological studies and clinical trials, than in routine clinical practice, where the time required to train-to-standard and for complete administration are frequently cited as barriers (Jensen & Weisz, 2002). However, the emerging emphasis on evidence-based practice in psychology has spurred recommendations for their use in routine clinical practice (APA Task Force, 2006). By design, structured interviews minimize the sources of variability that lead to unreliable psychiatric diagnoses (Summerfeldt & Antony, 2002). Like psychological tests, they have standardized content, format, and ordering of questions and provide algorithms for making a diagnostic decision. They should reduce unwarranted disparities in diagnosis among ethnic groups. Several researchers have shown that indeed the association between race and diagnosis found through a traditional interview can be attenuated or eliminated when the diagnosis is derived from structured interviews or other objective criteria (Craig, Goodman, & Hauglaund, 1982; Kashner et al., 2003; Mukherjee et al., 1983; Pavkov

et al., 1989; Neighbors et al., 2003; Whaley, 2004). Greater use of standardized interviews, which provide more consistent information, should be encouraged.

Psychological Testing

Psychological tests were developed to provide objective and standardized appraisals to support inferences about behavior or psychological processes. With any test used to measure psychopathology in ethnic groups, the assumption is implicit that an underlying disorder is expressed in the same way in each population and that the test in question adequately represents these various symptoms. If the disorder is manifest in different symptoms in different groups, this assumption is violated and the instrument is not equally appropriate for all groups. A second assumption is that the scores obtained represent true scores, whereas, in fact, each score measures the target construct with a certain level of error, and the amount of error may differ from one group to another (Choca, Shanley, & Van Denburg, 1992; Walters, Greene, Jeffrey, Kruzich, & Haskin, 1983). Further, as many psychological tests require interpretation, test use may also be subject to distortions similar to those affecting the clinical interview. All of these considerations are relevant to the most contentious issue in this debate, test fairness: whether psychological tests offer equally accurate assessment for minority groups, and, in particular, whether tests provide equally adequate basis for diagnosis, effective treatment, and for predicting level of adjustment.

Although there are scores of psychological tests that might be used to assess psychopathology, the number used with high frequency to assess adults in clinical practice and training settings is relatively small (Camara, Nathan, & Puente, 2000; Clemence & Handler, 2001). The Minnesota Multiphasic Personality Inventory (MMPI) and the Millon Clinical Multiaxial Inventory (MCMI) are the two broad-gauged self-report instruments used most frequently to assess adult personality and psychopathology.[2] Among instruments that assess specific disorders, the Beck Depression Inventory (BDI) is frequently used; however, little attention has been devoted to exploring its cross-ethnic utility (Okazaki & Tanaka-Matsumi, 2006). The most commonly used self-expressive or projective instruments are the Rorschach Inkblot Test, the Thematic Apperception Test (TAT), sentence completion tests (SCTs), and drawings (Watkins, Campbell, Nieberding, & Hallmark, 1995). For the most part, these commonly used instruments, which are reviewed below, are the same ones that have dominated psychological assessment for decades (Wade & Baker, 1977).

Self-Report Measures of Psychopathology
MINNESOTA MULTIPHASIC PERSONALITY INVENTORY-2 (MMPI-2)

Among self-report instruments used to assess psychopathology, the MMPI is most prominent and there is extensive research on its use with American ethnic groups. Greene (1987) summarized research published through 1985 that reported performance on MMPI as a function of ethnic group membership and which found meaningful scale differences (5 or more T-score points). Consonant with the view that the meaning of ethnic minority status cannot be equated across all ethnic groups, Greene found no consistent pattern for all minority samples. Hispanic–White comparisons yielded no consistent differences; however, there was a reliable pattern of higher scores for Native Americans and Asian-Americans. For comparisons between Blacks and Whites, he found that the greater the attention given to profile validity and the more stringent the controls for economic and educational levels, the less likely were there differences to be found. Since that review, substantial additional research has continued to explore the appropriate use of the MMPI-2 with ethnic minorities. The following review, focused primarily on MMPI-2, identifies the same four broad ethnic categories. We recognize, however, that each group encompasses a wide range of cultural or linguistic diversity.

American Indians

Previous research—MMPI and MMPI-2—with Native Americans has typically reported higher scale elevations, which because they were not well understood, led to warnings that differences between Native Americans and Caucasians on MMPI scale scores should be interpreted with caution (Forrey, 1996; Graham, 1993; Pollack & Shore, 1980). Recent studies attempt to bring greater clarity to scale elevation among American Indian tribes, but they also underscore the complexity of adequately addressing culture and ethnicity in test interpretation. Robin, Caldwell, and Goldman (2003) compared MMPI-2 profiles of non-patient samples from two American Indian tribes (one Southwestern and one Plains) to each other, as well as to the MMPI-2 normative sample. The authors hypothesized from previous research that Scales 4, 6, and 8 and their

corresponding content scales would be elevated; and that these differences would diminish when tribal members were matched by age, gender, and education with the normative group. The two Indian groups did not differ from one another, but both groups scored significantly higher than the normative group on five validity and clinical scales (L, F, 4, 8, and 9), six content scales (depression, health concern, antisocial practices, cynicism, bizarre mentation, and negative treatment indicators), and two supplementary scales (MacAndrews Alcoholism and addiction admission). Significant differences remained, but decreased in magnitude, when tribal members were matched with the normative sample by age, gender, and education. The authors suggested that these remaining differences reflect the greater hardships (economic, social, etc.) that tribal groups have endured as compared to the normative group; but they also acknowledged that mean differences alone cannot distinguish test bias from true differences in pathology. A companion study by the same authors (Greene, Albaugh, Robin, Caldwell, & Goldman, 2003) attempted to explore further the meaning of scale elevations by examining the empirical correlates of the MMPI-2 scores in the two Indian groups. As a criterion they used Diagnostic and Statistical Manual of Mental Disorders, 3rd edition (DSM-III) diagnoses derived from a modified Schedule for Affective Disorders and Schizophrenia-Lifetime version (SADS-L). The modification used a selection of "descriptive phrases" that the authors characterized as reflecting symptoms of substance use, antisocial behaviors, and negative affect, including depression and anxiety. In a quest for enhanced ecological validity of the criterion, the authors chose clinicians experienced with this population both to administer the SADS-L and to assign DSM-III diagnoses. Greene et al. (2003) found significant correlations between MMPI-2 elevations and DSM-III diagnoses based on the modified SADS-L, and concluded that we should not be so ready to assume test bias when significant elevations are observed among American Indian respondents.

Greene et al.'s efforts to enhance the cultural competency of SADS-L interviews and diagnoses by using clinicians familiar with the participant population did not forestall a challenge from Pace et al. (2006), who questioned the validity of using majority-created and -based criteria (i.e., SADS-L and DSM-III) to evaluate the validity of the MMPI-2 with this minority population. The essence of their challenge was that although the

DSM-III acknowledges cultural influences, it nevertheless assumes a cultural view of maladjustment that is difficult to apply without modification to minority cultures. Pace et al. (2006) also conducted their own investigation of the MMPI-2 with tribal members recruited from two distinct American Indian communities in Oklahoma, viz. Eastern Woodland Oklahoma (EWO) and Southwest Plains Oklahoma (SPO). Participants in this study were non-patients and volunteers attending tribal fairs or other tribal events. They found significant clinical elevations on the majority of MMPI-2 scales, even when education level was accounted for. Specifically, elevations near or above 5 T-points on Scales F, 1, 4, 5, 6, 7, and 8 were observed in both tribes, with elevations in the L scale among the SWPO but not the EWO (which the authors interpreted as reflecting the lower educational levels among the SWPO). The authors argue that such extensive elevation in a non-patient sample, after accounting for education, is at the very least problematic, and urged great caution in the use of MMPI-2 data in understanding personality among American Indians. For example, they argued, "unusual thinking" within the MMPI-2 may not necessarily be linked to distress or impairment within a particular tribal context. The authors urged researchers and clinicians to interpret MMPI-2 results using a cultural view consistent with the history of the particular tribes studied rather than to rely solely on the categorical, descriptive system on which the DSM is based.

African-Americans

Timbrook and Graham (1994) found no MMPI-2 validity scale differences among matched samples of Blacks and Whites; but on clinical scales Black men scored significantly higher than Whites on scales 8 and 9; among women, Blacks had higher scores on Scales 4, 5, and 9. Their comparison of unmatched samples revealed significant racial differences for both men and women on the validity scales. Additional research by Ben-Porath and his colleagues compared samples of Black and White forensic and psychiatric patients on clinical, validity, and content scales of the MMPI-2 (Arbisi, Ben-Porath, & McNulty, 1998; Ben-Porath, Shondrick, & Stafford, 1995; McNulty, Graham, Ben-Porath, & Stein, 1997). Ben-Porath et al. (1995) found no significant differences in clinical and validity scales in their forensic sample, though the other studies report some statistically significant differences that are less than five T-score points. By

contrast, Gironda (1998) reported a large number of significant differences, some exceeding five T-score points, in clinical and content scales for Black and White men and women referred for forensic assessment. Fortunately, these studies encompassed extra-test correlates of scale scores in their analyses. Correlates of MMPI-2 scale scores did not differ by race when cases from the normative sample were compared with special scales developed in 1993 by Long (Timbrook & Graham, 1994); nor, for the most part, when forensic clients' scores were compared with collateral information taken from their case files (Gironda, 1998); nor with therapists' ratings of personality and symptomatology (McNulty et al., 1997). The quality of the extra-test criteria used in these studies might be questioned as they do not represent a higher standard than the MMPI. In the aggregate, however, this body of research suggests comparable predictive validity of MMPI-2 for African-Americans who are matched for education and SES. This work is also consistent with a recent meta-analytic synthesis of 31 years of comparative MMPI research, which concluded that neither African-Americans nor Latinos were unfairly portrayed as pathological when tested with the MMPI-2 (Hall, Bansal, & Lopez, 1999). This finding is echoed in work by Arbisi, Ben-Porath, and McNulty (2002) who explored ethnic differences in MMPI-2 profiles between African-American and Caucasian psychiatric inpatients to determine whether the two ethnic groups produced differentially elevated profiles and if so, whether this reflects test bias (slope or intercept) or actual group differences. Mean differences on several validity and clinical scales were reported, and these were generally consistent with past research. Specifically, African-American men scored significantly higher than Caucasian men on anger, antisocial practices, bizarre mentation, cynicism, family problems, fears, depression, health concerns, negative treatment indicators, alcoholism and addiction acknowledgment. African-American women scored significantly higher on the first five, plus alcoholism. A step-down hierarchical multiple regression indicated the presence of prediction bias in 32 of the 65 comparisons among men, and 12 of the 65 among women. None, however, exceeded a small effect size, and the source of bias was differences in intercepts between the groups. When bias was present, it was consistently in the direction of underpredicting psychopathology in African-American males, which is inconsistent with past critiques of the MMPI as on overpredicting psychopathology in African-Americans. The authors suggest that this atypical finding warrants further study given the potential to overlook clinically relevant phenomena, but they concluded that relationships between MMPI-2 scale scores and clinically relevant phenomena were not significantly moderated by racial group membership in this inpatient psychiatric population.

In an effort to disentangle the contributions of oppression, culture, and psychopathology to MMPI-2 scores, Whatley, Allen, and Dana (2003) examined the association between MMPI-2 scale elevations and ethnic identity in a college sample. They contended that demographic variables such as ethnicity/race may serve as a proxy for more meaningful psychological constructs, for example, racial identity; and that use of such a proxy limits what is known about the meaning and magnitude of observed group differences on scores. The authors hypothesized that if MMPI scores are unrelated to cultural differences, they should be unrelated to measures of racial identity (racial identity attitude scale; Helms & Parham, 1996). However, racial identity was a significant predictor of select MMPI scale scores; specifically, scores on the (cultural) immersion–emersion subscale was a significant predictor of MMPI Scales 4 and 9, which are frequently associated with antisocial personality attributes. Because some variance in this 4–9 code type was associated with a normative identity sequence in African-American racial development, the authors argued that there is the potential for MMPI scores to pathologize individuals at this stage of identity development. Although the association was modest, the authors assert that it is comparable to the magnitude of relationships among MMPI scale scores and associated behaviors reported in the literature. The ultimate determination of whether racial identity measures tap processes associated with psychopathology or whether the MMPI pathologizes cultural difference is a key question that will require additional research. The message this preliminary study (there were 61 participants) aspires to convey for future research and assessment practice is clear: Include identity, acculturation, or other contextual measures in future MMPI research.

Hispanic-Americans

In general, fewer Hispanic–White than Black–White differences have been found on the MMPI. Campos's (1989) meta-analytic review of studies comparing Hispanics and Whites reported that a significantly higher mean L-score (approximately 4 T-score points) for Hispanics was the only consistent difference across studies. Comparisons of Hispanic-Americans and Caucasians on MMPI and MMPI-2 continue to reveal inconsistent results, with a seemingly equal likelihood that Hispanic samples will have lower or higher scores on clinical and validity scales in samples of psychiatric patients and university students (Velasquez & Callahan, 1990; Velasquez, Callahan, & Young, 1993; Whitworth & McBlaine, 1993; Whitworth & Unterbrink, 1994). Hall et al.'s (1999) meta-analytic synthesis reported aggregate effect sizes indicating higher scores on all three validity scales and lower scores on all clinical scales for Hispanics (mostly Mexican American) in comparison with Caucasians. However, only for Scales L and 5 were the differences considered robust. The L scale, which was higher for Hispanic American respondents, is typically interpreted as an index of socially desirable responding. It is unclear whether the higher score among Hispanic respondents is due to the intention to make a socially desirable presentation or to cultural difference in response style. Their finding of lower Scale 5 scores (heightened traditional masculine gender identity) among Hispanic men may also be interpreted as reflecting a culturally determined response rather than psychopathology. Thus there is little evidence that MMPI-2 scale scores portray Hispanics as excessively pathological. At present, there is inadequate research linking MMPI-2 scores to extra test behaviors among Hispanic populations. However, Butcher, Cabiya, Lucio, and Carrido's (2007) preliminary conclusion that the MMPI-2 provides valuable information about symptomatic behavior and future adjustment in Hispanic populations appears warranted.

Asian-Americans

Although the MMPI-2 standardization sample included a proportional representation of ethnic minorities, the small number of Asian-Americans in the sample made it unlikely that new norms would be sensitive to specific characteristics of these groups (Okazaki & Sue, 2000). An accumulating body of research suggests that acculturation level is associated with MMPI-2 scores for Asian-Americans (Stevens, Kwan, & Graybill, 1993). Tsai and Pike (2000) examined clinical and validity scores in an Asian-American college sample. Students at a low level of acculturation scored significantly higher than Caucasians on 9 of 13 clinical and validity scales, all differences were in the more deviant direction, and T-score differences were as great as 22 points. Low-acculturation Asian students also scored significantly higher on several scales than the medium- and high-acculturation groups, but the latter group did not differ from Caucasians. The caveat concerning ethnic identify measures is also relevant here: We do not know whether acculturation measures tap the process of psychopathology or the MMPI-2 pathologizes cultural difference. Nonetheless, MMPI-2 research with Asian-American populations dramatically highlights the potential importance of cultural factor in using psychological tests for diagnosis and treatment planning.

Our brief review of MMPI-2 use with four ethnic groups reveals quite disparate results. First, recent MMPI-2 research with African-Americans reveals little evidence of a systematic overestimation of psychopathology in samples of comparable social class. The improved picture with African-Americans may represent acculturative changes in the population, improved psychometric properties of the test, or a more inclusive normative sample of the MMPI-2 in comparison with original MMPI. There continues to be little evidence of systematic over- or under-prediction of psychopathology with Hispanic groups, and differences that are found (L scale and Scale 5) are readily understood as cultural, rather than pathological. Research with Asian-Americans is still sparse, but is suggestive of a very strong moderating influence of acculturation; whereas studies with Native Americans suggest strong caution in interpreting elevated profiles. Inter-ethnic differences highlight the distinctiveness of each group, while the association of MMPI-2 scale elevations with acculturation and ethnic identity within ethnicity underscores intra-group variability. Research incorporating both controls for SES and measures of ethnic and identity and acculturation would be useful in gauging their relative contribution MMPI-2 results in different ethnic groups.

THE MILLON CLINICAL MULTIAXIAL INVENTORY (MCMI)

There are important differences between the MCMI-I and the original MMPI in both theoretical underpinnings and construction. Unlike the original MMPI, the standardization sample for the MCMI-I included representative percentages of minority groups (a total of 19% comprising Asians, Blacks, Hispanics, and mixed ethnics). In addition, the procedures for converting raw scores into standard scores include separate conversion tables for men and women, for Blacks and Hispanics, and for the general population. Despite these efforts and evidence of similar factor structure for Blacks and

Whites, significant racial differences occurred not only at the level of item endorsement, but also in the standardized scale scores, as well as in the way the MCMI-I predicted DSM-III Axis I and Axis II disorders (Choca et al., 1992). For example, African-Americans received significantly higher scores on narcissistic, paranoid, and delusional disorder scales of the MCMI-I in a sample of psychiatric outpatients matched for age, education, and employment status (Hamberger & Hastings, 1992). In a study by Munley, Vacha-Haase, Busby, and Paul (1998), African-American inpatients scored higher than Caucasians on the same three scales in addition to scales of histrionic and drug dependence disorder on the MCMI-II; these differences were attenuated when Munley and colleagues matched their patients on primary diagnosis and comorbidity. Several investigators have used the MCMI-II with other ethnic minority samples or with samples that include ethnic minorities (Daly, 1998; Rudd & Orman, 1996; Stewart, 1999). However, there is exiguous comparative research or research on the predictive validity of the MCMI-I or -II with U.S. minority groups other than African-Americans (Craig & Bivens, 1998; Craig, Bivens, & Olson, 1997). One exception is the study by Glass, Bieber, and Tkachuk (1996) that reported significantly higher scores on several MCMI-II scores when comparing Alaskan natives with a primarily Anglo group of incarcerated offenders. Millon and Meagher (2004, p. 119) suggested that "it may be useful to develop separate norms for different ethnic groups" and Rossi and Sloore (2005) advocated for increased sensitivity to issues of equivalence in the cross-cultural and cross-national usage; however, little empirical work on the appropriate use of the MCMI with American ethnic populations has been published in recent years. Thus, Choca and colleagues' (1992) admonition to temper interpretation of MCMI scores for African-Americans until we understand more exactly the meaning of score elevations is still sound advice and is appropriate for other ethnic minority groups as well.

Projective Techniques: Self-Expressive Assessment of Psychopathology

Projective or self-expressive instruments are widely used in clinical practice, although Belter and Piotrowski (2001) reported a substantial decline in the number of clinical programs that offer training in projective instruments. Projective tests have been considered more culturally fair than self-report instruments because of their ambiguous stimuli, which are assumed to be culture-free, and also because there is minimal use of language in the presentation of test materials (Dana, 1993). When projective tests are used in an idiographic manner, they hold out the prospect of sensitivity to uniquely individual characteristics and processes. On the other hand, such use may also maximally activate the schemas and cognitive structures of the examiner. For this and other reasons, there has been considerable pressure to standardize administration, scoring, and interpretation of projective instruments. Such changes may improve psychometric properties, but may also produce instruments that paradoxically are more reflective of the normative group, and perhaps more culture-bound.

Self-expressive tests have typically been referred to as projective instruments, reflecting their association with psychoanalytic theory. The term self-expressive, to contrast with self-report, has been proposed as a less theoretically loaded and less pejorative description of projective instruments. Whether the relevant underlying process in such instruments is projection, visual representation, or some other perceptual or cognitive process is under debate (Hibbard, 2003; Leichtman, 2004). Traditionally, the value of projective instruments stemmed explicitly or implicitly from belief in the projective hypothesis, which argues that when people attempt to understand an ambiguous stimulus, their own needs, experiences, thought processes, and psychopathology are projected. Presumably, ambiguous stimuli force the respondent to organize and interpret, and this, in turn, provides an entree to the private world of the individual (Holtzman, 1980). Viglione's (1999) contention that the Rorschach has demonstrated versatility with diverse groups in the United States rested largely on endorsing assumptions underlying the projective hypothesis. Holtzman outlined three assumptions underlying the projective hypothesis: one, responses to projective stimuli provide an adequate sample on which to make judgments about personality and psychopathology; two, the determinants of the responses are basic and the same for all groups; and three, projective tests provide an equally adequate assessment for all groups. All three assumptions are important in assessing quality of projective tests with different groups. With regard to the first assumption, there are often implicit or explicit guidelines or agreement about what constitutes an adequate sample of responses for some projective tests. For example, with the Exner Comprehensive System a minimum of 15–20 responses is considered

scorable (Exner, 1993). Response production is an important subject in using self-expressive instruments with ethnic minority groups, whose members often give fewer responses than Caucasians (Dana, 1993; Glass et al., 1996; Howes & DeBlassie, 1989). Response production is related to educational level, but controlling educational level does not always eliminate the difference between African-Americans and Caucasians. Frank (1992) concluded that productivity was the one consistent difference between African-Americans and Caucasians, a finding he attributed to differences in self-disclosure rather than in intelligence or depression, which were controlled in studies on which his conclusions were drawn. Because of their lower responsiveness, protocols of ethnic minorities may be less valid or interpretable. The second assumption, that the determinants of responses are basic and universal, is more difficult to verify. It has long been known, however, that situational factors such as the examiner's sex and the quality of rapport can affect both the productivity of the patient and the type of projection (Abel, 1973). Recent research has offered some empirical support for the third assumption: that projective tests, at least in the form of the Rorschach, provide comparable assessment for different ethnic groups (Meyer, 2002; Presley, Smith, Hilsenroth, & Exner, 2001).

The Rorschach Inkblot Test

The Rorschach has been listed among the top 20 assessment instruments since 1935 (Camara et al. 2000). The development of Exner's (1993) Comprehensive System for scoring and interpreting the Rorschach, which created renewed interest, should be viewed as a pivotal point in Rorschach history. It should also be noted that the Exner Comprehensive Scoring System is not predicated on the projective hypothesis. The Rorschach resurgence has generated additional validation research as well as efforts to discredit the Rorschach in the name of science. Indeed the past decade has seen an unprecedented number of articles presenting conceptual and empirical vindication as well as the hyperbolic vilification found in such work as Lilienfeld, Wood, and Garb (2000) and Wood, Nezworski, Lilienfeld, and Garb's (2003) book, *What's wrong with the Rorschach?* (which has as a subtitle, *Science confronts the controversial inkblot test*). For vindicating arguments, see Hibbard (2003), the third and fourth issues of volume II of *Psychological Assessment* (1999), and the official statement of the board of the Society for Personality Assessment (Anonymous,

2005). Although this controversy addresses concerns about the reliability, validity, efficiency, and effectiveness of the Rorschach, per se, the debate has also touched on appropriateness of the Rorschach for use with members of minority groups, a topic that has a long history.

The Rorschach has been used extensively in anthropological studies of personality and culture (e.g., Hallowell, 1945). The first racial (Black–White) comparison on the Rorschach was conducted more than 50 years ago (Abel, 1973); a study involving Puerto Rican children occurred in 1966 (Ruse and Berkowitz, cited in Abel, 1973); and a number of studies were completed by Boyer and Klopfer and their associates with Apache children and adults (1963, 1964, 1968). Between 1970 and 1990, only a handful of studies addressed the performance of ethnic groups on the Rorschach (Howes & DeBlassie, 1989; Scott, 1981). A cursory examination of Exner's (1993) comprehensive scoring and interpretive guide revealed no systematic consideration of race and ethnicity in use of the Rorschach. In their Rorschach study of incarcerated Alaskan native and nonnative men, Glass et al. (1996) found a few predicted and several unpredicted differences between the groups. There were, however, no significant differences in Rorschach scores for three different levels of acculturation (traditional, bicultural, and assimilated) among the Alaskan native sample. Presley et al. (2001) formed a comparison group of 44 Whites and 44 African-Americans from the Comprehensive System normative sample ($N = 700$). They compared the two samples, which were matched on age, sex, education, and socioeconomic class on 23 variables, and found significant difference on only three. These three variables were suggestive of greater anger, higher schizophrenia index, and less cooperative responses among African-Americans, although only the last was considered large enough to suggest clinical significance. The authors interpreted the lower level of cooperative responses as suggesting that African-Americans expect cooperative reactions less routinely than Caucasians and perceive others to be less sensitive to their needs. The most striking finding, however, was similarity of the groups on the vast majority of variables studied in these matched samples. This study explored the question of mean differences on Rorschach scores and found little evidence that race moderated the scores. In a more in-depth study, Meyer (2002) used a large clinical "files" sample of 432 patients including 242 Whites, 157 African-Americans, and 33 members of other ethnic minority groups. He attempted to systematically test for bias by demonstrating a common factor structure for Whites, African-Americans, and a general minority group category; and by determining whether there was evidence of slope or intercept bias. The analyses generally supported Meyer's position that the Rorschach can be used effectively with majority and minority clients who are matched for age, education, marital, and inpatient status. As Meyer noted, however, a major limitation of the study was the fact that the criterion against which the Rorschach was measured was prior clinical diagnosis. The results should therefore be viewed in light of the limitations of clinical diagnosis noted above: Demonstrating that one instrument predicts another potentially biased one speaks about the correlation between the tests, but does not settle the question of their fairness. Nonetheless, the work of Presley et al. and Meyer makes an important beginning contribution and suggests that the Rorschach may have comparable utility for very carefully matched Caucasian and African-American groups. Research with other ethnic minority groups is still too scant to be conclusive.

Picture-Story Tests

The prototype of the picture-story test is Murray's Thematic Apperception Tests (TAT). The TAT was developed on the assumption that somewhat ambiguous, but emotionally suggestive, pictures will elicit personal narratives reflecting underlying needs and experiences. The scoring of the TAT with any population is problematic, and numerous scoring systems have been developed. Lilienfeld et al. (2000) describe some of the scoring systems as promising, but note that none has been adopted widely in clinical practice, and scant research has addressed the applicability of these scoring schemes to different cultural groups (Smith, Atkinson, McClelland, & Veroff, 1992). In clinical situations, few practitioners adhere to a standard system; instead, patients' stories are examined for themes and conflicts; and the scoring may be entirely impressionistic (Rossini & Moretti, 1997). For that reason, the scoring, and possibly the interpretation of the TAT, has been more variable than for the Rorschach, for which there are standard scoring systems. Despite the existence of a standard pool of stimuli, use of the TAT in common practice does not appear to constitute standardized assessment. It is not surprising then that serious questions have been raised about its reliability and validity for any group and about its incremental value in relation to self-report measures of personality and psychopathology (Lilienfeld et al., 2000).

Cultural and situational themes saturate the TAT. In the standard set of TAT card, the figures are of a certain race, a particular era, and the depicted themes may be culturally bound. These features may be ideal when they fit with the background of the examinee. If, on the other hand, the TAT stimuli are incongruent with the examinee's experience, there is greater potential for lack of identification that could inhibit verbal fluency and other important aspects of the test performance. Recognition of this limitation is apparent in articles published as long ago as the 1950s. Perhaps for that reason the TAT has a long history of being adapted for different ages, for example, the Senior Apperception Test and Children's Apperception Test (Bellak & Abrams, 1997); and for ethnic minority groups (Constantino, Dana, & Malgady, 2007; Dana, 2000; Henry, 1956; Snowden & Todman, 1982). Ethnic-specific versions of the test have been developed for several Native American tribes, African-Americans, and Hispanic groups.

Monopoli and Alworth (2000) noted that except for the Indian Research Project conducted in the 1940s, TAT research on Native American culture and psychological characteristics has been sparse and unsystematic. Apparently, numerous modifications of the TAT characters have been made to depict features closer to a variety of Native American tribes, but there are no systematic scoring systems for use with these pictures and thus interpretation is dependent on clinical inference. Some guidelines for use of the original TAT were provided by Henry (1956) for use with the Lakota people and by Monopoli (1984) for use with the Navaho, Hopi, and Zuni. Dana (1993) recommended that interpretation of TAT with Native Americans should not be solely predicated on expertise with the TAT, but that it also required extensive tribe-specific knowledge, often including tribal language. Reticence or low responding has also been found to be of concern in using the TAT with Native American groups. Whether this reticence is due to economic or educational factors, to cultural differences in the meaningfulness of the task or stimuli, or to reservations about the assessment process is undetermined.

The TAT was first adapted for use with African Americans by Thompson (1949), who modified facial features and darkened the skin color of characters on the cards to enhance identification with the stimulus figures. These modifications seemed to result in greater response production, but that finding is often disputed because word count was used as a measure of responsiveness. Bailey and Green (1977) developed another version of the TAT, the Black Thematic Apperception Test (B-TAT), which changed the hairstyle and clothing of the figures to enhance identification by African-Americans. Again, there was a suggestion of increased response production. (See Snowden and Todman, 1982, for a detailed critique of these TAT modifications.) Even with the modifications just mentioned, however, Black respondents remained relatively reserved in their response to TAT cards, raising the possibility that it is not the level of physical similarity with the stimulus that is critical, but the psychological meaning of the stimuli, and the projective assessment process itself differs between ethnic and racial groups. A slightly later development in this progression is a test developed by Williams (Williams & Johnson, 1981). The Themes Concerning Blacks (TCB) went further than its predecessors in trying to depict not only Black characters, but also features of Black life in different settings. There is also a scoring system, but comparisons with the TAT indicate that the TCB is essentially a different test; and its empirical correlates have not been fully tested (Dana, 1993). Each of these tests—T-TAT, B-TAT, and TCB—seems to facilitate responsiveness and can be considered an alternative to the original TAT. But none has yet found general use in clinical situations, and further psychometric development is needed.

By far the most fully developed adaptation of the TAT is TEMAS (Spanish for themes), originally developed for use with Hispanic children and adolescents (Constantino et al., 2007). Differences from the original TAT include ethnicity of the character and the use of color rather than achromatic pictures. The authors indicate that the TEMAS enhances self-disclosure in Hispanic clients, in comparison with traditional projective tests. They have also presented rudimentary evidence of criterion-related validity, a scoring system, and group-specific norms for African-Americans, Caucasians, and Hispanics. The test is available for general use in clinical situations. The authors have developed a parallel form for use with Asian-American populations (Constantino et al., 2007; Constantino & Malgady, 2000). With continued enhancement of its psychometric qualities, TEMAS promises to be useful in the assessment of psychopathology and already offers some improvements to the original TAT as it is commonly used.

Sentence Completion and Figure Drawing Tests

If one eliminates clinical interviews and intelligence and neurological tests from the list of commonly used procedures, SCTs and figure drawings are ranked among the top 10 (Camara et al., 2000; Watkins et al., 1995). Each of these procedures encompasses numerous strategies ranging from the use of a standard set of stimuli with a structured scoring system and interpretive guidelines through informal use in which the practitioner may select stimuli from a standard set or develop items and interpretations for each patient (Dana, 1998; Holaday, Smith, & Sherry, 2000). Sherry, Dahlen, and Holaday (2004) identified more than 40 different SCTs; however, only a few, viz. the Rotter Incomplete Sentences Blank and Washington University Incomplete Sentence Test of Ego Development, have been researched extensively. The scoring procedures developed for these SCT instruments are not used routinely in clinical practice (Holaday et al., 2000).

There are also several prominent graphic techniques. The best known are the Draw-A-Person (DAP), House-Tree-Person (HTP), and the Kinetic Family Drawing. The last of these is considered a kinetic technique because unlike the other two it directs the patient to draw a figure in action. Among the three, only the DAP is frequently used with adult populations. Like the Rorschach, graphic techniques have been the subject of intense recent controversy (Lilienfeld et al., 2000). Critics have demonstrated that there is no empirical evidence for the validity of specific quantitative indicators such as line thickness, figure size, and detail (e.g., Joiner, 1997; Joiner, Schmidt, & Barnett, 1996). Further, without strong interpretive guidelines, practitioners appear to carry over unsupported lay schemas about the meaning of drawings, for example, that a figure with broad shoulders indicates that the client feels burdened (Smith & Dumont, 1995), whereas empirical studies do not support such associations. Supporters of projective drawings have long held, however, that figure drawings are most meaningful when interpreted holistically in an approach that integrates the client's experience rather than from an enumeration of quantitative indicators (Handler & Riethmiller, 1998; Riethmiller & Handler, 1997; Tharinger & Stark, 1990). The appropriate use of projective drawings with ethnic minority clients in the United States has not typically been a part of this debate (see Naglieri, McNeish, & Bardos, 1991, for an exception).

However, there is evidence to indicate that drawings from both children and adults in other societies (German, Nigerian, Australian Aboriginal, and Mexican, among others) are different from those of Americans (Handler, Campbell, & Martin, 2004), suggesting that environment and culture exert an influence.

Comparative studies of the SCT and DAP have more often been directed at comparisons of cross-national groups than of ethnic subgroups within the United Sates (Handler et al., 2004; Sherry et al., 2004). Given variations in language use and physical characteristics among diverse U.S. groups, it is conceivable that clients of different ethnic minority groups may give distinctive responses to both the SCTs and projective drawings. When SCTs and projective drawings are employed in the informal manner common in present clinical practice, they might be thought of as adjunct to the clinical interview rather than as formal testing procedures and their utility with ethnic minority persons will depend on skill and cultural awareness of the practitioner. In view of the widespread use of these procedures, there is a great need for additional study of their basic psychometric qualities, their added value, their clinical utility, and their applicability to ethnic minority groups.

Conclusions

There have been many advances in the development of assessment instruments with applicability to diverse groups in the past decade. The MMPI-2 is a prime example. Some of the most extreme cautions about use of MMPI with African-Americans and Hispanic Americans have abated. Recent research with the Rorschach also holds out the likelihood that it is equally applicable to very closely matched groups of African-Americans and Whites. It bears repeating, however, that not all minority groups are alike. Findings that apply to one group are not necessarily applicable to all. For example, research with MMPI-2 suggests substantial similarity in mean scores for Hispanic and normative samples, but substantial and poorly understood overdiagnosis of psychopathology for Native American samples (Greene et al., 2003; Pace et al., 2006) and the applicability of the Rorschach to ethnic groups other than African Americans remains to be established. Thus, we have not reached the point of universal applicability of the major instruments used to assess psychopathology. Among other frequently used instruments such as the SCT and figure drawings, concerns about their reliability and validity continue to raise questions of their utility with all groups.

Despite the flaws of traditional instruments, the widespread development of ethnic-specific instruments seems impracticable because of the extensive effort and time that would be required to develop them and to establish their equivalence with existing instruments. Moreover, it is conceivable that instruments developed for persons with a very low level of acculturation might be inappropriate for highly acculturated members of the same ethnic group (Tsai & Pike, 2000). Similarly, the substantial intra-group variability, often including language, within such broad ethnic categories as Asian-American, suggests that multiple instruments might be required for those groups (Cervantes et al., 1991).

There are frequent admonitions to incorporate a measure of acculturation or ethnic identity to disentangle the manifestations of culture from pathology. At present, however, there are no universally accepted instruments to indicate when acculturation is sufficient to justify standard assessment procedures, or when ethnic identification is central to an understanding of psychopathology in a given patient. We do not know what dimensions of a particular culture produce distinctive emotional and behavioral manifestations, or when observed group differences are attributable to pathology rather than ethnic variations. Thus, subtracting or controlling for the effects of acculturation is conceptually appealing, but difficult to implement. In the case of ethnic minority groups with low average SES, we still need to know when differences on psychological tests are attributable to social class, when to the effects of minority status, and when to distinctive cultural features.

There is obviously a great need for continued development of instruments with desirable psychometric qualities that can be used with diverse groups. In view of the subtleties and complexities involved in culturally sensitive assessment, however, it is unlikely that we will find a satisfactory solution focused narrowly on testing instruments. In the absence of a formulaic solution, practitioners will need to take a textured approach that encompasses quality of the assessment instrument, ethnic identity, acculturation, cultural explanations of illness, and the patient's and examiner's reaction to the assessment situation (American Psychiatric Association, 2000; Dana, 2005; Whaley, 2001). These desirable qualities are captured in the construct of cultural competence, which has been discussed widely as a framework for approaching treatment of minority populations, and appears relevant to assessment as well (Arbisi et al., 2002; Pace et al., 2006). There are several models of cultural competence (Dana, Aguilar-Kitibutr, Diaz-Vivar, & Vetter, 2002; Sue & Sue, 2003). Allen (2007) presented a comprehensive model for multicultural assessment that depicts the many points in assessment, from the interview through testing to report writing, where cultural knowledge and understanding is necessary; the authors in Lim's (2006) recent book attempt to depict the ways in which knowledge about particular ethnic groups, their idioms of distress, and views on mental illness might be incorporated into all aspects of the clinical process, including assessment.

Whatever the distinctive features of the model presented, cultural competence is understood to include attitudes or values, knowledge, and skills that affect the assessment process. Recent models continue to emphasize that the attitudes, values, and behavior constituting the culture of the clinician are often unobserved, and, to a great extent, exist outside of conscious awareness (Westermeyer, 1987). Self-scrutiny, directed group discussions, reading, and supervised practice can be beneficial to the trainee and experienced clinician in the process of examining assessor bias. Required knowledge and skills include expertise regarding psychopathology and diagnosis in minority groups and greater sophistication in making clinical judgments, as well as expert knowledge of the strengths and limitations of the assessment instruments. In short, diagnostic accuracy may be enhanced when the assessor has an awareness of bias and ethnocentrism; an understanding of the processes of decision making and clinical judgment sufficient to mitigate cognitive processing errors; and enough knowledge of the cultural background and idioms of distress among their clients to provide a context for interpreting test data.

Notes

1. Despite the frequency of this finding, work by Mumford (1993) and Zhang and Snowden (1999) cast double on its generality.

2. A review for possible inclusive of the Big Five Inventory (BFI) revealed limited clinical use. Moreover, although the BFI has been used extensively in international comparisons, it has rarely been used to study interethinic variability in the United States (Leininger, 2002; Roesch, Wee, & Vaughn, 2006; Worrel & Cross, 2004) and has not been adopted for clinical use.

References

Abel, T. M. (1973). *Psychological testing in cultural contexts.* New Haven, CT: College and University Press.

Aldwin, C., & Greenberger, E. (1987). Cultural differences in the predictors of depression. *American Journal of Community Psychology, 15*(6), 789–813.

Allen, J. (2007). A multicultural assessment supervision model to guide research and practice. *Professional Psychology: Research and Practice, 38,* 248–258.

American Psychiatric Association. (2000). *Diagnostic and statistical manual of mental disorders* (4th Rev. ed.). Washington, DC: Author.

Anonymous. (2005). The status of the Rorschach in clinical and forensic practice: An official statement by the board of trustees of the Society for Personality Assessment. *Journal of Personality Assessment, 85,* 219–237.

APA Presidential Task Force on Evidence-Based Practice. (2006). Evidence-based practice in psychology. *American Psychologist, 61,* 271–285.

Arbisi, P., Ben-Porath, Y. S., & McNulty, J. L. (1998). *Impact of ethnicity on the MMPI-2 in inpatient settings.* Paper presented at the 106th annual meeting of the American Psychological Association, San Francisco.

Arbisi, P., Ben-Porath, Y., & McNulty, J. L. (2002). A comparison of MMPI-2 validity in African American and Caucasian psychiatric inpatients. *Psychological Assessment, 14,* 3–15.

Bailey, B. E., & Green, J. (1977). Black Thematic Apperception Test stimulus material. *Journal of Personality Assessment, 41,* 25–30.

Barry, D. T. (2007) Ethnicity, race, and men's mental health. In J. E. Grant & M. N. Potenza (Eds.), *Textbook of men's mental health* (pp. 343–361). Washington, DC: American Psychiatric Publishing.

Bellak, L., & Abrams, D. M. (1997). *The T.A.T., the C.A.T., and the S.A.T. in clinical use* (6th ed.). Needham, MA: Allyn & Bacon.

Belter, R., & Piotrowski, C. (2001). Current status of doctoral-level training in psychological testing. *Journal of Clinical Psychology, 57*(6), 717–726.

Beltran, I. (2006). The relation of culture to differences in depressive symptoms and coping strategies: Mexican American and European American college students. *Dissertation Abstracts, 67*(4-B), 2214.

Ben-Porath, Y. S., Shondrick, D. D., & Stafford, K. (1995). MMPI-2 and race in a forensic diagnostic sample. *Criminal Justice and Behavior, 22,* 12–32.

Blake, W. (1973). The influence of race on diagnosis. *Studies in Social Work, 43,* 184–192.

Boyer, L., Boyer, R. M., Brawer, F. R., Kawai, H., & Klopfer, B. (1964). Apache age groups. *Journal of Projective Techniques and Personality Assessment, 28,* 397–402.

Boyer, L., Boyer, R. M., Kawai, H., Scheiner, S. B., & Klopfer, B. (1968). Apache "learners" and "non-learners." *Journal of Projective Techniques and Personality Assessment, 32,* 147–159.

Boyer, L., Klopfer, B., Brawer, F. B., & Kawai, H. (1963). Comparisons of shamans and pseudoshamans of the Apaches of the Mescalero Indian Reservation. *Journal of Personality Assessment, 28,* 173–180.

Bruce, B. G., & Phelan, J. C. (2006). Fundamental social causes: The ascendancy of social factors as determinants of distributions of mental illnesses in populations. In W. W. Eaton (Ed.), *Medical and psychiatric comorbidity over the course of life* (pp. 77–94). Washington, DC: American Psychiatric Publishing.

Burlew, A. K., Bellow, S., & Lovett, M. (2000). Racial identity measures: A review and classification. In R. Dana (Ed.), *Handbook of cross-cultural and multicultural assessment* (pp. 173–196). Mahwah, NJ: Erlbaum.

Butcher, J. N., Cabiya, J., Lucio, E., Garrido, M. (2007). *Assessing Hispanic clients using the MMPI-2 and MMPI-A.* Washington, DC: American Psychological Association.

Camara, W., Nathan, J., & Puente, A. (2000). Psychological test usage: Implications in professional psychology. *Professional Psychology: Research and Practice, 31,* 141–154.

Campos, L. P. (1989). Adverse impact, unfairness, and bias in psychological screening of Hispanic peace officers. *Hispanic Journal of Behavioral Sciences, 11,* 122–135.

Cervantes, R. C., Padilla, A., & de Snyder, N. S. (1991). The Hispanic Stress Inventory: A culturally relevant approach to psychosocial assessment. *Psychological Assessment, 3,* 438–447.

Choca, J. P., Shanley, L. A., & Van Denburg, E. (1992). *Interpretive guide to the Millon Clinical Multiaxial Inventory.* Washington, DC: American Psychological Association.

Clemence, A. J., & Handler, L. (2001). Psychological assessment on internship: A survey of training directors and their expectations of students. *Journal of Personality Assessment, 76,* 18–47.

Constantino, G., & Malgady, R. G. (2000). Multicultural and cross-cultural utility of the TEMAS (Tell Me a Story) Test. In R. Dana (Ed.), *Handbook of cross-cultural and multicultural personality assessment* (pp. 481–513). Mahwah, NJ: Erlbaum.

Constantino, R., Dana, R. H., & Malgady, R. G. (2007). *TEMAS (Tell Me a Story) assessment in multicultural societies.* Mahwah, NJ: Erlbaum.

Costello, R. M. (1977). Construction and cross-validation of an MMPI Black–White scale. *Journal of Personality Assessment, 41,* 514–519.

Craig, R. J., & Bivens, A. (1998). Factor structure of the MCMI-III. *Journal of Personality Assessment, 70,* 190–196.

Craig, R. J., Bivens, A., & Olson, R. (1997). MCMI-III-derived typological analysis of cocaine and heroin addicts. *Journal of Personality Assessment, 69,* 583–595.

Craig, T., Goodman, A. B., & Hauglaund, G. (1982). Impact of DSM-III on clinical practice. *American Journal of Psychiatry, 139,* 922–925.

Cross, W. E. (1978). The Thomas and Cross models of psychological nigrescence: A review. *Journal of Black Psychology, 5,* 13–31.

Cuellar, I., Harris, I. C., & Jasso, R. (1980). An acculturation scale for Mexican American normal and clinical populations. *Hispanic Journal of Behavioral Science, 2,* 199–217.

Dahlstrom, W. G., Lachar, D., & Dahlstrom, L. E. (Eds.). (1986). *MMPI patterns of American minorities.* Minneapolis, MN: University of Minnesota Press.

Daly, J. E. (1998). Predicting compliance among men who batter: The contribution of demographics, violence-related factors and psychopathology. *Dissertation Abstracts International: Section B—The Sciences and Engineering, 59*(5-B), 2414.

Dana, R. H. (1993). *Multicultural assessment perspectives for professional psychology.* Boston: Allyn & Bacon.

Dana, R. H. (1998). Projective assessment of Latinos in the United States: Current realities, problems, and prospects. *Cultural Diversity and Mental Health, 3,* 165–184.

Dana, R. H. (2000). *Handbook of cross-cultural personality assessment.* Mahwah, NJ: Lawrence Erlbaum.

Dana, R. H. (2005). *Multicultural assessment: Principles, applications, and examples.* Mahwah, NJ: Lawrence Erlbaum.

Dana, R. H., Aguilar-Kitibutr, A., Diaz-Vivar, N., & Vetter, H. (2002). A teaching method for multicultural assessment: Psychological report contents and cultural competence. *Journal of Personality Assessment, 79,* 207–215.

Davis, G. L., Hoffman, R. G., & Nelson, K. S. (1990). Differences between Native Americans and Whites on the California Psychological Inventory. *Psychological Assessment: A Journal of Consulting and Clinical Psychology, 2,* 238–242.

Dohrenwend, B. P., Levav, I., Shrout, P. E., Schwartz, S., Naveh, G., Link, B. G., et al. (1998). Ethnicity, SES status and psychiatric disorders: The causation-selection issue. In B. Dohrenwend (Ed.), *Adversity, stress, and psychopathology* (pp. 285–318). New York: Oxford University Press.

Eaton, W. W. (1980). *The sociology of mental disorders.* New York: Praeger.

Exner, J., Jr. (1993). *The Rorschach: A Comprehensive System, Vol. 1: Basic Foundations* (3rd ed.). New York: John Wiley & Sons.

Fabrega, H., Rubel, A. J., & Wallace, C. A. (1967). Some social and cultural features of working-class Mexican psychiatric outpatients. *Archives of General Psychiatry, 16,* 704–712.

Fernando, S. (2002). *Mental health, race, and culture* (2nd ed.). New York: Palgrave.

Flaherty, J. A., & Meagher, R. (1980). Measuring racial bias in inpatient treatment. *American Journal of Psychiatry, 137,* 679–682.

Forrey, B. (1996). *MMPI-2 dissimulation with an America Indian sample.* Unpublished doctoral dissertation, University of South Dakota, Vermillion.

Frank, G. (1992). The response of African Americans to the Rorschach: A review of research. *Journal of Personality Assessment, 59,* 317–325.

Gironda, R. J. (1998). Comparative validity of MMPI-2 scores of African Americans and Caucasians in a forensic diagnostic sample (Unpublished doctoral dissertation, Kent State University, Kent, OH).

Glass, M., Bieber, S., & Tkachuk, M. (1996). Personality styles and dynamics of Alaska native and nonnative incarcerated men. *Journal of Personality Assessment, 66,* 583–603.

Graham, J. R. (1993). *MMPI-2: Assessing personality and psychopathology.* New York: Oxford University Press.

Greene, R. L. (1987). Ethnicity and MMPI performance: A review. *Journal of Consulting and Clinical Psychology, 55,* 497–512.

Greene, R. L., Albaugh, B., Robin, R., Caldwell, A., & Goldman, D. (2003). Use of the MMPI-2 in American Indians: II. Empirical correlates. *Psychological Assessment, 15,* 360–369.

Hall, G. C. N., Bansal, A., & Lopez, I. R. (1999). Ethnicity and psychopathology: A meta-analytic review of 31 years of comparative MMPI–MMPI-2 research. *Psychological Assessment, 11,* 186–197.

Hallowell, A. (1945). The Rorschach technique in the study of personality and culture. *American Anthropologist, 47,* 195–210.

Hamberger, L. K., & Hastings, J. E. (1992). Racial differences on the MCMI-II in an outpatient sample. *Journal of Personality Assessment, 58,* 90–95.

Handler, L., Campbell, A., & Martin, B. (2004). Use of graphic techniques in personality assessment: Reliability, validity, and clinical utility. In M. J. Hilsenroth, & D. L. Segal (Vol. Eds.), *Comprehensive handbook of psychological assessment, Vol. 2: Personality Assessment* (pp. 387–404). Hoboken, NJ: John Wiley & Sons.

Handler, L., & Riethmiller, R. (1998) Teaching and learning the administration and interpretation of graphic techniques. In L. Handler & M. Hilsenroth (Eds.), *Teaching and learning assessment* (pp. 267–294). Mahwah, NJ: Erlbaum.

Helms, J. E., & Parhams, T. (1996). The racial identity attitude scale. In R. L. Jones (Ed.), *Handbook of tests and measurements for Black populations* (pp. 164–174). Hampton, VA: Cobb & Henry.

Henry, W. E. (1956). *The analysis of fantasy.* New York: John Wiley & Sons.

Hibbard, S. (2003). A critique of Lilienfeld et al.'s (2000) The scientific status of projective techniques. *Journal of Personality Assessment, 80,* 260–271.

Holaday, M., Smith, D. A., & Sherry, A. (2000). Sentence completion tests: A review of the literature and results of a survey of members of the society for personality assessment. *Journal of Personality Assessment, 74,* 371–383.

Holtzman, W. H. (1980). Projective techniques. In H. C. Triandis & J. W. Berry (Eds.), *Handbook of cross-cultural psychology* (Vol. 2, pp. 245–278). Boston: Allyn & Bacon.

Howes, R. D., & DeBlassie, R. R. (1989). Modal errors in the cross cultural use of the Rorschach. *Journal of Multicultural Counseling and Development, 17,* 79–84.

Iwamasa, G. Y., Larrabee, A. L., & Merritt, R. D. (2000). Are *personality disorder* criteria ethnically biased? A card sort analysis. *Cultural Diversity and Ethnic Minority Psychology, 6,* 284–296.

Jensen, A., & Weisz, J. (2002). Assessing match and mismatch between practitioner-generated and standardized interview-generated diagnoses for clinic-referred children and adolescents. *Journal of Consulting and Clinical Psychology, 70,* 158–168.

Johnson, J., Cohen, P., Dohrenwend, B., Link, B. G., & Brook, J. S. (1999). A longitudinal investigation of social causation and social selection processes involved in the association between SES status and psychiatric disorders. *Journal of Abnormal Psychology, 108,* 490–499.

Joiner, T. E., Jr. (1997). Drawing conclusions—or not—from drawings. *Journal of Personality Assessment, 69,* 476–481.

Joiner, T. E., Jr., Schmidt, K. L., & Barnett, J. (1996). Size, detail, and line heaviness in children's drawings as correlates of emotional distress: (More) negative evidence. *Journal of Personality Assessment, 67,* 127–141.

Jones, R. L. (1996). *Handbook of tests and measurements for Black populations.* Hampton, VA: Cobb & Henry.

Kang, S. (2006). Measurement of acculturation, scale formats, and language competence: Their implications for adjustment. *Journal of Cross-cultural Psychology, 37,* 669–693

Kashner, T., Rush, A., Suris, A., Biggs, M., Gajewski, V., Hooker, D., et al. (2003). Impact of structured clinical interviews on physicians' practices in community mental health settings. *Psychiatric Services, 54,* 712–718.

Kessler, R. C., & Neighbors, H. W. (1986). A new perspective on the relationships among race, social class, and psychological stress. *Journal of Health and Social Behavior, 27,* 107–115.

Kunen, S., Niederhauser, R., Smith, P., Morris, J., & Marx, B. (2005). Race disparities in psychiatric rates in emergency departments. *Journal of Consulting and Clinical Psychology, 73,* 116–126.

Kwan, K. L., & Sodowsky, G. R. (1997). Internal and external ethnic identity and their correlates: A study of Chinese American immigrants. *Journal of Multicultural Counseling and Development, 25,* 51–67.

Lawson, W. B. (1986). Racial and ethnic factors in psychiatric research. *Hospital and Community Psychiatry, 37*, 50–54.

Lawson, W. B., Yesavage, J. A., & Werner, P. D. (1984). Race, violence, and psychopathology. *Journal of Clinical Psychiatry, 45*, 294–297.

Leichtman, M. (2004). Projective tests: The nature of the task. In M. Hersen (Series ed.) & M. J. Hilsenroth & D. L. Segal (Vol. eds.), *Comprehensive handbook of psychological assessment, Vol. 2: Personality assessment* (pp. 297–314). Hoboken, NJ: John Wiley & Sons.

Leininger, A. (2002). Vietnamese–American personality and acculturation: An exploration of relations between personality traits and cultural goals. In R. McCrae & J. Allik (Eds.), *The Five-Factor Model of personality across cultures* (pp. 197–225). New York: Kluwer Academic/Plenum.

Lilienfeld, S., Wood, J., & Garb, H. (2000). The scientific status of projective techniques. *Psychological Science in the Public Interest, 1*, 27–66.

Lim, R. (2006). *Clinical manual of cultural psychiatry.* Washington, DC: American Psychiatric Publishing.

Liss, J. L., Welner, A., Robins, E., & Richardson, M. (1973). Psychiatric symptoms in White and Black inpatients: I. Record study. *Comprehensive Psychiatry, 14*, 475–481.

Lopez, S., & Nunez, J. A. (1987). Cultural factors considered in selected diagnostic criteria and interview schedules. *Journal of Abnormal Psychology, 96*, 270–272.

Loring, M., & Powell, B. (1988). Gender, race, and DSM-III: A study of the objectivity of psychiatric diagnostic behavior. *Journal of Health and Social Behavior, 29*, 1–22.

Lu, F. (2004). Culture and inpatient psychiatry. In W.-S. Tseng & J. Streltzer (Eds.), *Cultural competence in clinical psychiatry* (pp. 21–36). Washington, DC: American Psychiatric Publishing.

Lyketsos, C., Aritzi, S., & Lyketsos, G. (1994). Effectiveness of office-based psychiatric practice using a structured diagnostic interview to guide treatment. *Journal of Nervous and Mental Disease, 182*, 720–723.

McNulty, J. L., Graham, J. R., Ben-Porath, Y. S., & Stein, L. A. R. (1997). Comparative validity of MMPI-2 scores of African American and Caucasian mental health center clients. *Psychological Assessment, 9*, 464–470.

Maduro, R. (1983). Curanderismo and Latino views of diseases and curing. *Western Journal of Medicine, 139*, 868–874.

Malgady, R. G., & Constantino, G. (1998). Symptom severity in bilingual Hispanics as a function of clinician ethnicity and language of interview. *Psychological Assessment, 10*, 120–127.

Manson, S. M. (1994). Culture and depression. Discovering variations in the experience of illness. In W. B. Lonner & R. S. Malpass (Eds.), *Psychology and culture* (pp. 285–290). Boston: Allyn & Bacon.

Marsella, A. J., Kinsie, D., & Gordon, P. (1973). Ethnic variations in the expression of depression. *Journal of Cross-cultural Psychology, 4*, 435–458.

Matsudaira, T. (2006). Measures of psychological acculturation: A review. *Transcultural Psychiatry, 43*, 462–483.

Mesquita, B., & Frijda, N. H. (1992). Cultural variations in emotions: A review. *Psychological Bulletin, 112*, 179–204.

Meyer, G. (2002). Exploring possible ethnic differences and bias in the Rorschach Comprehensive System. *Journal of Personality Assessment, 78*, 104–129.

Millon, T., & Meagher, S. E. (2004). The Millon Clinical Multiaxial Inventory-III (MCMI-III). In M. J. Hilsenroth & D. L. Segal (Eds.), *Comprehensive handbook of psychological assessment* (pp. 108–121). Hoboken, NJ: John Wiley & Sons.

Monopoli, J. (1984). A culture-specific interpretation of thematic test protocols for American Indians (Unpublished master's thesis, University of Arkansas, Fayetteville).

Monopoli, J., & Alworth, L. (2000). The use of the thematic apperception test in the study of Native American psychological characteristics: A review and archival study of Navaho men. *Genetic, Social, and General Psychology Monographs, 126*, 43–78.

Mukherjee, S., Shukla, S., Woodle, J., Rosen, A., & Olarte, S. (1983). Misdiagnosis of schizophrenia in bipolar patients: A multiethnic comparison. *American Journal of Psychiatry, 140*, 1571–1574.

Mumford, D. (1993). Somatization: A transcultural perspective. *International Review of Psychiatry, 5*, 231–242.

Munley, P. H., Vacha-Haase, T., Busby, R. M., & Paul, B. D. (1998). The MCMI-II and race. *Journal of Personality Assessment, 70*, 183–189.

Naglieri, J. A., McNeish, T. J., & Bardos, A. N. (1991). *Draw-a-Person: Screening procedures for emotional disturbance.* Austin, TX: ProEd.

Neighbors, H., Trierweiler, S., Ford, B., & Muroff, J. (2003). Racial differences in DSM diagnosis using a semi-structured instrument: The importance of clinical judgment in the diagnosis of African Americans. *Journal of Health and Social Behavior, 44*, 237–256.

Okazaki, S., & Sue, S. (2000). Implications of test revisions for Asian Americans. *Psychological Assessment, 12*, 272–280.

Okazaki, S., & Tanaka-Matsumi, J. (2006). Cultural considerations in cognitive-behavioral assessment. In P. Hays & G. Iwamasa (Eds.), *Culturally responsive cognitive-behavioral therapy: Assessment, practice, and supervision* (pp. 247–266). Washington, DC: American Psychological Association.

Pace, T., Robbins, R., Choney, S., Hill, J., Lacey, K., & Blair, G. (2006). A cultural-contextual perspective on the validity of the MMPI-2 with American Indians. *Cultural Diversity and Ethnic Minority Psychology, 12*, 320–333.

Park, B., & Rothbart, M. (1982). Perception of out-group homogeneity and levels of social categorization: Memory for the subordinate attributes of in-group and out-group members. *Journal of Personality and Social Psychology, 42*, 1051–1068.

Pavkov, T. W., Lewis, D. A., & Lyons, J. S. (1989). Psychiatric diagnoses and racial bias: An empirical investigation. *Professional Psychology: Research and Practice, 20*, 364–368.

Phinney, J., 1992. The Multigroup Ethnic Identity Measure: A new scale for use with diverse groups. *Journal of Adolescent Research, 7*, 156–176.

Poland, J., & Caplan, P. J. (2004). The deep structure of bias in psychiatric diagnosis. In P. J. Caplan & L. Cosgrove (Eds.), *Bias in psychiatric diagnosis* (pp. 9–23). Lanham, MD: Jason Aronson.

Pollack, D., & Shore, J. H. (1980). Validity of the MMPI with Native Americans. *American Journal of Psychiatry, 137*, 946–950.

Presley, G., Smith, C., Hilsenroth, M., & Exner, J. (2001). Clinical utility of the Rorschach with African Americans. *Journal of Personality Assessment, 77*, 491–507.

Raskin, A., Crook, T. H., & Herman, K. D. (1975). Psychiatric history and symptom differences in Black and White depressed inpatients. *Journal of Consulting and Clinical Psychology, 43*, 73–80.

Riethmiller, R. L., & Handler, L. (1997). The great figure drawing controversy: The integration of research and clinical practice. *Journal of Personality Assessment, 69,* 488–496.

Robin, R., Albaugh, B., Greene, R., Caldwell, A., & Goldman, D. (2003). Use of the MMPI-2 in American Indians: I. Comparability of the MMPI-2 between two tribes and with the MMPI-2 normative group. *Psychological Assessment, 15,* 351–359.

Roesch, S., Wee, C., & Vaughn, A. (2006). Relations between the Big Five personality traits and dispositional coping in Korean Americans: Acculturation as a moderating factor. *International Journal of Psychology, 41,* 85–96.

Rosenberg, M. (1984). A symbolic interactionist view of psychosis. *Journal of Health and Social Behavior, 25,* 289–302.

Rossi, G., & Sloore, H. (2005). International uses of the MCMI: Does interpretation change? In R. Craig (Ed.), *New directions in interpreting the Millon™ Clinical Multiaxial Inventory-III (MCMI-III™)* (pp. 144–161). Hoboken, NJ: John Wiley & Sons.

Rossini, E. D., & Moretti, R. J. (1997). Thematic Apperception Test (TAT) interpretation: Practice recommendations from a survey of clinical psychology doctoral programs accredited by the American Psychological Association. *Professional Psychology: Research and Practice, 28,* 393–398.

Roysircar-Sodowsky, G., & Maestas, M. (2000). Acculturation, ethnic identity, and acculturative stress: Evidence and measurement. R. H. Dana (Ed.), *Handbook of cross-cultural and multicultural personality assessment* (pp. 131–172). Mahwah, NJ: Lawrence Erlbaum Associates Publishers.

Rudd, M. D., & Orman, D. T. (1996). Millon Clinical Multiaxial Inventory profiles and maladjustment in the military: Preliminary findings. *Military Medicine, 161,* 349–351.

Rutter, M., & Tienda, M. (2005). *Ethnicity and causal mechanisms.* New York: Cambridge University Press.

Scott, R. (1981). FM: Clinically meaningful Rorschach index with minority children? *Psychology in the Schools, 18,* 429–433.

Sellers, R. M., & Nicole, S. J. (2003). The role of racial identity in perceived racial discrimination. *Journal of Personality and Social Psychology, 84,* 1079–1092.

Sherry, A., Dahlen, E., & Holaday, M. (2004). The use of sentence completion tests with adults. In M. J. Hilsenroth & D. L. Segal (Vol. Eds.), *Comprehensive handbook of psychological assessment, Vol. 2: Personality Assessment* (pp. 372–386). Hoboken, NJ: John Wiley & Sons.

Simon, R. J., Fleiss, J. L., Gurland, B. J., Stiller, P. R., & Sharpe, L. (1973). Depression and schizophrenia in hospitalized Black and White mental patients. *Archives of General Psychiatry, 28,* 509–512.

Smith, C., Atkinson, J., McClelland, D., & Veroff, J. (1992). *Motivation and personality: Handbook of thematic content analysis.* New York: Cambridge University Press.

Smith, D., & Dumont, F. (1995). A cautionary study: Unwarranted interpretation of the Draw-a-Person Test. *Professional Psychology, 26,* 298–303.

Snowden, L. R. (1999). African American folk idioms and mental health service use. *Cultural Diversity and Ethnic Minority Psychology, 5,* 364–370.

Snowden, L., & Todman, P. (1982). The psychological assessment of Blacks: New and needed developments. In E. Jones & S. Korchin (Eds.), *Minority mental health* (pp. 193–226). New York: Holt, Rinehart, & Winston.

Soloff, P. H., & Turner, S. M. (1981). Patterns of seclusion: A prospective study. *Nervous and Mental Disease, 169,* 37–44.

Stevens, J. M., Kwan, K., & Graybill, D. (1993). Comparison of MMPI-2 scores of foreign Chinese- and Caucasian-American students. *Journal of Clinical Psychology, 49,* 23–27.

Stewart, K. S. (1999). A study of a homeless population through the use of the MCMI-III. *Dissertation Abstracts International, Section B: The Sciences and Engineering, 59*(7-B), 3716.

Strawkowski, S. M., Lonczak, H. S., Sax, K., West, S. A., Crist, A., Mehta, R., et al. (1995). The effects of ethnicity on diagnosis and disposition from a psychiatric emergency service. *Journal of Clinical Psychiatry, 56,* 101–107.

Sue, D. W., & Sue, D. (2003). *Counseling the culturally diverse: Theory and practice.* New York: John Wiley & Sons.

Sue, S., & Morishima, J. K. (1982). *The mental health of Asian Americans.* San Francisco, CA: Jossey Bass.

Summerfeldt, L., & Antony, M. (2002). Structured and semi-structured diagnostic interviews. In M. Antony & D. H. Barlow (Eds.), *Handbook of assessment and treatment planning for psychological disorders* (pp. 3–37). New York: Guilford.

Tharinger, D. J., & Stark, K. (1990). A qualitative versus quantitative approach to evaluating the Draw-a-Person and Kinetic Family Drawing: A study of mood- and anxiety-disorder children. *Psychological Assessment, 2,* 356–375.

Thompson, C. E. (1949). The Thompson modification of the Thematic Apperception Test. *Rorschach Research Exchange and Journal of Projective Techniques, 13,* 469–478.

Timbrook, R. E., & Graham, J. R. (1994). Ethnic differences on the MMPI? *Psychological Assessment, 6,* 212–217.

Trierweiler, S., Munday, C., Thompson, E. E., Jackson, J., & Binion, V. J. (2006). Differences in patterns of symptom attribution in diagnosing schizophrenia between African American and non-African American clinicians. *American Journal of Orthopsychiatry, 76,* 154–160.

Trierweiler, S., Muroff, J., Jackson, J., Neighbors, H., & Munday, C. (2005). Clinician race, situational attributions, and diagnoses of mood versus schizophrenia disorders. *Cultural Diversity and Ethnic Minority Psychology, 11,* 351–364.

Trierweiler, S. J., Neighbors, H. W., Munday, C., Thompson, E. E., Binion, V. J., & Gomez, J. P. (2000). Clinician attributions associated with the diagnosis of schizophrenia in African American and non-African American patients. *Journal of Consulting and Clinical Psychology, 68,* 171–175.

Trierweiler, S., Neighbors, H., Munday, C., Thompson, E., Jackson, J., & Binion, V. (2006). Differences in patterns of symptom attribution in diagnosing schizophrenia between African American and Non-African American clinicians. *American Journal of Orthopsychiatry, 76*(2), 154–160.

Tsai, D. C., & Pike, P. L. (2000). Effects of acculturation on the MMPI-2 scores of Asian American students. *Journal of Personality Assessment, 74,* 216–230.

Urbina, S. (2004). *Essentials of psychological testing.* Hoboken, NJ: John Wiley & Sons.

Velasquez, R. J., & Callahan, W. J. (1990). MMPIs of Hispanic, Black, and White DSM-III schizophrenics. *Psychological Reports, 66,* 819–822.

Velasquez, R. J., Callahan, W. J., & Young, R. (1993). Hispanic–White MMPI comparisons: Does psychiatric diagnosis make a difference? *Journal of Clinical Psychology, 49,* 528–534.

Viglione, D. J. (1999). A review of recent research addressing the utility of the Rorschach. *Psychological Assessment, 11,* 251–265.

Wade, T. C., & Baker, T. B. (1977). Opinions and use of psychological tests: A survey of clinical psychologists. *American Psychologist, 32*, 874–882.

Walters, G. D., Greene, R. L., Jeffrey, T. B., Kruzich, D. J., & Haskin, J. J. (1983). Racial variations on the MacAndrew Alcoholism Scale of the MMPI. *Journal of Consulting and Clinical Psychology, 51*, 947–948.

Watkins, C. E., Campbell, V. L., Nieberding, R., & Hallmark, R. (1995). Contemporary practice of psychological assessment by clinical psychologists. *Professional Psychology, 26*, 54–60.

Weaver, C., & Sklar, D. (1980). Diagnostic dilemmas and cultural diversity in emergency rooms. *Western Journal of Medicine, 133*, 356–366.

Westermeyer, J. (1987). Cultural factors in clinical assessment. *Journal of Consulting and Clinical Psychology, 55*, 471–478.

Whaley, A. L. (1997). Ethnicity/race, paranoia, and psychiatric diagnoses: Clinician bias versus sociocultural differences. *Journal of Psychopathology and Behavioral Assessment, 19*, 1–20.

Whaley, A. (2001). Cultural mistrust: An important psychological constructs for diagnosis and treatment of African Americans. *Professional Psychology: Research & Practice, 32*(6), 555–562.

Whaley, A. L (2004). A two-stage method for the study of cultural bias in the diagnosis of schizophrenia in African Americans. *Journal of Black Psychology, 30*, 167–186.

Whatley, P., Allen, J., & Dana, R. (2003). Racial identity and the MMPI in African American male college students. *Cultural Diversity and Ethnic Minority Psychology, 9*, 345–353.

Whitworth, R. H., & McBlaine, D. D. (1993). Comparison of the MMPI and MMPI-2 administered to Anglo and Hispanic university students. *Journal of Personality Assessment, 61*, 19–27.

Whitworth, R. H., & Unterbrink, C. (1994). Comparison of MMPI-2 clinical and content scales administered to Hispanic and Anglo-Americans. *Hispanic Journal of Behavioral Sciences, 16*, 255–264.

Williams, D. R., Lavizzo-Mourey, R., & Warren, R. (1994). The concept of race and health status in America. *Public Health Reports, 109*, 26–41.

Williams, R. L., & Johnson, R. C. (1981). Progress in developing Afrocentric measuring instruments. *Journal of Non-White Concerns, 9*, 3–18.

Wood, J. M., Nezworski, M. T., Lilienfeld, S. O., & Garb, H. N. (2003). *What's wrong with the Rorschach?* San Francisco: Jossey Bass.

Worrell, F., & Cross, W. (2004). The reliability and validity of Big Five Inventory scores with African American college students. *Journal of Multicultural Counseling and Development, 32*, 18–32.

Zhang, A., & Snowden, L. (1999, May). Ethnic characteristics of mental disorders in five U.S. communities. *Cultural Diversity and Ethnic Minority Psychology, 5*, 134–146.

Issues in Clinical Assessment with Women

Judith Worell *and* Damon Ann Robinson

Abstract

This chapter aims to provide a framework for integrating gender-relevant issues with practical procedures for the psychological assessment of women in clinical practice. It reviews some historical and current approaches to gender in the assessment process, and provides suggestions for information-collection strategies that acknowledge the influence of gender-related variables on women's psychological health and well-being. Discussed are some of the concerns and research associated with gender bias in assessment, evidence for the influence of bias in the diagnostic process, and the important role of gender in selected clinically relevant topics. Finally, topics related to women's positive psychological health and well-being are proposed as essential elements of a competent assessment. Many of the topics discussed here are also relevent to assessment with preadolescent and adolescent girls. However, their concerns may differ developmentally and in substantial ways from those of adult women, and thus are not addressed here.

Keywords: assessment, biopsychosocial, diagnosis, empowerment, gender bias, ethnocultural, multiple identities, physical and sexual violence, trauma, women's health

A Biopsychosocial View

In this chapter, we use a biopsychosocial view of women's health that incorporates variables both within and outside the individual, including family, community, and culture (McDaniel, Johnson, & Sears, 2004; Worell & Goodheart, 2006). Overall, the importance of women's psychological health as an area of expansion is critical (U.S. Department of Health and Human Services, Office on Women's Health, 2001). According to a massive review of studies compiled in the 1996 world mental health report (Desjarlais, Eisenberg, Good, & Kleinman, 1996; as cited in Lopez & Guarnaccia, 2000), women's psychological health was identified as one of the five highest priorities for research worldwide. Lopez and Guarnaccia further concluded that gender, poverty, and social class are basic factors in the incidence and expression of psychological distress and dysfunction, both within and between ethnic and cultural groups. We also caution clinicians to attend to other variables that signal minority status, such as sexual orientation

and sexual identity, nationality and immigration status, aging, and physical (dis)ability. An emerging group of clients are women veterans, whose service-related concerns, such as posttraumatic stress disorder (PTSD), may differ in substantial ways from those of their male counterparts (Cloitre, Koenen, Gratz, & Jakupcak, 2002; Krause, DeRosa, & Roth, 2002). Throughout the chapter, clinicians are urged to examine their own knowledge base, attitudes, beliefs, and skills in the process of assessment with women from any of these diverse group identities.

Women represent the major portion of non-hospital client populations (Rhodes, Goering, & Williams, 2002). In a recent move to assist clinicians and other psychologists in conducting competent practice with women, the American Psychological Association (APA) approved a comprehensive set of Guidelines for Psychological Practice with Women (American Psychological Association, 2007). These guidelines are aspirational rather than mandated, but they offer a broad range of topics that are timely and relevant to assessment and intervention with girls and women. The guidelines were developed to coordinate with those for several other groups whose members include women, including lesbian, gay, and bisexual clients (American Psychological Association, 2000), clients with multicultural identities (American Psychological Association, 2003), and older adult clients (American Psychological Association, 2004). Clinicians who work with women clients from many diverse identities will find a rich source of research and practical applications within the guidelines for practice.

Purposes of Assessment

Clinical assessment typically serves the purpose of gathering multiple sources of information to assist in clinical conceptualization of presenting psychological problems and concerns. This conceptualization often drives decisions about types and directions of intervention made by the client and the clinician. Other types of clinical assessment may serve more circumscribed purposes, often with no expectation of further therapeutic intervention. Such examples include career and management decisions, Social security evaluations, forensic evaluations, child custody issues, competence to stand trial and "mental status" at the time of offense, and evaluations performed for the purpose of providing expert testimony. This chapter focuses primarily on assessment for the purposes of intervention and treatment, but many of the concepts presented are of importance in the consideration of gender variables in forensic and other types of evaluations.

A Woman-Centered Approach

Assessment does not occur in a vacuum. There is clearly no one set of questions for women or one model that is the "right" or "most complete" approach. The elements and focus of clinical assessment here are driven by at least four factors: (1) cultural knowledge, assumptions, and attitudes; (2) preferred theoretical or therapeutic orientations (Butcher, 1987; Lopez, 1989; MacDonald, 1984; McReynolds, 1989); (3) restrictions imposed on clinicians' decision making by the insurance industry; and (4) by the knowledge base of the clinician regarding issues specific to women and the significant contexts of their lives (Caplan & Cosgrove, 2004). Our purpose here is to reinforce and expand this knowledge base.

The suggestions we offer specifically for assessment with women derive from both theory and research on women's psychological health and treatment. However, it is essential to be aware that our

women clients are in many ways experts on their own lives and experiences. Our willingness to open doors to difficult and emotion-laden issues (e.g., physical or sexual abuse and violence) sends a message that such issues are acceptable and potentially important assessment and therapeutic areas. Indeed, for some women, a clinical psychological assessment may include questions that they have never before been asked. For individuals who identify with marginalized.ethnic or cultural groups, revealing such private information may be personally difficult or culturally proscribed (Greene, 2007; Nettles, 2007). Women who identify with a community that has been subjected to oppression and discrimination may believe that protection of their ethnic/cultural group is paramount; for others, shame and humiliation may prevent self-disclosure of sensitive material (Fisher, Daigle, Cullen, & Turner, 2003; Robinson & Howard-Hamilton, 2000; West, 2002).

We propose that clinical assessment with women be done within a culturally sensitive and woman-centered context. This approach considers the environmental factors that may impact women's psychological health concerns, including disadvantages and differential life experiences that create subtle and not so subtle gender, culture, and class inequities (American Psychological Association, 2007; Sue et al., 2007). Gender stratification, expressed as power imbalance and power assertion, can be seen as a direct contributing factor in some presenting problems (e.g., sexual harassment, rape, domestic violence), in women's socially gendered self-identity and self-worth (in many cultures women are considered as subordinate and "less than"), and in women's beliefs about their ability or feasibility to change their behaviors, feelings, and lives.

Multiple Identities

In the context of gender, we should be aware that assessment issues may also be related to other group identity characteristics for each woman, including but not limited to ethnoracial identity, culture, social class, (dis)ability, religious orientation, and sexual orientation. Simple comparisons between women and men in most of the extant research fail to capture the complexities that should be considered when clients other than White middle-class heterosexual women are being evaluated. Clients may be struggling with several intersecting identity concerns that become salient or brought into awareness depending on the situation (Marsella & Yamada, 2000; Stewart & McDermott, 2004; Williams, McCandless, & Dunlap, 2002).

For example, when a young Black attorney was experiencing sexual harassment from her supervisor, did she believe it was due to her race/ethnicity, her gender, her assertive interaction style, or perhaps her sexual orientation? When she subsequently testified against him before Congress, was she acting in a paranoid manner, in a self-serving mode, as angry retribution for his behavior, or was it evidence of her continuing anxiety, panic attacks, and depression? Possibly, untangling her awareness of her salient identity during the testimony would illuminate the degree of reality or fantasy in her accusations and the extent of her related distress. Were you the clinician recruited to evaluate her, it would be helpful to be aware of these possibilities in your assessment report. As an additional consideration, clients with multiple and intersecting identities that differ from those of your own may present a particular challenge. To the extent that you differ in substantial ways from the client you are assessing, self-monitoring for bias and limitations in cultural knowledge is essential (Sue & Sue, 1999). In particular, your knowledge and awareness of the possible power differentials between you and the client will be essential in your ability to gain client trust and thus to conduct a competent assessment.

Multimodal Approach

We conceptualize strategies for woman-centered assessment as a "multimodal approach," including observation, interviews, self-monitoring, collateral information (e.g., information from family or friends when applicable), psychological tests and inventories, prior psychological and medical records, and information regarding relevant life history. Such an approach continues to be a thorough method of assessment (Clark, 2007; Linn & Kessel, 2006). Choice of assessment instruments and procedures will vary depending on clinician assumptions about whether the behaviors reflect enduring personality traits or reflect a person–environment interaction (Harway & Hansen, 2004). However, in this time of managed care practices and dwindling resources in state and federal inpatient and outpatient settings, the demand for more rapid assessment is clear. We propose a model of critical areas of assessment with women that may serve to tap into gender-specific therapeutic areas in a timely manner. Gender-prevalent experiences also place a demand on the health professional to be cognizant of current and relevant issues regarding critical events in women's lives (e.g., the prevalence and expected outcomes of being physically and/or sexually abused), and to supplement traditional assessment methodology with an eye toward the contribution of gender bias. Although most assessment strategies seek evidence of disorder or pathology, our model includes the search for strengths such as positive coping skills, and personal/external resources (Folkman & Moskowitz, 2004; Goodheart, 2006; Worell & Remer, 2003; Worell, 2006).

Diagnosis in Context

The use of diagnostic labels has often been eschewed by feminist, woman-centered, and positive psychologists. Many of us prefer to speak of "problems in living" (Maddux, Snyder, & Lopez, 2004) or adaptive reactions to aversive and/or dangerous situations (Walker, 1994a; Worell & Remer, 2003). However, in the majority of clinical settings, *Diagnosis and Statistical Manual of Mental Disorders* (DSM) diagnoses are usually required either for third party payment or in disposition/treatment records. The proposed areas suggested for inquiry here can add a dimension that contextualizes the diagnosis. For example, a woman who presents with a hypervigilant interpersonal style, who reports marked anxiety, and who displays outbursts of anger might be considered to have paranoid interpersonal tendencies or elements of a borderline personality disorder (BPD). However, if we inquire more deeply, we may discover that she is living in a physically abusive relationship, such symptoms make sense as adaptive responses to a dangerous situation and may be considered more within the realm of an acute or posttraumatic stress disorder.

Gender Bias

Gender bias may occur in a variety of ways, although certainly not always overtly intended. Lopez (1989) offered a model of assessment bias that has usually implied a clinical judgment based on prejudice toward women or other groups. He identified four types of diagnostic errors: overpathologizing (in which women are perceived as more disturbed than a comparison group); minimizing (in which "clinicians may have dismissed the woman's presenting problems as more normative than they actually were" [Lopez, 1989, p. 186]); and overdiagnosing or underdiagnosing, with regard to the probability of assigning a particular diagnosis. Gender bias has also been suggested in the assumptions underlying the DSM criteria or category, which may disadvantage women with the assumption that the dysfunction is located primarily within the person rather than situated within a broader context (Caplan, 1995; Caplan & Cosgrove, 2004; Kuchins & Kirk, 1997; McReynolds, 1989).

In the present context, we use the term "gender bias" to denote a systematic error of commission or omission in any aspect of the assessment process based on lack of knowledge and/or stereotypical attitudes or beliefs about women in any of their diverse identities. Thus, clinicians' interpersonal behaviors with clients, choice and interpretation of assessment instruments, and diagnostic judgments are all potential targets for bias. There is no implication here that such bias, when it occurs, is intentional or within the individual's awareness. However, clinicians' appreciation of the possibilities for gender bias may enhance their sensitivity and consequent assessment strategies.

Early considerations of gender bias in assessment focused on whether women and men were evaluated differently as a result of gender-related stereotypical characteristics (Broverman, Broverman, Clarkson, Rosenkrantz, & Vogel, 1970). Cross-gendered behaviors (e.g., women demonstating stereotypical "male" traits or vice versa) were seemingly representative of more negative evaluations or seemed to have been considered more pathological behaviors. Similarly, more negativistic evaluations for women as a result of differential assessment of stereotypical "feminine" behaviors and characteristics were also demonstrated in studies during the 1970s (Cowan, 1976; Hayes & Wolleat, 1978).

As attention was focused on this issue of gender trait bias, it became more difficult simply to assess and demonstrate bias based on judgments about stereotypical behavior. These methodological difficulties suggested an increased awareness of the inappropriateness and limits of judging women (and men) on gross, stereotypical personality traits. That same increased attention to gender bias may have also hampered similar research in that mental health professionals were increasingly primed to respond in more socially desirable ways when faced with such overt decisions regarding gendered behaviors (Hare-Mustin, 1983; Phillips & Gilroy, 1985). However, other forms of gender bias began to emerge as research focused on more embedded and less obvious examples of such bias toward women. For example, in a simulated client interview, Buczek (1981) noted that among both female and male psychologists, less information could be recalled for the female versus the male simulated client. Differences were also found in the psychologists' choice of questions and topics noted in the interview which varied by sex of client, therapist, and topics raised. In sum, choices of information to be assessed, and information actually retained, may represent gender bias in clinical interviews.

In a different approach to gender bias, Sesan (1988) gathered data from 192 clients seen by 49 different therapists. These individuals were administered a 71-item questionnaire whose content was drawn from the APA Task Force on Sex Bias and Sex-Role Stereotyping in Psychotherapy (American Psychological Association, 1975, 1978). Results suggested that "error(s) of omission" occurred for those clients who had experienced sexual or physical abuse as a child or adult. The "omission" referred to clients' reports that pertinent information regarding such a history of violence was not explored. The study also found that therapists demonstrated more perceived bias for women who had less education, and who had children. In a similar vein, clinical histories frequently omit past and present experiences of trauma, although over half the women in the United States have been physically assaulted during their lives (Farley, 2004).

Although clinician training and education within the past 20 years has demonstrated significant strides in attention to gender sensitivity (e.g. American Psychological Association, 2007), gender bias may still exist. Several publications have reported that similar symptomatology was diagnosed differently when the clinician was led to believe that the client is a woman versus a man. For example, given the same set of symptoms, women were more likely than men to receive a diagnosis of depression (Potts, Burnam, & Wells, 1991). Similarly, Becker and Lamb (1994) surveyed 1,080 clinicians with a case example that provided an equal number of criteria for BPD or PTSD. Respondents rated the probability of a diagnosis on seven Axis I and seven Axis II categories. In this study, women were rated significantly higher for BPD, as well as for histrionic and self-defeating personality disorders, while men were rated higher for a diagnosis of antisocial personality disorder. The relationship of these biases to population prevalence is unknown, since the preponderance of women diagnosed with BPD may well be a reflection of clinician bias as well as actual population base rates.

Sex of Clinician

The sex of the clinician as a variable in gender bias of assessment and treatment has generally been found to be irrelevant (Davidson & Abramowitz, 1980; Sesan, 1988; Smith; 1980). However, the

Becker and Lamb (1994) study reported a gender bias in women clinicians' higher preference for assigning a diagnosis of PTSD for both the female and male cases. This bias may reflect the greater propensity of women clinicians to view behavior contextually rather than as a symptom of an internal or medical disorder. Such a finding might suggest that in those incidents of documented gender bias in assessment, both female and male clinicians may benefit from an examination of their knowledge base and decision-making process regarding case conceptualization. It might also suggest that both female and male clinicians can effectively use a woman-centered approach to assessment.

Psychiatric Diagnosis

One of the most controversial areas of gender bias in clinical practice has come from the use, inclusion and exclusion, and establishment of criteria of psychiatric diagnostic categories. In the United States, the compilation of psychiatric taxonomy is the DSM. The fourth edition (DSM-IV) was published in 1994, and a "text revision" (DSM-IV-TR) was published in 2000. This revision made no major changes to diagnoses and criteria but expanded research-based information, and inclusion of relevant information regarding cultural, gender, and age variables in category and course of illness.

The DSM defines criteria deemed necessary for a particular diagnostic category, and is frequently required for hospital records, treatment planning, and third-party reimbursement. The selected diagnoses and criteria have evolved over the various revisions, and there remains considerable disagreement on what might be, or if there is, a definitive definition of psychopathology, on which the theory and practice of categorical diagnosis is based (e.g., Bergner, 1997; Mechanic, 1997; Sarbin, 1997, Widiger & Trull, 1991, 2007) and the political nature of these decisions (Brown, 1990; Caplan, 1995, Caplan & Cosgrove, 2004; McReynolds, 1989). Among diagnoses considered more prevalent among women, some have argued that there has been a tendency to pathologize cultural expectations and culturally "approved" behaviors. Connections between the interplay of gender-role expectations and the process of diagnosis and mental health decisions may be found in numerous reviews (APA, 2007; Brown, 1990; Caplan, 1995; Hartung & Widiger, 1998; Landrine, 1989; Worell & Remer, 1992, 2003). It should also be noted that the possibility of gender bias related to DSM diagnoses, criteria, and applications has not been dismissed by principal authors and researchers (Hartung & Widiger, 1998; Spitzer, Williams, Kass, & Davies, 1989; Widiger, Frances, Spitzer, & Williams, 1988).

Specific Diagnosis and Criteria

As gender-bias research and literature abounded during the 1980s, the DSM-III-R (American Psychiatric Association, 1987) was released for use in clinical and research settings. This third and revised edition of the DSM drew considerable fire for diagnoses, and specific criteria necessary for diagnosis that were believed to reflect negative bias toward women. Such criticism focused on the overall reliability of the DSM diagnostic criteria for women clients. Proposed categories, such as the "Self-Defeating Personality Disorder" (SDPD), whose criteria could be in keeping with expected behaviors and thoughts of women in physically abusive situations (Walker, 1994a, 1994b), lacked empirical support and suggested a "blame the victim" mentality. While few would dispute that remaining in an abusive situation is not an optimum choice, the use of such a diagnosis implies pathology residing solely within the abused individual rather than an understanding of the complexities many abused women face when considering leaving a relationship (Harway & Hansen, 2004; Koss et al., 1994). This focus on the pathology of the individual (which has largely been the accepted focus of the DSM series) clearly decontextualizes a woman's experience of abuse and posits the "blame" for her life circumstances on her, rather than on the perpetrator of the abuse. In the wake of such criticism of this particular diagnosis, it is notable that it was not included in the DSM-IV and DSM-IV-TR.

According to prevalence rates of particular diagnoses by gender, differential diagnostic criteria have been found. For example, the criteria for personality disorders most frequently diagnosed in women contained more global and subjective personality traits, while those most often diagnosed in men used concise and behavioral terminology (Hamilton, Rothbart, & Dawes, 1986). Such findings have been debated by researchers, who note that the diagnostic criteria are not the source of bias but rather diagnostic names, which prompt biased diagnosing practices (Ford & Widiger, 1989). For example, histrionic personality disorder carries a legacy from the notion of a causative "wandering" uterus, to the "masochism" inherent in women, to being attention seeking and "inappropriately sexually seductive in appearance or behavior"

(American Psychiatric Association, 1987, p. 349). The editors of the DSM-IV and DSM-IV-TR did heed many of these criticisms, and substantially changed the nature of many of the criteria used in diagnoses, particularly in personality disorders.

Diagnostic criteria for personality disorders more frequently assigned to women include, for example, histrionic, dependent, and borderline disorders. In the evolution of these diagnostic categories, the subjective nature of criteria left the door quite open for gender-biased labeling. Criteria such as letting others make decisions for one's self and putting others' needs before one's own have been strong components of a dependent personality disorder diagnosis. However, these same behaviors parallel stereotypical gender-role behaviors for women (Jack & Ali, in press). BPD is not an uncommon diagnosis to assign when a client is angry and difficult in therapy and is not making expected progress (Kuchins & Kirk, 1997). However, as women are typically socialized to avoid expressions of anger, when anger does manifest itself it may seem severe and/or be expressed in less than assertive ways. To a large degree, the determination of the "appropriateness" of expression of anger lies with the clinician, who may experience some discomfort with such emotional display.

The DSM, with a focus on internal dynamics, may be considered to take problems in living and turn them into diseases that reside within individuals, and that have a medical or organic base as well (Maddux et al., 2004). Thus we treat only the individual, without identifying factors that may have contributed to her "disordered" diagnosis. For example, late luteal phase dysphoric disorder (originally introduced as a diagnostic category needing further study in DSM-III-R), a normal physiological change for women, is now buried as a disorder in the category "Depressive Disorders NOS" in the DSM-IV.

Changes made in the newer criteria for diagnoses in the DSM-IV and DSM-IV-TR represent an attempt to use more behavioral and less subjective terminology. It should also be noted that the emphasis on cultural norms and expectations should be factored into the decisions regarding whether a client fits the diagnostic thresholds. In particular, consideration of multicultural values is critical for assessing women from cultures other than the "mainstream" Caucasian-American perspective. As we suggested earlier, many of the behaviors identified as criteria for a disorder in DSM may be normative for cultures other than the dominant U.S. culture that reflects Western values. Whether a

woman is flamboyant and emotionally expressive or silent, passive, and accommodating with downcast eyes, may reflect the norms within her particular culture and should not be judged as deviant from the perspective of another culture (Canales, 2000; Landrine, 1995). Likewise, clinicians should be aware of the increased risks that women of double or multiple minority status face, both within the larger dominant culture and within their own communities. African-American women, for example, are at high risk for anxiety and panic (Neal-Barnett & Crowther, 2000), and are at even greater risk if they are also lesbian or bisexual (Greene, 2000).

Clinical Decisions

On a more positive note, there are many recent appeals for dimensional, rather than categorical, diagnostic decision making (Clark, 2007; Widiger & Trull, 2007; see also Chapter 18). In a cogent summary of continuing conceptual problems with the recent DSM-IV-TR, Widiger and Trull (2007) cite examples such as diagnostic overlap and comorbidity, arbitrary boundaries that overlap with normal functioning, and lack of sufficient scientific evidence for some categories. In addition, clinician selection of a particular subset of "symptoms" for certain categories opens the possibility that individuals with the same diagnosis demonstrate a completely different set of behaviors.

There is evidence to suggest that clinicians themselves do not follow diagnostic rules in their use of the DSM series. For example, Davis, Blashfield, and McElroy (1993) found that diagnoses were made as a result of a "weight" self-assigned to a given criterion rather than a presentation meeting all of the diagnostic criteria necessary. Clinicians have been demonstrated to be biased in a variety of analogous studies with a blend of criteria possible for several diagnoses. Ford and Widiger (1989) and Adler, Drake, and Teague (1990) found that psychologists more readily assigned a diagnosis of histrionic personality disorder to women whether or not the criteria in the case history were sufficient for diagnosis. Similarly, psychologists diagnosed women as having a histrionic personality disorder more frequently than they diagnosed men, even when presented with identical female and male cases. Potts, Burnam, and Wells (1991) found that clinicians more frequently diagnosed women as depressed when the diagnostic interview schedule did not meet criteria for a diagnosis of depression. Case histories representing women with stereotypical cross-gendered behaviors generated more attributions of greater pathology than when the stimulus client presented more stereotypical expected behavior (Waisberg & Page, 1988).

One possible reason for less than thorough clinician use of diagnostic categories and criteria may be higher base rates among women of particular symptoms and clinical syndromes. For example, it is well known that women tend more often than men to be depressed and anxious (Nolen-Hoeksema, 2002; Sprock & Yoder, 1997; Whiffen & Demidenko, 2006). While the reasons for this are multifaceted, clinicians and women clients alike may "expect" to see depressive and/or anxious symptomatology. Expanding the gender-related facets of higher base rates of depression are the coexisting factors that may increase the risk of depression. For example, higher rates of depression among battered women are predictive of low confidence to leave the abuser (Lerner & Kennedy, 2000). Similarly, gender-discrimination experiences were found to be more predictive of women's depression than generic stressors (Landrine, Klonoff, Gibbs, Manning, & Lund, 1995). In such examples, the depth and dimensions of gender-related variables are evident in assessing for diagnosis. To clarify the diagnostic picture, we would recommend strict use of criteria sufficient to meet an acceptable standard of diagnosis, along with being aware of the interplay of gender and multiple-identity variables when categorical decisions are required.

Contextual Assessment for Women

Virtually all clinical assessments will include queries regarding the client's presenting problems; the presence of and risk for suicidal or homicidal ideation; substance use; and the presence of psychotic symptomatology (e.g., auditory or visual hallucinations, delusional material, or other thought-disordered symptoms such as thought broadcasting or withdrawal). Screening for self-mutilation behaviors should be a standard part of the assessment process due to the high rates of such behaviors in clinical populations (Briere, 1998). In contrast, Wright and Lopez (2002) have argued that assets and deficits be given equal space in the assessment report. Admittedly, this suggestion presents a challenge to the interviewer, who is often less skilled in probing for strengths than in identifying pathology. Such strengths' assessment may be elicited from the client as well as by a variety of collateral informants and written reports. As a first step, it should be essential for all assessment reports to include a substantive section on the client's repertoire of personal strengths and environmental resources. Our suggestions for topics of inquiry with women clients, listed in Table 22.1, are not intended to supplant such

basic clinical information. Instead, they are intended to tap specifically into relevant gender variables that may shed light on presenting symptomatology and to address areas that may typically be overlooked.

Screening for Sexual and Physical Abuse

Clinical assessment with women must always consider the higher base rates of physical and sexual abuse for women. The literature has burgeoned with information regarding such abuse from a variety of sources. Prevalence rates continue to be high and noted in the literature. One of the more controversial areas has been in evaluation and treatment, particularly for childhood sexual abuse. Most notably, the debate over delayed memory for abuse (Cromer & Freyd, 2007; Enns, McNeilley, Corkery, & Gilbert, 1995; Freyd, DePrince, & Zurbriggen, 2001; Pope, 1996) has been an area of acrimonious dialog. In light of increased recognition of physical and sexual abuse as a significant gender-related factor in assessment (White & Frabutt, 2006), we emphasize issues related to screening for abuse. We maintain, however, that such screening is an elemental part of clinical assessment with women, and we encourage the clinician to develop strategies for screening that afford respect for clients as well as openness for the clinician to explore these issues.

PREVALENCE RATES

The prevalence of lifetime incidents of sexual and physical abuse for women is staggering. Among women seeking therapy, over half are estimated to have had episodes of interpersonal violence in a personally significant relationship (Ammerman & Hersen, 1992; Walker, 1989; Worell & Remer, 2003). According to several large surveys, over half the women respondents had experienced sexual victimization by the age of 24 (White & Frabutt, 2006); estimates of a lifetime experience of sexual assault have been estimated at 27% (Finkelhor, Hotaling, Lewis, & Smith, 1990). Adult rape or attempted rape was found to be just under 50% (Russell & Howell, 1983). The likelihood of a rape survivor being also an incest survivor was found to be approximately 65% in one study (Russell, 1986). In that same study, among women who had not experienced incest, 35% had experienced adult rape. Among a nonclinical sample, Koss (1985) found that 62% of the women sampled had had some variant of sexual victimization in their lifetime. Using path analysis, the experience of childhood sexual and physical abuse was associated with increased vulnerability to sexual

Table 22.1. Suggested areas for clinical assessment with women.

1. Violence, abuse, and trauma: Physical, sexual, and psychological abusive or traumatic experiences, either current or by history. Additionally, was there violence or abuse present in her family: for example, did she witness her mother being battered by her father, or other family violence? What messages did she learn about power differentials and violence in her family that affect her today? If she has had abusive or traumatic experiences, was she able to tell anyone, and what was the response? Has she experienced incidents of sexual harassment? As a woman of color and/or of diverse sexual orientations, how have experiences of racism, discrimination, violence, or exclusion affected her? How did her experiences as a veteran of distance or recent conflicts affect her?

2. Caretaking responsibilities: Many women find themselves caring for children, husbands, partners, relatives, and parents. For the single mothers, pressures resulting from financial insufficiency, isolation, and role overload may present additional stressors. The resulting exhaustion, frustration, and lack of caretaking of self may contribute to feelings of depression, anger, or anxiety.

3. Health—Medical conditions, medication prescribed, and medical concerns: Openly questioning about any reproductive or sexual problems is recommended. A history, or current symptoms of eating-disordered behaviors or weight-related concerns can be explored. Screening for substance abuse, either legal, illicit, or prescription drugs, should be a standard part of the assessment. Addressing physical disabilities or limitations on daily functioning and role responsibilities is also suggested.

4. Gender-role messages: Querying for underlying beliefs of traditional women's "roles," with her culture and her comfort with her real-life roles (e.g., boss, employee, wife, partner, single woman, mother, etc.), may help in understanding self-concept and self-worth issues. Understanding how these beliefs affect her day-to-day living in both negative and positive ways can enrich understanding of presenting symptomatology.

5. Relationship beliefs: The quality of her interpersonal relationships, including romantic, familial, and friendships, can shed light on the extent and quality of her social support network. Her evaluation of herself based on the presence or lack of a romantic relationship, and the quality of such prior relationships, is an area frequently impacted by stereotypical gender role and culturally driven messages. Finally, are her relationships the source of discrimination or additional stress (e.g., being a lesbian, bisexual, etc., especially if a member of a minority community)?

6. Previous therapy experiences: Obtaining an overview of prior therapy, including her judgment of its quality and helpfulness, and the type of therapy she received, can be useful information. Along these lines, her readiness to undertake therapy may be a factor, for example, in an involuntarily committed individual who feels she does not need hospitalization or treatment. In cases where she has previously explored abuse issues, an understanding of what type of therapy was used, particularly if high-risk interventions were used (e.g., hypnosis or detailed re-creations of traumatic events), are critical. Finally, the possibility of sexual touching or sexual relationships with former therapists should be noted.

7. Communication patterns. Does she have verbal access to her emotional life? How does she typically deal with strong feelings? Does she display explosive or inappropriate anger? Is she able to be assertive, or to express anger? Does she engage in unhealthy behaviors to deal with her feelings (e.g., overeating, substance use, self-injurious behaviors)? Finally, does she believe her communication styles are effective, or does she consider learning new methods as potentially helpful for her?

8. Attributional style: Does she attribute problems only to herself (self-blame), or is she able to see any external factors? Does she tend to expect negative outcomes, or engage in depressogenic thinking?

9. Ability to self-nurture: Does she actively take care of her needs, and value those needs, or does she tend to engage in caretaking of others with little or no attention to herself? Does she perceive that she is able to care for herself (e.g., an older widowed woman who has fears of living alone with financial concerns)? Are these perceived ideas pragmatically driven (e.g., does she lack adequate financial resources to care for her self)?

10. Career/employment concerns: Is her career a meaningful part of her life, or does she see herself working only to provide income? Does she feel isolated in her work, or does she have a support network that nurtures her in her profession? Does she face gender or ethnoracial discrimination or sexual harassment in her workplace? Are there stressors resulting from home–career conflicts?

continued

Table 22.1. (*continued*).

11. Resource assessment: Does she have adequate income to sufficiently manage her life? Does she receive child support, or has this been difficult to obtain? Does she have adequate insurance or financial resources to pay for medical care and medications? Has she ever been, or is is in danger of being, homeless? Does she have adequate friends and family, or community groups to whom she can turn for emotional support?
12. Expectations of therapy and perception of her needs: If the evaluation is performed in preparation for therapy, her expectations for therapy should be explored. In all cases, her perception of therapeutic needs and goals should be explored. Such questions validate her importance as a collaborator in therapy, and may be for many women the first time they have been so immediately included in the process of treatment planning. Are there obstacles to obtaining therapy (e.g., financial, feeling stigmatized, unsupported by friends or family)?

and physical assaults as adults, and more cumulative PTSD symptomatology (Nishith, Mechanic, & Resick, 2000). Adding to these accumulated data is evidence that survivors of sexual assault may not report their experiences at all due to fear of negative outcomes, such as reprisal or disbelief and blame by others (Ahrens, Campbell, Ternier-Thames, Wasco, & Sefl, 2007).

Adding the variable of vulnerability increased the likelihood of abuse. Among women who were frequently homeless and severely mentally distressed (predominately diagnosed as having schizophrenia, schizoaffective, bipolar, or major depressive disorder), the lifetime prevalence of physical and sexual assault was astronomical (Goodman, Dutton, & Harris, 1995). Of the 100 predominately single African-American women surveyed, 85% reported childhood physical abuse and 65% reported sexual abuse in childhood. The majority of these attacks were considered severe in nature. In adulthood, 87% of these women had experienced a severe physical assault, predominately by someone they knew well. Among these women, 76% had experienced sexual assault in adulthood. In sum, 97% of this sample of women had experienced physical or sexual abuse either during childhood or adulthood. The authors concluded that among this sample of women, the risk for "violent victimization is so high that rape and physical battery are normative experiences" (p. 474). Similarly, Buckner, Bassuk, and Zima (1993) concluded that a history of traumatic events across their lifetime is markedly common for homeless women, and many of their presenting psychological symptoms may well be representative of survival skills rather than of clinical pathology.

REACTIONS OF OTHERS

Finally, the reactions of others to reports of violence among psychologically disturbed individuals

may vary widely. Marley and Bulia (1999) questioned 234 adults who had previously received diagnoses of schizophrenia, bipolar, or schizoaffective disorder, about their experiences in reporting interpersonal violence to police. The women in this study reported rape or other adult sexual abuse by a known perpetrator or unknown perpetrators, as well as childhood sexual abuse. Abuse survivor variables leading to more police responses included higher levels of education, fewer lifetime victimization incidents, being married, having a higher income, having a home, and having no history of substance abuse. Subjectively, some respondents felt that they would not be believed because they had been diagnosed with a mental illness. In sum, hopelessness and psychological disturbance are variables that increase women's vulnerability to interpersonal violence, as well as level of belief by others to whom they may report the violence. Reliable data on incidence rates are thus conflated with reporting variables.

Barriers to Screening

Two major variables will affect the probability and effectiveness of screening for sexual and physical abuse, those associated with therapist and those connected to the client. For many mental health professionals, asking a client about a history of sexual or physical abuse is experienced as being uncomfortable or intrusive. Research indicates that the rates of querying for this information are quite low. For example, among a sample of psychologists, only 17% routinely inquired as to a history of lifetime sexual abuse (Pruitt & Kappius, 1992). In some instances, questions regarding lifetime abuse experiences are simply not asked (Craine, Hensen, Colliver, & MacLean, 1988; Pruitt & Kappius, 1992). Intuitively, a direct question about lifetime abuse must elicit more acknowledgment of such a history than addressing the issue only if the client spontaneously brings it up (Briere & Zaidi, 1989). In reviewing chart histories of 100 psychiatric inpatients, Jacobson, Koehler, and Jones-Brown (1987) found that 91% of assaults by history were not present in the chart information, but were reported when a structured interview assessed for such a history. Similarly, 100% of a lifetime history of sexual abuse and assault was not present in the standard chart, but was obtained through the structured interview. Additionally, even with direct screening for information regarding such violence in an intake interview, an underestimate of prevalence was found (35%) compared with 52% obtained in a written, self-report questionnaire that asked about sexual abuse. Clearly, assessing directly for sexual and physical abuse experiences yields more accurate information than expecting the client to report spontaneously.

As indicated previously, there are many reasons for client's failure to report current or past abuse—shame, guilt, self-blame, fear of retaliation by the abuser or rejection by family and community members, fear of breaking up the family, or believing that it is a private event. By not asking or assessing directly, therapists may unintentionally communicate that these are taboo topics, further reinforcing client reluctance to reveal abusive experiences. We have limited information about how these abuse experiences might differ among women from groups that vary in marital status, socioeconomic level, age, ethnicity, religious identity, or sexual orientation, but we assume that no groups of women are invulnerable to physical or sexual abuse during their lifetimes. Regardless of whether clients reveal "signs" of abuse, assessment for a history of abuse (or current abusive living conditions) should be a routine part of assessment with any woman client. It should be noted that we are not advocating an approach that attempts to "prove" a history of abuse regardless of the evidence. Nor do we suggest that extensive attempts be initiated to reconstruct an abuse history on the basis of a few symptoms. Rather, we are suggesting that routine screening for abusive experiences is warranted both by the high base rates for these events in women's lives and by the impact such a history may have on the diagnosis and the conceptualization of appropriate treatment strategies.

Hesitation to inquire about abusive experiences may be the result of many personal factors. For the therapist who has experienced her or his own history of traumatic events, questioning a client about her similar experiences may be threatening. Similarly, for therapists with a large caseload of abuse survivors, there may be fears of or experiences of secondary, or "vicarious traumatization" when the client discusses her experiences (Brady, Guy, Poelstra, & Brokaw, 1999). Among these authors' sample of 446 female therapists treating abuse survivors, secondary trauma symptomatology appeared to be relatively mild, and mediated by education, consultation and supervision, and spiritual well-being. In a similar vein, hospital staff members have been found to have feelings of alienation, to suffer, and to have questions about the "good and evil" of the world when working predominately with clients with abuse histories (Lyon, 1993). Again, supervision, continuing education, and opportunities for activities less stressful than intense therapy are suggested as ways for mediating the therapist's discomfort in dealing with this population.

The focus on education for mental health professionals regarding abuse issues was also a recommendation in a study involving medical students in Kuwait (Nayak, 2000). Among these students, 91.3% indicated that training in "interpersonal violence is necessary" (p. 127), but only 25% endorsed a routine assessment for such a history. Reasons cited for avoidance included fears that the client would become upset (73.5%), perceiving themselves to be untrained in this area (67.6%), "fear of offending" clients (67.6%), and viewing abuse as "a private issue" (68%) (p. 127). Even in a different cultural setting, abuse screening presents some difficulties for clinicians. Further research on cross-cultural components in addressing abuse histories would be helpful to provide recommendations in clinical training programs.

A strong deterrent to screening for sexual abuse history may also be the heated debate in the clinical arena regarding so-called "false memories" attributed to overzealous therapists. As Palm and Gibson (1998) stated most cogently, "direct questions about CSA [childhood sexual abuse] are appropriate, whereas pressure or repeated suggestions are not" (p. 260). Similarly, there has been considerable debate about appropriate clinical approaches for clients with a suspected history of childhood sexual abuse. The primary argument regarding therapist behavior has been the use of extreme techniques to "recreate" memories of abuse. Such techniques may include hypnosis, intense re-experiencing of possible traumatic events, and leading of a client toward a belief that she has experienced abuse on the basis of vague symptomatology that may be typical of abuse survivors.

In actual practice, the problems raised in working with possible recovered memories have directed a trend toward less controversial methods. For example, among psychologists with training in trauma issues, increased caution in "pursuing cases of recovered memories" was strongly endorsed (Palm & Gibson, 1998). Over half the sample did indicate that "acknowledging or remembering" abusive experiences was quite important (p. 258), although surprisingly few therapists reported actually seeing clients with a history of childhood sexual abuse. Among psychologists, a client's history of sexual abuse was more likely to be believed if memories were continuous rather than forgotten, vivid, and if the client were older at the time of the reported abuse (Gore-Felton et al., 2000). In an analogue study using abused client vignettes, psychologists did not immediately conclude that abuse had occurred, did not avoid current problems in favor of exploring possible past abuse experiences, and did not use leading techniques to establish possible abuse (Sullins, 1998).

Within recent years, professional literature has focused directly on recommendations for ethical and research-based approaches for abuse survivor clients, and for handling the issue of recovered memories and the mechanisms of memory itself. In general, such practice guidelines have focused on education and competence in the areas of trauma and memory, and the use of specific (and more conservative) techniques (Enns et al., 1998; Knapp & VandeCreek, 2000; Palm & Gibson, 1998). Additionally, some attention has been paid to motivations of clients (and their therapists) who later repudiate abuse memories. For example, de Rivera (2000) proposes models to explain the generation of "false" memories. The first is labeled "mind control" (p. 378), which refers to intense insistence by a therapist that her or his client has likely been abused, or must remember in great detail the events of abuse. De Rivera suggests that this is not a function of a malevolent therapist, but instead represents an extreme form of boundary violation with clients. In fact, among the sample of clients who later recanted abuse memories, therapists who unduly encouraged the construction of such memories also engaged in questionable behaviors such as going to a meal with the client, encouraging frequent contact between sessions, and making decisions for the client rather than assisting the client in making her own decisions. De Rivera's other models to explain repudiated memories included "self-narrative(s)," which referred to a client's self-construction of abuse memories as a likely explanation for current feelings

and behaviors. This may be a particularly important area for exploration in cases where the client has vague memories or feels her symptoms must be representative of a history of abuse. Finally, de Rivera's "role-enactment" referred to the possibility that a client will assume a victim/survivor role if placed in that role in therapy or in other situations. Interestingly, the participants in this study cited triggers for possible recovered memories as coming more frequently from media sources than from therapist behaviors.

In summation, the pendulum for blanket beliefs in childhood sexual abuse—often whether or not there are symptoms and behaviors suggestive of such abuse—has swung to a more conservative and research-based screening approach for lifetime abuse experiences. Ironically, part of our evaluation process may need to include details about previous therapy (e.g., if pressure was applied to help the client "recover" or reconstruct memories), and in cases of reported abuse, the client's knowledge base concerning symptoms and treatment. As any of us who have faced too many clients who initially report that they are "a multiple(s)" (having a dissociative disorder), understanding the mechanism of how they arrived at this conclusion is critical, as is understanding of the rare occurrence of that disorder.

Probing for Abuse Details

Having uncovered preliminary evidence of abuse in the client's life, the clinician will require further detailed information to make decisions relevant to an abuse history. Depending on the context of the assessment, a clinician may wish to evaluate the client further with formal interview schedules or scales, or may elect to allow the information to be revealed within the context of the subsequent therapy. If the client discloses information implying current risk, we believe that further assessment is essential. What kinds of preliminary information signal current risk? Any of the following acts toward the client should serve as cues: physical coercion or violence to persons or property, verbal abuse (yelling, blaming, belittling, degrading, etc.), sexual debasement or coercion, threats (verbal or use of weapons), isolation from friends and family, excessive jealousy and checking behavior, and a variety of other interpersonal control behaviors. For each identified category, therapists also need to inquire about frequency, severity, duration, and degree of physical injury. If physical violence is a concern, therapists should assess for lethality (dangerousness to self or partner), and for the woman's safety.

Because of the oppressive effects of sexual trauma, continued violence, and coercion on their victims, such clients may deny and minimize their experiences and may be better served with structured scales that survey specific acts and events. There are a number of measures that are designed to elicit more detailed information about physical or sexual abuse. For evidence of physical abuse, readers are referred to reviews by Saunders (1992), Tolman (1992), and Walker (1984). For evidence of child or adult sexual abuse, reviews by Briere (1992), Courtois (1988), and Jehu (1992) provide discussions of useful scales and interview formats. Finally, we suggest specific scales such as those by Fitzgerald et al. (1988) and Koss (1985) that assess a range of unwelcome sexual experiences, from mild gender harassment through violent sexual assault. Experiences of repeated sexual harassment have been shown to have negative effects on victims that are similar to those of other forms of sexual coercion (Coles, 1986), and these should be regarded with equal concern for the well-being of the client.

Assessing for Strength and Well-Being

From a woman-centered perspective, we believe it is insufficient to limit the assessment protocol to an evaluation of presenting symptoms, formal diagnosis, and a treatment plan that aims toward symptom remission and returning the client to her premorbid level of functioning. The ethical practice of psychological health care for women provides us with a rich arena for innovative woman-centered assessment and intervention. In concert with recent calls for a positive psychology emphasizing a focus on health and well-being over illness and despair (Seligman, 1996a, 1996b), it is timely to move away from paradigms that are concerned mainly with individual illness and internal pathology. Assessments for interventions that are designed to reduce the observed symptoms of a specific disorder are destined to return women in distress to the toxic environments within which their problems originated. Attention to individual pathology, to the exclusion of external and contextual factors contributing to women's distress, inevitably underestimates the pathogenic aspects of their life situations (Brown, 1994; Comas-Diaz & Greene, 1994; Sarbin, 1997; Worell, 2001; Worell & Remer, 1992, 2003).

In contrast, the hallmark of woman-centered practice has been its emphasis on attention to the context of women's lives, and to promoting strength,

well-being, and resilience rather than targeting only personal deficits (Johnson, Roberts, & Worell, 1999; Worell & Goodheart, 2006, Worell & Johnson, 1997). This positive approach encourages attention to personal assets as well as to liabilities, and to contributions as well as to concerns. Many woman-centered and contextual practitioners tend to view the indices of distress that motivate women to seek (or be hospitalized for) help as adaptive strategies in the context of disadvantage and adversity (Wyche & Rice, 1997).

In supplementing traditional assessment strategies that originate in models of illness and pathology, alternative measures are being developed that address the potential for positive growth toward well-being and resilience. Added to a traditional assessment protocol, measures of well-being can provide both diagnostic and treatment-focused information about positive and health-promoting client functioning. Several recently developed positive assessment tools, such as Ryff's (1989) Scales of Psychological Well-Being, Lambert and Burlingame's (1996) Outcome Questionnaire, and Worell and Chandler's (1996) Personal Progress Scale (PPS), have been undergoing validation. For example, to assess the utility of well-being in measuring positive therapy outcomes, a study with 45 women clients from eight university counseling centers found substantial positive correlations for both the PPS and two of Ryff's scales (autonomy and self-acceptance) with self-rater client improvement after seven or more therapy sessions, and also for a subset at 1-year follow-up (Chandler, Worell, Blount, & Lusk, 1997). In a more recent study (Johnson, Worell, & Chandler, 2005), a revised version of the PPS discriminated women trauma survivors with and without high levels of PTSD. That is, those survivors with higher PPS-R scores, reflecting a sense of personal empowerment, were less likely to demonstrate indices of PTSD.

Measures such as these are promising additions to assessment with women in mental health settings, many of whom may enter therapy with deficits in self-esteem, assertiveness, effective problem-solving skills, self-efficacy, and positive views of self as an agent of change. Rather than returning women to their prior functioning as indicative of remission, therapists may consider the dimension of well-being and its concomitants as important factors for contributing to client strength, effective coping, and resilience. In addition to symptom reduction, women clients will benefit from developing resilience in dealing with current and future stress and adversity. Given that many women still reside in poverty and have limited opportunities, the more resilient among them will be better equipped to maintain their sense of direction and effective coping (Todd & Worell, 2000). Although most women may not be able to make dramatic changes in their environments, they may be better equipped to deal effectively with the realistic context of their lives.

Summary and Conclusions

We have proposed that assessment strategies with women clients should be designed with five themes in mind: (1) women as a group have had a subordinate status in American society that encourages and "normalizes" certain socialized gender-related behaviors; (2) these gender-related behaviors may vary across cultures, ethnicity, ethnoracial identity, sexual orientation, socioeconomic status, and national or regional origins; (3) societal and concomitant psychologist expectations for women's behavior may frame and influence the assessment process; (4) women in all groups are at risk for repeated experiences of interpersonal violence and sexual abuse, which have significant and specific effects on their psychological health; and (5) client well-being, resilience, and strengths are equally important as indices of illness and disturbance in a comprehensive assessment process.

Gender bias has been a key variable in the literature regarding assessment and treatment of women clients. Untangling the nature of possible bias in assessment stems from many sources and may also include interaction effects. To some extent, all psychological assessment is contaminated with the subjectivity of diagnostic categories, diagnostic nomenclature, and clinicians' choice of, and blindness to, particular observations, questions, and their own understandings about psychological health and illness. We suggest that clinicians examine their potential for overt gender bias through (1) the examination of current research relative to understanding the interface between assessment and diagnosis with women's responses and expected behaviors following high-probability experiences (e.g., violence and victimization); (2) monitoring and challenging their own beliefs and expectations regarding the behavior of women from many diverse and intersecting identities; and (3) familiarizing themselves with the APA Guidelines on Counseling Women (2007).

Existing research and our awareness of specific women's issues in therapeutic practice should shape our skills in working with women clients. From this focus we have gained an awareness of the importance of assessing a woman's presenting issues, symptoms,

and strengths within the context of her life, including both internal psychological functioning and the external sociocultural framework in which she lives. We offer suggestions for target areas to be included in assessment with women clients (see Table 1). These areas reflect current knowledge regarding significant issues of inquiry with women but are certainly not an exhaustive list. It is our hope that future research on women's issues in therapeutic practice will (1) expand our knowledge about strategies for assessing the impact of women's diverse and intersecting identities (race, ethnicity, sexual orientation, etc.); (2) contribute to the development and refinement of measures that assess the positive variables associated with indices of strength and resilience; and (3) continue to expand the search for diagnostic categories or dimensions that view women's behaviors in the realistic context of their lives.

References

Adler, D. A., Drake, R. E., & Teague, G. B. (1990). Clinicians' practices in personality assessment: Does gender influence the use of DSM-II Axis II? *Comprehensive Psychiatry, 31,* 125–133.

Ahrens, C. E., Campbell, R., Ternier-Thames, N. K., Wasco, S. M., & Sefl, T. (2007). Deciding whom to tell: Expectations and outcomes of rape survivors' first disclosure. *Psychology of Women Quarterly, 31,* 38–49.

American Psychiatric Association. (1987). *Diagnostic and statistical manual of mental disorders* (3rd ed., Rev.). Washington, DC: Author.

American Psychiatric Association. (1994). *Diagnostic and statistical manual of mental disorders* (4th ed.). Washington, DC: Author.

American Psychiatric Association. (2000). *Diagnostic and statistical manual of mental disorders* (4th ed., Text rev.). Washington, DC: Author.

American Psychological Association. (1975). Report of the task force on sex bias and sex-role stereotyping in psychotherapeutic practice. *American Psychologist, 30,* 1169–1175.

American Psychological Association. (1978). Guidelines of therapy with women. *American Psychologist, 33,* 1122–1133.

American Psychological Association. (2000). Guidelines for psychotherapy with lesbian, gay, and bisexual clients. *American Psychologist, 55,* 1440–1451.

American Psychological Association. (2003). Guidelines on multicultural education, training, research, practice, and organizational change for psychologists. *American Psychologist, 58,* 377–402.

American Psychological Association. (2004). Guidelines for psychological practice with older adults. *American Psychologist, 59,* 236–260.

American Psychological Association. (2007). Guidelines for psychological practice with women. Retrieved from American Psychological Association web site htpc://www.apa.org/Women's Program Office.

Ammerman, R. T., & Hersen, M. (1992). *Assessment of family violence: A clinical and legal sourcebook.* New York: John Wiley & Sons.

Becker, D., & Lamb, S. (1994). Sex bias in the diagnosis of borderline personality disorder and post traumatic stress disorder. *Professional Psychology: Research and Practice, 25*, 55–61.

Bergner, R. M. (1997). What is psychopathology, and so what? *Clinical Psychology: Science and Practice, 4*, 235–248.

Brady, J. L., Guy, J. D., Poelstra, P. L., & Brokaw, B. F. (1999). Vicarious traumatization, spirituality, and the treatment of sexual abuse survivors: A national survey of women psychotherapists. *Professional Psychology: Research and Practice, 30*, 386–393.

Briere, J. N. (1992). Gender-based countertransference of female therapists in the psychotherapy of women. *Women and Therapy, 6*, 25–38.

Briere, J. N. (1998). Self-mutilation in clinical and general population samples: Prevalence, correlates, and functions. *American Journal of Orthopsychiatry, 68*, 609–620.

Briere, J. N., & Zaidi, L. Y. (1989). Sexual abuse histories and sequelae in female psychiatric emergency room patients. *American Journal of Psychiatry, 146*, 1602–1606.

Broverman, I. K., Broverman, D., Clarkson, F. E., Rosenkrantz, P. S., & Vogel, S. R. (1970). Sex-role stereotypes and clinical judgments of mental health. *Journal of Consulting and Clinical Psychology, 34*, 1–7.

Brown, L. S. (1990). Taking account of gender in the clinical assessment interview. *Professional Psychology: Research and Practice, 21*, 12–17.

Brown, L. S. (1994). *Subversive dialogues: Theory in feminist therapy.* New York: Basic Books.

Buckner, J. C., Bassuk, M. D., & Zima, B. T. (1993). Mental health issues affecting homeless women: Implications for intervention. *American Journal of Orthopsychiatry, 63*, 385–399.

Buczek, T. A. (1981). Sex biases in counseling: Counselor retention of the concerns of a female and male client. *Journal of Counseling Psychology, 28*, 13–21.

Butcher, J. N. (Ed.) (1987). Special series: Cultural factors in understanding and assessing psychology. *Journal of Consulting and Clinical Psychology, 55*, 459–512.

Canales, C. (2000). Gender as a subculture: The first division of multicultural diversity. In C. Cuellar & F. A. Paniagua (Eds.), *Handbook of multicultural mental health: Assessment and treatment of diverse populations* (pp. 3–26). San Diego, CA: Academic Press.

Caplan, P. J. (1995). *They say you're crazy: How the world's most powerful psychiatrists decide who's normal.* Reading, MA: Addison-Wesley.

Caplan, P. J., & Cosgrove, L. (2004). *Bias in psychiatric diagnosis.* Northvale, NJ: Jason Aronson.

Chandler, R., Worell, J., Blount, A., & Lusk, M. (1997). *What is unique about feminist therapy: Evaluation of the empowerment model.* Paper presented at the annual meeting of the American Psychological Association, Toronto, August 1997.

Clark, L. A. (2007). Assessment and diagnosis of personality disorders: Perennial issues and an emerging reconceptualization. In S. T. Fiske, A. E. Kazdin, & D. L. Schacter (Eds.), *Annual Review of Psychology* (Vol. 58, pp. 227–257). Palo Alto, CA: Annual Reviews.

Cloitre, M., Koenen, K. C., Gratz, K. L., & Jakupcak, M. (2002). Differential diagnosis of PTSD in women. In P. Kimmerling, P. Ouimette, & J. Wolfe (Eds.), *Gender and PTSD* (pp. 117–149). New York: Guilford Press.

Coles, F. S. (1986). Forced to quit: Sexual harassment complaints and agency response. *Sex Roles, 14*, 81–95.

Comas-Diaz, L., & Greene, B. (1994). *Women of color: Integrating ethnic and gender identities in psychotherapy.* New York: Guilford.

Courtois, C. A. (1988). *Healing the incest wound: Adult survivors in therapy.* New York: Norton.

Cowan, G. (1976). Therapist judgments of clients' sex-role problems. *Psychology of Women Quarterly, 1*, 15–24.

Craine, L. S., Hensen, C. E., Colliver, J. A., & MacLean, D. G. (1988). Prevalence of a history of sexual abuse among female psychiatric patients in a state hospital system. *Hospital and Community Psychiatry, 39*, 300–304.

Cromer, L. D., & Freyd, J. J. (2007). What influences believing child sexual abuse disclosures? The roles of depicted memory persistence, participant gender, trauma history, and sexism. *Psychology of Women Quarterly, 31*, 13–22.

Davidson, C., & Abramowitz, S. (1980). Sex bias in clinical judgments: Later returns. *Psychology of Women Quarterly, 4*, 377–395.

Davis, R. T., Blashfield, R. K., & McElroy, R. A. (1993). Weighing criteria in the diagnosis of a personality disorder: A demonstration. *Journal of Abnormal Psychology, 102*, 319–322.

de Rivera, J. (2000). Understanding persons who repudiate memories recovered in therapy. *Professional Psychology: Research and Practice, 31*, 378–386.

Desjarlais, R., Eisenberg, L., Good, B., & Kleinman, A. (1996). *World mental health: Problems and priorities in low-income countries.* Oxford: Oxford University Press.

Enns, C. Z., Campbell, J., Courtois, C. A., Gottlieb, M. C., Lese, K. P., Gilbert, M. S., et al. (1998). Working with adult clients who may have experienced childhood abuse: Recommendations for assessment and practice. *Professional Psychology: Research and Practice, 29*, 245–256.

Enns, C. Z., McNeilley, C., Corkery, J., & Gilbert, M. (1995). The debate about sexual abuse: A feminist perspective. *Journal of Counseling Psychology, 23*, 181–279.

Farley, H. S. (2004). *Prostitution, trafficking, and traumatic stress.* New York: Haworth.

Finkelhor, D., Hotaling, G., Lewis, I. A., & Smith, C. (1990). Sexual abuse in a national survey of adult men and women: Prevalence, characteristics, and risk factors. *Child Abuse and Neglect, 14*, 19–28.

Fisher, B., Daigle, L., Cullen, F., & Turner, M. (2003). Reporting sexual victimization to the police and others: Results from a national-level study of college women. *Criminal Justice and Behavior, 30*, 6–38.

Fitzgerald, L. F., Shullman, S. L., Bailey, M., Richards, H., Swecker, J., Gold, Y., et al. (1988). The incidence and dimensions of sexual harassment in academia and the workplace. *Journal of Vocational Behavior, 32*, 157–165.

Folkman, S., & Moskowitz, J. T. (2004). Coping: Pitfalls and promises. In S. T. Fiske, D. L. Schacter, & C. Zahn-Waxler (Eds.), *Annual review of psychology* (Vol. 55, pp. 745–774). Palo Alto, CA: Annual Reviews.

Ford, M. R., & Widiger, T. A. (1989). Sex bias in the diagnosis of histrionic and antisocial personality disorders. *Journal of Consulting and Clinical Psychology, 57*, 301–305.

Freyd, J. J., DePrince, A. P., & Zurbriggen, E. L. (2001). Self-reported memory for abuse depends upon perpetrator relationship. *Journal of Trauma and Dissociation, 2*, 5–17.

Goodheart, C. D. (2006). An integrated view of girls' and women's health: Psychology, physiology, and society. In J. Worell & C. D. Goodheart (Eds.), *Handbook of girls' and women's psychological* health: Gender and well-being across the lifespan. New York: Oxford University Press.

Goodman, L. A., Dutton, M. A., & Harris, M. (1995). Episodically homeless women with serious mental illness: Prevalence of physical and sexual assault. *American Journal of Orthopsychiatry, 65*, 468–478.

Gore-Felton, C., Koopman, C., Thoresen, C., Arnow, B., Bridges, E., & Spiegel, D. (2000). Psychologists' beliefs and clinical characteristics: Judging the veracity of childhood sexual abuse memories. *Professional Psychology: Research and Practice, 31*, 372–377.

Greene, B. (2000). African American lesbian and bisexual women in feminist psychodynamic psychotherapies. In L. D. Jackson & B. Green (Eds.), *Psychotherapy with African American women* (pp. 82–125). New York: Guilford.

Greene, B. (2007). Homophobia/heterosexism in communities of color. *Communique: Psychological perspectives on sexual orientation and communities of color* (pp. XXV–XXV11), August 2007. Washington, DC: American Psychological Association, Office of Ethnic Minority Affairs.

Hamilton, S., Rothbart, M., & Dawes, R. B. (1986). Sex bias, diagnosis and DSM III. *Sex Roles, 15*, 269–274.

Hare-Mustin, R. T. (1983). An appraisal of the relationship between women and psychotherapy, 80 years after the case of Dora. *American Psychologist, 44*, 455–464.

Hartung, C. M., & Widiger, T. A. (1998). Gender differences in the diagnosis of mental disorders: Conclusions and controversies of DSM-IV. *Psychological Bulletin, 123*, 260–278.

Harway, M., & Hansen, M. (2004). *Spouse abuse: Treating battered women, batterers, and their children* (2nd ed.). Sarasota, FL: Professional Resources Press.

Hayes, K. E., & Wolleat, P. L. (1978). Effects of sex in judgment of a simulated counseling interview. *Journal of Counseling Psychology, 25*, 164–168.

Jack, D. J. & Ali, A. (Eds.) (in press). *Cultural perspectives on women's depression: Self-silencing, psychological distress and recovery.* New York: Oxford University Press.

Jacobson, A., Koehler, J. E., & Jones-Brown, C. (1987). The failure of routine assessment to detect histories of assault experienced by psychiatric patients. *Hospital and Community Psychiatry, 38*, 786–792.

Jehu, D. (1992). Adult survivors of sexual abuse. In R. T. Ammerman & M. Hersen (Eds.), *Assessment of family violence: A clinical and legal sourcebook* (pp. 248–370). New York: John Wiley & Sons.

Johnson, N. G., Roberts, M. C., & Worell, J. (1999). *Beyond appearance: A new look at adolescent girls.* Washington, DC: American Psychological Association.

Johnson, D. M., Worell, J., & Chandler, R. (2005). Assessing psychological health and empowerment in women: The Personal Progress Scale Revised. *Women and Health, 41*, 109–129.

Knapp, S., & VandeCreek, L. (2000). Recovered memories of childhood abuse: Is there an underlying professional consensus? *Professional Psychology: Research and Practice, 31*, 365–371.

Koss, M. P. (1985). The hidden rape victim: Personality, attitudinal, and situational characteristics. *Psychology of Women Quarterly, 9*, 193–212.

Koss, M. P., Goodman, L. A., Browne, A., Fitzgerald, L. F., Keita, G. P., & Russo, N. F. (1994). *No safe haven: Male violence against women at home, at work, and in the community.* Washington, DC: American Psychological Association.

Krause, E. D., DeRosa, R. R., & Roth, S. (2002). Gender, Trauma themes, and PTSD: Narratives of male and female survivors. In R. Kimmerling, P. Ouimette, & J. Wolfe (Eds.), *Gender and PTSD* (pp. 349–381). New York: Guilford Press.

Kuchins, H., & Kirk, S. A. (1997). *Making us crazy—DSM: The psychiatric bible and the creation of mental disorders.* New York: Free Press.

Lambert, M. H., & Burlingame, G. M. (1996). *Outcome Questionnaire.* American Professional Credentialing Services: apes@erols.com

Landrine, H. (1989). The politics of personality disorder. *Psychology of Women Quarterly, 13*, 325–340.

Landrine, H. (1995). *Bringing cultural diversity to feminist psychology: Theory, research, and practice.* Washington, DC: American Psychological Association.

Landrine, H., Klonoff, E. A., Gibbs, J., Manning, V., & Lund, M. (1995). Physical and psychiatric correlates of gender discrimination. *Psychology of Women Quarterly, 19*, 473–492.

Lerner, C. F., & Kennedy, L. T. (2000). Stay-leave decision making in battered women: Trauma, coping and self-efficacy. *Cognitive Therapy and Research, 24*, 215–232.

Linn, M. C., & Kessel, C. (2006). Assessment and gender. In J. Worell & C. D. Goodheart (Eds.), *Girls' and women's psychological health: Gender and well-being across the lifespan* (pp. 40–50). New York: Oxford University Press.

Lopez, S. R. (1989). Patient variable biases in clinical judgment: Conceptual overview and methodological considerations. *Psychology Bulletin, 106*, 184–203.

Lopez, S. R., & Guarnaccia, P. J. (2000). Cultural psychopathology: Uncovering the social world of mental illness. In S. T. Fiske, D. L. Schacter, & A. Zahn-Waxler (Eds.), *Annual Review of Psychology* (Vol. 51, pp. 571–598). Palo Alto, CA: Annual Reviews.

Lyon, E. (1993). Hospital staff reactions to accounts by survivors of childhood abuse. *American Journal of Orthopsychiatry, 63*, 410–416.

MacDonald, M. M. (1984). Behavioral assessment of women clients. In E. A. Blechman (Ed.), *Behavior modification for women* (pp. 60–93). New York: Guilford Press.

Maddux, J. E., Snyder, C. R., & Lopez, S. J. (2004). Toward a positive clinical psychology: Deconstructing the illness ideology and constructing an ideology of human strengths and potential. In P. A. Linley & S. Joseph (Eds.), *Positive psychology in practice* (pp. 320–334). New York: John Wiley & Sons.

Marley, J. A., & Bulia, S. (1999). When violence happens to people with mental illness: Disclosing victimization. *American Journal of Orthopsychiatry, 69*, 398–402.

Marsella, A. J., & Yamada, A. M. (2000). Culture and mental health: An introduction and overview of foundations, concepts, and issues. In I. Cuellar & F. A. Paniagua (Eds.), *Handbook of multicultural mental health: Assessment and treatment of diverse populations* (pp. 3–26). San Diego, CA: Academic Press.

McDaniel, S. H., Johnson, B. S., & Sears, S. F. (2004). Psychologists promote biopsychosocial health for families. In R. H. Rozinsky, N. G. Johnson, C. D. Goodheart, & W. R. Hammond (Eds.), *Psychology builds a healthy world: Opportunities for research and practice* (pp. 49–75). Washington, DC: American Psychological Association.

McReynolds. P. (1989). Diagnosis and clinical assessment: Current status and major issues. In M. Rosenzwig & L. W.

Porter (Eds.), *Annual Review of Psychology* (pp. 83–108). Palo Alto, CA: Annual Reviews.

Mechanic, D. (1997). Psychopathology and public policy. *Clinical Psychology: Science and Practice, 4*, 272–275.

Nayak, M. B. (2000). Factors influencing hesitancy in medical students to assess history of victimization in patients. *Journal of Interpersonal Violence, 15*, 123–133.

Neal-Barnett, A. M., & Crowther, J. H. (2000). To be female, middle class, and Black. *Psychology of Women Quarterly, 24*, 129–136.

Nettles, R. (2007). Challenges to healthy African American lesbian, gay, bisexual or transgender status. In *Communique: Psychological perspectives on sexual orientation and communities of color* (pp. XIV–XVII), August 2007. Washington, DC: American Psychological Association, Office of Ethnic Minority Affairs.

Nishith, P., Mechanic, M. B., & Resick, P. A. (2000). Prior interpersonal trauma: The contribution to current PTSD symptoms in female rape victims. *Journal of Abnormal Psychology, 109*, 20–25.

Nolen-Hoeksema, S. (2002). Gender differences in depression. In L. H. Gotlib & C. Hammen (Eds.), *Handbook of depression* (pp. 492–509). New York: Guilford.

Palm, K. M., & Gibson, P. (1998). Recovered memories of childhood sexual abuse: Clinicians' practices and beliefs. *Professional Psychology: Research and Practice, 29*, 257–261.

Phillips, R. D., & Gilroy, F. D. (1985). Sex-role stereotypes and clinical judgments of mental health: The Broverman's findings revisited. *Sex Roles, 12*, 179–183.

Pope, K. S. (1996). Memory, abuse, and science: Questioning claims about the false memory syndrome epidemic. *American Psychologist, 51*, 957–974.

Potts, M. K., Burnam, M. A., & Wells, K. B. (1991). Gender differences in depression detection: A comparison of clinician diagnosis and standardized assessment. *Psychological Assessment, 3*, 609–615.

Pruitt, J. A., & Kappius, R. E. (1992). Routine inquiry into sexual victimization: A survey of therapists' practices. *Professional Psychology: Research and Practice, 23*, 474–479.

Robinson, T. L., & Howard-Hamilton, R. F. (2000). *The convergence of race, ethnicity, and gender: Multiple identities in counseling.* Upper Saddle River, NJ: Merrill.

Rhodes, A. E., Goering, P. N., & Williams, J. I. (2002). Gender and outpatient mental health service use. *Social Science and Medicine, 54*, 1–10.

Russell, D. E. H. (1986). *The secret trauma: Incest in the lives of girls and women.* New York: Basic Books.

Russell, D. E. H., & Howell, N. (1983). The prevalence of rape in the United States revisited. *Signs: Journal of Women in Culture and Society, 8*, 688–695.

Ryff, C. (1989). Happiness is everything, or is it? Explorations on the meaning of well-being. *Journal of Personality and Social Psychology, 57*, 1069–1081.

Sarbin, T. R. (1997). On the futility of psychiatric diagnostic manuals (DSMs) and the return of personal agency. *Applied and Preventative Psychology, 6*, 233–243.

Saunders, D. G. (1992). Woman battering. In R. T. Ammerman & R. M. Hersen (Eds.), *Assessment of family violence: A clinical and legal handbook* (pp. 208–235). New York: John Wiley & Sons.

Seligman, M. E. P. (1996a). Science as an alley of practice. *American Psychologist, 51*, 1072–1079.

Seligman, M. E. P. (1996b). A creditable beginning. *American Psychologist, 51*, 1086–1088.

Sesan, R. (1988). Sex bias and sex-role stereotyping in psychotherapy with women: Survey results. *Psychotherapy: Theory, Research, and Practice, 25*, 107–116.

Smith, M. (1980). Sex bias in counseling and psychotherapy. *Psychological Bulletin, 87*, 392–407.

Spitzer, R. L., Williams, J. B. W., Kass, F., & Davies, M. (1989). National field trial of the DSM-III-R diagnostic criteria for self-defeating personality disorder. *The American Journal of Psychiatry, 146*, 1561–1567.

Sprock, J., & Yoder, C. Y. (1997). Women and depression: An update on the report of the APA task force. *Sex Roles, 36*, 269–303.

Stewart, A. J., & McDermott, C. (2004). Gender in psychology. In S. T. Fiske, D. L. Schacter, & C. Zahn-Waxler (Eds.), *Annual review of psychology* (Vol. 55, pp. 519–544). Palo Alto, CA: Annual Reviews.

Sue, D. W., Capodilupo, C. M., Torino, G. C., Bucceri, J. M., Holder, A. M. B., Nadal, K. L., et al. (2007). Microaggressions in everyday life: Implications for clinical practice. *American Psychologist, 62*, 271–286.

Sue, D. W., & Sue, D. (1999). *Counseling the culturally different: Theory and practice.* New York: John Wiley & Sons.

Sullins, C. D. (1998). Suspected repressed childhood sexual abuse: Gender effects on diagnosis and treatment. *Psychology of Women Quarterly, 22*, 403–418.

Todd, J. L., & Worell, J. (2000). Resilience in low-income employed African American women. *Psychology of Women Quarterly, 24*, 119–128.

Tolman, R. M. (1992). Psychological abuse of women. In R. T. Ammerman & M. Hersen (Eds.), *Assessment of family violence: A clinical and legal handbook* (pp. 291–312). New York: John Wiley & Sons.

U.S. Department of Health and Human Services, Office on Women's Health (2001). *Women's health issues: An overview.* Washington, DC: National Women's Health Information Center.

Waisberg, J., & Page, S. (1988). Gender-role nonconformity and perception of mental illness. *Women and Health, 14*, 3–16.

Walker, L. E. A. (1984). *The battered woman syndrome.* New York: Springer.

Walker, L. E. A. (1989). Psychology and violence against women. *American Psychologist, 44*, 695–702.

Walker, L. E. A. (1994a). *Abused women and survivor therapy: A practical guide for the psychotherapist.* Washington, DC: American Psychological Association.

Walker, L. E. A. (1994b). Are personality disorders gender biased? In S. A. Kirk & S. D. Einbinder (Eds.), *Controversial issues in mental health* (pp. 21–29). New York: Allyn & Bacon.

West, C. M. (2002). Black battered women: New directions in research and Black feminist theory. In L. H. Collins, M. R. Dunlap, & J. C. Chrisler (Eds.), *Charting a new course for feminist psychology* (pp. 216–237). Westport, CT: Praeger.

Whiffen, V. E., & Demidenko, N. (2006). Mood disturbance across the lifespan. In J. Worell & C. D. Goodheart (Eds.), *Girls' and women's psychological health: Gender and well-being across the lifespan* (pp. 51–59). New York: Oxford University Press.

White, J. W., & Frabutt, M. (2006). Violence against girls and women: An integrative developmenala perspective. In J. Worell & C. D. Goodheart (2006). *Handbook of girls' and women's psychological health: Gender and well-being across the lifespan* (pp. 85–93). New York: Oxford University Press.

Widiger, T. A., Frances, A., Spitzer, R. L., & Williams, J. B. W. (1988). The DSM-II-R personality disorders: An overview. *The American Journal of Psychiatry, 135*, 786–795.

Widiger, T. A., & Trull, T. J. (1991). Diagnosis and clinical assessment. *Annual Review of Psychology, 42*, 109–133.

Widiger, T. A., & Trull, T. J. (2007). Plate tectonics in the classification of personality disorders. *American Psychologist, 62*, 71–83.

Williams, M. K., McCandless, T., & Dunlap, M. R. (2002). Women of color and feminist psychology: Moving from criticism and critique to integration and application. In L. H. Collins, M. R. Dunlap, & J. C. Chrisler (Eds.), *Charting a new course for feminist psychology* (pp. 65–90). Westport, CT: Praeger.

Worell, J. (2001). Feminist interventions: Accountability beyond symptom reduction. *Psychology of Women Quarterly, 25*, 335–343.

Worell, J. (2006). Pathways to healthy development: Sources of strength and empowerment. In J. Worell & C. D. Goodheart (Eds.), *Handbook of girls' and women's psychological health: Gender and well-being across the lifespan.* New York: Oxford University Press.

Worell, J., & Chandler, R. K. (1996). The Personal Progress Scale (Unpublished manuscript). University of Kentucky.

Worell, J., & Goodheart, C. D. (2006). *Handbook of girls' and women's psychological health: Gender and well-being across the lifespan.* New York: Oxford University Press.

Worell, J., & Johnson, N. (1997). *Shaping the future of feminist psychology: Education, research, and practice.* Washington, DC: American Psychological Association.

Worell, J., & Remer, P. (1992). *Feminist perspectives in therapy: An empowerment model for women.* New York: John Wiley & Sons.

Worell, J., & Remer, P. (2003). *Feminist perspectives in therapy: Empowering diverse women.* New York: John Wiley & Sons.

Wright, B. A., & Lopez, S. J. (2002). Widening the diagnostic focus: A case for including human strengths and environmental resources. In C. R. Snyder & S. J. Lopez (Eds.), *Handbook of positive psychology* (pp. 26–43). New York: Oxford University Press.

Wyche, K. F., & Rice, J. K. (1997). Feminist therapy: From dialogue to tenets. In J. Worell & N. Johnson (Eds.), *Shaping the future of feminist psychology: Education, research, and practice* (pp. 57–72). Washington, DC: American Psychological Association.

Use of the MMPI-2 in Neuropsychological Evaluations

Carlton S. Gass

Abstract

The measurement of personality and psychopathology in neuropsychological contexts is essential because brain injury affects psychological status and psychological problems can mimic brain dysfunction. The Minnesota Multiphasic Personality Inventory-2 (MMPI-2) is, by far, the most widely researched and clinically utilized test to meet this need. This chapter reviews special administrative and interpretive considerations that apply in neuropsychological settings. Recent and controversial developments in MMPI-2 research and application are also discussed.

Keywords: Alzheimer's disease, brain injury, cognitive test performance, correction factor, FBS, feedback of results, malingering, MMPI-2, neurological symptom reporting, neuropsychological deficits, post-concussive syndrome, Clinical Scales, seizure disorder, somatoform disorders

Clinical assessment in neuropsychological settings customarily involves the integration of numerous sources of information. These include "interview" data obtained directly from the examinee and, in many cases, people who are well-acquainted with the examinee. The "clinical history" of the presenting complaints or symptoms, as well as relevant background information, is often essential to accurate diagnostic formulation. "Observations" provide important data related to rapport, cooperation, attentiveness, affect and mood, energy level, stamina, task persistence, diverse aspects of speech, perceptual, and motor functioning, and executive functions such as initiation, sustaining a cognitive set, use of environmental feedback, insight, and review and verification of performance. "Cognitive test results" and "formal measures of perceptual and motor functions" are essential components in most neuropsychological assessments.

The final assessment component is a "measure of personality and emotional status." This domain is often overlooked, despite its importance in the assessment process. Whether endogenous or reactive in origin, changes in psychological status are very common

manifestations of brain dysfunction. In addition, because of their subjective nature, many seemingly neurological complaints actually represent somatic expressions of a psychiatric disorder. In many clinical settings, a very high percentage of neuropsychological referrals are made because of subjective complaints such as poor concentration, forgetfulness, and difficulties retaining new information. Such complaints are usually symptomatic of an emotional disorder and, less often, an underlying neurological condition (Gass & Apple, 1997; Gass & Russell, 1986a). In fact, a significant amount of the unique variance in performance on popular measures of attention and memory can be accounted for by Minnesota Multiphasic Personality Inventory (MMPI-2) indices of anxiety and depression in the absence of brain dysfunction (Gass, 1996a). Performance efficiency on some neuropsychological tests is lowered by emotional factors that, unless measured, cannot be accounted for (Gass, 1996a; Gass, Ansley, & Boyette, 1994). Accurate neuropsychological assessment often requires a valid measure of emotional and personality characteristics, because these can give a false appearance of central nervous system (CNS) dysfunction.

Brain injury commonly causes psychological symptoms, and psychological symptoms often masquerade as manifestations of neurological disease. In either scenario, clarification of psychological status is essential to proper diagnosis and treatment. Neuropsychologists are intent on using reliable and valid performance measures to assess neurobehavioral abilities. Unfortunately, a double standard is applied in selecting methods for assessing psychological status. A clinical interview is commonly the sole method used to evaluate emotional status. In some cases, clinicians combine the clinical interview with very limited data based on brief tests that narrowly address issues such as depression or anxiety.

The MMPI-2/MMPI (Butcher, Dahlstrom, Graham, Tellegen, & Kaemmer, 1989) has a long history of application within the field of neuropsychology. In fact, the MMPI was incorporated into a standardized and subsequently validated neuropsychological test battery by Ralph Reitan over 50 years ago (Reitan, 1955). The amount of past and present research efforts involving the MMPI-2 in the neuropsychological context is substantial and far exceeds that involving any other multidimensional measure of personality or psychopathology. This extensive research base is certainly one of the reasons for widespread use of the MMPI-2 by neuropsychologists (Butcher & Ben-Porath, 2004; Sharland & Gfeller, 2007). This chapter is a review of some important aspects of using the MMPI-2 specifically in clinical neuropsychological practice though some of this material lends itself to a broader application.

Special Administrative Issues in Neuropsychological Settings
Clarifying the Purpose of the MMPI-2

Many medical patients who are referred for neuropsychological assessment do not initially understand why they have been asked to take a test of psychological status. In addition, the content of MMPI-2 items includes occasional references to highly personal matters and other issues that might appear to be irrelevant to the reason for referral. This will sometimes elicit an uncooperative response set that yields inaccurate information. For example, some of these individuals respond to the test items defensively, feeling compelled to assert normalcy and deny any problems so as not to be mistaken as "crazy." Others may be offended and refuse to cooperate with the remainder of the assessment process.

The clinician can prevent these unfortunate outcomes by preparing the patient prior to administering the MMPI-2. This is part of the ethical requirement for clinicians to obtain informed consent. Patients should never be administered the MMPI-2 or other instruments without an adequate explanation of its function and the rationale for giving it. The MMPI-2 can be introduced as a routine part of the examination process designed to measure health-related feelings and attitudes. Although MMPI-2 administration is presented as a routine procedure, the clinician should be sensitive to the patient's needs and encourage questions or expressions of concern.

Administrative Format

The MMPI-2 can be used with most individuals who are at least 18 years old and have at least a sixth grade level of reading ability. The popularity of the MMPI-2 among neuropsychologists suggests that, in most clinical settings, administration is not a significant problem. However, patients who are substantially handicapped by cognitive impairment or behavioral disturbances are often unable to manage the requirements of the test, and are therefore unable to provide valid information. A wide variety of conditions can preclude a valid administration of the MMPI-2. These include impatience and low frustration tolerance, visual disturbances, confusion, dyslexia, impaired reading comprehension, inattention and distractibility, and florid psychotic symptoms. Burke, Smith, and Imhoff (1989), using a sample of 66 post-acute traumatic brain injury (TBI) patients, reported a 20% incidence of inconsistent responding to the MMPI. On the other hand, there is evidence suggesting that patients who have moderate neuropsychological impairment secondary to brain injury are typically able to produce profiles that are valid in regard to content-response consistency (Mittenberg, Tremont, & Rayls, 1996; Paniak & Miller, 1993).

Completion of the MMPI-2 sometimes requires breaking the session into several shorter periods. In testing the more severely impaired patients who are unable to manage its cognitive or sensorimotor demands, clinicians sometimes attempt to read the test items aloud to the patient and assume the task of filling out the answer sheet for the patient. The impact of the examiner's involvement in this situation is unknown. If this nonstandardized procedure is used (presumably as a last resort), caution must be exercised in interpreting the results. In many instances, a better alternative to this administrative procedure is to use an audiotape or a compact disk (CD) version released by Pearson Assessments. The CD first presents the general test instructions, followed by two readings of each item to ensure that examinees understand and have time to mark their response. If the standard MMPI-2 answer sheet proves too challenging for the examinee because of impaired visual and visuomotor function, a customized answer sheet with larger font can be made including the words "True" and "False" after each item number. The patient can then be instructed to circle the appropriate answer.

The selection of the written or audio administrative format is based on a consideration of time and examinee competency. Higher functioning individuals who can read without difficulty are best suited for the written format. Most examinees that can read the MMPI-2 booklet complete the inventory in about 90 min. Some take considerably longer and some cannot complete it. Those who have reading difficulties and require the audio format will need 135 min to complete the full MMPI-2. If an individual is ruminative and indecisive, the audio version might be preferable because of its constant pace, forcing a decision within a reasonable amount of time. The important point is that MMPI-2 administration is an intervention that requires clinician sensitivity and attentiveness. The audio and written formats yield equally valid results (Herrman, Dorfman, Roth, & Burns, 1997).

Monitoring the Examinee

Brain-impaired examinees should be monitored closely but unobtrusively to ensure that the instructions are properly followed as MMPI-2 administration begins. This is particularly critical in the case of those individuals who are more cognitively impaired, are more easily confused, and can lose track of the questions and their markings on the answer sheet. Most examinees that successfully complete the first several items are able to finish the remainder of the MMPI-2, though an additional session is sometimes required due to fatigue or time restrictions. In some instances, the examinee will have increasing difficulties as the testing continues, which may become apparent in several ways. First, the patient may inform the examiner directly by saying so. Unfortunately, neurologically impaired examinees sometimes "complete" the test, answering items without adequately understanding item content. The clinician can sometimes observe the quietly confused patient making unusual marks with the pen, writing in the wrong location on the answer sheet, skipping items, or not answering items at all. In any case, it is important for the clinician to monitor the patient throughout the course of the

administration, so that an appropriate intervention can be made if a problem arises.

The MMPI-2 should be completed by the examinee in a supervised setting where privacy can be assured and assistance is available if needed. There are two mistakes that clinicians sometimes make in MMPI-2 administration. The first is allowing the examinee to complete the MMPI-2 unsupervised or in the presence of friends or relatives. Some examinees are naturally inclined to solicit help in answering the test items. Caregivers of neurologically impaired individuals often insist on answering items on behalf of the patient. Even the presence of other examinees is a potential problem, as some examinees are predisposed to make the MMPI-2 a group experience, opting for a democratic process in answering test items. On one occasion, I entered a testing room where four or five examinees were voting on which answer to give for each MMPI item. Profile invalidity is the consequence. A second mistake is to allow patients to take the MMPI-2 home. In this scenario, one can never know who really completed the inventory, or what influences may have intervened (Pope, Butcher, & Seelen, 1993).

Use of a Short Form

In some cases, the MMPI-2 administration will have to be terminated because of various difficulties that emerge. If the first 370 MMPI-2 items are successfully completed by the examinee, this abbreviated form is perfectly adequate for scoring the L, F, K, and the basic Clinical Scales as well as the Harris–Lingoes subscales. A substantial loss of information is the unfortunate consequence. Short forms of the MMPI-2 have been proposed. Under certain circumstances an accurate short form might offer advantages that outweigh the loss of comprehensiveness (Dahlstrom & Archer, 2000). The proposed 180-item format has been shown to be very unreliable for predicting clinical code types, identifying the high-point scale, or predicting scores within 5–10 T-score points on most of the Clinical Scales (Gass & Luis, 2001a; Gass & Gonzalez, 2003). A standard interpretation of the 180-item short form is therefore likely to be inaccurate. However, in the event that a patient can complete only the first 180 items, the clinician can salvage some information that addresses the presence or absence of general problem areas without regard to their level of severity or specific symptom manifestations. If a prorated T-score on the 180-item short form basic clinical scale exceeds T65, it indicates that the full-form MMPI-2

T-score is also highly likely to be greater than T65 (Gass & Gonzalez, 2003).

Special Interpretive Issues in Neuropsychological Settings
Validity Scale Interpretation

In neuropsychological settings, the MMPI-2 validity scales hold special value in detecting manifestations of cognitive impairment that can result in profile invalidity or an undesirable response style. The inclusion of VRIN and TRIN in the MMPI-2 constitutes an important advantage over other psychological tests used by neuropsychologists. Many brain-injured examinees unintentionally provide inaccurate answers because they have acquired difficulties in areas such as reading, concentration, verbal comprehension, judgment, self-awareness, and decision making. Poor readers and cognitively impaired individuals who fail to adequately appreciate their limitations sometimes "complete" psychological inventories but produce inaccurate results. VRIN is optimal for detecting invalidity in these cases. Examinees who have frontal lobe dysfunction sometimes perseverate by giving the same "True" or "False" answer repeatedly, regardless of item content thereby elevating the scores on the TRIN scale.

The Lie Scale

The lie scale (L) is very important in evaluating people with brain dysfunction. The L scale measures the extent to which an examinee responds to the MMPI-2 items in order to give the impression of being exceptionally virtuous, moral, and in control over impulses. Examples include unrealistic claims of never being angry, never being dishonest, and never giving into temptations. Scores on the L scale have distinctive significance in brain-impaired individuals and have been linked with the extent and severity of cognitive impairment (Dikmen & Reitan, 1974, 1977; Gass & Ansley, 1994a). Higher scores on L—commonly observed in Alzheimer's disease and severe TBI—are more likely to occur in the presence of significant neuropsychological impairment. In a heterogeneous brain dysfunction sample, scores on the L scale were predictive of the degree of neuropsychological impairment on the Average Impairment Rating Scale, $r(144) = -.27$, $p < .005$ (Gass, 1997). This finding corroborates previous MMPI research that indicates that high scorers on L generally lack self-insight, fail to appreciate the effect of their behavior on other people, and overestimate their own abilities. Individuals who have brain damage and score high on the L scale typically underestimate their acquired cognitive deficits and make poor decisions such as taking on tasks that are beyond their capability.

Exaggerated Symptom Responding

A major societal trend is one of people seeking compensation for real, imagined, or faked injuries. Not surprisingly, a proliferation of research has focused on designing cognitive tests and MMPI-2 scales that address symptom exaggeration in personal injury cases (Greve, Bianchini, Love, Brennan, & Heinly, 2006). F scales (F, Fb, and Fp) primarily assess the extent of an individual's symptom reporting and/or exaggeration of psychopathology. Extremely high scores (T > 80) alert the clinician to the possibility of inaccurate self-report and an exaggeration or fabrication of problems. However, the F scales are sensitive to psychopathology and high scores do not provide an unambiguous indication of the extent to which an individual is exaggerating or feigning symptoms. Nevertheless, higher scores do indicate a greater probability of symptom exaggeration. This information is incorporated into a broader assessment context for evaluating symptom validity (Bordini, Chaknis, Ekman-Turner, & Perna, 2002; Vanderploeg & Curtiss, 2001).

All of the F scales consist of items that are sensitive but not specific to malingering. Honest self-reporting of problems associated with severe psychopathology commonly produces very high scores on F, Fb, and Fp. In clinical settings that have a high base rate of severe psychopathology, T-scores on F and Fb can exceed 110 in valid protocols. Graham (2006) cited an earlier study (Graham, Watts, & Timbrook, 1991) suggesting that "F-scale raw scores that are beyond the T-score ceiling for the scale (120) are optimal when trying to identify faking bad among psychiatric inpatients" (p. 50).

The Fake Bad Scale

The Fake Bad Scale (FBS; Lees-Haley, English, and Glenn, 1991) is used to detect "exaggerated disability and physiological suffering, particularly in the context of litigated minor head injury" (Greiffenstein, Fox, & Lees-Haley, 2007). This scale consists of 43 items that were selected for content based on observations of personal injury malingerers and unpublished frequency counts of malingerers' test responses. Unlike the other MMPI-2 F scales, the FBS measures somatic complaints more than reports of emotional difficulties or symptoms of severe psychopathology (Larrabee, 2003).

Empirical investigations of the FBS provide mixed findings that are not surprising given the variety of sampling characteristics across studies. A substantial body of evidence suggests that the FBS is highly sensitive to complaints of somatic discomfort and distress (Greiffenstein, Baker, Axelrod, Peck, & Gervais, 2004; Greiffenstein et al., 2007; Greve et al., 2006; Ross, Millis, Krukowski, Putnam, & Adams, 2004), whereas a number of studies suggest important limitations that qualify its use. For example, the FBS was not very sensitive to atypical presentations by litigating mild TBI (57%) using the widely recommended cutoff of 23 (Greiffenstein, Baker, Gola, Donders, & Miller, 2002). FBS was not very sensitive to identifying chronic pain litigants (42%) in a study by Meyers, Millis, and Volkert (2002). In a study of probable malingered neurocognitive dysfunction, FBS (cutoff = 25) had a sensitivity of .52 (Greve et al., 2006).

Variable support for FBS sensitivity to malingering extends to the issue of its specificity—that is, to its effectiveness in *not* misclassifying bona fide patients as malingerers. High scores on the FBS might lead clinicians to falsely conclude that an unacceptably high number of patients who have organic-based physical conditions or certain psychiatric disorders might be erroneously classified as malingerers (Butcher, Arbisi, Atlis, & McNulty, 2003). Studies have demonstrated that FBS scores are raised by objectively verified sources of physical discomfort (Iverson, Henrichs, Barton, & Allen, 2002; Meyers et al., 2002). Premorbid psychiatric history is associated with higher scores on FBS (Martens, Donders, & Millis, 2001). In TBI cases, scores on FBS appear to be significantly influenced by bona fide physical injury including anosmia and motor impairment (Greiffenstein et al., 2002). Collectively, the data suggest that physical injury combined with psychological distress can produce high scores on FBS in the absence of malingering.

A meta-analytic study (Nelson, Sweet, & Demakis, 2006) is often cited as support for the FBS without due consideration to its methodological limitations. For example, of the studies described in this investigation, the most dramatic effect size for FBS was, by far, that (3.52) found in the data reported in Guez, Brannstrom, Nyberg, Toolanen, and Hildingsson (2005). (The grand effect size using all 19 studies in the meta-analysis was substantially less—.96.) A whiplash subsample was extracted from the Guez et al. study and classified as a malingering group on the grounds that it "may have had reason to exaggerate symptoms"

(p. 43). In fact, Guez et al. were emphatic in stating that this sample was *not* malingering based on several lines of evidence including an absence of incentive (the majority of subjects were not involved in a compensation-seeking context), negative malingering test findings, and normal neuropsychological test results. Thus, although these data were cited as supportive of FBS, they actually raise concern regarding FBS validity and underscore its potential for misleading clinicians into erroneously suspecting malingering where none exists.

Larrabee (2007) reviewed numerous studies on psychological and physical symptom exaggeration pertinent to neuropsychological evaluation. Support for FBS as a malingering scale is largely based on studies that show its effectiveness in differentiating litigating from nonlitigating sample, as litigants typically score higher than nonlitigants on FBS. Compensation-seeking individuals in neuropsychological cases are more likely to have more symptomatic complaints and perform more poorly on neuropsychological tests. However, it should not be assumed that seeking compensation, in itself, causes a higher level of symptom reporting. The converse could be true: greater concern over acquired symptoms or deficits could precipitate the quest for compensation. The fact that litigants report more problems begs the question of the cause of their complaints. As Larrabee (2000) noted, additional evidence of malingering is required, such as clinically atypical presentations (Greiffenstein et al., 2002), in addition to a compensation-seeking context. Some studies that support FBS have used samples of subjects that had an improbable symptom presentation or produced evidence of incomplete effort. The limitations of FBS and its scope of application are described by Strauss, Sherman, and Spreen (2006).

Clinical Profile Interpretation

The long history of MMPI-2 use in neuropsychology has generated numerous areas of investigation designed specifically to enhance its application with individuals with known or suspected brain damage (see Table 23.1). The possibility that the MMPI could be used to diagnostically identify the presence of brain damage was one such area (Golden, Sweet, & Osmon, 1979). This pursuit failed. It was based on faulty presuppositions and flawed research methodologies. In neuropsychological or psychiatric settings, patient self-report of symptomatic complaints is an unreliable basis for identifying the presence of brain damage. Actual

Table 23.1. Neurologically sensitive MMPI-2 item content in brain-injured subjects.

Symptom	Item	Scale
Motor symptoms		
Paralysis or weakness (paresis)	295	Sc
Hand tremor	172	Hy
Manual clumsiness	177	Sc
Movement difficulties	182	Sc, Ma
Problems walking/balance	179	Hs, D, Hy
Slurred speech (dysarthria)	106	Sc, Ma
Sensory symptoms		
Numbness	247	Hs, Sc
Paresthesia	53	Hs
Diminished vision	349	Hs, Hy
Cognitive symptoms		
Poor concentration	325	Pt, Sc
Distractibility	31	D, Hy, Pt, Sc
Forgetfulness	165	D, Pt, Sc
Miscellaneous physical symptoms		
Generalized weakness	175	Hs, Hy, Pt
Rapid fatigue	152	Hs, Hy
Dizzy spells	164	Hs, Hy

Note: Gass, 1991, 1992, 1996b; Gass & Wald, 1997.

case history is much more reliable. Symptom questionnaires are ineffective and generally lack specificity in identifying brain dysfunction. Although people who have brain damage report their neurological symptoms on the MMPI-2, the test has many more items that assess psychopathology and personality characteristics. Numerous studies using carefully constructed samples found that the MMPI could be used to successfully discriminate brain-damaged subjects from those with specified forms of psychopathology (especially schizophrenia). In fact, early optimism about the MMPI in identifying brain damage was unwarranted, because the discriminative power was based almost completely on MMPI sensitivity to psychopathology and not on its ability to identify brain damage. For example, in a research sample that combines two discretely defined brain-damaged and schizophrenic individuals, it is not surprising that lower scorers on Scale 8 are more likely to be brain-injured subjects.

The objective of differentiating forensic TBI cases from normals was investigated by Senior, Lothrop, and Deacon (1999) using the 14-item correction for head injury (Gass, 1991b). The authors reported a sensitivity of .80 and specificity of .88, supporting the fact that the correction is effective in representing brain injury complaints. However, the correction was not designed to detect

brain injury in clinical settings. The MMPI-2 also has no utility in localizing brain lesions, which is an asset of many other neurodiagnostic techniques including neuropsychological testing (Gass & Russell, 1986b). More salient in recent MMPI-2 research is the fact that a very small number of MMPI-2 items are highly sensitive to brain dysfunction and pose an interpretive challenge when brain-injured individuals are examined (Gass, 1999).

Clinical Scale Interpretation

Analysis of the scores on the basic Clinical Scales is essential to MMPI-2 interpretation, because these scales have the advantage of decades of extensive empirical research upon which interpretive inferences are based. However, detailed information regarding the properties of these (and other) scales in brain-injured samples is relatively limited. Gass (1997) examined the MMPI-2 scoring characteristics of samples of 54 closed-head injury and 40 stroke patients (all males) who were referred for neuropsychological evaluation at the Miami Veterans Affairs Healthcare System. These and other research data (Gass, 2000), which will be alluded to throughout this section, were based exclusively on valid protocols. In addition, none of these referrals had a premorbid history of psychiatric treatment or addictive disorder. All had documented brain injuries, and none were seeking compensation benefits.

SCALE 1. HYPOCHONDRIASIS (HS)

This 32-item scale was originally referred to as the hypochondriasis scale because item selection was based on the responses of a group of neurotic patients who had multiple physical complaints and health-related preoccupations in the absence of any discernible medical condition or abnormal physical findings. In the neuropsychological context, elevations on Scale 1 are quite common. Brain-injured individuals commonly score moderately high on Scale 1 (65T to 75T) because of their frank endorsement of items that are highly sensitive to brain dysfunction. These include references to diminished general health status (45), paresthesias (53), tiredness and fatigue (152), weakness (175), pain (224), periodic dizzy spells (164), difficulty walking (179), and numbness (247). Although there are exceptions, empirical data suggest that scored responses to neurologically related items such as these account for an average increase of 10–15 T-score points on Scale 1, with a range of 0–30 points (Gass, 2000).

SCALE 2. DEPRESSION (D)

The 57-item depression scale assesses common symptoms of depression, including subjective dysphoria, sadness, low self-esteem, psychomotor retardation, a sense of hopelessness about the future, and vegetative features such as poor appetite, fatigue, and insomnia. High scorers (T > 70) are also socially withdrawn and often isolate themselves. They feel very inadequate, lack self-confidence, and are prone to feeling guilty. They experience cognitive inefficiency in daily living, such as poor concentration and forgetfulness, though their actual capability in these neurobehavioral domains may be intact (Gass & Russell, 1986a; Gass, Russell, & Hamilton, 1990). They are often indecisive and plagued by doubts about themselves. In inspecting the scores on these subscales, the clinician will frequently note that individuals who have neurological impairment score relatively high on mental dullness (D4) and physical malfunctioning (D3) as an expression of their cognitive and somatic difficulties (Gass & Lawhorn, 1991; Gass & Russell, 1991; Gass et al., 1990). High scores are also common on subjective depression (D1), which is consistent with the fact that symptomatic depression is probably the most common psychological sequelae of brain disease or injury.

Brain-injured individuals frequently produce marginal elevations (60T–70T) on Scale 2. Scores in this range are difficult to interpret because of its heterogeneous item content. Therefore, not all Scale 2 correlates necessarily apply. For this reason, an analysis of the scoring pattern on the Harris–Lingoes subscales is especially helpful in clarifying the meaning of marginally elevated scores on Scale 2. Individuals who have CNS impairment and report their neurological symptoms on the MMPI-2 typically increase their scores on the Scale 2 regardless of whether they are depressed. This occurs because the Scale 2 contains a subset of items that are related to bona fide physical and cognitive manifestations of brain damage. Included are items that refer specifically to problems with distractibility (31), convulsions (142), diminished reading comprehension (147), memory difficulty (165), generalized weakness (175), and walking or balance (179). Acknowledgment of these symptoms increases the T-score on the Scale 2 by an average of 5–10 points, with a range of 0–12 points (Gass, 2000). When protocols were not corrected for neurological item endorsement, half of the closed-head injury and 43% of the stroke patients comprising the Miami veterans referral sample scored above 65T on Scale 2. Scores on Scale 2 that exceed 75T in brain-injured individuals almost invariably reflect depressive symptoms in addition to any neurologic item-related artifact that might exist. In examining the protocols of brain-injured patients, more reliable information pertaining to depression can be obtained using the more homogeneous content scale DEP (depression).

Although depression is widely believed to affect adversely cognitive test performance, scores on Scale 2 are not usually predictive of neuropsychological test performance. Studies have suggested that Scale 2 scores in neuropsychological referrals are independent of the level of performance on measures of attention and memory (Gass, 1996a; Gass & Russell, 1986a; Gass et al., 1990), fluency or mazes (Gass et al., 1994), or alternating attention on the Trail-Making Test, Part B (Gass & Daniel, 1990).

SCALE 3. HYSTERIA (HY)

The hysteria scale is comprised of 60 items that were originally selected on the basis of their association with psychologically based sensory or motor abnormalities (conversion disorder). Accordingly, when a score on Scale 3 is high (T > 70) and has a prominently elevated position in the profile, individuals show a tendency to report a variety of somatic complaints and develop physical symptoms in response to psychological conflict or stressful circumstances. Behind these symptoms, in many cases, is secondary gain in the form of obtaining affectionate attention from others, or a reduction in stressful responsibilities (e.g., work). Neuropsychological referrals produce high scores on the lassitude-malaise and somatic complaints subscales far more commonly than on the other Scale 3 subscales, indicating a prominence of physical discomfort, fatigue, and various other physical complaints in this population. These two subscales include several items that are descriptive of neurological symptoms. Not surprisingly, these subscales are usually elevated to some degree in brain-injured patients, even in the absence of hysterical or histrionic personality characteristics (Gass & Lawhorn, 1991).

Due to the relatively high frequency of somatoform disorders in neuropsychological settings, Scale 3, like Scale 1, plays an important role in neuropsychological diagnosis. In numerous settings, individuals are referred for a neuropsychological evaluation because of symptoms that mimic a neurological condition. In some cases, these individuals have been misdiagnosed and prescribed inappropriate treatments over a period of many years. The most common example of this is nonepileptic seizure (NES) disorder, which occurs in approximately one-third of seizure cases. Although brain-impaired individuals often produce moderately high Scale 3 scores (60T–70T) without having symptoms of a somatoform disorder, very high scores on Scale 3 (T > 75) usually indicate the presence of somatoform symptomatology, somatic malingering, or a combination of the two. The same generalization applies to Scale 1. For example, scores on both Scales 1 and 3 are typically higher in nonepileptic seizure disorder than in epilepsy patients, who commonly exhibit primary elevations on Scales 2 and 8 (Ansley, Gass, Brown, & Levin, 1995).

Scale 3 scores are clearly increased when CNS symptoms are reported on the MMPI-2 by examinees who show no evidence of conversion hysteria or other somatoform characteristics. As is the case with Scales 1, 2, 7, and 8, the amount of the increase varies widely across individuals and possibly across neurological diagnoses. Neurologically relevant item content includes references to work capacity (10), distractibility (31), general health (45, 148), pain (47, 224), tiredness and fatigue (152, 173), periodic dizzy spells (164), tremor (172), weakness (175), and vision (249). The T-score on Scale 3 is increased by an average of 5–10 points as a result of reporting neurologically relevant items, though the potential increase ranges from 0 to 23 points (Gass, 2000). In the Miami veterans study of MMPI-2 profiles, 32% of the closed-head injury and 25% of the stroke sample had scores on Scale 3 exceeding 65T. However, a Massachusetts private practice sample of 54 male and female patients who had experienced more recent (less than 6 months) and milder head injuries produced high scores on Scale 3 (T > 65) with a frequency of 66%. It is significant that many of these patients had retained the services of an attorney in order to insure the maintenance of insurance benefits. Persisting symptoms following mild head injury are often associated with compensation-seeking behavior and with higher scores on Scale 3 (Youngjohn, Burrows, & Erdal, 1995; Youngjohn, Davis, & Wolf, 1997).

SCALE 4. PSYCHOPATHIC DEVIATE (PD)

Psychopathic or antisocial personality disorder characterized the clinical sample used by Hathaway and McKinley to construct the 50-item psychopathic deviate scale. A variety of asocial or antisocial behaviors and attitudes are associated with high scores (T > 65) on Scale 4. The interpretation of scores on Scale 4 in persons who have CNS impairment is not distinctive, as the items comprising this scale appear to have little or no neurological content bias. However, Scale 4 is sensitive to personality and behavioral changes that occur in a subset of brain-injured individuals, such as loss of self-control, outbursts of anger, and a diminished concern with other people's needs and interests. In most cases, however, elevated scores on Scale 4 reflect premorbid personality characteristics and not secondary effects of brain damage. Among the various neurodiagnostic groups, high scores on Scale 4 are most frequently produced by chronic substance abusers and victims of TBI (Gass & Russell, 1991). In the Miami veterans study, high scores (T > 65) on Scale 4 were produced by 34% of the closed-head injury and 18% of the stroke sample, though both groups had been screened for addictive disorders.

SCALE 5. MASCULINITY/FEMININITY (MF)

The masculinity–femininity scale was originally designed to identify problems in sex-role adjustment and particularly ego-dystonic impulses of a homo-erotic nature. In neuropsychological settings, Scale 5 scores do not appear to be affected by self-reported physical and cognitive symptoms of neurological dysfunction. In most clinical settings, the Scale 5 score typically falls well within the average range. The prevalence of elevated Scale 5 scores (T > 65) in the Miami male veterans sample was less than 4%, which is lower than would be expected in nonmilitary settings.

SCALE 6. PARANOIA (PA)

The criterion sample used by Hathaway to select the 40 items on paranoia scale consisted of individuals who had frank paranoid features or a diagnosed paranoid disorder. Scale 6 contains few, if any, items that refer directly to physical, cognitive, or health-related symptoms of brain dysfunction. Studies suggest that most neurologically impaired individuals score within the average range on Scale 6. However, traumatic brain-injured individuals endorse Scale 6 items with some frequency, particularly if they are examined very soon after injury. Their scores are sometimes sufficiently elevated (T > 65) to suggest suspiciousness, distrust, and a sense of having received a "raw deal" from life. Posttraumatic paranoia is not uncommon, particularly in acute head injury, though it rarely persists over a period of months (Grant & Alves, 1987). In the Miami veterans sample, 35% of the closed-head injury sample scored above 65T, whereas only 15% of the stroke patients scored this high (Gass, 1997). Personal injury claimants are more likely to report symptoms that increase scores on Scale 6. In the forensic neuropsychological context, mild head trauma litigants with late postconcussive syndrome (LPCS) commonly produce Scale 6 scores between 65T and 75T, with a mean T-score that is about 10 points higher than that found in the Miami veterans brain-damaged sample (Youngjohn et al., 1997).

SCALE 7. PSYCHASTHENIA (PT)

The 48 items that comprise this scale were intended to measure psychasthenia, which is roughly synonymous with obsessive compulsive disorder. High scorers (T > 65) on Scale 7 are very distressed, anxious, and worried, often an overabundance of seemingly minor issues. A substantial number of neurologically impaired individuals score above 65T on Scale 7. In the Miami veterans study, 50% of the closed-head injury and 33% of the stroke patients produced elevated (noncorrected) scores on this scale. Although many brain-injured individuals become highly distressed and worried about their health condition, the frequency of high scores in this population is partially due to the endorsement of items that fall within the larger cluster of empirically identified neurologically related items. These items include references to distractibility (31), reading problems (147), memory difficulty (165), generalized weakness (175), forgetfulness (308), and concentration difficulty (325). Acknowledgment of these symptoms increases the T-score on Scale 7 by an average of 5 points, although the effect can be as large as 12 points in an individual case (Gass, 1991b). Thus, slightly elevated scores on Scale 7 do not necessarily reflect anxiety and distress in individuals who have bona fide brain injury. Scores that exceed 70T, however, almost always indicate the presence of these symptoms.

Complaints of poor concentration, inattention, and forgetfulness are perhaps the most common reason for referral for neuropsychological evaluation. Scale 7 is the best single predictor of cognitive complaint severity in a comprehensive neuropsychological battery (Gass & Apple, 1997; Gass, Ardern, Howell, Dowd, Levy & McKenzie, 2005; Gass & Freshwater, 1999). Cognitive complaints are a reflection of anxiety and, in some cases, are also indicative of actual deficits (Gass & Apple, 1997).

No subscales exist for Scale 7, though the results of a factor analytic study suggest that the scale includes components of maladjustment, neuroticism, anxiety, psychotic tendencies, withdrawal, denial of antisocial behavior, poor concentration, agitation, and poor physical health (Comrey, 1958). To assist in making inferences about anxiety, fearfulness, or obsessional thinking, scores on Scale 7 can be compared with scores on several content scales that measure anxiety-related symptoms: generalized anxiety (ANX), obsessional thinking (OBS), specific phobias, apprehensions, and a general tendency to be fearful (FRS).

SCALE 8. SCHIZOPHRENIA (SC)

The schizophrenia scale consists of 78 items that were pooled by Hathaway and McKinley from several groups of items that were originally intended (but failed) to be specific to four subtypes of schizophrenia (paranoid, simple, hebephrenic, and catatonic). The resulting scale was both lengthy and heterogeneous in content. The heterogeneity of Scale 8 partially accounts for the fact that scores on it can be increased by factors that are largely unrelated to schizophrenia. For example, Graham (1993) reported that slightly higher scores frequently occur in adolescents, college students, African-American males, amphetamine users, and in people who have certain medical conditions, such as epilepsy. Butcher and Williams (1992) further observed that scores on Scale 8 are sometimes increased because of adherence to nontraditional or countercultural values, as well as in individuals who have severe sensory impairment or organic brain dysfunction. Additional sources of information, such as interview and observational data, relevant history, contextual considerations, and scores on Scales F and F(p), can be especially useful in interpreting high scores on Scale 8.

Despite the general association of schizophrenia with disordered thinking, it should be emphasized that Sc2 and Sc4 measure primarily "affective" components (depression and despair) that commonly exist as part of the symptom picture within the spectrum of schizophrenic disorders. In psychiatric settings, high scores on Sc3 and Sc6 suggest a more severe psychotic symptom picture than do scores on the other subscales. However, the characteristics that are measured by these two subscales are certainly not specific to psychosis or even psychopathology; they often reflect cognitive and sensorimotor complaints that are common in neurologically impaired individuals (Bornstein & Kozora, 1990; Gass, 1991b; Gass & Russell, 1991). The content scale bizarre mentation (BIZ) is a more specific measure of psychotic symptoms.

Neurological symptom reporting on the MMPI-2 increases scores on Scale 8. Items that are commonly endorsed include references to blank spells (229), distractibility (31, 299), speech changes (106), poor concentration (325), reading difficulty (147), memory problems (165), problems in walking (179), anosmia (299), tinnitus (255), numbness (247), and paralysis or weakness (177, 295). The endorsement of neurologically related symptoms on the MMPI-2 increases the T-score on Scale 8 by an average of 5–10 points, with a potential increase of as many as 20 points (Gass, 2000). There is some evidence that symptom reporting that is restricted to medically refractory seizure disorder has a minimal mean impact on Scale 8 and other MMPI-2 scores (Derry, Harnadek, McLachlan, & Sontrop, 1997), though the results of other studies suggest otherwise (Bornstein & Kozora, 1990). In the Miami veterans referral sample, uncorrected scores exceeding 65T on Scale 8 were produced by 48% of the closed-head injury and stroke patients. This figure approximates the 44% reported by Alfano, Finlayson, Stearns, and Neilson (1990) in an MMPI study of 115 heterogeneous brain-impaired patients, and the 55% reported by Bornstein and Kozora (1990) in a sample of 152 epilepsy patients (T > 70). Although scores in this range are not invariably associated with the presence of psychotic symptoms, these percentages still contrast sharply with the estimated 10% frequency of psychosis following brain injury secondary to trauma (Grant & Alves, 1987).

Individuals who feign TBI commonly produce mildly to moderately high scores on Scale 8, often because of their endorsement of MMPI-2 items that have content related to cognitive difficulties (Sc3)

and physical abnormalities (Sc6). The interpretation of high scores on Scale 8 should be made in the context of (a) knowledge of the examinee's history, (b) clinical observation, (c) the examinee's test-taking attitude as measured by the validity scales, and (d) understanding the medico-legal particulars surrounding the evaluation.

SCALE 9. HYPOMANIA (MA)

The 46 items on this scale measure characteristics of hypomania, including overactivity, heightened energy level, emotional excitement, and flight of ideas. Most brain-injured patients score well within the average range on Scale 9. In the Miami veterans study of MMPI-2 protocols, only 20% of the closed-head injury and 23% of the stroke patients scored higher than 65T. The incidence of elevated Scale 9 scores in a sample of milder and more recent head-injury cases undergoing rehabilitation was 4% (Gass & Wald, 1997). However, Gass, Luis, Rayls, and Mittenberg (1999) reported a 25% incidence of high (T > 65) Scale 9 scores in a sample of 67 acute nonlitigating head injury patients who averaged only 7 days post injury. High scorers on this scale are often referred for a neuropsychological assessment because of problems with distractibility and forgetfulness, and these symptoms are not uncommon in bipolar disorder, schizoaffective disorder, and schizophrenia. The phenomenon of secondary mania has been associated with damage to the right frontal and temporal brain regions (Starkstein, Pearlson, Boston, & Robinson, 1987; Van Reekum, Cohen, & Wong, 2000). Interestingly, scores on Scale 9 are positively correlated with degree of right hemisphere impairment (Gass & Russell, 1987).

SCALE 0. SOCIAL INTROVERSION (SI)

The social introversion scale was designed by L. E. Drake (1946) using a sample of female college students. It consists of 69 items that assess shyness, discomfort in and avoidance of social situations, and self-doubt. In neuropsychological settings, the interpretation of Scale 0 scores is straightforward. This scale contains very few neurologically related items and, as such, does not require a consideration of content bias or correction. High scores are more likely to be found in psychiatric referrals than in general medical patients. In the Miami veterans study of neurologic patients, none of whom had a premorbid psychiatric history, 23% of the closed-head injury and 20% of the stroke sample had high scores on Scale 0 (T > 65).

The RC Scales and the Restructured MMPI-2

The MMPI-2 Restructured Form (MMPI-2-RF, Ben-Porath & Tellegen, 2007) is a redesigned version of the MMPI-2 that has as its core the Restructured Clinical (RC) Scales (Tellegen et al., 2003). The RC Scales were developed to enhance the distinctiveness of the original Clinical Scales by removing a common "demoralization" factor that exists across the scales. The result is that they achieve greater homogeneity and discriminative validity in predicting specific behavioral criteria using fewer items. In neuropsychological settings, primary elevations are most likely to occur on RC1 because of its physical symptom and health-focused item composition. In contrast, RC3 is unlikely to be elevated as it no longer contains somatic item content and is quite different from its Hy counterpart (Butcher, Hamilton, Rouse, and Cumella, 2006).

The RC Scales are purer measures of a core construct underlying each of the original eight Clinical Scales (excluding Scales 5 and 0), but the core construct is narrower than that measured by the original scales. In evaluating the MMPI-2-RF, the critical issue is whether this 338-item inventory has sufficient advantages to offset its high cost in information loss based on decades of research on the behavioral correlates of the MMPI/MMPI-2 Clinical Scales, code-type patterns, and other aspects of score configuration. It is alleged that the RC Scales sacrifice a wealth of specific and dynamic interpretative predictions that are provided by their original Clinical Scale counterparts, particularly when well-established code-type information is utilized (Caldwell, 2006; Nichols, 2006). The radical alteration of Scale 3 (RC3), which is aptly described as a deconstruction by Butcher et al. (2006), is particularly disconcerting from a neuropsychological standpoint, given the original scale's sensitivity to conversion symptomatology. One example of this is psychogenic seizures, which account for almost one-third of seizure presentations (Ansley et al., 1995).

The RC Scales might have additional shortcomings. Nichols (2006) observed that the core constructs measured by the RC Scales, with the exception of RC9, show extremely high redundancy with existing MMPI-2 content scales (Butcher, Graham, Williams, & Ben-Porath, 1990) (rs between .80 and .95). More importantly, the RC Scales are more vulnerable to a defensive response style than are the Clinical Scales (Sellbom, Ben-Porath, McNulty, Arbisi, & Graham, 2006). Elsewhere, these authors attempted to dismiss this apparent weakness by attributing it to subtle item content on the standard Clinical Scales (Tellegen, Ben-Porath, Sellbom, Arbisi, McNulty, & Graham, 2006). However, if the subtle items constitute random noise, as the authors maintain, one would not expect their net effect to systematically increase (or decrease) standardized T-scores on the Clinical Scales. Anecdotal evidence that the RC Scales underestimate level of psychopathology received support in a recent study of substance abusers (Forbey & BenPorath, 2007). RC scores were consistently lower than their Clinical Scale counterparts.

The elimination of over 200 MMPI-2 items that are "working items" has additional implications for information loss and its potentially adverse impact on clinical use of the MMPI-2. Current interpretive practice uses the RC Scales to refine interpretation of the basic Clinical Scales by removing the common factor of "demoralization" that exists in the scales. This information can be quite helpful. Beyond this, it is unclear whether the potential benefits of the MMPI-2-RF outweigh the cost in information loss. The architects of the restructured MMPI-2 maintain that "profile configurations defined by well-chosen more homogeneous scales in principle should achieve a more accurate recognition of more distinctive syndromal response patterns. We believe the RC Scales will make it easier to explore true syndromal assessment" (Tellegen et al., 2006, p. 165). Whether this grand hope will be actualized remains to be seen. It is clear, however, that if clinicians abandon the original Clinical Scales and body of code-type information, they will sacrifice the most impressive body of empirically based interpretive material ever amassed in the history of personality assessment.

Diagnosing Neuropsychological Deficits

The diagnostic efficacy of neuropsychological tests depends, in part, on their specificity in detecting underlying brain dysfunction. To the extent that emotional and motivational factors interfere with neurobehavioral performance, inferences regarding brain-based abilities are more uncertain. Conation, which is "will power" or application of effort, can be adversely affected by neurological (Reitan & Wolfson, 2002) and non-neurological conditions. The latter include emotional states and situational factors in which optimal effort is expected to have a painful or unpleasant outcome. This is a common problem in the assessment of compensation claimants who stand to lose by performing well on tests of ability (Green, Rohling, Lees-Haley, & Allen, 2001).

Scores on the MMPI-2 or other measures of emotional status are often used as a basis for explaining deficient neuropsychological test performance. Paul is a 52-year-old airline worker who presented with symptoms of tinnitus, hyperacusis, depression, anxiety, and a narrowed visual field as well as periodic episodes of vertigo, dizziness, and motoric imbalance. He attributed these problems to noise exposure in his work place, claiming that his ear protection failed and that his employer was unresponsive to his complaints. He filed a lawsuit claiming complete disability. Formal testing cast strong doubt on his objective complaints, and some of his subjective claims were refuted by eyewitness testimony and photographic evidence.

The neuropsychological test findings revealed normal range performance in most domains with circumscribed deficits in nonverbal concept formation and visuoconstruction (see Figures 23.1, 23.2, and 23.3).

The MMPI-2 revealed that despite his attempt to appear highly proper and virtuous, he is anxious (ANX = T67) and reports many physical symptoms and concerns about his health (Hy = T79, Hs = T73, D3 = T83). His score on RC1 (T65) is lower than expected given his diagnosis of conversion, and this finding underscores concerns regarding RC Scale vulnerability to defensiveness and underestimation of psychopathology. What is

the likelihood that Paul's observed deficits are secondary to his depression? Many clinicians who view such cases place heavy diagnostic weight on high MMPI-2 scores, not only to identify psychological problems (which is appropriate), but also to infer an absence of underlying brain pathology. Not surprisingly, MMPI-2 scores that suggest high levels of depression, anxiety, or other problems of a psychological nature are often the basis for inferring an emotional impact on neuropsychological test performance. This common practice is based on logic and an appreciation of the fact that cognitive inefficiency can arise from emotional difficulties. Unfortunately, this interpretive approach has very little empirical foundation.

Research involving the widely used Halstead–Reitan Neuropsychology Battery (HRNB; Reitan & Wolfson, 1993), which includes concurrent administration of the MMPI, has examined correlations between performance on HRNB tests and MMPI scores on the basic Clinical Scales. Heaton and Crowley (1981) examined this issue in 561 patients who were referred to their laboratory for neuropsychological evaluation. Correlations between the Average Impairment Rating on the HRNB and the MMPI basic scales ranged from −.09 (K) to .33 (Scale 1), none accounting for as much as 11% of the variance in neuropsychological test performance. Calsyn, Louks,

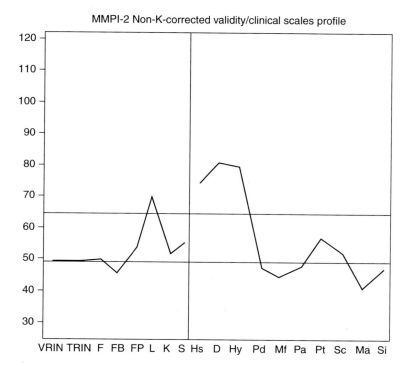

Fig. 23.1 Paul's basic validity and clinical MMPI-2 profile.

MMPI-2 Restructured clinical scales profile

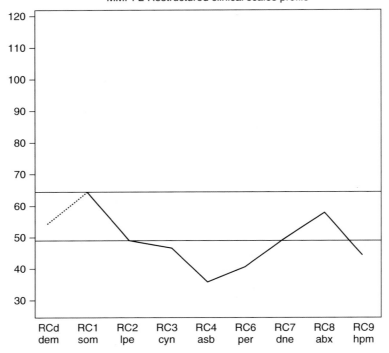

Fig. 23.2 Paul's MMPI-2 restructured clinical scales profile.

MMPI-2 Content scales profile

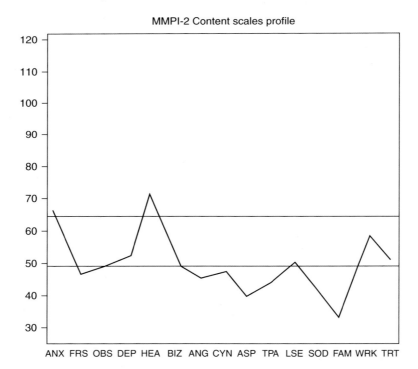

Fig. 23.3 Paul's MMPI-2 content scales profile.

and Johnson (1982) examined correlations between the MMPI and HRNB in a sample of normal individuals and found no statistically significant relationships. In stroke patients, only modest relationships were found between MMPI variables and neuropsychological test performance (Gass & Ansley, 1994a).

USE OF THE MMPI-2 IN NEUROPSYCHOLOGICAL EVALUATIONS

Gass (1991a) investigated the potential impact of MMPI variables on performance across each of the individual tests that comprise the HRNB. This sample consisted of 105 neuropsychological referrals who were judged to be neurologically intact by staff neurologists using interview data and any diagnostic procedures deemed necessary. The composite MMPI profiles of high and low scorers on each of the HRNB tests were contrasted, and they were found to be the same except in the analysis of high versus low scorers on the Speech Perception Test. In general, MMPI scores did not differ as a function of performance on the HRNB tests. However, errors on the Speech Perception Test were associated with higher anxiety measured on Scale 7. Zillmer and Perry (1996) factor analyzed the test scores of 225 psychiatric inpatients who had been administered the MMPI, the Rorschach, and a variety of neuropsychological tests. Their results showed that neuropsychological and personality assessment indices measure separate, relatively unrelated domains.

Although further investigation is warranted, existing studies on the relationship between MMPI scores and performance on the HRNB suggest that clinicians should be conservative in appealing to high scores on the MMPI-2 Clinical Scales as a basis for explaining poor performance on this battery of neuropsychological tests. Scores on the MMPI-2 are not reliable predictors of HRNB performance. In fact, even the relatively modest role of age and education was more powerful than MMPI scores in predicting HRNB scores (Gass, 1991a). In their review of this general topic, Reitan and Wolfson (1997) concluded, "As we have often said, clinical experience makes it quite clear that if it is possible to elicit the subject's cooperation and effort to do well, neuropsychological test results can be interpreted in a framework of brain–behavior relationships, even though the patient's MMPI results may be quite deviant" (p. 16).

Neuropsychologists frequently employ performance measures that are not part of the HRNB, and the manner in which emotional factors might influence scores on these tests warrants systematic investigation. The Logical Memory and Visual Reproduction subtests of the Wechsler Memory Scale are prime examples of popular tests that often play an important role in differential diagnosis. In order to be of diagnostic value, a memory test must be differentially sensitive to the effects of emotional factors and cerebral pathology. The relative influence of neurological versus emotional status on attention and memory test performance was examined by Gass (1996a) using a sample of neuropsychological referrals. These were 80 neurologically intact psychiatric patients and 48 patients with a recent history of TBI. The findings of this study can be summarized as follows. The unique variance accounted for by several MMPI-2 measures of confused or unusual thinking, anxiety, and fearfulness was 22% (Visual Reproduction), 16% (attention span), 13% (Logical Memory), and 5% (list learning, selective reminding format). Unlike previous findings pertaining to the HRNB, this study found evidence that psychological factors may exert a distinct and important impact on attention span and visuographic memory, and a significant though slightly more modest effect on verbal-narrative memory. The importance of MMPI-2 variables in predicting performance on tests of attention and verbal learning was recently corroborated by Ross, Putnam, Gass, Bailey, and Adams (2003) using a sample of 381 psychiatric and head-injured neuropsychological referrals. Attention and retentive memory were found to be strongly associated ($r = -.40$) with MMPI-2 measures of anxiety and depression in a study of 77 psychiatric inpatients (Gass & Ansley, 1994b).

The content scale FRS seems to have the strongest and most consistent association with neuropsychological test performance, especially in relation to nonverbal, visuospatial tasks. This scale measures the extent of highly specific fears, such as the sight of blood, high places, snakes, mice, and water, as well as a general disposition toward fearfulness. In the study already described (Gass, 1996a), FRS scores were predictive of performance on the Visual Reproduction subtest of the Wechsler Memory Scale-Revised ($r = -.40$). In another study FRS scores were predictive of performance on several measures of executive functioning. Using a sample of 70 neuropsychological referrals, all of whom were judged to be neurologically intact, Gass et al. (1994) found that higher scores on FRS predicted poorer performance on the Design Fluency Test ($r = -.48$), WISC-R Mazes ($r = -.40$), and the Controlled Oral Word Association Test ($r = -.36$, $ps < .01$). One possible explanation of these findings is that FRS measures a tendency toward situation-specific anxiety, and that this anxiety is elicited in the testing situation. Support for this hypothesis was found in a study of neuropsychological examinees who completed the Test Anxiety Profile (TAP; Oetting & Deffenbacher, 1980) in addition to a comprehensive neuropsychological test battery (Gass, 2002). TAP scores were associated with global performance on the WAIS-R (Full Scale IQ, $r = -.35$) and HRNB (Average Impairment Rating, $r = -.30$, $ps < .001$).

Controlling for Neurological Symptom Reporting

Scales 1, 2, 3, and 8 contain physical and cognitive symptom items that have been a source of confusion and controversy when the MMPI-2 is used with people in medical and medicolegal settings. In neuropsychological settings, group studies show that these scales typically show the highest elevations (Gass, 2000; Wooten, 1983). The interpretation of Scales 2, 3, and 8 is facilitated using scores on the Harris–Lingoes subscales. In brain-impaired and other medical samples, high scores on Scale 2 are most commonly associated with complaints of physical malfunctioning (D3) and mental dullness (D4). High scores on Scale 3 are associated with high scores on lassitude-malaise (Hy3) and somatic complaints (Hy4). On Scale 8, high scores are usually due, in part, to reports of cognitive difficulties (Sc3) and bizarre sensory experiences (Sc6). These types of somatic and cognitive complaints are common in brain-injured individuals who report their symptoms of CNS disease. Unfortunately, the extent to which scores on these subscales are reflective of psychological disturbance, as opposed to CNS symptom reporting is unknown. These subscales are not diagnostically sensitive or specific, nor are they uniformly reliable.

The architects of the MMPI (Starke Hathaway, PhD and J. Charnley McKinley, MD) were clinicians who had a strong interest in behavioral neurology. Hathaway, a clinical psychologist with a keen interest in engineering, published a textbook in 1942 entitled *Physiological Psychology*, in which he described and made artistic drawings to illustrate functional neuroanatomy. In fact, Hathaway's impetus for meeting the neuropsychiatrist, Dr. McKinley, was a shared interest in the measurement of CNS evoked potentials. According to Hathaway, McKinley "was an admirable neurologist . . . he was no psychiatrist at all." (Butcher, 1973). In constructing the MMPI, McKinley expressed an interest in measuring neurological as well as psychiatric symptoms, though the criterion groups used to compose the Clinical Scales were psychodiagnostic groups screened for brain dysfunction. After the test was developed, Hathaway and McKinley (1940) identified several item clusters of MMPI items reflecting "general neurologic" (19 items), "cranial nerve" (11 items), and "motility and coordination" (6 items). Using the empirical keying

method of scale construction with carefully defined psychodiagnostic groups, these CNS items were assigned along with other MMPI items to the various Clinical (psychopathology) Scales.

Psychometric principles are seriously challenged when these scales are applied to patients who, having bona fide CNS symptoms, differ in a relevant and systematic way from the psychiatric patients used in the criterion groups to construct the scales. In brain-injured samples, neurologically sensitive items constitute a distinctive source of variance in MMPI-2 responses (Gass, 1991b, 1992). At one extreme, some authors recommend ignoring the presence of these neurologically sensitive items or their potential profile effects when evaluating brain-impaired individuals. Some authors opt for a crystal ball approach, recommending a reliance upon vaguely defined "clinical judgment," but they fail to provide specific guidelines. At another extreme, some authors argue that the MMPI-2 as applied to brain-injured patients is essentially uninterpretable because of the confounding influence of neurological symptom reporting and the resulting inflation of scores across the Clinical Scales. They go so far as to recommend using rationally (not empirically) selected MMPI-2 items as a neurological symptom checklist.

A prudent approach to MMPI-2 use with brain-impaired patients requires a systematic examination of the potential impact of neurologically sensitive item endorsement on MMPI-2 profiles. However, the initial identification of neurologically sensitive items must be done empirically, not subjectively. Once the key items are identified, the clinician can inspect the examinee's responses to these items, singling out the items that were answered in the keyed direction, and calculating the effects of their endorsement on the clinical profile. The original MMPI-2 profile, scored in the standard way, can then be compared with the "corrected" profile (Arbisi & Ben-Porath, 1999; Gass, 1991b, 1992). To the extent that the two profiles are similar, the clinician can have greater certainty regarding the profile's accuracy as a reflection of emotional status and personality characteristics. To the extent that the two profiles differ, the clinician has to proceed more cautiously, knowing that there is a higher likelihood of artifactual score elevation. In either case, unless this interpretive method is followed, the clinician is left with the highest degree of uncertainty regarding the potential influence of neurological symptom reporting.

A fundamental question is, when assessing the brain-impaired patient, which items on the

MMPI-2 are most likely representative of neurological symptoms? Different approaches have been used to identify these items, but not all methods of item identification hold equal validity. For research purposes, the simplest approach has relied on expert opinion in item selection. However, this approach is inherently unreliable because experts disagree among themselves and may be biased by extraneous influences. An expert's opinion about any given item may change overnight. This is an empirical issue that requires an empirical solution. Although imperfect, a statistical approach is more objective than subjective judgments, and it makes much better sense. An optimal statistical solution to this problem was proposed by Kendall, Edinger, and Eberly (1978), who refined a previously devised MMPI correction for use with spinal cord injury patients. These authors outlined a rigorous empirical methodology for identifying MMPI items most sensitive to symptoms of spinal cord injury. This general strategy of item identification was adopted by Gass (1991b) for closed-head injury patients, and Gass (1992) with stroke victims. Using a sample of 75 TBI patients, none of whom were compensation seeking, 14 items were identified after they passed four successive empirical hurdles: discriminative power, frequency of positive endorsement, homogeneity, and face validity. First, responses to each item sharply distinguished the 75 patients from the MMPI-2 normative sample ($ps < .001$). Second, every item was endorsed by at least 25% of the head-injured patients. Third, the items comprised a unitary factor distinct from an emotional factor. Fourth, the content of the items showed face validity as representing physical consequences and cognitive symptoms related to brain damage.

The 14 items that emerged are 31, 101, 106, 147, 149, 165, 170, 172, 175, 179, 180, 247, 295, and 325. The scored direction appears in Table 23.2, which can be used to tabulate the influence of these items on the overall clinical profile. First, items that are answered in the keyed direction can be circled across their respective row. Second, in a columnwise manner, the number of circled items are added to obtain the raw score impact on each of the relevant Clinical Scales. These scores are then subtracted from the full scores on the Clinical Scales to provide an adjusted score for comparison. The neurologically sensitive items refer to distractibility, forgetfulness, headache, difficulties with speech, reading problems, tremor, imbalance, numbness, and motoric weakness. This set of items, as applied to bona fide TBI patients, has received empirical

support in several studies. The unitary nature of these items in a head injury sample was supported by Barrett, Putnam, Axelrod, and Rapport (1998), who reported a Cronbach's alpha coefficient of .80.

A mechanical application of the correction is unwarranted, precisely because one can never know whether the reported symptom is a reflection of a psychological factor, neurological influence, or a combination of the two. Proper use of the correction is aimed at reducing interpretive uncertainty by exploring the impact of an examinee's endorsement of neurologically sensitive items. This approach is based on empirically established item sensitivity to neurological symptoms. In contrast to prior conservative recommended guidelines, Youngjohn (2002, personal communication) observed that "the correction is equally as useful in providing empirical evidence of an absence of neurologically sensitive item endorsement as it is in showing positive evidence of item endorsement." Thus, in cases of alleged but unsubstantiated brain injury, negative MMPI-2 correction findings increase the certainty that the profile reflects psychological status and is not influenced by undetected brain injury. Positive correction findings, on the other hand, are uninterpretable in cases in which brain injury has not been established. Negative correction findings can also be informative in cases involving brain injury with a comorbid or premorbid emotional condition, substance abuse, and in compensation-seeking cases. In cases like these that show little or no profile correction, the clinician can have much greater confidence that the score elevations on Scales 1, 2, 3, 7, and 8 reflect psychological symptoms. Without the correction, the clinician is left to speculate.

Although this application of the correction is not predicated on an assumption of specificity, the issue of specificity was investigated by Edwards, Holmquist, Wanless, Wicks, and Davis (1998) using a sample of predominantly non-compensation-seeking TBI patients. These authors sought to determine whether the positive endorsement of these 14 items by head-injury patients might reflect preexisting psychological problems. After completing the MMPI-2, if an item was answered in the scored direction, each patient ($N = 20$) and a significant other ($N = 20$) was asked (independently) if the problem had been present before the head injury, or if was a result of the head injury. The authors went through each of the positively endorsed correction items and inquired about the origin of the symptom that was being reported. In nearly every instance, injury victims and their relatives independently

Table 23.2. MMPI-2 item table for evaluating traumatic brain injury.

Item	F	1	2	3	4	7	8	9	0
31 True	—	—	31T	31T	31T	31T	31T	—	31T
101 True	—	101T	—	101T	—	—	—	—	—
106 False	—	—	—	—	—	—	106F	106F	106F
147 True	—	—	147T	—	—	147T	147T	—	—
149 True	—	149T	—	—	—	—	—	—	—
165 False	—	—	165F	—	—	165F	165F	—	—
170 True	—	—	170T	—	—	170T	170T	—	—
172 True	—	—	—	172T	—	—	—	—	—
175 True	—	175T	175T	175T	—	175T	—	—	—
179 False	—	179F	—	179F	—	—	179F	—	—
180 True	180T	—	—	—	—	—	180T	—	—
247 True	—	247T	—	—	—	—	247T	—	—
295 False	—	—	—	—	—	—	295F	—	—
325 True	—	—	—	—	—	325T	325T	—	—
Sum									
	F	1	2	3	4	7	8	9	0

reported that the correction items were endorsed by the patient specifically because of problems resulting from the injury. Consider an example: Item 179, "I have had no difficulty in keeping my balance in walking." Thirteen of the patients answered "false" and, in the interview, all 13 of them attributed the imbalance to the head injury. Sixteen family members were interviewed independently and asked about the patient's answer to this item. All 16 family members attributed the symptom to the head injury. Across the 14 items, the patients were 10 times more likely to attribute the endorsed problem to the head injury than to their preinjury status. Similarly, their significant others independently attributed the item endorsements to the head injury about 13 times more often than to preinjury status. Overall, 109 of 119 endorsements of the 14 items were attributed to the head injury, supporting the specificity of the correction when applied to TBI patients. To date, no other study that has attempted to address the specificity of the correction has examined individual cases in this careful and detailed manner.

The 14-item correction was examined in a sample of 67 inpatients who were consecutive admissions to a general hospital immediately following a TBI (Gass et al., 1999). Exclusionary criteria included recent substance abuse, and a history of either neurological or psychiatric disorder. Upon admission, these patients were administered the Glasgow Coma Scale (GCS) and had CT scans. An incidental finding in this study was the fact that the endorsement frequency on the 14 MMPI-2

correction items was positively related to injury severity on the GCS ($r = .26$) and findings on the CT scan ($r = .26$, $ps < .05$). These findings provide empirical support for the 14-item correction. Nevertheless, they are unexpected and surprising given the well-established weak relationship between the number of symptom complaints and degree of brain injury, whether estimated on the basis of GCS scores, radiological findings, duration of loss of consciousness, or posttraumatic amnesia (Bornstein, Miller, & van Schoor, 1988). It is surprising to find a correlation between the amount of symptom reporting and estimates of injury severity, particularly when these estimates are typically crude and temporally separated from the time of symptom (MMPI-2) reporting by highly variable time periods, ranging from several weeks to many years. To complicate matters, mild head-trauma patients with questionable injuries commonly report more symptom complaints than bona fide brain injury patients (Berry et al., 1995; Youngjohn et al., 1995; Youngjohn et al., 1997). Furthermore, retrospective reports of injury severity made by mild head trauma litigants with large financial incentives and symptoms persisting up to 7 years post-incident (e.g., Brulot, Strauss, & Spellacy, 1997) have doubtful validity and are misleading and irrelevant for assessing the validity of an MMPI-2 correction.

Studies that use bona fide brain injury samples have supported the validity of the correction. Rayls, Mittenberg, Burns, and Theroux (2000) investigated the question of whether the 14 correction items are reflective of neurological versus emotional symptoms in the same sample of acute head injury cases described previously (Gass et al., 1999). They reported several major findings. First, the acutely injured patients endorsed correction items in a manner that was statistically independent of their measured level of distress surrounding their accident. Second, on retesting after several months, they endorsed the correction items much less frequently, commensurate with their recovery. Based on their data, these authors concluded that as applied to acute and mild head injury, the correction initially reflects an impact of neurological symptom reporting. However, in "mild" head injury patients, after several months have gone past, a continuing endorsement of these items probably reflects problems with psychological adjustment. This conclusion is consistent with the recommendation that the correction *not* be applied to adjust profile scores in uncomplicated mild head injury cases in whom persistent complaints exist well beyond the normal recovery period. The correction is applicable in this manner when brain damage exists, as in acute mild brain trauma, but not after the individual recovers and cerebral compromise has dissipated.

The manner in which the 14-item correction is used depends on whether the presence of TBI has been established. Responses to the 14 items cannot possibly be reflective of neurological symptoms unless there is an underlying neurological impairment. By implication, positive findings on the correction are meaningless in the majority of subjects who are involved in litigation or seeking compensation for symptoms that persist months or years following uncomplicated mild head injury. In most of these cases, there is ample reason to doubt the presence of brain dysfunction. Instead, the ongoing symptomatic complaints are usually related to psychological factors, motivational pressures, incentives to acquire compensation, and other important aspects of their medico-legal context (Binder, 1997; Binder, Rohling, & Larrabee, 1997; Reitan & Wolfson, 1997; Youngjohn et al., 1997). As previously noted, the correction is useful in these cases, however, if it yields negative findings (Youngjohn, 2002, personal communication). Interestingly, researchers who have recommended against using the correction based their conclusions on studies that employed highly questionable diagnostic samples in which brain injury was never established (Brulot et al., 1997; Dunn & Lees-Haley, 1995). In a clinical setting, once brain dysfunction is established, whether through clinical history,

neurological examination, or other neurodiagnostic methods, the correction factor can be used to gauge the potential impact of neurological symptom reporting on the MMPI-2 profile. Finally, the correction items are sensitive to various types of psychopathology and should be interpreted cautiously in individuals who have premorbid or comorbid emotional disturbances or substance abuse. In these cases, a minor or nil corrective impact increases the clinician's confidence in the validity of elevated scores on Scales 1, 2, 3, and 8, whereas a larger corrective impact is uninformative.

In contrast to closed head injury, the determination of structural brain damage is often more clearly made in cases of cerebrovascular disease, or stroke. Stroke is one of the most common neurological conditions that presents with a variety of physical and cognitive sequelae. Scores on the somatic-related scales of the MMPI-2 are commonly elevated in stroke patients to an extent suggestive of somatoform disorder, often contrary to any other evidence. The major source of variance distinguishing the MMPI-2 responses of stroke patients from normals is a cluster of items that refer, not to emotional problems, but to difficulties such as paresthesias, numbness, speech changes, reading difficulties, tremor, poor health, ataxia, weakness, and poor concentration. Using the same previously described statistical procedures, Gass (1992) identified 21 stroke-sensitive items that are most prominently represented on Scales 1 (12 items) and 3 (13 items). The association of these items with stroke was corroborated in a follow-up study of 50 CVA patients (Gass, 1996b). The influence of the endorsement of these items on the profiles of individual stroke patients can be examined systematically for the purpose of gauging the potential impact of neurological symptom endorsement on profile elevations (Gass, 2000). To the extent that the original profile and the "corrected" profile are similar, the clinician has greater confidence that traditional code-type and scale correlates apply. Conversely, if the two profiles are substantially different, then there is a greater likelihood that the traditional interpretive literature, based on psychiatric patients, will be inaccurate. In this case, very cautious interpretation is warranted.

Case Illustration

Amy is a 23-year-old woman who was involved in a jeep accident 2 years prior to testing. She reportedly sustained a closed-head injury with a 5-hour loss of consciousness. Serial brain scans were negative, as were other test results. She claimed that she was unable to concentrate well enough to handle any work during the 2 years following the accident. Neuropsychological testing revealed borderline performance across tasks of attention, concentration, and memory, and normal performance on the most sensitive indicators. She applied for medical discharge from the Navy, and sought compensation for her injury. At 1-year post injury, she began generating a very long list of vague physical complaints. She made numerous visits to neurology, orthopedics, and audiology. None of these services were able to find any physical basis for her complaints.

The Navy investigated her jeep accident and found her at fault. The board concluded that she was driving recklessly during a temper tantrum. In fact, the Navy brought her up on disciplinary charges. She then sought psychotherapy and attended three sessions. She avoided talking about emotional issues, focused entirely on physical complaints. She abruptly stopped showing up for appointments when she was informed that her request for a medical discharge was denied. Her MMPI-2 profile shown in Figure 23.4 revealed a test-taking attitude of admitting to significant problems of a circumscribed nature (Scale F)—in this case, physical—and at the same time attempting to

wave a flag of very strong moral integrity (Scale L). The 13/31 code type is suggestive of somatoform and specifically conversion symptoms.

The Harris–Lingoes subscales for Scale 3 revealed evidence of personality characteristics associated with hysteria, specifically the intense need for affection and the tendency to inhibit hostility in situations where anger is elicited. On the content scales, she revealed problems with anxiety, worry, and depression, all of which are less intense than her health concerns. The 14-item correction (Gass, 1991b) was applied to ascertain the profile effects of her answering items associated with TBI. The dotted line in her profile, which is the result after correction, is indicative that even if she sustained a brain injury (which is questionable), her MMPI-2 is a reflection of prominent somatoform symptoms.

MMPI-2, Mild Head Trauma, and Late Postconcussive Symptoms

The neurobehavioral effects of uncomplicated mild head trauma typically resolve within several weeks. When symptoms persist beyond several months—LPCS—an important role of psychological and motivational factors must be considered (Binder, 1997; Binder et al., 1997). Predisposing factors for development of LPCS appear to include a context for

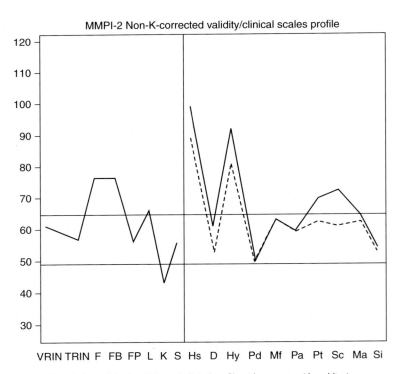

Fig. 23.4 Amy's basic validity and clinical profile with correction (dotted line).

potentially acquiring material benefit, preinjury somatoform symptoms, low socioeconomic status (SES), and fewer years of formal education (Greiffenstein & Baker, 2003). The premorbid MMPI-2 profiles of 23 LPCS claimants were uniformly abnormal and characterized by somatoform symptoms, with a dominant 13/31 configuration and secondary peaks on 2, 7, and 8 (Greiffenstein & Baker, 2001). Their post-injury MMPI-2 profiles revealed little change. The authors concluded that commonly observed somatoform post-injury MMPI-2 profiles in LPCS cases probably reflect preexisting psychopathology and, in specific, symptoms and characteristics of somatization and conversion disorder. Similarly, evidence suggests that individuals who have significant somatoform features are more likely than others to pursue financial compensation for minor/mild head injury (Putnam & Millis, 1994; Youngjohn et al., 1997). In these cases, the MMPI-2 correction can be used, as in the case of Amy, to unveil negative evidence of neurological impact on the MMPI-2. That is, if the correction fails to show an impact of neurologically sensitive item endorsement, the clinician can have greater certainty in the validity of a standard psychological interpretation of the clinical profile. However, if a significant correction impact is observed, it cannot be deemed valid or interpretable unless the presence of brain injury is first established. These same interpretive guidelines apply in cases involving premorbid or comorbid psychopathology, substance abuse, and compensation-seeking cases.

Incorporating MMPI-2 Results in Neuropsychological Reports

Report writing is more of an art than a science. Styles vary across clinicians and clinical settings. The major objective is to assist the referral source by addressing the referral question(s). The amount of space devoted to presenting the MMPI-2 results in a neuropsychological report might be small or large depending on the nature of the referral and the obtained findings. The potential contributions include (a) describing emotional status; (b) identifying relevant personality characteristics, as well as strengths and weaknesses relevant to treatment planning and rehabilitation; (c) describing test-taking attitude and possible response style bias; and (d) contributing to differential diagnosis. One challenge in report writing is incorporating the important descriptive detail from the MMPI-2 results that address the referral question and assist the client without providing additional excessive detail of questionable relevance. One of the most common complaints regarding psychological reports is excessive

length and overinclusion of descriptive information that is not directly relevant or brought to bear on treatment recommendations (Tallent, 1993). In some cases, information might be detrimental for inclusion in reports, particularly as examinees are increasingly accessing copies of their medical records including psychological reports. In legal settings, the reporting of nonessential details regarding personality can lead to embarrassing and troubling consequences. This problem is amplified when such reporting is cast in terminology or jargon that might be viewed as demeaning or otherwise offensive.

High-quality neuropsychological reports include MMPI-2-based information that is succinct, concise, relevant, and devoid of technical jargon or unnecessary language that is likely to offend the examinee or referral source. For example, reporting inferences of probable "immature heterosexual relations" in a nursing home resident with dementia is unlikely to be helpful, whereas the identification of depression and anxiety would be. In virtually all cases, issues such as suicidality, substance abuse, and impaired reality testing are critical issues. Stylistically, MMPI-2 inferences are reported with varying tones of definitiveness, depending on the strength of the supportive evidence. For example, the 27/72 code type strongly suggests symptoms of depression and anxiety, not that "*Some people* with this profile *might* have difficulties with depression and anxiety." Finally, the results of the MMPI-2 should be presented in a manner that prioritizes the major issues or problem areas, placing a proper amount of emphasis where it belongs.

Neuropsychological Intervention and Feedback Issues

Accurate assessment of emotional status is essential in neuropsychology because proper intervention is contingent on problem identification. In some cases, patients use self-report instruments such as the MMPI-2 as a vehicle to convey serious problems that they will not otherwise disclose. Bill was a 42-year-old inpatient who was 2 weeks post-left frontal stroke, with residual telegraphic speech. He had a prior left frontal CVA 2 years before, which left him with a mild right hemiparesis. Bill lived with his wife and was working as a mechanic. He was evaluated by the neurology service and referred for neuropsychological evaluation. In the interview, the patient stated that he was mildly depressed over having had a second stroke. However, when queried, he minimized the significance of this "disappointment."

On the MMPI-2, his results suggested a very different picture. He produced high scores on Scales 1, 2, 3, 7, and 8, and endorsed items that refer to suicidal behavior. Scores on Scales 1 and 3 were partially elevated because of his reported physical and health-related effects of stroke (Gass, 1992). An immediate follow-up feedback session and interview were conducted, in which he admitted having a clear and specific plan to shoot himself with his revolver out of a sense of hopelessness and frustration about his seemingly intractable medical condition. At this point, staff members were able to intervene to prevent a negative outcome. People often use self-report instruments to convey problems that they may not bring up or admit to in an initial interview.

The reverse phenomenon sometimes occurs, too. Some people adopt an exaggerated or defensive posture in answering MMPI-2 items, and the clinical interview provides more accurate information about the examinee. When psychological test protocols are either exaggerated or defensive, a feedback and follow-up interview session is often enlightening (Gass & Brown, 1992). Joe was a 57-year old combat veteran who was referred for a neuropsychological evaluation due to complaints of increasing forgetfulness and periodic "blank spells." He was applying for an increase in his disability rating for posttraumatic stress disorder (PTSD). His MMPI-2 profile revealed consistent (content-dependent) responding (TRIN and VRIN T-score < 80) with high scores on F (110T), Fb (108T), and Fp (92T). His profile showed an 86 code type, with high scores on Scale 8 (94T) and Scale 6 (86T) suggestive of psychotic symptoms and corroborated by an elevation on BIZ (76T). In the feedback session, he was queried regarding his endorsement of critical items suggestive of hallucinations and paranoid ideation. In every instance, he attributed his endorsement of these items to various experiences of flashbacks, nightmares, and drug intoxication. This interview helped to clarify that psychosis was not part of his clinical picture.

An excellent systematic and detailed approach to providing MMPI-2 feedback is presented by Butcher (1990). The feedback session is a two-way transaction between the clinician and the examinee perhaps accompanied by significant others. It a means for reviewing findings and providing clarification, and it is also an opportunity for additional assessment and intervention. Examinee's reactions to test feedback, such as conveyances of acceptance or rejection, can be informative and might be predictive of whether recommendations are followed. MMPI-2 feedback can be part of a structured intervention yielding positive therapeutic benefits including symptom reduction and enhancement of self-esteem (Finn, 1996). Many individuals who are referred for neuropsychological evaluation have untreated emotional difficulties and problematic behaviors that are made manifest through their MMPI-2 results. Through this process of feedback provision and discussion, the neuropsychologist can help individuals obtain the assistance they need.

Summary

- A neuropsychological evaluation is incomplete without an assessment of personality and emotional status.
- The use of a comprehensive self-report instrument such as the MMPI-2 holds many advantages. For example, some patients use the MMPI-2 to disclose significant problems that they will not bring up or acknowledge in a clinical interview.
- Profile invalidity can result from the ill-advised use of proposed short forms of the MMPI-2, inadequate preparation of the examinee, inadequate supervision over the testing session, or exclusive reliance on the standard written administration of the MMPI-2 with examinees who have limited reading ability. Reading difficulties can be circumvented through the use of the audiotape or CD format.
- High scores on the FBS (Lees-Haley, English, & Glenn, 1991) occur in cases involving the malingering of physical symptoms, but they also occur in a variety of other clinical conditions. FBS does not distinguish malingerers from individuals with somatoform disorders, which are commonplace in the personal injury arena.
- The MMPI-2 content scales, subscales, and RC Scales provide information that helps the clinician refine and supplement Clinical Scale interpretation.
- The RC Scales assess core constructs underlying most of the standard Clinical Scales. Reliance on the MMPI-2-RF as a replacement for the MMPI-2 entails a substantial loss of information, including the loss of important inferences based on Scale 3 (Hy).
- Most scores on the MMPI-2 are not reliable predictors of performance on neuropsychological tests. In the absence of corroborative evidence, clinicians should be reluctant to use elevated MMPI-2 scores as an explanatory basis for poor performance on neuropsychological tests.
- Scales 1, 2, 3, and 8 contain items that are not only sensitive to psychopathology, but also to

symptoms of brain dysfunction. A sensible approach to MMPI-2 use with brain-impaired patients requires a systematic examination of the potential impact of neurologically sensitive item endorsement on MMPI-2 profiles.

- The incorporation of MMPI-2-based information in neuropsychological reports and feedback requires special considerations based on the referral question and particular needs of the client. The feedback process includes elements of assessment and intervention.

References

Alfano, D. P., Finlayson, M. A., Stearns, G. M., & Neilson, P. M. (1990). The MMPI and neurological dysfunction: Profile configuration and analysis. *The Clinical Neuropsychologist, 4,* 69–79.

Ansley, J., Gass, C. S., Brown, M. C., & Levin, B. E. (1995). Epileptic and non-epileptic seizure disorder: A comparison of MMPI-2 profile characteristics [Abstract]. *Journal of the International Neuropsychological Society, 1,* 135–136.

Arbisi, P. A., & Ben-Porath, Y. S. (1999). The use of the Minnesota Multiphasic Personality Inventory-2 in the psychological assessment of persons with TBI: Correction factors and other clinical caveats and conundrums. *Neurorehabilitation, 13,* 51–59.

Barrett, P., Putnam, S. H., Axelrod, B. N., & Rapport, L. J. (1998). Some statistical properties of 2 MMPI neurocorrection factors for individuals with closed head injury [Abstract]. *Archives of Clinical Neuropsychology, 13,* 16.

Ben-Porath, Y. S., & Tellegen, A. (2007). *MMPI-2: Restructured Form (MMPI-2-RF).* Minneapolis, MN: University of Minnesota Press.

Berry, D. T. R., Wetter, M. W., Baer, R. A., Youngjohn, J. R., Gass, C. S., Lamb, D. G., et al. (1995). Overreporting of closed-head injury symptoms on the MMPI-2. *Psychological Assessment, 7,* 517–523.

Binder, L. M. (1997). A review of mild head trauma. Part II: Clinical implications. *Journal of Clinical and Experimental Neuropsychology, 19,* 432–457.

Binder, L. M., Rohling, M. L., & Larrabee, G. J. (1997). A review of mild head trauma. I: Meta-analytic review of neuropsychological studies. *Journal of Clinical and Experimental Neuropsychology, 19,* 421–431.

Bordini, E. J., Chaknis, M. M., Ekman-Turner, R. M., & Perna, R. B. (2002). Advances and issues. *Neurorehabilitation, 17,* 93–104.

Bornstein, R. A., & Kozora, E. (1990). Content bias of the MMPI Sc scale in neurologic patients. *Neuropsychiatry, Neuropsychology, and Behavioral Neurology, 3,* 200–205.

Bornstein, R. A., Miller, H. B., & van Schoor, T. (1988). Emotional adjustment in compensated head injury patients. *Neurosurgery, 23,* 622–627.

Brulot, M. M., Strauss, E., & Spellacy, F. (1997). Validity of the Minnesota Multiphasic Personality Inventory-2 correction factors for use with patients with suspected head injury. *The Clinical Neuropsychologist, 11,* 391–401.

Burke, J. M., Smith, S. A., & Imhoff, C. L. (1989). The response styles of post-acute traumatic brain-injured patients on the MMPI. *Brain Injury, 3,* 35–40.

Butcher, J. N. (1973). *A conversation with Starke Hathaway: Development of the MMPI.* Minneapolis, MN.

Butcher, J. N. (1990). *The MMPI-2 in psychological treatment.* New York: Oxford University Press.

Butcher, J. N., Arbisi, P. A., Atlis, M. M., & McNulty, J. L. (2003). The construct validity of the Lees–Haley Fake Bad Scale (FBS): Does this scale measure somatic malingering and feigned emotional distress? *Archives of Clinical Neuropsychology, 18,* 473–485.

Butcher, J. N., & Ben-Porath, Y. S. (2004). Use of the MMPI-2 in medico-legal evaluations: An alternative interpretation for the Senior and Douglas (2001) critique. *Australian Psychologist, 39,* 44–50.

Butcher, J. N., Dahlstrom, W. G., Graham, J. R., Tellegen, A., & Kaemmer, B. (1989). *MMPI-2 (Minnesota Multiphasic Personality Inventory-2): Manual for administration and scoring.* Minneapolis, MN: University of Minnesota Press.

Butcher, J. N., Graham, J. R., Williams, C. L., & Ben-Porath, Y. S. (1990). *Development and use of the MMPI-2 content scales.* Minneapolis, MN: University of Minnesota Press.

Butcher, J. N., Hamilton, C. K., Rouse, S. V., & Cumella, E. J. (2006). The deconstruction of the HY scale of MMPI-2: Failure of RC3 in measuring somatic symptom expression. *Journal of Personality Assessment, 87,* 186–192.

Butcher, J. N., & Williams, C. L. (1992). *Essentials of MMPI-2 and MMPI-A interpretation.* Minneapolis, MN: University of Minnesota Press.

Caldwell, A. B. (2006). Maximal measurement or meaningful measurement: The interpretive challenges of the MMPI-2 Restructured Clinical (RC) Scales. *Journal of Personality Assessment, 87,* 193–201.

Calsyn, D. A., Louks, J. L., & Johnson, J. S. (1982). MMPI correlates of the degree of generalized impairment based on the Halstead–Reitan battery. *Perceptual and Motor Skills, 55,* 1099–1102.

Comrey, A. L. (1958). A factor analysis of items on the MMPI psychasthenia scale. *Educational and Psychological Measurement, 18,* 99–107.

Dahlstrom, G. W., & Archer, R. P. (2000). A shortened version of the MMPI-2. *Assessment, 7,* 131–137.

Derry, P. A., Harnadek, M. C. S., Mclachlan, R. S., & Sontrop, J. (1997). Influence of seizure content on interpreting psychopathology on the MMPI-2 in patients with epilepsy. *Journal of Clinical and Experimental Neuropsychology, 19,* 396–404.

Dikmen, S., & Reitan, R. M. (1974). Minnesota Multiphasic Personality Inventory correlates of dysphasic language disturbances. *Journal of Abnormal Psychology, 83,* 675–679.

Dikmen, S., & Reitan, R. M. (1977). MMPI correlates of adaptive ability deficits in patients with brain lesions. *Journal of Nervous and Mental Disease, 165,* 247–254.

Drake, L. E. (1946). A social I.E. scale for the MMPI. *Journal of Applied Psychology, 30,* 51–54.

Dunn, J. T., & Lees-Haley, P. R. (1995). The MMPI-2 correction factor for closed-head injury: A caveat for forensic cases. *Assessment, 2,* 47–51.

Edwards, D. W., Holmquist, L., Wanless, R., Wicks, J., & Davis, C. (1998). Comparing three methods of "neuro-correction" for the MMPI-2 [Abstract]. *Journal of the International Neuropsychological Society, 4,* 27–28.

Finn, S. E. (1996). *Manual for using the MMPI-2 as a therapeutic intervention.* Minneapolis, MN: University of Minnesota Press.

Forbey, J. D., & Ben-Porath, Y. S. (2007). A comparison of the MMPI-2 Restructured Clinical (RC) and Clinical Scales in a substance abuse treatment sample. *Psychological Services, 4,* 46–58.

Gass, C. S. (1991a). Emotional variables in neuropsychological test performance. *Journal of Clinical Psychology, 47*, 100–104.

Gass, C. S. (1991b). MMPI-2 interpretation and closed-head injury: A correction factor. *Psychological Assessment, 3*, 27–31.

Gass, C. S. (1992). MMPI-2 interpretation of patients with cerebrovascular disease: A correction factor. *Archives of Clinical Neuropsychology, 7*, 17–27.

Gass, C. S. (1996a). MMPI-2 variables in attention and memory test performance. *Psychological Assessment, 8*, 135–138.

Gass, C. S. (1996b). MMPI-2 interpretation and stroke: Cross-validation of a correction factor. *Journal of Clinical Psychology, 52*, 569–572.

Gass, C. S. (1997). *Assessing patients with neurological impairments.* Presented at the University of Minnesota MMPI-2 Clinical Workshops & Symposia, Minneapolis, MN, June 5.

Gass, C. S. (1999). Assessment of emotional functioning with the MMPI-2. In G. Groth-Marnat (Ed.), *Neuropsychological assessment in clinical practice: A practical guide to test interpretation and integration* (chap. 14). New York: John Wiley & Sons.

Gass, C. S. (2000). Personality evaluation in neuropsychological assessment. In R. D. Vanderploeg (Ed.), *Clinician's guide to neuropsychological assessment* (2nd ed., pp. 155–194). Mahwah, NJ: Lawrence Erlbaum Associates.

Gass, C. S. (2002). Does test anxiety impede neuropsychological test performance? *Archives of Clinical Neuropsychology, 17*, 860.

Gass, C. S., & Apple, C. (1997). Cognitive complaints in closed-head injury: Relationship to memory test performance and emotional disturbance. *Journal of Clinical and Experimental Neuropsychology, 19*, 290–299.

Gass, C. S., & Ansley, J. (1994a). MMPI correlates of poststroke neurobehavioral deficits. *Archives of Clinical Neuropsychology, 9*, 461–469.

Gass, C. S., & Ansley, J. (1994b). *Neuropsychological correlates of MMPI-2 scores in an inpatient psychiatric sample.* Paper presented at the 29th Annual Symposium on Recent Developments in the Use of the MMPI (MMPI-2 and MMPI-A), May 24, Minneapolis, Minnesota.

Gass, C. S., Ansley, J., & Boyette, S. (1994). Emotional correlates of fluency test and maze performance. *Journal of Clinical Psychology, 50*, 586–590.

Gass, C. S., Ardern, H., Howell, S., Dowd, A., Levy, S., & McKenzie, K. (2005). Cognitive complaints in relation to test performance and emotional status in a neuropsychological referral sample [Abstract]. *Archives of Clinical Neuropsychology, 20*, 893.

Gass, C. S., & Brown, M. C. (1992). Neuropsychological test feedback to patients with brain dysfunction. *Psychological Assessment, 4*, 272–277.

Gass, C. S., & Daniel, S. K. (1990). Emotional impact on Trail Making Test performance. *Psychological Reports, 67*, 435–438.

Gass, C. S., & Freshwater, S. (1999). MMPI-2 symptom disclosure and cognitive complaints in a head injury sample [Abstract]. *Archives of Clinical Neuropsychology, 14*, 29–30.

Gass, C. S., & Gonzalez, C. (2003). MMPI-2 short form proposal: CAUTION. *Archives of Clinical Neuropsychology, 18*, 521–527.

Gass, C. S., & Lawhorn, L. (1991). Psychological adjustment following stroke: An MMPI study. *Psychological Assessment, 3*, 628–633.

Gass, C. S., & Luis, C. A. (2001a). MMPI-2 short form: Psychometric characteristics in a neuropsychological setting. *Assessment, 8*, 213–219.

Gass, C. S., Luis, C. A., Rayls, K. R., & Mittenberg, W. (1999). MMPI-2 profiles in acute traumatic brain injury: Impact of demographic variables and neurological symptom reporting. *Journal of the International Neuropsychological Society, 5*, 140.

Gass, C. S., & Russell, E. W. (1986a). Differential impact of brain damage and depression on memory test performance. *Journal of Consulting and Clinical Psychology, 54*, 261–263.

Gass, C. S., & Russell, E. W. (1986b). MMPI-2 correlates of lateralized cerebral lesions and aphasic deficits. *Journal of Consulting and Clinical Psychology, 54*, 359–363.

Gass, C. S., & Russell, E. W. (1987). MMPI correlates of performance–intellectual deficits in patients with right hemisphere lesions. *Journal of Clinical Psychology, 43*, 484–489.

Gass, C. S., & Russell, E. W. (1991). MMPI profiles of closed-head trauma patients: Impact of neurologic complaints. *Journal of Clinical Psychology, 47*, 253–260.

Gass, C. S., Russell, E. W., & Hamilton, R. A. (1990). Accuracy of MMPI-based inferences regarding memory and concentration in closed-head trauma. *Psychological Assessment, 2*, 175–178.

Gass, C. S., & Wald, H. (1997). MMPI-2 interpretation and closed-head trauma: Cross-validation of a correction factor. *Archives of Clinical Neuropsychology, 12*, 199–205.

Golden, C. J., Sweet, J. J., & Osmon, D. C. (1979). The diagnosis of brain damage by the MMPI: A comprehensive evaluation. *Journal of Personality Assessment, 43*, 138–142.

Graham, J. R. (1993). *MMPI-2: Assessing personality and psychopathology* (2nd ed.). New York: Oxford University Press.

Graham, J. R. (2006). *MMPI-2: Assessing personality and psychopathology* (4th ed.). New York: Oxford University Press.

Graham, J. R., Watts, D., & Timbrook, R. E. (1991). Detecting fake-good and fake-bad MMPI-2 profiles. *Journal of Personality Assessment, 57*, 264–277.

Grant, I., & Alves, W. (1987). Psychiatric and psychosocial disturbances in head injury. In H. S. Levin, J. Grafman, & H. M. Eisenberg (Eds.), *Neurobehavioral recovery from head injury* (pp. 232–261). New York: Oxford University Press.

Green, P., Rohling, M. L., Lees-Haley, P. R., & Allen, L. M. (2001). Effort has a greater effect on test scores than severe brain injury in compensation claimants. *Brain Injury, 15*, 1045–1060.

Greiffenstein, M. F., & Baker, W. J. (2001). Comparison of premorbid and postinjury MMPI-2 profiles in late postconcussive claimants. *The Clinical Neuropsychologist, 15*, 162–170.

Greiffenstein, M. F., & Baker, W. J. (2003). Premorbid clues? Preinjury scholastic performance and present neuropsychological functioning in late postconcussive syndrome. *The Clinical Neuropsychologist, 17*, 561–573.

Greiffenstein, M. F., Baker, W. J., Axelrod, B., Peck, E. A., & Gervais, R. (2004). The Fake Bad Scale and MMPI-2 F-family in detection of implausible psychological trauma claims. *The Clinical Neuropsychologist, 18*, 573–590.

Greiffenstein, M. F., Baker, W. J., Gola, T., Donders, J., & Miller, L. J. (2002). The FBS in atypical and severe closed head injury litigants. *Archives of Clinical Neuropsychology, 19*, 333–336.

Greiffenstein, M. F., Fox, D., & Lees-Haley, P. R. (2007). The MMPI-2 Fake Bad Scale in detection of noncredible brain injury claims. In K. B. Boone (Ed.), *Detection of noncredible cognitive performance.* New York: Guilford Press.

Greve, K. W., Bianchini, K. J., Love, J. M., Brennan, A., & Heinly, M. T. (2006). Sensitivity and specificity of MMPI-2 validity scales and indicators to malingered neurocognitive dysfunction I traumatic brain injury. *Clinical Neuropsychologist, 20,* 491–512.

Guez, M., Brannstrom, R., Nyberg, L, Toolanen G., & Hildingsson, C. (2005). Neuropsychological functioning and MMPI-2 profiles in chronic neck pain: A comparison of whiplash and non-traumatic groups. *Journal of Clinical and Experimental Neuropsychology, 27,* 151–163.

Hathaway, S. R., & McKinley, J. C. (1940). A multiphasic personality schedule (Minnesota): I. Construction of the schedule. *Journal of Psychology, 10,* 249–254.

Heaton, R. K., & Crowley, T. J. (1981). Effects of psychiatric disorders and their somatic treatments on neuropsychological test results. In S. B. Filskov & T. J. Boll (Eds.), *Handbook of clinical neuropsychology* (pp. 481–525), New York: John Wiley & Sons.

Herrman, E. J., Dorfman, W. I., Roth, L., & Burns, W. J. (1997). Utility of the MMPI-2 with a geropsychiatric population: Comparison of four formats (Unpublished manuscript).

Iverson, G. L., Henrichs, T. F., Barton, E. A., & Allen, S. (2002). Specificity of the MMPI-2 Fake Bad Scale as a marker for personal injury malingering. *Psychological Reports, 90,* 131–136.

Kendall, P. C., Edinger, J., & Eberly, C. (1978). Taylor's MMPI correction for spinal cord injury: Empirical endorsement. *Journal of Consulting and Clinical Psychology, 46,* 370–371.

Larrabee, G. J. (2000). Forensic neuropsychological assessment. In R. D. Vanderploeg (Ed.), *Clinician's guide to neuropsychological assessment* (2nd ed., pp. 301–336). Mahwah, NJ: Erlbaum.

Larrabee, G. J. (2003). Detection of symptom exaggeration with the MMPI-2 in litigants with malingered neurocognitive deficit. *The Clinical Neuropsychologist, 17,* 54–68.

Larrabee, G. J. (2007). Evaluation of exaggerated health and injury symptomatology. In G. J. Larrabee (Ed.), *Assessment of malingered neuropsychological deficits.* New York: Oxford University Press.

Lees-Haley, P. R., English, L. T., & Glenn, W. J. (1991). A Fake Bad Scale on the MMPI-2 for personal injury claimants. *Psychological Reports, 68,* 203–210.

Martens, M., Donders, J., & Millis, S. (2001). Evaluation of invalid response sets after traumatic head injury. *Journal of Forensic Neuropsychology, 2,* 1–18.

Meyers, J. E., Millis, S. R., & Volkert, K. (2002). A validity index for the MMPI-2. *Archives of Clinical Neuropsychology, 17,* 157–169.

Mittenberg, W., Tremont, G., & Rayls, K. R. (1996). Impact of cognitive function on MMPI-2 validity in neurologically impaired patients. *Assessment, 3,* 157–163.

Nelson, N. W., Sweet, J. J., & Demakis, G. J. (2006). Meta-analysis of the MMPI-2 Fake Bad Scale: Utility in forensic practice. *The Clinical Neuropsychologist, 20,* 39–58.

Nichols, D. S. (2006). The trials of separating bath water from baby: A review and critique of the MMPI-2 Restructured Clinical Scales. *Journal of Personality Assessment, 87,* 121–138.

Oetting, E. R., & Deffenbacher, J. L. (1980). *The Test Anxiety Profile (TAP) manual.* Fort Collins, CO: Rocky Mountain Behavioral Sciences Institute.

Paniak, C. E., & Miller, H. B. (1993). Utility of the MMPI-2 validity scales with brain injury survivors [Abstract]. *Archives of Clinical Neuropsychology, 9,* 172.

Pope, K. S., Butcher, J. N., & Seelen, J. (1993). *The MMPI, MMPI-2, and MMPI-A in court.* Washington, DC: American Psychological Association.

Putnam, S. H., & Millis, S. R. (1994). Psychosocial factors in the development of and maintenance of chronic somatic and functional symptoms following mild traumatic brain injury. *Advances in Medical Psychotherapy, 7,* 1–22.

Rayls, K. R., Mittenberg, W., Burns, W. J., & Theroux, S. (2000). Prospective study of the MMPI-2 correction factor after mild head injury. *The Clinical Neuropsychologist, 14,* 546–550.

Reitan, R. M. (1955). Affective disturbances in brain-damaged patients: Measurements with the Minnesota Multiphasic Personality Inventory. *Archives of Neurology and Psychiatry, 73,* 530–532.

Reitan, R. M., & Wolfson, D. (1993). *The Halstead–Reitan neuropsychological test battery: Theory and clinical interpretation* (2nd ed.). Tucson, AZ: Neuropsychology Press.

Reitan, R. M., & Wolfson, D. (1997). Emotional disturbances and their interaction with neuropsychological deficits. *Neuropsychology Review, 7,* 3–19.

Reitan, R. M., & Wolfson, D. (2002). The differential effect of conation on intelligence test scores among brain-damaged and control subjects. *Archives of Clinical Neuropsychology, 19,* 29–35.

Ross, S. R., Millis, S. R., Krukowski, R. A., Putnam, S. H., & Adams, K. M. (2004). Detecting incomplete effort on the MMPI-2: An examination of the Fake Bad Scale in mild head injury. *Journal of Clinical and Experimental Neuropsychology, 26,* 115–124.

Ross, S. R., Putnam, S. H., Gass, C. S., Bailey, D. E., & Adams, K. M. (2003). MMPI-2 indices of psychological disturbance and attention and memory test performance in head injury. *Archives of Clinical Neuropsychology, 18,* 905–916.

Sellbom, M., Ben-Porath, Y. S., McNulty, J. L., Arbisi, P. A., & Graham, J. R. (2006). Elevation differences between MMPI-2 Clinical Scales and Restructured Clinical (RC) Scales. *Assessment, 13,* 430–441.

Senior, G., Lothrop, P., & Deacon, S. (1999). *TBI(F): An MMPI-2 scale for assessing traumatic brain injury in a forensic setting.* Poster, 19th Annual Conference of the National Academy of Neuropsychology.

Sharland, M. J., & Gfeller, J. D. (2007). A survey of neuropsychologists' beliefs and practices with respect to the assessment of effort. *Archives of Clinical Neuropsychology, 22,* 213–223.

Starkstein, S., Pearlson, G., Boston, J., & Robinson, R. (1987). Mania after brain injury: A controlled study of causative factors. *Archives of Neurology, 44,* 1069–1073.

Strauss, E., Sherman, E., & Spreen, O. (2006). *A compendium of neuropsychological tests* (3rd ed.). New York: Oxford University Press.

Tallent, N. (1993). *Psychological report writing* (4th ed.). Englewood Cliffs, NJ: Prentice-Hall.

Tellegen, A., Ben-Porath, Y. S., Sellbom, M., Arbisi, P., McNulty, J., & Graham, J. R. (2006). Further evidence on the validity of the MMPI–2 restructured clinical (RC) scales: Addressing questions raised by Rogers, Sewell, Harrison, and Jordan and Nichols. *Journal of Personality Assessment, 87,* 48–71.

Tellegen, A., Ben-Porath, Y. S., McNulty, J., Arbisi, P., Graham, J. R., & Kaemmer, B. (2003). *The MMPI-2 Restructured Clinical (RC) Scales: Development, validation,* and *interpretation*. Minneapolis, MN: University of Minnesota Press.

Vanderploeg, R. D., & Curtiss, G. (2001). Malingering assessment: Evaluation of validity of performance. *NeuroRehabilitation, 16*, 245–251.

Van Reekum, R., Cohen, T., & Wong, J. (2000). Can traumatic brain injury cause psychiatric disorders? *Journal of Neuropsychiatry and Clinical Neuroscience, 12*, 316–327.

Wooten, A. J. (1983). MMPI profiles among neuropsychology patients. *Journal of Clinical Psychology, 39*, 392–406.

Youngjohn, J. R., Burrows, L., & Erdal, K. (1995). Brain damage or compensation neurosis? The controversial postconcussive syndrome. *The Clinical Neuropsychologist, 9*, 595–598.

Youngjohn, J. R., Davis, D., & Wolf, I. (1997). Head injury and the MMPI-2: Paradoxical severity effects and the influence of litigation. *Psychological Assessment, 9*, 177–184.

Zillmer, E. A., & Perry, W. (1996). Cognitive-neuropsychological abilities and related psychological disturbance: A factor model of neuropsychological, Rorschach, and MMPI indices. *Assessment, 3*, 209–224.

Assessing Couples

Douglas K. Snyder, Richard E. Heyman, *and* Stephen N. Haynes

Abstract

Couple distress has a high prevalence as well as high comorbidity with a broad range of emotional, behavioral, and physical health problems. Relationship problems also influence individuals' response to treatment for a wide range of psychological disorders. Hence, clinicians need to be skilled in assessing relationships in order to provide effective interventions whether working primarily with individuals, couples, or the broader family system. This chapter first introduces brief screening measures and clinical methods for diagnosing couple distress in clinical as well as research applications. The bulk of the chapter is devoted to conceptualizing and assessing couple distress for the purpose of planning and evaluating treatment. Emerging technologies for assessing intimate relationships are presented, along with recommendations for future research.

Keywords: assessment, couples, couple distress, marriage, relationships

Individuals rate having a satisfying marriage or relationship as one of their most important goals in life (Roberts & Robins, 2000). Indeed, marital happiness exceeds satisfaction in other domains (e.g., health, work, or children) as the strongest single predictor of overall life satisfaction (Fleeson, 2004). When intimate relationships become distressed, the negative effects on partners' emotional and physical well-being can be far-reaching. Moreover, failure to address clients' relationship well-being can compromise the effectiveness of individual therapies targeting a broad range of psychological disorders (Snyder & Whisman, 2004). Hence, it behooves mental health practitioners to gain expertise in assessing couples as a prerequisite to planning and implementing effective interventions—whether conducting individual- or couple-based treatments.

Assessment of couples shares basic principles of assessing individuals—viz. (a) the foci of assessment methods be empirically linked to target problems and constructs hypothesized to be functionally related; (b) selected assessment instruments and

methods demonstrate evidence of reliability, validity, and cost-effectiveness; and (c) findings be linked within a theoretical or conceptual framework of the presumed causes of difficulties, as well as to clinical intervention or prevention.

Couple assessment differs from individual assessment in that couple assessment strategies (a) focus specifically on relationship processes and the interactions between individuals; (b) provide an opportunity for direct observation of target complaints involving communication and other interpersonal exchange; and (c) must be sensitive to potential challenges unique to establishing a collaborative alliance when assessing highly distressed or antagonistic partners, particularly in a conjoint context. Our discussion of strategies for assessing couples is necessarily selective—emphasizing dimensions empirically related to couple distress, identifying alternative methods and strategies for obtaining relevant assessment data, and highlighting specific techniques within each method.

We begin this chapter by defining couple distress and noting its prevalence and comorbidity with emotional, behavioral, and physical health problems of individuals in both clinical and community populations. Both brief screening measures and clinical methods are presented for diagnosing couple distress in clinical as well as research applications. The bulk of the chapter is devoted to conceptualizing and assessing couple distress for the purpose of planning and evaluating treatment. Toward this end, we review empirical findings regarding behavioral, cognitive, and affective components of couple distress and specific techniques derived from clinical interview, behavioral observation, and self-report methods. In most cases, these same assessment methods and instruments are relevant to evaluating treatment progress and outcome. Also included is a discussion of emerging technologies for assessing intimate relationships. We conclude with general recommendations for assessing couple distress and directions for future research.

Conceptualizing Couple Relationship Distress

Defining Couple Distress

The fourth edition of the *Diagnostic and statistical manual of mental disorders—text revision* (DSM-IV-TR; American Psychiatric Association, 2000) defines a "partner relational problem" as a pattern of interaction characterized by negative or distorted communication, or "noncommunication (e.g., withdrawal)," that is associated with clinically significant impairment in individual or relationship functioning or the development of symptoms in one or both partners. The acknowledgment of relational problems as a "frequent focus of clinical attention," but their separation from other emotional and behavioral disorders, comprises only a marginal improvement over earlier versions of the DSM that all but ignored the interpersonal context of distressed lives.

What are the limitations to this conceptualization of partner relational problems? First is an almost exclusive emphasis on the etiological role of communication in the impairment of functioning or development of symptoms in one or both partners. Although group comparisons document differences in communication between clinic versus community couples (Heyman, 2001), and "communication problems" comprise the most frequent presenting complaint of couples (Geiss & O'Leary, 1981), evidence that communication differences precede, rather than follow, from relationship distress is weak or nonexistent. Moreover, research with community samples indicates that some forms of "negative" communication predict *better* rather than worse relationship

outcomes longitudinally (Gottman, 1993). In addition, positive changes in relationship satisfaction following couple therapy correspond only weakly or nonsignificantly with actual changes in communication behavior (Jacobson, Schmaling, & Holtzworth-Munroe, 1987; Sayers, Baucom, Sher, Weiss, & Heyman, 1991).

In proposing a broadened conceptualization of relationship disorders for the DSM-V, First et al. (2002, p. 161) defined relational disorders as "persistent and painful patterns of feelings, behavior, and perceptions involving two or more partners in an important personal relationship ... marked by distinctive, maladaptive patterns that show little change despite a great variety of challenges and circumstances." Still lacking in this conceptualization (as well as in the DSM-IV-TR) is a recognition of "nonsymptomatic" deficiencies that couples often present as a focus of concern, including those that detract from optimal individual or relationship well-being. These include deficits in feelings of security and closeness, shared values, trust, joy, love, and similar positive emotions that individuals typically value in their intimate relationships.

Heyman, Feldbau-Kohn, Ehrensaft, Langhinrichsen-Rohling, and O'Leary (2001) proposed and evaluated criteria for relationship distress modeled loosely on the DSM major depressive disorder (MDD) diagnosis. Their definition of relationship distress required that "during the past month, a subjective sense of relationship dissatisfaction was noted by one or both partners and was accompanied by at least one significant symptom in the interactional, cognitive, or affective domains" (see Table 24.1). Heyman et al.'s original criteria were expanded to include additional interactional indicators of relationship distress by a task force of psychologists and psychiatrists examining the role of relational processes in revisions to the DSM (Beach & Wamboldt, 2007). Overall, these criteria emphasize both (a) a subjective global indicator of the construct's core (relationship dissatisfaction as noted by reports of a sense of unhappiness, thoughts of divorce, or need for professional help for the relationship), and (b) specific indicators of distress (at least one behavioral, cognitive, or affective symptom).

Items for Criterion A, overall dissatisfaction, were based on a rational approach to conceptualizing significant relationship distress. Items for Criteria B, C, and D were based on scientific literature demonstrating the linkage between low relationship satisfaction and each of the following: higher likelihood of reciprocating or escalating negativity during

Table 24.1. Criteria for partner relational discord syndrome.

During the past month, a subjective sense of relationship dissatisfaction (Criterion A) was noted by one or both partners and was accompanied by at least one significant symptom in the interactional, cognitive, or affective domains (Criteria B–D).

A. Relationship dissatisfaction

   (1) Pervasive sense of unhappiness with the relationship
   (2) Thoughts of divorce/separation that are more than transitory
   (3) Perceived need for professional help for the relationship

B. Interactional symptoms

   (1) Conflict resolution difficulties
      a. Marked escalation of negative behavior or affect (e.g., "little" disputes quickly and frequently evolve into heated arguments)
      b. Pervasive withdrawal from interaction so that resolution is impeded. Withdrawal can be either through leaving a discussion before it is resolved or through more pervasive disconnectedness that impedes bringing up or resolving problems.
   (2) Other coercive exchanges
      Coercing partner by:
      a. Widespread withholding of vital relationship behaviors (e.g. contributing to childcare, household responsibilities, affection)
      b. Engaging in frequent nonverbal negative behaviors not including physical aggression (e.g. "cold shoulder," angry looks)
   (3) Notable lack of positive exchanges
      a. Notable lack of sharing thoughts and feelings
      b. Notable lack of sexual and nonsexual physical intimacy
      c. Notable lack of positive shared activities
      d. Notable lack of emotional and tangible social support

C. Cognitive symptoms

   (1) Perceived negative intentions
      a. Negative behaviors of the partner are pervasively attributed to negative personality traits or are perceived to be done voluntarily, intentionally, or with negative intent
      b. Positive behaviors of the partner are pervasively attributed to temporary states or are perceived to be done accidentally, unintentionally, or with hidden negative intentions
   (2) Low relationship efficacy
      Low sense of efficacy that the relationship can improve (without professional help)

D. Affective symptoms

   Interactions with or thoughts about the partner are frequently marked by intense and persistent levels of
   (1) Anger or contempt
   (2) Apathy
   (3) Sadness

---

conflict and of withdrawal (see review by Heyman, 2001), distressed attributional patterns (e.g., Bradbury & Fincham, 1990), low sense of efficacy that the relationship can improve (e.g., Vanzetti, Notarius, & NeeSmith, 1992), and intense or persistent levels of anger/contempt or sadness (e.g., Gottman, 1999). Overall dissatisfaction accompanied by apathy was included to make the symptom criteria exhaustive and because apathy or emotional detachment is a primary presenting complaint of some couples (O'Leary, Heyman, & Jongsma, 1998).

Prevalence and Comorbid Conditions

Clinical interventions targeting couple distress continue to gain in stature as vital components of mental health services. Three factors contribute to this growing recognition: (a) the prevalence of couple distress in both community and clinic samples; (b) the impact of couple distress on both the emotional and physical well-being of adult partners and their offspring; and (c) increased evidence of the effectiveness of couple therapy, not only in treating couple distress and related relationship problems, but also as a primary or adjunct treatment for a variety of individual emotional, behavioral, or physical health disorders (Snyder, Castellani, & Whisman, 2006).

Couple distress is prevalent in both community epidemiological studies and in research involving clinical samples. In the United States, the most salient indicator of couple distress remains a divorce rate of approximately 50% among married couples (Kreider & Fields, 2002), with about half of these occurring within the first 7 years of marriage. Independent of divorce, the research literature suggests that many, if not most, marriages experience periods of significant turmoil that place partners at risk for dissatisfaction, dissolution, or symptom development (e.g., depression or anxiety). Data on the effects of stigma, prejudice, and multiple social stressors experienced by lesbian, gay, transgender, and bisexual populations suggest that same-sex couples may experience additional challenges (Meyer, 2003).

In a previous national survey, the most frequently cited causes of acute emotional distress were relationship problems including divorce, separation, and other marital strains (Swindle, Heller, Pescosolido, & Kikuzawa, 2000). Other studies have indicated that maritally discordant individuals are overrepresented among individuals seeking mental health services, regardless of whether or not they report marital distress as their primary complaint (Lin, Goering, Offord, Campbell, & Boyle, 1996). In a study of 800 employee assistance program (EAP) clients, 65% rated family problems as "considerable" or "extreme" (Shumway, Wampler, Dersch, & Arredondo, 2004).

Data from the National Comorbidity Survey indicated that, in comparison to happily married persons, maritally distressed partners are 3 times more likely to have a mood disorder, 2.5 times more likely to have an anxiety disorder, and 2 times more likely to have a substance use disorder (Whisman, 1999). Additional findings from an epidemiological survey in Ontario showed that, even when controlling for distress in other relationships with relatives and close friends, marital distress was significantly correlated with major depression, generalized anxiety disorder, social and simple phobia, panic disorder, and alcohol dependence or abuse (Whisman, Sheldon, & Goering, 2000). Moreover, couple distress—particularly negative communication—has direct adverse effects on cardiovascular, endocrine, immune, neurosensory, and other physiological systems that, in turn, contribute to physical health problems (Kiecolt-Glaser & Newton, 2001). Nor are the effects of couple distress confined to the adult partners. Gottman (1999) cites evidence indicating that "marital distress, conflict, and disruption are associated with a wide range of deleterious effects on children, including depression, withdrawal, poor social competence, health problems, poor academic performance, a variety of conduct-related difficulties, and markedly decreased longevity" (p. 4).

In brief, couple distress has a markedly high prevalence, has a strong linkage to emotional, behavioral, and health problems in the adult partners and children, and is among the most frequent primary or secondary concerns reported by individuals seeking assistance from mental health professionals.

Etiological Considerations and Implications for Assessment

Both the aforementioned comorbidity findings and clinical observations suggest that couple distress likely results from, as well as contributes to, emotional and behavioral problems in one or both partners as well as their children. Understanding a given couple's distress requires extending beyond individual considerations to pursue a broader assessment of the relational and socioecological context in which couple distress emerges. Snyder, Cavell, Heffer, and Mangrum (1995) proposed a multitrait, multilevel assessment model for assessing couple and family distress comprising five overlapping construct domains (cognitive, affective, behavioral, interpersonal, and structural/developmental) operating at five system levels (individuals, dyads, the nuclear family, the extended family, and community/cultural systems). Table 24.2 (from Snyder & Abbott, 2002) provides a modest sampling of specific constructs relevant to each domain at each system level.

The relevance of any specific facet of this model to relationship distress for either partner varies dramatically across couples; hence,

Table 24.2. Sample assessment constructs across domains and levels of couple and family functioning.

	Individual	Dyad (Couple, parent–child)	Nuclear family system	Extended system (Family of origin, friends)	Culture/community
Cognitive	Intelligence; memory functions; thought content; thought quality; analytic skills; cognitive distortions; schemas; capacity for self-reflection and insight	Cognitions regarding self and other in relationship; expectancies, attributions, attentional biases, and goals in the relationship	Shared or co-constructed meanings within the system; family ideology or paradigm; thought sequences between members contributing to family functioning	Intergenerational patterns of thinking and believing; co-constructed meaning shared by therapist and family or other significant friends or family	Prevailing societal and cultural beliefs and attitudes; ways of thinking associated with particular religious or ethnic groups that are germane to the family or individual
Affective/ emotional	Mood; affective range, intensity, and valence; emotional lability and reactivity	Predominant emotional themes or patterns in the relationship; cohesion; range of emotional expression; commitment and satisfaction in the relationship; emotional content during conflict; acceptance and forgiveness	Family emotional themes of fear, shame, guilt, or rejection; system properties of cohesion or emotional disaffection; emotional atmosphere in the home— including humor, joy, love, and affection as well as conflict and hostility	Emotional themes and patterns in extended system; intergenerational emotional legacies; patterns of fusion or differentiation across generations	Prevailing emotional sentiment in the community, culture, and society; cultural norms and mores regarding the expression of emotion
Behavioral	Capacity for self-control; impulsivity; aggressiveness; capacity to defer gratification; substance abuse; overall health, energy, and drive	Recursive behavioral sequences displayed in the relationship; behavioral repertoire; reinforcement contingencies; strategies used to control other's behavior	Repetitive behavioral patterns or sequences used to influence family structure and power; shared recreation and other pleasant activities	Behavioral patterns displayed by the extended system (significant friends, family of origin, therapist) used to influence the structure and behaviors of the extended system	Cultural norms and mores of behavior; behaviors which are prescribed or proscribed by the larger society

continued

Table 24.2. (*continued*)

	Individual	Dyad (Couple, parent–child)	Nuclear family system	Extended system (Family of origin, friends)	Culture/community
Interpersonal/ communication	Characteristic ways of communicating and interacting across relationships or personality (e.g. shy, gregarious, narcissistic, dependent, controlling, avoidant)	Quality and frequency of the dyad's communication; speaking and listening skills; how couples share information, express feelings, and resolve conflict	Information flow in the family system; paradoxical messages; family system boundaries, hierarchy, and organization; how the family system uses information regarding its own functioning; family decision-making strategies	Degree to which information is shared with and received from significant others outside the nuclear family system or dyad; the permeability of boundaries and the degree to which the family or couple is receptive to outside influences	Information that is communicated to the family or individual by the community or culture in which they live; how the family or individual communicates their needs and mobilizes resources
Structural/ developmental	All aspects of physiological and psychosocial development; personal history that influences current functioning—including psychosocial stressors; intrapersonal consistency of cognitions, affect, and behavior	History of the relationship and how it has evolved over time; congruence of partners' cognitions, affect, and behavior	Changes in the family system over time; current stage in the family life cycle; stressors related to childrearing; congruence in needs, beliefs, and behaviors across family members	Developmental changes across generations; significant historical events influencing current system functioning (e.g. death, illness, divorce, abuse); congruence of beliefs and values across extended social support systems	The cultural and political history of the society in which the family or individual lives; current political and economic changes; congruence of the individual's or couple's values with those of the larger community

Note: From Snyder, D. K., & Abbott, B. V. (2002). Couple distress. In M. M. Antony & D. H. Barlow (Eds.), *Handbook of assessment and treatment planning for psychological disorders* (pp. 341–374). New York: Guilford. Copyright 2002 by Guilford Press. Reprinted with permission.

although providing guidance regarding initial areas of inquiry from a nomothetic perspective, the relation of any specific component to relationship distress for a given individual or couple needs to be determined from a functional analytic approach and applied idiographically (Cone, 1988; Haynes, Leisen, & Blaine, 1997; Haynes & O'Brien, 2000). Moreover, interactive effects occur within domains across levels, within levels across domains, and across levels and domains. For example, individual differences in emotion regulation could significantly impact how partners interact when disclosing personal information or attempting to resolve conflict (Snyder, Simpson, & Hughes, 2006). Later in this chapter, we highlight more salient components of this assessment model operating primarily at the dyadic level as they relate to case conceptualization and treatment planning.

Assessment for Diagnosis and Screening

A diagnosis of couple distress is based on the subjective evaluation of dissatisfaction by one or both partners with the overall quality of their relationship. By comparison, "relationship dysfunction" may be determined by external evaluations of partners' objective interactions (as observed by the assessor or reported by the partners). Although subjective and external evaluations frequently converge, partners may report being satisfied with a relationship that—by outsiders' evaluations—would be rated as dysfunctional due to observed deficits in conflict resolution, emotional expressiveness, management of relationship tasks involving finances or children, interactions with extended family, and so forth. Similarly, partners may report dissatisfaction with a relationship that to outsiders appears characterized by effective patterns of interacting in these and other domains. Discrepancies between partners' subjective reports and outside observers' evaluations may result, in part, from raters' differences in personal values, gender, ethnicity, or cultural perspectives (Tanaka-Matsumi, 2004) or from a lack of opportunity to observe relatively infrequent behaviors (e.g., physical abuse, or cruel comments when drunk).

Partners may also disagree in their relationship accounts—either because of actual differences in subjective experiences of their relationship or because of differences in ability or willingness to convey these experiences via interview or self-report measures. Various methods for combining partners' self-reports have been proposed including "weak

link," "strong link," and "averaged report" models. The "weak link" approach emphasizes partner reports denoting higher levels of distress based on the premise that relationships come under duress and may be dissolved even if only one partner is significantly dissatisfied. Alternatively, the "strong link" approach asserts that one partner's relatively higher levels of satisfaction or commitment may lead to resilience and maintenance of a relationship through particularly difficult or stressful times. The "averaged report" method, although the most common approach to combining partners' reports in couple research prior to multilevel modeling techniques, may be the least justifiable approach because it obscures partner differences and provides no information about either resilience or vulnerability (i.e., couples wherein both partners report "moderate" distress are regarded as equivalent to couples wherein one partner reports extensive distress and the other little or no distress).

For screening purposes, a brief structured interview may be used to assess overall relationship distress and partner violence. Heyman et al.'s (2001) distress interview (see Table 24.1) has demonstrated high inter-rater reliability and convergent validity with observed interactions. Heyman and Slep (2006) have developed an interview for partner and child maltreatment that resulted in over 90% agreement on diagnostic decisions between community assessors and master reviewers.

An alternative approach to detecting relationship distress builds on taxometric analyses by Whisman, Beach, and Snyder (2008) identifying a "marital distress taxon" reliably distinguishing clinic from community couples based on partners' self-reports across five domains of relationship functioning assessed by the Marital Satisfaction Inventory-Revised (MSI-R; Snyder, 1997). Incorporating both taxometric findings and item analytic procedures, Whisman and colleagues subsequently constructed a 10-item interview with high sensitivity and specificity for detecting relationship distress; the same items can be administered in a self-report format with different cutoffs for tailoring sensitivity and specificity to specific assessment purposes (Whisman, Snyder, & Beach, 2009).

The emphasis on partners' subjective evaluations of couple distress has led to development of numerous self-report measures of relationship satisfaction and global affect. There is considerable convergence across measures purporting to assess such constructs as marital "quality," "satisfaction," "adjustment," "happiness," "cohesion," "consensus," "intimacy," and the like, with correlations between measures often approaching the upper bounds of their reliability. Differentiation among such constructs at a theoretical level often fails to achieve the same operational distinction at the item-content level (cf., Fincham & Bradbury, 1987, for an excellent discussion of this issue). Hence, selection among such measures should be guided by careful examination of item content (i.e., content validity) and empirical findings regarding both convergent and discriminant validity. In Table 24.3, we have listed several assessment instruments

having strong empirical evidence of reliability, construct validity, and potential clinical utility. Those instruments with the strongest psychometric evidence across multiple studies are denoted as "highly recommended."

Relatively short measures of overall relationship satisfaction may be useful as diagnostic and screening strategies for couple distress. The most frequently used global measure of relationship satisfaction in couple research is the Dyadic Adjustment Scale (DAS; Spanier, 1976), a 32-item instrument purporting to differentiate among four related subscales reflecting cohesion, satisfaction, consensus,

---

Table 24.3. Evidence-based couple assessment methods.

Assessment Methods for Screening and Diagnosis
Interview
Couple Distress Taxon Interview (Whisman et al., 2009)
*Structured Diagnostic Interview for Marital Distress and Partner Aggression (Heyman et al., 2001)

Self-report measures
Couple Distress Taxon Scale (Whisman et al., 2009)
Couple Satisfaction Index (Funk & Rogge, 2007)
*Dyadic Adjustment Scale (Spanier, 1976)
Kansas Marital Satisfaction Scale (Schumm et al., 1986)
Relationship Disharmony and Disaffection Scales (Herrington et al., 2008)

Observational methods
Rapid Couples Interaction Scoring System (Krokoff et al., 1989)
*Rapid Marital Interaction Coding System (Heyman, 2004)

Assessment Methods for Case Conceptualization and Treatment Planning
Self-report measures
Specific relationship behaviors
Communication Patterns Questionnaire (Christensen, 1987)
*Conflict Tactics Scale-Revised (Straus et al., 1996)
Frequency and Acceptability of Partner Behavior Inventory (Doss & Christensen, 2006)

Relationship cognitions
Relationship Attribution Measure (Fincham & Bradbury, 1992)

Multidimensional relationship inventories
Evaluating and Nurturing Relationship Issues, Communication, Happiness (Olson & Olson, 1999)
*Marital Satisfaction Inventory-Revised (Snyder, 1997)

Observational methods
Affect
Behavioral Affective Rating System (Johnson, 2002)
*Specific Affect Coding System (Gottman et al., 1996)
Behavioral engagement
Conflict Rating System (Heavey et al., 1995)
General communication skills
*Clinical Rating of Adult Communication Scale (Basco et al., 1991)
Interactional Dimensions Coding System (Kline et al., 2004)
Kategoriensystem für Partnerschaftliche Interaktion (Partner Interaction Coding System; Hahlweg, 2004)
Power
*System for Coding Interactions in Dyads (Malik & Lindahl, 2004)

continued

Table 24.3. (*continued*)

Problem solving
Codebook of Marital and Family Interaction (Notarius et al., 1991)
*Communication Skills Test (Floyd, 2004)
Dyadic Interaction Scoring Code (Filsinger, 1983)
Living In Family Environments Coding System (Hops et al., 1995)
Verbal Tactics Coding Scheme (Sillars, 1982)
Support/intimacy
*Social Support Interaction Coding System (Pasch et al., 2004)

Assessment Methods for Treatment Monitoring and Evaluation
Self-report measures
*Dyadic Adjustment Scale (Spanier, 1976)
Goal Attainment Scaling (Kiresuk et al., 1994)
Kansas Marital Satisfaction Scale (Schumm et al., 1986)
*Marital Satisfaction Inventory—Revised (Snyder, 1997)

Observational methods
*Rapid Marital Interaction Coding System (Heyman, 2004)

Note: *denotes highly recommended based on overall psychometric characteristics and demonstrated utility.

and affectional expression. For abbreviated screening measures of couple distress, several alternatives are available, including a brief (7-item) version of the DAS (Hunsley, Best, Lefebvre, & Vito, 2001). An even briefer measure, the Kansas Marital Satisfaction Scale (KMSS; Schumm et al., 1986), includes three Likert items assessing satisfaction with marriage as an institution, the marital relationship, and the character of one's spouse. New global measures of relationship sentiment continue to be developed for both research and clinical purposes. These include a new set of three Couple Satisfaction Index (CSI) scales constructed using item response theory (IRT) and comprising 32, 16, and 4 items each (Funk & Rogge, 2007), and two factor scales derived from the MSI-R distinguishing overt conflict (disharmony) from emotional distance or isolation (disaffection) (Herrington et al., 2008).

Despite its widespread use, a review of psychometric properties reveals important limitations to the DAS. Factor analyses have failed to replicate its four subscales (Crane, Busby, & Larson, 1991), and the internal consistency of the affectional expression subscale is weak. There is little evidence that the full-length DAS and similar longer global scales offer incremental validity above the 3-item KMSS—although preliminary evidence suggests that the new CSI scales may offer higher precision of measurement and greater sensitivity for detecting differences in relationship satisfaction.

Because partners frequently present for treatment together, clinicians have the rare opportunity to observe the reciprocal social determinants of problem behaviors without venturing outside the therapy office. Structured observations constitute a useful assessment method because they minimize inferences needed to assess behavior, can facilitate formal or informal functional analysis, can provide an additional method of assessment in a multimethod strategy (e.g., integrated with interview and questionnaires), and can facilitate the observation of otherwise difficult to observe behaviors (Haynes & O'Brien, 2000; Heyman & Slep, 2004). We discuss analog behavioral observation of couple interactions and describe specific observational coding systems at greater length in the following section on case conceptualization and treatment planning. However, for purposes of initial screening and diagnosis, we advocate two approaches to assessing partners' descriptions of relationship problems, expression of positive and negative feelings, and efforts to resolve conflicts and reach decisions—specifically, the Rapid Marital Interaction Coding System (RMICS; Heyman, 2004) and the Rapid Couples Interaction Scoring System (RCISS; Krokoff, Gottman, & Hass, 1989). Even when not formally coding couples' interactions, clinicians' familiarity with the behavioral indicators for specific communication patterns previously demonstrated to covary with relationship accord or distress should facilitate empirically informed screening of partners' verbal and nonverbal exchanges.

When a couple presents for therapy with primary complaints of dissatisfaction in their relationship, screening for the mere presence of couple distress is unnecessary. However, there are numerous other situations in which the practitioner may need to screen for relationship distress as a contributing or exacerbating factor in patients' presenting complaints—including mental health professionals treating individual emotional or behavioral difficulties; physicians evaluating the interpersonal context of such somatic complaints as fatigue, chronic headaches, or sleep disturbance; or emergency room personnel confronting persons with severe relationship distress culminating in physical violence and injuries. We advocate a sequential strategy of progressively more detailed assessment when indicators of relationship distress emerge (cf. Snyder & Abbott, 2002, pp. 366–367):

1. Clinical inquiry as to whether relationship problems contribute to individual difficulties such as feeling depressed or anxious, having difficulty sleeping, abusing alcohol or other substances, or feeling less able to deal with such stresses as work, children and family, or health concerns. When indicated by this initial inquiry, conducting a brief structured interview to screen for overall relationship distress (e.g., Table 24.1) and partner violence (e.g., Heyman & Slep, 2006).

2. Alternatively, in place of a face-to-face interview, use of an initial brief screening measure (e.g., the KMSS or DAS-7) having evidence of both internal consistency and construct validity to assess overall relationship distress.

3. For individuals reporting moderate to high levels of global relationship distress, following up with more detailed assessment methods such as semistructured interviews, analog behavioral observation, and multidimensional relationship satisfaction questionnaires to differentiate among levels and sources or domains of distress.

Overall Evaluation

When screening for either clinical or research purposes, we advocate assessment strategies favoring sensitivity over specificity to minimize the likelihood of overlooking potential factors contributing to individual or relationship distress. This implies the initial use of broad screening items in clinical inquiry or self-report measures—along with direct observation of partner interactions whenever possible—and subsequent use of more extensive narrow-band or multidimensional measures described in the following section on treatment planning to pinpoint specific sources

of concern. Initial assessment findings indicating overall relationship distress need to be followed by functional analytic assessment strategies to delineate the manner in which individual and relationship concerns affect each other and relate to situational factors (Floyd, Haynes, & Kelly, 1997).

Assessment for Case Conceptualization and Treatment Planning

Conceptualizing couple distress for the purpose of planning treatment requires extending beyond global sentiment to assess specific sources and levels of relationship difficulties, their individual and broader socioecological determinants, and their potential responsiveness to various clinical interventions. We begin our consideration of assessing couple relationships for case conceptualization and treatment planning with a discussion of construct domains particularly relevant to couple distress— including relationship behaviors, cognitions, and affect—as well as individual and broader cultural factors. We follow this with a discussion of various assessment methods and techniques for evaluating specific constructs in these domains.

Domains to Target When Evaluating Couple Distress

RELATIONSHIP BEHAVIORS

Research examining behavioral components of couple distress has emphasized two domains: the rates and reciprocity of positive and negative behaviors exchanged between partners, and communication behaviors related to both emotional expression and decision making. Regarding the former, distressed couples are distinguished from nondistressed couples by (a) higher rates of negative verbal and nonverbal exchanges (e.g., disagreements, criticism, hostility); (b) higher levels of reciprocity in negative behavior (i.e., the tendency for negativity in partner A to be followed by negativity in partner B); (c) lengthier chains of negative behavior once initiated; (d) higher ratios of negative to positive behaviors, independent of their separate rates; and (e) lower rates of positive verbal and nonverbal behaviors (e.g., approval, empathy, smiling, positive touch) (Weiss & Heyman, 1997). Findings suggest a stronger linkage for negativity, compared to positivity, to overall couple distress.

Given the inevitability of disagreements arising in long-term relationships, numerous studies have focused on specific communication behaviors that exacerbate or impede the resolution of couple conflicts. Most notable among these are difficulties in articulating thoughts and feelings related to specific relationship concerns and deficits in decision-making strategies for containing, reducing, or eliminating conflict. Gottman (1994) observed that expression of criticism and contempt, along with defensiveness and withdrawal, predicted long-term distress and risk for relationship dissolution. Christensen and Heavey (1990) found that distressed couples were more likely than nondistressed couples to demonstrate a demand → withdraw pattern in which one person seeks or asks for change and the partner withdraws, with respective approach and retreat behaviors progressively intensifying.

Given findings regarding the prominence of negativity, conflict, and ineffective decision-making strategies as correlates of relationship distress, couple assessment must address specific questions regarding relationship behaviors—especially communication behaviors. We list these below, along with sample assessment methods; in subsequent sections specifying interview, observational, and self-report strategies for assessing couple distress, we describe these and related methods in greater detail.

1. How frequent and intense are the couple's conflicts? How rapidly do initial disagreements escalate into major arguments? For how long do conflicts persist without resolution? Both interview and self-report measures may yield useful information regarding rates and intensity of negative exchanges as well as patterns of conflict engagement. Commonly used self-report measures specific to communication include the Communication Patterns Questionnaire (CPQ; Christensen, 1987) (see Table 24.3). Couples' conflict-resolution patterns may be observed directly by instructing partners to discuss problems of their own choosing representative of both moderate and high disagreement, and then either formally or informally coding these interactions using one of the behavioral coding systems described later in this chapter.

2. What are the common areas of conflict or distress? For example, interactions regarding finances, children, sexual intimacy, use of leisure time, or household tasks; involvement with others including extended family, friends, or coworkers; differences in preferences or core values? In addition to the clinical interview, numerous self-report measures sample sources of distress across a variety of relationship domains. Among those having evidence of both reliability and construct validity are the Frequency and Acceptability of Partner Behavior

Inventory (FAPBI; Doss & Christensen, 2006) and the Marital Satisfaction Inventory-Revised (MSI-R; Snyder, 1997)—both of which are described in greater detail later along with other self-report measures.

3. What resources and deficits do partners demonstrate in problem identification and conflict resolution strategies? Do they engage couple issues at adaptive levels (i.e., neither avoiding nor dwelling on relationship concerns)? Do partners balance their expression of feelings with decision-making strategies? Are problem resolution efforts hindered by inflexibility or imbalances in power? Do partners offer each other support when confronting stressors from within or outside their relationship? As noted by others (Bradbury, Rogge, & Lawrence, 2001; Cutrona, 1996), most of the interactional tasks developed for use in couple research have emphasized problem solving and conflict resolution to the exclusion of tasks designed to elicit more positive relationship behaviors such as emotional or strategic support. Hence, when designing interaction tasks for couples, both clinicians and researchers should include tasks specifically designed to sample potential positive as well as negative exchanges. For example, couples might be asked to discuss a time when one partner's feelings were hurt by someone outside the relationship (e.g., a friend or coworker), in order to assess behaviors expressing understanding and caring—although few templates with these foci have been developed and psychometrically evaluated (Mitchell et al., 2008).

RELATIONSHIP COGNITIONS

Social learning models of couple distress have expanded to emphasize the role of cognitive processes in moderating the impact of specific behaviors on relationship functioning (Baucom, Epstein, & LaTaillade, 2002). Research in this domain has focused on such factors as selective attention, attributions for positive and negative relationship events, and specific relationship assumptions, standards, and expectancies. For example, findings indicate that distressed couples often exhibit a bias toward selectively attending to negative partner behaviors and relationship events and ignoring or minimizing positive events (Sillars, Roberts, Leonard, & Dun, 2000). Compared to nondistressed couples, distressed partners also tend to blame each other for problems and to attribute each other's negative behaviors to broad and stable traits (Bradbury & Fincham, 1990). Distressed couples are also more likely to have unrealistic standards and assumptions about how relationships should work, and lower expectancies regarding their partner's willingness or ability to change their behavior in some desired manner (Epstein & Baucom, 2002). Based on these findings, assessment of relationship cognitions should emphasize the following questions:

1. Do partners demonstrate an ability to accurately observe and report both positive and negative relationship events? For example, partners' descriptions and interpretations of couple interactions observed directly in therapy can be compared to the clinician's own assessment of these same exchanges. Partners' response sets when completing self-report relationship measures can also be assessed; for example, the Conventionalization (CNV) scale on the MSI-R (Snyder, 1997) assesses the tendency to distort relationship appraisals in an overly positive direction.

2. What interpretation or meaning do partners impart to relationship events? Clinical interviews are particularly useful for eliciting partners' subjective interpretations of their own and each other's behaviors; such interpretations and attributions are also frequently expressed during conflict resolution or other interactional tasks. To what extent are partners' negative relationship behaviors attributed to stable, negative aspects of the partner versus to external or transient events? Self-report measures assessing relationship attributions include the Relationship Attribution Measure (RAM; Fincham & Bradbury, 1992).

3. What beliefs and expectancies do partners hold regarding both their own and the other person's ability and willingness to change in a manner anticipated to be helpful to their relationship? What standards do they hold for relationships generally?

RELATIONSHIP AFFECT

Similar to findings regarding behavior exchange, research indicates that distressed couples are distinguished from nondistressed couples by higher overall rates, duration, and reciprocity of negative relationship affect and, to a lesser extent, by lower rates of positive relationship affect. Nondistressed couples show "less reciprocity" of positive affect, reflecting partners' willingness or ability to express positive sentiments spontaneously independent of their partner's affect (Gottman, 1999). By contrast, partners' influence on each other's negative affect has been reported for both proximal and distal outcomes. For example, Pasch, Bradbury, and Davila (1997) found that partners' negative mood prior to discussion of a personal issue predicted lower levels of emotional

support they provided to the other during their exchange. From a longitudinal perspective, couples who divorce are distinguished from those who remain married by partners' premarital levels of negative affect and by the persistence of negative reciprocity over time (Cook et al., 1995). Gottman (1999) determined that the single best predictor of couples' eventual divorce was the amount of contempt partners expressed in videotaped interactions. Hence, assessment of couple distress should evaluate the following:

1. To what extent do partners express and reciprocate negative and positive feelings about their relationship and toward each other? Partners' reciprocity of affect is best evaluated using either structured or unstructured interactions and coded (either formally or informally) using one of the behavioral observation systems described later in this section. Although much of the couple literature emphasizes negative emotions, positive emotions such as smiling, laughter, expressions of appreciation or respect, comfort or soothing, and similar expressions are equally important to assess through observation or clinical inquiry.

2. What ability does each partner have to express his or her feelings in a modulated manner? Problems with emotion self-regulation may be observed either in overcontrol of emotions (e.g., an inability to access, label, or express either positive or negative feelings) or in undercontrol of emotions (e.g., the rapid escalation of anger into intense negativity approaching rage, progression of tearfulness into sobbing, or deterioration in quality of thought secondary to emotional overload) (cf. Snyder et al., 2006). Unregulated negativity culminating in either verbal or physical aggression can be assessed through self- or partner report using either the original or revised versions of the Conflict Tactics Scale (CTS/CTS2; Straus, 1979; Straus, Hamby, Boney-McCoy, & Sugarman, 1996).

3. To what extent does partners' negative affect generalize across occasions? Generalization of negative affect, or "negative sentiment override" (Weiss, 1980), can be observed in partners' inability to shift from negative to either neutral or positive affect during the interview or in interactional tasks, or in reports of distress across most or all domains of relationship functioning assessed using self-report. In research applications, ratings of affect by partners observing their videotaped interactions may provide an additional means of assessing sentiment override. For example, in a study of the effects of relationship

sentiment override on couples' perceptions, partners used an affect-rating dial to indicate how positively or negatively they felt during a previously videotaped interaction and how they thought their partner felt during the interaction (Hawkins, Carrère, & Gottman, 2002).

COMORBID INDIVIDUAL DISTRESS

As noted earlier when discussing comorbid conditions, there is growing evidence that relationship difficulties covary with, contribute to, and result from individual emotional and behavioral disorders (Snyder & Whisman, 2003). Both clinician reports and treatment outcome studies suggest that individual difficulties render couple therapy more difficult or less effective (Allgood & Crane, 1991; Northey, 2002; Sher, Baucom, & Larus, 1990; Snyder, Mangrum, & Wills, 1993; Whisman, Dixon, & Johnson, 1997). Hence, when evaluating couple distress, additional attention should be given to disorders of individual emotional or behavioral functioning to address the extent to which either partner exhibits individual emotional or behavioral difficulties, potentially contributing to, exacerbating, or resulting in part from couple distress. Given the association of couple distress with affective disorders and alcohol use, initial interviews of couples should include questions regarding depressive symptoms, suicidality, and alcohol or other substance use—as well as brief screening for previous treatment of emotional or behavioral disorders.

When clinical interview suggests potential interaction of relationship and individual dysfunction, focused and brief measures (e.g., the Beck Depression Inventory-II [BDI-II]; Beck, Steer, & Brown, 1996, or the Symptom Checklist-90-Revised [SCL-90-R]; Derogatis & Savitz, 1999) should be considered. It is equally important to assess couples' strengths and resources across intrapersonal, relationship, and broader social system levels. These include partners' ability to limit the impact of individual or couple dysfunction despite overwhelming stressors, or containing the generalization of distress to other family members.

Finally, establishing the direction and strength of causal relations among individual and relationship disorders, as well as their linkage to situational stressors or buffers, is crucial for determining both the content and sequencing of clinical interventions. This includes the linkage of marital conflict to child behavior problems (Gerard, Krishnakumar, & Buehler, 2006).

In many cases, such functional relations are reciprocal—supporting interventions at either end of the causal chain.

CULTURAL DIFFERENCES IN COUPLE DISTRESS

Consistent with our conceptual framework, cultural differences in the development, subjective experience, overt expression, and treatment of couple distress are critical to evaluate. By this we refer not only to cross-national differences in couples' relationships, but also to cross-cultural differences within nationality and consideration of nontraditional relationships including gay and lesbian couples. There are important differences among couples as a function of their culture, religious orientation, economic level, and age. These dimensions can affect the importance of the couple relationship to a partner's quality of life, their expectancies regarding marital and parenting roles, typical patterns of verbal and nonverbal communication and decision making within the family, the behaviors that are considered distressing, sources of relationship conflict, the type of external stressors faced by a family, and the ways that partners respond to couple distress and divorce (e.g., Diener, Gohm, Suh, & Oishi, 2000; Gohm, Oishi, Darlington, & Diener, 1998; Jones & Chao, 1997). For example, Haynes et al. (1992) found that parenting, extended family, and sex were less strongly related to marital satisfaction whereas health of the spouse and other forms of affection were more important factors in marital satisfaction in older (i.e., over 55 years) compared to younger couples. Similarly, Bhugra and De Silva (2000) suggested that relationships with extended family members might be more important in some cultures. Also, when partners are from different cultures, cultural differences and conflicts can be a source of relationship dissatisfaction (e.g., Baltas & Steptoe, 2000). An important implication of such findings is that measures shown to be valid for one population may be less so for another.

Assessment Methods and Specific Techniques for Evaluating Couple Distress

Assessment strategies for evaluating relationships vary across the clinical interview, observational methods, and self- and other-report measures. In the sections that follow, we discuss empirically supported techniques within each of these assessment methods. Although specific techniques within any method could target diverse facets of individual, dyadic, or broader system functioning, we emphasize those more commonly used when assessing couples.

THE COUPLE ASSESSMENT INTERVIEW

After a couple has been identified as a candidate for treatment, the next step in the assessment-treatment process is a clinical assessment interview with the couple. This initial interview is usually conducted with both partners together and has multiple goals (see Birchler & Fals-Stewart, 2006, for an example of a couple interview, and Sayers & Tomcho, 2006, for a discussion of behavioral interviewing). First, the clinical interview is an important method for identifying a couple's concerns, areas of distress and satisfaction, behavior problems, and strengths. Second, it is an important source of information about the couple's commitment, motivation for treatment, and treatment goals. Third, the assessment interview should be conducted in a manner that strengthens the client–clinician relationship. Fourth, it helps the clinician identify potential barriers to subsequent assessment and treatment and the strategies that might be useful for managing or overcoming those barriers. Fifth, it is the main source of historical data on the couple's marriage and previous therapies. Finally, it is essential for gaining a couple's informed consent about, and cooperation with, the assessment-treatment process.

The initial couple assessment interview also helps the clinician select additional assessment strategies. For example, Gordis, Margolin, and John (2001) used a couple assessment interview to select topics for discussion during an analog behavioral observation of couple communication patterns. Data from the couple assessment interview also lead to initial hypotheses about ways in which the couple's behaviors, emotions, cognitions, and external stressors contribute to their distress. These hypotheses contribute to the eventual case formulation that, in turn, affects decisions about the best treatment strategy for a particular couple (see Haynes & Williams, 2003, and Haynes, Yoshioka, Kloezeman, & Bello, 2008, for examples of how a couple assessment interview guides subsequent assessment strategies and case formulation).

Assessment interviews continue throughout the couple assessment-treatment process. Subsequent interviews help the clinician refine the case formulation, identify new barriers and challenges to treatment, clarify treatment goals, and evaluate treatment outcome and process.

The interview is perhaps the most versatile couple assessment method because it can provide information across multiple domains and response modes. For example, it can provide information on the specific behavioral interactions of the couple such as positive and negative behavioral exchanges, problem-solving skills, sources of disagreement, expectations, automatic negative thoughts, beliefs and attitudes about the partner and relationship, and related emotions. The couple assessment interview can also provide information on broader family system or cultural factors that might affect the couple's functioning, treatment goals, and response to interventions. Examples of such areas of concern include problems with in-laws and extended family members, difficulties with the couple's children, economic strains, and poor health. The initial assessment interview can also provide information on potentially important causal variables for couple distress at an individual level, such as a partner's substance use, mood disorder, or problematic behavior traits.

The couple assessment interview should be sensitive to sources of individual differences. Many studies have indicated that clients' behavior problems, social interactions, beliefs, goals, and external stressors can differ as a function of their ethnicity, age, education, religiosity, sexual orientation, intellectual abilities, and other sources of individual differences (see overviews of cross-cultural assessment and assessment with ethnic minorities in Tanaka-Matsumi, 2004, and assessment with older adults in Edelstein, Woodhead, Bower, & Lowery, 2006).

The couple assessment interview is also one of the most useful methods of hypothesizing about the "functional relations" that account for a couple's relationship difficulties. That is, information from the interview can help "explain" a couple's distress. The functional relations of greatest interest in couple assessment are those that are strongly related to a couple's problem behaviors and feelings and those that might be relevant for relationship enhancement. Identifying functional relations allows the assessor to hypothesize about "why" a partner is unhappy or what behavioral sequences lead to angry exchanges. Clinicians are interested, for example, in finding out what triggers a couple's arguments, which communication patterns lead to their escalation, why positive relationship events are often overlooked by a couple, and how behaviors, cognitions, and emotions are affected by outside stressors. What does one partner do, or not do, that leads the other partner to feel unappreciated or angry or to withdraw from the relationship? The case studies noted earlier (Haynes et al., 2008; Haynes & Williams, 2003) illustrate a focus on identifying important functional relations for distressed couples.

Several formats for the couple assessment interview have been proposed. In the previous section on screening and diagnosis, we identified brief structured interviews for identifying overall relationship distress and partner aggression. Various formats for organizing and conducting more extensive assessment interviews with couples have been proposed (cf., Birchler & Fals-Stewart, 2006; Epstein & Baucom, 2002; Gottman, 1999; Halford, 2001; Karpel, 1994; L'Abate, 1994; Snyder & Abbott, 2002). For example, Snyder and Abbott (2002) recommended an extended initial conjoint assessment interview lasting about 2 hr; Karpel (1994) suggested an initial meeting with the couple together, followed by individual sessions with each partner, followed by another meeting with the couple together; Gottman (1999) conducted a brief conjoint interview followed by separate interviews with each partner; Birchler, Magana, and Fals-Stewart (2003) and Birchler and Fals-Stewart (2006) recommended two conjoint interviews and questionnaire assessment followed by separate interviews with each partner focusing on personal history and the partner's views of the relationship.

Recommended foci of the initial couple assessment interviews vary across clinicians but have common elements. For example, Snyder and Abbott (2002) outlined several broad targets and goals of the interview: (a) the structure and organization of the marriage; (b) current relationship difficulties and their development; (c) previous efforts to address relationship difficulties; (d) the personality and characteristics of each partner; (e) deciding whether or not to proceed with couple therapy; and (f) expectations about the therapy process.

Other foci frequently included in couple assessment interviews include (a) cultural/ethnic contexts of the relationship (expected roles for each partner, and the role of the extended family); (b) external stressors faced by the couple (e.g., economic stressors or health-related concerns); (c) the couple's communication and problem-solving skills; (d) each partner's level of distress and commitment to continuing the relationship; (e) areas of disagreement and agreement; (f) positive aspects and strengths of the relationship; (g) social supports available to each partner and the couple; (h) each partner's behavioral traits that may contribute to couple distress; (i) each partner's goals and expectations regarding the relationship; and (j) violence in the relationship.

There is considerable discussion (and some disagreement) in the clinical literature regarding the benefits and potential risks of conducting interviews with partners separately. Some studies (Haynes, Jensen, Wise, & Sherman, 1981; Whisman & Snyder, 2007) have found that the convergent validity of self-reports about "sensitive" issues such as sex, infidelity, and violence is higher from individual interview or alternative individual-response formats than conjoint interviews. Also, a client may not disclose violence in an initial couple assessment interview because of embarrassment, minimization, or fear of retribution (Ehrensaft & Vivian, 1996; see Rathus & Feindler, 2004, for a discussion of the assessment of partner violence).

Although separate interviews with partners can result in more valid data on sensitive issues and are included in many couple assessment protocols, they have several drawbacks. First, how is sensitive information disclosed to the therapist in separate interviews handled during joint interviews? What if one partner discloses information (e.g., about infidelity, violence) to the therapist that has not been disclosed to the other partner or reported in joint sessions? Most clinicians (e.g., Birchler & Fals-Stewart, 2006; Snyder & Abbott, 2002; Snyder & Doss, 2005) recommend explicit discussion with the couple about the conditions under which information disclosed by one partner in a separate interview will be shared with the other partner.

A major drawback to couple assessment interviews is that none of the comprehensive formats has undergone rigorous psychometric evaluation. All have face validity but little empirical evidence regarding their test–retest reliability, internal consistency, inter-rater agreement, content validity, concurrent and predictive convergent and discriminant validity, sources of error, and generalizability across sources of individual differences such as ethnicity and age.

OBSERVATIONAL METHODS

As noted previously in this chapter, couple assessment offers the unique opportunity to observe partners' complaints involving communication and other interpersonal exchanges directly. Like interviews and self-report methods, analog behavioral observation (ABO) describes a method of data collection; specifically, it involves a situation designed by, manipulated by, or constrained by a clinician that elicits both verbal and nonverbal behaviors of interest such as motor actions, verbalized attributions, and observable facial reactions (Heyman &

Slep, 2004, p. 162). We earlier identified both the RMICS and RCISS as rapid observational methods particularly useful for initial screening and diagnosis of couple distress. Detailed descriptions and psychometric reviews of additional couple coding systems have been published previously (cf., Heyman, 2001; Kerig & Baucom, 2004). Although these systems vary widely, in general they target six major a priori classes of targeted behaviors:

1. *Affect* (e.g., humor, affection, anger, criticism, contempt, sadness, anxiety). Examples include the Behavioral Affective Rating System (BARS; Johnson, 2002) and the Specific Affect Coding System (SPAFF; Gottman, McCoy, Coan, & Collier, 1996; Shapiro & Gottman, 2004).

2. *Behavioral engagement* (e.g., demands, pressures for change, withdrawal, avoidance). An example is the Conflict Rating System (CRS; Heavey, Christensen, & Malamuth, 1995).

3. *General communication skills* (e.g., involvement, verbal and nonverbal negativity and positivity, information and problem description). Examples include the Clinician Rating of Adult Communication (CRAC; Basco, Birchler, Kalal, Talbott, & Slater, 1991), the Interactional Dimensions Coding System (IDCS; Kline et al., 2004), and the *Kategoriensystem für Partnerschaftliche Interaktion* (Partner Interaction Coding System; KPI; Hahlweg, 2004).

4. *Problem solving* (e.g., self-disclosure, validation, facilitation, interruption). Examples include the Codebook of Marital and Family Interaction (COMFI; Notarius, Pellegrini, & Martin, 1991), the Communication Skills Test (CST; Floyd, 2004), the Dyadic Interaction Scoring Code (DISC; Filsinger, 1983), the Living in Family Environments (LIFE) coding system (Hops, Davis, & Longoria, 1995), and the Verbal Tactics Coding Scheme (VTCS; Sillars, 1982).

5. *Power* (e.g., verbal aggression, coercion, attempts to control). An example is the System for Coding Interactions in Dyads (SCID; Malik & Lindahl, 2004).

6. *Support/intimacy* (e.g., emotional and tangible support, attentiveness). An example is the Social Support Interaction Coding System (SSICS; Pasch, Harris, Sullivan, & Bradbury, 2004).

Psychometric characteristics for the 15 couple coding systems summarized in Table 24.3 demonstrate considerable variability in the extent to which information regarding reliability, validity, and treatment sensitivity for each system has been accrued. For example, only 3 of 15 coding systems report data concerning internal consistency—although this likely reflects many coding systems' emphasis on specific behaviors rather than considering behavior codes as markers of broader constructs. When superordinate classes of behavior (e.g., positive or negative) are of interest, internal consistency should be evaluated by using either Cronbach's alpha or indices derived from factor analysis (Heyman, Eddy, Weiss, & Vivian, 1995). Stable estimates of behavioral frequencies may require extended observation depending on the base-rate of their occurrence—as few as 2 min for frequent behaviors, but 30 min or longer for infrequent behaviors (Heyman et al., 2001). Inter-rater reliability for nearly all coding systems reviewed here was adequate or better following coder training—although the more comprehensive or complicated the system, the more difficult it is to obtain high inter-rater reliability. Few studies have been conducted on the temporal stability of observed couple behaviors across tasks or settings. However, the limited evidence suggests that couples' interactions likely vary across topic (e.g., high vs. low conflict), setting (e.g., home vs. clinic or research laboratory), and length of marriage (with longer married couples exhibiting more enduring patterns; Gottman & Levenson, 1999; Lord, 1999; Wieder & Weiss, 1980).

Although varying in their emphasis, each of the couple coding systems reviewed here clearly assesses constructs related to communication and other domains of partner interaction relevant to relationship functioning and couple distress. Many of the coding systems can trace their origins to the Family Interaction Coding System (Patterson, Ray, Shaw, & Cobb, 1969; Reid, 1978) that was developed from naturalistic observations of family members' behaviors in the home. Nearly all coding systems have accrued evidence of discriminative and convergent validity, and only the most recently developed systems have yet to accrue evidence of validity generalization across groups varying in sociodemographic characteristics or assessment setting. Pre- and posttreatment data for couple behavioral coding systems are limited, in part because of fewer funded clinical trials of couple therapy during recent years in which these systems were developed. However, the Marital Interaction Coding System (MICS) and Couples Interaction Scoring System (CISS) have evidence of treatment sensitivity; it is reasonable to infer that their quicker versions

(RMICS and RCISS) and coding systems that measure similar constructs (i.e., most of the communication-oriented systems) would demonstrate similar levels of treatment sensitivity.

Concerns have been raised about the clinical utility of analog behavioral observations (e.g., Mash & Foster, 2001), because nearly all coding systems require extensive observer training to reach adequate levels of inter-observer agreement. Even after observers are certified as reliable, a great deal of energy is required to maintain reliability (e.g., weekly meetings with regular feedback on agreement). Thus, even if clinicians expended a great deal of time learning a system to the point of mastery (i.e., meeting the reliability criterion), their reliability would naturally decay without ongoing efforts to maintain agreement. Such a requirement is likely not reasonable for most clinicians.

However, even if not striving to code behavioral observations in the manner required for scientific study of couple interactions, the empirically informed use of behavioral observations should be standard in clinicians' assessment of couple distress. That is, collecting communication samples is an important part of couple clinical assessment because "communication is the common pathway to relationship dysfunction because it is the common pathway for getting what you want in relationships. Nearly all relationship-relevant conflicts, emotions, and neuroses are played out via observable communication—either verbally or nonverbally" (Heyman, 2001, p. 6).

If questionnaires or interview assessments suggest that an interactive task may place one or both partners in danger (e.g., if there is a history of serious physical or emotional abuse, indications of severe power or control dynamics, or threats conveyed to the assessor), analog behavioral observation would be contraindicated (Aldarondo & Straus, 1994). However, if it seems reasonable that it is safe to proceed, then the clinician should hypothesize which classes of behaviors seem most highly connected to the target problems. Wherever possible, analog behavioral observations should be video-recorded so that the sample can be reviewed later with an eye toward a class of behaviors other than what was the assessor's primary focus during the in vivo ABO. Furthermore, unless the clinician can rule out a plausible connection between conflict communication and the couple's problems, we recommend that a conflict communication ABO be collected. This is done by choosing at least two topics of interest (at least one topic for which partner A desires

change and at least one for partner B), asking the couple to discuss the selected topic for 5–10 minutes while the assessor watches silently, and then switching to a new topic and discussing that one. Based on findings from observational research with couples, Heyman (2001) suggested that clinicians use behavioral observations in assessing couple distress to address the following:

1. How does the conversation start? Does the level of anger escalate? What happens when it does? Does the couple enter repetitive negative loops?

2. Do partners indicate afterward that what occurred during the conversations is typical? Is their behavior stable across two or more discussions?

3. Do partners' behaviors differ when it is her topic versus his? Do they label the other person or the communication process as the problem?

4. What other communication behaviors—either positive (e.g., support, empathic reflection) or negative (e.g., criticism, sneers, turning away)—appear functionally related to partners' ability to discuss relationship issues effectively?

SELF- AND OTHER-REPORT METHODS

The rationale underlying self-report methods in couple assessment is that such methods (a) are convenient and relatively easy to administer, (b) are capable of generating a wealth of information across a broad range of domains and levels of functioning germane to clinical assessment or research objectives including those listed in Table 24.2, (c) lend themselves to collection of data from large normative samples which can serve as a reference for interpreting data from individual respondents, (d) allow disclosure about events and subjective experiences respondents may be reluctant to discuss with an interviewer or in the presence of their partner, and (e) can provide important data concerning internal phenomena opaque to observational approaches including thoughts and feelings, values and attitudes, expectations and attributions, and satisfaction and commitment.

However, the limitations of traditional self-report measures also bear noting. Specifically, data from self-report instruments can (a) reflect bias (or "sentiment override") in self- and other-presentation in either a favorable or unfavorable direction; (b) be affected by differences in stimulus interpretation and errors in recollection of objective events, (c) inadvertently influence respondents' nontest behavior in unintended ways (e.g., by sensitizing respondents and increasing their reactivity to specific issues), and (d) typically provide few fine-grained details concerning moment-to-moment interactions compared to analog behavioral observations. Because of their potential advantages and despite their limitations, self-report techniques of couple and family functioning have proliferated, with published measures numbering well over 1,000 (Touliatos, Perlmutter, Straus, & Holden, 2001). However, relatively few of these measures have achieved widespread adoption. Chun, Cobb, and French (1975) found that 63% of measures they reviewed had been used only once, with only 3% being used 10 times or more. Fewer than 40% of couple and family therapists regularly use *any* standardized instruments (Boughner, Hayes, Bubenzer, & West, 1994). Contributing to these findings is the inescapable conclusion that the majority of measures in this domain demonstrate little evidence regarding the most rudimentary psychometric features of reliability or validity, let alone clear evidence supporting their clinical utility (Snyder & Rice, 1996).

We describe below, and summarize in Table 24.3, a small subset of self-report instruments selected on the basis of their potential clinical utility and at least moderate evidence of their reliability and validity. In some domains (e.g., relationship cognitions and affect), well-validated measures are few. Additional measures identified in previous reviews (cf., Epstein & Baucom, 2002; Sayers & Sarwer, 1998; Snyder, Heyman, & Haynes, 2005) or in comprehensive bibliographies of self-report couple and family measures (e.g., Corcoran & Fischer, 2000; Davis, Yarber, Bauserman, Schreer, & Davis, 1998; Fredman & Sherman, 1987; Grotevant & Carlson, 1989; Jacob & Tennenbaum, 1988; L'Abate & Bagarozzi, 1993; Touliatos et al., 2001) may be considered as additional clinical resources; however, the data they generate should generally be regarded as similar to other self-reports derived from interview—namely, as subject to various biases of observation, recollection, interpretation, and motivations to present oneself or one's partner in a favorable or unfavorable light.

A variety of self-report measures have been developed to assess couples' behavioral exchanges including communication, verbal and physical aggression, and physical intimacy. The FAPBI (Doss & Christensen, 2006) assesses 20 positive and negative behaviors in four domains (affection, closeness, demands, and relationship violations) and possesses excellent psychometric characteristics. As a clinical tool, the FAPBI has the potential to delineate relative strengths and weaknesses in the relationship, transforming diffuse negative complaints into specific requests for positive change.

Among self-report measures specifically targeting partners' communication, one that demonstrates good reliability and validity is the CPQ (Christensen, 1987). The CPQ was designed to measure the temporal sequence of couples' interactions by soliciting partners' perceptions of their communication patterns before, during, and following conflict. Scores on the CPQ can be used to assess characteristics of the demand → withdraw pattern frequently observed among distressed couples.

Assessing relationship aggression by self-report measures assumes particular importance because of some individuals' reluctance to disclose the nature or extent of such aggression during an initial conjoint interview. By far the most widely used measure of couples' aggression is the CTS. The original CTS (Straus, 1979) included 19 items assessing three modes of conflict resolution including reasoning, verbal aggression, and physical aggression. The revised instrument (CTS2; Straus, Hamby, Boney-McCoy, & Sugarman, 1996) randomly ordered the items (which appears to have increased rates of reported aggression), adds scales of sexual coercion and physical injury as well as additional items to better differentiate between minor and severe levels of verbal and physical aggression. An additional measure of relationship aggression, the Aggression (AGG) scale of the Marital Satisfaction Inventory-Revised (MSI-R; Snyder, 1997), comprises 10 items reflecting psychological and physical aggression experienced from one's partner. Advantages of the AGG scale as a screening measure include its relative brevity and its inclusion in a multidimensional measure of couples' relationships (the MSI-R) described below.

Earlier we noted the importance of evaluating partners' attributions for relationship events. The Relationship Attribution Measure (RAM; Fincham & Bradbury, 1992) presents hypothetical situations and asks respondents to generate responsibility attributions indicating the extent to which the partner intentionally behaved negatively, was selfishly motivated, and was blameworthy for the event. Both causal and responsibility attributions assessed by the RAM have evidence of good internal consistency and test–retest reliability, as well as convergence with partners' self-reported overall relationship satisfaction and observed affect.

For purposes of case conceptualization and treatment planning, well-constructed multidimensional measures of couple functioning are useful for discriminating among various sources of relationship strength, conflict, satisfaction, and goals. Widely used in both clinical and research settings is the Marital Satisfaction Inventory-Revised (MSI-R; Snyder, 1997), a 150-item inventory designed to identify both the nature and intensity of relationship distress in distinct areas of interaction. The MSI-R includes two validity scales, one global scale, and 10 specific scales assessing relationship satisfaction in such areas as affective and problem-solving communication, aggression, leisure time together, finances, the sexual relationship, role orientation, family of origin, and interactions regarding children. Two broad-band factor scales assessing disharmony and disaffection have recently been developed as well (Herrington et al., 2008). More than 20 years of research have supported the reliability and construct validity of the MSI-R scales (cf., Snyder & Aikman, 1999). The instrument boasts a large representative national sample, good internal consistency and test–retest reliability, and excellent sensitivity to treatment change. The Global Distress (GDS) subscale of the MSI-R has been shown to predict couples' likelihood of divorce 4 years following therapy (Snyder, 1997). A validation study using a national sample of 60 marital therapists supported the overall accuracy and clinical utility of the computerized interpretive report for this instrument (Hoover & Snyder, 1991). Recent studies suggest the potential utility of Spanish and German adaptations of the MSI-R for cross-cultural application with both clinic and community couples (Snyder et al., 2004), as well as use of the original English version with non-traditional (e.g., gay and lesbian) couples (Means-Christensen, Snyder, & Negy, 2003).

Additional multidimensional measures obtaining fairly widespread use include the PREPARE and ENRICH inventories (Fowers & Olson, 1989, 1992; Olson & Olson, 1999), developed for use with premarital and married couples, respectively. Both of these measures include 165 items in 20 domains reflecting personality (e.g., assertiveness, self-confidence), intrapersonal issues (e.g., marriage expectations, spiritual beliefs), interpersonal issues (e.g., communication, closeness), and external issues (e.g., family and friends). A computerized interpretive report identifies areas of "strength" and "potential growth" and directs respondents to specific items reflecting potential concerns. The ENRICH inventory has a good normative sample and has ample evidence supporting both its reliability and validity. Two other somewhat similar measures, FOCCUS (156 items; Markey,

Micheletto, & Becker, 1997) and RELATE (271 items; Busby, Holman, & Taniguchi, 2001), have established validity (content, construct, concurrent, and predictive), and good test–retest reliability and internal consistency (Larson, Newell, Topham, & Nichols, 2002).

Overall Evaluation

Couples presenting for therapy vary widely in both the content and underlying causes of their individual and relationship problems. Conceptualizing partners' distress and planning effective treatment requires careful assessment of behavioral, cognitive, and affective components of relationship functioning conducted across multiple modalities including interview, analog behavioral observation, and self-report measures. Effective intervention depends upon assimilating assessment findings within an overarching theoretical framework linking individual and relationship difficulties to presumed etiologies as well as to clinical intervention. Toward this end, assessment of couple distress requires going beyond nomothetic conclusions derived from standardized measures of relationship functioning to integrate idiographic findings from clinical interview and behavioral observation in a functional analytic approach (Floyd et al., 1997; Haynes et al., 1997).

Assessment for Treatment Monitoring and Treatment Outcome

In principle, assessment strategies relevant to case conceptualization and treatment planning are also germane to monitoring treatment progress and evaluating outcome. It would be difficult to imagine adequate assessment of partners' changes in individual and relationship functioning that do not include clinical inquiry about alterations in behavioral, cognitive, and affective domains outside of treatment sessions; repeated analog behavioral observations to track the acquisition and use of targeted communication skills; and integration of self-report measures profiling changes across diverse domains and providing information in sensitive areas.

Several caveats moderate this general conclusion. First, the use of repeated assessments to evaluate changes attributable to treatment requires measures demonstrating temporal reliability in the absence of clinical intervention (presuming the phenomena being evaluated are otherwise stable across time). Although obvious as a precondition for interpreting change, information regarding the temporal reliability of couple-based assessment techniques is remarkably sparse. Second, treatment effects are best assessed by using measures both relevant and specific to aspects of individual and relationship functioning targeted by clinical interventions. Finally, treatment monitoring across sessions imposes pragmatic constraints on measures' length, thus suggesting enhanced utility for reliable and valid measures distinguished by their brevity (e.g., the KMSS as a measure of global affect or the FAPBI to assess more specific dyadic behaviors).

Changes in individualized treatment goals can be quantified using "goal attainment scaling" (GAS; Kiresuk, Smith, & Cardillo, 1994) as described previously for use in couple therapy by Whisman and Snyder (1997). When adopting the GAS method, the issues that will be the focus of treatment are first identified, and then each problem is translated into one or more goals. The expected level of outcome is then specified for each goal, along with the "somewhat more" and "much more" than expected levels of outcome, as well as the "somewhat less" and "much less" expected levels. Each level of outcome is assigned a value on a 5-point measurement scale ranging from −2 for much less than expected level of outcome, to +2 for much more than expected level of outcome. Levels of outcome can then be rated during or following treatment, and the ratings across goals can be averaged to provide a summary score for evaluating the degree to which treatment helped the couple attain their own individualized goals.

Overall Evaluation

Gains or deterioration in individual and relationship functioning should be evaluated using techniques sensitive and specific to treatment effects across assessment modalities incorporating interview, behavioral observation, and self-report methods. Conclusions drawn from nomothetic approaches (such as the DAS or MSI-R) should be complemented by idiographic methods, ideally incorporating observational assessment as well as goal attainment scaling or similar procedures.

Emerging Assessment Technologies

Most of what we know about how distressed couples interact in their daily lives comes from interview, questionnaire, and observational data collected in clinics or laboratories (see reviews by Birchler & Fals-Stewart, 2006; Floyd et al., 1997; Snyder, Heyman, & Haynes, 2005). These assessment methods have provided important insights about some of the negative and positive behavioral exchanges as well as the attendant thoughts and emotions that are associated with couple distress (e.g. Gottman & Notarius, 2000). However, left unanswered is the degree to which these data reflect the behavior, thoughts, and emotions of couples in their daily lives. Although data have been derived from real-time daily interactions or retrospective daily recordings by couples (e.g., Halford, Gravestock, Lowe, & Scheldt, 1992), as well as from observations by external observers in the home (e.g., Margolin, Burman, & John, 1989), data from self-monitoring and natural-setting observations can be affected by bias, memory deficits, problems of adherence (e.g., to schedules of real-time self-monitoring), and reactive effects of the assessment process. Moreover, such daily interaction data can be quite expensive to obtain (see overviews of behavioral observation in Hartmann, Barrios, & Wood, 2004, and of self-monitoring in Sigmon & LaMattina, 2006).

One promising method of obtaining data regarding couples in their daily lives, and that addresses some of these drawbacks, is self-monitoring through electronic diaries (EDs)—the use of palm-top computers to collect real-time data on couple behavior, emotions, thoughts, and the contexts in which they occur in the natural environment (see a review of EDs by Piasecki, Hufford, Solhan, & Trull, 2007). With EDs, originally pioneered as "ecological momentary sampling" by Shiffman and colleagues (e.g., Shiffman et al., 1997), a hand-held computer prompts the respondent at random or preset times to enter data about the multimodal aspects of dependent variables of interest (e.g., couple conflict or positive exchanges), along with contextual information such as the social setting, antecedent exchanges, and environmental stressors. The assessor later downloads stored data for real-time tabular or graphic presentation and to examine functional relations among events.

In an example of the application of EDs to assess couple interaction, Janicki, Kamarck, Shiffman, and Gwaltney (2006) examined the degree to which spousal conflict and positive interactions, reported by 245 older couples (averaging 61 years old) using EDs, were related to their level of marital satisfaction. Each partner monitored interactions with their spouse (and others) for 2 days. The data on positive and negative interactions were significantly correlated, in expected directions, with ambulatory cardiovascular measures (see a review of ambulatory biomeasures in Haynes & Yoshioka, 2007) and with questionnaire measures of marital adjustment.

Although EDs have multiple sources of potential error (see reviews by Piasecki et al., 2007; Sigmon & LaMattina, 2006), the use of EDs to monitor couple interactions is promising in several respects: (a) it reduces the error associated with retrospective reports; (b) it reduces the likelihood of missing data through nonadherence with the assessment protocol; (c) it allows for measuring the rate of, and functional relations among, multiple variables; (d) sampling rates and times can be individually programmed; and (e) it is less costly than using external observers. Alternatively, interactive voice response systems can be relatively inexpensive and easy to implement; moreover, these have many of the same advantages of EDs but use a simpler and ubiquitous technology (i.e., telephones) (e.g., Tucker, Foushee, Black, & Roth, 2007).

Conclusions and Future Directions
Recommendations for Assessing Couple Distress

Assessment strategies and specific methods for assessing couple distress will necessarily be tailored to partners' unique constellation of presenting difficulties, as well as specific resources of both the couple and the clinician. However, regardless of the specific context, the following recommendations for assessing couple distress will generally apply.

1. Given empirical findings linking couple distress to individual disorders and their respective impact in moderating treatment outcome, assessment of couple functioning should be standard practice when treating individuals. Screening for couple distress when assessing individuals may involve a brief interview format shown to relate to relevant indicators of couple interactions or a brief self-report measure exhibiting prior evidence of discriminative validity. Similarly, when treating couples, partners should be screened for individual emotional or behavioral difficulties potentially contributing to, exacerbating, or resulting in part from couple distress.

2. Assessment foci should progress from broad to narrow—first identifying relationship concerns at the broader construct level and then examining more specific facets of couple distress and its correlates using a finer-grained analysis. The specific assessment methods described in this review vary considerably in their overall breadth or focus within any specific construct domain and, hence, will vary both in their applicability across couples and their placement in a sequential exploratory assessment process. Consistent with this guideline,

assessment should begin with nomothetic approaches but then progress to idiographic methods facilitating functional analysis of factors related to target concerns.

3. Within clinical settings, certain domains (communication, aggression, substance use, affective disorders, emotional or physical involvement with an outside person) should always be assessed with every couple either because of their robust linkage to relationship difficulties (e.g., communication processes involving emotional expressiveness and decision making) or because the specific behaviors, if present, have particularly adverse impact on couple functioning (e.g., physical aggression or substance abuse).

4. Couple assessment should integrate findings across multiple assessment methods. Self- and other-report measures may complement findings from interview or behavioral observation in generating data across diverse domains both central or conceptually related to the couple's difficulties, or across those domains potentially more challenging to assess because of their sensitive nature or their not being amenable to direct observation. However, special caution should be exercised when adopting self- or other-report measures in assessing couple distress. Despite their proliferation, most measures of couple functioning described in the literature have not undergone careful scrutiny of their underlying psychometric features. Among those instruments for which some evidence concerning reliability and validity has been garnered, evidence often exists only for overall scores and not at the level of subscales or smaller units of analysis at which interpretations may be made.

5. At the same time, assessment of couple distress should be parsimonious. This objective can be facilitated by choosing evaluation strategies and modalities that complement each other and by following a sequential approach that uses increasingly narrow-band measures to target problem areas that have been identified by other assessment techniques.

6. Psychometric characteristics of any assessment technique—whether from interview, analogue behavioral observation, or self-report measure—are conditional upon the specific population and purpose for which that assessment method was developed. Given that nearly all measures of couple distress were developed and tested on White, middle-class, married couples, their relevance to and utility for assessing ethnic couples, gay and lesbian couples, and low-income couples is unknown. This caveat extends to content- as well as criterion-related

validity. Hence, any assessment measure demonstrating evidence of validity with some couples may not be valid, in part or in whole, for any given couple, thus further underscoring the importance of drawing upon multiple indicators across multiple methods for assessing any specific construct.

7. Assessment related to treatment should be ongoing—not only to evaluate change, but also to incorporate emerging data regarding hypothesized linkages between target concerns and potential antecedents and consequences.

Recommendations for Further Research

Future directions for assessment research germane to the field generally also apply to research in assessing couple distress specifically, including the need for greater attention to (a) psychometric underpinnings of various measurement methods and instruments, (b) factors moderating reliability and validity across populations differing in sociocultural characteristics as well as in clinical functioning, (c) the assessment process including initial articulation of assessment goals, selection of assessment method and instruments, and methods of interpreting data and providing feedback, and (d) the functional utility of assessment findings in enhancing treatment effectiveness (Hayes, Nelson, & Jarrett, 1987).

In considering the implications of these directives for assessing couple distress, considerably more research is needed before a comprehensive, empirically based couple assessment protocol can be advocated. For example, despite the ubiquitous use of couple assessment interviews, virtually no research has been conducted to assess their psychometric features. Observational methods, although a rich resource for generating and testing clinical hypotheses, are less frequently used and present significant challenges to their reliable and valid application in everyday practice. Questionnaires—despite their ease of administration and potential utility in generating a wealth of data—frequently suffer from inadequate empirical development and, at best, constitute only part of a multimethod assessment strategy.

We would recommend, as a research roadmap, that clinical researchers consider adapting the Institute of Medicine stages of intervention research cycle (Mrazek & Haggerty, 1994). Stage 1 involves identifying the disorder and measuring its prevalence. Despite being so basic a need, there currently exists no gold standard for discriminating distressed from nondistressed couples; the questionnaires typically used for such classifications are of limited

sensitivity and specificity (Heyman et al., 2001). Stage 2 involves delineating specific risk and protective factors. As noted above, some replicated factors have been identified, although this research could be sharpened by defining groups more carefully (via Stage 1 above). Stage 3 (efficacy trials) would involve tightly controlled trials of the efficacy of a multimethod assessment in clinical practice. Stage 4 (effectiveness trials) would involve controlled trials of the outcome of this assessment in more real-world clinical environments. Only then would testing broad-scale dissemination (Stage 5) of empirically based couple assessment be appropriate.

This research roadmap reflects an ambitious agenda unlikely to be met by any single investigator or group of investigators. However, progress toward evidence-based assessment of couple distress will be enhanced by research on specific components targeting more notable gaps in the empirical literature along the lines recommended below.

1. Greater attention should be given to expanding the empirical support for promising assessment instruments already detailed in the literature than to the initial (and frequently truncated) development of new measures. Proposals for new measures should be accompanied by compelling evidence for their incremental utility and validity and a commitment to programmatic research examining their generalizability across diverse populations and assessment contexts.

2. Research needs to delineate optimal structured and semi-structured interview formats for assessing couples. Such research should address (a) issues of content validity across populations and settings; (b) organizational strategies for screening across diverse system levels and construct domains relevant to couple functioning (similar to branching strategies for the Structured Clinical Interview for the DSM [First, Gibbon, Spitzer, & Williams, 1997] and related structured interviews for individual disorders); (c) relative strengths and limitations to assessing partners separately versus conjointly; (d) factors promoting the disclosure and accuracy of verbal reports; (e) relation of interview findings to complementary assessment methods (as in generating relevant tasks for analog behavioral observation); and (f) the interview's special role in deriving functional analytic case conceptualization.

3. Although laboratory-based behavioral observation of couple interaction has considerably advanced our understanding of couple distress, generalization of these techniques to more common

clinical settings has lagged behind. Hence, researchers should develop more macro-level coding systems for quantifying observational data that promote their routine adoption in clinical contexts while preserving their psychometric fidelity.

4. Research needs to attend to the influences of culture at several levels. First, there has been little attention to developing measures directly assessing domains specific to relationship functioning at the community or cultural level (e.g., cultural standards or norms regarding emotional expressiveness, balance of decision-making influence, or boundaries governing the interaction of partners with extended family or others in the community). Hence, assessment of such constructs currently depends almost exclusively on the clinical interview, with no clear guidelines regarding either the content or format of questions. Second, considerably more research needs to examine the moderating effects of sociocultural factors on measures of couple functioning, including the impact of such factors as ethnicity, age, socioeconomic status, or sexual orientation. Third, work needs to proceed on adapting established measures to alternative languages. In the United States, the failure to adapt existing instruments to Spanish or to examine the psychometric characteristics of extant adaptations is particularly striking given that (a) Hispanics are the largest and fastest-growing ethnic minority group, and (b) among U.S. Hispanic adults age 18–64, 28% have either limited or no ability to speak English (Snyder et al., 2004).

Adapting existing measures to alternative contexts (i.e., differing from the original development sample in language, culture, or specific aspects of the relationship such as sexual orientation) should proceed only when theoretical or clinical formulations suggest that the construct being measured does not differ substantially across the new application. Detailed discussions of both conceptual and methodological issues relevant to adapting tests to alternative languages or culture exist elsewhere (Butcher, 1996; Geisinger, 1994). Because clinicians and researchers may fail to recognize the inherent cultural biases of their conceptualization of couple processes, the appropriateness of using or adapting tests cross-culturally should be evaluated following careful empirical scrutiny examining each of the following:

- Linguistic equivalence including grammatical, lexical, and idiomatic considerations.
- Psychological equivalence of items across the source and target cultures.

- Functional equivalence indicating the congruence of external correlates in concurrent and predictive criterion-related validation studies of the measure across applications.
- Scalar equivalence ensuring not only that the slope of regression lines delineating test-criterion relations be parallel (indicating functional equivalence) but also that they have comparable metrics and origins (zero points) in both cultures.

5. Finally, research needs to examine the process, as well as the content, of couple assessment. For example, little is known regarding the impact of decisions about the timing or sequence of specific assessment methods, the role of the couple in determining assessment objectives, or the provision of clinical feedback on either the content of assessment findings or their subsequent effect on clinical interventions.

Although assessment of couples has shown dramatic gains in both its conceptual and empirical underpinnings over the past 25 years, much more remains to be discovered. Both clinicians and researchers need to avail themselves of recent advances in assessing couples and collaborate in promoting further development of empirically based assessment methods.

Acknowledgments

Portions of this chapter were adapted from Snyder, Heyman, and Haynes (2005), "Evidence-based approaches to assessing couple distress," *Psychological Assessment, 17*, 288–307. Richard Heyman's work on this chapter was supported by National Institute of Child Health and Human Development grant R01HD046901.

References

Aldarondo, E., & Straus, M. (1994). Screening for physical violence in couple therapy: Methodological, practical, and ethical considerations. *Family Process, 33*, 425–439.

Allgood, S. M., & Crane, D. R. (1991). Predicting marital therapy dropouts. *Journal of Marital and Family Therapy, 17*, 73–79.

American Psychiatric Association. (2000). *Diagnostic and statistical manual of mental disorders—text revision* (4th ed.). Washington, DC: Author.

Baltas, Z., & Steptoe, A. (2000). Migration, culture conflict and psychological well being among Turkish-British married couples. *Ethnicity and Health, 5*, 173–180.

Basco, M. R., Birchler, G. R., Kalal, B., Talbott, R., & Slater, A. (1991). The Clinician Rating of Adult Communication (CRAC): A clinician's guide to the assessment of interpersonal communication skill. *Journal of Clinical Psychology, 47*, 368–380.

Baucom, D. H., Epstein, N., & LaTaillade, J. J. (2002). Cognitive-behavioral couple therapy. In A. S. Gurman &

N. S. Jacobson (Eds.), *Clinical handbook of couple therapy* (3rd ed., pp. 26–58). New York: Guilford Press.

Beach, S. R. H., & Wamboldt, M. (2007, May). *Relational processes and DSM-V: Revising current nosology and improving assessment.* Second National Conference on Relational Processes and DSM-V, La Jolla, CA.

Beck, A. T., Steer, R. A., & Brown, G. K. (1996). *Manual for the Beck Depression Inventory-II.* San Antonio, TX: Psychological Corporation.

Bhugra, D., & De Silva, P. (2000). Couple therapy across cultures. *Sexual and Relationship Therapy, 15,* 183–192.

Birchler, G. R., & Fals-Stewart, W. (2006). Marital dysfunction. In M. Hersen (Ed.), *Clinician's handbook of adult behavioral assessment* (pp. 297–323). San Diego, CA: Academic Press.

Birchler, G. R., Magana, C., & Fals-Stewart, W. (2003). Marital dyads. In M. Hersen & S. M. Turner (Eds.), *Diagnostic interviewing* (3rd ed., pp. 365–391). New York,: Kluwer Academic/Plenum.

Boughner, S. R., Hayes, S. F., Bubenzer, D. L., & West, J. D. (1994). Use of standardized assessment instruments by marital and family therapists: A survey. *Journal of Marital and Family Therapy, 20,* 69–75.

Bradbury, T. N., & Fincham, F. D. (1990). Attributions in marriage: Review and critique. *Psychological Bulletin, 107,* 3–33.

Bradbury, T. N., Rogge, R., & Lawrence, E. (2001). Reconsidering the role of conflict in marriage. In A. Booth, A. C. Crouter, & M. Clements (Eds.), *Couples in conflict* (pp. 59–81). Mahwah, NJ: Erlbaum.

Busby, D. M., Holman, T. B., & Taniguchi, N. (2001). RELATE: Relationship evaluation of the individual, family, cultural, and couple contexts. *Family Relations, 50,* 308–316.

Butcher, J. N. (1996). Translation and adaptation of the MMPI-2 for international use. In J. N. Butcher (Ed.), *International adaptations of the MMPI-2: A handbook of research and clinical applications* (pp. 26–43). Minneapolis, MN: University of Minnesota Press.

Christensen, A. (1987). Detection of conflict patterns in couples. In K. Hahlweg & M. J. Goldstein (Eds.), *Understanding major mental disorder: The contribution of family interaction research* (pp. 250–265). New York: Family Process Press.

Christensen, A., & Heavey, C. L. (1990). Gender and social structure in the demand/withdraw pattern of marital conflict. *Journal of Personality and Social Psychology, 59,* 73–81.

Chun, K., Cobb, S., & French, J. R. P. (1975). *Measures for psychological assessment: A guide to 3,000 original sources and their applications.* Ann Arbor, MI: University of Michigan, Survey Research Center of the Institute for Social Research.

Cone, J. D. (1988). Psychometric considerations and the multiple models of behavioral assessment. In A. S. Bellack & M. Hersen (Eds.), *Behavioral assessment: A practical handbook* (3rd ed., pp. 42–66). New York: Pergamon.

Cook, J., Tyson, R., White, J., Rushe, R., Gottman, J. M., & Murray, J. (1995). The mathematics of marital conflict: Qualitative dynamic mathematical modeling of marital interaction. *Journal of Family Psychology, 9,* 110–130.

Corcoran, K., & Fischer, J. (2000). *Measures for clinical practice: A sourcebook, Vol. 1: Couples, families, and children.* New York: Free Press.

Crane, D. R., Busby, D. M., & Larson, J. H. (1991). A factor analysis of the Dyadic Adjustment Scale with distressed and nondistressed couples. *American Journal of Family Therapy, 19,* 60–66.

Cutrona, C. (1996). *Social support in couples: Marriage as a resource in times of stress.* Thousand Oaks, CA: Sage.

Davis, C. M., Yarber, W. L., Bauserman, R., Schreer, G., & Davis, S. L. (1998). *Handbook of sexuality-related measures.* Thousand Oaks, CA: Sage.

Derogatis, L. R., & Savitz, K. L. (1999). The SCL-90-R, Brief Symptom Inventory, and matching clinical rating scales. In M. E. Maruish (Ed.), *The use of psychological testing for treatment planning and outcomes assessment* (2nd ed., pp. 679–724). Mahway, NJ: Erlbaum.

Diener, E., Gohm, C. L., Suh, E., & Oishi, S. (2000). Similarity of the relations between marital status and subjective well-being across cultures. *Journal of Cross-cultural Psychology, 31,* 419–436.

Doss, B. D., & Christensen, A. (2006). Acceptance in romantic relationships: The Frequency and Acceptability of Partner Behavior Inventory. *Psychological Assessment, 18,* 289–302.

Edelstein, B. A., Woodhead, E. L., Bower, E. H., & Lowery, A. J. (2006). Evaluating older adults. In M. Hersen (Ed.), *Clinician's handbook of adult behavioral assessment* (pp. 497–527). San Diego, CA: Academic Press.

Ehrensaft, M., & Vivian, D. (1996). Spouses' reasons for not reporting existing physical aggression as a marital problem. *Journal of Family Psychology, 10,* 443–453.

Epstein, N. B., & Baucom, D. H. (2002). *Enhanced cognitive-behavioral therapy for couples: A contextual approach.* Washington, DC: American Psychological Association.

Filsinger, E. E. (1983). A machine-aided marital observation technique: The Dyadic Interaction Scoring Code. *Journal of Marriage and the Family, 45,* 623–632.

Fincham, F. D., & Bradbury, T. N. (1987). The assessment of marital quality: A reevaluation. *Journal of Marriage and the Family, 49,* 797–809.

Fincham, F. D., & Bradbury, T. N. (1992). Assessing attributions in marriage: The Relationship Attribution Measure. *Journal of Personality and Social Psychology, 62,* 457–468.

First, M. B., Bell, C. C., Cuthbert, B., Krystal, J. H., Malison, R., Offord, D. R., et al. (2002). Personality disorders and relational disorders: A research agenda for addressing crucial gaps in DSM. In D. J. Kupfer, M. B. First, & D. A. Regier (Eds.), *A research agenda for DSM-V* (pp. 123–199). Washington, DC: American Psychiatric Association.

First, M. B., Gibbon, M., Spitzer, R. L., & Williams, J. B. W. (1997). *Structured Clinical Interview for DSM-IV Axis I disorders—clinician version.* Washington, DC: American Psychiatric Association.

Fleeson, W. (2004). The quality of American life at the end of the century. In O. G. Brim, C. D. Ryff, & R. C. Kessler (Eds.), *How healthy are we: A national study of well-being at midlife* (pp. 252–272). Chicago, IL: University of Chicago Press.

Floyd, F. J. (2004). Communication Skills Test (CST): Observational system for couples' problem-solving skills. In P. K. Kerig & D. H. Baucom (Eds.), *Couple observational coding systems* (pp. 143–158). Mahwah, NJ: Erlbaum.

Floyd, F., Haynes, S. N., & Kelly, S. (1997). Marital assessment: A dynamic and functional analytic perspective. In W. K. Halford & H. J. Markman (Eds.), *Clinical handbook of marriage and couples intervention* (pp. 349–378). New York: Guilford Press.

Fowers, B., & Olson, D. (1989). ENRICH marital inventory: A discriminant validity study. *Journal of Marital and Family Therapy, 15,* 65–79.

Fowers, B., & Olson, D. (1992). Four types of premarital couples: An empirical typology based on PREPARE. *Journal of Family Psychology, 6*, 10–12.

Fredman, N., & Sherman, R. (1987). *Handbook of measurements for marriage and family therapy.* New York: Brunner/Mazel.

Funk, J., & Rogge, R. (2007). Testing the ruler with item response theory: Increasing precision of measurement for relationship satisfaction with the Couples Satisfaction Index. *Journal of Family Psychology, 21*, 572–583.

Geisinger, K. F. (1994). Cross-cultural normative assessment: Translation and adaptation issues influencing the normative interpretation of assessment instruments. *Psychological Assessment, 6*, 304–312.

Geiss, S. K., & O'Leary, D. (1981). Therapist ratings of frequency and severity of marital problems: Implications for research. *Journal of Marital and Family Therapy, 7*, 515–520.

Gerard, J. M., Krishnakumar, A., & Buehler, C. (2006). Marital conflict, parent–child relations, and youth maladjustment: A longitudinal investigation of spillover effects. *Journal of Family Issues, 27*, 951–975.

Gohm, C. L., Oishi, S., Darlington, J., & Diener, E. (1998). Culture, parental conflict, parental marital status, and the subjective well-being of young adults. *Journal of Marriage and the Family, 60*, 319–334.

Gordis, E. B., Margolin, G., & John, R. S. (2001). Parents' hostility in dyadic marital and triadic family settings and children's behavior problems. *Journal of Consulting and Clinical Psychology, 69*, 727–734.

Gottman, J. M. (1993). The roles of conflict engagement, escalation, and avoidance in marital interaction: A longitudinal view of five types of couples. *Journal of Consulting and Clinical Psychology, 61*, 6–15.

Gottman, J. M. (1994). *What predicts divorce? The relationship between marital processes and marital outcomes.* Hillsdale, NJ: Erlbaum.

Gottman, J. M. (1999). *The marriage clinic: A scientifically-based marital therapy.* New York: Norton.

Gottman, J. M., & Levenson, R. W. (1999). How stable is marital interaction over time? *Family Process, 38*, 159–165.

Gottman, J. M., McCoy, K., Coan, J., & Collier, H. (1996). The specific affect coding system (SPAFF). In J. M. Gottman (Ed.), *What predicts divorce? The measures* (pp. 1–169). Hillsdale, NJ: Erlbaum.

Gottman, J. M., & Notarius, C. I. (2000). Decade review: Observing marital interaction. *Journal of Marriage and the Family, 62*, 927–947.

Grotevant, H. D., & Carlson, C. I. (1989). *Family assessment: A guide to methods and measures.* New York: Guilford.

Hahlweg, K. (2004). *Kategoriensystem für Partnerschaftliche Interaktion* (KPI): Interactional Coding System (ICS). In P. K. Kerig & D. H. Baucom (Eds.), *Couple observational coding systems* (pp. 127–142). Mahwah, NJ: Erlbaum.

Halford, W. K. (2001). *Brief therapy for couples.* New York: Guilford Press.

Halford, W. K., Gravestock, F. M., Lowe, R., & Scheldt, S. (1992). Toward a behavioral ecology of stressful marital interactions. *Behavioral Assessment, 14*, 199–217.

Hartmann, D. P., Barrios, B. A., & Wood, D. D. (2004). Principles of behavioral observation. In S. N. Haynes & E. M. Heiby (Eds.), *Comprehensive handbook of psychological assessment, Vol. 3: Behavioral assessment* (pp. 108–127). Hoboken, NJ: John Wiley & Sons.

Hawkins, M. W., Carrère, S., & Gottman, J. M. (2002). Marital sentiment override: Does it influence couples' perceptions? *Journal of Marriage and Family, 64*, 193–201.

Hayes, S. C., Nelson, R. O., & Jarrett, R. B. (1987). The treatment utility of assessment: A functional approach to evaluating assessment quality. *American Psychologist, 42*, 963–974.

Haynes, S. N., Floyd, F. J., Lemsky, C., Rogers, E., Winemiller, D., Heilman, N., et al. (1992). The Marital Satisfaction Questionnaire for older persons. *Psychological Assessment, 4*, 473–482.

Haynes, S. N., Jensen, B., Wise, E., & Sherman, D. (1981). The marital intake interview: A multimethod criterion validity evaluation. *Journal of Consulting and Clinical Psychology, 49*, 379–387.

Haynes, S. N., Leisen, M. B., & Blaine, D. D. (1997). Design of individualized behavioral treatment programs using functional analytic clinical case models. *Psychological Assessment, 9*, 334–348.

Haynes, S. N., & O'Brien, W. H. (2000). *Principles and practice of behavioral assessment.* New York: Kluwer.

Haynes, S. N., & Williams, A. W. (2003). Case formulation and design of behavioral treatment programs: Matching treatment mechanisms to causal variables for behavior problems. *European Journal of Psychological Assessment, 19*, 164–174.

Haynes, S. N., & Yoshioka, D. T. (2007). Clinical assessment applications of ambulatory biosensors. *Psychological Assessment, 19*, 44–57.

Haynes, S. N., Yoshioka, D., Kloezeman, K., & Bello, R. (2008). Behavioral assessment. In J. N. Butcher (Ed.), *Handbook of personality assessment.* New York: Oxford University Press.

Heavey, C. L., Christensen, A., & Malamuth, N. M. (1995). The longitudinal impact of demand and withdrawal during marital conflict. *Journal of Consulting and Clinical Psychology, 63*, 797–801.

Herrington, R. L., Mitchell, A. E., Castellani, A. M., Joseph, J. I., Snyder, D. K., & Gleaves, D. H. (2008). Assessing disharmony and disaffection in intimate relationships: Revision of the Marital Satisfaction Inventory factor scales. *Psychological Assessment, 20*, 341–350.

Heyman, R. E. (2001). Observation of couple conflicts: Clinical assessment applications, stubborn truths, and shaky foundations. *Psychological Assessment, 13*, 5–35.

Heyman, R. E. (2004). Rapid Marital Interaction Coding System (RMICS). In P. K. Kerig & D. H. Baucom (Eds.), *Couple observational coding systems* (pp. 67–94). Mahwah, NJ: Erlbaum.

Heyman, R. E., Chaudhry, B. R., Treboux, D., Crowell, J., Lord, C., Vivian, D., et al. (2001). How much observational data is enough? An empirical test using marital interaction coding. *Behavior Therapy, 32*, 107–123.

Heyman, R. E., Eddy, J. M., Weiss, R. L., & Vivian, D. (1995). Factor analysis of the Marital Interaction Coding System (MICS). *Journal of Family Psychology, 9*, 209–215.

Heyman, R. E., Feldbau-Kohn, S. R., Ehrensaft, M. K., Langhinrichsen-Rohling, J., & O'Leary, K. D. (2001). Can questionnaire reports correctly classify relationship distress and partner physical abuse? *Journal of Family Psychology, 15*, 334–346.

Heyman, R. E., & Slep, A. M. S. (2004). Analogue behavioral observation. In E. M. Heiby & S. N. Haynes (Eds.), *Comprehensive handbook of psychological assessment, Vol. 3:*

Behavioral assessment (pp. 162–180). New York: John Wiley & Sons.

Heyman, R. E., & Slep, A. M. S. (2006). Creating and field-testing diagnostic criteria for partner and child maltreatment. *Journal of Family Psychology, 20*, 397–408.

Hoover, D. W., & Snyder, D. K. (1991). Validity of the computerized interpretive report for the Marital Satisfaction Inventory: A customer satisfaction study. *Psychological Assessment, 3*, 213–217.

Hops, H., Davis, B., & Longoria, N. (1995). Methodological issues in direct observation: Illustrations with the Living in Family Environments (LIFE) coding system. *Journal of Clinical Child Psychology, 24*, 193–203.

Hunsley, J., Best, M., Lefebvre, M., & Vito, D. (2001). The seven-item short form of the Dyadic Adjustment Scale: Further evidence for construct validity. *American Journal of Family Therapy, 29*, 325–335.

Jacob, T., & Tennenbaum, D. L. (1988). *Family assessment: Rationale, methods, and future directions.* New York: Plenum.

Jacobson, N. S., Schmaling, K. B., & Holtzworth-Munroe, A. (1987). Component analysis of behavioral marital therapy: 2-year follow-up and prediction of relapse. *Journal of Marital and Family Therapy, 13*, 187–195.

Janicki, D. L., Kamarck, T. W., Shiffman, S., & Gwaltney, C. J. (2006). Application of ecological momentary assessment to the study of marital adjustment and social interactions during daily life. *Journal of Family Psychology, 20*, 168–172.

Johnson, M. D. (2002). The observation of specific affect in marital interactions: Psychometric properties of a coding system and a rating system. *Psychological Assessment, 14*, 423–438.

Jones, A. C., & Chao, C. M. (1997). Racial, ethnic and cultural issues in couples therapy. In W. K. Halford & H. J. Markman (Eds.), *Clinical handbook of marriage and couples interventions* (pp. 157–176). New York: John Wiley & Sons.

Karpel, M. A. (1994). *Evaluating couples: A handbook for practitioners.* New York: Norton.

Kerig, P. K., & Baucom, D. H. (Eds.) (2004). *Couple observational coding systems.* Mahwah, NJ: Erlbaum.

Kiecolt-Glaser, J. K., & Newton, T. L. (2001). Marriage and health: His and hers. *Psychological Bulletin, 12*, 472–503.

Kiresuk, T. J., Smith, A., & Cardillo, J. E. (Eds.). (1994). *Goal attainment scaling: Applications, theory, and measurement.* Hillsdale, NJ: Erlbaum.

Kline, G. H., Julien, D., Baucom, B., Hartman, S. Gilbert, K, Gonzalez, T., et al. (2004). The Interactional Dimensions Coding System (IDCS): A global system for couple interactions. In P. K. Kerig & D. H. Baucom (Eds.), *Couple observational coding systems* (pp. 113–126). Mahwah, NJ: Erlbaum.

Kreider, R. M., & Fields, J. M. (2002). Number, timing, and duration of marriages and divorces: 1996. *Current Population Reports, P70-80.* Washington, DC: U.S. Census Bureau.

Krokoff, L. J., Gottman, J. M., & Hass, S. D. (1989). Validation of a global rapid couples interaction scoring system. *Behavioral Assessment, 11*, 65–79.

L'Abate, L. (1994). *Family evaluation: A psychological approach.* Thousand Oaks, CA: Sage.

L'Abate, L., & Bagarozzi, D. A. (1993). *Sourcebook of marriage and family evaluation.* New York: Brunner/Mazel.

Larson, J. H., Newell, K., Topham, G., & Nichols, S. (2002). A review of three comprehensive premarital assessment questionnaires. *Journal of Marital and Family Therapy, 28*, 233–239.

Lin, E., Goering, P., Offord, D. R., Campbell, D., & Boyle, M. H. (1996). The use of mental health services in Ontario: Epidemiologic findings. *Canadian Journal of Psychiatry, 41*, 572–577.

Lord, C. C. (1999). Stability and change in interactional behavior in early marriage (Unpublished doctoral dissertation, State University of New York, Stony Brook, NY).

Malik, N. M., & Lindahl, K. M. (2004). System for coding interactions in dyads. In P. K. Kerig & D. H. Baucom (Eds.), *Couple observational coding systems* (pp. 173–190). Mahwah, NJ: Erlbaum.

Margolin, G., Burman, B., & John, R. S. (1989). Home observations of married couples reenacting naturalistic conflicts. *Behavioral Assessment, 11*, 101–118.

Markey, B., Micheletto, M., & Becker, A. (1997). *Facilitating open couple communication, understanding, and study (FOCCUS).* Omaha, NE: Family Life Office, Archdiocese of Omaha.

Mash, E. J., & Foster, S. L. (2001). Exporting analogue behavioral observation from research to clinical practice: Useful or cost-defective? *Psychological Assessment, 13*, 86–98.

Means-Christensen, A. J., Snyder, D. K., & Negy, C. (2003). Assessing nontraditional couples: Validity of the Marital Satisfaction Inventory-Revised (MSI-R) with gay, lesbian, and cohabiting heterosexual couples. *Journal of Marital and Family Therapy, 29*, 69–83.

Meyer, I. (2003). Prejudice, social stress, and mental health in lesbian, gay, and bisexual populations: Conceptual issues and research evidence. *Psychological Bulletin, 129*, 674–697.

Mitchell, A. E., Castellani, A. M., Sheffield, R. L., Joseph, J. I., Doss, B. D., & Snyder, D. K. (2008). Predictors of intimacy in couples' discussions of relationship injuries: An observational study. *Journal of Family Psychology, 22*, 21–29.

Mrazek, P. J., & Haggerty, R. J. (Eds.). (1994). *Reducing risks for mental disorders: Frontiers for preventive intervention research.* Washington, DC: National Academy Press.

Northey, W. F., Jr. (2002). Characteristics and clinical practices of marriage and family therapists: A national survey. *Journal of Marital and Family Therapy, 28*, 487–494.

Notarius, C. I., Pellegrini, D., & Martin, L. (1991). Codebook of Marital and Family Interaction (COMFI) (Unpublished manuscript, Catholic University of America, Washington, DC).

O'Leary, K. D., Heyman, R. E., & Jongsma, A. E. (1998). *The couples psychotherapy treatment planner.* Hoboken, NJ: John Wiley & Sons.

Olson, D. H., & Olson, A. K. (1999). PREPARE/ENRICH program: Version 2000. In R. Berger & M. T. Hannah (Eds.), *Preventive approaches in couples therapy* (pp. 196–216).

Pasch, L. A., Bradbury, T. N., & Davila, J. (1997). Gender, negative affectivity, and observed social support behavior in marital interaction. *Personal Relationships, 4*, 361–378.

Pasch, L. A., Harris, K. W., Sullivan, K. T., & Bradbury, T. N. (2004). The Social Support Interaction Coding System. In P. K. Kerig & D. H. Baucom (Eds.), *Couple observational coding systems* (pp. 319–334). Mahwah, NJ: Erlbaum.

Patterson, G. R., Ray, R. S., Shaw, D. A., & Cobb, J. A. (1969). Manual for coding of family interactions (Unpublished coding manual). New York: Microfiche Publications.

Piasecki, T. M., Hufford, M. R., Solhan, M., & Trull, T. J. (2007). Assessing clients in their natural environments with electronic diaries: Rationale, benefits, limitations, and barriers. *Psychological Assessment, 19*, 25–43.

Rathus, J. H., & Feindler, E. L. (2004). *Assessment of partner violence: A handbook for researchers and practitioners.* Washington, DC: American Psychological Association.

Reid, J. B. (Ed.). (1978). *A social learning approach: Vol. 2. Observation in home settings.* Eugene, OR: Castalia.

Roberts, B. W., & Robins, R. W. (2000). Broad dispositions, broad aspirations: The intersection of personality traits and major life goals. *Personality and Social Psychology Bulletin, 26*, 1284–1296.

Sayers, S. L., Baucom, D. H., Sher, T. G., Weiss, R. L., & Heyman, R. E. (1991). Constructive engagement, behavioral marital therapy, and changes in marital satisfaction. *Behavioral Assessment, 13*, 25–49.

Sayers, S. L., & Sarwer, D. B. (1998). Assessment of marital dysfunction. In A. S. Bellack & M. Hersen (Eds.), *Behavioral assessment: A practical handbook* (4th ed., pp. 293–314). Boston, MA: Allyn and Bacon.

Sayers, S. L., & Tomcho, T. J. (2006). Behavioral interviewing. In M. Hersen (Ed.), *Clinician's handbook of adult behavioral assessment* (pp. 63–84). San Diego, CA: Academic Press.

Schumm, W. R., Paff-Bergen, L. A., Hatch, R. C., Obiorah, F. C., Copeland, J. M., Meens, L. D., et al. (1986). Concurrent and discriminant validity of the Kansas Marital Satisfaction Scale. *Journal of Marriage and the Family, 48*, 381–387.

Shapiro, A. F., & Gottman, J. M. (2004). The Specific Affect Coding System (SPAFF). In P. K. Kerig & D. H. Baucom (Eds.), *Couple observational coding systems* (pp. 191–208). Mahwah, NJ: Erlbaum.

Sher, T. G., Baucom, D. H., & Larus, J. M. (1990). Communication patterns and response to treatment among depressed and nondepressed maritally distressed couples. *Journal of Family Psychology, 4*, 63–79.

Shiffman, S., Hufford, M., Hickcox, M., Paty, J. A., Gnys, M., & Kassel J. D. (1997). Remember that? A comparison of real-time versus retrospective recall of smoking lapses. *Journal of Consulting and Clinical Psychology, 65*, 292–300.

Shumway, S. T., Wampler, R. S., Dersch, C., & Arredondo, R. (2004). A place for marriage and family services in employee assistance programs (EAPs): A survey of EAP client problems and needs. *Journal of Marital and Family Therapy, 30*, 71–79.

Sigmon, S. T., & LaMattina, S. M. (2006). Self assessment. In M. Hersen (Ed.), *Clinician's handbook of adult behavioral assessment* (pp. 145–164). San Diego, CA: Academic Press.

Sillars, A. L. (1982). Verbal Tactics Coding Scheme: Coding manual (Unpublished manuscript, Ohio State University).

Sillars, A., Roberts, L. J., Leonard, K. E., & Dun, T. (2000). Cognition during marital conflict: The relationship of thought and talk. *Journal of Social and Personal Relationships, 17*, 479–502.

Snyder, D. K. (1997). *Manual for the Marital Satisfaction Inventory-Revised.* Los Angeles: Western Psychological Services.

Snyder, D. K., & Abbott, B. V. (2002). Couple distress. In M. M. Antony & D. H. Barlow (Eds.), *Handbook of assessment and treatment planning for psychological disorders* (pp. 341–374). New York: Guilford.

Snyder, D. K., & Aikman, G. G. (1999). The Marital Satisfaction Inventory-Revised. In M. E. Maruish (Ed.), *Use of psychological testing for treatment planning and outcomes assessment* (2nd ed., pp. 1173–1210). Mahwah, NJ: Erlbaum.

Snyder, D. K., Castellani, A. M., & Whisman, M. A. (2006). Current status and future directions in couple therapy. *Annual Review of Clinical Psychology, 57*, 317–344.

Snyder, D. K., Cavell, T. A., Heffer, R. W., & Mangrum, L. F. (1995). Marital and family assessment: A multi-faceted, multilevel approach. In R. H. Mikesell, D. D. Lusterman, & S. H. McDaniel (Eds.), *Integrating family therapy: Handbook of family psychology and systems theory* (pp. 163–182). Washington, DC: American Psychological Association.

Snyder, D. K., Cepeda-Benito, A., Abbott, B. V., Gleaves, D. H., Negy, C., Hahlweg, K., et al. (2004). Cross-cultural applications of the Marital Satisfaction Inventory-Revised (MSI-R). In M. E. Maruish (Ed.), *Use of psychological testing for treatment planning and outcomes assessment* (3rd ed., pp. 603–623). Mahwah, NJ: Erlbaum.

Snyder, D. K., & Doss, B. D. (2005). Treating infidelity: Clinical and ethical directions. *Journal of Clinical Psychology, 61*, 1453–1465.

Snyder, D. K., Heyman, R. E., & Haynes, S. N. (2005). Evidence-based approaches to assessing couple distress. *Psychological Assessment, 17*, 288–307.

Snyder, D. K., Mangrum, L. F., & Wills, R. M. (1993). Predicting couples' response to marital therapy: A comparison of short- and long-term predictors. *Journal of Consulting and Clinical Psychology, 61*, 61–69.

Snyder, D. K., & Rice, J. L. (1996). Methodological issues and strategies in scale development. In D. H. Sprenkle & S. M. Moon (Eds.), *Research methods in family therapy* (pp. 216–237). New York: Guilford Press.

Snyder, D. K., Simpson, J. A., & Hughes, J. N. (Eds.) (2006). *Emotion regulation in couples and families: Pathways to dysfunction and health.* Washington, DC: American Psychological Association.

Snyder, D. K., & Whisman, M. A. (Eds.) (2003). *Treating difficult couples: Helping clients with coexisting mental and relationship disorders.* New York: Guilford.

Snyder, D. K., & Whisman, M. A. (2004). Treating distressed couples with coexisting mental and physical disorders: Directions for clinical training and practice. *Journal of Marital and Family Therapy, 30*, 1–12.

Spanier, G. B. (1976). Measuring dyadic adjustment: New scales for assessing the quality of marriage and similar dyads. *Journal of Marriage and the Family, 38*, 15–28.

Straus, M. A. (1979). Measuring intrafamily conflict and violence: The Conflict Tactics (CT) Scales. *Journal of Marriage and the Family, 41*, 75–88.

Straus, M. A., Hamby, S. L., Boney-McCoy, S., & Sugarman, D. B. (1996). The revised Conflict Tactics Scales (CTS2): Development and preliminary psychometric data. *Journal of Family Issues, 17*, 283–316.

Swindle, R., Heller, K., Pescosolido, B., & Kikuzawa, S. (2000). Responses to nervous breakdowns in America over a 40-year period: Mental health policy implications. *American Psychologist, 55*, 740–749.

Tanaka-Matsumi, J. (2004). Individual differences and behavioral assessment. In S. N. Haynes & E. M. Heiby (Eds.), *Comprehensive handbook of psychological assessment, Vol. 3: Behavioral assessment* (pp. 128–139). Hoboken, NJ: John Wiley & Sons.

Touliatos, J., Perlmutter, B. F., Straus, M. A., & Holden, G. W. (Eds.) (2001). *Handbook of family measurement techniques* (Vols. 1–3). Thousand Oaks, CA: Sage.

Tucker, J. A., Foushee, H. R., Black, B. C., & Roth, D. L. (2007). Agreement between prospective interactive voice response self-monitoring and structured retrospective reports of drinking and contextual variables during natural resolution attempts. *Journal of Studies on Alcohol and Drugs, 68,* 538–542.

Vanzetti, N. A., Notarius, C. I., & NeeSmith, D. (1992). Specific and generalized expectancies in marital interaction. *Journal of Family Psychology, 6,* 171–183.

Weiss, R. L. (1980). Strategic behavioral marital therapy: Toward a model for assessment and intervention. In J. P. Vincent (Ed.), *Advances in family intervention, assessment, and theory* (Vol. 1, pp. 229–271). Greenwich, CT: JAI Press.

Weiss, R. L., & Heyman, R. E. (1997). A clinical-research overview of couples interactions. In W. K. Halford & H. J. Markman (Eds.), *Clinical handbook of marriage and couples intervention* (pp. 13–41). New York: John Wiley & Sons.

Whisman, M. A. (1999). Marital dissatisfaction and psychiatric disorders: Results from the National Comorbidity Survey. *Journal of Abnormal Psychology, 108,* 701–706.

Whisman, M. A., Beach, S. R. H., & Snyder, D. K. (2008). Is marital discord taxonic and can taxonic status be assessed reliably? Results from a national, representative sample of married couples. *Journal of Consulting and Clinical Psychology, 76,* 745–755.

Whisman, M. A., Snyder, D. K., & Beach, S. R. H. (2009). Screening for marital and relationship discord. *Journal of Family Psychology, 23.*

Whisman, M. A., Dixon, A. E., & Johnson, B. (1997). Therapists' perspectives of couple problems and treatment issues in couple therapy. *Journal of Family Psychology, 11,* 361–366.

Whisman, M. A., Sheldon, C. T., & Goering, P. (2000). Psychiatric disorders and dissatisfaction with social relationships: Does type of relationship matter? *Journal of Abnormal Psychology, 109,* 803–808.

Whisman, M. A., & Snyder, D. K. (1997). Evaluating and improving the efficacy of conjoint couple therapy. In W. K. Halford & H. J. Markman (Eds.), *Clinical handbook of marriage and couples interventions* (pp. 679–693). New York: John Wiley & Sons.

Whisman, M. A., & Snyder, D. K. (2007). Sexual infidelity in a national survey of American women: Differences in prevalence and correlates as a function of method of assessment. *Journal of Family Psychology, 21,* 147–154.

Wieder, G. B., & Weiss, R. L. (1980). Generalizability theory and the coding of marital interactions. *Journal of Consulting and Clinical Psychology, 48,* 469–477.

Assessing Adolescents with the MMPI-A

Edward J. Cumella *and* Jennifer Lafferty O'Connor

Abstract

The Minnesota Multiphasic Personality Inventory-Adolescent (MMPI-A) was developed using adolescent norms and adolescent-specific content to offer clinicians an objective assessment instrument of adolescent psychopathology across many settings. The MMPI-A includes Validity Scales that measure the extent to which an adolescent responds to questions in a cooperative and truthful manner. The MMPI-A also includes 10 basic Clinical Scales, 15 Content Scales, 31 Content Component Scales, and 42 Supplementary Scales. MMPI-A profiles require specialized knowledge and training to correctly interpret adolescent functioning and psychopathology. Computer-driven scoring and reporting may assist clinicians in accurate, comprehensive, and integrated interpretation of the MMPI-A's many scales. The MMPI-A can be used to provide feedback to adolescents about their self-reported psychopathology and gain their cooperation with the therapeutic process.

Keywords: adolescent, assessment, Clinical Scales, Content Component Scales, Content Scales, MMPI, MMPI-A, psychopathology, Supplementary Scales, Validity Scales

Before the original Minnesota Multiphasic Personality Inventory (MMPI; Hathaway & McKinley, 1943) was published in 1943, it was already being used in personality research with adolescents (Capwell, 1945). Large longitudinal MMPI studies with adolescents continued through the 1950s and 1960s, demonstrating that the MMPI could well predict later juvenile delinquency and schizophrenia in boys and girls (Hanson, Gottesman, & Heston, 1990; Monachesi & Hathaway, 1969). However, this research revealed differences in item endorsement patterns between adolescents and adults, and longitudinally as subjects moved from middle to late adolescence. To address these issues and open MMPI access more broadly to adolescent assessment, Marks and Briggs developed adolescent norms (Marks, Seeman, & Haller, 1974). These norms derived from the MMPI responses of 1,800 normal adolescents and were provided separately for males and females ranging from ages 12 to 18. Marks and Briggs further used external criteria to develop 29 adolescent specific scale elevation patterns known as "code types," differentially describing both high and low scores. *The Actuarial Use of the MMPI with Adolescents and Adults* (Marks et al., 1974) established the reliability, validity, and broad utility of the MMPI with adolescents across multiple settings. Later research offered adolescent norms using larger samples (Gottesman, Hanson, Kroeker, & Briggs, 1987) or more recent test dates (Colligan & Offord, 1989), extended norms to Content and Special Scales, and examined the clinical correlates of additional single-scale and two-point code types (Archer, Gordon, Giannetti, & Singles, 1988; Williams & Butcher, 1989).

Over time, the extensive MMPI research with adolescents suggested that the original MMPI, although often employed in assessing adolescent psychopathology, was burdened with several limitations among teenage subjects. Archer (2005, p. 38) summarized the following issues: (a) need for a revised item pool, eliminating offensive and developmentally inappropriate items, rewriting items for easier readability, and adding items with adolescent specific content; (b) need for a universally accepted set of contemporary adolescent norms based on a nationally and ethnically representative adolescent sample; (c) need to create scales to assess adolescent specific problems and developmental issues; and (d) need for clear test interpretation guidelines for adolescent MMPI profiles. During the MMPI Restandardization Project, the University of Minnesota Press determined that the most effective way to address these limitations was to develop an adolescent specific version of the MMPI (Butcher & Williams, 2007, p. 6). The MMPI-Adolescent (MMPI-A) was completed and published in 1992 (Butcher et al., 1992).

To develop the MMPI-A, 154 newly written adolescent specific items along with the original MMPI items, some reworded, were administered to approximately 2,500 adolescents in eight states across the United States during the late 1980s. Approximately one-third of the tests were excluded due to invalidity or age, leaving 1,620 adolescents comprising the adolescent normative sample. The average age of the sample was 15.6 years. The sample closely matched the ethnic distribution of the U.S. population at the time, but overrepresented adolescents from college educated families, suggesting an upward socioeconomic skew (Butcher et al., 1992).

The MMPI-A was developed using this adolescent normative sample. The MMPI-A contains 478 items. Only the first 350 items are needed to score the basic Validity and Clinical Scales. The remaining items are necessary to score the additional Validity, Supplementary, and Content Scales. Thus, the MMPI-A is shorter than the MMPI or MMPI-2—a feature deemed important based on experience with adolescents taking the original MMPI (e.g., Archer, Maruish, Imhof, & Piotrowski, 1991). By design, the MMPI-A maintains substantial continuity with the original MMPI and MMPI-2. It embellishes these adult-oriented instruments by adding adolescent specific Content and Supplementary Scales, and refines Scales F, Mf, and Si by deleting items that did not meet statistical criteria for inclusion in the adolescent sample (Butcher et al., 1992).

The MMPI-A is a sophisticated self-report instrument that allows clinicians to assess psychopathology in adolescent clients despite complex developmental, clinical, and methodological issues that can interfere with the psychological assessment of teens. MMPI-A is designed to assess psychopathology among adolescents aged 14–18 in outpatient, residential, and inpatient general and mental health settings, as well as academic and forensic settings.

The MMPI-A provides an objective assessment of an adolescent's level of functioning in relation to standardized dimensions of psychopathology. The MMPI-A can serve as an index of therapeutic change if administered repeatedly during treatment. The ability to accurately assess changes in psychopathology over time is particularly useful with adolescents, as they undergo significant developmentally related psychological transitions.

The MMPI-A has rapidly become the most widely used objective personality assessment instrument with adolescents (Archer & Newsom, 2000). Since its publication, hundreds of books, book chapters, and research articles have appeared covering the MMPI-A's use and performance in a range of settings and populations. These investigations have continued to refine our knowledge of MMPI-A interpretation.

MMPI-A Interpretation

A strength of the MMPI-A is its ability to detect invalid response patterns, which occur frequently in adolescents (Archer, 2005). MMPI-A Validity Scales can be used to detect a variety of response styles that may distort a respondent's clinical profile. Under-reporting and over-reporting of psychopathology, random and haphazard responding, extreme responding, and defensive or guarded response styles can all be detected by MMPI-A Validity Scales.

Validity Scales

MMPI-A Validity Scales must be carefully examined by clinicians prior to interpreting a client profile. The Validity Scales provide information about whether or not the adolescent responded to test items in a cooperative, consistent, and accurate manner. Validity Scales provide information not only about the technical validity of the response pattern, but also about behavioral correlates and personality features that likely apply to the respondent.

CANNOT SAY SCALE

The Cannot Say Scale consists of the total number of items that a respondent fails to answer. Adolescents typically omit 10 or fewer items when completing the MMPI-A. When 11 or more items are omitted, the Cannot Say score is considered elevated.

Elevated Cannot Say Scale scores can occur for a variety of reasons. Higher Cannot Say Scale scores have been found to be inversely related to intelligence and academic success (Archer, 2005), suggesting that poor reading ability or vocabulary level may contribute to higher rates of item omission due to difficulty comprehending items. This underscores the importance of assessing for reading level before administering the MMPI-A. A seventh grade reading level is required for adequate comprehension of items on the MMPI-A.

Cannot Say scores can also be elevated due to clinical issues. Excessive indecisiveness or obsessive thinking can contribute to item omission. Defiant or uncooperative attitudes may also contribute to elevated Cannot Say Scores. Clinical judgment may be required to determine the cause of excessive item omission.

If respondents have a Cannot Say Scale raw score of 11–29, they are omitting more items than is typical. However, it is unlikely that fewer than 30 omissions will result in significant profile distortions unless the omitted items are concentrated within a few scales. If an adolescent omits 30 or more items, the profile must be considered invalid (Butcher & Williams, 2007). In this case, if the respondent's reading level appears adequate, then the adolescent should be asked to go back and complete the unanswered items so that the profile can be scored and interpreted.

THE FREQUENCY (F) SCALE AND THE F1 AND F2 SUBSCALES

The F scale was designed to identify respondents who are endorsing atypical and unusual thoughts, feelings, attitudes, and experiences. The F scale includes items that are rarely endorsed by a normal population of teens. The 66 items selected for the MMPI-A F scale were endorsed by less than 20% of adolescents in the normative sample. F scale item content includes paranoid ideation, bizarre sensory experiences, and antisocial behaviors and attitudes.

Adolescents who produce elevations ($T = 66$ or above) on the MMPI-A F scale may be suffering from severe psychiatric illness or acute psychiatric distress, in which case their profiles are valid. On the other hand, adolescents with elevated F scores may be over-reporting or exaggerating their symptoms. Adolescents are most likely to over-report psychopathology as a plea for help in an effort to communicate their desire for attention and support (Archer, 2005). T-scores of 100 and above invalidate the profile (Butcher & Williams, 2007). Such highly elevated F scale scores can reflect either over-

reporting or random responding (Baer, Kroll, Rinaldo, & Ballenger, 1999).

The F1 scale consists of 33 items from the first 350 items in the MMPI-A, and can therefore be interpreted when the MMPI-A is given in its abbreviated format. The F1 scale provides information concerning the validity of the adolescent's responses to the basic MMPI-A Clinical Scales, whose items fall within the first portion of the test. The F2 scale consists of 33 items that occur after item 242. The F2 scale provides information concerning the adolescent's responses to the items that contribute to Content and Supplementary Scale scores. If the adolescent's F1 score is within acceptable limits, but the F2 score is extremely elevated ($T > 90$), random responding during the latter portion of the test is likely. In this case, MMPI-A Basic Scales can be interpreted, but Content and Supplementary Scales should not be interpreted due to the high likelihood that they are invalid (Butcher & Williams, 2007).

THE LIE (L) SCALE

The L scale was created to identify respondents who are deliberately attempting to present themselves in an overly positive light by denying common human faults and weaknesses. Moderate L scale elevations ($T = 60–65$) suggest use of denial as a primary defense mechanism and tendencies toward being overly conventional and conforming. Marked elevations ($T > 65$) suggest a "fake-good" response set in which the respondent is attempting to create an unrealistically favorable impression of being well adjusted. Marked L scale elevations typically result in artificially low ($T \leq 60$) Clinical and Content Scale scores (Archer, 2005).

THE DEFENSIVENESS (K) SCALE

The MMPI-A K scale was empirically designed to identify respondents who experience significant symptoms of psychopathology, but produce profiles that are within normal limits. Adolescents in psychiatric settings who produce K scale T-scores of 65 and above are typically unwilling to admit to their psychiatric problems and tend to deny their need for treatment or psychiatric help. They typically have a poor prognosis for treatment due to refusal or inability to cooperate with treatment efforts (Archer, 2005). Adolescents may under-report psychopathology when they have been involuntarily placed in treatment, and therefore have a strong desire to present as though they do not have problems and are not in need of help.

In one study, a full 19% of adolescents in an inpatient psychiatric setting produced K+ profiles—where only the K scale is elevated at T = 65 or greater. Patients with this profile were found to be extremely defensive. On the other hand, markedly low elevations on the K scale (T < 40) suggest a conscious or unconscious exaggeration of symptoms. This type of exaggeration may involve a deliberate attempt to "fake bad," or may be a "cry for help" in response to acute psychological distress.

VARIABLE RESPONSE INCONSISTENCY (VRIN) AND TRUE RESPONSE INCONSISTENCY (TRIN) SCALES

The VRIN and TRIN scales provide information about a respondent's tendency to endorse MMPI-A items in an inconsistent manner. VRIN consists of 50 pairs of items that have either similar or opposite content. Each time a respondent answers an item pair in a contradictory manner, a point is added to the VRIN scale raw score. VRIN scale T-scores of 75 or above suggest that the adolescent has responded to items in an inconsistent, careless, or random manner (Butcher & Williams, 2007).

The TRIN scale was designed to detect an adolescent's tendency to respond to most items as true or most as false, regardless of item content. The scale consists of 24 pairs of items that are opposite in content. TRIN scale T-scores of 75 or above indicate unacceptable levels of response inconsistency (Butcher & Williams, 2007). Inconsistent item endorsement patterns measured by VRIN and TRIN can be caused by inadequate reading ability, a noncompliant or defiant attitude, thought disorganization, active psychosis, or substance intoxication. The clinician must use clinical judgment to determine the most likely cause.

Norms and T-scores

Adolescent MMPI-A Scales should be interpreted using adolescent norms. Use of adult norms tends to produce profiles that overestimate psychiatric symptoms in adolescent respondents (Williams, Butcher, Ben-Porath, & Graham, 1992). However, use of adolescent norms has also been found to produce profiles that may underestimate an adolescent's true level of psychopathology (Archer, Handel, & Lynch, 2001). To accommodate this concern, on MMPI-A Clinical, Content, and Supplementary Scales, T-scores of 60 to 64 represent a moderate level of psychopathology and can be interpreted cautiously as indicating that the respondent may show some, but not necessarily all, of the correlates associated with a given scale. T-scores of

65 and higher suggest greater certainty that the psychopathology measured by a particular scale is present. Nevertheless, perhaps as much as 25–30% of adolescents in clinical samples still appear to produce within-normal-limits MMPI-A profiles, where none of the basic Clinical Scales are elevated (Hand, Archer, Handel, & Forbey, 2007). As such, clinicians should not assume that within-normal-limits MMPI-A profiles indicate an absence of psychopathology, even where Validity Scales do not suggest denial or defensiveness.

Clinical Scales

The MMPI-A contains 10 Clinical Scales that provide an objective assessment of an adolescent's level of functioning in specific areas of psychopathology. To assess the degree to which a respondent's level of functioning differs from that which is typically reported by adolescents, the respondent's test scores are compared against those obtained by the MMPI-A normative sample of adolescents.

SCALE 1 (HS: HYPOCHONDRIASIS)

Scale 1 consists of 32 items that include vague physical complaints and bodily ailments. Respondents who produce T-scores of 60 or above on Scale 1 tend to be preoccupied with bodily functioning, illness, and disease. These individuals are likely to develop somatic symptoms in response to stress, to present with internalizing disorders such as anxiety and depression, and to display poor insight in therapy.

SCALE 2 (D: DEPRESSION)

Scale 2 consists of 57 items with content areas including general apathy, social withdrawal, dissatisfaction, pessimistic thinking, and poor morale. Several items also address physical symptoms commonly associated with clinical depression, such as sleep disturbance. Adolescents with Scale 2 T-scores of 60 or above tend to experience a general dissatisfaction with life and lack hope for the future. They typically exhibit low self-confidence and struggle with self-criticism and feelings of inadequacy, guilt, and shame. Butcher et al. (1992) found that adolescent inpatients with Scale 2 elevations were likely to be characterized as depressed and to evidence suicidal ideation and/or suicidal gestures. Respondents for whom Scale 2 is the highest scale score, known as spike 2 profiles, tend to be good psychotherapy candidates because their relatively high degree of emotional distress may serve as a positive motivator to engage in the therapeutic process (Archer, 2005).

SCALE 3 (HY: HYSTERIA)

Scale 3 consists of 60 items that were intended to identify respondents who react hysterically to stressful situations. Item content includes somatic complaints and concerns, as well as items related to presenting oneself as being well socialized and well adjusted. Adolescents with high Scale 3 of T ≥ 60 tend to have heightened needs for affection, attention, and approval from others. They tend to be psychologically naive and may have limited psychological insight (Archer, 2005). Butcher et al. (1992) found that female adolescent patients with elevations on Scale 3 tend to express stress or anxiety through somatic complaints; Cumella, Wall, and Kerr-Almeida (1999) found a relationship between Scale 3 elevations and eating disorders among adolescent girls.

SCALE 4 (PD: PSYCHOPATHIC DEVIATE)

Scale 4 consists of 49 items intended to identify respondents who have a pattern of delinquent behaviors and/or antisocial attitudes/traits. Scale 4 item content covers a variety of issues including delinquent behaviors, social isolation, family conflicts, problems with authority, and dissatisfaction with life. Adolescents with high Scale 4 profiles of T ≥ 60 tend to have poor impulse control and are likely to engage in thrill-seeking and high risk behaviors that may include substance abuse and sexual promiscuity. They typically have conduct problems at school and significant parent–teen conflict at home. They are likely to have rebellious or hostile attitudes toward authority figures. Butcher et al. (1992) found that adolescents with Scale 4 elevations are prone to acting out and externalizing behaviors, with girls more likely to engage in sexual promiscuity and boys more likely to run away.

SCALE 5 (MF: MASCULINITY–FEMININITY)

The MMPI-A Mf scale serves as a measure of gender role identification. It contains 44 items with broad content including recreational interests, interpersonal relationships, fears, and sensitivity. Male respondents with high Mf scores of T ≥ 60 are described as having a pattern of stereotypically feminine interests, whereas female respondents with high Mf scores are seen as having stereotypically masculine interests. Meunier and Bodkins (2005) found that elevations on Scale 5 may be associated with aggressiveness and behavioral acting out among females. Male and female respondents with low Mf scores, T ≤ 40, tend to strongly identify with the traditional or stereotyped gender roles of their own sex.

SCALE 6 (PA: PARANOIA)

Scale 6 was intended to identify patients with paranoid thinking patterns. This scale consists of 40 items that cover overt psychotic symptoms such as feelings of persecution, suspiciousness, ideas of reference, and other disturbances in reality testing. This scale also contains a large number of items not directly related to psychosis, including interpersonal sensitivity, cynicism, rigidity, and moral self-righteousness. Adolescents with moderate elevations, T = 60–69, evidence hostility, resentfulness, and argumentativeness. They tend to struggle with distrust in their interpersonal relationships and experience significant interpersonal sensitivity (Archer, 2005). Adolescents who produce marked elevations on Scale 6, T ≥ 70, may have a thought disorder associated with psychosis or schizophrenia. Butcher et al. (1992) found that Scale 6 elevations were related to hostile/withdrawn behaviors and neurotic/dependent behaviors among adolescent male inpatients.

SCALE 7 (PT: PSYCHASTHENIA)

Scale 7 was intended to measure symptoms associated with obsessive compulsive disorder, including excessive doubt and worry, high levels of tension and anxiety, obsessive thinking, and compulsive behaviors. Scale 7 consists of 48 items that address a variety of symptoms, including obsessive thoughts, anxiety, poor concentration, feelings of unhappiness, physical complaints, and feelings of inadequacy. Adolescents who produce high Scale 7 scores of T ≥ 60 are typically anxious, tense, preoccupied, and obsessional. They tend to be overly conscientious, self-critical, and perfectionistic, and may struggle with feelings of insecurity, self-doubt, and inferiority (Archer, 2005). Wrobel and Lachar (1992) reported that high Scale 7 scores were related to an increase in nightmares for both male and female MMPI-A respondents.

SCALE 8 (SC: SCHIZOPHRENIA)

Scale 8 was intended to identify patients with schizophrenia. Scale 8 consists of 77 items, the largest MMPI-A scale. Scale 8 item content includes unusual and bizarre thinking, disturbances in mood and behaviors, poor impulse control, and problems with social isolation. Respondents who produce high Scale 8 scores of T ≥ 60 are typically withdrawn, socially isolated, and reclusive, and may display schizoid features. They are likely to struggle with feelings of inferiority, low self-worth, and unhappiness. Adolescents who produce marked elevations on Scale 8, T ≥ 70, may be experiencing delusions, hallucinations, and other schizophrenic symptoms. Wrobel and Lachar (1992) found that adolescents with high Scale 8 scores were often teased or rejected as children. Butcher et al. (1992) found that Scale 8 elevations were associated with acting out, schizoid, and psychotic behaviors among adolescent inpatient males.

SCALE 9 (MA: HYPOMANIA)

Scale 9 was intended to identify patients who are manifesting hypomanic symptoms at the time of assessment. This scale consists of 46 items with relatively diverse content areas, including irritability, elevated mood, cognitive and behavioral overactivity, egocentricity, grandiosity, and impulsivity. Adolescents with high Scale 9 scores of $T \geq 60$ tend to be outgoing, socially extroverted, talkative, and energetic. They are often described by others as impulsive, restless, and distractible, and have a higher likelihood of school conduct problems and delinquent behaviors. They may be egocentric, self-centered, insensitive, and self-indulgent (Archer, 2005).

Although individuals who score high on Scale 9 may display manic features such as flight of ideas, delusions of grandeur, and hyperactivity, this does not necessarily suggest a diagnosis of bipolar disorder. For example, adolescents who abuse amphetamines are also likely to score high on Scale 9 (Butcher et al., 1992). Furthermore, low Scale 9 scores do not necessarily suggest an absence of bipolar disorder. Lumry, Gottesman, and Tuason (1982) found that individuals with bipolar disorder may produce very different profiles depending on which phase of the disorder they are currently experiencing. Adolescents with bipolar disorder who are currently experiencing a depressive episode are more likely to produce high scores on Scales 2 and 7, rather than Scale 9. In fact, markedly low Scale 9 scores, $T < 40$, can be suggestive of serious depressive symptoms including vegetative signs such as lethargy, apathy, and decreased motivational states.

SCALE 0 (SI: SOCIAL INTROVERSION)

The Si scale consists of 62 items and was intended to identify individuals with significant social introversion. Scale 0 contains two broad content clusters, one addressing degree of social participation and one addressing self-deprecation and low self-confidence. High Si scores can result from item endorsement in either or both of these content areas (Graham, 2000). Adolescents who score high on Scale 0, $T \geq 60$, typically have tendencies toward social introversion and social discomfort. They

tend to be insecure and lacking in self-confidence. They are likely to be overcontrolled, inflexible, and conventional (Butcher & Williams, 2007).

Additional MMPI-A Scales

The MMPI-A also includes 15 Content Scales, 6 Supplementary Scales, and 5 Personality Dimension Scales. In addition, 28 Harris–Lingoes subscales and three Si subscales provide detailed information about the content of item endorsement. These additional MMPI-A scales can be used by clinicians to supplement and refine interpretation of the Clinical Scales.

CONTENT SCALES

The MMPI-A Content Scales were initially based on the MMPI-2 Content Scales, with adjustments made for an adolescent population (Williams & Lachar, 1992). These scales were created through a multistep approach that included rational, empirical, and construct-oriented techniques. The Content Scales assess homogeneous themes that have been externally validated in clinical samples (Butcher & Williams, 2007).

Several important changes were made to the MMPI-2 Content Scales in order to create MMPI-A Content Scales applicable to adolescents and adolescent development (Williams & Lachar, 1992). The MMPI-2 Work Interference Scale was removed and the School Problems Scale was added to address behaviors, attitudes, and relational problems that may be interfering with an adolescent's ability to function in academic settings. The Low Aspirations Scale was added to address adolescents who dislike learning or studying, and lack interest in being successful. The Alienation Scale was added to assess an adolescent's experience of feeling misunderstood by others and reluctance to express thoughts/feeling to others.

The Content Scales are composed of items that are face-valid and are relatively obvious in terms of their psychopathological content. Content Scale scores are therefore heavily influenced by a respondent's motivation to over-report or under-report symptoms. Careful evaluation of the validity of an adolescent's response style is very important before drawing any conclusions based on Content Scale scores.

The MMPI-A Content Scales consist of: A-anx (Anxiety), A-obs (Obsessiveness), A-dep (Depression), A-hea (Health), A-aln (Alienation), A-biz (Bizarre Mentation), A-ang (Anger), A-cyn (Cynicism), A-con (Conduct Problems), A-lse (Low Self-Esteem), A-las (Low Aspirations), A-sod (Social Discomfort), A-fam (Family Problems), A-sch (School Problems), and A-trt (Negative Treatment Indicators).

The MMPI-A Content Scales can be used to refine the interpretation of the Clinical Scales by suggesting which of the various descriptors for each Clinical Scale should be emphasized. For example, when Scale 4 is elevated, a rather wide variety of behaviors and symptoms are suggested, including acting out and delinquent behaviors, familial discord, and poor social adjustment. By examining which Content Scales are also elevated, the clinician can determine which descriptors best apply in a given case. In addition, the Content Scales can be used to gather information about certain issues not directly addressed in the Clinical Scales. For example, the Clinical Scales do not directly assess low self-esteem, anger, or family problems, but the Content Scales do address these issues.

Forbey and Ben-Porath (2003) investigated the degree to which the MMPI-A Content Scales provide incremental gains in clinically useful information beyond what is already provided by the MMPI-A Clinical Scales. They utilized regression analysis techniques to estimate the additional or incremental variance accounted for by the Content Scales in predicting clinicians' ratings of psychological symptoms among adolescents in a residential mental health setting. Several of the MMPI-A Content Scales demonstrated significant incremental validity beyond the Clinical Scales in predicting clinicians' ratings of adolescent behavior and personality characteristics. This underscores the importance of fully utilizing Content Scale scores.

To supplement the Content Scales, Sherwood, Ben-Porath, and Williams (1997) empirically developed the Content Component Scales—subscales for each parent Content Scale representing a highly delimited problem area within the parent scale. The MMPI-A Content Component Scales can only be interpreted if the parent Content Scale is elevated at $T = 60$ or greater, but may add refinement to interpretation of the parent Content Scales.

SUPPLEMENTARY SCALES

The MMPI-A Supplementary Scales consist of six measures, three adopted from the original MMPI, and three created by researchers specifically for use in the MMPI-A. Similar to the Content Scales, these scales can be used to refine the interpretation of the Clinical Scales.

MacAndrew Alcoholism Scale-Revised (MAC-R)

The MAC-R scale contains 49 items, 45 identical to the original MAC scale items selected on an empirical basis. High MAC-R scores among adolescents suggest the possibility of substance abuse problems, including abuse of alcohol and a variety of other drugs. Elevated MAC-R scores have also been associated with increased delinquent behaviors and antisocial personality characteristics such as self-indulgence, egocentrism, and lack of concern over the consequences of one's actions (Archer, 2005).

Alcohol and Drug Problem Proneness (PRO) Scale

The PRO Scale was created specifically for the MMPI-A. It consists of 36 items that were empirically selected based on item endorsement differences between adolescents in inpatient psychiatric treatment versus alcohol and drug treatment programs. These items cover a variety of content areas including antisocial attitudes, familial characteristics, peer group features, and other beliefs and behaviors associated with alcohol and drug problems among teens. T-score values of 65 and greater are associated with increased potential for development of alcohol and drug abuse problems (Butcher et al., 1992).

The Alcohol/Drug Problem Acknowledgment Scale (ACK) Scale

This scale was developed specifically for the MMPI-A to assess an adolescent's willingness to acknowledge alcohol and drug use, as well as certain symptoms, attitudes, and beliefs associated with substance abuse. High scorers endorse a variety of current alcohol and/or drug related problems. Tirrell (2005) found that among the MAC-R, ACK, and PRO scales of the MMPI-A, the ACK scale demonstrated the highest level of effectiveness in differentiating adolescent substance abusers from non-substance-abusing psychiatric inpatients.

The Immaturity (IMM) Scale

This scale was specifically developed for the MMPI-A to assess psychological maturation during adolescence using Loevinger's (1976) concept of ego development as a conceptual basis. Items were selected using both rational and statistical methods. Based on Loevinger's (1976) model, immature adolescents would be expected to be impulsive, egocentric, and lacking in self-awareness and interpersonal insight. Their cognitive processes would be expected to be concrete and relatively simplistic. In terms of moral development, adolescents who are "immature" would be expected to externalize blame and lack concern for the consequences of their actions. Adolescents who score high on this scale at $T \geq 65$ have been found to be irresponsible, defiant, easily angered, impatient, and impulsive (Archer, 2005).

Welsh's Anxiety (A) and Repression (R) Scales

Welsh originally designed the MMPI Anxiety and Repression Scales to assess the two major factors that typically emerge when the MMPI has undergone factor analyses. The first factor, assessed by the Anxiety Scale, has been referred to as "general maladjustment" and accounts for a large proportion of variance in MMPI Clinical Scales. The second major factor, assessed by the Repression Scale, has been referred to as "ego control or inhibition."

The MMPI-A Anxiety Scale contains 35 items that assess general psychological maladjustment and emotional distress associated with internalizing disorders such as anxiety and depression. The Anxiety Scale highly correlates with Scale 7 on the MMPI (Archer, Gordon, Anderson, & Giannettii, 1989). Adolescents with high scores on the Anxiety Scale tend to be maladjusted, tense, fearful, anxious, self-critical, guilty, and easily overwhelmed. Elevations on the Anxiety Scale have been associated with presenting problems related to suicidal ideation and attempts (Archer & Slesinger, 1999).

The MMPI-A Repression Scale highly correlates with Scales L, K, and the "neurotic triad," which includes Scales 1, 2, and 3 (Archer & Krishnamurthy, 2002). Adolescents with high Repression Scale scores tend to be overcontrolled, inhibited, constricted, and pessimistic, and tend to show little emotion (Archer & Krishnamurthy, 2002).

The Personality Psychopathology Five (PSY-5) Scales

The Personality Psychopathology Five were developed for the MMPI-2 to assess personality adjustment factors not addressed by the symptom-oriented Clinical Scales. The PSY-5 Scales differ theoretically from other MMPI scales in their intent to emphasize specific personality traits or dispositional features rather than psychopathological factors. A similar set of scales was developed and validated for the MMPI-A by McNulty, Harkness, Ben-Porath, & Williams (1997).

The Aggressiveness Scale addresses instrumental or offensive aggression and high-scorers display assaultive, aggressive, and delinquent behaviors. The Psychoticism Scale addresses the type of mental disconnection or distance from reality associated with psychosis. The Disconstraint Scale assesses tendencies toward impulsivity, and risk-taking, antisocial, and delinquent behaviors. The Negative Emotionality/Neuroticism Scale assesses a predisposition to unpleasant emotions such as anxiety, guilt, and worry. The Introversion/Low Positive Emotionality Scale assesses the inability to experience joy or other positive emotions, with high scorers tending toward shyness and social withdrawal.

The Harris–Lingoes and Si subscales

Harris and Lingoes (1955) constructed 27 subscales for six of the Clinical Scales. They created these subscales on a rational basis by grouping together items from each Clinical Scale that appeared similar in content. These subscales were intended to assist clinicians in understanding the particular items that resulted in a Clinical Scale elevation.

These subscales should only be used to supplement and refine interpretations derived from the Validity and Clinical Scales. Butcher and Williams (2007) recommend that Harris–Lingoes subscales should only be interpreted when the parent Clinical Scale is elevated at T ≥ 60. Because validity data for these scales are limited, caution should be used in interpreting them (Archer, 2005).

Ben-Porath, Hostetler, Butcher, & Graham (1989) developed Si subscales for the MMPI-2 using factor analytic techniques. Three subscales emerged: shyness/self-consciousness, social avoidance, and alienation—self and others. These subscales were carried over to the MMPI-A without modification. These subscales can be used to refine and individualize the interpretation of Si scale elevations for a particular respondent.

Interpretive Strategies

MMPI-A interpretation begins with an examination of the Validity Scales. Such examination enables the clinician to determine whether the profile can be meaningfully interpreted. If the profile appears valid and interpretable, the Clinical Scales are then examined.

Clinical Scales with T-scores of 60 to 64 are interpreted cautiously, and those with higher T-scores are interpreted with greater confidence, to indicate the presence of the behaviors, attitudes, and traits measured individually by each Clinical Scale.

When more than one Clinical Scale is elevated, the clinical correlates of each scale are likely to be present in the adolescent. Some correlates will overlap. Others will incrementally produce a more robust and fleshed out picture of a particular symptom cluster. Some correlates will interact synergistically, such as depressive symptoms (Scale 2) and efforts to repress and deny such symptoms (Scale 3). It takes advanced assessment and MMPI-A training, sufficient knowledge of adolescent psychopathology, and specific knowledge of the presenting problems and environmental context of the adolescent being assessed for a clinician to accurately interpret MMPI-A scale elevations.

In MMPI and MMPI-2 interpretation, specific two and three point Clinical Scale elevation patterns with known clinical correlates have been used extensively. These patterns are called code types. Archer (2005) offers 29 different two-point code-type descriptors for the MMPI-A. However, Williams and Butcher (1989) found that traditional code-type classification lacks adequate validity when applied to adolescent populations. The use of code types with the MMPI-A is therefore controversial and not currently recommended by University of Minnesota researchers and publications.

After examination of the MMPI-A Clinical Scales, MMPI-A Supplementary Scales should be reviewed to support and refine Clinical Scale interpretations. Welsh's A scale can be applied to estimate the overall level of maladjustment, and Welsh's R scale to examine use of repression as a primary defense mechanism. The respondent's overall level of psychological maturity can be assessed through the Immaturity Scale. Substance abuse screening information can be obtained through interpretation of the MAC-R, ACK, and PRO scales. The PSY-5 scales can then be assessed to obtain information about personality dimensions for the respondent.

Next, the 15 Content Scales can be examined to improve and refine profile interpretation. Furthermore, information not directly provided by the Clinical Scales, such as the adolescent's probable initial approach to therapy, can be determined through examination of the Content Scales. For any Content Scale elevated at $T = 60$ or greater, its corresponding Content Component Scales may assist with interpretation.

Next, the clinician can selectively examine the Harris–Lingoes and Si subscales to refine or clarify hypotheses already developed based on interpretation of Clinical, Content, and Supplementary Scale scores. These subscales should only be interpreted when the parent Clinical Scales are elevated at $T \geq 60$. Due to limited validity data, interpretation should be done cautiously with these scales, exercising care not to dramatically alter or amend the interpretation developed from prior steps in the process.

Item-level indicators, including omitted and critical items, should be examined last. Responses to single items are less reliable than scores on scales that are comprised of multiple items. For example, a respondent may accidentally mark or misread a single item. Therefore, clinicians should be extremely cautious about making significant statements based on single-item endorsements.

As a special interpretive note, it is important for clinicians to know that boys in clinical settings whose MMPI-A profiles include elevations on Scales 7, 8, A-dep, A-ang, A-lse, A-fam, and A-sch, and girls in clinical settings who elevate on Scales 4, 8, and A-fam, are more likely to have experienced sexual abuse. Additionally, boys in clinical settings who elevate on Pd only may have experienced physical abuse (Butcher et al., 1992; Williams & Lachar, 1992).

MMPI-A interpretative data developed through the steps delineated above should be used in conjunction with data from other sources, including clinical interview findings, clinical observations, collateral history from parents, schools, and other sources, and additional psychometric tests. When used in conjunction with these additional data sources, the MMPI-A can provide valid and reliable information about the type, nature, and extent of psychiatric symptoms for an adolescent respondent. The MMPI-A can yield important information about an adolescent's current level of distress, level of psychological maturation, characteristic defense mechanisms, typical relationship patterns, problematic personality traits, and openness to treatment and behavior change. In addition, the MMPI-A will often allow the clinician to make initial diagnostic impressions, hypotheses for treatment, and a determination of the specific types and modalities of treatment that are likely to be effective with a particular client.

The Minnesota Report: Adolescent Interpretive System

The University of Minnesota Press publishes the *Minnesota Report: Adolescent interpretive system* (Butcher & Williams, 2007). Now in its second edition, this computer-based report follows the interpretive steps outlined above and offers client-specific MMPI-A interpretations using sophisticated algorithms grounded in MMPI-A research. This report can save valuable clinician time and, because of its comprehensiveness, reduces clinician error or oversight in MMPI-A interpretation. Nevertheless, computerized reports are not substitutes for trained clinician judgment. The adequacy and relevance of the Minnesota Report must be assessed by a clinician who is familiar with the adolescent's presentation, background, environment, limitations, and needs.

Case Example

Collectively, the authors have assessed approximately 1,200 adolescents using the MMPI-A in conjunction with clinical interview, collateral histories, and other psychometrically reliable and valid tests. We have selected one case history to illustrate key aspects of MMPI-A interpretation in a mental health setting. Potentially identifying case details have been changed. For further case studies, a collection of 16 MMPI-A cases can be accessed in Ben-Porath and Davis (1996), and 5 case examples appear in Archer (2005).

Emily was a 14-year-old Korean-American female being treated in an inpatient program for anorexia nervosa. Emily's parents emigrated from South Korea when she was a small child. Her parents indicated that they came to the United States so that Emily could receive the best education. Emily's father had been a successful businessman in his home country, but had difficulty finding work in the United States. The family was struggling financially, so Emily's father decided to return to South Korea to work and send money to the States where Emily and her mother remained. Emily's eating disorder began approximately 1 year after her father returned to Asia. Emily had always been close to her mother, until her eating disorder emerged. Along with the eating disorder came increasingly rude, angry, defiant, and even aggressive behavior toward her mother. Emily's physical and mental condition eventually became so severe that her mother felt unable to manage Emily on her own, and Emily's father retuned from South Korea to place Emily in inpatient treatment.

Following admission, Emily was angry about being placed in treatment and insisted that she did not want to recover from her eating disorder. She refused to eat all food and became angry when providers attempted to speak with her in any way. Nevertheless, she did complete a battery of psychological tests, including the MMPI-A, from which the Minnesota Report was produced. Despite Emily's negative attitude toward treatment, MMPI-A validity indicators suggested that Emily responded to test items in a cooperative manner and her profile was likely to be an accurate representation of her current psychological functioning.

Emily's MMPI-A profile was elevated on Clinical Scales 7 and 2, in that order. This suggested prominent symptoms of anxiety and depression in the context of significant psychological maladjustment indicated by an elevated Welsh Anxiety Scale. Examination of Content Scales indicated that she endorsed many symptoms of depression, such as sadness, fatigue, crying spells, and self-deprecatory thoughts (elevated A-dep). She also endorsed many symptoms of anxiety, including tension, worry, sleep difficulties, concentration problems, intrusive thoughts, and obsessional thinking (A-obs, A-anx). These anxiety symptoms were not initially evident due to the prominence of Emily's anger and hostility early in treatment, but her anxiety and depressive symptoms soon became the primary focus of treatment as her treatment team discovered that these issues were closely tied to her eating disorder.

Emily's MMPI-A profile was also elevated on Scale 4, suggesting that Emily may rely on acting out behaviors as a primary defense mechanism. Her Scale 4 score suggested self-centeredness, poor impulse control, rebellious attitudes, and a high probability of aggressive or hostile behavior. Content Scale scores further suggested considerable anger control problems such as aggressive behaviors and temper tantrums (A-ang), which supported her mother's reports of behaviors at home. Elevation on the Family Problems Content Scale (A-fam) also highlighted the significant conflict and discord in the parent–child relationship reported by Emily's mother.

Further examination of the Scale 4 Harris–Lingoes subscales suggested that Emily was likely feeling misunderstood, alienated, isolated, lonely, and unhappy. This information offered a hypothesis to explain her hostility and anger. By exploring this hypothesis with Emily in psychotherapy, the treatment team learned that Emily was feeling misunderstood by her parents, who still identified with Korean culture, and by her peers, who had "American families." In fact, it was by reflecting this theme to Emily during a therapy session that an initial connection was established with her. She felt understood by her therapist, a true departure from her feelings of being misunderstood by everyone else in her world. Her feelings of alienation and isolation also became the anchoring point by which the team was able to explore Emily's anxiety and depressive symptoms, which were intimately related to her experience of being a cultural misfit. As Emily was offered empathy and supportive validation during the early days of treatment, her hostile attitude diminished considerably and she became increasingly willing to work toward recovery from her eating disorder.

Emily's MMPI-A also revealed a slight elevation on the Immaturity Scale, which, along with the Scale 4 elevation, suggested that Emily might be avoiding responsibility for her problems and externalizing blame. Indeed, Emily would try to make excuses or blame others for any problem that arose in the treatment setting. In light of this information, the use of behavioral modification plans, in which consequences were clear and consistent, proved to be very helpful in moving Emily toward accepting ownership of her behaviors during treatment. Emily's mother also needed education and support in developing effective limit-setting skills so that she was prepared to manage Emily's rebellious tendencies in the home environment.

Emily's high score on the MMPI-A PRO scale suggested possible involvement with a peer group that uses alcohol or drugs. However, she did not endorse alcohol or drug use problems herself on the ACK scale. As Emily opened up in treatment, she admitted to hanging out with a different crowd recently, as part of her desire to rebel against her parents' view of her as a "good girl." She was able to recognize that this peer group was not a good fit for her, and was able to identify other ways through which she might begin to form her own identity apart from her parents' expectations.

As treatment progressed, Emily acknowledged that she felt angry at her parents' high expectations for her academic achievement and resented that they had moved to the States for her benefit. She also resented the fact that her father left her alone with her mother, after which she felt responsible for taking care of her mother. This latter attribution explained why her once close relationship with her mother had deteriorated during the past year.

Emily wanted to have the freedom to explore her own identity. She was able to acknowledge that her eating disorder served to separate from her mother and form her own identity, because the eating and exercise choices she was making in her eating disorder deviated substantially from her parents' counsel. She also believed that her weight loss might help her to feel more accepted by her peers. Emily further reflected that her eating disorder was allowing her to hurt her parents, at whom she was quite angry. Emily was therefore taught assertive communication skills during treatment, allowing her to express these feelings and needs to her parents without resorting to aggressive or passive aggressive techniques. In response, her parents were willing to make adjustments to allow Emily more freedom and less pressure to achieve. Emily was also engaged in substantial amounts of group therapy, in which her feelings of alienation from peers were addressed.

Emily's anxiety and obsessionality diminished during treatment, as she became more optimistic about her relationships with her parents and peers, felt more understood, and believed that her parents' expectations of her were becoming more realistic. However, through school history and parental reports, the treatment team learned about long-term obsessional tendencies predating Emily's eating disorder. As a result, the team psychiatrist prescribed an anti-obsessional medication and Emily was enrolled in an anxiety group where she was educated about anxiety and obsessions and engaged in cognitive-behavioral treatments designed to address anxiety symptoms.

The MMPI-A data gathered during the first week of treatment were very helpful, because Emily was hostile, angry, and noncooperative at the start of treatment and unwilling to discuss the nature of her problems. The MMPI-A provided the information that was needed to develop hypotheses about Emily's experiences in relation to her overt psychopathology, to explore psychopathology that was otherwise less apparent, to select appropriate treatment strategies and goals, and to identify potential barriers to successful treatment. This information enabled Emily's treatment team to tailor their therapeutic approaches to minimize resistance and maximize progress toward the goals of treatment.

Providing Test Results Feedback

Butcher (1990) provided general guidelines for MMPI-2 feedback that are applicable to MMPI-A feedback. Butcher recommends that the clinician provide a brief description of the meaning of the Clinical Scales. The client's T-scores can be reviewed in relation to test norms. Responses should be encouraged from the client during the feedback process. This may be particularly helpful in eliciting active involvement from adolescent clients who may feel less invested in treatment due to parental initiation of treatment. Butcher emphasizes the importance of assessing clients' acceptance of feedback by asking them to restate the major findings in their own words and provide initial reactions to these findings. Butcher suggested that the clinician carefully assess how much feedback the client can realistically handle without becoming overwhelmed or overly defensive, and limit feedback if necessary.

As with all test feedback, clinicians need to rely on their clinical training to express sensitivity for the client's dignity, cultural background, education, and intelligence. The use of psychological jargon to explain the meaning of Clinical Scales should generally be avoided, along with terminology that could be perceived as a negative identity label (e.g., depressive, psychotic, hysterical, antisocial, borderline). Clinical Scale correlates should be presented with compassion and a focus on the adolescent's efforts to cope with difficult life experiences. For example, in addressing a Scale 6 elevation, rather than a negatively focused and potentially labeling statement, such as, "you appear very distrusting of other people," one could say, "it appears that perhaps you are not sure if you can trust other people." The latter emphasizes the client's choice, suggests compassion for the pain this choice may entail, and implies the client's ability to examine this choice in light of life experience and make possible changes in coping style that promote greater intimacy.

Presented with clinical sensitivity and judgment, MMPI-A testing feedback can be a highly effective way to elicit input into, and encourage ownership of, the treatment process for adolescents who have been involuntarily placed in treatment by their parents or courts. This feedback can assist adolescent clients in developing greater awareness of the thoughts, feelings, behaviors, and relationship patterns that they themselves have endorsed, and may provide an opportunity for the clinician to align with clients in identifying relevant treatment goals. In this manner, the treatment process can focus on the problems and issues that have been self-reported by the client through the MMPI-A, rather than problems that an authority figure, such as a parent, has identified. The MMPI-A can therefore assist the clinician in developing rapport with an adolescent client early in treatment, while also providing relevant information for strategic treatment planning.

Conclusion

The MMPI-A is a sophisticated instrument by which clinicians can assess psychopathology in adolescent clients aged 14–18 across outpatient, residential, and inpatient general and mental health settings, as well as academic and forensic settings. The MMPI-A includes Validity Scales that assist clinicians in determining the extent to which an adolescent responds to MMPI-A questions in an open, truthful, and cooperative manner. Valid MMPI-A profiles offer objective assessment of adolescent functioning in relation to standardized dimensions of psychopathology and serve as a measure of therapeutic change if administered repeatedly during treatment. Computer-driven scoring and reporting assist clinicians in accurate, comprehensive, and integrated interpretation of the MMPI-A's

many scales. The MMPI-A can be used to provide feedback to adolescents about their self-reported psychopathology and to gain their cooperation with the therapeutic process.

Future Directions

The MMPI-A is now being used with a variety of clinical populations outside the United States. Butcher et al. (2000) presented a qualitative cross-cultural comparison of the Minnesota Report for adolescents in 15 different countries. Clinicians in each of these 15 countries administered the MMPI-A to their clients and provided detailed case descriptions. In general, the clinicians who participated in the study found that the Minnesota Report accurately reflected their clients' issues, providing useful and accurate information. However, further research is needed in the area of cross-cultural generalizability of the MMPI-A. It might be important to create specific norms for populations outside the United States where the MMPI-A is being used with frequency.

Another area of future investigation involves assessment of adolescent clients with autism spectrum disorders. While low functioning autistic spectrum disorders may be apparent from an early age, higher functioning presentations such as Asperger's disorder often remain undiagnosed until adolescence. Clients with Asperger's disorder often first appear for treatment as teens with presenting behaviors suggestive of depression, anxiety, and eating disorders (Atwood, 2007). Adolescents with Asperger's may be incorrectly diagnosed with a variety of disorders, resulting in inappropriate and ineffective treatment approaches. Identification of typical Asperger's MMPI-A profiles or indicators may help clinicians to screen for this issue in adolescent clients, allowing for earlier detection and treatment for these individuals. Ozonoff, Garcia, Clark, and Lainhart (2005) studied the MMPI-2 profiles of 20 adults with autism spectrum disorders who fell in the average to above average range of intelligence. When compared to a control group, large group differences emerged, with the autism spectrum group scoring higher on the L scale, Clinical Scales 2 and 0, Content Scale Social Discomfort, Supplementary Scale Repression (R), and PSY-5 scale Introversion. The proportion of autism spectrum adults scoring in the clinical range on these scales was between 25% and 35%. It will be important to expand these initial findings in studies of adolescents using the MMPI-A. This is a timely issue given that the diagnosis of Asperger's disorder among teens has been rising substantially in the past decade (Latif & Williams, 2007).

Future development with the MMPI-A would also benefit from (1) a focus on improved methods of detecting defensive or fake good profiles, or reducing within-normal-limits profiles in clinical samples; (2) continued evaluation of the reliability and validity of both the newer MMPI-A scales such as the Content Component Scales and the less well explored scales such as the Harris–Lingoes and Si subscales; (3) further investigation to assess the utility of MMPI-A code types for enhanced interpretation; (4) additional research to improve algorithms and produce computerized reports of maximal validity; and (5) possible item modification to reduce the reading level of the MMPI-A and extend its usage to ages below 14.

References

Archer, R. P. (2005). *MMPI-A: Assessing adolescent psychopathology*. Mahwah, NJ: Lawrence Erlbaum.

Archer, R. P., Gordon, R. A., Anderson, G. L., & Giannettii, R. A., (1989). MMPI special Scale correlates for adolescent inpatients. *Journal of Personality Assessment, 53,* 654–664.

Archer, R. P., Gordon, R. A., Giannetti, R. A., & Singles, J. M. (1988). MMPI Scale clinical correlates for adolescent inpatients. *Journal of Personality Assessment, 52,* 707–721.

Archer, R. P., Handel, R. W., & Lynch, K. D. (2001). The effectiveness of MMPI-A items in discriminating between normative and clinical samples. *Journal of Personality Assessment, 77*(3), 420–435.

Archer, R. P., & Krishnamurthy, R. (2002). *Essentials of MMPI-A assessment.* New York: John Wiley & Sons.

Archer, R. P. Maruish, M., Imhof, E. A. & Piotrowski, C. (1991). Psychological test usage with adolescent clients: 1990 survey findings. *Professional Psychology, 22,* 247–252.

Archer, R. P. & Newsom, C. R. (2000). Psychological test usage with adolescent clients: Survey update. *Assessment, 7,* 227–235.

Archer, R. P., & Slesinger, D. (1999). MMPI-A patterns related to the endorsement of suicidal ideation. *Assessment, 6*(1), 51–59.

Atwood, T. (2007). *The complete guide to Asperger's syndrome.* London: Kingsley.

Baer, R. A., Kroll, L. S., Rinaldo, J., & Ballenger, J. (1999). Detecting and discriminating between random responding and overreporting on the MMPI-A. *Journal of Personality Assessment, 72*(2), 308–320.

Ben-Porath, Y. S. & Davis, D. L. (1996). *Case studies for interpreting the MMPI-A.* Minneapolis, MN: University of Minnesota Press.

Ben-Porath, Y. S., Hostetler, K., Butcher, J. N., & Graham, J. R. (1989). New subscales for the MMPI-2 Social Introversion (Si) scale. *Psychological Assessment, 1,* 169–174.

Butcher, J. N. (1990). *MMPI-2 in psychological treatment.* New York: Oxford University Press.

Butcher, J. N., Ellertsen, B., Ubostad, B., Bubb, E, Lucio, E., Lim, J., et al. (2000). *International case studies on the MMPI-A: An objective approach.* Minneapolis, MN: University of Minnesota Department of Psychology. Retrieved November 30, 2007, from http://www1.umn.edu/mmpi/reprints.php.

Butcher, J. N., & Williams, C. L. (2007). *User's guide to the Minnesota Report: Adolescent interpretive system.* Minneapolis, MN: National Computer Systems.

Butcher, J. N., Williams, C. L., Graham, J. R., Archer, R., Tellegen, A., Ben-Porath, Y. S., et al. (1992). *MMPI-A manual for administration, scoring, and interpretation.* Minneapolis, MN: University of Minnesota Press.

Capwell, D. F. (1945). Personality patterns of adolescent girls: II. Delinquents and nondelinquents. *Journal of Applied Psychology, 29,* 284–297.

Colligan, R. C. & Offord, K. P. (1989). The aging MMPI: Contemporary norms for contemporary teenagers. *Mayo Clinic Proceedings, 64,* 3–27.

Cumella, E. J., Wall, A. D., & Kerr-Almeida, N. (1999). MMPI-A in the inpatient assessment of adolescents with eating disorders. *Journal of Personality Assessment, 73*(1), 31–44.

Forbey, J. D., & Ben-Porath, Y. S. (2003). Incremental validity of the MMPI-A Content Scales in a residential treatment facility. *Assessment, 10*(2), 191–202.

Gottesman, I. I., Hanson, D. R., Kroeker, T. A., & Briggs, P. F. (1987). New MMPI normative data and power-tranformed T-score tables for the Hathaway–Monachesi Minnesota cohort of 14,019 fifteen-year-olds and 3,674 eighteen-year-olds. In R. P. Archer (Ed.), *Using the MMPI with adolescents* (pp. 241–297). Hillsdale, NJ: Lawrence Erlbaum.

Graham, P. (2000). *MMPI-2: Assessing personality and psychopathology* (3rd ed.). New York: Oxford University Press.

Hand, C. G., Archer, R. P., Handel, R. W., & Forbey, J. D. (2007). The classification accuracy of the Minnesota Multiphasic Personality Inventory-Adolescent: Effects of modifying the normative sample. *Assessment, 14*(1), 80–85.

Hanson, D. R., Gottesman, I. I., & Heston, L. L. (1990). Long-range schizophrenia forecasting: Many a slip twixt cup and lip. In J. E. Rolf, A. Masten, D. Cicchetti, K. Neuchterlein, & S. Weintraub (Eds.), *Risk and protective factors in the development of psychopathology* (pp. 424–444). New York: Cambridge University Press.

Harris, R. E., & Lingoes J. C. (1955). *SubScales for the MMPI : An aid to profile interpretation.* Department of Psychiatry, University of California School of Medicine and the Langley Porter Clinic. Mimeographed materials.

Hathaway, S. R., & McKinley, J. C. (1943). *The Minnesota Multiphasic Personality Inventory* (Rev. ed.). Minneapolis, MN: University of Minnesota Press.

Latif, A. H., & Williams, W. R. (2007) Diagnostic trends in autism spectrum disorders. *Autism: The International Journal of Research and Practice, 11*(6), 479–487.

Loevinger, J. (1976). *Ego Development: Conceptions and theories.* San Francisco: Jossey-Bass.

Lumry, A. E., Gottesman, I. I., & Tuason, V. B. (1982). MMPI state dependency during the course of bipolar psychosis. *Psychiatric Research, 7,* 59–67.

Marks, P. A., Seeman, W., & Haller, D. L. (1974). *The actuarial use of the MMPI with adolescents and adults.* Baltimore, MD: Williams & Wilkins.

McNulty, J. L., Harkness, A. R., Ben-Porath, Y. S. & Williams, C. L. (1997). Assessing the Personality Psychopathology Five (PSY-5) in adolescents: New MMPI-A scales. *Psychological Assessment, 9,* 250–259.

Meunier, G., & Bodkins, M. (2005). Interpretation of MMPI-A Scale 5 with female patients. *Psychological Reports, 96,* 545–546.

Monachesi, E. D., & Hathaway, S. R. (1969). The personality of delinquents. In J. N. Butcher (Ed.), *MMPI: Research developments and clinical applications* (pp. 207–219). Minneapolis, MN: University of Minnesota Press.

Ozonoff, S., Garcia, N., Clark, E., & Lainhart, J. E. (2005) MMPI-2 personality profiles of high-functioning adults with autism spectrum disorders. *Assessment, 12*(1), 86–95.

Sherwood, N. E., Ben-Porath, Y. S., & Williams, C. L. (1997). *Further refinements in content assessment with the MMPI-A: Development and application of the MMPI-A Content Component Scales.* Minneapolis, MN: University of Minnesota Press.

Tirrell, C. A. (2005). Concurrent validity of the MMPI-A substance abuse scales: MAC-R, ACK, and PRO. *Dissertation*

Abstracts International, Section B: The Sciences and Engineering, 65(9-B), 4893.

Williams, C. L., & Butcher, J. N. (1989). An MMPI study of adolescents: II. Verification and limitations of code type classifications. *Psychological Assessment, 1*, 260–265.

Williams, C. L., Butcher, J. N., Ben-Porath, Y. S., & Graham, J. R. (1992). *MMPI-A Content Scales: Assessing psychopathology in adolescents.* Minneapolis, MN: University of Minnesota Press.

Wrobel, N. H., & Lachar D. (1992) Refining adolescent MMPI interpretations: Moderating effects of gender in prediction of descriptions from parents. *Psychological Assessment, 4*, 375–381.

PART 6

Specific Settings and Problems

Assessment of Suicide Risk

Ronald A. Stolberg and Bruce Bongar

Abstract

The assessment of suicide risk remains one of the most important, complex, and difficult tasks performed by clinicians. Because suicide is one of the few fatal consequences of a psychiatric illness, accurate assessment of suicide risk is essential. Therefore, the purpose of this chapter is to present the assessment of suicide risk from a clinically balanced and research-informed standpoint. The optimal risk assessment integrates a sound clinical interview with actuarial instruments providing supplementary or clarifying information.

Keywords: suicide, risk assessment, self-harm, suicide risk, assessment, MMPI-2, MCMI-III, suicide attempts, suicide potential, Rorschach, BDI, suicidal ideation, suicidal intent, hopelessness

There are many reasons why the assessment of suicide risk is one of the most important aspects of clinical work. The fact that the majority (up to two-thirds) of those who commit suicide have had contact with a health-care professional in the month before their death (Kutcher & Chehil, 2007) illustrates this point profoundly. Because suicide is one of the few fatal consequences of psychiatric illness, accurate assessment of suicidal risk is essential (Packman, Marlitt, Bongar, & Pennuto, 2004). It is estimated that there are about a quarter million nonfatal suicide attempts each year in the United States. About 15% of those who attempt suicide will eventually take their own lives, and one-third of those who complete suicide have had nonfatal attempts in their past (Yufit & Lester, 2005). Suicide was the 11th leading cause of death in the United States in 2000, when an estimated 29,350 deaths were attributed to it (National Institute of Mental Health, 2003).

The purpose of this chapter is to present the assessment of suicide risk from a clinically balanced and research informed standpoint. There is no question that clinicians are increasingly faced with decisions about what to do when a patient reports suicidal ideation or when assessment data lead to the same conclusion (Wingate, Joiner, Walker, Rudd, & Jobes,

2004). Unfortunately, many suicidal individuals do not voluntarily report their thoughts or plans for self-harm to the professionals who are trained to act accordingly. If we work from the premise that not all patients are willing to admit their suicidal ideation to their health-care provider (Glassmire, Stolberg, Greene, & Bongar, 2001; Johnson, Lall, Bongar, & Nordlund, 1999), then we must utilize other resources, namely the psychological assessment and a sound clinical review of risk factors, to guide our intervention starategies.

A wide array of instruments have been developed for the measurement of various aspects of suicidality. These actuarial instruments can be a helpful supplement in risk elevation (Bryan & Rudd, 2006) but they have a notoriously high false-positive rate. Thus, optimal risk assessment integrates a sound clinical interview with actuarial instruments providing supplementary or clarifying information.

A recent trend is to focus on new empirically based strategies in the assessment of suicide potential (Bongar, 2000; Bryan & Rudd, 2006). Some researchers have turned their attention away from making predictions of patient behavior to clinicians' own views of critical factors when assessing for suicide (Bongar, 1991; Bruno, 1995; Bryan & Rudd, 2006;

Greaney, 1995; Kutcher & Chehil, 2007; Mahrer, 1993), attempting to identify the standards of care for this practice situation. This approach seeks to bridge the study of patient characteristics with that of clinician education, training, and experience in hope of describing reasonable and prudent practitioner behaviors. A profile of these behaviors not only is useful in identifying the standard of care, but can also help identify professional myths and deficiencies in practice, both essential to training and education efforts.

The assessment of suicide risk remains among the most important, complex, and difficult tasks performed by clinicians (Bongar, Maris, Berman, Litman, & Silverman, 1993; Chemtob, Bauer, Hamada, Pelowski, & Muraoka, 1989; Motto, 1991; Reinecke & Franklin-Scott, 2005). Because suicidology literature is voluminous, diverse, and sometimes contradictory, clinicians may have difficulty determining the relative importance of various factors when assessing the individual. Some researchers have emphasized particular charts of variables. Gutheil and Appelbaum (1982), for example, stated that the best approach to gathering data "focuses on previous psychiatric history; recent behavior or behavioral change; significant alteration of circumstances (e.g., loss of job); bizarreness of ideation or action; threats to self or others, or related behavior such as the purchase of poison, rope, or a gun; history of substance abuse and the like" (p. 52). These authors pointed out that the central clinical and legal concerns involve negligence in evaluation and in involuntary interventions (i.e., hospitalization). Brent, Kupfer, Bromet, and Dew (1988) noted that an accurate diagnostic assessment is necessary with regard to primary and comorbid psychiatric disorder, alcohol and drug abuse, personality disorders, and attendant medical disorders. In addition, they pointed out that a proper assessment mobilizes the families and significant others in order to improve compliance with treatment and decrease the chance of a relapse.

Much of the difficulty in the assessment of suicide risk comes from the psychometric weaknesses of existing suicide scales and measures (Rogers & Oney, 2005). We suggest that all measures of suicide risk (e.g., scales, tests, and critical items) need to be reviewed in context of the assessment itself. What is the referral question, why is this person here with me at this time, and how previous experiences or cognitions may impact the current presentation are all vital to consider. Recent advances in risk assessment research show areas that have been empirically demonstrated to be essential to the risk assessment (Rudd, Joiner, & Rajab, 2001). Bryan and Rudd

(2006) present a clear outline for a thorough risk assessment which includes an examination of:

1. predispositions to suicidal behavior (diagnosis, history of attempts, gender, etc.);
2. identifiable precipitant or stressors (loss, health problems, relationship problems, etc.);
3. symptomatic presentation (specific diagnosis with elevated risk factors);
4. presence of hopelessness (severity and duration);
5. the nature of suicidal thinking (intensity, duration, intent, means, lethality, etc.);
6. previous suicidal behavior (opportunity, frequency, and context of attempts, etc.);
7. impulsivity and self-control (subjective and objective control); and
8. protective factors (support, religion, children life satisfaction, etc.).

Kutcher and Chehil (2005) authored a quick structured approach to assessing suicide risk levels called the Tool for Assessment of Suicide Risk (TASR). Readers interested in a copy of the instrument and direction for its use are directed to Kutcher and Chehil (2007). One of the other useful components of the TASR is a list of important questions to ask. A few of those questions are listed here:

1. Do you have thoughts of death or suicide?
2. Do you have a specific plan?
3. What methods have you considered?
4. Do you have access to a plan?
5. Do you have a date and place in mind?
6. If you were alone now would you try to kill yourself?

Along these lines Fremouw, de Perczel, and Ellis (1990), as well as Bassuk (1982), noted that the assessment of a patient's potential suicide risk necessitates the gathering and weighing of a variety of information and data—and the importance of this particular assessment has led these psychologists to construct an impressive decision model that integrates and formalizes the steps for a thorough and reasonable decision about the risk for suicide for a particular patient. Somewhat like Bassuk's 1982 checklist system, their decision model involves seven steps for the psychologist:

1. *The collection of demographic information* (e.g., age, sex, race, marital status, and living situation) to determine whether the patient is in a high-risk or low-risk group.
2. *The examination of clinical and historical indicators* as the more specific information that

increases or decreases the patient's risk for suicide (e.g., unique historical, environmental, and psychological features that a patient presents in the intake interview, or during ongoing therapy).

a. Questions about general historical-situational factors (which begin to lead the clinician to be concerned about a higher risk).

b. Very specific clinical indicators and warning signs that often are the precursors of an imminent attempt (e.g., having a definite plan, strong self-destructive impulses).

c. Psychological indicators such as recent losses, depression-anxiety, isolation-withdrawal, hopelessness, disorientation-disorganization, alcohol and drug use, change in clinical features, suicide plan, and final arrangements for his or her own death.

3. *An initial screening for risk*, that is, after examining historical-situational, demographic, and clinical indicators, the clinician must make a decision about whether the potential risk for suicide warrants any further assessment. If there appears to be no risk, assessment and treatment proceed in a routine fashion. However, if there are risk factors in the demographic or clinical-situational-historical matrix, the clinician should assess the current risk for suicide through two formats, initially through interview, and if indicated, by self-report.

4. *Direct assessment of risk* using:

a. *The clinical interview* (which includes the patient's reasons for feeling suicidal, as well as his or her reasons for living), and, where risk appears mild, moderate, or unknown.

b. *Assessment by self-report* (e.g., the use of standardized assessment instruments such as the Beck Depression and Hopelessness scales to facilitate a thorough understanding).

5. *Determination of the level of risk and the implementation of a response* (e.g., none to low risk, mild, moderate, high).

6. *Determination of the imminence of risk* (e.g., assessment and documentation of rationale, consultation).

7. *Implementation of treatment strategies* (e.g., intensified outpatient care, voluntary hospitalization, involuntary hospitalization, etc.).

Although the above model is an important contribution as a systematic decision-making tool for the practicing clinician (and may very well represent the future general shape of standard models of assessment/intervention for suicide potential), Motto (1989), in a review of general problems in suicide risk assessment, pointed out one of the concerns is that to date we have no established and generally accepted procedure for clinicians to follow.

Motto (personal communication, July 1998) also noted that the accurate assessment of imminent risk does improve with clinical experience, and that supervision in working with suicidal patients should be a crucial element in all clinical training programs—"there is just no substitute for experience." Rosenberg (1997) pointed out that the suicide prevention literature primarily focuses on action-based interventions (e.g., assessment of risk factors and the use of direct interventions, such as hospitalization) for preventing suicide and that it lacks specific strategies to deal with the patient's emotional pain associated with suicidal ideation. In response to this need, Rosenberg (1997) designed a suicide assessment and intervention training model.

The clinical training approach suggested here differs from present training in several important ways. First, a systematic training model was developed and sequenced with respect to expertise and cognitive psychology principles (see Rosenberg, 1997). Few current training models utilize principles gleaned from this body of literature. Second, this model provides training in basic assessment skills, whereas most other programs focus on teaching basic interviewing or specific counseling skills (e.g., asking open-ended questions and learning reflection-of-feeling responses). Third, affective or feeling-based intervention strategies (intended to address underlying thoughts or feelings of suicide) are highlighted in this approach and supplement action-based strategies that are more commonly used.

Simon (1988) remarked that providing a reasonable standard of care in assessing and diagnosing suicidal patients preempts "the very problematic issue of prediction of suicide for which standards do not exist. Psychiatrists have not been held legally liable for inaccurate predictions of suicide per se" (pp. 86–87). When discussing what clinicians can do to reduce their legal liability when treating a suicidal patient, Simon (1992) identified "failure to diagnose" (assess the risk of suicide) (p. 274) as one of the three broad categories of negligence of which clinicians should be aware. Only when they "have failed to collect necessary data and logically assess it in making a prediction of suicide have lawsuits against psychiatrists prevailed" (Simon, 1988, pp. 86–87).

However, Lewinsohn, Garrison, Langhinrichsen, and Marsteller (1989) pointed out that the low base rate of suicide makes it very difficult for screening instruments to predict accurately the degree of suicidal risk for any specific individual. Specifically, the low base rate results in a very large number of false-positive assessments relative to the number of true positives, even when the most effective screening instruments are used.

More recently, however, Bongar (2002) has constructed a comprehensive and integrated decision checklist that draws upon and recognizes the important contributions of Beck, Kovacs, and Weissman's (1979) empirical model (e.g., hopelessness, helplessness, negative cognitions), Fawcett and colleagues' (Fawcett, Scheftner, Clark, Hedeker, Gibbons, & Coryell, 1987) empirical model (e.g., chronic vs. acute, the social matrix, communication of intent), Hirschfeld and Davidson's (1988) epidemiological model, Simon's checklist model, Shneidman's psychological model, and Yufit's suicide assessment team/Suicide Assessment Battery/Suicide Screening Checklist (SAT/SAB/SSC) protocols (1988). This clinical and legal formulation of a standard of care for the assessment of elevated risk (Bongar, 2002) follows the decision checklist tradition and puts forward a large number of specific steps and detection-decision points. However, practitioners should be cautious: Such approaches often offer a possible set of known risk factors and often are not meant to be definitive or exhaustive. Mental health professionals will almost certainly tailor the assessment of elevated risk to what Motto (1989) has shown to be the uniqueness of every decision on suicide probability. Fawcett et al. (1987), using data from a large-scale prospective study of patients with major affective disorders, found that 25 patients (of a total of 954) committed suicide; hopelessness, loss of pleasure or interest, and mood cycling during the index episode differentiated the suicide group. These researchers noted that, although suicide is a relatively frequent event in depressed patients, it still has a statistically low base rate and, therefore, may be statistically unpredictable on an individual basis using cross-sectional measures. Fawcett (1988) did offer a model that, while acknowledging the limitations of the current knowledge base, enumerates a variety of both short-term (acute predictors) and long-term suicide risk features (chronic predictors).

In recognition of the methodological and clinical difficulties in predicting suicide, the core of this chapter on assessment of suicide risk will focus on the collection of critical data and decision points in the clinical formulation, detection, and documentation of "imminent and elevated risk" in the usual and customary populations seen in professional psychological practice. In view of publications that focus specifically on the issues of youth suicide and suicide among the elderly (Berman, Jobes, & Silverman, 2006; Groholt, Ekeberg, & Haldorsen, 2006; Gutierrez, 2006; Heisel & Flett, 2006; McIntosh, Santos, Hubbard, & Overholser, 1994; Wise & Spengler, 1997), this chapter will emphasize more general personality, clinical, and legal issues with regard to the formulation of a standard of care for adult clinical populations.

A clinical approach to the assessment of suicidal patients

1. recognizes the probabilistic nature of risk detection versus risk prediction;

2. acknowledges the strengths and limitations of the traditional diagnostic categories (e.g., DSM (Diagnostic and statistical manual)), as well as the various theories of psychotherapy and psychopathology;

3. understands epidemiologic and clinical risk factors within specific groups, taking into consideration the data on both acute and chronic predictors of risk;

4. remembers when consultation, supervision, and referral are necessary; and

5. integrates a careful clinical history, mental status examination, ongoing clinical evaluations, consultations, information from significant others, and data from psychological assessment and suicide risk estimators/scales into a broad-spectrum information-gathering procedure for systematic assessment and management of detected risk.

Recently, seven factors relevant to suicide risk were identified by Joiner, Walker, Rudd, and Jobes (1999): previous suicidal behavior, type of current suicidal symptoms, precipitant stressors, symptomatic presentation, self-control and impulsivity, predispositions, and protective factors. When present, these seven factors have different implications for overall risk of suicide and are influenced by the patient's status as either a suicide ideator, single attempter, or multiple attempter.

The Modified Scale for Suicidal Ideation (Joiner, Rudd, & Rajab, 1997) identified two factors, "resolved plans and preparation" and "suicidal desire and ideation," as highly indicative of increased suicide risk. "Resolved plans and preparation" include the following symptoms: "a sense of courage to make an attempt, availability of means to and opportunity for attempt, duration of suicidal ideation, and intensity of suicidal ideation" (Joiner et al., 1999, p. 448). The authors suggest that a patient who presents with these symptoms should be considered as at least a moderate risk for suicide. The second factor, "suicidal desire and ideation," includes the following symptoms: "reasons for living, wish to die, frequency of ideation, wish not to live, passive attempts, desire for attempt, expectancy of attempt, lack of deterrents to attempt, and talk of death and/or suicide" (Joiner et al., 1999, p. 448). In the absence of symptoms associated with the "resolved plans and preparation" factor and the other five factors listed above, and if the patient is not a multiple attempter, then the patient would not be considered at risk for suicide. The patient's past history of suicide attempts is used in conjunction with specific current suicidal symptoms, such as "resolved suicide plans and preparation," and is interpreted in relationship with the other five factors to produce a model for assessment of suicidal risk.

For example, a patient who expresses a wish to die, who talks of suicide, and who reports frequent suicidal ideation can be worrisome to the clinician. In the absence of symptoms from the resolved plans and preparation factor, however (and in the absence of multiple attempt status or complicating factors from other domains), these symptoms do not warrant a high-risk designation. As an additional example, a patient who expresses little desire for death and relatively infrequent suicidal ideation, but who senses high competence and courage to attempt to suicide, who has means and opportunity, and who reports details of a suicide plan, is at high risk, regardless of other factors (Joiner et al., 1999, p. 448).

However, before proceeding, it is essential to emphasize once again that hard and fast actuarial data on the long-term prediction of attempted or completed suicide—predictions that can be directly translated to the emergent clinical moment—do not presently exist. Currently, "there are no pathognomic predictors of suicide" (Simon, 1987, p. 259). Further, we will be following a tradition set by Monahan (1981) in his superb treatise on the clinical prediction of violent behavior, another clinical dilemma suffused with uncertainty and a lack of hard and fast actuarial data, namely, that this chapter represents "nothing more (or less) than the professional judgment of persons experienced at the task of prediction" (Monahan, 1981, p. 101) and that clinicians would do well to follow Meehl's advice that, "when actuarial data do not exist, we must use our heads" (Monahan, 1981, p. 108).

Recent Empirical Evidence on Risk Assessment Practices

In 1990, the Risk Assessment Committee of the American Association of Suicidology (AAS) reported the results of their survey on suicide risk assessment procedures among a random sample of practicing psychologists, psychiatrists, and clinical social workers (including members and nonmembers of the AAS). Although the results of this survey should be interpreted with caution due to the small sample size ($n = 5414$) and relatively low response rate (38%), they do provide at least an initial glimpse into the assessment practices of practitioners (Jobes, Eyman, & Yufit, 1990). Also of interest was the amount of assessment activity carried out by the respondents, many of whom appeared to be psychologists—they reported evaluating, on the average, 1.9 suicidal adolescents and 2.8 suicidal adults per month.

Specifically, Jobes, et al. (1990) found that:

1. Suicide assessment instruments appear to be used infrequently and are rated as having limited usefulness. For adolescents, the most frequently used were the Beck Hopelessness Scale (BHS) (28%) and the Beck Suicide Intent Scale (SIS) (23%). For adults the most frequently used were BHS (34%) and SIS (28%). These two scales were rated as "somewhat useful" for both adults and adolescents.

2. Although traditional psychological tests are used more frequently, they are not rated as very useful. The most commonly used tests were the Minnesota Multiphasic Personality Inventory (MMPI, 47%), Beck Depression Inventory (BDI, 46%), the Rorschach (44%), and the Thematic Apperception Test (TAT, 42%). Of these, only the BDI received a rating of "somewhat useful."

3. With a few exceptions, there are few major differences in the approaches used to assess acute versus chronic risk, and limited differences in the assessment of adults compared with the assessment of adolescents. Instead, most clinicians clearly rely primarily on the clinical interview to assess suicide (specifically, on certain valued questions and observations).

Linehan (Linehan, Rizvi, Welch, & Page, 2000) updated her 1981 model for analyzing risk factors associated with suicidal behaviors in an effort to determine whether risk factors among patients diagnosed with a personality disorder differ from those among individuals in the general population. Linehan noted that although many of the risk factors are the same, a few factors are actually not significant for individuals with borderline personality disorder. Linehan et al. (2000) also explored why age, marital status, and gender did not appear to indicate a heightened risk for suicidal behavior. They reported that the absence of an effect for marital status may be due to low variance in that individuals meeting criteria for this diagnosis are less likely to be married. The absence of an effect for age may have to do with the follow-up period in the studies reported. None of the studies followed elderly people meeting criteria for borderline personality disorder. The absence of gender difference in suicide parallels findings reported by Kreitman (1977) showing similar rates of suicide for males and females with histories of repeated parasuicidal acts—a criterion for borderlines.

Recent empirical studies of psychologists' reported practice behaviors confirm the primary reliance on the clinical interview as the major risk assessment tool in clinical practice (Card-Strong, 1998; Greaney, 1995; Peruzzi & Bongar, 1999). New empirically based strategies may well be needed to approach the assessment of suicidal potential. Some researchers have turned their attention away from making predictions of patient behavior to clinicians' own views of critical factors when assessing for suicide (Bongar, 1991; Bruno, 1995; Greaney, 1995; Mahrer, 1993), attempting to identify the standards of care for this practice situation. This approach seeks to bridge the study of patient characteristics with that of clinician education, training, and experience in hopes of describing "reasonable and prudent" practitioner behaviors. A profile of these behaviors not only is useful in identifying the standard of care, but can also help identify professional myths and deficiencies in practice, both essential to training and education efforts.

To shed some light on the preferences of active practitioners and their primary reliance on interview and observational data, this chapter will examine the historical and contemporary literature on the use of psychological tests, suicide scales, and risk estimators, as well as the epidemiological and clinical data on risk factors. This leads to the importance of formulation of clinical judgment via important clinical observations and key elements in the clinical interview, as integral components of a model of comprehensive clinical assessment and risk management.

Psychological Testing

The psychological assessment of suicidal risk is a process fraught with personal uneasiness and anxiety on the part of the mental health professional. The burden is awesome, and the responsibility is frightening (Neuringer, 1974a). Neuringer remarked that if all of the methodological problems associated with valid assessment of suicidal risk can be overcome, then the occurrence of false negatives will be severely diminished, which is the aim of suicide assessment.

Motto (1991) stated that because each individual is a unique entity, the nature of assessment and measurement is difficult. He noted that a measure and observation that may determine suicide risk in one person may have different significance or no relevance at all for another person. He concluded that if clinicians are given the opportunity to establish a level of trust that ensures candor and openness, then the clinician is in the optimal position to assess risk in individual cases.

Kaplan, Asnis, Sanderson, and Keswani (1994) reported that there is a high level of agreement between patients disclosing the same information about suicidal behaviors on a self-report measure compared with face-to-face communications with a clinician in a clinical interview. Kaplan found the one exception is that many patients tend to disclose more information regarding recent suicidal ideation on self-report forms. He did not find any discrepancies between self-report and verbal communication on suicidal information that was historical in nature.

However, it should be emphasized that the assessment of a patient's risk for suicide should never be based on a single score or scale. A complete evaluation of risk factors, such as the patient's psychiatric diagnosis, substance abuse, previous suicide attempts, a family history of suicide, and current level of functioning, should be considered in conjunction with psychological assessment results (Bongar, 1992; Maris, Berman, Maltsberger, & Yufit, 1992).

The Rorschach Inkblot Technique

While there has been little agreement on a single assessment tool that can adequately predict suicide, there is agreement that a thorough evaluation includes both a clinical interview and available psychological tests. The Rorschach Comprehensive System (Exner, 2003) is one of the psychological tests frequently used in clinical settings for this purpose (Ganellen, 2005). The following is a review of current approaches and a review of the historical literature on thistopic.

There are several ways to analyze a Rorschach Inkblot method protocol. The traditional method is that of the single sign approach. This approach hinges on the identification of Rorschach variables thought to be associated with suicide. Fowler, Hilsenroth, and Piers (2001) remind us to be cautious of this approach because individual variables are almost always less reliable and have less statistical power than approaches including multiple variables.

The best known single Rorschach variable claimed to be associated with suicidality is the color-shading blend (Ganellen, 2005). An early study by Applebaum and Holtzman (1962) found an association between one or more color-shading blends and a vulnerability to suicidal behavior. The results have been replicated throughout the years with and without success (Applebaum & Colson, 1968; Fowler et al., 2001; Hansell, Lerner, Milden, & Ludolph, 1988; Silberg & Armstrong, 1992). Most recently Fowler et al. (2001) found that a near-lethal suicide group of subjects produced significantly more color-shading blend responses than two other control groups.

Another single sign approach is that of examining the record for transparencies or cross-sectional responses. The first significant findings came from a study by Blatt and Ritzler (1974). They compared their small sample ($n = 12$) of patients who had committed suicide with a matched control group and found that the best differentiating variable was the number of transparencies/cross-sectional responses. These results have been studied and expanded upon by several authors (Fowler et al., 2001; Hansell et al., 1988; Silberg & Armstrong, 1992). A consistent problem with this approach is the relatively high occurrence of transparencies and cross-sectional responses in the protocols of nonsuicidal patients.

A progressive approach to identifying suicide risk with the Comprehensive System was developed by Exner and Wylie (1977). Their pursuit resulted in a cluster of Rorschach variables associated with suicidal behavior. With this cluster of variables, they were initially able to correctly identify 75% of the suicide completes from a sample of both patients and non-patients. This cluster of variables became known as the Rorschach Suicide Constellation (S-CON). It was found to have a high rate of true positives while maintaining a low rate of false positives (Ganellen, 2005). S-CON was eventually revised in 1993 but Wood, Nezworski, and Stejskal (1996) still questioned the validity and reliability of the measure and pointed out that many of the original statistical findings remained unpublished. Fowler et al. (2001) responded to the criticisms by conducting a large-scale study. They found the revised S-CON to do well in distinguishing suicidal and near-lethal suicidal behavior from parasuicidal behavior. Fowler, Hilsenroth, and Piers (2001) did recommend that lowering the S-CON cutoff score would increase its sensitivity. The current recommendation is to use a cut off score of 7 or above.

An articulate and well-structured summary of Rorschach data useful in the identification of individuals at elevated risk for suicide is presented by Ganellen (2005). He identifies five high-risk affective states and the corresponding Rorschach data for each.

Hopelessness/Despair: Lambda $< .45$; D-score < 0; $M = 0$ or FC + CF + C = 0; $m > 2$ and/or $Y > 2$.

Guilt/Self-Hatred: $V > 0$; FD > 2; Fr > 0; egocentricity index $< .33$ or $> .44$ with Fr + 0.

Loss/Abandonment: $T >$ or $= 2$; Food > 0; $p > a + 1$; Mp $>$ Ma

Loneliness/Isolation: Isolation index $> .33$; CDI $>$ or $= 4$; $H < (H) + Hd + (Hd)$

Impulsivity: $D < 0$; FM $<$ or $= 2$; $C > 0$; Zd $<$ or $= -.35$; M– or Formless M > 0

Other interesting studies have been completed recently looking at using the Rorschach in non-traditional ways. Lundback et al. (2006) investigated the link between Cerebrospinal fluid 5-hydroxyindoleacetic acid CSF 5-HIAA and scores on the Rorschach of patient with recent suicide attempts. They found a strong relationship between low CSF 5-HIAA levels and high S-CON and vista scores on the Rorschach for these patients. Grava, Ceroni, Rucci, and Scudellari (2006) found that by using some of Klopfer and Davidson's (1962) indexes they were able to identify the quality of mood, the degree of bad impulse management, and the degree of aggression. These personality structures were linked to a "pathway of suicide" by the authors.

Historically, the Rorschach technique was the most commonly used method for estimating the risk of suicide, although it has been supplanted by more sophisticated psychometric instruments such as the MMPI and various suicide lethality scales (Neuringer, 1974b). Neuringer noted that there has not been any particular determinant, sign, or set of signs, or content which appears to be associated with suicide under all or even most conditions.

However, the Rorschach may still be a potent tool for assessing the risk of suicide, if it is used correctly. Meyer (1989) argued that Exner's (1978) research provided an elegant and effective tool for the prediction for suicide potential. He cited a large number of specific factors from Exner's seminal contribution *The Rorschach: A Comprehensive System* (Exner, 1978) (e.g., FV + VF + V + FD is greater than 2; occurrence of a color-shading response; Zd is greater than or equal to 3.5; 3r + (2)/R is less than 0.30, experience potential is greater than experience actual; CF1C is greater than FC; S is greater than 3; X1% is less than 0.70; pure H is less than 2; P is greater than 8, or less than 3; R is less than 17). Meyer (1989) noted that a number of authors concur with Exner that the number of responses is low in suicidals, especially when they are depressed, that less integrated color responses are more common, and that the number of popular responses are either very high or low (Swiercinsky, 1985).

Meyer (1989) also pointed out the importance of content that suggests decay or geographic depression as indicators of suicidal ideation. He noted that "responses that suggest hanging or drowning or other direct means of suicide should obviously alert the examiner to further consideration" (p. 319). Here he is in agreement with Neuringer (1974b), who suggested that the clinician rely most on content from the Rorschach. Neuringer wrote that if suicidal content appears on the Rorschach, it should be taken very seriously since its manifestation could be an indication that self-destructive behavior is close to the surface and that the patient is trying communicate to the examiner.

Meyer (1993) examined the effect of the response frequency (R) on the suicide constellation to determine the effects of the constellation's ability to discriminate among groups when reports deviate from the average length. He determined that within the suicide constellation, longer protocols are significantly more likely to have more than two vista or form dimension scores, a color-shading blend, more than three morbid scores, and more than three space responses. He concluded that more frequent responses are associated with higher scores on the S-CON. Frank (1994) warned that if a person manifests suicidal ideation or behavior and has a Rorschach with indicators of poor form quality (CF5C.FC and X1%, 70), this individual should be considered at risk for suicide.

Eyman and Eyman (1991) maintained that although single signs on the Rorschach have been used to predict suicide potential (e.g., transparency responses and color shading), the results of studies on single signs have been mixed. There is some clinical support for the use of these variables to assess suicide risk but, thus far, the research is insufficient to allow a clinician to feel confident in their use (Eyman & Eyman, 1991).

Silberg and Armstrong (1992) sought to determine the usefulness of the Rorschach in uncovering suicidal potential in hospitalized adolescents. They compared severely depressed nonsuicidal patients with severely depressed suicidal patients to isolate the factors unique to suicidal behavior and unrelated to diagnostic variables. They had 138 subjects with ages ranging from 12 to 18 and carrying a wide variety of diagnoses. They concluded that the adult suicidal constellation did not significantly discriminate among the groups. However, they found that four of the six features of the index selected 64% of suicidal subjects. This indicated that suicidal adolescents are painfully introspective (with FV + VF + V > 0), exhibit painful arousal (color-shading blends .1), are morbidly preoccupied (MOR > 0), are impulsive (CF1C.FC), and have misperceptions of people (M– and distorted reasoning skills, weighted special scores > 9) (Silberg & Armstrong, 1992).

Perhaps the Rorschach can be most useful in the assessment of suicide risk if it is combined with appropriate and sound clinical judgment (Eyman & Eyman, 1991). Eyman and Eyman (1991) cautioned that suicide is too complex a behavior to be adequately captured by a single sign. They suggested that the configurational or constellation approach also shows promise for the use of the Rorschach for the assessment of risk. They noted that "characterological features can be found among people who are seriously suicidal that differentiate them from mild-attempters and these characteristics can be assessed using the Rorschach and the TAT" (p. 48).

Neuringer (1974b) further cautioned that the clinician should not make an inference about suicidal intention from the Rorschach by itself; that case history material, and data from other psychometric instruments, can help to maximize the accuracy of the decision-making process. He concluded that "the clinician should strive to have all the data possible available to him. The presence of previous suicidal attempts and threats should compound the danger associated with the presence of suicidal Rorschach content" (p. 91). For additional information on use of the Rorschach with the suicidal patient, the reader is directed to Exner (1978, 1986), Eyman and Eyman (1991), Meyer (1989), and Neuringer (1974b).

Minnesota Multiphasic Personality Inventory (MMPI, MMPI-2, and MMPI-A)

The MMPI-2 (Butcher, Dahlstrom, Graham, Tellegen, & Kaemmer, 1989) and its corresponding adolescent version, the MMPI-A (Butcher et al., 1992), are the most widely used instruments for assessing psychopathology in clinical practice (Greene, 2000) and are the most widely used objective personality assessment measures in the world (Archer & Newsom, 2000; Friedman, Lewak, Nichols, & Webb, 2001).

Inconsistent findings among retrospective comparisons of suicide attempters and nonattempting comparison groups have led some researchers (e.g., Eyman & Eyman, 1991) to conclude that, despite considerable research effort, no MMPI item, scale, or profile configuration has been found to consistently differentiate suicidal and nonsuicidal patients. They did concede that the restandardized MMPI-2 may provide more valid indicators of suicidality.

An articulate decription of the current trend in MMPI suicide research is presented by Friedman, Archer, and Handel (2005) who wrote:

> The move to a risk assessment model from dangerousness prediction per se can also be applied to MMPI interpretation. Numerous factors influence an individual to think and behave in a suicidal (homocidal) manner. . . . The exacerbation of severe psychiatric symptoms may also increase suicidal risk such as common hallucinations, intolerable depressive symptoms, or alcohol and/or drug intoxication. The value of the MMPI lies in being part of a risk assessment mosaic that includes interview data, collateral sources of information, and other psychometric data to help serve the mission of estimating suicide potential rather than the prediction of actual suicide. In this fashion, the test data can help inform and guide a risk management strategy. (p. 65)

With the release of the MMPI-2, there became available to practitioners the Koss–Butcher Critical Item Set-Revised, listing 22 items that are related specifically to depressed suicidal ideation. However, Butcher (1989) noted that these critical items are not "designed to operate as scales. They are used to highlight item content that might be particularly significant in the individual's case. As sources of clinical hypotheses, the critical items might be used to key the clinician into problem areas or concerns the patient may have" (Butcher, 1989, p. 17). (For additional information on the specifics of these critical items, the reader is directed to the work of Butcher, 1989; Butcher et al., 1989).

Although the majority of studies investigating the utility of the MMPI instruments during suicide assessment focused on the original version of the test, two recent studies evaluated the utility of the revised version of the test (the MMPI-2: Butcher et al., 1989) for the assessment of suicide potential. Sepaher, Bongar, and Greene (1999) found that approximately 20% of psychiatric patients endorsed items 506 and 520 among nine different well-defined MMPI-2 code types. These items were referred to as the "I mean business" items by Sepaher et al. because both directly inquire about a recent history of suicidal ideation or intent. Glassmire et al. (2001) found that these and four additional similar items (150, 303, 524, and 530) were often endorsed by psychotherapy patients who had recently denied a history of suicidality during an intake interview. The authors found that a large percentage of patients who endorsed at least one of the MMPI-2 suicide items also denied suicidal ideation or behavior during a telephone intake interview. The authors found that these six items could be grouped together to provide a highly face-valid and internally consistent scale of self-reported suicide potential they called the Suicide Potential Scale (SPS). The reader is referred to this article by Glassmire et al. for a table containing linear T-score conversions for this scale based on a large clinical sample.

Additionally, a study (Stolberg, Glassmire, Ricci, Greene, & Bongar, 1999) designed to establish practice guidelines and a standard of care for the use of the MMPI-2 with suicidal patients examined how a select group of specialists used the MMPI/MMPI-2 to assess risk. Delphi methodology was used, which resulted in expert consensus on the following questions: (a) How (if at all) do you use the Validity Scales to assess for suicide potential? (b) How (if at all) do you use the Clinical Scales to assess for suicide potential? (c) Which specific items, or questions, if any, do you use when assessing for suicide potential? (d) "How (if at all) do you use other Scales (e.g., Content, Supplementary, Research Scales) to assess for suicide potential?

Clopton (1974), in an extensive review of the MMPI and the assessment of suicide risk, pointed to the findings of Dahlstrom, Welsh, and Dalhstrom (1972) that the degree of the person's depression, that is, an elevated score on Scale 2 (D) of the MMPI, was a mood state frequently associated with a preoccupation with death and suicide. He continued:

> The implication of high scores on scale 2 depend on other features of the MMPI and upon the behavior of the person taking the test. For instance, it is their conclusion (Dahlstrom et al., 1972) that suicidal risk is greater when a person's MMPI results show a significant elevation on scale 2 but his behavior does not give any indication of depression, and he denies depressive thoughts and feelings, than when the depression indicated by a scale 2 elevation is clearly reflected in the person's behavior. (p. 118)

Clopton also noted that the one standard MMPI scale found the most frequently to differentiate suicidal and nonsuicidal groups was Scale 2. Meyer (1989) agreed, and stated that the prototypical pattern for suicidal individuals is the 2-7/7-2 combination on the MMPI. He felt that this code specifically indicates the presence of suicidal ideation, and that whenever Scale 2 is elevated above 80T, the clinician should raise the possibility suicidal ideation.

Meyer also pointed out that the critical items on the MMPI concerning suicide should always be carefully checked and that the likelihood of suicidal ideation "being actualized increases as scores on scale 4, 8, and 9 rise, reflecting greater loss of control over impulses, a rise in energy available for behavior, and an increasing sense of isolation and resentment toward other people" (p. 317), respectively. Specifically, a rise in Scale 8 indicates that suicidal patients may actually kill themselves whether or not they want to succeed; their impaired judgment may bring about an inadvertent suicide. He also noted that people can become suicidal following a severe loss in their psychosocial world and that a high spike on Scale 2 is characteristic of these circumstances. Meyer believes that the "2-4/4-2 code is more likely to reflect a manipulative suicide. Where both scales 4 and 6 are elevated, in addition to at least a moderate elevation on scales 2 and 7, repressed anger and interpersonal hostility are as basic to a suicide attempt as manipulation" (p. 318).

Craig and Olsen (1990) compared drug addicts without a history of suicide attempts to drug addicts with a history of suicide attempts. They found that suicide attempters were characterized by higher levels of maladjustment (mostly in the areas of depression) and feelings of alienation, were more prone to utilize projection and externalization, and were more emotionally withdrawn. Significant differences were found on scales F, K, Depression, Hysteria, Psychopathic Deviance, Masculinity/Femininity, Paranoia, Psychasthenia, Schizophrenia, and Social Introversion.

Except for K, the suicidal attempters obtained higher mean scores. The modal profile of the suicide attempter group (excluding scales Mf and Si) had an average T-score elevation of 73.12 compared with 66.12 of the nonsuicidal group. In addition, suicidal ideators scored highest on the Pd scale compared with nonattempters and attempters. Suicide attempters scored higher on content scales DEP, ORG, and MOR compared with the no-history of attempt group. Attempters and ideators scored higher on the FAM content scale compared with the no-history group. Code types found to be unique to the suicide attempt group were 1-8/8-1, 2-9/9-2, 4-3, and 5-9. Code types that were specific to the no-history group were 2, 5, 9, 1-9, 6-2, and 8-9. In the suicide attempt group, 42% of the codes comprised the 2-4/4-2, 4-9/9-4, 4-8/8-4, and 6-8/8-6 code types.

Finally, Osborne (1985), after reviewing the use of the MMPI in psychiatric practice, argued that the MMPI is best used within the context of other information-gathering techniques and should be viewed as providing the clinician with hypotheses that can be verified with other methods. Such other methods could include the use of other psychological tests, suicide scales, and risk estimators, and a comprehensive clinical interview and history (Hendren, 1990).

In addition to the extensive research on the MMPI/MMPI-2 there are several MMPI-A studies that can guide the interested clinician. Forbey and Ben-Porath (1998) developed a critical item set for the MMPI-A using a combination of empirical and rational procedures. Their six-item set includes two items (177 and 283) that explicitly inquire about suicidal ideation. Archer and Slesinger (1999) included one additional item (399) which asks about hopelessness and explored the endorsement frequency of these three items in relation to MMPI-A mean clinical scale elevations and code-type classifications (Friedman et al., 2005). They found that adolescents who endorsed these three items more frequently produced spike 2 or spike 8 profiles, and 4-8/8-4, 8-9/9-8, 6-8/8-6 profiles.

16-PF

Meyer and Deitsch (1996) noted that on the Sixteen Personality Factors (16-PF), suicide attempters appear consistently to show themselves as shy, tense, suspicious, expedient, emotionally unstable, apprehensive, self-sufficient, somewhat introverted, and extremely anxious: "Translated into 16 PF scales, this means high scores on Q4, O, 1, Q2 and lower scores on G, H, and C. Furthermore, repeat attempters typically score lower on scales Q3 and C than do first-time attempters, indicating less stability and more impulsivity" (p. 318).

Millon Clinical Multiaxial Inventory: MCMI-III and MACI

McCann and Suess (1988) examined the Millon Clinical Multiaxial Inventory (MCMI) profiles of 131 psychiatric inpatients to identify 1-2-3-8 code types on the basic personality scales. This profile reflects a schizoid, avoidant, dependent, and passive–aggressive blend of personality traits. Approximately 25% of the subjects obtained the 1-2-3-8 code type. The authors' analyses of the diagnoses and clinical records of these patients suggested that this profile reflects an affect/mood disturbance with prominent depressive features and suicidal ideation or suicide attempt prior to admission in the hospital. Summarizing, Meyer and Deitsch (1996) wrote of the MCMI that:

> As might be expected, elevations on the MCMI of 85 or higher on D and CC, and a high score on the Desirability Scale would be indicative of suicide potential

(Choca, 1992). If N begins to increase and a very high D begins to decrease on repeated testing, the patient may be acquiring the necessary resolve and energy to complete the act; thus suicide potential may be high. Those personality patterns most likely to exhibit suicide potential are indicated by elevated scores on 2, 8A, 5, and/or C. These patterns are the most inconsistent and they are particularly susceptible to poorly developed support systems. High scores on scale 8A are particularly associated with manipulative suicide potential. (pp. 382–383)

McCann and Gergelis (1990) compared MCMI-II profiles of 40 psychiatric inpatients admitted for suicidal ideation with those of 40 patients admitted for a suicide attempt. They concluded that suicide attempters scored significantly higher on Scale Y (desirability) compared with ideators. Elevations on Scale Y indicate suicide attempters have a higher tendency to deny problem areas, generate socially desirable response sets, and conceal psychological and interpersonal difficulties. Ellis, Rudd, Rajab, and Wehrly (1996) cluster-analyzed MCMI scores from 299 suicidal psychiatric outpatients. Four personality profiles emerged from their cluster analysis: negativistic/avoidant/schizoid, avoidant/dependent/negativistic, antisocial, and histrionic/narcissistic.

The Millon Adolescent Personality Inventory (MACI) 1993 includes scales not found on its parent inventory, the MCMI-III. Most importantly, the MACI contains two points of reference for identification of suicidal ideation. Scale GG (Suicidal Tendency) assesses suicidal ideation and planning. Adolescents who score high on this scale may contemplate suicide as an option to end their pain and suffering. Their depressive states are described as severe even to the point of losing sight of reasons to live (Strack, 2002). Additionally, the MACI contains a scale named Borderline Tendency (Scale 9). Adolescents who score high on this scale experience periods of marked behavioral and emotional dysregulation. Scale 9 has four content scales, one of which is called Suicidal Impulsivity. This content scale highlights the self-destructive ideations and suicide attempts that are associated with the borderline personality structure (Strack, 2002).

The Personality Assessment Instrument

The Personality Assessment Instrument (PAI; Morey, 1991) is another commonly used personality assessment instrument that has been used for the identification of suicidal ideation and hopelessness. The PAI contains a treatment scale called Suicidal

Ideation (SUI). The SUI includes items that range from thinking about death, to contemplating suicide to a current serious consideration of suicide (Morey, 2003). High scores on this scale indicate that a person is thinking about suicide, it is not a prediction of suicide completion tool. As scores on this scale go up, so does the level of risk. Scores above 100T indicate a morbid preoccupation of death and suicide. Potential for suicide must be assessed immediately and interventions should be implemented without delay (Morey, 2003). The SUI scale has been found to correlate with suicide precaution status in clinical patients who have conveyed suicidal ideation (Morey, 1991). Similarly, Rogers, Ustad, and Salekin (1998) found correlations between the PAI SUI scale and suicidal symptoms as assessed via structured clinical interview.

Similar to the MACI, the PAI has a scale which measures borderline features (Borderline Features, BOR). It has a subscale appropriately called Self-Harm (BOR-S). This scale reflects a tendency to act impulsively, without concern of the consequences. High scores on BOR-S reflect levels of recklessness that may include self-mutilation and suicidal behavior (Morey, 2003). Appropriate steps should be taken to evaluate the level of dangerousness for individuals who score high on this scale.

Thematic Apperception Test

After a review of the literature on the TAT as a diagnostic instrument for the assessment of suicide risk, McEvoy (1974) concluded that the literature on the use of the TAT as an estimator of suicide risk is clearly disappointing. He stated that the research is scarce and not easily compared. Perhaps the only general conclusion is that the test has not proved to be useful for this purpose.

Since that time there have been numerous studies on the utility of the TAT for identifying suicidal ideation (Adkins & Parker, 1996; Junuwine, 2001; Litinsky & Haslam, 1998; Ngai, 2001; Yufit, 2005). Despite a body of literature on the topic there has always been strong "clinical lore" that specific TAT cards could be used for the assessment of suicide risk. The "suicide cards" (3BM and 14) were thought to offer ambiguous scenarios that elicited responses from patients that were contemplating suicide. Card 3BM shows a figure sitting on the floor with what can be perceived as either a set of keys or a gun on the floor next to the individual. Card 14 shows a male figure in silhouette in a window frame. Clinical tradition indicates that people contemplating suicide more often tell a story in which the figure jumps out the open window (Litinsky & Haslam, 1998). Other cards that have shown promise in the assessment of risk include cards 1 and 12BG (Yufit, 2005) A thorough review of any suicidal content is always recommended, regardless of the card.

Beck Depression Inventory and Beck Hopelessness Scale

Although the BDI is a widely accepted measure of face valid depression, it has not escaped criticism (Reinecke & Franklin-Scott, 2005). These concerns lead to the development of a revised BDI, the Beck Depression Inventory-II (BDI-II; Beck, Steer, & Brown, 1996). Overall, 23 changes were made to the existing scale. The changes included dropping items (4), adding items (4), and rewording 17 questions. The BDI-II still consists of 23 items rated on a 0–3 scale. Total scores range from 0 to 63. While the two instruments have a high correlation (.93), the mean BDI-II score appears to be 1.54 times higher than the mean BDI score (Reinecke & Franklin-Scott, 2005). Thus, it is suggested that a higher cutoff score is needed. Little research with suicidal patients has been done with this instrument and a large number of clinicians still rely heavily on the tried and true BDI.

As Beck and Steer (1987) themselves observed, during the last 26 years the "BDI has become one of the most widely accepted instruments in clinical psychology and psychiatry for assessing the intensity of depression in psychiatric patients (Piotrowski, Sherry, & Keller, 1985) and for detecting possible depression in normal populations (Beck, Steer, Kovacs, & Garrison, 1985)" (p. 1). A BDI total score can provide an estimate of the severity of the overall depression. Yet Beck and Steer stressed that it is also important to attend to specific item content.

In particular, special attention should be given to those symptoms relevant to suicide ideation (p. 7). Beck et al. (1985) have pointed out that that the BDI's pessimism item (Item 2) "was nearly as predictive of eventual suicide in 211 suicide ideators as the 20 item Hopelessness Scale (HS)" (Beck, Weissman, Lester, & Trexler, 1974). Patients admitting to suicide ideation (Item 9) and hopelessness (Item 2) with ratings of 3 or 4 should be closely scrutinized for suicide potential.

It is also important to observe the overall pattern of the depression symptoms that the patient is describing. The BDI reflects not only cognitive and affective symptoms, but also somatic and vegetative symptoms. For example, some suicidal patients will not express suicide ideation, but have actually stopped eating and sleeping (Beck & Steer, 1987, pp. 7–8).

Because scores on the BHS produce only an estimate of the overall severity of hopelessness (i.e., the severity of an individual's negative attitudes about the future), Beck and Steer (1988) pointed out that it is clinically important to pay attention to other aspects of psychological functioning, in particular the patient's levels of suicidal ideation and depression. They noted the study by Beck and coworkers (1985) which reported that BHS scores of nine or more were predictive of eventual suicide in 10 out of 11 depressed suicide ideators who were followed for 5–10 years after discharge from the hospital, pointing to earlier findings that hopelessness has repeatedly been found to be a better predictor of suicidal intention than depression per se (Beck, 1986). Beck and Steer (1988) concluded that patients describing moderate to severe levels of hopelessness should be closely scrutinized for suicide potential.

Furthermore, Beck et al. (1985) found that, in a 10-year prospective follow-up of 165 psychiatric patients who had been hospitalized for suicidal ideation, hopelessness was highly predictive of eventual suicide. Of the 11 patients in their study who went on to complete suicide, 10 (90.9%) had BHS scores greater than or equal to 9. Beck and colleagues recently extended this investigation to an outpatient population and found that in a prospective study of 1,958 outpatients seen at the Center for Cognitive Therapy, hopelessness (as measured on the BHS) was significantly related to completed suicide (Beck, Brown, Berchick, Stewart, & Steer, 1990). Beck and colleagues specifically found that a BHS cutoff score of 9 or above identified 16 (94.2%) of the 17 eventual suicides, thus replicating a previous study with hospitalized patients. The high-risk group identified by this cutoff score was 11 times more likely to commit suicide than the rest of the outpatients. The BHS thus may be used as a sensitive indicator of suicidal potential (p. 190).

Bongar (2002) reviewed research by Beck and colleagues and concluded that a score of 9 or more on the BHS is a useful cutoff for elevated risk. However, it is important to note that Beck and Steer (1988) also gave several case examples to demonstrate the complexities involved in using the BHS and BDI as predictors of suicide during therapy. They cited the case of a patient who, at the time of his evaluation, showed on his self-report and interview report the signs of severe depression, but no suicidal ideation.

His BDI score, for example, was 45. He endorsed Item 9 as "I don't have thoughts of killing myself."

Similarly, the Scale for Suicide Ideation (SSI) did not indicate current suicidal thoughts or plans. However, his BHS score was 20. He came in for three consecutive sessions, cancelled the fourth, and did not show up for the next scheduled appointment. Scores on the BDI during the three sessions he had kept dropped from 45 at admission to 35, 37, and 37, respectively. During the sessions the patient denied verbally and on self-report forms any suicidal thoughts or plans. However, his BHS remained high (again a score of 20; Beck & Steer, 1988, p. 22).

The case of this patient, who killed himself 3 days prior to the next scheduled appointment, demonstrates that "in the presence of a high BHS and dropping BDI, a psychotherapist should be alert to the possibility of a suicide attempt" (Beck & Steer, 1988, p. 22). Here, Beck and Steer noted that the BHS accurately reflected suicidal risk "whereas the patient's self report of suicidal ideation or suicidal item on the BDI did not" (p. 22). Beck and Steer also emphasized the need to inquire about reasons for any specific hopeless responses to BHS items, as the clinical exploration of these responses may lead to the patient's acknowledging suicidal wishes. They noted that the BHS is also a valuable tool for indicating that the patient is still pessimistic (and possibly suicidal) even though significant improvement in symptoms has occurred. By discussing the specifically endorsed items on the BHS with the patient, the therapist can pinpoint some of the particular situational and psychological factors contributing to a therapeutic impasse. Focusing on specific relevant items on the BHS can help to break up a pervasive hopelessness and foster collaboration (Beck & Steer, 1988, pp. 24–25).

For the purposes of risk detection, a score of 9 or higher on the BHS is of particular importance, because the BHS attempts to identify the "potential for fatal suicide attempts and not the behavior itself. . . . In interpreting the results of the present studies, hopelessness may best be construed as a risk factor, perhaps analogous to a history of smoking or elevated blood pressure as a predispositional factor in heart disease" (Beck et al., 1990, p. 194). Young et al. (1996) reported that stable levels of hopelessness over time may be more predictive of suicide attempts than a high level of current hopelessness at any one point in time, in patients with remitted depression.

Beck, Brown, Steer, Dahlsgaard, and Grisham (1999) designed a study to calculate odds ratios and to determine the usefulness of using the BHS for suicide ideation at its worst point in the patient's life (SSI-W), for measuring current suicide ideation (SSI-C), and for identifying patients at higher risk for suicide. They found that patients who scored in the "higher risk" category for "suicide ideation at its worst point in their lives" had 14 times higher odds of committing suicide than patients who scored in the "lower risk" category. In contrast, patients who scored in the "higher risk" category for current suicide ideation or for hopelessness had approximately 6 times higher odds of committing suicide (p. 7).

The SSI-W was found to be a significant predictor of eventual suicide and there was a "significant trend for the unique contribution" of hopelessness, as captured by the BHS. Current suicide ideation (SSI-C) was not found to be a significant predictor of suicide. This study indicated that clinicians should assess for the severity of past suicide ideation and for stable levels of hopelessness over a continued period of time as opposed to focusing solely on the patient's current suicidal ideation (Beck et al., 1999). It was noted that outpatients with high scores on the SSI-W and consistently high scores on the BHS who do not respond to therapy should be considered as a high-risk group for eventual suicide (Beck et al., 1999).

Assessment of Suicidal Ideation, Intent, and Behavior

A number of years ago, the Suicide and Suicidal Behavior Program of the Mood, Affective, and Personality Disorders Research Branch of the Division of Clinical Research at the National Institute of Mental Health convened a workshop to discuss and address "common problems and issues in research methodology with emphasis on developing a common core of assessment tools and standardized terminology (e.g., suicide versus attempted suicide)" (Alcohol, Drug Abuse, and Mental Health Administration, 1989, pp. 1–81) for use in the study of suicide. Also, the Child and Adolescent Disorders Research Branch of the Division of Clinical Research commissioned an exhaustive study that reviewed scales suitable for epidemiological and clinical research for the assessment of suicidal behavior in adolescents (Lewinsohn et al., 1989). Although these activities are certainly an important step toward promoting comparative nationwide clinical research efforts for the study of suicide via the use of a standardized set of assessment instruments, it is important to note that these recommendations and workshops have as their purpose the optimization of efforts toward collaborative and comparative clinical research, rather than the setting of "standards for frontline clinical practice."

This ambitious attempt to standardize the assessment of suicide risk for the purposes of clinical research follows a long tradition of efforts at estimating and assessing the risk of attempted and completed suicide. These efforts have included assessment protocols that contain both standardized psychological tests and suicide risk estimator and lethality scales.

Motto (1989) noted that methodological and practical problems have plagued the development of scales of suicide risk. Some of the important obstacles have been small samples, limited data, a low base rate, nongeneralizabilty of critical stressors, and the individual uniqueness of suicidal persons.

Lewinsohn and colleagues (1989), after comprehensively evaluating all available assessment instruments used to study suicidal behaviors in adolescents and young adults for the NIMH, concluded that the success of the various instruments to determine which individuals are at high risk for suicidal behavior or other forms of self-destructive action has not been determined (pp. 97–98).

As can be seen from the ongoing efforts of the NIMH, there continues to be enormous interest in the development of suicide risk scales and estimators. Motto (1989) stated that historically the only well-known measure was a little-used suicide risk scale of the MMPI and that contemporary efforts at scale construction began in 1963 when the Los Angeles Suicide Prevention Center developed a special scale for assessing callers to their center (Farberow, Helig, & Litman, 1968). Motto noted that this scale has been widely used by suicide prevention and crisis centers.

The Los Angeles Suicide Prevention Center Scale focuses on demographic and clinical characteristics of patients. Bassuk (1982) noted that, in this regard, it is similar to Tuckman and Youngman's 1968 Scale for Assessing Suicide Risk (SASR). The SASR is a scale used to identify among suicide attempters those persons with a high potential to commit suicide. However, citing problems of replication, Eyman and Eyman (1991) conclude that the "scale [SASR] is not useful for a psychiatric population and [we] also believe its use is premature in a general population as the original finding has not been replicated" (p. 23).

Also, the Index of Potential Suicide (Zung, 1974), which measures potential suicide risk and includes both clinical and social-demographic variables, has been shown to distinguish adequately between patients with no suicidal behavior and those with a history of suicidal behavior. However, this scale does not seem to have good predictive validity (Eyman & Eyman, 1991).

With regard to the evaluation of an actual suicide attempt scale, there have been several important developments. The Firestone Assessment of Self-Destructive Thoughts (FAST) was developed by Firestone and Seiden (1990) and is based on the concept that suicide and self-destructive behavior are influenced by an inner "voice" (e.g., a negative thought process). The voice process represents a well-integrated pattern of thoughts, attitudes, and beliefs, antithetical to self and hostile toward others, that is at the core of the patient's self-limitations and self-defeating actions. The voice varies along a continuum of intensity ranging from mild self-criticism to angry self-attacks and suicidal thoughts.

The FAST is a self-report questionnaire designed to be used as a screening instrument (Firestone & Firestone, 1996). The patient endorses frequency of negative thoughts on a 5-point Likert-type scale. These self-destructive thoughts can be conceptualized along the Continuum of Negative Thought Patterns and help clinicians direct their interventions toward the areas where their patients are experiencing psychological pain (Firestone & Firestone, 1996; Firestone & Seiden, 1990). Knowledge of where a patient score falls on the continuum can also assist clinicians in identifying patients who are at increased risk for suicide. Table 26.1 presents some of the items on the FAST.

The Suicidal Ideation Questionnaire (SIQ) (Reynolds, 1987, 1988), the Adult Suicidal Ideation Questionnaire (ASIQ) (Reynolds, 1991), and the Suicidal Behavior History Form (SBHF) (Reynolds & Mazza, 1992) were developed in response to the growing demand by clinicians for an effective and efficient way to assess for suicide ideation and systematically obtain information on a patient's history of suicidal behavior (Reynolds, 1987, 1988, 1991; Reynolds & Mazza, 1992). The ASIQ is a derivation of the 30-item SIQ that was initially developed for the assessment of suicidal ideation in adolescents. The ASIQ consists of 25 items that measure a specific suicidal thought or behavior. The patient rates each ASIQ item on a 7-point scale, ranging from general wishes of death to specific thoughts or plans, which assess the frequency of occurrence within the past month. High scores indicate frequent suicidal thoughts. The SBHF provides a format for the evaluation and documentation of previous suicidal behaviors. It can be used with adults and adolescents.

One historically important scale is the Risk-Rescue Scale developed by Weissman and Worden (1974), which defines a suicide attempt as an "event

Table 26.1. Selected items from the Firestone Assessment of Self-Destructive Thoughts.

Level 1: Self-depreciating thoughts of everyday life
You just don't fit in.
You're different from other people.

Level 2: Thoughts rationalizing self-denial
You're too shy to make any new friends.
Look at all you have to do.
You're never going to get finished.
You can't take any time off.

Level 3: Cynical attitudes toward others
Can't you see he (she) is just taking advantage of you?
He (She) is such an exploitative person.
You can't trust men (women). Just depend on yourself.

Level 4: Thoughts influencing isolation
Just stay in the background.
Don't make waves.
Just look normal, don't let anybody know how you really feel.

Level 5: Self-contempt: vicious self-abusive thoughts
You can't do anything right!
You're disgusting!
You're a failure, a total failure.

Level 6: Thoughts that support the cycle of addiction
Have another drink (cookie).
You need to relax.
Go ahead and drink, you deserve it.

Level 7: Thoughts contributing to a sense of hopelessness
Your future is hopeless; things will never get better.
You're a burden to your family.
They'd be better off without you.

Level 8: Giving up on oneself
Nothing makes any difference anymore.
Why go on living?
The world is not a place that you can live in.

Level 9: Injunctions to inflict self-harm
Step off the curb, walk in front of that car.
Smash yourself, get yourself off this earth.

Level 10: Thoughts planning details of suicide
Pick a time, find a time when nobody will notice you're missing.
You're so miserable; you can't stand it anymore.
Just get out of it.
Get the pills to do it.

Level 11: Injunctions to carry out suicide plans
Why don't you end it all?
Go ahead! It'll be over in a minute.
Just do it. Kill yourself!

where the risk of death is extremely high and probability of rescue is extremely low" (Shneidman, 1985, p. 20). Smith, Conroy, and Ehler developed an 11-point scale, the Lethality of Suicide Attempt Rating Scale (LSARS), to measure the degree of lethality of a suicide attempt. Eyman and Eyman

(1991), in their review of the assessment of suicide using psychological tests, found that the LSARS was a valuable tool in assessing the lethality of intent and method from a previous suicide attempt.

However, despite the development of a number of alternative instruments (Beck, Schuyler, & Herman, 1974; Cohen, Motto, & Seiden, 1966; Poeldinger, Gehring, & Blaser, 1973; Weissman & Worden, 1972; Yufit & Benzies, 1973; Zung, 1974), such instruments remain primarily useful "as research tools rather than aids for front-line clinicians" (Motto, 1989, p. 249).

As Motto (1989) noted, an alternative approach to the search for generalized indicators of risk has been to examine precisely defined populations and settings and to develop scales that would be "situation-specific" (p. 249), as, for example, the attempt by Litman (1975) to provide:

"An estimate of risk for nineteen different patient populations, such as suicide attempters seen in the hospital (moderate risk), depressed alcoholic middle-aged male callers to Suicide Prevention Center (high risk), and young female suicide attempters (low risk). Subsequent work continues to focus on "clinical models," defined in terms of personality characteristics or clinical picture; for example, "stable with forced change," "alienated," "nice person," "alcohol abuse," "drug abuse" (Motto, 1977, 1979), or "suicide attempter" (Pallis, Barraclough, Levey, Jenkins, & Sainsbury, 1982; Pallis, Gibbons, & Pierce, 1984) . . . as with earlier studies, these reports generated interest among researchers but did not have a demonstrable impact on clinical practice (p. 249)."

To the appraisal contained in the above list, Eyman and Eyman (1991) would add the work of Buglass and McCulloch (1970) and their Scale for Predicting Subsequent Suicidal Behavior, as well as Miskimins, DeCook, Wilson, and Maley's (1967) Suicide Potential Scale.

One probable explanation for the lack of impact of such scales, collectively or individually, is that in their development, "little attention was paid to providing clinicians with a simple brief procedure that could be quickly translated into a clear indication of suicide risk" (Motto, 1989, p. 250). However, there have been recent attempts to construct clinically useful screening instruments for utilization by the clinician. The following examples are meant to be representative of this approach to the assessment of suicide, rather than an exhaustive list of all available instruments. (For a model of such lists, the reader is directed to Eyman and Eyman [1991], and to Lewinsohn et al. [1989].)

Fremouw and colleagues (1990) noted the utility of the Reasons for Living Inventory (Linehan, 1985), a self-report measure with 48 items, including items that reveal the belief systems of a patient that "may serve as mediators of suicidal behaviors" (n.b., psychometric properties are still under investigation, and cutoff scores for the scale are currently unavailable). They pointed out that this self-report measure has been found to discriminate between suicidal and nonsuicidal individuals; specifically, Linehan's (1985) findings indicated "the absence of strong positive reasons to live are most indicative of suicidal behavior" (Fremouw et al., 1990, p. 56).

Eyman and Eyman (1991) noted that the Hillson Adolescent Profile (Inwald, Brobst, & Morrissey, 1987), which contains 310 true/false items, appears to be a promising tool for distinguishing suicidal and nonsuicidal adolescents in school and offender populations. They also noted that the Suicidal Ideation Questionnaire (SIQ; Reynolds, 1988), which was developed to assess adolescents' thoughts about death and suicide, may be more appropriate and useful for school populations than for psychiatric ones.

The Suicide Probability Scale (SPS) is a short self-report measure designed to assist in the assessment of suicide risk in both adults and adolescents. This 36-item self-report measure asks patients to rate their present and past behaviors on a 4-point Likert scale. Cull and Gill (1982) pointed out that the assessment of suicide risk can be shown in three summary scores: a total weighted score, a normalized T-score, and a suicide probability score that can be adjusted to accommodate different a priori base rates for particular clinical populations.

This instrument, although serving as a useful model for interesting future directions in the development of assessment instruments, has a number of limitations. The intent of the scale is not particularly disguised, and it assesses an individual's reported feelings and behaviors only at one point in time. However, as the authors themselves recognized, further research on this instrument is needed to establish predictive validity, replicate findings with a wider range of representative samples, and assess the incremental validity of the SPS "in predicting suicidal behaviors beyond what could be predicted on the basis of commonly available patient demographic and clinical characteristics alone" (Cull & Gill, 1982, p. 61).

Beck and colleagues developed two important scales for the measurement of suicidal ideation and intent. These are the SSI and the Suicide Intent Scale (SIS) (Beck, Kovacs, & Weissman, 1979; Beck et al., 1974). The SSI has been used in several studies to measure intensity, duration, and specificity of psychiatric patients' wishes to commit suicide (Beck, Steer, & Ranieri, 1988). The SSI is a 19-item instrument that a trained clinician may use to rate the severity of a patient's suicidal thoughts and plans on a 3-point scale that ranges from 0 to 2. Rather than employing cutoff scores, a clinician who detects any positive ideation on Item 4 (Active Wish-to-Die) or Item 5 (Passive Wish-to-Die) rates the patients on the remaining 14 items of the scale. The Center for Cognitive Therapy recommends that SSI total scores be used only as measures of suicide ideation in "true" ideators and not in general clinical populations. From a clinical standpoint, the Center for Cognitive Therapy considers an SSI score of 10 or higher as indicating suicidal risk and suggests that patients be followed closely.

Lewinsohn et al. (1989) recognized the SSI as a carefully developed, reliable instrument for measuring suicidal ideation. Beck et al. (1988) also reported that the SSI, in a self-report version, can be a reliable method for measuring the severity of suicide ideation in both outpatients and inpatients. However, they noted that "although the present study indicates that the SSI represents a valid and reliable method for rapidly estimating suicide ideation in psychiatric patients, it is not recommended that the self-report version of the SSI replace clinical interviewing as a method for evaluating a patient's suicide plans and thoughts. The self-report version represents another tool for multimethod assessment of suicide ideation" (p. 504).

Lewinsohn and coworkers (1989) concluded: "given that intentionality is an important construct in the study of suicide, the SIS represents the only rationally derived scale to evaluate suicidal intent" (p. 15). They cited Steer and Beck's (1988) belief that "the information elicited by this test can help clinicians judge how serious the attempt was and might be again, while noting that its use is restricted to people who have made a previous attempt which is a high risk group" (Lewinsohn et al., 1989, p. 15). The SSI and the SIS represent important directions for future clinical research efforts and further the cause of combining clinical interview with clinical assessment protocols such that suicidal ideation and intent may be assessed more systematically. From a general clinical assessment perspective, Bassuk (1982) concluded that "by using the scale for suicidal ideation, the hopelessness scale, and the suicide intent scale, the interviewer can assess either directly or indirectly the seriousness of the patient's intent or subjective wish to die" (p. 29).

Hirschfeld and Russell (1997) designed an Algorithm for Assessing the Risk of Suicide to be used in conjunction with identified risk factors for suicide and attempted suicide. If the patient is found to be at risk for suicide, they recommend that the Algorithm for the Management of Suicidal Thoughts or Behavior be used by the clinician. The authors note that once treatment is started for patients identified as high risk there should be close follow-up and continued assessment, as "some patients are at even greater risk for suicide for the first few days after treatment has been started" (Hirschfeld & Russell, 1997, pp. 912–913). For individuals with chronic suicidal ideation, the goal of the clinician is to change risk factors that can be modified in an effort to increase patient safety. The authors note that a person who is determined to kill himself or herself will probably prevail despite the best efforts of family members and health-care professionals. However, the overwhelming majority of people who desire to kill themselves at one time will feel very different after improvement in their depression or after receiving help with other problems (Hirschfeld & Russell, 1997, p. 914).

Motto, Heilbron, and Juster (1985) developed an empirical suicide risk scale for adults hospitalized due to a depressive or suicidal state. Their study of 2,753 suicidal patients prospectively examined 101 psychosocial variables. After a 2-year follow-up, 136 (4.94%) of the subjects had committed suicide. The authors employed rigorous statistical analysis, including a validation procedure, to identify 15 variables as significant predictors of suicidal outcome. Their findings were translated into a paper-and-pencil scale that gives an estimated risk of suicide within 2 years. Motto (1989) noted that instruments such as these can provide a valuable supplement to clinical judgment, as well as the kind of quantitative expression of suicide risk that represents to many clinicians "fine tuning" of their clinical judgment.

However, Clark, Young, Scheftner, Fawcett, and Fogg (1987) undertook a field test of Motto and colleagues' Risk Estimator for Suicide (Motto et al., 1985) that "raised questions" about the instrument though without invalidating the scale (Clark et al., 1987, p. 926). Clark and colleagues selected a subset of psychiatric patients with major or chronic affective disorders that corresponded to those in Motto's sample. The subjects in their sample exhibited distinctly lower suicide rates over a 2-year follow-up

(2.4%) than the sample reported by Motto (4.9%). What the 1987 study does highlight is the critical need to understand the limitations of all such scales particularly the likelihood that suicide scales derived by multivariate analysis of a large number of clinical, psychosocial, and demographic variables may tend to be arbitrary and sample-specific. They propose that serial assessments which pay attention to clinical symptoms, changing stress levels, and long-standing character structure in concert (Smith, 1985) would provide a better method of estimating suicide risk.

Assessing Suicide through Structured Interviews and a Psychological Battery

Yufit (1988, 2005) proposed that the assessment of suicidal behavior is best conducted through the use of a SAT and a battery of specific assessment measures termed the Suicide Assessment Battery (SAB). Such a team would be composed of a multi-disciplinary staff of psychologists, social workers, nurses, and psychology graduate students, specially trained in the use of a focused screening interview format and other assessment techniques for the identification and evaluation of suicide potential. SAT assessment would involve three levels: a focused interview (Level I), this interview plus specialized rating scales (Level II), and an extended psychological assessment (Level III) including the above interviews and ratings as well as special psychological assessment techniques, the SAB (Yufit, 2005).

The SAB would be used to make an extended evaluation of suicide potential beyond interview ratings (Level I) and the scores on the specialized suicide rating scales (Level II). Before proceeding to Level III, the clinician already would have conducted the structured interview and used rating scales such as the BDI, as well as the Risk-Rescue Scale and the Los Angeles SPC Assessment of Suicide Potential to evaluate the patient. As Yufit noted, Level III techniques "would most likely be used with inpatients who make suicidal threats or attempts, or where suicide can be inferred" (1988, p. 26).

One of the most important elements in the SAB is the Time Questionnaire (TQ). The TQ, a semi-projective personality assessment technique, has been found to correlate with suicide potential (Yufit & Benzies, 1979). The TQ has been administered to "over 1,500 persons, including clinical and non-clinical samples, as well as matched sample populations; it has consistently differentiated high lethal suicidal persons from lower levels of suicide lethality and nonsuicidal persons as well as a variety of psychiatric diagnostic groups, on the basis of uniquely different time perspectives . . . the TQ is a key technique in the SAB" (Yufit, 1988, p. 27). Yufit (personal communication, April 1990) added the Coping Abilities Questionnaire, a 15-item instrument that measures the range of coping ability (from excellent to minimal).

In addition to the TQ and Coping Abilities Questionnaire, other possible key elements in a SAB include the following:

1. Q-sort set, a 22-item set representative of "descriptive items relating to variables often associated with suicidal behavior" (Yufit, 1988, p. 28);

2. Suicide Assessment Checklist, a 36-item checklist to provide a supplement to clinical judgment;

3. Experience Inventory, in which the patient is asked to list 10 most important experiences (Cottle, 1976);

4. Motto Suicide Risk Assessment, an empirically derived instrument using significant items from a large-scale prospective study of a clinic instrument used to assess suicide (Motto et al., 1985);

5. A specially devised sentence completion, a 32-item form with sentence stems especially selected to elicit affect related to morbid thoughts, self-destruction, hope, trust, the future, and so on;

6. Draw-A-Person, DAP in the Rain, a variation of the "Draw-A-Person in the Rain projective technique in which rain is an ambiguous stimulus . . . Scoring is subjective in nature, but the work of Machover and other exponents of DAP can be utilized" (Yufit, 1988, p. 30);

7. autobiography, in which the patient is asked to write his or her life history in any way that he or she wishes;

8. Rorschach, primarily used for associational content;

9. TAT, quantitative analysis of story themes related to isolation, hopelessness, mistrust, morbid content, and future orientation;

10. Object Relations Technique, a variant of the TAT that usually gives more elaborate data than the more structured TAT;

11. Erikson Questionnaire, a multiple-choice instrument giving scores on Erikson's developmental model of stages related to intimacy-isolation, trust–mistrust, autonomy-shame, and doubt;

12. Humor Test, a 104-item, objectively scored questionnaire that gives polar opposite scores on 13 factor analytically determined scales;

13. Hope Scale, a Fawcett–Sussman scale of items relating to the evaluation of hope as personality variable.

These 13 assessment techniques represent a broad array of available and useful measures from which a SAB can be derived, usually including five or six of the techniques (e.g., the core SAB battery might include the suicide checklist, Coping Questionnaire, TQ, and Q-sort) (Yufit, personal communication, August, 1990).

Yufit (1988) pointed out that the use of the SAB, which includes a number of scales still in experimental form, "may be questioned, but they are considered very useful to trying to fill the lacunae and tap the nuances in the complex task of identification and assessment of suicide potential" (p. 32). He concluded that at this stage of development, these techniques are not necessarily conclusive, nor are they often objective, but they very often do serve as important "guidelines" to assist in the identification and the assessment of the components of suicide potential. They should supplement clinical judgment, not substitute for it (p. 33).

Recently the Question, Persuade, Refer, and/or Treat (QPRT) was developed by Quinnett and Bratcher (1996) to help clinicians evaluate, counsel, and treat suicidal patients. This structured risk assessment interview can be used in conjunction with other scales, such as the BDI or the BHS. The QPRT is a "tactical interview guide" created to help the clinician obtain dynamic and critical information regarding the urgency, nature, and context of a suicidal crisis, as well as to assess the current level of immediate risk. A decision tree format is used to guide the clinician and patient in creating a crisis management plan.

In an effort to formalize and distill the elements of risk detection (as well as to try to increase the accuracy of diagnosing suicide risk), Yufit (1989) developed and field-tested a new integrated instrument, the SSC. The SSC is used by a clinician or interviewer to assess an individual for the "purpose of identification of suicidal potential. Suicidal potential (or suicide risk) refers to the likelihood that such a person will engage in behavior that will directly or indirectly lead to self-destruction" (p. 4-129). The SSC is a screening instrument constructed from empirical data and utilizing known and presumed correlates of suicidal behavior, is designed to complement and improve "the validity of clinical judgment" (p. 4-139). In short, instruments such as the SSC (as well as batteries such as the SAB) may allow clinicians to supplement their own clinical intuition with a systematized approach to collecting assessment information (Yufit, personal communication, August 1990). An accurate (and widely accepted) model for the assessment of elevated risk in the suicidal patient may require a future research effort that would involve a large-scale collaborative multicenter study designed to evaluate *all* of the existing assessment procedures for both efficacy and significance (Yufit, personal communication, August 1990).

Limitations of Theoretical Orientation and DSM-IV Diagnosis

When clinicians select assessment criteria and then implement an appropriate intervention strategy with suicidal patients, they may find that traditional theories of psychotherapy, and traditional psychiatric diagnostic categories, are of limited practical value in precisely assessing suicidal risk. As Beutler (1989) pointed out, "the descriptive dimensions embodied in the current diagnostic system bear little relationship to the selection of the mode or frequency of psychosocial interventions . . . while it would be unthinkable in any practice of medicine for the mode of treatment to be independent of patient diagnosis, this is precisely the case in the assignment of psychotherapy modes and formats" (p. 272).

An integrated perspective on assessment and treatment of the suicidal patient must be maintained (Simon, 1988). For example, psychoanalytic approaches may tend to deemphasize discussion of the suicidal patient's condition with family members, or deemphasize an evaluation for the efficacy of organic therapies—in which case vital information can be lost. Conversely, biologically based approaches may not place enough emphasis on the need for an ongoing treatment relationship, that is, may diminish the role of the therapeutic alliance as an essential element of sound psychopharmacologic intervention. Finally, Simon (1988) noted the danger of medications being prescribed in lieu of the patient being seen more frequently.

Jacobs (1989) asserted that the clinician must go beyond formal psychiatric diagnosis, because many suicides occur in individuals who have not been labeled as psychiatrically ill. He cited Mack and Hickler's research (1981), which found that the problem of suicide cuts across all diagnoses; many of those who take their own lives are mentally ill, but some are not; some are psychotic, but most are not; and some act impulsively, but most do not. Jacobs (1989) also noted that the next concern for the clinician with regard to assessment relates to an understanding of demographic and clinical risk factors.

Linehan and colleagues (2000) noted that the limited research associating Axis II disorders with suicide is largely attributable to the fact that Axis II disorders were not formally diagnosed before 1980. In hierarchical and principal diagnosis systems, Axis II diagnoses are typically assigned only when an Axis I disorder is absent. In this context, suicidal ideation or behavior is viewed as a symptomatic response to an Axis I disorder. The high comorbidity of Axis I and Axis II disorders guarantees a significant underestimate of the prevalence of personality disorders.

Furthermore, personality disorders are typically represented by dimensional rather than categorical measures. That is, a specific number of criterion behavior patterns need to be present, and typically the greater the number of behaviors the greater the disorder. Linehan, Rizvi, Welsh, and Page (2000) noted that while studies have attempted to examine the relationship of personality disorders the methods used have been inconsistent. In the absence of clear methodology, we are left with information obtained from categorical diagnostic systems. Widiger and Frances (1987) point out that criterion behaviors are at times used as indicators of some underlying pathology (diagnostically), and at other times, they are used as operational criteria of a disorder (definitionally). Research, in many cases, does not sufficiently distinguish which criteria are definitional and which (if any) diagnostic.

Clark (1990) believed that there are a number of different types of suicide, based on different demographics, motives, or diagnoses. He thought that developing specific risk profiles for each of these different types of patients would be prudent. Clark and Fawcett (1992) advocated the formulation of diagnosis-specific suicide risk profiles. Clark (1990) provided four reasons for why diagnosis-specific profiles may be useful. First, he noted the relationship between mental illness and suicide (e.g., psychological autopsy studies). These studies indicate that most people who die from suicide suffered from some form of mental illness.

Second, Clark described follow-up mortality studies of patients with major affective disorders, alcoholism, and schizophrenia that indicated an elevated risk of death by suicide for each of these diagnoses. Third, he pointed out that different diagnoses (e.g., major depression, alcoholism, and schizophrenia) have different clinical presentations, courses, prognoses, and treatments, so the risks for suicide in patients with these diagnoses are also likely to differ. Fourth, Clark believed that the advent of structured interviews and well-delineated diagnostic categories would make reliable research of these categories possible.

Along these lines, Peruzzi and Bongar (1999) identified eight critical risk factors for suicide in patients with major depression: the medical serious-ness of previous attempts, history of suicide attempts, acute suicidal ideation, severe hopeless-ness, attraction to death, family history of suicide, acute overuse of alcohol, and the experience of recent loss or separation. Additionally, Canapary (1999) found a two-tier series of suicide risk factors with an alcoholic population. The first tier of risk factors includes the seriousness of previous attempts, past suicide attempts, and the communication of suicidal ideation; the second tier includes feelings of hope-lessness, a family history of suicide, and the current use of alcohol.

Suicide is not a psychopathological entity that is recognized by the DSM (Lewinsohn et al., 1989). Indeed, major depression and borderline personality disorder are the only diagnoses in the DSM-IV for which suicidality is a criterion. Zubin (1974) noted that suicide is the final stage of a very complex process that encompasses a heterogeneous set of phenomena and that occurs in people who are anything but homogeneous (Lewinsohn et al., 1989, p. 1).

In summary, at the level of a diagnostic and initial assessment of the suicidal patient, we believe that the psychologist should concentrate primarily on dispo-sitional assessment and on the formulation and doc-umentation of "risk detection" in the assessment and diagnostic stage, rather than on specific behavior prediction (Maris et al., 1992; Murphy, 1988b). However, the mental status examination, clinical interview, and DSM-IV diagnostics are essential and critical elements in a comprehensive clinical evaluation process (see also Lester, 2005) and, for the purposes of the present chapter, are important tools in the detection of suicide risk.

General Formulation of Clinical Judgment in the Clinical Interview

Maltsberger (1988) believed that there are five specific components in the general formulation of suicide risk:

1. assessing the patient's past responses to stress, especially losses;

2. assessing the patient's vulnerability to three life-threatening affects—aloneness, self-contempt, and murderous rage;

3. determining the nature and availability of exterior sustaining resources;

4. assessing the emergence and emotional importance of death fantasies;

5. assessing the patient's capacity for reality testing (p. 48).

He added that "what is sometimes called the 'formulation of suicide risk' offers the clinician a disciplined method for assessing suicide danger that integrates and balances the presenting clinical mate-rial from the patient's past history, his present illness, and the present mental status examination" (p. 48).

Another approach to the formulation of clinical judgment and the assessment of risk is a clinical checklist method of conducting the assessment (Bassuk, 1982). In this approach, one uses combina-tions of structured interviews, checklists, standard psychological instruments, and suicide risk scales and estimators to ensure a comprehensive evalua-tion. (For additional information on comprehensive assessment and interviewing strategies, see Hendren, 1990.)

Yufit (1988) noted that the assessment of suicide potential will often be accomplished through the initial focused interview (based on either a referral from the emergency room, inpatient service, or out-patient clinician). The Level I (focused interview) would explore:

1. the patient's conscious intent of actually ending his/her own life;

2. risk of rescue or possible interruption during suicide attempt;

3. degree of planning;

4. behavior level (e.g., threats, ideation, gestures, overt attempt);

5. lethality of attempt made;

6. extent of physical injury and/or toxicity;

7. precipitant factors;

8. intensity of current life stress;

9. history of previous attempts, gestures, threats, and ideation;

10. degree of depression;

11. the patient's ability to relate to the examiner during the interview, overt dress and grooming, posture, degree of agitation, ability to discuss the problem, and so on;

12. changes in the patient's behavior during the initial contact;

13. overall psychological status (e.g., the examination of any DSM-IV disorders).

The majority of patients at the Center for Cognitive Therapy at the University of Pennsylvania carry a diagnosis of depression, and therefore hopelessness and suicidal ideation will often be ongoing therapeutic issues. The center's policy manual indicates that when the patient's suicidal ideation is either continuous or intermittent, that is to say consists of low to moderate levels of purely ideational symptoms, it can be dealt with as with any other depressive symptom, that is, primarily by the treating therapist with regular supervision (R. J. Berchick, personal communication, September 20, 1989). However, the center's special procedure for suicidal patients is:

> The therapist should maintain especially close monitoring of *all* suicidal thoughts as well as concomitant levels of hopelessness and depression. Regular administration of the first five items of the SSI (and the rest of the scales if any of these are positive), the BHS, and BDI at each session is strongly recommended, because these scales will provide a reliable means of monitoring any changes in these variables over time.

Richman and Eyman (1991), citing the previous work of Smith (1985), Eyman (1987), and Smith and Eyman (1988), have developed a model for understanding why a person chooses to commit suicide based on the data from the Suicide Research Project at Menninger's. This model posits three conditions for suicide:

1. a narrowly defined, unrealistic, and fragile identity;
2. an event that jeopardizes the individual's identity;
3. deficits in the management of affect and difficulties in problem solving (Richman & Eyman, 1991, p. 2).

Motto (1989) held that the central clinical task is to "determine and monitor the patient's threshold for pain (either physical or psychological)." This would take into consideration the person's pathology, strengths, and available defensive patterns. If the pain level exceeds the pain threshold (even briefly), Motto saw suicide as imminent. Therefore, the psychologist must carefully assess and monitor the patient's threshold for pain and estimate how close the current level of pain comes to it. "The better we know the patient, the more sensitive we can be to the influences that can alter these two critical determinants of a suicidal act. Treatment aims ideally at both raising the threshold by maturational development, and decreasing the pain level by providing emotional support and by resolution of pain-generating conflicts" (Motto, 1989, p. 254).

Shneidman (1987) likewise believed that:

"The central feature of suicide is pain, and that the key to suicide prevention lies in the reduction of that individual's psychological pain. All else—demographic variables, family history, previous suicidal history—is peripheral except as those factors bear on the presently felt pain. Ultimately, suicide occurs when there is the co-existence of intolerable pain, intense negative press, and extreme perturbation with perceptual constriction and an irresistible penchant for life-ending action (pp. 176–177)."

Clinicians must also, according to Shneidman (1984, 1986a), exercise extreme caution with any patient who is perturbed and who has a lethal means available. This would include clinical work with patients with poor impulse control who are in crisis and are unable to decrease their level of perturbation in the therapeutic encounter. Shneidman (1987) presented a theoretical cubic model of suicide that includes the combined effects of psychological pain, perturbation, lethality, and what he termed "press" to attempt to identify those individuals most at risk for suicide. Here "press" is similar to what Murray (1938) called pressure—that is, those aspects of the inner or outer world or environment that touch, move, impinge on, or affect an individual, and to which he or she reacts. "Press" can be either positive or negative.

Practically speaking, Pokorny (1983) noted that the identification and care of the suicidal patient in clinical practice is made up of a *sequence of small decisions*, a point we wish to underscore. Murphy (1988a) expanded on this dictum by noting that:

The first decision might be based on some alerting sign or clinical configuration, and the decision would be to investigate further. After further investigation, one might stop, if no additional alerting or confirming indicator were found. Or one might decide to explore the situation even further; perhaps even to hospitalize, for example. In each case, the decision is not what to do for all time, but rather what to do next, for the near future (Pokorny, 1983) . . . there is continuing opportunity for feedback, and thus for modification of risk assessment and intervention (p. 53).

From the standpoint of any potential malpractice action, the most crucial element in the formulation of clinical judgment is that the psychologist's professional behavior not significantly deviate from what is usual and customary for the care of patients with these particular signs and symptoms. That is to say, the psychologist will have demonstrated the behavior of a reasonable and prudent practitioner and not made any significant omissions in assessment, as well as have taken appropriate precautions to minimize the risk of a patient suicide (Berman & Cohen-Sandler, 1982, 1983). The importance of thorough documentation cannot be overstated.

Patient suicide is not a tragedy that exclusively confronts the mental health professions, but "the incidence of its occurrence is such a frequent issue, both professionally and sometimes legally, that it demands special consideration" from mental health professionals (Smith, 1986, p. 62). Authorities who investigate suicidal phenomena have not reached consensus on the key risk factors, whether short term and long term, that distinguish suicide completers. Ironically, for the practicing clinician, this lack of consensus offers some protection from a legal perspective. Courts and juries have often held that when it comes to suicide, there is no single correct or perfect solution in the management of the suicidal patient. Rather, both courts and juries tend to judge the clinician's actions in comparison with what seemed reasonable in compliance with the accepted standards of their profession (Simon, 1988).

Finally, the psychologist must understand that the final decision as to suicide risk is an intuitive judgment, that "we are obliged to accept that no matter how much information is gathered, sooner or later all the data must be weighed together and an intuitive estimate of risk recorded. That it is only an educated guess does not diminish its importance or its value as a consideration in management and treatment planning" (Motto, 1989, p. 2).

Notes

Portions of this chapter are adapted from B. Bongar, *The suicidal patient: Clinical and legal standards of care* (2nd ed.), 2002. Washington, DC: American Psychological Association. Copyright: American Psychological Association.

References

Adkins, K. K., & Parker, W. (1996). Perfectionism and suicidal preoccupation. *Journal of Personality, 64*, 529–543.

Alcohol, Drug Abuse, and Mental Health Administration. (1989). *Report of the secretary's task force on youth suicide* (Vols. 1–4). DHSS Publication No. ADM 89-1621-1624). Washington, DC: U.S. Government Printing Office.

Applebaum, S. A., & Colson, D. B. (1968). A re-examination of the color shading Rorschach test response. *Journal of Projective Techniques and Personality Assessment, 32*, 160–164.

Applebaum, S. A., & Holtzman, P. S. (1962). The color shading response and suicide. *Journal of Projective Techniques, 26*, 155–161.

Archer, R. P., & Newsom C. R. (2000). Psychological test usage with adolescent clients: Survey update. *Assessment, 7*, 227–235.

Archer, R. P., & Slesinger, D. (1999). MMPI-A patterns related to the endorsement of suicidal ideation. *Assessment, 6*, 51–59.

Bassuk, E. L. (1982). General principles of assessment. In E. L. Bassuk, S. C. Schoonover, & A. D. Gill (Eds.), *Lifelines: Clinical perspectives on suicide* (pp. 17–46). New York: Plenum.

Beck, A. T. (1986). Hopelessness as a predictor of eventual suicide. In J. J. Mann & M. Stanley (Eds.), *Psychobiology* (pp. 90–96). New York: New York Academy of Sciences.

Beck, A. T., Brown, G., Berchick, R. J., Stewart, B. L., & Steer, R. A. (1990). Relation of hopelessness to ultimate suicide: A replication with psychiatric outpatients. *American Journal of Psychiatry, 147*(2), 190–195.

Beck, A. T., Brown, G. K., Steer, R. A., Dahlsgaard, K. K., & Grisham, J. R. (1999). Suicide ideation at its worst point: A predictor of eventual suicide in psychiatric outpatients. *Suicide and Life-Threatening Behavior, 29*, 1–9.

Beck, A. T., Kovacs, M., & Weissman, A. (1979). Assessment of suicidal intention: The scale for suicide ideation. *Journal of Consulting and Clinical Psychology, 47*, 343–352.

Beck, A. T., Schuyler, D., & Herman, I. (1974). Development of suicidal intent scales. In A. T. Beck, H. L. P. Resnik, & D. J. Lettieri (Eds.), *The prediction of suicide* (pp. 45–56). Bowie, MD: Charles Press.

Beck, A. T., & Steer, R. A. (1987). *Beck Depression Inventory: Manual.* San Antonio, TX: The Psychological Corporation.

Beck, A. T., & Steer, R. A. (1988). *Beck Hopelessness Scale: Manual.* San Antonio, TX: The Psychological Corporation.

Beck, A. T., Steer, R. A., & Brown G. K. (1996). *Manual for the Beck Depression Inventory-II.* San Antonio, TX: Psychological Corporation.

Beck, A. T., Steer, R. A., Kovacs, M., & Garrison, B. (1985). Hopelessness and eventual suicide: A 10 year prospective study of patients hospitalized with suicidal ideation. *American Journal of Psychiatry, 142*, 559–563.

Beck, A. T., Steer, R. A., & Ranieri, W. F. (1988). Scale for Suicide Ideation: Psychometric properties of a self-report version. *Journal of Clinical Psychology, 44*, 500–505.

Beck, A. T., Weissman, A., Lester, D., & Trexler, L. (1974). The measurement of pessimism: The Hopelessness Scale. *Journal of Consulting and Clinical Psychology, 42*, 861–865.

Berman, A. L., & Cohen-Sandler, R. (1982). Suicide and the standard of care: Optimal vs. acceptable. *Suicide and Life-Threatening Behavior, 12*, 114–122.

Berman, A. L., & Cohen-Sandler, R. (1983). Suicide and malpractice: Expert testimony and the standard of care. *Professional Psychology: Research and Practice, 14*, 6–19.

Berman, A. L., Jobes, D. A., & Silverman, M. M. (2006). *Adolescent suicide: Assessment and intervention* (2nd ed.). Washington, DC: American Psychological Association.

Beutler, L. E. (1989). Differential treatment selection: The role of diagnosis in psychotherapy. *Psychotherapy, 26*, 271–281.

Blatt, S. J., & Ritzler, B. (1974). Suicide and the representation of transparency and cross-section on the Rorschach. *Journal of Consulting and Clinical Psychology, 42*, 280–287.

Bongar, B. (1991). *The suicidal patient: Clinical and legal standards of care.* Washington, DC: American Psychological Association.

Bongar, B. (1992). *Suicide: Guidelines for assessment, management, and treatment.* New York: Oxford University Press.

Bongar, B. (2000). Suicide. In C. W. Edward & C. B. Nemeroff (Eds.), *The Corsini encyclopedia of psychology and the behavioral sciences* (3rd ed.). New York: John Wiley & Sons.

Bongar, B. (2002). *The suicidal patient: Clinical and legal standards of care* (2nd ed.). Washington, DC: American Psychological Association.

Bongar, B., Maris, R. W., Berman, A. L., Litman, R. E., & Silverman, M. M. (1993). Inpatient standards of care and the suicidal patient: General clinical formulations and legal considerations. *Suicide and Life-Threatening Behavior, 23*(3), 245–256.

Brent, D. A., Kupfer, D. J., Bromet, E. J., & Dew, M. A. (1988). The assessment and treatment of patients at risk for suicide. In A. J. Frances & R. E. Hales (Eds.), *American Psychiatric Press Review of Psychiatry* (Vol. 7, pp. 353–385). Washington, DC: American Psychiatric Press.

Bruno, G. (1995). Suicide assessment practices among psychologists (Unpublished doctoral dissertation, Pacific Graduate School of Psychology, Palo Alto, CA).

Bryan, C. J., & Rudd, M. D. (2006). Advances in the assessment of suicide risk. *Journal of Clinical Psychology, 62*, 185–200.

Buglass, D., & McCulloch, J. W. (1970). Further suicidal behaviour: the development and validation of predictive scales. *British Journal of Psychiatry, 116*, 483–491.

Butcher, J. N. (1989). The *Minnesota Report: Adult Clinical System MMPI-2*. Minneapolis, MN: University of Minnesota Press.

Butcher, J. N., Dahlstrom, W. G., Graham, J. R., Tellegen, A., & Kaemmer, B. (1989). *MMPI-2: Manual for administration and scoring*. Minneapolis, MN: University of Minnesota Press.

Butcher, J. N., Williams, C. L. Graham, J. R., Archer, R. P., Tellegan, A., Ben-Porath, Y. S., et al. (1992). *Minnesota multiphasic personality inventory-adolescent: Manual for administration, scoring, and interpretation*. Minneapolis, MN: University of Minnesota Press.

Canapary, A. (1999). Suicidal risk factors with an alcoholic population (Unpublished doctoral dissertation, Pacific Graduate School of Psychology, Palo Alto, CA).

Card-Strong, L. (1998). A national survey of psychologists' practice behaviors when diagnosing and treating major depressive disorder (Unpublished doctoral dissertation, Pacific Graduate School of Psychology, Palo Alto, CA).

Chemtob, C. M., Bauer, G. B., Hamada, R. S., Pelowski, S. R., & Muraoka, M. Y. (1989). Patient suicide: Occupational hazard for psychologists and psychiatrists. *Professional Psychology: Research and Practice, 20*, 294–300.

Choca, J. P. (1992). *Interpretative guide to the Millon Clinical Multiaxial Inventory*. Washington, DC: American Psychological Association.

Clark, D. C. (1990). Panic disorder: Summary and editor's commentary. *Suicide Research Digest, IV*, 3–4.

Clark, D. C., & Fawcett, J. (1992). Review of empirical risk factors for evaluation of the suicidal patient. In B. Bongar (Ed.), *Suicide: Guidelines for assessment, management and treatment* (pp. 16–48). New York: Oxford University Press.

Clark, D. C., Young, M. A., Scheftner, W. A., Fawcett, J., & Fogg, L. (1987). A field test of Motto's Risk Estimator for Suicide. *American Journal of Psychiatry, 144*, 923–926.

Clopton, J. R. (1974). Suicidal risk via the Minnesota Multiphasic Personality Inventory (MMPI). In C. Neuringer (Ed.), *Psychological assessment of suicide risk* (pp. 118–133). Springfield, IL: Charles C. Thomas.

Cohen, E., Motto, J., & Seiden, R. (1966). An instrument for evaluating suicide potential. *American Journal of Psychiatry, 122*, 886–891.

Cottle, T. J. (1976). *Perceiving time*. New York: John Wiley & Sons.

Craig, R. J., & Olson, R. E. (1990). MMPI characteristics of drug abusers with and without histories of suicide attempts. *Journal of Personality Assessment, 55*, 717–728.

Cull, J. G., & Gill, W. S. (1982). *Suicide Probability Scale (SPS) manual*. Los Angeles: Western Psychological Services.

Dahlstrom, W. G., Welsh, G. S., & Dahlstrom, L. E. (1972). *An MMPI handbook* (Vol. 1). Minneapolis, MN: University of Minnesota Press.

Ellis, T. E., Rudd, M. D., Rajab, M. H., & Wehrly, T. E. (1996). Cluster analysis of MCMI scores of suicidal psychiatric patients: Four personality profiles. *Journal of Clinical Psychology, 52*, 411–422.

Exner, J. (1978). *The Rorschach: A comprehensive system, Vol. 2: Current research and advanced interpretation*. New York: John Wiley & Sons.

Exner, J. (1986). *The Rorschach: A comprehensive system* (2nd ed., Vol. 1). New York: John Wiley & Sons.

Exner, J. E. (2003). *The Rorschach: A comprehensive system, Vol.1: Basic foundations* (4th ed.). New York: John Wiley & Sons.

Exner, J. E., & Wylie, J. (1977). Some Rorschach data concerning suicide. *Journal of Personality Assessment, 41*, 339–348.

Eyman, J. R. (1987). *Unsuccessful psychotherapy with seriously suicidal borderline patients*. Paper presented at the joint meeting of the American Association of Suicidology and the International Association of Suicidology, San Francisco.

Eyman, J. R., & Eyman, S. K. (1991). Personality assessment in suicide prediction. *Suicide and Life-Threatening Behavior, 21*, 37–55.

Farberow, N. L., Helig, S., & Litman, R. (1968). *Techniques in crisis intervention: A training manual*. Los Angeles: Suicide Prevention Center.

Fawcett, J. (1988, May 7). Interventions against suicide. In D. G. Jacobs & J. Fawcett (Chairs), *Suicide and the psychiatrist: Clinical challenges*. Symposium presented by the Suicide Education Institute of Boston, in collaboration with The Center of Suicide Research and Prevention, at the American Psychiatric Association Annual Meeting, Montreal.

Fawcett, J., Scheftner, W., Clark, D., Hedeker, D., Gibbons, R., & Coryell, W. (1987). Clinical predictors of suicide in patients with major affective disorders: A controlled prospective study. *American Journal of Psychiatry, 144*, 35–40.

Firestone, R. W., & Firestone, L. A. (1996). *Firestone Assessment of Self-Destructive Thoughts manual*. San Antonio: Harcourt Brace & Company.

Firestone, R. W., & Seiden, R. H. (1990). Suicide and the continuum of self-destructive behavior. *Journal of American College Health, 38*, 207–213.

Forbey, J. D., & Ben-Porath, Y. S. (1998). *A critical item set for the MMPI-A*. Minneapolis, MN: University of Minnesota Press.

Fowler, J. C., Hilsenroth, M. J., & Piers, C. (2001). An empirical study of seriously disturbed suicidal patients. *Journal of the American Psychoanalytic Association, 49*, 161–186.

Frank, G. (1994). On the prediction of suicide from the Rorschach. *Psychological Reports, 74*, 787–794.

Fremouw, W. J., de Perczel, M., & Ellis, T. E. (1990). *Suicide risk: Assessment and response guidelines*. New York: Pergamon.

Friedman, A. F., Archer, R. P., & Handel, R. W. (2005). Minnesota Multiphasic Personality Inventories (MMPI/MMPI-2, MMPI-A) and suicide. In R. I. Yufit & D. Lester (Eds.), *Assessment, treatment, and prevention of suicidal behavior*. Hoboken, NJ: John Wiley & Sons.

Friedman, A. F., Lewak, R., Nichols, D. S., & Webb, J. T. (2001). *Psychological Assessment with the MMPI-2*. Mahwah, NJ: Erlbaum.

Ganellen, R. J. (2005). Rorschach contributions to assessment of suicidal risk. In R. I. Yufit & D. Lester (Eds.), *Assessment, treatment, and prevention of suicidal behavior*. Hoboken, NJ: John Wiley & Sons.

Glassmire, D. M., Stolberg, R. A., Greene, R. L., & Bongar, B. (2001) The utility of suicide items for assessing suicide potential: Development of a suicide potential scale. *Assessment, 8,* 281–290.

Grava, G. Ceroni, G. B., Rucci, P., & Scudellari, P. (2006). Suicidal behaviors and personality structure. *Suicide and Life-Threatening Behavior, 36,* 569–577.

Greaney, S. (1995). Psychologists behavior and attitudes when working with the non-hospitalized suicidal patient (Unpublished doctoral dissertation, Pacific Graduate School of Psychology, Palo Alto, CA).

Greene, R. L. (2000). *The MMPI-2: An interpretive manual* (2nd ed.). Boston: Allyn & Bacon.

Groholt, B., Ekeberg, O., & Haldorsen, T. (2006). Adolescent suicide attempters: What predicts future suicidal acts? *Suicide and Life-Threatening Behavior, 36,* 638–650.

Gutheil, T. G., & Appelbaum, P. S. (1982). *Clinical handbook of psychiatry and the law.* New York: McGraw-Hill.

Gutierrez, P. M. (2006). Integratively assessing risk and protective factors for adolescent Suicide. *Suicide and Life-Threatening Behavior, 36,* 129–135.

Hansell, A. G., Lerner, H. D., Milden, R. S., & Ludolph, P. S. (1988). Single sign Rorschach indicators: A validity study using a depressed inpatient population. *Journal of Personality Assessment, 52,* 658–669.

Heisel, M. J., & Flett, G. L. (2006). The development and initial validation of the Geriatric Suicide Ideation Scale. *American Journal of Geriatric Psychiatry, 14,* 742–751.

Hendren, R. L. (1990). Assessment and interviewing strategies for suicidal patients over the life cycle. In S. J. Blumenthal & D. J. Kupfer (Eds.), *Suicide over the life cycle: Risk factors, assessment, and treatment of suicidal patients* (pp. 235–252). Washington, DC: American Psychiatric Press.

Hirschfeld, R. M. A., & Davidson, L. (1988). Risk factors for suicide. In A. J. Frances & R. E. Hales (Eds.), *American Psychiatric Press Review of Psychiatry* (Vol. 7, pp. 307–333). Washington, DC: American Psychiatric Press.

Hirschfeld, R. M. A., & Russell, J. M. (1997). Assessment and treatment of suicidal patients. *New England Journal of Medicine, 333,* 910–915.

Inwald, R. E., Brobst, K. E., & Morrissey, R. F. (1987). *Hillson Adolescent Profile Manual.* Kew Gardens, NY: Hillson Research.

Jacobs, D. G. (1989). Psychotherapy with suicidal patients: The empathic method. In D. G. Jacobs & H. N. Brown (Eds.), *Suicide: Understanding and responding: Harvard Medical School perspectives on suicide* (pp. 329–342). Madison, CT: International Universities Press.

Jobes, D. A., Eyman, J. R., & Yufit, R. I. (1990). *Suicide risk assessment survey.* Paper presented at the annual meeting of the American Association of Suicidology, New Orleans.

Johnson, W. B., Lall, R., Bongar, B., & Nordlund, M. D. (1999). The role of objective personality assessment inventories in suicide risk assessment: An evaluation and proposal. *Suicide and Life-Threatening Behavior, 29,* 165–185.

Joiner, T. E., Jr., Rudd, M. D., & Rajab, M. H. (1997). The Modified Scale for Suicidal Ideation: Factors of suicidality and their relation to clinical and diagnostic variables. *Journal of Abnormal Psychology, 106,* 260–265.

Joiner, T. E., Walker, R. L., Rudd, M. D., & Jobes, D. A. (1999). Scientizing and routinizing the assessment of suicidality in outpatient practice. *Professional Psychology: Research and Practice, 30,* 447–453.

Junuwine, M. J. (2001). Narratives of suicidal adolescents. *Dissertation Abstracts International, Section B: The Sciences and Engineering, 61*(10-B), 5567.

Kaplan, M. L., Asnis, G. M., Sanderson, W. C., & Keswani, L. (1994). Suicide assessment: Clinical interview vs. self-report. *Journal of Clinical Psychology, 50,* 294–298.

Klopfer, B., & Davidson, H. H. (1962). *The Rorschach Technique: An Introductory Manual.* New York: Harcourt, Brace & World, Inc.

Kreitman, N. (Ed.) (1977). *Parasuicide.* New York: John Wiley & Sons.

Kutcher, S., & Chehil, S. (2005). Tool for Assessment of Suicide Risk (TASR). In S. Kutcher & S. Chehil (2007). *Suicide risk management: A manual for health professionals.* Malden, MA: Blackwell.

Kutcher, S., & Chehil, S. (2007). *Suicide risk management: A manual for health professionals.* Malden, MA: Blackwell.

Lester, D. (2005) The classic systems of psychotherapy and suicidal behavior. In R. I. Yufit & D. Lester (Eds.), *Assessment, treatment, and prevention of suicidal behavior.* Hoboken, NJ: John Wiley & Sons.

Lewinsohn, P. M., Garrison, C. Z., Langhinrichsen, J., & Marsteller, F. (1989). *The assessment of suicidal behavior in adolescents: A review of scales suitable for epidemiological and clinical research* (Report prepared under contract nos. 316774, 316776). Rockville, MD: Child and Adolescent Disorders Research Branch DCR, National Institute of Mental Health.

Linehan, M. M. (1985). The reasons for living inventory. In P. Keller & L. Ritt (Eds.), *Innovations in clinical practice* (pp. 321–330). Sarasota, FL: Professional Resource Exchange.

Linehan, M. M., Rizvi, S. L., Welch, S. S., & Page, B. (2000). Suicide and personality disorders. In K. Hawton & K. van Heeringen (Eds.), *International handbook of suicide and attempted suicide.* Chichester, West Sussex, UK: John Wiley & Sons.

Litinsky, A. M., & Haslam, N. (1998). Dichotomous thinking as a sign of suicide risk on the TAT. *Journal of Personality Assessment, 71,* 368–378.

Litman, R. E. (1975). The assessment of suicidality. In R. Pasnau (Ed.), *Consultation-liaison psychiatry.* New York: Grune and Stratton.

Lundback, E., Forslund, K., Rylander, G., Jokinen, J., Nordstrom, P., & Asberg, M. (2006). CSF 5-HIAA and the Rorschach test in patients who have attempted suicide. *Archives of Suicide Research, 10,* 339–345.

McCann, J. T., & Gergelis, R. E. (1990). Utility of the MCMI-II in assessing suicide risk. *Journal of Clinical Psychology, 46,* 764–770.

McCann, J. T., & Suess, J. F. (1988). Clinical applications of the MCMI: The 1-2-3-8 codetype. *Journal of Clinical Psychology, 44,* 181–186.

McEvoy, T. L. (1974). Suicidal risk via the Thematic Apperception Test. In C. Neuringer (Ed.), *Psychological assessment of suicide risk* (pp. 3–17). Springfield, IL: Charles C. Thomas.

McIntosh, J. L., Santos, J. F., Hubbard, R. W., & Overholser, J. C. (1994). *Elder suicide: Research, theory and treatment.* Washington, DC: American Psychological Association.

Mack, J. E., & Hickler, H. (1981). *Vivienne: The life and suicide of an adolescent girl.* Boston, MA: Little Brown.

Mahrer, J. (1993). The use of "no-suicide contracts" and agreements with suicidal patients. *Dissertation Abstracts International, 54*(6B), 3345.

Maltsberger, J. T. (1988). Suicide danger: Clinical estimation and decision. *Suicide and Life-Threatening Behavior, 18*, 47–54.

Maris, R. W., Berman, A. L., Maltsberger, J. T., & Yufit, R. I. (Eds.) (1992). *Assessment and prediction of suicide*. New York: Guilford Press.

Meyer, R. G. (1989). *The clinician's handbook: The psychopathology of adulthood and adolescence* (2nd ed.). Boston: Allyn & Bacon.

Meyer, R. G. (1993). *The clinician's handbook: Integrated diagnostics, assessment, and intervention in adult and adolescent psychopathology* (3rd ed.). Boston: Allyn & Bacon.

Meyer, R. G., & Deitsch, S. E. (1996). *The clinician's handbook: Integrated diagnostics, assessment, and intervention in adult and adolescent psychopathology* (4th ed.). Boston: Allyn & Bacon.

Miskimins, R. W., DeCook, R., Wilson, L. T., & Maley, R. F. (1967). Prediction of suicide in a psychiatric hospital. *Journal of Clinical Psychology, 23*, 296–301.

Monahan, J. (1981). *The clinical prediction of violent behavior* (DHSS Publication No. ADM 81-921). Washington, DC: National Institute of Mental Health.

Morey, L. C. (1991). *The Personality Assessment Inventory professional manual*. Odessa, FL: Psychological Assessment Resources.

Morey, L. C. (2003). *Essentials of PAI Assessment*. Hoboken, NJ: John Wiley & Sons.

Motto, J. A. (1977). The estimation of suicide risk by use of clinical models. *Suicide and Life-Threatening Behavior, 7*, 236–245.

Motto, J. A. (1979). The psychopathology of suicide: A clinical approach. *American Journal of Psychiatry, 136*(4-B), 516–520.

Motto, J. A. (1989). Problems in suicide risk assessment. In D. G. Jacobs & H. N. Brown (Eds.), *Suicide: Understanding and responding: Harvard Medical School perspectives on suicide* (pp. 129–142). Madison, CT: International Universities Press.

Motto, J. A. (1991). An integrated approach to estimating suicide risk. *Suicide and Life-Threatening Behavior, 21*, 74–89.

Motto, J. A., Heilbron, D. C., & Juster, R. P. (1985). Development of a clinical instrument to estimate suicide risk. *American Journal of Psychiatry, 142*, 680–686.

Murphy, G. E. (1988a). The prediction of suicide. In S. Lesse (Ed.), *What we know about suicidal behavior and how to treat it* (pp. 47–58). Northvale, NJ: Jason Aronson.

Murphy, G. E. (1988b). Prevention of suicide. In A. J. Frances & R. E. Hales (Eds.), *American Psychiatric Press review of psychiatry* (Vol. 7, pp. 403–421). Washington, DC: American Psychiatric Press.

National Institute of Mental Health. (April, 2003). *Suicide Deaths, U.S., 2000*. Retrieved from http://nimh.nih.gov/research.suifact.cfm

Neuringer, C. (1974a). Problems in assessing suicide risk. In C. Neuringer (Ed.), *Psychological assessment of suicide risk* (pp. 3–17). Springfield, IL: Charles C. Thomas.

Neuringer, C. (1974b). Rorschach inkblot test assessment of suicidal risk. In C. Neuringer (Ed.), *Psychological assessment of suicide risk* (pp. 74–94). Springfield, IL: Charles C. Thomas.

Ngai, A. (2001). Representational world of the suicidal youth as depicted on the TAT. *Dissertation Abstracts International, Section B: The Sciences and Engineering, 61*(7-B), 3854.

Osborne, D. (1985). The MMPI in psychiatric practice. *Psychiatric Annals, 15*, 542–545.

Packman, W. L., Marlitt, R. E., Bongar, B., & Pennuto, T. O. (2004). A comprehensive and concise assessment of suicide risk. *Behavioral Sciences and the Law, 22*, 667–680.

Pallis, D. J., Barraclough, B., Levey, A., Jenkins, J., & Sainsbury, P. (1982). Estimating suicide risk among attempted suicides: The development of new clinical scales. *British Journal of Psychiatry, 141*, 37–44.

Pallis, D. J., Gibbons, J. S., & Pierce, D. W. (1984). Estimating suicide risk among attempted suicides: Efficiency of predictive scales after the attempt. *British Journal of Psychiatry, 144*, 139–148.

Peruzzi, N., & Bongar, B. (1999). Assessing risk for completed suicide in patients with major depression: Psychologists' views of critical factors. *Professional Psychology: Research and Practice, 30*, 576–580.

Piotrowski, C., Sherry, D., & Keller, J. W. (1985). Psychodiagnostic test usage: A survey of the Society for Personality Assessment. *Journal of Personality Assessment, 49*, 115–119.

Poeldinger, W. J., Gehring, A., & Blaser, P. (1973). Suicide risk and MMPI scores, especially as related to anxiety and depression. *Suicide and Life-Threatening Behavior, 3*, 147–153.

Pokorny, A. D. (1983). Prediction of suicide in psychiatric patients. *Archives of General Psychiatry, 40*, 249–257.

Quinnett, P., & Bratcher, K. (1996). *Question Persuade Refer Treat: Suicide risk management inventory user's manual*. Spokane, WA: Greentree Behavioral Health, a division of Spokane Mental Health.

Reinecke, M. A., & Franklin-Scott, R. L. (2005). Assessment of suicide: Beck's scales for assessing mood and suicidality. In R. I. Yufit & D. Lester (Eds.), *Assessment, treatment, and prevention of suicidal behavior*. Hoboken, NJ: John Wiley & Sons.

Reynolds, W. M. (1987). *Suicidal Ideation Questionnaire*. Odessa, FL: Psychological Assessment Resources.

Reynolds, W. M. (1988). *Suicidal Ideation Questionnaire: Professional manual*. Odessa, FL: Psychological Assessment Resources.

Reynolds, W. M. (1991). *Adult Suicidal Ideation Questionnaire: Professional manual*. Odessa, FL: Psychological Assessment Resources.

Reynolds, W. M., & Mazza, J. J. (1992). *Suicidal behavior history form: Clinician's guide*. Odessa, FL: Psychological Assessment Resources.

Richman, J., & Eyman, J. R. (1991). Psychotherapy of suicide: Individual, group and family approaches. In D. Lester (Ed.), *Understanding suicide: The state of the art*. Philadelphia: Charles Press.

Rogers, J. R., & Oney, K. M. (2005). Clinical use of suicide assessment scales: Enhancing reliability and validity through the therapeutic relationship. In R. I. Yufit & D. Lester (Eds.), *Assessment, treatment, and prevention of suicidal behavior*. Hoboken, NJ: John Wiley & Sons.

Rogers, R., Ustad, K. L., & Salekin, R. T. (1998). Convergent validity of the personality assessment inventory: A study of emergency referrals in a correctional setting. *Assessment, 5*, 3–12.

Rosenberg, J. I. (1997) Expertise research and clinical practice: A suicide assessment and intervention training model. *Educational Psychology Review, 9*, 279–296.

Rudd, M. D., Joiner, T. E., & Rajab, H. (2001). *Treating suicidal behavior: An effective time-limited approach*. New York: Guilford Press.

Sepaher, I., Bongar, B., & Greene, R. L. (1999). Codetype base rates for the "I Mean Business" suicide items on the MMPI-2. *Journal of Clinical Psychology, 55*, 1167–1173.

Shneidman, E. S. (1985). *Definition of suicide*. New York: John Wiley & Sons.

Shneidman, E. S. (1987). A psychological approach to suicide. In G. R. VandenBos & B. K. Bryant (Eds.), *Cataclysms, crises, and catastrophes: Psychology in action* (pp. 147–183). Washington, DC: American Psychological Association.

Silberg, J. L., & Armstrong, J. G. (1992). The Rorschach test for predicting suicide among depressed adolescent inpatients. *Journal of Personality Assessment, 59,* 290–303.

Simon, R. I. (1987). *Clinical psychiatry and the law.* Washington, DC: American Psychiatric Press.

Simon, R. I. (1988). *Concise guide to clinical psychiatry and the law.* Washington, DC: American Psychiatric Press.

Simon, R. I. (1992). *Concise guide to psychiatry and the law for clinicians.* Washington, DC: American Psychiatric Press.

Smith, J. (1986). *Medical malpractice psychiatric care.* Colorado Springs, CO: Shepards/McGraw-Hill.

Smith, K. (1985). Suicide assessment: An ego vulnerabilities approach. *Bulletin of the Menninger Clinic, 48,* 489–499.

Smith, K., & Eyman, J. R. (1988). Ego structure and object differentiation in suicidal patients. In H. D. Lerner & P. M. Lerner (Eds.), *Primitive mental states and the Rorschach* (pp. 175–202). Madison, CT: International Universities Press.

Steer, R. A., & Beck, A. T. (1988). Use of the Beck Depression Inventory, Hopelessness Scale, Scale for Suicide Ideation, and Suicidal Intent Scale with adolescents. *Advances in Adolescent Mental Health, 3,* 219–231.

Stolberg, R. A., Glassmire, D. M., Ricci, C. M., Green, R. L., & Bongar, B. (1999). *Using the MMPI-2 to increase the accuracy of identifying suicidal clients.* Poster presented at the 34th Annual Symposium on Recent Developments in the Use of the MMPI-2 & MMPI-A, Huntington Beach, CA, April 17, 1999.

Strack, S. (2002). *Essentials of Millon inventories assessment* (2nd ed.). New York: John Wiley & Sons.

Swiercinsky, D. (1985). *Testing adults.* Kansas City, MO: Test Corporation of America.

Tuckman, J., & Youngman, W. F. (1968). Assessment of suicide risk in attempted suicides. In H. L. Resnik (Ed.), *Suicidal behaviors: Diagnosis and Management.* Boston: Little Brown.

Weissman, A. D., & Worden, J. W. (1972). Risk-rescue in suicide assessment. *Archives of General Psychiatry, 26,* 553–560.

Weissman, A. D., & Worden, J. W. (1974). Risk-rescue in suicide assessment. In A. T. Beck, H. L. Resnik, & D. L. Lettieri (Eds.), *The prediction of suicide.* Bowies, MD: Charles Press.

Widiger, T., & Francis, A. (1987). Interviews and inventories for the measurement of personality disorders. *Clinical Psychology Review, 7,* 49–75.

Wingate, L. R., Joiner, T. E., Walker, R. L., Rudd, M. D., & Jobes, D. E. (2004). Empirically informed approaches to topics in suicide assessment. *Behavioral Sciences and the Law, 22,* 651–665.

Wise, A. J., & Spengler, P. M. (1997). Suicide in children younger than age fourteen: Clinical judgement and assessment issues. *Journal of Mental Health Counseling, 19,* 4, 318–335.

Wood, J. M., Nezworski, M. T., & Stejskal, W. J. (1996). The comprehensive system for the Rorschach: A critical examination. *Psychology Science, 7,* 3–10.

Young, M. A., Fogg, L. F., Scheftner, W., Fawcett, J., Akiskal, H., & Maser, J. (1996). Stable trait components of hopelessness: Baseline and sensitivity to depression. *Journal of Abnormal Psychology, 105,* 155–165.

Yufit, R. I. (1988). Manual of procedures—assessing suicide potential: Suicide assessment team. (Unpublished manual; Available from Robert I. Yufit, PhD, Department of Psychiatry and Behavioral Sciences, Division of Clinical Psychology, Northwestern University Medical School, Chicago, IL).

Yufit, R. I. (1989). *Developing a suicide screening instrument for adolescents and young adults.* In Alcohol, Drug Abuse, and Mental Health Administration Report of the Secretary's Task Force on Youth Suicide (DHSS Publication No. ADM 89-1621-1624). Washington, DC: U.S. Government Printing Office.

Yufit, R. I., & Benzies, B. (1973). Assessing suicide potential by time perpective. *Suicide and Life-Threatening Behavior, 3,* 270–282.

Yufit, R. I., & Benzies, B. (1979). *Preliminary manual Time Questionnaire: Assessing suicide potential.* Palo Alto, CA: Consulting Psychologists Press.

Yufit, R. I. (2005). Assessing the vital balance in evaluating suicidal potential. In R. I. Yufit & D. Lester (Eds.), *Assessment, treatment, and prevention of suicidal behavior.* Hoboken, NJ: John Wiley & Sons.

Yufit, R. I. & Lester, D. (Eds.) (2005). *Assessment, treatment, and prevention of suicidal behavior.* Hoboken, NJ: John Wiley & Sons.

Zubin, J. (1974). Observations on nosological issues in the classification of suicidal behavior. In A. T. Beck, H. L. Resnik, & D. L. Lettieri (Eds.), *The prediction of suicide* (pp. 3–25). Bowies, MD: Charles Press Publishers.

Zung, W. W. K. (1974). Index of Potential Suicide (IPS). In A. T. Beck, H. L. Resnik, & D. L. Lettieri (Eds.), *The Prediction of Suicide* (pp. 221–249). Bowies, MD: Charles Press Publishers.

Use of Self-Report Measures in Assessing Alcohol and Drug Abuse

Joseph A. Banken *and* Roger L. Greene

Abstract

This chapter provides a conceptual framework for the use of self-report measures in assessing alcohol and drug abuse. The chapter reviews the use of self-report measures for assessing a number of different issues: screening for substance abuse; traditional scales used to identify alcohol or drug abuse; timing of assessment within an alcohol/drug treatment program; specific tests that have particular utility within the area; and identification of patients with dual disorders. The Minnesota Multiphasic Personality Inventory-2 (MMPI-2) is emphasized throughout the chapter, but the results can be generalized to other self-report measures. Self-report measures continue to show promise in addressing alcohol/drug abuse. Research still is needed to address more comprehensively these issues.

Keywords: Addiction Admission Scale (AAS), Addiction Potential Scale (APS), Alcohol Use Inventory (AUI), AUDIT, CAGE, MacAndrew Alcoholism Scale-Revised (MAC-R), MAST, Millon Multiaxial Clinical Inventory (MCMI/MCMI-II/MCMI-III), Minnesota Multiphasic Personality Inventory (MMPI/MMPI-2), Rapid Alcohol Problems Screen 4–Quantity Frequency (RAPS4-QF)

The use of any form of psychological assessment in alcohol/drug abuse has been hampered by the traditional bias in this field against any form of assessment, which has stated more or less explicitly that once the person stops drinking/drugging the other problems will go away. It is only in the last few decades that progress has been made in the use of psychological assessment in this field with the recognition of the (a) specific contributions that can be made by psychological assessment in planning interventions and treatment; (b) existence of persons with dual disorders that must be diagnosed and treated concurrently; and (c) need for screening for alcohol/drug abuse in many areas of our society that has increased public awareness of the role of assessment. This chapter will focus on the use of self-report measures in several areas of assessing alcohol/drug abuse: (a) issues involved in screening for substance abuse; (b) traditional scales used to identify alcohol or drug abuse; (c) timing of psychological assessment within an alcohol/drug

treatment program; (d) specific tests that have particular utility within the area; and (e) identification of patients with dual disorders. The primary emphasis in this chapter will be on the Minnesota Multiphasic Personality Inventory-2 (MMPI-2) (Butcher, Dahlstrom, Graham, Tellegen, & Kaemmer, 1989), although the results can be generalized easily to any self-report measures.

Preliminary Considerations

A number of potential issues must be given explicit consideration in understanding research on alcohol or drug abuse. The parameters of the person's use of substances need to be reported explicitly. These data can be as simple as whether the person uses substances constantly, only on weekends, or during binges. The type of substance(s) used also is important, at least as to generic class, for example, sedative-hypnotics, stimulants, and so on, as well as whether the person uses only one substance or multiple substances. The work of Skinner and his colleagues (cf. Morey & Skinner, 1986; Morey, Skinner, & Blashfield, 1984; Skinner, Jackson, & Hoffmann, 1974) may be very useful in this area in terms of identifying patterns of use that can be compared with psychological test performance.

The social-interpersonal aspects of the alcohol or drug use should be identified. Persons may use substances only alone, withdraw and isolate themselves as the result of the use of substances, only use in social contexts, or some combination of these behaviors. Misuse of alcohol is not only associated with multiple physical and mental health problems, but also increases risk factors related to criminal behavior. Psychosocial aspects of substance use is particularly important in women, younger persons, and older persons who may start drinking at a later time in their life, all of whom generally have shorter periods of substance use history. The use and misuse of alcohol among college students has been widely documented (e.g., O'Malley & Johnston, 2002; Perkins, 2002) and more recently has been an area of public concern.

The factors that have led the person to receive treatment need to be identified. Although persons enter treatment as a result of "hitting bottom," the factors that lead to that bottom are very different. Persons may be entering treatment because of the "encouragement" of the legal system, employers, spouses, and so on. The increased use of substance use testing in the workplace may result in persons being identified and referred for treatment before "hitting bottom," that is, at an earlier stage of substance abuse.

Any comparisons that are made between polydrug and alcoholic patients must consider the potential effects of age since polydrug patients average 15–20 years younger than alcoholics. Another consideration is that persons dependent on alcohol are 3 times more likely than those in the general population to use tobacco, and people dependent on tobacco are 4 times more likely than the general population to be dependent on alcohol (Grant, Hasin, Chou, Stinson, & Dawson, 2004). The influence of socioeconomic class and education, which have significant effects on self-report personality test performance, also must be considered. The general failure to even consider the role of such moderator variables, which is so characteristic of research in this area, must be corrected if meaningful data are to be obtained.

One of the most significant needs in this entire area is to focus on treatment process and outcome issues, that is, whether subgroups of patients who use specific substances respond better to one type of treatment and whether they have differential recovery rates. Project MATCH Research Group (1993) has provided a comprehensive overview of this topic that should be consulted by anyone who is working in this area. The time is long past when delineating whether alcoholics or drug addicts are a unitary group is a viable question; the data are clear that substance users are very heterogeneous. Research questions need to be more sharply focused; such as, do alcoholics with both a 2-4/4-2 codetype and an elevated score on the MacAndrew Alcoholism Scale-Revised (MAC-R) have better recovery rates in a confrontational-based AA program? Or, are attrition rates across the course of treatment within this codetype higher or lower than in a 4-9/9-4 codetype, and if so, how can this problem be addressed? It also would be informative to determine whether patients within these specific subgroups have different histories of personal and familial substance use. Consequently, it is mandatory that researchers do more than simply report that the patients are in some unspecified treatment program. Detailed databases that encompass both the individual's and his/her familial history of substance use as well as social and environmental factors that may be involved must be reported as well as the patient's MMPI-2 performance. Substance use is a complex process; it is time that research designs start to appreciate this complexity and report data that can begin to give some insight into the multitude of factors that are involved.

The point in time at which the data are collected is very important. If the data are collected too early in treatment the patients may be too toxic to report accurately. This specific issue will be discussed below.

How the persons respond after they entered treatment also must be considered, particularly in any study that is evaluating treatment effectiveness or outcome. Some persons will continue to deny or minimize their use of substance(s) throughout treatment, and/or leave treatment prematurely. Clinicians, who collect their data early in treatment and do not consider that some patients may leave before completing treatment, will have different results than those who collect data later or toward the end of treatment.

Finally, the basis on which the diagnosis is made must be given careful consideration. All too often it appears that the only criterion for the diagnosis is the person's presence in a treatment facility with little regard for whether the diagnosis is appropriate or whether other psychiatric diagnoses are present. The assumption appears to be that false-positive diagnoses do not occur in these facilities, which may be fairly safe given the denial and minimization that are characteristic of the misuse of substance(s). However, it is important to be aware of the variety of social, interpersonal, and legal factors that resulted in this person being identified as needing treatment. These issues/factors may be less important within a given facility because people may be referred for similar reasons, but they clearly are important when patients are compared across a variety of facilities. Individuals who receive treatment in a state or Veterans Administration (VA) hospital may differ in a number of important ways from persons in a private hospital or who are maintained in an outpatient setting (cf. English & Curtin, 1975; Krauthamer, 1979; Pattison, Coe, & Doerr, 1973). The consideration of special populations such as that of adolescents, older persons, pregnant women, college students, and minority populations will need additional consideration in the design of substance use research. Evidence shows that even low-risk drinking, such as fewer than seven drinks per week or three or fewer standard drinks per drinking day during pregnancy, can cause adverse fetal effects, although the direct reasons for such damage remains elusive (Bearer, 2001). The prevalence of any alcohol use by pregnant women was 12.8% in 1999 and 3.3% % reported binge drinking (five or more drinks per episode) (Centers for Disease Control and Prevention, 2002).

It should be apparent that until researchers start addressing the issues described above, it will be very difficult to reach any definitive conclusions about work in this area.

Screening for Substance Abuse

There has been increasing concern over the last decade for the identification of persons whose substance abuse may potentially interfere with their job functions, and screening for substance abuse now is required in a number of industries. The importance of such screening cannot be overestimated when it is considered that the lifetime prevalence rate for substance abuse disorders in adults approaches 16% (Regier et al., 1988), and at least 20% of adults who visit a physician have had an alcohol problem at one time (Cleary et al., 1988). The clinician must keep in mind that screening is used to identify people who are likely to have a substance abuse disorder. Screening is not the same as diagnostic assessment, which attempts to establish a specific diagnosis, usually that which meets specific DSM-IV (Diagnostic and Statistical Manual of Mental Disorders, 4th edition) criteria.

Over the last several years, there has been increased interest in detection and treatment of less severe alcohol problems such as hazardous alcohol consumption, which is understood as a quantity or pattern of alcohol use that places the person at risk for adverse consequences in the workplace (Saunders, Aasland, Babor, De La Fuente, & Grant, 1993) or primary medical care settings (Reid, Fiellen, & O'Connor, 1999). Extant screening tools for substance abuse generally lack sensitivity to hazardous alcohol consumption that complicates the implementation of this approach. According to the National Institute on Alcohol Abuse and Alcoholism (NIAAA, 2000), alcohol use disorders are a major contributor to morbidity and mortality despite the knowledge that effective treatments for these disorders are available (Saitz, 2005).

Similar concerns arise in clinical settings where prevalence rates for substance abuse have been estimated to range from 12% to 30% (Moore et al., 1989). Clinicians frequently fail to recognize that the patient's symptoms may reflect substance abuse or dependence rather than, or in addition to, psychiatric symptomatology. Additionally, current screening tools such as the CAGE (Mayfield, McLeod, & Hall, 1974) may not be effective in populations that have not had the opportunity to develop severe substance use problems (cf. Heck, 1991).

The critical need to identify individuals who may be abusing substances in the workplace and in clinical settings has resulted in the failure to consider the multitude of variables that may impact these assessments, particularly in disadvantaged groups. Investigators frequently overlook the relationship between sensitivity, specificity, and the prevalence of a given disorder, and the potential loss of predictive power when a test or procedure is used in a given setting (Baldessarini, Finkelstein, & Arana, 1983). Item 264, which inquires about excessive alcohol use, and 489, which inquires whether alcohol or drugs are a problem, from the MMPI-2 (Butcher et al., 1989) can be used as examples of two different types of screening "tests" to illustrate these points.

"Sensitivity," or how well the test identifies persons who abuse alcohol, is a critical variable in a screening instrument, because a test with low sensitivity will produce a large number of false negatives. In a sample of 291 inpatients at the Southwest Institute for Addictive Diseases in the Department of Psychiatry at Texas Tech University, Item 264 on the MMPI-2 had a sensitivity of 77% in men ($N = 174$) and 59% in women ($N = 117$), while Item 489 had a sensitivity of 80% in men and 72% in women. Thus, these two screening "tests" missed about 20% of the male patients and 30–40% of the women patients who already are in a treatment program or have otherwise been identified as being substance-dependent. The substantial effects of gender are not usually discussed in the use of these screening instruments, and the effects of ethnicity are even less well understood. It should be clear that the sensitivity of Items 264 and 489 would decrease in settings such as the workplace where the person may be motivated not to report problems with or excessive use of alcohol. Unfortunately, it is in such settings where increased sensitivity is very desirable that the natural outcome is for decreased sensitivity.

If both MMPI-2 Items 264 and 489 are used in conjunction with one another, there is a sensitivity of 59% in men and 32% in women in the above inpatient sample, while only 9% of the men and 15% of the women are classified as false negatives. This false-negative rate, however, should be kept in mind when prevalence rates are discussed below.

"Specificity," or how well the test identifies persons who do not abuse alcohol, is equally important as sensitivity, since a test with low specificity will produce a large number of false positives. In the MMPI-2 normative sample (Butcher et al., 1989), Item 264 has a specificity of 53% in White men ($N = 933$) and 76% in White women ($N = 1184$), while Item 489 has a specificity of 95% in White men and 97% in White women. Again, the substantial effects of gender are apparent on Item 264. In the MMPI-2 normative sample, Item 264 has a specificity of 73% in Black men ($N = 126$) and 89% in Black women ($N = 188$), while Item 489 has a specificity of 93% in Black men and 96% in Black women. There also appear to be substantial gender difference in Blacks on Item 264. It should be readily apparent that depending upon which of these two "tests" was used to screen individuals, a different sample would be identified.

It should be readily apparent that Items 264 and 489 have much better specificity than sensitivity in White women and the relationship between sensitivity and specificity varies between these two "tests" in White men. Only Item 489 appears to have similar specificities across gender and ethnic groups in the MMPI-2 normative group, and it has reasonably good sensitivity.

Overall accuracy is an additional measure of a screening test's utility, but it is much less useful than sensitivity and specificity. Accuracy is defined as the proportion of people correctly classified by the screening test. Specifically, accuracy is the sum of true positives and true negatives over the entire population. In most populations, the prevalence of an alcohol use disorder is significantly less than 50%. With this prevalence rate, overall accuracy is nearly equal to specificity, and therefore overall accuracy does not provide additional value in estimating the validity of a screening test (Alberg, Park, Hager, & Brock, 2004).

As noted above, the lifetime "prevalence rate" for substance abuse disorders approaches 16% in men and 8% in women (Regier et al., 1988). Given these low prevalence rates for alcoholism in the general population, it is difficult for any screening instrument to improve upon the base rate prediction that everyone is not alcoholic because it will be 84% accurate in men and 92% accurate in women. Gottesman and Prescott (1989) recently summarized the issues involved in the use of the MAC (MacAndrew, 1965) in settings in which the prevalence rate is so low. Sensitivity and specificity also change as a function of prevalence rate that is too complex to be explored here. Baldessarini et al. (1983) provide a thorough discussion of this issue.

The cost benefits between sensitivity and specificity can be visually illustrated by using a receiver operator characteristic (ROC) curve. ROCs are rarely used in the social sciences, but can give researchers and clinicians improved methods to assess the validity of a screening test. ROC curves post the number of true positives (sensitivity) on the ordinate (y-axis), against the number of false positives (calculated as 1 – specificity value) on the abscissa (x-axis). With ROC graphics, clinicians and researchers can identify the cutoff value with the best possible combination of specificity and sensitivity for the target population of interest.

The specific criteria that are used to define a substance abuse disorder can vary widely and have substantial effects on the patients that are identified. Whether a test's validity has been properly established for a specific population and as related to a specific disorder can be a matter of debate. Criteria that emphasize liver function, for example, will identify a different set of alcoholics than criteria that emphasize social and occupational functioning. There are laboratory values and clinical conditions that have been related to alcohol abuse. Clinically high levels of gamma glutamyl transpepsidose

(GGT) and mean corpuscular volume (MVP) can be associated with alcohol abuse. However, there are problems of low specificity with the use of such measures. Currently, no single laboratory test can identify and quantify alcohol use that takes place over a protracted period. Some clinicians have suggested the use of multiple biomarkers to screen for suspected alcohol use, but important problems of sensitivity and specificity remain. New biomarkers for assessing alcohol intake and alcohol abuse are being researched, including the plasma sialic acid index of apolipoprotein J (SIJ), total serum sialic acid (TSA), 5-hydroxytryptophol (5-HTOL), and various fatty acid ethyl esters (FAEEs) (Peterson, 2004).

Researchers and clinicians frequently assume that an alcoholic is an alcoholic without considering how alcoholism is being defined in the development of a specific screening test. The specific criteria used to define alcoholism also place inherent limits on how well a screening test can identify such individuals. For example, a test that is designed to assess alcohol dependence in an inpatient setting will not perform in a similar manner in the workplace where the interest may be in the identification of persons who abuse substances or have hazardous consumption of substances. In addition, a critical hurdle for a screening test involves how well it can assess individuals who should be diagnosed as alcoholic by the specific criteria being employed, but who for whatever reason are not being identified, rather than alcoholics in a treatment program. A long-standing problem with many screening instruments is that they have been validated with groups likely to have a high base rate of alcohol problems (Ewing, 1984). Unlike screening for alcohol problems, little research has been devoted to developing screening tools for drug problems that are brief enough to be used in a wide variety of treatment settings (Rost, Burnam, & Smith, 1993).

Gender differences are rarely considered with standard screening instruments for substance abuse problems such as the Michigan Alcohol Screening Test (MAST: Selzer, 1971) or the CAGE (Mayfield et al., 1974). It is obvious that women who have scores of 10 or higher on the MAST or 2 or higher on the CAGE are reporting significant problems with alcohol. However, the few studies that have examined gender differences on the MAST routinely report that women have lower scores (Rivers, Rivers, & Newman, 1991), which clearly limits the utility of the MAST as a screening instrument in women. Even more serious are the findings of Babor, Kranzler, and Lauerman (1989), who found that women with high scores on the MAST differed from women with low scores only in their number of lifetime problems with alcohol, and that no screening scale worked well with women.

It frequently is conjectured that hidden or secretive drinking in women (Gearhart, Beebe, Milhorn, & Meeks, 1991) makes it more difficult to screen for their alcohol problems (Celentano, McQueen, & Chee, 1980). A number of potential explanations are provided for this hidden drinking: (a) women are more likely to drink at home and by themselves; (b) society (friends, law enforcement personnel) is more likely to "protect" women from the consequences of their drinking; and (c) the role of the housewife makes it easier to conceal drinking. As Celentano et al. (1980) noted, however, most prevalence estimators of problem drinking have been developed in men and the questions do not appear to be relevant to the areas of concern in women. Hence, "hidden" drinking in women may more accurately reflect that screening instruments do not ask the appropriate questions. Also, differences in prevalence rates for problem drinking for men and women need to be considered in evaluating "hidden" drinking. Osterling, Nilsson, Berglund, Moberg, and Kristenson (1992) found that unidentified problem drinking is proportional to problem drinking in men and women which argues rather strongly against hidden drinking being exclusively a characteristic of women.

Gender differences also need to be examined when specific items are under consideration for use in a screening test. Two items are frequently recommended in this literature as being equally appropriate for men and women: (1) five or more drinks on a given day and (2) getting into fights while drinking. These conclusions, however, do not take into consideration the differences in base rates with which these behaviors occur in men and women. For example, 49% of men and only 23% of women reported five or more drinks on any day in the last year (United States National Center for Health Statistics, 1985). The data on arrests and drug use among persons arrested also reveal substantial gender differences. Men are much more likely to be arrested (81.6%), yet drug use is nearly comparable for men and women if the person is arrested (Federal Bureau of Investigation, 1991). However, Petroni, Allen-Byrd, and Lewis (2003) found that endorsement of the Koss and Butcher and Lachar and Wrobel critical items on the MMPI-2 became more similar between men and women over the ensuing years of the recovery process.

Given the propensity for alcoholics to deny or minimize the seriousness of their disease, it could be argued that the identification of an individual via some screening instrument is of little practical value unless the person is willing to acknowledge that alcohol is a problem. It is important to understand whether screening is intended to identify individuals who need some type of intervention, which is the case in the clinical setting, or who needs to be excluded from some high-risk occupation, which is more likely to be the case in the work setting. In the clinical setting, denying or minimizing alcohol problems has a different set of implications than in the workplace, and clinicians need to be aware of these issues.

Traditional Self-Report Scales Used to Identify Alcohol or Drug Problems

A number of self-report scales have been developed to identify individuals with alcohol or drug problems. Several scales have been developed specifically to screen persons who may abuse substances: MAST (Selzer, 1971); Self-Administered Alcoholism Screening Test (Swenson & Morse, 1975); and Mortimer–Filkins Test (Mortimer, Filkins, Kerlan, & Lower, 1973), which have been reviewed rather frequently (cf. Jacobson, 1983, 1989; National Institute on Alcohol Abuse and Alcoholism, 1990). Because of the limitations of space only a limited number of MMPI-2 scales will be examined here: MAC-R, Addiction Admission Scale (AAS), and Addiction Potential Scale (APS) (Weed, Butcher, McKenna, & Ben-Porath, 1992), and Scales B and T from the Millon Multiaxial Clinical Inventory (MCMI/MCMI-II). Each of these scales will be examined in turn.

MacAndrew Alcoholism Scale

A number of MMPI scales have been developed to identify persons who have alcohol and drug problems. The interested reader should consult an earlier edition of this chapter (Greene & Banken, 2001) for those references. This chapter will be limited to those scales that are scored routinely on the MMPI-2 (AAS, APS, and MAC/MAC-R). There are several extensive reviews of the MAC/MAC-R that can be consulted by the interested reader (Craig, 2005; Gottesman & Prescott, 1989; Greene & Garvin, 1988; MacAndrew, 1981), and Weed, Butcher, and Ben-Porath (1995) have provided a thorough review of all MMPI-2 measures of substance abuse.

The MAC-R identifies White males who have a propensity to use substances with 70–75% hit rates

and false negatives around 20%. Data on adolescents and White females who use substances are less reliable because of the limited research. Second, when White males who use substances must be discriminated from other psychiatric patients, hit rates' decrease, and the percentage of false positives increases. These discriminations become even more difficult when patients have dual disorders (a substance abuse/dependence diagnosis and some other DSM-IV-TR Axis I or II diagnosis), which will be explored in more detail below. Finally, the MAC-R should be used very cautiously with Black males because of the extremely low hit rates and high percentages of false positives in psychiatric patients. It is unclear whether similar problems occur in other ethnic groups and with Black females because there is no research on which to make any conclusions.

The research on the MAC-R with polydrug patients clearly is less complete than with alcoholic patients. Several conclusions still can be drawn and a number of recommendations can be made for future research in this area. First, the elevated scores on the MAC-R in polydrug patients indicate that the MAC-R is sensitive to the misuse of all types of substances including alcohol. The MAC-R could be called more appropriately a "substance abuse" scale rather than an "alcoholism" scale. The "substances" that are misused do not have to be "street" drugs either, since legally prescribed medications are equally prone to such misuse. Second, there do not appear to be any ethnic differences between Black and White male polydrug patients in terms of their mean performance on the MAC-R. Yet the finding that Black, male, psychiatric patients score nearly in the same range as Black polydrug and alcoholic patients suggests that the MAC-R probably is less effective with members of minority groups. Finally, data are needed on the performance of the MAC-R in other samples of polydrug patients such as women, adolescents, and so on. Until such information is available, the MAC-R should be used cautiously in these groups, too.

Addiction Admission and Addiction Potential Scales

Butcher and his colleagues (Weed et al., 1992) developed two new substance abuse scales that are scored routinely with the MMPI-2. The AAS, a 13-item scale, differs significantly from the MAC in that it focuses on simple denial or acknowledgement of substance abuse problems. The APS, a 39-item scale, was designed to identify personality features and lifestyle patterns that are related to alcohol and drug abuse. The APS was constructed by contrasting item responses of the MMPI-2 normative group (Butcher et al., 1989), psychiatric patients (Graham & Butcher, 1988), and alcoholics (McKenna & Butcher, 1987). Greene, Weed, Butcher, Arredondo, and Davis (1992) cross-validated AAS and APS in a sample of substance abusers and psychiatric inpatients, and they found nearly identical results to Weed et al. (1992).

Despite the existence of the AAS and APS scales for nearly 15 years, there is limited research on them. Several studies (Aaronson, Dent, & Kline, 1996; Greene et al., 1992; Svanum, McGrew, & Ehrmann, 1994) have documented the usefulness of the AAS to identify substance abuse. These studies routinely found that the AAS was better able to identify individuals who abused substances than less direct measures such as the APS and MAC-R. The APS does appear to be more accurate at discriminating between substance abusers and psychiatric patients than the MAC-R. These scales appear to have utility in identifying individuals who have problems with alcohol or drugs. These scales do not show significant specificity in discriminating alcohol from drug abuse, but are sensitive to the identification of substance abuse in general.

Scales B and T (MCMI-III)

The MCMI-III, an updated version of the earlier MCMI and MCMI-II, was designed for use in clinical settings (Millon, 1983). The MCMI-III contains two substance abuse scales: the alcohol dependence scale (Scale B) was developed to assess the presence of alcoholism, and the drug dependence scale (Scale T) was designed to assess recurrent or recent history of drug abuse. B, a 46-item scale, assesses a history of excessive drinking that has produced problems in the home and workplace. T, a 58-item scale, is associated with a history of drug use pronounced enough to cause difficulties in either home or the work situation. According to Millon (1983), both Scales B and T contain numerous indirect items that may be useful in identifying psychiatric patients who are not eager to admit substance abuse problems. However, there have been few studies using the MCMI with alcoholics (Bartsch & Hoffman, 1985; Craig, Verinis, & Wexler, 1985). Only Millon's validation studies specifically assessed the relationship between the MAC and Scales B and T using the MMPI and MCMI with correlations of .44 and .51, respectively (Millon, 1983, p. 52).

The performance of the MCMI substance scales has been disappointing when used in substance-abusing populations (Gilbertini & Retzlaff, 1988; Miller & Streiner, 1990). Miller and Streiner (1990) reported that Scale B is not as accurate as the MAC and that the scale should not be used.

Additional Screening Scales

In the past few years several self-report screening scales have been developed that are variations on existing screening scales. Allen, Maisto, and Connors (1995) provide an informative review of screening tools for alcohol problems in primary care treatment settings.

The TWEAK, a five-item screening tool that is a variation on the CAGE, is designed to be a brief interview instrument to allow increased sensitivity to identify alcohol problems in pregnant women and women of child-bearing age (Flynn, Marcus, Barry, & Blow, 2003; Russell, 1994). Recent research has shown that the TWEAK identifies the level of "at-risk" drinking at twice the currently accepted definition of one drink per day (Sokol, Delaney-Black, & Nordstrom, 2003). The Tolerance, Annoyed, Cut down, Eye-Opener (T-ACE) is a brief questionnaire that can be used as an effective screening instrument to assess prenatal alcohol consumption, and is based on the more familiar CAGE.

The Alcohol Use Disorders Identification Test (AUDIT; Babor, DeLa Fuente, Saunders, & Grant, 1989) is a 10-question instrument that detects a broad spectrum of alcohol disorders. Several validity studies (Saunders et al., 1993) have reported encouraging results. In addition to the 10 AUDIT questions, an eight-item AUDIT clinical procedure assesses trauma history, abnormal physical findings, and GGT level (Bohn, Babor, & Kranzler, 1995). Steinbauer, Cantor, Holzer and Volk (1998) found the AUDIT to have better operating characteristics than the Self-Administered Alcoholism Screening Test and the CAGE across a variety of clinical groups. It is possible that the AUDIT may currently represent the most effective screening methodology to identify patients with a variety of alcohol problems. The interested reader is referred to Allen, Litten, Fertig, and Babor (1997) and Reinert and Allen (2002) for a review of research on use of the AUDIT.

The Rapid Alcohol Problems (RAP: Cherpitel, 1998) and its revision, the Rapid Alcohol Problems Screen 4 (RAPS4: Cherpitel, 2000), is a screening tool that has combined optimal questions from the CAGE, Brief Michigan Alcoholism Screening Test

(BMAST), AUDIT, and TWEAK and has shown sensitivity for identification of problem drinkers across ethnic groups and among women in emergency room populations. However, additional validation is needed before using these screening scales routinely in diverse ethnic groups and diverse clinical settings. In subsequent work, Cherpitel et al. (2005) have modified the RAPS4 to the RAPS4-QF which includes the questions from the RAPS4 screening questions plus additional items of quantity (five or more drinks on at least one occasion during the last year) and frequency (drink as often as once a month). A positive response on both the quantity and frequency of drinking or with a positive response of any one of the four RAPS items is defined as "at-risk" drinking. The RAPS4 has been shown to outperform other screening instruments for the general population (Cherpitel, 2002).

Screening Test Used with College Students

The Young Alcohol Screening Test (YAAPST) is a 27-item scale that has shown acceptable reliability and validity with 92% sensitivity and 57% specificity (Hurlbut & Sher, 1992). The College Alcohol Problems Scale (CAPS-r) is an eight-item scale that has shown acceptable reliability and concurrent validity among college students (Maddock, Laforge, Rossi, & O'Hare, 2001). The Rutgers Alcohol Problem Index (RAPI) has two versions: the original 23-item and an 18-item version. The RAPI demonstrates acceptable internal consistency (Neal & Carrey, 2004) and test–retest reliability using 1-, 6-, and 12-month time frames (Miller et al., 2002). All of these screening tests are characterized by the existence of one or two studies validating their use.

The NIAAA's alcohol question sets and the AUDIT can also be used to assess alcohol problems in the past year. However, the NIAAA alcohol questions are used for research rather than clinical settings, and the appropriate cutoff score for the AUDIT among college students has been controversial.

At present, there is very little research on brief screening instruments for other drug dependence and abuse. Cherpitel (2004) has expanded earlier research from problems drinkers with the RAPS and has developed a four-item screening instrument, called the Rapid Drugs Problem Screener (RDPS). An advantage of the RDPS is that its utility has been evaluated against DSM-IV and International Classification of Diseases, 9th edition (ICD-9) criteria for drug dependence and abuse and therefore may have particular utility for clinicians.

Unfortunately, current research on the RDPS needs to be evaluated in larger populations of females and diverse ethnic groups and geographic locations.

The Timing of Psychological Assessment

The primary dilemma regarding the timing of psychological assessment is that early assessment can provide information that is crucial for effective patient treatment planning, but psychological assessment conducted too soon after admission may be distorted by the consequences of toxicity or withdrawal. Many studies have demonstrated that when psychological testing is conducted during the first few days of treatment and later repeated, the second assessment reveals much less distress, agitation, and confusion (Bean & Karasievich, 1975; Craig, 1983; Graf, Baer, & Comstock, 1977; Libb & Taulbee, 1971).

Clinicians who treat alcoholics and other substance-dependent patients are well aware of the need to delay psychological assessment when the patient who enters the treatment program has withdrawal or other toxic effects. Despite the awareness of the need to delay assessment to allow for detoxification and withdrawal, clear guidelines for the optimal time to administer the initial psychological assessment are lacking. Although Sherer, Haygood, and Alfano (1984) suggested that a 10-day delay after admission is sufficient for some psychological testing, other investigators have recommended longer delays. For example, Nathan (1991, p. 359) concluded that patients with depression, anxiety, or psychotic behavior need to be drug-free for 4 to 6 weeks "before they can be reliably diagnosed with a psychiatric disorder exclusive of the effects of their drug use." Recommendations regarding the optimal time for testing may vary depending on such factors as the drug abused by the patient, the severity and length of the abuse, and the type of psychological testing (neuropsychological vs. personality). The significantly decreased inpatient stays that have become a reality in the last several years with managed care for substance use treatment makes the issue of the appropriate timing for psychological assessment even more critical. Research clearly is needed that addresses this issue.

Self-Report Tests Traditionally
Used in Alcohol or Drug Treatment Programs
MINNESOTA MULTIPHASIC PERSONALITY INVENTORY

There have been a number of reviews of the use of the MMPI in alcohol- and drug-abusing samples

(Clopton, 1978; Graham & Strenger, 1988; Greene & Garvin, 1988; Morey & Blashfield, 1981), with most of the research focused on alcoholics. Several conclusions can be drawn from the performance of alcoholic patients on the standard MMPI validity and clinical scales. First, it is clear that there is no unitary alcoholic personality. Instead there seems to be a number of smaller, more discrete subgroups of alcoholics, although the composition of these subgroups depends upon the method used to identify them. The codetype research would suggest several subgroups (2-4/4-2, 2-7/7-2, 4-9/9-4) in both male and female alcoholics, and additional codetypes that are specific to males (1-2/2-1) and females (3-4/4-3, 4-6/6-4, and 4-8/8-4). Empirical methods such as cluster analysis also identify subgroups of alcoholic patients (2-7-8-4, 4-9, and 1-2-3-4) that have some degree of overlap with those identified by codetype research. These subgroups, however, only account for 25–35% of the alcoholic patients. Second, there has been only limited work to examine whether these subgroups of alcoholics have different treatment outcomes/processes and/or drinking histories. It would be interesting to know whether specific subgroups of alcoholic patients are more successful in a particular type of treatment or that they have a particular history of substance use. Finally, more research is needed on groups other than the typical White, male alcoholic, and it is important to include psychiatric and normal reference groups in order to better understand the actual role of alcohol and drug abuse.

The research on the MMPI with polydrug patients has been very similar to the research on alcoholics, except that it has received limited attention until the last few years. One of the first questions examined was whether there was a polydrug "personality," and whether polydrug patients differed from alcoholics, that is, did some personality types have a specific drug of choice? These initial studies usually involved a comparison of polydrug patients with alcoholics, and they demonstrated that groups of polydrug patients were experiencing more emotional distress than alcoholic patients. There appear to be a number of conclusions that can be drawn from the MMPI performance of polydrug patients. First, it is clear that there is not a unitary polydrug personality, just as there is not a unitary alcoholic personality. Instead there seems to be a number of smaller, more discrete subgroups of polydrug patients, although the composition of these subgroups differs from those seen in alcoholic patients. The codetype research

would suggest several subgroups (4-8/8-4 and 4-9/9-4) that are seen frequently in both male and female, White polydrug patients, and additional codetypes that are specific to white males (6-8/8-6, 7-8/8-7, and 8-9/9-8). Second, Black, male polydrug patients appear to be less emotionally disturbed than White males. Third, and again similar to the alcoholic patients, there has been virtually no work to examine whether these subgroups of polydrug patients have different treatment outcomes and/or histories of drug abuse. It would be interesting to know whether specific subgroups of polydrug patients are more successful in a particular type of treatment or that they have a particular history of substance abuse. The influence of the multitude of moderator variables described above as they impact upon these subgroups of polydrug patients must be considered in any research in this area. Finally, more research is needed on groups other than the typical White and Black, male polydrug patient.

MILLON MULTIAXIAL CLINICAL INVENTORY

There are no specific reviews of the MCMI in substance abuse samples as with the MMPI, or studies that investigate its use in treatment planning. Choca, Shanley, and Van Denburg (1992) have provided a short section on substance abuse (pp. 122–125) in their *Interpretive guide to the Millon Clinical Multiaxial Inventory*. This lack of research is somewhat surprising given the high frequencies of psychiatric disorders that are generally found in substance abuse settings (see section on dual diagnosis).

The primary research with the MCMI has been to identify groups or clusters of alcoholic patients (Bartsch & Hoffman, 1985; Craig et al., 1985; Gibertini & Retzlaff, 1988; Mayer & Scott, 1988). These studies typically identify groups of patients who elevate the following scales, although the exact percentage will vary across studies: antisocial and narcissistic; avoidant and dependent; passive–aggressive/negativistic; and compulsive. There has been little attempt to relate these groups of MCMI profiles to aspects of treatment other than the patient's style of alcohol or drug abuse. It should be apparent that there is plenty of opportunity to investigate the usefulness of the MCMI in substance abuse settings.

ALCOHOL USE INVENTORY

The Alcohol Use Inventory (AUI) originally was developed from research that analyzed the manner in which people described drinking problems (Horn & Wanberg, 1969). They identified common factors among these statements of individuals seeking assistance for alcoholism, which they used in developing the AUI.

The current version of the AUI (Horn, Wanberg, & Foster, 1987) consists of 24 heterogeneous scales that assess a variety of features associated with "alcohol" use. Since the AUI does not assess the use of other substances, it is limited to patients who only use alcohol or whose drug of choice is alcohol. Seventeen primary scales assess the benefits, styles, consequences, and concerns and acknowledgments related to alcohol use. Seven second-order scales were derived from factor analyses of the primary scales. These second-order scales assess enhanced functioning associated with alcohol use, degree of sustained drinking, life disruption, worry about drinking, and acknowledgment and awareness of drinking problems. One third-order scale assesses broad involvement with alcohol and is believed to reflect alcoholism.

The primary use of the AUI has been to describe the drinking patterns of patients who have been classified into groups or typologies based on age of onset of drinking (Lee & DiClimente, 1985); diagnosis (Hyer, Leach, Boudewyns, & Davis, 1991); family history (Alterman, 1988; Jones-Saumty, Hochhaus, Dru, & Zeiner, 1983); gender (Olenick & Chalmers, 1991); level or amount of alcohol impairment (Rohsenow, 1982a, 1982b; Williams, Gutsch, Kazelskis, Verstegen, & Scanlon, 1980); locus of control (Donovan & O'Leary, 1978; O'Leary, Donovan, & O'Leary, 1978); MCMI (Corbisiero & Reznikoff, 1991); MMPI (Donovan, Chaney, & O'Leary, 1978; Kline & Snyder, 1985; Robyak, Donham, Roy, & Ludenia, 1984); and reason for referral for treatment (Calsyn, Reynolds, O'Leary, & Walker, 1982). The diverse nature of the groupings that have been used in a variety of settings precludes any real generalizations about drinking patterns as assessed by the AUI.

No studies have used the AUI to assess treatment process or treatment outcome. Such research would seem to be the logical next step in the use of the AUI.

Presence of a Dual Diagnosis

The increased attention to dual disorders—some form of psychopathology in conjunction with substance abuse—also reflects the awareness of the comorbidity of these disorders.

For example, Ross, Glaser, and Germanson (1988) reported that most patients (84%) in their substance abuse treatment facility had a lifetime prevalence of another psychiatric disorder with diagnoses of antisocial personality disorder, generalized anxiety disorder, and phobias being most frequent. It should be more difficult to screen for substance abuse in psychiatric patients because they will share some symptoms with alcoholics as a result of their psychopathology and may have comorbid disorders.

When psychological assessments are conducted during the first few days of treatment, many patients may appear anxious, depressed, or psychotic, and it is difficult to determine whether those psychopathological patterns reflect the effects of toxicity or more enduring personality characteristics. Therefore, it often is difficult to use early assessment data to differentiate between those patients who have a dual diagnosis and those patients whose symptoms are residuals of substance abuse (Nathan, 1991). That uncertainty is a major roadblock because of the need to initiate specific treatments for those patients with dual disorders and within a relatively short period of time because of the constraints imposed by managed health care.

Substance abuse patients frequently meet the DSM-IV-TR criteria for an additional mental disorder, such as anxiety disorder, mood disorder, or schizophrenia (Regier et al., 1990). Antisocial personality disorder is also a common additional diagnosis for substance abuse patients, although substance abuse patients have also been found to have a variety of other personality disorders (Hasselbrock, Meyer, & Keener, 1985; Kosten, Kosten, & Rounsaville, 1989; Kosten, Rounsaville, & Kleber, 1982; Kroll & Ryan, 1983; Nace, 1989; Nace, Saxon, & Shore, 1983; Poldrugo & Forti, 1988; Rounsaville, Dolinsky, Babor, & Meyer, 1987; Vaglum & Vaglum, 1985).

The presence of a dual diagnosis in a substance abuse patient has important treatment implications because the additional problems can affect the patient's responses to substance abuse treatment, as well as the length and outcome of treatment, and can require that substance abuse treatment be supplemented with additional treatment components designed to respond to the individual needs of the patient (Blume, 1989; Nace, Davis, & Gaspari, 1991; Osher & Kofoed, 1989). For example, substance abuse patients with antisocial or borderline personality disorders have poorer treatment outcomes than other substance abuse patients (Cadoret, Troughton, & Widmer, 1984; Kosten et al., 1989; Poldrugo & Forti, 1988; Rounsaville et al., 1987; Shuckit, 1985). An outcome study of alcoholics with schizotypal personality disorder found that even though their drinking had ceased after treatment, they were still impaired by anxiety, paranoia, and social problems (Kroll & Ryan, 1983). Another outcome study of substance abuse patients found the likelihood of relapse increased significantly with the comorbid diagnosis of personality disorder (Thomas, Melchert, & Banken, 1999).

Accurate psychological assessment in substance abuse programs is complicated by the neuropsychological deficits that result from prolonged drug and alcohol abuse (Grant, 1987; Kleinknecht & Goldstein, 1972; Ryan & Butters, 1982, 1984; Tarter & Edwards, 1985). Some deficits may be permanent, such as impairments in abstract thinking, problem solving, and complex motor skills. For other deficits, such as short-term memory, concentration and attention, and visual memory, recovery begins soon after abstinence begins, and after two weeks of abstinence markedly improved functioning generally occurs (Allen, Faillace, & Markley, 1971; Bean & Karasievich, 1975; Goldman, Williams, & Klisz, 1983; Parsons & Farr, 1981). However, alcoholics over the age of 40 do not show the same recovery in neuropsychological functioning as younger alcoholics (Goldman et al., 1983; Grant, Adams, & Reed, 1984).

Summary

Only recently has significant progress been seen in the use of self-report measures in assessing alcohol and drug abuse. This progress can be summarized within two major areas: screening and treatment planning and outcome.

Screening for substance use and abuse has become widespread in our society with the increased concern about the accurate identification of individuals whose substance use may interfere with job performance. However, the low prevalence of substance use and the need for appropriate diagnostic specificity make meaningful research in this area difficult at best. Gender and ethnic differences in reporting substance abuse must be given careful consideration in designing and interpreting these screening instruments. However, research using the AUDIT and other screening instruments are beginning to address these considerations (cf. Steinbauer et al., 1998).

In order to enhance the contributions to treatment planning and outcome in substance abuse settings, a number of practical considerations need to be addressed. First, the parameters of the person's use of substance(s) needs to be reported explicitly. Social and interpersonal aspects of substance use and factors leading the person to enter treatment must be identified, and consideration needs to be given to moderating factors such as socioeconomic class and education. Second, self-report measures need to be focused on treatment process and outcome rather than simply reporting a set of scores as being descriptive of a specific sample of patients. It should be evident that persons who use and abuse substances are a heterogeneous group, and research should examine for differences within specific MMPI-2 codetypes, MCMI-III profile patterns, or AUI profiles, rather than reporting mean results for an entire group of patients. Third, the timing of psychological assessment following detoxification is a critical issue that needs empirical investigation. The development of guidelines for the optimal time for the administration for various types of self-report measures is needed. Finally, the presence of dual psychiatric disorders in patients who abuse substances and the problems of drug abuse on college campus is only beginning to be recognized. The presence of dual diagnoses has important treatment implications that need to be examined explicitly. Although newer scales continue to be developed, continued research will be essential to find the best evidence for use of screening scales for substance abuse disorders, in the particular settings in which they are employed.

References

Aaronson, A. L., Dent, O. B., & Kline, C. D. (1996). Cross-validation of MMPI and MMPI-2 predictor scales. *Journal of Clinical Psychology, 52*, 311–315.

Alberg, A. J., Park, J. W., Hager, B. W., & Brock, M. V. (2004). The use of "overall accuracy" to evaluate the validity of screening and diagnostic tests. *Journal of General Internal Medicine, 19*, 460–465.

Allen, J. P., Litten, R. Z., Fertig, J. B., & Babor, T. (1997). A review of the research on the Alcohol Use Disorders Identification Test (AUDIT). *Alcoholism: Clinical and Experimental Research, 21*, 613–619.

Allen, J. P., Maisto, S. A., & Connors, G .J. (1995). Self-report screening tests for alcohol problems in primary care. *Archives of Internal Medicine, 155*, 1726–1729.

Allen, R. P., Faillace, L. A., & Markley, H. C. (1971). Recovery of memory functioning in alcoholics following prolonged intoxication. *Journal of Nervous and Mental Diseases, 153*, 417–423.

Alterman, A. I. (1988). Patterns of familial alcoholism severity and psychopathology. *Journal of Nervous and Mental Disease, 176*, 167–175.

Babor, T. F., De La Fuente, J. R., Saunders, J., & Grant, M. (1989). The Alcohol Use Disorders Identification Test: Guidelines for use in the primary health Care. *WHO Publication*, No.89.4. Geneva: World Health Organization.

Babor, T. F., Kranzler, H. R., & Lauerman, R. J. (1989). Early detection of harmful alcohol consumption: Comparison of clinical, laboratory, and self-report screening procedures. *Addictive Behaviors, 14*, 139–157.

Baldessarini, R. J., Finkelstein, S., & Arana, G. W. (1983). The predictive power of diagnostic tests and the effect of prevalence of illness. *Archives of General Psychiatry, 40*, 569–573.

Bartsch, T. W., & Hoffman, J. J. (1985). A cluster analysis of Millon Clinical Multiaxial Inventory (MCMI) profiles: More about a taxonomy of alcoholic subtypes. *Journal of Clinical Psychology, 41*, 707–713.

Bearer, C. F. (2001). Markers to detect drinking during pregnancy. *Alcohol Research and Health, 25*, 210–218.

Bean, K. L., & Karasievich, G. O. (1975). Psychological test results at three stages of inpatient alcoholism treatment. *Journal of Studies on Alcohol, 36*, 838–852.

Blume, S. B. (1989). Dual diagnosis: Psychoactive substance dependence and the personality disorders. *Journal of Psychoactive Drugs, 21*, 139–144.

Bohn, M. J., Babor, T. F., & Kranzler, H. R. (1995). The Alcohol Use Disorders Identification Test (AUDIT): Validation of a screening instrument for use in medical settings. *Journal of Studies on Alcohol, 56*, 423–432.

Butcher, J. N., Dahlstrom, W. G., Graham, J. R., Tellegen, A., & Kaemmer, B. (1989). *Minnesota Multiphasic Personality Inventory-2 (MMPI-2): Manual for administration and scoring.* Minneapolis, MN: University of Minnesota Press.

Cadoret, R., Troughton, E., & Widmer, R. (1984). Clinical differences between antisocial and primary alcoholics. *Comprehensive Psychiatry, 25*, 1–8.

Calsyn, D. A., Reynolds, F. D., O'Leary, M. R., & Walker, R. D. (1982). Differential drinking patterns, personality characteristics, and field articulation of court-referred and non-court-referred male alcoholics in treatment. *International Journal of the Addictions, 17*, 249–257.

Celentano, D. D., McQueen, D. V., & Chee, E. (1980). Substance abuse by women: A review of the epidemiologic literature. *Journal of Chronic Diseases, 33*, 383–394.

Centers for Disease Control and Prevention. (2002). Alcohol use among women of childbearing age: United States 1991–1999. *Morbidity and Mortality Weekly Report, 51*, 273–276.

Cherpitel, C. (1998). Differences in performance of screening instruments for problem drinking among Blacks, Whites, and Hispanics in an emergency room population. *Journal of Studies on Alcohol, 59*, 420–426.

Cherpitel, C. (2000). A brief screening instrument for problem drinking the emergency room: The RAPS4. *Journal of Studies on Alcohol, 61*, 447–449.

Cherpitel, C. (2002). Screening for alcohol problems in the U.S. general population: Comparison of the CAGE, RASS4, and RAPS4-QF by gender, ethnicity, and services utilization. *Alcoholism Clinical and Experimental Research, 26*, 1686–1691.

Cherpitel, C. (2004). Screening for drug use disorders in the emergency department: Performance of the Rapid Drug Problems Screen (RDPS). *Drug and Alcohol Dependence, 74*, 171–175.

Cherpitel, C., Yu, Y., Bond, J., Borges, G., Cremonte, M., Marais, S., et al. (2005). Cross-national performance of the RAPS4/RAPS4-QF for tolerance and heavy drinking: Data from 13 countries. *Alcohol Research Group, 66*, 428–432.

Choca, J. P., Shanley, L. A., & Van Denburg, E. (1992). *Interpretive guide to the Millon Clinical Multiaxial Inventory.* Washington, DC: American Psychological Association.

Cleary, P. D., Miller, M., Bush, B. T., Warburg, M. W., Delbanco, T. L., & Aronson, M. D. (1988). Prevalence and recognition of alcohol abuse in a primary care population. *American Journal of Medicine, 85*, 466–471.

Clopton, J. R. (1978). Alcoholism and the MMPI: A review. *Journal of Studies on Alcohol, 39*, 1540–1558.

Corbisiero, J. R., & Reznikoff, M. (1991). The relationship between personality type and style of alcohol use. *Journal of Clinical Psychology, 47*, 291–298.

Craig, R. J. (1983). Effects of opiate withdrawal on MMPI profile scores. *International Journal of the Addictions, 18*, 1187–1193.

Craig, R. J. (2005). Assessing contemporary substance abusers with the MMPI MacAndrews alcoholism scale: A review. *Substance Use and Misuse, 40*, 427–450.

Craig, R. J., Verinis, J. S., & Wexler, S. (1985). Personality characteristics of drug addicts and alcoholics on the Millon Clinical Multiaxial Inventory. *Journal of Personality Assessment, 49*, 156–160.

Donovan, D. M., Chaney, E. F., & O'Leary, M. R. (1978). Alcoholic MMPI subtypes: Relationship to drinking styles, benefits, and consequences. *Journal of Nervous and Mental Disease, 166*, 553–561.

Donovan, D. M., & O'Leary, M. R. (1978). The drinking-related locus of control scale: Reliability, factor structure and validity. *Journal of Studies on Alcohol, 39*, 759–784.

English, G. E., & Curtin, M. E. (1975). Personality differences in patients at three alcoholism treatment agencies. *Journal of Studies on Alcohol, 36*, 52–61.

Ewing, J. A. (1984). Detecting alcoholism: The CAGE questionnaire. *Journal of the American Medical Association, 252*, 1905–1907.

Federal Bureau of Investigation. (1991). *Crime in the United States.* Washington, DC: Author.

Gearhart, J. G., Beebe, D. K., Milhorn, H. T., & Meeks, G. R. (1991). Alcoholism in women. *American Family Physician, 44*, 907–913.

Gibertini, M., & Retzlaff, P. (1988, August). *Personality and alcohol use patterns among inpatient alcoholics.* Paper presented at the 96th Annual Convention of the American Psychological Association, Atlanta, GA.

Goldman, M. S., Williams, D. L., & Klisz, D. K. (1983). Recoverability of psychological functioning following alcohol abuse: Prolonged visual-spatial dysfunction in older alcoholics. *Journal of Consulting and Clinical Psychology, 51*, 310–324.

Gottesman, I. I., & Prescott, C. A. (1989). Abuses of the MacAndrew MMPI alcoholism scale: A critical review. *Clinical Psychology Review, 9*, 223–242.

Graf, K., Baer, P. E., & Comstock, B. S. (1977). MMPI changes in briefly-hospitalized non-narcotic drug users. *Journal of Nervous and Mental Diseases, 165*, 126–133.

Graham, J. R., & Butcher, J. N. (1988, March). *Differentiating schizophrenic and major affective disorders with the revised form of the MMPI.* Paper presented as the 23rd Annual Symposium on Recent Advances in the Use of the MMPI, St. Petersburg, FL.

Graham, J. R., & Strenger, V. E. (1988). MMPI characteristics of alcoholics: A review. *Journal of Consulting and Clinical Psychology, 56*, 197–205.

Grant, I. (1987). Alcohol and the brain: Neuropsychological correlates. *Journal of Consulting and Clinical Psychology, 55*, 310–324.

Grant, B. F., Hasin, D. S., Chou, S. P., Stinson, F. S., & Dawson, D. A. (2004). Nicotine dependence and psychiatric disorders in the United States: Results from the National Epidemiologic

Survey of Alcohol and Related Conditions. *Archives of General Psychiatry, 61,* 1107–1115.

Grant, I., Adams, K. M., & Reed, R. (1984). Aging, abstinence, and medical risk factors in the prediction of neuropsychological deficit among long-term alcoholics. *Archives of General Psychiatry, 41,* 710–718.

Greene, R. L., & Banken, J. A. (2001). Use of objective psychological procedures in assessing alcohol/drug abuse problems. In J. N. Butcher (Ed.), *Practical considerations in clinical personality assessment* (2nd ed., pp. 491–507). New York: Oxford University Press.

Greene, R. L., & Garvin, R. D. (1988). Substance abuse/dependence. In R. L. Greene (Ed.), *The MMPI: Use in specific populations* (pp. 159–197). San Antonio: Grune & Stratton.

Greene, R. L., Weed, N. C., Butcher, J. N., Arredondo, R., & Davis, H. G. (1992). A cross-validation of MMPI-2 abuse scales. *Journal of Personality Assessment, 58,* 405–410.

Flynn, H. A., Marcus, S. M., Barry, K. L., & Blow, F. C. (2003). Rates and correlates of alcohol use among pregnant women in obstetrics clinics. *Alcoholism: Clinical and Experimental Research, 27,* 81–87.

Hasselbrock, M. N., Meyer, R. E., & Keener, J. J. (1985). Psychopathology in hospitalized alcoholics. *Archives of General Psychiatry, 42,* 1050–1055.

Heck, E. J. (1991). Developing a screening questionnaire for problem drinking in college students. *Journal of American College Health, 39,* 227–231.

Horn, J. L., & Wanberg, K. W. (1969). Symptom patterns related to excessive use of alcohol. *Quarterly Journal of Studies on Alcohol, 30,* 35–38.

Horn, J. L., Wanberg, K. W., & Foster, F. M. (1987). *Guide to the Alcohol Use Inventory.* Minneapolis, MN: National Computer Systems.

Hurlbut, S. C., & Sher, K. J. (1992). Assessing alcohol problems in college students. *Journal of American College Health, 41,* 49–58.

Hyer, L., Leach, P., Boudewyns, P. A., & Davis, H. (1991). Hidden PTSD in substance abuse patients among Vietnam veterans. *Journal of Substance Abuse Treatment, 8,* 213–219.

Jacobson, G. R. (1983). Detection, assessment, and diagnosis of alcoholism: Current techniques. In M. Galanter (Ed.), *Recent developments in alcoholism* (Vol. 1, pp. 377–413). New York: Plenum.

Jacobson, G. R. (1989). A comprehensive approach to pretreatment evaluation: I. Detection, assessment, and diagnosis of alcoholism. In R. K. Hester & W. R. Miller (Eds.), *Handbook of alcoholism treatment approaches* (pp. 17–53). New York: Pergamon.

Jones-Saumty, D., Hochhaus, L., Dru, R., & Zeiner, A. (1983). Psychological factors of familial alcoholism in American Indians and Caucasians. *Journal of Clinical Psychology, 39,* 783–790.

Kleinknecht, R. A., & Goldstein, S. G. (1972). Neuropsychological deficits associated with alcoholism. *Quarterly Journal of Studies on Alcohol, 137,* 928–931.

Kline, R. B., & Snyder, D. K. (1985). Replicated MMPI subtypes for alcoholic men and women: Relationship to self-reported drinking behaviors. *Journal of Consulting and Clinical Psychology, 53,* 70–79.

Kosten, T. A., Kosten, T. R., & Rounsaville, B. J. (1989). Personality disorders in opiate addicts show prognostic specificity. *Journal of Substance Abuse Treatment, 6,* 163–168.

Kosten, T. A., Rounsaville, B. J., & Kleber, H. D. (1982). DSM-III personality disorders in opiate addicts. *Comprehensive Psychiatry, 23,* 572–581.

Krauthamer, C. (1979). The personality of alcoholic middle-class women: A comparative study with the MMPI. *Journal of Clinical Psychology, 35,* 442–448.

Kroll, P., & Ryan, C. (1983). The schizotypal personality on an alcohol treatment unit. *Comprehensive Psychiatry, 24,* 262–270.

Lee, G. P., & DiClimente, C. C. (1985). Age of onset versus duration of problem drinking on the Alcohol Use Inventory. *Journal of Studies on Alcohol, 46,* 398–402.

Libb, J. W., & Taulbee, E. S. (1971). Psychotic-appearing MMPI profiles among alcoholics. *Journal of Clinical Psychology, 27,* 101–102.

MacAndrew, C. (1965). The differentiation of male alcoholic outpatients from nonalcoholic psychiatric outpatients by means of the MMPI. *Quarterly Journal of Studies on Alcohol, 26,* 238–246.

MacAndrew, C. (1981). What the MAC scale tells us about men alcoholics: An interpretive review. *Journal of Studies on Alcohol, 42,* 604–625.

McKenna, T., & Butcher, J. N. (1987, April). *Continuity of the MMPI with alcoholics.* Paper presented at the 22nd Annual Symposium on Recent Developments in the Use of the MMPI, Seattle, WA.

Maddock, J. E., Laforge, R. G., Rossi, J. S., & O'Hare, T. (2001). The College Alcohol Problems Scale. *Addictive Behaviors, 26,* 385–398.

Mayer, G. S., & Scott, K. (1988). An exploration of heterogeneity in an inpatient male alcoholic population. *Journal of Personality Disorders, 2,* 243–255.

Mayfield, D. G., McLeod, G., & Hall, P. (1974). The CAGE questionnaire: Validation of a new alcoholism screening instrument. *American Journal of Psychiatry, 131,* 1121–1123.

Miller, E. T., Neal, D. J., Roberts, L. J., Baer, J. S., Cressler, S. O., Metrik, J., et al. (2002). Test–retest reliability of alcohol measures: Is there a difference between Internet-based assessment and traditional methods? *Psychology of Addictive Behaviors, 16,* 56–63.

Miller, H. R., & Streiner, D. L. (1990). Using the Millon Clinical Multiaxial Inventory's Scale B and the MacAndrew Alcoholism Scale to identify alcoholics with concurrent psychiatric diagnoses. *Journal of Personality Assessment, 54,* 736–746.

Millon, T. (1983). *Millon Clinical Multiaxial Inventory manual* (3rd ed.). Minneapolis: Interpretive Scoring Systems.

Moore, R. D., Bone, L. R., Geller, G., Mamon, J. A., Stokes, E. J., & Levine, D. M. (1989). Prevalence, detection, and treatment of alcoholism in hospitalized patients. *Journal of the American Medical Association, 261,* 403–407.

Morey, L. C., & Blashfield, R. K. (1981). Empirical classification of alcoholism: A review. *Journal of Studies on Alcohol, 42,* 925–937.

Morey, L. C., & Skinner, H. A. (1986). Empirically derived classifications of alcohol-related problems. In M. Galanter (Ed.), *Recent developments in alcoholism* (Vol. IV, pp. 145–168). New York: Plenum Press.

Morey, L. C., Skinner, H. A., & Blashfield, R. K. (1984). A typology of alcohol abusers: Correlates and implications. *Journal of Abnormal Psychology, 93,* 408–417.

Mortimer, R. G., Filkins, L. D., Kerlan, M. W., & Lower, J. S. (1973). Psychometric identification of problem drinkers. *Quarterly Journal of Studies on Alcohol, 34,* 1322–1335.

Nace, E. P. (1989). Personality disorder in the alcoholic patient. *Psychiatric Annals, 19*, 256–260.

Nace, E. P., Saxon, J. J., & Shore, N. (1983). A comparison of borderline and nonborderline alcoholic patients. *Archives of General Psychiatry, 40*, 54–56.

Nace, E. P., Davis, C. W., & Gaspari, J. P. (1991). Axis II comorbidity in substance abusers. *Archives of General Psychiatry, 48*, 118–120.

Nathan, P. E. (1991). Substance use disorders in the DSM-IV. *Journal of Abnormal Psychology, 100*, 356–361.

National Institute on Alcohol Abuse and Alcoholism. (1990). *Screening for alcoholism.* Alcohol Alert, No. 8, PH285.

National Institute on Alcohol Abuse and Alcoholism (2000). *Tenth Special Report to the U.S. Congress on alcohol and health.* Bethesda, MD: National Institutes of Health, NIAAA.

Neal, D. J., & Carrey, K. B. (2004). Developing discrepancy within self-regulation theory: Use of personalized normative feedback and personal strivings with heavy-drinking college students. *Addictive Behaviors, 29*, 281–297.

O'Leary, M. R., Donovan, D. M., & O'Leary, D. E. (1978). Drinking patterns of alcoholics differing in levels of perceived and experienced control. *Journal of Studies on Alcohol, 39*, 1499–1505.

Olenick, N. L., & Chalmers, D. K. (1991). Gender-specific drinking styles in alcoholics and nonalcoholics. *Journal of Studies on Alcohol, 52*, 325–330.

O'Malley, P. M., & Johnston, L. D. (2002). Epidemiology of alcohol and other drug use among American college students. *Journal of Studies in Alcohol, 14*, 23–39.

Osher, F. C., & Kofoed, L. L. (1989). Treatment of patients with psychiatric and psychoactive substance abuse disorders. *Hospital and Community Psychiatry, 40*, 1025–1030.

Osterling, A., Nilsson, L. H., Berglund, M., Moberg, A. L., & Kristenson, H. (1992). Sex differences in problem drinking among 42-year-old residents of Malmo, Sweden. *Acta Psychiatria Scandanavia, 85*, 435–439.

Parsons, O. A., & Farr, S. P. (1981). The neuropsychology of alcohol and drug use. In S. B. Filskov & T. J. Boll (Eds.), *Handbook of clinical neuropsychology* (pp. 320–365). New York: John Wiley & Sons.

Pattison, E. M., Coe, R., & Doerr, H. O. (1973). Population variation among alcoholism treatment facilities. *International Journal of the Addictions, 8*, 199–229.

Perkins, H. W. (2002). Surveying the damage: A review of research on consequences of alcohol misuse in college populations. *Journal of Studies on Alcohol (Supplement), 14*, 91–100.

Peterson, K. (2004). Biomarkers for alcohol use and abuse. *Alcohol Research and Health, 28*, 30–37.

Petroni, D. C., Allen-Byrd, L., & Lewis, V. M. (2003). Indicators of the alcohol recovery process: Critical items from Koss–Butcher and Lachar–Wrobel analysis of the MMPI-2. *Alcoholism Treatment Quarterly, 21*, 41–56.

Poldrugo, R., & Forti, B. (1988). Personality and alcoholism treatment outcome. *Drug and Alcohol Dependence, 21*, 171–176.

Project MATCH Research Group. (1993). Project MATCH: Rationale and methods for multisite clinical trial matching alcoholism patients to treatment. *Alcoholism: Clinical and Experimental Research, 17*, 1130–1145.

Regier, D. A., Boyd, J. H., Burke, J. D., Jr., Rae, D. S., Myers, J. K., Kramer, M., et al. (1988). One-month prevalence of mental disorders in the United States. *Archives of General Psychiatry, 45*, 977–986.

Regier, D. A., Farmer, M. E., Rae, D. S., Locke, B. Z., Keith, S. J., Judd, L. L., et al. (1990). Comorbidity of mental disorders with alcohol and other drug abuse: Results from the epidemiologic catchment area (ECA) study. *Journal of the American Medical Association, 264*, 2511–2518.

Reid, M. C., Fiellen, D. A., & O'Connor, P. G. (1999). Hazardous and harmful alcohol consumption in primary care. *Archives in Internal Medicine, 159*, 1681–1689.

Reinert, D. F., & Allen, J. P. (2002). Alcohol Use Disorders Identification Test (AUDIT): A review of recent research. *Alcoholism: Clinical and Experimental Research, 26*, 272–279.

Rivers, P. C., Rivers, L. S., & Newman, D. L. (1991). Alcohol and aging: A cross-gender comparison. *Psychology of Addictive Behavior, 5*, 41–47.

Robyak, J. E., Donham, G. W., Roy, R., & Ludenia, K. (1984). Differential patterns of alcohol abuse among normal, neurotic, psychotic, and characterological types. *Journal of Personality Assessment, 48*, 132–136.

Rohsenow, D. J. (1982a). Social anxiety, daily moods, and alcohol use over time among heavy social drinking men. *Addictive Behaviors, 7*, 311–315.

Rohsenow, D. J. (1982b). The Alcohol Use Inventory as predictor of drinking by male heavy social drinkers. *Addictive Behaviors, 7*, 387–395.

Ross, H. F., Glaser, F. B., & Germanson, T. (1988). The prevalence of psychiatric disorders in patients with alcohol and other drug problems. *Archives of General Psychiatry, 45*, 1023–1031.

Rost, K., Burnam, M. A., & Smith, G. R. (1993). Development of screeners for depressive disorders and substance disorder history. *Medical Care, 31*, 189–200.

Rounsaville, B. J., Dolinsky, Z. S., Babor, T. F., & Meyer, R. E. (1987). Psychopathology as a predictor of treatment outcome in alcoholics. *Archives of General Psychiatry, 44*, 505–513.

Russell, M. (1994). New assessment tools for risk drinking during pregnancy: T-ACE, TWEAK, and others. *Alcohol Health & Research World, 18*, 55–61.

Ryan, C., & Butters, N. (1982). Cognitive effects in alcohol abuse. In B. Kissin & H. Begleiter (Eds.), *The biology of alcoholism* (Vol. 6, pp. 485–538). New York: Plenum Press.

Ryan, C., & Butters, M. (1984). Alcohol consumption and premature aging: A critical review. In M. Galanter (Ed.), *Recent developments in alcoholism* (Vol. 1, pp. 223–250). New York: Plenum Press.

Saitz, R. (2005). Clinical practice. Unhealthy alcohol use. *New England Journal of Medicine, 352*, 596–607.

Saunders, J. B., Aasland. O. G., Babor, T. F., De La Fuente, J. R., & Grant, M. (1993). Development of the Alcohol Use Disorders Identification Test (AUDIT): WHO collaborative project on early detection of persons with harmful alcohol consumption. *Addiction, 88*, 791–804.

Selzer, M. L. (1971). The Michigan Alcoholism Screening Test: The quest for a new diagnostic instrument. *American Journal of Psychiatry, 127*, 89–94.

Sherer, M., Haygood, J. M., & Alfano, A. M. (1984). Stability of psychological test results in newly admitted alcoholics. *Journal of Clinical Psychology, 40*, 855–857.

Shuckit, M. A. (1985). The clinical implications of primary diagnostic groups among alcoholics. *Archives of General Psychiatry, 42*, 1043–1049.

Skinner, H. A., Jackson, D. N., & Hoffmann, H. (1974). Alcoholic personality types: Identification and correlates. *Journal of Abnormal Psychology, 83,* 658–666.

Sokol, R. J., Delaney-Black, V., & Nordstrom B. (2003). Fetal alcohol spectrum disorder. *JAMA, 290,* 2996–2999.

Steinbauer, J. R., Cantor, S. B., Holzer, C. E., & Volk, R. J. (1998). Ethnic and sex bias in primary care screening tests for alcohol use disorders. *Annals of Internal Medicine, 129,* 353–362.

Svanum, S., McGrew, J., & Ehrmann, L. C. (1994). Validity of the substance abuse scales of the MMPI-2 in a college student sample. *Journal of Personality Assessment, 62,* 427–439.

Swenson, W. M., & Morse, R. M. (1975). The use of a Self-Administered Alcoholism Screening Test (SAAST) in a medical center. *Mayo Clinic Proceedings, 50,* 204–208.

Tarter, R. E., & Edwards, K. L. (1985). Neuropsychology of alcoholism. In R. E. Tarter & D. H. Van Thiel (Eds.), *Alcohol and the brain: Chronic effects* (pp. 217–244). New York: Plenum.

Thomas, V. H., Melchert, T. P., & Banken, J. A. (1999). Substance dependence and personality disorders: Comorbidity and treatment outcome in an inpatient treatment population. *Journal of Studies on Alcohol, 60,* 271–277.

United States National Center for Health Statistics. (1985). *Health promotion and disease prevention, United States 1985, Vital and health statistics.* Washington, DC: Author.

Vaglum, S., & Vaglum, P. (1985). Borderline and other mental disorders in alcoholic female psychiatry patients: A case control study. *Psychopathology, 18,* 50–60.

Weed, N. C., Butcher, J. N., & Ben-Porath, Y. S. (1995). MMPI-2 measures of substance abuse. In J. N. Butcher & C. D. Spielberger (Eds.), *Advances in personality assessment* (Vol. 10, pp. 121–145). Hillsdale, NJ: Erlbaum.

Weed, N. C., Butcher, J. N., McKenna, T., & Ben-Porath, Y. S. (1992). New measures for assessing alcohol and drug abuse with the MMPI-2: The APS and AAS. *Journal of Personality Assessment, 58,* 389–404.

Williams, R. L., Gutsch, K. U., Kazelskis, R., Verstegen, J. P., & Scanlon, J. (1980). An investigation of relationships between level of alcohol use impairment and personality characteristics. *Addictive Behaviors, 5,* 107–112.

Understanding and Assessing Aggression and Violence

Edwin I. Megargee

Abstract

This chapter considers the issues involved in understanding and, especially, assessing, human aggression and violence. After defining aggression and discussing a broad range of factors that influence its assessment, it differentiates individualized from generalized assessments. In the former, the clinician analyzes the factors influencing aggressive behavior in a particular individual. A conceptual framework, the "algebra of aggression," is offered for analyzing physiological and psychological factors such as instigation, inhibitions, and habit strength that influence the relative response strength of different aggressive and nonaggressive acts.

Generalized assessments are focused on identifying which members of a group, such as applicants for parole, are most likely to be aggressive. A number of subjective and objective rationally and actuarially derived risk assessment instruments are described and evaluated.

Keywords: aggression and violence, individual assessments, generalized assessments, risk assessment

On August 1, 1966, a "false negative" shot 38 people on the University of Texas's (UT) Austin campus, killing 14. Several weeks earlier, Charles Whitman, a UT student, had gone to the student health center complaining of headaches and uncontrollable urges to shoot people at random from the 22-story tower that dominates the campus. The psychiatrist whom Whitman consulted prescribed an analgesic for the headaches and suggested that he return for another session the following week. Instead, on the night of July 31, Whitman killed his mother and, later that evening, his wife. The following morning, he donned the uniform of a maintenance worker, packed a trunk full of guns and ammunition, and wheeled it to a tower elevator. Ascending to the top floor, he shot and killed the attendant, sealed off the elevators, and took his weapons to the balustrade overlooking the campus. When he thought classes were about to change, flooding the campus with students, he opened fire. Along with hundreds of others UT faculty and students, I was pinned down for over 90 minutes until a police officer and an armed civilian ascended the tower stairs and fatally shot Whitman.

When assessing the risk of aggression and violence, it is the possibility of missing false negatives, such as Whitman, that most worries clinicians. However, it is the false positives, namely individuals incorrectly diagnosed as being aggressive, who are far more numerous (Otto, 1992; Wollert, 2006).

The consequences of being labeled dangerous can be severe. They can include prolonged imprisonment, revocation of probation or parole, involuntary commitment to a mental health facility, and loss of parental rights in custody disputes. In Texas, people convicted of capital crimes who are assessed as being a continuing threat to society often end up on death row (Cunningham & Reidy, 1999; Dorland & Krauss, 2005; Edens, Buffington-Vollum, Keilen, Roskamp, & Anthony, 2005). In many states, sex offenders regarded as dangerous may be civilly committed, subjected to preventive detention, or effectively barred from living in some communities (Alexander, 2004; Mercado & Ogloff, 2007).

Defining Aggression and Violence

Johnson (1972, p. 8) wrote that, "the most important thing that can be said about defining aggression" is that, "there is no single kind of behavior that can be called 'aggressive' nor is there any single process which represents 'aggression'." Indeed, it would be possible, although not very helpful, to devote this entire chapter to a discussion of the difficulties encountered in formulating a universally acceptable definition of aggression (Baron, 1977; Johnson, 1972; Megargee, 1993).

Several important issues must be considered when one tries to define aggression or violence. The first is "intentionality." I am sure everyone agrees that Charles Whitman's deliberately planned and well-executed mass murder constituted aggression and violence. However, was it also aggression or violence in February 2006 when Vice President Cheney accidentally sprayed a hunting partner with birdshot? Some behaviorists attempted to avoid this issue by defining aggression as any behavior that, "delivers noxious stimulation to another organism" regardless of whether or not it was intended (Buss, 1961, p. 1). However, today most authorities insist that the perpetrator must intend to harm the target for the behavior to be considered aggressive (Anderson & Bushman, 2002).

Assuming intent is a necessary component of aggression, the next question is whether harmful intent alone is sufficient to constitute aggression. If a woman who plans to commit a suicide bombing in a crowded market is arrested before she can carry out her attack, is her scheme alone enough to be considered aggression?

"Legality" is yet another issue. Charles Whitman and the two men who shot him to death all committed homicide on that hot August afternoon. Were all three engaging in violent aggression? Some authorities reserve the terms "aggression" or "violence" for illegal or criminal behavior while others include any act that harms another human being, regardless of its legality.

The "target" of the aggressive behavior is another concern. Anderson and Bushman (2002, p. 28) regard human aggression as harmful "behavior directed toward another individual," but what of harm inflicted on other targets such as animals, objects, or property? Is someone who deliberately sets a forest fire aggressive if no people are injured? What about a worker who slaughters animals at a meatpacking plant? In my seminars on aggression, discussions of these issues could go on for hours, even days, if left unchecked.

In this chapter, which is limited to human behavior, "aggression" refers to overt verbal or physical behavior that can harm people and other living creatures by causing them distress, damage, pain, or injury, or by damaging their property or reputation. "Violence" is severe physical aggression that is likely to cause serious damage or injury. To be considered aggression, the harm must be intended or the possibility of such harm accepted by the perpetrator. Such behavior will be viewed as aggressive whether or not hurting the victim was the aggressor's primary intention and regardless of whether the behavior is classified as legal or illegal in the particular society in which it occurs.

This definition includes instrumental aggression where the primary intent is not necessarily to harm someone but in which a person's pain or suffering is an acceptable outcome, as well as the legal aggression or violence that might occur in military combat. It does not include accidental or unintentionally harmful behavior, or unavoidable pain inflicted for altruistic reasons such as might occur in medical or dental treatment.[1]

Heterogeneity of Aggression and Violence

Just as there is no simple definition of aggression, there is also no single prototype for those who behave aggressively or who engage in violence. After Seung-Hui Cho shot and killed 32 people on the Virginia Tech campus in April 2007, I was asked how closely he resembled Charles Whitman, whom I had studied four decades earlier. The two could hardly have been more different. Whitman, a former altar boy and Eagle Scout, was a hard-working, well-regarded, achievement-oriented married veteran with a temporal lobe tumor. Cho was an estranged, alienated, under-achieving misfit with no known physical impairment whose agitated behavior and bizarre writings frightened his teachers and fellow students.

In the 1960s, many social psychologists thought that, although the causes of the milder forms of aggressive behavior that they studied in the laboratory could be quite complex, violent crimes were typically committed by offenders who had inadequate controls and inhibitions against aggressive acting out (Berkowitz, 1962; Buss, 1961). Such undercontrol could result from (a) a failure to incorporate society's moral codes and prohibitions against aggression, (b) being socialized into a subculture of violence in which aggression or violence was expected and rewarded in certain circumstances, or (c) impairment of normal inhibitions against aggression by organic conditions, toxic substances, or functional psychopathology.

Although many aggressive and violent people clearly do lack adequate inhibitions or controls, we discovered that some extremely violent offenders are, paradoxically, overcontrolled individuals whose rigid and excessive inhibitions against any type of aggressive behavior allow aggressive instigation to accumulate until it is unleashed in one often cataclysmic act, after which they revert to their typical overcontrolled pattern (Megargee, 1966, 1982). In addition to these under- and overcontrolled assaultive types, it is also possible for normally socialized people with culturally appropriate values systems to engage in violence. This includes law enforcement officers and military personnel whose jobs may require them to behave aggressively. Normally socialized people may also engage in aggression in response to being attacked, severely provoked, extremely frustrated, or if they are caught up in the contagious chaos of a riot or rebellion (Berkowitz, 1970).

This heterogeneity makes it unlikely that any single global device for the assessment or prediction of aggression or violence will be universally effective. For example, Hare's Psychopathy Checklist-Revised (PCL-R; Hare, 2003) might be very useful in detecting poorly socialized criminal offenders who have inadequate inhibitions against aggressive behavior or violence, but it is unlikely to identify the normally socialized people driven to aggression by extreme situational factors.

Issues and Factors Influencing Assessments of Aggression and Violence

In addition to the complexity of aggressive behavior, there are a number of other issues that influence its assessment. They include the type of appraisal required, the context and setting in which the assessment takes place, and whether an individual or a group is being assessed.

Type of Appraisal

Most assessments of aggressive behavior fall into one of two general categories: "retrospective" or "diagnostic" assessments in which individuals who have already been violent are evaluated, and "prospective" or "prognostic" assessments in which their potential for future aggression or violence is estimated.

In retrospective assessments, psychologists are typically confronted with aggression that has already occurred and are asked to explain it. Criminal liability might depend on the mental status of the perpetrator at the time of offense. For example, Mary Winkler, a minister's wife who shot and killed her sleeping husband in March 2006, was convicted of a reduced charge of voluntary manslaughter and sentenced to only 210 days of confinement after a psychologist for the defense testified that her husband's abusiveness resulted in a mental disorder that made it impossible for her to form criminal intent (Grinberg, 2007). Retrospective evaluations are especially important in program planning. For example, the management and treatment needs of undercontrolled and overcontrolled assaultive offenders obviously differ greatly (Megargee, 1966).

In prospective or prognostic evaluations or "risk assessments," psychologists are asked whether a person, group, or even a nation is likely to commit aggression in the future. If so, what form is the aggressive behavior likely to take? Against whom or what is the aggressive behavior likely to be directed? Under what conditions is such aggression most likely to occur? What circumstances or interventions are likely to increase or decrease the risk of such behavior (Borum, Fein, Vossekuil, & Berglund, 1999; Heilbrun & Heilbrun, 1995)? The answers to these questions might be used to help determine whether patients or prisoners are ready for release or if a child should be returned to the custody of a possibly abusive parent. As anyone who has ever bet on a sporting event knows, it is much more difficult to predict what will happen in the future than it is to explain what has happened in the past.

Some assessment techniques work much better in retrospective than in prospective assessments. Retrospectively, the overcontrolled hostility (O-H) scale for the Minnesota Multiphasic Personality Inventory-2 (MMPI-2; Megargee, Cook, & Mendelsohn, 1967) can help identify overcontrolled assaultive offenders, but prospectively the O-H scale is of limited utility in predicting violent behavior because of the rarity of this syndrome.

Context and Setting

The context of the assessment and the setting in which it is carried out are also important considerations. Assessments of aggression and violence may take place in jails, prisons, or closed psychiatric wards. Security considerations may dictate that the client is in a cell or even in some sort of restraints, and other people, such as attorneys, correctional officers, or psychiatric aides, may be present. The impact of these factors on the subject's performance need to be considered in such appraisals.

Psychologists who are doing appraisals for third parties, such as pre-sentence evaluations or custody assessments for the courts, may be viewed as adversaries by those being assessed. Professional ethics require that, before they participate in an evaluation, subjects should be told for whom the clinician is working and informed of any limitations on confidentiality (American Association for Correctional Psychology, Standards Committee, 2000; American Psychological Association, 2002; Megargee, 2003, 2006a; Monahan, 1972; Pope, Butcher, & Seelen, 2006).

Criminal offenders and others whose aggressive or violent propensities are being assessed often have a strong stake in the outcome of the evaluation. They may be highly motivated to manipulate the results so that they appear sick or well, incompetent or competent. The assessor must be alert to the subjects' possible efforts to dissimulate or malinger and interpret the findings accordingly (see Chapter 32).

Individualized versus Generalized Assessments

It is also important to distinguish between "individualized" and "generalized" evaluations. In individualized or "idiographic" risk assessments, the task is to evaluate a particular person. This may involve a retrospective evaluation of someone like Mary Winkler who has already committed an aggressive act, or a prognostic assessment to determine if someone is likely to pose a threat in the future. Sometimes this involves a "targeted" risk assessment, that is, estimating the likelihood that a person will aggress against a specific target, such as a spouse, coworker, schoolmate, or public figure (Borum et al., 1999). In addition to a personality evaluation, targeted risk assessment may require us to assess the potential perpetrator's ability to formulate and carry out a plan of attack, and to assess his or her technical skills, access to weapons, and ability to gain access to the would-be victim (Cohen & Felson, 1979).

In individualized assessments, we typically have access to a much broader array of more detailed information than we do in generalized evaluations. This often includes a detailed case history, psychological testing, and the opportunity to interview the subject as well as others who are familiar with the subject's behavior and attitudes. It is much easier for clinicians to obtain information about situational factors in individualized than in generalized assessments. Interviews conducted in the subject's home are especially valuable because they enable us to evaluate an individual's environment as well as his or her personality.

Generalized or "nomothetic" assessments typically take place in the context of risk prediction. Here our task is to identify which members of a group or class of people are most likely to be involved in aggression or violence. Such generalized assessments often take place in mental health facilities or correctional institutions as a guide to management planning or release decisions. For example, in a federal prison for youthful offenders, Bohn (1979) used our MMPI-based offender classification system (Megargee, Bohn, Meyer, & Sink, 1979; Megargee, Carbonell, Bohn & Sliger, 2001) to identify those prisoners who were (a) most likely to prey on others and (b) most likely to be victimized. By assigning these groups to separate living quarters, the rate of serious assaults was reduced 46%.

In generalized risk assessments, clinicians typically have to rely on a more limited array of data than they have available in individualized appraisals. They may have no personal contact with those being assessed, relying instead on demographic or file-based information or test scores. Information about environmental and situational factors that may facilitate or impede aggressive behavior is often lacking.

Individualized appraisals should enable clinicians to formulate contingent evaluations, specifying the conditions and circumstances under which the person being evaluated is more or less likely to engage in various types of aggressive behavior directed toward certain targets. Generalized assessments are more likely to result in probability statements specifying the likelihood that individuals belong in mutually exclusive "aggressive" or "nonaggressive" groups.

In the sections that follow, I will separately discuss strategies for individualized and generalized assessments of aggression and violence. I will first present a conceptual framework designed to guide individual appraisals. Dubbed the "algebra of aggression" by the U.S. Secret Service agents to whom I taught the system in the 1980s, it considers the various factors that interact to cause someone to choose an aggressive response. I will then describe approaches to nomothetic predictions of aggression, concentrating on the many objective instruments that have been devised in forensic and correctional settings in the last 15 years.

Individualized Assessment of Aggression
The Algebra of Aggression: A Conceptual Framework for the Analysis of Aggressive Behavior

In his recent Sutherland Award address, Nagin (2007) proposed that the concepts of choice and decision making should occupy "center stage" in criminological theory and research. Choices are central to my conceptual framework for understanding human aggression. According to this formulation, every act of human aggression results from the interaction of numerous factors and involves dozens of implicit and explicit choices. This is true whether the act is planned and deliberate or spontaneous and impulsive. These choices involve emotions as well as cognitions, physiology as well as psychology, and situational as well as personal factors.

Although we may not be consciously aware of it, at any given time we are confronted with dozens of alternative behaviors; some of which may be aggressive. These potential aggressive responses may be verbal or physical, mild or extreme, direct or indirect. How do we make these choices? According to the algebra of aggression, we typically select the response that appears to offer us the most satisfactions and the fewest dissatisfactions in that particular situation.

This simple statement conceals a rapid but complex internal bargaining process in which we weigh the capacity of each response to fulfill various competing drives and motives against the discomforts or disappointments we might suffer from choosing that response. By means of this "internal algebra," we calculate the net strength of each possible response, compare it with all the other responses, and select the strongest.

What determines the net strength of a potential response? We must consider both "personal" and "situational" factors. In the case of an aggressive or violent act, we can isolate three personal factors that interact to determine its response strength. The first two induce us to act aggressively while the third deters us from aggressive behavior.

The first personal factor which promotes aggression is "instigation to aggression." Instigation to aggression is the sum of all the forces that can motivate us to commit a violent or aggressive act. It includes both "intrinsic or angry" instigation, which is our conscious or unconscious desire to harm the victim in some fashion, and "extrinsic or instrumental" instigation, which is our wish for other desirable outcomes that the aggressive act in question might achieve for us, such as economic gain or

in the case of a robbery or political benefits from an act of terrorism.

The second personal factor contributing to aggressive behavior is "habit strength," the extent to which a given response has been rewarded or punished in the past. Other things being equal (which they rarely are), the more often we have been reinforced for aggressive behavior in the past, or the more we have observed others being rewarded for aggression, the more likely we are to aggress in the future.

Instigation to aggression and habit strength both induce us to act aggressively. What deters us? Opposing the motivational factors is the third set of personal variables, namely "inhibitions against aggression." Inhibitions include all the reasons we might refrain from a given aggressive act directed at a particular target. They include both moral prohibitions, which cause us to feel that this act of aggression is wrong, and practical considerations, such as our fear of retaliation. Inhibitions can be general or specific and can vary as a function of the act, the target, and the circumstances.

Instigation, habit strength, and inhibitions are all personal characteristics, but behavior results from individuals interacting with their milieus. The next set of variables is comprised of "situational factors" which encompass all those external factors that may influence the likelihood that we will engage in aggressive behavior. These include "environments," "settings," "situations," and "stimuli," and they may either facilitate or impede aggressive behavior.

"Reaction potential," my last major construct, consists of the net strength of any given response after all the inhibitory factors, both personal and situational, have been balanced against the excitatory ones. A response will be blocked and cannot occur whenever the inhibitions exceed the instigation. A response is "possible" (i.e., has a positive reaction potential) if the forces favoring the aggressive response exceed those opposing it. After all the possible responses compete with one another, the one with the highest reaction potential—that is, the capacity to satisfy the most needs at the least cost—should be chosen (Megargee, 1993).

Given this overall conceptual framework, we can then ask salient questions such as, "What are the causes of anger? What happens to instigation once it is aroused? What factors increase or decrease our inhibitions? How might environmental factors be manipulated to increase or decrease the likelihood of aggressive behavior?" General questions such as these can guide psychological research on aggression.

When appplied to individual clients in clinical settings, these issues can help us understand our clients' individual dynamics of aggression and suggest interventions that may be useful dealing with their aggressive behaviors.

Given this brief overview of the conceptual framework, let us examine how we can use it in assessment and treatment. We will begin with the personal factors promoting aggressive behavior, intrinsic and extrinsic instigation to aggression and habit strength, inquiring how each of these constructs develop, and how they can be diminished. Next, we will discuss the personal factors deterring aggression, namely inhibitions. After discussing these internal or personal factors, we will move on to the external or situational factors that may facilitate or suppress aggressive behavior and violence.

Intrinsic Instigation to Aggression

Intrinsic instigation to aggression is the conscious or unconscious desire to injure or harm the target in some fashion. Depending on its duration and intensity, we refer to these motives as "anger," "hostility," "rage," or "hatred." It is important for both assessment and treatment to understand the role of instigation in aggressive behavior.

SOURCES OF INTRINSIC INSTIGATION

The first question is the origins of an individual's anger. An understanding of the determinants, both physiological and psychological, can assist in both retrospective and prospective assessment as well as in the management of aggressive behavior patterns.

Physiological sources of instigation include (a) genetic predispositions including temperament and gender; (b) diseases or disorders of the central nervous system such as Whitman's' brain tumor; (c) the influence of hormones including thyroxin, testosterone, and adrenaline; (d) physical illnesses such as encephalitis as well as their associated pain and discomfort; (e) drugs such as phencyclidine (PCP) and steroids as well as toxic factors such as lead paints and pollutants; (f) fatigue, stress and pain; and (g) generalized autonomic arousal. (See Megargee, 1993, pp. 621–624, for a detailed discussion of physiological sources of intrinsic instigation.)

There are also numerous psychological sources of instigation, including (a) frustration (Dollard, Doob, Miller, Mowrer, & Sears, 1939); (b) aversive events and provocations (Berkowitz, 1989, 1990, 2003); (c) physical or verbal attacks (Azrin, Hake, & Hutchinson, 1965); and (d) territorial

intrusions (Ardrey, 1966). Frustration was one of the earliest causes of anger to be studied (Dollard et al., 1939). Researchers learned that the number of frustrations, the strength of the frustrated drive, and the arbitrariness of the frustration all increased the amount of instigation, and that the instigation from several sources could summate (Berkowitz, 1962, 1989). The phenomenon of "road rage" (Novaco, 1991) is a good example of frustration-induced angry aggression.

Over the years, the concept of frustration expanded from the simple blocking of an ongoing goal response postulated by Dollard and his associates (1939) to include interference with learned attitudes and cognitive expectancies about how people should behave and how we should be treated. When these expectations are frustrated, instigation to aggression can result.

In the wake of mass shootings in high schools in the United States and elsewhere, there has been an increased appreciation of the role that ostracism and bullying play in creating instigation to aggression and violence (Jimerson & Furlong, 2006; Vossekuil, Fein, Reddy, Borum & Modzeleski, 2002).

Some societies and religions teach their members to be angry when they witness behaviors that they regard as disrespectful, as evidenced by the widespread Islamic protests over the publication of cartoons depicting the prophet Mohammed in the Danish newspaper *Jyllands-Posten* on September 30, 2005. Indeed, some honor codes require lethal retribution for perceived affronts, not only of perceived enemies such as Salman Rushdie, but even of relatives who might have disgraced the family or tribe (Anderson & Bushman, 2002; Baumeister, Smart, & Boden, 1996; Berkowitz, 1990, 2003; Cohen, Nisbett, Bowdle, & Schwarz, 1996, Tawfeeq & Todd, 2007).

REDUCING INTRINSIC INSTIGATION

How people deal with anger or hostility is another important consideration. According to "catharsis" theory, intrinsic instigation should be depleted by attacking the source of the provocation. If this is impossible, angry individuals may reduce instigation by attacking someone else (displacement), choosing an alternative response (response substitution), or observing someone else's aggressive behavior, either in real life or the media (vicarious aggression) (Berkowitz, 1962; Buss, 1961). Hokanson (1970), however, has shown that the instigation-reducing effects of counter-aggression appear to depend on previous learning and cultural values.

ASSESSING AND TREATING INTRINSIC INSTIGATION

Obviously, the more intense and long-lasting the instigation, the easier it is to assess. Because anger and rage are transitory, we may not observe them in a single session. As with the assessment of other emotions, the more often we interact with a subject, the greater the range of emotions, including anger, we are likely to observe.

Our primary assessment questions are the amount, the duration, and the direction of instigation to aggression: "Is the subject angry?" "How angry?" "How long does he stay angry?" "At whom is she angry?" The secondary questions are what causes this instigation and how does the subject deal with it: "What angers him?" "What does she do when she is angry?"

One of the best ways to assess anger and hostility is also the simplest: asking subjects, using a variety of synonyms, what makes them angry or annoyed, who aggravates them, what they would like to do when they are provoked, to whom they would like to do it, and what it is they actually do and why. Anger is a strong emotion; given the opportunity, many people will express it quite openly, even when it is not in their best interests to do so. Because anger and hostility are difficult to conceal, their friends and associates should also be able to comment on a client's temper.

A number of self-report tests and scales have been constructed to assess anger and hostility. The Buss–Durkee Hostility Guilt Inventory (Buss & Durkee, 1957) features seven scales designed to assess various aspects of hostility and aggression, plus one for assessing guilt over its expression, a potential measure of inhibitions. Spielberger's (1996) State Trait Anger Expression Inventory (STAXI) has three standard scales, "Anger out" (Ax/out), "Anger in" (Ax/in), and "Anger control" (Ax/con), as well as two experimental subscales, "Anger control in" (Ax/con-in) and "Anger control out" (Ax/con-out). Novaco and his colleagues have devised several measures related to anger and its causes, including the Novaco Anger Scale (NAS; Novaco, 1994, 2003), the Novaco Provocation Inventory (NPI; Novaco, 1975, 1988), and the Dimensions of Anger Reaction Scale (DAS and DAS-5; Hawthorne, Mouthaan, Forbes, & Novaco, 2006).

Scales designed to assess anger and hostility are also included on self-report inventories such as the MMPI-2 (Butcher, Dahlstrom, Graham, Tellegen, & Kaemmer, 1989). Since instigation to aggression has been implicated as a factor in cardiovascular and gastrointestinal disorders, a number of measures of anger and hostility have been devised for use in behavioral medicine (Chesney & Rosenman, 1985). Most of these scales have obvious content and can easily be dissembled.

Researchers have also devised observational rating instruments such as the Ward Anger Rating Scale (WARS; Novaco, 1994; Novaco & Taylor, 2004) designed to allow staff members to record and quantify inpatients' angry and aggressive behavior over the course of a week.

Ascertaining the sources of instigation to aggression can have important clinical implications for assessment and for treatment. The court that sentenced Mary Winkler to the time she had already served in jail plus some additional counseling probably concluded that she was unlikely to engage in further violence since, by killing her abusive husband, she had already eliminated her major source of instigation to aggression.

With regard to treatment, a clinician might investigate whether a client's frustration and resulting anger stems from unreasonable expectations. If so, cognitive therapy designed to correct these beliefs might be effective (Feindler & Ecton, 1986; Goldstein & Keller, 1987). On the other hand, if the grievance is genuine and the anger justified, a better solution might be to help the client find a more constructive way of coping with the frustrating situation, such as seeking redress in the courts. Cognitive redefinition, especially through humor, is another effective mechanism for reducing instigation (Megargee, 1993).

Extrinsic (Instrumental) Instigation to Aggression

People aggress not only because they want to hurt the victim, but also because they hope aggression may help them attain other goals. As Al Capone reportedly said, "You can get much farther with a kind word and a gun than you can with a kind word alone" (Peter, 1977, p. 141).

SOURCES OF EXTRINSIC INSTIGATION

There is a vast array of possible extrinsic motives, both primary and secondary. Primary motives include (a) personal gains and satisfactions, such as acquisition of property or enhancement of self-esteem; (b) removal of problems or impediments, such eliminating enemies or witnesses to crimes; (c) achieving social goals, such as power or respect from others; and (d) the attainment of political or religious goals, as exemplified by the conflicts in the Middle East and elsewhere (Megargee, 1982, 1993). And, of course, aggression is part of the job description for many people, including professional athletes, police officers, and military personnel. (See Megargee, 1982, for a detailed discussion of extrinsic motives.)

We need to be alert to secondary as well as primary motives. Although he had robbed banks mainly for the money, a reformed robber told me that he had also enjoyed the adrenaline rush he had experienced playing "cops and robbers" with real guns and cars. Although we psychologists often focus on intrinsic motives such as anger and hostility when working with aggressive people, extrinsic motivation probably leads to as much if not more aggression, especially when we consider large-scale conflicts between groups and nations.

REDUCING EXTRINSIC INSTIGATION

The best way to reduce extrinsic instigation is to eliminate the payoff for the aggressive behavior. If aggression is ineffective in achieving the extrinsic goals, other strategies are more likely to be adopted during the response competition. This is the basic principle underlying the imposition of severe criminal sanctions for violent crimes. Unfortunately, in our society, as well as in many others, it is difficult if not impossible to eliminate all the rewards for aggression.

ASSESSING AND TREATING EXTRINSIC INSTIGATION

Not being a personality trait, extrinsic motivation is much more difficult to assess than intrinsic. Lacking tests to assess instrumental motivation, we must often rely on self-reports elicited in response to probing questions in an interview. We can also infer how aggressive behavior is reinforced from case history data. Obviously, this works better in retrospective than prospective assessments.

The first step in dealing with instrumental aggression is to analyze the contingencies in the client's milieu. What are the payoffs for behaving aggressively? Many cultures and families reward and model aggression (Bandura, 1973; Bandura & Walters, 1963). Moreover, extrinsic instigation can generalize from one situation to another. Parents who berate the umpire at Little League games should not be surprised when their children emulate them and disrespect other adults.

Once we have determined the contingencies reinforcing the undesired aggressive behavior, we should

attempt to reduce the reinforcements for that behavior as much as possible. At the same time, we should create nonaggressive opportunities for clients to attain their legitimate goals. While this does not eliminate the aggressive responses from their repertoires, it should make the nonaggressive alternatives more likely to be selected in the response competition.

The effectiveness of this two-pronged approach was demonstrated in an experiment with nursery school children who were misbehaving in order to obtain attention. Brown and Elliott (1965) reduced the students' verbal and physical aggressive behavior by having their teachers systematically reinforce prosocial responses that were incompatible with aggression while minimizing the attention they paid to aggressive responses.

Habit Strength

Reinforcement of aggressive responses increases their habit strength, the last personal factor leading to aggression. Angry aggression is reinforced by the pain or discomfort inflicted on the victim, instrumental by attaining extrinsic goals through aggressive behavior. The stronger the habit strength for a particular aggressive response, the more likely that act and similar behaviors will be selected in the future.

SOURCES OF HABIT STRENGTH

Direct reinforcement of our own aggression is the most effective way to increase habit strength. The rewards are strongest for the actual response and generalize to others that are similar to it. A schoolchild motivated to punch an obnoxious playmate in the nose receives stronger reinforcement for doing so successfully than he does for calling his opponent names or telling tales about him to the teacher. If, however, the nose-punching response is blocked, he should obtain some satisfaction from the other lesser responses. Displacement may also take place. If he is unable or unwilling to attack his antagonist, perhaps because the other lad is bigger or is accompanied by his friends, he may take out his anger on another boy who is smaller or weaker.

The more a family, reference group, or culture approves of aggressive behavior, the more secondary reinforcement a person will receive. The boy who punches his obnoxious opponent in the nose is likely to get additional reinforcement from his peers (and, perhaps, not entirely unwelcome attention from his teacher). Girls, who are less likely to be reinforced for physical aggression, are less likely to develop as much aggressive habit strength as boys.

Although direct reinforcement of our own aggressive responses is most effective, we can also develop habit strength indirectly by observing role models successfully engage in aggressive behavior. Children can learn aggressive scripts from observing domestic violence, from watching countless portrayals of aggressive behavior in the media, and from playing violent video games. These aggressive scripts, once learned, can then serve as guides for future aggressive behavior in real-life situations (Anderson & Bushman, 2002; Bandura, 1973; Huesmann, 1986, 1998; Huesmann & Eron, 1986). For example, in the videos Seung-Hui Cho mailed to NBC the day of his multiple killings at Virginia Tech, he acknowledged the influence of Dylan Klebold and Eric Harris's killing spree at Columbine High School in 1999, referring to them as "martyrs" (Healy, 2007).

REDUCING HABIT STRENGTH

Once acquired, aggressive habits and scripts are extraordinarily difficult to eliminate. As we all learned in Psychology 101, extinction is the only certain technique for eliminating habits. However, extinction requires the elimination of any reinforcement for aggressive behavior, which is virtually impossible in our culture. Although punishment may temporarily suppress aggressive behavior, it does not eliminate aggressive responses from our repertoires. Moreover, to the extent that punishment is frustrating or perceived as an attack, it can also increase intrinsic instigation. This is one reason prisons are often ineffective.

ASSESSING AND TREATING HABIT STRENGTH

Of all the constructs in the algebra of aggression, habit strength should be the easiest to assess, based as it is on the individual's reinforcement history as documented in the case history. Habit strength is the variable that most strongly predicts aggression; the longer and stronger the history of aggression, the more likely an individual will behave similarly in the future. One can infer strong habit strength from a long history of aggressive behavior, especially if the aggression appears to have been successful. A history of aggressive behavior is a key element in diagnosing Megargee's (1966) undercontrolled assaultive type, and is central to the objective prediction devices used in many mental health and correctional risk assessments (Borum, 1996; Otto, 2000). However, as in the case of the overcontrolled assaultive type, the fact that some people have no known history of aggression or violence is no guarantee that they will never aggress in the future.

With regard to treatment, Brown and Elliott's (1965) experiment also demonstrated how difficult it is to eliminate habits once they have been formed. As we noted, both verbal and physical aggression diminished during their experiment when their nursery school teachers were instructed to minimize the amount of attention they paid to aggressive students. Unfortunately, fighting resumed once the experiment was over, presumably because the teachers could not bring themselves to continue ignoring physical aggression while rewarding only prosocial behavior.

Inhibitions against Aggression

Opposing instigation and habit strength are inhibitions against aggression. Inhibitions include both moral prohibitions and pragmatic concerns. They can be general or specific, lasting or temporary, and they vary as a function of the aggressive act, the target, and the circumstances.

SOURCES OF INHIBITIONS

Moral prohibitions go by various terms such as "taboos," "conscientiousness," and "superego." In the course of normal development, we all learn that certain aggressive acts directed at particular people are morally wrong. For example, in most societies aggression against one's parents, especially one's mother, is considered wrong, while attacking an enemy, especially one who is from an alien culture, is more acceptable.

Pragmatic issues are another source of internal inhibitions. One practical concern is the fear that bad things, such as punishment or retribution, may occur following a particular aggressive act. Fearing he might be attacked by a mob following his planned assassination of President James A. Garfield in 1881, Charles Guiteau hired a cab to wait and take him to the DC prison as soon as he had shot the president (Clark, 1982).

Another concern is the fear that the proposed act might fail to accomplish its objective. On several occasions in 1972, Arthur Bremer set out to assassinate President Richard Nixon, but was deterred when he was unable to get close enough to get a clear shot at the President. In a classic case of displacement, he next targeted and eventually shot Gov. George Wallace, who was running for the Democratic nomination for president (Clark, 1982).

REDUCING INHIBITIONS

Unfortunately, it is much easier to decrease inhibitions than it is to foster them. Physiological factors that reduce inhibitions include (a) injuries or diseases affecting the central nervous system; (b) certain endocrinological disorders; and (c) the chemical actions of disinhibiting substances such as alcohol.

Among the many psychological causes of inadequate inhibitions against aggression are (a) the failure to develop adequate inhibitions because of deficient socialization or abuse during childhood; (b) growing up in a society that approves of certain acts of aggression or violence; (c) being exposed to social influences, including the media, that model aggressive behavior; (d) conflicting values (i.e., it is wrong to attack someone but right to defend your honor); (e) rationalizations (i.e., aggression is wrong but this is anticipatory self-defense rather than aggression); (f) peer pressure; and (g) contagion. (See Megargee, 1997, for a detailed discussion of inhibitions.) A full assessment of inhibitions must explore whether people's inhibitions against aggression are easily overcome.

ASSESSING INHIBITIONS

It is much more difficult to measure inhibitions against aggression than it is to assess instigation to aggression or habit strength (Megargee, 1997). The mere absence of a history of aggressive behavior or failure to express animosity toward others does not necessarily indicate that people have strong inhibitions. A more parsimonious explanation would be that they simply lacked instigation.

To assess inhibitions directly, one must look for circumstances in which people should be motivated to aggress but fail to do so. While such situations can be created in the laboratory, they are difficult to contrive in the clinic. Role playing, group therapy, and direct confrontations in an interview may afford opportunities to observe inhibitions. More often, we have to ask people about what aggressive behaviors they find acceptable or unacceptable under various circumstances. Inhibitions are easier than anger to dissimulate, and potentially self-serving reports need to be cross-checked with the case history and reports by people who have had an opportunity to observe a client's behavior in provocative circumstances.

Often we must rely on indirect evidence. One source of indirect evidence is whether the familial and social history is conducive to the development of well-socialized values. Is a person cautious or impulsive? This involves consideration of stakes as well as risks. The more people have to lose through aggressive behavior, the less likely they are to risk it (Gottfredson, 1987). This is one reason so-called "white collar criminals" are more likely to rob you

with a fountain pen than with a pistol, to paraphrase Woody Guthrie's "Ballad of Pretty Boy Floyd."

Personality tests are another indirect source of data on inhibitions. While there are no adequate tests of inhibitions against aggression per se, there are measures designed to measure overall conscientiousness and socialization. Although Hartshorne and May's (1928, 1929) classic studies demonstrated the specificity of moral prohibitions, other things being equal well-socialized people with strong values are more likely to have inhibitions against those forms of aggression that are censured by their culture than those who are poorly socialized.

Hogan and Ones (1997) describe several personality tests designed to assess "conscientiousness" as one of the so-called basic or "Big Five" personality traits. Chief among them is the NEO PI (Costa & McRae, 1992). The California Psychological Inventory (CPI; Gough & Bradley, 1996) has three scales relevant to inhibitions: Socialization (So), Responsibility (Re), and Self Control (Sc). These scales, which have been validated in many cultures, assess the degree to which individuals have assimilated (So) and understand (Re) their cultural values, and also measure their ability to control their behavior and abide by these precepts (Sc) (Megargee, 1972). Although I use the CPI in nonclinical populations, I prefer to use the MMPI-2 with more deviant or pathological groups. A clinically elevated O-H scale score suggests a conflict between expression or suppression of hostility, but low scores are meaningless (Megargee et al., 1967). Elevations and high points on basic Scales 4, 6, 8, and 9; on supplementary scale MAC-R; and on content scale ASP suggest deficient inhibitions and controls.

No one is more lacking in inhibitions than the psychopath, and Hare's (2003) PCL-R has been related to violent criminal behavior in a number of studies. The PCL-R will be discussed in the section on risk assessment.

Situational Factors and External Conditions
HOW SITUATIONAL FACTORS INFLUENCE AGGRESSION

Aggression results from the interaction of the personal factors discussed above with external conditions that can either facilitate or impede aggressive behavior or violence. These situational factors can be divided into environments, settings, situations, and stimuli to demarcate a rough continuum from widespread to focal influences. Among the external factors that might promote aggressive behavior are

(a) living in a society that encourages aggressive behavior (environment); (b) being in a war zone such as any of a number of Middle Eastern trouble spots (setting); (c) being caught up in the general chaos of a firefight or riot (situation); and (d) being attacked by an antagonist (stimulus).

Factors that might inhibit violence include (a) living in a peaceful and harmonious society (environment); (b) attending a Quaker religious service (setting); (c) being in the presence of loved ones or authorities who disapprove of aggression (situation); and (d) being lovingly embraced by a potential target of aggression (stimulus). The boundaries between these terms are not significant; the point is that a wide range of external factors and events helps determine whether or not an aggressive act takes place. The common denominator for these events, according to Monahan and Klassen (1982), is that they all occur outside our skins.

Situational influences involve times as well as places; much more violence occurs in New York City's Central Park between 2:00 and 4:00 A.M. on Sunday morning than from 2:00 to 4:00 P.M. on Sunday afternoon. Of course, personality and situational factors are not independent. Those peaceful people who flock to Central Park on a sunny afternoon generally shun it in the early morning hours, leaving it to the predators and police.

Contagion effects are also important. Berkowitz (1970) demonstrated an increase in violence following highly publicized aggressive crimes. We have already noted the fact that Seung-Hui Cho was influenced by the Columbine High School killings. In addition to his Virginia Tech massacre, there have been at least 25 high school shootings involving multiple victims in the United States as well as at least 9 mass school shootings in other countries (Infoplease.com, 2007).

The circumstances and stimuli to which clients are exposed and the conditions in which they live are extremely important determinants of aggression. Cognitive expectancies interacting with situational realities can cause frustration, the major source of intrinsic instigation (Dollard et al., 1939). Environmental factors can moderate the relation of personality factors, such as empathy, to aggression (Rose & Feshbach, 1990). Given strong enough threat or provocation, almost anyone may become violent.

Since this book is about personality assessment, space does not permit a discussion of all the external factors that influence aggression. Among those that have been emphasized in the literature are ambient temperature (Anderson & Bushman, 2002; Baron & Ransberger, 1978; Megargee, 1977); architectural design (Newman, 1972); crowding (Megargee, 1977; Russell, 1983); the family, peer, and job environments; the availability of alcohol and of potential victims (Monahan & Klassen, 1982); and the behavior of antagonists, victims, associates, and bystanders (Megargee, 1993; Wolfgang, 1958). Perhaps the most widely discussed variable is access to weapons by either or both antagonists (Cook, 1982; MacDonald, 1975; Monahan & Klassen, 1982).

ASSESSING SITUATIONAL FACTORS

In both prospective and retrospective assessments, clinicians must consider the influence of situational as well as personality factors. There is no substitute for familiarity with a client's various environments and living conditions. First-hand appraisals are the best source of information. This is done most easily in hospitals and prisons in which one is attempting to predict institutional violence. It is more difficult in community settings, but if home visits can be arranged they are invaluable. In most cases, however, we must rely on descriptions in case history material, police reports, and information gained in interviews with clients.

Compared with personality measures, there are few instruments for systematically assessing situational influences. An exception is the Correctional Institution Environment Scale (CIES; Moos, 1975), a 90-item instrument scored on nine environmental scales that is designed to be administered to inmates and staff. The CIES has been used more to evaluate the the effects of various program changes on the social climate of prisons rather than as a measure to be considered in analyzing the causes of institutional aggression.

In recent years, several instruments have been devised to assess bullying and identify bullies in schools using both self- and peer reports. However, their reliability and validity have not yet been well established (Cornell, Sheras, & Cole, 2006).

Bjørkly (1993, 1994) devised a situational "Scale for the Prediction of Aggression and Dangerousness in Psychotic Patients," which is designed to predict the frequency and intensity of psychiatric patients' aggressive behavior in 29 different situations, both on the ward and off. Recent research (Bjørkly, Havik, & Løberg, 1996) has attested to its interrater reliability, but its validity is yet to be established, as is its applicability outside of Norway. Monahan and Klassen (1982) suggested that we investigate the circumstances that led people to commit aggressive acts in the past and determine whether they correspond to the situations they are likely to encounter in the future. We might also ascertain the environmental and situational factors associated with peaceful periods to help guide recommendations for future treatment or environmental manipulation.

The less we know about the settings in which clients will find themselves or the situations and stimuli they will face, the more difficult it is to make accurate predictions. Only in institutional settings, such as prisons and inpatient mental health units, where the environmental factors are relatively constant for all subjects, does it appear possible to make reasonably accurate predictions based only on personality factors (McGuire & Megargee, 1976).

Response Competition and Reaction Formation

An aggressive or violent act will be blocked if inhibitory factors exceed motivating ones. However, if all the forces favoring a particular response exceed those opposing it, that act is possible, at least as long as those conditions prevail. Before it can be carried out, however, all the possible responses, both violent and nonviolent, must compete with one another. The one with the highest reaction potential—that is, the greatest capacity to satisfy the most needs at the least cost—should be chosen.

ASSESSING REACTION POTENTIAL

In a retrospective analysis of aggressive behavior, it is obvious that the act that was actually performed had the highest reaction potential. If that act was socially or personally undesirable, and the clinical goal is to decrease the likelihood of a recurrence, other more satisfactory alternatives should be investigated. Why were these acts not selected? Were the inhibitions too great? Their chance of success too low? Did cognitive beliefs suggest that the aggressive act was the more honorable alternative? Did friends or onlookers encourage the aggressive behavior? The answers to such questions might indicate how the reaction potential of the objectionable behavior may be decreased and that of more acceptable responses increased.

In prospective assessments, the clinician's task is to try to determine the range of possible responses and estimate their relative reaction potential. Situational circumstances, such as whether or not certain interventions are attempted, may be critical.

Instead of affixing a blanket label, such as "dangerous," these analyses should help clinicians make more sophisticated contingent predictions of the likelihood that clients will engage in specified aggressive behaviors under various sets of circumstances.

Generalized Assessments of Aggression and Violence

While retrospective assessments entail detailed clinical evaluations of aggressive events and individuals, prospective studies typically involve screening groups of patients or offenders to identify those who are most likely to aggress in the future. Originally referred to as predicting "dangerousness," these evaluations are now termed "risk assessment."

Approaches to Risk Prediction
SUBJECTIVE JUDGMENT

In the 1950s and 1960s, diagnoses of dangerousness were made clinically by psychiatrists, psychologists, and case workers using whatever criteria their training and experience suggested. In the 1970s, researchers began examining the accuracy of these diagnoses by conducting follow-ups of psychiatric patients who had been labeled dangerous and subsequently released into the community. Official records such as arrest reports indicated that only 20–35% of these patients actually engaged in aggressive behavior after they had been released (Kozol, Boucher, & Garafalo, 1972; Steadman & Cocozza, 1974). More recent studies using more sophisticated assessments and improved research methods now suggest that the accuracy of short-term clinical predictions of violence among acute psychiatric patients may be as high as 50% (Borum, 1996; Monahan, 1996; Otto, 1992). This improved accuracy still risks classifying many nonaggressive people as potentially violent ("false positives"), especially in settings in which aggressive behavior is infrequent.

Clinical risk assessment has been criticized as being overly subjective and potentially influenced by illusory correlation, stereotypes, and hindsight bias (Towl & Crighton, 1995). This was illustrated by Cooper and Werner's (1990) investigation of the abilities of 10 psychologists and 11 case workers to predict institutional violence based on 17 variables in a sample of 33 male federal correctional institution inmates, 8 of whom (24%) were violent and 25 of whom (76%) were not. They found that interjudge reliabilities were quite low, averaging only .23 among pairs of judges. Pooled judgments were substantially more reliable than individual assessments. Accuracy was appalling; the psychologists' predictive accuracy averaged only –.08 (range = –.25 to +.22), while the case workers' mean accuracy was +.08 (range = –.14 to + .34). The main reason for the inaccuracy appeared to be illusory correlation, with judges often using cues that proved to be unrelated to the criterion.

Subjective classification procedures are difficult to document, which can result in a lack of oversight and accountability. Correctional facilities relying on subjective appraisals have been plagued by chronic "overclassification," with prisoners being assigned to more restrictive conditions of confinement than necessary. In a series of cases, the courts held that subjective classifications were too often arbitrary, capricious, inconsistent, and invalid (Austin, 1993; Solomon & Camp, 1993). In Laaman v. Helgemoe (437 F. Supp. 318, D.N.H. 1977, quoted by Solomon & Camp, 1993, p. 9), the court stated that prison classification systems, "cannot be arbitrary, irrational, or discriminatory," and in Alabama the court took over the entire correctional system and ordered every inmate reclassified (Fowler, 1976).

PERSONALITY TESTS

Psychological tests developed in other contexts and for other purposes have also been used in risk assessment. The original MMPI and its successor, the MMPI-2, are the world's most widely used and researched clinical inventories.[2] Megargee and Mendelsohn (1962) found that extremely violent and moderately violent male applicants for probation did not differ from nonviolent criminals and noncriminals on a dozen original MMPI scales especially designed to measure hostility and aggression. Megargee and Carbonell (1995) correlated a number of MMPI scales with measures of institutional adjustment and violence. The correlations, while significant, were generally too low to be of much value in prospective risk assessment, and multiple regression equations were not much better.

Bohn (1979) was able to reduce the incidence of serious assaults in a federal correctional institution 46% by using the MMPI-based offender classification system (Megargee et al., 1979, 2001) to identify those inmates most likely to be predatory and those most likely to be preyed upon so they could be housed in different dormitories. However, the MMPI-2 is better at assessing offenders' attitudes, mental health, emotional adjustment, and need for treatment or other professional interventions ("needs assessment") than it is at estimating how dangerous they are (Megargee, 2006b).

The psychological test with the best track record with regard to violence risk assessment is Hare's (2003) PCL-R. The PCL-R was devised to assess the construct of psychopathy as originally delineated by Cleckley (1941/1976). Since 1980, an impressive array of empirical evidence from personality, physiological, and cognitive psychological research as well as from criminology and corrections has attested to the construct validity of the PCL-R. Barone (2004, p. 113) recently referred to the PCL-R as the "gold standard" for the measurement of psychopathy.

PCL-R assessments require a thorough review of the clinical, medical, and legal records, followed by a clinical interview in which a complete chronological case history is obtained. For research purposes, it is possible to compute PCL-R scores based only on (extensive) file data (Grann, Långström, Tengström & Kullgren, 1999), but this is not recommended (Meloy & Gacono, 1995).

The PCL-R consists of 20 symptoms of psychopathy, each of which is scored on a 3-point scale from 0 (absent) to 2 (clearly present). Inter-rater reliabilities average .86, and users are advised to base assessments on the average of two or more independent ratings whenever possible (Hare et al., 1990). Although Hare et al. (1990) regard the PCL-R as a homogeneous, unidimensional scale based on its average alpha coefficient of .88, there are two well-defined factors. The first reflects an egocentric, selfish interpersonal style with its principal loadings from such items as glibness/superficial charm (.86), grandiose sense of self-worth (.76), pathological lying (.62), conning/manipulative (.59), shallow affect (.57), lack of remorse or guilt (.53), and callousness/lack of empathy (.53). The items loading on the second factor suggest the chronic antisocial behavior associated with psychopathy: impulsivity (.66), juvenile delinquency (.59), and need for stimulation, parasitic lifestyle, early behavior problems, and lack of realistic goals (all loading .56) (Hare et al., 1990).

Reviewing a number of empirical investigations, both retrospective and prospective, Hart (1996) reported that psychopaths, as diagnosed by the PCL-R, had higher rates of violence in the community and in institutions than nonpsychopaths, and that psychopathy, as measured by the PCL-R, was predictive of violence after admission to a hospital ward and also after conditional release from a hospital or correctional institution. He estimated that the average correlation of PCL-R scores with violence in these studies was about .35. In their follow-up of 618 men discharged from a maximum security psychiatric institution, Harris, Rice, and Quinsey (1993) reported that, of all the variables they studied, the PCL-R had the highest correlation (+.35) with violent recidivism, and they included psychopathy as defined by PCL-R scores >25, as a predictor in their Violent Risk Appraisal Guide. Rice and Harris (1997) reported that the PCL-R was also associated with sexual reoffending by child molesters and rapists. In their meta-analysis of 18 studies relating the original and revised PCLs to violent and nonviolent recidivism, Salekin, Rogers, and Sewell (1996) found 29 reports of effect sizes ranging from 0.42 to 1.92 with a mean of 0.79. They reported, "We found that the PCL and PCL-R had moderate to strong effect sizes and appear to be good predictors of violence and general recidivism "(p. 203).[3] Hart summarized it best when he concluded, "predictions of violence using the PCL-R are considerably better than chance, albeit far from perfect" (1996, p. 64). The Psychopathy Checklist-Screening version (PCL-SV; Hart, Hare, & Forth, 1994), a reduced 12-item version of the PCL-R more suitable for screening, has also been shown to relate to violent behavior (Douglas, Yeomans, & Boer, 2005).

OBJECTIVE ASSESSMENT TOOLS: RATIONALLY DERIVED

A number of objective classifcation instruments have been created in recent years to eliminate the unreliability and subjectivity associated with clinical decision making (see Table 28.1). Some have been constructed rationally, others empirically. Authors of rationally constructed devices select variables that they believe are associated with aggression, violence, misconduct, or recidivism on the basis of clinical experience, psychological theories, and the findings in the empirical literature. For example, the Dangerous Behavior Rating Scale (Webster & Menzies, 1993) was based on the algebra of aggression model (Megargee, 1976) discussed earlier in this chapter, while the Level of Supervision Inventory (LSI) was guided by social learning theory (Bonta & Motiuk, 1985). Variable selection is also strongly influenced by practical concerns such as the types of data available in the client files and whether it is feasible to interview or test those being screened. Once the variables are selected and operationally defined, a coding scheme needs to be constructed that deals with issues such as missing data and personnel must be trained to code records reliably. Next, a scoring system must be devised that considers such

issues as how to weight and combine the variables. Should an overall global score be computed or should a decision tree approach be used? Finally, cutting scores must be selected, or decision rules formulated, to assign subjects to categories differing in their estimated propensity for aggression and violence. Regardless of the methods employed, in a purely objective system the final decisions are based on the outcome of the instrument. If, as is often the case, staff can override the objective classification, subjective elements have reentered the system.[4]

As might be expected, the validity and utility of rationally derived devices varies greatly. The Federal Bureau of Prisons (BOP) and a number of state departments of corrections created objective instruments to indicate appropriate custody and supervision levels in correctional institutions (Austin, 1993; Brennan, 1987, 1993; Glaser, 1987). While not specifically designed to predict aggression per se, the potential for violence was, obviously, an important consideration. The model based security level classifications on the expected length of incarceration, offense severity, type of prior commitment, history of violence or escape attempts, and types of detainers (Kane, 1993). However, Proctor (1994), who evaluated Nebraska's adaptation of the BOP model, noted it accounted for only 3% of the variance in institutional adjustment and concluded, "The results regarding the predictive validity of the Nebraska model suggest that the classification model was not a valid instrument for predicting institutional adjustment" (p. 267).

Much better results have been obtained with the LSI (Bonta & Motiuk, 1985) and its successor, the Level of Service Inventory-Revised (LSI-R; Andrews & Bonta, 1995). Originally designed to screen inmates for possible placement in Canadian correctional halfway houses, it is now widely used in probation offices and prisons throughout Canada and has been researched and utilized in Australia (Daffern, Ogloff, Ferguson, & Thomson, 2005), England and Wales (Hollin & Palmer, 2006; Palmer & Hollin, 2007), Germany (Dahle, 2006), and even the US (Schlager & Simourd, 2007) despite the fact that Gendreau, Goggin and Smith (2002, p. 423) complained that American psychologists "have generally not heard of it."

The LSI and LSI-R are interview-based instruments that evaluate offenders on 54 two-point scales covering 10 areas: (a) criminal history, (b) education/employment, (c) finances, (d) family/marital, (e) accommodations, (f) leisure/recreation,

Table 28.1. Objective devices.

1. Instruments devised for use in adult correctional and forensic settings

ASSESS-LIST	A 10-item clinical scale that combines with the VRAG to form the VPS (Webster & Polvi, 1995)
Dangerous Behavior Rating Scale	Based on Megargee's (1982, 1993) algebra of aggression model (Webster & Menzies, 1993)
HCR-20	Comprised of 20 ratings in three categories: historical, clinical, and risk management (Webster, Douglas, Eaves, & Hart, 1997; Douglas & Webster, 1999)
Level of Supervision Inventory (LSI and LSI-R)	Interview-based instruments that evaluate offenders in 10 areas for probation and halfway house placement (Bonta & Motiuk, 1985)
Lifestyle Criminality Screening Form (LCSF)	A 14-item scale designed to identify those career criminals who account for an excessive amount of antisocial behavior (Walters, White, & Denney, 1991)
Offender Group Reconviction Scale (OGRS)	A criminogenic reoffending scale based on criminal history and demographic variables (Copas & Marshall, 1998)
Risk Assessment Scale for Prisons (RASP)	Devised to forecast violence in US prisons (Cunningham & Sorenson, 2006; Cunningham, Sorenson, & Reidy, 2005)
Self-Appraisal Questionnaire (SAQ)	A 72-item yes/no instrument aimed at predicting violent and nonviolent recidivism (Loza, Dhaliwal, Kroner, & Loza-Fanous, 2000; Loza & Loza-Fanous, 2003)
Short-Term Assessment of Risk and Treatability (START) scale	Designed to guide the multidisciplinary assessment of forensic mental health inpatients (Nicholls, Brink, Desmarais, Webster, & Martin, 2006; Webster, Nicholls, Martin, Desmarais, & Brink, 2006)
Violence Prediction Scheme (VPS)	Comprised of the ASSESS-LIST and the VRAG (Webster, Harris, Rice, Cormeier, & Quinsey, 1994)
Violence Risk Assessment Guide (VRAG)	A record-based assessment tool used to sort mentally disordered offenders into nine categories based on their propensity for violence (Harris, Rice, & Quinsey, 1993)
Violence Risk Scale (VRS)	Combines both static and dynamic variables including ratings of clients' treatment progress (Wong & Gordon, 2006)

2. Instruments devised for risk assessments with juveniles and youths

Early Assessment Risk List for Boys (EARL-B) and Early Assessment Risk List for Girls (EARL-G)	Structured clinical checklists designed for the professional judgment of risk for aggressive and disruptive behaviors among boys (Augimeri, Koegl, Webster, & Levene, 2001) and girls (Levene, Augimeri, Pepler, Walsh, Webster, & Koegl, 2001)
Structured Assessment of Violence Risk Level in Youth (SAVRY)	Based on the HCR-20 for adults (Borum, Bartel, & Forth, 2002; Catchpole & Gretton, 2003)
Youth Level of Service/Case Management Inventory	Based on the LSI, has 42 items assessing eight criminogenic factors (Hoge & Andrews, 2002)

3. Instruments designed to assess violence among psychiatric inpatients

Classification of Violence Risk (COVR)	An interactive software program that provides a statistical estimate of the likelihood of violence based on chart and interview data (Monahan et al., 2006)
Multiple Iterative Classification Tree (ICT)	An actuarial decision-tree approach based on the MacArthur risk assessment studies for use in planning discharge with acutely ill civil inpatients (Monahan et al., 2005)
Suicide and Aggression Survey (SAS)	An interview-based instrument for adolescent and adult psychiatric patients (Korn et al., 2006)
Violence Screening Checklist (VSC)	Uses of demographic, case history, and diagnostic data to predict physical attacks among civilly committed inpatients (McNiel, 1988; McNiel & Binder, 1994)

continued

Table 28.1. (*continued*)

4. Tools devised to predict sexual reoffending and recidivism

These tools were constructed following the passage of legislation allowing for the continued post-sentence detention and treatment of sex offenders deemed likely to offend:

Estimate of Risk of Adolescent Sexual Offence Recidivism (ERASOR)	Actuarial instrument aimed at adolescents (Worling & Curwen, 2001),
Minnesota Sex Offender Screening Tool-Revised (MnSOST-R)	Actuarial instrument based on file information. Better at predicting general than sexual recidivism (Epperson, Kaul, & Hesselton, 1998)
Multifactorial Assessment of Sex Offender Risk for Recidivism (MASORR)	Clinical ratings of factors empirically associated with sexual reoffending in literature including PCL-R (Barbaree, Seto, Langston, & Peacock, 2001)
Rapid Risk Assessment for Sexual Offender Recidivism (RRASOR)	Brief actuarial scale (Hanson, 1997)
Risk for Sexual Violence Protocol (RSVP)	(Hart, Kropp, Laws, Klaver, Logan, & Watt, 2003)
Sex Offender Risk Appraisal Guide (SORAG)	(Quinsey, Harris, Rice, & Cormier, 1998)
Sexual Violence Risk-20 (SVR-20)	Instrument used to assist structured professional judgment (Boer, Hart, Kropp, & Webster, 1997)
STATIC-99	Ten items designed for adult males who have committed at least one prior sex offense (Barbaree, Seto, Langston, & Peacock, 2001; Hanson & Thornton, 1999)

5. Instruments designed to identify potential perpetrators of domestic violence

Ontario Domestic Assault Risk Assessment (ODARA)	Designed to predict further assaults against domestic partners by known male batterers (Hilton et al., 2004)
Spousal Assault Risk Assessment Guide (SARA)	Based on VRAG and ASSESS-LIST (Kropp, Hart, Webster, & Eaves, 1994).

(g) companions, (h) alcohol/drug, (i) emotional/personal, and (j) attitude/orientation. It thus utilizes both static and dynamic information. Studies of the LSI have reported adequate reliability and significant associations of LSI total scores with success or failure in institutional settings, on probation and parole, and with general recidivism among both male and female offenders (Catchpole & Gretton, 2003; Girard & Wormith, 2004; Hollin & Palmer, 2006; Kroner & Mills, 2001; Palmer & Hollin, 2007; Simourd, 2004). However, the LSI-R's associations with violent recidivism are less robust than those with general recidivism (Daffern et al., 2005; Gendreau et al., 2002). Girard and Wormith (2004) recently added a new specific/risk section to the latest "Ontario" revision of the LSI to improve its assessment of aggressive behavior.

OBJECTIVE ASSESSMENT TOOLS: ACTUARIALLY DERIVED

Whereas rationally constructed instruments try to capture the judgments of classification experts and apply them in a standard fashion, actuarial tools are derived by selecting items that previous research has shown are empirically related to the behavior in question, such as institutional misbehavior or recidivism. These "risk factors" are then combined into a predictive scheme. Some investigators use multiple regression equations or weighted discriminant functions, some use simple additive models in which points are assigned for each risk factor, and some use decision trees. These schemes seem to work best in correctional mental health facilities, which typically have more data available, including psychological evaluations, than ordinary correctional institutions. It is generally agreed that, as a group, actuarially derived objective instruments outperform those that are rationally constructed (Barbaree, Seto, Langston, & Peacock, 2001; Dawes, Faust, & Meehl, 1989; Grove & Meehl, 1996; Grove, Zald, Hallberg, Lebow, Snitz, & Nelson, 2000; Kroner et al., 2007). However, in the area of risk assessment, it appears that the best rational and actuarial devices are comparable in their validity (Grann, Belfrage, & Tengström, 2000).

The best-established actuarial instrument for the prediction of violent recidivism is the Violence Risk Appraisal Guide (VRAG; Harris et al., 1993), which was derived from a population of 618 violent offenders at a maximum-security psychiatric institution, 191 of whom (31%) engaged in further violence after their eventual release. The clinical records of these "violent failures" were combed, coded, and compared with those of the 427 violent offenders who did not subsequently engage in violent recidivism. Multivariate analyses identified 12 variables from the 50 or so studied which significantly differentiated the two criterion groups. They included three history variables (elementary school maladjustment, separation from parents before age 16, and never marrying), four clinical history variables (history of alcohol abuse, DSM-III diagnoses of schizophrenia or personality disorder, and score on the PCL-R), two overall criminal history variables (record of property offenses and prior failures on conditional release), and three factors regarding the index offense (injuries to the victim, gender of victim, and age of offender at the time of the offense). Interestingly, the PCL-R was the variable most closely related to violent recidivism. These 12 variables were differentially weighted (with the PCL-R receiving the highest weight) and combined to yield a total VRAG score which was used to assign the subjects to nine categories ranging from the lowest to the highest chance of recidivism (Harris et al., 1993).

Because the VRAG consists only of unchanging static items, Webster and Polvi (1995) created the ASSESS-LIST, a device consisting of 10 more dynamic clinical variables: antecedent history, self-presentation, social and psychosocial adjustment, expectations and plans, symptoms, supervision, life factors, institutional management, sexual adjustment, and treatment progress. Together, the VRAG and ASSESS-LIST comprise the Violence Prediction Scheme (VPS; Webster, Harris, Rice, Cormier, & Quinsey, 1994).

Actuarially derived tools should be cross-validated on new independent samples before being used, and instruments devised in one setting or locale should be checked for accuracy before they are adopted elsewhere (Craig, Beech, & Brown, 2007). The VRAG has been successfully cross-validated on new samples of serious mentally disordered offenders by its creators and independent researchers (Douglas et al., 2005; Grann et al., 2000; Harris, Rice, & Cormier, 2002; Harris et al., 1993; Kroner & Mills, 2001; Loza & Dhaliwal, 1997; Quinsey, Harris, Rice, & Cormier, 1998; Rice & Harris, 1994, 1995).

Given its reliance on psychiatric diagnoses and psychological factors involved in previous violence,

it is questionable whether the VPS could be applied in many correctional settings or to patients who have no prior history of violence.

STRUCTURED PROFESSIONAL JUDGMENT

Whether they are rationally or actuarially derived, the essence of objective assessment tools such as the LSI-R and the VRAG is that decisions regarding the risks for aggression posed by those being assessed are based entirely on the scores they obtain on the instruments or the classifications they receive from the decision tree. In "structured professional judgment" (SPJ), objective tools are used to guide clinical judgments to a greater or lesser degree (Douglas et al., 2005).

A number of SPJ instruments have been developed (Douglas et al., 2005).[5] Of these, the best known and most widely used is the rationally constructed HCR-20 (Douglas & Webster, 1999; Webster, Douglas, Eaves, & Hart, 1997). The HCR-20 is comprised of 20 records-based ratings in three categories: historical, clinical, and risk management. The ten historical (H) items are similar to the items on the VRAG. They include history of (a) previous violence, (b) young age at first violent incident, (c) relationship instability, (d) employment problems, (e) substance abuse (f), history of major mental illness, (g) psychopathy as measured by the PCL-R, (h) early maladjustment, (i) personality disorder, and (j) prior supervision failure (Douglas & Webster, 1999).

The five clinical (C) items reflecting current emotional status are (a) lack of insight, (b) negative attitudes, (c) active symptoms of major mental illness, (d) impulsivity, and (e) unresponsiveness to treatment.

The five risk management (R) items are (a) plans lacking feasibility, (b) exposure to destabilizers, (c) lack of personal support, (d) lack of compliance with remediation attempts, and (e) stress (Douglas & Webster, 1999). These dynamic C and R items, which can change to reflect a client's current situation, are the clearest difference between the HCR-20 and instruments that are based exclusively on historical or file data.

Because it is designed to guide structured clinical judgments, the HCR-20 does not have recommended cutting scores or algorithms that categorize people. Instead, it produces numerical scores on each of its three scales as well as a total score that clinicians are encouraged to consider when deciding whether people are at low, medium, or high risk of violent offending (Douglas et al., 2005). Nevertheless, a number of researchers have investigated the relationship between HCR-20 scores and various measures of institutional misconduct and recidivism as well as both sexual and nonsexual violent offending and reoffending. These studies indicate that the HCR-20 scales have areas under the curve (AUCs), correlations, and effect sizes comparable to the LSI-R, PCL-R, and VRAG (Douglas & Webster, 1999; Douglas et al., 2005; Grann et al., 2000; Kroner & Mills, 2001). In some of these studies, the static historical items have the highest relations to the criteria, in others the dynamic clinical and risk factors.

Douglas et al. (2005) also investigated how successfully the HCR-20 guided structured judgments of low, moderate, or high risk for violence. They reported that 19.1% of the low, 58.8% of the moderate, and 85.7% of the high groups were subsequently violent.

Issues in Prospective Risk Assessment

The development of objective risk assessment tools has made the prediction of aggressive behavior and violence much more accurate than was the case with the previously employed subjective appraisals (Borum, 1996; Monahan, 1996). That said, how useful are these devices in applied settings?

Clearly, there are limitations on their ability to predict dangerous behavior. First, these instruments are not specific to aggression and violence. The PCL-R assesses psychopathy, but not all psychopaths are violent and not all violent individuals are psychopathic. The HCR-20, LSI-R, and the VRAG/VPS all reflect other types of antisocial or illegal behavior such as general recidivism and insitutional misconduct as well as the aggressive or violent behavior which is the focus of this chapter.

Second, the best objective instruments, including the HCR-20, LSI-R, PCL-R, and VRAG/VPS, all require an extensive array of up-to-date information about each person being assessed including mental health data and an individual interview.[6] This limits their utility to settings with the records and resources required to rate the various items. With the exception of the LSI-R, they generally appear to have been used in clinical settings on emotionally disturbed inpatients with a history of violent behavior.

A third limitation is the fact that these devices all focus on the characteristics of those being assessed, their past behavior, demographic characteristics, emotional adjustment and the like, while ignoring the situational factors that might influence their behavior (Klassen & O'Connor, 1988; Moos, 1975). Thus

they are better able to identify habitually violent, mentally disturbed, or undercontrolled aggressive individuals than those who are overcontrolled or responding to situational provocations.

Fourth, objective instruments typically omit "protective" or ameliorative data that might mitigate the risk of aggression (Douglas et al., 2005). They typically include variables, such as prior felonies, that are associated with negative outcomes while overlooking positive factors, such as marketable employment skills or a positive family situation, which might decrease the risk of antisocial behavior.

Fifth, until proven otherwise, objective risk assessment devices, especially those that were actuarially derived, should only be used in those settings in which they were created. For example, Borum (1996, p. 994) noted that a diagnosis of schizophrenia is positively associated with violence in one model and negatively in another. He suggested the discrepancy stems from differences in the settings where the devices were developed. Kroner et al. (2007, p. 907) stated that, "traditional risk-assessment instruments might not adequately predict sexual recidivism in some offenders." They concluded that specialized instruments are required to predict sexual reoffending.

When it comes to predicting aggressive or violent behavior, it is generally agreed that these objective tools should only be applied to individuals who are at a high risk for violent offending because they have already behaved violently or threatened violence (Klassen & O'Connor, 1988; Otto, 2000), and most of the research with these instruments has been conducted in such populations (Borum, 1996; Kroner et al., 2007). The purpose of this caveat is to guarantee a sufficiently high incidence or "base rate" of violence to permit reasonably accurate prediction. The closer the incidence of aggressive behavior is to 50%, the greater the potential contribution that a predictive tool can make. However, the more infrequent the behavior, the greater the number of false positives—nonviolent individuals incorrectly labeled violent—we can expect. Indeed, when violence rates are as low as 5% or 10%, we will make more errors using an instrument with a high false-positive rate than we would by simply assuming no one will be violent (Brennan, 1993; Kamphuis & Finn, 2002; Klassen & O'Connor, 1988; Meehl & Rosen, 1955; Megargee, 1976, 1981; Wollert, 2006; see Chapter 8).

As Otto (1992, p. 128) noted, when assessing dangerousness, incorrect predictions are inevitable, the most common errors being false positives. For this reason, it is important to consider the consequences of incorrect classifications (Megargee, 1976). In Bohn's (1979) study, those prisoners labeled "potential predator" or "potential prey" based on their MMPI-based classifications were simply separated by being assigned to different dormitories. Their designations had no impact on their programming or other conditions of confinement. With such a benign outcome, Bohn could tolerate large numbers of false positives in both categories. However, in many cases, the consequences for false positives can be quite serious. For example, those diagnosed as dangerous sex offenders may be civilly committed or subjected to preventive detention over and above their criminal sentence; those released may be forced to register with the police, denied certain types of employment, and restricted with regard to where they can live (Janus, 2003; Kroner et al., 2007).

Although the emphasis in risk assessment is on diagnosing the most dangerous offenders, the greater contribution of these classification tools has been to identify low-risk individuals (true negatives) who can be placed in less secure settings or released to the community (Austin, 1993; Glaser, 1987; Solomon & Camp, 1993). When making subjective predictions of violence, assessors are often overly conservative, placing too many individuals in higher-than-necessary risk categories (Heilbrun & Heilbrun, 1995; Monahan, 1981, 1996; Proctor, 1994; Solomon & Camp, 1993). This is not surprising. There is little public concern over false positives who may be retained in overly restrictive mental health or correctional facilities, but there is an understandable outcry when a future mass murderer such as Charles Whitman or Seung-Hui Cho is assessed as not dangerous.

Reducing the extent of overclassification is especially important in criminal justice and correctional settings. First, it is the correct thing to do. The courts have consistently ruled that criminal offenders have the right to be maintained in the least restrictive settings consistent with maintaining safety, order, and discipline. Second, less restrictive settings are more economical. Confining a criminal offender in a maximum-security institution costs $3,000 a year more than a minimum-security facility and $7,000 more than a community setting. Third, all residents benefit because more programming is possible in less restrictive correctional settings, and the deleterious effects of crowding are diminished (Proctor, 1994).

Perhaps the greatest limitation on the utilization of objective risk assessment devices is the reluctance of clinicians to rely on such tools. The more complex the statistical procedures, the less likely decision makers are to use them (Brennan, 1993). In his classic paper, "Why I no longer attend case conferences," Paul Meehl (1977) lamented the tendency for clinicians to place more faith in their subjective impressions than they do in base rates or the results of objective instruments. In a recent risk assessment study, Kroner and Mills (2001) found that experienced clinicians provided with base rate data apparently ignored them when estimating the likelihood of violent offending. As a result, they did no better than a contrast group of clinicians who had no information on base rates.

Hilton and Simmons (2001) reviewed the factors associated with decisions made by the Ontario Review Board on whether mentally disordered offenders charged with serious, usually violent, offenses should be detained in maximum security. VRAG scores, which were provided to the members of the board, were not related to the eventual security-level decisions. The most important single variable was the testimony of the senior clinician, although criminal history, psychotropic medication, institutional behavior, and even the physical attractiveness of the patient also played a role. They concluded, "contrary to current optimism in the field, actuarial risk assessment had little influence on clinical judgments and tribunal decisions about mentally disordered offenders in this maximum security setting.... It is apparent ... that simply creating actuarial instruments and making the results available to decision makers does not alter long-established patterns of forensic decision making" (Hilton & Simmons, 2001, pp. 402, 406).

Notes

1. Although we have only considered human aggression, there is also a vast literature on animal aggression, which further complicates definitional issues. Because this book concerns clinical personality assessment, discussion has been limited to human aggression and violence, but readers should keep in mind that a comprehensive theory of aggressive behavior should be applicable to animal as well as human behavior.

2. Gendreau et al. (2002, p. 422) recently complained, "Is there an offender anywhere in North America who has not at some point been administered the MMPI/MMPI-2?"

3. Salekin et al. (1996, p. 211) hailed the PCL-R as being "unparalleled as a measure for making risk assessments." Gendreau et al. (2002) took umbrage at this effusive praise and took 30 journal pages to explain why the LSI-R was superior to the PCL-R. Hemphill and Hare (2004) took offense at Gendreau et al.'s (2002) criticisms and spent 41 pages explaining why the PCL-R was at least as good as the LSI-R for predicting criminal justice criteria, even though the PCL-R was designed to assess the construct of psychopathy rather than predict recidivism.

4. The issue of when or if clinicians should be able to override the objective classification has been hotly debated for over half a century beginning with Meehl's (1957) classic article, "When shall we use our heads instead of the formula?"

5. According to Douglas et al. (2005), the instruments designed for SPJ include the EARL-20B and EARL-20G, the HCR-20, the RSVP, the SARA, the SAVRY, and the SVR-20 (see Table 28.1).

6. The LSI-R and PCL-R both require interviews, and the HCR-20 and the VRAG both include the PCL-R.

References

Alexander, R. (2004). The United States Supreme Court and the civil commitment of sex offenders. *Prison Journal, 84,* 361–378.

American Association for Correctional Psychology, Standards Committee. (2000). Standards for psychological services in jails, prisons, correctional facilities, and agencies (2nd ed.). *Criminal Justice and Behavior, 27,* 433–494.

American Psychological Association. (2002). Ethical principles for psychologists and code of conduct. *American Psychologist, 57,* 1060–1073.

Anderson, C. A., & Bushman, B. J. (2002). Human aggression. *Annual Review of Psychology, 53,* 27–51.

Andrews, D. A., & Bonta, J. (1995). *The Level of Service Inventory-Revised.* Toronto, ON: Multi-Health Systems.

Ardrey, R. S. (1966). *The territorial imperative.* New York: Athenaeum.

Augimeri, L. K., Koegl, C. J., Webster, C. D., & Levene, K. S. (2001). *Early Assessment Risk List for Boys (EARL-B), Version 2.* Toronto, ON: Earl's Court Child and Family Centre.

Austin, J. (1993). Objective prison classification systems: A review. In American Correctional Association (Ed.), *Classification: A tool for managing today's offenders* (pp. 108–123). Laurel, MD: American Correctional Association.

Azrin, N. H., Hake, D. F., & Hutchinson, R. R. (1965). Elicitation of aggression by physical blows. *Journal of the Experimental Analysis of Behavior, 8,* 55–57.

Bandura, A. (1973). *Aggression: A social learning analysis.* Englewood Cliffs, NJ: Prentice-Hall.

Bandura, A., & Walters, R. H. (1963). *Social learning and personality development.* New York: Holt, Rinehart & Winston.

Barbaree, H. E., Seto, M. C., Langston, C. M., & Peacock, E. J. (2001). Evaluating the predictive accuracy of six risk assessment instruments for adult sex offenders. *Criminal Justice and Behavior, 28,* 490–521.

Baron, R. A. (1977). *Human aggression.* New York: Plenum.

Baron, R. A., & Ransberger, V. (1978). Ambient temperature and the occurrence of collective violence: The "long hot summer" revisited. *Journal of Personality and Social Psychology, 36,* 351–360.

Barone, N. (2004). Review of the Hare Psychopathy Checklist-Revised (PCL-R), 2nd edition. *Journal of Psychiatry and Law, 32,* 113–114.

Baumeister, R. F., Smart, L., & Boden, J. M. (1996). Relation of threatened egotism to violence: The dark side of self-esteem. *Psychological Review, 103,* 5–33.

Berkowitz, L. (1962). *Aggression: A social psychological analysis.* New York: McGraw-Hill.

Berkowitz, L. (1970). The contagion of violence: An S-R mediational analysis of the effects of observed aggression. *Nebraska Symposium on Motivation, 18,* 9–135.

Berkowitz, L. (1989). Frustration-aggression hypothesis: Examination and reformulation. *Psychological Bulletin, 106,* 59–73.

Berkowitz, L. (1990). On the formation and regulation of anger and aggression: A cognitive-neoassociationistic analysis. *American Psychologist, 45,* 494–503.

Berkowitz, L. (2003). Affect, aggression, and antisocial behavior. In R. J. Davidson, K. Scherer, & H. H. Goldsmith (Eds.), *Handbook of affective sciences* (pp. 804–832). New York: Oxford University Press.

Bjørkly, S. (1993). The Scale for the Prediction of Dangerousness and Aggression in Psychotic Patients: An introduction. *Psychological Reports, 73,* 1363–1377.

Bjørkly, S. (1994). The Scale for the Prediction of Dangerousness and Aggression in Psychotic Patients: A prospective pilot study. *Criminal Justice and Behavior, 21,* 341–356.

Bjørkly, S., Havik, O. E., & Løberg, T. (1996). The interrater reliability of the Scale for the Prediction of Dangerousness and Aggression in Psychotic Patients (PAD). *Criminal Justice and Behavior, 23,* 440–454.

Boer, D. P., Hart, S. D., Kropp, P. R., & Webster, C. D. (1997). *Manual for the Sexual Violence Risk-20.* Odessa, FL: Psychological Assesment Resources.

Bohn, M. J., Jr. (1979). Inmate classification and the reduction of violence. In *Proceedings of the 109th Annual Congress of Correction* (pp. 63–69). College Park, MD: American Correctional Association.

Bonta, J., & Motiuk, L. L. (1985). Utilization of an interview-based classification instrument: A study of correctional halfway houses. *Criminal Justice and Behavior, 12,* 333–352.

Borum, R. (1996). Improving the clinical practice of violence risk assessment: Technology, guidelines, and training. *American Psychologist, 51,* 945–956.

Borum, R., Bartel, P., & Forth, A. (2002). *Manual for the Structured Assessment of Violence Risk in Youth (SAVRY).* Tampa, FL: University of South Florida.

Borum, R., Fein, R., Vossekuil, B., & Berglund, J. (1999). Threat assessment: Defining an approach for evaluating risk of targeted violence. *Behavioral Sciences and the Law, 17,* 323–337.

Brennan, T. (1987). Classification: An overview of selected methodological issues. In D. M. Gottfredson & M. Tonry (Eds.), *Prediction and classification in criminal justice decision-making* (pp. 201–248). Chicago: University of Chicago Press.

Brennan, T. (1993). Risk assessment: An evaluation of statistical classification methods. In American Correctional Association (Ed.), *Classification: A tool for managing today's offenders* (pp. 46–70). Laurel, MD: American Correctional Association.

Brown, P., & Elliott, R. (1965). Control of aggression in a nursery school class. *Journal of Experimental Child Psychology, 2,* 103–107.

Buss, A. H. (1961). *The psychology of aggression.* New York: John Wiley & Sons.

Buss, A. H., & Durkee, A. (1957). An inventory for assessing different kinds of hostility. *Journal of Consulting Psychology, 21,* 343–348.

Butcher, J. N., Dahlstrom, W. G., Graham, J. R., Tellegen, A. M., & Kaemmer, B. (1989). *Minnesota Multiphasic Personality Inventory-2 (MMPI-2): Manual for administration and scoring.* Minneapolis, MN: University of Minnesota Press.

Catchpole, R. E. H., & Gretton, H. M. (2003). The predictive validity of risk assessment with violent young offenders: A 1-year examination of criminal outcomes. *Criminal Justice and Behavior, 30,* 688–708.

Chesney, M. A., & Rosenman, R. H. (Eds.). (1985). *Anger and hostility in cardiovascular and behavior disorders.* Washington, DC: Hemisphere.

Clark, J. W. (1982). *American assassins.* Princeton, NJ: Princeton University Press.

Cleckley, H. (1976). *The mask of sanity.* St. Louis, MO: C. V. Mosby (Original work published in 1941).

Cohen, D, Nisbett, R. E. Bowdle, B. F., & Schwarz, N. (1996). Insult, aggression, and the southern culture of honor: An "experimental ethnography." *Journal of Personality and Social Psychology, 70,* 945–960.

Cohen, L. E., & Felson, M. (1979). Social change and crime rate trends: A routine activity approach. *American Sociological Review, 44,* 588–608.

Cook, P. I. (1982). The role of firearms in violent crime: An interpretative review of the literature. In M. E. Wolfgang & N. A. Weiner (Eds.), *Criminal violence* (pp. 236–291). Beverly Hills, CA: Sage.

Cooper, R. P., & Werner, P. D. (1990). Predicting violence in newly admitted inmates. A lens model of staff decision making. *Criminal Justice and Behavior, 17,* 431–447.

Copas, J., & Marshall, P. (1998). The Offender Group Reconviction Scales: A statistical reconviction scale for use by probation officers. *Applied Statistics, 47,* 159–171.

Cornell, D. G., Sheras, P. L., & Cole, J. C. (2006). Assessment of bullying. In S. R. Jimerson & M. Furlong (Eds.), *Handbook of school violence and school safety: From research to practice* (pp. 191–209). Mahwah, NJ: Lawrence Erlbaum.

Costa, P. T., Jr., & McRae, R. R. (1992). *NEO-PI-R professional manual.* Odessa, FL: Psychological Assessment Resources.

Craig, L. A., Beech, A. R., & Brown, K. D. (2007). The importance of cross-validating actuarial measures. *Forensic Update, 40,* 34–39.

Cunningham, M. D., & Reidy, T. J. (1999). Don't confuse me with the facts: Common errors in risk assessment at capital sentencing. *Criminal Justice and Behavior, 26,* 20–43.

Cunningham, M. D., & Sorenson, J. R. (2006). Actuarial models for assessing prison violence risk: Revision and extension of the Risk Assessment Scale for Prison (RASP). *Assessment, 13,* 253–265.

Cunningham, M. D., Sorenson, J. R., & Reidy, T. J. (2005). An actuarial model for prison violence risk among maximum security inmates. *Assessment, 12,* 40–49.

Daffern, M., Ogloff, J. R. P., Ferguson, M., & Thomson, L. (2005). Assessing risk for aggression in a forensic psychiatric hospital using the Level of Service Inventory-Revised: Screening version. *International Journal of Forensic Mental Health, 4,* 201–206.

Dahle, K.-P. (2006). Strength and limitations of actuarial prediction of criminal reoffence in a German prison sample: A comparative study of LSI-R, HCR-20, and PCL-R. *International Journal of Law and Psychiatry, 29,* 431–442.

Dawes, R. M., Faust, D., & Meehl, P. E. (1989). Clinical versus actuarial judgment. *Science, 243,* 1668–1674.

Dollard, J., Doob, L. W., Miller, N. E., Mowrer, O. H., & Sears, R. R. (1939). *Frustration and aggression.* New Haven, CN: Yale University Press.

Dorland, M., & Krauss, D. (2005). The danger of dangerousness in capital sentencing: Exacerbating the problem of arbitrary and capricious decision-making. *Law and Psychology Review, 29,* 63–105.

Douglas, K. S., & Webster, C. D. (1999). The HCR-20 violence risk assessment scheme: Concurrent validity in a sample of incarcerated offenders. *Criminal Justice and Behavior, 26,* 3–19.

Douglas, K. S., Yeomans, M., & Boer, D. P. (2005). Comparative validity analysis of multiple measures of violence risk in a sample of criminal offenders. *Criminal Justice and Behavior, 32,* 479–510.

Edens, J. F., Buffington-Vollum, J. K., Keilen, A., Roskamp, P., & Anthony, C. (2005). Predictions of future violence in capital murder trials: Is it time to disinvent the wheel? *Law and Human Behavior, 29,* 55–86.

Epperson, D. L., Kaul, J. D., & Hesselton, D. (1998). *Final report of the development of the Minnesota Sex Offender Screening Test-Revised: MnSOST-R.* Paper presented at the 17th Annual Conference of the Association for the Treatment of Sexual Abusers, Vancouver, BC.

Feindler, E. L., & Ecton, R. B. (1986). *Adolescent anger control: Cognitive behavioral techniques.* New York: Pergamon.

Fowler, R. (1976). Sweeping reforms ordered in Alabama prisons. *APA Monitor, 7*(4), 1, 15.

Gendreau, P., Goggin, D. S., & Smith, P. (2002). Is the PCL-R really the "unparalleled" measure of offender risk? *Criminal Justice and Behavior, 29,* 397–426.

Girard, L., & Wormith, J. S. (2004). The predictive validity of the Level of Service Inventory-Ontario Revision on general and violent recidivism among various offender groups. *Criminal Justice and Behavior, 31,* 150–181.

Glaser, D. (1987). Classification for risk. In D. M. Gottfredson & M. Tonry (Eds.), *Prediction and classification in criminal justice decision making* (pp. 249–291). Chicago: University of Chicago Press.

Goldstein, A. P., & Keller, H. (1987). *Aggressive behavior: Assessment and intervention.* New York: Pergamon.

Gottfredson, D. M. (1987). Prediction and classification in criminal justice decision making. In D. M. Gottfredson & M. Tonry (Eds.), *Prediction and classification in criminal justice decision making* (pp. 1–20). Chicago: University of Chicago Press.

Gough, H. G., & Bradley, P. (1996). *CPI manual* (3rd ed.). Palo Alto, CA: Consulting Psychologists Press.

Grann, M., Belfrage, H., & Tengström, A. (2000). Actuarial assessment of risk for violence: The predictive validity of the VRAG and the historical part of the HCR-20. *Criminal Justice and Behavior, 27,* 97–114.

Grann, M., Långström, N., Tengström, A., & Kullgren, G. (1999). Psychopathy (PCL-R) predicts violent recidivism among criminal offenders with personality disorders in Sweden. *Law and Human Behavior, 23,* 205–217.

Grinberg, E. (2007). Jury convicts Mary Winkler of voluntary manslaughter in husband's shooting death. *Court Radio/TV,* June 12, 2007, 11:16 a.m. ET.

Grove, W. M., & Meehl, P. E. (1996). Comparative efficiency of informal (subjective, impressionistic) and formal (mechanical, algorithmic) prediction procedures: The clinical-statistical controversy. *Psychology, Public Policy, and the Law, 2,* 293–323.

Grove, W. M., Zald, D. H., Hallberg, A. M., Lebow, B., Snitz, E., & Nelson, C. (2000). Clinical versus mechanical judgment: A meta-analysis. *Psychological Assessment, 12,* 19–30.

Hanson, R. K. (1997). *Development of a brief scale for sexual offender recidivism.* Ottawa, ON: Public Works and Government Services of Canada.

Hanson, R. K., & Thornton, D. (1999). *STATIC-99: Improving actuarial risk assessments for adult sex offenders.* User report 1999–2002. Ottawa, ON: Department of the Solicitor General of Canada.

Hare, R. D. (2003). *The Hare Psychopathy Checklist-Revised (PCL-R)*. Toronto, Canada: Multi-Health Systems.

Hare, R. D., Harpur, T. J., Hakstian, A. R., Forth, A. E., Hart, S. D., & Newman, J. P. (1990). The Revised Psychopathy Checklist: Reliability and factor structure. *Psychological Assessment: A Journal of Consulting and Clinical Psychology, 2,* 338–341.

Harris, G. T., Rice, M. E., & Cormier, C. A. (2002). Prospective replication of the Violence Risk Appraisal Guide in predicting violent recidivism among forensic patients. *Law and Human Behavior, 26,* 377–394.

Harris, G. T., Rice, M. E., & Quinsey, V. L. (1993). Violent recidivism of mentally disordered offenders: The development of a statistical prediction instrument. *Criminal Justice and Behavior, 20,* 315–335.

Hart, S. D. (1996). Psychopathy and risk assessment. In D. J. Cooke, A. E. Forth, J. Newman, & R. D. Hare (Eds.), *International perspectives on psychopathy, Issues in criminological and legal psychology* (Vol. 24, pp. 63–67). Leicester, UK: The British Psychological Society, Division of Criminological and Legal Psychology.

Hart, S. D., Hare, R. D., & Forth, A. E. (1994). Psychopathy as a risk marker for violence: Development and validation of a screening version of the revised Psychopathy Checklist. In J. Monahan & H. Steadman (Eds.), *Violence and mental disorder: Developments in risk assessment* (pp. 81–98). Chicago: University of Chicago Press.

Hart, S. D., Kropp, R., Laws, D. R., Klaver, J., Logan, C., & Watt, K. (2003). *The Risk for Sexual Violence Protocol (RSVP)—Structured professional guidelines for assessing risk of sexual violence.* Burnaby, BC: Simon Fraser University Mental Health, Law and Policy Institute.

Hartshorne, H., & May, M. A. (1928). *Studies in the nature of character, Vol. 1: Studies in deceit.* New York: Macmillan.

Hartshorne, H., & May, M. A. (1929). *Studies in the nature of character, Vol. 2: Studies in service and self control.* New York: Macmillan.

Hawthorne, G., Mouthaan, J., Forbes, D., & Novaco, R. W. (2006). Response categories and anger management: Do fewer categories result in poorer measurement? *Social Psychiatry and Psychiatric Epidemiology, 41*(2), 164–172.

Healy, R. (2007, April 18). Echoes of Columbine. *Time.com.* http://www.time.com/time/nation/article/0,8599,1612346, 00.html

Heilbrun, K., & Heilbrun, A. B. (1995). Risk assessment with the MMPI-2 in forensic evaluations. In Y. S. Ben-Porath, J. R. Graham, G. C. N. Hall, R. D. Hirschman, & M. S. Zaragoza (Eds.), *Forensic applications of MMPI-2* (pp. 127–159). Thousand Oaks, CA: Sage.

Hemphill, J. F., & Hare, R. D. (2004). Some misconceptions about the Hare PCL-R and risk assessment: A reply to Gendreau, Goggin, & Smith. *Criminal Justice and Behavior, 31,* 203–243.

Hilton, N. Z., Harris, G. T., Rice, M. E., Lang, C., Cormier, C. A., & Lines, K. J. (2004). A brief actuarial instrument for the prediction of wife assault recidivsim: The Ontario Domestic Assault Risk Assessment. *Psychological Assessment, 16,* 267–275.

Hilton, N. Z., & Simmons, J. L. (2001). The influence of actuarial risk assessment in clinical judgments and tribunal decisions about mentally disordered offenders in maximum security. *Law and Human Behavior, 25,* 393–408.

Hogan, J., & Ones, D. S. (1997). Conscientiousness and integrity at work. In S. R. Briggs, R. Hogan, & W. H. Jones (Eds.), *Handbook of personality psychology* (pp. 849–870). New York: Academic Press.

Hoge, R., & Andrews, D. (2002). *The Youth Level of Service/Case Management Inventory.* Toronto, ON: Multi-Health Systems.

Hokanson, J. (1970). Psychophysiological evaluation of the catharsis hypothesis. In E. I. Megargee & J. E. Hokanson (Eds.), *The dynamics of aggression* (pp. 74–86). New York: Harper & Row.

Hollin, C. R., & Palmer, E. J. (2006). The Level of Service Inventory-Revised profile of English prisoners: Risk and reconviction analysis. *Criminal Justice and Behavior, 33,* 347–366.

Huesmann, L. R. (1986). Psychological processes promoting the relation between exposure to media violence and aggressive behavior by the viewer. *Journal of Social Issues, 42,* 125–140.

Huesmann, L. R. (1998). The role of social information processing and cognitive schema in the acquisition and maintenance of habitual aggressive behavior. In R. G. Geen & E. Donnerstein (Eds.), *Human aggression: Theories, research, and implications for policy* (pp. 73–109). New York: Academic Press.

Huesmann, L. R., & Eron, L. D. (1986). *Television and the aggressive child: A cross-national comparison.* Hillsdale, NJ: Lawrence Erlbaum.

Infoplease.com. (2007). Time line of recent worldwide school shootings. *Information Please* online almanac. Pearson Education, June 29, 2007.

Janus, E. S. (2003). Legislative responses to sexual violence: An overview. *Annals of New York Academy of Sciences, 989,* 247–264.

Jimerson, S. R., & Furlong, M. (Eds.) (2006). *Handbook of school violence and school safety: From research to practice.* Mahwah, NJ: Lawrence Erlbaum.

Johnson, R. N. (1972). *Aggression in man and animals.* Philadelphia: W. B. Saunders.

Kamphuis, J. H., & Finn, S. E. (2002). Incorporating base rate information in daily clinical decision making. In J. N. Butcher (Ed.), *Clinical personality asessessment: Practical approaches* (2nd ed., pp. 257–268). New York: Oxford University Press.

Kane, P. R. (1993). Classification: Its central role in managing the Federal Bureau of Prisons. In American Correctional Association (Ed.), *Classification: A tool for managing today's offenders* (pp. 124–134). Laurel, MD: American Correctional Association.

Klassen, D., & O'Connor, W. A. (1988). A prospective study of predictors of violence in adult male mental patients. *Law and Human Behavior, 12,* 143–158.

Korn, M. L., Botsis, A. J., Kotler, M., Plutchik, R., et al. (2006). The Suicide and Aggression Survey: A semistructured instrument for the measurement of suicidality and aggression. *Comprehensive Psychiatry, 33,* 359–365.

Kozol, H., Boucher, R., & Garafalo, R. (1972). The diagnosis and treatment of dangerousness. *Crime and Delinquency, 18,* 371–392.

Kroner, D. G., & Mills, J. F. (2001). The accuracy of five risk appraisal instruments in predicting institutional misconduct and new convictions. *Criminal Justice and Behavior, 28,* 471–479.

Kroner, D. G., Mills, J. F., Reitzel, L. R., Dow, E., Aufderheide, D., & Railey, M. G. (2007). Directions for violence and sexual risk assessment in correctional psychology. *Criminal Justice and Behavior, 34,* 906–918.

Kropp, P. R., Hart, S. D., Webster, C. D., & Eaves, D. (1994). *Manual for the Spousal Assault Risk Assessment Guide.* Vancouver, BC: Canada Institute on Family Violence.

Levene, K. S., Augimeri, L. K., Pepler, D. J., Walsh, M. M., Webster, C. D., & Koegl, C. J. (2001). *Early Assessment Risk List for Girls (EARL-G), Version 2.* Toronto, ON: Earl's Court Child and Family Centre.

Loza, W., & Dhaliwal, G., (1997). Psychometric evaluation of the Risk Appraisal Guide (RAG): A tool for assessing violent recidivism. *Journal of Interpersonal Violence, 12,* 779–793.

Loza, W., Dhaliwal, G., Kroner, D., & Loza-Fanous, A. (2000). Reliability, construct and concurrent validities of the Self Appraisal Questionnaire. *Criminal Justice and Behavior, 27,* 356–374.

Loza, W., & Loza-Fanous, A. (2003). More evidence for the validity of the Self-Appraisal Questionnaire for predicting violent and non-violent recidivism. *Criminal Justice and Behavior, 30,* 709–721.

MacDonald, J. (1975). *Armed robbery: Offenders and their victims.* Springfield, IL: Charles C. Thomas.

McGuire, J. S., & Megargee, E. I. (1976, September). Prediction of dangerous and disruptive behavior in a federal institution for youthful offenders. In C. S. Moss (Chair), *Objective studies on violence in correctional settings.* Symposium presented at the meeting of the American Psychological Association, Washington, DC.

McNiel, D. E. (1988). Empirically based evaluation and management of the potentially violent patient. In P. K. Kleespie (Ed.), *Emergencies in mental health practice: Evaluation and management* (pp. 95–116). New York: Guilford.

McNiel, D. E., & Binder, R. L. (1994). Screening for risk of inpatient violence: Validation of an actuarial tool. *Law and Human Behavior, 18,* 579–586.

Meehl, P. E. (1957). When shall we use our heads instead of the formula? *Journal of Counseling Psychology, 4,* 268–273.

Meehl, P. E. (1977). Why I do not attend case conferences. In *Psychodiagnosis: Selected papers* (pp. 255–302). New York: Norton.

Meehl, P. E., & Rosen, A. (1955). Antecedent probability and the efficiency of certain psychometric signs, patterns, and cutting scores. *Psychological Bulletin, 52,* 194–216.

Megargee, E. I. (1966). Undercontrolled and overcontrolled personality types in extreme antisocial aggression. *Psychological Monographs, 80* (3, whole No. 611).

Megargee, E. I. (1972). *The California Psychological Inventory handbook.* San Francisco: Jossey-Bass.

Megargee, E. I. (1976). The prediction of dangerous behavior. *Criminal Justice and Behavior, 3,* 3–22.

Megargee, E. I. (1977). The association of population density, reduced space and uncomfortable temperatures with misconduct in a prison community. *American Journal of Community Psychology, 5,* 289–298.

Megargee, E. I. (1981). Methodological problems in the prediction of violence. In J. R. Hays, T. K. Roberts, & K. S. Solway (Eds.), *Violence and the violent individual* (pp. 179–191). New York: S. P. Scientific and Medical Books.

Megargee, E. I. (1982). Psychological correlates and determinants of criminal violence. In M. Wolfgang & N. Wiener (Eds.), *Criminal violence* (pp. 81–170). Beverly Hills, CA: Sage.

Megargee, E. I. (1993). Aggression and violence. In H. Adams & P. Sutker (Eds.), *Comprehensive handbook of psychopathology* (2nd ed., pp. 617–644). New York: Plenum.

Megargee, E. I. (1997). Internal inhibitions and controls. In S. R. Briggs, R. Hogan, & W. H. Jones (Eds.), *Handbook of personality psychology* (pp. 581–614). New York: Academic Press.

Megargee, E. I. (2003). Psychological assessment in correctional settings. In J. R. Graham & J. A. Naglieri (Eds.), *Handbook of psychology, Vol. 10: Assessment psychology* (pp. 365–388). New York: John Wiley & Sons.

Megargee, E. I. (2006a). Using the MMPI-2 in correctional settings. In J. N. Butcher (Ed.), *MMPI-2: A handbook for practitioners* (pp. 327–360). Washington, DC: American Psychological Association.

Megargee, E. I. (2006b). *Using the MMPI-2 in criminal justice and correctional settings: An empirical approach.* Minneapolis, MN: University of Minnesota Press.

Megargee, E. I., Bohn, M. J., Jr., Meyer, J., Jr., & Sink, F. (1979). *Classifying criminal offenders: A new system based on the MMPI.* Beverly Hills, CA: Sage.

Megargee, E. I., & Carbonell, J. L. (1995). Use of the MMPI-2 in correctional settings. In Y. S. Ben-Porath, J. R. Graham, G. C. N. Hall, R. D. Hirschman, & M. S. Zaragoza (Eds.), *Forensic applications of MMPI-2* (pp. 127–159). Thousand Oaks, CA: Sage.

Megargee, E. I., Carbonell, J. L., Bohn, M., & Sliger, G. L. (2001). *Classifying criminal offenders with MMPI-2: The Megargee system.* Minneapolis, MN: University of Minnesota Press.

Megargee, E. I., Cook, P. E., & Mendelsohn, G. A. (1967). Development and validation of an MMPI scale of assaultiveness in overcontrolled individuals. *Journal of Abnormal Psychology, 72,* 519–528.

Megargee, E. I., & Mendelsohn, G. A. (1962). A cross-validation of 12 MMPI indices of hostility and control. *Journal of Abnormal and Social Psychology, 65,* 431–438.

Meloy, J. R., & Gacono, C. (1995). Assessing the psychopathic personality. In J. N. Butcher (Ed.), *Clinical personality assessment: Practical approaches* (2nd ed., pp. 410–422). New York: Oxford University Press.

Mercado, C. C., & Ogloff, J. R. P. (2007). Risk and the preventive detention of sex offenders in Australia and the United States. *International Journal of Law and Psychiatry, 30,* 49–59.

Monahan, J. (Ed.) (1972). *Who is the client? The ethics of psychological intervention in the criminal justice system.* Washington, DC: American Psychological Association.

Monahan, J. (1981). *The clinical prediction of violent behavior.* Rockville, MD: National Institute of Mental Health.

Monahan, J. (1996). Violence prediction: The past twenty years. *Criminal Justice and Behavior, 23,* 107–120.

Monahan, J., & Klassen, D. (1982). Situational approaches to understanding and predicting criminal violence. In M. Wolfgang & N. Wiener (Eds.), *Criminal violence* (pp. 292–319). Beverly Hills, CA: Sage.

Monahan, J., Steadman, H. J., Applebaum, P. S., Grisso, T., Mulvey, E. P., Roth, L. H., et al. (2006). The classification of violence risk. *Behavioral Science and the Law, 24,* 721–730.

Monahan, J., Steadman, H. J., Robbins, P. C. Applebaum, P., Banks, S., Grisso, T., et al. (2005). An actuarial model of risk assessment for persons with mental disorders. *Psychiatric Services, 56,* 810–815.

Moos, R. H. (1975). *Evaluating correctional and community settings.* New York: John Wiley & Sons.

Nagin, D. S. (2007). Moving choice to center stage in criminological research and theory: The American Society of Criminology 2006 Sutherland Award address. *Criminology, 45*, 259–272.

Newman, O. (1972). *Defensible space*. New York: Macmillan.

Nicholls, T. L., Brink, J., Desmarais, S. L., Webster, C. D., & Martin, M. (2006). The Short-Term Assessment of Risk and Treatability (START): A prospective validation in a forensic psychiatric sample. *Assessment, 13*, 313–327.

Novaco, R. W. (1975). *Anger control: The development and evaluation of an experimental treatment*. Lexington, MA: D.C. Heath.

Novaco, R. W. (1988). Novaco Provocation Inventory. In M. Hersen & A. S. Bellack (Eds.), *Dictionary of behavioral assessment techniques* (pp. 315–317). New York: Pergamon.

Novaco, R. W. (1991). Aggression on roadways. In R. Baenniger (Ed.), *Targets of violence and aggression* (pp. 257–306). Hillsdale, NJ: Lawrence Erlbaum.

Novaco, R. W. (1994). Anger as a risk factor for violence among the mentally disordered. In J. Monahan & H. J. Steadman (Eds.), *Violence and mental disorder: Developments in risk assessment* (pp. 21–58). Chicago: University of Chicago Press.

Novaco, R. W. (2003). *The Novaco Anger Scale and Provocation Inventory (NAS-PI)*. Los Angeles: Western Psychological Services.

Novaco, R. W., & Taylor, J. L. (2004). Assessment of anger and aggression in male offenders with developmental disabilities. *Psychological Assessment, 16*, 42–50.

Otto, R. (1992). The prediction of dangerous behavior: A review and analysis of "second generation" research. *Forensic Reports, 5*, 103–133.

Otto, R. (2000). Assessing and managing violence risk in outpatient settings. *Journal of Clinical Psychology, 56*, 1239–1262.

Palmer, E. J., & Hollin, C. (2007). The level of service inventory-revised with English women offenders. *Criminal Justice and Behavior, 34*, 971–984.

Peter, L. J. (1977). *Peter's quotations: Ideas for our time*. New York: William Morrow.

Pope, K. S., Butcher, J. N., & Seelen, J. (2006). *MMPI/MMPI-2/MMPI-A in court: A practical guide for expert witnesses and attorneys* (3rd ed.) Washington, DC: American Psychological Association.

Proctor, J. L. (1994). Evaluating a modified version of the federal prison system's inmate classification model: An assessment of objectivity and predictive validity. *Criminal Justice and Behavior, 21*, 256–272.

Quinsey, V. L., Harris, G. T., Rice, M. E., & Cormier, C. A., (1998). *Violent offenders: Appraisals and managing risks*. Washington, DC: American Psychological Association.

Rice, M. E., & Harris, G. T. (1994). *The actuarial prediction of violent recidivism among sex offenders*. Paper presented at the Conference on the Assesment and Management of Risk in the Sex Offender, Clarke Institute of Psychiatry, Toronto, ON, May 1994.

Rice, M. E., & Harris, G. T. (1995). Violent recidivism: Assessing predictive validity. *Journal of Consulting and Clinical Psychology, 63*, 737–748.

Rice, M. E., & Harris, G. T. (1997). Cross-validation and extension of the Violence Risk Appraisal Guide for child molesters and rapists. *Law and Human Behavior, 21*, 231–241.

Rose, A., & Feshbach, N. (1990). *Empathy and aggression revisited: The effects of context*. Paper presented at the IXth Biennial World Meeting of the International Society for Research on Aggression, Banff, AB, June 1990.

Russell, G. W. (1983). Crowd size and density in relation to athletic aggression and performance. *Social Behavior and Personality, 11*, 9–15.

Salekin, R. T., Rogers, R., & Sewell, K. W. (1996). A review and meta-analysis of the Psychopathy Checklist and Psychoapthy Checklist-Revised: Predictive validity of dangerousness. *Clinical Psychology: Science and Practice, 3*, 203–205.

Schlager, M. D., & Simourd, D. J. (2007). Validity of the Level of Service Inventory-Revised (LSI-R) among African American and Hispanic male offenders. *Criminal Justice and Behavior, 34*, 545–554.

Simourd, D. J. (2004). Use of dynamic risk/need assessment instruments among long-term incarcerated offenders. *Criminal Justice and Behavior, 31*, 306–323.

Solomon, L., & Camp, A. T. (1993). The revolution in correctional classification. In American Correctional Association (Ed.), *Classification: A tool for managing today's offenders* (pp. 1–16). Laurel, MD: American Correctional Association.

Spielberger, C. D. (1996). *State-Trait Anger Expression Inventory: STAXI professional manual*. Odessa, FL.: Psychological Assessment Resources.

Steadman, H., & Cocozza, J. (1974). *Careers of the criminally insane*. Lexington, MA: D.C. Heath.

Tawfeeq, M., & Todd, B. (2007). Four arrested in Iraq honor killing.*CNN.com, Int. ed.* May 21, 2007, 12:30 p.m.

Towl, G., & Crighton, D. (1995). Risk assessment in prison: A psychological critique. *Forensic Update, 40*, 6–14.

Vossekuil, B., Fein, R. A., Reddy, M., Borum, R., & Modzeleski, W. (2002). *The final report and findings of the Safe School Initiative: Implications for the prevention of school attacks in the United States*. Washington, DC: U.S. Secret Service and U. S. Department of Education.

Walters, G. D., White, T. W., & Denney, D. (1991). The Lifestyle Criminality Screening Form. *Criminal Justice and Behavior, 18*, 406–418.

Webster, C. D., Douglas, K. S., Eaves, D., & Hart, S. D. (1997). *HCR-20: Assessing risk for violence, Version 2*. Burnaby, BC: Mental Health, Law, & Policy Institute, Simon Frazier University.

Webster, C. D., Harris, G. T., Rice, M. E., Cormier, C., & Quinsey, V. L. (1994). *The Violence Prediction Scheme: Assessing dangerousness in high risk men*. Toronto, ON: University of Toronto.

Webster, C. D., & Menzies, R. J. (1993). Supervision in the deinstitutionalized community. In S. Hodgins (Ed.), *Mental disorder and crime* (pp. 22–38). Newbury Park, CA: Sage.

Webster, C. D., Nicholls, T., Martin, M., Desmarais, S. L., & Brink, J. (2006). The Short-Term Assessment of Risk and Treatability (START): The case for a new structured professional judgment scheme. *Behavioral Science and the Law, 24*, 747–766.

Webster, C. D., & Polvi, N. H. (1995). Challenging assessments of dangerousness and risk. In J. Ziskind (Ed.), *Coping with psychiatric and psychological testimony* (pp. 221–240). Marina del Rey, CA: Law and Psychology Press.

Wolfgang, M. (1958). *Patterns of criminal homicide*. Philadelphia: Unversity of Pennsylvania Press.

Wollert, R. (2006). Low base rates limit expert certainty when current actuarials are used to identify sexually violent predators: An application of Bayes's theorem. *Psychology, Public Policy, and the Law, 12*, 56–85.

Wong, S. C. P., & Gordon, A. (2006). The validity and reliability of the Violence Risk Scale: A treatment-friendly violence risk assessment tool. *Psychology, Public Policy, and the Law, 12*, 279–309.

Worling, J. R., & Curwen, T. (2001). *The "ERASOR": Estimate of Risk of Adolescent Sexual Offense Recidivism, Version 2.* Toronto, ON: SAFE T Program, Thistletown Regional Centre.

Assessing Antisocial and Psychopathic Personalities

Carl B. Gacono *and* J. Reid Meloy

Abstract

The assessment of antisocial and psychopathic personalities presents special challenges for the forensic evaluator. This chapter emphasizes use of the Hare Psychopathy Checklist-Revised (PCL-R), Rorschach, and Minnesota Multiphasic Personality Inventory (MMPI) for a comprehensive evaluation of these patients. These measures lend incremental validity to understanding these difficult patients, especially when combined with testing of intelligence and cognitive functioning. Integrating data from multiple domains is essential to answering the psycholegal and forensic treatment questions surrounding the antisocial and psychopathic patient. The forensically trained clinical psychologist is best suited to assess psychopathy, a task that historically has been overlooked or avoided in traditional mental health settings.

Keywords: antisocial, forensic evaluation, psychopathy, PCL-R, Rorschach, MMPI

Understanding that antisocial personality disorder and psychopathy are distinct but related constructs is crucial to clinical and forensic assessment of these patients. While antisocial personality disorder (ASPD; DSM-IV; American Psychiatric Association [APA], 1994, 2000) evolved from a social deviancy model (Robins, 1966) and the term sociopathy (DSM; American Psychiatric Association (APA), 1952),[1] the construct of psychopathy can be traced to the more traditional psychiatric conceptualizations originating in late nineteenth-century Germany (Cleckley, 1976). ASPD criteria are primarily *behavioral,* while psychopathy criteria include both *behaviors and traits* that significantly overlap with most of the DSM-IV Cluster B syndromes (narcissistic, histrionic, borderline, and antisocial personality disorders; Gacono, Nieberding, Owen, Rubel, & Bodholdt, 2001). A clinician arrives at a diagnosis of ASPD by verifying that the patient meets specific criteria outlined in the DSM-IV-TR (APA, 2000), which include (a) a pervasive pattern of disregard for and violation of the rights of others since age 15; (b) a history of conduct disorder prior to the age of 15; and, (c) age 18 or older. In contrast, the diagnosis of

psychopathy requires a formal assessment with the Psychopathy Checklist-Revised (PCL-R; Hare, 1991, 2003) that typically involves a review of collateral information and a semistructured interview (Gacono, 2005).

Two additional findings support the need to differentiate between these terms. First, base rates for ASPD and psychopathy are not the same. Although most psychopathic subjects will meet criteria for ASPD, at most one-third of ASPD samples in maximum-security prisons will meet the PCL-R criteria for "psychopathy" (Hare, 1991, 2003). The clinical importance of this fact can be stated differently. Most ASPD adults, male or female, are not psychopathic and will not meet the factor analytic definition of this construct, in particular the personal qualities and behavior characterized by a callous and remorseless disregard for the rights and feelings of others and a chronic antisocial lifestyle (Hare, 1991, 2003).

Second, an ASPD diagnosis provides far less predictive utility in clinical/forensic decision making than PCL-R scoring (Hare, 2003; Lyon & Ogloff, 2000). An impressive body of literature (see Hare, 2003) has demonstrated that, when compared with low scorers, prisoners with high PCL-R scores

- commit a greater quantity and variety of offenses (Hare & Jutai, 1983);
- commit a greater frequency of violent offenses in which predatory violence (Meloy, 1988, 2006) is used against male strangers (Hare & McPherson, 1984; Williamson, Hare, & Wong, 1987);
- have lengthier criminal careers (Hare, McPherson, & Forth, 1988);
- have a poorer response to therapeutic intervention (Ogloff, Wong, & Greenwood, 1990), which, in some cases, may be followed by an increase in their subsequent arrest rates for violent crimes (Rice, Harris, & Cormier, 1992); and
- are at high risk for problematic and disruptive behavior while in treatment (Gacono, Meloy, Sheppard, Speth, & Roske, 1995; Gacono, Meloy, Speth, & Roske, 1997; Young, Justice, Erdberg, & Gacono, 2000).

Additionally, PCL-R item analysis provides valuable information for treatment planning with offenders (Gacono, 1998; Gacono, Jumes, & Grey, 2008). These robust findings make psychopathy assessment a useful, and in some cases essential, tool for clinical/forensic examiners evaluating antisocial and/or psychopathic patients (Gacono & Bodholdt, 2001; Gacono, Loving, Evans, & Jumes, 2002).

Forensic Assessment and Issues

In all cases the forensic psychologist, as *evaluator* rather than *therapist*, is performing an *investigation* to gather data. He is not an agent of change. Confusion between these two fundamentally different roles may lead to misuse of information and unethical behavior (Meloy, 1989; Goldstein, 2007). The psychologist must have a clear conception of his or her role before the assessment begins.

The psychologist must also consider that psychopathic individuals are chronically deceptive and will lie to and mislead the assessor at every turn. Deceptive behaviors often include projection of blame, malingering or exaggeration of psychiatric symptoms, and/or conscious denial: all important behaviors to be noted as part of the assessment process (Kosson, Gacono, & Bodholdt, 2000). The goal of the psychopathic patient, and to a lesser degree the nonpsychopathic antisocial patient, is usually to gain a more dominant or pleasurable position in relation to his objects, whether a person, an institution, or legal proceeding (Meloy, 1988, 2001).

The forensic psychologist must always *evaluate the validity all data, particularly unsubstantiated self-reports, obtained from antisocial and psychopathic patients.* Gathering data from three different sources—face-to-face interviews, independent historical information, and testing—aids the evaluator in addressing potential deception and combines to form the foundation of the evaluation (Meloy, 1989). *Interviewing* involves a face-to-face contact with the individual long enough to complete a mental status exam, assess specifically targeted areas (malingering, psychopathy level, and so forth), and gather self-reported problems and historical data. Additionally, face-to-face interviewing may provide the interviewer with adumbrations of possible transference and countertransference reactions, which in turn may inform or "flesh out" the interpersonal section of the evaluation (Kosson et al., 2000). Independent *historical or contemporaneous information* refers to any data that are not self-reported by the examinee, and includes such things as other psychiatric and psychological records, medical records, school and military records, employment records, criminal records, and interviews with historical and contemporary observers of the examinee (parents, siblings, legal, and health care professionals). *Testing* refers to psychological, neuropsychological, and medical tests, historical or contemporary, that provide objective reference points to further understand the psychology or psychobiology of the examinee. All three sources of information are necessary when assessing antisocial and psychopathic patients.

When evaluating antisocial and psychopathic patients, the psychologist must have a clear understanding of his or her purpose for assessing psychopathy level or the presence or absence of a psychopathic syndrome. The need to "assess" psychopathy varies with the nature of the setting and the function of the evaluation (Bodholdt, Richards, & Gacono, 2000; Gacono, 2000a; Gacono, Loving, & Bodholdt, 2001; Gacono, Loving et al., 2002). For example, prior to sentencing the psychologist is usually called upon to aid the trier of fact, the judge or jury, in answering a psycholegal question, such as intent, motivation, dangerousness, or sanity. Subsequent to institutional commitment, referral questions stem from institutional concerns and may involve severity of antisocial personality disorder, malingering, treatment amenability or planning, sanity, violence risk, threat management, sadism, sexual sadism, recommendation for outpatient treatment, and other issues related to diagnosis, treatment, or risk management (Bodholdt et al, 2000; Gacono, 1998, 2000a; Gacono, Jumes et al., 2008).

Having clarified the psycholegal issue and context of the evaluation, the forensic psychologist will next have to determine what historical and personality information is needed to address the referral issues and which methods are most efficacious in obtaining the desired information. With this in mind, Monahan and Steadman's (1994) risk assessment model provides a useful guide for matching appropriate assessment domains and methods (Gacono, 2002). Monahan et al. (2001) emphasized gathering data from four primary domains that included dispositional factors, clinical or psychopathological factors, historical or case history variables, and contextual factors. The psychologist determines which domains are relevant to the referral question and then chooses reliable and valid methods and/or instruments for obtaining data from each (Acklin, 2002; Beutler, Harwood, & Holaway, 2002; Weiner, 2002). Results are subsequently integrated into opinions that address the referral question.

Key forensic issues essential for the forensic psychologist assessing antisocial and psychopathic patients include:

• Be clear as to one's professional role and the referral question
• Be skeptical and evaluate the validity of all data (particularly self-report)
• Gather data from multiple sources and always include collateral information
• Have a clear rationale for assessing psychopathy level
• Have a clear rationale for choosing assessment methods

In this chapter we focus on several methods and instruments, such as the PCL-R (Hare, 1991, 2003), Rorschach, and Minnesota Multiphasic Personality Inventory-2 (MMPI-2), that are of considerable value when assessing antisocial and psychopathic patients.

The Psychopathy Checklist-Revised

With specialized experience and training, the forensic evaluation of psychopathy is relatively straightforward (Gacono, 2000a, b; Gacono & Hutton, 1994; Hare, 1991). The only published reliable and valid method to date for arriving at a psychopathic "designation (taxon)" with adult patients is the PCL-R (Hare, 1991, 2003).[2] The PCL-R is a 20-item, 40-point scale completed following a review of independent historical and contemporaneous data and completion of a semistructured interview (see Gacono, 2005). Additional psychological testing is not necessary to determine a patient's psychopathy level or to arrive at a designation of psychopathy.

A growing body of research has demonstrated the PCL-R's reliability and validity for prison and forensic psychiatric populations (Hare, 2003). Psychologists may be called upon to demonstrate their knowledge of PCL-R reliability and validity studies, the demographics of these studies, validation groups, normative scores with male, female, and delinquent incarcerated samples, criticism of the test and its psychometric properties, and clear and simple explanations of the test to the trier of fact, judge or jury (Gacono et al., 2002a). Several caveats are essential to these ends (see Gacono, 2000; Gacono & Gacono, 2006). First, it is very important to remember that the lay person may misconstrue the terms antisocial, psychopathic, and sociopathic as synonymous, essentially describing a bad person for whom they have little empathy and less compassion. Psychologists must be able to educate the court concerning the relevance of these distinctions. Second, methodological issues, such as the use of lowered PCL-R cutoffs or use of an instrument other than the PCL-R for designating psychopathy groups, severely impact the generalizability of studies and make cross-study comparisons problematic (Gacono & Gacono, 2006; Gacono, Nieberding et al., 2001). The most glaring, and unfortunately too frequently occurring, problem occurs when inferences are formed about psychopathy from samples that contain no primary or severe psychopaths. Given multiple problems in the published literature, what at first appear to be discrepant research findings are easily explained as artifacts of the divergent methodologies (Gacono & Gacono, 2006; Gacono, Nieberding et al., 2001).

Finally, it is essential to understand that "psychopathy" is used as both a categorical (PCL-R $\geq$ 30) and a dimensional construct (Gacono & Gacono, 2006). Categorical designations are appropriate and preferred for comparative research when the concern is how psychopaths (PCL-R $\geq$ 30) nomothetically differ from nonpsychopaths (PCL-R $<$ 30). Dimensional uses are idiographically favored in the vast majority of clinical/forensic settings (Bodholdt et al., 2000). In these contexts, psychopathy is conceptualized on a continuum, such that individuals who obtain moderate or high PCL-R scores exhibit more serious and pervasive behavioral problems than those with lower PCL-R scores. One is more clinically interested in finding out the psychopathy ranges and scores that are best at predicting behavior in a given setting, than whether or not a given individual's score meets the traditional threshold for a designation of psychopathy (PCL-R ≥ 30; also see Quinsey, Harris, Rice, & Cormier, 1998). Psychopathy level or degree (dimensional) rather than a "diagnosis" of psychopathy (categorical) becomes one of several weighted factors in clinical and forensic decision making (Gacono, Nieberding et al., 2001; Gacono, Loving et al., 2002).

Several key issues related to PCL-R administration and scoring are also worth highlighting (Gacono, 2000a). Prior to administering the psychopathy checklists, the following should be ensured:

• The evaluator is a licensed mental health professional with forensic experience (the exception to this is the P-SCAN, a nonclinical measure of psychopathy developed for law enforcement)
• The evaluator has participated in adequate training which has included his or her demonstrated ability to reliably score the instrument (see Bodholdt et al., 2000; Kosson et al., 2000)
• The evaluator is familiar with the current psychopathy research (Patrick, 2006)
• The patient is similar to a sample upon which the instrument has been validated
• There is available independent historical information
• Collateral information is always reviewed before the interview (Gacono, 2000a)

The examiner establishes a mind set for conducting the interview, geared toward reducing scoring bias and halo effects (Gacono, 2000a). Throughout the PCL-R administration process the following should be foremost in the evaluator's mind:

• Conduct the PCL-R interview as a separate part of the overall psychological evaluation
• Use a semistructured interview schedule, such as the Clinical and Forensic Interview Schedule for the Hare Psychopathy Checklist-Revised and Screening version (CFIS; Gacono, 2000c, 2005),[3] to aid in systematically recording essential information and facilitating the development of rapport with, and a sense of empathy for, the patient
• Rate items based on lifelong patterns and typical functioning

• Focus on scoring each item separately; avoid letting speculation about the total score influence individual item scoring (confirmatory bias)
• Avoid introspection about etiology or preconceived notions of psychopathy
• Frequently refer directly to the PCL-R Rating Booklet (Hare, 2003) to maintain the scoring prototype (Gacono, 2000a)

Additionally, when testifying, the evaluator should be prepared to provide evidence concerning his qualifications and training, the appropriateness of the instruments used with this particular patient or defendant (normative samples), the adequacy of collateral information available for scoring, and the rationale for arriving at conclusions (Gacono, Loving et al., 2002).

Since the term *psychopathy* is not an official diagnostic label, it is recommended that it be defined as a constellation of behaviors and traits (Bodholdt et al., 2000; Meloy & Gacono, 2000). Most criminal psychopaths meet the criteria for ASPD and should be diagnosed as such, but some will not be. The severity of the ASPD diagnosis can be determined by the patient's PCL-R score, with ranges designating the ASPD diagnosis as mild (≤19), moderate (20–29), or severe (≥30) (Meloy, 1988, 1992). This parallels what is used in the DSM-IV diagnosis of conduct disorder. Since the ASPD criteria are primarily behavioral, the use of secondary, more trait-based, Axis II diagnoses allows the clinician to more accurately reflect the patient's personality. Additionally, research has demonstrated that PCL-R Factor I items correlate with narcissistic and histrionic personality disorders (NPD and HPD, respectively) and Factor II correlates more strongly with ASPD. Consequently, a patient who is diagnosed with ASPD and NPD, while *not necessarily* psychopathic, will elevate on the PCL-R and likely have a severe or moderate ASPD diagnosis. An ASPD patient, on the other hand, with a concurrent avoidant personality disorder diagnosis will likely carry an ASPD (mild) diagnosis. The patient's clinical picture is further clarified in the report's finding section by using factor scores and item analysis as a basis for describing existing traits and behaviors (Gacono, 1998, 2000c; Gacono & Hutton, 1994). The ASPD criteria, when conceptualized as an ordinal scale, correlates with severity of psychopathy as measured by the PCL-R (Hare, 2003).

Although the PCL-R alone suffices to determine the presence or absence of psychopathy, assessment generally involves more than arriving at a simple label (Gacono, Nieberding et al., 2001). Other personality instruments such as the MMPI-2 (Butcher, 2006; Butcher, Dahlstrom, Graham, Tellegen, & Kaemmer, 1989; Hathaway & McKinley, 1943) and Rorschach Inkblot method (Exner, 2003; Exner & Erdberg, 2005; Rorschach, 1942) add to our clinical understanding of the ASPD diagnosed or psychopathic individual. While these instruments were not specifically designed to "diagnose" psychopathy, and not surprisingly fail to do so (Gacono, Nieberding et al., 2001), neither do the Psychopathy Checklist-Screening Version (PCL:SV; Hart, Cox, & Hare, 1995) nor the newer experimental self-report measures of psychopathy (Hare, 1991; Lilienfeld & Andrews, 1996).[4] We recommend that several other tests be employed to further delineate the *individualized* behavioral and intrapsychic characteristics (dimensional aspects) of antisocial and psychopathic subjects.

The Rorschach

The assessment of antisocial and psychopathic patients begins as a gross categorization of chronic antisocial behavior (DSM-IV), moves to a determination of the degree of psychopathic disturbance (PCL-R), and is further refined through the Rorschach to measure the internal structure and dynamics of the particular patient. The Rorschach is ideally suited for contributing to this assessment (Cunliffe & Gacono, 2008; Gacono & Meloy, 1994; Gacono, Gacono, & Evans, 2008; Meloy, 1988), as it avoids the face validity of self-report measures, yet provides reliable and valid information about the individual's personality structure and function (Exner, 2003; Exner & Erdberg, 2005).

While the Rorschach is generally scored in a reliable manner (Viglione & Meyer, 2007), if scoring questions arise, consultations should be sought, informing the colleague that his or her name may be referenced in pending litigation as a consultant before the talk begins. Despite the importance of reliable scoring, improper administration rather than scoring issues are more likely to impact the validity of an individual Rorschach protocol (Gacono, Evans, & Viglione, 2002). Although the Rorschach can be malingered, we have found that the test is usually only "beaten" by the antisocial or psychopathic patient who sufficiently constricts his response frequency (Ganellan, 1994, 2008; Perry & Kinder, 1990). Such a psychometrically invalid protocol (Exner, 1988), however, may still yield worthwhile psychodiagnostic information (Weiner, 1998). We have found that ASPD males in general produce normative response

frequencies (Gacono & Meloy, 1992, 1994), at least in research settings. Rorschachs taken for forensic purposes in pre-trial criminal cases may be constricted; however, the examiner should aggressively pursue a valid protocol ($R \geq 14$; according to Exner's (2003) guidelines).

Although the clinician should administer and interpret the Rorschach according to the Comprehensive System (Exner, 1993, 2003), other psychoanalytically informed empirical measures of the Rorschach are also quite valuable. Two methods having acceptable interrater reliability that complement the Comprehensive System are an object relations measure (Kwawer, 1980) and two measures of defenses (Cooper & Arnow, 1986; Lerner & Lerner, 1980). Kwawer (1979) found that his 10 categories of "primitive interpersonal modes" (1980) were able to significantly differentiate between a borderline and an age- and gender-matched control sample of patients' Rorschachs. Cooper, Perry, and Arnow (1988) reported interrater reliabilities for each of their 15 defense categories ranging from .45 to .80, with a median of .62 (intraclass correlation coefficients). Inter-rater reliability for borderline defenses as a group, most commonly seen in psychopathic protocols, was .81. The authors did not, however, find any particular defense mechanism related to the presence of antisocial personality disorder (DSM-III-R), and speculated, consistent with high frequencies in forensic settings (50–75%), that the diagnosis of ASPD may be too psychodynamically heterogeneous.

Evaluators should also be familiar with a growing database of forensic Rorschach samples (Bannatyne, Gacono, & Greene, 1999; Cunliffe & Gacono, 2008; Gacono & Gacono, 2008; Gacono & Meloy, 1994; Gacono, Meloy, & Bridges, 2000, 2008; Gacono, Gacono, & Evans, 2008; Singer, Hoppe, Lee, Olesen, & Walters, 2008), keeping in mind how these samples differ from Exner's non-patient and clinical norms (Exner & Erdberg, 2005). A series of studies with antisocial and psychopathic patients (Gacono, 1988, 1990; Gacono & Meloy, 1991, 1992, 1994; Gacono, Meloy, & Heaven, 1990; Meloy & Gacono, 1992; Meloy, Gacono, & Kenney, 1994; Young et al., 2000) have validated the use of the Rorschach as a nomothetically sensitive instrument in discriminating between psychopathic ASPD and nonpsychopathic ASPD subjects (also see Smith, Gacono, & Kaufman, 1995, and Loving & Russell, 2000, for an extension of these findings to conduct-disordered adolescents), and supported the assertion that these individuals function at a borderline level of personality organization (Kernberg, 1984; Meloy, 1988, 2001). Compared to nonpsychopathic ASPDs, psychopathic ASPDs exhibit more pathological narcissism (Gacono et al., 1990; Young et al., 2000), less anxiety, less capacity for attachment (Gacono & Meloy, 1991), and some indications of increased sadism (Meloy & Gacono, 1992). Their Rorschach protocols indicate a virtual absence of idealization and higher-level neurotic defenses, coupled with a reliance on primitive defenses such as devaluation, denial, projective identification, omnipotence, and splitting (Gacono, 1990; Gacono, Meloy, & Berg, 1992). Object relations are also preoedipal, with psychopathic ASPDs evidencing significantly more Rorschach measures of narcissistic mirroring, boundary disturbance, and violent symbiosis when compared to nonpsychopathic ASPD Rorschachs (Gacono & Meloy, 1992). A typical psychopathic Rorschach protocol can be expected to reflect these findings and contain a certain number of abnormal structural characteristics (see Table 29.1).

Deviations from these typical findings should deepen the understanding of the individual differences within any one patient, but do not necessarily rule out a psychopathic disturbance. For example, a more histrionic psychopath might produce a protocol with some idealizing defenses, a color projection (CP) response, a low lambda (L), and an elevated affective ratio (Afr). On the other hand, a paranoid psychopath might produce a constricted protocol, elevated Dd responses, a low H+A:Hd+Ad ratio, and a positive hypervigilance index (HVI). A psychopathic patient with schizophrenia or bipolar disorder might significantly depart from the above-identified structural characteristics, and may instead produce severe reality distortion (X-% > 30) and an elevated PTI (for SCZI data, see Gacono & Gacono, 2008).

Forensic evaluators should be thoroughly familiar with recent Rorschach studies (Weiner, 1996) and their relationship to legal standards for admissibility of scientific evidence (McCann, 1998). *The Handbook of Forensic Rorschach Assessment* (Gacono, Evans, Kaser-Boyd, & Gacono, 2008) provides essential guidelines for the use of the Rorschach in various forensic contexts. Other articles have guided the manner in which Rorschach data can be presented in court (Meloy, 1991; Weiner, 2008), the admissibility of Rorschach data in court (Weiner, Exner, & Sciara, 1996), and the weight of Rorschach data in court (Meloy, 2008; Meloy, Hansen, & Weiner, 1997). Psychologists

Table 29.1. Select Rorschach variable means from a sample of 33 male prisoners identified as psychopathic.

Responses	21
Core characteristics	
Lambda	>.99
D	0
Adj D	0
Affects	
FC:CF+C	1:4
Afr	<.50
Pure C	>0
T	0
Y	0
Space	>2
Interpersonal relations	
Pure H	2
(H)+Hd+(Hd)	2.5
Good COP	0
Ag	0
Sx	1
Self-perception	
Rf	1
PER	>2
W:M	>3:1
Cognitions	
X+%	54
F+%	56
X-%	22

Note: From Gacono, C. B., & Meloy, J. R. (1994). *Rorschach assessment of aggressive and psychopathic personalities*. Hillsdale, NJ: Erlbaum.

should be thoroughly familiar with these resources when using the Rorschach in the assessment of antisocial and psychopathic personalities.

The MMPI-2

Our overview of psychopathy assessment next turns to the psychometric workhorse of the profession, the MMPI-2. Although self-report measures in criminal populations must be interpreted with a keen awareness of the possibility of attempts at deception or willful distortion, the MMPI-2 should be used with other instruments in the assessment of antisocial and psychopathic patients for the following reasons:

• To provide convergent validity for the other sources of data
• To measure self-report of psychopathology with an instrument that is sensitive to distortion
• To measure domains of behavior that are not empirically abnormal

- To support evidentiary standards for admissibility as a scientific method or procedure (Daubert *v.* Merrell Dow Pharmaceuticals, 113 Sup. Ct. 2786)

The latter standard, applicable in all federal and some state jurisdictions in the United States, is met through the court's determination that the measure is relevant to the case and scientifically valid (the court uses the term reliable when it actually means valid). The evaluator must always remember that if the instrument is unreliable, it cannot be valid.

The clinical scale most sensitive to "a variation in the direction of psychopathy" (McKinley & Hathaway, 1944, p. 172) is, of course, Scale 4 (Pd). Most criminal populations will show homogeneity by elevating on this scale. Scale 4, however, does not significantly correlate with PCL-R scores, and is more related to Factor II (chronic antisocial behavior or social deviancy) and ASPD than to Factor I (aggressive narcissism or affective-interpersonal deficiencies). MMPI-2 Scale 4 alone should never be used in isolation for determining the presence or absence of psychopathy, no matter how extreme. Scale 4 *is not measuring psychopathy*, but does correlate with the more heterogeneous ASPD diagnosis.

McKinley and Hathaway (1944) developed the original MMPI Scale 4 by contrasting two normative groups, married adults and college applicants, with a sample of female and male delinquents (ages 17–22) referred by the Minnesota courts to a psychiatric setting. These young adults had a long history of minor criminal behavior: stealing, lying, truancy, sexual promiscuity, alcohol abuse, and forgery. There were no homicide offenses in the histories of these subjects, *of whom the majority were girls.* Cross-validation indicated that a T-score of ≥70 on Scale 4 was achieved by 59% of a sample of 100 male federal prisoners (McKinley & Hathaway, 1944). This original criterion group was already incarcerated and had been selected for psychiatric study. Temporal reliability of this scale ranges from .49 to .61 for intervals up to a year in this population (Dahlstrom, Welsh, & Dahlstrom, 1975), compared to .71 in normals (McKinley & Hathaway, 1944).

Scale 4 is composed of 50 items, of which the deviant response is answered "true" on 24 items, and "false" on 26 items. Factor analysis has generally yielded five factors: shyness, hypersensitivity, delinquency, impulse control, and neuroticism (Greene, 1980). Several texts are relevant for validation and interpretation of Scale 4 (Butcher, 2006; Dahlstrom et al., 1975; Friedman, Lewak, Nichols, & Webb, 2001; Graham, 1978; Greene, 1980; Nichols, 2001). The Harris and Lingoes (1955) Pd subscales help to further understand Scale 4 nuances (Caldwell, 1988).

The Scale 4 items underwent virtually no changes between the MMPI and the MMPI-2. The 50 items remained, and 4 were reworded. Norms for the revised scale show a drop of 10 T-score points for males and 5 T-score points for females. The Pd scale, moreover, is not affected by educational level in either the MMPI-2 male or female normative samples (Butcher, 1990).

The Harris and Lingoes subscales were substantially changed on the MMPI-2. The Pd3 subscale, social imperturbability, lost half its items. This measure of what Nichols (personal communication, April, 1993) calls *insouciance* has received consistently high negative loadings on anxiety and may best capture the social aggression of antisocial and psychopathic personalities. The MMPI-2 deletions may have affected the subscales' meanings. Further, scale reliability has declined as a function of these item eliminations. Although these subscales were compromised and may be less adequate than they were, we still think they deserve clinical attention since the MMPI-2 changes eliminated off scale items and better organized the content of Scale 4 into homogeneous subscales to aid in interpretation. Further research is necessary.

Several MMPI-2 content and component scales that relate to external aggressive tendencies (Butcher, 2002)—antisocial practices (ASP), anger (ANG), cynicism (CYN), aggression (AGG), and disconstraint (DISC)—may also be useful in understanding the attitudes and predictable behaviors of antisocial and psychopathic patients. Sellbom, Ben-Porath, Lilienfeld, Patrick, & Graham (2005) examined various MMPI-2 scales and subscales and their relationship to psychopathy as measured by the psychopathic personality inventory (PPI) in a large sample of male and female college students. They found that AGG and DISC both significantly correlated with the affective-interpersonal and social deviance factors of the PPI (essentially equivalent to Factor 1 and Factor 2 of the PCL-R, respectively). Certain scales measuring introversion (INTR), negative emotionality (NEGE), and fears (FRS) also had significant *negative* correlations with Factor 1 of the PPI.

The ASP content scale has two facets: antisocial attitudes and antisocial behaviors. In the Sellbom et al. (2005) study, it significantly correlated with the social deviance factor of the PPI (0.52), but had no significant relationship to the affective-interpersonal factor (–0.07). In an earlier study, Lilienfeld (1996) found the ASP did demonstrate incremental validity for global indices of psychopathy in undergraduate students utilizing the PPI over and above Scale 4.

The AGG scale was specifically designed to measure grandiosity, dominance, and instrumental (predatory) aggression (Nichols, 2001), and may show promise as an important measure that validates other research indicating that psychopaths are more predatorily violent than other criminals (Meloy, 2006). Williams (2002) found that both instrumental and reactive violent offenders were significantly different from nonviolent offenders on Scale 4, ASP, and CYN. All of these scales need further research with psychopathic subjects in prison utilizing the PCL-R as the independent measure of psychopathy.

The most useful MMPI typology for classifying criminals was developed by Megargee and Bohn (1979), and has been reformulated utilizing the MMPI-2 in a large sample of incarcerated men ($N = 2,619$ inmates) and women ($N = 797$ inmates) (Megargee, 2006a). In their original sample of 1,214 federal inmates, 96% of the MMPI profiles could be assigned to one of their 10 subtypes. Early research supported the typology's concurrent validity (Booth & Howell, 1983; DiFrancesca & Meloy, 1989; Hutton, Miner, & Langfeldt, 1993; Nieberding et al., 2003), but questioned its predictive validity (Louscher, Hosford, & Moss, 1983). The revised typology represents a substantial improvement, and classifies 95% of inmates across 10 neutrally worded types (Able, Baker, Charlie, etc.). The classification system is available in a computer-based software program (Megargee, 2000), and provides both concurrent and predictive validity data for each subtype. Many of the dependent findings that emerged when the classification system was originally developed with the MMPI are quite similar to the findings with the MMPI-2, and provide a superior interpretation system to the typical 1-point and 2-point profile interpretations for criminal offenders (Megargee, 2006a, b).

How do Scale 4 and its subscales contribute to a clinical understanding of psychopathy in forensic psychiatric samples? The PCL-R, MMPI Scale 4, and MMPI-2 Scale 4 scores were compared in two samples of male subjects who had been found not guilty by reason of insanity and were committed to an involuntary outpatient treatment program (Meloy, Haroun, & Schiller, 1990). Most of these

Table 29.2. Pearson product-moment correlations between PCL-R scores and MMPI, MMPI-2 Pd scores in samples of NGI acquittees.

		N = 40	N = 34
		MMPI	MMPI-2
Pd		.21	.20
Pd1	Family discord	.00	.10
Pd2	Authority problems	.34*	.31*
Pd3	Social imperturbability	.20	.23
Pd4	Social alienation	−.17	−.10
Pd5	Self-alienation	−.05	−.22

Note: * $p < .05$ (one-directional test).

subjects were Caucasian males diagnosed with paranoid schizophrenia, and had committed a violent crime. The data are presented in Table 29.2.

Whereas the data suggest that there is a positive relationship between elevations on MMPI and MMPI-2 Pd and the PCL-R, the product moment correlations are modest and nonsignificant (as noted in Table 29.2). Our findings are consistent with Hare (1991, 2003), who found that correlations between the MMPI Pd scale and the PCL-R ranged from .19 to .25. We think this is primarily due to the Pd scale's measurement of Factor II of the PCL-R (chronic antisocial behavior) rather than Factor I (interpersonal and affective deficiency). If the PCL-R factors are separately correlated with Pd, Factor I ranges between .05 and .11 and Factor II ranges between .28 and .31 (Hare, 1991).

The Harris and Lingoes subscale correlations with the PCL-R indicate that Pd2, authority problems, are highest, and Pd1, family discord, are virtually nonexistent. Pd3, social imperturbability, is not significantly correlated, but increases slightly on the MMPI-2 version. Most compelling is the negative correlation between the PCL-R and the MMPI-2 Pd5, self-alienation, which we mentioned earlier as a measure of guilt. This is consistent with the psychopath's lack of guilt, self-blame, or remorse concerning his antisocial acts (Caldwell, 1988; Hare, 2003). These findings also suggest that correlations between the PCL-R and Pd, although modest, do not appear to change between criminal and forensic psychiatric samples.

The Restructured Clinical (RC) Scales were developed by Tellegen et al. (2003) to improve the convergent and discriminant validity of the original Clinical Scales. Items were removed which measured a common affect-laden construct they called *demoralization*. The RC Scales are more homogeneous and less intercorrelated than the original Clinical Scales. Sellbom et al. (2005) found that RC4 and RC9 were optimal predictors of the social deviance factor of psychopathy among college students, and when coupled with low scores on RC2 and RC7 (purportedly measuring the affective-interpersonal factor of psychopathy), they accounted for nearly all of the PPI variance predicted by the MMPI-2.

Megargee (2006a) found considerable redundancy, however, between the RC Scales and the MMPI-2 content and PSY-5 scales in his large sample of male and female inmates. Over half of the RC Scales *also fell below the mean* of the MMPI-2 normative sample, and none of the RC Scale scores reached clinical significance (T > 65): findings that are grossly inconsistent with what is known about psychopathology among inmates. The mean RC4 score for male inmates was 55.74 and for female inmates was 53.99. The highest correlation for RC4 was not Pd, but instead Addiction Admission Scale (AAS), a validated measure of substance abuse (.78). The RC4 correlation with Scale 4 was 0.52. In a large analysis of multiple criminal forensic samples, RC4 correlations with AAS ranged from .68 to .82, but RC4 correlations with Pd only ranged from .51 to .61 (Rouse, Greene, Butcher, Nichols, & Williams, 2008).

Although these data do not address the relationship between RC4 and psychopathy—again, we emphasize that Pd has a nonsignificant relationship with PCL-R scores—the RC scales in criminal populations appear to be problematic as measures of both psychopathology in general and antisocial behavior in particular.

Since response style should be considered (Bannatyne et al., 1999; Gacono & Gacono, 2008), and distortion should be assumed in all forensic evaluations (Meloy, 1989), the MMPI-2 validity scales take on special importance when assessing psychopathy. It appears that Scales L and F remain the most useful in classifying fake-bad and fake-good profiles (Timbrook, Graham, Keillor, & Watts, 1993), but attention must be paid to the relative configurations of VRIN, TRIN, Fb, Ds, and F(p). Megargee (2006b) has also developed a criminal infrequency scale (Fc) which may prove to be helpful in identifying problematic profiles among criminal offenders. The clinician is referred to the extensive work of both Butcher et al. (1989) and Caldwell (1988, 1997) for their interpretive refinements concerning deviant responding to the MMPI-2, and the texts of Friedman et al. (2001), Nichols (2001), and Megargee (2006a).

Measures of Cognition and Intelligence

Although not central to the assessment of personality, a standardized measure of intelligence, such as the Wechsler Adult Intelligence Scale-IV or the Kaufman Adolescent and Adult Intelligence Test, should be incorporated into the battery when assessing psychopathy. In the absence of time to do a complete intelligence battery, the Quick Test (Ammons & Ammons, 1977) gives a reliable estimate of intelligence, and it has been validated in forensic settings (Husband & DeCato, 1982; Randolph, Randolph, Ciula, Padget, & Cuneo, 1980; Sweeney & Richards, 1988). An estimate of general intelligence provides a baseline for interpretive performance on other instruments, although IQ has repeatedly been shown to not to correlate with psychopathy (Hare, 1991, 2003). Neuropsychological measures may provide useful information to the clinician, but gross differences between psychopathic and nonpsychopathic subjects have yet to be consistently demonstrated (Hare, 1991, 2003).

Some neuropsychological tests are also useful for suggesting malingering because of their limited face validity. Psychopathic malingerers will often perform worse than the expected norms for neurologic or psychiatric patients. They will also evidence more impairment than observed behavioral functioning would suggest. Dependent on the context of the examination and nature of the referral question, clinicians are frequently called upon to assess malingering when evaluating antisocial and psychopathic personalities. The reader is referred to Rogers (1988) and Rogers & Cruise (2000) for a more detailed discussion of assessing malingering.

Two points are most salient to the use of neuropsychological instruments in the assessment of psychopathy. First, any measures of performance are subject to motivational factors, and psychopathic patients may quickly realize that decrements in their performance on neuropsychological tests will contribute to their "disability" and perhaps avoidance of personal responsibility. Second, the genuine presence of neuropsychological impairment does not rule out psychopathy, and may in fact be consistent with cognitive and emotional deficits already established in research with psychopaths (Hare, 1991, 2003).

Neuropsychological impairments that appear genuine, moreover, may warrant further neurobiological workup with methods that eliminate motivational factors and measure brain structure or function (these procedures could include magnetic resonance imaging [MRI], functional MRI [fMRI], computed tomography [CT], positron emission tomography [PET], or electroencephalography [EEG] studies). For example, one sexual murderer (PCL-R = 37) produced generally invalid psychological test results due to malingering, and was diagnosed with both ASPD and NPD on Axis II. He was found, moreover, to have an abnormal visual evoked potential test using EEG technology and an abnormal PET scan indicating decreased metabolic uptake in certain areas of his prefrontal cortex and midbrain. Based on these findings, and corollary behaviors, he received an additional Axis I diagnosis of organic personality syndrome, explosive type (DSM-III-R).

Raine and his colleagues originally conducted a series of studies (Raine & Buchsbaum, 1996; Raine, Buchsbaum, & LaCasse, 1997; Raine et al., 1994; Raine et al., 1998) which investigated differences in prefrontal cortical *function* when comparing murderers referred for neuroimaging to various comparison groups, and when comparing affective and predatory murderers. A recent meta-analysis of 43 neuroimaging studies of psychopathic, antisocial, and criminal subjects indicated that both structural (reduced gray matter) and functional (hypofrontality) problems are present, but functional abnormalities predominate. Research interest is focusing upon the orbital-frontal area and middle gyrus of the prefrontal cortex. There is a large effect size for the differences between such samples and normals (Yang, Glenn, & Raine, 2008), and a large heritability for severe psychopathy (Viding et al., 2005). Studies such as these which empirically support a relationship between neurobiology and criminal behavior are not probative of criminal responsibility in any one case, but provide directions for future research and the possible use of neuroimaging in forensic cases. Raine (1993) has also reviewed and contributed to a substantial body of work that strongly suggests biological loadings for what he refers to as "habitually violent criminality," including physiological measures that indicate a biological trait of *chronic cortical underarousal* in the habitually violent criminal.

Research findings such as these extend the original work of Hare (1970) which found peripheral autonomic hypo-reactivity to aversive stimuli among psychopaths, and suggest that biological measures, broadly or discretely defined, will eventually play a role in the psychodiagnosis of psychopathy. Until that time, the evaluator should treat the neurobiological findings concerning psychopaths as a large patchwork quilt that is just beginning to be woven, but will eventually help us further understand brain–behavior relationships within psychopathy.

Integration of Findings

Perhaps the most difficult task of the psychologist is to integrate the findings from various assessment procedures into an empirically accurate and theoretically consistent clinical picture of the patient (Gacono, 2002). In the case of the psychopath in a forensic setting, findings will also need to withstand the rigors of cross-examination (Gacono, Evans, & Viglione, 2008; Meloy, Hansen, & Weiner, 1997; Pope, Butcher, & Seelen, 1993). Again, we cannot overstate the importance of the history and clinical interview and their usefulness to validate, or invalidate, test findings. Test results, moreover, provide contemporaneous and objective reference points for the support or refutation of developing clinical hypotheses, as well as data relevant to the management of psychopathic patients in an institution (Gacono & Evans, 2008; Gacono, Loving et al., 2001; Meloy, 2007).

In forensic evaluations the specific psycholegal question(s) to be addressed should be clear to the examiner before work begins on the case. In evaluating insanity, a diagnosis may be only the first step in determining whether or not there is a mental disease or defect, and then questions of responsibility or culpability are the next step in the causal chain, refocusing the examiner on the facts of the crime and any test findings that might support or refute certain states of mind in the perpetrator at the time of the criminal act. Then again, test results that address unstable emotional conditions, such as depression, may be irrelevant to prospective or retrospective hypothesis formulation. In most cases, however, psychopathy as a character or personality disorder has the temporal stability to cast an illuminating light on the historical propensities of the individual.

The tests we have emphasized—the PCL-R, the Rorschach, and the MMPI-2—are central to understanding antisocial and psychopathic patients. The PCL-R is based on observed attitudes and documented behavior (history) of the individual. PCL-R total scores nomothetically inform conclusions due to their correlations with risk for recidivism, including violent recidivism, institutional misconduct, and poor treatment outcome. Idiographically, PCL-R item analysis is useful to understand specific vulnerabilities to risk and areas to target for intervention (Gacono, 1998). Combined with findings from the Rorschach (which accesses personality structure and functioning) and the MMPI-2 (which measures conscious self-report of psychopathology and its distortion), these instruments provide both discriminant and convergent data and allow for a more incisive and individualized understanding of antisocial and psychopathic patients.

For example, a patient is scored 2 on the PCL-R Item 13, lack of realistic or long-term goals, partially arrived at on the basis of a series of frequent job changes in the subject's employment record. The MMPI-2 indicates a Pd2 (authority problems) T-score of 75, providing insight into one of the reasons for frequent job changes, which is further confirmed through the subpoena of employer records. The Rorschach is scrutinized and yields $S > 2$ (H: chronic anger), Lambda $> .99$ (H: a simple, item-by-item approach to problem solving), and FC:CF + C of 1:4, with two Pure C responses (H: unmodulated affect with a marked propensity to emotional explosiveness). Further study of the employment records indicates several incidents of angry outbursts toward employers. A look at the long sought after military record also indicates a less than honorable discharge. The evaluator then compares these findings with his clinical interview with the patient and recalls his countertransferential feelings of anxiety as the patient aggressively questioned his credentials before the interview began. Taken together, these approaches to understanding this hypothetical patient provide clinical understanding that is at once broader and more meaningful than the yield from any one test. It is the culmination of inference building (both convergent and divergent findings) across the three primary sources of data: the clinical interview, independent historical and contemporaneous data, and test results.

The clinical assessment of antisocial and psychopathic personalities is a complex task that involves both nomothetic comparison and idiographic delineation. While it is most frequently needed in criminal forensic settings, where an assessment is almost always linked to a psycholegal issue or forensic treatment planning, it is equally important to remember that these disorders may also appear in any healthcare practice and require nonforensically oriented clinicians to have some familiarity with the detection and management of these patients. The forensically trained clinical psychologist, however, is best suited to assess psychopathy, a task that historically has been overlooked or avoided in traditional mental health settings.

Notes

1. Appearing in the first DSM (APA, 1952), sociopathy included a variety of conditions such as sexual deviation, alcoholism, and "dyssocial" and "antisocial" reactions. While only the antisocial reaction was similar to traditional conceptualizations of psychopathy (Jenkins, 1960), the replacement of "Sociopathy" with ASPD in DSM-II (APA, 1968) and the subsequent increased focus on behavioral criteria widened the gap between ASPD and psychopathy.

2. Forth, Kosson, and Hare (2003) have developed a Psychopathy Checklist Youth version (PCL:YV) and Paul Frick and others have developed instruments for assessing psychopathic traits in children (Frick, Barry, & Bodin, 2000). These instruments show promise of applied usage with younger patients.

3. The CFIS (Gacono, 2005) facilitates a rapid accumulation of PCL:SV and PCL-R data similar to the format of other semistructured interview schedules. It links data to individual items, allows for an easy check of inter-rater reliability, is tailored to individual evaluations, and eliminates the need to purchase multiple forms (use with PCL-R and PCL:SV). The CFIS reduces administration time by a third to a half of what is accomplished with the existing PCL-R schedule and is appropriate for clinical, forensic, and research settings. The first author developed this semistructured interview.

4. While the Psychopathy Checklist-Screening version (Hart et al., 1995) is diagnostically useful as a screening instrument, it is most appropriately used in acute care settings and should not be utilized by itself in forensic evaluations due to its high false-positive rate. Although the majority of MMPI Clinical Scales were developed by extracting items endorsed differentially by psychiatric patients belonging to distinct diagnostic groups, the correspondence between Clinical Scale elevations and formal diagnosis was found to be less than originally promised; thus, with considerably greater assessment information, the MMPI-2 can be seen as informing diagnosis, not establishing it (see Friedman et al., 2001; Hathaway & McKinley, 1943).

References

Acklin, M. (2002). How to select personality tests for a test battery. In J. Butcher (Ed.), *Clinical personality assessment: Practical approaches* (2nd ed., pp. 13–23). New York: Oxford University Press.

American Psychiatric Association. (1952). *Diagnostic and statistical manual of mental disorders*. Washington, DC: Author.

American Psychiatric Association. (1968). *Diagnostic and statistical manual of mental disorders* (2nd ed.). Washington, DC: Author.

American Psychiatric Association. (1994). *Diagnostic and statistical manual of mental disorders* (4th ed.). Washington, DC: Author.

American Psychiatric Association. (2000). *Diagnostic and statistical manual of mental disorders* (4th ed., Rev.). Washington, DC: Author.

Ammons, R., & Ammons, C. (1977). The Quick Test: Provisional manual. *Psychological Reports Monograph Supplement, 11*(I–VII), 111–161 (Originally published 1962).

Bannatyne, L., Gacono, C., & Greene, R. (1999). Differential patterns of responding among three groups of chronic psychotic forensic outpatients. *Journal of Clinical Psychology, 55,* 1553–1565.

Beutler, L., Harwood, M., & Holaway, R. (2002). How to assess clients in pretreatment planning. In J. Butcher (Ed.), *Clinical personality assessment: Practical approaches* (2nd ed., pp. 76–95). New York: Oxford University Press.

Bodholdt, R., Richards, H., & Gacono, C. (2000).Assessing psychopathy in adults: The Psychopathy Checklist-Revised and Screening version. In C. B. Gacono (Ed.), *The clinical and forensic assessment of psychopathy: A practitioner's guide* (pp. 55–86). Mahwah, NJ: Lawrence Erlbaum.

Booth, R., & Howell, R. (1983). Classification of prison inmates with the MMPI: An extension and validation of the typology. *Criminal Justice and Behavior, 7,* 407–422.

Butcher, J. (1990). Education level and MMPI-2 measured psychopathology: A case of negligible influence. *MMPI-2 news and profiles, 1,* 3.

Butcher, J. (2002). Item content in the interpretation of the MMPI-2. In J. Butcher (Ed.), *Clinical personality assessment: Practical approaches* (2nd ed., pp. 319–334). New York: Oxford University Press.

Butcher, J. (Ed.) (2006). *MMPI-2: The practitioner's handbook.* Washington, DC: American Psychological Association.

Butcher, J., Dahlstrom, G., Graham, J., Tellegen, A., & Kaemmer, B. (1989). *MMPI-2 manual for administration and scoring.* Minneapolis, MN: University of Minnesota Press.

Caldwell, A. (1988). *MMPI supplemental scale manual.* Los Angeles: Caldwell Report.

Caldwell, A. (1997). *Forensic questions and answers on the MMPI-2.* Los Angeles: Caldwell Report.

Cleckley, H. (1976). *The mask of sanity.* St Louis: C. V. Mosby (Originally published 1941).

Cooper, S., & Arnow, D. (1986). An object relations view of the borderline defenses: A Rorschach analysis. In M. Kissen (Ed.), *Assessing object relations phenomena* (pp. 143–171). Madison, CT: International Universities Press.

Cooper, S., Perry, J., & Arnow, D. (1988). An empirical approach to the study of defense mechanisms: I. Reliability and preliminary validity of the Rorschach defense scales. *Journal of Personality Assessment, 52,* 187–203.

Cunliffe, T., & Gacono, C. B. (2008). A Rorschach understanding of antisocial and psychopathic women. In C. Gacono, B. Evans, N. Kaser-Boyd, & L. Gacono (Eds.), *The handbook of forensic Rorschach assessment* (pp. 361–378). Mahwah, NJ: Lawrence Erlbaum.

Dahlstrom, G., Welsh, G., & Dahlstrom, L. (1975). *An MMPI handbook, Vol. II: Research applications* (Rev. ed.). Minneapolis, MN: University of Minnesota Press.

DiFrancesca, K., & Meloy, J. R. (1989). A comparative clinical investigation of the "How" and "Charlie" MMPI subtypes. *Journal of Personality Assessment, 53,* 396–403.

Exner, J. (1988). Problems with brief Rorschach protocols. *Journal of Personality Assessment, 52,* 640–647.

Exner, J. (1993). *The Rorschach: A comprehensive system, Vol. 1: Interpretation* (3rd ed.). New York: John Wiley & Sons.

Exner, J. (2003). *The Rorschach: A comprehensive system, Vol. 1: Basic foundations of interpretation* (4th ed.). New York: John Wiley & Sons.

Exner, J., & Erdberg, P. (2005). *The Rorschach: A comprehensive system, Vol. 2: Advanced interpretation* (3rd ed.). New York: John Wiley & Sons.

Forth, A., Kosson, D., & Hare, R. (2003). *The Psychopathy Checklist: Youth version.* New York: Multi-Health Systems.

Frick, P., Barry C., & Bodin, S. (2000). Applying the concept of psychopathy to children: Implications for the assessment of antisocial youth. In C. B. Gacono (Ed.), *The clinical and forensic assessment of psychopathy: A practitioner's guide* (pp. 3–24). Mahwah, NJ: Lawrence Erlbaum.

Friedman, A., Lewak, R., Nichols, D., & Webb, J. (2001). *Psychological assessment with the MMPI-2.* Mahwah, NJ: Lawrence Erlbaum.

Gacono, C. B. (1988). A Rorschach analysis of object relations and defensive structure and their relationship to narcissism and psychopathy in a group of antisocial offenders (Unpublished doctoral dissertation, United States International University, San Diego, CA).

Gacono, C. B. (1990). An empirical study of object relations and defensive operations in antisocial personality disorder. *Journal of Personality Assessment, 54,* 589–600.

Gacono, C. B. (1998). The use of the Psychopathy Checklist-Revised (PCL-R) and Rorschach in treatment planning with antisocial personality disordered patients. *International Journal of Offender Therapy and Comparative Criminology, 42,* 49–64.

Gacono, C. B. (2000a). Suggestions for implementation and use of the psychopathy checklists in forensic and clinical practice. In C. B. Gacono (Ed.), *The clinical and forensic assessment of psychopathy: A practitioner's guide* (pp. 175–202). Mahwah, NJ: Lawrence Erlbaum.

Gacono, C. B. (2000b). *The clinical and forensic assessment of psychopathy: A practitioner's guide.* Mahwah, NJ: Lawrence Erlbaum.

Gacono, C. B. (2000c). Appendix A: PCL-R clinical and forensic interview schedule. In C. B. Gacono (Ed.), *The clinical and forensic assessment of psychopathy: A practitioner's guide* (pp. 409–421). Mahwah, NJ: Lawrence Erlbaum.

Gacono, C. B. (2002). Introduction to a special series: Forensic psychodiagnostic testing. *Journal of Forensic Psychology Practice, 2,* 1–10.

Gacono, C. B. (2005). *The clinical and forensic interview schedule for the Hare Psychopathy Checklist: Revised and Screening version.* Mahwah, NJ: Lawrence Erlbaum.

Gacono, C. B., & Bodholdt, R. (2001). The role of the Psychopathy Checklist-Revised (PCL-R) in risk assessment. *Journal of Threat Assessment, 1,* 65–79.

Gacono, C. B., & Evans, B. (2008). Preface. In C. Gacono, B. Evans, N. Kaser-Boyd, & L. Gacono (Eds.), *The handbook of forensic Rorschach assessment* (pp. xi–xix). Mahwah, NJ: Lawrence Erlbaum.

Gacono, C. B., Evans, B., Kaser-Boyd, N., & Gacono, L. A. (2008). *The handbook of forensic Rorschach assessment.* Mahwah, NJ: Lawrence Erlbaum.

Gacono, C. B., Evans, B., & Viglione, D. (2002). The Rorschach in forensic practice. *Journal of Forensic Psychology Practice, 2,* 33–53.

Gacono, C. B., Evans, B., & Viglione, D. (2008). Essential issues in the forensic use of the Rorschach. In C. Gacono, B. Evans, N. Kaser-Boyd, & L. Gacono (Eds.), *The handbook of forensic Rorschach assessment* (pp. 3–20). Mahwah, NJ: Lawrence Erlbaum.

Gacono, C. B., & Gacono, L. A. (2006). Some caveats for evaluating the research on psychopathy. *The Correctional Psychologist, 38,* 7–9.

Gacono, L. A., & Gacono, C. B. (2008). Some considerations for the Rorschach assessment of forensic psychiatric patients. In C. Gacono, B. Evans, N. Kaser-Boyd, & L. Gacono (Eds.), *The handbook of forensic Rorschach assessment* (pp. 421–444). Mahwah, NJ: Lawrence Erlbaum.

Gacono, C. B., Gacono, L. A., & Evans, F. B. (2008). The Rorschach and antisocial personality disorder. In

C. Gacono, B. Evans, N. Kaser-Boyd, & L. Gacono (Eds.), *The handbook of forensic Rorschach assessment* (pp. 323–360). Mahwah, NJ: Lawrence Erlbaum.

Gacono, C. B., & Hutton, H. (1994). Suggestions for the clinical and forensic use of the Hare Psychopathy Checklist-Revised (PCL-R). *International Journal of Law and Psychiatry, 17*, 303–317.

Gacono, C. B., Jumes, M., & Grey, T. (2008). Use of the Rorschach in forensic treatment planning. In C. Gacono, B. Evans, N. Kaser-Boyd, & L. Gacono (Eds.), *The handbook of forensic Rorschach assessment* (pp. 211–232). Mahwah, NJ: Lawrence Erlbaum.

Gacono, C., Loving, J., & Bodholdt, R. (2001). The Rorschach and psychopathy: Toward a more accurate understanding of the research findings. *Journal of Personality Assessment, 77*(1), 16–38.

Gacono, C. B., Loving, J., Evans, B., & Jumes, M. (2002). The psychopathy checklist-revised: PCL-R testimony and forensic practice. *Journal of Forensic Psychology Practice, 2*, 11–32.

Gacono, C. B., & Meloy, J. R. (1991). A Rorschach investigation of attachment and anxiety in antisocial personality disorder. *Journal of Nervous and Mental Disease, 179*, 546–552.

Gacono, C. B., & Meloy, J. R. (1992). The Rorschach and the DSM-III-R antisocial personality: A tribute to Robert Lindner. *Journal of Clinical Psychology, 48*, 393–405.

Gacono, C. B., & Meloy, J. R. (1994). *Rorschach assessment of aggressive and psychopathic personalities*. Hillsdale, NJ: Erlbaum.

Gacono, C. B., Meloy, J. R., & Berg, J. (1992). Object relations, defensive operations, and affective states in narcissistic, borderline, and antisocial personality disorder. *Journal of Personality Assessment, 59*, 32–49.

Gacono, C. B., Meloy, J. R., & Bridges, M. R. (2000). A Rorschach comparison of psychopaths, sexual homicide perpetrators, and nonviolent pedophiles. *Journal of Clinical Psychology, 56*, 757–777.

Gacono, C. B., Meloy, J. R., & Bridges, M. R. (2008). A Rorschach understanding of psychopaths, sexual homicide perpetrators, and nonviolent pedophiles. In C. Gacono, B. Evans, N. Kaser-Boyd, & L. Gacono (Eds.), *The handbook of forensic Rorschach assessment* (pp. 379–402). Mahwah, NJ: Lawrence Erlbaum.

Gacono, C. B., Meloy, J. R., & Heaven, T. (1990). A Rorschach investigation of narcissism and hysteria in antisocial personality disorder. *Journal of Personality Assessment, 55*, 270–279.

Gacono, C. B., Meloy, J. R., Sheppard, K., Speth, S., & Roske, A. (1995). A clinical investigation of malingering and psychopathy in hospitalized insanity acquittees. *Bulletin of the American Academy of Psychiatry and the Law, 23*, 387–397.

Gacono, C. B., Meloy, J. R., Speth, S., & Roske, A. (1997). Above the law: Escapees from maximum security forensic hospital and psychopathy. *Journal of the American Academy of Psychiatry and the Law, 25*, 547–550.

Gacono, C. B., Nieberding, R., Owen, A., Rubel, J., & Bodholdt, R. (2001). Treating juvenile and adult offenders with conduct-disorder, antisocial, and psychopathic personalities. In J. Ashford, B. Sales, & W. Reid (Eds.), *Treating adult and juvenile offenders with special needs* (pp. 99–129), Washington, DC: American Psychological Association.

Ganellan, R. (1994). Attempting to conceal psychological disturbance: MMPI defensive response sets and the Rorschach. *Journal of Personality Assessment, 63*, 423–437.

Ganellan, R. (2008). Rorschach assessment of malingering and defensive response sets. In C. Gacono, B. Evans, N. Kaser-Boyd, & L. Gacono (Eds.), *The handbook of forensic Rorschach assessment* (pp. 89–120). Mahwah, NJ: Lawrence Erlbaum Publishers.

Goldstein, A. (Ed.). (2007). *Forensic psychology: Emerging topics, expanding roles*.New York: John Wiley & Sons.

Graham, J. (1978). *The MMPI: A practical guide*. New York: Oxford University Press.

Greene, R. (1980). *The MMPI: An interpretive manual*. New York: Grune & Stratton.

Hare, R. D. (1970). *Psychopathy: Theory and research*. New York: John Wiley & Sons.

Hare, R. D. (1991). *Manual for the Psychopathy Checklist-Revised*. Toronto, ON: Multi-Health Systems.

Hare, R. D. (2003). *Manual for the Psychopathy Checklist-Revised* (2nd ed.). Toronto, ON: Multi-Health Systems.

Hare, R. D., & Jutai, J. (1983). Criminal history of the male psychopath: Some preliminary data. In K. Van Dusen & S. Mednick (Eds.), *Prospective studies of crime and delinquency*. Boston: Kluner Mijhoff.

Hare, R. D., & McPherson, L. (1984). Violent and aggressive behavior by criminal psychopaths. *International Journal of Law and Psychiatry, 7*, 35–50.

Hare, R. D., McPherson, L., & Forth, A. (1988). Male psychopaths and their criminal careers. *Journal of Consulting and Clinical Psychology, 56*, 710–714.

Harris, R., & Lingoes, J. (1955). Subscales for the MMPI: An aid to profile interpretation (Unpublished manuscript, University of California).

Hart, S., Cox, D., & Hare, R. (1995). *Manual for the Psychopathy Checklist: Screening version (PCL:SV)*. Toronto, ON: Multi-Health Systems.

Hathaway, S. R., & McKinley, J. C. (1943). *The minnesota multiphasic personality inventory manual*. Minneapolis, MN: University of Minnesota Press.

Husband, S., & DeCato, C. (1982). The Quick Test compared with Wechsler Adult Intelligence Scale as measures of intellectual functioning in a prison clinical setting. *Psychological Reports, 50*, 167–170.

Hutton, H., Miner, M., & Langfeldt, V. (1993). The utility of the Megargee–Bohn typology in a forensic psychiatric hospital. *Journal of Personality Assessment, 60*, 572–587.

Jenkins, R. (1960). The psychopathic or antisocial personality. *Journal of Nervous and Mental Disease, 131*, 318–334.

Kernberg, O. (1984). *Severe personality disorders*. New Haven, CT: Yale University Press.

Kosson, D., Gacono, C., & Bodholdt, R. (2000). Assessing psychopathy: interpersonal aspects and clinical interviewing. In C. B. Gacono (Ed.), *The clinical and forensic assessment of psychopathy: A practitioner's guide* (pp. 203–230). Mahwah, NJ: Lawrence Erlbaum.

Kwawer, J. (1979). Borderline phenomena, interpersonal relations, and the Rorschach test. *Bulletin of the Menninger Clinic, 43*, 515–524.

Kwawer, J. (1980). Primitive interpersonal modes, borderline phenomena and Rorschach content. In J. Kwawer, P. Lerner, H. Lerner, & A. Sugarman (Eds.), *Borderline phenomena and the Rorschach test* (pp. 89–109). New York: International Universities Press.

Lerner, P., & Lerner, H. (1980). Rorschach assessment of primitive defenses in borderline personality structure. In J. Kwawer, P. Lerner, H. Lerner, & A. Sugarman (Eds.), *Borderline* phenomena and the Rorschach test (pp. 257–274). New York: International Universities Press.

Lilienfeld, S. (1996). The MMPI-2 antisocial practices content scale: Construct validity and comparison with the Psychopathic Deviate Scale. *Psychological Assessment, 8*, 281–293.

Lilienfeld, S., & Andrews, B. (1996). Development and preliminary validation of a self-report measure of psychopathic personality traits in noncriminal populations. *Journal of Personality Assessment, 66*, 488–534.

Louscher, P., Hosford, R., & Moss, C. (1983). Predicting dangerous behavior in a penitentiary using the Megargee typology. *Criminal Justice and Behavior, 10*, 269–284.

Loving, J., & Russell, W. (2000). Selected Rorschach variables of psychopathic juvenile offenders. *Journal of Personality Assessment, 75*, 126–142.

Lyon, D., & Ogloff, J. (2000). Legal and ethical issues in psychopathy assessment. In C. B. Gacono (Ed.), *The clinical and forensic assessment of psychopathy: A practitioner's guide* (pp. 139–174). Mahwah, NJ: Lawrence Erlbaum.

McCann, J. T. (1998). Defending the Rorschach in court: An analysis of admissibility using legal and professional standards. *Journal of Personality Assessment, 70*, 125–144.

McKinley, C., & Hathaway, S. (1944). The Minnesota Multiphasic Personality Inventory V. Hysteria, hypomania, and psychopathic deviate. *Journal of Applied Psychology, 28*, 153–174.

Megargee, E. (2000). *User's guide: MMPI-2 criminal justice and correctional report for men.* Minneapolis, MN: Pearson/NCS Assessments.

Megargee, E. (2006a). *Using MMPI-2 in criminal justice and correctional settings: An empirical approach.* Minneapolis, MN: University of Minnesota Press.

Megargee, E. (2006b). Use of the MMPI-2 in correctional settings. In J. N. Butcher (Ed.), *MMPI-2: The practitioner's handbook* (pp. 327–460). Washington, DC: American Psychological Association.

Megargee, E., & Bohn, M. (1979). *Classifying criminal offenders.* Beverley Hills, CA: Sage.

Meloy, J. R. (1988). *The psychopathic mind: Origins, dynamics, and treatment.* Northvale, NJ: Jason Aronson.

Meloy, J. R. (1989). The forensic interview. In R. Craig (Ed.), *Clinical and diagnostic interviewing* (pp. 323–344). Northvale, NJ: Jason Aronson.

Meloy, J. R. (1991). Rorschach testimony. *Journal of Psychiatry and Law, 19*, 221–235.

Meloy, J. R. (1992). *Violent attachments.* Northvale, NJ: Aronson.

Meloy, J. R. (2001). *The mark of Cain.* Hillsdale, NJ: The Analytic Press.

Meloy, J. R. (2006). Empirical basis and forensic application of affective and predatory violence. *Australian and New Zealand Journal of Psychiatry, 40*, 539–547.

Meloy, J. R. (2007). Antisocial personality disorder. In G. Gabbard (Ed.), *Gabbard's treatments of psychiatric disorders* (4th ed., pp. 775–790). Washington, DC: American Psychiatric Press.

Meloy, J. R. (2008). The authority of the Rorschach: An update. In C. Gacono, B. Evans, N. Kaser-Boyd, & L. Gacono (Eds.) *The handbook of forensic Rorschach assessment* (pp. 79–87). Mahwah, NJ: Lawrence Erlbaum.

Meloy, J. R., & Gacono, C. B. (1992). The aggression response and the Rorschach. *Clinical Psychology, 48*, 104–114.

Meloy, J. R., & Gacono, C. B. (2000). Assessing psychopathy: Psychological testing and report writing. In C. B. Gacono (Ed.), *The clinical and forensic assessment of psychopathy: A practitioner's guide* (pp. 231–250). Mahwah, NJ: Lawrence Erlbaum.

Meloy, J. R., Gacono, C. B., & Kenney, L. (1994). A Rorschach investigation of sexual homicide. *Journal of Personality Assessment, 62*, 58–67.

Meloy, J. R., Hansen, T., & Weiner, I. (1997). Authority of the Rorschach: Legal citations during the past fifty years. *Journal of Personality Assessment, 69*, 53–62.

Meloy, J. R., Haroun, A., & Schiller, E. (1990). *Clinical guidelines for involuntary outpatient treatment.* Sarasota, FL: Professional Resource Exchange.

Monahan, J., & Steadman, H. (1994). Toward a rejuvenation of risk assessment research. In J. Monahan & H. Steadman (Eds.), *Violence and mental disorders: Developments in risk assessment* (pp. 1–17). Chicago: The University of Chicago Press.

Monahan, J., Steadman, H., Silver, E., Appelbaum, P., Robbins, P., Mulvey, E., et al. (2001). Rethinking risk assessment: The MacArthur study of mental disorder and violence. New York: Oxford University Press.

Nichols, D. (2001). *Essentials of MMPI-2 assessment.* New York: John Wiley & Sons.

Nieberding, R., Gacono, C., Pirie, M., Bannatyne, L., Viglione, D., Cooper, B., et al. (2003). MMPI-2 based classification of forensic psychiatric outpatients: An exploratory cluster analytic study. *Journal of Clinical Psychology, 59*, 907–920.

Ogloff, J., Wong, S., & Greenwood, A. (1990). Treating criminal psychopaths in a therapeutic community program. *Behavioral Sciences and the Law, 8*, 81–90.

Patrick, C. (Ed.) (2006). *Handbook of psychopathy.* New York: Guilford Press.

Perry, G., & Kinder, B. (1990). The susceptibility of the Rorschach to malingering: A critical review. *Journal of Personality Assessment, 54*, 47–57.

Pope, K., Butcher, J., & Seelen, J. (1993). *The MMPI, MMPI-2, and MMPI-A in court.* Washington, DC: American Psychological Association.

Quinsey, V., Harris, G., Rice, M., & Cormier, C. (1998). *Violent offenders: Appraising and managing risk.* Washington, DC: American Psychological Association.

Raine, A. (1993). *The psychopathology of crime.* San Diego, CA: Academic Press.

Raine, A., & Buchsbaum, M. (1996). Violence and brain imaging. In D. M. Stoff & R. B. Cairns (Eds.), *Neurobiological approaches to clinical aggression research* (pp. 195–218). Mahwah, NJ: Erlbaum.

Raine, A., Buchsbaum, M., & LaCasse, L. (1997). Brain abnormalities in murderers indicated by positron emission tomography. *Biological Psychiatry, 42*, 495–508.

Raine, A., Buchsbaum, M., Stanley, J., Lottenberg, S., Abel, L., & Stoddard, S. (1994). Selective reductions in prefrontal glucose metabolism in murderers. *Biological Psychiatry, 36*, 365–373.

Raine, A., Meloy, J. R., Bihrle, S., Stoddard, J., LaCasse, L., & Buchsbaum, M. (1998). Reduced prefrontal and increased subcortical brain functioning assessed using positron emission tomography in predatory and affective murderers. *Behavioral Sciences and the Law, 16*, 319–332.

Randolph, G., Randolph, J., Ciula, B., Padget, J., & Cuneo, D. (1980). Retrospective comparison of Quick Test IQs of new admissions and a random sample of patients in a maximum security mental hospital. *Psychological Reports, 46*, 1175–1178.

Rice, M., Harris, T., & Cormier, C. (1992). An evaluation of a maximum security therapeutic community for psychopaths and other mentally disordered offenders. *Law and Human Behavior, 16*, 399–412.

Robins, L. N. (1966). *Deviant children grownup*. Baltimore, MD: Williams & Wilkins.

Rogers, R. (1988). *Clinical assessment of malingering and deception*. New York: The Guildford Press.

Rogers, R., & Cruise, K. (2000). Malingering and deception among psychopaths. In C. B. Gacono (Ed.), *The clinical and forensic assessment of psychopathy: A practitioner's guide* (pp. 269–284). Mahwah, NJ: Lawrence Erlbaum.

Rorschach, H. (1942). *Psychodiagnostics*. New York: Grune & Stratton.

Rouse, S., Greene, R., Butcher, J., Nichols, D., & Williams, C. (2008). What do the MMPI-2 restructured clinical scales reliably measure? Answers from multiple research settings. *Journal of Personality Assessment, 90*, 435–442.

Sellbom, M., Ben-Porath, Y., Lilienfeld, S., Patrick, C., & Graham, J. (2005). Assessing psychopathic personality traits with the MMPI-2. *Journal of Personality Assessment, 85*, 334–343.

Singer, J., Hoppe, C., Lee, M., Olesen, N., & Walters, M. (2008). Child custody litigants: Rorschach data from a large sample. In C. Gacono, B. Evans, N. Kaser-Boyd, & L. Gacono (Eds.), *The handbook of forensic Rorschach assessment* (pp. 445–464). Mahwah, NJ: Lawrence Erlbaum.

Smith, A., Gacono, C., & Kaufman, L. (1995). A Rorschach comparison of psychopathic and nonpsychopathic conduct disordered adolescents. *Journal of Clinical Psychology, 53*, 289–300.

Sweeney, D., & Richards, H. (1988, March). *The Quick Test, the WAIS and the WAIS-R: Normative data, cultural bias, and psychometric properties in a forensic psychiatric population*. Paper presented at the midwinter meeting of the Society for Personality Assessment, New Orleans.

Tellegen, A., Ben-Porath, Y., McNulty, J., Arbisi, P., Graham, J., & Kraemmer, B. (2003). *MMPI-2 Restructured Clinical (RC) Scales: Development, validation, and interpretation*. Minneapolis, MN: University of Minnesota Press.

Timbrook, R., Graham, J., Keillor, S., & Watts, D. (1993). Comparison of the Wiener–Harmon subtle-obvious scales and the standard validity scales in detecting valid and invalid MMPI-2 profiles. *Psychological Assessment, 5*, 53–61.

Viding, E., Blair, R., Moffitt, T., & Plomin, R. (2005). Evidence for substantial genetic risk for psychopathy in 7-year olds. *Journal of Child Psychology and Psychiatry, 46*, 592–597.

Viglione, D., & Meyer, G. (2007). In C. Gacono, B. Evans, N. Kaser-Boyd, & L. Gacono (Eds.), *The handbook of forensic Rorschach assessment* Mahwah, NJ: Lawrence Erlbaum.

Weiner, I. (1996). Some observations on the validity of the Rorschach Inkblot method. *Psychological Assessment, 8*, 206–213.

Weiner, I. (1998). *Principles of Rorschach interpretation*. Mahwah, NJ: Lawrence Erlbaum.

Weiner, I. (2002). How to anticipate ethical and legal challenges in personality assessments. In J. Butcher (Ed.), *Clinical personality assessment: Practical approaches* (2nd ed., pp. 126–134). New York: Oxford University Press.

Weiner, I. (2008). Presenting and defending Rorschach testimony. In C. Gacono, B. Evans, N. Kaser-Boyd, & L. Gacono (Eds.), *The handbook of forensic Rorschach assessment* (pp. 121–137). Mahwah, NJ: Lawrence Erlbaum.

Weiner, I., Exner, J., & Sciara, A. (1996). Is the Rorschach welcome in the courtroom? *Journal of Personality Assessment, 67*, 422–424.

Williams, J. (2002). Psychopathy in instrumental and reactive violent offenders using MMPI-2 scales as predictors (Unpublished doctoral dissertation, Louisville, KY: Spalding University).

Williamson, S., Hare, R. D., & Wong, S. (1987). Violence: Criminal psychopaths and their victims. *Canadian Journal of Behavioral Science, 19*, 454–462.

Yang, Y., Glenn, A., & Raine, A. (2008). Brain abnormalities in antisocial individuals: Implications for the law. *Behavioral Sciences and the Law, 26*, 65–84.

Young, M., Justice, J., Erdberg, P., & Gacono, C. (2000). The incarcerated psychopathy in psychiatric treatment: Management or treatment? In C. B. Gacono (Ed.), *The clinical and forensic assessment of psychopathy: A practitioner's guide* (pp. 313–332). Mahwah, NJ: Lawrence Erlbaum.

Clinical Personality Assessment in the Employment Context

James N. Butcher, Donald K. Gucker, *and* Lowell W. Hellervik

Abstract

Clinical personality assessment is not widely used in industrial/organizational (I/O) psychology for employment selection. The assessment of clinical symptoms, emotional instability, and personality problems in personnel evaluations is primarily used in evaluating applicants for positions such as law enforcement, fire department, nuclear power plant, and airline pilot positions in which high emotional stability, successful stress skills, and high responsibility are considered important to the performance of a high-risk job. The clinical personality assessment is characteristically conducted post hire and seen as analogous to the pre-employment medical examination. The most widely used psychological test in this application is the Minnesota Multiphasic Personality Inventory-2 (MMPI-2) which has a substantial research base (more than 600 studies) supporting its use. This chapter provides interpretive guidelines for the MMPI-2 in personnel screening and suggests an effective strategy (retest method) for dealing with defensive applicants.

Keywords: fitness-for-duty evaluation, industrial and organizational psychology, K scale, Minnesota report, personnel, RC Scales, retest method, test defensiveness

The term "clinical personality assessment" is not familiar to many industrial/organizational (I/O) psychologists. They might assume its meaning to be an evaluation of personality by a trained clinician using direct observations, interview, and psychological testing of an individual's behavior to explore psychopathology rather than the broader personality appraisal of characteristics considered to be related to work functioning. Whatever meaning is attached to the term, personality constructs are central to the application. Many I/O academics and other researchers have avoided the use of personality measures in personnel evaluations for many years and have only recently begun to incorporate them for use in personnel assessments as potential significant contributors to their models of performance prediction in the workplace. After a number of years of low visibility, in the 1990s, personality variables have experienced a renaissance with a phoenix-like rise to prominence as psychology has found great interest

in the "Five Factor Model" (FFM; see Costa & McCrae, 1985; Hough, Eaton, Dunnette, Kamp, & McCloy, 1990).

Although, "clinical" personality tests such as the MMPI/MMPI-2 have been largely ignored by I/O psychologists, they have continued to be used by a minority of psychologists (clinical or counseling psychologists) working in some personnel screening settings. Clinical assessments have been primarily incorporated into employment screening as part of the medical/mental health evaluation for assessing job applicants for positions that are considered to be unusually stressful or requiring a high degree of emotional stability or high responsibility such as police officers, nuclear power plant employees, airline pilots, or air traffic controllers. The more limited use of clinical assessment instruments in I/O psychology results, in part, because most employment decisions do not require a clinical personality evaluation (i.e., positions in sales, managerial, etc.), since a "specific personality type" or a "spotless" mental health adjustment is not necessary for successful performance of most jobs. Moreover, there has been concern in the past over whether employers can "invade the privacy" of applicants through the use of personality measures (Ervin, 1965).

Evolution of Industrial/Organizational Psychology

The evolution of the I/O assessment model provides a clear perspective on testing practices in this context. Psychological assessment of people in organizations has recently passed its 100th birthday. As noted in Chapter 1, the first personality assessment evaluation research was published by Heymans and Wiersma (1906), who used a rating strategy in which the professional observer evaluated the individual on a set of personality dimensions. The first self-report personality assessment was developed a few years later by Robert Woodworth (1919, 1920) to obtain self-reported symptoms and personality characteristics of draftees into the army during World War I.

I/O psychology was broadly influenced by the work of psychologists such as Hugo Munsterberg (1913), at Harvard, who promoted applied psychology, especially mental testing, as a solution to the assessment problems of industry. He developed tests for the hiring of traveling salesmen, ship captains, and trolley drivers, and followed up with studies evaluating the tests' effectiveness. At Northwestern University and, later, at the Carnegie Institute of Technology, Walter Dill Scott applied psychological principles to advertising, hiring, and motivation. He developed many now-standard assessment tools: the scored personal history blank, interview guide, performance rating form, and standardized measures of an applicant's intelligence, alertness, carefulness, imagination, resourcefulness, and verbal facility.

Psychological testing as a professional activity expanded during America's entry in World War I. A group of psychologists responded to a patriotic appeal from the American Psychological Association by developing and administering an intelligence test to more than 1,700,000 recruits. A performance test based on the work done by Paterson and Pintner (see Paterson, 1936) at Ohio State was administered to recruits with limited language skills. A second group of psychologists, led by Walter Dill Scott (see Scott & Clothier, 1923; Scott & Hayes, 1921), created and administered a personnel system that rated recruits according to their abilities, education, and experience and placed them in appropriate positions.

For example, an early test examined whether truck drivers had the skills necessary to deliver ammunition and supplies to the front under battle conditions. By the war's end, this second group of psychologists had developed 80 standardized tests. Their motto was "the right man in the right job." After the war, Walter Dill Scott formed the Scott Company, the first modern psychological consulting organization. It was dedicated to the application of scientific methods to personnel problems in business and industry.

The ensuing four decades saw modest expansion of psychological consulting corporations such as Scott's, as well as similar consulting performed by academics. Job analysis studies began to have impact on carefully measuring requirements for each job. During World War II, millions of recruits were assessed by thousands of psychologists and assigned a military job category based on the results. In the 1960s, Professor Marvin Dunnette, at the University of Minnesota, following the "dust-bowl empiricist" tradition (see Dunnette, 1966), acknowledged successful work in analyzing specific jobs, but he said comparisons among large numbers of jobs were still a matter of subjective judgment and guesswork. Dunnette and his colleagues conducted empirical research on the relationship between personality characteristics and job performance (Kirchner, Dunnette, & Mousley, 1960). In addition, he called for the application of empirical information, developed, perhaps, by clustering and factor analysis and the use of "electronic computers." Selection tests were of "limited usefulness and questionable validity" in Dunnette's view, in part, because he found that they were being used by people who were "ill-equipped" either to appreciate the tests' shortcomings or to do research. The use of the job interview, without more research, "had best be rationalized on the basis of its utility as a public relations device rather than as a personnel procedure." Predictions of job success, he said, were no more sophisticated than the model presented by Munsterberg 60 years before.

As Dunnette was critiquing this state of affairs, a new development was occurring that would shape the I/O field substantially. Douglas Bray (Bray, 1964), the personnel research psychologist at American Telephone and Telegraph (AT&T), was conducting what was to become a highly influential study of "management progress." In addition to standardized tests of intelligence, personality, and other characteristics, he created "work samples" or simulations of management work. Thus, management candidates were required to participate in these "exercises" while being observed and evaluated by psychologists. Typically 12 candidates participated in these centers along with 6 psychologists. In the meetings conducted about each candidate, each of approximately 24 "dimensions" or characteristics were evaluated by each psychologist, along with an overall estimate of how high the candidate would ascend in AT&T's management hierarchy. Ratings and discussions were based on the entire array of data interviews, tests, and simulations.

Typical simulations were:

1. *An "in-basket" exercise*. This was a stack of paperwork typical of what a manager might find on his desk; a fictional organization chart of subordinates, peers, and superiors; and a calendar. The paperwork included reports from subordinates, requests from peers, demands from the boss, complaints from customers, etc. The candidate was required to do whatever he thought appropriate— respond, ignore, delegate, etc.—but he also had to keep track of his actions to assure no mis-scheduling occurred and to enable follow-up. This simulation, then, had rich potential for evaluating many "dimensions" such as planning, organization, delegating, interpersonal skill, etc.

2. *A leaderless group discussion*. This often required the participant to present a "candidate for promotion" (a paper candidate judged to be equal but different from the other five) to the other five persons in his group. After all six presentations were completed, the group discussed and rank-ordered them. This simulation allowed evaluation of such dimensions as oral communications skills, impact, decision making, etc.

3. *A cooperative group task*. This was an exercise in which the group of six served as an investment committee and traded stocks on a miniature stock exchange. This measured many of the dimensions already mentioned in addition to problem solving, collaboration, flexibility, etc.

Information thus obtained was integrated with test and background information in meetings of the staff at the conclusions of each "assessment center." The ratings by the staff were done for research purposes only. So when the follow-up data revealed that the staff judgments were highly predictive of the candidates' ultimate corporate progress, there was considerable excitement over the "assessment center method."

Indeed, two consulting companies, Personnel Decisions International (PDI) and Development Dimensions, began offering the assessment center as a significant component of their services in about 1970. By the mid-1970s, PDI had created a hybrid assessment method by adding nongroup simulations, such as an In-Basket, to its more traditional tests and interview assessment for individuals. PDI also adopted the "dimension" ratings as a method for integrating all available data (Personnel Decisions International Corporation, 1991). Such integration enabled reports to organizational clients to speak more directly in their language rather than the language of psychological tests and test scale labels. However, the traditionally large number of dimensions, coupled with high inter-correlations within clusters, resulted in creating a hierarchical structure of dimensions within "factors." For example, dimensions such as planning, organizing, delegating, and follow-up were subsumed under the factor label "administrative skills." Thus, personality test constructs and information contained in the MMPI or CPI served as input into ratings of dimensions although the specific scale scores were to some extent ignored. While a significant loss in the eyes of many, narrative reports and oral feedback to both assessees and their organizations typically made significant use of test scores (as both partial evidence for a dimensional rating and as content for counseling discussions on matters too subtle to be overtly identified in the simulations, interviews, and dimensions).

Further, each of the factors in the FFM of personality has been shown to be in reality, what had been referred to as a "compound variable" much like the "dimensions" described above. Hough noted that the FFM yields information about the higher-order factor structure of personality; however, it ignores, confounds, or otherwise obscures understanding of variables combined into five broad factors (Hough, 1998; Schneider, Hough, & Dunnette, 1996).

Both assessment centers and their hybrid derivative are expensive in comparison with test or test and interview assessments. However, research suggests that ratings have significant incremental validity over both cognitive and personality variables when predicting management performance. Although others have disagreed with these findings (e.g., Goffin, Rothstein, & Johnston, 1996), the processes continue to thrive, in part because of predictive validity and in part because of their face validity. Most assessees see simulations as requiring the same kind of behavior as their jobs require.

Assessment center acceptance and popularity was aided by US governmental intrusion into private sector hiring and promotion practices. Beginning in the late 1970s, The Equal Employment Opportunity Commission and subsequent Affirmative Action initiatives were created to provide oversight into ensuring that there was no unfair discrimination against certain identified groups. Testing, especially intelligence testing, became a major target of their concern and employers became fearful of any use of tests Equal Employment Opportunity Commission, Civil Service Commission, U.S. Department of Labor, and U.S. Department of Justice (1978).

Meanwhile, many I/O psychologists considered personality testing to be unimportant for employment decisions. Hough and Ones (2002) commented that, with a few notable exceptions, the period from the 1960s to the mid-1980s was a dark age for personality. Clinically oriented personality tests, such as the MMPI, were limited in application among I/O because the general assessments they performed were thought to have little to do with work-related emotional maladjustment. In addition, item pools of the tests (particularly the original MMPI contained some content thought to be offensive in the employment context) were often inflammatory in the new world required by government agencies—job relatedness. (The objectionable items on the MMPI were removed in the revision of the test that was published in 1989; see Butcher, Dahlstrom, et al., 1989.) However, even strong validity in predicting important job variables was often insufficient to outweigh the real and imagined risks of asking job candidates questions about personal matters or about matters that were not clearly relevant to the job. There have been exceptions. In situations in which emotional maladjustment was considered to have job relevance, for example, among nuclear power plant employees, psychologists from PDI provided recommendations to the nuclear regulatory commission for providing an assessment of psychological adjustment (based in part on the MMPI-2) since this was considered to be relevant to safety on the job.

In the 1980s, organizations began to demand even greater "fidelity" to their company, though, for example, retail organizations found it difficult to use simulations set in a manufacturing environment. So, considerable work began to be done around customizing both dimensions—now often under the label "competencies" and the simulations. While the term competency and the resulting variables seem to many to be quite similar to dimensions, the connotation, at least, is more that of a job-related capability than a personal characteristic such as a personality trait. Consequently, personality testing, while still useful as an input to evaluating competencies, became less central to the evaluation of an individual.

Most recently, some organizations are using the assessment center method to go beyond simply evaluating people into deploying these high-fidelity simulations into helping them shape and implement strategy changes for their business. This innovation is requiring psychologists to deploy themselves on the boundary of business planning à la MBAs and more traditional psychological measurement of individuals. Such an engagement with an organization begins with in-depth interviews with the line executives responsible for overall organizational success. These interviews are designed to reveal the strategy of the business—often the "change" in strategy deemed required to succeed—and the perceived requirements/competencies of "people" to enable the strategy to succeed.

From the strategy discussions emerge the competencies to be measured, especially at higher levels of management. The executive strategy interviews also provide insights into critical behavioral events that need to be handled in a particular way to assure uniform execution of the overall strategy. Such events become the kernel for creation of simulations designed specifically to help evoke behaviors relevant to evaluating managers on the new competencies. Those newly designed simulations are combined into an assessment center (along with traditional tests and interviews) and incumbent managers are scheduled to go through the process. Feedback on their performance subsequent to each exercise gives them concrete examples of what they need to do to execute on the CEO's view about change in the strategy. Further, the final integrative report is useful for "talent management" purposes—deciding who is the best fit for which positions and when.

In this latest evolution of management assessment, personality testing is less central than earlier versions. Further, participants in the process have often stood the test of time in their organizations, so in the few cases where they exist, the organization has adopted coping strategies to accommodate for them (see discussion by Klimoski & Zukin, 2003).

As we have seen, management selection has evolved to the point that it employs a complex set of assessment strategies. With the extensive development in the field of assessment research it is likely that personality testing is underweighted, and deserves more careful consideration in I/O programs than is currently given.

For the special high-risk occupations—police, fire department, nuclear power industry, and airline pilot selection—it remains important to incorporate a risk assessment that continues to benefit from clinical personality assessment strategies that have their roots in early personality assessment history. In addition to evaluations before they become employed, a clinical personality assessment might be required for a current employee who encountered mental health or behavioral problems during his/her employment. Clinical evaluation may be required as a component in "fitness for duty evaluations" for employees in high-risk occupations who encounter work-related difficulties. For example, a police officer who has been suspended for excessive force or an airline pilot who behaved inappropriately while working (Butcher, 2002) might be required to undergo an evaluation before returning to work.

We next turn to a closer examination of personality assessment that addresses the appraisal of potential mental health or personality problems that are potential risks for problems on the job.

Assessing Personality and Mental Health Problems in Employment Settings

Psychologists working in industrial settings have long been aware of the potential work problems that can result when crucial employees develop mental health problems that interfere with their job performance. This is particularly of concern for occupations that have a high degree of public responsibility such as for airline pilots or police applicants. The importance of identifying those who are at increased risk for aberrant behavior in the work context has been addressed by a number of authorities (see discussions by Blau, 1994; Enelow, 1991; Sperry, Kahn, & Heidel, 1994; Thomas & Hersen, 2004).

A number of researchers have provided support for using personality assessment in the workplace to identify problem employees at the point of entry of the job (Goodstein & Lanyon, 1999; Hough et al., 1990; Irving, 1993; Robertson, 1994a, b). Important work-related personality characteristics have been identified as being critical factors in high-stress or high-public-responsible occupations (Butcher, Ones, & Cullen, 2006). The personal characteristics that can be addressed in an MMPI-2-based evaluation will be described in the sections that follow.

The MMPI-2: History and Validation Research

There is a well-established tradition of using personality questionnaires in making personnel decisions. Woodworth (1920) developed the first inventory for assessing personality characteristics. The Personal Data Sheet was designed especially for a personnel decision context for the purpose of eliminating individuals from the military who were psychologically unfit. In the years that followed, a number of personality inventories were used for personnel decisions, for example, Bernreuter (1931) (see also the discussion by Ingle, 1934), and more broadly in mental health settings.

Personality assessment with the MMPI in personnel applications had its start shortly after the test was published in 1943. Abramson first conducted research on the applicability of the MMPI in a military screening setting in assessing specialized personnel samples (Abramson, 1945). Subsequent research has provided a rich database for using the MMPI or MMPI-2 in a number of personality evaluation settings,[1] for example, police (Bartol, 1982; Burbeck & Furnham, 1985; Carpenter & Raza, 1987; Cauthen, 1988; Cimbura, 2000; Corey, 1989; Cortina, Doherty, Schmitt, & Kaufman, 1992; Costello, Schoenfeld, & Kobos, 1982; FitzGerald, 1987; Wells, 1992; Wright, 1988), firefighters (Johnson, 1983; Matarazzo, Allen, Saslow, & Wiens, 1964), clergy (Brenneis, 2000; Camargo, 1997a, b; Dittes, 1962; Putnam, Adams, & Butcher, 1992; Putnam, Kurtz, & Houts, 1996), and pilots (Butcher, 1994; Caldwell, O'Hara, Caldwell, & Stephens, et al. 1993; Fulkerson, 1956, 1957, 1958a, b; Fulkerson & Sells, 1958; Geist & Boyd, 1980; Sparvieri & de Angelis, 1971; Usenko, 1992). Overall, more than 600 research studies have emerged to support this test use.

Special problems of particular vulnerabilities in employees have been addressed in research. Bartol (1991) found that the Pd and Ma scales were associated with termination from the police force. Cimbura (2000) studied the effects of stress on police officers. Job performance as a police officer was significantly related to some MMPI scores (Scogin, Schumacher, Gardner, & Chaplin, 1995). Beutler, Nussbaum, and Meredith (1988) tested police officers after they were recruited and then 4 years later. They noted that there was an increased expression of health, mental health, and substance abuse symptoms at the retest. The authors suggested that the increased symptom expression likely related to the stress or police work. The MMPI-2 has been used to assess potential work impacting problems. For example, Liao, Arvey, Nutting, and Butler (2001) found two MMPI-2 scales (Pd and Sc) associated with accidents and injury among firefighters. Rozanov, Mokhavikov, and Stiliha (2002) reported that the MMPI-2 was effective at detecting suicide in a military environment.

In order to clarify the psychometric characteristics of the MMPI/MMPI-2 in employment settings, a number of studies have addressed the psychometric properties of the test with personnel applications. The MMPI-2 has been shown to be reliable in employment assessments (Colotla, Bowman, & Shercliffe, 2001; Putnam et al., 1996). The MMPI-2, particularly well-defined scores, has been shown to be a stable assessment instrument among injured workers (Livingston, Jennings, Colotla, Reynolds, & Shercliffe, 2006). Carpenter and Raza (1987) examined the performance of police applicants with other occupational groups and Butcher (1994) provided a psychometric appraisal of airline pilot applicants.

Assessing Test Defensiveness

Research has demonstrated that applicants for employment tend to respond to psychological tests in a defensive and self-enhancing manner (Butcher, 1994; Caldwell et al., 1993; Detrick, Chibnall, & Rosso, 2001; Ganellen, 1994; Hough, 1998 Paulhus, Harms, Bruce, & Lysy, 2003). The defensiveness or the tendency to present oneself as highly virtuous and void of problems (even minor problems most people admit to) is common among applicants. For example, in a study of airline pilot applicants, Butcher (1994) found that a group of applicants to a major air carrier obtained extremely defensive scores on Scale K of the MMPI-2 (T = 66). A large number of applicants respond in such a nondisclosing way that their personality profiles may not be usable in the evaluation. Two strategies for understanding and/or reducing the applicant's defensive stance have been developed. One approach has been to broaden our understanding of the applicant's response pattern through an additional defensiveness scale (Scale S) and subscales to assess possible source of defensiveness. The second approach, retesting under altered instructions, has been an effective strategy of actually reducing test defensiveness in applicants. Both of the strategies will be described.

Detecting Defensive Responding—the Superlative Self-Presentation Scale

Butcher and Han (1995) developed a validity scale, the Superlative Self-Presentation or S scale to assess the test defensiveness often found among applicants. In developing the S scale, Butcher and Han used samples of 274 male airline applicants and the MMPI-2 normative sample ($N = 1,138$ men and 1,462 women) for selecting items. In addition, external information on a subset of the normative sample (i.e., 822 normal couples who had taken the MMPI-2 and had rated each other on 110 personality variables was used to identify potential correlates for the S scale).

The items for the S scale were initially selected by examining the item responses of airline pilots compared with those in the normative sample. Items that were endorsed differently reflected the tendency for airline pilot applicants to describe themselves in superlative terms in order to impress examiners compared with the normative men from the MMPI-2 restandardization sample. In the next phase, the provisional scale was refined by using internal consistency methods (coefficient alpha) to assure high scale homogeneity. The S scale was validated next using the rating data available from the MMPI-2 standardization project noted above. The scale was shown to have a number of behavioral correlates reflecting the presentation of oneself as a well-controlled, virtuous, and problem-free person.

The final stage involved the development of a set of subscales in order to enable the evaluation of specific motivations to deny problems. The items on the S scale were item-factored to obtain the five clusters that were named: beliefs in human goodness, serenity, contentment with life, patience\denial of irritability and anger, and denial of moral flaws.

Several studies have been published showing that the S scale is one of the strongest indicators of defensive responding (Bagby et al., 1997; Bagby, Marshall, Bury, Bacchiocci, & Miller, 2006; Cooper, 2003; Lim & Butcher, 1996). For example, one study found differences between different settings on the S subscales: A group of airline pilot applicants tended to show elevations on all of the S subscales while parents who were involved in child custody evaluations showed elevations on only two of the subscales: S4 (patience\denial of irritability and anger) and S5 (denial of moral flaws) (Butcher, 1998).

Retesting with Altered Instructions—an Effective Strategy to Deal with the Defensive Invalid, and Thus Unusable, Applicant MMPI-2 Profile

Defensive invalid (DI) MMPI-2 profiles are relatively common in personnel assessments and result in psychological evaluations that provide limited or no information. Butcher, Morfitt, Rouse, and Holden (1997) hypothesized that applicants would be more forthcoming in personality evaluations if they were aware that their assessment was invalid and unusable and would likely be more open and cooperative if they were given an opportunity to retake the test. They employed a test readministration strategy with revised instructions to lower test defensiveness. Those instructions informed the applicant with an invalid profile that the initial test result was not acceptable due to excessive defensiveness, and also provided brief information about the tests' ability to evaluate applicant test-taking attitudes. Profiles were classed as DI if T-scores on L and K exceeded 65 and 70, respectively. In the retest, the obtained results clearly showed that most applicants would respond more appropriately in the second administration. Of those initial DI applicant profiles (26% of the total sample) who were retested with revised instructions, only 15% or 20% remained defensive in the second administration.

The readministration strategy was replicated in a study by Cigrang and Staal (2001) in a military setting where the MMPI-2 was administered as part of an applicant screening process. DI profiles were obtained in 48% of the initial administrations, and retesting with revised instructions produced valid profiles with 83% of the applicants that initially produced DI profiles. Cigrang and Staal summarized the core issue, stating that profiles that are "excessively defensive create a dilemma for psychologists working in personnel selection settings. Clinical guidelines recommend the profile be considered uninterpretable, but the absence of usable testing data could lead to the elimination of otherwise qualified candidates." The retest strategy for defensive profiles was further evaluated in a recent study in a medical setting. Walfish (2007) conducted a study of potential bariatric surgery patients who often tend to be defensive over concern that they will be denied the operation if they prove to be psychologically disturbed. He found that the majority (94%) of patients produced valid profiles on the second testing. He recommended that this procedure be used in assessing clients for such surgical procedures.

The Butcher et al. readministration procedure was further evaluated in a study by Gucker and McNulty (2004) in a personnel security setting. The MMPI-2 was administered as part of a psychological evaluation, among other procedures, to reduce the amount of time required to obtain a high-level security clearance with a government agency. Individuals seeking such a security clearance have traditionally been required to await the results of a lengthy background investigation (BI); however, it became possible for an applicant to volunteer for a fast-track interim clearance program that, if successfully accomplished, would permit rapid access to sensitive work-essential information (good only until the BI is completed and evaluated). Successful completion of this fast-track interim security clearance program permitted an applicant access to sensitive work-essential material without the customary delay usually associated with the BI process.

The fast-track security assessment program included a semistructured clinical interview and administration of the MMPI-2. DI MMPI-2 profiles clearly posed a problem in that an important piece of decision-essential data could not be utilized. To deal with this problem, the Butcher et al. readministration strategy was initiated utilizing invalidity criteria relative to L and K. The following readministration instructions are a modified version of those used in the earlier study:

> Because of test defensiveness, your first test results were not valid and, thus, cannot be used as part of your evaluation.
>
> When people take the Minnesota Multiphasic Personality Inventory-2 (MMPI-2) in employment settings, they sometimes respond to the questions in a manner that will create a favorable self-impression, emphasizing their strengths and de-emphasizing what they perceive to be their weaknesses.
>
> The MMPI-2 contains several measures that were constructed to allow the interpreter to evaluate test-taking attitudes, and test protocols that are invalid, unfortunately cannot be used as part of the ... evaluation.
>
> We hope that you will consent to retake the MMPI-2. If you do so, please answer all the items unless they really do not apply to you, and be as accurate as possible about yourself in terms of your responses to the test questions.

As part of the readministration procedure, the applicant must read the standard administration instructions after reading the above modified instructions.

The 2004 study by Gucker and McNulty was based upon a sample of 512 applicants with a mean age of 36 years. A total of 77% of the group produced valid profiles on initial administration, while 23% produced DI profiles. Of the initial DI group, 82% produced valid profiles upon readministration with the above modified instructions. The changes in validity scale scores from the initial DI to the retest condition were impressive. On retest, the L scale dropped from a mean T of 72 to 53, K from 66 to 54, and S from 69 to 55, showing predominantly valid, nondefensive profiles. In general, initial disparate validity values move toward more normalized values, and L, K, & S deltas are at the >.001 level of confidence.

In a 2006 study, updating the original Gucker and McNulty sample, the sample size was expanded from the original N of 512 by adding 879 cases, thus producing a total N of 1390. The resulting validity scale values are almost identical to those of the earlier study (Gucker & McNulty, 2004). On initial administration, 21% presented as DI, and 79% produced initial valid profiles. Upon readministration using the modified instructions, the initial DI group ($N = 297$) produced valid profiles in 84% of the applicants that initially produced DI profiles. Of the retest group, only 15% ($N = 47$) remained defensive/invalid. This study demonstrates almost identical validity scale values to the earlier study, in spite of the total N increasing from 512 to 1,390 applicants.

In order to illustrate the change in symptom disclosure on retest, the clinical and content scales' mean T-scores derived from the expanded study data were examined. The content scale data clearly demonstrate a strong inverse relationship in mean T-values as defensiveness increases. The more open the applicant's test-taking approach, the more symptoms are acknowledged. The initial DI content scales' mean is 40.08, the initially valid mean is 44.28, and the retest valid mean is 49.48. The retest valid mean scores demonstrate the most "normal" scores in that they approach T50, whereas the initial DI means are associated with a general reduction in T-score elevations, clustering about T40. Paired t-test values between the initial DI means and the retest means are at .001 or greater.

The effect on the MMPI-2 content scales with increasingly open self-appraisal is informative. Applicants are clearly more willing to acknowledge mental health symptoms under the readministration strategy, enabling the assessment psychologist to gain additional usable personality information.

Most MMPI-2 scales behave as the content scales do when defensiveness is present, that is, scale elevations are inverse to the degree of defensiveness; however, the clinical scales do not seem to be as subject to defensive manipulation as the other major scale groups. The clinical scales evidence a notable reduction in mean differences between the three group means, and when compared to content scale data, the clinical scales seem significantly less subject to defensive manipulation than the content scales, and thus likely present a less distorted picture of the individual who responds defensively. Interestingly, Scales 2, 4, 5, and 8 display minimal differences between these three sets of data, and when the retest valid data are compared to the initial valid data, there are no statistically significant differences between Scales 2, 4, 5, and 8, further demonstrating the value of the clinical scales.

In the majority of cases, the applicant produces an open and valid validity configuration along with normal range clinical and content scale profiles. In a small percentage of the retest cases, the applicant shows possible personality problems or mental health symptoms that require further follow-up or consideration. In a small number of cases, there is a "confession effect" on some scales, particularly FRS and CYN. That is, the applicant during retest is much more open to divulging problems, particularly relatively common fears (FRS) or some cynical attitudes toward others (CYN). The retest with revised instructions strategy proved to be advantageous in that only 4% (47 cases) of the total N (1,093 cases) of the expanded study produced profiles that remained defensively invalid on retest, as opposed to the 21% (297 cases) initial DI number. The proportion of applicant profiles exceeding T65 on one or more of the MMPI-2 clinical, content, or supplementary scales moved from 40.3% in the DI group to 64.8% in the retest valid group, and from 6.4% in the DI content scale group to 47.2% in the retest valid group.

The data indicate that the retest with revised instructions strategy is effective at reducing the number of uninterpretable records; not only are a majority of the initial invalid and thus unusable cases salvaged but the valid retest data demonstrate a substantial increase in the number of scale elevations present, likely representing problems that were masked in the initial testing.

Strategies for MMPI-2 Interpretation

Once the possibility of test defensiveness is considered and resolved, either by retesting or by adjusting one's expectations of the information that can be obtained in the profiles, then the clinical scales and supplemental measures can be addressed. For further information on the interpretation of MMPI-2 scales, see Butcher (2005) and Graham (2006). If the applicant's performance is considered to present a sufficiently valid self-portrayal as to share personality information, the clinical, personality, and symptom scales can be addressed. For a detailed summary of job-related personality characteristics associated with MMPI scores, see Butcher et al. (2006).

Exclusion versus Inclusion Rules in the Evaluation

Unlike the use of test indices to select specific characteristics that are considered to enhance job performance (such as selecting individuals with high IQ score for positions involving complicated intellectual tasks), clinical personality assessment addresses personality characteristics or symptomatic behavior or interpersonal attitudes that are thought to likely interfere with or be a detriment to the occupation. For example, extreme scores on introversion for positions that require social interaction or high scores on substance abuse indicators for positions that require stability and reliability can signal problems in the workplace.

Personality Information Available through Personality Assessment

Butcher et al. (2006) provided a number of personality characteristics/traits that can be associated with high MMPI-2 scores and can provide information for personality-based hiring decisions. Some of these qualities are listed below:

• *Defensive approach to dealing with conflicts/relationships.* The person tends to be defensive, rigid, and evasive in dealing with others; is ineffective in dealing with conflict; or tends to be self-defensive under pressure (as shown by score elevations such as high K and S).
• *Low stress tolerance/low emotional control.* The person may panic under stress; may make inappropriate decisions under pressure; or may react to stress with negative behaviors such as alcohol abuse, and show physical symptoms (as shown by high scores such as high Hy, Pt, D, Addiction

Proneness Scale [APS], and MacAndrew Alcoholism Scale-Revised [MAC-R]).
• *Low acceptance of feedback, supervision.* The person may tend to externalize blame; become defensive when criticized. He/she may not accept authority (as shown by score elevations such as high Pa, Pd, Ma, and CYN).
• *Low impulse control.* The person may fail to think situations through before acting; may make rash decisions (as shown by score elevations such as high Pd, Ma, ASP or Antisocial Personality, and DISC or Disconstraint).
• *Presence of negative attitudes.* The applicant demonstrates low positive social skills; holds an overly cynical view of others; shows low trust (as shown by elevated scores such as high Si, CYN, and Pa).
• *Low dependability/reliability.* Shows characteristics of a procrastinator; is likely not to be careful at tasks; may show personality problems, such as impulsivity, that could create difficulties on the job (as shown by scale elevations such as high Pd, Ma, Sc, ASP, and CYN).
• *Shows low initiative/low achievement motivation.* The person may need careful supervision; is low in energy; and may show disabling psychopathology (as shown by score elevations such as high Sc, D, and WRK) or Work Interference.
• *Fails to conform to rules and regulations.* May not follow rules and regulations; shows low respect for authority; may not follow recommended testing procedures (as shown by elevations on scales such as high Pd, Ma, and ASP).
• *Low anger control.* May not be controlled; under stress; shows interpersonal relationship problems; has tendencies toward reactive aggression (as shown by score elevations such as high ANG or Anger, ASP, DISC, Pd, and Ma).
• *Low adaptability/low flexibility.* The person shows a low capacity to change behavior to meet new demands; likely has difficulty accepting new job demands; may not be able to work on more than one task at a time (as shown by high elevations such as Pt, Si, and WRK).
• *Possible problems with teamwork/working with others.* Shows a low capacity to develop and maintain good working relationships; has a low acceptance of authority and supervision; does not show a positive approach to problems (as shown by score elevations such as Pd, Sc, ANG, and ASP).

MMPI-2 Clinical Profile Information

Of key importance in MMPI-2-based decisions are the eight clinical scales of the basic profile. These scales possess the most extensive research support.

If the applicant's scores on these measures are in the clinically interpretable range, they suggest potential problems that can affect work performance. The research-based correlates for the MMPI-2 scales apply for this application. For example, an elevation of or greater than 65 on the Pa scale suggests problems such as suspicious mistrust, tendency to blame others for their problems, oversensitivity to interpersonal slights, and aloofness from others. If Pd is the highest point in the profile and elevated above a T-score of 65, then characteristics such as that the applicant tends to be impulsive and aggressive, breaks rules, engages in self-oriented and hedonistic behavior, and has relationship problems may characterize his/her functioning in the workplace. See Butcher (2005) and Graham (2006) for a fuller discussion of the meanings of clinical scale elevations.

Case of John W., Airline Pilot Applicant

John W., a 34-year-old corporate jet charter pilot, was evaluated in a psychological screening program for an airline pilot position at a major passenger airline. He had a 4-year college degree and a 6-year experience in the U.S. Navy flying fighter jets. For the past 3 years, he has been flying as a corporate charter pilot. His driving record indicated that he had two speeding tickets and one careless driving citation over the past 5 years.

In the interview, he denied having used illegal substances and reported that he only used alcohol once or twice a month and "never to excess." He did, however, acknowledge that, as a teenager, he was given a ticket for having an open bottle in his car. He denied having had any mental health treatment in the past. In the interview, the most stressful experience he noted was when he was going through a divorce 2 years earlier. However, he quickly indicated that his life was "smoother" now and that he was engaged to be married in 3 months.

MMPI-2-BASED HYPOTHESES TO CONSIDER

The MMPI-2 scores presented in Table 30.1 provide hypotheses about several possible problems with the applicant's personality adjustment. First, his validity scores, while within the interpretable range, suggests that the applicant is likely to be underreporting or masking problems. His K-score was elevated at a T-score of 70, indicating a high degree of test defensiveness and marginally invalid results. Thus, his clinical and content scale scores are likely to be lower than if he had been more forthcoming in his self-report. The applicant's clinical

Table 30.1. MMPI-2 Validity, clinical, and supplemental scale T-scores for John W., an airline pilot applicant.

Name validity scales	Scale elevation (T-score)
VRIN (Inconsistency)	38
TRIN (Inconsistency)	50T
F (Infrequency)	39
F(B) (Infrequency, Back)	46
F(p) (Infrequency–Psychopathology)	56
L (Lie)	43
K (Defensiveness)	70
S (Superlative Self-Presentation)	61
Clinical Scales	
Hs (Hypochondrasias)	64
D (Depression)	50
Hy (Hysteria)	64
Pd (Psychopathic Deviation)	74
Mf (Masculinity–Femininity)	46
Pa (Paranoia)	61
Pt (Psychasthenia)	57
Sc (Schizophrenia)	65
Ma (Hypomania)	53
Si (Social Introversion–Extraversion)	30
Supplemental Scales	
MAC-R (MacAndrew Scale)	62
APS (Addiction Potential Scale)	71
AAS (Addiction Acknowledgment Scale)	56
Pk (Keane PTSD Scale)	43
Do (Dominance)	61
Re (Responsibility)	47

scale scores, specifically his elevation on both the Pd scale and the Sc scale, suggests the strong possibility of personality-based problems that include the following characteristics: impulsivity, poor judgment, the strong possibility that the applicant disregards rules. High elevations on Pd and Sc suggest a somewhat unconventional lifestyle that centers on self-oriented and hedonistic behavior. Substance abuse problems are also noted in the supplemental scales; both the MAC-R and the APS scales are elevated in the range to suggest possible substance abuse problems.

Example Write-up John W.'s MMPI-2 Profile Evaluation

In his MMPI-2 performance, the applicant presented himself in an overly virtuous manner, which raises questions about possible underreporting of symptoms or other relevant personality issues. His marginally invalid MMPI-2 profile raises questions about whether his clinical and content scale scores are lower than what they would be if he were more forthcoming. However, he did produce noteworthy elevations on some of the MMPI-2 clinical and supplementary scales that provide sufficient information to alert the personnel decision makers about potential personality adjustment problems needing additional evaluation.

He should be assessed further for a history of immature, impulsive, and selfish actions. Pleasure seeking and risk taking are possible strong motivators for his behavior. He shows low tolerance for frustration and is likely to be manipulative. Many people with similar profiles tend to blame others rather than accept responsibility for their own actions. His likely pattern of immature and unreliable behaviors may have contributed to a history of poor work performance or achievement record, as well as other work difficulties.

His performance on the substance abuse scales (MAC-R and APS) suggests a personality style that is consistent with a substance use or abuse problem. Some individuals with a previous history of substance abuse problems who are no longer abusing drugs or alcohol can produce these scores. Therefore, careful evaluation of his "current" lifestyle factors, including alcohol and drug usage, should be further evaluated in the job-screening context. In addition, he may have experienced conflicts with authority and could become quite resentful. His MMPI-2 patterns suggest that he tends to have antisocial beliefs and attitudes. Others may view him as aggressive and hostile at times.

On the other hand, he is likely to be quite outgoing and sociable, and creates a good first impression. He may frequently be seen as spontaneous and fun loving. It would not be unusual for him to seek to be the center of attention. Although he seems to need to be around others, he may not have actual interest in or concern for them, and may use others for his own gains.

Based on his MMPI-2 scores, this applicant should be carefully evaluated for a history of acting out problems, substance abuse issues, impulsive behavior, and poor judgment. He may have problems with authority and may ignore rules, which could cause interpersonal problems and other problems at work. His likelihood of becoming easily bored and being a thrill seeker may be incompatible with performance as an airline pilot. People with this MMPI-2 pattern are likely to be considered unreliable at times. His past behavior and likely personality problems should be evaluated with careful background or reference checks.

Computer-based Interpretation as an Alternate Approach

Most employment assessment programs require comprehensive processing of the test results in a time-efficient manner in order to meet the schedule demands of the selection program. Computer-based assessment evaluations provide objective evaluations in a time-efficient manner (Atlis, Hahn, & Butcher, 2006). The most widely used personnel assessment computer-based report is the Minnesota Reports offered by Pearson Assessments.[2] The Minnesota Report for Personnel Settings provides two options for the assessment practitioner: a computer-derived narrative report and an adjustment rating report or a rating scale that ranks the applicant on several personality dimensions such as Openness to Evaluation, Addiction Potential, Stress Tolerance, and Overall Adjustment.

These MMPI-2 scoring options provide profiles for the validity scales and clinical scales, the content scales, and the PSY-5 scales along with scores for the widely used MMPI-2 supplemental scales such as the Addiction Proneness Scale or APS, Mac Andrew Alcoholism Scale or MAC-R, Addiction Acknowledgment Scale or AAS, the Hostility Scale or Ho, and Marital Distress Scale or MDS. The validity and clinical profiles, in addition to showing the applicant's scores plotted on the MMPI-2 norms, also shows the mean scores of a large sample of job applicants, and the mean scores of applicants from a selected database, for example, can be compared with those of airline pilots, police officers, nuclear power plant operators, etc. This information is provided in order to enable the practitioner to gain a perspective on the applicant's profiles by examining other applicants from similar populations (often referred to as "local norms"). The report also includes a description of the client's relevant content in the form of pertinent content themes and responses to the Negative Work Attitudes (WRK) scale items.

Role of the MMPI-2 in Personnel Decisions

The MMPI-2 can give the assessment psychologist a perspective on the applicant's adjustment or, more specifically, possible problems in relationships, substance use, self-confidence, emotional stability, and so forth that can be integrated with other information to obtain a complete picture. The MMPI-2, or any personality test, is not a stand alone instrument for making personnel decisions. Rather, the personality test results provide one set of hypotheses to include with other pertinent information from interview, behavioral observations, BI, etc.

The type of personnel selection setting decisions required can influence the way in which the MMPI-2-based information is incorporated into the evaluation. Two personnel evaluation settings are described below to illustrate how clinically based decisions are important to work-related evaluations. See Butcher et al. (2006) for information about other settings.

1. *Airline pilot selection program at a major air carrier.* The airline selection program typically proceeds as follows: After the applicant has applied and documented his/her qualifications through references, FAA licensing documents, military records, etc., they are invited (if aviation qualified) for a 2-day on-site interview, flight simulator check ride, and medical-psychological examination. The psychological evaluation includes several qualifying examinations such as an aviation knowledge exam. The MMPI-2 is group-administered during the first day of procedures. Applicants who pass the flight experiences, simulator check ride, and aviation knowledge exam are sent to the medical exam and psychological interviews. Prior to the medical and psychological examination, the applicant is extended a provisional offer of employment. Before the psychological evaluation is undertaken, the MMPI-2 is scored and the validity scale criteria are evaluated to determine if the test is interpretable. In the event that the protocol is invalid due to test defensiveness, the applicant is given the opportunity to retake the MMPI-2 at that point. Instructions are provided to reduce defensiveness as described above. After reviewing the MMPI-2 and conducting a psychological evaluation, the psychologist provides an assessment of the applicant's psychological adjustment. In the event that the recommendation is to withdraw the provisional offer based on findings of the medical or psychological examination, the applicant's file is reviewed by an Airline Pilot Review Board comprised of a senior airline captain, an OEO administrator, and a senior assessment psychologist. In some instances, the panel members may need to obtain additional information from other sources such as references, present employer, etc. A final decision to affirm of disconfirm the offer is made by the review panel.

2. *Security determination assessment procedures.* In order to comply with The Americans with Disabilities Act (ADA) of 1990, Titles I and V, no applicant is permitted to initiate the psychological assessment component of the fast-track examination procedure unless an offer of employment has been tendered by a prospective employer. The ADA considers preoffer medical examinations to be discriminatory; consequently, letters of offer, conditional or otherwise, are required to be produced prior to examination.

In the clearance assessment context, applicants for a security clearance proceed through a sequence that includes a general program briefing followed by the signing of consent to participate documents associated with each component of the program. Once these activities are accomplished, the applicant takes the standard computer version of the MMPI-2 in a setting designed for computer test administration. A video camera monitors room activity and transmits that information for real-time observation.

Most applicants use the English-language computer-administered version of the MMPI-2; however, the Spanish audiotape version, as well as the Spanish booklet version, is available. In addition, if the applicant has marginal reading ability, the appropriate audio-taped version is offered, using either the computer or the booklet answer form to record responses. Each applicant is apprised of these options prior to test administration. Applicant responses are computer scored, and two reports are produced, including the MMPI-2 Extended Score Report and the MMPI-2 Personnel Adjustment Rating Report.[3] The profile is immediately examined for validity issues, and if DI, the readministration instructions are presented. Applicants may decide not to retest; however, that decision is rare. MMPI-2 data are available to the interviewing psychologist prior to interview.

The final psychological report is based on both historical, interview, and test data. If issues of concern arise as a result of the psychological evaluation, the case is reviewed by at least one external quality assurance (QA) psychologist. In addition, every 10th case is also sent for external QA review, thus providing additional layers of external independent review.

Importance of Using Well-Developed and Research Measures for Personnel Decisions

Personnel decisions need to be based upon the most acceptable and defensible (in court) instruments and procedures available. The use of any assessment instrument in employment-related evaluation requires that the procedure is valid and research based. Since the MMPI was published in 1940, there have been hundreds of different scales developed from the item pool. In fact, more scales have been published for the MMPI/MMPI-2 than there are items in the inventory. Several scale development procedures have followed. The original empirical approach used by Hathaway and McKinley (1940), in which items were included on the measure based upon actual differentiation between a clinical group and a normative sample, was the flagship approach to scale construction with the MMPI. However, other approaches have resulted in scales such as the content-based measures in which the item clusters were obtained from a rational review of the item pool; or through factor analysis, a statistical procedure that also results in homogeneous, content similar item make-up. The publication of a scale based on MMPI-2 items does not automatically qualify it for personnel selection.

Although some scales, such as the Superlative Self-Presentation Scale (S) by Butcher & Han (1995) that was derived from a sample of job applicants to assess test defensiveness, used both an empirical (item differentiation between applicants and the normative population) and refined approach using correlational statistics (the alpha coefficient), most new personality measures are not developed for or tested out in employment settings and may have less applicability for this setting than for mental health settings.

Several new procedures and scales have been recently introduced for the MMPI-2 and will be described briefly below. Although they are not recommended for personnel screening because no research for the personnel setting has been developed, they are prominently advertised and might be considered as possible resources for personnel applications.

NON-K-CORRECTED CLINICAL SCALE PROFILES

The K scale of the MMPI was developed by Meehl and Hathaway to correct for defensiveness as a means of improving the discrimination of cases in a psychiatric setting by correcting some clinical scales to detect psychopathology in patients who were overly defensive during the administration. Five MMPI scales (Hy, Pd, Pt, Sc, and Ma) were found to work more effectively by adding a portion of the K scale to the raw score. Subsequent research has shown that the K scale is effective at detecting defensive responses and problem denial (Graham, 2006; Greene, 2000), but the use of the K correction weights has not been proven to add much (Archer, Fontaine, & McCrae, 1998; Sines, Baucom, & Gruba, 1979). For example, Weed (1993) evaluated different possible weights but

found no combination of weights was effective at increasing the discrimination. However, most MMPI studies since 1946 have been conducted using K-corrected T-scores and no research on scale validity has produced a sufficient validity database to support the interpretation of non-K-corrected scores for most applications. Thus, contemporary applications in personnel settings use the K-corrected scores, in part, because there is very little difference between K-corrected and non-K-corrected profiles in the majority of instances. In some cases, however, non-K-corrected profiles can appear different from the K-corrected profile and can result in a different code type. At present, the practice of correcting for K in interpreting profiles still continues in MMPI-2 use, because virtually all of the empirical research supporting test interpretation of the clinical scales involves K-corrected scores. In personnel screening particularly, the non-K-corrected profile has not been sufficiently researched to serve as a confident basis for interpretation and the test interpreter has a much more extensive database for interpreting the K-corrected profile than the non-K-corrected.

The interpreter needs to carefully attend to the T-score on K. If the K scale score is in the range of 68–71, the protocol is marginally valid; if it exceeds 72 T, then the profile is unlikely to be useful in providing reliable self-reported personality information. Thus, defensive profiles in this range should not be interpreted.

THE RESTRUCTURED CLINICAL OR RC SCALES

The RC Scales were developed by Tellegen et al. (2003) as a means of refining or clarifying interpretation of the traditional clinical scales. These measures were developed using existing data sets and no new norms or validity data were included. The scales were developed as follows: Initially, the scale developers constructed a "Demoralization scale" to identify items that were thought to adversely affect the clinical scales because of their heavy loading by general maladjustment. Next, they removed the demoralization items from the clinical scales to develop "seed" scales for the eight clinical scales that were thought to represent the basic "core" of the constructs. Next, the RC core constructs were expanded by obtaining items from the remainder of the item pool by taking items that correlated highly with the core constructs Finally, the authors conducted internal and external validity analyses to further explore the RC Scales' psychometric functioning. The authors used three existing databases to verify the internal validity and predictive validity of the RC Scales (see discussion in Chapters Chapter 7 and 14 for further information on the RC Scale development).

Limited information was made available on the scales when they were initially published and a number of questions were raised about their functioning and contribution to interpretation. The RC Scales have come under considerable criticism for several reasons:

1. Their "core" has been thought to have drifted too far from the original clinical scales to serve in a clarifying role for elevations on the traditional scales (Butcher, Hamilton, Rouse, & Cumella, 2006; Gordon, 2006; Nichols, 2006).

2. The RC Scales have been shown to be largely redundant measures of existing content and supplemental scales and not providing new, valid measures of the clinical scale constructs (Rogers, Sewell, Harrison, & Jordan, 2006; Rouse, Greene, Butcher, Nichols, & Williams, 2008).

3. Several articles have raised questions about the sensitivity of the RC Scales to psychopathology. For example, Rogers et al. (2006) reported that in a large clinical sample, almost half of the RC Scales showed no elevations for patients. Similarly, Wallace and Liljequist (2005) reported that 56% of mental health patients had normal range RC Scale profiles. More recently, Megargee (2006) found that the sensitivity of the RC Scales at detecting adjustment problems was low. Contrary to what one might expect, the average MMPI-2 scores for the RC Scales for the prisoners showed no mental health or personality problems; over half of the average RC mean scores were actually below the average scores of the MMPI-2 normative sample (see also discussion in Cox et al., in Chapter 4).

The MMPI-2 RF

The test publisher recently announced a new shortened version of the MMPI-2 in an effort to provide an abbreviated version of several new scales. The developers of the new short form of the MMPI-2 made no efforts to maintain continuity with the original MMPI or MMPI-2 clinical or content scales but focused upon the Restructured or RC Scales (Tellegen et al., 2003). The scale authors have not included the traditional MMPI-2 constructs in favor of new, shorter scales, which have a sparse research base. These scales have not been vetted in personnel selection situations and are not supported for such applications. For further discussion of the problems with the RC scales and MMPI-2 RF see Butcher and Williams (2009).

Summary

This chapter provides an overview of the use of clinical personality measurement techniques in employment applications. Major goals of the chapter include the following areas of emphasis. First a rationale for the inclusion of clinical personality assessment measures in personnel decisions such as employment screening, fitness for duty evaluations, and reliability screenings for making recommendations for promotion to responsible positions or for the issuance of security clearances for sensitive applications are provided. A number of contemporary issues pertaining to clinical personnel screening are presented. Next, a historical summary of the use of the most widely used personality measure in clinical settings, the MMPI-2, is presented along with a strategy for the interpreting instruments used in employment settings. The chapter provides practical examples of clinically based assessments in employment settings. It also includes descriptive information on the MMPI-2 and contains up-to-date references and resources that interested readers wishing more thorough information can follow up.

Notes

1. For a more complete listing of MMPI/MMPI-2 research in personnel settings, see: Rouse, S. V. & Butcher, J. N. (1995). *Annotated bibliography on the use of the MMPI/MMPI-2 in personnel and educational selection.* Minneapolis, MN: University of Minnesota Press and web site http://www.umn.edu/mmpi

2. Pearson Assessments (formerly NCS), 5601 Green Valley Drive, 5th floor, Bloomington, MN 55437. Phone: 800-627-7271, Fax: 952-681-3259.

3. The Minnesota Report[TM]: Revised Personnel System, 3rd ed., James N. Butcher, PhD.

References

Abramson, H. A. (1945). The Minnesota personality test in relation to selection of specialized military personnel. *Psychosomatic Medicine, 7,* 178–184.

The Americans with Disabilities Act of 1990 (ADA). (1990). United States Public Law 101-336, 104 Stat. 327 (July 26, 1990).

Atlis, M. M., Hahn, J., & Butcher, J. N. (2006). Computer-based assessment with the MMPI-2. In J. N. Butcher (Ed.), *MMPI-2: The practitioner's handbook* (pp. 445–476). Washington, DC: American Psychological Association.

Archer, R. P., Fontaine, J., & McCrae, R. R. (1998). Effects of two MMPI-2 validity scales on basic scale relations to external criteria. *Journal of Personality Assessment, 70,* 87–102.

Bagby, R. M., Marshall, M. B., Bury, A., Bacchiocci, J. R., & Miller, L. (2006). Assessing underreporting and overreporting styles on the MMPI-2. In J. N. Butcher (Ed.), *MMPI-2: The practitioner's handbook* (pp. 39–69). Washington, DC: American Psychological Association.

Bagby, R. M., Nicholson, R. A., Rogers, R., Buis, T., Seeman, M. V., & Rector, N. A. (1997). Effectiveness of the MMPI-2 validity indicators in the detection of defensive responding in clinical and nonclinical samples. *Psychological Assessment, 7,* 406–413.

Bartol, C. R. (1982). Psychological characteristics of small-town police officers. *Journal of Police Science and Administration, 10,* 58–63.

Bartol, C. R. (1991). Predictive validation of the MMPI for small-town police officers who fail. *Professional Psychology: Research and Practice, 22,* 127–132.

Bernreuter, R. G. (1931). *The Personality Inventory.* Palo Alto, CA: Consulting Psychologists Press.

Beutler, L. E., Nussbaum, P. D., & Meredith, K. E. (1988). Changing personality patterns of police officers. *Professional Psychology: Research and Practice, 19,* 503–507.

Blau, T. H. (1994). *Psychological services for law enforcement.* New York: John Wiley & Sons.

Bray, D. W. (1964). The Management Progress Study. *American Psychologist, 19,* 419–420.

Brenneis, M. J. (2000). Personality and demographic factors predicting conflicted attitudes toward authority in clergy who have completed residential psychiatric treatment. *Dissertation Abstracts International, 61,* 558.

Burbeck, E., & Furnham, A. (1985). Police officer selection: A critical review of the literature. *Journal of Police Science and Administration, 13,* 58–69.

Butcher, J. N. (1994). Psychological assessment of airline pilot applicants with the MMPI-2. *Journal of Personality Assessment, 62,* 31–44.

Butcher, J. N. (1998). *Analysis of S subscales to refine interpretation of "good impression".* Paper presented at the 33rd Annual Symposium on Recent Developments in the Use of the MMPI-2/MMPI-A Workshop and Symposia, Clearwater Beach, FL, March 1998.

Butcher, J. N. (2001). *The Minnesota Report: Revised Personnel System* (3rd ed.). Minneapolis, MN: NCS Assessments.

Butcher, J. N. (2002). Assessing pilots with "the wrong stuff:" A call for research on emotional health factors in commercial aviators. *International Journal of Selection and Assessment, 10,* 1–17.

Butcher, J. N. (2005). *MMPI-2: A beginner's guide* (2nd ed.). Washington DC: The American Psychological Association.

Butcher, J. N., Dahlstrom, W.G., Graham, J. R., Tellegen, A., & Kaemmer, B. (1989). *Minnesota multiphasic personality inventory-2 (MMPI-2): Manual for administration and scoring.* Minneapolis, MN: University of Minnesota Press.

Butcher, J. N., Hamilton, C. K., Rouse, S. V., & Cumella, E. J. (2006). The Deconstruction of the Hy scale of MMPI-2: Failure of RC3 in measuring somatic symptom expression. *Journal of Personality Assessment, 87,* 199–205.

Butcher, J. N., & Han, K. (1995). Development of an MMPI-2 scale to assess the presentation of self in a superlative manner: The S scale. In J. N. Butcher & C. D. Spielberger (Eds.), *Advances in personality assessment* (Vol. 10, pp. 25–50). Hillsdale, NJ: LEA Press.

Butcher, J. N., Morfitt, R. C., Rouse, S. V., & Holden, R. R. (1997). Reducing MMPI-2 defensiveness: The effect of specialized instructions on retest validity in a job applicant sample. *Journal of Personality Assessment, 68,* 385–401.

Butcher, J. N., Ones, D. S., & Cullen, M. (2006). Personnel screening with the MMPI-2. In J. N. Butcher (Ed.), *MMPI-2:*

The practitioner's handbook (pp. 381–406). Washington, DC: American Psychological Association.

Butcher, J. N., & Williams, C. L. (2009). Personality assessment with the MMPI-2: Historical roots, international adaptations, and current challenges. *Applied Psychology, Health and Well-Being,* 1, 105–135.

Caldwell, J. A., O'Hara, C., Caldwell, J., & Stephens, R. L. et al. (1993). Personality profiles of U.S. Army helicopter pilots screened for special operations duty. *Military Psychology, 5,* 187–199.

Camargo, R. J. (1997a). Factor, cluster, and discriminant analyses of data on sexually active clergy: Erratum. *American Journal of Forensic Psychology, 15,* 64.

Camargo, R. J. (1997b). Factor, cluster, and discriminant analyses of data on sexually active clergy: The molesters of youth identified. *American Journal of Forensic Psychology, 15,* 5–24.

Carpenter, B. N., & Raza, S. M. (1987). Personality characteristics of police applicants: Comparisons across subgroups and with other populations. *Journal of Police Science and Administration, 15,* 10–17.

Cauthen, D. (1988). Urban police applicant MMPI score differences due to employment classification and gender. *Dissertation Abstracts International, 48,* 3148.

Cigrang, J. A., & Staal, M. A. (2001). Readmission of the MMPI-2 following defensive invalidation in a military job applicant sample. *Journal of Personality Assessment, 76,* 472–481.

Cimbura, J. A. (2000). An exploration of stress in police officers: A study of the predictive value of pre-employment psychological measures in the development of stress reactions in a sample of Ontario police officers. *Dissertation Abstracts International, 60,* 4291.

Colotla, V. A., Bowman, M. L., & Shercliffe, R. J. (2001). Test–retest stability of injured workers' MMPI-2 profiles. *Psychological Assessment, 13,* 572–576.

Cooper, J. E. (2003). Identifying the superlative self-presentation of Christian clergy clients: An investigation of the MMPI-2 S scale factor structure and client typologies. *Dissertation Abstracts International, Section B: The Sciences and Engineering, 60*(7-B), 3505.

Corey, D. M. (1989). The psychological suitability of police officer candidates. *Dissertation Abstracts International, 49,* 3433.

Cortina, J. M., Doherty, M. L., Schmitt, N., & Kaufman, G. (1992). The "Big Five" personality factors in the IPI and MMPI: Predictors of police performance. *Personnel Psychology, 45,* 119–140.

Costa, P.T., Jr., & McCrae, R. E. (1985). *The NEO Personality Inventory manual.* Odessa, FL: Psychological Assessment Services.

Costello, R. M., Schoenfeld, L. S., & Kobos, J. (1982). Police applicant screening: An analogue study. *Journal of Clinical Psychology, 38,* 216–221.

Detrick, P., Chibnall, J. T., & Rosso, M. (2001). Minnesota Multiphasic Personality Inventory-2 in police officer selection: Normative data and relation to the Inwald Personality Inventory. *Professional Psychology—Research and Practice, 32,* 484–490.

Dittes, J. (1962). Research on clergymen: Factors influencing decisions for religious serves and effectiveness in the vocation. *Religious Education, 57,* 141–165.

Dunnette, M. D. (1966). *Personnel selection and placement.* Oxford: Wadsworth Publishing.

Enelow, A. (1991). Psychiatric disorders and work function. *Psychiatric Annals, 21,* 27–35.

Equal Employment Opportunity Commission, Civil Service Commission, U.S. Department of Labor, & U.S. Department of Justice. (1978). Uniform guidelines on employee selection procedures. *Federal Register, 43,* 38290–38315.

Ervin, S. J., Jr. (1965). Why Senate hearings on psychological tests in government. *American Psychologist, 20,* 879–880.

FitzGerald, P. R. (1987). The prediction of police performance using the MMPI and CPI. *Dissertation Abstracts International, 47*(8-B), 3519.

Fulkerson, S. C. (1956). Adaptability screening of flying personnel: Development of a preliminary screening battery. *United States Air Force School of Aviation Medicine Report, no.v56-84,* 21.

Fulkerson, S. C. (1957). Adaptability screening of flying personnel: Research on the Minnesota Multiphasic Personality Inventory. *United States Air Force School of Aviation Medicine Report, no.v57-106,* 17.

Fulkerson, S. C. (1958a). An acquiescence key for the MMPI. *United States Air Force School of Aviation Medicine Report, no. v58–71, 11.*

Fulkerson, S. C. (1958b). The use of the MMPI in the psychological evaluation of pilots. *Journal of Aviation Medicine, 29,* 122–129.

Fulkerson, S. C., & Sells, S. B. (1958). Adaptation of the MMPI for aeromedical practice norms for military pilots. *United States Air Force School of Aviation Medicine Report, no.v58-128,* 6.

Ganellen, R. J. (1994). Attempting to conceal psychological disturbance: MMPI defensive response sets and the Rorschach. *Journal of Personality Assessment, 63*(3), 423–437.

Geist, C. R., & Boyd, S. T. (1980). Personality characteristics of Army helicopter pilots. *Perceptual and Motor Skills, 51,* 253–254.

Goffin, R. D., Rothstein, M. G., & Johnston, N. G. (1996). Personality testing and the assessment center: Incremental validity for managerial selection. *Journal of Applied Psychology, 81,* 746–756.

Goodstein, L. D., & Lanyon, R. I. (1999). Applications of personality assessment to the workplace: A review. *Journal of Business and Psychology, 13,* 291–322.

Gordon, R. M. (2006). False assumptions about psychopathology, hysteria and the MMPI-2 Restructured Clinical Scales. *Psychological Reports, 98,* 870–872.

Graham, J. R. (2006). *MMPI-2: Assessing personality and psychopathology* (4th ed.). New York: Oxford University Press.

Greene, R. L. (2000). *The MMPI-2: An interpretive manual* (2nd ed.). Needham Heights, MA: Allyn & Bacon.

Gucker, D., & McNulty, J. L. (2004). *The MMPI-2, defensiveness and an analytic strategy.* Paper presented at the 39th Annual Symposium on Recent Developments in the Use of the MMPI-2 and the MMPI-A, Minneapolis, MN, May 2004.

Hathaway, S. R., & McKinley, J. C. (1940). A multiphasic personality schedule (Minnesota): Construction of the schedule. *Journal of Psychology, 10,* 249–254.

Heymans, G., & Wiersma, E. (1906). Beitrage zur spezillen psychologie auf grund einer massen-unterschung. *Zeitschrift fur Psychologie, 43,* 81–127.

Hough, L. (1998). Personality at work: Issues and evidence. In M. D. Hakel (Ed.), *Beyond multiple choice: Evaluating alternatives to traditional testing for selection* (pp. 131–166). Mahwah, NJ: Lawrence Erlbaum.

Hough, L. M., Eaton, N. K., Dunnette, M. D., Kamp, J. D., & McCloy, R. A. (1990). Criterion-related validities of personality constructs and the effect of response distortion on those validities. *Journal of Applied Psychology, 75,* 581–595.

Hough, L. M., & Ones, D. S. (2002). The structure, measurement, validity, and use of personality variables in industrial, work, and organizational psychology. In N. Anderson, D. S. Ones, H. K. Sinangil, & C. Viswesvaran (Eds.), *Handbook of industrial, work and organizational psychology,* Vol. 1: Personnel psychology (pp. 233–277). Thousand Oaks, CA: Sage Publications.

Ingle, D. J. (1934). A test of mental instability. *Journal of Applied Psychology, 18,* 252–266.

Irving, P. G. (1993). On the use of personality measures in personnel selection. *Canadian Psychology, 34,* 208–214.

Johnson, E. E. (1983). Psychological tests used in assessing a sample of police and fire fighter candidates. *Journal of Police Science and Administration, 11,* 430–433.

Kirchner, W. K., Dunnette, M. D., & Mousley, N. (1960). Use of the Edwards Personal Preference Schedule in the selection of salesmen. *Personnel Psychology, 13,* 421–424.

Klimoski, R. J., & Zukin, L. B. (2003). Psychological assessment in industrial/organizational settings. In J. R. Graham & J. A. Naglieri (Eds.), *Handbook of psychology* (Vol. 10, pp. 317–344). New York: John Wiley & Sons.

Liao, H., Arvey, R. D., Nutting, S. M., & Butler, R. (2001). Correlates of work injury frequency and duration among firefighters. *Journal of Occupational Health Psychology, 6,* 229–242.

Lim, J., & Butcher, J. N. (1996). Detection of faking on the MMPI-2: Differentiation between faking-bad, denial, and claiming extreme virtue. *Journal of Personality Assessment, 67,* 1–25.

Livingston, R. B., Jennings, E., Colotla, V. A., Reynolds, C. R., & Shercliffe, R. J. (2006). MMPI-2 code-type congruence of injured workers. *Psychological Assessment, 18,* 126–130.

Matarazzo, J. D., Allen, B. V., Saslow, G., & Wiens, A. N. (1964). Characteristics of successful policemen and firemen applicants. *Journal of Applied Psychology, 48,* 123–133.

McKenna, T., & Butcher, J. N. (1987). *Continuity of the MMPI with alcoholics.* Paper presented at the 23rd Annual Symposium on Recent Developments in the Use of the MMPI, Seattle, WA.

Megargee, E. I. (2006). Use of the MMPI-2 in correctional settings. In J. N. Butcher (Ed.), *MMPI-2: The practitioner's handbook* (pp. 327–460). Washington, DC: American Psychological Association.

Munsterberg, H. (1913). *Psychology and industrial efficiency.* Boston: Houghton-Mifflin.

Nichols, D. S. (2006). The trials of separating bath water from baby: A review and critique of the MMPI-2 Restructured Clinical Scales. *Journal of Personality Assessment, 87,* 121–138.

Paterson, D. G. (1936). *Men, women, and jobs: A study in human engineering; a review of the studies of the Committee on Individual Diagnosis and Training.* Minneapolis, MN: University of Minnesota Press.

Paulhus, D. L., Harms, P. D., Bruce, M. N., & Lysy, D. C. (2003). The over-claiming technique: Measuring self-enhancement independent of ability. *Journal of Personality and Social Psychology, 84,* 890–904.

Personnel Decisions International Corporation. (1991). *The profiler*. Minneapolis, MN: Author.

Putnam, S., Adams, K., & Butcher, J. N. (1992, May). *A comparative MMPI-2 study of three professional samples: Attorneys, insurance case managers, and clergy*. Paper presented at the 27th Annual Symposium on Recent Developments in the Use of the MMPI-2/MMPI-A Workshop and Symposia, Minneapolis, MN.

Putnam, S. H., Kurtz, J. E., & Houts, D. C. (1996). Four-month test–retest reliability of the MMPI-2 with normal male clergy. *Journal of Personality Assessment, 67*, 341–353.

Robertson, I. T. (1994a). Personality assessment and personnel selection. *European Review of Applied Psychology/Revue Européenne de Psychologie Appliquée, 43*, 187–194.

Robertson, I. T. (1994b). Personality and personnel selection. In C. Cooper & D. M. Rousseau (Eds.), *Trends in organizational behavior* (Vol. 1, pp. 75–89). Oxford: John Wiley & Sons.

Rogers, R., Sewell, K. W., Harrison, K. W., & Jordan, M. J. (2006). The MMPI-2 Restructured Clinical Scales: A paradigmatic shift to scale development. *Journal of Personality Assessment, 87*, 139–147.

Rouse, S. V., Greene, R. L., Butcher, J. N., Nichols, D. S., & Williams, C. L. (2008). What do the MMPI-2 Restructured Clinical Scales reliably measure? Answers from multiple research settings. *Journal of Personality Assessment, 90*, 435–422.

Rozanov, V. A., Mokhavikov, A. N., & Stiliha, R. (2002). Successful model of suicide prevention in the Ukraine military environment. *Crisis, 23*, 171–177.

Schneider, R. J., Hough, L. M., & Dunnette, M. D. (1996). Broadsided by broad traits: How to sink science in five dimensions or less. *Journal of Organizational Behavior, 17*, 639–655

Scogin, F., Schumacher, J., Gardner, J., & Chaplin, W. (1995). Predictive validity of psychological testing in law enforcement settings. *Professional Psychology: Research and Practice, 26*, 68–71.

Scott, W. D., & Clothier, R. C. (1923). *Personnel management*. Chicago: Shaw.

Scott, W. D., & Hayes, M. H. S. (1921). *Science and common sense in working with men*. New York: Ronald.

Sines, L. K., Baucom, D. H., & Gruba, G. H. (1979). A validity scale sign calling for caution in the interpretation of MMPIs among psychiatric inpatients. *Journal of Personality Assessment, 43*, 604–607.

Sparvieri, F., & de Angelis, E. (1971). On the problem of the psychological selection of student pilots: Preliminary results of the use of the MMPI in a group of student pilots. *Rivista de Medicina Aeronautica e Spaziale, 34*, 101–110.

Sperry, L., Kahn, J. P., & Heidel, S. H. (1994). Workplace mental health consultation: A primer of organizational and occupational psychiatry. *General Hospital Psychiatry, 16*, 103–111.

Spiro III, A., Butcher, J. N., Levenson, M. R., Aldwin, C. M., & Bosse, R. (2000). Change and stability in personality: A 5-year study of the MMPI-2 in older men. In J. N. Butcher (Ed), *Basic sources for the MMPI-2* (pp. 443–463). Minneapolis, MN: University of Minnesota Press.

Tellegen, A., Ben-Porath, Y. S., McNulty, J., Arbisi, P., Graham, J. R., & Kaemmer, B. (2003). *MMPI-2: Restructured Clinical (RC) Scales*. Minneapolis, MN: University of Minnesota Press.

Thomas, J. C., & Hersen, M. (2004). *Psychopathology in the workplace: Recognition and adaptation*. New York: Brunner-Routledge.

Usenko, G. (1992). Psychosomatic status and flying skill during geomagnetic disturbances [Russian]. *Aviakosmicheskaia i Ekologicheskaia Meditsina, 26*, 23–27.

Walfish, S. (2007). Reducing Minnesota Multiphasic Personality Inventory defensiveness: Effect of specializecd instructions on retest validity in a sample of preoperative bariatric patients. *Surgery for Obesity and Related Diseases, 3*, 184–188.

Wallace, A., & Liljequist, L. (2005). A comparison of the correlational structures and elevation patterns of the MMPI-2 Restructured Clinical (RC) and Clinical Scales. *Assessment, 12*, 290–294.

Weed, N. C. (1993). An evaluation of the efficacy of MMPI-2 indicators of validity. *Dissertation Abstracts International, 53*, 3800.

Wells, V. K. (1992). The MMPI and CPI as predictors of police performance. *Dissertation Abstracts International, 53*, 597.

Woodworth, R. S. (1919). Examination of emotional fitness for war. *Psychological Bulletin, 15*, 59–60.

Woodworth, R. S. (1920). *The Personal Data Sheet*. Chicago: Stoelting.

Wright, B. S. (1988). Psychological evaluations as predictors of police recruit performance. *Dissertation Abstracts International, 49*, 1585.

Anticipating Ethical and Legal Challenges in Personality Assessments

Irving B. Weiner

Abstract

Despite their best intentions, practitioners of personality assessment sometimes painfully discover they have paid insufficient attention to what they should or should not have done. This chapter addresses ways in which personality assessors can anticipate ethical and legal challenges and by so doing avoid them. The overriding consideration in this regard is adherence to the APA Ethical Principles and Code of Conduct and relevant state statutes and regulations. Practitioners can additionally protect themselves against ethical and legal recriminations by following some recommended procedures for establishing clearly the identity of the client when they accept a referral; selecting measures that are commonly used, well substantiated, and familiar to them; conducting their evaluations in standard ways and recording the data carefully; writing and presenting their reports in an appropriately denotative and circumspect manner; and maintaining the confidentiality and availability of their records for an appropriate length of time.

Keywords: ethics, forensics, personality assessment, psychological testing, risk management

Personality assessors rarely intend to break the law or violate the ethical standards of their profession. Likewise, few psychologists wish to look insensitive in their consulting rooms or foolish in the courtroom. At times, however, practitioners painfully discover that, despite their best intentions and wishes, they have paid insufficient attention to what they should or should not have done. This chapter addresses ways in which personality assessors can anticipate ethical and legal challenges and, by taking arms against them, avoid a sea of troubles.

As an overriding consideration in minimizing risk, psychologists can protect themselves against ethical and legal quagmires by adhering to the "Ethical Principles and Code of Conduct" of the American Psychological Association (APA, 2002) and the relevant statutory laws and professional regulations in the state in which they are practicing. Additional protections are specified in "Record Keeping Guidelines" (APA, 1993), "Guidelines for Child Custody Evaluations" (APA, 1994), "Guidelines on Multicultural Education, Training, Research, Practice, and Organizational

Change for Psychologists" (APA, 2003), and "Specialty Guidelines for Forensic Psychologists" (Committee on Ethical Guidelines for Forensic Psychologists, 1991). Information about state laws and regulations is available in a series of APA books devoted to the individual states (e.g., for Florida, see Petrila & Otto, 1996).

Other contemporary elaborations on ethical practice in psychology include books by Bennett et al. (2006), Bucky, Callan, and Stricker (2007), Kitchener (2000), Knapp and VandeCreek (2006), Nagy (2005), Pope, Butcher, and Seelen (2006), and Pope and Vasquez (2007) (see also http://www.kspope.com). For further general information about ethical and legal risk in personality assessment, readers are referred to Weiner and Greene (2008, chap. 3) and specific attention by Koocher (2006) to forensic assessment of children and adolescents, by Barnett and Dunning (2005) to assessing the elderly, and by Brabender and Bricklin (2001) and Turchik, Karpenko, Hammers, and McNamara (2007) to conducting assessments in diverse settings.

A few additional introductory comments about adherence to ethical and legal standards are in order. First, as elaborated by Barnett, Behnke, Rosenthal, and Koocher (2007), ethical codes furnish principles that guide clinicians in practicing ethically, but they do not supply solutions to every ethical uncertainty that may arise in clinical practice. Hence clinicians must often rely on their judgment as well as on formal codes of conduct in resolving ethical dilemmas, and their decisions must also take into account the context of each situation. A satisfactory solution to an ethical issue in one situation may not be a sensitive or discreet way of resolving a similar issue emerging in a different setting and involving different types of people with different types of problems.

Second, as discussed by Knapp, Gottlieb, Berman, and Handelsman (2007), clinicians may at times encounter legal demands or expectations that run counter to their ethical convictions. Practitioners are obliged to abide by the laws of their state, whatever the ethical principles of their profession. Yet there may be times when ethical principles warrant objections by psychologists to what they are being asked to do, and in these instances they may attempt to reconcile with the court a conflict between what is legal and what they see as violating a patient's or client's rights.

Third, awareness of ethical and legal issues should not be a now-and-then event occasioned by an unexpectedly problematic case or a complaint filed in civil court or with a licensing board. Instead, to minimize their risk of professional peril, practitioners need to be continuously and proactively alert to the ethical and legal implications of what they do or omit to do.

Fourth, as a seemingly obvious matter but one that nevertheless must be made explicit, psychologists who provide assessment services should protect themselves and the public by obtaining and maintaining licensure in the state in which they practice and by carrying appropriate malpractice insurance. In some locales, psychologists working in state agencies or other specified facilities may be exempted from licensing requirements, and some institutions may provide adequate malpractice coverage for their psychology staff. It behooves assessment psychologists to be certain of their particular circumstances in both of these respects.

The present chapter discusses five sequential phases of clinical personality assessment, in each of which lurk some ethical and legal hazards: (1) accepting a referral; (2) selecting the test battery; (3) conducting the psychological evaluation; (4) preparing and presenting a report; and (5) managing case records. As they proceed through these phases of an assessment, psychological examiners can sustain a high level of anticipation, and thereby sidestep any lurking hazards, by following the recommendations in this chapter and by imagining three scenarios:

1. Whatever you do, imagine that a knowledgeable and unfriendly critic is looking over your shoulder.
2. Whatever you say, imagine that it will be taken in the most unfavorable light possible and used against you.
3. Whatever you write, imagine that it will be read aloud, sarcastically, in a court of law.

Although these scenarios may suggest an unseemly paranoia, colleagues who have encountered the kinds of unpleasant situations illustrated in this chapter will surely think otherwise. However, as a less pathological construction than paranoia on how clinicians should conduct their practice, hypervigilance at least is in order. Practitioners can also be comforted by appreciating that the APA ethics code rests on the fundamental requirement for psychologists to be knowledgeable and responsible professionals who respect the rights and dignity of others, show concern for the welfare of their clients and colleagues, and present themselves fairly and honestly to their patients and their communities. These features of being a competent clinician and a decent person usually suffice to carry personality assessors with propriety through the several phases of conducting a psychological evaluation. In each phase, however, there are certain steps that can be taken to restrict ethical and legal jeopardy.

Accepting a Referral

From an ethical and legal perspective, a key consideration in accepting a referral for diagnostic consultation is knowing who the client is. The client in personality assessment has traditionally been regarded as the person who is examined, receives a report of the findings, pays for the services rendered, and commands the clinician's primary allegiance. A self-referred examinee who expects to receive feedback concerning the psychologist's conclusions and recommendations and to pay the bill can usually be identified as the client with little difficulty. Often, however, as elaborated by Monahan (1980), there are other circumstances in the delivery of assessment services that make clienthood a more complex matter than this.

Frequently, for example, people being examined share their clienthood with other parties or agencies to which the clinician also has some responsibility. In the case of a minor child, there are typically parents who will be paying the bill and rightfully expecting to be informed of the results of the evaluation. In the case of individuals referred for a diagnostic consultation, other professionals who will not be paying for the service will be the primary recipient of the psychologist's report, although the person being examined is ordinarily entitled under the Health Insurance Portability and Accountability Act (HIPAA) regulations to receive a copy of the report as well. On occasion, however, particularly in examinations to assist in personnel selection or fitness-for-duty determinations, third parties paying the bill and receiving a full report may require the person being examined to waive access to the content of the report.

In still other instances, managed care organizations and other health insurers may pay at least in part for an evaluation but request and receive only minimal information, like the date of testing, the measures used, a formal diagnosis, and perhaps a treatment recommendation. In this and the other referral circumstances just mentioned, examiners have dual or even multiple obligations to meet the expectations and entitlements of both the person being tested and the parties paying for and being informed about the evaluation.

As a further consideration relevant to proper procedure, psychological examinations may occur in response to either a "clinical" referral or an "administrative" referral. A clinical referral comes from someone who is concerned about a patient's welfare and attempting to be helpful to the person. An administrative referral comes from a person or entity seeking assistance in making a judgment about the individual to be evaluated. The results of administrative evaluations may or may not be helpful to an examinee, and referring parties are concerned mainly with the welfare of the entities they represent, not the welfare of the person being examined. Common types of administrative referrals include the previously mentioned personnel selection and fitness-for-duty evaluations, requests from employers or insurance companies to evaluate employees for disability, court-ordered assessments to help determine the competence or sanity of criminal defendants, and school-based referrals to assist in class placement or disciplinary decisions. Bennett et al. (2006, chap. 6) aptly refer to such administrative evaluations as "testing with external consequences," as a way of distinguishing them from clinical testing for purposes of differential diagnosis and treatment planning.

In further contrast to the usual situation in clinical evaluations, persons seen for administrative purposes are usually involuntary examinees. Were parties with control over their destiny not requiring an examination, they would not be in the psychologist's office. Administratively referred persons can of course refuse to be examined, or they can go through the motions of participating in an examination without being fully cooperative. However, they are usually aware that refusal or recalcitrance is likely to be viewed negatively by the referring entity and work against them in whatever decisions are made about them.

In addition, administratively referred persons, unlike self-referred and clinically referred patients, are not the examiner's clients. The client in these instances is the entity who has asked to have the person examined. The examiner's report of findings and recommendations goes to the entity, and the examiner is not obliged to provide feedback to the person examined. Moreover, in these administrative evaluations, examiners may be contractually constrained by the referral source from sharing their opinions with an examinee or providing any information about the test results. Yet these administratively referred individuals are sometimes responsible for paying for their examination, as in the case of impaired professional persons seeking reinstatement of a license that was suspended because of substance abuse or emotional problems. Sharing of information aside, moreover, examiners do have an ethical and legal obligation to treat administratively referred individuals with respect, to assess them competently, and to report the implications of their test responses accurately and without bias.

To safeguard against an inadvertent violation of anyone's rights or an accidental failure to meet someone's appropriate expectations, personality assessors should be certain in advance who their client is and what obligations they have to whom. Three questions in particular should be asked prior to conducting an evaluation: Who is requesting the evaluation and why? Who is to be informed of the results of the examination? Who will be paying the psychologist's fee? Diagnostic consultants who obtain clear answers to these questions protect themselves against four potential sources of ethical and legal unpleasantness: (1) assessing irrelevant or unasked questions; (2) using inappropriate or inadequate measures; (3) giving too little feedback to the person being examined or too much information to other interested parties, and vice versa; and (4) getting into disputes over unexpected or unpaid bills.

Selecting the Test Battery

To anticipate possible ethical and legal pitfalls in selecting a test battery, and especially in forensic cases, assessors should keep in mind the following five considerations:

1. The test battery should be limited to measures that are warranted by the referral question, and clinicians should recognize when to keep some of their favorite tests on the sidelines. If a referral question concerns neuropsychological impairment, for example, examiners should have a good reason for including the Rorschach Inkblot Method in their test battery, such as an explicit request for assessment of personality as well as neuropsychological functioning. Absence of such a request makes it difficult to justify administering and billing for a personality assessment instrument that rarely contributes to identifying central nervous system disorder. Similarly, examiners who include a Wechsler Adult Intelligence Scale-III (WAIS-III) in a test battery designed to answer questions about personality style may be challenged to defend the utility of the WAIS-III for this purpose.

2. The test battery should consist of widely used and well-known measures. This consideration is not intended to discourage the development of new tests or the clinical application of respectable measures that have not yet become widely used or well known. However, evaluations with forensic implications are ill suited for relying on experimental or esoteric measures. The APA ethics code cautions as well against including obsolete or outdated versions of tests in a test battery, and using short forms of standard measures can also put examiners in potential forensic jeopardy (see Crespi & Politikos, 2005).

Examiners who administer obsolete, outdated, or abbreviated measures may be challenged to justify such questionable practice if they appear on the witness stand or before a regulatory board. To avoid potential unpleasantness when there is a possibility of having to testify about their data, assessors should limit their battery to tests that judges, juries, and attorneys, as well as fellow psychologists, are likely to recognize by name, that are reasonably invulnerable to challenge, or that can at least be shown to represent standard professional practice.

Should psychologists decide for some reason to administer a highly specialized or rarely used measure or a controversial new form of a test, they should be prepared to make a case for having done so—a case that goes beyond saying, "I sometimes get good information from this test" (which may give the unintended impression that most other professionals do not get much information from it, or else it would be more widely used). Assessors who cannot justify the composition of their test battery are at risk for having their credibility challenged, either for being cavalier about their work (throwing in measures on a whim) or for not conforming to standard practices in conducting a psychodiagnostic evaluation. Published surveys of the relative frequency with which various tests are used in clinical practice can help assessors select batteries with this consideration in mind (see Archer, Buffington-Vollum, Stredny, & Handel, 2006; Archer & Newsom, 2000; Camara, Nathan, & Puente, 2000; Cashel, 2002; Hogan, 2005; Quinnell & Bow, 2001).

3. Psychological assessors concerned about ethical and legal hazards should limit their test batteries to measures that have a solid psychometric foundation. This recommendation is not intended to be prejudicial to measures of uncertain or undetermined psychometric status that clinicians find helpful in their work and rely on for generating hypotheses, not as a basis for drawing conclusions. However, when examiners anticipate that a case may go to court, it is advisable for them to exclude from their battery any measures for which there are limited data concerning their reliability, validity, and normative expectations.

Avoiding psychometrically soft measures in cases that could elicit ethical or legal questions about an assessment does not mean merely refraining from mentioning them in one's report. Assessors may be tempted at times to administer an extensive battery that includes some personal favorites or "interesting" but empirically untested measures, and then prepare a report based only on the psychometrically sound measures in the test battery. Surrendering to such temptation can buy a ticket to trouble. Should the slightest hint emerge in the courtroom that more tests were administered than are being testified to, what can happen next to an expert witness is not a pretty sight. After having said "Yes" when asked if other tests not mentioned in the report were also given, assessors must not only discuss but also defend these other tests (which were probably kept out of the report because they would be difficult to discuss and defend). They must also explain why information about these tests was excluded from the original report or testimony. Few expert witnesses can navigate such a storm without losing some of their credibility and respect overboard.

4. Assessors should use tests with which they are familiar. Expert witnesses who cannot cite some chapter and verse from the literature concerning the measures in their test battery are risking an embarrassing turn on the witness stand: "So, Doctor, you really don't know much at all about the tests you have used, do you?" Aside from being exposed by such a question as not having done their homework, assessors who use tests with which they are not well acquainted are also treading treacherous ethical ground. Practicing one's profession ethically requires maintaining competence in doing so (see Weiner, 1989). Psychological assessors who do not keep up with developments in the field, who have not learned new methods that are demonstrably better than older methods, who lack familiarity with revised norms that have superseded previous norms, and who are unaware of contemporary research findings and refinements in test interpretation have not maintained their competence as psychodiagnostic consultants. Lacking competence as assessors, they cannot practice assessment psychology in a responsible and ethical manner.

5. Psychological assessors should be culturally and linguistically sensitive in selecting their tests. If they are evaluating a person with limited English-language skills and using tests that have been translated into that person's native tongue, they should make sure that these translated tests have been assessed for their equivalence to the original. As pointed out by Bennett et al. (2006, chap. 6), this equivalence extends both to the specific meaning of individual words and phrases, especially slang expressions, and to item content with culture-specific referents that make little sense to examinees from diverse cultural backgrounds. The equivalence of translated tests should have been examined at least in part by back-translation from the new to the original language, as in translating an English-language test into Spanish and then back into English from the Spanish translation and noting how the two English versions compare (see Allen & Walsh, 2000). Translated tests that have not been adequately assessed for their equivalence are fair game for legal challenge, and examiners who use such tests are risking discomfort in the courtroom.

Conducting the Psychological Evaluation

Adequately trained and conscientious psychologists need little additional guidance in conducting psychological evaluation in ways that will pass ethical and legal muster. Knowing and following standardized instructions for test administration and treating examinees with dignity and respect should prepare examiners adequately for any questions that might be raised concerning the propriety of their procedures. However, two considerations that are sometimes overlooked in the press of doing business merit mention.

First, assessors who employ technicians to administer tests should always meet and talk with the person being examined, and it is advisable as well for them to administer at least a portion of the battery. Clinical reasons for proceeding in this way are well known. Blind interpretation of test data has its place, for research and teaching purposes and when expert consultants are retained specifically to comment on test protocols produced by individuals to whom they have no obligation other than to be accurate and unbiased. However, when clinicians accept a referral to "see" someone for a psychodiagnostic evaluation, they should do just that—see the person. The information that skilled professionals can glean from observing how people look, talk, dress, and comport themselves, as well as from their behavior while they are taking various tests, adds a valuable dimension to the evaluation. Technicians' observations can be helpful, but they are rarely a satisfactory replacement for firsthand observation by the person who will be preparing a report of the findings.

From an ethical perspective, people who are billed for a psychological examination by someone they saw briefly or not at all while they were being examined may rightly believe that they have been treated shabbily. Feeling shortchanged, they may decline to pay the bill, and they may also complain to a third-party payer or regulatory agency that they did not receive the services for which they were charged. In addition to exposing themselves to this kind of ethical jeopardy, psychological examiners who do not see an individual they are evaluating are vulnerable to criticism in the courtroom. Attorneys have little to lose by asking, "Which of these tests did you actually administer yourself, Doctor?" or "How much total time did you spend face-to-face with Mr. X?" If assessors must answer that they did little or none of the actual testing or spent very little face-to-face time with Mr. X, no amount of explanation can completely eliminate the impression that they are not very committed or conscientious in their work, or that they do not know as much as they should about the person who was examined, or both. Such undesirable ethical and legal outcomes can be anticipated and avoided simply by taking an active and visible role in the evaluation of all referred individuals.

As a second consideration, assessors should make sure that their test forms will stand up to inspection and give every appearance that the tests were administered, scored, and evaluated in a careful, proper, and thoroughly professional manner. Standard recording forms should be used for each test, and all of the information requested by the forms should be entered. Examiners who have their own preferred ways of recording test responses and entering scores should exercise their preferences only when they do not anticipate ethical or legal inquiry concerning their examination. Whenever ethical or legal issues do arise, idiosyncratic deviations from standard practice expose examiners to questions about why they proceeded as they did. No matter how adequately examiners believe they can answer such questions, and thereby defend their methods, the very fact of their having to defend nonstandard methods can raise doubts in others' minds about the appropriateness of the procedures that were used and the reliability of the results that were obtained.

As for entering all of the requested data, completed test forms convey thoroughness and competence. WAIS-III forms in which the index scores are omitted look naked to the trained eye, on the other hand, as do other frequently used test forms in which spaces for inserting numbers or drawing profiles have been left blank. Whether experienced examiners feel they need to fill in test forms completely in order to interpret the data is beside the point. To spare themselves aggravation when their test data are inspected in an ethical or legal context, psychological assessors should collect and prepare raw test data in a manner that is beyond reproach.

A perhaps pedestrian but potentially problematic aspect of having adequate test forms for appropriate parties to inspect is their legibility. Examiners should ensure that whatever they have written down can be read by others, should it become necessary. Having legible records signifies a sense of professional responsibility and openness to sharing information as appropriate; examiners whose records cannot be read by other people or, worse yet, cannot be read by the examiners themselves, are at risk for appearing careless and indifferent to their clients' welfare. Psychologists whose handwriting is difficult to read

should consider copying their test protocols over or having them typed. In so doing, however, they should preserve the original protocols in their own handwriting, to document who took the record and the accuracy of the transcription.

For assistance in avoiding some of these potential problems with the quality of test records, examiners are advised to generate computerized scoring and data printouts when suitable software programs are available. These programs reduce scoring errors, which if discovered reflect poorly on an examiner whose work is being reviewed, and they ensure being able to present neat, complete, and legible summaries of test scores, scales, and indices. Computer printouts also have the indirect benefit of attesting an examiner's familiarity with and utilization of available assessment technology.

Preparing and Presenting a Report

For examiners to prepare and present accurate, useful, and effective reports, they must (a) be competent with respect to determining from the test data what a report should say in response to a particular referral question and (b) have some facility in phrasing reports, whether for oral or written delivery.

Competency in psychological assessment was mentioned previously in discussing the ethical necessity for examiners to be familiar with the tests they use and the literature concerning them. Sufficient competence in assessment to sustain ethical practice involves more than knowing how to select, administer, and score tests, however. Ethicality calls as well for proficiency in interpreting the test data that are obtained. Graduate and postgraduate education and training, participation in continuing education workshops, and perusal of assessment textbooks are among the routes to proficiency in test interpretation. The core components of psychological assessment competency are detailed further by Krishnamurthy et al. (2004). Also of note is a position statement by the Society for Personality Assessment Board of Trustees (2006) on the requirements for becoming a competent assessment psychologist, which begins as follows: "It is the position of the Society that psychological assessment is a specialty that requires intensive and ongoing education and training to be practiced competently and ethically and in order to protect the public" (p. 355).

Being expert in collecting and interpreting personality assessment data is still not enough to ensure competence in responding to a referral question, however. In order to provide helpful conclusions and recommendations and confine their reports to relevant findings, examiners must also be knowledgeable about the domain in which a referral question has been formulated. For example, to help in distinguishing between bipolar and borderline personality disorder, personality assessors must be conversant with the nature of these disorders and differences between them. If asked for a treatment recommendation, they must be familiar with the implications of various personality characteristics for differential treatment planning. Evaluating a criminal defendant for competence to stand trial or insanity at the time of an offense requires acquaintance with the legal definitions of these terms. Conducting a fitness-for-duty or personnel selection assessment calls for familiarity with the particular demands of the person's duty or the position being sought and the implications of personality characteristics for an individual's ability to meet these demands.

With respect to facility in phrasing, numerous authors have delineated guidelines for writing clinical and forensic reports (see Heilbrun, 2001, chap. 10; Groth-Marnat & Horvath, 2006; Harvey, 2006; Lichtenberger, Mather, Kaufman, & Kaufman, 2004; Michaels, 2006; Weiner, 2006). Considerable advice on preparing and presenting testimony in the courtroom is also available in the literature (e.g., Bank & Packer, 2007; Blau, 1998; Brodsky, 2004; Ewing, 2003; Hess, 2006; Heilbrun, 2001, chap. 11; Shapiro, 1991). The following brief comments do not cover the same ground as these previous contributions, nor are they intended to provide a comprehensive discussion of report writing. Instead, for the purposes of the present chapter, they offer four specific suggestions for communicating assessment results in ways that can help psychological examiners gain respect for their efforts and minimize the impact of subsequent ethical or legal challenges to their work.

1. Reports of psychological evaluations should focus explicitly on what the tests show and distinguish test findings from general inferences about the person who was examined. Test reports that consist only of general inferences (e.g., "This person appears to have a schizophrenic disorder") leave the reader in the dark about what led the psychologist to the conclusions drawn and how the test findings contributed to them, if at all. Easier to follow and more convincing are reports that describe the implications of the test findings for particular psychological characteristics (e.g., "Mr. A's Rorschach responses indicated a marked propensity

for illogical thinking and considerable difficulty perceiving events in his life in a realistic manner"); that identify specific findings with special diagnostic or prognostic significance (e.g., "On both the MMPI-2 and the Rorschach, Mr. A. showed abnormal elevations on indices associated with the presence of a schizophrenic disorder"); and that only in conclusion draw general inferences based on the test findings and, as appropriate, other available information as well (e.g., "On the basis of these test findings, and in light of Mr. A's family history of schizophrenia, it seems likely that his recent adjustment difficulties reflect the onset of a schizophrenic disorder").

As counterpoint to specifying the basis for a positive finding of disorder, examiners should be similarly denotative but also circumspect in reporting negative findings. Whether a referral question concerns schizophrenia, psychopathy, suicidal risk, or any other impairment of adaptive capacity, examiners should avoid ruling out the possibility of disorder or risk, no matter how free from indices of disorder or dangerous propensities the test data appear to be. Psychometrically, this caution against ruling out possibilities reflects the fact that psychological tests always produce some frequency of false-negative findings. Clinically, absolute assertions that a condition is not present, like any unqualified statement about a probabilistic event, expose psychological assessors to potential embarrassment. Having overstated a negative finding, they can easily be made to admit being less than 100% certain that a person they examined does not have a particularly condition or behavioral tendency, as well as the possibility that a person with this condition or behavioral tendency may not always show it on psychological tests. Admitting to overstatements can make examiners appear reckless in their judgments and not fully believable—a situation best avoided by restraint in making assertions.

As a way of presenting present negative findings with scientific accuracy and professional caution, examiners can indicate what the tests show, as just illustrated, and then couch their conclusions in relative rather than absolute terms. In the case of the hypothetical Mr. A, referred for evaluation of possible schizophrenia, a report of negative findings might parallel the above example with the following statement:

> The tests do not contain any evidence of illogical thinking or impaired reality testing. Mr. A did not elevate on any of the commonly used MMPI-2 or

Rorschach indices of schizophrenia. Accordingly, although the possibility of schizophrenia cannot be ruled out on the basis of these findings, the test results make it unlikely that his adjustment difficulties are attributable to the onset of a schizophrenic disorder.

Presenting negative findings in this way protects examiners not only against unwarranted overstatement, but also against professional embarrassment and possible liability should subsequent events document an instance of false negative findings.

2. Reports should concentrate on describing what people are probably like and comment only cautiously on what they have probably done or are likely to do (see Weiner, 2003). Specific and unqualified predictions from psychological test findings to behavior puts examiners in a precarious position in which their conclusions will be difficult to justify. On the other hand, referrals for psychodiagnostic consultation often call for behavioral predictions, and psychological assessors are expected to provide them. Common examples in contemporary practice include requests to assess suicide potential, violence risk, and having been a victim or perpetrator of sexual abuse.

As an alternative in such instances to offering definite opinions about an individual's past or future behavior, examiners are advised to construct conclusions based on comparisons between the firm findings in the case (i.e., test indications of what the person is probably or most certainly like) and empirical evidence concerning how people with personality characteristics similar to those of the examinee generally tend to behave or what they tend to have experienced. This evidence-based nomothetic approach in preparing reports helps examiners avoid unwarranted assertions about an individual's future behavior or past experiences and has two related advantages in personality assessment.

First, an evidence-based nomothetic approach facilitates formulating conclusions with an appropriate degree of qualification. If an individual's personality test responses (and other assessment findings as well) are very similar to those of individuals who very often behave aggressively toward other people, it is reasonable to conclude that "This person shows a high level of violence potential" or "This person is much more likely than most people to become violent if provoked." If, on the other hand, the assessment data indicate a few personality characteristics that are sometimes associated with aggressive behavior, the examiner is justified in reporting that "This

person shows some but not a high level of violence potential" or "This person is somewhat but not substantially more likely than most people to respond aggressively if provoked."

Second, in addition to avoiding unwarranted assertions, this recommended approach to prediction or postdiction insulates examiners against courtroom insinuations that they have overstated their case. Suppose an attorney asks, "Are you saying that this man is going to go out in the street and start hurting people if he's not put in jail?" Pychologists who have expressed their conclusions in nomothetic terms can reply, "No, I'm not saying that; I'm just saying that he shows a lot of the personality characteristics commonly found in people who behave violently, which means that he is at greater risk than most people for becoming violent himself." Testimony presented in this way usually serves to get across the point that examiners are trying to make without putting them at risk for appearing to have drawn conclusions that go beyond their data.

3. Assessors should avoid describing people in unfavorable or prejudicial terms. Reports of a psychological evaluation may be read by many people who are not mental health professionals, including family members and examinees themselves. In assessments for administrative purposes, reports are likely to fall as well into the hands of lawyers, judges, health-care managers, employers, teachers, and principals. Comments that have traditionally seemed appropriate for entry into clinical records may strike non–mental health professionals as harsh, critical, judgmental, and pejorative. Examinees who feel they have been unfairly disadvantaged by what a psychologist has said or written about them may seek recourse by challenging the propriety of the examiner's conduct. It therefore behooves personality assessors to find ways of saying what needs to be said about individuals who are disturbed or impaired without seeming to lack sympathy and understanding.

For example, in describing a resistive examinee who was difficult to evaluate, an assessor could say, "Ms. B was uncooperative, and she invalidated some of the tests by refusing to respond to many items." Or, describing the same person, the assessor could say, "Apparently because of her considerable anxiety about being evaluated, Ms. B found it difficult to comply with the examination procedures and was unable to respond to many of the test items." A disgruntled client or an independent observer could well consider the first of these comments prejudicial, whereas even a person disappointed with the results of the examination or dismayed by its influence on subsequent events could find little fault with the second comment.

Examiners should similarly appreciate the importance of describing individuals' personality strengths and assets as well as their limitations and shortcomings. Especially in writing clinical reports, psychologists tend to emphasize what is wrong with people they have examined, mainly because this is typically what they have been asked to assess. Moreover, assessors schooled in measures designed for differential diagnosis and standardized on patient groups may be unsure where to look in their test protocols for indications of personality strengths and assets. Where such positive indications are to be found is in those test data that are often labeled "negative findings" and passed over because they do not identify any adjustment difficulty or behavioral risk. In the service of preparing a balanced report, features of the test data that do not suggest psychological disorder or impaired coping capacity can usually be reappraised as positive rather than negative findings and described as probable strengths or assets.

For example, examinees who show little evidence of thought disorder or impaired reality testing can be described as people who appear capable of thinking logically and coherently and perceiving people and events accurately. Those whose responses do not suggest social passivity, discomfort, or withdrawal can be described as outgoing individuals who are capable of seeking out and enjoying the company of others. Absence of indications of impulsivity may speak to good capacities for self-control, absence of indications of low self-esteem may point to a satisfying self-concept, and so on. Psychologists who take care to write and speak positively as well as negatively about the people they examine, and who express what is maladaptive in a sympathetic and understanding manner, minimize their vulnerability to malpractice allegations from persons who feel they have been damaged by improper professional conduct.

4. Examiners who generate computer-based test interpretations (CBTIs) should use them judiciously in preparing their reports. Judicious use of CBTIs begins with not relying entirely on what they say. Computer-generated narratives do not describe the person who has been examined; they describe people in general whose pattern of test responses resembles the response pattern of the person who has been examined. Because of individual differences among people who in many ways resemble each other, and as a reflection of variance around average levels, CBTI printouts usually include some statements that do not apply to the particular examinee, and even some statements that are inconsistent with each other—caveats that are noted in most CBTI narratives.

Examiners should therefore regard CBTI narratives as an assist to interpretation, not as a source of definitive conclusions; they should integrate the CBTI statements with other available information in deciding what to write in their reports; and they should be prepared to account for CBTI statements that are misleading, inaccurate, or inconsistent. Once printed out, CBTI narratives are discoverable in legal proceedings, and they can be subject to word-by-word cross-examination if an assessor testifies in court.

Being judicious in using computer-generated narratives also calls for resisting temptation to insert well-crafted CBTI statements into one's report. Integrity requires examiners who are so tempted to find ways of expressing these incisive statements in their own words, or else to copy them in quotation marks and with identification of their source. Assessment psychologists who are exposed as having put extensive portions of a CBTI narrative into their report without an appropriate attribution can face ethical sanctions along with public appearance of deviousness and diminished credibility as a capable and knowledgeable professional. For further discussion of these and other considerations in using computer-generated interpretive reports, readers are referred to Butcher (2003), Chapter 36, Butcher, Perry, and Hahn (2004), and Lichtenberger (2006).

Managing Case Records

The most important ethical and legal consideration in managing case records is maintaining their confidentiality. Confidentiality has been widely discussed and extensively taught over the years, and guidelines for its maintenance can be found in the APA ethics code and elsewhere (Bennett et al., 2006, chap. 4; Kitchener, 2000, chap. 8). Less widely discussed but also important in anticipating ethical and legal challenges in personality assessment is careful attention to how case records are compiled and stored. As one aspect of managing their case records carefully, psychological examiners should regard them as they do any other personal property that may be inspected by strangers, sometimes unexpectedly. Records that are complete, orderly, and in reasonably pristine form reflect well on the competence and conscientiousness of the assessor. Those that are disorganized and dog-eared suggest that examiners are paying insufficient attention to the rights and dignity of their clients.

Examiners must also take care to maintain the availability of their case records for an adequate period of time. Long after the fact of a psychological examination, clients and those concerned about them have a right to expect that the records will be available if needed for any purpose. The obligations of examiners in this regard are often specified in statutory regulations concerning the practice of psychology. In Florida, for example, the Administrative Code of the Board of Psychology requires complete psychological records to be maintained for at least 3 years following an examination and a summary of the records for an additional 4 years.

Furthermore, the ethical obligations of examiners to maintain records extend not only as long as they practice but beyond as well. The APA Ethical Standards specify that psychologists should plan in advance to preserve the confidentiality and availability of their records after they discontinue practice and in the event of their incapacity or death. Accordingly, psychological assessors should make provisions for the maintenance of their case records in future times when they will no longer be available or capable themselves to share this information with appropriate parties.

To summarize this chapter, psychologists who conduct personality evaluations can protect themselves against ethical and legal recriminations by establishing clearly the identity of the client when they accept a referral; by selecting for their test battery measures that are commonly used, well substantiated, and familiar to them; by conducting their evaluations in standard ways and recording the data carefully; by writing and presenting their reports in an appropriately denotative and circumspect manner; and by maintaining the confidentiality and availability of their records for an appropriate length of time.

References

Allen, J., & Walsh, J. A. (2000). A construct-based approach to equivalence: Methodologies for cross-cultural/multicultural personality assessment research. In R. H. Dana (Ed.), *Handbook of cross-cultural and multicultural personality assessment* (pp. 63–86). Mahwah, NJ: Lawrence Erlbaum.

American Psychological Association. (1993). Record keeping guidelines. *American Psychologist, 48*, 984–986.

American Psychological Association. (1994). Guidelines for child custody evaluations in divorce proceedings. *American Psychologist, 49*, 677–680.

American Psychological Association. (2002). Ethical principles of psychologists and code of conduct. *American Psychologist, 57*, 1060–1073.

American Psychological Association. (2003). Guidelines on multicultral education, training, research, practice, and organizational change for psychologists. *American Psychologist, 58*, 377–401.

Archer, R. P., Buffington-Vollum, J. K., Stredny, R. V., & Handel, R. W. (2006). A survey of psychological test use patterns among forensic psychologists. *Journal of Personality Assessment, 87*, 84–94.

Archer, R. P., & Newsom, C. R. (2000). Psychological test usage with adolescent clients: Survey update. *Assessment, 7*, 227–235.

Bank, S. C., & Packer, I. K. (2007). Expert witness testimony: Law, ethics, and practice. In A. M. Goldstein (Ed.), *Forensic psychology: Emerging topics and expanding roles* (pp. 421–445). Hoboken, NJ: John Wiley & Sons.

Barnett, J. E., Behnke, S. H., Rosenthal, S. L., & Koocher, G. P. (2007). In case of ethical dilemma, break glass: Commentary on ethical decision making in practice. *Professional Psychology: Research and Practice, 38*, 7–12.

Barnett, J. E., & Dunning, C. B. (2005). Assessment and treatment of the elderly: Clinical and ethical issues. In L. VandeCreek (Ed.), *Innovations in clinical practice: Focus on adults* (pp. 19–32). Sarasota, FL: Professional Resources Press.

Bennett, B. E., Bricklin, P. M., Harris, E., Knapp, S., VandeCreek, L., & Youunggren, J. N. (2006). *Assessing and managing risk in psychological practice*. Rockville, MD: The Trust.

Blau, T. H. (1998). *The psychologist as expert witness* (2nd ed.). New York: John Wiley & Sons.

Brabender, V., & Bricklin, P. (2001). Ethical issues in psychological assessment in different settings. *Journal of Personality Assessment, 77*, 192–194.

Brodsky, S. L. (2004). *Coping with cross-examination and other pathways to effective testimony*. Washington, DC: American Psychological Association.

Bucky, S., Callan, J., & Stricker, G. (Eds.) (2007). *Ethical and legal issues for mental health professionals: In forensic settings*. New York: Haworth Press.

Butcher, J. N. (2003). Computerized psychological assessment. In I. B. Weiner (Ed.), *Handbook of psychology, Vol. 11: Assessment psychology* (pp. 141–164). Hoboken, NJ:John Wiley & Sons.

Butcher, J. N. (in press). How to use computer-based reports. In J. N. Butcher (Ed.), *Oxford handbook of clinical and personality assessment*. New York: Oxford University Press.

Butcher, J. N., Perry, J., & Hahn, J. (2004). Computers in clinical assessment: Historical developments, present status, and future challenges. *Journal of Clinical Psychology, 60*, 331–345.

Camara, W. J., Nathan, J. S., & Puente, A. E. (2000). Psychological test usage: Implications in professional psychology. *Professional Psychology, 31*, 141–154.

Cashel, M. L. (2002). Child and adolescent psychological assessment: Current clinical practices and the impact of managed care. *Professional Psychology: Research and Practice, 33*, 1446–1453.

Committee on Ethical Guidelines for Forensic Psychologists (1991). Specialty guidelines for forensic psychologists. *Law and Human Behavior, 15*, 655–665.

Crespi, T. D., & Politikos, N. N. (2005). Short forms in psychological assessment—ethical and forensic concerns for school psychology: Comment on Thompson, LoBello, Atkinson, Chisholm, and Ryan (2004). *Professional Psychology, 35*, 517–518.

Ewing, C. P. (2003). Expert testimony: Law and practice. In I. B. Weiner (Ed.), *Handbook of psychology. Vol. 11, Forensic psychology* (pp. 55–66). Hoboken, NJ: John Wiley & Sons.

Groth-Marnat, G., & Horvath, L. S. (2006). The psychological report: A review of current controversies. *Journal of Clinical Psychology, 62*, 73–82.

Harvey, V. S. (2006). Variables affecting the clarity of psychological reports. *Journal of Clinical Psychology, 62*, 5–18.

Heilbrun, L. (2001). *Principles of forensic mental health assessment.* New York: Kluwer Academic/Plenum.

Hess, A. K. (2006). Serving as an expert witness. In I. B. Weiner & A. K. Hess (Eds.), *Handbook of forensic psychology* (3rd ed., pp. 652–607). Hoboken, NJ: John Wiley & Sons.

Hogan, T. P. (2005). 50 widely used psychological tests. In G. P. Koocher, J. C. Norcross, & S. S. Hill, III (Eds.), *Psychologists' desk reference* (2nd ed., pp. 101–104). New York: Oxford University Press.

Kitchener, K. S. (2000). *Foundations of ethical practice, research, and teaching in psychology.* Mahwah, NJ: Erlbaum.

Knapp, S., Gottlieb, M., Berman, J., & Handelsman. M. M. (2007). When laws and ethics collide: What should psychologists do? *Professional Psychology: Research and Practice, 38*, 54–59.

Knapp. S. J., & VandeCreek, L. D. (2006). *Practical ethics for psychologists: A positive approach.* Washington, DC: American Psychological Association.

Koocher, G. P. (2006). Ethical issues in forensic assessment of children and adolscents. In S. N. Sparta & G. P. Koocher (Eds.), *Forensic mental health assessment of children and adolescents* (pp. 46–63). New York: Oxford University Press.

Krishnamurthy, R., VandeCreek, L., Kaslow, N. J., Tazeau, Y. N., Miville, M. L., Kerns, R., et al. (2004). Achieving competence in psychological assessment: Directions for education and training. *Journal of Clinical Psychology, 60*, 725–739.

Lichtenberger, E. E., Mather, N., Kaufman, N. L., & Kaufman, A. S. (2004). *Essentials of assessment report writing.* Hoboken, NJ: John Wiley & Sons.

Lichtenberger, E. O. (2006). Computer utilization and clinical judgment in psychological assessment reports. *Journal of Clinical Psychology, 62*, 19–32.

Michaels, M. H. (2006). Ethical considerations in writing psychological assessment reports. *Journal of Clinical Psychology, 62*, 47–58.

Monahan, J. (Ed.) (1980). *Who is the client?* Washington, DC: American Psychological Association.

Nagy, T. F. (2005). *Ethics in plain English: An illustrative casebook for psychologists* (2nd ed.). Washington, DC: American Psychological Association.

Petrila, J., & Otto, R. K. (1996). *Law and mental health professionals: Florida.* Washington, DC: American Psychological Assocation.

Pope, K. S., & Vasquez, M. J. T. (2007). *Ethics in psychotherapy and counseling: A practical guide* (3rd ed.). San Francisco, CA: Jossey-Bass.

Pope, K. S., Butcher, J. N., & Seelen, J. (2006). *The MMPI, MMPI-2, & MMPI-A in court* (3rd ed.). Washington, DC: American Psychological Association.

Quinnell, F. A., & Bow, J. N. (2001). Psychological tests used in child custody evaluations. *Behavioral Sciences and the Law, 19*, 491–501.

Shapiro, D. L. (1991). *Forensic psychological assessment.* Boston: Allyn & Bacon.

Society for Personality Assessment Board of Trustees. (2006). Standards for education and training in psychological assessment: Position of the Society for Personality Assessment. *Journal of Personality Assessment, 87*, 355–357.

Turchik, J. A., Karpenko, V., Hammers, D., & McNamara, J. R. (2007). Practical and ethical assessment issues in rural, impoverished, and managed care settings. *Professional Psychology: Research and Practice, 38*, 158–168.

Weiner, I. B. (1989). On competence and ethicality in psychodiagnostic assessment. *Journal of Personality Assessment, 53*, 827–831.

Weiner, I. B. (2003). Prediction and postdiction in clinical decision making. *Clinical Psychology: Science and Practice, 10*, 335–338.

Weiner, I. B. (2006). Writing forensic reports. In I. B. Weiner & A. K. Hess (Eds.), *Handbook of forensic psychology* (3rd ed., pp. 631–651). Hoboken, NJ: John Wiley & Sons.

Weiner, I. B., & Greene, R. L. (2008). *Handbook of personality assessment.* Hoboken, NJ: John Wiley & Sons.

PART 7

Interpretation and Reporting of Assessment Findings

Assessment of Feigned Psychological Symptoms

David T. R. Berry, Myriam J. Sollman, Lindsey J. Schipper, Jessica A. Clark, *and* Anne L. Shandera

Abstract

Feigned symptom reports have become of increasing interest in recent years, in part because the results of psychological evaluations are more widely accepted in legal proceedings. This chapter reviews several pertinent issues regarding assessment of malingering, including methodological concerns, base rates of feigning, and coaching to avoid detection. Several frequently used measures of malingering, including the Minnesota Multiphasic Personality Inventory-2 (MMPI-2), Personality Assessment Inventory (PAI), Millon Clinical Multiaxial Inventory-III (MCMI-III), Structured Inventory of Malingered Symptomatology (SIMS), Miller Forensic Assessment of Symptoms Test (M-FAST), and Structured Interview of Reported Symptoms (SIRS), are reviewed. Cutting scores, sensitivity, specificity, and positive and negative predictive powers are provided at various base rates of feigning. After the SIRS, the feigning scales of the MMPI-2 have the most support for malingering detection, followed by the PAI scales. Generally, all measures reviewed showed greater negative predictive power rates; thus, a two-stage sequential process for malingering detection is discussed.

Keywords: malingering, MMPI-2, PAI, MCMI-III, SIMS, M-FAST, SIRS

Normal people frequently attempt to manage the impressions they make on others to achieve their personal goals. For example, individuals meeting their prospective spouse's parents for the first time are typically quite attentive to making the "right" impression. Classified advertisements placed to market an automobile or other merchandise usually highlight the positive qualities of the item. Students contacting their instructors to indicate that they will miss an examination or turn in an assignment late due to illness are often quite intent on communicating the severity of their symptoms. Everyday examples of impression management abound, suggesting that deliberate manipulation of the opinions of others is a pervasive phenomenon in contemporary society.

Indirect acknowledgements of the frequency of impression management, including its extreme form, lying, are also numerous. Parents of a child who has told a lie usually emphatically stress the

need to tell the truth, and may shame or physically discipline for such offenses. Clients of physicians, attorneys, and psychotherapists are told that the confidentiality of their communications with the professional is protected by law (with exceptions duly noted) in order to encourage the candor that is felt to be in the client's best interest but apparently not thought to occur spontaneously in all cases. Before testifying in a legal proceeding, witnesses are asked to swear that they will tell the truth, the whole truth, and nothing but the truth, a rather elaborate formulation that indirectly acknowledges the many forms that distortions of the truth may take. Clearly, a wide range of everyday habits in society, professional standards, and institutional procedures implicitly acknowledge that individuals may withhold or misrepresent information for their perceived advantage, sometimes to the point of outright lies.

Curiously, despite the widespread appreciation in society at large that individuals may misrepresent information for their own perceived benefit, psychologists and other mental health professionals have traditionally devoted relatively little formal attention or resources to assessing objectively the accuracy of information presented by clients. Instead, clinicians typically depend on a global clinical judgment of uncertain validity that may be casually summarized along the lines of "the present results are judged representative of the client's current functioning" with little or no substantive evidence offered in support.

This "ignorant bliss," however, has been challenged as the results of psychological assessments have become increasingly accepted in legal and administrative proceedings determining the assignment of substantial benefits such as disability pensions, workers' compensation awards, and monetary damages, as well as the adjudication of criminal offenses. Through vigorous cross-examinations, often aided by sources such as *Coping with Psychiatric and Psychological Testimony* (Ziskin, 1995) and widespread public discontent with "insanity pleas," psychologists and other mental health clinicians have become increasingly aware of the need to evaluate carefully and routinely the veracity of information obtained from testing, clinical interviews, and related methods that are based ultimately on self-report. To address the issue of feigned symptom reports reliably, it is necessary to have well-validated, objective indicators of the phenomenon.

This chapter will provide an overview of the current status of structured psychological methods used to evaluate the possibility of one extreme type of impression management that may occur in psychological assessments. Deliberate exaggeration or fabrication of problems or misattribution of symptoms to obtain a desired external goal is behavior that, in the context of a psychological or psychiatric evaluation, is commonly known as "faking bad" or "malingering." Psychologists have generally conceptualized feigned psychological complaints as a "response set," and readers should be aware that it is only one of several possible response sets such as random responding, yea-saying or nay-saying, and faking good that may affect self-reports. Response sets such as random responding and yea-saying at times constitute important confounds that must be ruled out before a determination of faking bad is reached. In this chapter, other response sets will be addressed only as they bear on the detection of feigned reports, with relevant sources of information on the alternative response sets provided as appropriate.

Conceptual and Practical Issues
Criteria

False symptom reports are part of the criteria for identifying three conditions in the DSM-IV-TR (American Psychiatric Association [APA], 2000). Perhaps the most blatant example of feigned symptom reports involves malingering. Strictly speaking, malingering is not a diagnosis in DSM-IV-TR (APA, 2000). Instead, DSM-IV-TR treats malingering as a "V-code," more specifically as one of several "additional conditions that may be the focus of clinical attention" (APA, 2000, p. 739). The essential feature of malingering is "the intentional production of false or grossly exaggerated physical or psychological symptoms, motivated by external incentives such as avoiding military duty, avoiding work, obtaining financial compensation, evading criminal prosecution, or obtaining drugs" (p. 739). Although no formal criteria are given for arriving at a determination of malingering, the clinician is told to strongly suspect malingering if two or more of the following are present: medico-legal context, discrepancy between subjective and objective information, lack of cooperation with assessment or treatment, or presence of antisocial personality disorder. In the DSM-IV-TR system, malingering is distinguished from similar conditions by two factors: whether or not conscious control is exerted over false symptom reports and whether apparent goals are external (money, narcotics, avoiding criminal prosecution, etc.) as opposed to intrapsychic (fulfill the sick role, resolve unconscious conflicts). The resulting hypothetical two-by-two table includes malingering (conscious feigning for external goals), factitious disorder (conscious feigning for internal goal; i.e., to achieve the sick role), and conversion disorder (unconscious production of signs and symptoms to resolve psychological conflicts). Oddly, the fourth quadrant of the hypothetical table resulting from crossing the two major factors (unconscious production of signs and symptoms for external goals) is not addressed in the DSM-IV-TR system, but might constitute a potentially important condition for future exploration.

The omission in the DSM-IV-TR entries on malingering and related disorders of explicit guidance for making the crucial and intrinsically difficult distinctions required by the system is particularly problematic. For example, reliable discrimination of conscious versus unconscious motivation and control of behavior requires a high level of inference in all but exceptional circumstances, yet DSM-IV-TR provides no definitive directions for making such a decision. In fact, comparison of the entries on malingering from DSM-III (APA, 1980) and DSM-IV-TR (APA, 2000) indicates little substantive change in the relevant text, despite the passage of 20 years between the publications of these two editions. This suggests that the nosology has been essentially unresponsive to two decades of empirical and theoretical work in the area of malingering, a remarkable omission that would surely be inconceivable for other important conditions or behaviors addressed by the text.

The failure to update the DSM-IV-TR entry on malingering to be responsive to progress in the area is particularly egregious in light of serious criticisms leveled over the years. Rogers (1997, p. 7) has characterized the DSM definition of malingering as a "criminological model" focusing on bad people (with antisocial personality disorder), in bad circumstances (legal difficulties), doing bad things (misleading clinicians). Rogers (1990) found that use of the DSM criteria for "strongly suspecting" malingering (presence of two or more of the four conditions discussed above) resulted in poor classification rates when applied to a forensic sample. Thus, clinicians evaluating the possibility of malingering are left with the two key components of malingering: (a) deliberate fabrication or gross exaggeration of symptoms (to which might be added deliberate misattribution of symptoms) and (b) pursuit of an external goal, but virtually no direction for establishing their presence in a patient. This means that DSM-IV-TR de facto leaves clinicians to their own devices for determining the presence or absence of the key criteria for identifying malingering in individual cases, a void remarkably similar to that which drove the massive revision of the psychiatric nosology leading to the DSM-III (APA, 1980).

Methodological Issues

Because DSM-IV-TR does not provide explicit criteria for the determination of malingering, clinicians must decide for themselves which techniques to use to address the issue. Perhaps the most critical factor in this choice should be the research base supporting each instrument, particularly the quality of the underlying work. Thus, clinicians must evaluate the methodological rigor of the published literature supporting a malingering test as part of the process of identifying appropriate instruments. Failure to do so may leave the clinician vulnerable during Daubert hearings (*Daubert vs. Merrell, Dow Pharmaceuticals, Inc.*, 1993), in which the presiding judge determines whether expert testimony is admissible on the basis of several "prongs" outlined in the Supreme Court decision in this and subsequent cases.

One important issue in evaluating the quality of a malingering study is the experimental design utilized. Published research on malingering has included case studies, simulation (analog) studies, known-groups comparisons, and differential prevalence designs. Case studies, which involve detailed descriptions of single cases of known malingerers, while useful for stimulating hypotheses and as training examples, are of unknown generalizability and hence of limited utility.

The most common design in the area of detection of malingering has been the simulation study, in which groups are instructed to malinger or answer honestly, and compared on one or more feigning scales. This type of design is particularly useful in the initial stages of validating a malingering test and it offers the possibility of inferring causality on the basis of the experimental instruction manipulation. However, simulation designs are limited in that it is not clear if results from the analog malingerers apply to "real world" malingerers. Additionally, participants in the "honest" group should be clinically relevant patients. In general, the closer the characteristics of the analog subjects come to those of the actual referral stream in which the possibility of malingering is being considered, the more generalizable results from such designs are likely to be. Thus, the common "Introduction to Psychology" subjects participating only for research credit included in many simulation studies (including some work by the present authors) may severely restrict generalizability of findings.

An alternative design for validation of malingering detection instruments is the "known-groups" study, in which independently identified feigners are compared to patients classified as answering honestly on a malingering test or scale. Although the validity of the independent classification technique puts a ceiling on the potential validity of the malingering scale undergoing testing, results from this type of design are much more likely to be generalizable than simulation designs. However, one potential limitation to known-groups designs is that those in the malingering group, by virtue of having been detected by the independent technique, may not be representative of all malingerers, as only blatant malingerers might have been identified. Another often neglected issue is the determination of the honesty of patients in the control group. Their approach to testing should be documented, not merely presumed, so that the known-groups design does not reduce to a differential prevalence design (see below). A final potential issue with known-groups designs is that they do not include experimental manipulations and random assignments to groups, with the ability to infer causality that accompanies such a methodology. Thus, known groups of malingerers and honest patients may be different in many ways beyond simply the presence or absence of the response set.

Differential prevalence designs involve forming groups based on a characteristic thought to be related to the likelihood of malingering and comparing them on a malingering instrument or scale. Thus, patients undergoing psychiatric disability evaluations might be contrasted with those being seen for a psychotherapy intake and who are not compensation-seeking. While this methodology cannot speak to the accuracy of the malingering test as the status of individual group members is unknown, the compensation-seeking group should have, on average, higher scores on the malingering measure than the non-compensation-seeking group. If no differences are found on the malingering test, serious questions must be raised about the construct validity of the test. However, it must be emphasized that differential prevalence designs cannot substitute for known-groups or simulation designs in determining the classification parameters of the test.

Rogers (1997) suggests that the strongest support for a malingering test comes from positive findings across multiple designs. Minimally, a malingering test or scale should have support from both simulation and known-groups designs. The greater the number of successful cross-validations, the more confident the clinician may be in the effectiveness of the test or scale. Successful cross-validations in different settings and by independent research groups are also desirable. It should be noted that cross-validation must encompass specific cutting scores or decision rules, and not be restricted simply to significant group differences on the test or scale in question. Continual derivation of new optimal cutting scores in successive studies fails to provide stable sensitivity and specificity estimates for specific cutting scores, which in turn greatly hampers or even precludes establishment of clinically important positive predictive power (PPP) and negative predictive power (NPP) values discussed below and elsewhere in this text (Chapter 8).

Rogers (1997) has provided a detailed review of methodological issues in malingering research. Table 32.1 highlights particularly important issues for the clinician reviewing the literature supporting

Table 32.1. Methodological quality issues in validation of malingering detection tests and scales.

Simulation designs

Are participant characteristics similar to those with whom the test will be used in clinical practice?
Are analog malingerers given a plausible "scenario" that they understand and may identify with?
Are analog malingerers instructed to be "believable" in their feigning (try to avoid detection)?
Are analog malingerers given time and resources to prepare to malinger successfully?
Are analog malingerers provided with information on symptoms and detection strategies to reflect knowledge that is probably easily available to "real world" malingerers?
Are analog malingerers provided with an incentive powerful enough to motivate them to attempt to feign successfully?
Are analog malingerers "debriefed" at the end of the study to determine if they recalled, comprehended, and complied with their instructions?
Are nonmalingering measures included in the experimental protocol, replicating clinical practice in which both malingering and standard tests are given?
Is a clinically relevant patient control group included?
Is the honesty of the patient control group verified through post-test debriefing or other independent means?
Are the numbers of participants in the malingering and honest groups adequate to detect an effect?

Known-groups Designs

How valid is the criterion used to assign group membership (criterion validity will place a ceiling on predictor validity)?
How representative of malingerers are those assigned to the malingering group (if only flagrant malingerers are "caught," results, may misrepresent the ability of the test to identify malingering)?
Is the honesty of the patient control group verified through post-test debriefing or other independent means?
How representative of honest patients are those assigned to the nonmalingering control group?

Differential prevalence

Does the criterion chosen to select groups have demonstrated validity for producing different base rates of malingering?

a malingering detection technique. In general, as a study includes more of these characteristics, greater confidence may be placed in the findings. However, it should be noted that certain "fatal flaws," such as absence of a relevant clinical control group, may dramatically reduce the quality of the study in spite of the presence of many of these features in a given research design.

Base Rates of Feigned Psychological Symptoms

As Finn (Chapter 8), and others have pointed out, the accuracy of a technique for predicting the presence or absence of any condition ultimately rests on the sensitivity and specificity of the method as determined on groups of individuals known to have or not have the condition, respectively, as well as the base rates of the condition. Sensitivity is the percentage of the group known to have a condition which receives a positive test sign (suggestive of presence of the condition). Specificity is the percentage of the group known not to have the condition which receives a negative test sign (suggestive of absence of the condition). Sensitivity provides the probability that an individual known to have the condition will have a positive test sign, whereas specificity provides the probability that an individual known not to have the condition will have a negative test sign. Obviously, if an individual is known to have, or not have, the condition, it is unnecessary to give a test to make this determination. However, when combined with the base rate of the condition in question, sensitivity and specificity may be used to calculate the more clinically relevant statistics of PPP and NPP. PPP and NPP communicate, respectively, the probability that an individual who is predicted to have the condition (positive test sign) actually has the condition, and the probability that an individual who is predicted not to have the condition (negative test sign) does not in fact have the condition.

The distinction between sensitivity and specificity on the one hand, and positive and negative predictive power on the other hand, is more than an academic one. For example, consider a scale for the detection of malingering that has a sensitivity of .90 and a specificity of .90 at a given cutting score. Applied in a setting with a base rate of malingering of 50%, the PPP of the scale is .90, as is NPP. However, when the same scale is applied in a setting where the base rate of malingering is very low at 5%, PPP falls to .32 whereas NPP climbs to .99. This means that in the low base rate setting, there is only about 1 chance in 3 that an individual who is classified as malingering by the scale (positive test sign) is in fact feigning symptoms. In contrast, if an evaluee has a negative test sign in these circumstances, it is very unlikely that he or she is malingering symptoms.

Thus, under certain conditions, positive and negative test signs may have very divergent associated predictive powers. Additionally, across tests, some procedures may generate strong PPP for ruling in feigning, whereas others may provide strong NPP for ruling out the condition. Therefore it is vital that clinicians generate an estimate of the base rate of feigning in their local settings and estimate predictive powers before applying malingering scales. If it is logistically difficult or impossible to establish such local base rate estimates, the clinician may consider published estimates of the base rates of malingering in various settings. These estimates can then be used, in combination with published sensitivity and specificity values, to estimate PPP and NPP in the local setting.

Determining the base rates of feigned psychological symptoms has generally been undertaken using two methods: asking clinicians to estimate the frequency of feigning in their settings, or administering objective feigning detection instruments to consecutive evaluees. Rogers, Sewell, and Goldstein (1994) surveyed 320 forensic psychologists to obtain a subjective estimate of the base rates of malingering in forensic and nonforensic settings. These authors reported that their clinician subjects estimated that about 15.7% of forensic evaluees malingered, as opposed to 7.4% of patients in nonforensic settings. When 221 forensic experts were similarly surveyed by Rogers, Salekin, Sewell, Goldstein, and Leonard (1998), their average estimates were that 17.4% of forensic patients and 7.2% of nonforensic patients malingered. Although a useful starting point, it may be argued that these estimates are likely to be lower than is actually the case, because the successful malingerer, by definition, would not have been detected by the clinician and thus would not be included in the subjective base rate estimates.

More recent estimates based on objective methods have appeared. Strong, Greene, and Schinka (2000) used taxometric analysis of items from two Minnesota Multiphasic Personality Inventory-2 (MMPI-2) malingering scales to estimate the base rate of symptom over-reporting in psychiatric inpatient units ($n = 626$) and heterogeneous Veteran's Affairs (VA) clinical service units ($n = 1,455$). Their results suggested that about 27% of psychiatric inpatients and 19% of the VA medical patients were overreporting problems. Frederick, Crosby, and Wynkoop (2000) reported data from the Validity Index Profile (VIP), a well-validated test of motivation and effort on cognitive testing, given to 737 male pretrial defendants referred to the U.S. Medical Center for Federal Prisoners for questions involving competency to stand trial, criminal responsibility, risk assessments, general psychological evaluations, and commitments for restoration to competency to stand trial. More than 43% of these forensic evaluees turned in a performance on the VIP that was classified as "invalid." However, this does not translate directly into a base rate of feigned symptoms, as the classification system used by the VIP includes random responding and "careless" responding in the invalid category (although some researchers have found that a subset of analog malingerers report that their strategy for faking explicitly involved random responding; Arbisi & Ben-Porath, 1998). Using the Structured Interview of Reported Symptoms (SIRS; see below), Norris and May (1998) found that 45.3% of 75 adult inmates from jails in a rural southeastern county with psychological complaints were malingering. Lewis, Simcox, and Berry (2002) used the SIRS to evaluate 51 individuals undergoing pretrial evaluations to determine competency to stand trial and mental state at the time of a crime in the federal justice system. They found that 31.4% of their subjects were classified as malingering. Miller (2004) indicated that 28% of a sample of male criminal defendants who had been placed in forensic units of a state hospital because of a determination of incompetency to stand trial were classified as feigning by the SIRS. Guy and Miller (2004) administered the SIRS to 50 males in a maximum-security prison who had requested mental health services and found evidence that 42% were feigning symptoms. Thus, available data suggest that the base rate of feigned symptoms in general psychological evaluations may fall somewhere between 7.3 and 27%, whereas the base rate in explicitly forensic settings appears to climb to the range of 28–45%. These prevalence estimates imply that as the "stakes" involved in a psychological evaluation increase, the base rate of false symptom reports probably climbs accordingly, a factor that should be incorporated in base rate estimates.

Coaching

Given the important outcomes determined in many forensic examinations, Victor and Abeles (2004) raised concern that some parties might "coach" individuals to avoid being identified by feigning instruments. Earlier, Wetter and Corrigan (1995) surveyed law students and attorneys and reported that the majority believed they had an ethical obligation to warn their clients about validity indices used in psychological assessments. Although the base rate of coaching is unknown, it may be very common in some settings (Lees-Haley, 1997). In a case report, Youngjohn (1995) documented attorney coaching in a personal injury trial. Allen and Green (2001) described a steady decline in detection rates on the Computerized Assessment of Response Bias, given to forensic evaluees over a 6-year period, suggesting diffusion of knowledge about the procedure.

The Internet provides a rich source of information on psychological tests, including feigning detection instruments. Ruiz, Drake, Glass, Marcotte, and van Gorp (2002) reported that up to 5% of sites with information on psychological testing were a "direct threat to test security" (p. 294). In a warning to customers, Multi-Health Systems, Inc., publisher of the Test of Memory Malingering (TOMM), suggested hiding the test's acronym from evaluees to protect against individuals searching the Internet for information about motivational tests, including the TOMM (Multi-Health Systems, Inc., Letter to TOMM users, January 8, 2003). Clinicians doubting the easy availability of relevant information may wish to run a search of their own; the results are likely to be eye-opening.

Costs of Misdiagnosis

Failure to consider and rule out the possibility of malingering of psychological and psychiatric disorder potentially carries high costs for insurers, disability systems, and ultimately society at large. Thus, we suggest that the possibility of feigned symptoms should be carefully considered in any assessment for which diagnoses of psychopathology carry important external positive contingencies for the patient.

There are potentially serious consequences for false positive errors in the identification of malingering as well.[1] The falsely labeled malingerer may be denied treatment, may lose access to needed financial resources, and may even be legally prosecuted for fraud. Thus, we suggest that identifying an evaluee as a malingerer should not be done without thorough consideration of all available evidence as well as acknowledgment that the presence of malingering does not rule out the possibility of psychopathology. We recommend caution and a thorough understanding of the limits of available techniques.

With rare exceptions, a patient should never be labeled a malingerer on the basis of a single finding. Rather, increasing confidence may be gained as multiple lines of evidence from varied sources and diverse methods converge on the conclusion that self-reported symptoms are being exaggerated, fabricated, or misattributed. A two-stage process for maximizing confidence in identifying malingerers is presented later in this chapter.

Suggested Strategy for Clinical Practice

Despite the many conceptual and practical complexities in the identification of malingering reviewed above, clinicians are commonly faced with cases in which this issue should be considered. Because of the difficulties in predicting a low base rate condition reviewed above and by Finn (Chapter 8), it is probably not desirable to address in depth the possibility of malingering in clinical situations in which the clinician's and patient's interests are closely aligned, such as psychological testing at the beginning of psychotherapy. Such situations probably constitute a "low base rate" environment which minimizes the potential positive predictive power of a malingering scale. An important exception to this occurs when a "routine" evaluee obtains a score on a validity scale from an omnibus inventory such as the MMPI-2 that is at or above the highest score typically obtained by cooperative patients in the setting. Thus, even in a nonforensic evaluation, extreme scores on malingering scales, for example, a T-score of 95 or higher on the MMPI-2 F(p) scale (see below) combined with negative evidence for the presence of random responding should trigger consideration of the possibility of exaggeration or fabrication of psychological problems. This should be followed by a search for undiscovered possible external incentives. If no potential external positive contingencies are found for feigned symptoms, the patient may be "crying for help" in order to avoid being overlooked (Berry et al., 1996), and this issue might be discussed with the client.

As clinical practice moves to settings in which there are commonly powerful external incentives for feigning psychological problems, routine consideration of the possibility of malingering becomes important. Disability evaluations, personal injury examinations, criminal responsibility hearings, and similar referrals signal a likely higher base rate of malingering that potentially increases the PPP of malingering scales as well as the need to address this condition routinely. If the evaluee has important positive consequences hinging on a finding of psychopathology, it is imperative to use inventories that include validity scales with demonstrated sensitivity to malingering, as reviewed below. However, with rare exceptions, results from these multiscale inventories are unlikely to offer sufficient PPP for confidently documenting feigned symptom reports. Thus, positive findings from malingering scales on multiscale inventories, from the interview, behavioral observations, available records, or collateral sources of information should trigger the use of additional instruments specialized for the detection of malingering, as also reviewed below. Multiple and converging lines of evidence suggestive of malingering will constitute the strongest basis for identification of this response set. It should be noted that failure to address the possibility of malingering in such a setting may even be conceived of as a disservice to the patient, as ruling out malingering in an honest patient may allow the clinician to make a stronger statement regarding the presence of psychopathology.

Malingering Screening and Detection Scales

In order to provide useful information for clinicians faced with the problem of detection of false symptom reports, the characteristics of validity scales from several multiscale inventories as well as instruments specialized for the detection of malingering will be presented. This review will not be exhaustive, but rather will focus on structured instruments commonly used in clinical settings for assessing psychopathology and personality, as well as on tests specifically developed and validated to detect malingered psychological disorder. In light of the importance ascribed earlier to the classification accuracy and methodological characteristics of the research base supporting each scale or instrument, several of these factors will be covered in the review. Because comparison of normals who are feigning with normals who are answering honestly is not particularly clinically relevant, only those studies that included both a malingering group and a control group of psychiatric patients known or reasonably presumed to be answering honestly are reviewed. Additionally, reviewed studies were required to present classification accuracy statistics at clearly specified cutting scores, or to provide enough information to extract or infer these data. In each table, reported sensitivity and specificity data at specific cutting scores are provided, along with positive and negative predictive power values at the two base rates identified by Strong et al. (2000), which represent midrange estimates of the base rate of malingering. These statistics will allow a clinician to obtain a realistic perspective on the potential accuracy of various feigning detection scales, as well as facilitate comparison across instruments. It should be noted that a large literature on the detection of malingering during neuropsychological assessment is available, and the interested reader might wish to consult relevant review sources (Larrabee, 2007; Pope, Butcher, & Seelen, 2006; Sweet, 1999; Vickery, Berry, Inman, Harris, & Orey, 2001).

Minnesota Multiphasic Personality Inventory-2

The MMPI and its successor, the MMPI-2 (Butcher, Dahlstrom, Graham, Tellegen, & Kaemmer, 1989), have been the most widely utilized self-report measures of personality and psychopathology of their time (Pope et al., 2006). The MMPI-2 includes 567 true/false questions written at a sixth-grade reading level combined to form many validity, clinical, content, and supplementary scales measuring various domains of psychological functioning, as well as response sets. These validity scales are a primary strength of the MMPI-2, indicating the extent to which an individual attends to item content, distorts in a favorable or unfavorable light, and has a tendency toward either yea- or nay-saying.

The primary validity scale of the original MMPI, the infrequency (F) scale, was carried over nearly intact to the MMPI-2, with the intent of identifying atypical patterns of responding. As such, the original scale was developed using items endorsed by less than 10% of the MMPI normative sample. The F scale of the MMPI-2 contains 60 of the original 64 items, each of which is embedded in the first part of the test. In addition to the F scale, the MMPI-2 included several other validity scales to enhance feigning detection. The back infrequency (Fb) scale is conceptually similar to F, but includes 40 items embedded in the latter portion of the test to assess for differences in test-taking style across items. The F − K index is another scale designed to assess malingering by subtracting the K (defensiveness) raw score from the raw F scale score. It is thought that individuals attempting to present false symptoms will elevate the F scale, while depressing the K scale. Thus, the more positive the F − K score, the greater the tendency to exaggerate or fabricate symptoms. A more recent addition to the MMPI-2 validity scales is the infrequency-psychopathology—F(p)—scale developed by Arbisi and Ben-Porath (1995) after observation that elevations

on the F scale were sometimes due to severe psychopathology rather than false symptom reports. Thus, they created the F(p) scale with 27 items shown to be rarely endorsed by not only the MMPI-2 normative sample, but also by a large group of psychiatric inpatients. Because all infrequency scales, including F, F − K, and F(p), are vulnerable to random responding, it is necessary to rule this response set out using additional MMPI-2 validity scales (Gallen & Berry, 1996, 1997; Wetter, Baer, Berry, Smith, & Larsen, 1992).

The variable response inconsistency (VRIN) scale includes 47 pairs of conceptually similar or opposite items and assesses the individual's consistency in responding to item content. Lack of attention to item content or completely random responding should be suspected if many item pairs are endorsed in conflicting ways. The true response inconsistency (TRIN) scale assesses an individual's tendency toward yea- or nay-saying on the test, based on responses to items paired for opposite content. Greene (2000) recommends a systematic approach to determining if any response biases are present. He suggests first examining the VRIN scale for lack of attention to item content and TRIN scale for yea- or nay-saying response sets. Should either of these scales be significantly elevated, it is likely that elevations on infrequency scales are not due specifically to false symptom reports or exaggeration, but rather to a lack of attention to item content.

Over the past several decades, the MMPI and MMPI-2 validity scales have been the focus of many empirical studies, with several meta-analyses summarizing the published literature (Berry, Baer, & Harris, 1991; Rogers, Sewell & Salekin, 1994; Rogers, Sewell, Martin, & Vitacco, 2003). Overall, these studies have suggested that F and F(p) are the best scales for detecting psychiatric malingering on the MMPI and MMPI-2, although ambiguity exists with regard to the specific cutting scores to be used in order to optimize classification rates. It is also noteworthy that although F and F(p) have been found best suited for detecting feigned psychiatric symptoms, these scales are not necessarily suitable for detecting feigned physical or cognitive symptoms, such as after a traumatic brain injury (Larrabee, 2007). However, the focus of this review will remain on feigned psychiatric symptoms, and thus primarily on the F and F(p) scales, as well as the F − K index. Fb is not covered here due to its conceptual similarity to F.

Table 32.2 presents the results from published patient-controlled studies assessing the MMPI-2

Table 32.2. Results from patient-controlled malingering detection studies using the MMPI-2.

Study	Group	N	Sample	Design	Inc	Warn	Comp Check	Scale	Cutoff	Sn	SP	BR = .27 PPP	BR = .27 NPP	BR = .19 PPP	BR = .19 NPP
Graham, Watts, & Timbrook, 1991	FB	30	Male Stud	Sim	N	N	N	F	$T \geq 120$	.90	.97	.92	.96	.88	.98
	Hon	30	Male Pt			N	N	F-K	≥ 23	.90	.97	.92	.96	.88	.98
Lees-Haley, 1991	FB	20	Fem Stud	Sim	N	N	N	F	$T \geq 120$	.95	.95	.88	.98	.82	.99
	Hon	20	Fem Pt			N	N	F-K	≥ 25	.90	.95	.87	.96	.81	.95
Lees-Haley, 1991	Mal	26	Pers Inj	KG	n/a	n/a	n/a	F	$T \geq 65$	.81	1.00	1.00	.93	1.00	.96
	Hon	21	Pers Inj		n/a	n/a	n/a								
Lees-Haley, 1992	Mal	55	Pers Inj	KG	n/a	n/a	n/a	F	$T \geq 62$	.89	.98	.94	.96	.91	.97
	Hon	64	Pers Inj		n/a	n/a	n/a	F-K	≥ -4	.82	.98	.94	.94	.91	.96
Rogers, Bagby, & Chakraborty, 1993	FBNC	15	CV	Sim	Y	N	N	F	$T > 120$	.60	.97	.88	.87	.83	.91
	Hon	37	Pt			N	N	F-K	> 14	.67	.81	.57	.87	.45	.91
	FBSC	15	CV	Sim	Y	Y	N	F	$T > 120$	.73	.97	.90	.91	.85	.94
	Hon	37	Pt			Y	N	F-K	> 14	.67	.81	.57	.87	.45	.91
	FBVC	14	CV	Sim	Y	Y	N	F	$T > 120$	.21	.97	.72	.77	.62	.84
	Hon	37	Pt			Y	N	F-K	> 14	.29	.81	.36	.76	.26	.83
	FBCB	15	CV	Sim	Y	Y	N	F	$T > 120$	.47	.97	.85	.83	.79	.89
	Hon	37	Pt			Y	N	F-K	> 14	.48	.81	.48	.81	.37	.87
Wetter et al., 1993	FB	20	CV	Sim	Y	N	Y	F	$T \geq 96$	.85	.70	.51	.93	.40	.95
	Hon	20	PTSD			N	N	F-K	≥ 15	.75	.85	.65	.90	.54	.94
	FB	22	CV	Sim	Y	N	Y	F	$T \geq 104$	1.00	.90	.79	1.00	.70	1.00
	Hon	20	PASC			N	N	F-K	≥ 16	.95	.95	.88	.98	.82	.99

continued

Table 32.2. (*continued*)

Study	Group	N	Sample	Design	Inc	Warn	Comp Check	Scale	Cutoff	Sn SP	BR = .27		BR = .19	
											PPP	NPP	PPP	NPP
Bagby, Rogers, & Buis, 1994	FB	58	Stud	Sim	Y	Y	N	F	$T > 104$	.88	.63		.52	
	Hon	184	Fsc Pt				N			.81		.95		.97
								F-K	>11	.88	.64		.53	
										.82		.95		.97
Bagby, Rogers, Buis & Kalemba, 1994	FB	58	Stud	Sim	Y	Y	N	F	$T > 89$	.91	.64		.53	
	Hon	95	Pt				N			.81		.96		.97
								F-K	>7	.95	.64		.53	
										.80		.98		.98
Iverson, Franzen, & Hammond, 1995	FB	28	Corr	Sim	N	Y	N	F	$T \geq 92$	.89	.94		.91	
	Hon	51	Pt				N			.98		.96		.97
								F-K	>9	.86	.94		.91	
										.98		.95		.97
Rogers, 1995	FB	33	Pt	Sim	Y	Y		F	$T > 120$	.94	.81		.73	
	Hon	38	Pt							.92		.98		.98
								F-K	>18	.88	.67		.56	
										.84		.95		.97
								F(p)	$T > 110$	.88	.87		.81	
										.95		.96		.97
Sivec, Hilsenroth, & Lynn, 1995	FB	65	Stud	Sim	Y	Y	Y	F	$T > 99$	.95	.78		.69	
	Hon	40	Pt				N			.90		.98		.99
Pensa et al., 1996	FB	20	Stud	Sim	Y	N	N	F	$T \geq 95$	.93	.95		.92	
	Hon	20	Pt				N			.98		.97		.98
								F-K	≥8	1.00	.76		.66	
										.88		1.00		1.00
Arbisi & Ben-Porath, 1998	FB	33	Pt	Sim	Y	N	Y	F	$T \geq 100$	.97	.64		.53	
	Hon	41	Pt				Y			.80		.99		.99
								F(p)	$T \geq 100$	.97	.95		.92	
										.98		.99		.99
Elhai et al., 2000	FB	79	Stud	Sim	Y	Y	N	F	$T > 120$	.75	.55		.43	
	Hon	124	Pt				N			.77		.89		.93
								F-K	≥17	.71	.46		.35	
										.69		.87		.91
Storm & Graham, 2000	FBNC	67	Male Stud	Sim	Y	N	Y	F	$T > 120$	.67	.93		.89	
	Hon	192	Male Pt				N			.98		.89		.93
								F-K	>23	.63	.92		.88	
										.98		.88		.92
								F(p)	$T > 106$	.98	.85		.78	
										.75		.91		.91
	FBNC	124	Fem Stud	Sim	Y	N	Y	F	$T > 120$	.95	.91		.87	
										.82		.91		.94

Study	Sample	N	Group	Method				Index	Cutoff						
	Hon	160	Fem Pt				N	F-K	>17	.97	.84	.84	.94	.77	.96
	FBVC	93	Male Stud	Sim	Y		Y	F(p)	T >120	.94	.86	.91	.94	.87	.96
	Hon	192	Male Pt				N	F	T >101	.97	.54	.54	.95	.43	.97
								F-K	>16	.83	.35	.62	.83	.51	.89
								F(p)	T >94	.92	.59	.69	.79	.58	.86
	FBVC	156	Fem Stud	Sim	Y		Y	F	T >85	.90	.78	.44	.86	.34	.90
	Hon	160	Fem Pt				N	F-K	>−2	.64	.90	.39	.89	.29	.93
								F(p)	T >89	.49	.69	.60	.93	.49	.95
Archer et al., 2001	FB	60	Male S&C	Sim	N		N	F	T ≥90	.83	.62	.52	.88	.41	.92
	Hon	329	Male Pt				N	F(p)	T ≥70	.79	.53	.54	.85	.42	.90
	FB	143	Fem S&C	Sim	N		N	F	T ≥90	.83	.50	.43	.83	.32	.88
	Hon	288	Fem Pt				N	F(p)	T ≥70	.75	.39	.46	.80	.35	.86
Lewis, Simcox, & Berry, 2002	Mal	24	Corr	KG	n/a		n/a	F	T >107	.83	.67	1.00	.79	1.00	.85
	Hon	31	Corr				n/a	F(p)	T >100	1.00	.50	1.00	.89	1.00	.93
								F-K	>10	1.00	.79	.83	.84	.76	.90
Heinze, 2003	Mal	33	Corr	KG	n/a		n/a	F	T ≥100	.94	.73	.69	.92	.59	.95
	Hon	33	Corr				n/a	F(p)	T ≥100	.88	.52	.56	.90	.45	.93
								F-K	≥16	.85	.70	.68	.83	.58	.88

continued

Table 32.2. *(continued)*

Study	Group	N	Sample	Design	Inc	Warn	Comp Check	Scale	Cutoff	Sn SP	BR = .27		BR = .19	
											PPP	NPP	PPP	NPP
Ross, Millis, Krukowski, Putnam, & Adams, 2004	Mal	59	Fsc Pt	KG	n/a	n/a	n/a	F	$T \geq 65$	.66	.40		.30	
	Hon	59	TBI							.64		.84		.89
							n/a	F-K	≥ -6	.58	.33		.24	
										.56		.78		.85
Heinze & Vess, 2005	Mal	6	Corr	KG	n/a	n/a	n/a	F	$T \geq 100$	.33	.64		.53	
	Hon	47	Corr				n/a			.93		.79		.86
								F-K	>15	.17	.44		.33	
										.92		.75		.83
								F(p)	$T \geq 100$	.33	1.00		1.00	
										1.00		.80		.86
Arbisi, Ben-Porath, & McNulty, 2006	FB	35	PTSD Pt	Sim	Y	Y	Y	F	$T \geq 120$	.49	1.00		1.00	
	Hon	55	PTSD Pt				Y			1.00		.84		.89
								F(p)	$T \geq 100$	.49	1.00		1.00	
										.80		.77		.84
Eakin et al., 2006	FB	29	PTSD Pt	Sim	Y	Y	N	F	>11	.71	.47		.36	
	Hon	23	Stud				N			.70		.87		.91
								F(p)	>4	.52	.60		.48	
										.87		.83		.89

Note. For studies, only first author is listed. Sn/Sp column indicates sensitivity in top line and specificity in bottom line for each comparison. n/a = not applicable. Inc = incentive for successful faking. Warn = warning to fake believably, Comp Check = check for compliance with faking instructions, Sn = sensitivity, Sp = specificity, BR = base rate, PPP = positive predictive power, NPP = negative predictive power. For Group: FB = fake bad, Hon = honest, FBCB = fake bad with coaching on symptoms and validity scales, FBNC = fake bad with no coaching, FBSC = fake bad with coaching on symptoms, FBVC = fake bad with coaching on validity scales, Mal = malingering. For Sample: Corr = correctional, CST = competency to stand trial evaluees, CV = community volunteers, Fem = female, Fsc = forensic, IPt = inpatient, Pers Inj = workers compensation or personal injury claimant, PASC=paranoid schizophrenia, PTSD = post traumatic stress disorder, S&C = student and community volunteers, Stud = student, TBI = traumatic brain injury. For Design: Sim = Simulation, KG = Known-groups. Sn/Sp column indicates sensitivity in top line and specificity in bottom line for each comparison. For cut score: M = male, F = female. In cases where results using more than one cutting score were reported, data from the cutting score with the highest overall hit rate are presented.

feigning scales, including data on sample characteristics, study methodology, cutting scores, sensitivity, specificity, and positive and negative predictive powers at two hypothetical base rates of malingering (.19 and .27). The most notable aspect of these data is the sheer number of studies that have been published utilizing psychiatric control groups, as also illustrated in a comprehensive listing by Pope et al. (2006). Several known-groups studies are present, as well as simulation designs. The majority of simulation designs used the recommendations of Rogers (1997) and incorporated incentives for accurate feigning and warning to be believable, although very few utilized a compliance check for understanding and adherence to instructions. This remains true even with more recent studies, which raises methodological concerns given the specific recommendations provided by Rogers (1997). Although this table highlights the tremendous number of studies available on the MMPI-2 validity scales, it is difficult to glean specific information on cutting scores and operating characteristics here. Thus, Table 32.8 provides a summary of the aggregated MMPI-2 studies as well as results from other instruments and scales to be reviewed below.

Table 32.8 provides mean cutting scores, sensitivity, specificity, and positive and negative predictive powers across the MMPI-2 studies presented in Table 32.2. It should be noted that these cannot be taken as exact estimates of operating characteristics, but rather as a rough approximation of the values based on available studies. Overall, considerable variability exists for cutting scores for all these scales. The F scale shows the best operating characteristics across studies, with high specificity and moderate sensitivity. Additionally, F showed the highest sensitivity overall, whereas F(p) had the highest overall specificity. Considering the clinically relevant predictive powers, none of these indices had impressive PPP. In contrast, NPP was generally at .90 or higher for almost all these scales at both base rates, suggesting better ability to rule out than to rule in feigning. The modest PPP for these scales suggests that a positive test sign on the MMPI-2 is insufficient, on its own, for identifying feigning. These results suggest that to identify feigning, data from an additional indicator, such as the SIRS, should be used to supplement MMPI-2 validity scales in a determination of feigning. An example combining results from the MMPI-2 and the SIRS for detecting feigning will be presented later in this chapter.

An important caveat that should be noted for the MMPI-2 validity scales is the subtle problem resulting from the availability of multiple validity scales embedded in the measure. Routine consideration of all possible feigning scales on the MMPI-2 (F, Fb, F-K, F(p), Ds, FBS, RBS, etc.), with positive results from any one held as suggestive of feigning, will result in an overall elevated false positive rate because as Greene (2000) indicates, these scales are imperfectly correlated and thus tap somewhat different aspects of false symptom presentation. Thus, in order to minimize potential Type I error, only two or possibly three of these scales should be routinely utilized and taken as evidence of malingering. Further, as noted previously, elevations on these scales should only be considered possible indicators of malingering after VRIN and TRIN have been examined and other response styles ruled out.

Personality Assessment Inventory

The Personality Assessment Inventory (PAI; Morey, 1991, 2007) is an objective self-report measure of personality and psychopathology that has steadily grown in popularity. The PAI is intended for use with adults 18 years and older. It is written at a fourth-grade reading level and consists of 344 items answered in a 4-point Likert format. Responses are arranged into 22 non-overlapping scales covering four domains: validity scales (4), clinical scales (11), treatment indication scales (5), and interpersonal style scales (2).

Of the original PAI validity indices, two assess inconsistent and random response styles and two assess positive and negative self-presentation styles. The inconsistency (ICN) scale consists of paired questions selected due to content similarity and the infrequency (INF) scale includes eight items that are either very rarely or nearly always endorsed, but which are not indicative of psychopathology. Both these scales are elevated by random responding.

The presence of the ICN and INF scales on the PAI facilitates Greene's (2000) recommended systematic approach to evaluating profile validity. Therefore, the infrequency and inconsistency scales should be consulted first before addressing the possibility of symptom feigning.

The original PAI validity scales assessing self-presentation styles included a positive impression (PIM) scale and a negative impression (NIM) scale. The NIM scale includes nine items, which, when endorsed, suggest a tendency to report a greater degree of symptomatology than would be predicted by objective evidence. A NIM elevation therefore suggests an exaggerated, unfavorable impression or feigning.

In addition to the original validity indices, at least two others have been developed to assess feigned symptom reports. These include the malingering (MAL) index and the Rogers discriminant function (RDF). The MAL index was created by Morey and Lanier (1998) using configural features, or scoring rules, of PAI profiles that tend to be more frequently observed in simulations of severe mental illness than in actual clinical cases. The configural features are based upon T-score patterns involving the INF, ICN, and NIM validity scales, as well as subscales of five clinical scales. Eight features or rules are reviewed, for which each is weighted one raw score point when present. Zero features correspond to a MAL T-score of 44.

As with the MAL index, the RDF (Rogers, Sewell, Morey, & Ustad, 1996) was developed to separate profiles of true clinical cases from those of simulated mental illness. Discriminant function analysis was employed to identify an optimal combination of subscales and weights separating these groups. The resulting algorithm (available in the original publication and the revised 2007 test manual) included 20 scales and subscales. The regression basis of a discriminant function means that generalization to other samples is sometimes difficult, and hand calculation is often tedious. However, reliable discriminant functions are thought to have the benefit of being resistant to coaching.

Table 32.3 presents the PAI's fake-bad index results from published malingering studies meeting inclusion criteria noted earlier. Of the 16 qualifying studies, 11 used simulation designs and 5 used known-groups evaluations. The availability of data from this number of simulation, and particularly known-groups evaluations, is an important strength for the PAI. An additional strength is that all known-groups evaluations used the SIRS (Rogers, Bagby, & Dickens, 1992) as a classification criterion. The consistent use of one criterion allows an easier comparison between studies. Simulation studies were also relatively consistent, as the majority of authors reported offering incentives to feigners and providing an admonition to fake believably. Use of a compliance check to ensure participants understood and followed instructions was much less commonly reported, however, and present for only four feigning groups and two honest groups.

Table 32.8 presents estimated classification values for the PAI NIM, MAL, and RDF indices. For all three indices, a fairly wide range of cutting scores have been used. NIM has most balanced sensitivity and specificity as well as the highest sensitivity values. MAL has the highest specificity value. Translating these into predictive powers, it can be seen that even at the higher base rate, none of these indices has satisfactory PPP. In contrast, NPP is close to, or above, .90 for both NIM and RDF. These results suggest that positive test signs on the PAI faking indices are inadequate for identification of feigning on their own, and should, like the MMPI-2, be followed up with a dedicated malingering test to identify feigned symptom reports with confidence. In contrast, the strong NPPs for NIM and RDF suggest they may be used to rule out feigning in the presence of negative test signs. Overall, given that many more studies have evaluated NIM, with generally positive results, it appears to be the preferred index for identifying feigned symptom reports on the PAI, although, as noted, a second stage instrument is required for confidence.

Millon Clinical Multiaxial Inventory-III

The Millon Clinical Multiaxial Inventory is now in its third edition (MCMI-III: Millon, Davis, & Millon, 1997), and has long been among the more popular instruments when concern about personality disorders is high. The newest version of this test includes 175 true/false items scored on 24 content scales tapping clinical personality patterns, severe personality pathology, basic clinical syndromes, and severe syndromes. Additionally, four scales provide information on response sets. The test is intended to coordinate with major DSM-IV-TR Axis I disorders as well as Axis II personality disorders. Rather than T-scores, raw scores are transformed to base rate scores which are intended to incorporate varying prevalences of the disorders tapped by the MCMI-III, offering a potential advantage over the fixed prevalences implicitly assumed by most standard scores.

Response set indicators on the MCMI-III include a validity index (V) and three modifying indices: disclosure (X), desirability (Y), and debasement (Z). The validity index includes three items with extreme endorsement rates and is sensitive to random responding of various etiologies. The disclosure index assesses the tendency of the test taker "to be frank and self-revealing or reticent and secretive" (Millon et al., 1997, p. 118). This index is "calculated from the degree of positive or negative deviation from the midrange of an adjusted composite raw score for Scales 1 to 8B" (p. 118), apparently derived from the normative patient sample and used to adjust scores on other scales, in addition to serving

Table 32.3. Results from patient-controlled malingering detection studies using the PAI.

Study	Group	N	Sample	Design	Inc	Warn	Comp Check	Scale	Cutoff	Sn / Sp	BR = .27		BR = .19	
											PPP	NPP	PPP	NPP
Rogers, Sewell, Morey, & Ustad, 1996	FB	182	Stud	Sim	Y	Y	N	NIM	$T \geq 77$	.56	.52		.41	
	Hon	221	Pt				N			.81		.83		.89
Liljequist, Kinder, & Schinka, 1998	FB	27	Stud	Sim	Y	Y	Y	Mal I	≥ 3	.32	.52		.43	
	Hon	29	Pt-PTSD				N			.90		.78		.85
	FB	27	Stud	Sim			Y	Mal I	≥ 3	.44	1.00		1.00	
	Hon	30	Pt-alcoh				N			1.00		.83		.88
								Mal I	≥ 3	.97	.84		.77	
										1.00		.82		.88
Morey & Lanier, 1998	FB	44	Stud	Sim	Y	N	N	NIM	$T > 80$	.89	.75		.65	
	Hon	45	Pt				N			.89		.96		.97
								RDF	$T > 65$[a]	.95	.90		.85	
										.96		.98		.99
Rogers et al., 1998	Mal	16	Corr	KG[b]	n/a	n/a	n/a	NIM	$T > 80$	.63	.82		.75	
	Hon	43	Corr IPt		n/a	n/a	n/a			.95		.87		.92
Rogers et al., 1998	Mal	57	Corr	KG[b]	n/a	n/a	n/a	NIM	$T \geq 77$	.84	.54		.43	
	Hon	58	Corr IPt		n/a	n/a	n/a			.74		.94		.95
								Mal I	> 4	.47	.55		.44	
										.86		.81		.87
								RDF	$T > 65$[a]	.51	.40		.30	
										.72		.80		.86
Calhoun et al., 2000	FB	23	Stud	Sim	Y	Y	N	NIM	$T \geq 73$[c]	.83	.32		.23	
	Hon	23	Pt-PTSD				N			.35		.85		.90
								NIM	$T \geq 84$[d]	.74	.32		.23	
										.43		.82		.88
								NIM	$T \geq 92$[e]	.61	.39		.29	
										.65		.82		.88

continued

Table 32.3. (*continued*)

Study	Group	N	Sample	Design	Inc	Warn	Comp Check	Scale	Cutoff	Sn	Sp	BR = .27 PPP	BR = .27 NPP	BR = .19 PPP	BR = .19 NPP
Scragg, Bohr, & Menhdam, 2000	FB	25	CV	Sim	Y	Y	N	Mal I	≥3	.56	.78	.48	.83	.37	.88
	Hon	19	Pt-Psy				N	NIM	$T \geq 84$[f]	.54	1.00	1.00	.85	1.00	.90
								Mal I	≥3	.45	.94	.74	.82	.64	.88
								RDF	$T \geq 60$[g]	.63	.94	.80	.87	.71	.92
Blanchard et al., 2003	FB[l]	28	Stud-PF	Sim	Y	Y	N	NIM	$T \geq 110$	.54	.99	.93	.90	.95	.85
	FB[l]	24	Stud-FF		Y	Y	N	Mal I	≥5	.48	1.00	1.00	.84	1.00	.89
	Hon[l]	432	Psy IPt				N	RDF	$T \geq 75$[h]	.60	.99	.96	.87	.93	.91
Samra, 2004	FB	41	Stud	Sim	Y	Y	Y	NIM	$T > 91$	.05	1.00	1.00	.74	1.00	.82
	Hon	16	MDD OPt				N	NIM	$T > 81$	.21	1.00	1.00	.77	1.00	.84
Neher, 2005	FB	43[j]	Psy IPt[j]	Sim[i]	Y	N	N	Mal I	≥3	.17	1.00	1.00	.77	1.00	.84
	Hon				Y	N	N								
Boccaccini, Murrie, & Duncan, 2006	Mal[m]	45	Corr	KG[b]	n/a	n/a	n/a	NIM	$T \geq 92$	.78	.84	.64	.91	.53	.94
	Hon[l,m]	109	Corr		n/a	n/a	n/a	NIM	$T \geq 84$	.89	.73	.55	.95	.44	.97
								NIM	$T \geq 81$	.91	.72	.55	.96	.43	.97
								NIM	$T \geq 77$	.91	.91	.49		.38	

Study	Group	N	Sample	Design				Scale	Cut						
Eakin et al., 2006	FB[m]	29	Stud	Sim	Y	Y	Y	MAL I	≥5	.65	.13	.62	.95	.50	.97
	Hon[m]	23	Stud-PTSD		Y	Y	Y	MAL I	≥3	.97	.53	.55	.75	.44	.83
								MAL I	≥2	.84	.89	.75	.83	.65	.88
								NIM	msg	.89	.90	.29	.96	.20	.97
								MAL I	msg	.17	1.00	.27	.82	.19	.88
								RDF	msg	.00	.76	.32	.00	.23	.00
Kucharski & Duncan, 2006[g]	Mal[m]	32	Corr-CST	KG[b]	n/a	n/a	n/a	NIM	T ≥ 84	.39	.88	.59	.81	.47	.87
	Hon[m]	108	Corr-CST		N	N	N								
Baity et al., 2007	FB	20	Psy IPt	Sim				NIM	T > 77	.77	.67	.71	.95	.61	.96
	Hon[j]	21	Psy IPt					NIM	T ≥ 73	.90	.78	.67	.88	.57	.92
								NIM	T > 65	.86	.86	.49	.91	.38	.94
								RDF	T > 80	.67	.29	.68	.93	.58	.95
								RDF	T > 60	.95	.71	.58	.78	.47	.85
								RDF	T > 50	.81	.86	.38	.88	.28	.92
Edens, Poythress, & Watkins-Clay 2007	FB[l]	30	Corr	Sim	Y	Y	Y	NIM	T ≥ 77	.48	.76	.36	.90	.26	.94
						Y	Y	MAL	≥5	.52	.73	.42	.80	.31	.87
								RDF	T ≥ 70	.90	.73	.55	.95	.44	.97

continued

Table 32.3. (continued)

Study	Group	N	Sample	Design	Inc	Warn	Comp Check	Scale	Cutoff	Sn Sp	BR = .27 PPP	BR = .27 NPP	BR = .19 PPP	BR = .19 NPP
Kucharski et al., 2007[k]	Mal[m]	31	Corr-CST	KG[b]	n/a	n/a	n/a	NIM	$T \geq 73$	.90	.49		.38	
	Hon[m]	85	Corr-CST				n/a			.66		.95		.97
								NIM	$T \geq 77$	.90	.59		.48	
										.77		.95		.97
								NIM	$T \geq 81$	.87	.61		.49	
										.79		.94		.96
								NIM	$T \geq 84^{o}$	.84	.63		.52	
										.82		.93		.96
								NIM	$T \geq 88$	.81	.68		.58	
										.86		.92		.95
								NIM	$T \geq 92$	.71	.70		.60	
										.89		.89		.93

Note: Group: For studies, only first author is listed unless additional authors required to identify reference. n/a = not applicable. Inc = incentive for successful faking. Warn = warning to fake believably, Comp Check = check for compliance with faking instructions, Sn = sensitivity, Sp = specificity, BR = base rate, PPP = positive predictive power, NPP = negative predictive power. For sample: FB = fake bad, FG = fake good, Hon = Honest, Mal = Malingering. For sample: alcoh = alcohol dependence, Corr = correctional, CST = competency to stand trial evaluee, CV = community volunteer, FF = forensic feigning condition, IPt = inpatient, MDD = major depressive disorder, OPt = outpatient, PF = psychiatric feigning condition, Pt = patient, Psy = psychiatric (mixed or unspecified), PTSD = post-traumatic stress disorder, Stud = student. For Design: Sim = simulation, KG = known groups. For Scales: CDF = Cashel Discriminant Function Scale, Mal I = Malingering Index, NIM = Negative Impression Management, RDF = Rogers Discriminant Function. Sn/Sp column indicates sensitivity in top line and specificity in bottom line for each comparison.

[a]Cutoff given in paper was >.57 raw; this was converted to an approximate T-score for the purpose of this table. [b]Formed using SIRS as criteria. [c]Cutoff given in paper was 8 raw. d Cutoff given in paper was 11 raw. [e]Cutoff given in paper was 13 raw. [f]Cutoff determined a priori. [g]Cutoff given in paper was >.06 raw; this was converted to an approximate T-score for the purpose of this table. [h]Cutoff given in paper was ≥1.70 raw; this was converted to an approximate T-score for the purpose of this table. [i]Within-subjects design where individuals took test under standard instructions and under instructions to fake good (both within 2–24 hour period); order was randomized. [j]Note that the same Hon comparison group was used for both FB and FG analyses. [k]Personal communication with the first author indicated that the 2006 and 2007 studies had overlapping data sets; both are provided to illustrate test characteristics at various cutting scores. [l]The Hon group was comprised of those scoring in the Indeterminate range (N = 44) and those producing valid SIRS results. [m]Random responders were eliminated from this group prior to data analysis. [n]The operating characteristics at this cutoff score did not contribute to the operating characteristic summary table, as the 2006 Kucharski et al. study provides data for this score based upon the more inclusive sample.

as a validity indicator. The desirability index taps the "inclination to appear socially attractive, morally virtuous, or emotionally well composed" (p. 118) and thus should be sensitive to a "fake good" approach to the test. The debasement index is the most directly applicable to detection of over-reporting of psychological problems. It assesses a tendency to "devalue oneself by presenting more troublesome emotional and personal difficulties than are likely" (p. 118).

Significant potential issues exist with regard to the MCMI-III validity scales. First, given the presence of only three items, the V scale may "miss" a significant proportion of random responders, possibly leading to erroneous conclusions regarding the presence of over-reporting of symptoms on the basis of other scales. Charter and Lopez (2002) reported that approximately 50% of entirely random MCMI-III protocols received scores of 0 or 1 on the V scale and thus would have avoided proper identification. Thus, the stepwise approach to evaluating protocol validity possible for the MMPI-2 is potentially much less powerful for the MCMI-III. Another issue is that the BR scores of 75 and 85 for the X, Y, and Z scales were set simply to demarcate percentile rankings of 75 and 90 in the normative patient sample without regard to any independent determination of presence or absence of response sets (pp. 61–62). This is a rather weak developmental method for scales used to make important decisions regarding response sets. Yet another potential concern is that BR score thresholds of 75 and 85 are used to signal the presence of a trait or condition on clinical scales. Thus, this metric may be confusing to clinicians who do not closely read the manual as they may misinterpret elevated scores on Scales X, Y, and Z as clearly indicating the presence of the target response set. A concern specific to Scales Y and Z is that they were developed based on the responses of a small number of graduate students ($n = 12$; Millon, 1987) who were asked to respond under "fake good" and "fake bad" instructions, and only minimal detail (group means) is offered regarding results from two small-scale validation studies reported in the MCMI-II manual. Although the scales were apparently modified somewhat in the transition from the MCMI-II to III, no further empirical work on the scales was presented in the MCMI-III manual, raising questions about the robustness and generalizability of results from these scales. Craig (1999), in a review paper on forensic applications of the MCMI, states "readers should be aware that the validity scales of the MCMI remain

the least researched and least validated of all MCMI scales and hence could be subject to extensive cross-examination" (p. 295). Morgan, Schoenberg, Dorr, and Burke (2002) reported that the MCMI-III feigning scales were much less sensitive to feigning than the comparable MMPI-2 scales. In their study of 191 psychiatric inpatients, nearly 31% of protocols classified as invalid by the MMPI-2 F(p) scale were categorized as valid by the MCMI-III Scale X. Thus, there are a number of reasons to fear that the MCMI-III validity scales are too inaccurate for cases where malingering is a significant concern.

Table 32.4 presents results from published malingering detection studies of the MCMI-III that included a patient control group. Perhaps the most striking aspect here is the paucity of studies. Only three published studies were found that included a patient control group for the MCMI-III using traditional interpretative indices, all of which used simulation designs. These simulation studies each have minor methodological weaknesses, especially when a student population is used to "fake bad." Table 32.4 shows generally low to moderate sensitivity values but somewhat stronger specificity statistics. Classification statistics from these studies suggest a low to moderate PPP, depending on the base rate (.29–.43 at a base rate of .19, and .39–.76 at a base rate of .27). In contrast to PPP, NPP results are generally stronger with values ranging from .81 to .93 at a base rate of .19, and from .73 to .89 at a base rate of .27.

Given the many questions raised earlier about the acceptability of the MCMI-III feigning indices, as well as the small number of patient-controlled studies, this test does not appear to be an ideal choice in settings characterized by higher base rates of malingering. In particular, given the modest PPP noted in Table 32.4, the MCMI-III appears inadequate to document feigned symptom reports without data from an additional malingering test, and thus no summary results are reported in Table 32.8.

Dedicated Malingering Tests

In addition to malingering detection scales embedded in multiscale inventories of personality and psychopathology, there are several tests devoted solely to the detection of feigned symptom reports. Although routine use of tests providing only information about malingering may be appropriate in settings with moderate to high base rates of malingering, in other settings they are likely to be used only for evaluees who have provided evidence for feigned symptoms on multiscale inventories or in

Table 32.4. Results from patient-controlled malingering detection studies using the MCMI-III.

Study	Group	N	Sample	Design	Inc	Warn	Comp Check	Scale	Cutoff	Sn Sp	BR = .27 PPP	BR = .27 NPP	BR = .19 PPP	BR = .19 NPP
Daubert & Metzler, 2000	FB	80	OPt	Sim	Y	N	N	X	≥85BR	.61	.54		.43	
	Hon	80	OPt							.81		.85		.90
								Y	≤35BR	.58	.47		.36	
										.76		.83		.89
								Z	≥85BR	.55	.49		.38	
										.79		.83		.88
								X*	≥80BR	.76	.49		.36	
										.71		.89		.93
								Y*	≤39BR	.64	.48		.37	
										.74		.85		.90
								Z*	≥81BR	.64	.52		.41	
										.78		.85		.90
Schoenberg, Dorr, & Morgan, 2003	Mal	106	Stud	Sim	Y	N	Y	X*	>89BR	.35	.52		.41	
	Hon	181	IPt							.88		.79		.85
								Y*	<21BR	.33	.45		.34	
										.85		.77		.84
								Z*	>82BR	.59	.39		.29	
										.66		.81		.87
								X	>178r	.00	.00		.00	
										1.00		.73		.81
Schoenberg, Dorr, & Morgan, 2006	FB	18	Stud	Sim	Y	Y	Y	DisFxA	n/a*	.51	.76		.67	
	Hon	21	Ipt							.94		.84		.89
								DisFxB		.64	.58		.47	
										.83		.86		.91
	FB	55	Stud	Sim	Y	Y	Y	DisFxA	n/a*	.45	.62		.51	
	Hon	88	Ipt							.90		.82		.87
								DisFxB		.71	.61		.49	

Note: For studies, only first author is listed. Sn/Sp column indicates sensitivity in top line and specificity in bottom line. Sn/Sp column indicates sensitivity in top line and specificity in bottom line. Warn = warning to fake believably, Comp Check = check for compliance with faking instructions, Sn = sensitivity, Sp = specificity, PPP = positive predictive power, NPP = negative predictive power, NPP = negative predictive power. n/a = not applicable. Inc = incentive for successful faking. Inc = incentive for successful faking. For Group: FB = fake bad, Hon = Honest, Mal = Malingering. For Sample: IPt = inpatient, OPt = outpatient, Stud = student. For Design: Sim = Simulation. For Scale: X = Disclosure, Y = Desirability, Z = Debasement; * = optimal cutting score in samples; DisFxA/DisFxB = Discriminant Function A/B.

other aspects of their presentations. The tests reviewed in this section include only those with adequate independent evaluation of their operating characteristics including patient control groups.

Structured Inventory of Malingered Symptomatology

The Structured Inventory of Malingered Symptomatology (SIMS) was developed by Smith (1992) with the goal of producing a brief malingering screening instrument that was easily administered, capable of high rates of detection, and written at a low reading level (fifth grade). It was recently published by Psychological Assessment Resources (Widows & Smith, 2005). In addition to using a self-report true/false format, the 75-item SIMS was designed to include scales sensitive to several specific forms of malingering, including psychosis (P), amnesia (Am), neurologic impairment (N), affective disorder (Af), and low intelligence (Li) (Smith & Burger, 1997). The total score, summed across all scales on the SIMS, appears to be the most commonly used variable for predicting the presence or absence of malingering. One limitation of the SIMS is that it does not have a scale for addressing the possibility of random responding. A totally random approach to the test would likely cause mid-range elevations on all the malingering scales, a potentially misleading finding.

Table 32.5 presents results from the five published studies of the SIMS that included an appropriate control group. Strengths of the available studies of the SIMS include the use of both known-groups and simulation designs, and the provision of incentives for successful feigners in the analog studies. Another noteworthy aspect of the available data is the use of a fairly consistent cutting score for predicting malingering, with all studies but one using the same cutoff score. In addition, there has been increased variety in control groups used in recent years, with adolescent, correctional, student, personal injury, and psychiatric populations all being studied. In spite of this progress, the number of nonforensic adult psychiatric inpatients studied is still quite low. An additional weakness of the available studies is the failure to check compliance in supposedly honest patient groups. A final potential concern is the lack of a random responding scale, although presumably the examiner would note such an approach.

Table 32.8 presents mean classification values summarizing data from the SIMS. It can be seen that the SIMS is characterized by moderately high

sensitivity and moderate specificity. Translated into predictive powers, at both base rates NPP is excellent (>.90), although PPP is rather modest. This profile suggests that the SIMS might make an excellent brief screening tool for feigned symptom reports, as a negative test sign on the instrument is highly predictive of honest responding. In contrast, the relatively weak PPP makes the SIMS a poor candidate for following up a positive test sign from a multiscale inventory such as the MMPI-2 or the PAI. At that stage, high PPP is critical as labeling an evaluee a malingerer should never be done lightly. Thus, another instrument with stronger PPP should probably be preferred to the SIMS for ruling in psychiatric feigning.

Miller Forensic Assessment of Symptoms Test

The Miller Forensic Assessment of Symptoms Test (M-FAST; Miller, 2001) is a 25-item structured interview for psychiatric feigning. The M-FAST is intended to be a brief screening instrument, taking only 5 min to administer. Based on malingering detection strategies identified by Rogers (1997), the M-FAST consists of seven subscales: unusual hallucinations (UH), reported versus observed behavior (RO), rare symptom combinations (RC), extreme symptoms (ES), negative image (NI), unusual symptom course (USC), and suggestibility (S). The total score is obtained by summing the scale scores, and a cutting score of 6 or above suggests feigning.

Table 32.6 presents available published data on patient-controlled studies of the M-FAST. The M-FAST has been validated in a number of published studies with college students (Miller, 2001), forensic psychiatric inpatients (Jackson, Rogers, & Sewell, 2005; Miller, 2001), criminal defendants found incompetent to stand trial (Miller, 2004), prisoners (Guy & Miller, 2004; Jackson et al., 2005), and civil forensic populations (Alwes, Clark, Berry & Granacher, 2008). Favorable findings independent of the scale's author have been reported, as have supporting results from both known-groups and simulation designs using a single recommended cutting score.

Table 32.8 shows mean values summarizing M-FAST findings. Mean sensitivity is moderate at .79, whereas mean specificity is somewhat stronger at .84. These parameters translate into low to moderate PPP, but NPP values which are strong (≥.90). This profile suggests that the M-FAST is best used as a screen to rule out feigning. However, individuals with positive test signs on the M-FAST should

Table 32.5. Results from patient-controlled malingering detection studies using the SIMS.

Study	Group	N	Sample	Design	Inc	Warn	Comp Check	Scale	Cutoff	Sn Sp	BR = .27		BR = .19	
											PPP	NPP	PPP	NPP
Rogers, Hinds & Sewell, 1996	FB	53	Adol IPt	Sim	Y	N	N	Total	>16	.44[a]	.71		.61	
	Hon	53	Adol IPt							.94[a]		.82		.88
Lewis, Simcox, & Berry, 2002	Mal	20	Corr	KG[b]	n/a	n/a	n/a	Total	>16	1.00	.45		.30	
	Hon	31	Corr							.55		1.00		1.00
Merckelbach & Smith, 2003	FB	57	Stud	Sim	N	Y	N	Total	>16	.93	.95		.92	
	Hon	10	Psy IPt							.98		.97		.98
	Hon	231	Stud											
Alwes et al., 2008	PsyM	23	Pers Inj	KG	n/a	n/a	n/a	Total	>16	.96	.52		.40	
	PsyH	172	Pers Inj							.97		.98		.99
	Neu M	75	Pers Inj	KG	n/a	n/a	n/a	Total	>16	.75	.41		.31	
	Neu H	178	Pers Inj							.60		.87		.91
Edens et al., 2007	FB	30	Corr	Sim	Y	Y	Y	Total	>14	.90	.36		.26	
	Hon	30	Corr IPt		Y					.40		.92		.94

Note: For studies, only first author is listed. Sn/Sp column indicates sensitivity in top line and specificity in bottom line for each comparison. Sn/Sp column indicates sensitivity in top line and specificity in bottom line for each comparison. n/a = not applicable. Inc = incentive for successful faking. Warn = warning to fake believably. Comp Check = check for compliance with faking instructions. Sn = sensitivity. Sp = specificity. BR = base rate. PPP = positive predictive power. NPP = negative predictive power. For Group: FB = fake bad. Hon = Honest. Mal = Malingering. PsyM = psychiatric malingering. PsyH = psychiatric honest. Neu H = neurocognitive honest. Neu M = neurocognitive malingering. For Sample: Adol = Adolescent. Corr = correctional. IPt = inpatient. Stud = student. Pers Inj = Workers Compensation or Personal Injury claimant. For Design: Sim = Simulation. KG = Known-groups. For Scale: Tot = SIMS Total Score. [a] Sensitivity and Specificity estimated from PPP, NPP, and base rate of 50%. [b] The SIRS was used as criterion for individual classification.

Table 32.6. Results from patient-controlled malingering detection studies using the M-FAST.

Study	Group	N	Sample	Design	Inc	Warn	Comp Check	Scale	Cutoff	Sn/Sp	BR = .27		BR = .19	
											PPP	NPP	PPP	NPP
Guy & Miller, 2004	Mal	21	Corr IPt	KG	N	N	N	Total	≥6	.86	.65		.54	
	Hon	29	Corr IPt							.83		.94		.96
Miller, 2004	Mal	14	Psy CST	KG	N	N	N	Total	≥6	.93	.67		.56	
	Hon	36	Psy CST							.83		.97		.98
Jackson & Rogers, 2005	FB	43	Corr	Sim	N	Y	Y	Total	≥6	.76	.74		.64	
	Hon	96	Corr							.90		.91		.94
Veazey, Miller, & Hays, 2005	Mal	8	Psy CST	KG	N	N	N							
	Hon	41	Psy CST											
	Mal	5	Psy IPt	KG	N	N	N	Total	≥6	.80	.66		.56	
	Hon	39	Psy IPt							.85		.92		.95
Guy, Kwartner, & Miller, 2006	FB	48	Stud	Sim	Y	Y	Y	Total	≥6	.88	.64		.53	
	Hon	48	Scz							.82		.95		.97
	FB	41	Stud	Sim	Y	Y	Y	Total	≥6	.84	.60		.48	
	Hon	20	BP							.79		.93		.95
	FB	51	Stud	Sim	Y	Y	Y	Total	≥6	.62	.52		.41	
	Hon	25	MDD							.79		.85		.90
	FB	50	Stud	Sim	Y	Y	Y	Total	≥6	.63	.61		.50	
	Hon	47	PTSD							.85		.86		.91
Alwes, 2008	PsyM	23	Pers Inj	KG	n/a	n/a	n/a	Total	≥6	.83	.77		.68	
	PsyH	172	Pers Inj							.91		.94		.96

Note: For studies, only first author is listed unless others required to identify reference. Sn/Sp column indicates sensitivity in top line and specificity in bottom line for each comparison. n/a = not applicable. Inc = incentive for successful faking, Warn = warning to fake believably, Comp Check = check for compliance with faking instructions, Sn = sensitivity, Sp = specificity, BR = base rate, PPP = positive predictive power, NPP = negative predictive power. For Group: FB = fake bad, Hon = Honest, Mal = Malingering, PsyM = psychiatric malingering, PsyH = psychiatric honest. For Sample: BP = bipolar disorder, Corr = correctional, CST = competency to stand trial evaluees, IPt = inpatient, MDD = major depressive disorder, Pers Inj = workers compensation or personal injury claimant, PTSD = post traumatic stress disorder, Scz = schizophrenia, Stud = student. For Design: Sim = Simulation, KG = Known-groups.

receive another procedure to confirm presence of feigning, as the M-FAST's PPP values are far too low to rule in false symptom reports with sufficient confidence.

Structured Interview of Reported Symptoms

The SIRS (Rogers et al., 1992) was developed to assess malingered psychological symptoms as well as other response sets in a structured interview format. The 172 items are organized into eight primary scales, which have consistently shown the ability to discriminate between malingerers and honest responders, and five supplementary scales which have not proven as effective in detecting malingering or are intended to assess other response sets (inconsistency, defensiveness). Three of the primary scales focus on very unusual symptom presentations (rare symptoms, symptom combinations, improbable and absurd symptoms), four assess the range and severity of symptoms (blatant symptoms, subtle symptoms, selectivity of symptoms, severity of symptoms), and the final primary scale examines discrepancies between self-reports of overt symptoms and interviewer observations (reported vs. observed symptoms). The structured interview format adds an additional dimension to data considered for identification of malingering beyond the traditional methods (unstructured clinical interview, self-report test results, behavioral observations, and record reviews). Additionally, this format standardizes the interviewer's behavior and serves to minimize inadvertent examiner clues regarding the implausibility of symptom endorsements. Finally, structured clinical interviews have facilitated improved reliability and validity of psychiatric diagnoses and offer the same potential for the detection of malingering (Rogers, 1995).

Raw scores from each of the SIRS scales are classified as honest, indeterminate, probable feigning, or definite feigning based on extensive data from patients, prisoners, analog malingerers, and independently identified malingerers (Rogers et al., 1992). Overall results are interpreted as suggestive of feigned psychological symptoms if one or more primary scales are in the definite feigning range, if three or more primary scales are in the probable feigning range, or if the total raw score exceeds 76. Reports published by the test's authors as well as independent investigators have supported the accuracy of the SIRS for detection of malingering. Inter-rater reliability, a key concern for interview-based data, has been reported to be quite strong (mean reliability = .96). Although the SIRS includes

a supplementary consistency scale (INC), it does not appear to have been extensively validated for detection of random responding. Presumably, however, random answers would be noted by the interviewer.

Table 32.7 presents results from malingering detection studies using the SIRS and including an appropriate control group. It should be noted that the manual summarizes data from several published studies on the SIRS which have been collapsed for the sake of convenience in Table 32.7 as Rogers et al. (1992). Thus, both simulation and known-groups designs have been utilized to evaluate the SIRS. Groups of simulators have been offered incentives to malinger and given warnings to respond believably, and subjects' compliance with the instructions has been checked, and coached subjects have not been found to avoid detection on the SIRS.

Classification data in Table 32.8 indicate that, using the primary scale (PS) with a cutoff of ≥3 in the probable feigning range, the SIRS has high PPP for identifying malingering at both base rates used in Table 32.8, and respectable NPP values also have been reported. The major strength of the SIRS appears to be its high PPP. Thus, when ruling in feigning, the SIRS appears to be the instrument of choice. Its major limitation may be the requirement for more direct clinician time for administration than necessary for self-report procedures.

Hypothetical Classification Rates for a Two-Stage Malingering Detection Strategy

Considering the available data on the classification rates of various malingering detection scales and tests in Table 32.8, it is clear that almost all available indices, with one exception, have much stronger NPP than PPP. This situation points to a need to explore the accuracy of sequential application of these indicators, or the "successive hurdles approach" described by Meehl and Rosen (1955). A simple model would involve a first-stage deployment of an indicator with high NPP to rule out malingering in the subset of evaluees with a negative test sign, and a second stage consisting of administration of an additional malingering detection procedure with high PPP to the subset of individuals with a positive test sign from stage one. This strategy potentially maximizes the utility of information obtained from tests with divergent NPP and PPP as well as benefits from the heightened base rate of malingering among second stage evaluees.

Implementing this sequential strategy requires identification of a test with high NPP for Stage 1

Table 32.7. Results from patient-controlled malingering detection studies using the SIRS.

Study	Group	N	Sample	Design	Inc	Warn	Comp Check	Scale	Cutoff	Sn Sp	BR = .27		BR = .19	
											PPP	NPP	PPP	NPP
Rogers et al., 1992	Mal	206	Mixed	KG+Sim	Y	Y	Y	Ps	≥3Feign	.48	.97		.96	
	Hon	197	Pt/Cor/ Com				n/a			.99		.84		.89
Gothard et al., 1995	Mal	37	For/Cor	KG+Sim	Y	Y	Y	Ps	≥3Feign	.97	.93		.90	
	Hon	78	For/Cor				Y			.97		.99		.99

Note: For studies, only first author is listed. Inc = incentive for successful faking, Warn = warning to fake believably, Comp Check = check for compliance with faking instructions, Sn = sensitivity, Sp = specificity, BR = base rate, PPP = positive predictive power, NPP = negative predictive power. For Group: Mal = malingering, Hon-honest. For Sample: Mixed = forensic, correctional, community, & student, Pt = patient, Cor = correctional, Com = community. For Design: KG+Sim = includes both known groups and simulation designs. For Scale: PS = Primary Scales. For Cutoff: Feign = in probable feigning range. Sn/Sp column indicates sensitivity in top line and specificity in bottom line for each comparisons.

Table 32.8. Means across studies for cutting score, sensitivity, specificity, PPP, and NPP for detection of malingering using the MMPI-2 PAI, SIMS, M-FAST & SIRS.

	MMPI-2 F	MMPI-2 F–K	MMPI-2 F(p)	PAI NIM	PAI MAL	PAI RDF	SIMS Total	M-FAST Total	SIRS PS
Cutting score									
Mean	102.38	13.55	94.54	82.2	3.5	66.0	15.7	>6	>3
Range	62–100	(−4)–25	70–120	66–110	2–5	51–81	14–16	n/a	n/a
SD	17.46	7.10	15.83	8.9	1.0	9.3	.82	0	n/a
Sensitivity									
Mean	.74	.73	.62	.73	.53	.69	.83	.79	.73
Range	.21–1.00	.17–1.00	.33–97	.05–.91	.13–1.00	.29–.95	.44–1.00	.62–.93	.48–.97
SD	.20	.23	.20	.22	.27	.21	.21	.11	.33
Specificity									
Mean	.89	.86	.90	.75	.84	.77	.74	.84	.98
Range	.64–1.00	.49–.98	.75–1.00	.17–1.00	0–1.00	.39–.99	.40–.98	.79–.91	.97–.99
SD	.11	.12	.08	.21	.27	.22	.25	.04	.01
PPP BR = .27									
Mean	.77	.68	.77	.62	.67	.62	.57	.65	.95
Range	.43–1.00	.35–.94	.46–1.00	.29–1.00	.27–1.00	.32–.96	.36–.95	.52–.77	.93–.97
SD	.18	.19	.20	.21	.24	.23	.22	.04	.02
NPP BR = .27									
Mean	.91	.90	.87	.89	.76	.87	.93	.92	.91
Range	.77–1.00	.75–1.00	.79–.99	.74–.96	0–.96	.78–.98	.82–1.00	.85–.97	.84–.97
SD	.06	.07	.06	.06	.23	.07	.07	.07	.03
PPP BR = .19									
Mean	.68	.60	.70	.53	.60	.53	.47	.64	.93
Range	.32–1.00	.26–.91	.35–1.00	.20–1.00	.19–1.00	.23–.93	.26–.92	.41–.68	.90–.96
SD	.22	.21	.25	.24	.28	.25	.26	.08	.02
NPP BR = .19									
Mean	.94	.93	.91	.92	.81	.91	.95	.95	.94
Range	.84–1.00	.83–1.00	.85–.99	.82–.97	0–.97	.85–.99	.88–1.00	.90–.98	.89–.99
SD	.04	.05	.09	.04	.25	.05	.05	.03	.04
# comparisons	29	22	13	26	13	9	6	9	2[a]

Note: Cutting score = point at or above which scale value interpreted as a positive test sign. All cutting scores given in T-scores except F–K which is given in raw scores. See text for definition of sensitivity, specificity, Positive Predictive Power (PPP) and Negative Predictive Power (NPP). BR = base rate of feigning.
[a] = Many published studies summarized in SIRS manual.

screening and a test with high PPP for Stage 2 classification of malingering. Although the PAI is a significant rival, the multiscale MMPI-2 has slightly more to recommend it for use in a first stage of malingering screening, including extensive documentation of the accuracy of its validity scales, relatively widespread use in forensic settings, and the availability of several indices with high NPP. Of the three MMPI-2 fake-bad indices reviewed above, the F scale has the highest NPP in Table 32.8. Thus, the MMPI-2 F scale will be used in the hypothetical two-stage process provided below as an example.

Because the second stage of evaluation here is aimed at identifying malingerers with a high level of confidence, high PPP is required for an instrument used at this stage. Of the three dedicated malingering detection instruments discussed above, the SIRS has the highest average PPP for the detection of malingering, relatively extensive empirical evaluation, and the theoretical advantage of assessing malingering in a different format (structured interview) than the self-report MMPI-2. Thus, the SIRS will be employed in the second stage of the example evaluation process.

Table 32.9 presents results from a hypothetical two-stage screening process using the MMPI-2 F scale at Stage 1 and the SIRS at Stage 2. The table includes Stage 1 data from the MMPI-2 F scale for 1,000 evaluees. Given average sensitivity and specificity results for the F scale using a cutting score of >102T, 280 evaluees would have a positive F sign. However, the associated PPP, given a malingering base rate of .27, would be about 71%. This means that there would be almost 1 chance in 4 that an individual with a positive MMPI-2 F sign was not malingering, but rather answering honestly. This level of certainty is judged by the present authors to be inadequate for labeling an individual as malingering. Therefore, the 280 evaluees with a positive F sign would have to undergo further evaluation as described shortly.

Table 32.9 also indicates that 720 evaluees would have a negative MMPI-2 F sign. Although some of these individuals would in fact be malingering, the NPP for this group is roughly 90%. This level of certainty is judged to be adequate for ruling out malingering, and the prevalence of 10% malingering in this group means that it would be difficult to improve on predicting with the base rates. Thus all evaluees with a negative F sign would be predicted to be honest and not further evaluated in Stage 2.

As mentioned above, the 280 evaluees with a positive F sign would go on to be given the SIRS in Stage 2. It is important to note that the base rate of malingering in those with a positive MMPI-2 F sign is roughly 71%, a rather high base rate environment that will boost PPP. Using the average sensitivity and specificity values for the SIRS at a criterion of three or more primary scales in the probable feigning range, the second part of Table 32.9 shows resulting predictive powers. Although NPP is modest here, the PPP for a positive SIRS result is 98.6%. Thus, those who reach Stage 2 of this process and obtain a positive SIRS sign are overwhelmingly likely to be malingerers.

Table 32.9 also includes a summary of the overall hit rate at both stages. It can be seen that the two-stage process slightly increases the overall hit rate as well as featuring high NPP and PPP at the crucial points in the process. Thus, this two-stage model has much to recommend it for the detection of feigned symptom reports.

This two-stage model is not impervious to potential criticisms, however. First, it must be noted that judgments regarding the adequacy of various levels of predictive power are subjective, and some clinicians may disagree with the decision made by the present authors to minimize false positive errors. If so, they may use the overall model to adopt decision-making strategies using different subjective weights. Second, the sensitivity and specificity values used in the example are based on averages across multiple studies, and require cross-validation in large samples before they may be confidently used in clinical work. Finally, should additional well-validated tests of malingering become available, the group with a negative SIRS test sign at Stage 2, which has a base rate of malingering close to 40%, might be given the additional procedure for greater confidence in ruling out malingering.

Conclusions

The possibility of exaggerated, feigned, or misattributed psychological symptoms should be routinely considered in evaluations for which significant incentives exist for findings of psychopathology. Although the overall base rate of malingered psychological problems is not yet known, it is clear from several published studies that the frequency of feigning may increase to between 30% and 50% of individuals tested in compensation-seeking or forensic contexts. Among the multiscale personality and psychopathology inventories reviewed above, the MMPI-2 has the greatest support for its malingering detection scales, closely followed by the PAI. However, the PPP of fake-bad scales from these inventories is not high enough in most cases to justify a conclusion of malingering on the basis of

Table 32.9. Classification Parameters of One- and Two-Stage Feigning Detection Strategies.

One-stage feigning detection strategy using F

Cutting score	F > 102T		Reality		
Sensitivity	.740		Mal	Hon	
Specificity	.890	F +	200	80	200/280 = .714 (PPP)
Base rate	.270	F −	70	650	650/720 = .903 (NPP)
Hit rate	.850 (850/1000)		270	730	

Two-stage feigning detection strategy using F and SIRS (only those with F+ receive SIRS)

Cutting score	SIRS ≥3 Primary Scales +		Reality		
Sensitivity	.730		Mal	Hon	
Specificity	.980	SIRS +	146	2	146/148 = .986 (PPP)
Base Rate	.714	SIRS −	54	78	78/132 = .591 (NPP)
			200	80	
Hit Rate	.874 (650 + 224/1000)				

Note: Mal = malingering, Hon = honest.

their results alone. For those who are not "screened out" on the basis of a negative test sign from these indices, it is recommended that a second stage of testing involving the SIRS be undertaken to raise certainty for a conclusion of malingering. Given the reported relatively high prevalences of feigned symptoms in certain settings, it will be important to continue research into the detection of malingering and develop additional tests and procedures. Clinicians working in relevant settings should closely but critically monitor new literature as it is published, and adjust their practices to the evolving knowledge base as appropriate.

Notes

1. For example, Butcher, Arbisi, Atlis, and McNulty (2003) suggested that application of the Lees-Haley Fake Bad Scale (FBS; Lees-Haley, English, & Glenn, 1991) may lead to excessive false positive findings of psychological feigning when applied to disability evaluations and to female evaluees.

References

Note: * = data summarized in one or more tables in this chapter.

Allen, L. M., & Green, P. (2001). Declining CARB failure rates over 6 years of testing: What's wrong with this picture? *Archives of Clinical Neuropsychology, 16*, 846.

*Alwes, Y. R., Clark, J. A., Berry, D. T. R., & Granacher, R. P. (2008). Screening for feigning in a civil forensic setting. *Journal of Clinical and Experimental Neuropsychology, 30*, 1–8.

American Psychiatric Association. (1980). *Diagnostic and statistical manual of mental disorders* (3rd ed.). Washington, DC: Author.

American Psychiatric Association. (2000). *Diagnostic and statistical manual of mental disorders* (4th ed., Text rev.). Washington, DC: Author.

*Arbisi, P. A., & Ben-Porath, Y. S. (1995). An MMPI-2 infrequent response scale for use with psychopathological populations: The infrequency-psychopathology scale, F(p). *Psychological Assessment, 4*, 424–431.

*Arbisi, P. A., & Ben-Porath, Y. S. (1998). The ability of the Minnesota Multiphasic Personality Inventory-2 validity scales to detect fake-bad responses in psychiatric inpatients. *Psychological Assessment, 10*, 221–228.

Arbisi, P. A., Ben-Porath, Y. S., & McNulty, J. (2006). The ability of the MMPI-2 to detect feigned PTSD within the context of compensation seeking. *Psychological Services, 3*, 249–261.

*Archer, R. P., Handel, R. W., Greene, R. L., Baer, R. A., & Elkins, D. E. (2001). An evaluation of the usefulness of the MMPI-2 F(p) scale. *Journal of Personality Assessment, 76*, 282–295.

*Bagby, R. M., Roger, R., & Buis, T. (1994). Detecting malingered and defensive responding on the MMPI-2 in a forensic inpatient sample. *Journal of Personality Assessment, 62*, 191–203.

*Bagby, R. M., Rogers, R., Buis, T., & Kalemba, V. (1994). Malingered and defensive response styles on the MMPI-2: An examination of validity scales. *Assessment, 1*, 31–38.

*Baity, M. R., Siefert, C. J., Chambers, A., & Blais, M. A. (2007). Deceptiveness on the PAI: A study of naïve faking with psychiatric inpatients. *Journal of Personality Assessment, 88*, 16–24.

*Berry, D. T. R., Adams, J. F., Clark, C. D., Thacker, S. R., Burger, T. L., Wetter, M. W., et al. (1996). Detection of a cry for help on the MMPI-2: An analog investigation. *Journal of Personality Assessment, 67*, 26–36.

Berry, D. T. R., Baer, R. A., & Harris, M. J. (1991). Detection of malingering on the MMPI: A meta-analytic review. *Clinical Psychology Review, 11*, 585–598.

*Blanchard, D. D., McGrath, R. E., Pogge, D. L., & Khadivi, A. (2003). A comparison of the PAI and MMPI-2 as predictors of faking bad in college students. *Journal of Personality Assessment, 80*, 197–205.

*Boccaccini, M., Murrie, D. C., & Duncan, S. A. (2006). Screening for malingering in a criminal forensic sample with the Personality Assessment Inventory. *Psychological Assessment, 18*, 415–423.

Butcher, J. N., Arbisi, P. A., Atlis, M. M., & McNulty, J. L. (2003). The construct validity of the Lees-Haley Fake Bad Scale: Does this scale measure somatic malingering and feigned emotional distress? *Archives of Clinical Neuropsychology, 18*, 473–485.

Butcher, J. N., Dahlstrom, W. G., Graham, J. R., Tellegen, A., & Kaemmer, B. (1989). *MMPI-2: Manual for administration and scoring.* Minneapolis, MN: University of Minnesota Press.

*Calhoun, P. S., Earnst, K. S., Tucker, D. D., Kirby, A. C., & Beckham, J. C. (2000). Feigning combat-related posttraumatic stress disorder on the Personality Assessment Inventory. *Journal of Personality Assessment, 75*, 338–350.

Charter, R. A., & Lopez, M. N. (2002). Millon Clinical Multiaxial Inventory (MCMI-III): The inability of the validity conditions to detect random responding. *Journal of Clinical Psychology, 58*, 1615–1617.

Craig, R. J. (1999). Testimony based on the Millon Clinical Multiaxial Inventory: Review, commentary, and guidelines. *Journal of Personality Assessment, 73*, 290–304.

Daubert vs. Merrell, Dow Pharmaceuticals, Inc. (1993). 113 S. Ct. 2786.

*Daubert, S. D., & Metzler, A. E. (2000). The detection of fake-bad and fake-good responding on the Millon Clinical Multiaxial Inventory III. *Psychological Assessment, 12*, 418–424.

*Eakin, D. E., Weathers, F. W., Benson, T. B., Anderson, C. F., & Funderbunk, B. (2006). Detection of feigned posttraumatic stress disorder: A comparison of the MMPI-2 and PAI. *Journal of Psychopathology and Behavioral Assessment, 28*, 145–155.

*Edens, J. F., Poythress, N. G., & Watkins-Clay, M. M. (2007). Detection of malingering in psychiatric unit and general population prison inmates: A comparison of the PAI, SIMS, and SIRS. *Journal of Personality Assessment, 88*, 33–42.

*Elhai, J. D., Gold, P. B., Frueh, B. C., & Gold, S. N. (2000). Cross-validation of the MMPI-2 in detecting malingered Posttraumatic Stress Disorder. *Journal of Personality Assessment, 75*, 449–463.

Frederick, R. I., Crosby, R. D., & Wynkoop, T. F. (2000). Performance curve classification of invalid responding on the Validity Index Profile. *Archives of Clinical Neuropsychology, 15*, 281–300.

Gallen, R. T., & Berry, D. T. R. (1996). Detection of random responding in MMPI-2 protocols. *Assessment, 3*, 171–178.

Gallen, R. T., & Berry, D. T. R. (1997). Partially random MMPI-2 protocols: When are they interpretable? *Assessment, 4*, 61–68.

*Gothard, S., Viglione, D. J., Meloy, J. R., & Sherman, M. (1995). The detection of malingering in competency to stand trial evaluations. *Law and Human Behavior, 19*, 493–505.

*Graham, J. R., Watts, D., & Timbrook, R. E. (1991). Detecting fake good and fake bad MMPI-2 profiles. *Journal of Personality Assessment, 57,* 264–277.

Greene, R. L. (2000). *The MMPI-2: An interpretive manual* (2nd ed.). Boston: Allyn & Bacon.

*Guy, L. S., Kwartner, P. P., & Miller, H. A. (2006). Investigation of the M-FAST: Psychometric properties and utility to detect diagnostic specific malingering. *Behavioral Sciences and the Law, 24*(5), 687–702.

*Guy, L. S., & Miller, H. A. (2004). Screening for malingered psychopathology in a correctional setting: Utility of the Miller-Forensic Assessment of Symptoms Test (M-FAST). *Criminal Justice and Behavior, 31*(6), 695–716.

*Heinze, M. C. (2003). Developing sensitivity to distortion: Utility of psychological tests in differentiating malingering and psychopathology in criminal defendants. *The Journal of Forensic Psychiatry and Psychology, 14,* 151–177.

*Heinze, M. C., & Vess, J. (2005). The relationship among malingering, psychopathy, and the MMPI-2 validity scales in maximum security forensic psychiatric inpatients. *Journal of Forensic Psychology Practice, 5,* 35–53.

*Iverson, G. L., Franzen, M. D., & Hammond, J. A. (1995). An examination of inmates' ability to malinger on the MMPI-2. *Psychological Assessment, 7,* 118–121.

*Jackson, R.L., & Rogers, R. (2005). Forensic applications of the Miller Forensic Assessment of Symptoms Test (MFAST): Screening for feigned disorders in competency to stand trial evaluations. *Law and Human Behavior, 29*(2), 199–210.

*Jackson, R. L., Rogers, R., & Sewell, K. W. (2005). Forensic applications of the Miller forensic assessment of symptoms (M-FAST): Screening for feigned disorders in competency to stand trial. *Law and Human Behavior, 29,* 199–210.

*Kucharski, L., & Duncan, S. (2006). Clinical and demographic characteristics of criminal defendants potentially misidentified by objective measures of malingering. *American Journal of Forensic Psychology, 24,* 5–20.

*Kucharski, L. T., Toomey, J. P., Fila, K., and Duncan, S. (2007). Detection of malingering of psychiatric disorder with the Personality Assessment Inventory: An investigation of criminal defendants. *Journal of Personality Assessment, 88,* 25–32.

Larrabee, G. J. (Ed.). (2007). *Evaluation of malingered neuropsychological deficits.* New York: Oxford University Press.

*Lees-Haley, P. R. (1991). MMPI-2 F and F − K scores of personal injury malingerers in vocational neuropsychological and emotional distress claims. *American Journal of Forensic Psychology, 9,* 5–14.

*Lees-Haley, P. R. (1992). Efficacy of MMPI-2 validity scales and MCMI-II modifier scales for detecting spurious PTSD claims: F, F − K, Fake Bad Scale, ego strength, subtle-obvious subscales, DIS & DEB. *Journal of Clinical Psychology, 48,* 681–688.

Lees-Haley, P. R. (1997). Attorneys influence expert evidence in forensic psychological and neuropsychological cases. *Assessment, 4,* 321–324.

Lees-Haley, P. R., English, L. T., & Glenn, W. J. (1991). A fake bad scale on the MMPI-2 for personal injury claimants. *Psychological Reports, 68,* 203–210.

*Lewis, J. L., Simcox, A. J., & Berry, D. T. R. (2002). Screening for feigned psychiatric symptoms in a forensic sample by using the MMPI-2 and the Structured Inventory of Malingered Symptomatology. *Psychological Assessment, 14,* 170–176.

*Liljequist, L., Kinder, B. N., & Schinka, J. A. (1998). An investigation of malingering posttraumatic stress disorder on the Personality Assessment Inventory. *Journal of Personality Assessment, 71,* 322–336.

Meehl, P. E., & Rosen, A. (1955). Antecedent probability and the efficiency of psychometric signs, patterns or cutting scores. *Psychological Bulletin, 52,* 194–216.

*Merckelbach, H., & Smith, G.P. (2003). Diagnostic accuracy of the Structured Inventory of Malingered Symptomatology (SIMS) in detecting instructed malingering. *Archives of Clinical Neuropsychology, 18,* 145–152.

Miller, H. A. (2001). *Miller-Forensic Assessment of Symptoms Test (M-FAST): Professional manual.* Odessa, FL: Psychological Assessment Resources.

*Miller, H. A. (2004). Examining the use of the M-FAST with criminal defendants incompetent to stand trial. *International Journal of Offender Therapy and Comparative Criminology, 48*(3), 268–280.

Millon, T. (1987). *Manual for the MCMI-II.* Minneapolis, MN: National Computer Systems.

Millon, T., Davis, R., & Millon, C. (1997). *Millon Clinical Multiaxial Inventory-III manual* (2nd ed.). Minneapolis, MN: National Computer Systems.

Morey, L. C. (1991). *Personality Assessment Inventory professional manual.* Odessa, FL: Psychological Assessment Resources.

Morey, L. C. (2007). *Personality Assessment Inventory (PAI): Professional manual* (2nd ed.). Lutz, FL: Psychological Assessment Resources.

*Morey, L. C., & Lanier, V. W. (1998). Operating characteristics of six response distortion indicators for the Personality Assessment Inventory. *Assessment, 5,* 203–214.

*Morgan, C. D., Schoenberg, M. R., Dorr, D., & Burke, M. J. (2002). Overreport on the MCMI-III: Concurrent validation with the MMPI-2 using a psychiatric inpatient sample. *Journal of Personality Assessment, 78,* 288–300.

Neher, J. A. (2005). *The effects of honest versus fake-good response sets by a psychiatric population on the Personality Assessment Inventory* (doctoral dissertation, 2005). *Dissertation Abstracts International, 66*(05B), 2834. Abstract retrieved spring 2007 from PsychInfo/Dissertation Abstracts International database.

*Norris, M. P., & May, M. C. (1998). Screening for malingering in a correctional setting. *Law and Human Behavior, 22,* 315–323.

*Pensa, R., Dorfman, W. J., Gold, S. N., & Schneider, B. (1996). Detection of malingered psychosis with the MMPI-2. *Psychotherapy in Private Practice, 14,* 47–62.

Pope, K. S., Butcher, J. N., & Seelen, J. (2006). Some final thoughts. In J. N. Butcher & K. S. Pope (Eds.), *The MMPI, MMPI-2, and MMPI-A in court: A practical guide for expert witnesses and attorneys* (3rd ed., pp. 203–209). Washington, DC: American Psychological Association.

Rogers, R. (1990). Development of a new classificatory model of malingering. *Bulletin of the American Academy of Psychiatry and Law, 18,* 323–333.

Rogers, R. (1995). *Diagnostic and structured interviewing: A handbook for psychologists.* Odessa, FL: Psychological Assessment Resources.

Rogers, R. (Ed.). (1997). *Clinical assessment of malingering and deception* (2nd ed.). New York: Guilford.

*Rogers, R., Bagby, R. M., & Chakraborty, D. (1993). Feigning schizophrenic disorders on the MMPI-2: Detection of coached simulators. *Journal of Personality Assessment, 60,* 215–226.

Rogers, R., Bagby, R. M., & Dickens, S. E. (1992). *SIRS—Structured Interview of Reported Symptoms: A professional manual.* Odessa, FL: Psychological Assessment Resources.

*Rogers, R., Hinds, J. D., & Sewell, K. W. (1996). Feigning psychopathology among adolescent offenders: Validation of the SIRS, MMPI-A, and SIMS. *Journal of Personality Assessment, 67*, 244–257.

*Rogers, R., Kropp, P. R., Bagby, M. R., & Dickens, S. E. (1992). Faking specific disorders: A study of the Structured Interview of Reported Symptoms (SIRS). *Journal of Clinical Psychology, 48*, 643–648.

Rogers, R., Salekin, R. T., Sewell, K. W., Goldstein, A., & Leonard, K. (1998). A comparison of forensic and nonforensic malingerers: A prototypical analysis of explanatory models. *Law and Human Behavior, 22*, 353–367.

*Rogers, R., Sewell, K. W., Cruise, K. R., Wang, E. W., & Ustad, K. L. (1998). The PAI and feigning: A cautionary note on its use in forensic-correctional settings. *Assessment, 5*, 399–405.

Rogers, R., Sewell, K. W., & Goldstein, A. (1994). Explanatory models of malingering: A prototypical analysis. *Law and Human Behavior, 18*, 543–552.

Rogers, R., Sewell, K. W., Martin, M. A., & Vitacco, M. J. (2003). Detection of feigned mental disorders: A meta-analysis of the MMPI-2 and malingering. *Assessment, 10*, 160–177.

*Rogers, R., Sewell, K. W., Morey, L. C., & Ustad, K. L. (1996). Detection of feigned mental disorders on the Personality Assessment Inventory: A discriminant analysis. *Journal of Personality Assessment, 67*, 626–640.

Rogers, R., Sewell, K. W., & Salekin, R. T. (1994). A meta-analysis of malingering on the MMPI-2. *Assessment, 1*, 227–237.

*Rogers, R., Sewell, K. W., & Ustad, K. L. (1995). Feigning among chronic outpatients on the MMPI-2: A systematic examination of fake-bad indicators. *Assessment, 2*, 81–89.

*Rogers, R., Ustad, K. L., & Salekin, R. T. (1998). Convergent validity of the Personality Assessment Inventory: A study of emergency referrals in a correctional setting. *Assessment, 5*, 3–12.

Ross, S. R., Millis, S. R., Krukowski, R. A., Putnam, S. H., & Adams, K. M. (2004). Detecting incomplete effort on the MMPI-2: An examination of the Fake Bad Scale in mild head injury. *Journal of Clinical and Experimental Neuropsychology, 26*, 115–124.

Ruiz, M. A., Drake, E. B., Glass, A., Marcotte, D., & van Gorp, W. G. (2002). Trying to beat the system: Misuse of the Internet to assist in avoiding the detection of psychological symptom dissimulation. *Professional Psychology: Research and Practice, 33*, 294–299.

Samra, J. (2004). The impact of depression on multiple measures of malingering. *Dissertation Abstracts International: Section B: The Sciences and Engineering, 64*(8-B) 4061.

*Scragg, P., Borr, R., & Menhdam, M. (2000). Assessment of feigning post-traumatic stress disorder on the PAI. *Clinical Psychology and Psychotherapy, 7*, 155–160.

*Schoenberg, M., Dorr, D., & Morgan, C. (2003). The ability of the Millon Clinical Multiaxial Inventory-third edition to detect malingering. *Psychological Assessment, 15*(2), 198–204.

*Schoenberg, M., Dorr, D., & Morgan, C. (2006). Development of discriminant functions to detect dissimulation for the Millon Clinical Multiaxial Inventory (3rd edition). *Journal of Forensic Psychiatry and Psychology, 17*(3), 405–416.

*Sivec, H. J., Hilsenroth, M. J., & Lynn, S. J. (1995). Impact of simulating borderline personality disorder on the MMPI-2: A cost-benefits model employing base rates. *Journal of Personality Assessment, 64*, 295–311.

Smith, G. P. (1992). Detection of malingering: A validation study of the SLAM test (Unpublished doctoral dissertation), University of Missouri, St. Louis, MO.

Smith, G. P., & Burger, G. K. (1997). Detection of malingering: Validation of the Structured Inventory of Malingered Symptomatology (SIMS). *Journal of the American Academy of Psychiatry and the Law, 25*, 183–189.

*Storm, J., & Graham, J. R. (2000). Detection of coached general malingering on the MMPI-2. *Psychological Assessment, 12*, 158–165.

Strong, D. R., Greene, R. L., & Schinka, J. A. (2000). A taxometric analysis of MMPI-2 infrequency scales [F and F(p)]. *Psychological Assessment, 12*, 166–173.

Sweet, J. J. (1999). *Forensic neuropsychology.* Exton, PA: Swets & Zeitlinger.

*Veazey, C. H., Miller, H. A., & Hays, J. R. (2005). Validity of the Miller Forensic Assessment of Symptoms Test in psychiatric inpatients. *Psychological Reports, 96*(3), 771–774.

Vickery, C. D., Berry, D. T. R., Inman, T. H., Harris, M. J., & Orey, S. A. (2001). Detection of inadequate effort on neuropsychological testing: A meta-analytic review of selected procedures. *Archives of Clinical Neuropsychology, 16*, 45–73.

Victor, T. L., & Abeles, N. (2004). Coaching clients to take psychological and neuropsychological tests: A clash of ethical obligations. *Professional Psychology: Research and Practice, 35*, 373–379.

*Wetter, M. W., Baer, R. A., Berry, D. T. R., Robeson, L. H., & Sumpter, J. (1993). MMPI-2 profiles of motivated fakers given specific symptom information: A comparison to matched patients. *Psychological Assessment, 5*, 317–323.

Wetter, M. W., Baer, R. A., Berry, D. T. R., Smith, G. T., & Larsen, L. H. (1992). Sensitivity of MMPI-2 validity scales to random responding and malingering. *Psychological Assessment, 4*, 369–374.

Wetter, M. W., & Corrigan, S. (1995). Providing information to clients about psychological tests: A survey of attorney's and law students' attitudes. *Professional Psychology: Research and Practice, 26*, 474–477.

Widows, M. R., & Smith, G. P. (2005). *Structured Inventory of Malingered Symptomatology: Professional manual.* Odessa, FL: Psychological Assessment Resources.

Youngjohn, J. (1995). Confirmed attorney coaching prior to neuropsychological evaluation. *Assessment, 2*, 279–283.

Ziskin, J. (1995). *Coping with psychiatric and psychological testimony* (5th ed.). Los Angeles, CA: Law and Psychology Press.

Assessment of Clients in Pretreatment Planning

T. Mark Harwood *and* Larry E. Beutler

Abstract

Pretreatment planning is an essential element in psychotherapy. Constraints imposed by managed care, efficiency of treatment/cost-effectiveness issues, and increased likelihood of change and increased magnitude of change are obvious justifications for the provision of individualized and comprehensive pretreatment assessment. Relatedly, quality pretreatment assessment is essential for accurate patient–treatment matching. In this vein, systematic treatment selection (STS), prescriptive psychotherapy (PT), systematic treatment (ST) and Innerlife are variants of an overriding empirically supported model of patient–treatment matching. More specifically, STS, PT, ST, and Innerlife employ accurate, comprehensive pretreatment assessment to help guide the clinician in the selection and matching of specific psychotherapeutic strategies and principles. These research-informed strategies and principles of change, selected based on pretreatment data, efficiently and effectively address the unique treatment needs of the patient and their presenting problem(s).

Keywords: assessment, treatment planning, patient predisposing variables, prescriptive psychotherapy, pretreatment planning, referral, principles, strategies, interventions, systematic treatment

The first and most central question facing the clinician who is assessing a client is, "How will these findings be used?" A focused and meaningful evaluation requires that one keeps the ultimate uses of the report in mind. It is our experience that clinicians frequently fail to obtain a clear understanding of the referral question and may respond out of habit to certain inferred questions, thus providing results and information that are routine and overly general.

With the advent of managed health care, there has been decreasing support for the use of systematic psychological assessment in many clinical practices. Reliance on the clinical interview has largely replaced the use of reliable and valid psychological tests. This, we believe, is a serious mistake and places too many decisions on a method that suffers from poor reliability and uncertain validity. In a related way, much debate has occurred between those who believe that standard procedures and reports can be applied to the process of psychological assessment and those who maintain that each assessment should be specifically tailored to each client's needs and each referent's requests (Beutler & Groth-Marnat, 2003; Clarkin & Hurt, 1988; Cohen & Swerdlik, 2005; Sweeney, Clarkin, & Fitzgibbon, 1987). The epitome of the standard assessment approach is embodied in computer-generated reports. This approach utilizes a uniform set of one or more instruments, assesses a uniform set of dimensions, and applies standard descriptive statements to the evaluation of all patients. While this approach is satisfactory as a screening procedure, we believe that even if the same procedures are being used in different cases, an individually focused approach to interpreting and reporting the results makes better sense than a standard report in those instances when the clinician is asked to provide consultation to someone else.

Psychological assessment is a method for obtaining answers to questions. Without explicitly defining the questions in advance, the conclusions that one reaches and the report that one creates may be needlessly complex, general, uninformative, or inaccurate. Hence, the first task of the clinician is to determine what questions are being asked. Asking the referent for clarification of the question being asked is an obvious first step when the clinician is functioning as a consultant to another professional. In this role, the questions asked by a referring professional usually fall within five categories: (a) What "diagnosis" fits this person's current presentation? (b) What is the "prognosis" for this person's condition? (c) How impaired is this person's "current functioning"? (d) What "treatment" will be most likely to yield positive effects? (e) What factors are contributing to or "causing" this client's disturbance?

While the report is tailored to the specific question or questions asked, there is some degree of consistency to the nature of the information that is needed in order to answer all of these questions. That is, there are common domains of patient functioning that must be addressed in order to adequately answer any of the questions that might be posed by a referent. These common areas include: (a) an assessment of current level, strengths, and limitations of intellectual, memory, and other cognitive functions; (b) an evaluation of mood, affect, and level of emotional control; (c) a determination of events, conflicts, and needs that trigger the problematic responses for which the patient is seeking help; and (d) a narrative formulation of the patient's resources and deficits. This latter domain entails providing a conceptual formulation of the patient that is distilled from the information available from the other domains of functioning. This formulation usually includes a description of the nature of the patient's interaction with the environments that both evoke and alleviate the problem behaviors, including levels of motivation for treatment, styles of coping with external and internal stressors, levels and types of social support, and a description of common interpersonal themes or patterns that characterize the patient's functioning.

While an integration of descriptive and inferred information on these domains of functioning provide a common framework for responding to referral questions, different questions require more or less attention and detail to one or more of the different domains. For example, to answer a question that asks if the patient's behavior is representative of a central nervous system disorder (a diagnosis question), the clinician will need to focus more on an assessment of cognitive functions (judgment, intelligence, short- and long-term memory, concept formation, sensory

and perceptual functions, etc.) than would be required if the clinician were responding to question about the severity of the patient's depression (a question of current functional level). Likewise, a question regarding whether or not cognitive therapy would be helpful (a treatment question) would require the clinician to formulate an opinion regarding the patient's motivation level and coping styles to a greater extent than a question asking if a history of child abuse is related to the child's subsequent anxiety and social disturbance (a question of etiology).

Unfortunately, the questions actually asked on written referral forms are seldom as clearly framed as one would like. Often, these written questions are much more specific than the ones really motivating the referral and if responded to naively may cause the clinician to omit information the referent really desires and needs. For example, instead of asking for a "diagnosis," the referring professional may ask for "an MMPI" or a "Rorschach." At other times, the questions asked may be too broad to direct the clinician's inquiry. Thus, instead of asking for the desired treatment recommendations directly, the referent may ask for "personality testing."

In each of these cases, the referring professional may be using a shorthand method of attempting to get information from the consultant. Unless the consultant can decode the question, however, a response to the referent's shorthand will not be found to be helpful. Each cryptically written request for consultation hides some assumptions and specific but unstated questions that the referring clinician is attempting to address. For example, the referent who makes a written request for "neuropsychological testing" may be seeking confirmation of organic etiology in order to allow the patient to receive insurance compensation, or he/she may be trying to predict whether the symptoms are likely to dissipate enough over time to allow the patient to go back to work. Obviously, the responding clinician will want either to undertake a different form of evaluation or to write the report differently in these two instances.

Unless the clinician is very familiar with the referent's habits, he/she must clarify what decisions are being contemplated and what types of questions and dilemmas are facing the referent in order to have prompted this referral. Reframing requests in terms of questions that reflect one of the five aforementioned categories is desirable in order to provide the most reliable and useful information for the referent.

In the final analysis, all questions that are asked of the consulting clinician have implications for treatment and prognosis. This is true even when the clinician is functioning as an intake evaluator for an individual who has come to him or her as a patient for treatment. To the degree that this is true, the questions asked of a consulting clinician fall within the same categories as those that clinicians ask themselves when evaluating a potential psychotherapy client. That is, to the clinician-therapist, the questions that must be first addressed when the patient requests assistance is whether treatment is needed and if so, what treatment is likely to produce the most positive effects. A treatment-related question invokes one or more additional and more specific questions. For example, in the case of an intake evaluation of a person who is seeking treatment, all of the following related questions must be addressed:

1. Should this person be treated?
2. What are the long-term objectives of treatment?
3. Where should this person be treated?
4. Over what period of time and with what frequency should treatment occur?
5. Should the treatment be medical/pharmacological, psychological, or both?
6. Should others be included in the client's treatment (group or family or couple intervention)?
7. What type of relationship should the treating clinician provide?
8. How should the client be prepared for treatment?
9. What should the mediating goals of treatment be?
10. What strategy will have the greatest likelihood of succeeding with this person?
11. What specific procedures and techniques are indicated or contraindicated to implement this strategy?
12. How should treatment procedures and goals be changed over time?

Obviously, the methods of responding to these questions range in complexity and preference. Moreover, a description of ways to assess all of the dimensions on which answers to the myriad specific questions that can be asked is well beyond the scope of this chapter. However, we will attempt to define some of the most important and frequently useful dimensions that should be considered by the clinician in attempting to outline a treatment plan, and will explore some of the implications of these dimensions for selecting among alternative treatments with

a specific focus on questions of applying psychotherapeutic strategies.

A Problem-Solving Approach to Pretreatment Planning

Pretreatment planning entails an evaluation that is specifically crafted to meet the patients' needs and/or the referents' requests. Thus, assessment must be focused, meaningful, and attentive to expected changes over time. The complexity of treatment must also be acknowledged. Beutler and Clarkin (1990) suggest that there are four domains in which the clinician makes decisions. The first of these is in the selection of the dimensions of patient functioning that are to be assessed. These variables must be carefully selected to ensure relevance to the questions asked and to possess both concurrent and predictive validity. These "patient predisposing variables" provide the window through which one views subsequent treatment decisions. Hence, these subsequent treatment decisions are only as good as the dimensions and the methods of assessing them that are chosen at this first level.

Empirically and psychometrically sound assessment of relevant patient characteristics serves as the basis for recommending three subsequent and sequentially defined levels of treatment: the "context" in which treatment will be offered, the nature of the "relationship" that will be fostered, and the "specific strategies and techniques" that will be applied by the psychotherapist or counselor. Thus, when initially considering the nature of the referral, one must carefully select procedures that provide information on characteristics that "predispose" the patient to respond differentially to aspects of each of these three domains.

1. The "patient predisposing variables" that are relevant to the most frequently asked questions of treatment planning include such aspects of the patient and the patient's problems as formal diagnosis, probable etiology, target problems, demographic characteristics, personality and response dispositions, relevant environmental circumstances, and nature of available support systems.
2. The "context" of treatment refers to the setting in which treatment will be offered (e.g., inpatient or outpatient), the relative use of medical and psychosocial modalities, the format through which treatment will be conducted (e.g., individual, couples, group), and the intensity of

treatment to be offered (i.e., the duration and frequency).

3. Determining the nature of the "relationship" that will optimize treatment outcomes requires a consideration of several factors. These include the assignment of the therapist to fit the patient (i.e., patient-therapist matching), the use and nature of role induction procedures, and methods for enhancing the therapist's influence or role.

4. The "strategies and techniques" of psychotherapy are those goals and activities of the therapist that initiate and direct the processes of change. Assuming that psychotherapy has been selected as the treatment of choice, decisions at this level entail a specific and detailed determination of the objectives and mediating goals of treatment, the selection of strategies of change, and the selection of specific techniques through which these strategies will be implemented in order to achieve optimal treatment results.

Obviously, the determination of what patient predisposing dimensions to evaluate will limit the degree to which one can assign selectively treatment context variables, relationship variables, and specific interventions. The areas deemed to be indicated for assessment, the purpose of the evaluations, the intended use of results, and the historical information obtained will affect the decisions made at each subsequent level and will ultimately come to bear on how one develops the treatment plan. That is, both the needs of the client and the requests of the referent determine the specific instruments and techniques used in selecting components of a treatment plan.

Information gathered at one point in time is insufficient for treatment planning; assessment must be a continual process reflecting the mercurial nature of patient dimensions and dependent therapy focus. Only after a concise, comprehensive, and relevant clinical picture has been rendered may patients be assigned to the therapist and type of therapy, with the duration, frequency, and setting that will achieve optimal results. Again, assessment should be an ongoing process with adjustments in treatment made whenever indicated.

The reader should have gathered that careful pretreatment planning is an important practice that is intended to benefit patients by providing maximal efficiency and results; however, pretreatment planning is a necessary endeavor for other reasons as well. Four closely related observations have converged, highlighting the need to engage in selective, focused, targeted, and efficient selection of patient dimensions for all psychotherapeutic endeavors:

1. There is a growing recognition that conventional diagnosis is not sufficient in and of itself for establishing a focused plan of treatment.

2. There is a virtual endless list of patient variables (personality traits and states as well as demographic, philosophical, and environmental variables) that have been touted as important for enhancing treatment efficacy (i.e., quality of therapeutic alliance, patient–therapist compatibility, patient and therapist investment in therapy and outcome, nature of support systems, etc.).

3. There is a burgeoning array of treatments, at least some of which have proven to be differentially efficacious for various presenting problems (e.g., pharmacotherapy for certain depressive states versus *in vivo* exposure for phobic avoidance; cognitive-behavioral vs. insight approaches for patients with different personal styles).

4. There are increasing pressures from insurance companies, managed health-care systems, and the present state of the economy to limit the cost of and access to services. This translates to reduced coverage for what may be considered by one or another gatekeeper in the system as unnecessary or ineffective treatments. Health services have become less able to tolerate the inefficiencies and ineffectiveness that has characterized a large portion of psychiatric and psychological practice. Assuming that the health-care enterprise will continue to consider patients as being entitled to necessary and effective services, clinicians must carefully direct their assessment efforts to dimensions and qualities that are relevant to assigning efficient and effective treatment planning, and must do so in a way that conserves time and resources.

As the role of managed health care has become increasingly present in the decision-making process with respect to provision of services, the focus of treatment protocols has shifted from one designed around effective and reliable health care to one prioritized to lower cost. The emphasis on time-limited, standardized, and symptom-focused treatment exerts a cost on both patient and clinician. To the therapist the cost is giving up or abandoning the use of what may be effective procedures because they do not fit the prevailing models. To patients, the cost may be the failure to take the time to individualize and tailor treatments to make them fit their own particular needs and dispositions (Beutler, 2000).

Though mental health care (MHC) programs purport to provide consumers with effective and reliable health care, the satisfaction of recipients has long taken a backseat to economic objectives. The problems that develop when the economic bottom line takes precedence over the patient's bottom line have been exacerbated by the proliferation of therapies. With more than 400 brand name treatments in use today, both the clinician and MHC case manager may find it difficult to select the particular approach that can be applied most effectively to treat each patient in a cost-efficient and time-limited fashion. The aforementioned situation has prompted the proliferation of treatment guidelines and structured treatment manuals to aid both clinicians and MHC case managers in simplifying treatment decision-making processes. Indeed, over the last few years, and driven by converging trends toward evidenced-based medicine and cost containment, the health-care industry has become involved in the development of treatment guidelines (Clay, 2000). In addition, scientific organizations such as National Institute of Mental Health (NIMH) are diverting greater amounts of funding resources to investigations that focus on effectiveness research (Foxhall, 2000). NIMH hopes to bring research and practice closer together by providing practitioners with evidence for the most promising treatments across diagnoses and settings.

As clinicians are faced with the constraints imposed by MHC programs, the role of research becomes essential in providing both efficient and effective treatments. Researchers must rise to the current challenges and provide evidence-based approaches that clinicians can effectively apply in a time-limited and cost-efficient fashion. Systematic yet flexible approaches designed to meet the unique needs of each patient may be the most successful in providing promising care given the present circumstances.

A therapist is forced to practice under a premise that fosters imprecise clinical reasoning when patients are treated without consideration of the accumulation of factors that affect treatment efficacy. The blind application of therapies and other interventions, solely as a function of the therapist's proclivities and familiarity, without regard to the suitability of the patient's unique characteristics and problems to those procedures is wrong—wrong for the patient because substandard services are provided and wrong for mental health professionals because it wastes precious resources and is professionally irresponsible (Clarkin & Hurt, 1988). One could argue that such practice violates ethical considerations by increasing the likelihood of delivering varying degrees of inappropriate or ineffective treatment. This is not to say that pretreatment planning guarantees that the best treatment or results will be delivered or recommended in the individual case; however, decisions based upon patient and treatment qualities that have established relationships to outcomes increases the likelihood and magnitude of positive results.

Normatively and empirically developed assessment instruments have proven invaluable in deriving useful information for the skilled administrator. Clinical psychologists, by virtue of their expertise in using formal assessment instruments, are wonderfully poised to respond to the pressures for improving efficient treatment assignment. Assurance of reliable and valid measurement (both formal and informal) provides a sound basis for confidence in the inferences made when responding to questions of diagnosis, prognosis, and subsequent treatment decisions.

In sum, careful consideration of a small number of carefully selected and validated patient dimensions can provide the clinician with more valuable and comprehensive information on which to select appropriate treatment components than a plethora of ill-defined opinions based upon nonempirical theories. The derivation of valid information both from formal and informal pretreatment assessment procedures is an endeavor that will greatly aid achieving maximum compatibility of patient with treatment.

The following section describes eight patient variables that appear to bear a significant relationship to decisions that are invoked at one or more of the levels of treatment selection (Beutler, Malik, Talebi, Fleming, & Moleiro, 2004). In this section, we will identify the domains of treatment decision making to which these variables are most closely related. However, we will provide only an introduction to how these variables may be used in subsequent decisions about treatment context, defining the appropriate means of developing the therapeutic relationship, and selecting treatment strategies and techniques. Further clarification of the relationships between patient predisposing characteristics and subsequent decisions will be reserved for separate discussions of each of the sequential levels of treatment decision making.

Patient Predisposing Variables

Patient predisposing variables are defined as those qualities that characterize the patient and his or her environment at the time he or she enters treatment;

these variables have important implications for treatment planning. For example, patient diagnosis is a predisposing variable that has bearing on the setting, modality, and intensity of treatment. In addition, a patient's expectations about treatment represent important considerations with respect to the therapeutic relationship, treatment compliance, and retention. We will briefly discuss the role of diagnosis and expectations in terms of pretreatment planning; however, a set of more refined and empirically supported patient dimensions will comprise the lion's share of the remainder of this chapter.

More specifically, Beutler, Clarkin, and Bongar (2000), Beutler & Hodgson (1993), Beutler and Groth-Marnat (2003), & Beutler et al. (2003, 2004) extracted from extant research and then cross-validated through empirical test a series of hypotheses that were then used to construct cross-cutting treatment guidelines. These guidelines emphasized the role of seven predisposing patient dimensions: (a) problem complexity and chronicity, (b) level of functional impairment, (c) social support, (d) patient coping style, (e) level of trait-like resistance, (f) subjective distress, and (g) readiness for/stage of change, on how one selects the aspects and characteristics of treatment. Beutler et al. (2004) added an eighth dimension, attachment style, which is closely related to coping style, based on the findings from a task force on relationships, techniques, and technique factors organized by Division 29 of the American Psychological Association (Castonguay & Beutler, 2006a).

The following treatment guidelines have received empirical support:

- A careful examination of problem severity, functional impairment, and available support systems can inform the clinician as to whether treatment is warranted or not.
- An examination of diagnosis, functional impairment, and problem severity can be used to determine if restrictive or nonrestrictive treatment settings are indicated.
- Information on diagnosis, expectations, and severity can also suggest how treatment should balance psychosocial and medical aspects.
- Data on problem complexity, patient expectations, and subjective distress or severity can indicate the probable value of short- versus long-term intervention.
- An understanding of the complexity of the problem can also be used to delineate whether treatment should be symptom- or conflict-focused.

- An assessment of coping style can suggest the probable value of cognitive, behavioral, or affectively oriented procedures.
- Information on interpersonal resistance propensities can provide guidance as to the degree of therapist directiveness to be used.
- Attachment style may have implications with respect to adapting and tailoring the therapeutic relationship to specific patient characteristics and needs (Norcross, 2002).

In practice, treatment recommendations are more complex than these simple relationships would suggest. Each of the patient predisposing variables interacts with one another. Acknowledging this complexity will ensure that the clinician considers the patient from a comprehensive multifactorial perspective rather than a narrow and simplistic diagnostic one. Beutler and Clarkin (1990) observe that any rigid adherence to decisions made on the basis of any single dimension, including diagnosis, is likely to be ill informed, incomplete, and overly simplistic. Thus, no matter how empirically valid, any proposed relationships among patient predisposing variables and treatment assignment are still far from direct and are to be seen as means of prioritizing interventions in terms of probable success, not rigid decisions to be mindlessly applied.

While we cannot do justice to the complexity of clinical decisions in the brief space allotted to us here, in the following paragraphs we will describe some of the specific patient qualities that guide pretreatment planning. We will also review some of the mediating effects that treatments exert on the relationships among these variables and treatment outcomes. As long as the reader is aware that our consideration of these variables as representing independent classes is an oversimplification performed in the service of clarity, the conclusions and recommendations should be informative for the clinician who attempts to translate assessment results into meaningful answers to meaningful questions. For more detailed information on patient predisposing variables and treatment planning, the interested reader is directed to Beutler et al. (2000) and to Beutler and Harwood (2000).

Diagnostic Variables

The first group of patient predisposing variables that merit evaluation in treatment planning are made up of diagnostically based symptom clusters. Included here are syndromes and specific problems that bear attention. An assessment of these symptoms requires a determination of cognitive level and activity, an evaluation of moods and affects, and a descriptive formulation of problematic, interpersonal, and social behaviors. The assignment of a formal diagnosis implies the existence of a given pattern of signs and symptoms and reflects on treatment assignment from two perspectives.

First, these diagnostic and problem identifiers serve as markers for change. In other words they provide a baseline measurement by which to judge progress in treatment. Second, formal diagnoses serve as shorthand indicators of severity and chronicity of the problem and for interrelated symptom clusters. These diagnoses serve as relatively specific indicators assigning aspects of the treatment context.

At the very least, earning a diagnosis suggests that the condition is one deserving of treatment. For example, a pattern of intellectual deficits accompanying a diagnosis of mental retardation is likely to result in a very different decision about whether treatment will be valuable than a similar pattern of cognitive deficits that coexists with a diagnosis of acute intoxication, dementia secondary to depression (i.e., pseudodementia), or dissociative disorder. Beyond this, diagnoses that suggest the presence of a chronic condition indicate the need for long-term or continuing treatment, whereas transient disturbances suggest that short-term and supportive treatments are indicated. Likewise, the diagnoses of decompensated conditions, such as dementia of the Alzheimer's type, bipolar disorder, and schizophrenia, suggest the need for pharmacotherapy and, in many instances, selecting a controlled environment in which to see the patient.

Frequently, diagnosis provides some guidelines for the selection and application of pharmacological interventions. For example, a diagnosis of major depression may inform the clinician to consider one class of medications while a diagnosis of schizophrenia may lead the clinician to consider another. However, diagnoses tell us little about aspects of the patient's personal characteristics, sociodemographic background, willingness to cooperate in treatment, and other aspects of personality that are so central to selecting among psychotherapeutic goals and procedures (e.g., Barlow & Waddell, 1985; Beutler, 1989). An evaluation that extends diagnostic considerations to the domain of nondiagnostic variables (personal characteristics of the patient and his or her environment) will elicit more complete and necessary information for these latter decisions. Only by extending the evaluation to a consideration of these nondiagnostic areas will one be able to make and implement decisions about the selection of a therapist, enhancing and facilitating patient motivation, and selecting specific psychotherapy strategies and techniques.

To complement the role of diagnosis in treatment planning, the nondiagnostic characteristics of the person as well as the characteristics of the environment must be assessed. Collectively, the variables in these general classes provide the foundation for selectively matching treatment to patient needs.

Nondiagnostic Patient Variables

Patients enter treatment with preconceived notions regarding therapy, possible treatments, and the nature of expected outcomes that either enhance or abate their levels of treatment motivation. The task of assigning treatments differentially involves identifying those differences that correspond with variations in the situational and interpersonal demands and characteristics of treatment settings, therapists, and procedures. Some of these differences represent enduring traits that are identified as characteristic of the person while others are more transient or state-like and are usually characterized as situationally responsive. This distinction, while somewhat arbitrary, is an important one and provides a convenient framework for identifying those variables of each type that may be or appear to be important to treatment planning. In the following paragraphs, we will review some of the most obvious or important patient traits and response states that we believe should be considered when questions of treatment planning in psychological assessment are addressed.

State-Like Qualities

While there are many qualities of problems that vary as a function of specific situations and circumstances, in this section we will describe three that appear to be of major importance to the differential assignment of treatment: patient expectations, subjective distress, and functional impairment.

PATIENT EXPECTATIONS

Patients enter treatment with preconceived and motivational notions regarding therapy, possible treatments, and the nature of expected outcomes. These same patients carry with them "social role expectations" that extend beyond the therapeutic relationship but are nonetheless influential in how they will respond to certain interventions. An assessment and understanding of these expectations allows the practitioner to modify treatment and increase patient–therapist compatibility (Garfield, 1986).

It is important that patient expectations either be met or changed to correspond with treatment format, structure, and duration in order to facilitate and enhance both therapeutic engagement and outcome. Treatment outcome is likely to be unsatisfactory when a patient's expectations do not match his or her treatment experiences. Evidence for this conclusion is to be found among the many studies on therapist–patient matching as well as those on pretreatment preparation. This literature (e.g., Beutler & Mitchell, 1981; Beutler & Bergan, 1991; Lorion & Felner, 1986) suggests that the likelihood of positive outcome increases when therapist attributes and therapeutic processes are consistent with the patient's global beliefs about psychotherapy, or when patient beliefs are brought into line with therapy demand characteristics.

A patient's life history (e.g., social and demographic variables) creates a unique phenomenal life view that shapes his or her beliefs about self and others. In a more limited way, these life events predispose the development of certain attitudes and beliefs about therapeutic processes, therapists, and therapy efficacy. As applied to this specific domain of psychotherapy, these expectations are changeable but apparently correlated with how long one will stay in treatment, one's motivation for change, and the effectiveness of therapy itself. These expectations may be thought of as belonging to three general domains: treatment expectations, social role expectations, and changes in treatment expectations.

Treatment expectations include assumptions about the therapist (e.g., attributes, credibility, and expertness), therapeutic process (e.g., philosophies that govern therapy, beliefs regarding confidentiality, and the issues that should be addressed in therapy), and the nature of outcomes. As already stated, these assumptions are motivational. That is, they initially determine a person's willingness to enter therapy and also provide the inclination toward effective involvement in the therapeutic process.

Social role expectations are concealed in the patient's history of social roles and functions. A broad review of the patient's background, historical experiences, and social relationships is necessary to distill these types of expectations as they color the view of the psychotherapeutic process. It is important that the therapists have a familiarity with the response variations and outlooks likely to be associated with different sexual, age, ethnic, religious, socioeconomic, and educational backgrounds to help in ferreting out social role expectations.

Nuclear family dynamics (structure, overt and covert rules and attitudes) must also be discussed to get an understanding of the patient's development of attitudes toward themselves and others.

Therapeutic involvement (as indicated by expressed motivation, compliance, commitment, and retention in treatment) will usually be enhanced if patients' preferences for therapist sex, age, and ethnicity are met and if they share some level of common cultural experiences. While these similarities may be implicated indirectly in treatment efficacy, they seem quite certainly to be implicated in the process of entering and staying in treatment (Bergin & Garfield, 1994; Lambert, 2004). Because of the importance of congruence between patient's expected and experienced exposure to certain therapist attributes, therapeutic roles, and processes, when patients' expectations and preferences are disparate with treatment, the therapist has several choices in applying treatment. She may choose to modify treatment, refer the patient to someone else, shape or change patient expectations to be more consistent with what happens in therapy, or hope that the patient will come to adopt more compatible roles and expectations with time and experience.

As this would suggest, the relationship between therapist and patient backgrounds, expectations, and beliefs is important in determining the nature of the therapeutic relationship. Similarity of ethnic and social backgrounds increases the likelihood that the level of necessary correspondence exists between the views of patients and therapists about therapy and therapeutic process. Thus, whenever possible, it is advantageous to consider patient and therapist compatibility during treatment planning and to assign patients to therapists accordingly. At the same time, patients apparently look to therapists for different perspectives on aspects of interpersonal relationships, suggesting that some disparity of attitudes toward making and maintaining intimacy and friendships may also bear on therapist compatibility. When patient and therapist backgrounds and interpersonal attitudes "fit" or correspond, fewer treatment modifications may be necessary, thereby increasing the possibility of positive therapeutic outcome (Beutler, Crago, & Arizmendi, 1986).

It should be remembered that patient expectations are state-like qualities. That is, they are dynamic and constantly changing with the confirming and disconfirming effect of each new experience. This requires the therapist to constantly assess the patient's expectations and alter interventions accordingly. While initially setting treatment formats and anticipated length to fit patient expectations is important for retaining patients in treatment, ongoing adaptation of the treatment to fit changing preferences and modified expectations will be likely to enhance treatment outcome. Therefore, therapists are well advised to give careful and close attention to the expressed wishes and desires of those whom they serve (Beutler & Clarkin, 1990).

Subjective Distress and Arousal

A long history of research on cognitive efficiency and coping suggests that arousal and distress can both motivate change and impair effective functioning, depending upon their level. In some patients, subjective distress is weakly associated with external measures of impairment (Strupp, Horowitz, & Lambert, 1997); therefore, one must quantify both subjective and functional (objective) dimensions of distress. Additionally, subjective distress is mercurial in nature, reflecting a variety of symptom states that are transitory and changeable. While moderate distress appears to activate, orient one's response, and motivate engagement in behaviors that may alleviate distress, either very low or very high levels may impair the patient's ability or willingness to attend, introduce either rigidity or inconsistency to problem-solving efforts, and result in ineffective engagement.

Levels of distress reflect the patient's degree of success in warding off anxiety. In this sense, patient distress may be taken as indicators of one's ability to cope (Beutler & Clarkin, 1990), as distinct from their "coping style." That is, a patient's distress level indicates how well coping methods work to keep the patient protected from anxiety. At extreme levels, distress may impair functioning; at low levels it may retard progress; however, at moderate levels stress or anxiety may provide focus and motivation to support and initiate change. Thus, the STS principles that corresponds to Subjective Distress are: (a) the likelihood of positive therapeutic change is greatest when the patient is experiencing moderate levels of distress, and (b) positive therapeutic change is greatest when a patient is stimulated to manageable levels of emotional arousal in a safe and trusting environment until their problematic responses diminish or extinguish.

A patient's expectations and anxiety level interact to produce a person's unique level of therapeutic motivation and compliance with treatment demands. In turn, the patient's motivation and compliance level sets limitations on the type and degree of psychotherapeutic intervention accepted. Acceptance may be enhanced by the establishment of clear expectations, the encouragement of overtly explicit commitments to comply, and the provision of reasonable incentives.

It is also important to consider the patient's mood, intellectual level, orientation within the environment, cognitive efficiency, cognitive control of imaginal processes, affect and affective control, and intensity of experienced conflict during the assessment of subjective distress and an associated patient dimension, problem severity. Evaluation of these dimensions informs decisions regarding the format and duration of treatment, and directs the clinician in selecting the immediate goals of treatment and the intervention strategies to be used. The Beck Depression Inventory-II (BDI-II; Beck, Steer, & Brown 1996), the Symptom Checklist Revised (SCL-90-R; Derogatis, 1994), and the State-Trait Anxiety Inventory (STAI; Spielberger, Gorsuch, Lushene, Vagg, & Jacobs, 1983) represent the measures employed most often to assess levels of subjective distress. The state portion of the STAI is well suited to assessing presession levels of distress throughout the therapy process. With respect to research-informed treatment guidelines, the higher the distress, the more protection and support are required, both in selecting the setting and the frequency of treatment and in determining the methods of intervention to be used. Therapists should remain vigilant to distress levels and endeavor to maintain moderate levels of arousal; manageable levels of arousal will provide both adequate motivation and allow effective participation in the therapeutic process.

Empirical support for Subjective Distress comes from at least eleven investigations that support the use of this patient dimension in both pretreatment planning and the selection of specific interventions (Beutler et al., 2000). The combined sample size, comprised of both in-patients and out-patients, totaled to more than 1,250. A variety of diagnoses were represented in these eleven studies and several psychosocial and pharmacological treatments were delivered.

FUNCTIONAL IMPAIRMENT

Functional impairment is often related to one's level of subjective distress, especially when social support, environmental circumstances, and personal resources are considered. The level of dysfunction or severity of a problem has long been thought to be an indicator of treatment intensity. Managed care programs typically assign varying levels of care (e.g., number of treatment sessions, restrictiveness of settings, and length of care) based on the degree of impairment observed to be present. Functional impairment is typically gauged through an assessment of the degree to which one can perform the basic functions of self-care, work activities, social relationships, and maintenance of intimate relationships (e.g., Sperry, Brill, Howard, & Grissom, 1996).

The clinical rating scale most often employed to quantify a patient's level of functional impairment is the Global Assessment of Functioning scale from the *Diagnostic and statistical manual of mental disorders, 4th ed., Text revision* (GAF, DSM-IV-TR)—this rating is based on the integration of information gathered from a comprehensive clinical interview and any appropriate collaterals. Specific problem-focused instruments such as the Anxiety Disorders Interview Schedule (ADIS; DiNardo, O'Brien, Barlow, Waddell, & Blanchard, 1983) and the Hamilton Rating Scale for Depression (HRSD; Hamilton, 1967) may also be employed when warranted to quantify functional impairment.

A consideration of a patient's level of FI results in a principle that impacts on the magnitude of patient change. Additionally, FI is a prognostic indicator—the greater the level of functional impairment, the poorer the prognosis; this is especially true when FI is severe, social support is problematic, and patient distress level is mild. The STS principle that pertains to FI is "[b]enefit corresponds with treatment intensity among high functionally impaired patients" (Beutler & Harwood, 2000, p. 149). In other words, as a patient's functional impairment increases, so should the number of treatment sessions that the patient receives on a weekly basis. Further, the length of treatment sessions may be increased, or therapy may involve a form of multi-person treatment (e.g., any combination of individual, group, family, couple, or pharmacological treatments). In addition to an indicator of prognosis, the STS principle that corresponds to FI may be characterized as a Level of Care Principle.

FI has been identified by the division 29 Task Force as a Participant Factor (Castonguay & Beutler, 2006a, Beutler, Blatt, Alamohamed, Levy, & Angtuaco, 2006); however, it has also been identified by the dysphoria work group of the Task Force on Empirically Based Principles of Therapeutic Change (Castonguay & Beutler, 2006b). Empirical support for the assessment of functional impairment and application of this information in treatment planning can be found in more than 45 investigations (Beutler et al., 2000). The combined sample size from these studies sums to more than 7,700 participants from both in-patient and out-patient settings. Almost all diagnostic categories were represented in the foregoing studies and myriad types of psychosocial treatments, including a variety of modes and formats, were administered.

READINESS FOR CHANGE

Personal readiness and motivation to change are important considerations in any treatment plan. Prochaska and colleagues (Prochaska & DiClemente, 1984; Prochaska, DiClemente, & Norcross, 1992; Prochaska & Norcross, 2002) have suggested that progress in treatment may be enhanced if a patient's readiness for change is commensurate with the intervention method employed. Patient readiness for change exists along a continuum with five stages: precontemplation, contemplation, preparation, action, and maintenance. The Stages of Change Questionnaire (McConnaughy, DiClemente, & Velicer, 1983) provide specific information with respect to the patient's location along this continuum.

Two hypotheses have been proposed by Prochaska and his colleagues. First, more advanced stages of readiness for change are indicators of greater likelihood for improvement. Second, specific psychotherapeutic interventions are associated with each stage of change/readiness—matching intervention/procedure with stage will maximize the effectiveness of these procedures.

Trait-Like Qualities

"Personality is a description of recurrent but dynamic patterns that are enacted in the face of new and often threatening experience rather than as a collection of static qualities" (Beutler & Clarkin, 1990, p. 66). The things we define as personality are usually restricted to those that are trait-like. That is, they endure across situations and are perceived as existing within the person rather than as being primarily determined by the situation. Beutler (1990), Beutler et al. (2000), and Beutler and Clarkin (1990) have reviewed the many such dimensions that have been considered and have extracted those that seem to be most closely related to the selection of psychotherapeutic strategies and to the efficacy of specific psychotherapeutic interventions.

Among the many trait-like characteristics of patients that have been proposed to determine the efficacy of different interventions, problem complexity, interpersonal resistance or reactance, and coping ability are the most frequently studied. As with most of the variables and dimensions in this chapter, these three patient traits are interactive and reciprocal; however, convenience and clarity require that we treat them as separate aspects of response.

PROBLEM COMPLEXITY/CHRONICITY (PCC)

One of the ways that patient problems are most distinctive in their relationship to the selection of psychotherapeutic goals is in their level of complexity and chronicity. Some problems are primarily manifest in a single symptom cluster or in a well-defined set of evoking circumstances while other problems cross-environments, are made up of varied and often unrelated symptoms, and appear to represent complex recurrences or themes that characterize the person's life. Often the only similarity one can find in the events that evoke these recurrent themes is very abstract, suggesting that a symbolic rather than an objective similarity among situations provides the evocation for the onset of problems.

Another way of thinking about problem complexity is to view some problems as being state-like and others as trait-like in their manifestation. This distinction can be clarified by comparing the nature of complex problems to the concept of subjective distress discussed earlier. Subjective distress is a state-like quality and serves as an index of degree of acute impairment. In contrast, complex problems are more stable and less situation-specific than level of arousal or distress. Indeed, complex problems are manifest by the traditional "neurotiform" behaviors characterized by symbolic (unconscious or preconscious) repetitive and unpleasant reenactments of previously cathected conflictual themes.

In an analysis of variables that might serve to indicate the use of treatments that vary in level of intensity, Beutler et al. (2000) determined that both characteristics of the problem itself and of the patient's relationship to significant others exerted similar influence on types and levels of treatment. PCC, indexed by such things as the number of prior episodes of clinical problems, the durable nature of major disorders over time, the presence of comorbid conditions, the presence of personality disorders, the level of overall social support, and the degree of disruption to family interactions, is indicative of a patient who would best benefit from an intensive, long-term treatment regimen that included multi-person therapy and considered the use of psychoactive medication (Beutler et al., 2004). In other words, the assignment of treatment setting, duration, frequency, mode, and format may be dictated, or partially guided, by an accurate assessment of patient PCC.

Patients whose problems are complex (i.e., widespread, recurrent, and chronic), especially in the absence of a significant other who provided support and in the absence of family contacts, all bode poorly for good outcomes. In turn, these factors suggest

that the patient would be best served if the treatment included some form of family or group psychotherapy in which one could develop social support systems. These same factors were found to portend the likelihood that psychoactive medication would be beneficial and contraindicated the use of short-term treatment efforts.

On the other hand, noncomplex problems are habitual, unidimensional, and transient in nature. These problems probably result from inadequate or faulty learning histories and are maintained by subjectively felt situational reward. Though more state- than trait-like, introducing the concept here emphasizes the importance of this distinction in selecting the long-term goals and objectives of treatment.

Comprehending how the symptoms developed and are maintained will provide clues to the nature and degree of problem complexity. A careful evaluation of patient predisposing variables will indicate if relatively enduring, repetitive, and symbolic manifestations of characterological struggles are at work or if transient, situation-specific, and unidimensional habitual patterns of behavior are present. This determination will provide a focus for symptomatic, conflictual, or combined therapeutic interventions.

Problem complexity, with respect to psychiatric comorbidity, may be determined most reliably through structured or semistructured interview based on the most current version of the DSM (American Psychiatric Association). Using broader definitions of problem complexity, omnibus measures such as the Minnesota Multiphasic Personality Inventory-2 (MMPI-2; Butcher, 1990) are useful instruments for gauging chronicity and for predicting likely treatment response/outcome and assigning certain specific treatment strategies (e.g., insight vs. symptom focus, treatment intensity, amount of focus on social support; Beutler et al., 2004).

One limitation of omnibus measures in assessing problem complexity is that they are not well suited for identifying the significance of pervasive themes or dynamic conflicts, an important component of complexity. The core conflictual relationship theme (CCRT; Crits-Christoph & Demorest, 1991; Crits-Christoph, Demorest, & Connelly, 1990) is a promising method for highlighting the thematic/dynamic conflicts that patients typically reenact at some point in treatment and within the rich medium of the therapeutic relationship. Additionally, the STS Clinician Rating Form has been developed specifically to provide an efficient clinician-derived assessment of PCC.

Designating some problems as noncomplex in nature and others as dynamic efforts to resolve an unconscious struggle does not mean that treating one is any less difficult than treating the other; however, it does suggest that different paths to change may be necessary for these two types of problem presentation. Generally, complex problems indicate that outcomes should partially be judged by the resolution of thematic patterns rather than simply by symptom change. In contrast, the success of treating noncomplex problems can legitimately be assessed on the basis of symptom rather than lifestyle measures and criteria. Thus, intensive, long-term treatments are often indicated for complex problems (Freebury, 1984; Thorpe, 1987), while symptom-focused and short-term therapies are advocated for noncomplex problems. Additionally, highly complex problems should favor psychosocial treatments over pharmacological treatments and psychotherapy should be insight-focused instead of symptom-focused (Beutler et al., 2000, 2004).

To the degree that a patient presents with problems that have both complex and secondary reactive qualities, as occurs frequently, the treatment indicated may combine multiple goals. Beutler and Clarkin (1990) point out that since symptom-focused treatments are more rapid, cost-efficient, and easy to apply, a convenient rule of thumb is to treat all problems as situational or noncomplex initially and until it becomes obvious that the problem supersedes situations and represents a recurrent interpersonal theme-of-life pattern.

This patient dimension is often related to functional impairment; however, some patients are able to function adequately, in various aspects of their lives, even when dealing with complex/chronic problems (Beutler, Brookman, Harwood, Alimohamed, & Malik, 2002). For example, some alcoholics are functional and their disorder may actually operate as a coping mechanism for a period of time. The STS principle that corresponds to PCC indicates that highly complex problems respond best to broad-band treatment. Such an approach would employ various combinations of multidisciplinary/multiperson treatment tailored to the patient and their presenting problem. Within the domain of psychotherapy, systemic and dynamic treatments should perform better than symptom-focused treatments. Among medical treatments, electroconvulsive therapy would be generally favored over pharmacotherapy (Beutler et al., 2000; Gaw & Beutler, 1995; Harwood & Beutler, 2008).

In sum, complexity and chronicity may be assessed clinically and identified by patterns of recurrence, persistence of problems, co-morbidity, and broadly generalized disturbances in interpersonal relationships (Beutler & Harwood, 2000). As a general rule, prognosis is attenuated by problem complexity/chronicity and by the absence of patient distress (Beutler et al., 2000). Facilitating social support increases the likelihood of positive change among patients with complex/chronic problems (Harwood & Williams, 2003).

The treatment matching dimension of problem complexity and chronicity has received empirical support in at least 23 investigations (Beutler et al., 2000). The aggregated participant pool for these 23 investigations totaled nearly 2,000 and was comprised of both in-patient and out-patient populations. Diagnoses varied across studies as did treatment modalities and treatment formats. Relatedly, a variety of psychosocial treatments and pharmacological treatments were examined by investigators.

INTERPERSONAL RESISTANCE

Interpersonal resistance may be defined as one's sensitivity and resistance to the influence of others. As with problem complexity, this concept has both state- and trait-like features. While a person's tendency to resist influence may largely depend upon the environmental circumstance and the relationship that he or she has with the one who is exerting the influence, most researchers (Brehm, 1976; Dowd & Pace, 1989; Shoham-Salomon, 1991) also emphasize that tolerance for external influence varies from person to person in a consistent and stable fashion. It is this state-like resistance that has the most implications for treatment planning (Beutler et al., 2004).

Reactance is an extreme form of resistance in which the respondent (patient) reacts to suggestion or guidance by doing the opposite of what is suggested. This concept is extracted from the social psychology literature that has striking applications and parallels to clinical literature. In its clearest form, reactance represents not just a defense against, but an oppositional reaction to, authority. In psychotherapy, it is parallel in meaning to the interpersonal (though not the intrapsychic) aspects of the concept of resistance (e.g., Barlow & Waddell, 1985). Essentially, reactance and therapeutic resistance as used here are measured by the degree to which one is disposed, by nature of personal traits, to engage in activities that resist the control of others, including a potential therapist.

Having a low tolerance for being controlled by others is a special problem for patients in psychotherapy since psychotherapy is inherently an experience that threatens one's sense of self control. Mental health treatment often operates paradoxically by creating temporary dependence on the therapist in the service of encouraging ultimate disengagement and lasting independence.

Interpersonal resistance may prevent one from gratifying needs for nurturance, support, attachment, and social or interpersonal regard. Thus the balance between the need for attachment and the need for independence and autonomy may be disrupted in those who are highly reactant. Hence, whatever homeostasis is maintained through the adoption of defenses against the anxiety of either attachment or separation needs is likely to be unstable and excessive in these people. In the psychotherapy relationship itself, this instability may be manifest by withdrawal from treatment, failure to comply with treatment expectations, and resistance to improvement.

One's level of state resistance is best assessed via observing a patient's moment-by-moment response to the demand characteristics of the therapy environment. Once observed, the therapist is well advised to counterbalance the patient's level of resistance to the use of procedures that deemphasize the therapist's power and efforts to change the patient. The use of nondirective, supportive, self-management, and paradoxical interventions are examples of procedures that may serve this function. The appropriate adjustments in therapeutic strategy and specific interventions can be made by attending both to the trait-like and in-session or state-like aspects of patient reactance/resistance.

Trait resistance is best assessed with the Therapeutic Reactance Scale (TRS; Dowd, Milne, & Wise, 1991) or specific subscales or combinations of subscales from various personality tests such as the MMPI-2 (e.g., TRT (Treatment Readiness), AUT (Problems with Authority), Taylor Manifest Anxiety Scale, and Edwards Social Desirability Scale). Patients who are low in resistance tendencies respond well to either directive or nondirective interventions; however, directive interventions generally appear to produce the best response among low-resistance patients (Beutler et al., 2003). As a general rule, patients high in trait resistance respond poorly to highly therapist controlled and directive therapies—these patients should be treated with nondirective client-driven forms of therapy (e.g., client centered).

The careful reader will have noticed the interactive role of defensive behavior and interpersonal resistance. The patient's configuration of interpersonal, ritualized defensive styles of response provides the targets of conflict-oriented treatment strategies—the thematic focus.

Resistance was recently identified by the Division 29 Task Force as a participant factor (Castonguay & Beutler, 2006b). The STS principles specific to resistance are "[t]herapeutic change is most likely when the therapeutic procedures do not evoke patient resistance" and "[t]herapeutic change is greatest when the directiveness of the intervention is either inversely correspondent with the patient's current level of resistance or authoritatively prescribes a continuation of the symptomatic behavior" (Beutler & Harwood, 2000, pp. 116–117). As the foregoing indicates, resistance has implications for both the likelihood of change and the magnitude of change (Beutler et al., 2003).

Empirical support for the assessment of reactance and the application of reactance level information in treatment planning comes from more than 30 investigations (Beutler et al., 2000). The aggregated participant pool from the aforementioned studies totals to more than 8,000 inpatients and outpatients. The psychosocial treatment formats employed included individual, family, group, and parent training with a variety of psychotherapies and pharmacological agents employed among myriad diagnostic categories.

COPING STYLES

Each person has his or her unique configuration of defenses that can be partially described by a listing of specific defense mechanisms. These defense mechanisms have traditionally been considered to lie outside of conscious awareness and to endure across situations. In addition, however, it is also apparent that people select and adopt certain behaviors in a conscious and thoughtful effort to adapt to stress and to avoid discomfort. Coping styles are the collection of conscious and unconscious methods one uses both to manage anxiety or threat and to compensate for problems in everyday functioning.

Aside from threats from the environment, these constellations of behavior reflect dominant and relatively consistent behaviors which collectively constitute efforts to avoid either recognizing or confronting the contradictions in one's internal experience— opposing wishes, injunctions, contradictory values, unwanted impulses, and discordant beliefs—or even disconfirming information about valued beliefs and self-views (Beutler & Clarkin, 1990).

While much theory and research has been devoted to describing and distinguishing among various coping styles, most of this literature agrees that at least a good share of the variation among people in this characteristic can be defined as existing along a continuum ranging from internalizing (characterized by self-constraint and emotional withdrawal) to externalizing (characterized by extraversion and impulsivity). Internalizing coping styles consist of the specific defense mechanisms of self-criticism, sensitization, and compartmentalization, while those associated with externalization include acting out, projection, and direct avoidance of threat (Beutler et al., 2000; Beutler & Harwood, 2000; Miller & Eisenberg, 1988).

We have found that a variety of MMPI-2 Clinical Scales, configured in a ratio format, is the best way to assess a patient's dominant style of coping. An internalization ratio (IR), an empirically supported index of coping style, is rendered based on the following MMPI-2 scales:

$$IR = Hy + Pd + Pa + Ma/Hs + D + Pt + Si$$

An IR greater than 1.0 is considered high and characteristic of an externalizing coping style; the patient is likely to project his or her own feelings and motives onto others and tend to be more undercontrolled and impulsive than the average patient. On the other hand, a ratio score that is less than 1.0 indicates that the patient is less impulsive, more self-critical, and more introspective than the average patient—his or her dominant style of coping is characterized as internalizing.

Patients with different styles of coping with intrapsychic or interpersonal threats will often require different treatments. An accumulating body of research evidence has suggested that coping styles have particular implications for the effectiveness of strategies that are designed to change cognitions and behaviors versus those designed to foster insight and awareness.

The STS principle that corresponds to coping style states that patients who possess introverted/internalizing/restricted coping styles will receive the greatest benefit from treatment if the therapist employs interventions designed to directly affect insight and awareness (Beutler et al., 2000). Conversely, patients with extroverted, impulsive, externalizing coping styles will receive the greatest benefit from treatment if the clinician employs therapeutic procedures that are specifically designed to directly foster symptom-change. Recently, coping style was identified as a participant factor by the Division 29 Task Force and the foregoing STS principle is considered an empirically based

principle due to "a preponderance of the available evidence" (Castonguay & Beutler, 2006a, p. 634) as evaluated by the Division 12 or Division 29 Task Force. As the careful reader will have gathered, coping style is a patient factor that, if addressed properly in treatment, has the potential to increase the magnitude of positive change (Beutler et al., 2000, 2003). The guiding principle specific to coping style states, "Therapeutic change is greatest when the relative balance of interventions either favors the use of skill building and symptom removal procedures among patients who externalize or favors the use of insight and relationship-focused procedures among patients who internalize" (Beutler et al., 2000, p. 204).

Empirical support for the identification of a patient's dominant coping style and the application of this information in treatment selection comes from at least 30 investigations involving both in-patient and out-patient populations (Beutler et al., 2000). Aggregating the samples from the foregoing investigations totals to more than 5,600 participants suffering from a wide variety of disorders. Depression was a primary diagnostic category represented; however, co-morbidity was a prominent feature in many studies with substance abuse, anxiety disorders, personality disorders, and severe psychopathology well represented among the samples. Various treatment formats were employed including individual, group, and both married and cohabiting couples.

ATTACHMENT STYLE

The concept of an interpersonal attachment style is similar to the concept of coping style and attachment style appears to be associated with aspects of the therapeutic alliance. Some evidence suggests that tailoring or adapting the therapeutic relationship to patient needs and characteristics, such as attachment style and diagnosis, produces benefit in treatment outcome (Norcross, 2002).

Adult attachment may be assessed via the Adult Attachment Interview (AAI; George, Kaplan, & Main, 1985), a semistructured interview designed to explore the patient's current perception of childhood experiences. Other instruments and methods for assessing attachment style have been developed and investigated (see Brennan, Clark, & Shaver, 1998; Mallinckrodt, Gantt, & Coble, 1995); however, convergent validity among all measures of adult attachment has not exceeded moderate levels, suggesting that each of these measures may be quantifying differing aspects of attachment (Beutler et al., 2004).

ENVIRONMENTAL VARIABLES

The third major category of patient predisposing variables contains those that exist independently of the patient and that provide either sources of stress or sources of support. These are environmental variables and represent both the stressors and resources in the patient's present environment (e.g., personal support systems, work/school environments, family patterns, the setting or relationship in which dominant conflicts occur, and the social forces that apply pressure and support). These environmental qualities are important considerations that have etiologic and/or mediating/exacerbating significance for the development of one's symptoms and problems (e.g., Flaherty & Richman, 1986; Cohen & Sokolovsky, 1978; Horowitz et al., 1988).

Identification and evaluation of environmental characteristics of the patient's environment bears most directly on the selection of treatment context (mode/format, duration/frequency, and setting). Consideration of the patient's salient environment(s) can also help generate hypotheses about how circumstances and conditions may interact with other treatment-relevant variables to influence the treatment plan. That is, treatment settings and relationships constitute environments that exist with various degrees of similarity to the patient's usual environment. Assessment of the immediate family (and family history) can help provide insight into etiology and maintaining pathology as well as guidelines for what to avoid and what to recommend as a treatment setting to provide a corrective experience for the patient. A thorough history of common environments and social systems (sociodemographics) may also be relevant to predicting the likely compatibility of patient and therapist.

The relationship between diagnosable symptoms and types of family contextual stressors needs careful clinical assessment in the process of planning treatments. For example, some family members may manifest or directly contribute to a diagnosable condition in other family members while others may discourage pathological or maladaptive responses. An assessment of a patient's family and social support systems will indicate how and if the symptomatic and nonsymptomatic family members should be included as an integral part of the treatment plan. Moreover, expanding and enhancing sources of social support is critical in planning for long-term maintenance of gains.

Even diagnostically similar patients require distinctly different treatments, dependent in part upon the nature of the family support system and the multicausality of psychological difficulties (e.g., Schulberg & McClelland, 1987). Beutler and Clarkin (1990) have emphasized this point in suggesting that "a functional analysis of similar symptoms will often reveal quite different causal patterns and every patient's unique strengths and family environment will serve as enabling or restraining conditions upon which to predict differential treatment responses" (p. 38).

Family characteristics (relationship dimensions, personal growth dimensions, and system maintenance dimensions) may be assessed with the Family Environment Scale (FES; Moos & Moos, 1986). Work environment (social climate of work unit with a focus upon relationships between employees and supervisors and among employees, with respect to personal growth and basic organizational structure and functioning) may be assessed with the Work Environment Scale (WES; Moos & Insel, 1974). Characteristics of a patient's social support network may be assessed via the Social Support Questionnaire (SSQ; Sarason, Levine, Basham, & Sarason, 1983).

One's perceived level of social support is a positive prognostic indicator in the STS model (Beutler et al., 2000, 2003; Beutler & Harwood, 2000). Treatment benefit is correspondent with social support suggesting that improvement in the quality of social support may also be a specific treatment factor (Castonguay & Beutler, 2006a). Indeed, social support has been identified as a patient prognostic indicator by the dysphoria work group of the Task Force on Empirically Based Principles of Therapeutic Change (Castonguay & Beutler, 2006c).

The STS principles associated with social support are "[a] certain level of experienced or felt support may be necessary to activate the power of interpersonal and relationship therapies" (Beutler et al., 2000, p. 190), social support may be enhanced through multi-person treatment, and enhancing one's system of social support may result in a greater magnitude and likelihood of positive change. Social support levels are typically assessed through clinical interview or via self-report measures such as the Sarason Social Support Questionnaire (Sarason, Levine, Basham, & Sarason, 1983).

The patient-treatment matching dimension of social support has received empirically-based endorsement in at least 37 investigations involving a combined sample comprised of more than 7,700 in-patients and out-patients (Beutler et al., 2000). A variety of diagnoses, treatment formats, treatment modalities, and psychosocial treatments were represented in the 37 investigations involving social support and its importance to psychosocial and pharmacological treatment.

Treatment context variables, relationship variables, and therapeutic interventions have been mentioned throughout this chapter. However, the roles of the several patient predisposing variables that we advocate assessing in order to answer treatment questions in psychological assessment can be further illustrated by brief but separate discussion of these domains of treatment decision making, and may further clarify the relevance of patient assessment in treatment planning.

Treatment Context
Treatment Setting

Treatment settings range from inpatient to outpatient and differ in the degree to which the situation is monitored or unstructured. Most patients seeking psychological intervention present problems that are amenable to treatment in relatively unrestrictive settings, that is, in the psychologist's office or in the natural environment in which the problems occur; however, patients exhibiting acute and serious symptoms, for example, suicidal behavior or psychotic symptoms, require restrictive settings such as hospitals. Information obtained from the patient predisposing dimension, such as PCC, FI, SS, and SD, determines the optimal setting (providing the most appropriate treatment with the least restriction).

The presence of a life-threatening condition, as represented both in the identification of the diagnosis and the availability of external supports, is an indicator for restrictive and structured treatment settings. When supports are available in the environment and when the condition is not life threatening, decompensating, and endangering, less restrictive treatment options may be advantageously made available.

For example, Frances, Clarkin, and Perry (1984) observe that acute suicidal intent/self-destructive behaviors or any complex, chronic condition that results in an inability to effectively manage independent living (e.g., schizophrenia, Alzheimer's disease, other forms of dementia, psychosis, severe major depression) would constitute some indicators that may necessitate placement in restrictive settings. These authors propose that nonrestrictive settings are indicated for individuals that do not pose a threat to self or others and who maintain an acceptable level of general functioning. Most anxiety states, nonpsychotic depression, simple phobias, dysfunctional family problems, and personality disorders are examples of indicators for nonrestrictive treatment settings.

Treatment Mode/Format

Treatment modes may be psychosocial (e.g., individual, group, marital and family therapy formats) and/or medical/somatic (e.g., formats such as pharmacotherapy, surgical procedures, or electroconvulsive therapy). Some patients may require a single treatment format while others may respond best to various format combinations. The nature and complexity of the presenting problem are the major determinants in the selection of treatment mode and format.

Psychosocial treatment formats are indicated for problems requiring behavioral, psychodynamic, and/or person-centered treatment strategies. Family/marital and group treatment formats fall under this rubric as well. Individual treatment formats are usually called for to alleviate complex (neurotiform) and noncomplex problems. Phobic avoidance, anxiety/panic disorders, depression, and personality disorders are examples of problems that may respond well to various individual treatment formats. Group therapy may be indicated for patients experiencing interpersonal conflicts. Support groups are specifically indicated for clients who can benefit from contact with other persons with similar difficulties. Family/marital therapy is appropriate when the dyad or family unit is dysfunctional due to pathogenic interpersonal interactions. Family/marital therapy may be necessary when the dysfunction perpetuates undesirable symptoms or behaviors, for example, when problematic alcohol consumption is the result of internalized negative affect.

On the other hand, psychosocial treatments are usually contraindicated, at least as primary treatments, for those suffering from various neurological disorders, bipolar I disorder, schizophrenia, or other forms of severe psychoses; however, psychosocial treatment formats may be quite helpful in maximizing treatment compliance and reducing patient relapse, especially if family members or significant others who are responsible for the care of these severely impaired persons are a focus of the psychosocial treatment. Group therapy would be contraindicated when the patient does not possess adequate ego strength to withstand powerful group dynamics. Of course, family/marital therapy is usually contraindicated whenever the presenting problem is not the result of, or maintained by, the interactions between members in the dyad or unit.

Medical/somatic treatment formats are indicated for conditions requiring psychotropic medication, electroconvulsive shock therapy (ECT), and invasive procedures (i.e., injections, surgeries). An ECT format is often advocated for elderly patients with severe depression and delusions (Murphy & Macdonald, 1992). Psychotherapeutic drug formats may be indicated for various diagnoses such as certain depressions, psychoses, anxiety disorders, and mania. Formats requiring invasive procedures are indicated less often; however, high surgical success rates with certain aberrant neuroanatomical anomalies (e.g., severe forms of epilepsy) may warrant such a format.

Medical treatment formats are contraindicated for problems where the potential side effects or risks involved in drug therapy, ECT, or surgical procedures outweigh the potential benefits to the patient. For example, pharmacokinetic and pharmacodynamic unpredictability warrants careful consideration in matters where psychotropics are in question (e.g., many antidepressants induce postural hypotension, a potentially disastrous side effect in the elderly). The severity of the presenting problem(s), an awareness of various alternative medical and/or psychosocial treatments, and an evaluation of the indications/contraindications involved, informs the course of action regarding medical/somatic interventions from a patient cost–benefit perspective.

In certain cases, combined psychosocial and medical treatments are particularly effective. For example, a diagnosis of severe major depression may require pharmacotherapy or ECT to alleviate immediate symptoms (Murphy & Macdonald, 1992), and cognitive-behavioral interventions to produce greater improvement and reduce the probability of recurring depressive episodes (Hollon & Beck, 1979).

Treatment Intensity

The selection of treatment duration and frequency (i.e., the components of treatment intensity) is guided by the assessment of problem severity/chronicity, problem complexity, and patient resources (Beutler & Clarkin, 1990; Beutler et al., 2000, 2003; Beutler & Harwood, 2000; Frances et al., 1984). While there are no hard and fast rules regarding how patients will respond to various treatment intensities, research and accepted theory have provided some broad guidelines in the selection of treatment intensity.

As indicated previously, complex problems generally require long-term intensive treatments.

Indicators for long-term intensive therapies include chronic conditions such as bipolar disorder and schizophrenia (Beutler & Clarkin, 1990), recurring conditions (e.g., depression), or disorders of the self, for example, narcissistic personality disorders (Kohut & Wolf, 1978). A willingness on the part of the patient to remain in therapy (Beutler & Clarkin, 1990) and adequate income to shoulder the cost are necessary conditions for long-term intensive treatments.

Short-term symptom-focused treatments are usually indicated for habitual patterns or noncomplex problems. Additional indicators for short-term treatments include minority status, low socioeconomic status (SES)/formal education level (Baekeland & Lundwall, 1975; Garfield, 1986), and the presence of somatic and externalized symptoms (Beutler et al., 2003; Dubrin & Zastowny, 1988).

Relationship Variables

Relationship variables (demographic and interpersonal) either enhance or hinder the establishment and maintenance of the therapeutic alliance. Patient and therapist compatibility (among attributes and expectations) must be assessed and treatment should be modified accordingly. It is the responsibility of the clinician to identify potential problems, stemming from background or expectation incompatibility, and take the appropriate palliative steps. Attention to relationship variables will reduce interferences caused by incompatibilities, help the therapist overcome patient resistances, and enlist the client as an active participant in therapy.

The therapeutic relationship may be enhanced in myriad ways. Patient–therapist matching is one relationship-enhancing endeavor that requires the consideration of demographic similarity and interpersonal response patterns (i.e., interpersonal striving, personal beliefs, and attributions).

Important demographic characteristics include gender (Jones, Krupnick, & Kerig, 1987), age (Luborsky, Crits-Christoph, Alexander, Margolis, & Cohen, 1983), ethnicity (Jones, 1978), and socioeconomic background (Carkhuff & Pierce, 1967). These studies indicate that patient–therapist demographic similarity enhances perceptions and feelings regarding therapists and increases the likelihood that the therapeutic relationship and outcome will be perceived favorably.

Interpersonal response patterns may be conceptualized as enduring dispositions to action (Beutler & Clarkin, 1990). Observable behaviors, attitudes, beliefs, needs/striving, and habits make up one's repertoire of interpersonal response patterns. The response patterns of both therapist and patient interact to influence the therapeutic process. Dissimilarity among any aspect of patient–therapist response patterns are potential sources of conflict that may create barriers in the therapeutic process (Luborsky, 1984).

Practitioners should be aware of the patients with whom they work well and the patients they should refer. Dissimilarity within any single demographic or interpersonal response characteristic does not preclude successful therapeutic outcome; however, dissimilarities (especially among several characteristics) may prove problematic. The therapist should be aware of any potential conflicts and adjust themselves accordingly. When several dissimilarities between therapist and patient exist, it may be necessary to refer the patient elsewhere.

Role induction procedures can enhance the therapeutic relationship while enlisting the patient as an active participant in the therapeutic process. Role induction prepares the client for treatment; that is, therapists educate clients in terms of therapeutic roles and outcomes before actual treatment per se. Patients may be educated with direct written or verbal information, pretherapy modeling (Truax & Carkhuff, 1967; Truax & Wargo, 1969) and therapeutic contracting (Beck, Rush, Shaw, & Emery, 1979).

Direct written or verbal information about the nature of therapy and the expected roles of patients can facilitate symptomatic change, strengthen the therapeutic alliance, and influence the establishment of positive feelings about treatment (Turkat, 1979; Mayerson, 1984; Zwick & Attkisson, 1985). Of course, written and/or verbal fluency is a must for these procedures to be effective.

Pre-therapy information can be used to provide a model to help patients develop skills that facilitate a positive treatment response. Videotapes (Truax & Carkhuff, 1967; Truax & Wargo, 1969) and films (Mayerson, 1984; Wilson, 1985) have been used to model appropriate treatment behaviors and representative sessions with positive results. That is, dropout rates decreased and therapeutic involvement and outcome was enhanced. Therapeutic contracting is a role induction method involving agreements between the client and therapist regarding treatment. The content contained in therapeutic contracts varies. However, some important ingredients have been identified (Beutler & Clarkin, 1990); that is, contracts should contain (1) explicit

time limits for treatment (or contract renewals and progress evaluations), (2) treatment goals, (3) therapist and patient roles, and (4) consequences of failing to comply with the terms of the contract.

Strategies and Techniques

The selection of appropriate psychotherapeutic strategies and techniques should take place after evaluating patient predisposing variables, considering treatment contextual elements (implications and ramifications), and developing a working relationship. Wide-ranging complex problems (neurotiform) require conflict-oriented treatments of great breadth and intensity (duration and frequency). Psychotherapeutic procedures target unconscious motivations and wishes when treating neurotiform problems. In other words, the presence of neurotiform problems indicates a need to achieve the resolution of internal conflicts. "Recurrent symptom patterns that have long since departed from their original and adaptive form, that are evoked in environments that bear little relationship to the original evoking situations, or which exist with little evidence of specific, external reinforcers, represent complex symptom patterns indicative of underlying conflict" (Beutler & Clarkin, 1990, p. 226). Complex problems require therapeutic interventions and strategies with conflict-oriented foci, that is, psychodynamic or other insight-oriented intensive therapies.

Simple unidimensional problems indicate symptom-focused, narrow-breadth, short-term treatments. Overt behaviors are the major targets for psychotherapeutic interventions when unidimensional problems are treated. Patient's presenting with unidimensional (noncomplex) problems requires therapies that focus on symptomatic change. Identifying characteristics of noncomplex problems include isolated symptoms (i.e., environment-specific and environment-reinforced) that are easily traced or related to their original adaptive form and etiology. Unidimensional problems often respond well to cognitive-behavioral short-term therapies.

In sum, the goals and strategies/interventions of treatment may be conflict or symptom focused, depending on the complexity of the presenting problem(s). The specific nature of the intended therapeutic outcome and strategies/interventions depends on the unique circumstances and complaints surrounding the problem(s). Specific treatment activities and techniques may be chosen to accommodate the patient's defensive style. The quality of therapeutic transactions should be monitored and present patient resistance levels should partially govern the selection and use of techniques.

Levels of patient arousal and activity can be therapeutically managed to maximize positive treatment results. This technique facilitates successful outcome with either conflictual (complex) or symptomatic (noncomplex) problems by encouraging self-observation, cognitive reorganization, and disconfirmation of pathognomic beliefs. Therapeutic arousal may be introduced through confrontation, empty-chair techniques, directed fantasies, analysis of transference and defenses, interpretation, silence, and open-ended questions. Therapeutic arousal may be decreased with breathing control procedures, attention to somatic sensations, cognitive control strategies, reflection, reassurance, advice and teaching, relaxation and distraction, yes/no or closed-ended questions, and managed exposure (e.g., Rapee, 1987).

Optimal levels of therapeutic arousal depend on anxiety levels (both state and trait) and patient resistance levels (which may vary across time, situations, and patients); however, some general indicators and contraindicators in the regulation of arousal level have been identified (Blau, 1988). Patients exhibiting high levels of resistance to therapist interventions require the use of relatively unintrusive therapeutic techniques, that is, encouragement, empathic reflection, unconditional positive regard, and restatement. Patients who are moderately secure in therapy and exhibiting intermediate levels of resistance will generally benefit from moderately intrusive interventions, that is, structuring, direct questions, exploring patient feelings, setting limits, and providing guidance and advice. Intensive probing interventions, such as analysis of resistance and transference, confrontation of behaviors and fears, dream analysis, guided fantasy, and magnification of patient or therapist gestures, are indicated only with patients that are low in resistance and very secure with their therapist.

Coping style (one's conscious and unconscious pattern of defense against internal conflicts) must also be considered when selecting appropriate therapeutically arousing interventions. To date, a plethora of studies in diverse populations have suggested that this may be among the more powerful predictors of differential response to various types or models of psychotherapy. For example, Sloane and colleagues (Sloane, Staples, Cristol, Yorkston, & Whipple, 1975) were among the first to observe, in a post-hoc analysis, that patients whose MMPI profiles were weighted toward indicators of behavioral acting out, impulsivity, and aggression (externalizers) were more likely to respond to behavior therapies than to psychoanalytic ones. In contrast, those whose MMPIs were marked by anxiety, self-criticism, and social withdrawal (internalizers) were found to be more responsive to psychoanalytic than behavioral therapies. Beutler and Mitchell (1981) found a similar interaction effect in a correlational study of therapists who held experiential, dynamic, and behavioral allegiances. Such findings led Beutler (1983) to propose that patients who were characterized by externalizing coping styles and those who were characterized by internalizing coping styles were likely to show a differential response to insight-oriented and behavior-change therapies.

In more systematic studies of this proposition among groups of anxious and depressed patients, Beutler and his colleagues (Beutler et al., 1991, 2000, 2003; Beutler, Machado, Engle, & Mohr, 1993; Beutler, Mohr, Grawe, Engle, & MacDonald, 1991; Calvert, Beutler, & Crago, 1988) conducted a series of prospective and comparison studies of this proposition with consistent findings in support of the hypothesis. These findings complement those obtained in controlled clinical trials research conducted in other laboratories and with other populations (Cooney, Kadden, Litt, & Getter, 1991; Kadden, Cooney, Getter, & Litt, 1990). Collectively, these studies suggest that patient coping style is an important variable to consider when assigning various types of psychotherapeutic strategies and interventions.

Future Directions

A careful examination of the extant research literature and recent research results indicate that the most effective approaches for a patient's particular problem(s) are not always contained in one specific theory (Beutler et al., 2000, 2003; Beutler & Harwood, 2000; Beutler, Moleiro, Malik & Harwood, 2003; Harwood & Beutler, 2008). Because patients respond in unique ways to any given intervention, it is essential that we apply what investigations into the interaction effects between patient predisposing variables and corresponding therapy procedures elicit. Prescriptive psychotherapy (PT; Beutler & Harwood, 2000) is just such an endeavor representing the most recent research-driven derivative of systematic treatment selection (Beutler & Clarkin, 1990)—a systematic eclectic treatment model that matches key patient dimensions with treatment strategies and principles.

These patient dimensions have been found in previous research to be effective mediators of treatment outcome (Beutler & Clarkin, 1990; Beutler et al., 2000, 2003; Beutler & Harwood, 2000; Gaw & Beutler, 1995; Harwood & Beutler, 2008).

This systematic eclectic approach to treatment maintains that matching patient, therapist, psychotherapeutic strategies and interventions, and diagnostic variables appropriately can greatly enhance the effectiveness and predictive value of a psychotherapeutic approach. In a recent randomized clinical trial (RCT) with comorbid patients (substance abuse with depression), we examined the outcomes for prescriptive, narrative, and cognitive therapies with respect to the contributions of patient qualities, interventions, the therapeutic alliance, and the match between patient and treatment qualities. Results of this study add to the increasing body of research literature indicating that what the therapist does matters. Indeed, patient variables (resistance, coping style, subjective distress, and functional impairment), specific interventions, and good matches between patient and therapeutic strategy and principle were found to be strong predictors of outcome. The predictive power of these variables became even greater at follow-up accounting for more than 90% of the variance in outcome at 6 months post treatment. As expected, the therapeutic alliance was also found to be an important predictor; however, a large portion of the variance attributable to the alliance was captured by matches between therapist intervention and patient resistance levels, coping style, and levels of distress and impairment. In sum, good fits between patient and treatment qualities predicted good outcomes across a variety of outcome dimensions and among very complex, comorbid patient groups.

A computerized application of the prescriptive therapy model, systematic treatment selection (Beutler & Groth-Marnat, 2003) has been shown to provide patients with an easily accessible method for assessing each of the empirically supported PT patient dimensions. A second and expanded version of this model, InnerLife, (Webpsych, 2009) is currently under development. The interested reader may wish to access the InnerLife website (www.innerlife.com) to obtain a description and overview of this cutting-edge, technologically advanced program for patient-treatment matching. This version will be activated directly by patient reports via the Internet and will include an array of research-based self-help options to supplement psychotherapeutic interventions. All recommendations will follow both the principles articulated by Beutler et al. (2000) and by the Task Force on Principles of Therapeutic Change

That Work (Castonguay & Beutler, 2006b). Patients take an interactive online assessment, modified from the original clinician-based evaluation procedure (i.e., the Clinician Rating Form, CRF; Fisher, Beutler, & Williams, 1999), specifically designed to efficiently quantify the STS patient–treatment matching dimensions. A wealth of treatment information, including recommended treatment(s) and strategies, empirically supported treatment manuals, self-help materials, therapists who have demonstrated good treatment response with similar patients, projected treatment trajectory (prognosis), and treatment progress evaluation (actual patient change trajectory), is rendered by the InnerLife program.

Summary

Questions regarding diagnosis, prognosis, current level of functioning, most effective treatment, and causation/maintenance are answerable through an evaluation of relevant patient predisposing variables. In matters of conventional diagnosis, the clinician must determine the degree to which signs and symptoms fit a defined syndrome. The DSM-IV-TR provides a fairly comprehensive guide for conventional diagnostic classification. Clinical skill and experience in the selection and use of formal and informal diagnostic measures facilitates this determination.

Questions about prognosis ordinarily require an evaluation of problem chronicity, personality/defensive style, problem complexity, and environmental circumstances. In some cases, an exploration of available and acceptable environmental/behavioral patient alternatives may be necessary. An assessment of the appropriate patient predetermining variables will elicit the information needed to answer these types of questions.

A patient's current level of functioning may be assessed in a variety of ways; however, only a few will be relevant to the specific situation or problem prompting the assessment. Generally, an evaluation for present level of functioning involves formal and informal measures of cognitive ability and/or a determination of problem severity. In some cases, diagnosis, personality, and problem complexity may be relevant in light of the presenting problem and/or patient circumstances.

Treatment questions are best answered through a comprehensive evaluation of the relevant patient predisposing variables, for example, diagnosis, personality/defensive style, coping ability, problem complexity, problem severity, environmental circumstances/social support, and level of functional impairment. A comprehensive, meaningful, and clear clinical picture must be rendered before treatment questions can be answered competently.

Questions regarding causation (i.e., etiology and maintenance) may require an assessment of environmental circumstances, prior treatment history, family and personal history, current relationships, personality, and medical status and history. The patient's unique circumstances and diagnosis coupled with the specificity of the referral question will determine the patient variables that must be explored in order to answer these question types.

The questions confronting clinicians during referral or treatment planning may be answered through an assessment of predisposing patient dimensions. Referral questions, once properly specified, may be addressed competently by focusing on the appropriate patient variables. In matters of treatment planning, a comprehensive treatment model (an integration of the information gathered from the patient predisposing dimensions) facilitates the sequential consideration of the remaining treatment variables and the hierarchical selection of appropriate interventions.

Patients are unique, and their problems, defensive styles, treatment expectations, and environmental conditions are unique as well. Idiosyncratic patient qualities and novel circumstances represent unique psychotherapeutic needs that necessarily require treatment plans crafted to fit the individual. Each patient must be evaluated comprehensively and frequently for therapy to be effective and efficient. Indeed, every patient predisposing variable has treatment ramifications and it is professionally irresponsible to treat patients without consideration of these therapeutically relevant variables.

Pretreatment Planning Conclusions

According to Beutler et al. (2004), an ideal treatment will

1. focus directly on highly disruptive social symptoms such as those involving drug abuse or acting out behaviors;
2. attempt to enhance emotional arousal processing;
3. adjust emotional focus to the level of patient subjective distress;
4. adjust symptomatic versus insight/awareness focus of treatment to match coping style; and
5. match confrontation and directiveness levels to patient level of trait resistance.

More specifically,

Functional impairment level serves as an index of progress in treatment as well as a predictor of outcome (prognosis). Highly impaired patients may be contraindicated for insight or relationship-oriented therapies. Pharmacological interventions or problem-oriented approaches seem indicated for those patients suffering from highly impairing symptoms. Mild to moderate impairment may be predictive of a positive response to numerous psychotherapies.

Subjective distress, a prognostic indicator with utility for assessing outcome, is directly related to improvement among nonsomatic depressed and anxious patients. Among those with somatic complaints, distress is complexly related to improvement. High levels of distress indicate the utility of self-directed treatment among nonsomatic patients while somatic symptoms may augur well for patients low in distress—additional research is needed to clarify the role of distress in the context of psychotherapy.

Readiness for change may be an indicator of prognosis. That is, the higher the readiness for change, the more positive the treatment outcome. Moreover, interventions that raise consciousness and facilitate self-exploration are most effective for those patients at the precontemplative and contemplative stages. Similarly, action-oriented symptom-focused interventions may be best suited for those patients in preparation and action stages.

Problem complexity is indicated by the presence of multiple diagnoses (i.e., comorbidity and/or personality disorders) and by the chronicity and pervasiveness of problems. Longer-term treatments are indicated for those with diagnostic complexity; however, among those whose conditions are acute, or relatively uncomplicated by concomitant Axis II disorder and interpersonal distress associated with internal symbolic conflicts, symptom-focused pharmacotherapy and symptom-focused psychological interventions are indicated. Further, treatment efficacy is enhanced if the breadth of interventions used corresponds with the complexity of the problem.

Resistance potential, in its trait-like form, is a reasonably good predictor of the differential efficacy of directive and nondirective therapies. Among resistance-prone individuals, therapist guidance, use of professional status, and control are contraindicated; however, paradoxical and nondirective interventions are very effective.

Patients low on resistance potential respond best to directive interventions and guidance. In-session resistance status informs the moment-by-moment process of psychotherapy.

Social support has implications for treatment planning and may serve as an index and predictor of differential treatment response to various psychosocial interventions. Long-term and intensive treatment is indicated for patients with low levels of objective or subjective social support—improvement corresponds with intensity of treatment; however, those with good social support do not respond well to intensive or long-term treatments.

Coping style or level of impulsivity is a consistent predictor of differential treatment response to cognitive-behavioral or relationship/insight-oriented treatments. Specifically, externalizing, impulsive patients respond well to behaviorally oriented symptom-focused therapies while overcontrolled and introspective patients (internalizers) tend to respond well to insight/relationship-oriented therapies.

Attachment style appears to influence the patient's ability to establish a therapeutic relationship and ultimately impacts outcome. Secure attachment appears associated with overall better functioning and prognosis; however, pre- to posttreatment improvement may be greater among dismissive patients.

Acknowledgment

Work on this chapter was partially supported by NIAAA grant no. RO1-AA 08970 to the second author.

References

Baekeland, F., & Lundwall, M. A. (1975). Dropping out of treatment: A critical review. *Psychological Bulletin, 82,* 738–783.

Barlow, D. H., & Waddell, M. T. (1985) Agoraphobia. In D. H. Barlow (Ed.), *Clinical handbook of psychological disorders: A step-by-step treatment manual* (pp. 1–68). New York: Guilford.

Beck, A. T., Rush, A. J., Shaw, B. F., & Emery, G. (1979). *Cognitive therapy of depression.* New York: Guilford.

Beck, A. T., Steer, R. A., & Brown, G.K. (1996). *Manual for the Beck Depression Inventory II.* San Antonio, TX: Psychological Corporation.

Bergin, A. E., & Garfield, S. L. (Eds.) (1994). *Handbook of psychotherapy and behavior change* (4th ed.). New York: John Wiley and Sons.

Beutler, L. E. (1983). *Eclectic psychotherapy: A systematic approach.* Elmsford, NY: Pergamon.

Beutler, L. E. (1989). Differential treatment selection: The role of diagnosis in psychotherapy. *Psychotherapy, 26,* 271–281.

Beutler, L. E. (2000). David and Goliath: When psychotherapy research meets health care delivery systems. *American Psychologist, 55,* 997–1007.

Beutler, L.E., & Bergan, J. (1991). Value change in counseling and psychotherapy: A search for scientific credibility. *Journal of Counseling Psychology, 38,* 16–24.

Beutler, L. E., Blatt, S. J., Alamohamed, S., Levy, K. N., & Angtuaco, L. A. (2006). Participant factors in treating dysphoric disorders. In L. G. Castonguay & L. E. Beutler (Eds.), *Principles of therapeutic change that work* (pp. 13–63). New York: Oxford University Press.

Beutler, L. E., Brookman, L., Harwood, T. M., Alimohamed, S., & Malik, M. M. (2002). Functional impairment and coping style. *Psychotherapy, 38,* 437–442.

Beutler, L. E., & Clarkin, J. (1990). *Systematic treatment selection: Toward targeted therapeutic interventions.* New York: Brunner/Mazel.

Beutler, L. E., Clarkin, J. F., & Bongar, B. (2000). *Guidelines for the systematic treatment of the depressed patient.* New York: Oxford University Press.

Beutler, L. E., Crago, M., & Arizmendi, T. G. (1986). Therapist variables in psychotherapy process and outcome. In S. L. Garfield & A. E. Bergin (Eds.), *Handbook of psychotherapy and behavior change* (3rd ed., pp. 257–310). New York: John Wiley & Sons.

Beutler, L. E., Engle, D., Mohr, D., Daldrup, R. J., Bergan, J., Meredith, K., et al. (1991). Predictors of differential and self directed psychotherapeutic procedures. *Journal of Consulting and Clinical Psychology, 59,* 333–340.

Beutler, L. E., & Groth-Marnat, G. (2003). *Integrative assessment of adult personality* (2nd ed.). New York: Guilford.

Beutler, L. E., & Harwood, T. M. (2000). *Prescriptive psychotherapy.* New York: Oxford University Press.

Beutler, L. E., & Hodgson, A. B. (2003). Prescriptive psychotherapy. In G. Striker & J. Gold (Eds.), *Comprehensive handbook of psychotherapy integration* (pp. 151–164). New York: Plenum.

Beutler, L. E., Machado, P. P. P., Engle, D., & Mohr, D. (1993). Differential patient X treatment maintenance of treatment effects among cognitive, experiential, and self-directed psychotherapies. *Journal of Psychotherapy Integration, 3,* 15–31.

Beutler, L. E., Malik, M., Talebi, H., Fleming, J., & Moleiro, C. (2004). Use of psychological tests/instruments for treatment planning. In M. E. Maruish (Ed.), *The use of psychological testing for treatment planning and outcomes assessment, Vol. 1: General considerations* (3rd ed., pp. 111–145). Mahwah, NJ: Lawrence Erlbaum.

Beutler, L. E., & Mitchell, R. (1981). Psychotherapy outcome in depressed and impulsive patients as a function of analytic and experiential treatment procedures. *Psychiatry, 44,* 297–306.

Beutler, L. E., Mohr, D. C., Grawe, K., Engle, D., & MacDonald, R. (1991). Looking for differential effects: Cross-cultural predictors of differential psychotherapy efficacy. *Journal of Psychotherapy Integration, 1,* 121–142.

Beutler, L. E., Moleiro, C., Malik, M., & Harwood, T. M. (2003). A new twist on empirically supported treatments. *Revista Internacional de Psicologia Clinica de la Salud/International Journal of Clinical and Health Psychology, 3,* 423–437.

Beutler, L. E., Moleiro, C., Malik, M., Harwood, T.M., Romanelli, R., Gallagher-Thompson, D., et al. (2003). A comparison of the Dodo, EST, and ATI factors among co-morbid stimulant dependent, depressed patients. *Clinical Psychology and Psychotherapy, 10,* 69–85.

Blau, T. H. (1988). *Psychotherapy tradecraft: The technique and style of doing therapy*. New York: Brunner/Mazel.

Brehm, S. S. (1976). *The application of social psychology to clinical practice*. Washington, DC: Hemisphere press.

Brennan, K. A., Clark, C. L., & Shaver, P. R. (1998). Self-report measurement of adult attachment: An integrative overview. In J. A. Simpson & W. S. Rholes (Eds.), *Attachment theory and close relationships* (pp. 46–76). New York: Guilford Press.

Butcher, J. N. (1990). *The MMPI-2 in psychological treatment*. New York: Oxford University Press.

Calvert, S. J., Beutler, L. E., & Crago, M. (1988). Psychotherapy outcome as a function of therapist–patient matching on selected variables. *Journal of Social and Clinical Psychology, 6*, 104–117.

Carkhuff, R. R., & Pierce, R. (1967). Differential aspects of therapist race and social class upon patient depth of self-exploration in the initial clinical interview. *Journal of Consulting Psychology, 31*, 632–634.

Castonguay, L. G., & Beutler, L. E. (2006a). Principles of therapeutic change: A task force on participants, relationships, and technique factors. *Journal of Clinical Psychology, 62*, 631–638.

Castonguay, L. G., & Beutler, L. E. (2006b). Common and unique principles of therapeutic change: What do we know and what do we need to know? In L. G. Castonguay & L. E. Beutler (Eds.), *Principles of therapeutic change that work* (pp. 353–369). New York: Oxford University Press.

Castonguay, L.G., & Beutler, L.E. (2006c). Therapeutic factors in dysphoric disorders. *Journal of Clinical Psychology, 62*, 639–647.

Clarkin, J. D., & Hurt, S. W. (1988). Psychological assessment: Tests and rating scales. In J. A. Talbot, R. E. Hales, & S. C. Yudofsky (Eds.), *Textbook of psychiatry*. Washington, DC: American Psychiatric Press.

Clay, R. A. (2000). Treatment guidelines: Sorting fact from fiction. *APA Monitor on Psychology, 31*, 44–46.

Cohen, C. I., & Sokolvosky, J. (1978). Schizophrenia and social networks: Ex-patients in the inner city. *Schizophrenia Bulletin, 4*, 546–560.

Cohen, J. R., & Swerdlik, M. E. (2005). *Psychological testing and assessment* (6th ed.). New York: McGraw-Hill.

Cooney, N. L., Kadden, R. M., Litt, M. D., & Getter, H. (1991). Matching alcoholics to coping skills or interactional therapies: Two-year follow-up results. *Journal of Consulting and Clinical Psychology, 59*, 598–601.

Crits-Christoph, P., & Demorest, A. (1991). Quantitative assessment of relationship theme components. In M. J. Horowitz (Ed.), *Person schema and maladaptive interpersonal patterns* (pp. 197–212). Chicago, IL: University of Chicago Press.

Crits-Christoph, P., Demorest, A., & Connolly, M. B. (1990). Quantative assessment of interpersonal themes over the course of psychotherapy. *Psychotherapy, 27*, 513–521.

Derogatis, L. R. (1994). *SCL-90: Administration, scoring, and procedures manual* (3rd ed.). Minneapolis, MN: National Computer Systems.

DiNardo, P. A., O'Brien, G. T., Barlow, D. H., Waddell, M. T., & Blanchard, E. B. (1983). Reliability of DSM-III anxiety disorders categories using a new structured interview. *Archives of General Psychiatry, 40*, 1070–1075.

Dowd, E. T., Milne, C. R., & Wise, S. L. (1991). The Therapeutic Reactance Scale: A measure of psychological reactance. *Journal of Counseling and Development, 69*, 601–613.

Dowd, E. T., & Pace, T. F. (1989). The relativity of reality: Second order change in psychotherapy. In A. Freeman,

K. M. Simon, L. E. Beutler, & H. Arkowitz (Eds.), *Comprehensive handbook of Cognitive Therapy* (pp. 213–226). New York: Plenum.

Dubrin, J. R., & Zastowny, T. R. (1988). Predicting early attrition from psychotherapy: An analysis of a large private-practice cohort. *Psychotherapy, 25*, 393–408.

Fisher, D., Beutler, L. E., & Williams, O. B. (1999). STS clinician rating form: Patient assessment and treatment planning. *Journal of Clinical Psychology, 55*(7), 825–842.

Flaherty, J. A., & Richman, J. A. (1986). Effects of childhood relationships on the adult's capacity to form social supports. *American Journal of Psychiatry, 143*, 851–855.

Foxhall, K. (2000). Research for the real world: NIMH is pumping big money into effectiveness research to move promising treatments into practice. *Monitor on Psychology, 31*, 28–36.

Frances, A., Clarkin, J., & Perry, S. (1984). *Differential therapeutics in psychiatry*. New York: Brunner/Mazel.

Freebury, M. B. (1984). The prescription of psychotherapy. *Canadian Journal of Psychiatry, 29*, 499–503.

Garfield, S. L. (1986). Research on client variables in psychotherapy. In S. L. Garfield & A. E. Bergin (Eds.), *Handbook of psychotherapy and behavior change* (3rd ed., pp. 213–256). New York: John Wiley and Sons.

Gaw, K. F., & Beutler, L. E. (1995). Integrating treatment recommendations. In L. E. Beutler & M. Berren (Eds.), *Integrative assessment of adult personality* (pp. 280–319). New York: Guilford Press.

Harwood, T. M., & Beutler, L. E. (2008). EVTs, EBPs, ESRs, and RIPs: Inspecting the varieties of research based practices. In L. L'Abate (Ed.), *Toward a science of clinical psychology*. New York: Nova Science Publishers, Inc.

Harwood, T. M., & Williams, O. B. (2003). Identifying treatment-relevant assessment: Systematic treatment selection. In L. E. Beutler & G. Groth-Marnat (Eds.), *Integrative assessment of adult personality* (2nd ed., pp. 65–81). New York: Guilford Press.

Hamilton, M. (1967). Development of a rating scale for primary depressive illness. *British Journal of Social and Clinical Psychology, 6*, 278–296.

Hollon, S. D., & Beck, A. T. (1979). Cognitive therapy of depression. In P. E. Kendall & S. D. Hollon (Eds.), *Cognitive-behavioral interventions: Theory, research, procedures* (pp. 153–202). New York: Academic Press.

Horowitz, L. M., Rosenberg, S. E., Baer, B. A., Ureño, G., & Villaseñor, V. S. (1988). Inventory of personal problems: Psychometric properties and clinical applications. *Journal of Consulting and Clinical Psychology, 56*, 885–892.

Jones, E. E. (1978). Effects of race on psychotherapy process and outcome: An exploratory investigation. *Psychotherapy: Theory, Research and Practice, 15*, 226–236.

Jones, E. E., Krupnick, J. L., & Kerig, P. K. (1987). Some gender effects in brief psychotherapy. *Psychotherapy, 24*, 336–352.

Kadden, R. M., Cooney, N. L., Getter, H., & Litt, M. D. (1990). Matching alcoholics to coping skills or interactional therapies: Posttreatment results. *Journal of Consulting and Clinical Psychology, 57*, 698–704.

Kohut, H., & Wolf, E. S. (1978). The disorders of the self and their treatment: An outline. *International Journal of Psychoanalysis, 59*, 413–425.

Lambert, M. J. (Ed.). (2004), *Handbook of psychotherapy and behavior change* (5th ed., pp. 227–306). New York: John Wiley and Sons.

Lorion, R. P., & Felner, R. D. (1986). Reseach on psychotherapy with the disadvantaged. In S. L. Garfield & A. E. Bergin (Eds.), *Handbook of psychotherapy and behavior change* (3rd ed., pp. 739–776). New York: John Wiley and Sons.

Luborsky, L. (1984). *Principles of psychoanalytic psychotherapy: A manual for supportive-expressive treatment.* New York: Basic Books.

Luborsky, L., Crits-Christoph, P., Alexander, L., Margolis, M., & Cohen, M. (1983). Two helping alliance methods for predicting outcomes of psychotherapy: A counting signs vs. a global rating method. *Journal of Nervous and Mental Disease, 171,* 480–491.

Mallinckrodt, B., Gantt, D. L., & Coble, H. M. (1995). Attachment patterns in the psychotherapy relationship: Development of the client attachment to therapist scale. *Journal of Counseling Psychology, 42,* 307–317.

McConnaughy, E. A., DiClemente, C. C., & Velicer, W. F. (1983). Stages of change in psychotherapy: Measurement and sample profiles. *Psychotherapy, 20,* 368–375.

Mayerson, N. H. (1984). Preparing clients for group therapy: A critical review and theoretical formulation. *Clinical Psychology Review, 4,* 191–213.

Miller, P. A., & Eisenberg, N. (1988). The relation of empathy to aggressive and externalizing/antisocial behavior. *Psychological Bulletin, 103,* 324–344.

Moos, R. H., & Insel, P. M. (1974). *Work Environment Scale.* Palo Alto, CA: Consulting Psychologists Press.

Moos, R. H., & Moos, B. S. (1986). *Family Environment Scale manual* (2nd ed.). Palo Alto, CA: Consulting Psychologists Press.

Murphy, E., & Macdonald, A. (1992). Affective disorders in old age. In E. S. Paykel (Ed.), *Handbook of Affective Disorders* (pp. 601–618). New York: Guilford Press.

Norcross, J. C. (Ed.). (2002). *Psychotherapy relationships that work.* New York: Oxford University Press.

Prochaska, J. O., & DiClemente, C. C. (1984). *The transtheoretical approach: Crossing traditional boundaries of change.* Homewood, IL: Dow Jones/Irwin.

Prochaska, J. O., DiClemente, C. C., & Norcross, J. C. (1992). In search of how people change: Applications to addictive behaviors. *American Psychologist, 47,* 1102–1114.

Prochaska, J. O., & Norcross, J. C. (2002). Stages of change. In J. C. Norcross (Ed.), *Psychotherapy relationships that work.* New York: Oxford University Press.

Rapee, R. (1987). The psychological treatment of panic attacks: Theoretical conceptualization and review of evidence. *Clinical Psychology Review, 7,* 427–438.

Sarason, I. G., Levine, H. M., Basham, R. B., & Sarason, B. R. (1983). Assessing social support: The Social Support Questionnaire. *Journal of Personality and Social Psychology, 44,* 127–139.

Schulberg, H. C., & McClelland, M. (1987). Depression and physical illness: The prevalence, causation, and diagnosis of comorbidity. *Clinical Psychology Review, 7,* 145–167.

Shoham-Salomon, V. (1991). Introduction to special section on client-therapy interaction research. *Journal of Consulting and Clinical Psychology, 59,* 203–204.

Sloane, R. B., Staples, F. R., Cristol, A. H., Yorkston, N. J., & Whipple, K. (1975). *Psychotherapy versus behavior therapy.* Cambridge, MA: Harvard University Press.

Sperry, L., Brill, P. L., Howard, K. I., & Grissom, G. R. (1996). *Treatment outcomes in psychotherapy and psychiatric interventions.* New York: Brunner/Mazel.

Spielberger, C. D., Gorsuch, R. L., Lushene, R., Vagg, P. R., & Jacobs, G. A., (1983). *Manual for the state-trait anxiety inventory.* Palo Alto, CA: Consulting Psychologists Press.

Strupp, H. H., Horowitz, L. M., & Lambert, M. J. (1997). *Measuring patient changes in mood, anxiety, and personality disorders: Toward a core battery.* Washington, DC: American Psychological Association.

Sweeney, J. A., Clarkin, J. F., & Fitzgibbon, M. L. (1987). Current practice of psychological assessment. *Professional Psychology: Research and Practice, 18,* 377–380.

Thorpe, S. A. (1987). An approach to treatment planning. *Psychotherapy, 24,* 729–735.

Truax, C. B., & Carkhuff, R. R. (1967). *Toward effective counseling and psychotherapy: Training and practice.* Chicago: Aldine.

Truax, C. B., & Wargo, D. G. (1969). Effects of vicarious therapy pretraining and alternate sessions on outcome in group psychotherapy with outpatients. *Journal of Consulting and Clinical Psychology, 33,* 440–447.

Turkat, D. M. (1979). Psychotherapy preparatory communications: Influences upon patient role expectations. *Dissertation Abstracts International, 39,* 4059B.

Webpsych (2009). InnerLife. A proprietary software program.

Wilson, D. O. (1985). The effects of systematic client preparation, severity, and treatment setting on dropout rate in short-term psychotherapy. *Journal of Social and Clinical Psychology, 3,* 62–70.

Zwick, R., & Attkisson, C. C. (1985). Effectiveness of a client pre-therapy orientation videotape. *Journal of Counseling Psychology, 32,* 514–524.

Assessment of Treatment Resistance
via Questionnaire

Julia N. Perry

Abstract

This chapter examines how evaluating traitlike resistance with objective personality assessment instruments can assist therapists in better anticipating, understanding, and responding to their clients' signs of therapeutic resistance. Beginning with a brief review of the data regarding gender-influenced attitudes toward psychological treatment, it then presents and discusses specific Minnesota Multiphasic Personality Inventory (MMPI/MMPI-2) validity, clinical, and content scales that measure elements of treatment resistance. A review of clinical and normative data on the Butcher Treatment Planning Inventory (BTPI), a measure that was created specifically for treatment planning purposes, is discussed. Finally, a case example to illustrate specific methods of informing psychotherapy with objective test data is presented.

Keywords: personality assessment, resistance, treatment planning

There has been considerable study and commentary within the field of psychology regarding the range of factors affecting psychotherapy process and outcome. Myriad therapist qualities and client qualities have been investigated (e.g., Corey, 1991; Hersen & Ammerman, 1994). Establishing a maximally serviceable relationship between clients and therapists requires that both parties be genuinely engaged in the psychotherapy process. In order for that to happen, therapists need to be willing to "treat" their clients, typically using evidence-based methods that are matched to clients' presenting difficulties. In addition, clients need to be open to and accepting of the "treatment" that they receive. Although both of these elements are necessary for therapeutic change, neither is sufficient. This chapter will focus on client factors by examining ways in which objective assessment can assist providers in understanding the sources of treatment resistance affecting their clients.

The Concept of "Resistance"

Broadly speaking, clients must be willing to involve themselves in psychotherapy to at least a minimal degree in order to achieve therapeutic

benefit. Unwillingness on their part to do so is viewed as "psychotherapeutic resistance." The "resistance" concept is rooted in psychoanalysis. Freud's writings delineate several types of resistance, such as that relating to unwillingness to examine associations and to interpret dreams. But, he theorized, an even more fundamental type occurred "when we [psychoanalysts] undertake to cure a patient of his symptoms [and] he opposes against us a vigorous and tenacious *resistance* throughout the entire course of the treatment" (Freud, 1973, p. 297). This phenomenon was so important to psychoanalysis that Freud concluded that overcoming resistance was the most time-consuming and difficult element of all psychoanalytic work.

Freud's conceptualization held that resistance was unconscious; thus, it went unrecognized by the person experiencing it. In fact, his theory was based on the idea that resistance could be manifested whenever an analyst attempted to bring an analysand's unconscious material to the level of consciousness. However, in its present iteration, there is no presumption that clients' resistive behavior is unconscious or goes unrecognized by them. In fact, resistance can be a willful phenomenon. Whether it is purposeful or not, it can bear significantly on the therapeutic relationship and exert its influence at various points in time over the treatment course.

Resistance to Initiating Psychological Treatment

Resistance can begin quite early in the psychotherapeutic process. For example, the idea of immersing oneself in psychotherapy actually begins even before clients embark upon their treatment experiences. Frank and Frank (1991) outlined this idea in their discussion of the client's "assumptive world," in which suppositions are organized in attitudes that potentially determine behavior. This "behavior" may be whether to engage in psychological treatment at all.

Data indicate that a substantial proportion of individuals who may require psychological treatment never receive it. In recent decades, estimates of people who meet criteria for at least one mental disorder have run as high as 14% (e.g., Regier et al., 1993), whereas the portion of Americans who actually received formal psychological intervention have been estimated at around only 6% (Castro, 1993). The gaps between these figures indicate that a sizable proportion of individuals with psychological problems are going untreated (or at least undertreated). This phenomenon may be due, in part, to what has been characterized as the "unappealing if not unacceptable" nature of many psychological treatments, from a client's point of view (Cowen, 1982, p. 385). Thus, large numbers of people may choose not to "bring their personal troubles to mental health professionals at *any* point in their unfolding" (Cowen, 1982, p. 385).

A number of other studies have examined this phenomenon. Back in 1958, Rosenthal and Frank identified low levels of education and income as predictors of which individuals held negative attitudes toward psychotherapy and, consequently, would reject offered treatment. By 1971, Raynes and Warren had examined such variables as race and age and had found that Blacks younger than age 40 were the least likely group in their sample to initiate treatment. Decades later, Furnham and Wardley (1990) found older age to be predictive of negative beliefs about psychological interventions, likely in keeping with Brody's (1994) conclusion that negative attitudes about treatment would be found among individuals with "conservative," "old-fashioned," and "traditional" points of view.

Gender also has been implicated as an important determining factor, with research generally demonstrating greater willingness to engage in psychotherapy among women than among men. This finding has been supported by the work of such individuals as Ryan (1969); Cheatham, Shelton, and Ray (1987); Johnson (1988); and Butcher, Rouse, and Perry (1998). Ryan's (1969) research demonstrated that the therapy clients being studied were twice as likely to be women as men, underscoring the gender disparity with regard to psychotherapy involvement. More recent research has confirmed this phenomenon and also has provided possible explanations for it. A study by Cheatham et al. (1987) uncovered a decreased willingness for men to seek psychotherapy, as compared to women. Johnson (1988) also found that female college students were more willing than their male counterparts to recognize a need for professional help and to be open to sharing their difficulties with other people.

Butcher et al. (1998) also looked at men's and women's attitudes toward experiences in therapy, using a seven-item "Survey of Treatment Attitudes" that was composed for their study. They asked 388 university students (213 women and 175 men) such questions as, "Have you ever been in psychological counseling in the past?", and "Do you think that you would be willing to seek assistance from a psychologist or psychiatrist if you were experiencing problems in psychological adjustment?" They found that the women in their sample were more likely than the men to have participated in counseling and also to have considered participating in some kind of psychological treatment. The female participants also reported being more willing than the male participants to recommend psychological interventions to a family member or friend.

In explaining findings such as these, several theorists have implicated not the biological category of sex but the attitudes that men and women frequently hold, which are shaped by psychological and sociological factors,. For example, research by Robertson and Fitzgerald (1992) showed that high scores on measures of masculinity predicted negative attitudes toward psychotherapy on the Fisher–Turner Attitudes Toward Seeking Professional Help Scale. Moreover, although women tended to prefer traditional forms of psychotherapy, men who possessed more stereotypically masculine attitudes demonstrated a preference for alternative, nontraditional interventions. Johnson's (1988) study attributed male–female differences to sex role differences, not sex category, per se. Specifically, individuals who were classified as "feminine" or "androgynous" according to the Bem Sex Role Inventory were most likely to recognize a need for psychological intervention, irrespective of sex classification or category.

However, other research has failed to find such a relationship between gender and resistance to initiating treatment (e.g., Garfield, 1994, 1995; Noonan, 1973). Noonan's early work determined that sex was not related to a client's likelihood of failing to keep an initial appointment for psychotherapy. Garfield has contended that only social class and education affect which individuals will decide to initiate psychotherapy. He has indicated that all other demographic variables are largely unrelated to this behavior and that research uncovering male–female differences in resistance to psychotherapy is flawed by inadequate operationalization of terms (including "psychotherapy"). This implication that sex differences wash out if a wider and less traditional definition of psychotherapy is used is supported by others (e.g., Robertson & Fitzgerald, 1992).

Regardless of one's position, there generally is not an assumption of a direct relationship between demographic variables and openness to initiating psychological treatment. Rather, the variables are generally considered to influence one's expectations about the potential helpfulness and usefulness of psychotherapy (Norcross & Beutler, 1997). It stands to reason that individuals who do not expect such services to be beneficial will be less willing to take part in them. However, even if clients do have positive expectations about psychotherapy, there remains the potential for attitudes and behaviors to affect treatment negatively once it is underway. This creates further potential for problematic outcomes. Therefore, it is important to look at the specific factors that may affect clients' ability to engage actively in psychological treatment and to consider the potential ramifications of those factors.

Resistance and Ongoing Psychological Treatment

Many issues have been implicated when examining the potential resistance encountered in ongoing psychotherapy, which is often operationalized as something relating to poor treatment response. It is possible to examine trends by diagnostic category, but they are often viewed more broadly, across groups of disorders or problems. In the latter case, one conceptual distinction is between statelike and traitlike resistance (e.g., Beutler et al., 1991).

Statelike resistance presumes that obstacles being encountered somehow can be removed or altered and that situational factors are key. At a general level, clients' readiness to undertake psychological treatment is itself a mutable and statelike factor. Using the Stages of Change Questionnaire (Prochaska, Velicer, DiClemente, & Fava, 1988), it is possible to determine the extent to which clients are prepared and willing to exert effort to make changes in their lives. The questionnaire holds that individuals who are undertaking psychological treatment go through some or all of a series of progressive stages (typically conceptualized as precontemplation, contemplation, preparation, action, and maintenance). Whatever stage they are in at a given time reflects their current readiness to modify thoughts and behavior. Encountering client "resistance" may indicate that the individual has not yet advanced to a stage of readiness to embark upon the change process. Although it could be a therapist's impression that this is the case, drawing the conclusion more systematically could allow the therapist to understand how best to prepare the client to move to a stage that is more conducive to active change. In other words, it could point the client and therapist toward methods for addressing the "resistance" being encountered.

Traitlike resistance, on the other hand, could affect treatment response in a more ongoing and persistent way. A number of instruments have demonstrated themselves to be useful in capturing the nature of this type of resistance, especially as it is manifested by clients during a course of psychological treatment. Chief among these instruments are the Minnesota Multiphasic Personality Inventory (MMPI) and its revised counterpart, the MMPI-2.

The MMPI/MMPI-2

Providers can glean a wealth of information about clients' attitudes toward treatment from MMPI/MMPI-2 profiles (e.g., Butcher, 2005a; Butcher & Perry, 2008; Finn & Kamphuis, 2006; Graham, 2006). Some scales look specifically at treatment resistance issues, whereas others were developed for different purposes but also provide important information about resistance. The ego strength supplementary scale (Es; Barron, 1953) was developed to measure the ability of clients to benefit from psychotherapy. It was constructed by contrasting the MMPI item responses of "successful" and "unsuccessful" psychotherapy clients, to determine which items distinguished between the two groups. However, the scale has been found to measure one's ability to withstand stress, rather than one's potential for psychotherapy success (Butcher & Williams, 2000). Another measure, the Therapeutic Reactance Scale (TRS; Dowd, Milne, & Wise, 1991), has demonstrated greater potential to predict therapy response, at least among individuals with acute and transitory difficulties (Beutler, Goodrich, Fisher, & Williams, 1999).

Other MMPI-2 scales measure elements of treatment resistance as well. The Negative Treatment Indicators (TRT) content scale specifically examines clients' attitudes toward accepting psychotherapy and other types of treatment (Butcher & Williams, 2000). It also measures their attitudes toward making behavioral changes. Individuals who produce elevated scores on TRT are thereby acknowledging negative attitudes toward health-care professionals, unwillingness to change their behavior, and lack of belief that change is possible (see study by Craig & Olson, 2003).

Elevated scores on several of the other MMPI-2 scales also have implications with regard to treatment resistance (e.g., Butcher, 1990; Butcher & Williams, 2000; Greene & Clopton, 1999). The instrument's validity indicators provide information about individuals' willingness to be forthcoming during the assessment process, which has logical implications for their willingness to be open and honest in any psychotherapy that may be undertaken. Therefore, elevated scores on several measures can be indicators of resistance: cannot say (Cs), indicating the number of items not answered; the lie scale (L), assessing the tendency to claim excessive virtue; the infrequency scales (F and F_B), which look at deviant and random responding; the suppressor scale (K), which is another, subtler measure of problem denial; true response inconsistency (TRIN), measuring yea-saying and nay-saying response sets; and variable response inconsistency (VRIN), which assesses response inconsistency that possibly is due to random responding. Among these, L, K, and TRIN may be most important, given that individuals who produce elevated scores on these scales may be attempting to "put their best foot forward" in a manner that leads them to deny or minimize their difficulties. It stands to reason that clients who are unwilling to complete the MMPI-2 fully and accurately are less apt to comply fully with other facets of assessment and intervention (Greene & Clopton, 1999). However, it should also be noted that individuals may produce elevations on one or more of the

validity indicators for other reasons (e.g., being unable to read English well enough to produce a valid profile); such clients will not necessarily come across as resistant to psychological interventions (see discussion in Butcher, Cabiya, Lucio, & Garrido, 2007).

Elevated (T ≥ 65) and even low (T < 45) scores on MMPI-2 clinical scales also have implications for the individual's attitudes in treatment (e.g., Butcher & Williams, 2000; Greene & Clopton, 1999), although the relationships are not necessarily uniformly robust. Elevated scores on Scale 1 (Hs) are associated with a tendency to be difficult to engage in psychotherapy, in part due to likely pessimism about the benefits of treatment. Low scorers on Scale 2 (D) tend to have little internal motivation to undertake any kind of psychological treatment. High scorers on Scales 3 (Hy) may be resistant to psychological interpretations of their problems; although they initially may seem enthusiastic about their treatments, their eagerness is unlikely to persist. Individuals who produce elevated scores on Scale 4 (Pd) tend to demonstrate poor prognosis for change in therapy. Moreover, those who score low on Pd generally have little psychological insight and need motivation in order to make specific behavioral changes.

High scorers on Scale 6 (Pa) are also likely to have poor prognosis for treatment-related change. They often are so suspicious of others that they have difficulty in forming solid therapeutic relationships. Like those who score high on Hy, individuals who produce elevations on Scale 7 (Pt) may refuse to accept psychological interpretations of their problems; they may also be so tense and anxious that it is necessary to reduce their anxiety levels before psychological treatment is initiated. On the other hand, a low Pt score suggests that the individual is so comfortable with himself or herself that there does not appear to be a need for treatment or change.

A tendency to resist psychological interpretations of problems is associated with high scores on Scale 8 (Sc) as well. However, the individuals who produce such scores may remain in psychotherapy for longer than most patients. Finally, individuals who score in the elevated range on Scale 9 (Ma) are inclined to attend their therapy sessions irregularly, and they may terminate therapy prematurely as well.

Similar problems are associated with elevated scores on the MMPI-2 content scales (Greene & Clopton, 1999). High scorers on anxiety (ANX) may be so anxious that it is actually ineffective to initiate psychotherapy prior to reducing their anxiety levels via other means, including medication. Those whose cynicism (CYN) or social discomfort (SOD) scores are elevated are apt to have difficulty in establishing trusting relationships with their therapists, which is likely to be a significant impediment to any psychotherapy that they undertake.

Butcher, Rouse, and Perry (2000) examined MMPI-2 scale correlates in a slightly different manner. They surveyed 64 psychotherapists from around the country and obtained data on 460 psychotherapy clients (271 women and 189 men). Within the sample, the most common psychotherapy orientation was cognitive-behavioral. Each therapist completed a client information form, specifying demographic information and diagnostic details, on each client participant. Next, clients completed the MMPI-2 and another objective psychological measure, the Butcher Treatment Planning Inventory (BTPI; results from that measure will be discussed later in this chapter). The clients, who were mostly White, female, and self-referred for treatment, were assigned diagnoses according to the fourth edition of the *Diagnostic and statistical manual of mental disorders* (DSM-IV; American Psychiatric Association [APA], 1994). On Axis I, the most common diagnoses were dysthymic disorder, major depressive disorder, and adjustment disorder. Nearly one-quarter of clients also met criteria for an Axis II personality disorder, most often personality disorder not otherwise specified, borderline personality disorder, or dependent personality disorder. The majority of the client participants attended weekly or biweekly therapy sessions.

On the client information forms, therapists listed the psychological problems and symptoms that they regarded each client to be experiencing, resulting in a list of 100 descriptive words and phrases (such as "low self-esteem," "isolation," and "fatigue"). Overall, there were no significant correlations between scores on the clinical scales or content scales and descriptors predicting poor therapy prognosis. However, when examining well-defined, single-point code types or "spikes" (i.e., for any one clinical scale, $T \geq 65$ and at least 5 points higher than T-score for any other clinical scale), the results differed. "Problems disclosing information to others" was reported for 28.6% of individuals with a T-score spike on Hs ($N = 514$), 29.0% of those with a spike on D ($N = 531$), 38.9% of those with a spike on Pt ($N = 518$), and 43.5% of those with a spike on Sc ($N = 523$). In addition, "relationship conflicts" were reported for 29.3% of the individuals with a spike on Pd ($N = 541$) and 30.8% of those with a spike on Ma ($N = 513$). The presence of

difficulties with establishing and maintaining interpersonal relationships clearly has implications for an individual's ability to develop and sustain a strong psychotherapeutic bond with a psychotherapist.

Treatment resistance has been assessed in other ways as well, again using the MMPI-2. In their study of college students, Butcher et al. (1998) compared the MMPI-2 profiles of individuals who answered "yes" and "no" to the following question: "Have you ever thought that you would like to talk with a psychologist or psychiatrist about something that bothers you?" Those who answered "yes" scored significantly higher on Sc (with a mean T-score of just over 65) than those who answered "no" (who had a mean T-score of nearly 55). Individuals who answered "yes" to this question also scored significantly higher than those who answered "no" on F, F_B, Hs, D, Pd, Pa, Pt, Sc, Scale 0 (Si), and a number of content scales. Though at first glance these findings seem to contradict the aforementioned information about correlates, it should be noted that they are not based on *elevated* clinical and content scores.

Regarding the question, "Do you think that you would be willing to seek assistance from a psychologist or psychiatrist if you were experiencing problems in psychological adjustment?", there were no significant differences in MMPI-2 scale scores between those who answered "yes" and those who answered "no." There also were no individuals who produced an elevated score on any of the MMPI-2 scales.

The MMPI-2 has been subjected to extensive study with respect to treatment resistance issues, and it clearly is a useful method of assessing such matters. Nevertheless, the instrument itself was not designed to guide treatment planning and psychological intervention issues. It is worthwhile to examine the information that can be gleaned from measures that were created specifically for the purpose of treatment planning. As noted by Groth-Marnat (1999), promising instruments have been introduced within recent years, including the Systematic Treatment Selection Clinician Rating Form (Fisher, Beutler, & Williams, 1999). The following section of this chapter will focus on another example, the BTPI.

The Butcher Treatment Planning Inventory

The BTPI (see Butcher, 2005b; see also Ben-Porath, 1997, and Perry & Butcher, 1999) evolved from a merger of objective personality assessment principles and psychological intervention. It was derived on the basis of a combination of rational and empirical means. It is intended to be behaviorally oriented and fundamentally atheoretical in nature. The BTPI seeks to assess not only clients' psychological symptomatology, but also those specific qualities that are likely to impede psychological treatment, making it an ideal candidate for research into treatment resistance issues.

The measure consists of 210 true-or-false items. Through their responses to these items, respondents can directly communicate key information with regard to the nature and process of psychotherapy. The content of each item assigns it to one or more of the instrument's 14 scales, as summarized in Table 34.1.

The four scales that make up Cluster 1 assess the validity of the individual's self-report on the instrument. Inconsistent responding (INC) consists of 21 pairs of items and looks at the degree to which individuals endorse each pair's items in a semantically logical way. "I am very hard to get to know" and "I am very hard to get to know, and I prefer it that way" should both be answered either true or false. If a respondent indicates that one statement is true and the other is false, then his or her raw INC score would reflect that inconsistency. The 15 overly virtuous self-views (VIR) items look at respondents' tendency to

try to present themselves to others in an unrealistically positive manner and indicate that they are better adjusted than most people are. The 61 exaggerated problem presentation (EXA) items look at the degree to which individuals endorse an unrealistically high number of symptoms that tend not to be endorsed by mental health patients. The closed-mindedness (CLM) scale's 19 items evaluate the individual's tendency to resist disclosing personal information and making cognitive and behavioral changes.

The five scales comprising Cluster 2 assess personality-related issues that could make a significant impact on treatment. Problems in relationship formation (REL) is composed of 18 items that measure a lack of interpersonal trust as well as problems in relating to others. The 16 somatization of conflict (SOM) items look at the extent to which individuals try to cope with their psychological problems by developing new or worsening physical symptoms. Low expectation of therapeutic benefit (EXP) consists of 25 items that examine respondents' skepticism about the appropriateness and value of making cognitive and behavioral changes through therapy. The 19 items that constitute the self-oriented/narcissism (NAR) scale look at the extent to which individuals are self-indulgent in their interpersonal styles and

Table 34.1. BTPI scale and composite information.

Scales	Abbreviation	Information Provided
Cluster 1: Validity scales		
Inconsistent responding	INC	Contradictory or random item responses
Overly virtuous self-views	VIR	Presentation of an unrealistically positive self-image
Exaggerated problem presentation	EXA	Overendorsement of symptoms
Closed-mindedness	CLM	Resistance to new ways of thinking and behaving
Cluster 2: Treatment issues scales		
Problems in relationship formation	REL	Difficulties in forming relationships
Somatization of conflict	SOM	Channeling of psychological problems into physical ones
Low expectation of therapeutic benefit	EXP	Negative attitudes toward treatment
Self-oriented/narcissism	NAR	Self-centeredness
Perceived lack of environmental support	ENV	Impression of the social environment as negative or punishing
Cluster 3: Current symptom scales		
Depression	DEP	Standard depression symptoms
Anxiety	ANX	Standard anxiety symptoms
Anger-out	A-O	Hostile attitudes, tendency toward outward expressions of anger
Anger-in	A-I	Internalization of anger, self-blame
Unusual thinking	PSY	Strange, magical, or delusional beliefs, unusual behaviors
Composites	*Abbreviation*	*Included Scales*
General pathology composite	GPC	DEP, ANX, A-O, A-I
Treatment difficulty composite	TDC	PSY, REL, SOM, EXP, NAR, ENV

selfish in their relationships with others. Perceived lack of environmental support (ENV) contains 17 items, which assess people's impressions of the extent to which they feel emotionally distant from others.

The five Cluster 3 scales look at specific psychological symptoms currently being experienced. The 18-item depression (DEP) scale evaluates such attributes as depressed affect and lack of energy. The 15-item anxiety (ANX) scale measures feelings of anxiousness, nervousness, and tension. Each of the two anger-related scales contains 16 items. Anger-out (A-O) looks at hostile and aggressive outward expressions of anger, whereas and anger-in (A-I) assesses the tendency to internalize anger and engage in self-blame. Finally, the 15 items that comprise the unusual thinking (PSY) scale gauge the degree to which respondents currently exhibit unusual behaviors and hold atypical beliefs that may even be delusional in nature.

In addition to the individual scales, the instrument contains two composite scores. The raw score for the general pathology composite (GPC) is calculated via the respondent's scores on DEP, ANX, A-O, and A-I. The other Cluster 3 scale, PSY, is included in the treatment difficulty composite (TDC), due to the nature of its content. The remaining TDC scales come from Cluster 2: REL, SOM, EXP, NAR, and ENV.

The BTPI was constructed so as to assess the "nonspecific" or common factors in psychotherapy (Butcher, 2005b). As Butcher contends, many of these factors are related to clients' attitudes toward treatment, personality characteristics and qualities

that affect relationship formation, and motivational elements that could interfere with an intended goal of some type of cognitive and/or behavioral change. Therefore, all of the BTPI scales relate to the concept of treatment resistance, given their evaluation of negative factors that could interfere with a client's ability to gain maximum benefit from treatment. Table 34.2 summarizes the possible treatment implications of elevated (i.e., $T \geq 65$) scores. Four recent studies have demonstrated the potential usefulness of the type of treatment resistance information derived from the BTPI.

Two College Student Samples

In 1998, Butcher and colleagues looked at the relationship between BTPI scale scores and attitudes toward psychological treatment among 379 college students. Each student participant completed the same seven-item treatment attitudes survey that was referenced previously in this chapter. They also completed the BTPI.

Results indicated that the students who had not previously participated in counseling had lower expectations of therapeutic benefit (i.e., higher scores on EXP) than did individuals who had participated in counseling at some prior time in their lives. In addition, as compared with students who were willing to seek counseling, individuals who reported being unwilling to seek counseling indicated lower expectation of benefiting from treatment (through producing higher scores on EXP), less openness to new ways of thinking and behaving (higher scores on CLM), less consistency in their self-reports (higher scores on INC), greater difficulty

Table 34.2. Treatment resistance indicators on the BTPI scales.

Scale	Treatment Correlates of Elevated Scores
INC	Difficulty in cooperating with treatment
VIR	Avoidance of self-disclosure
EXA	Inability to focus on specific symptoms
CLM	Irritation when criticized, poor reaction to personal feedback
REL	Reluctance to trust, difficulty establishing therapeutic alliance
SOM	Unwillingness or inability to deal directly with psychological problems
EXP	Doubt that change is desirable or possible, reluctance to comply with treatment recommendations
NAR	Sense of entitlement, unwillingness to alter behavior in order to suit others
ENV	Opposition to making life changes because of perceived lack of emotional support
DEP	Inability to comply with treatment due to depression severity
ANX	Inability to comply with treatment due to anxiety severity
A-O	Irritability or hostility toward the therapist
A-I	Passivity, self-punishing behavior, self-blame if treatment does not go well
PSY	Irrational beliefs, trouble processing stimuli accurately, mistrust of the therapist

in forming relationships with others (higher scores on REL), and greater tendency to be self-punitive (higher scores on A-I).

There were some gender differences as well. Specifically, male participants produced higher scores than women on CLM, REL, and EXP, suggesting that male students were more closed-minded, reported more problems in forming relationships, and had lower expectations of benefiting from psychotherapy, as compared to female students. The data from this college student sample support the notion that treatment resistance can be measured using an objective measure. These individuals' BTPI scores were largely consistent with the attitudes conveyed via the seven-item survey.

Hatchett, Han, and Cooker (2002) considered another operationalization of treatment resistance by examining the degree to which premature termination from counseling could be predicted on the basis of BTPI data. As part of the intake evaluation process at a university counseling center, 95 new clients agreed to complete the BTPI. According to the demographic information that they gathered, their typical participant was female and Caucasian, with a median age of 21. Termination status was considered "premature" if a client missed a scheduled appointment and made a unilateral decision to discontinue care.

Results showed that the BTPI scales assessing lack of openness about new ways of thinking and behaving (CLM), tendency to channel psychological distress into physical symptoms (SOM), and perception of having limited social support were the most useful predictors of premature termination, along with the two composite measures (GPC and TDC). Higher scores were associated with premature termination for all of those scales, with the exception of the GPC, which was found to enhance the prediction of termination status by suppressing extraneous variance in the other measures. When faced with the failure of EXP (as a measure of low expectation of benefit from psychotherapy) to predict premature termination, the researchers implicated the restricted range of scores on the scale within their sample; they further hypothesized that individuals whose expectations of benefit were very low perhaps never became involved in counseling in the first place. The authors concluded that their findings supported the theory and rationale underlying the BTPI and also its ability to identify college students at increased risk of early termination of counseling. The following sections extend these clinical findings by examining BTPI trends within other client samples.

A Heterogeneous Sample of Psychotherapy Clients

In the Butcher et al. study (2000; see also Butcher 2005b) described previously in this chapter, the same group of 460 psychotherapy clients who completed the MMPI-2 also completed the BTPI. Within that sample, there were elevated scores on each of the BTPI scales for at least a portion of the participants (see Table 34.3).

For those of their clients who were still involved in psychotherapy 3 months after the initial data were collected, the study's therapist participants provided

Table 34.3. Percentage of individuals with elevated scale scores in a heterogeneous clinical sample.

Scale	Total Sample	Women	Men
INC	6	4	8
VIR	10	11	10
EXA	26	28	24
CLM	19	19	20
REL	16	13	19
SOM	28	34	21
EXP	3	3	3
NAR	3	3	2
ENV	27	31	21
DEP	37	41	31
ANX	28	35	19
A-O	13	13	13
A-I	18	23	11
PSY	14	14	12

Note: Based on data from Butcher (2005b).

follow-up information about treatment progress (see Butcher, 2005b). The psychotherapists addressed such factors as clients' ability to follow treatment plans, their ability to make changes, and their ability to attain treatment goals. The GPC scores of the clients were then examined, providing a way to capture depression, anxiety, and anger that could affect treatment progress and resistance to change (unfortunately, TDC scores were also not examined).

Clients who were rated by their therapists as being unable to set realistic treatment goals produced significantly higher GPC scores than clients who were rated as being able to set realistic treatment goals. There also were higher GPC scores among individuals who, according to their therapists, were unable to follow treatment plans, left treatment prematurely, did not have the type of interpersonal network necessary to provide emotional support during therapy, and were unable to think "psychologically" in therapy. In contrast, the GPC scores were significantly lower among clients who were rated as having reached maximum benefit from therapy, gained a great deal of insight and been able to make important changes, met most of the important treatment goals, left treatment feeling much improved, and received significant relief from their symptoms.

These data add support to the BTPI scales' usefulness in providing information about receptivity to psychological intervention. The therapist ratings

corroborated the fact that treatment attitudes reflected in BTPI profiles could correspond closely to treatment attitudes observed by therapists during psychotherapy.

A Homogeneous Sample of Individuals with Anxiety Disorders

BTPI score patterns were also examined in a more diagnostically uniform group of individuals who were all diagnosed with anxiety disorders (Perry, 1999; see Table 34.4). Each of that study's 105 participants (53 women and 52 men) had been diagnosed with at least one anxiety disorder (according to DSM-IV criteria) prior to the time of participation in the study, and each participant was either already engaged in or about to begin psychological treatment for the anxiety. In addition to the BTPI, each participant provided demographic and other background information. Therapists provided information about their clients' diagnoses and treatment and rated such treatment factors as the amount of progress that had been made at the point of study.

The most common primary anxiety disorder diagnosis among the participants was obsessive compulsive disorder (diagnosed in almost 30% of the participants), followed by panic disorder with agoraphobia and posttraumatic stress disorder (both of which were present in just over 25% of the sample). At least one other DSM-IV Axis I diagnosis was present in almost 45% of the sample as well, with

Table 34.4. Mean BTPI scale scores in a sample of individuals with anxiety disorder diagnoses.

Scale	Total Sample	Women	Men
INC	42.48	40.25	44.75
VIR	58.27	56.43	60.13
EXA	56.21	55.00	57.44
CLM	47.26	48.66	45.83
REL	54.83	55.66	53.98
SOM	62.08	58.36	65.87
EXP	45.51	43.86	47.21
NAR	45.93	46.60	45.25
ENV	54.96	55.09	54.83
DEP	59.12	58.79	59.46
ANX	62.67	61.75	63.60
A-O	54.92	55.32	54.52
A-I	54.76	54.53	55.00
PSY	55.62	54.09	57.17
GPC	60.46	59.97	60.98
TDC	54.48	53.32	55.65

Note: Based on data from Perry (1999).

depressive disorders occurring most commonly. In addition, just over 17% of participants were diagnosed with an Axis II disorder, most commonly personality disorder not otherwise specified. The typical participant was a Caucasian, never-married woman whose psychological treatment was cognitive-behavioral in nature. Approximately half of the sample was self-referred for treatment. The mean number of previous courses of treatment was roughly 3. At the time of the study, the participants had completed an average of 39 psychotherapy sessions in their current courses of care and had an average of 17 sessions remaining in the initial treatment "contracts." The mean Global Assessment of Functioning (GAF) rating was nearly 61.

For the sample as a whole, there were no scale scores at $T \geq 65$. However, there were a number of scores falling in the $T = 60$–64 range (see Table 34.4). Predictably, the highest scores were found on the ANX scale ($T = 62.67$). When the sample was broken down by gender, results showed that the men in the group produced a mean T-score of just over 65 on the SOM scale, indicating high likelihood of expressing psychological problems through physical symptoms. Male participants' scale scores were also significantly higher than those for female participants on EXP, SOM, ANX, PSY, and the TDC.

The participants' primary anxiety diagnoses were also more broadly categorized by type, in order to examine trends among individuals with significantly overlapping symptoms. Among the notable findings were elevations on Scales SOM, ANX, and PSY, as well as on the GPC, among the 17 individuals who were diagnosed with either posttraumatic stress disorder or acute stress disorder.

Elevations and high scores ($T = 60$–64) on the BTPI scales were found more frequently among individuals with comorbid Axis II disorders than among individuals without them. In the total sample, individuals with personality disorder diagnoses produced high scores on EXA, SOM, ANX, PSY, and the GPC, as well as an elevated score (i.e., $T \geq 65$) on DEP. This is in contrast to individuals without such additional diagnoses, for whom there were no elevated scores and high scores (i.e., $T = 60$–64) only on SOM and ANX. These findings indicate the potential for greater treatment resistance among individuals with Axis II disorders, in keeping with the interpersonal difficulties associated with such disorders.

If the BTPI scales are intended to point to potential treatment resistance issues among therapy clients, the data indicated a good deal of openness

to psychological intervention in this sample of individuals with anxiety disorders. The relative lack of score elevations suggested that the participants were not experiencing many of the difficulties tapped by the BTPI scales. Therefore, one could expect their treatments to be less vulnerable to treatment resistance difficulties. Indeed, most anxiety disorders are considered to be highly amenable to treatment, particularly with behavioral and cognitive-behavioral therapies (e.g., Barlow, 1990; Chambless & Gillis, 1993; Foa, 1996). Thus, the types of individuals with these disorders may be open to interventions in a way that promotes successful treatment.

The notion of the relatively high level of functioning among this sample also is supported by the mean GAF rating of nearly 61. According to the DSM-IV, a score of 61 is associated with "mild symptoms" or "some difficulty in social, occupational, or school functioning"; individuals are to be assigned a GAF score of at least 61 if they are "generally functioning pretty well" and have "some meaningful interpersonal relationships" (American Psychiatric Association, 1994, p. 32). Assuming that these study participants likely would have been rated lower at the onset of their treatments (as it is unlikely that highly functioning individuals would have sought or been referred for psychological treatment), it could be hypothesized that their openness to therapy facilitated their doing so well by the time of the study; however, this conclusion cannot be made definitively on the basis of the available data.

That fact notwithstanding, there were noteworthy trends in the data that bear on the issue of treatment resistance. As stated previously, analyses revealed that male participants' scale scores significantly exceeded those of female participants on EXP, SOM, ANX, PSY, and the TDC. Moreover, compared with the female participants, the men in the study were rated by their therapists as having made significantly less treatment progress to that point. Such data suggest the potential for greater treatment resistance among the men than among the women. The significantly higher scores on EXP and the TDC are of special interest, particularly when they are coupled with therapists' judgments of male clients' progress. It could be that the men had made less progress than the women in part because their expectations were lower, creating the potential for a self-fulfilling prophecy. Difficulties in making behavioral and attitudinal changes also may have been influenced by qualities (such as somatization of psychological problems, unusual thinking) that impede the process of making meaningful and systematic treatment progress.

The data also highlight another factor in potential male–female discrepancies in openness to change. There were several significant negative correlations between the male participants' estimated number of supportive individuals in their lives (collected as part of the background information on them) and their scores on BTPI scales and composites. That is, having fewer people on whom they felt that they could rely for emotional support was associated with higher BTPI scores among the men. Interestingly, this same relationship was not found among female participants, as the women's data did not indicate significant associations between the quantity of their social supports and their BTPI scores. Although the number of one's relationships alone does not tell the whole story (as it does not speak about the quality of those relationships), these data do underscore how important to treatment it might be for individuals to perceive that they have meaningful interpersonal relationships. Findings from previous studies support the notion that the subjective experience of support has implications for differential treatment response (Beutler et al., 1999).

Each of the aforementioned studies highlights the potential usefulness of gauging resistance-related factors using objective assessment methods. The case outlined in the following section provides an example to illustrate the practical applications of the process.

Case Example
Presenting Complaint and Background Information

Lisa was a 54-year-old, Caucasian, divorced, employed high school graduate who was receiving mental health services in an outpatient clinic. She was referred for psychological evaluation by a social worker who was providing psychotherapy services and by a treating psychiatrist, with a goal of assisting them in revising Lisa's current treatment plan. Lisa had been meeting with both providers for the previous year, carrying a primary diagnosis of recurrent major depressive disorder and a secondary diagnosis of pathological gambling. Although she had experienced some treatment gains (including limited reduction in depressive symptoms and brief periods of abstinence from gambling) within the first 6 months, both she and her treatment providers had been frustrated by her overall lack of progress. Just prior to the evaluation, she had identified increased

distress about multiple health issues, including joint pain and obstructive sleep apnea. She had begun describing herself as a "medical disaster." At the time of the evaluation, her identified goals for psychotherapy were to "get a better sense" of herself, to be better able to recognize her accomplishments, and to "be able to move ahead in life." She had a long-standing history of feeling inadequate and isolated, in part due to having grown up in a remote area and having had few supportive role models as a child. She reported having a limited support network in her adult years as well. As part of an evaluation that included a clinical interview, Lisa completed the MMPI-2 and BTPI.

MMPI-2 RESULTS

Lisa's raw CS score was 0, indicating that she had responded to all inventory items and had not declined to answer any of them (Table 34.5). However, her score on the L scale suggested that she had not responded to the items in a fully candid way. Her L score ($T = 71$) indicated that she had presented herself in an unrealistically virtuous fashion and had claimed to have fewer negative qualities than most people have. Elevated scores on L are very likely to reduce respondents' scores on the MMPI-2 clinical scales to an artificial degree, making the individuals appear to be better psychologically adjusted than is actually true (Graham, 2006). Nonetheless, Lisa also seemed to have exaggerated her responses to items on the latter portion of the inventory ($T_{FB} = 93$). She may have responded to those items carelessly, randomly, or with the intention of embellishing her problems. As a result, her scores on the MMPI-2 content scales (including $T_{TRT} = 69$) were not interpreted.

Lisa did produce elevations on several MMPI-2 clinical scales, with the highest scores on D ($T = 94$) and Pt ($T = 90$). She also produced elevations on Pa ($T = 81$), Hy ($T = 77$), Sc ($T = 72$), and Hs ($T = 71$). Overall, the clinical picture was of someone who was in intense psychological distress and was experiencing major problems with depression and anxiety. Descriptors associated with the profile included being high-strung, insecure, unconfident, and incapable in the face of problems. The profile was also associated with passivity and dependency in relationships, a tendency to blame oneself for interpersonal problems, and avoidance of confrontation.

BTPI RESULTS

Consistent with her pattern in the latter portion of the MMPI-2, Lisa appeared to have over-reported symptoms and problems on the BTPI ($T_{EXA} = 67$).

Table 34.5. MMPI-2 Validity, clinical, and content scale T scores for Lisa.

Name	Scale elevation (T-score)
Validity Scales/Indexes	
? (Cannot Say Score)	0
VRIN (Inconsistency)	38
TRIN (Inconsistency)	58T
F (Infrequency)	65
F(B) (Infrequency, Back)	93
F(p) (Infrequency-Psychopathology)	41
L (Lie)	71
K (Defensiveness)	46
S (Superlative Self-Presentation)	43
Clinical Scales	
Hs (Hypochondrasias)	71
D (Depression)	94
Hy (Hysteria)	77
Pd (Psychopathic Deviation)	60
Mf (Masculinity-Femininity)	45
Pa (Paranoia)	81
Pt (Psychasthenia)	90
Sc (Schizophrenia)	72
Ma (Hypomania)	53
Si (Social Introversion-Extraversion)	75
Content Scales	
ANX (Anxiety)	81
FRS (Fears)	72
OBS (Obsessiveness)	71
DEP (Depression)	78
HEA (Health Concerns)	68
BIZ (Bizarre Mentation)	52
ANG (Anger Control Problems)	56
CYN (Cynicism)	53
ASP (AntiSocial Personality)	47
TPA (Type-A Behavior)	50
LSE (Low Self Esteem)	86
SOD (Social Distrust)	80
FAM (Family Problems)	42
WRK (Work Adjustment Problems)	71
TRT (Treatment Planning)	69

She had also responded to the BTPI items in a manner suggesting the she was not receptive to new ideas or suggestions from others, including those about the significance of her behavior ($T_{CLM} = 69$).

Lisa's treatment issues scales showed that she was very likely to channel emotional distress into physical symptoms ($T_{SOM} = 71$). Her profile was associated with avoidance of dealing directly with emotional conflict. It was also indicative of such intense worry about physical health that substantial reduction in activity level could result. The treatment issues pattern was suggestive of poor self-concept and low self-esteem as well.

Lisa's current symptoms scales were notable primarily for high scores on A-I ($T = 87$) and ANX ($T = 83$). Her profile was suggestive of turning one's anger inward and being unreasonably self-punishing.

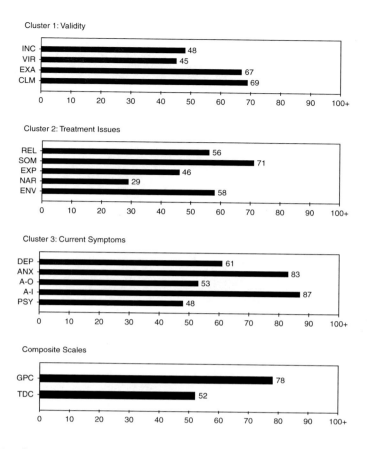

Cluster 1: Validity

INC	48
VIR	45
EXA	67
CLM	69

Cluster 2: Treatment Issues

REL	56
SOM	71
EXP	46
NAR	29
ENV	58

Cluster 3: Current Symptoms

DEP	61
ANX	83
A-O	53
A-I	87
PSY	48

Composite Scales

GPC	78
TDC	52

Fig. 34.1 Lisa's Scale and composite T-scores on the BTPI. Reproduced by permission

It also suggested high likelihood of interpersonal problems caused by one's taking a subservient role in relationships. The profile was further indicative of anxiety, worry, and indecision that could interfere with daily functioning.

INDICATIONS OF RESISTANCE AND TREATMENT IMPLICATIONS

Lisa's psychological evaluation results provided several pieces of helpful information bearing on her potential to demonstrate resistance in working with her care providers. The findings from both the MMPI-2 and BTPI suggested reluctance to disclose personal information, whether due to unwillingness to be cooperative, intentional distortion of her problems, lack of psychological sophistication, or other factors. Therefore, it would likely be hard at times for Lisa to talk openly with her providers, particularly about subjects that she regarded as highly sensitive. The evaluation results also indicated that she could be quite unreceptive to new ways of thinking. Such an attitude could interfere significantly with her willingness to hear

and accept others' suggestions and interpretations. Her tendency to channel psychological stress into physical symptoms might be especially hard for her to acknowledge and address in working with her therapist.

Computerized BTPI Report for Lisa (Reproduced with permission of MHS)
VALIDITY OF THE REPORT

Most patients in psychological treatment are more open than Lisa in their responses to the BTPI items. Only 8% of clients in the Minnesota Psychotherapy Assessment Project attained peak CLM T-scores >64. Figure 34.1 contains Lisa's computer-generated BTPI report.

She has responded to the BTPI in a manner that suggests she is generally closed to new ideas or suggestions from others as to possible meanings of her behavior. She endorses content that suggests she is not very open to new ways of thinking. It is likely that her lack of openness will influence her behavior in psychological therapy. She is not likely to be very receptive to psychological interpretation about her behavior and may resent pressure on her to consider alternatives to her comfortable ways of behaving. The therapist should be aware of the need for confronting her lack of openness or defensiveness if it is observed in the treatment process.

Other response attitudes she showed on the BTPI items should be evaluated further in order to more fully understand potential problems with her treatment process.

She has endorsed a number of extreme items on the BTPI and claims to be experiencing a great deal of symptoms and attitudes that are unlikely to be endorsed by most people. The individual's current situation should be evaluated to determine the reason(s) for the exaggerated symptom endorsement.

Other response attitudes she showed on the BTPI items should be evaluated further in order to more fully understand potential problems with her treatment attitudes.

She has endorsed a number of extreme items on the BTPI and claims to be experiencing a great deal of symptoms and attitudes that are unlikely to be endorsed by most people. The individual's current situation should be evaluated to determine the reason(s) for the exaggerated symptom endorsement.

TREATMENT ISSUES

Lisa has attained a very high score on the SOM scale, suggesting that she is experiencing a considerable amount of physical distress at this time. She seems to feel that her problems are based on physical causes, and she does not like to deal with emotional conflict in a direct way. She tends to channel emotional conflict into physical symptoms such as headache, pain, or stomach distress. Moreover, she worries about her health to such an extent that she is reducing her activities substantially. She tends to view herself as tired and is worried that her health is not better.

The use of somatic defenses and the development of physical problems under psychological conflict are prominent mechanisms in outpatient therapy. Over a quarter (28%) of the clients in the Minnesota Psychotherapy Assessment Project produced high scores (T > 64) on the SOM scale. In addition, SOM led other Cluster 2 scales as the most frequent peak score (with 19% of the clients having a peak SOM T-score >64).

CURRENT SYMPTOMS

Lisa appears to have very low self-esteem and negative views about her ability to function in many situations. She usually takes a subservient role in interpersonal situations and readily takes blame for problems she has had no part in originating in order to placate other, more dominant persons. She turns anger inward and appears to punish herself unreasonably at times. A moderate percentage of outpatient psychotherapy clients in the Minnesota Psychotherapy Assessment Project (18%) obtained A-I T-scores >64. However, only 8% of these had A-I as the peak current symptom scale score, with T > 64.

In addition, she has also reported other psychological symptoms on the BTPI items that need to be taken into consideration in evaluating her mood state. She also appears to be very anxious at this time. She is reporting great difficulty as a result of her tension, fearfulness, and inability to concentrate effectively. She seems to worry even over small matters to the point that she cannot seem to sit still. Her daily functioning is severely impaired because of her worries and an inability to make decisions.

TREATMENT PLANNING

Her somatization defenses need to be a central focus in early treatment sessions. Therapists should be aware of her potential difficulty to think psychologically in treatment sessions.

There is some possibility that she is experiencing low self-esteem, which could impact her functioning in interpersonal contexts.

Extremely negative self-views were noted in her self-appraisal. Treatment planning should incorporate strategies designed to increase her self-esteem and reduce her tendency to view herself in such a negative light. The practitioner might find it valuable in treatment sessions to be aware of her extreme tendency to accept blame in situations for which the client bears no responsibility.

The therapist needs to keep in mind that she appears to be prone to react to stressful situations with catastrophic reactions.

PROGRESS MONITORING

Lisa obtained a GPC T-score of 78. She has endorsed a broad range of mental health symptoms on the BTPI. Her elevated GPC index score indicates that she acknowledged a number of mental health symptoms that require attention in psychological treatment. For a statistically significant change, based on a 90% confidence interval, a subsequent GPC T-score must be above 84 or below 72.

Lisa obtained a TDC T-score of 52. Overall, her TDC index score is well within the normal range indicating that she has not acknowledged many of the personality-based symptoms addressed by the BTPI to assess difficult treatment relationships. For a statistically significant change, based on a 90% confidence interval, a subsequent TDC T-score must be above 59 or below 45.

Use of Testing Results by Lisa's Providers

Lisa's scores on the BTPI treatment issues scales of ENV (T = 58) and EXP (T = 46) were in the average range. These suggested room for optimism, as Lisa appeared to view her social environment as at least minimally supportive and to have some hope about experiencing benefit on the basis of her providers' interventions. In addition, her average-range score on REL (T = 56) suggested that she had a basic capacity to form therapeutic relationships with both of her care providers. Nevertheless, her current symptoms profile was associated with taking a subservient role in relationships, readily taking the blame for problems that were not of her doing, and punishing herself unreasonably at times. The multiple indications of poor self-concept suggested that Lisa was vulnerable to feeling easily criticized and hurt. All of these factors had the potential to affect her relationships with her providers and to hinder her progress in working with them. Her providers therefore would need to be particularly sensitive in communicating with her, if they wished to maintain momentum in moving toward the treatment goals. Because Lisa might be unlikely to speak up for herself, even when others were taking advantage of her, she likely would need considerable assistance with assertiveness training. Such skills would have the potential not only to help her stand up to potentially abusive individuals, but also to communicate her needs more openly to her care providers.

One of the treatment targets identified by Lisa and her therapist was behavioral activation, which had been suggested in order as a means of managing Lisa's depression. However, prior to the assessment, Lisa's therapist had been frustrated by Lisa's frequent failure to complete related homework assignments and inability to identify plausible explanations for her behavior. According to the evaluation findings, Lisa's experience of worse physical symptoms during times of stress and her overall concerns about her physical functioning were potential culprits.

Interestingly, in the face of feedback about the MMPI-2's and BTPI's indications that she was closed-minded, Lisa had responded, "That's me!" She stated that she had not previously acknowledged this quality openly in working with her therapist and

may not have fully realized its impact prior to the time of the assessment. She expressed hope that psychotherapy could assist her in identifying new ways of thinking and behaving. However, she was at a loss as to how to begin working toward these goals. Providing feedback about the evaluation results opened the door to discussing such issues with her. Finn's therapeutic model of assessment (e.g., Finn & Kamphuis, 2006; Finn & Tonsager, 1992, 1997) and concept of "assessment therapy" (Finn & Martin, 1997) were useful ones in this instance, promoting discussion of psychological assessment information with Lisa in a manner encouraging behavioral change. Using this approach, the evaluation not only provided a means of highlighting the potential "resistance" issues affecting Lisa's care, but it also created opportunities for further discussions of these factors among Lisa and her care providers.

Conclusions

According to Frank and Frank (1991, p. 167):

> The personal qualities and attitudes that patients bring to psychotherapy seem to have a greater effect on their response to therapy than does the technique their therapist uses. Patients' own world-views or personal attributes predispose them to accept some therapeutic conceptualizations and procedures more readily than others.

As such, ascertaining the nature of those "qualities and attitudes" is clearly important in determining who is and who is not likely to benefit from psychological interventions at a given time. Gaining some understanding of these factors helps both clients and therapists to recognize why treatment may not be progressing in the manner that they (and those who are funding their psychological services) would like. It also has implications for how resources are allocated and how decisions are made with regard to the length of psychotherapy "contracts" and courses of care.

As the data outlined in this chapter demonstrate, there is great potential usefulness in solidly understanding how and why "resistance" is manifested by therapy clients. To the extent that objective measures of treatment resistance factors, including the MMPI-2 and the BTPI, can help to shed light on resistance-related difficulties, it is advisable to employ them at the earliest stages of the therapy. They also can and should be repeated as appropriate throughout the course of treatment. In this way, their results can assist clients and therapists in anticipating problems and in reacting to them, such that the two can deviate from prescribed therapy plans in order to address resistance issues head on.

References

American Psychiatric Association. (1994). *Diagnostic and statistical manual of mental disorders* (4th ed.). Washington, DC: Author.

Barlow, D. H. (1990). Long-term outcome for patients with panic disorder treated with cognitive-behavioral therapy. *Journal of Clinical Psychiatry, 51*, 17–23.

Barron, F. (1953). An ego strength scale which predicts response to psychotherapy. *Journal of Consulting Psychology, 17*, 327–333.

Ben-Porath, Y. S. (1997). Use of personality assessment instruments in empirically guided treatment planning. *Psychological Assessment, 9*, 361–367.

Beutler, L. E., Engle, D., Mohr, D., Daldrup, R. J., Bergan, J., Meredith, K., et al. (1991). Predictors of differential and self-directed psychotherapeutic procedures. *Journal of Consulting and Clinical Psychology, 59*, 333–340.

Beutler, L. E., Goodrich, G., Fisher, D., & Williams, O. B. (1999). Use of psychological tests/instruments for treatment planning. In M. E. Maruish (Ed.), *The use of psychological testing for treatment planning and outcomes assessment* (2nd ed., pp. 81–113). Mahwah, NJ: Erlbaum.

Brody, S. (1994). Traditional ideology, stress, and psychotherapy use. *Journal of Psychology, 128*, 5–13.

Butcher, J. N. (1990). *The MMPI-2 in psychological treatment.* New York: Oxford University Press.

Butcher, J. N. (2005a). *MMPI-2: A beginner's guide* (2nd ed.). Washington DC: American Psychological Association.

Butcher, J. N. (2005b). *Butcher Treatment Planning Inventory (BTPI): Technical manual.* Toronto, ON: Multi-Health Systems.

Butcher, J. N., Cabiya, J., Lucio, E. M., & Garrido, M. (2007). *Assessing Hispanic clients using the MMPI-2 and MMPI-A.* Washington, DC: American Psychological Association.

Butcher, J. N., & Perry, J. N. (2008). *Personality assessment in psychological treatment: Use of the MMPI-2 and BTPI.* New York: Oxford University Press.

Butcher, J. N., Rouse, S. V., & Perry, J. N. (1998). Assessing resistance to psychological treatment. *Measurement and Evaluation in Counseling and Development, 31*, 95–108.

Butcher, J. N., Rouse, S. V., & Perry, J. N. (2000). Empirical description of psychopathology in therapy clients: Correlates of the MMPI-2 scales. In J. N. Butcher (Ed.), *Basic sources on the MMPI-2* (pp. 487–500). Minneapolis, MN: University of Minnesota Press.

Butcher, J. N., & Williams, C. L. (2000). *Essentials of MMPI-2 and MMPI-A interpretation* (2nd ed.). Minneapolis, MN: University of Minnesota Press.

Castro, J. (1993, May 31). What price mental health? *Time,* 59–60.

Chambless, D. L., & Gillis, M. M. (1993). Cognitive therapy of anxiety disorders. *Journal of Consulting and Clinical Psychology, 61*, 248–260.

Cheatham, H. E., Shelton, T. O., & Ray, W. (1987). Race, sex, causal attribution, and help-seeking behavior. *Journal of College Student Personnel, 26*, 559–568.

Corey, G. (1991). *Theory and practice of counseling and psychotherapy* (4th ed.). Pacific Grove, CA: Brooks/Cole.

Cowen, E. L. (1982). Help is where you find it: Four informal helping groups. *American Psychologist, 37*, 385–395.

Craig, R. J., & Olson, R. E. (2003). Predicting the outcome of methadone maintenance treatment with the negative treatment indicators content scale from the MMPI-2. *Psychological Reports, 93*, 1056–1058.

Dowd, E. T., Milne, C. R., & Wise, S. L. (1991). The therapeutic reactance scale: A measure of psychological reactance. *Journal of Counseling and Development, 69*, 541–545.

Foa, E. B. (1996). The efficacy of behavioral therapy with obsessive-compulsives. *The Clinical Psychologist, 49*, 19–22.

Finn, S. E., & Kamphuis, J. H. (2006). Therapeutic assessment with the MMPI-2. In J. N. Butcher (Ed.), *MMPI-2: The practitioner's handbook* (pp. 165–191). Washington, DC: American Psychological Association.

Finn, S. E., & Martin, H. (1997). Therapeutic assessment with the MMPI-2 in managed health care. In J. N. Butcher (Ed.), *Personality assessment in managed health care: Using the MMPI-2 in treatment planning* (pp. 131–152). New York: Oxford University Press.

Finn, S. E., & Tonsager, M. E. (1992). Therapeutic effects of providing MMPI-2 test feedback to college students awaiting therapy. *Psychological assessment, 4*, 278–287.

Finn, S. E., & Tonsager, M. E. (1997). Information-gathering and therapeutic models of assessment: Complementary paradigms. *Psychological Assessment, 9*, 374–385.

Fisher, D., Beutler, L. E., & Williams, O. B. (1999). Making assessment relevant to treatment planning: The STS Clinician Rating Form. *Journal of Clinical Psychology, 55*, 825–842.

Frank, J. D., & Frank, J. B. (1991). *Persuasion and healing: A comparative study of psychotherapy* (3rd ed.). Baltimore, MD: Johns Hopkins University Press.

Freud, S. (1973). *A general introduction to psychoanalysis* (25th printing). New York: Pocket Books.

Furnham, A., & Wardley, Z. (1990). Lay theories of psychotherapy: I. Attitudes toward, and beliefs about, psychotherapy and therapists. *Journal of Clinical Psychology, 46*, 878–890.

Garfield, S. L. (1994). Research on client variables in psychotherapy. In S. L. Garfield & A. E. Bergen (Eds.), *Handbook of psychotherapy and behavior change* (4th ed., pp. 190–228). New York: John Wiley & Sons.

Garfield, S. L. (1995). *Psychotherapy: An eclectic-integrative approach* (2nd ed.). New York: John Wiley & Sons.

Graham, J. R. (2006). *MMPI-2: Assessing personality and psychopathology.* New York: Oxford University Press.

Greene, R. L., & Clopton, J. R. (1999). Minnesota Multiphasic Personality Inventory-2 (MMPI-2). In M. E. Maruish (Ed.), *The use of psychological testing for treatment planning and outcomes assessment* (2nd ed., pp. 1023–1049). Mahwah, NJ: Erlbaum.

Groth-Marnat, G. (1999). Current status and future directions of psychological assessment: Introduction. *Journal of Clinical Psychology, 55*, 781–785.

Hatchett, G. T., Han, K., & Cooker, P. G. (2002). Predicting premature termination from counseling using the Butcher Treatment Planning Inventory. *Assessment, 9*, 156–163.

Hersen, M., & Ammerman, R. T. (Eds.) (1994). *Handbook of prescriptive treatment for adults.* New York: Plenum.

Johnson, M. E. (1988). Influences of gender and sex role orientation on help-seeking attitudes. *Journal of Psychology, 122*, 237–241.

Noonan, J. R. (1973). A follow-up of pre-therapy dropouts. *Journal of Community Psychology, 1,* 43–45.

Norcross, J. C., & Beutler, L. E. (1997). Determining the therapeutic relationship of choice in brief therapy. In J. N. Butcher (Ed.), *Objective psychological assessment in managed health care: A practitioner's guide* (pp. 42–60). New York: Oxford University Press.

Perry, J. N. (1999). Assessment of psychological treatment planning issues in clients with anxiety disorders (Unpublished doctoral dissertation), University of Minnesota, Minneapolis, MN.

Perry, J. N., & Butcher, J. N. (1999). Butcher Treatment Planning Inventory (BTPI): An objective guide to treatment planning. In M. E. Maruish (Ed.), *The use of psychological testing for treatment planning and outcomes assessment* (2nd ed., pp. 1157–1171). Mahwah, NJ: Erlbaum.

Prochaska, J. O., Velicer, W. F., DiClemente, C. C., & Fava, J. (1988). Measuring process of chance: Applications to the cessation of smoking. *Journal of Consulting and Clinical Psychology, 56,* 520–528.

Raynes, A. E., & Warren, G. (1971). Some distinguishing features of patients failing to attend a psychiatric clinic after referral. *American Journal of Orthopsychiatry, 41,* 581–589.

Regier, D. A., Boyd, J. H., Burke, J. D., Rae, D. S., Myers, J. K., Kramer, M., et al. (1993). One-month prevalence of mental disorders in the United States and sociodemographic characteristics: The Epidemiological Catchment Area study. *Acta Psychiatrica Scandinavica, 88,* 35–47.

Robertson, J. M., & Fitzgerald, L. F. (1992). Overcoming the masculine mystique: Preferences for alternative forms of assistance among men who avoid counseling. *Journal of Counseling Psychology, 39,* 240–246.

Rosenthal, D., & Frank, J. D. (1958). Psychotherapy and the placebo effect. *Psychological Bulletin, 53,* 294–302.

Ryan, W. (1969). *Distress in the city.* Cleveland, OH: Press of Case Western Reserve University.

Writing Clinical Reports

Raymond L. Ownby

Abstract

Psychological assessment is a key aspect of professional practice and one that distinguishes psychology from other disciplines. Reporting the results of assessments is thus an important professional function but surveys suggest that many consumers of reports are dissatisfied. This chapter reviews problems with reports and discusses the expository process model. This model uses insights from basic psycholinguistic research to inform reporting practices.

Keywords: psychological reports, psycholinguistics, given-new contract, expository process model, computer-based assessment

Introduction

In 1997, Ownby noted that much of any review on report writing in psychology of necessity had to focus on discussion of expert opinion because little empirical research on reports existed (Ownby, 1997). The situation has changed little in the intervening time, although investigations continue to appear sporadically. Empirical investigations are relatively rare. More common are papers that review consumer's complaints about reports and, based on the authors' opinions, make recommendations on how to write reports. With the rise of interest in empirically supported treatments in psychology (Chambless & Hollon, 1998) and evidence-based practice in medicine (Guyatt, Cairns, & Churchill, 1992), the absence of empirical research to guide clinical practice is brought into even sharper focus. The situation, however, is unsurprising since almost any review of any clinical practice in psychology concludes that recommendations can only be made tentatively because of the absence of solid research on the topic. In other fields of endeavor, practitioners have often drawn on research in related areas or on basic science research to guide their clinical practice. Psychologists have been remiss in this approach, even though a large body of research

and practice in such related fields as psycholinguistics, reading, and technical writing exists. It is unfortunate that the insular view promoted within psychological specialties is not more often supplemented by insights from other related areas.

In the past, Ownby (1997) suggested that the application of basic psycholinguistic concepts, especially the concept of the given-new contract in discourse comprehension, would promote hypothesis-driven research in report writing and provide an empirical basis for practice. Basic science research on discourse comprehension can provide better guidance on how to write reports that readers can understand than merely continuing to follow expert recommendations. In this chapter, this suggestion will be explained and expanded as a basis for making specific recommendations on how to present results of psychological assessments in written reports.

The Current Situation

Psychological assessment is an endeavor in which psychologists apply highly technical and usually well-researched evaluation techniques to understand individuals' behavioral and cognitive characteristics. The utility of such an assessment, however, inheres not so much in the completion of the assessment procedures as in the communication of the assessment results to others. The demands of the task, especially for psychologists in training, dominate the assessor's experience. The mechanics of performing a standardized administration, for example, are seen as the proper focus of educational efforts. Conceptually integrating the results of diverse assessment measures and communicating them in a useful way to a reader, while perhaps acknowledged as part of the task, are given less attention. This orientation is revealed in assessment textbooks, which devote most of their chapters to domain-specific assessment techniques but perhaps one to the arguably more cognitively complex task of taking assessment data and integrating them into a coherent narrative account of the reason for the assessment, its results, and what should be done about them. While understandable in the context of the history of psychology and the qualifications of textbook writers (who are generally senior psychologists with extensive experience), the situation inevitably gives rise to a test-administration orientation when what is arguably needed is a communication orientation. The key problem in assessment is to communicate the information obtained in a useful way, but an early focus during training on the mechanics of test administration, scoring, and interpretation is not followed by a later focus on communicating the information thus derived in ways that are helpful.

Report writers can readily find advice on how to write reports. One common piece of advice is to "write clearly." While it's hard to argue with this, it's not clear how useful this advice is to novice or troubled report writers. It's akin to saying "Feel better!" to an anxious or depressed individual. It's not that it's a bad idea, but the recommendation lacks specificity and does not provide clear guidance about a course of action to remedy a problem. Far more useful would be help with a concrete set of procedures that can be followed in order to feel better, or in the case of reports, to write better. Exhortation to do good things leaves the individual who makes the recommendations personally satisfied and gives the impression that something important has been communicated, but may leave the reader with little concrete advice with which to guide his or her behavior. Writers thus need concrete strategies for writing reports, as well as to tailor reports to specific purposes, contexts, and readers, rather than exhortations to write clearly or succinctly. Impediments to report readability are readily identified (e.g., Harvey, 2006), but writers' recommended remedies are often unintentionally vague or difficult to implement.

A failure to focus on conceptualization and communication in graduate coursework can be rationalized as the work of clinical practica and internships, but this is analogous to teaching someone to ski on one occasion and asking them to actually face a slope months or years later. The situation merits examination since habits acquired early in one's career are likely to persist. Writing the clinical report is thus much more than recording results of test administration, and the higher-level cognitive skills required for integrating and communicating results deserve more explicit attention. The remainder of this chapter provides a guide by which psychologists can improve their ability to conceptualize and communicate results of their psychological assessments.

Problems in Psychological Reports

An area in which empirical data exist on reports concerns the complaints voiced by consumer of reports. Readers of reports consistently complain that writers use jargon, write unclearly, and do not provide specific report elements that are often requested in certain report contexts or by certain report consumers (Groth-Marnat & Horvath, 2006).

Psycholinguistic Concepts

Although little noticed by psychologists writing about how to write reports, a substantial body of research exists on how to make writing easier for the reader to understand (Gopen & Swan, 1990). In the absence of specific empirical research on clinical report writing, concepts from the more general field of technical writing and the basic science study of discourse comprehension processes in psycholinguistics may help writers communicate more effectively. Three concepts from psycholinguistics are particularly relevant to writing clinical reports: (a) the given-new contract, (b) coherence, and (c) cohesion.

The *given-new contract* refers to a core principle in discourse comprehension that states that to effectively communicate one tells the listener or reader something new about something he or she already knows about. This means that the person initiating the communication must establish common ground with the listener or reader before going forward with new information, and implies that the person who initiates communication must have some idea of what the message's intended recipient already knows. In writing reports, this means that to effectively communicate the writer of a report must have a fairly good idea of what his reader already knows about the likely substance of the assessment. As will be discussed below, this means that the writer must be able to link common terms used to describe abilities and personality (e.g., "intelligence," "visuospatial skills," "dependence," or "anxiety") to concrete behavioral descriptions or specific test scores. Following recommendations drawn from the given-new contract means that the writer must clearly establish what he or she is writing about before relating new information about the client assessed.

Coherence is a property of a written report that conveys to the reader a sense that statements are conceptually related to one another and the account of the assessment makes sense. The ideas, concepts, interpretations, and recommendations should all have clear conceptual links in order to leave the reader with the impression that all the elements discussed in the report are relevant and help lead the reader to understanding the author's interpretation and recommendations.

Cohesion is a property of discourse in which individual elements such as clauses and paragraphs are logically related or linked. While coherence may be thought of as a property in which ideas are logically related, cohesion refers to the mechanical linking of ideas through grammatical devices such as coordination and subordination. *Coordination*, for example, is a grammatical device that allows the writer to link two distinct ideas that might be able to stand alone. This is often accomplished with words called conjunctions ("and," "but," "therefore"): *The client arrived at the office promptly and did not fatigue excessively during the course of the assessment.* Both clauses, or major sections, of this sentence can stand separately. They are linked in a coordinate fashion with the word "and." Subordination is another grammatical device that allows the author to links clauses in instances in which one of the clauses would not stand independently: *After completing the MMPI-2, the client insisted on returning home for the day.* The clause "After completing the MMPI-2" would not make sense by itself, nor is it a complete sentence. It is grammatically as well as conceptually linked to the clause that follows it. Employed properly, these devices allow the author of a report give an account of the assessment in which key ideas are presented in a way that makes the reader feel as though the ideas fit together.

The Purpose of Reports

Elsewhere it has been argued that any attempt to empirically examine psychological reports requires a definition of the purpose of reports (Ownby, 1997).

The following statement is a postulate that will allow an ongoing evaluation of what makes reports effective:

> The purpose of psychological reports is to communicate the results of an evaluation in a way that is credible and persuasive.

Here, credible means that after reading a statement or a report, the reader would say, if asked, that he or she believes the assertion it contains. Credibility can be established by referencing assertions to basic assessment data that the reader is likely to accept based on the psychologist's basic training in administering assessment tools. For example, a statement that the patient is depressed might be supported by reference to an elevation on Scale 2 of the Minnesota Multiphasic Personality Inventory-2 (MMPI-2), to a score on a self-report measure such as the Beck Depression Inventory, or to behavioral observations of psychomotor slowing or sad affect. Although the reader may be skeptical of or even explicitly disagree with the writer's conclusions, credibility demands that raw assessment data be used to substantiate assertions that are one step removed from raw data but employ intermediate explanatory concepts such as "depression" (see the next section for more on these explanatory concepts).

Persuasive means that after reading a statement or a report, the reader would be more likely to follow a recommended course of action. Persuasive statements must be based in credible data but the recommendations for behavior contained in them must also be logically linked to the credible data. A recommendation for psychotherapy for depression, for example, might follow from a credible conclusion that a patient is depressed, but would be more persuasive if accompanied by data showing that the client or patient is interested in obtaining psychotherapy and that he or she is likely to benefit from it. Unless the report is only written for archival purposes (and thus is merely a clerical exercise), the writer should give the reader guidance not only on the assessment data but also on the implications of those data.

The idea that psychological reports and the statements, conclusions, and recommendations they contain should be both credible and persuasive is a postulate. In the context of this chapter, this means that it is an assertion that is taken as basic, without other empirical support. A brief consideration of the role that reports play will for most readers support a conclusion that this postulate is reasonable. It does not exclude the possibility that reports may have other purposes as well. Reports in organizational contexts such as the legal system or the schools may serve the purpose of documenting that required procedures have been followed, for example, and may provide a record of assessment results useful in future encounters with the client or patient.

Jargon versus Middle-Level Constructs

Virtually every author who has researched or written about problems with reports notes that the use of jargon limits the effectiveness of reports. Perhaps the obvious solution to the problem is to avoid jargon. This is obvious, yes, but ultimately uninformative for report writers as it avoids a definition of jargon and leaves the writer without clear alternatives for explaining assessment results. Appelbaum (1970) reviewed the process of writing psychological reports and suggested that writers may use *middle-level constructs* to link basic assessment data such as test scores and behavioral observations to broader interpretive hypotheses. Examples of these middle-level constructs are commonlyused terms such as "intellectual abilities," "memory," "anxiety," or "narcissism." An analysis of reports shows that these middle-level constructs are probably precisely the same words that others criticize. Some writers' middle-level constructs are thus readers' jargon.

Further consideration of this issue shows that readers may not object so much to the terms themselves but to the fact that they do not know what they mean. If psychologists find middle-level constructs useful in interpreting assessments, but readers do not understand them, what is the report writer to do? Ownby (1997) suggests a simple but effective remedy: make sure that all middle-level constructs are linked to data. This practice will help ensure that the reader knows what the writer is trying to communicate and will therefore improve the credibility and persuasiveness of the report.

Expository Process Model

The expository process model (EPM) is a simple conceptual tool that links psycholinguistic concepts and the postulated purpose of reports to concrete strategies for writing them. A more extensive discussion is available in Ownby (1997). The EPM takes research on problems on reports into account and provides a solution that can guide report writing at micro (i.e., how to write sentences) to macro (i.e., how to organize the report) levels.

The key postulate of the EPM is:

Every statement in a psychological report must be linked to information shared by the reader and the writer (a "given"); if not, the statement must be converted into given information through reference to concrete data such as behavioral observations or specific test scores.

The EPM is not so much new as it is a codification of the intuitions of others. As long ago as 1960, Klopfer (1960) for example argued that rather than saying a person was "narcissistic," the writer should say something such as, "The patient is so intensely preoccupied with himself that he finds it very difficult to become interested in other people." While the reader might not understand what the writer meant by the term "narcissistic" and thus complain about the author's use of jargon, if the term is made into a shared referent by linking it to a behavioral description the problem of jargon is removed. Appelbaum (1970) also argued some time ago that the problem with jargon in reports was that writers used "middle-level constructs" whose meanings were not clear to the reader. These authors thus argue that clarity in reporting at this very basic level requires referencing assessment-relevant abstractions, such as "narcissism" or "visuospatial abilities" to data that will ensure that the reader understands them. Failing to take the reader's understanding of key psychological constructs, however familiar to the writer, will lead to lack of comprehension of what the writer intends.

The Sentence

As just illustrated, a key problem at the sentence level of report is jargon. Jargon is likely to be the pejorative term readers assign to middle-level constructs they don't understand. "Executive functions," for example, may be jargon to some readers (and worse, it may not seem unclear to some readers until they stop and think about what "executive" really means), but a concrete reference to "the ability to coordinate two problem-solving processes at one time" is much less likely to be labeled jargon. Concepts about personality should be used judiciously as well, especially since some concepts are in common use in everyday language, such as "paranoid" and "schizophrenic." As noted above, even a multifaceted concept such as "narcissism" can be rendered more intelligible by explaining it in simple terms.

Linking this analysis of middle-level constructs with the requirements of the given-new contract leads to a concrete formula for writing sentences in reports. The sentence should refer to given information (the client, a specific measure, or previously discussed ideas) and provide new information about the given. The new information will often be expressed in the form of an evaluation of a middle-level construct, such as "*severe* depression," or "*low* self-esteem." At the sentence level, the middle-level construct must be linked to observable data or a concrete explanation.

The Paragraph

The EPM also provides guidance about paragraph structure as well. Many writers have been taught that each paragraph should contain a "topic sentence" that states the main idea of the paragraph. Other sentences in that paragraph should elaborate upon or substantiate whatever is said in the topic sentence. If the writer has written an outline prior to writing (a task that many writers experience as yet more unpleasant work), then topics from the outline can become topic sentences. This approach will help the writer provide a sense of coherence to what is written. The outline allows the writer to see the overall organization of the planned report and detect potential illogical transitions or extraneous material. Writers who approach writing the report by beginning with the first paragraph and simply proceed through the narrative deprive themselves of this method for ensuring the coherence of their narrative. Two small studies support the hypothesis that using the EPM can result in sentences and paragraphs that are more credible and persuasive (Ownby, 1990a, b) than are non-model-based alternatives. A more extensive discussion of alternative paragraph structures is available elsewhere (Ownby, 1997).

Key Elements of Reports

The requirements of the given-new contract and coherence mean that some elements must be included in virtually all reports. The basic given information of the assessment must be established, and the path from given to the author's interpretations and recommendations must be logical and clear. Further, the task of presenting credible and persuasive reports of assessments requires that the person assessed be identified, the reason why he or she was assessed should be established, the methods used in the assessments be reported, results be discussed, and recommendations be made. The core elements that must be included in any psychological report are thus (a) identifying information, (b) reason for evaluation, (c) procedures employed, (d) procedure results, (e) implications of the results,

(f) specific answers to the referral question, and (g) recommendations for follow-up action. Inclusion of these elements is essential, and failure to do so is likely to render the report ineffective in communicating results. Failing to include any of these elements is likely as well to leave the reader dissatisfied. As discussed in the next section, reporting models will dictate how and in what order the key elements are presented, but even in the shortest report these key elements should be addressed.

Report Sections

How the writer creates sections of the report will depend to some extent on his or her preferences and the model chosen for the report (e.g., hypothesis-, test-, or ability-oriented; see the next section). Here again, the requirements of the given-new contract, coherence, and cohesion provide guidance. The given-new contract suggests that the first section of the report should establish the given—usually the client. Most reports intuitively or by tradition follow this dictate and begin with a section of "identifying information." Having established who the report is about, the requirement for coherence suggests that the next section of the report establish why the evaluation was conducted. Here again, most writers intuitively follow this practice and provide a description of why the client was seen for the evaluation. This section may also include some elaboration of relevant history about the client to substantiate or elaborate the reason for the referral. For example, the reason for evaluation might most simply be stated as "personality and cognitive evaluation." Such a brief statement might be inadequate to many readers, failing to establish the necessary given information. If the writer includes, "Ms. X's personality and memory are said to have changed after she was involved in a car crash earlier this year," the reader may have a much better understanding of the assessment report that follows.

Overall Report Organization

Before writing, the writer should decide which of several models he or she should employ in reporting the assessment results. Reporting models provide guidance about how the essential elements of a report are organized in the report as well as about in what level of detail and in what portion of the report they are presented. The choice of reporting model should be guided by an explicit evaluation of (a) the referral source and his or her characteristics (psychologist, judge, physician, teacher, administrator); and (b) the context in which the assessment and its reporting occur (e.g., psychiatric hospital, medical hospital, outpatient clinic, forensic facility, school, or community mental health center). A consideration of the possible combinations of just these two domains shows the potential complexity of this decision. The best practice is for the report writer to explicitly assess these issues, along with consumers' preferences when practical. The worst practice is for the writer to base his or her reporting on personal preference, habit, or convenience alone.

Report models refer to one of several possible general strategies in reporting the evaluation. These include (a) the professional letter, (b) the test-oriented report, (c) the ability domain-oriented report, and (d) the hypothesis-oriented report.

THE PROFESSIONAL LETTER REPORT

In this report format, the author conveys the result of the assessment in a one- to two-page letter. Use of this abbreviated format is based on the existence of a professional relation between the referral source and the psychologist, so that it is not necessary to establish the credibility and persuasiveness of the conclusions in the same way that might be required in other contexts. This format may be useful in many medical contexts, where both writer's and reader's time is at a premium and a working relation already exists.

Identifying information and the reason for assessment should be communicated briefly at the beginning of the letter in a sentence following the salutation of the letter, thus: "I saw your patient/client Ms. Black on your referral for evaluation of her cognitive and emotional status." The assessment procedures completed can be reported as a statement such as "We completed a battery of cognitive and emotional measures," that may go on to list specific measures if they are particularly relevant, "including the Wechsler Adult Intelligence Scale-III and the Minnesota Multiphasic Personality Inventory-2." Assessment results might then report the outcome of the assessment as conclusions with minimal supporting data, such as "Our assessment shows that Mr./Ms. Black is depressed/has a personality disorder." A DSM-IV diagnosis may be useful as part of the conclusion. Recommendations should derive logically from the diagnosis and may also be brief: "We discussed a trial of interpersonal psychotherapy with the client/patient, and referred him/her to our colleague Dr. Green."

THE TEST-ORIENTED REPORT

The test-oriented report will include sections that establish identifying information and reason for referral. The key element of assessment procedures is addressed through a list of tests administered. The body of the report then proceeds with a test-by-test description that lists the tests, the client's or patient's score or performance on each, and perhaps a more general interpretation of the performance in terms of a middle-level construct. Such a sequence might be created as follows. "Test name: MMPI-2. Score on relevant scale(s) showed a pattern of 2-4-8, suggestive of personality pathology." If employed, it is critical that a report based on this model include an integrating section in which potentially diverse and apparently conflicting test results are integrated into a coherent account of the psychologist's view of the client's functioning. Failure to do so makes this report little more than a listing of tests and scores that is unlikely to be useful to the reader.

THE ABILITY- OR DOMAIN-ORIENTED REPORT

In this model, reports are written with paragraphs discussing ability domains such as "language," "visuospatial," and "psychomotor" abilities. This model may be particularly useful for neuropsychological reports, since the neuropsychological assessment often includes a detailed evaluation of cognitive abilities. An analog of this model in personality assessment might be a report organized according to the domains of personality functioning as conceived by the assessor and thought to be useful to the report's intended recipient. A psychodynamically oriented report, for example, might include headings such as "intrapsychic conflicts" and "defense mechanisms." A cognitively oriented evaluation might include sections on "automatic thoughts" and "core beliefs."

THE HYPOTHESIS-ORIENTED REPORT

This is an apparently underused reporting model but one which has much to recommend it. This format may be particularly useful if, in fact, the purpose of reports is to provide credible and persuasive communication because it directly focuses on these goals and reduces the inevitable emphasis on assessment mechanics that results from ability-oriented and test-oriented reports. The hypothesis-oriented report simply states the referral purpose as a question and lists hypotheses that are responsive to the question. Hypotheses can then be sequentially evaluated in the context of assessment results. Conclusions logically flow from these evaluations, and the links from referral question to assessment data, conclusions, and recommendations will be apparent to the reader.

Specific Issues about Reports

Groth-Marnat and Horvath (2006) review controversies that arise in considering psychological reports, several of which merit discussion here as well.

Length

Most reports are too long, but the appropriate length for any report must be determined after consideration of the purpose of the report, the needs of the intended recipient, and the possibility that the report may have multiple readers over many years. Reports are too long because their writers focus on mechanical reporting of the assessment rather than a well thought out presentation of relevant data in a way that will assist the reports reader in making clinical decisions. Donders (2001), for example, found that neuropsychologists said that their average report length was 5–10 pages. Psychologists who write reports of this length should consider the need for this report length and whether the report's recipients find their reports useful. Merely following clinical practice tradition without a critical consideration of it is inadvisable.

Readability

Readability refers to the overall difficulty which the content and format of written text present to readers. It is perhaps most familiar to both readers and writers in its assessment through grade equivalent scores, so that one can refer to a passage of text as having been written at a fourth grade level or one can say that a person reads proficiently material at an eighth grade level. A typical recommendation is to write material for a general audience at an eighth grade level. This recommendation is based on the observation that most persons read independently at levels about four years less than their highest level of education. Since most people in the United States complete 12 years of education, material should thus be written four years below this level.

No readily available study has reported on readability of psychological reports in the grade equivalent metric. It is well known, however, that much professional material is written at levels of much greater difficulty. Professionals often underestimate the degree of difficulty their written communications present for readers (Ownby, 2006), however, and by inference it is possible that psychologists may underestimate the difficulty their reports present.

Assessment of readability has often been based on fairly simple formulas that use average word and sentence length in a passage of a given length to evaluate readability. Although in the past this task was tedious, most modern word processors will now provide readability estimates on demand. Improving readability as assessed by these formulas can be accomplished by using shorter words and limiting sentence length. In general, using shorter words helps the writer focus on using simpler concepts, and using shorter sentences reduces the grammatical complexity of sentences. Although evaluation of a report in this way can increase writers' awareness of how difficult their prose is for readers to understand, using these indices to improve readability can be problematic if done uncritically. In many instances, for example, it may be important for conceptual precision to use a polysyllabic technical term, and emphasizing short and simple sentences can make the writing seem choppy.

Validity of Measures

Measures used in assessments may vary in the degree to which their use is based in research that establishes reliability, validity, and appropriate norms. The judicious use of any psychological measure is the responsibility of the psychologist who chooses, administers, and interprets it. The use of measures with limited validity is inadvisable, but when such a use is undertaken it is ethically mandatory that any interpretation based on such an instrument be labeled as based on a measure of unknown or limited validity (Michaels, 2006). The reader is referred to Standard 9 of the Ethical Principles of Psychologists for further guidance (American Psychological Association, 2003).

Inclusion of Test Scores

A number of authors have weighed in on the subject of including test scores in reports. Several issues arise in considering whether and how to report scores on specific measures in a report. The first is whether reporting a score places the client in any way at unwarranted risk. The second is whether the person who receives the test score will be able to interpret it meaningfully. Finally, if the score is written into a report that may persist in someone's records for many years, will future readers of the report be able to interpret it? Even a cursory examination of these issues must lead psychologists to be cautious about releasing test scores.

Reporting test scores about clients' intellectual abilities may facilitate attempts to help them receive needed services or provide appropriate career guidance, but might also be used to justify denying them important opportunities. Although few data are available on consumers' ability to understand scores on ability measures, it is easy to imagine that misunderstandings on the meaning of intellectual ability scores could be detrimental to clients. These concerns, however, must be balanced against the need to accurately report assessment results. When the psychologist chooses to report specific test scores, he or she should report them in ways that help guard against misinterpretation. In the case of ability test scores, it may be helpful to report a score as having fallen in a range with an interpretation related to the confidence the psychologist has in the estimate. One can say "Mr. Brown's score on the Wechsler Adult Intelligence Scale-III fell in the high average range," or "Mr. Brown's score fell in the range of 112–124, indicating a high probability that if he took the test again his score would fall in this range." Reporting specific scores on personality measures can be similarly reported with appropriate caution and with immediate reference to empirically supported interpretations. One could say, for example, "Mr. Brown's score on Scale 6 of the MMPI-2 was 72; persons who respond to MMPI-2 items in this manner often are very sensitive to the opinions of others and may feel as though they get a raw deal from life." Writers should also take precautions when interpreting differences between subtest scores on the same measures, differences between scores on different measures standardized on different populations, and when basing interpretations on patterns of test scores.

An impediment to this approach to test interpretation and reporting is the uncertainty many psychologists have about key psychometric concepts such as standard error and when differences between test scores are unusual and when they are common. Various authors have provided guides to the practical implications of test scores and how to interpret them in light of their inherent measurement imprecision and normal variability (Donders, 2006; Dori & Chelune, 2004; Hunsley & Meyer, 2003; Schretlen, Munro, Anthony, & Pearlson, 2003).

Use of Computer-Based Narratives

Given the usefulness of computer-based test administration and interpretation, it is unsurprising that this approach has received a great deal of attention. Questions arise, however, about how to integrate results of computerized test interpretations into the psychological reports. Since Meehl's provocative observation that statistically based interpretations were often at least as good as those made by clinicians (Meehl, 1954), the computer has become a natural ally of those interested in using empirical data to interpret test results (Butcher, Perry, & Hahn, 2004). Since Meehl's time, many studies have shown that test interpretations based on empirical research are at least as accurate as those based on clinical judgment (Grove, Zald, Lebow, Snitz, & Nelson, 2000).

A number of narrative reports are available for commonly used psychological measures, and it is understandable that psychologists might want to integrate such a narrative into their reports and thus facilitate writing the assessment report. This is a temptation that psychologists should resist, however, for a number of reasons. At the very least, copying material verbatim from a computer-based interpretive report is plagiarism and thus is ethically unacceptable on that basis alone. More significantly, copying material from a narrative means that the psychologist writing the report has abdicated his or her professional responsibility to evaluate a person's performance on psychological measures and provide an interpretation based on not only empirical prediction rules but also on a sensitive appraisal of the assessment context, the client's situation, and the needs of the report's likely readers. Computer-generated narratives should thus be used as adjuncts rather than replacements for reporting assessment results (Butcher, Perry, & Atlis, 2000).

Conclusion

Psychological assessment is a key role that distinguishes psychology from other professions. Although much training focuses on the mechanics of administering, scoring, and interpreting results of measures used in assessments, greater attention to the communication of assessment results is needed. While only sporadic attention has been paid by researchers to how reports should be written, deficits in the research base may be addressed by turning to applied studies on professional writing and basic psycholinguistic research on discourse comprehension. An analysis of report problems from these perspectives leads to the EPM, a method for structuring report at the sentence, paragraph, section, and overall report levels.

Future Directions

1) Is it possible to systematically assess the contexts into which reports are sent and develop guidelines about the most appropriate reporting models, content, and organization for each context based on this assessment? For example, is it possible that the report of a forensic

evaluation should include specific elements, be a specific length, and be organized in specific sections that all might be different from an assessment report sent to a psychiatrist colleague in private practice?

2) Empirical investigations are needed of how report variables such as content, length, and organization are received by consumers of reports and how these variables influence their subsequent behavior.

3) How can psychologists be better trained to understand the psychometric properties of measures and how these properties should affect the way they present assessment results in reports?

References

American Psychological Association. (2003). *The ethical principles of psychologists*. Washington, DC: Author.

Appelbaum, S. (1970). Science and persuasion in the psychological test report. *Journal of Consulting and Clinical Psychology, 35*, 349–355.

Butcher, J. N., Perry, J. N., & Atlis, M. M. (2000). Validity and utility of computer-based test interpretation. *Psychological Assessment, 12*, 6–18.

Butcher, J. N., Perry, J., & Hahn, J. (2004). Computers in clinical assessment: Historical developments, present status, and future challenges. *Journal of Clinical Psychology, 60*, 331–345.

Chambless, D. N., & Hollon, S. D. (1998). Defining empirically supported therapies. *Journal of Consulting and Clinical Psychology, 66*, 7–18.

Donders, J. (2001). A survey of report writing by clinical neuropsychologists: II. Test data, report format, and document length. *The Clinical Neuropsychologist, 15*, 150–161.

Donders, J. (2006). Performance discrepancies on the California Verbal Learning Test—second edition (CVLT—II) in the standardization sample. *Psychological Assessment, 18*, 453–463.

Dori, G. A., & Chelune, G. J. (2004). Education-stratified baserate information on discrepancy scores within and between Wechsler Adult Intelligence Scale—third edition and the Wechsler Memory Scale—third edition. *Psychological Assessment, 16*, 146–154.

Gopen, G. D., & Swan, J. A. (1990). The science of scientific writing. *American Scientist, 78*, 550–558.

Groth-Marnat, G., & Horvath, L. S. (2006). The psychological report: A review of current controversies. *Journal of Clinical Psychology, 62*, 73–81.

Grove, D. M., Zald, D. H., Lebow, B. S., Snitz, B. E., & Nelson, C. (2000). Clinical versus mechanical prediction: A meta-analysis. *Psychological Assessment, 12*, 19–30.

Guyatt, G., Cairns, J., & Churchill, D. f. t. E.-B. M. W. G. (1992). Evidence-based medicine: A new approach to teaching the practice of medicine. *JAMA, 268*, 2420–2425.

Harvey, V. S. (2006). Variables affecting the clarity of psychological reports. *Journal of Clinical Psychology, 62*, 5–18.

Hunsley, J., & Meyer, G. J. (2003). The incremental validity of psychological testing and assessment: Conceptual, methodological, and statistical issues. *Psychological Assessment, 15*, 446–455.

Klopfer, W. G. (1960). *The psychological report: Use and communication of psychological findings*. New York: Grune & Stratton.

Meehl, P. A. (1954). *Clinical versus statistical prediction: A theoretical analysis and a review of the evidence*. Minneapolis, MN: University of Minnesota Press.

Michaels, M. H. (2006). Ethical considerations in writing psychological assessment reports. *Journal of Clinical Psychology, 62*, 47–58.

Ownby, R. L. (1990a). A study of the expository process model in mental health settings. *Journal of Clinical Psychology, 46*, 366–371.

Ownby, R. L. (1990b). A study of the expository process model in school psychological reports. *Psychology in the Schools, 27*, 353–358.

Ownby, R. L. (1997). Psychological reports: A guide to report writing in professional psychology (3rd ed.). New York: John Wiley & Sons.

Ownby, R. L. (2006). Readability of consumer-oriented geriatric depression information on the Internet. *Clinical Gerontologist, 29*, 17–32.

Schretlen, D. J., Munro, C. A., Anthony, J. C., & Pearlson, G. D. (2003). Examining the range of normal intraindividual variability in neuropsychological test performance. *Journal of the International Neuropsychological Society, 9*, 864–870.

How to Use Computer-Based Reports

James N. Butcher

Abstract

The first computer program to interpret a psychological test, the original version of the Minnesota Multiphasic Personality Inventory (MMPI), was developed in the 1960s. Computers have become an indispensable component in psychological assessment in most health-care, forensic, mental health, and personnel settings. This chapter addresses several aspects of the use of computer-based psychological test reports. The rationale and value of using computer-based reports is described and reasons for the widespread use of computerized test interpretation detailed. Computer-based interpretation systems can usually provide a more comprehensive and objective summary of relevant test-based hypotheses than practitioners have the time and resources to develop. Use of computer-based test results avoids or minimizes subjectivity in selecting and emphasizing interpretive material. Computer-based psychological test results can be obtained quite rapidly saving practioner's valuable time for use in early clinical sessions. Finally, a broad range of computer-based assessment services is available for the practitioner to incorporate into his or her practice. The methods of computer test data processing that practitioners can employ are varied and include the following data entry methods: mail-in service, in-office computer processing, fax processing option, and Internet-based test applications.

Keywords: abbreviated forms, actuarial prediction, computer adaptive tests, computer-based reports, MMPI-2, test feedback

Almost half a century has now passed since the first computer was programmed to interpret a psychological test, the original version of the Minnesota Multiphasic Personality Inventory (MMPI), at the Mayo Clinic (Rome et al., 1962). Today computers have become an indispensable partner in psychological assessment in health-care, forensic, mental health, and other settings (Butcher, Perry, & Atlis, 2000; Atlis, Hahn, & Butcher, 2006). One survey of clinical practitioners found that 67.8% of respondents used computer scoring of psychological tests and 43.8% also used computer-derived reports in their clinical practice (Downey, Sinnett, & Seeberger, 1998). Computers can be used to aid the psychological practitioner in a number of ways in performing clinical evaluations. For example, they can be used to administer test items, to rapidly score and profile test results, and to interpret test scores and

generate a complete sophisticated report that describes and classifies problems. Moreover, the use of the computer, with its extensive memory and rapid combination capability, allows the psychologist to synthesize vast amounts of information and provide interpretations related to very complete results such as determining prognosis and treatment planning and aid in tracking symptom change in therapy.

This chapter will address several facets of the use of computer-based psychological test reports. First, the rationale and value of using computer-based reports will be explored. Then important factors to consider in using computer-based reports will be described and illustrated. Next, the clinical use of one computer-based test report, the Minnesota Report for the MMPI-2, will be described. The importance of profile base rates will be described (see Chapter 8). In this example, the use of the

MMPI-2 in providing test feedback to clients in psychological treatment will be illustrated. After this practical case example is described, the use of computer reports in forensic testimony will be explored. The chapter concludes with an examination of several possible problems with computer-based psychological test reports and provides a perspective on appropriate uses.

Value of Using Computer-Based Psychological Tests in Clinical Assessment

Several reasons can be found for the widespread use of computer-based test interpretation in clinical assessment. First, computer-based interpretation systems can usually provide a more comprehensive and objective summary of relevant test-based hypotheses than the clinical practitioner has the time and resources to develop (Atlis et al., 2006). In interpreting profiles, a computer will attend to all relevant scores and not ignore or fail to consider important information, as sometimes happens when human beings face a large array of complicated data. Computer-assisted test interpretations are usually more thorough and better documented than those typically derived by clinical assessment procedures.

Second, use of computer-based test results avoids or minimizes subjectivity in selecting and emphasizing interpretive material. Biasing factors, such as halo effects, can creep into less structured procedures such as the clinical interview. The computer can carry out the "look up and combine function" involved in test interpretation in an unbiased manner compared with most human interpreters.

Third, computer-based psychological test results can be obtained quite rapidly, thereby being available for the clinician to use in early clinical sessions. One can often have a summary of test results within minutes of the time the client has completed the testing. The summary information, as we will discuss later, can actually be used in the initial clinical contact with the client instead of a week or two later, as was common for psychological test evaluations in the precomputer era.

Fourth, computer interpretation systems are considered to be almost completely reliable; that is, they always produce the same results on the same set of scores. Moreover, tests that are computer administered have been shown to be equivalent to those administered by the traditional booklet form (Finger & Ones, 1999).

Finally, a broad range of computer-based assessment services is available for the practitioner to incorporate into his or her practice. Generally, the practitioner can have a great deal of confidence in most commercially available test scoring and interpretation programs, since the testing industry usually maintains high standards for computerized assessment. In his review of computerized psychological assessment programs, Bloom (1992) concluded that "the very high level of professional vigilance over test administration and interpretation software undoubtedly accounts for the fact that computerized assessment programs have received such high marks" (p. 172).

Factors to Consider in Test Scoring and Interpretation Services

Many factors will determine which of the commercially available computer scoring and interpretation services best fit one's assessment needs. Foremost in the decision, of course, will be whether a particular test interpretation company provides the range and quality of test scoring and interpretation services that are needed. Testing services are usually dedicated to particular tests and not to others. No test interpretation companies offer all tests that a practitioner might wish to use in his or her practice. Some services have limited publication or distribution arrangements and are unable to provide scoring of some tests due to copyright restrictions. For example, a company might not have permission to computer-score the scales contained on a test, yet it might offer computer-based interpretive reports. In such cases, the tests must be scored manually and the scale scores entered into the computer to obtain interpretations. It is important for the practitioner to ensure that the testing company has the type of data processing option that the practitioner needs. Inquiries need to be made about the exact nature of the test scoring and processing options provided.

Methods of Computer Test Data Processing

The methods of computer test data processing that practitioners can employ are varied. The following are several possible data entry methods and test factors that the practitioner might consider in deciding which computer application best fits his or her practice requirements.

Mail-In Service

The oldest type of scoring and interpretation service commercially available is the mail-in test processing option. For the most part, this service is provided to practitioners who have limited in-house computer facilities or who may process large numbers of tests in batches. The tests in this scoring option are usually administered to clients in a paper-and-pencil format. The answer sheets are then mailed to the testing service for processing.

In-Office Computer Processing

If the practitioner has a computer available for test processing, there are several test processing options to consider. First, a computer program to administer the items online might be available. In this situation, the client is presented the items on a TV screen and endorses them by typing his or her answers on the computer keyboard. A second scoring option involves administering the items using the paper-and-pencil form and key-entering the items into the computer—a procedure that usually takes a clerical assistant about 10 min for an inventory the length of the MMPI-2. A third approach to response processing involves administering the items using the paper-and-pencil version of the test with an optically readable answer form. The practitioner or a staff member would process the answer sheet by using an optical scanner, a type of copier that reads blackened marks directly into a computer. The optical scanner usually costs $3,000 or $4,000 dollars in addition to the cost of the computer. However, this procedure is considered to be quite cost-effective if about eight or more tests are administered in a week.

Fax Processing Option

This approach to test scoring is available for practitioners who want a rapid processing for a protocol but do not have a computer-based test processing option available to them; the practitioner does not need a computer. This option is relatively simple: the practitioner simply administers the test using the paper-and-pencil format and faxes the answer sheet to the test scoring company for processing. Because of the length of the MMPI-2 and to assure reliability, the test scoring service will manually enter responses from the faxed answer sheet. In terms of simplicity, this procedure is similar to the older mail-in service option except that there is usually immediate turnaround of the report.

Internet-Based Test Applications

Technological developments in psychological assessment are advancing rapidly today, particularly applications on the Internet. In fact, computer applications are developing at a much faster rate than the psychological technology in the testing industry. However, test publishers are being faced with pressures to provide psychological test services such as scoring and interpretation through the Internet and some commercial services have begun to make these services available. Providing testing services through the Internet, however, presents several problems that psychologists will need to address. The ethics of psychological test usage and the standards of care, as well as the basic psychological test research, have not kept up with the spurt in growth of the Internet. Questions pertaining to such issues as test security, and the reliability and validity of expanding test use to different settings than those in which the tests were originally developed, will need to be addressed (see also Atlis et al., 2006).

Shortened or Abbreviated Forms

There are several abbreviated versions of personality scales for the MMPI-2 available; however, these forms provide only limited information and do not sufficiently assess the traditional measures that psychologists typically include in their interpretations (Butcher & Hostetler, 1990). For example, Dahlstrom and Archer (2000) published a shortened form of the MMPI-2 that was comprised simply of the first 180 items in the booklet. This approach to abbreviating the test failed to produce an effective measure of the existing scales (Gass & Gonazalez, 2003; Gass & Luis, 2001).

A new shortened version of the MMPI-2, the MMPI-2 RF, has recently been published by Pearson Assessments to provide test users with a new version of the MMPI-2. No effort was made to maintain continuity of the original instrument or to capture traditional MMPI-2 constructs as other short forms have attempted (Butcher & Williams, 2009). Rather, this version includes new and shorter scales such as the Restructured Clinical or RC Scales (Tellegen et al., 2003). These measures, however, have not been validated sufficiently in the field or published in scientific literature to substitute for the original instrument. These shortened measures do not provide the validity and reliability that would be required for inclusion in court cases should that be necessary.

Computer Adaptive Testing (CAT)

The computer adaptive approach to psychological testing involves a computer administering the items to clients in a "tailor-made" version rather than a fixed item format. That is, the test protocol varies for each client based upon their responses to earlier items on the test. This computer-administering approach has focused upon "tailoring" the test to the client by only administering items that were needed to assess the major symptom pattern(s) rather than having a fixed format of administering all the items (Weiss, 1985). Two strategies for item selection have been studied: the item response theory approach, which is applied most effectively with homogeneous item scales, and the "count-down" method (Butcher, Keller, Bacon, 1985; Handel, Ben-Porath, Watt, 1999), which attempts to provide an estimate of the total score based upon a set number of items. The computer-adapted MMPI-2 has been found to save about half an hour of testing time at the cost of a full evaluation of the client's problems with the full version. In most cases, this small time saving does not warrant an abbreviated administration (see Atlis et al., 2006, for a fuller discussion).

Several questions to consider in selecting a computer-based test interpretation service to process psychological tests are outlined in Table 36.1.

This chapter will focus on practical considerations in using one type of computer-based psychological test interpretive report that is widely used in clinical evaluation settings. The case illustration involves the MMPI-2, since the MMPI and its derivatives have been the most widely used clinical instrument in most settings (Lubin, Larsen, & Matarazzo, 1984; Piotrowski & Keller, 1989) and have the most extensive history of computer adaptation for a psychological test. One survey of mental health professionals reported that the MMPI-2 was ranked as being the most frequently administered test (Frauenhoffer, Ross, Gfeller, Searight, & Piotrowski, 1998). Other surveys have reported similar conclusions (Borum & Grisso, 1995; Lees-Haley, 1992; Lees-Haley, Smith, Williams, & Dunn, 1996). In fact, 100% of frequent

assessors surveyed in one study used the MMPI or MMPI-2 in personal injury cases (Boccaccini & Brodsky, 1999). The idea of computer-based MMPI-2 (MMPI) interpretation is based on the view that tests can more effectively be interpreted in an actuarial manner than through clinical interpretation strategies (see Grove & Meehl, 1996; Grove, Zald, Lebow, Smith, & Nelson, 2000; Meehl, 1954). A report made up of objective applied personality and clinical symptom descriptions that have been established for the test scales or patterns can more accurately be combined by machine than can reports derived by clinical means. For the most part, computer-generated clinical reports can be viewed as predetermined or canned statements that are applied to individuals who obtain particular psychological test scores. The statements or paragraphs contained in the computerized report, which is often in narrative form, are stored in computer memory and automatically retrieved to match a case when it meets particular scale elevations, profile types, or scale indices. The behavioral correlate information for MMPI-2 scales and code types can be found in a number of sources (see Archer, Griffin, & Aiduk, 1995; Butcher, Graham, Williams, & Ben-Porath, 1990; Butcher, Rouse, & Perry, 2000; Butcher & Williams, 2000; Graham, 2006; Graham, Ben-Porath, & McNulty, 1999; Gilberstadt & Duker, 1963; Lewandowski & Graham, 1972; Marks, Seeman, & Haller, 1975). Computer interpretation requires that test scores be used to access appropriate specific symptoms, behaviors, and so on, that are stored in the computer.

The actuarial combination of data from the MMPI-2 scales has been well established. However, empirical research has not provided correlates for all

Table 36.1. Questions to consider in evaluating the adequacy of computerized psychological testing services.

Does the test on which the computer interpretation system is based have an adequate network of established validity research?

Do the system developers have the requisite experience with the particular test(s) to provide reliable valid information?

Is there a sufficient amount of documentation available on the system of interest? Is there a published user's guide to explain the test and system variables?

Is the computer-based report based on the most widely validated measures available on the test?

Is the system flexible enough to incorporate new information as it becomes available?

How frequently is the system revised to incorporate new empirical data on the test?

Was the interpretation system developed following the APA guidelines for computer-based tests?

Do the reports contain a sufficient evaluation of potentially invalidating response conditions?

How closely does the system conform to empirically validated test correlates? Is it possible to determine from the outputs whether the reports are consistent with interpretive strategies and information from published resources on the test?

Does the company providing computer interpretation services have a qualified technical staff to deal with questions or problems?

Are the reports sufficiently annotated to indicate appropriate cautions?

possible scale combinations. Consequently, no MMPI or MMPI-2 interpretation system is fully actuarial. Rather, some interpretations will be based on expert conclusions about the meaning of and the interpretation strategy for single scale scores. The term 'automated clinician' more accurately describes the computer-based interpretive systems available, since they are based to some extent on clinical judgments as well as on pure actuarial data (Fowler, 1969). The validity of an automated test report will depend on the extent of replicable personality information available for the psychological test on which the interpretive system is based. The validity of the computerized system will also depend on how closely the developer of the system has conformed to the actuarial data and whether clearly replicated correlates have been used to develop descriptors.

There is some debate about how computer-based reports are to be incorporated in the clinical assessment (Fowler & Butcher, 1986; Garb, 1992; Matarazzo, 1986; Rubenzer, 1991). It is important that computerized interpretive reports be used in conjunction with other clinical information about the patient obtained from other sources. Automated MMPI-2 clinical reports are designed for use by professionals who are knowledgeable in the interpretive background of the MMPI-2.

Clinical Use of a Computerized MMPI-2 Report

This section illustrates the use of a computer-based test report in pretreatment planning. The MMPI-2 has been used extensively in assessing patients in pretreatment psychological evaluation (see Butcher & Perry, 2008). Potential therapy patients are administered the test early in the treatment process or before therapy begins. The therapist, or in some cases the clinician evaluating the client in pretreatment planning, may also conduct a test feedback session with the client. In this session, the individual's test-taking attitude and its implication for appraising treatment motivation and readiness for therapy can be discussed. The extent and character of the individual's problems, symptoms, and so on, can be described. Finally, recommendations and predictions about prognosis for resolving problems can be explored with potential strategies for problem resolution being suggested. This approach to providing MMPI-2 feedback in pretreatment planning has been discussed in more detail by Finn and Kamphuis (2006) and Butcher and Perry (2008).

Before presenting MMPI-2 results to clients, several factors need to be taken into account. First, the current psychological status of the client receiving the feedback information needs to be appraised. In providing test information, the clinician needs to assess the capacity of the client to understand and utilize the information. For example, the process requires that the client have sufficient reality contact and a "receptive" attitude toward the session in order to be able to understand and integrate the test information accurately. The client's level of intellectual functioning and educational background also need to be considered. For example, if the client is intelligent and well educated, more specific and detailed information can be discussed than if the individual is less well educated or less capable intellectually. The presentation should be varied to suit the individual's general fund of information. The type of setting in which the test was given is an important variable to take into account. Published sources such as Butcher (2005), Butcher and Williams (2000), Graham (2006), and Greene (2000) contain information about relevant MMPI-2 scale descriptors for varied groups.

Steps in Providing Test Feedback to Clients

The suggestions presented in Table 36.2 (Butcher & Perry, 2008) might serve as a useful strategy for providing test feedback to clients in pretreatment planning.

MMPI-2 Feedback as an Intervention

What effect does test feedback have on the patient's behavior and adjustment? Finn and Tonsager (1992) showed that the test feedback process itself can be a powerful clinical intervention. They conducted a clinical study in which one group of patients from a therapy waiting list ($N = 537$) was provided MMPI-2 test feedback according to a model developed by Finn (1990) (see also Finn & Kamphuis, 2006). The second group of patients ($N = 529$) from the waiting list was administered the MMPI-2 but not given test feedback. The results of the study were very informative: individuals who were provided feedback on their MMPI-2, compared with the control group, showed a significant decline in reported symptoms and an increase in measured self-esteem. Finn and Tonsager reported:

> This study provides support for the therapeutic impact of sharing MMPI-2 test results verbally with college age clients. Clients who completed an MMPI-2 and

Table 36.2. Steps in providing test feedback to clients.

Step 1. Explain why the test was administered
- Explain the rationale behind your giving test feedback to the client.
- Indicate that you want to provide information about the problem situation that is based on how the client responds to various questions.
- Explain that personality characteristics and potential problems revealed in the test scores are compared to those of other people who have taken the test, and that feedback gives the client perspective on his or her problems that can be used as a starting point in therapy.

Step 2. Describe what the test is and its uses
- Describe the MMPI-2 and provide the patient with an understanding of how valid and accurate the test is for clinical problem description. Explain, for example, that the MMPI-2 was originally developed as a means of obtaining objective information about patients' problems and personality characteristics.
- Indicate that the MMPI-2 is the most widely used clinical test in the United States, which has been translated into many languages and which is used in many other countries for evaluating patient problems.
- Explain that it has been developed and used with many different patient problems and provides accurate information about problems and issues the client is dealing with.

Step 3. Describe how the personality test works
- Begin this step in the feedback process by providing a description of several elements of the MMPI-2. Use the patient's own test profiles to provide a basis for visualizing the information you are going to provide.
- Explain that a scale is a group of items or statements that measure certain characteristics or problems such as depression or anxiousness.
- Describe what an "average" score is on the profile. Show how scores are compared on the profile, and indicate that higher scores reflect "more" of the characteristics involved and problems the patient is experiencing.
- Point out where the elevated score range is and what a score at T = 65 or T = 80 means in terms of the number of people obtaining scores in this range.
- If available, use an average profile from a relevant clinical group from the published literature to illustrate how people with particular problems score on measure. For example, if the patient has significant depression, showing a group mean profile of depressed clients provides a good comparison group.

Step 4. Describe how the validity scales on the test work
Discuss the strategies the patient used in approaching the test content. Focus on the person's self-presentation and on how he or she is viewing the problem situation at this time. Discussion of the client's validity pattern is one of the most important facets of test feedback because it provides the therapist with an opportunity to explore the patient's motivation for and accessibility to treatment.

Step 5. Point out the client's most significant departures from the norm on the Clinical Scales
Indicate that the client's responses have been compared with those of thousands of other individuals who have taken the test under different conditions. Describe your patient's highest ranging clinical scores in terms of prevailing attitudes, symptoms, or problem areas. It is also valuable to discuss the individual's low points on the profile to provide a contrast with other personality areas in which he or she does not seem to be having problems. But avoid descriptions that are low in occurrence, and avoid using psychological jargon.
- Emphasize the individual's highest point(s) on the test profiles.
- Point out where the scores fall in relation to the "average" scores.
- Provide understandable descriptions of the personality characteristics revealed by the prominent scale elevations.

Step 6. Seek responses from the client during the feedback session
Encourage the client to ask questions about the scores and clear up any points of concern.

Step 7. Appraise client acceptance of the test feedback
Ask the client to summarize how he or she feels the test characterized personal problems to evaluate whether there were aspects of the test results that were particularly surprising or distressing, and whether there were aspects of the interpretation to which the patient objected.

later heard their MMPI-2 test results reported a significant increase in their self-esteem immediately following the feedback session, an increase that continued to grow over the 2-week follow-up period. In addition, after hearing their MMPI-2 test results, clients showed a significant decrease in their symptomatic distress, and distress continued to decline during the subsequent 2-week period. Last, compared with clients receiving attention only from the examiner, clients who completed the MMPI-2 and received a feedback session showed more hopefulness about their problems immediately following the feedback session, and this persisted at the final follow-up.
(p. 284)

The results of this study suggest that information from psychological tests can be effectively used as a direct therapeutic intervention. We now turn to a discussion of a case in which the MMPI-2 was administered and used in the pretreatment planning evaluation.

Case History

The patient, a 46-year-old department store sales manager, was initially referred to the medical clinic by her supervisor because she had been absent from work on numerous occasions in recent months. In the medical examination she told the doctor that she would like to get treatment for her severe headaches and fatigue that she felt were causing her to miss a lot of work. She also complained about an "inability to sleep and general restlessness." She indicated to the doctor that she had been going through a lot of stress lately after the breakup of a long-term relationship. In her medical examination, the doctor began to suspect that many of her symptoms were psychological and referred her to see the staff psychologist.

In the psychological examination, she was interviewed by the clinical psychologist and administered the MMPI-2 after the initial session. The patient had been divorced by her husband 5 years earlier after he discovered that she had been having an affair with a prominent man in the community. Her husband had been given custody of their two teenage children, who had now grown up and living independently. The patient did not seek custody at the time of the divorce. She has had no relationship with her former husband during the past 5 years and sees the two children only every few months.

During the 1½-hour session with the psychologist, the patient said that she was undergoing a great deal of stress over the breakup of a long-time relationship with a man whom she had been seeing for several years. She expressed considerable anger over the breakup of the relationship and reported that she was experiencing many physical problems and lately was having difficulty at times making it to work when she felt weak or tired. She also indicated that she had been drinking more since the breakup; however, she did not feel that alcohol was a big problem for her. A follow-up session was planned for her 2 days later.

MMPI-2 SCALE SCORES AND REPORT

The MMPI-2 validity scale pattern, the Clinical and supplemental scale pattern, and the MMPI-2 content scale pattern are provided in Tables 36.4, 36.5 and 36.6. The computer-based narrative report is summarized in Table 36.3.

FOLLOW-UP INTERVIEW AND TEST FEEDBACK SESSION

The second interview with the psychologist began with the psychologist asking the client if anything important to her situation had occurred since her last visit to the clinic. He also asked whether she had any questions about the previous session before discussing the results of the testing.

In structuring the feedback session, the psychologist was aware (from the MMPI-2 report) of the possibility that she might be reluctant to accept personality test feedback as a result of her general mistrust and tendency to blame others for her problems (see Table 36.3). He wanted to provide her with important personality information without raising her defensiveness to the point that she would be unable to accept the feedback. He began the test feedback session by reminding her of the initial reasons for the psychological evaluation. He next provided her with background as to the reasons for administering the MMPI-2 and that he had hoped the test would be able to add to an understanding of her situation. First, the practitioner discussed her general cooperativeness with the evaluations, referring to the validity scale elevations in the profile.

Her validity scale scores suggested that she appeared to be very open to the evaluation and did not seem to be engaging in problem denial. She reported a number of problems in a straightforward manner. The psychologist also told her that some of the test information might not seem appropriate to her (because of her tendency to externalize blame), and she was encouraged to ask questions if she did not see the relevance to her.

Next, using the Clinical and content scale profiles, the therapist explained how the MMPI-2 scores

Table 36.3. Descriptive summary of the Minnesota Report on the MMPI-2 for a 46-year-old department store manager.

The computer-based Minnesota Report addressed a number of problems the client faced and described the personality characteristics likely to be present. An initial section was included that gave information about the client's approach to the testing in a profile validity paragraph. She produced a clinical profile that was likely valid. The report suggested that she was cooperative with the evaluation.

The pattern of clinical and personality symptoms shown by the report appeared to provide a good summary of the client's current personality functioning. The clinical narrative used in the report incorporated features of her two high points, Pd and Pa, which showed high-profile definition. The report noted that persons with this MMPI-2 clinical profile tend to show an extreme pattern of chronic psychological maladjustment including immaturity and alienation, and tendencies to manipulate others for their own gratification. The client also seems quite self-indulgent, hedonistic, and narcissistic, with grandiose ideas of herself and her abilities. The report noted that she is likely to be quite aggressive with others and very impulsive, and likely tends to act out her problems rather than resolve them. She seems to rationalize her difficulties and takes no direct responsibility for her actions, but tends to blame other people for her problems. The report also noted that she may resort to hostile, resentful, and irritable behvior.

The computer report also pointed out that she appears to be a tense and high-strung person who believes that she experiences more intensely than other people do and feels lonely and misunderstood.

The report also provides information as to the relative frequency of Clinical Scale symptoms that clients with similar patterns show. Her high-point scale score on Pd occurs in over 9.5% of the MMPI-2 normative sample of women. However, only 4.7% of the sample have Pd scale peak scores at or above a T-score of 65, and only 2.9% of clients have well-defined Pd spikes. This particular MMPI-2 profile pattern is relatively rare in samples of normals, occurring in fewer than 1% of normative women. In medical samples, this high-point Clinical Scale score (Pd) is found in about 6.8% of women.

The client scored high on APS and AAS. This indicated that there is a possibility of a drug or alcohol abuse problem that should be carefully evaluated. The narrative report also noted hat this profile pattern is generally stable over time and that if she is retested at a later date she is likely to produce similiar results.

In terms of being able to get along with other people, the narrative report indicated that she has a great deal of difficulty in her social relationships. She often feels that others do not respect her or give her enough sympathy. She tends to be aloof from others and uncompromising in conflict sitations. Divorce is relatively common for such clients. The report noted that she is often hypersensitive about what others think of her and is concerned about her relationships with others. She likely has difficulty expressing her feelings toward others.

In terms of clinical diagnosis, persons attaining this patern of scores are usually viewed as having a severe personality disorder. Antisocial features are present and the possibility of paranoid personality is highlighted. In addition, the report concludes that she responds in a manner similar to that of clients who have paranoid disorder, a possibility that should be ruled out.

She appears to have a number of personality characteristics that are associated with substance abuse or substance use problems and she has acknowledged some problems with excessive use or abuse of addictive substances.

The Minnesota Report also provides some treatment suggestions. Persons with this pattern of scores tend to avoid psychological treatment and are usually not good candidates for psychotherapy. The report notes that they tend to resist psychological interpretation and rationalize their own input and tend to blame others for their problems. The report suggests that she has acknowledged problems with alcohol or drug use, a factor that should be addressed more fully in therapy.

Source: Adapted summary of the clients' Minnesota Report.

provided summaries of her present feelings, symptoms, and attitudes. Her Clinical Scale scores reflected a great deal of anger and hurt on her part. She seemed to be feeling mistrustful of others and showed a tendency to blame others for her own problems. The MMPI-2 scales reflect immaturity in behavior and relationships that have probably persisted for some time. The psychologist pointed out that she was clearly experiencing a great deal of physical distress and tension at this time and that perhaps many of the problems centered around relationship difficulties.

One of the greatest problems she seemed to be experiencing, although she tended to minimize it in the initial interview, was that of alcohol abuse. The MMPI-2 substance abuse indicators (as well as her acknowledged pattern of alcohol use reported in the initial session) suggested a strong likelihood that alcohol abuse was a much more significant problem than she had been willing to discuss before. The remainder of the interview was oriented toward highlighting her major problems and encouraging her to enter an alcohol treatment program. She acknowledged that her life had been going downhill

Table 36.4. MMPI-2 Validity and Clinical Scale T-scores for a 46-year-old department store manager.

Scale name	Scale elevation (T-score)
VRIN (Inconsistency)	58
TRIN (Inconsistency)	58
F (Infrequency)	61
F(B) (Infrequency, Back)	58
L (Lie)	38
K (Defensiveness)	54
S (Superlative Self-Presentation)	43
Hs (Hypochondriasis)	74
D (Depression)	72
Hy (Hysteria)	73
Pd (Psychopathic Deviation)	97
Mf (Masculinity–Femininity)	30
Pa (Paranoia)	85
Pt (Psychasthenia)	79
Sc (Schizophrenia)	76
Ma (Hypomania)	45
Si (Social Introversion–Extraversion)	60

Table 36.5. MMPI-2 Content Scale T-scores for a 46-year-old department store manager.

Scale name	Scale elevation (T-score)
ANX (Anxiety)	66
FRS (Fears)	59
OBS (Obsessiveness)	48
DEP (Depression)	62
HEA (Health Concerns)	68
BIZ (Bizarre Mentation)	64
ANG (Anger Control Problems)	47
CYN (Cynicism)	46
ASP (Anti-Social Personality)	54
TPA (Type-A Behavior)	60
LSE (Low Self-Esteem)	57
SOD (Social Distrust)	56
FAM (Family Problems)	57
WRK (Work Adjustment Problems)	57
TRT (Treatment Planning)	51

Table 36.6. MMPI-2 Supplemental Scale T-Scores for a 46-year-old department store manager.

Scale name	Scale elevation (T-score)
MAC-R (MacAndrew Scale)	62
APS (Addiction Potential Scale)	69
AAS (Addiction Acknowledgment Scale)	73
Pk (Keane PTSD Scale)	68
O-H (Overcontrolled–Hostility)	59
MDS (Marital Distress)	N/A

for some months and that her most recent relationship was one that seemed to center on using (and abusing) alcohol; also her alcohol use had been increasing as the relationship broke up. At the end of the session she acknowledged that she had received a DWI citation a year before and had lost her driving privileges for 6 months. She reported that one of the reasons that she missed some work was that she was unable to drive and relied on her friend to drive her. Although she acknowledged being usually somewhat mistrustful and "private," she was currently feeling "pretty bad about life" and felt that she needed help for her problems, which she felt were getting worse.

Several possible treatment options were discussed with her. There were a number of inpatient programs that could be recommended and it was also possible to obtain alcohol problem treatment on an outpatient basis under some conditions. Because of her involvement with alcohol, however, it was strongly recommended that she consider a 4-week inpatient treatment program. She was initially very reluctant to agree to inpatient treatment since she felt the absence from work would be detrimental to her job. She asked about the possibility of an outpatient program that would allow her to work during the day. She agreed to returning for a third session to discuss various alcohol treatment program options that were open to her. She was encouraged to discuss the possibility of a leave of absence with her employer before the next session.

In the follow-up session the practitioner initially inquired about her present thinking about the treatment program for her. She reported that her discussion with her employer had been very encouraging and she felt that her supervisor was very supportive of her. Her supervisor (an abstinent alcoholic himself) was very understanding of her situation and urged her to take a leave of absence to participate in the inpatient program as he had done several years before. He gave her assurances that she was a valuable employee and that her job would not be threatened by her absence. She used the session to discuss other possible problems she might encounter by being in an inpatient program. She ended the session with a clear plan to initiate inpatient treatment on the following Monday.

Forensic Use of Computer-Based Reports

It is becoming more and more important for psychologists to employ clinical procedures that will hold up under rigorous cross-examination in court, because more cases today are becoming the subject of litigation. Psychologists testifying in court might consider using computer-based test reports that provide results in an objective manner, reducing the possibility of subjectivity and bias in interpretation (Pope, Butcher, & Seelen, 2006). Computerized psychological test reports can lend considerable objectivity and credibility to a forensic psychological study. The use of a computer to analyze test score patterns can remove subjective bias from the interpretation process.

The value of using objective psychological measures in court testimony was described by Ziskin (1981):

> I would recommend for forensic purposes the utilization of one of the automated MMPI services. One obvious advantage is the minimizing or eliminating of the possibility of scoring errors or errors in transposition of scores (Allard, Butler, Faust, & Shea, 1995). Also these systems are capable of generating more information about an individual than the individual clinician is usually capable of simply by virtue of their ability to deal with greater amounts of information. Another advantage is the reduction of the problems of examiner effects, such as biases entering into the collection, recording, and interpretation of the data.
> (p. 9)

Psychologists developing reports in forensic settings might consult Pope et al. (2006).

Points to Consider

Several issues concerning the use of computer-based personality test evaluations in forensic assessments need to be addressed. Pope and colleagues (2006) point out that when forensic testimony involves the use of computer-based testing, it is very important to be able to establish the chain of custody for the test protocol in question, to document that the computer-based report is actually the report for the client in the case. The forensic psychologist should be prepared to explain how the answer sheet was obtained and to show that the computer-based results are actually those for the client in question. There have been cases in which the MMPI was excluded from evidence because the psychologist was unable to establish that the test interpretation was actually the one that the client completed. For example, allowing the client to take the test somewhere other than in the clinician's office may well lead to exclusion of the results from testimony.

It is also important to ensure that the particular interpretation in the computer-based report is an appropriate match for the patient's test scores. In cross-examination, an attorney might ask questions about how the psychologist knows that the computer report actually fits the client. As noted earlier, computer-based psychological tests are usually prototypes. Therefore, some of the report descriptions might not apply for a particular case. The psychologist should be prepared, on cross-examination, to deal with descriptive statements in the report that are considered not appropriate for the particular client.

Psychologists who use computer-based MMPI-2 reports in court typically are able to establish the objectivity and utility of the instrument for understanding the client's problems and personality. Most people have found that the MMPI (MMPI-2) is relatively easy to explain to lay people such as juries or to judges. Moreover, judges and juries are often found to be interested in the idea that computers can be programmed to provide an objective appraisal of the test.

Cautions or Questions Regarding Use of Computerized Psychological Reports

Some problems or pitfalls can occur with the use of computerized psychological evaluations. Computer-based test users need to be vigilant about problems that can enter into blind reliance on computer-based personality assessment and implement remedies to avoid such problems. To have an effective practice the clinician must be alert to and avoid the following potential problems with computer-based testing:

Computerized assessment can promote an overly passive attitude toward clinical evaluation. Professionals who allow the computer to do all the work of gathering and summarizing clinical data may fail to pay sufficient attention to the patient in the assessment process to gain a thorough understanding of the patient's problems. A great deal can be learned about a patient by carefully observing and keeping in close touch with the test data, and in thoughtfully summarizing the results. Having computerized results should not be considered a substitute for clinical observation and astute integration of a broad range of pertinent information.

Computerized assessments can introduce a mystical aura into the assessment process. Clinicians who become overly enthralled with the marvels of computer-based test results may have difficulty questioning whether interpretations are appropriate or sufficiently tied to research. There is nothing magical or mysterious about a computer-based psychological test report. Computer or automated test results should be qualitatively no different from what a well-trained expert with the test could do if he or she had sufficient time and the available resource information about the test. Essentially, the same sources of information are available and typically used by computer interpretation system developers and by clinicians. The main difference is that the computer system development is usually more extensive and comprehensive than the clinician is able to develop on a single case with limited time available.

The computer may lead to an unwarranted impression of scientific precision in test interpretation through the use of impressive-looking printouts. Computerized psychological test results can lure individuals into feeling satisfied that they are finding out the most important and most accurate information about patients. However, the results provided by computers can be trivial, irrelevant, meaningless, or downright wrong. Keep in mind that one could program computers to generate nonsense syllables or horoscopes that have no empirical foundation or predictive value. Any report based on weak or meaningless test interpretations, even though computer-generated, will still be meaningless.

Computer interpretations may not be specific enough to provide differential descriptions of clients. Most clinical psychology students are aware of the phenomenon known as the "P. T. Barnum effect," that is, using general statements in personality description that are so vague and nonspecific that they apply to virtually anyone. O'Dell (1972) conducted a study showing that P. T. Barnum-type interpretations in a computer report would be accepted by people as accurate information about them even though the descriptions apply to all people. Although they may sound insightful and descriptive, reports that include a large number of P. T. Barnum-type statements are not very useful in making clinical decisions. Computerized-test users need to be on the alert for Barnum-type statements in the report and avoid making important clinical decisions based on them.

Some information included in a computer-based assessment report may not match every patient. Personality test reports are basically prototypal descriptions. That is, they are generic summaries that are developed for a particular set of scores, configuration, or profile type. Some of the prototypal information that is printed out may not be relevant or appropriate for a particular case. For example, some correlates for a particular scale pattern that are reported in research articles or textbooks on the test might not apply for all cases that have the test pattern. It is up to the clinician to determine if the test hypotheses from the report are relevant and appropriate for the case. Any interpretations or hypotheses that are not appropriate, judged by what is known about the client from other sources of information, should be ignored in the conclusions of the report (see the discussion in Pope et al., 2006).

It is also important for the practitioner to ensure that the particular interpretation in the computer-based report is an appropriate prototypal match between the patient's scores on the test and the statements generated by the computer. The closer the match between the client's scores and those of the prototype pattern, the more appropriate the report will be.

Failure to maintain control over computer-based reports can lead to problems. Practitioners need to ensure that computer-derived test reports are appropriately controlled and are not misused (Pope et al., 2006). Computer-based psychological reports, as usually noted on the narrative, were developed for professional use. This generally implies that the consumer has a background in psychopathology and psychological measurements and is knowledgeable about the particular test in use. Computer printouts that become a part of a patient's file should be properly labeled to prevent them from being mistaken for the final report on the patient.

Computerized test reports are raw test data, not final products. One important point to consider is that computer-based reports do not usually "stand alone" as a psychological report. The computer printout, if kept in a patient's file, should contain annotation as to how the information was used in the final report (Butcher & Williams, 2000) to ensure that future users of the file will not mistake the computer-based hypotheses for the clinician's final report. It is up to the clinician conducting the evaluation to see that the information is properly labeled.

Relative Accuracy of Computer-Based Systems

An important point to consider in determining whether to use a computer-based interpretive report is that two different computer interpretation services providing interpretations of the same test might actually produce somewhat different results for the same protocol. Theoretically, any computer-based interpretation of a test should be quite similar to any other, since all are based on the same correlate research literature. Interpretation of test scores can vary; however, computer interpretation systems that are based closely on research-validated indices tend to have similar outputs. Yet, research has shown that test interpretation services may differ with respect to their amount of information and the accuracy of the interpretations (Eyde, Kowal, & Fishburne, 1991). Practitioners using an all-automated interpretation system should be familiar with the issues of computerized test interpretation generally and the validity research on the particular system used (see Butcher et al., 1998; Eyde, 1993; Eyde et al., 1991; Moreland, 1987; Williams & Weed, 2004).

Are Computer-Based Psychological Assessments Ethical and Appropriate?

The psychological profession accepts computer interpretation as an appropriate means of evaluating test data on clients (see the American Psychological Association Guidelines for computer-based assessment, 1986): "A long history of research on statistical and clinical prediction has established that a well-designed statistical treatment of test results and ancillary information will yield more valid assessments than will an individual professional using the same information" (p. 9).

A survey of practitioners found that applied psychologists have substantially endorsed computer-based psychological assessment as an ethical practice (McMinn, Buchanan, Ellens, & Ryan, 1999).

Who Can Purchase and Use Computerized Reports?

Are the test reports available only to qualified psychologists or can other professionals, such as physicians and social workers, buy the services? The question of who can purchase and use computerized psychological test reports is frequently asked. The American Psychological Association (1986) has established guidelines for determining user qualifications for psychological test interpretation services. Psychological tests are grouped into different categories on the basis of purpose and use of the test. Recommendations for test user qualifications differ according to the different types of tests involved. For example, clinical personality tests (such as the MMPI-2) and computerized reports on them are considered B1-level instruments and are available to fellows, members, and associate members of the American Psychological Association as well as to psychologists, physicians, and marriage and family therapists who are licensed by the regulatory board of the state in which they practice.

Summary

Computerized psychological testing, originally developed in the 1960s, has evolved substantially over the past three decades. Computer-based psychological test reports can add significantly to the practitioner's clinical evaluations in terms of providing valuable, thorough, and accurate information that is processed in a timely manner. Many reasons account for the widespread use of computerized reports in clinical practice today: computer-based test interpretations are an objective and comprehensive means of interpreting psychological tests; they can be rapidly processed and made available early in the treatment session; and they have a high degree of reliability.

This chapter provided a discussion of how clinicians can incorporate computer-based information into their clinical practice. A case example was included to illustrate the types of information available and the ways it can be incorporated into treatment planning. The use of computer-based interpretive reports in forensic settings was also discussed and some guidelines for their use in court testimony were provided.

Several possible pitfalls that can accompany the use of computer-based psychological tests were discussed. It is important for practitioners to be aware of and to avoid the potential problems that can occur with the incorporation of automated assessment into clinical practice. Ways of avoiding problems were discussed in order to provide the practitioner with assurance that computer-derived information from psychological tests can be readily incorporated into a clinical practice, making it more appropriate and effective.

References

Allard, G., Butler, J., Faust, D., & Shea, M. T. (1995). Errors in hand scoring objective personality tests: The case of the personality diagnostic questionnaire-revised (PDQ-R). *Professional Psychology: Research and Practice, 26,* 304–308.

American Psychological Association. (1986). *American Professional Association Guidelines for computer-based tests and interpretations.* Washington, DC: Author.

Archer, R. P., Griffin, R., & Aiduk, R. (1995). Clinical correlates for ten common code types. *Journal of Personality Assessment, 65,* 391–408.

Atlis, M. M., Hahn, J., & Butcher, J. N. (2006). Computer-based assessment with the MMPI-2. In J. N. Butcher (Ed.), *MMPI-2: The practitioner's handbook* (pp. 445–476). Washington, DC: American Psychological Association.

Bloom, B. L. (1992). Computer assisted psychological intervention: A review and commentary. *Clinical Psychology Review, 12*, 169–198.

Boccaccini, M. T., & Brodsky, S. L. (1999). Diagnostic test use by forensic psychologists in emotional injury cases. *Professional Psychology: Research and Practice, 31*(1), 251–259.

Borum, R., & Grisso, T. (1995). Psychological test use in criminal forensic evaluations. *Professional Psychology, 26*, 465–473.

Butcher, J. N. (2005). *MMPI-2: A beginner's guide* (2nd ed.). Washington, DC: American Psychological Association.

Butcher, J. N., Berah, E., Ellersten, B., Miach, P., Lim, J., Nezami, E., et al. (1998). Objective personality assessment: Computer-based MMPI-2 interpretation in international clinical settings. In C. Belar (Ed.), *Comprehensive clinical psychology: Sociocultural and individual differences* (pp. 277–312). New York: Elsevier.

Butcher, J. N., Graham, J. R., Williams, C. L., & Ben-Porath, Y. S. (1990). *Development and use of the MMPI-2 content scales.* Minneapolis, MN: University of Minnesota Press.

Butcher, J. N., & Hostetle, K. (1990). Abbreviating MMPI item administration: Past problems and prospects for the MMPI-2. *Psychological Assessment: A Journal of Consulting and Clinical Psychology, 2*, 12–22.

Butcher, J. N., Keller, L. S., & Bacon, S. F. (1985). Current developments and future directions in computerized personality assessment. *Journal of Consulting and Clinical Psychology, 53*, 803–815.

Butcher, J. N., & Perry, J. N. (2008). *Personality assessment in treatment planning: Use of the MMPI-2 and BTPI.* New York: Oxford University Press.

Butcher, J. N., Perry, J. N., & Atlis, M. M. (2000). Validity and utility of computer-based test interpretation. *Psychological Assessment, 12*(1), 6–18.

Butcher, J. N., Rouse, S. V., & Perry, J. N. (2000). Empirical description of psychopathology in therapy clients: Correlates of MMPI-2 scales. In J. N. Butcher (Ed.), *Basic sources on the MMPI-2* (pp. 487–500). Minneapolis, MN: University of Minnesota Press.

Butcher, J. N., & Williams, C. L. (2000). *MMPI-2 and MMPI-A: Essentials of clinical interpretation.* Minneapolis, MN: University of Minnesota Press.

Butcher, J. N., & Williams, C. L. (2009). Personality Assessment with the MMPI-2: Historical roots, international adaptations, and current challenges. *Applied Psychology Health and Well-Being.*

Dahlstrom, W. G., & Archer, R. P. (2000). A shortened version of the MMPI-2. *Assessment, 7*, 131–137.

Downey, R. B., Sinnett, E. R., & Seeberger, W. (1998). The changing face of MMPI practice. *Psychological Reports, 83*(3, Pt. 2), 1267–1272.

Eyde, L. (1993). Tips for clinicians using computer based test interpretations (CBTIs). In B. Schlosser & K. Moreland (Eds.), *Taming technology: Issues, strategies and resources for the mental health practitioner* (pp. 97–99). Washington, DC: American Psychological Association.

Eyde, L., Kowal, D., & Fishburne, F. J. (1991). The validity of computer-based test interpretations of the MMPI. In T. B. Gutkin & S. L. Wise (Eds.), *The computer and the decision making process* (pp. 75–123). Hillsdale, NJ: LEA Press.

Finger, M. S., & Ones, D. S. (1999). Psychometric equivalence of the computer and booklet forms of the MMPI: A meta-analysis. *Psychological Assessment, 11*(1), 58–66.

Finn, S. E. (1990). *A model for providing test feedback with the MMPI and MMPI-2.* Paper presented at the 25th Annual Symposium on Recent Developments in the Use of the MMPI (MMPI-2), Minneapolis, MN, June 1990.

Finn, S. E., & Kamphuis, J. H. (2006). Therapeutic assessment with the MMPI-2. In J. N. Butcher (Ed.), *MMPI-2: The practioner's handbook* (pp. 165–191). Washington, DC: American Psychological Association.

Finn, S. E., & Tonsager, M. (1992). Therapeutic effects of providing MMPI-2 test feedback to college students awaiting therapy. *Psychological Assessment, 4*, 278–287.

Fowler, R. D. (1969). Automated interpretation of personality test data. In J. N. Butcher (Ed.), *MMPI: Research developments and clinical applications* (pp. 105–175). New York: McGraw-Hill.

Fowler, R. D., & Butcher, J. N. (1986). Critique of Matarazzo's views on computerized testing: All sigma and no meaning. *American Psychologist, 41*, 94–96.

Frauenhoffer, D., Ross, M. J., Gfeller, J., Searight, H. R., & Piotrowski, C. (1998). Psychological test usage among licensed mental health practitioners: A multidisciplinary survey. *Journal of Psychological Practice, 4*, 28–33.

Garb, H. (1992). The debate over the use of computer-based test reports. *The Clinical Psychologist, 45*, 95–100.

Gass, C. S., & Gonazalez, C. (2003). MMPI-2 short form proposal: CAUTION. *Archives of Clinical Neuropsychology, 18*, 521–527.

Gass, C. S., & Luis, C. A. (2001). MMPI-2 short form: Psychometric characteristics in a neuropsychological setting. *Assessment, 8*, 213–219.

Gilberstadt, H., & Duker, J. (1963). *A handbook of clinical and actuarial MMPI interpretation.* Philadelphia: Saunders.

Graham, J. R. (2006). *MMPI-2: Assessing personality and psychopathology* (4th ed.). New York: Oxford University Press.

Graham, J. R., Ben-Porath, Y. S., & McNulty, J. (1999). *Using the MMPI-2 in outpatient mental health settings.* Minneapolis, MN: University of Minnesota Press.

Greene, R. (2000). *The MMPI-2/MMPI: An interpretive manual* (2nd ed.). Needham Heights, MA: Allyn & Bacon.

Grove, W. M., & Meehl, P. E. (1996). Comparative efficiency of information (subjective, impressionistic) and formal (mechanical, algorithmic) prediction procedures: The clinical-statistical controversy. *Psychology, Public Policy, and Law, 2*, 293–323.

Grove, W. M., Zald, D. H., Lebow, B., Smith, E., & Nelson, C. (2000). Clinical versus mechanical prediction: A meta-analysis. *Psychological Assessment, 12*(1), 19–30.

Handel, R. W., Ben-Porath, Y. S., & Watt, M. (1999). Computerized adaptive assessment with the MMPI-2 in a clinical setting. *Psychological Assessment, 11*, 369–380.

Lees-Haley, P. R. (1992). Psychodiagnostic test usage by forensic psychologists. *American Journal of Forensic Psychology, 10*, 25–30.

Lees-Haley, P. R., Smith, H. W., Williams, C. W., & Dunn, J. T. (1996). Forensic neuropsychologial test usage: An empirical survey. *Archives of Clinical Neuropsychology, 11*, 45–51.

Lewandowski, D., & Graham, J. R. (1972). Empirical correlates of frequently occurring two-point code types: A replicated study. *Journal of Clinical Psychology, 39*, 467–472.

Lubin, B., Larsen, R., & Matarazzo, J. D. (1984). Patterns of psychological test usage in the United States: 1935–1982. *American Psychologist, 39*, 451–454.

McKenna, T., & Butcher, J. *Continuity of the MMPI with alcoholics.* (1987, April). *Paper given at the 22nd Annual Symposium on Recent Developments in the Use of the MMPI.* Seattle, Washington.

McMinn, M. R., Buchanan, T., Ellens, B. M., & Ryan, M. (1999). Technology, professional practice, and ethics: Survey findings and implications. *Professional Psychology: Research and Practice, 30,* 165–172.

Marks, P. A., Seeman, W., & Haller, D. (1975). *The actuarial use of the MMPI with adolescents and adults.* Baltimore, MD: Williams & Wilkins.

Matarazzo, J. (1986). Computerized clinical psychological test interpretations: Unvalidated plus all mean and no sigma. *American Psychologist, 41*, 14–24.

Meehl, P. (1954). *Clinical versus statistical prediction: A theoretical analysis and a review of the evidence.* Minneapolis, MN: University of Minnesota Press.

Moreland, K. (1987). Computerized psychological assessment: What's available. In J. N. Butcher (Ed.), *Computerized psychological assessment* (pp. 26–49). New York: Basic Books.

O'Dell, J. (1972). P. T. Barnum explores the computer. *Journal of Consulting and Clinical Psychology, 38*, 270–273.

Piotrowski, C., & Keller, J. W. (1989). Psychological testing in outpatient mental health facilities: A national study. *Professional Psychology Research and Practice, 20,* 423–425.

Pope, K., Butcher J. N., & Seelen J. (2006). *The MMPI/MMPI-2/MMPI-A in court: Assessment, testimony, and cross-examination for expert witnesses and attorneys* (3rd ed.). Washington, DC: American Psychological Association.

Rubenzer, S. (1991). Computerized testing and clinical judgment: Cause for concern. *The Clinical Psychologist, 4,* 63–66.

Rome, H. P., Swenson, W., Mataya P., McCarthy, C. E. Pearson J. S., Keating F. R., et al. (1962). Symposium on automation technics in personality assessment. *Proceedings of the Staff Meetings of the Mayo Clinic, 37,* 61–82.

Tellegen, A., Ben-Porath, Y. S., McNulty, J., Arbisi, P., Graham, J. R., & Kaemmer, B. (2003). *MMPI-2: Restructured Clinical (RC) Scales.* Minneapolis, MN: University of Minnesota Press.

Weiss, D. J. (1985). Adaptive testing by computer. *Journal of Consulting and Clinical Psychology, 53,* 774–789.

Williams, J. E., & Weed, N. C. (2004). Review of computer-based test interpretation software for the MMPI-2. *Journal of Personality Assessment, 83*(1), 78–83.

Ziskin, J. (1981). The use of the MMPI in forensic settings. In J. N. Butcher, W. G. Dahlstrom, M. D. Gynther, & S. Schofield (Eds.), *Clinical notes on the MMPI* (No. 9, entire issue). Nutley, NJ: Hoffman-LaRoche Laboratories/NCS.

Overview and Future Directions

James N. Butcher

Abstract

Personality assessment emerged during the early twentieth century largely through two avenues: development of personality questionnaires for assessing characteristics considered pertinent to screening draftees in the military in World War I, and early experiments with inkblot perception. Personality assessment broadened into other areas of applied and research psychology including clinical, forensic, and personnel applications as psychologists' professional roles expanded during the twentieth century. Personality assessment methods and applications have evolved successfully over the past century even though changes in social and professional practices have altered somewhat the focus of assessment during some periods. The contributions in this volume, providing a cross section of personality assessment techniques and instruments, have been extensively described and illustrated. Current challenges for personality assessment were highlighted and the potential for assessment to contribute further to understanding of personality and adjustment by various approaches was explored by the contributors. New directions for personality assessment have been suggested. The international expansion or globalization of Western-based personality assessment methodology was described and the fact that we are experiencing an increasingly broadened and effective cross-cultural collaborative environment for study of personality and psychopathology with the growing development of personality psychology internationally has been noted.

Keywords: history, cross-cultural, ethnicity, computer-based, invasion of privacy, high stakes testing

A look backward in time at the development of personality assessment over the past 100 years gives one an interesting perspective on the diverse methodology and effective applications that occurred in the field. As described in Chapter 1, personality assessment emerged in the early twentieth century and expanded substantially until the close of century. Researchers and practitioners in applied psychology incorporated early personality assessment strategies originated by Herman Rorschach (1921) and Robert Woodworth (1920) to develop instruments to evaluate personality. The 1930s and 1940s witnessed a strong merger between applied psychology and personality assessment as new effective instruments and techniques became available. Two distinct tracks in personality assessment evolved during this period—the diverse development of personality

questionnaires (Cattell & Stice, 1957; Meehl, 1945) and the use of ambiguous visual stimuli such as inkblots and pictures as a mode for eliciting "projective" responses from which personality characteristics are inferred (Exner, 1983; Lerner, 2007; Rapaport, Gill, & Schafer, 1945; Schafer, 1948).

As noted in Chapter 1, assessment psychology proceeded for years without a comprehensive underlying theoretical basis and instrument development and acceptance was sporadic at best. In the 1930s, Gordon Allport and Henry Murray provided a needed perspective and theoretical rationale for many types of personality assessments, particularly instruments that were "projective" in nature. The empirical approach by Hathaway and McKinley (1940), though without a theoretical "flag" until Meehl's thoughtful "empiricist manifesto" in 1945, provided a strong empirical rationale and justification for instruments like the Minnesota Multiphasic Personality Inventory (MMPI). These "trait-oriented" approaches to understanding personality characteristics provided the theoretical grounding for a functional perspective needed in personality assessment. After the 1940s, personality assessment psychology continued to be central in personnel screening but also merged extensively with clinical and counseling psychology and became oriented toward assessing personality and mental health problems. Later, forensic psychology, with assessment as a primary vehicle, came to address varied problems ranging from correctional assessment to family custody evaluations, and assessing litigants in personal injury cases.

Past Challenges to Personality Assessment

Personality assessment methodology and evolving techniques have not been without critics. Some of the problems will be noted in order to give the reader a view on past difficulties that assessment psychologists have faced during the evolution of the field. A number of psychologists raised concerns about personality assessment methods or tests (e.g., Ellis, 1946; Ellis & Conrad, 1948). Some criticism has been directed at the theoretical bases of assessment by questioning the existence of "traits" (Mischel, 1968). Some criticism of testing has come from outside of psychology, for example, criticisms that the use of personality inventories was an "invasion of privacy" (Ervin, 1965) or Annie Paul's general critique of "the cult of personality" (Paul, 2004). Other critics have more directly raised questions about specific instruments. For example, Jackson and Messick (1969) questioned aspects of self-report questionnaires in tests like the MMPI by viewing client's responses to the items as largely driven by response sets. Others have taken different strategies in their critiques, for example, Helmes and Reddon (1993) provided a number of blanket criticisms of the MMPI psychometrics including such factors as a perceived lack of a consistent measurement model, heterogeneous scale content, and suspect diagnostic criteria, item overlap among scales, lack of cross-validation of the scoring keys, inadequacy of measures of response styles, and suspect norms. Other critics viewed the original MMPI as outdated and incomplete and provided criticisms that would eventually lead to revising the instrument (Butcher, 1972). Other instruments have also been criticized; for example, there has been a substantial controversy surrounding the Rorschach Inkblot technique as well as the Exner

Comprehensive System and its norms for interpreting the test (Garb, 1999; Lilienfeld, Wood, & Garb, 2000).

In spite of these criticisms, personality assessment has continued to contribute to understanding of personality characteristics and problems of clients in numerous settings. In many ways, responses to these criticisms have actually improved interpretation strategies or strengthened the use of the instruments like the Rorschach (see Chapter 15). For example, a recent issue of the *Journal of Personality Assessment* provided a series of articles reporting an extensive normative base for the Rorschach Comprehensive System from many countries (see Shaffer, Erdberg, & Meyer, 2007). In addition, the criticisms of the possibility of response sets affecting MMPI assessment prompted further research and development of validity scales (such as VRIN, TRIN, S scales) that provide valuable pictures of the client's approach to the assessment. In another example, Mischel's (1968) critique of personality assessment and trait conceptualizations was influential although the viewpoint received considerable opposition and continued development. Trait theorists have actively pursued the trait approach to personality and the past 20 years have witnessed an extensive development of trait-oriented research, specifically what has been described as the "Big Five" model from which a number of personality measures have evolved (see Chapters 9 and 16).

Broader developments in the field have also impacted assessment development of trait constructs in personality. During the 1970s, psychological assessment in mental health settings came to be viewed by some as less important in clinical settings because of the widespread popularity of behavioral therapy. There was a sharp reduction in the use of traditional assessment techniques in the clinical setting as shown by the dip in the total amount of research in psychological assessment across test instruments compared with the 1960s (Butcher, Atlis, & Hahn, 2003). Even some clinical and counseling training programs deemphasized personality assessment and focused upon providing behavioral treatment without training in traditional assessment methods. During this period some assessment psychologists began to move into settings other than mental health, particularly into medical, forensic, and personnel applications (Butcher, Ones, & Cullen, 2006).

The clinical practice of psychological assessment (particularly objective assessment methods) made a comeback with studies being conducted on more varied topics and broader clinical application in the 1980s. In the 1990s, assessment research regained some of its earlier emphasis. For example, one review during this period found that there were about 250 articles published a year on the MMPI-2 and about 50 articles a year on the Rorschach, the two most widely used assessment instruments (Butcher & Rouse, 1996).

Personality assessment practice in mental health settings encountered further difficulties during the late 1990s as the managed care system began to assert control over the types and amounts of funding available for mental health services (see Butcher, 1997; Harwood et al., 1997). Psychological assessment was, in some contexts, relegated a minor role in the provision of mental health psychological services because payment was often not provided for the evaluation. Piotrowski (1999) reviewed findings from several surveys conducted in the 1990s pointing out that managed care has constrained both practice and training in clinical psychology. Managed care adversely affected testing and assessment practices and resulted in psychologists performing less testing and restricted their pool of assessment instruments to brief, symptom-focused testing measures and away from the more difficult to interpret measures such as projective instruments. Reimbursement for psychological assessment in clinical settings has, however, been improving in recent years with mental health services being more consistently provided for psychological assessment (see American Psychological Association Practice Directorate, 2006). The extent to which this practice will result in broader assessment use in mental health settings awaits further development.

Developments in Assessment: The Current Scene

The field of personality assessment is one that is rich in variety and extensive in application. One of our primary goals in the development of this handbook on personality assessment was to provide a comprehensive and detailed examination of the rich array of personality assessment approaches that are available today and the methodological issues that can impact instrument development. As anticipated, the contributors to this volume have provided a very substantial picture of the history, current status, and illustrative applications in personality assessment. The reader can obtain a valuable perspective on contemporary issues and an appreciation of the growing methodological strategies and test applications that have evolved. Both the traditional

and newer approaches to personality assessment are showcased in this book.

Broad Acceptance of Personality Assessment Strategies in Applied Psychology

The varied content of this handbook attests to the extent to which personality assessment has become an integral part of contemporary psychology. Assessment techniques are widely used in clinical activities such as assessment of potential suicide (Chapter 26), assessment of head injury patients (Chapter 23), evaluation of criminal offenders (Chapter 28; psychopathic personality in Chapter 29), assessment of marital couples in distress (Chapter 24), evaluations for therapy (Chapters 33 and 34), and personnel screening (Chapter 30), to mention only a few applications. Psychologists in many settings rely upon personality assessments to assist them in their decisions about people.

Evidence of Validity and Utility of Available Assessment Methods

Assessment-oriented psychologists can be reassured that the psychological assessment procedures available today validly address clinical problems in mental health settings as effectively as many trusted medical procedures. The validity and utility of psychological tests were highlighted in a study that underscored the value of psychological assessment in clinical settings (Meyer et al., 2001). These authors compared the accuracy of psychological tests with that of medical tests (such as X-rays or CT scans) for symptomatic evaluation. They found that psychological tests were as valid and reliable as most medical tests used in medical practice today (Meyer et al., 2001).

CLASSIC APPROACHES TO ASSESSMENT

Any comprehensive assessment volume, in order to be thorough and to reflect reality of our time, needs to incorporate the "old standards" as well as highlighting new methods. Several chapters in the handbook have been devoted to providing an updated overview of contemporary uses in the techniques that are widely used in assessment settings: clinical observation (see Chapter 11 on behavioral observations), behavioral assessment (as viewed in Chapter 13) and procedures for conducting interview (as described in Chapter 12) were reviewed. Two instruments that have been on the table for 70 or more years, the MMPI/MMPI-2 (Chapter 14 and the Rorschach as viewed in Chapter 15), were summarized and current developments in techniques described.

An Increasing Variety of Personality Inventories and Behavioral Assessment Strategies Are Available for Use in Clinical Assessment

Most of these newer personality inventories follow somewhat different theoretical viewpoints and test construction strategies than was used with the MMPI and, consequently, address different aspects of personality. For example, the Millon Clinical Multiaxial Inventory (and revised versions such as the MCMI-II and MCMI-III) (Millon, 1977) were developed from Millon's general theory of personality and standardized on patients undergoing mental health care. He did not use a general normative population as was used in the development of instruments such as the MMPI. The MCMI and the revised versions, the MCMI-II and MCMI-III inventories (Millon, 1996), are intended to evaluate patients undergoing psychotherapy and follow the Diagnostic and Statistical Manual (DSM) criteria. The use of psychotherapy patients as the reference sample is both a strength and a limitation for some applications. That is, comparing a protocol with patients gives the practitioner a perspective on his or her client's problems that is not provided with other tests. However, use of a patient reference group (instead of "normals") weakens use in settings such as personnel selection or forensic evaluations in which reference samples need to be drawn from the normal population to be informative.

Another instrument, the NEO PI (Costa & McCrae, 1992), was developed as a measure of "normal range" personality characteristics but is sometimes used in clinical assessment. The authors constructed the NEO PI based upon the five-factor theory of personality (see Digman, 1990) in order to appraise the five major trait domains underlying this theoretical approach. Some inventories address highly specialized assessment tasks such as the Psychopathy Checklist (PCL) by Hare (2002) as a means for typifying psychopathic personalities. In applying psychological tests with clients, it is important for the practitioner to review the test manual for the instrument to ascertain proper administration, scoring, and interpretation guidelines to ensure that a test is properly used.

In addition to psychological tests, there are a number of formal behavioral assessment methods and rating scales that have evolved over the last half of the twentieth century to provide valuable information in clinical evaluations (see discussions by Goldfried & Kent, 1972; in Chapter 13; and by Haynes & O'Brien, 2000). These instruments are usually completed by the clinician or an observer rather than the client and address different aspects of the patient's behavior than those addressed by traditional assessment methods, such as self-report. There is also a range of interview formats that are used both for research and clinical applications (see Chapter 12).

Assessment Has Been Successfully Integrated into Psychological Treatment

In the past 20 years, a clinical treatment approach has evolved that has taken the strengths of psychological assessment methods and incorporated assessment data into psychotherapy as a behavioral change strategy through providing test feedback to the client (Butcher, 1990). This approach, referred to as "therapeutic assessment" (Finn & Tonsager, 1992), has been shown to effectively provide clients with personality information based on their test results early in treatment—a tactic that leads to improved self-esteem and reduced symptoms. A recent survey by Smith, Wiggins, and Gorske (2007) reported the results of a survey from 719 psychologist members of the International Neuropsychological Society, the National Academy of Neuropsychology, and the Society for Personality Assessment who regularly conducted assessments as part of their professional activities. They found that the majority of respondents (71%) frequently provided in-person assessment feedback to their clients and/or their clients' families. Moreover, they reported that most respondents (72%) indicated that clients found this information to be helpful and positive in the clinical process.

The Wide Availability of Electronic Computers Enhance Personality Assessment Today

Computer scoring and test interpretation make psychological testing results more readily available and cost-effective for incorporating into psychological assessment. Moreover, computer interpretation provides the practitioner with an objective framework for a clinical evaluation (Atlis, Hahn, & Butcher, 2006; Chapter 10). A number of resources are available that demonstrate the utility of computer-based assessment in clinical evaluations (see Butcher et al., 1998, 2000; Butcher & Cheung, 2006).

METHODOLOGICAL DEVELOPMENTS IN PERSONALITY ASSESSMENT

Psychologists developing personality assessment instruments today, or those interested in evaluating existing instruments for their use, are blessed with a plethora of psychometric strategies, methods for approaching the scale construction task or evaluating psychometric utility, and software incorporating the programs necessary for statistical analyses of test data. For example, procedures are available for assessing item characteristics such as alpha coefficients (Streiner, 2003; item reponse theory or IRT [Weiss & Suhdolnik, 1985]). Scale construction strategies such as factor analysis (Jöreskog, 2007) that are valuable for developing scales or refining measures have been explored. Several strategies are now widely used in evaluating the effectiveness and validity of psychological measures such as meta-analysis (Hunter & Schmidt, 1990) and reliability generalization (Rouse, 2007; Vacha-Haase, Henson, & Caruso, 2002). This book includes several methodological papers that address issues in validity (Chapters 4 and 5) and includes several chapters that provide guidelines for assuring that personality tests operate according to high professional standards (Chapters 6 and 7).

NEW TECHNOLOGIES IN PERSONALITY EVALUATION

New technological developments hold promise for expanding information in personality and psychological symptom assessment. Chapter 19 provides an overview of new developments in the use of neuroimaging for predicting clinical states, with particular attention to clinical assessment. The authors describe the underpinnings of the blood oxygenation level–dependent responses that are used in functional magnetic resonance imaging (fMRI). They provide background for understanding the development and use of models based on brain data to examine latent states, such as deception, and latent traits, such as the diagnosis of schizophrenia. Although neuroimaging is not, at present, a practical tool for clinical assessment, Chapter 19 concludes that it likely will provide an important avenue to pursue, for example, the study of depression and anxiety.

The Need for Objective Evaluations of a Client's Personality Characteristics in Applied Settings

The use of personality measures in nonmental health settings has increased the role that assessment psychologists play in contemporary psychology. Assessment-oriented forensic psychologists often contribute to the evaluation of clients, for example, to aid in determining a parent's suitability in parenting for custody of minor children, or to assess a client who alleges to be psychologically injured as a result of an accident in personal injury claims, or to assist in the evaluation of criminal offenders, for example, in the sentencing phase of a trial (see Megargee, 2006; Pope, Butcher, & Seelen, 2006) or to assesss dangerousness (see Chapter 28).

Personality tests have continued to contribute to assessing suitability in some personnel selection settings for positions, such as airline pilots, police personnel, and nuclear power plant employees, in which emotional stability is an important concern to safe job performance (Butcher et al., 2006; Chapter 30).

Attending to Cultural and Racial Factors in Personality Assessment

This handbook includes several chapters that focus attention on the importance of tailoring or adapting personality assessment methods and strategies to a multicultural society. The importance of continued vigilance for assuring nonbiased assessment is highlighted in Chapter 21. The author has pointed out that "Detecting and mitigating racial bias in assessment is a profoundly complex challenge" and provided a perspective on several conceptual issues central to assessing U.S. minority groups besides reviewing efforts to address ethnic and racial sensitivity in frequently used adult assessment instruments. She has pointed out that the MMPI-2 is a prime example of progress in this area, for example, in use with African-Americans, to the point that earlier controversy in its use has abated. In addition, she noted that recent research with the Rorschach also holds out the likelihood that it is equally applicable to very closely matched groups of African-Americans and Whites. However, in spite of such changes, serious concerns remain. For example, the MMPI-2 appears to show excess pathology in Asian-Americans (particularly those who are in the process of acculturating to a new culture) and reminds the reader that we have not reached the point of universal applicability of the major instruments used to assess psychopathology. Similarly, Chapter 20 points out that although there is ongoing research on the relationship between race-related measures and psychopathology, there is no consistent effort to develop and validate a clinical assessment measure that can tap into this critical aspect of many Asian-Americans' experience. The authors have noted that although a set of variables that are as complex, dynamic, and historically situated as racial discrimination affect Asian-American individuals, further efforts need to address these variables. Clinical personality assessment with

Asian-Americans is a field that continues to face many challenging problems that require attention. The authors call for continued programmatic research on clinical personality instruments with Asian-American populations to ensure that the most effective procedures be used. Recent developments in test interpretation with Hispanic clients (see Butcher, Cabiya, Lucio, & Garrido, 2007; Garrido & Velasquez, 2006; Geisinger, 1992) show both a broad research base and effective interpretive guidelines in applying the MMPI-2 with Latino clients.

With respect to another demographic variable that requires careful consideration in assessment, Chapter 22 provides an important perspective on the historical and current approaches to gender in the assessment process, and provides suggestions for effective information collection strategies that acknowledge the influence of gender-related variables on women's psychological health and well-being. They discuss several concerns and available research associated with gender bias in assessment, and examine the evidence for the influence of bias in the diagnostic process.

INTERNATIONAL DEVELOPMENTS IN ASSESSMENT RESEARCH AND APPLICATIONS

The use of well-established and demonstrated equivalent assessment instruments can serve as an effective vehicle for gaining a broader understanding of personality factors in other cultures. Opportunities now exist for psychologists to broaden our knowledge of psychopathology through gaining a more global perspective of mental health problems. Psychological test adaptations in cultures that are different from the country of origin are not novel. In fact, two of the most widely used assessment techniques, the Rorschach and Binet Intelligence Scale, were initially cross-cultural adaptations from other countries to the United States. Several important differences in today's test adaptation are addressed.

Cross-cultural personality assessment research is more viable today than ever before (see research on cross-cultural comparisons of personality dimensions by Cheung, Cheung, Zhang, Leong, & Yeh, 2008). The capability of collecting comparable data describing similar clinical patterns in different countries can contribute to our general understanding of personality and adds cumulative information to the field of personality. An illustration of the gains to be made in the field of personality can be seen in using the large number of well-developed translations of

the MMPI-2 that are presently available—over 33 (Butcher, 1996). These adapted versions of the test enable research on clinical problem areas across many countries and can serve as a basis for cross-national psychopathology research (Butcher, 2006). A number of studies have shown highly similar clinical patterns on the available translations of MMPI clinical measures (Manos, 1985; Savacir & Erol, 1990). Clinical research on the MMPI-2 has been expanding greatly in other countries, for example, in Europe (Butcher, Derksen, Sloore, & Sirigatti, 2003), and in China (Cheung, 2004; Cheung, Cheung, & Zhang, 2004). Three recent MMPI-2 research projects have been conducted by teams of psychologists in several countries in order to assess the effectiveness of computer-based assessment across cultures (Butcher et al., 1998, 2000; Butcher & Cheung, 2006).

With the growth in applied psychology in other countries there is an increasing number of trained personality researchers who have both the interest in and expertise for conducting collaborative international personality assessment research. International research programs to study personality processes are much more efficiently developed today. International research collaboration on personality projects is more efficient with the rapid communication that is available through the high-speed Internet (Butcher, 2006). And most researchers have ready access to the extensive body of published research that can be a great advantage to collaborating researchers today; finally, the use of email to transport data and communicate findings or problems makes the collaborative process more time-efficient.

Current Challenges Facing Contemporary Personality Assessment Psychologists

There are a number of continuing challenges that can result in diminished effectiveness in assessment psychology today if they are not resolved and improved; six problem areas that can impact future test applications or procedures will be described here.

Diminished Assessment Training in Professional Programs

As noted earlier, one challenge facing psychological assessment today is the reduced emphasis upon training graduate students in assessment (Merenda, 2007). There has been a noticeable reduction of assessment training in many graduate programs, particularly with respect to projective techniques. Graduate students from some training programs often find it difficult to obtain placements in desired internship programs or find that their lack of assessment skills disadvantages them in being accepted in their placement of choice. Clemence and Handler (2001) pointed out that major discrepancies exist between what is being taught in graduate school and what experiences are expected by internship programs.

Fortunately, some of the professional associations are committed to providing continuing education training in areas of clinical practice, for example, the American Psychological Association, the Society for Personality Assessment, and some state psychological associations. Their programs aim to update and "refresh" professionals but this is generally insufficient for providing the basic graduate education in assessment methods and techniques.

The challenge: In order for the field to continue to have highly qualified researchers and practitioners, it is necessary for educational institutions to provide objective, balanced educational experiences in assessment research methodology and applied assessment techniques.

Lag in Development of New Assessment Procedures

Greene (2006) recently noted, "It also behoves us as specialists in assessment to realize that if it were 1940 and we were discussing state of the art in assessment, we would be talking about the MMPI, Rorschach, and TAT.... The fact that in 2005 we still are using the same techniques is mind-boggling. There are few fields in which the advances have been so limited" (p. 254). In a similar vein, over 35 years ago, Hathaway (1972), in an evaluation of the progress of personality assessment methods entitled "Where have we gone wrong? The mystery of missing progress," noted that the field of personality assessment has made little progress toward developing newer personality tests.

The hopeful view that the computer revolution held promise for providing more realistic visual environments such as enhanced "lifelike" test stimuli and more advanced and effective computer-based administrative formats has not materialized. It simply takes too much developmental work and costly validation effort in order for an instrument to gain trust and acceptance for clinical decisions. Moreover, the use of modern technologies in processing test results, such as Internet applications of psychological tests, has encountered a number of problems that require resolution (see discussion by Atlis et al., 2006) for this media to be effective and professionally acceptable. For example, the potential

lack of test item security makes test publishers reluctant to expose successful and well-established tests to the perils of poor security of the web. Thus, psychological assessment relies substantially on traditional instruments and new innovations are not in sight.

The challenge: Over the past 60 years, new personality assessment approaches have not moved substantially beyond what the earlier assessment test developers produced. Technology exists to provide "lifelike" interpersonal situations that could be used effectively as stimuli but will the next generation find approaches that move the field further or in a different direction?

Practitioners Often Use Psychological Tests in the Applications for Which They Are Not Intended or Are Not Psychometrically Appropriate

Psychological tests have limits that need to be understood before they are applied with clients. Any psychological test will have limitations, depending upon factors such as restriction of the stimuli, specific nature of the test structure, the reference populations used to develop the norms, the research validation, and so forth. Or, a procedure that was developed for assessing a specific problem area might fall short or be irrelevant for assessing another. As noted earlier, the MCMI instruments were developed for assessing clients in psychotherapy and have items and reference groups designed for that population. Yet, the test is applied in settings such as forensic or personnel when results can only be puzzling given the test goals and norms.

The challenge: Psychological tests need to be clearly described to assure that tests are appropriately used and their limitations clearly understood. Practitioners need to be more cognizant of test limitations and not ask the test to perform tasks for which there are insufficient supportive data.

Abbreviating or Shortening Well-Established Instruments Can Have Undesirable Side Effects

Less is not more. In 1975, Hathaway pointed out, "If you choose to for any reason to administer only part of the test, you should be aware of how this would affect the interpretations and the consequences which you would subsequently find through your interpretation. I, for one, would never administer only part of the test. I suspect the increment of new information would fall short." The MMPI/MMPI-2 were devised to assess a broad range of characteristics for use in general personality assessment settings and have a substantial research base in support of their varied applications. It takes only an hour and a half (with an MMPI-2) to obtain an extensive review of a client's symptoms, attitudes, test-taking behaviors, etc., that typically provides valuable information in giving a perspective on a client's problems. In the majority of settings this is not an overbearing commitment of time.

The abbreviation of established tests in order to provide a seemingly more "user-friendly" option can result in misleading interpretations or results. That is, a shortened test may require less testing time but can result in lowered validity and reliability or even a completely different set of results for the shortened measure than the practitioner was expecting based on the reputation of the original instrument. The clearest examples of this problem were found in the popular strategy for developing MMPI short forms during the 1970s and 1980s when there were several attempts made such as the Mini-Mult (Kincannon, 1968), the Faschingbauer (FAM; Faschingbauer, 1974), and the MMPI 168 (Overall & Gomez-Mont, 1974) (see discussion in Chapter 14). These short forms, however, did not completely capture the meanings of the full MMPI scale scores (see reviews by Butcher & Hostetler, 1990; Dahlstrom, 1980), and, for the most part, disappeared from the assessment scene. Two efforts to develop shortened MMPI-2 forms were published. For example, Dahlstrom and Archer (2000) published a shortened form of the MMPI-2 that comprised simply the first 180 items in the booklet. This abbreviated form resulted in similar problems as the earlier efforts (Gass & Luis, 2001). The other recent shortened version by McGrath, Terranova, Pogge, and Kravic (2003), the MMPI-297, proved more successful than the Dahlstrom and Archer version; however, it still produced T-scores that are substantially different (discrepancies of $T > 5$) from those derived from the full form of the MMPI-2, and its convergent validity is also weaker across a number of settings (McGrath et al., 2003).

Recently, there has been an effort to promote a shortened version of the MMPI-2 referred to as the MMPI-2-RF that takes a very different approach to abbreviating the test than past efforts. This 338-item, extremely altered version includes as its core the Restructured Clinical or RC Scales (Tellegen et al., 2003) in lieu of the traditional and well-established Clinical Scales. In addition, there are a number of other short measures that have not been previously published and the inclusion of one scale, the Lees-Haley Fake Bad Scale (FBS), has been at the center of a great controversy recently (see discussion below) as a result of bias. This RF approach to assessment uses the traditional name and reputation (MMPI) to provide a completely new instrument in its place. The test user needs to be aware that the RC Scales bear little psychometric resemblance to the traditional clinical scales (see Butcher, Hamilton, Rouse, & Cumella, 2006; Butcher & Williams, 2009; Nichols, 2006; Rouse, Greene, Butcher, Nichols, & Williams, 2008) and thus cannot effectively replace their functioning although the implication in the name, MMPI-2-RF, is that it does just that (see also the discussion in Chapter 23).

The challenge: Abbreviated versions of standard tests are typically not substitutes for the original form but are different tests and are often not equivalent to the original. Clear differentiation of new versions from the original needs to be carefully made to avoid confusion and test misuse.

Erosion of Standards for Assessment Instruments

It is important for the profession to guard against the dissemination of assessment instruments that do not perform psychometrically as promised or that perform in a biased manner and unfairly disadvantage clients. Professional vigilance to maintain quality assurance in assessment techniques is required, especially in "high stakes" evaluations such as personal injury forensic or work compensation cases.

Geisinger (2005) provided cautionary recommendations for psychologists using psychological tests in evaluations that can impact whether a client will or will not receive benefits based on a psychologist's test-based recommendations. See also Chapters 6 and 7 which discuss the importance of maintaining high standards in personality assessment instruments; new or modified assessment procedures need to meet high standards in order to assess personality variables with accuracy and reliability, and to be consistent with the expectations of qualified and ethical test users. Both chapters provide illustrations of problem situations that can occur in the field.

When high standards are ignored in the construction of instruments, the field of personality assessment is diminished, and clients, instead of being helped, can suffer consequences from an unfair evaluation (see Armstrong, 2008). The distribution of flawed assessment devices under the guise of "high standards" has recently occurred in changes made in the use of the MMPI-2. A scale that was developed several years ago from the MMPI-2 item pool (the FBS by Lees-Haley, English, & Glenn, 1991)—even with a documented proclivity to discriminate against women and against some persons with somatic problems (Butcher, Arbisi, Atlis, & McNulty, 2003)—was included in an MMPI-2 scoring program and made available across all settings. This formal, broad dissemination of the FBS was implemented even though the scale developer (see Lees-Haley & Fox, 2004) actually indicated that the FBS was designed for personal injury litigation *only* and not for broad clinical settings. This scale was included on the test scoring service by the test distributor in 2007 (see the rationale provided by Ben-Porath & Tellegen, 2007). The scale has not been shown to effectively detect malingering in any setting yet it has now become a widely disseminated "standard" option that could potentially result in patients with somatic symptoms being ignored or denied services if the practitioner uses this measure routinely or without careful attention to the limitations of the scale.

A recent review and analysis of the performance of the FBS in both forensic and clinical settings was conducted by Butcher, Gass, Cumella, Kally, and Williams (2008). The study further details the psychometric weakness of the FBS, the highly variable interpretive strategies used to interpret it, and the bias that occurs in using this scale to assess people. Butcher et al. also demonstrated the potentially damaging consequences of using the FBS in general mental health settings. They reported the high misclassification rate as "faking" in a sample of women eating disorder inpatients—a group with extremely unlikely malingering attitudes in taking the test. Using Lees-Haley's original cut off scores, 62% of the inpatient women with severe mental health problems (1,275 out of the sample of 2,054) would be classified as malingering; using the more conservative cutoff score suggested by Ben-Porath and Tellegen (2007), 11% of the women (235) were considered to be faking their symptoms.

The continued use of this scale for assessing litigants in personal injury cases is problematic in that many people with genuine physical or psychological symptoms would be characterized in a derogatory fashion (i.e., faking their symptoms).

The FBS has faired poorly in court cases in which their adequacy for admission into evidence has been challenged. Judges in four recent Frye hearings have not allowed the FBS into testimony (Davidson *v.* Strawberry Petroleum et al., 2007; Vandergracht *v.* Progressive Express et al., 2005; Williams *v.* CSX Transportation, Inc., 2007; *Stith v State Farm Insurance*, 2008) because it is baised against women

and people with physical symptoms, thereby prohibiting the defense experts from testifying in court that the FBS showed the plaintiff had been malingering.

It is likely that damaging results could be obtained as the FBS is used in broader assessment contexts such as medical assessments and outpatient and inpatient mental health evaluations, because as both Butcher, Arbisi et al. (2003) and Butcher, Gass et al. (2008) have shown, a high percentage of mental health clients are characterized as "faking" using the generally recommended cutoff scores suggested by Ben-Porath and Tellegen (2007). Thus, people with genuine problems could be denied services or payment for medical services.

The challenge: There is a need to eliminate test bias in "high stakes" measures. If this is not possible for a particular measure, then such instruments need to be avoided in assessing clients in applications where potentially damaging consequences can occur.

The Challenge of Increasing Diversity in the Client Population of the United States

The United States is a multicultural society with the largest minority population of Spanish-speaking immigrants increasing at a fast rate. Practitioners need to be vigilant about possible cultural factors that can affect psychological assessment. Research needs to provide useful assessment for multicultural mental health services because of the increasing diversity in U.S. populations and the importance of assuring valid and reliable adaptations of existing psychological measures. The need to provide culturally sensitive psychological assessment instruments has been an increasing concern of psychologists (Garrido & Velasquez, 2006; Hall, Bansal, & Lopez, 1999; Hays, 2001) and progress has been made with some instruments, such as the MMPI-2 (Butcher et al., 2007) for providing appropriate interpretive strategies. The MMPI-2, for example, has been shown to result in comparable findings between Hispanic and Anglo populations (Hall et al., 1999); however, further evaluation is needed for all clinical procedures that are used in clinical assessment of diverse client populations (e.g., some scale differences on scale L might occur) if the goal of fair and effective multicultural assessment is to be attained.

The challenge: Demonstrating and assuring that personality assessment measures are appropriate when used with clients from diverse backgrounds.

Future Directions

As the field of personality assessment ends its first century with a strong record of success that is reflected in the range of contributions featured in this book, we anticipate the evolution in the next 100 years with several questions: Will there be novel, improved, and more effective approaches to carry the field forward? Or, will there be a persistence of past successes with further refinements made to old standards? Will the new technological advances we highlight here be followed by further broadening of personality assessment methodology? Will contemporary society continue to rely upon available personality assessment instruments as it currently does? Will personality assessment keep pace with society's advances and expectations?

Whatever avenues are pursued, it is likely that the demands of current applications and the general acceptance of well-established techniques will continue to encourage development in applied settings. Along with the successes come the challenges: Can we meet these expectations?

Given the challenges that personality assessment psychologists are facing today, as described above, we may wonder about the best strategies to take with regard to the question that where do we go from here. In my view, we can be very optimistic about the future pathways that personality assessment will follow. As we saw in this handbook, we have a very rich history and substantially contemporary database from which to proceed over the coming years. Some well-traveled paths will likely continue in use while other avenues will emerge as exploration proceeds. As the chapters here attest, we are well equipped methodologically to assure a fruitful passage. Perhaps the most effective approach to progress in personality assessment would be to confront the challenges we currently face, as described in this book, through further research while maintaining the strengths of past successes. With problems ameliorated, we can advance into the next generation of personality assessment technology with confidence.

It is my view that the challenges we have noted in various places in this book can be overcome and that sounder steps can be taken to insure that the future of personality assessment will be successful. I hope the accomplishments and the visions our personality assessment forebearers held will be maintained and the hopes they had for the future of the field will be fulfilled.

References

American Psychological Association Practice Directorate. (2006). *Testing codes toolkit.* Washington, DC: American Psychological Association.

Armstrong, D. (2008). PERSONALITY CHECK Malingerer Test roils personal-injury law 'Fake Bad Scale' bars real victims, its critics contend. *Wall Street Journal,* March 5, 2008.

Atlis, M. M, Hahn, J., & Butcher, J. N. (2006). Computer-based assessment with the MMPI-2. In J. N. Butcher (Ed.), *MMPI-2: The practitioner's handbook* (pp. 445–476). Washington, DC: American Psychological Association.

Ben-Porath, Y. S., & Tellegen, A. (2007). MMPI-2 Fake Bad Scale (FBS). Retrieved December 4, 2007, from http://www.upress.umn.edu/tests/mmpi2_fbs.html

Butcher, J. N. (Ed.). (1972). *Objective personality assessment: Changing perspectives.* New York: Academic Press.

Butcher, J. N. (1990). *The MMPI-2 in psychological treatment.* New York: Oxford University Press.

Butcher, J. N. (1996). *International adaptations of the MMPI-2: Research and clinical applications.* Minneapolis, MN: University of Minnesota Press.

Butcher, J. N. (Ed.) (1997). *Personality assessment in managed care: Using the MMPI-2 in treatment planning.* New York: Oxford University Press.

Butcher, J. N. (2006). Assessment in clinical psychology: A perspective on the past, present challenges, and future prospects. *Clinical Psychology: Science and Practice, 13*(3), 205–209.

Butcher, J. N., & Cheung, F. M. (2006, May). *Workshop on the MMPI-2 and Forensic Psychology.* Hong Kong: Chinese University of Hong Kong and the Hong Kong Social Welfare Department.

Butcher, J. N., & Hostetler (1990). Abbreviating MMPI item administration: Past problems and prospects for the MMPI-2. *Psychological Assessment: A Journal of Consulting and Clinical Psychology, 2,* 12–22.

Butcher, J. N., & Rouse, S. V. (1996). Personality: Individual differences and clinical assessment. *Annual Review of Psychology, 47,* 87–111.

Butcher, J. N., Arbisi, P. A., Atlis, M. M., & McNulty, J. L. (2003). The construct validity of the Lees-Haley Fake Bad Scale: Does this scale measure somatic malingering and feigned emotional distress? *Archives of Clinical Neuropsychology, 18,* 473–485.

Butcher, J. N., Atlis, M., & Hahn, J. (2003). Assessment with the MMPI-2: Research base and future developments. In D. Segal (Ed.), *Comprehensive handbook of psychological assessment* (pp. 30–38). New York: John Wiley & Sons.

Butcher, J. N., Berah, E., Ellertsen, B., Miach, P., Lim, J., Nezami, E., et al. (1998). Objective personality assessment: Computer-based MMPI-2 interpretation in international clinical settings. In C. Belar (Ed.), *Comprehensive clinical psychology: Sociocultural and individual differences* (pp. 277–312). New York: Elsevier.

Butcher, J. N., Cabiya, J., Lucio, E. M., & Garrido, M. (2007). *The MMPI-2 and MMPI-A with Hispanic clients in the United States.* Washington, DC: American Psychological Association Books.

Butcher, J. N., Derksen, J., Sloore, H., & Sirigatti, S. (2003). Objective personality assessment of people in diverse cultures: European adaptations of the MMPI-2. *Behavior Research and Therapy, 41,* 819–840.

Butcher, J. N., Ellertsen, B., Ubostad, B., Bubb, E., Lucio, E., Lim, J., et al. (2000). *International case studies on the MMPI-A: An objective approach.* Minneapolis, MN: MMPI-2 Workshops.

Butcher, J. N., Gass, C. S., Cumella, E., Kally, Z., & Williams, C. L. (2008). Potential for bias in MMPI-2 assessments using the Fake Bad Scale (FBS). *Psychological Injury and Law, 1*(3), 191–209.

Butcher, J. N., Gass, C. S., Cumella, E., Kally, Z., & Williams, C. L. (2008). Potential for bias in MMPI-2 assessments using the Fake Bad Scale (FBS). *Psychological Injury and the Law*. Advanced online publication. Retrieved July 14, 2008. doi:10.1007/s12207-007-9002-z

Butcher, J. N., Hamilton, C. K., Rouse, S. V., & Cumella, E. J. (2006). The Deconstruction of the Hy scale of MMPI-2: Failure of RC3 in measuring somatic symptom expression. *Journal of Personality Assessment, 87*(1), 199–205.

Butcher, J. N., Ones, D. S., & Cullen, M. (2006). Personnel screening with the MMPI-2. In J. N. Butcher (Ed.), *MMPI-2: The practioner's handbook* (pp. 381–406). Washington, DC: American Psychological Association.

Butcher, J. N., & Williams, C. L. (2009). Personality assessment with the MMPI-2: Historical roots, international adaptations, and current challenges. *Applied Psychology, Health and Well-Being, 1*, 105–135.

Cattell, R. B., & Stice, G. E. (1957). *The Sixteenth Personality Factors Questionnaire*. Champaigne, IL: Institute for Personality and Ability Testing.

Cheung, F. M. (2004). Use of Western and indigenously developed personality tests in Asia. *Applied Psychology: An International Review, 53*(2), 173–191.

Cheung, F. M., Cheung, S., & Zhang, J. (2004). Convergent validity of the Chinese Personality Assessment Inventory and the Minnesota Multiphasic Personality Inventory-2: Preliminary findings with a normative sample. *Journal of Personality Assessment, 82* (1), 92–103.

Cheung, F. M., Cheung, S. F., Zhang, J., Leong, F., & Yeh, K. H. (2008). Relevance of openness as a personality dimension in Chinese culture. *Journal of cross-Cultural Psychology, 39*(1), 81–108.

Clemence, A. J., & Handler, L. (2001). Psychological assessment on internship: A survey of training directors and their expectations of students. *Journal of Personality Assessment, 76*, 18–47.

Costa, P. T., Jr., & McCrae, R. R. (1992). *Revised NEO Personality Inventory (NEO PI-R) and NEO Five Factor Inventory (NEO-FFI)*. Okesa, FL: Psychological Assessment Resources.

Dahlstrom, W. G. (1980). Altered forms of the MMPI. In W. G. Dahlstrom & L. E. Dahlstrom (Eds.), *Basic readings on the MMPI* (pp. 386–393). Minneapolis, MN: University of Minnesota Press.

Dahlstrom, W. G., & Archer, R. P. (2000). A shortened version of the MMPI-2. *Assessment, 7*, 131–137.

Davidson *v.* Strawberry Petroleum et al. (2007). Case #05-4320, Hillsborough County, FL.

Digman, J. M. (1990). Personality structure: Emergence of the Five Factor Model. *Annual Review of Psychology, 41*, 417–440.

Ellis, A. (1946). The validity of personality questionnaires. *Psychological Bulletin, 43*(5), 385–440.

Ellis, A., & Conrad, H. S. (1948). The validity of personality inventories in military practice. *Psychological Bulletin, 45*(5), 385–426.

Ervin, S. J., Jr. (1965). Why Senate hearings on psychological tests in government. *American Psychologist, 20*, 879–880.

Exner, J. E., Jr. (1983). *The Exner report for the Rorschach Comprehensive System*. Minneapolis, MN: National Computer Systems.

Faschingbauer, T. R. (1974). A 166 item short form for the group MMPI: The FAM. *Journal of Consulting and Clinical Psychology, 42*, 645–655.

Finn, S. E., & Tonsager, M. E. (1992). Therapeutic effects of providing MMPI-2 feedback to college students awaiting therapy. *Psychological Assessment, 4*, 278–287.

Garb, H. N. (1999). Call for a moratorium on the use of the Rorschach Inkblot Test in clinical and forensic settings. *Assessment, 6*, 311–318.

Garrido, M., & Velasquez, R. (2006). Interpretation of Latino/Latina MMPI-2 profiles: Review and application of empirical findings and cultural-linguistic considerations. In J. N. Butcher (Ed.), *MMPI-2: The practioner's handbook* (pp. 477–504). Washington, DC: American Psychological Association.

Gass, C. S., & Luis, C. A. (2001). MMPI-2 short form: Psychometric characteristics in a neuropsychological setting. *Assessment, 8*, 425–429.

Geisinger, K. F. (Ed). (1992). *Psychological testing of Hispanics*. Washington, DC: American Psychological Association.

Geisinger, K. F. (2005). The testing industry, ethnic minorities, and individuals with disabilities. In R. P. Philps (Ed.), *Defending standardized testing*. Mahwah, NJ: LEA Press.

Goldfried, M. R., & Kent, R. N. (1972). Traditional versus behavioral assessment: A comparison of methodological and theoretical assumptions. *Psychological Assessment, 77*, 409–420.

Greene, R. L. (2006). Use of the MMPI-2 in outpatient mental health settings. In J. N. Butcher (Ed.), *The MMPI-2 A practitioner's guide* (pp. 253–271). Washington, DC: American Psychological Association.

Hall, G. C. N., Bansal, A., & Lopez, I. R. (1999). Ethnicity and psychopathology: A meta-analytic review of 31 years of comparative MMPI/MMPI-2 research. *Psychological Assessment, 11*(2), 186–197.

Hare, R. S. (2002). The Psychopathy Check List-Revised. Toronto, ON: Multi-Health Systems.

Harwood, T. M., Beutler, L. E., Fisher, D., Sandowicz, M., Albanese, A. L., & Baker, M. (1997). Clinical decision making and managed care. In J. N. Butcher (Ed.), *Personality assessment in managed health care*. New York: Oxford University Press.

Hathaway, S. R. (1972). Where have we gone wrong? The mystery of missing progress. In J. N. Butcher (Ed.), *Objective personality assessment: Changing perspectives* (pp. 24–44). New York: Academic Press.

Hathaway, S. R. (1975). Comment on MMPI abbreviated forms. In *Who owns test items? Present confusions and anxieties about 1984*. Symposium on Recent Developments in the Use of the MMPI, St. Petersburg, FL, February 1975.

Hathaway, S. R., & McKinley, J. C. (1940). A multiphasic personality schedule (Minnesota): I. Construction of the schedule. *Journal of Psychology: Interdisciplinary and Applied, 10*, 249–254.

Haynes, S. N., & O'Brien, W. O. (2000). *Principles of behavioral assessment*. New York: Kluwer Academic/Plenum.

Hays, P. (2001). *Addressing cultural complexities in practice: A framework for clinicians and counselors*. Washington, DC: American Psychological Association.

Helmes, E., & Reddon, J. R. (1993). A perspective on developments in assessing psychopathology: A critical review of the MMPI and MMPI-2. *Psychological Bulletin, 113*, 453–471.

Hunter, J. E., & Schmidt, F. L. (1990). *Methods for meta-analysis: Correcting error and bias in research findings*. Newbury Park, CA: Sage.

Jackson, D. N., & Messick, S. (1969). A distinction between judgments of frequency and of desirability as determinants of response. *Educational and Psychological Measurement,* *29*, 273–293.

Jöreskog, K. G. (2007). Factor analysis and its extensions. In R. Cudeck & R. C. MacCallum (Eds.), *Factor analysis at 100: Historical developments and future directions* (pp. 47–77). Mahwah, NJ: Lawrence Erlbaum.

Kincannon, J. (1968). Prediction of the standard MMPI scale scores from 71 items: The Mini-Mult. *Journal of Consulting and Clinical Psychology, 32*, 319–325.

Lees-Haley, P. R., & Fox, D. D. (2004). Commentary on Butcher, Arbisi, Atlis, and McNulty (2003) on the Fake Bad Scale. *Archives of Clinical Neuropsychology, 19*, 333–336.

Lees-Haley, P. R., English L. T., & Glenn W. J. (1991). A Fake Bad Scale on the MMPI-2 for personal injury claimants. *Psychological Reports, 68*, 203–210.

Lerner, P. M. (2007). On preserving a legacy: Psychoanalysis and psychological testing. *Psychoanalytic Psychology, 24*, 208–230.

Lilienfeld, S. O., Wood, J. M., & Garb, H. N. (2000). The scientific status of projective techniques. *Psychological Science in the Public Interest, 1*, 27–66.

Manos, N. (1985). Adaptation of the MMPI in Greece: Translation, standardization, and cross-cultural comparisons. In J. N. Butcher & C. D. Spielberger (Eds.), *Advances in personality assessment* (Vol. 4). Hillsdale, NJ: Lawrence Erlbaum.

McGrath, R. E., Terranova, R., Pogge, D. L., & Kravic, C. (2003). Development of a short form for the MMPI-2 based on scale elevation congruence. *Assessment, 10*(1), 13–28.

Meehl, P. E. (1945). The dynamics of "structured" personality tests. *Journal of Clinical Psychology, 1*, 296–303.

Megargee, E. I. (2006). Use of the MMPI-2 in correctional settings. In J. N. Butcher (Ed.), *MMPI-2: The practioner's handbook* (pp. 327–460). Washington, DC: American Psychological Association.

Merenda, P. F. (2007). Update on the decline in the education and training in psychological measurement and assessment. *Psychological Reports, 101*(1), 153–155.

Meyer, G. J., Finn, S. E., Eyde, L. D., Kay, G.G., Moreland, K. L., Dies, R. R., et al. (2001). Psychological testing and psychological assessment: A review of evidence and issues. *American Psychologist, 56*(2), 128–165.

Millon, T. (1977). *Millon Clinical Multiaxial Inventory.* Minneapolis, MN: National Computer Systems.

Millon, T. (1996). *The Millon Inventories.* New York: Guilford Press.

Mischel, W. (1968). *Personality and assessment.* Hoboken, NJ: John Wiley & Sons.

Nichols, D. S. (2006). The trials of separating bath water from baby: A review and critique of the MMPI-2 restructured clinical scales. *Journal of Personality Assessment, 87*, 121–138.

Overall, J. E., & Gomez-Mont, F. (1974). The MMPI-168 for psychiatric screening. *Educational and Psychological Measurement, 34*, 315–319.

Paul, A. M. (2004). *The cult of personality—how personality tests are leading us to miseducate our children, mismanage our companies and misunderstand ourselves.* New York: Free Press.

Piotrowski, C. (1999). Assessment practices in the era of managed care: Current status and future directions. *Journal of Clinical Psychology, 55*(7), 787–796.

Pope, K. S., Butcher, J. N., & Seelen, J. (2006). *The MMPI/ MMPI-2/MMPI-A in court* (3rd ed.). Washington, DC: American Psychological Association.

Rapaport, D., Gill, M., & Schafer, R. (1945). *Diagnostic psychological testing* (2 vols.). Chicago: World Book.

Rorschach, H. (1921). *Psychodiagnostik.* Bern: Hans Huber.

Rouse, S. V. (2007). Using reliability generalization methods to explore measurement error: An examination of the MMPI-2 PSY-5 scales. *Journal of Personality Assessment, 88*, 264–275.

Rouse, S. V., Greene, R. L., Butcher, J. N., Nichols, D. S., & Williams, C. L. (2008).What do the MMPI-2 Restructured Clinical Scales reliably measure? Answers from multiple research settings. *Journal of Personality Assessment, 90*, 435–442.

Savacir, I., & Erol, N. (1990). The Turkish MMPI: Translation, standardization, and validation. In J. N. Butcher & C. D. Spielberger (Eds.), *Advances in personality assessment* (Vol. 8, pp. 49–62). Hillsdale, NJ: Lawrence Erlbaum.

Schafer, R. (1948). *The clinical application of psychological tests: Diagnostic summaries and case studies.* New York: International Universities Press.

Shaffer, T. W., Erdberg, P., & Meyer, G. J. (2007). Introduction to the JPA Special Supplement on international reference samples for the Rorschach Comprehensive System. *Journal of Personality Assessment, 89*, S2–S6.

Smith, S. R., Wiggins, C. M., & Gorske, T. T. (2007). A survey of psychological assessment feedback practices. *Assessment, 14*(3), 310–319.

Stith v State Farm Mutua Insurance, Case No. 50-2003 CA 010945AG, Palm Beach County, Florida, 2008.

Streiner, D. L. (2003). Starting at the beginning: An introduction to coefficient alpha and internal consistency. *Journal of Personality Assessment, 80*, 99–103.

Tellegen, A., Ben-Porath, Y. S., McNulty, J., Arbisi, P., Graham, J. R., & Kaemmer, B. (2003). *MMPI-2: Restructured Clinical (RC) Scales.* Minneapolis, MN: University of Minnesota Press.

Vacha-Haase, T., Henson, R. K., & Caruso, J. C. (2002). Reliability generalization: Moving toward improved understanding and use of score reliability. *Educational and Psychological Measurement, 62*, 562–569.

Vandergracht v. Progressive Express et al. (2007). Case #02-04552, Hillsborough County, FL.

Weiss, D., & Suhdolnik, D. (1985). Robustness of adaptive testing to multidimensionality. In D. J. Weiss (Ed.), *Proceedings of the 1982 item response theory and computerized adaptive testing conference* (pp. 248–280). Minneapolis, MN: University of Minnesota, Department of Psychology, Computerized Adaptive Testing Laboratory.

Williams v. CSX Transportation, Inc. (2007). Case #04-CA-008892, Hillsborough County, FL.

Woodworth, R. S. (1920). *Personal data sheet.* Chicago: Stoelting.

Index of Psychological Tests and Procedures

Alcohol Use Inventory (AUI)

Characteristics Assessed

The client's perceptions about four dimensions of alcohol use and abuse, including benefits derived from drinking; styles of drinking; consequences of drinking; and concerns associated with alcohol use.

John Horn, PhD., Kenneth W. Wanberg, PhD, and F. Mark Foster, MS.

The Alcohol Use Inventory (AUI) provides a basis for describing different ways in which individuals use alcohol, the benefits they derive from such use, the negative consequences associated with its use, and the degree of concern individuals express about the use of alcohol and its consequences.

Publisher:
Pearson Assessments
5601 Green Valley Drive
Bloomington, MN 55437-1099
Sales: 800.227.7271
Support: 800.627.7271 ext. 3235
General Info: 877.242.6767
Call: 800.627-7271
Fax: 800.632.9011 or 952.681.3299
E-Mail: pearsonassessments@pearson.com

For More Information:
www.pearsonassessments.com/tests/aui.htm

Alzheimers's Disease Assessment Scale

Characteristics Assessed

Cognitive functions including memory, language and praxis; noncognitive functions including mood state and behavioral changes.

Where Test Can Be Obtained
Dr. Richard C. Mohs, Affiliated with Eli Lily & Co.
Psychiatry Services (116A)
VA Medical Center
130 West Kingsbridge Road
Bronx, NY 10468

The test is not self-administered and usually takes about 45 min.

The administration cannot be delegated to clerical or nursing staff.

For More Information:
www.acnp.org/g4/GN401000133/CH130.html

Key Reference
Rosen, W. G., Mohs, R. C., & Davis, K. L. (1984). A new rating scale for Alzheimer's disease. *American Journal of Psychiatry, 141*, 1356–1364.

Anxiety Disorders Interview Schedule-Revised

Characteristics Assessed

Assesses the severity of anxious syndromes and their accompanying mood states.

Publisher:
Graywind Publications
Executive Park Drive
1535 Western Ave.
Albany, NY 12203

The test is not self-administered and usually takes about 3–3.5 hr.

The administration procedure cannot be delegated to clerical or nursing staff.

The test is not computer scorable and cannot be interpreted by computer.

Key References
DiNardo, P. A., & Barlow, D. H. (1988). *Anxiety disorders interview schedule-revised (ADIS-R)*. Albany, NY: Graywind.
DiNardo, P. A., O'Brien, G. T., Barlow, D. H., Waddell, M. T., & Blanchard, E. B. (1983). Reliability of DSM-III anxiety disorder categories using a new structured interview. *Archives of General Psychiatry, 40*, 1070–1074.

Anxiety Sensitivity Index (ASI)

Characteristics Assessed

Assesses the negative consequences of the experience of anxiety.

The test is self-administered and usually takes about 10 min.

The administration procedure can be delegated to clerical or nursing staff.

The test is not computer scorable and cannot be interpreted by computer.

To Obtain the Test
IDS Publishing Corporation
PO Box 389
Worthington, OH, 43085
614-885-2323
Email: sales@idspublishing.com

Key References
McNally, R. J. (2002). Anxiety sensitivity and panic disorder. *Biological Psychiatry, 52*, 938–994.
Reiss, S. (1997). Trait anxiety: It's not what you think it is. *Journal of Anxiety Disorders, 11*, 201–214.
Reiss, S., Peterson, R. A., Gursky, D. M., & McNally, R. J. (1986). Anxiety sensitivity, anxiety frequency and the prediction of fearfulness. *Behavior Research and Therapy, 24*, 1–8.
Taylor, S., Koch, W. J., & Crokett, D. J. (1991). Anxiety sensitivity, trait anxiety, and the anxiety disorders. *Journal of Anxiety Disorders, 5*, 293–311.

Basic Personality Inventory (BPI)

Characteristics Assessed

Dimensions of psychopathology (hypochondriasis, anxiety, depression, thinking disorder, etc.) divided into 11 clinical scales.

Publisher:

Sigma Assessment Systems, Inc.
PO Box 610984
Port Huron, MI 48061-0984
1-800-265-1285

The test is self-administered and usually takes about 35–40 min. The administration can be delegated to clerical or nursing staff. The test is computer scorable and can be interpreted by computer. The address of the official computer scoring and interpretation service is
Sigma Assessment Systems, Inc.
PO Box 610984
Port Huron, MI 48061-0984
1-800-265-1285

Key Reference

Jackson, D. N. (1988, 1995, 1997). *Basic Personality Inventory: BPI manual.* MI: Sigma Assessment Systems, Inc.

Beck Anxiety Inventory (BAI)

Characteristics Assessed

Self-report measure of anxiety symptomatology.

Publisher:

Pearson Assessments
5601 Green Valley Drive
Bloomington, MN 55437-1099
Sales: 800.227.7271
Support: 800.627.7271 ext. 3235
General Info: 877.242.6767
Call: 800.627.7271
Fax: 800.632.9011 or 952.681.3299
E-Mail: pearsonassessments@pearson.com

For More Information:

www.pearsonassessments.com/tests/aui.htm
The test is self-administered and usually takes about 10 min. The administration can be delegated to clerical or nursing staff. The test is not computer scorable and cannot be interpreted by computer.

Key References

Beck, A. T., Epstein, N., Brown, G., & Steer, R. A. (1988). An inventory for measuring clinical anxiety: Psychometric properties. *Journal of Consulting and Clinical Psychology, 56*, 893–897.
Eydrich, T., Dowdall, D., & Chambless, D. L. (1992). Reliability and validity of the Beck anxiety inventory. *Journal of Anxiety Disorders, 6*, 55–61.

Beck Depression Inventory (BDI)

Characteristics Assessed

Depression.

Publisher:

Pearson Assessments
5601 Green Valley Drive
Bloomington, MN 55437-1099

Sales: 800.227.7271
Support: 800.627.7271 ext. 3235
General Info: 877.242.6767
Call: 800.627.7271
Fax: 800.632.9011 or 952.681.3299
E-Mail: pearsonassessments@pearson.com

For More Information:

www.pearsonassessments.com/tests/aui.htm
The test is self-administered and usually takes about 10–15 min. The administration can be delegated to clerical or nursing staff. The test is computer scorable and can (a brief narrative) be interpreted by computer.
Other Important Features
21 four-choice statements

Key References

Beck, A. T. (1987). *Beck depression inventory: manual.* San Antonio, TX: Psychological Corporation.
Beck, A. T., Ward, C. H., Mendelson, M., Mock, J., Erbaugh, J. (1961). An inventory for measuring depression. *Archives of General Psychiatry, 4*, 561–571.

Butcher Treatment Planning Inventory (BTPI)

Characteristics Assessed

The Butcher Treatment Planning Inventory (BTPI) was developed as a means of providing personality information on clients involved in personality information on clients involved in psychological intervention. It was derived on the basis of a combination of rational and empirical means. Through its construction, it was created to be behaviorally oriented and fundamentally, atheoretical in nature. The BTPI is intended to assess not only clients' psychological symptoms, but also those specific qualities that are likely to impede the psychological treatment process. The scale consists of 210 true/false items, each of whose content assigns it to one or more of the instrument's 14 scales. Four scales are included to assess the validity of the individual's self-report on the instrument: Inconsistent Responding (INC), the Overly Virtuous Self-Views (VIR), the Exaggerated Problem Presentation (EXA), and the Closed-Mindedness (CLM). There are five scales that assess treatment issues: There are five symptom scales: Depression (DEP) assessing proneness to low mood; Anxiety (ANX) measuring the experience of tension and nervousness; Anger-Out (A-O) assessing hostile attitudes and exhibiting of anger; Anger-In (A-I), measuring internalization of anger and self-blame; and Unusual Thinking (PSY) assessing strange or delusional beliefs and demonstrating of unusual behaviors.

Characteristics Assessed

Personality characteristics and process variables in treatment planning.

Publisher:

Multi-Health Systems Inc.
908 Niagara Falls Blvd.
North Tonawanda, NY 14120-2060
800-496-8324
Fax: 800-540-4484
Multi-Health Systems Inc. (MHS)
3770 Victoria Park Ave.
Toronto, ON M2H 3M6
416-492-2627 (Ext. 330)
Fax: 416-492-3343

Further Information can also be Obtained at:
www.umn.edu/mmpi

Key References

Butcher, J. N. (2005). *The Butcher treatment planning inventory (BTPI): Test manual and interpretive guide.* Toronto, ON: Multi-Health Systems.

Butcher, J. N., Rouse, S. V., & Perry, J. N. (1998). Assessing resistance to psychological treatment. *Measurement and Evaluation in Counseling and Development, 31*, 95–108.

Butcher, J. N., Rouse, S. V., & Perry, J. N. (2000). Empirical description of psychopathology in therapy clients: Correlates of the MMPI-2 scales. In J. N. Butcher (Ed.), *Basic sources on the MMPI-2* (pp. 487–500). Minneapolis, MN: University of Minnesota Press.

Perry, J. N., & Butcher, J. N. (1999). Butcher treatment planning inventory (BTPI): An objective guide to treatment planning. In M. E. Maruish (Ed.), *The use of psychological testing for treatment planning and outcomes assessment* (2nd ed., pp. 1157–1171). Mahwah, NJ: Erlbaum.

Clinician Administered PTSD Scales (CAPS)

Characteristics Assessed

Assesses the severity and frequency of PTSD symptoms.
Where Test Can Be Obtained.
Dr. Dudley David Blake
Psychology Services (116B)
Boston VAMC
150 South Huntington Ave.
Boston, MA 02130
The test is not computer scorable and cannot be interpreted by computer.

For Further Information:
www.ntis.gov/pdf/programbrochure.pdf

Key Reference

Blake, D. D., Weathers, F. W., Nagy, L. M., Kaloupek, D. G., Klauminzer, G., Charney, D., & Keane, T. (1990). A clinician rating scale for assessing current and lifetime PTSD: The CAPS-1. *The Behavior Therapist, 13*, 137–188.

Clinical Frequencies Recording System (CFRS)

Characteristics Assessed

Low-frequency critical events and totally setting-dependent behavior of clients and staff in inpatient and residential treatment settings.

Publisher:
Research Press
Dept. 27W
Main: 217-352-3273
PO Box 9177
Toll Free: 800-519-2707
Champaign, IL 61826
Fax: 217-352-1221
The test is computer scorable but cannot be interpreted by computer.

Other Important Features

A set of forms for completion by clinical staff as part of ongoing service delivery, specifically for a comprehensive social-learning program, but adaptable to other programs.

Functioning scores are derived across forms to provide weekly "rate-per-opportunity."

Key Reference

Redfield, J. P. (1979). Clinical frequencies recording systems: Standardizing staff observations by event recording. *Journal of Behavioral Assessment, 1*, 211–219.

Cognitive Coping Strategy Inventory (CCSI)

Characteristics Assessed

Various reactions for coping with pain.
Where Test Can Be Obtained
See Butler et al. (1989).
The test is self-administered and usually takes about 10–12 min. The administration can be delegated to clerical or nursing staff. The test is not computer scorable and cannot be interpreted by computer.

Key Reference

Butler, R. W., Damarin, F. L., Beauliu, C., Schwebel, A. I., & Thorn, B. F. (1989). Assessing cognitive coping strategies for acute post-surgical pain. *Psychological Assessment, 1*, 41–45.

Columbia University Scale for Psychopathology

Characteristics Assessed

(Designed for Alzheimer patients): Delusions, hallucinations, illusion, behavioral disturbance (aggression, wandering away, restlessness, and confusion), vegetative symptoms of depression.
Where Test Can Be Obtained
Dr. D. P. Devarand
New York State Psychiatric Institute
722 West 168th Street
New York, NY 10032
The test is not self-administered and usually takes about 10–25 min. The test can be administered by a trained lay interviewer.
The test is not computer scorable and cannot be interpreted by computer.

Other Important Features

This is a semistructured interview instrument that focuses on symptoms occurring during the past year.

Key Reference

Devarand, D. P., Miller, L., Richards, M. Marder, K., Bell, K., Mayeux, R., et al. (1992). The Columbia University Scale for Psychopathology in Alzheimer's disease. *Archives of Neurology, 49*, 371–376.

Comprehensive Assessment and Referral Evaluation (CARE)

Characteristics Assessed

Psychiatric, medical, nutritional, economic, and social problems of the older person.
The test is not computer scorable and cannot be interpreted by computer.

Other Important Features

Clinician rating scale

Key Reference

Gurland, B., Kuriansky, J., Sharpe, L., Simar, R., Stiller, P., & Birkett, P. (1977–1978). The Comprehensive Assessment and Referral Evaluation (CARE)—Rationale, development and reliability. *International Journal of Aging and Human Development, 8*, 9–42.

Computerized TSBC/SRIC Planned-Access Observational Information System

Characteristics Assessed

Incorporates all characteristics assessed by component direct observational coding (DOC) instruments—the Time-Sample Behavioral Checklist (TSBC) and the Staff–Resident Interaction Chronograph (SRIC)—as well as biographical data for ongoing assessment of functioning and effectiveness of clients, staff, and treatment programs in inpatient/residential facilities.

Publisher:

Research Press
Dept. 27W
Main: 217-352-3273
PO Box 9177
Toll Free: 800-519-2707
Champaign, IL 61826
Fax: 217-352-1221

The test is not self-administered.

The administration can be delegated to clerical or nursing staff (see below).

The test is computer scorable but cannot be interpreted by computer.

Paul (1994b) contains all computer programs and file-management procedures for retrieving and scoring standard reports on an ongoing basis.

Other Important Features

Uses full-time technician-level observers and clerical staff for data collection. An ongoing system, with integrated training materials and procedures for all levels of staff to support collection, monitoring, processing, retrieval, distribution, and interpretation of information on clients, staff, and treatment programs in mental hospitals and community facilities.

Key References

Paul, G. L. (Ed.) (1994a). *Observational assessment instrumentation for service and research—The Computerized TSBC/SRIC Planned-Access Information System: Assessment in residential treatment settings* (Part 4). Champaign, IL: Research Press.

Paul, G.L. (Ed.) (1994b). *Observational assessment instrumentation for service and research—The TSBC/SRIC system implementation package: Assessment in residential treatment settings* (Part 5). Champaign, IL: Research Press.

Constructive Thinking Inventory (CTI)

Characteristics Assessed

Six coping dimensions: emotional coping, behavioral coping, categorical thinking, superstitious thinking, naive optimism, and negative thinking.

Where Test Can Be Obtained
Dr. Seymour Epstein
Department of Psychology
University of Massachusetts
Amherst, MA 01003

For Further Information Contact:

sepstein@psych.umass.edu

The test is self-administered and usually takes about 15 min.

The administration can be delegated to clerical or nursing staff.

The test is not computer scorable and cannot be interpreted by computer.

Key Reference

Epstein, S., & Meier, P. (1989). Constructive thinking: A broad coping variable with specific components. *Journal of Personality and Social Psychology, 57*, 332–350.

Cope Scale

Characteristics Assessed

13 basic coping styles.
Where Test Can Be Obtained
Dr. Charles S. Carver
PO Box 248185
University of Miami
Coral Gables, FL 33124
Fax: 305-284-3402

For Further Information:

http://www.psy.miami.edu/faculty/ccarver/CCscales.html

The test is self-administered and usually takes about 15 min.

The administration can be delegated to clerical or nursing staff.

The test is not computer scorable and cannot be interpreted by computer.

Key Reference

Carver, C. S., Scheier, M. F., & Weintraub, J. K. (1989). Assessing coping strategies: A theoretically based approach. *Journal of Personality and Social Psychology, 56*, 267–283.

Coping Inventory for Stressful Situations (CISS)

Characteristics Assessed

Task-oriented coping style, emotion-oriented coping style, and avoidance-oriented coping style.

Publisher:

Multi-Health Systems Inc.
908 Niagara Falls Blvd.
North Tonawanda, NY 14120-2060
800-496-8324
Fax: 800-540-4484

The test is self-administered and usually takes about 10 min.

The administration can be delegated to clerical or nursing staff.

The test is computer scorable and can be interpreted by computer.

The address of the official computer scoring and interpretation service is

Multi-Health Systems Inc.
908 Niagara Falls Blvd.
North Tonawanda, NY 14120-2060
800-496-8324
Fax: 800-540-4484
Multi-Health Systems Inc. (MHS)
3770 Victoria Park Ave.
Toronto, ON M2H 3M6
416-492-2627 (Ext. 330)
Fax: 416-492-3343

Other Important Features

Adult and adolescent versions of the CISS are available.

Key Reference

Endler, N. S., & Parker, J. D. A. (1990). *Coping Inventory for Stressful Situations (CISS): Manual.* Toronto, ON: Multi-Health Systems.

Coping Resources Inventory (CRI)

Characteristics Assessed

Five "personal resources" variables: cognitive resources, social resources, emotional resources, spiritual/philosophical resources, and physical resources.

Publisher:

Consulting Psychologist Press
3803 E. Bayshore Road
Palo Alto, CA 94303-9608
800-624-1765
Fax: 650-623-9273
Email: knw@cpp-db.com
Web: www.cpp-db.com

The test is self-administered and usually takes about 10 min.

The administration can be delegated to clerical or nursing staff.

The test is not computer scorable and cannot be interpreted by computer.

Key Reference

Hamer, A. L., & Marting, M. S. (1988). *Manual for the coping resources inventory.* Palo Alto, CA: Consulting Psychologists Press.

Coping Strategy Indicator (CSI)

Characteristics Assessed

Three basic coping reactions or strategies that may be used in a cross section of stressful situations (problem-solving coping, seeking social-support coping, and avoidance coping).

Where Test Can Be Obtained
Dr. James H. Amirkhan
Department of Psychology
California State University
Long Beach, CA 90840
INIST Diffusion S.A.
Service Clients/Customer Service
2, allée du parc de Brabois
F-54514 Vandoeuvre Cedex France
Tél : +33 (0) 3.83.50.46.64
Fax : +33 (0) 3.83.50.46.66
Email: infoclient@inist.fr

The test is self-administered and usually takes about 8–10 min.

The administration can be delegated to clerical or nursing staff.

The test is not computer scorable and cannot be interpreted by computer.

Key Reference

Amirkhan, J. H. (1990). A factor analytically derived measure of coping: The coping strategy indicator. *Journal of Personality and Social Psychology, 59,* 1066–1074.

The Daily Hassles Scale

Characteristics Assessed

This "life event scale" focuses on day-to-day stressors people encounter that might result in difficulties in coping.

Publisher:

Mind Garden, Inc.
1690 Woodside Road, Suite 202
Redwood City, CA 94061
Email: info@mindgarden.com

There is no computer scoring or interpretation available for the scale.

Other Important Features

Although primarily a research instrument, this scale might have clinical applications as well. The scale is a 117-item self-report questionnaire. All items represent frequently reported daily hassles.

Key Reference

Lazarus, R. S., & Folkman, S. (1989). *Manual: Hassles and uplifts scale, research edition.* Palo Alto, CA: Mind Garden.

Defense Style Questionnaire (DSQ)

Characteristics Assessed

Three defense mechanism clusters: mature defenses, immature defenses, and neurotic defenses.

Where Test Can Be Obtained

Included as an appendix in Vaillant, G. E. (1986). *Empirical studies of ego mechanisms of defense.* Washington, DC: American Psychiatric Press.

The test is not self-administered and usually takes about 15 min.

The administration can be delegated to clerical or nursing staff.

The test is not computer scorable and cannot be interpreted by computer.

Key References

Andrews, G., Singh, M., & Bond, M. (1993). The defense style questionnaire. *Journal of Nervous and Mental Disease, 181,* 246–256.

Bond, M. (1986). An empirical study of defense styles. In G. E. Vaillant (Ed.), *Empirical studies of ego mechanisms of defense* (pp. 1–29). Washington, DC: American Psychiatric Press.

Dementia Rating Scale

Characteristics Assessed

Attention, perseveration (both verbal and motor), drawing ability, verbal and nonverbal abstraction, and verbal and nonverbal short-term memory.

Where Test Can Be Obtained
Dr. Steven Mattis
Department of Neurology
Weill Medical College of Cornell University
Bronx, NY 10475

The test is not self-administered and usually takes about 10–15 min with normal elderly patients, 30–45 min with dementia patients.

The administration cannot be delegated to clerical or nursing staff.

Key References

Coblentz, J. M., Mattis, S., Zingesser, L. H., Kasoff, S. S., Wisniewski, H. H., & Katzman, R. (1973). Pre-senile dementia: Clinical aspects and evaluations of cerebrospinal fluid dynamics. *Archives of Neurology, 29,* 299–308.

Montgomery, K. M. (1982). A normative study of neuropsychological test performance of a normal elderly sample (Unpublished master's thesis). University of Victoria, BC, Canada.

Diagnostic Interview for Narcissism

Characteristics Assessed

Narcissistic personality disorder.
Where Test Can Be Obtained
Dr. John Gunderson

McLean Hospital
115 Mill Street
Belmont, MA 02178

The test is not self-administered and usually takes about 1–3 hr. The administration cannot be delegated to clerical or nursing staff.

The test is not computer scorable and cannot be interpreted by computer.

Other Important Features

Semistructured interview

Key Reference

Gunderson, J. G., Ronningstam, E., & Bodkin, A. (1990). The diagnostic interview for narcissistic patients. *Archives of General Psychiatry, 47*, 676–680.

Diagnostic Interview for Personality Disorders

Characteristics Assessed

Personality disorders.
Where Test Can Be Obtained
Dr. John Gunderson
McLean Hospital
115 Mill Street
Belmont, MA 02178

The test is not self-administered and usually takes about 1–3 hr. The administration cannot be delegated to clerical or nursing staff.

The test is not computer scorable and cannot be interpreted by computer.

Other Important Features

Semistructured interview

Key Reference

Zanarini, M., Frankenburg, F. R., Chauncey, D. L., & Gunderson, J. G. (1987). The diagnostic interview for personality disorders: Interrater and test–retest reliability. *Comprehensive Psychiatry, 28*, 467–480.

Dimensional Assessment of Personality Pathology—Basic Questionnaire

Characteristics Assessed

Maladaptive personality traits.
Where Test Can Be Obtained
Dr. John W. Livesley
Department of Psychiatry
University of British Columbia
2255 Wesbrook Mall
Vancouver, BC V6T 2A1 Canada

The test is not self-administered and usually takes about 45 min.

The administration cannot be delegated to clerical or nursing staff.

The test is computer scorable and cannot be interpreted by computer.

Key Reference

Schroeder, M. L., Wormworth, J. A., & Livesley, W. J. (1992). Dimensions of personality disorder and their relationship to the Big Five dimensions of personality. *Psychological Assessment, 4*, 47–53.

Early Memories Procedure

Characteristics Assessed

Contents: Five spontaneous early memories; the clearest or most important memory in lifetime; 15 directed memories (some early, some lifetime), including most traumatic memories. Assesses: Major unresolved issue currently in process.

Publisher:

Dr. Arnold R. Bruhn
4400 E West Hwy.
Bethesda, MD 20814-4524
Website: www.arbruhn.com/home.html

The test is self-administered and usually takes about 5 min for psychologists.

The test is not computer scorable and cannot be interpreted by computer.

Other Important Features

Assesses clinically relevant aspects of autobiographical memory. Functions as a "hub" technique for other "spare" procedures, such as Memories of Spouse procedure.

Key References

Bruhn, A. R. (1990). *Earliest childhood memories: Theory and application to clinical practice.* New York: Praeger.

Bruhn, A. R. (1992a). The early memories procedure: A projective test of autobiographical memory, Part 1. *Journal of Personality Assessment, 58*, 1–15.

Bruhn, A. R. (1992b). The early memories procedure: A projective test of autobiographical memory, Part 2. *Journal of Personality Assessment, 58*, 326–346.

Fear Survey Schedule—III (FSS-III)

Characteristics Assessed

Self-report inventory of fears common among phobics.
EdITS/EDUCATIONALAND INDUSTRIALTESTING SERVICE
PO 7234, SAN DIEGO, CA 92167
619-222-1666, 800-416-1666
Fax: 619-226-1666
Email: customerservice@edits.net
http://www.edits.net/pdfs/FSS.pdf

The test is self-administered and usually takes about 20 min.

The administration can be delegated to clerical or nursing staff.

The test is not computer scorable and cannot be interpreted by computer.

Key References

Wolpe, J., & Lang, P. J. (1974). A fear survey schedule for use in behavior therapy. *Behavior Research and Therapy, 2*, 27–30.

Arrindell, W. A., & van der Ende, J. (1986). Further evidence for cross-sample invariance of phobic factors: Psychiatric inpatient ratings on the Fear Survey Schedule. *Behavior Research and Therapy, 24*, 289–297.

Functional Assessment Inventory (FAI)

Characteristics Assessed

Functional information in five domains—social resources, economic resources, mental health, physical health, and ADL status.

The test is not self-administered and usually takes about 30 min.

Key References

Carl, R., Pfeiffer, E., Keller, D. M., Burke, H., & Samis, H. V. (1983). An evaluation of the validity of the functional assessment inventory. *Journal of the American Geriatric Society, 31*, 606–612.

Pfeiffer, E., Johnson, T., & Chiofolo, R. (1981). Functional assessment of elderly subjects in four service settings. *Journal of the American Geriatric Society, 10*, 433–437.

General Temperament Survey (GTS)

Characteristics Assessed

Three broad dimensions of temperament: negative affectivity, positive affectivity, and disinhibition.

Publisher:

Available as part of the Schedule for Nonadaptive and Adaptive Personality (SNAP)
University of Minnesota Press
2037 University Avenue SE
Minneapolis, MN 55455
Where Test Can Be Obtained
Dr. L.A. Clark & Dr. D. Watson (unlisted)
Department of Psychology
Seashore Hall
University of Iowa
Iowa City, IA 52242-11407

The test is self-administered and usually takes about 20 min.
The administration cannot be delegated to clerical or nursing staff.
The test is computer scorable and cannot be interpreted by computer.

Other Important Features

May be available through University of Minnesota Press in the future.

Key References

Watson, D., & Clark, L. A. (1993). Behavioral disinhibition versus constraint: A dispositional perspective. In D. M. Wegner & J. W. Pennebaker (Eds.), *Handbook of mental control* (pp. 506–527). New York: Prentice-Hall.

Watson, D., & Clark, L. A. (1992). On traits and temperament: General and specific factors of emotional experience and their relations to the Five-Factor Model. *Journal of Personality, 60*, 443–476.

Geriatric Depression Scale

Characteristics Assessed

Measures depression in the elderly.
Where Test Can Be Obtained
Dr. T. L. Brink
1044 Sylvan Doctor
San Carlos, CA 94070
or
Dr. Jerome Yesavage
VA Medical Center
3801 Miranda Avenue
Mail Code 151-Y
Palo Alto, CA 94304

The test (both oral and written format) is self-administered and is about 30 items long.
The administration can be delegated to clerical or nursing staff.

Other Important Features

Translation available in Spanish and French.

Key Reference

Yesavage, J. A., Brink, T. L., Rose, T. L., & Leirer, V. O. (1983). Development and validation of a geriatric depression screening scale: A preliminary report. *Journal of Psychiatric Research, 17*, 37–49.

Geriatric Mental Status Interview

Characteristics Assessed

Contains almost 500 items considered relevant for assessing psychopathology in a geriatric psychiatric population.
The test is not self-administered and usually takes an average of 1.5 hr.
The administration cannot be delegated to clerical or nursing staff.

Other Important Features

Semistructured interview guide—1500 items.

Key Reference

Gurland, B., Copeland, J., Sharpe, L., & Kelleher, M. (1976). The geriatric mental status interview (GMS). *International Journal of Aging and Human Development, 7*, 303–311.

Halifax Mental Status Scale

Characteristics Assessed

Orientation, memory for a single phrase, concentration, comprehension of commands, naming objects manual praxis, visual constructional ability.
Where Test Can Be Obtained
Dr. John Fisk
Neuropsychology Service
Department of Psychology
Camp Hill Medical Center
Halifax, NS B3H 362

The test is not self-administered and usually takes less than 15 min.
The administration cannot be delegated to clerical or nursing staff.

Key Reference

Fisk, J. D., Braha, R. E., & Walker, A. (1991). The Halifax mental status scale: Development of a new test of mental status for used with elderly clients. *Psychological Assessment: A Journal of Consulting and Clinical Psychology, 3*, 162–167.

Hamilton Anxiety Rating Scale (HARS)

Characteristics Assessed

A clinician-administered scale designed to measure the severity of anxiety symptoms. Originally designed for use with patients diagnosed with anxiety neuroses.
The test is not self-administered and usually takes about 30 min.

The administration cannot be delegated to clerical or nursing staff.

The test is not computer scorable and cannot be interpreted by computer.

Key References

Hamilton, M. (1959). The assessment of anxiety states by rating. *British Journal of Medical Psychology, 32*, 50–55.

Maier, W., Buller, R., Philipp, M., & Heuser, I. (1988). The Hamilton anxiety scale: Reliability, validity and sensitivity to change in anxiety and depressive disorders. *Journal of Affective Disorders, 14*, 61–68.

Hare Psychopathy Checklist-Revised

Characteristics Assessed

Rating scale for the assessment of psychopathy in male forensic populations. It yields dimensional scores concerning behavior and inferred personality traits.

Publisher:

Multi-Health Systems Inc.
908 Niagara Falls Blvd.
North Tonawanda, NY 14120-2060
800-496-8324
Fax: 800-540-4484
Multi-Health Systems Inc. (MHS)
3770 Victoria Park Ave.
Toronto, ON M2H 3M6
416-492-2627 (Ext. 330)
Fax: 416-492-3343

The test is not self-administered and usually takes about 2 hr.

The administration cannot be delegated to clerical or nursing staff.

The test is not computer scorable and cannot be interpreted by computer.

Other Important Features

Clinical interview and review of collateral information necessary; can also be used to classify and diagnose individuals for research and clinical purposes.

Key Reference

Hare, R. D., Hart, S. D., & Harpur, T. J. (1991). Psychopathy and the DSM-IV criteria for antisocial personality disorder. *Journal of Abnormal Psychology, 100*, 391–398.

Hopelessness Scale

Characteristics Assessed

Hopelessness.

Publisher:

Pearson Assessments
5601 Green Valley Drive
Bloomington, MN 55437-1099
Sales: 800.227.7271
Support: 800.627.7271 ext. 3235
General Info: 877.242.6767
Call: 800.627.7271
Fax: 800.632.9011 or 952.681.3299
E-Mail: pearsonassessments@pearson.com

For More Information:

www.pearsonassessments.com/tests/aui.htm

The test is not self-administered but is based on self-report. It usually takes a few minutes.

The administration cannot be delegated to clerical or nursing staff.

Key References

Beck, A. T., Weissman, A., Lester, D., & Trexler, L. (1974). The measurement of pessimism: The hopelessness scale. *Journal of Consulting and Clinical Psychology, 42*, 861–865.

Beck, A. T., Steer, R. A., Kovacs, M., & Garrison, B. (1985). Hopelessness and eventual suicide: A ten year prospective study of patients hospitalized with suicide ideation. *American Journal of Psychiatry, 142*, 559–563.

Individualism–Collectivism (INDCOL) Scale

Characteristics Assessed

Degree of individualism–collectivism (set of feelings, beliefs, behavioral intentions, and behaviors related to solidarity and concern for others).

Where Test Can Be Obtained
Dr. C. Harry Hui
Department of Psychology
University of Hong Kong
Pokfulam Road
Hong Kong

The test is self-administered and usually takes about 15–30 min.

The administration cannot be delegated to clerical or nursing staff.

The test is not computer scorable and cannot be interpreted by computer.

Key References

Hui, C. H. (1988). Measurement of individualism–collectivism. *Journal of Research in Personality, 22*, 17–36.

Robert, C., Lee, W. C., & Chan, K.-Y. (2006). An empirical analysis of measurement equivalence with the INDCOL measure of individualism and collectivism: Implications for valid cross-cultural inference. *Personnel Psychology, 59*(1), 65–99.

Interviewer-Rated Defense Mechanism Scales

Characteristics Assessed

12 basic defense mechanisms.

Where Test Can Be Obtained
Dr. Alan Jacobson
Joslin Diabetes Center
1 Joslin Place
Boston, MA 02215

The test is not self-administered and takes several hours (depending on the type of clinical material used). The administration cannot be delegated to clerical or nursing staff.

The test is not computer-scorable and cannot be interpreted by computer.

Other Important Features

The Jacobson et al. measure is an observer-rated defense mechanism measure developed for use with adolescent population.

Key Reference

Jacobson, A. M., Beardslee, W., Hauser, S. T., Noam, G. G., Powers, S. I., Houlihan, J., et al. (1986). Evaluating ego defense mechanisms using clinical interviews: An empirical study of adolescent diabetic and psychiatric patients. *Journal of Adolescence, 9*, 303–319.

Inventory of Interpersonal Problems (IIP)

Characteristics Assessed

This self-report inventory provides information about interpersonal problems based on the circumplex interpersonal model of Timothy Leary. It is a 117-item scale that usually takes about half an hour to administer.

Publisher:

Pearson Assessments
5601 Green Valley Drive
Bloomington, MN 55437-1099
Sales: 800.227.7271
Support: 800.627.7271 ext. 3235
General Info: 877.242.6767
Call: 800.627-7271
Fax: 800.632.9011 or 952.681.3299
E-Mail: pearsonassessments@pearson.com

For More Information:

www.pearsonassessments.com/tests/aui.htm

Key Reference

Horowitz, L. M. (1996). The study of interpersonal problems: A Leary legacy. *Journal of Personality Assessment, 66,* 283–300.

Life Experiences Survey (LES)

Characteristics Assessed

This survey was constructed from the theoretical perspective that subjective ratings of life changes are critical in determining the impact of life events. The survey includes 47 specified items and 3 items that the subject completes.

Publisher:

Sarason, Johnson, & Siegel (1978)
It takes approximately 10 min to complete the LES.
The survey is not computer scorable or interpretable.

Key Reference

Sarason, I. B., Johnson, J. H., & Siegel, J. M. (1978). Assessing the impact of life changes: Development of the life experiences survey. *Journal of Consulting and Clinical Psychology, 46,* 932–946.

Loss of Face Measure

Characteristics Assessed

Areas in which face-threatening concerns are salient.
Where Test Can Be Obtained
Dr. Nolan Zane
Graduate School of Education
University of California, Santa Barbara
Santa Barbara, CA 93106
The test is not self-administered and takes about 10 min.
The administration can be delegated to clerical or nursing staff.
The test is not computer scorable and cannot be interpreted by computer.

Key Reference

Zane, N. W. S. (1991). *An empirical examination of Loss of Face among Asian Americans.* Paper presented at the 99th annual convention of the American Psychological Association, San Francisco, CA, August 1991.

The M Test

Characteristics Assessed

Malingering of schizophrenia.
Where Test Can Be Obtained
**Dr. Rex Beaber
Dr. Rex Beaber
Division of Family Medicine
1875 Century Park East, Suite 700
Room BH-134 CHS
Los Angeles, CA 90067
UCLA Medical Center
Los Angeles, CA 90024
The test is self-administered and takes about 10 min.
The administration cannot be delegated to clerical or nursing staff.
The test is not computer scorable and cannot be interpreted by computer.

Key References

Beaber, R., Marston, A., Michelli, J., & Mills, M. (1985). A brief test for measuring malingering in schizophrenic individuals. *American Journal of Psychiatry, 142,* 1478–1481.
Gillias, J., Rogus, R., & Bagby, M. (1991). Validity of the M Test. *Journal of Personality Assessment, 57,* 130–140.

Maudsley Obsessional-Compulsive Inventory (MOCI)

Characteristics Assessed

Self-report measure to assess the existence and extent of different obsessive compulsive complaints.
Where Test Can Be Obtained
Dr. R. J. Hodgson
Addition Research Unit
Institute of Psychiatry, 101
Denmark Hill, London
SE5 9AF England
The test is self-administered and takes about 10–15 min.
The administration can be delegated to clerical or nursing staff.
The test is not computer scorable and cannot be interpreted by computer.

Key References

Hodgson, R. J., & Rachman, S. (1977). Obsessional-compulsive complaints. *Behavior Therapy, 15,* 389–395.
Sternberger, L. G., & Burns, G. L. (1990). Compulsive activity checklist and the Maudsley obsessional-compulsive inventory: Psychometric properties of two measures of obsessive-compulsive disorder. *Behavior Therapy, 21,* 117–127.

Marital Satisfaction Inventory-Revised

Characteristics Assessed

This 150-item inventory assesses the extent to which the respondent considers his or her marriage to be satisfactory. The inventory is used with premarital couples as well as married couples. The scale contains two validity scales and 10 specific scales measuring relationship satisfaction.

Publisher:

Western Psychological Services
12031 Wilshire Boulevard
Los Angeles, CA 90025

Key Reference

Snyder, D. R., & Aikman, G. G. (1999). The marital satisfaction inventory-revised. In M. E. Maruish (Ed.), *Use of psychological tests for treatment planning and outcomes assessment* (pp. 1173–1210). Mahwah, NJ: Erlbaum.

Memories of Spouse

Characteristics Assessed

Contents: 15 spontaneous memories of spouse, beginning with first meeting, and several directed memories. Assesses: Problem areas in relationship. Provides an overview of the marriage, beginning with first meeting.

Publisher:

Arnold R. Bruhn
The Topaz House
4400 E. West Highway #28
Bethesda, MD 20814

The test is self-administered and takes about 5 min for psychologists.
The administration can be delegated to clerical or nursing staff.
The test is not computer scorable and cannot be interpreted by computer.

Key Reference

Bruhn, A. R., & Feigenbaum, K. (1993). The interpretation of autobiographical memories (Unpublished manuscript).

Miller Behavioral Style Scale (MBSS)

Characteristics Assessed

Two basic coping styles: information distractors (blunters) and information seekers (monitors).
Where Test Can Be Obtained
Dr. Suzanne M. Miller
Department of Psychology, Weiss Hall
Temple University
113th and Columbia Streets
Philadelphia, PA 19122
The test is self-administered and takes about 10–15 min.
The administration can be delegated to clerical or nursing staff.
The test is not computer scorable and cannot be interpreted by computer.

Key References

Miller, S. M. (1987). Monitoring and blunting: Validation of a questionnaire to assess styles of information seeking under threat. *Journal of Personality and Social Psychology, 52*, 345–353.

Miller, S. M., Brody, D. S., & Summerton, S. (1988). Styles of coping with threat: Implications for health. *Journal of Personality and Social Psychology, 54*, 142–148.

Michigan Alcoholism Screening Test (MAST)

Characteristics Assessed

This instrument provides a quantifiable assessment of alcohol use problems. The inventory is a 25-item measure that is administered by an interviewer.

Publisher:

Melvin Selzer
6967 Paseo Laredo
LaJolla, CA 92037

Key Reference

Selzer, M. L. (1971). The Michigan alcoholism screening test: The quest for a new diagnostic instrument. *American Journal of Psychiatry, 127*, 1653–1658.

Million Clinical Multiaxial Inventory-III (MCMI-III)

Characteristics Assessed

A measure of 22 personality disorders and clinical syndromes for adults undergoing psychological or psychiatric assessment or treatment.

Publisher:

Pearson Assessments
5601 Green Valley Drive
Bloomington, MN 55437-1099

The test is self-administered and takes about 45–60 min.
The administration can be delegated to clerical or nursing staff.
The test is computer scorable and is interpreted by computer.
The address of the official computer scoring and interpretation service is:
Pearson Assessments
5601 Green Valley Drive
Bloomington, MN 55437-1099

Key References

Craig, R. J. (Ed.) (1993). *The million clinical multiaxial inventory: A clinical research information synthesis.* Hillsdale, NJ: Erlbaum.

Choca, J., Shanty, L., & Van Denberg, E. (1991). *Interpretive guide to the million multiaxial inventory.* Washington, DC: American Psychological Association.

Millon, T. (Ed.) (1997). *The million inventories: Clinical and personality assessment.* New York: Guilford Press.

Mini-Mental State (MMS)

Characteristics Assessed

Orientation; memory; attention; ability to name, follow verbal and written commands, and constructional ability.
Where Test Can Be Obtained
Dr. Marshal F. Folstein
Department of Psychiatry and Behavioral Science
Johns Hopkins Hospital
Baltimore, MD 21205
The test is not self-administered and usually takes about 5–10 min.
The administration cannot be delegated to clerical or nursing staff.
The test is not computer scorable and cannot be interpreted by computer.

Key References

Folstein, M. F., Folstein, S. E., & McHugh, P. (1975). "Mini-mental state": A practical method for grading the cognitive state of patients for the clinician. *Journal of Psychiatric Research, 12*, 189–198.

Anthony, J. C., LeResche, L., Niaz, W., Von Korff, M. R., & Folstein, M. F. (1982). Limits of the mini-mental state as a screening test for dementia and delirium among hospital patients. *Psychological Medicine, 12*, 397–408.

The Multicenter-Panic Anxiety Scale (MC-PAS)

Characteristics Assessed

Clinician-rated composite symptom rating scale for panic disorder.

Where Test Can Be Obtained

Dr. Katherine Shear

Anxiety Disorders Clinic

Western Pyschiatric Institute & Clinic

3811 O'Hara Street

Pittsburgh, PA 15213

The test is not self-administered and usually takes about 20 min.

The administration cannot be delegated to clerical or nursing staff.

The test is not computer scorable and cannot be interpreted by computer.

Key Reference

Shear, M. K., Brown, T. A., Barlow, D. H., Money, R., Sholomskas, D. E., Woods, S. W., Gorman, J. M., & Papp, L. A. (1997). Multicenter collaborative panic disorder severity scale. *American Journal of Psychiatry, 154*(11), 1571–1575.

The Multidimensional Function Assessment Questionnaire (OARS)

Characteristics Assessed

Individual functioning—provides functional information in five domains of social resources, economic resources, mental health, physical health, and ADL status.

Older Americans Resources and Services Programs

Duke University Center for Study of Aging and Human Development

Durham, NC 27710

The test is not self-administered and usually takes about 45 min–1 hr.

The administration cannot be delegated to clerical or nursing staff.

The test is (computer-assigned ratings available in key reference) computer scorable but cannot be interpreted by computer.

Key Reference

Duke University Center for the Study of Aging. (1978). *Multidimensional functional assessment: The OARS methodology* (2nd ed.) Durham, NC: Duke University.

Multilevel Assessment Instrument (MAI)

Characteristics Assessed

Health, activities of daily living, cognition, time use, social interaction, psychological well-being (personal adjustment—moral and psychiatric symptoms), and perceived quality of life (perceived environment—housing quality, neighborhood quality, and personal security).

Where Test Can Be Obtained

**Jana M. Mosley, PhD, MPH, MSN

**Dr. M. Powell Lawton (deceased January 2001)

Philadelphia Geriatric Center

301 Old York Road

Philadelphia, PA 19141

The test is not self-administered and usually takes about 50 min (15–60 min).

The administration cannot be delegated to clerical or nursing staff.

The test is computer scorable but cannot be interpreted by computer.

Other Important Features

Interview format

Key References

Lawton, M. P., Kleban, M. H., & Moss, M. (1980). *The Philadelphia geriatric center multilevel assessment instrument.* Final report to the National Institute of Aging. Philadelphia, Philadelphia Geriatric Center, Philadelphia, PA.

Lawton, M. P., Moss, M., Fulcomer, M., & Kleban, M. (1982). A research and service oriented multilevel assessment instrument. *Journal of Gerontology, 37,* 91–99.

Minnesota Multiphasic Personality Inventory (MMPI-2)

Characteristics Assessed

The MMPI-2 is a revised version of the original MMPI and was published in 1989. A broad range of personality characteristics and clinical symptoms are addressed by the MMPI-2, for example, anxiety and somatization disorders, antisocial patterns, mood disorders, thought disorder, relationship problems, and potential problems with alcohol and drug abuse. There are eight validity measures available to aid in the detection of invalidating conditions. The traditional empirically based MMPI Clinical Scales are continuous with MMPI-2, and a number of new content and special scales to detect alcohol and drug abuse and marital problems have been published.

Publisher:

University of Minnesota Press

University of Minnesota

2037 University Avenue SE

Minneapolis, MN 55455-3082

Where Test Can Be Obtained

Pearson Assessments

5601 Green Valley Drive

Bloomington, MN 55437-1099

Sales: 800-227-7271

Support: 800-627-7271 (Ext. 3235)

General info: 877-242-6767

Call: 800-627-7271

Fax: 800-632-9011 or 952-681-3299

Email: pearsonassessments@pearson.com

Information on the MMPI-2 can be obtained at www.umn.edu/mmpi

The test is self-administered and usually takes about 1.5 hr.

The administration can be delegated to clerical or nursing staff.

The test is computer scorable and can be interpreted by computer.

The address of the official computer scoring and interpretation service is provided by Pearson Assessments

5601 Green Valley Drive

Bloomington, MN 55437-1099

Sales: 800-227-7271

Support: 800-627-7271 (Ext. 3235)

General info: 877-242-6767

Call: 800-627-7271

Fax: 800-632-9011 or 952-681-3299

Email: pearsonassessments@pearson.com

Key References

Butcher, J. N., Cabiya, J., Lucio, E. M., & Garrido, M. (2007). *Assessing Hispanic clients using the MMPI-2 and MMPI-A.* Washington, DC: American Psychological Association.

Butcher, J. N., Dahlstrom, W. G., Graham, J. R., Tellegen, A., & Kaemmer, B. (2001). *MMPI-2 (Minnesota Multiphasic Personality Inventory-2): Manual for administration and scoring* (Rev. ed.). Minneapolis, MN: University of Minnesota Press.

Butcher, J. N., & Williams, C. L. (2000). *Essentials of MMPI-2 and MMPI-A interpretation* (2nd ed.). Minneapolis, MN: University of Minnesota Press.

Graham, J. R. (2000). *MMPI-2: Assessing personality and psychopathology* (3rd ed.). New York: Oxford University Press.

Minnesota Multiphasic Personality Inventory (MMPI-A)

Characteristics Assessed

The MMPI-A is a revised version of the original MMPI for adolescents and was published in 1992. A broad range of personality characteristics, clinical symptoms, and adolescent behavioral problems are addressed by the MMPI-A, for example, anxiety and somatization disorders, conduct problems, mood disorders, thought disorder, and potential problems with alcohol and drug abuse. There are seven validity measures available to aid the detection of invalidating conditions. The traditional empirically based MMPI clinical scales are continuous with MMPI-A, and a number of new content scales have been developed to address adolescent problems. Special scales to detect alcohol and drug abuse have been published.

Publisher:

University of Minnesota Press
University of Minnesota
2037 University Avenue SE
Minneapolis, MN 55455-3082

Where Test Can Be Obtained
Pearson Assessments
5605 Green Circle Drive
Minnetonka, MN 55437-1099

The test is self-administered and usually takes about 1 hr.

The administration can be delegated to clerical or nursing staff.

The test is computer scorable and can be interpreted by computer.

The address of the official computer scoring and interpretation service is

Pearson Assessments
5605 Green Circle Drive
Minnetonka, MN 55437-1099
Information on the MMPI-A can be obtained at: www.umn.edu/mmpi

Key References

Butcher, J. N., Cabiya, J., Lucio, E. M., & Garrido, M. (2007). *Assessing Hispanic clients using the MMPI-2 and MMPI-A.* Washington, DC: American Psychological Association.

Butcher, J. N., & Williams, C. L. (2000). *Essentials of MMPI-2 and MMPI-A interpretation* (2nd ed.). Minneapolis, MN: University of Minnesota Press.

Butcher, J. N., Williams, C. L., Graham, J. R., Archer, R., Tellegen, A., Ben-Porath, Y. S., et al. (1992). *MMPI-A (Minnesota Multiphasic Persoality Inventory for Adolescents): Manual for administration and scoring.* Minneapolis, MN: University of Minnesota Press.

Neo Personality Inventory-Revised (NEO PI-R)

Characteristics Assessed

Five major dimensions of personality: neuroticism, extraversion, openness, agreeableness, and conscientiousness.

Publisher:

Psychological Assessment Resources, Inc.
PO Box 998
Odessa, FL 33556

The test is self-administered and usually takes about 30–40 min. The administration can be delegated to clerical or nursing staff. The test is computer scorable and can be interpreted by computer. The address of the official computer scoring and interpretation service is

Psychological Assessment Resources, Inc.
PO Box 998
Odessa, FL 33556

Other Important Features

Test has three forms: Form S for self-reports, Form R for observer ratings, and a shortened version of Form S, the NEO FFI.

Key References

Costa, P., & McRae, R. (1990). Personality disorders and the Five-Factor Model of personality. *Journal of Personality Disorders, 4,* 362–371.

Costa, P., & McRae, R. (1992). Normal personality assessment in clinical practice. *Psychological Assessment, 4,* 5–13, 20–22.

Neurobehavioral Rating Scale

Characteristics Assessed

Behavioral, emotional, and cognitive sequelae of head injury.
Where Test Can Be Obtained
**Dr. Harvey Levin

Former Address:

University of Maryland Baltimore
Division of Neurosurgery
Division of Neurological Surgery
D73
22 S. Greene Street Room S12D09B
University of Texas Medical Branch
Baltimore, MD 21201
Galveston, TX 77555-0641
Fax: 410-328-0756
Phone: 410-328-0938

The test is not self-administered and usually takes about 10 min.

The administration cannot be delegated to clerical or nursing staff.

The test computer scorable but cannot be interpreted by computer.

Other Important Features

Clinician ratings using 27 7-point scales.

Key References

Levin, H. S., High, W. M., Goethe, K. E., Sisson, R. A., Overall, J. E., Rhoades, H. M., et al. (1987). The Neurobehavioral Rating Scale: Assessment of the behavioral sequelae of head injury by the clinician. *Journal of Neurology, Neurosurgery, and Psychiatry, 50,* 183–193.

Grant, I., & Alves, W. (1987). Psychiatric and psychosocial disturbances in head injury. In H. S. Levin, J. Grafman, &

H. M. Eisenberg (Eds.), *Neurobehavioral recovery from head injury*, 232–261. New York: Oxford University Press.

Neuropsychology Behavior and Affect Profile

Characteristics Assessed

Indifference, mania, depression, behavioral inappropriateness, and communication problems (pragnosia).

Where Test Can Be Obtained:

Dr. Linda Nelson

UCLA/Semel Institute

760 Westwood Plaza, Rm. C8-749

Los Angeles, CA 90095.

The test is not self-administered.

The test is not computer scorable and cannot be interpreted by computer.

Other Important Features

The instrument consists of 106 statements and five scales, and has self- and other-rater versions.

Key Reference

Nelson, L. D., Satz, P., Mitushina, M., Van Gorp, W., Cicchetti, D., Lewis, R., & Van Lancker, D. (1989). Development and validation of the neuropsychology behavior and affect profile. *Psychological Assessment, 1*, 225–272.

Penn State Worry Questionnaire (PSWQ)

Characteristics Assessed

Brief self-report measure of trait worry.

Where Test Can Be Obtained

Dr. Thomas D. Borkovec

Penn State University

417 Bruce Moore Bldg.

University Park, PA 16802

The test is self-administered and usually takes about 10 min. The administration can be delegated to clerical or nursing staff.

The test is not computer scorable and cannot be interpreted by computer.

Key References

Meyer, T. J., Miller, M. L., Metzger, M., & Borkovec, T. D. (1990). Development and validation of the Penn state worry questionnaire. *Behavior Research and Therapy, 28*, 487–495.

Brown, T. A., Antony, M. M., & Barlow, D. H. (1992). Psychometric properties of the Penn state worry questionnaire: In a clinical anxiety disorders sample. *Behavior Research and Therapy, 30*, 33–37.

Personality Adjective Checklist (PACL)

Characteristics Assessed

Assesses personality traits as conceptualized by Theodore Millon using a 153-word adjective checklist.

Publisher:

21st Century Assessment

PO Box 608

South Pasadena, CA 91031-0608

The test is self-administered and usually takes about 15 min. The administration can be delegated to clerical or nursing staff.

Other Important Features

Easy to use; short; inexpensive

Key References

Strack, S. (1987). Development and validation of an adjective checklist to assess the millon personality types in a normal population. *Journal of Personality Assessment, 51*, 572–587.

Strack, S. (1991). *Manual for the personality adjective checklist (PACL)* (Rev. ed.). South Pasadena, CA: Stephen Strack.

Personality Assessment Form

Characteristics Assessed

Personality disorders.

Where Test Can Be Obtained

Dr. Paul Pilkonis

Western Psychiatric Institute & Clinic

3811 O'Hara Street

Pittsburgh, PA 15213

The test is self-administered and usually takes about 1–2 hr. The administration cannot be delegated to clerical or nursing staff.

The test is not computer scorable and cannot be interpreted by computer.

Other Important Features:

Unstructured to semistructured interview.

Key Reference

Pilkonis, P. A., Heape, C. L., Ruddy, J., & Serrano, P. (1991). Validity in the diagnosis of personality disorders: The use of the LEAD standard. *Psychological Assessment, 3*, 46–54.

Personality Assessment Inventory (PAI)

Characteristics Assessed

Dimensions of psychopathology (e.g., somatic complaints, anxiety, paranoia, alcohol problems, stress, warmth, etc.) divided into 11 clinical scales, five treatment scales, and two interpersonal scales.

Publisher:

Psychological Assessment Resources, Inc. (PAR)

PO Box 998

Odessa, FL 33556

The test is self-administered and usually takes about 45–55 min. The administration can be delegated to clerical or nursing staff. The test is computer scorable and can be interpreted by computer. The address of the official computer scoring and interpretation service is

Psychological Assessment Resources, Inc. (PAR)

PO Box 998

Odessa, FL 33556

Key Reference

Morey, L. C. (1991). *The personality assessment inventory: Professional manual*. Odessa, FL: Psychological Assessment Resources.

Personality Diagnostic Questionnaire-4

Characteristics Assessed

Personality disorders.

Where Test Can Be Obtained

Dr. Steve Hyler

New York State Psychiatric Institute
722 West 168th Street
New York, NY 10032

The test is self-administered and usually takes about 30 min.

The administration can be delegated to clerical or nursing staff.

The test is computer scorable but cannot be interpreted by computer.

Publisher:

Dr. A. W. Loranger
New York Hospital CMC
White Plains, NY 10605

The test is not self-administered and usually takes about 1–4 hr.

The administration cannot be delegated to clerical or nursing staff.

The test is not computer scorable and cannot be interpreted by computer.

Other Important Features

Semistructured interview

Key Reference

Loranger, A. W., Susman, V. L., Oldham, J. M., & Russakoff, L. M. (1987). The personality disorder examination: A preliminary report. *Journal of Personality Disorders, 1*, 1–13.

Personality Interview Questions-II

Characteristics Assessed

Personality disorders.
Where Test Can Be Obtained
Dr. Thomas A. Widiger
Department of Psychology
College of Arts and Sciences
University of Kentucky
115 Kastle Hall
Lexington, KY 40506-0044

The test is not self-administered and usually takes about 1–3 hr.

The administration cannot be delegated to clerical or nursing staff.

The test is not computer scorable and cannot be interpreted by computer.

Other Important Features

Semistructured interview

Key References

Widiger, T. A., Frances, A. J., & Trull, T. J. (1989). Personality disorders. In R. Craig (Ed.), *Clinical and diagnostic interviewing* (pp. 221–236). Northvale, NJ: Jason Aronson.

Widiger, T. A., Freiman, K., & Bailey, B. (1990). Convergent and discriminate validity of personality disorder prototypic acts. *Psychological Assessment, 2*, 107–113.

Psychological Test Battery to Detect Faked Insanity

Characteristics Assessed

Detection of simulated insanity.
Where Test Can Be Obtained
**Dr. David Schretlen (unlisted)
Department of Psychiatry
Johns Hopkins School of Medicine

Meyers 218
600 North Wolfe Street
Baltimore, MD 21205

The test is self-administered and usually takes about 15 min.

The administration can be delegated to clerical or nursing staff.

The test is not computer scorable and cannot be interpreted by computer.

Key References

Schretlen, D., Wilkins, S., Van Gort, W., & Bobholz, J. (1992). Cross-validation of a psychological test battery to detect faked insanity. *Psychological Assessment, 4*, 77–83.

Schretlen, D., & Arkowitz, H. (1990). A psychological test battery to detect prison inmates who fake insanity or mental retardation. *Behavioral Sciences and the Law, 8*, 75–84.

PTSD Symptom Scale (PSS)

Characteristics Assessed

Self-report measure of the major symptom areas of PTSD including re-experiencing, avoidance and numbing, and hyperarousal.

Where Test Can Be Obtained
Dr. Edna Foa
Medical College of Pennsylvania at EPPI
3535 Market Street, 6th floor
Philadelphia, PA 19104

The test is self-administered and usually takes about 15 min.

The administration can be delegated to clerical or nursing staff.

The test is not computer scorable and cannot be interpreted by computer.

Key Reference

Foa, E. B., Riggs, D. S., Dancu, C. V., & Rothbaum, B. O. (1993). Reliability and validity of a brief instrument for assessing post-traumatic stress disorder. *Journal of Traumatic Stress, 6*, 459–473.

Revised Diagnostic Interview For Borderlines

Characteristics Assessed

Borderline personality disorder.
Where Test Can Be Obtained
Dr. John Gunderson
McLean Hospital
115 Mill Street
Belmont, MD 02478

The test is not self-administered and usually takes about 1–3 hr.

The administration cannot be delegated to clerical or nursing staff.

The test is not computer scorable and cannot be interpreted by computer.

Other Important Features

Semistructured interview

Key Reference

Zanarini, M. C., Gunderson, J. G., Frankenburg, F. R., & Chauncey, D. L. (1989). The revised diagnostic interview for borderlines: Discrimination of BPD from other Axis-II disorders. *Journal of Personality Disorders, 3*, 10–18.

Where Test Can Be Obtained
Dr. Gary W. Small
UCLA Neuropsychiatric Institute
760 Westwood Plaza
Los Angeles, CA 90024
The test is not self-administered and usually takes less than 1 hr. The administration cannot be delegated to clerical or nursing staff.

Other Important Features
Semistructured interview

Key References
Hachinski, V. C., Iliff, L. D., Phil, M., Zihka, E., Duboulay, G. H., McAllister, V. L., et al. (1975). Cerebral blood flow in dementia. *Archives of Neurology, 32,* 632–637.
Small, G. W. (1985). Revised ischemic score for diagnosing multi-infarct dementia. *Journal of Clinical Psychiatry, 46,* 514–517.

Romantic Relationship Procedure
Characteristics Assessed
Contents: Four longest-lasting or most important romantic relationships—three memories of each relationship. Assesses: Problem areas and unresolved issues in romantic relationships.

Publisher:
Dr. Arnold R. Bruhn
4400 E. West Highway
Bethesda, MD 20814
The test is self-administered and usually takes about 5 min for psychologists.
The administration can be delegated to clerical or nursing staff.
The test is not computer scorable and cannot be interpreted by computer.

Key Reference
Bruhn, A. R., & Feigenbaum, K. (1993). *The interpretation of autobiographical memories.* (Self-published). 7910 Woodmont Avenue #1300, Bethesda, MD 20814.

Rorschach
Characteristics Assessed
A perceptual-associative-judgmental task that infers certain current psychological states and traits; personality characteristics related to cognitive and perceptual functioning.

Publisher:
Hans Huber
Langgasstrasse 76
POB CH-3000
Bern 9 Switzerland
The test is not self-administered and usually takes about 45 min–1 hr.
The administration procedures cannot be delegated to clerical or nursing staff.
The test is not computer scorable but can be interpreted by computer.
The address of the official computer interpretation service is RSP-2, RIAP-2
Rorschach Workshops
2149 Riceville Road
Asheville, NC 28805

Other Important Features
Extensive norms now available for various nonpatient and clinical populations if Comprehensive System used for scoring an interpretation.

Key References
Exner, J. (1993). *The Rorschach: A comprehensive system* (3rd ed., Vols. 1 & 2). New York: John Wiley & Sons.
Lerner, P. (1991). *Psychoanalytic theory and the Rorschach.* Hillsdale, NJ: Analytic Press.

Schedule for Affective Disorders and Schizophrenia-Lifetime Version (SADS-LA)
Characteristics Assessed
The SADS-LA provides a comprehensive assessment of anxiety and related disorders across lifetime.
Where Test Can Be Obtained
Dr. Abby J. Fyer
Anxiety Disorders Clinics
New York State Psychiatric Institute
722 West 168th Street
New York, NY 10032
The test is not self-administered and usually takes about 3.5 hr. The administration cannot be delegated to clerical or nursing staff.
The test is not computer scorable and cannot be interpreted by computer.

Key References
Fyer, A. J., Mannuzza, S., Martin, L. Y., Gallops, M. S., et al. (1989). Reliability of anxiety assessment: II. Symptom agreement. *Archives of General Psychiatry, 46,* 1102–1110.
Mannuzza, S., Fyer, A. J., Martin, L. Y., Gallops, M. S., et al. (1989). Reliability of anxiety assessment: I. Diagnostic agreement. *Archives of General Psychiatry, 46,* 1093–1101.

Schedule for Nonadaptive and Adaptive Personality (SNAP)
Characteristics Assessed
12 primary traits (e.g., aggression, dependency) and three broad temperaments (e.g., negative affectivity) that are relevant to personality disorder. Also contains 6 validity indices and 13 DSM-II-R Axis II PD diagnostic scales.

Publisher:
University of Minnesota Press
2037 University Avenue SE
Minneapolis, MN 55455
The test is self-administered and usually takes about 1 hr.
The administration can be delegated to clerical or nursing staff.
The test is computer scorable but cannot, at the present time, be interpreted by computer.

Other Important Features
Supplement for scoring the DSM-IV Axis II personality disorders will be available in the future; adolescent version is being tested.

Key References
Clark, L. A., McEwen, J. L., Collard, L. M., & Hickok, L. G. (1993). Symptoms and traits of personality disorder: Two new methods for this assessment. *Psychological Assessment, 5,* 81–91.
Clark, L. A., Vorhies, L., & McEwen, J. L. (1994). Personality disorder symptomatology from the five-factor perspective. In

P. T. Costa, Jr., & T. Widiger (Eds.), *Personality disorders and the Five-Factor Model of personality* (pp. 95–116). Washington, DC: American Psychological Association.

The Short-Care

Characteristics Assessed

Depression, dementia, and disability in elderly persons.
Where Test Can Be Obtained
Dr. Barry Gurland
Columbia University Geriatrics & Gerontology/Stroud Center
100 Haven Avenue, Tower I III-297
New York, NY 10032
The test is not self-administered and usually takes about 30 min per session.
The administration cannot be delegated to clerical or nursing staff.

Other Important Features

Semistructured interview

Key Reference

Gurland, B., Golden, R. R., Teresi, J., & Challop, J. (1984). The SHORT-CARE: An efficient instrument for the assessment of depression, dementia and disability. *Journal of Gerontology, 39*, 166–169.

Social Interaction Anxiety Scale (SIAS)

Characteristics Assessed

Measures cognitive, affective, and behavioral reactions to a variety of situations involving social interactions.
Where Test Can Be Obtained
Dr. Richard G. Heimberg
Center for Stress and Anxiety Disorders
1535 Western Avenue
Albany, NY 12203
The test is self-administered and usually takes about 10 min.
The administration can be delegated to clerical or nursing staff.
The test is not computer scorable and cannot be interpreted by computer.

Key Reference

Heimberg, R. G., Mueller, G. P., Holt, C. S., & Hope, D. A. (1992). Assessment of anxiety in social interaction and being observed by others: The social interaction anxiety scale and the social phobia scale. *Behavior Therapy, 23*, 53–73.

The Staff–Resident Interaction Chronograph (SRIC)

Characteristics Assessed

The nature, amount, content, and interactions provided to clients by staff inpatient and residential settings (including context).

Publisher:

Research Press
Dept. 26W
Main: 217-352-3273
PO Box 9177
Toll Free: 800-519-2707
Champaign, IL 61826
Fax: 217-352-1221

The test is not self-administered and usually takes 10 min of direct observational samples.
The administration can be delegated to fulltime technician-level observers for data collection.
The test is computer scorable but cannot be interpreted by computer.
The address of the official computer scoring and of the official computer scoring and interpretation service is
Research Press
PO Box 9177
Champagne, IL 61826

Other Important Features

Key references provide videotape observer training materials and procedures and a summary of all technical development, reliability and validity evidence, and generalizability/feasibility data on 679 staff (aide-level to doctoral-level), 35 treatment programs (psychodynamic through biological) in adult treatment units (8–120 biological) in adult treatment units (8–120 beds) covering mentally retarded, alcohol/substance abuse, and mentally ill populations in mental hospitals and community facilities.

Key References

Paul, G. L. (1988). *Observational assessment instrumentation for service and research—The Staff–Resident Interaction Chronograph: Assessment in residential treatment settings* (Part 3). Champaign, IL: Research Press.
Paul, G. L. (1994). *Observational assessment instrumentation for service and research—The TSBC/SRIC system implementation package: Assessment in residential treatment settings* (Pt. 5). Champaign, IL. Research Press.

State-Trait Anger Scale (STAS)

Characteristics Assessed

The STAS is a true–false inventory to measure both trait anger and state anger in a manner analogous to the trait-state anxiety measures published by Spielberger. The inventory measures the intensity of anger and the manner of expression.

Publisher:

Psychological Assessment Resources (PAR)
PO Box 998
Odessa, FL 33556

Key Reference

Spielberger, C. C., Johnson, E. H., Russell, S. F., Crane, R. J., Jacobs, G. A., & Worden, T. J. (1985). The experience and expression of anger: Construction and validation of an anger expression scale. In M. A. Chesney & R. H. Rosenman (Eds.), *Anger and hostility in cardiovascular and behavioral disorders* (pp. 5–30). New York: Hemisphere.

State-Trait Anxiety Inventory (STAI)

Characteristics Assessed

State form: Measure of state anxiety; sensitive to changes in transitory anxiety.
Trait form: Measure of relatively stable individual differences in anxiety proneness.

Publisher:

Consulting Psychological Press
3803 East Bayshore Road
Palo Alto, CA 94303

The test is not self-administered and usually takes 20 min.
The administration can be delegated to clerical or nursing staff.
The test is computer scorable but cannot be interpreted by computer.

Key Reference

Spielberger, C. D. (1983). *Manual for the state-trait anxiety inventory (Form Y)*. Palo Alto, CA: Consulting Psychological Press.

Structured Clinical Interview for DSM-IV

Characteristics Assessed

Structured clinical interview designed to assess DSM-IV diagnosable conditions.

Publisher:

American Psychiatric Press
750 First Street NE
Washington, DC 20002-4242
The test is not self-administered and usually takes about 3 hr.
The administration cannot be delegated to clerical or nursing staff.
The test is not computer scorable and cannot be interpreted by computer.

Key References

American Psychiatric Association. (1994). *The diagnostic and statistical manual of mental disorders* (4th ed.). Washington, DC: American Psychiatric Press.
Spitzer, R. L., & Williams, J. B. (1988). Revised diagnostic criteria and a new structured interview for diagnosing anxiety disorders. *Journal of Psychiatric Research, 22,* 55–85.

Structured Clinical Interview for DSM-IV Personality Disorders

Characteristics Assessed

Personality disorders.

Publisher:

American Psychiatric Press
750 First Street NE
Washington, DC 20002-4242
The test is not self-administered and usually takes about 1–3 hr.
The administration cannot be delegated to clerical or nursing staff.
The test is not computer scorable and cannot be interpreted by computer.

Other Important Features

Semistructured interview

Key References

American Psychiatric Association. (1994). *The diagnostic and statistical manual of mental disorders* (4th ed.). Washington, DC: American Psychiatric Press.
Spitzer, R. L., Williams, J. B. W., Gibbon, M., & First, M. B., (1972). The structured clinical interview for DSM-III-R (SCID): I. History, rationale, and description. *Archives of General Psychiatry, 49,* 624–629.

Structured Inventory of Malingered Symptomatology (SIMS)

Characteristics Assessed

This 75-item true–false inventory was designed to detect malingering in forensic samples. It addresses faking of neurologic as well as mental health symptoms.

Publisher:

See Smith & Burger (1997)

Key Reference

Smith, G. P., & Burger, G. K. (1997). Detection of malingering: Validation of the Structured Inventory of Malingered Symptomatology (SIMS). *Journal of the American Academy of Psychiatry and the Law, 23,* 183–189.

Structured Interview of Reported Symptoms (SIRS)

Characteristics Assessed

Malingering and deception.

Publisher:

PAR, Inc.
PO Box 998
16204 N. Florida Avenue
Odessa, FL 33556
Lutz, FL 33549
The test is not self-administered and usually takes about 30–60 min.
The administration cannot be delegated to clerical or nursing staff.
The test is not computer scorable and cannot be interpreted by computer.

Key References

Roger, R. (1997). *Clinical assessment of malingering and deception* (2nd ed.). New York: Guilford Press.
Rogers, R., Gillis, R., & Bagby, R. (1990). The SIRS as a measure of malingering: A validation study with a correctional sample. *Behavioral Science and the Law, 8,* 85–92.
Rogers, R., Gillis, R., Bagby, R., & Moneiro, E. (1991). Detection of malingering on the SIRS: A study of coached and uncoached malingerers. *Psychological Assessment, 3,* 673–677.

Structured Interview Schedules for Clients and Significant Others (SISCSO)

Characteristics Assessed

Present and historical level of functioning, psychiatric symptomotology, role functioning, and expectations of adult mental patients at entry, predischarge, and follow-up for inpatient-residential facilities.

Publisher:

Research Press
PO Box 9177
Champagne, IL 61826
The test is not self-administered and usually takes abut 2 hr each.
The administration cannot be delegated to clerical or nursing staff.
Selected instruments derived from the interview responses can be computer-scored; users must write their own programs. Test cannot be interpreted by computer.

Other Important Features

A set of six structured interview protocols originally used with severely disabled chronic mental patients; Paul & Mariotto (1986) provides details and recommendations for expansion as a generic set for adult populations.

Key Reference

Paul, G. L., & Mariotto, M. J. (1986). Potential utility of the sources and methods: A comprehensive paradigm. In G. L. Paul (Ed.), *Principles and methods to support cost-effective quality operations: Assessment in residential treatment settings* (Part 1). Champaign, IL: Research Press.

The Suicide Intent Scale

Characteristics Assessed

Suicide risk.

Publisher:

The Charles Press Publishers, Inc.
Bowie, MD 20715

The test is not self-administered, but is based on self-report and usually takes a few minutes. The administration cannot be delegated to clerical or nursing staff.

Key References

Beck, A. T., Schuyler, D., & Herman, I. (1974). Development of suicidal intent scales. In A. T. Beck, H. L. P. Resnick, & D. J. Lettieri (Eds.), *The prediction of suicide* (pp. 45–56). Oxford: Charles Press Publishers.

Beck, R. W., Morris, J. B., & Beck, A. T. (1974). Cross validation of the suicide intent scale. *Psychological Reports, 34*, 445–446.

The Suicide Risk Assessment Scale

Characteristics Assessed

Suicide risk.

Publisher:

American Journal of Psychiatry
American Psychiatric Association
1400 K Street, NW
Washington, DC 20005

The test is not self-administered but is based on patient self-report. It takes about 30 min. The administration cannot be delegated to clerical or nursing staff.

Other Important Features

This is one of the very few tests for estimating suicide risk with empirically weighted items.

Key Reference

Motto, J. A. (1989). Problems in suicidal risk assessment. In D. Jacobs & H. N. Brown (Eds.), *Suicide: Understanding and responding: Harvard Medical School perspectives* (pp. 129–142). Madison, CT: International Universities Press, Inc.

Suinn–Lew Asian Self-Identity and Acculturation Scale (SL-ASIA)

Characteristics Assessed

Level of acculturation among Asian-Americans.
Where Test Can Be Obtained
Dr. Richard M. Suinn
Department of Psychology
Colorado State University
Fort Collins, CO 80523

The test is self-administered and usually takes about 10–15 min.

The administration can be delegated to clerical or nursing staff.

The test is not computer scorable and cannot be interpreted by computer.

Key References

Suinn, R. M., Ahuna, C., & Khoo, G. (1992). The Suinn–Lew Asian self-identity acculturation scale: Concurrent and factorial validation. *Educational and Psychological Measurement, 52*, 1–6.

Suinn, R. M., Rikard-Figueroa, K., Lew, S., & Virgil, P. (1987). The Suinn–Lew Asian self-identity acculturation scale: An initial report. *Educational and Psychological Measurement, 47*, 401–407.

Symptom Checklist-90-Revised

Characteristics Assessed

Somatization, obsessive behavior, interpersonal sensitivity, depression, anxiety, hostility, phobic anxiety, paranoid ideation, and psychoticism.

Publisher:

Pearson Assessments
5601 Green Valley Drive
Bloomington, MN 55437-1099

The test is self-administered and usually takes about 15 min.
The administration can be delegated to clerical or nursing staff.
The test is computer scorable and can be interpreted by computer.
The address of the official computer scoring and interpretation service is
Pearson Assessments
5601 Green Valley Drive
Bloomington, MN 55437-1099

Other Important Features

Norms available for non-patient adults and adolescents as well as psychiatric inpatients and outpatients.

Key Reference

Derogatis, L. R. (1977). *SCL-R administration, scoring, and procedures manual.* Baltimore, MD: Clinical Psychometrics Research Unit, Johns Hopkins University School of Medicine.

Temas (Tell-Me-A-Story) Thematic Apperception Test

Characteristics Assessed

Personality/psychopathology in Hispanics, Blacks, and Whites.

Publisher:

Technical Manual
Western Psychological Services
12031 Wilshire Blvd.
Los Angles, CA 90025

The test is not self-administered and usually takes a variable amount of time.

The administration cannot be delegated to clerical or nursing staff.

The test is not computer scorable and cannot be interpreted by computer.

Key Reference

Constantino, G., Malgady, R. G., & Rogler, L. H. (1988). *TEMAS (Tell-Me-A-Story) manual.* Los Angeles: Western Psychological Services. Williams, R. L. (1972). *Themes concerning blacks.* St. Louis, MO: Williams & Associates.

Themes Concerning Blacks (TCB)

Characteristics Assessed

Personality/psychopathology in Blacks.

Publisher:

Williams & Associates
Department of Psychology
Washington University
St. Louis, MO

The test is not self-administered and usually takes a variable amount of time.

The administration cannot be delegated to clerical or nursing staff.

The test is not computer scorable and cannot be interpreted by computer.

Key References

Williams, R. L. (1972). *Themes concerning blacks*. St. Louis, MO: Williams & Associates.

Williams, R. L., & Johnson, R. C. (1981). Progress in developing Afro-centric measuring instruments. *Journal of Non-White Concerns, 9*, 3–18.

The Time-Sample Behavioral Checklist (TSBC)

Characteristics Assessed

Assets, deficits, and excesses in functioning of clients in inpatient and residential settings (including context); how and where clients and staff spend their time.

Publisher:

Research Press
PO Box 9177
Champagne, IL 61826

The test is not self-administered and usually takes 1 hr for direct observational time samples.

The administration can be delegated to full-time technician-level observers for data collection.

The test is computer scorable but cannot be interpreted by computer.

Other Important Features

Key references provide videotape observer training materials and procedures and a summary of all technical development, reliability and validity evidence, and normative data ($n = 1205$) for adult populations (ages 18–99) in mental hospitals and community facilities (covering mentally retarded, alcohol/substance abuse, acute and chronic mentally ill in all diagnostic categories).

Key References

Paul, G. L. (1987a). *Observational assessment instrumentation for service and research—The Time-Sample Behavioral Checklist: Assessment in residential treatment settings* (Part 2). Champaign, IL: Research Press.

Paul, G. L. (1987b). *Observational assessment instrumentation for service and research—The TSBC/SRIC system implementation package: Assessment in residential treatment settings* (Part 5). Champaign, IL: Research Press.

Tweak Test

Characteristics Assessed

The TWEAK test is a 5-item self-report measure that is usually administered in a clinician interview. The acronym

TWEAK is made up from the names of the five items in the test. This measure is designed to assess heavy past or current drinking.

Publisher:

Copies of the TWEAK may be obtained by writing at
**Dr. Marcia Russell (formerly)
Research Institute of Addiction
1021 Main Street
Buffalo, NY 14203-1016

Key Reference

Chan, A. W. K., Pristach, E. A., Welte, J. W., & Russell, M. (1993). Use of the TWEAK test in screening for alcoholism in heavy drinking populations. *Alcohol Clinical Experience Research, 17*, 1188–1192.

Washington Psychosocial Seizure Inventory (WPSI)

Characteristics Assessed

Emotional and interpersonal adjustment and psychosocial functioning. (Also family background, financial status, medical management, intelligence.)

Where Test Can Be Obtained
Dr. Carl B. Dodrill
Epilepsy Center ZA-50
325 Ninth Avenue
Harborview Hospital
Seattle, WA 98104

The test is self-administered.

The test is not computer scorable and cannot be interpreted by computer.

Key Reference

Dodrill, C. B., Batzel, L. W., Queissel, H. R., & Temkin, N. R. (1980). An objective method for the assessment of psychological and social problems among epileptics. *Epilepsia, 21*, 123–135.

Ways of Coping Questionnaire (WCQ)

Characteristics Assessed

Eight basic coping reactions or strategies that may be used in a cross section of stressful situations.

Publisher:

Consulting Psychologists Press
3803 E. Bayshore Road
Palo Alto, CA 94303-9608

The test is self-administered and usually takes about 10–12 min.

The administration can be delegated to clerical or nursing staff.

The test is not computer scorable and cannot be interpreted by computer.

Key References

Folkman, S., & Lazarus, R. S. (1988). *Manual for the ways of coping questionnaire*. Palo Alto, CA: Consulting Psychologists Press.

Folkman, S., Lazarus, R. S., Dunkel-Schetter, C., DeLongis, A., & Gruen, R. (1986). The dynamics of a stressful encounter. *Journal of Personality and Social Psychology, 50*, 992–1003.

Wisconsin Personality Disorders Inventory

Characteristics Assessed

Personality disorders.

Where Test Can Be Obtained

Dr. Marjorie Klein

Department of Psychiatry

University of Wisconsin Medical School

1300 University Ave.

Madison, WI 53706

The test is self-administered and usually takes about 1 hr.

The administration can be delegated to clerical or nursing staff.

The test is computer scorable but cannot be interpreted by computer.

Key Reference

Klein, M. H., Benjamin, L. S., Rosenfeld, R., Treece, L., Husted, J., & Greist, J. H. (1993). The wisconsin personality disorders inventory: I. Development, reliability, and validity. *Journal of Personality Disorders, 7*(4), 285–303.

Yale-Brown Obsessive Compulsive Scale (Y-BOCS)

Characteristics Assessed

Clinician-rated measure of the severity of symptoms of obsessive compulsive disorder.

Contains separate subscales for obsessions and compulsions.

Where Test Can Be Obtained

Wayne K. Goodman

Department of Psychiatry

Yale University School of Medicine

The Connecticut Mental Health Center

34 Park Street

New Haven, CT 06508

The test is not self-administered and usually takes about 20 min.

The administration cannot be delegated to clerical or nursing staff.

The test is not computer scorable and cannot be interpreted by computer.

Key References

Goodman, W., Price, L. H., Rasmussen, S. A., Mazure, C., et al. (1989a). The Yale-Brown obsessive compulsive scale: I. Development, use, and reliability. *Archives of General Psychiatry, 46*, 1006–1011.

Goodman, W., Price, L. H., Rasmussen, S. A., Mazure, C., et al. (1989b). The Yale-Brown obsessive compulsive scale: II. Validity. *Archives of General Psychiatry, 46*, 1012–1016.

INDEX

Note: The letter 't' denotes tables

McGrath, R. E., 88
McKinley, J. Charnley, 9, 250, 446, 573
Magnetic resonance imaging (MRI). *See*
    Functional magnetic resonance
    imaging
Magnetoencephalography (MEG),
    369–70, 370f
Malgady, R. G., 109–10
Malingering, 435–6, 575, 613–14,
    639–40. *See also* Feigned
    psychological symptoms
  conceptual and practical issues
    coaching, 618
    cost of misdiagnosis, 618–19
    definition and diagnostic criteria,
      614–15
    methodological issues, 615–17
  DSM-IV-TR and, 614–15
  strategy for clinical practice, 619
Malingering detection strategy, hypothetical
    classification rates for a two-stage,
    636, 638t, 638–9, 639t
Malingering detection tests and scales,
    methodological quality issues in
    validation of, 616t, 616–17
Malingering (MAL) index, 626
Malingering screening and detection scales,
    619–20
  MCMI-III, 626, 631, 632t
  MMPI-2, 620, 625, 638t, 638–9
    results from patient-controlled
      malingering detection studies, 620,
      621t–4t, 625
  Personality Assessment Inventory (PAI),
    625–6, 627t–30t, 638t
Malingering tests, dedicated, 631, 633,
    636, 638–9
Maltsberger, J. T., 520
Management. *See* Industrial/organizational
    (I/O) psychology
Mania. *See* Hypomania (Ma) scale
Marginal maximum likelihood (MML), 73
Marital distress. *See* Couple distress
Marital Distress (MDS) scale, 267
Marital distress taxon, 463
Marital problem questionnaires, 230
Marital Satisfaction Inventory-Revised
    (MSI-R), 475
Markon, K. E., 156–7
Masculine Gender Role (GM) scale, 268
Masculinity-Femininity (Mf) scale, 258,
    439, 489
Matarazzo, J. D., 201
Meehl, Paul E., 84, 85, 148, 260
Mental health care (MHC) programs, 647
Mentally retardation, 105
Mental status exams, 210–12, 222
  content areas, 211t–12t
Merrill, M., 192
Meyer, Gregory J., 292, 293
Meyer, R. G., 509–10
Michigan Alcohol Screening Test (MAST),
    531, 533–4

Miller, W. R., 212
Miller Forensic Assessment of Symptoms Test
    (M-FAST), 633, 635t, 636, 638t
Millon Adolescent Personality Inventory
    (MACI), 511
Millon Clinical Multiaxial Inventory
    (MCMI), 10
  CBTI systems for, 169
  malingering screening and detection
    scales, 626, 631, 632t
  minority groups and, 404
  personality disorders and, 341–3, 346t,
    347, 348t–50t, 352–3
  substance abuse scales (B and T), 533
  substance abuse settings and, 535
  suicide risk and, 510–11
Minnesota Multiphasic Personality
    Inventory. *See* MMPI
Minnesota Report: Adolescent Interpretive
    System (Butcher & Williams), 493
Minnesota Reports, 168, 592
Minority groups. *See* Ethnic and racial
    minority clients in U.S.; Race,
    ethnicity, and minority status
MMPI (Minnesota Multiphasic
    Personality Inventory)
  computer-assisted interpretive systems,
    168–9
  development, 9–10, 250–1
  international application, 44–5, 48–51,
    271, 593. *See also* Asian
    Americans, personality assessment
    with; Asian populations, MMPI-2
    studies with
  providing test results feedback, 495–6,
    697, 698t, 699–701
    as an intervention, 697, 699
  reasons for restandardization, 112, 251
    deficiency changes, 113, 114
    growth changes, 119–30
  resistance and, 669–71, 677
  restandardization project, 251–2
  short forms, 271–2
  substance abuse and, 528–30, 534–6
  suicide risk and, 508–10
  validity scales, 251, 252, 254t, 254–6,
    435–6
    malingering and, 620, 621t–4t, 625,
      638–9
  violence risk and, 554
MMPI-2 (Minnesota Multiphasic
    Personality Inventory-2nd
    edition), 9–10, 48, 49, 273.
    See also MMPI; Personality
    Psychopathology Five (PSY-5)
    scales; Personnel decisions
  abbreviated versions and short forms,
    271–2, 434–5, 695
  Clinical Scales, 251, 256–9, 438–41.
    See also Restructured Clinical (RC)
    Scales; *specific scales*
    identifying the "core" components of,
      115

computer-based test interpretation,
    168–9, 272–3, 592
  case history, 699–701, 700t, 701t
  clinical use of computerized report,
    697, 699–701
  computerized adaptive testing with,
    174–6, 272, 696–7
  limitations of, 176
  content interpretation of, 260, 261
    advantages of, 261
    limitations of, 260–1
  content scales, 262–6, 263t, 444f, 573
  critical items, 266
  First Factor, 124–6. *See also* Anxiety (A)
    scale
  Harris-Lingoes subscales, 261–2, 446,
    492, 573, 574
  history of, 251–2, 586
    timeline of developments in, 253t–4t
  international adaptations, 271, 379–81
  Internet-based testing, 176–7
  minority clients and, 270–1, 401–4
  personality disorders and, 341, 346t, 347
  personnel applications, 586–7
    strategies for interpretation, 590–1
  psychopathy and, 572–5, 574t
  supplemental scales, 266, 267t. *See also*
    Personality Psychopathology Five
    (PSY-5) scales
    factor scales, 266
    scales of adjustment, 267
    scales of anger, 267–8
    scales of gender role identification, 268
    scales of personal resources, 266–7
    scales of substance abuse, 268
MMPI-2 RF (MMPI-2 Restructured
    Form), 114, 595. *See also*
    Restructured Clinical (RC) Scales
MMPI-297, 272
MMPI-A (Minnesota Multiphasic
    Personality Inventory-Adolescent),
    10, 380–1, 496
  case example, 494–5
  development, 486
  future directions, 496–7
  interpretation, 486
    adolescent interpretive system, 493
    Clinical Scales, 488–90
    Content Component Scales, 491
    Content Scales, 490–1
    interpretive strategies, 492–3
    norms and T-scores, 488
    Supplementary Scales, 491–2
    validity scales, 486–8
Molecular genetics
  clinical assessment and, 36–9
  future directions in, 38–9
Molecular genetic studies, 33–4
  evidence for polygenic influence, 33–4
  mechanisms of polygenic influence, 34–6
Monoamine oxidase A (MAOA) gene, 35,
    38, 39
Motivational interviews, 212